DEVELOPMENTAL SCIENCE

An Advanced Textbook

SIXTH EDITION

DEVELOPMENTAL SCIENCE

AN ADVANCED TEXTBOOK

SIXTH EDITION

Edited by

Marc H. Bornstein
Editor, Parenting: Science and Practice
Eunice Kennedy Shriver National Institute of Child Health and
Human Development

and

Michael E. Lamb
University of Cambridge

Psychology Press
Taylor & Francis Group
NEW YORK AND HOVE

Published in 2011
by Psychology Press
270 Madison Avenue
New York, NY 10016
www.psypress.com

Published in Great Britain
by Psychology Press
27 Church Road
Hove, East Sussex BN3 2FA

Psychology Press is an imprint of the Taylor & Francis Group, an Informa business

Copyright © 2011 by Psychology Press

Typeset in Times by RefineCatch Limited, Bungay, Suffolk
Printed in the USA by Sheridan Books, Inc. on acid-free paper
Cover design by Andrew Ward

10 9 8 7 6 5 4 3 2 1

Library of Congress Cataloging-in-Publication Data
Developmental science: an advanced textbook / [edited by] Marc H. Bornstein, Michael E. Lamb—6th ed.
  p. cm
ISBN 978-1-84872-871-4 (hardcover: alk. paper) 1. Developmental psychology—Textbooks.   I. Bornstein,
Marc H.   II. Lamb, Michael E., 1953–
  BF713.D465 2011
  155—dc22   2010011849

ISBN: 978-1-84872-871-4

Visit the Taylor & Francis Web site at http://www.taylorandfrancis.com and the Psychology Press Web site at
http://www.psypress.com

CONTENTS

PREFACE

Developmental science constitutes a unique, comprehensive, and significant domain of intellectual endeavor for three main reasons. First, developmental scientists offer an essential perspective on psychological theory and research. When, for example, psychologists conduct experiments in perception, investigate language, or study personality, they usually concentrate on perception, language, or personality in individuals of a particular age—infants, children, adolescents, adults, or the elderly. In so doing, they gain important knowledge about perception, language, or personality. To study psychological phenomena at only one point in the life cycle, however, is to limit our knowledge of them by failing to consider such factors as their stability and continuity through time that are the province of developmental study. Indeed, it could be argued that, when we undertake a comprehensive analysis of any psychological phenomenon, we necessarily incorporate a developmental perspective. The question is, how well is that perspective addressed? The chapters in this textbook on substantive areas of psychology—neuroscience, perception, cognition, language, emotion, and social interaction—all demonstrate that the developmental perspective transcends and enriches any narrow focus on particular points in the life span. One purpose of this textbook, then, is to furnish inclusive developmental perspectives on all substantive areas in psychology, and the substantive chapters included in this edition underscore the dynamic and exciting status of contemporary developmental science.

Second, developmental science is a major subdiscipline in its own right. It has its own history and systems, its own perspectives, and its own methodologies and approaches to measurement and analysis, as each of the contributions to this textbook illustrates. If studying psychology comprehensively involves attending to development, then there are special traditions, perspectives, and methodologies to which students of psychology must also attend. These traditions, perspectives, and methods are masterfully introduced and reviewed in the chapters that follow.

Third, many aspects of developmental science have obvious and immediate relevance to real-world issues and problems. Each of the chapters in this textbook exemplifies the everyday relevance of developmental science through reviews of the history, theory, and substance of the subdiscipline. Furthermore, one chapter focuses directly and explicitly on the application of developmental research to policy and practice.

In summary, developmental science provides a perspective that illuminates substantive phenomena in psychology, applies across the life span, has intrinsic value, and manifest relevance to daily life. It is for these reasons that we undertook the study of developmental science and subsequently prepared this advanced introduction to the field.

This volume can be used at the advanced undergraduate and introductory graduate levels. It is hardly possible today for any single individual to convey, with proper sensitivity and depth, the breadth of contemporary developmental science at this level. For that reason, we invited experts to prepare original, comprehensive, and topical treatments of the major areas of developmental science. We then organized and edited their contributions, with the cooperation and good will of our contributors, into a single coherent volume. The success of several previous editions encouraged us to prepare, update, revise, and reorganize this sixth edition. For this edition, all chapters have been extensively revised to ensure that they represent faithfully the current status of scholarly efforts in all aspects of developmental science. In some cases, dramatic progress or change in orientation over the last decade also led us to include completely original chapters. The sixth edition is now supported by resources developed by Trey Buchanan of Wheaton College. The password protected website at http://-www.psypress.com/textbook-resources/ features material for students and material that is accessible only to instructors. Students will find chapter outlines, topics to think about before reading the chapters, a glossary, and suggested readings with active reference links. Instructors will have access to this material as well as electronic access to all of the text figures and tables, suggestions for classroom assignments and/or discussion, and a test bank with multiple-choice, short-answer, and essay questions for each chapter. *Developmental Science: An Advanced Textbook* provides the only comprehensive and up-to-date introduction to the field for advanced students.

Developmental Science has many purposes. We hope that readers of this textbook will obtain a new perspective on psychology, a greater appreciation of the varied phenomena that constitute psychology, and a fundamental grounding in developmental science itself.

We also wish to thank many reviewers for thoughtful ideas about this new edition: Trey Buchanan (Wheaton College), Annie M. Cardell (Mountain State University), Lisa K. Hill (Hampton University), and Rebecca Wood (Central Connecticut State University). In addition, we are grateful to Mandy Collison, Erin Flaherty, and Debra Riegert at Psychology Press for their excellent production support.

Marc H. Bornstein
Michael E. Lamb

FOUNDATIONS OF DEVELOPMENTAL SCIENCE

The three chapters in this first section of *Developmental Science: An Advanced Textbook* summarize the intellectual history of developmental science, review the cultural orientation to thinking about human development, and introduce the manner in which empirical research on development is conducted.

In Chapter 1, Richard M. Lerner, Selva Lewin-Bizan, and Amy Eva Alberts Warren present the philosophical origins and history of systems in developmental science. They place great emphasis on the contextual systems view of contemporary developmental study. Developmental science has been the primary battleground for theorists attempting to explain development. Lerner and his colleagues explain shifts over time both in the definitions of development proposed within multiple theories and in the manner in which central issues in development (e.g., nature versus nurture, continuity versus discontinuity, stability versus instability) are portrayed in each. Lerner and colleagues conclude with a discussion of the articulation of theory to application in developmental science.

In Chapter 2, Michael Cole and Martin Packer provide a sweeping account of the understanding and wisdom gained when scholars adopt a cultural perspective on development. Cole and Packer review central issues in the psychology of culture, including alternative definitions of culture before proceeding to recount specific relations between culture and different stages of development, from prenatal to adulthood. As Cole and Packer show convincingly, culture infuses virtually every facet of human growth, and therefore developmental scientists must be constantly attentive to its pervasive and diverse influences.

Finally in Chapter 3, Donald P. Hartmann, Kelley E. Pelzel, and Craig B. Abbott discuss the diverse ways in which evidence should be gathered, analyzed, interpreted, and understood by developmental scientists. Developmental scientists are methodologically eclectic and rely on observations, interviews, questionnaires, and experiments to obtain data. They marshal an array of descriptive and inferential statistical techniques to analyze data and reach conclusions. The authors also offer a unique review of qualitative approaches to data analysis. Because most studies conducted by developmentalists involve children, a unique set of ethical issues also attends developmental research, and these too are discussed by Hartmann, Pelzel, and Abbott.

❖ **1** ❖

CONCEPTS AND THEORIES OF HUMAN DEVELOPMENT

Richard M. Lerner
Tufts University
Selva Lewin-Bizan
Tufts University
Amy Eva Alberts Warren
Institute for Applied Research in Youth Development

INTRODUCTION

The meaning of the term "development" continues to engage scholars in philosophical and theoretical debate (e.g., Collins, 1982; Featherman, 1985; Ford & Lerner, 1992; Harris, 1957; Kaplan, 1983; Lerner, 2002, 2006; Overton, 1998, 2003, 2006; Reese & Overton, 1970). The existence of the debate is itself indicative of a key feature of the meaning of the term: Development is not an empirical concept. If it were, inspection of a set of data would indicate to any observer whether development was present. However, different scientists can look at the same data set and disagree about whether development has occurred.

In this chapter, we discuss the concept of development as it has been and currently is used within human developmental science. We review both the philosophical foundations and the historical roots of the concept and explain how its use within contemporary, cutting-edge theoretical models of human development finds its basis in this philosophical and historical record.

Past concepts of development were predicated on Cartesian philosophical ideas about the character of reality that separated, or "split," what was regarded as real from what was relegated to the "unreal" or epiphenomenal (Overton, 1998, 2003, 2006). In human development, major instances of such splitting involved classic debates about nature versus nurture as "the" source of development, continuity versus discontinuity as an appropriate depiction of the character of the human developmental trajectory, and stability versus instability as an adequate means to describe developmental change. Today, most major developmental theories eschew such splits, and use concepts drawn from **developmental systems theories** (e.g., Lerner, 2006; Overton, 1998, 2003, 2006) to depict the basic developmental process as involving relations—or "fusions" (Thelen & Smith, 2006; Tobach & Greenberg, 1984)—among variables from the multiple levels of organization that comprise the ecology of human development (e.g., see Bronfenbrenner, 2001, 2005). In contemporary developmental science, the basic process of development involves mutually influential (i.e., bidirectional) relations between levels of organization ranging from biology through individual and social functioning to societal, cultural, physical, ecological, and, ultimately, historical levels of organization (e.g., Baltes, Lindenberger, & Staudinger, 1998, 2006; Elder & Shanahan, 2006; Ford & Lerner, 1992).

As a consequence, contemporary developmental theory transcends another split that has characterized the field of human developmental science—a split between basic science and application (Fisher & Lerner, 1994; Lerner, 2006). The relational character of development means that some degree of change is always possible within the developmental system, as the temporality of history imbues each of the other levels of organization within the developmental system with the potential for change. Temporality means that at least relative **plasticity** (the potential for systematic change) exists within the integrated (fused) developmental system. Temporality creates changes in the mutually influential relations between individuals and their contexts. These mutually influential relations may be represented as individual ↔ context relations.

Theoretically predicated attempts to change the course of development—the trajectory of individual ↔ context relations—constitute both tests of the basic, relational process of human development *and* (given ethical mandates to act only to enhance human development) attempts to improve the course of life. These interventions into the life course may be aimed at individuals, families, communities, or the institutions of society, and may involve such actions as instituting community based programs or enacting broad rules (i.e., social policies) governing the structure or function of such programs (Lerner, 2002, 2006). Thus, from the viewpoint of the developmental systems theories that define the cutting edge of contemporary developmental science, there is no necessary distinction between research on the basic, relational process (relational development) linking individuals to their multi-tiered ecological systems and applications aimed at promoting positive individual ↔ context relations.

How did developmental science traverse a conceptual course from split conceptions of the bases and course of development to integrative concepts and models that emphasize the relational character of human development and the synthesis of basic and applied foci? To answer this key question, which in essence tells the story of past and contemporary defining features of human developmental science, we need to consider first what developmental scientists may or may not assume about the nature of their subject matter.

THE ASSUMPTIONS OF HUMAN DEVELOPMENTAL SCIENTISTS

Scientists begin their study of development with some implicit or explicit concept of what development is. Then, when they inspect a given set of data, they can determine whether the features of the data fit with their concepts. Thus, debates among scientists about the meaning of development arise because different scientists have different conceptual templates. These conceptual differences exist because different scientists are committed to distinct philosophical and theoretical beliefs about the nature of the world and of human life.

Nevertheless, despite the philosophical and theoretical differences that exist among scientists in their conceptions of development, there is some agreement about the minimal features of any concept of development. In its most general sense, development refers to change. But "change" and "development" are not equivalent terms. Whenever development occurs there is change, but not all changes are developmental ones. Changes must have a systematic, organized character for them to be labeled as developmental. But systematicity, or organization, does not suffice to define development. For organized, or systematic, changes to be developmental ones, they have to have a *successive* character. The idea of successive changes indicates that the changes seen at a later time are at least in part influenced by the changes that occurred at an earlier time, if only to the extent that the range of changes probable at the later time is limited by earlier occurrences.

Despite a relatively high degree of consensus about the point that development is a theoretical concept that, at least, connotes systematic and successive change in an organization, there is a good deal of disagreement among developmental scientists about what particular ideas need to be added to define the term adequately. These differences in definitions are associated with theoretical differences that, ultimately, are based on their commitments to different philosophical positions (Kuhn, 1962; Lerner, 2002; Overton, 2003, 2006; Pepper, 1942). These philosophical positions involve implicit and explicit assumptions that scientists make regarding their theories, hypotheses, and the methods they use to design their research or to make observations.

The philosophical models of the world used by scientists have a pervasive effect on the scientific positions they adopt. In developmental science, they specify the basic characteristics of humans, and of reality itself, and thus function either to include or to exclude particular features of humans and/or of the world's events in the realm of scientific discourse. Hence, science is relative rather than absolute. Facts are not viewed as naturally occurring events awaiting discovery. According to Kuhn (1962), science "seems an attempt to force nature into [a] preformed and relatively inflexible box . . . No part of the aim of normal science is to call forth new sorts of . . . phenomena; indeed those that will not fit the box are often not seen at all. Nor do scientists normally aim to invent new theories, and they are often intolerant of those invented by others" (p. 24).

As we explain below, a range of models exist within developmental science. As such, full understanding of human development cannot be obtained from any one theory or methodology, nor can it be obtained from a cataloging of empirical "facts." The integration of philosophy, theory, method, and research results is required to attain a complete understanding of any instance of scientific scholarship. Within such an integration, theory and research are given meaning. They are developed and interpreted within the context of a given philosophical perspective. Thus, it is necessary to understand the different philosophical assumptions on which the study of development can be based and to examine the models, or world views, that are used today in the study of human development.

CONCEPTUAL SPLITS IN THE HISTORY OF DEVELOPMENTAL SCIENCE

Have people always believed that humans develop? Have people always said that infants are different from children and that both are different from adolescents and adults? Have "special" portions of the life span, such as adolescence or the aged years, always been held to exist? Have people always believed that there is such a phenomenon as human development, and if not, when and why did such a belief arise?

Focusing on the Western world, many of the central questions and controversies about human development are quite old, with roots in ancient Greece and the traditions of Western philosophy. In both the 2,000 years of this philosophy and about 150 years of pertinent science, the ideas advanced to explain development have revolved around the same few issues. These issues represent the core concepts in any discussion of development, and differences among philosophers and scientists can be understood by looking at the stances they take in regard to such basic conceptual issues. These pertain most directly to one issue: the **nature–nurture** controversy.

In its most extreme form, the nature–nurture controversy pertains to whether behavior and development derive from nature (or in modern terms, heredity, maturation, or genes) or, at the other extreme, whether behavior and development derive from nurture (or in more modern terms, environment, experience, or learning). However, whatever terms are used, the issue raises questions about how nature characteristics (for example, genes) may contribute to development and/or how nurture characteristics (for example, stimulus–response connections, education, or socialization) may play a role in development.

Once the analysis of development is framed in such a split fashion, it is generally further assumed that some set of empirical investigations will ultimately record a definitive answer to the either/or question. The simple empirical observation that generations of empirical investigations have failed to resolve any of these issues demonstrates the inadequacy of the assumption that research done will resolve controversies about splits. As a consequence, the fundamental conceptual prejudice of seeing the world in **conceptual splits** continues to hold the controversies in place as controversies (Overton, 1998). For instance, despite decades of evidence from biology and comparative psychology that genes function as fused entities within an integrated organism ↔ context relational system (e.g., see Gottlieb, 1992, 1997, 2004; Gottlieb, Wahlsten, & Lickliter, 2006), there exist repeated appeals to partition variance associated with genes from variance associated with the context (e.g., Plomin, 2000; Rowe, 1994; Rushton, 2000).

In fact, one can regard the history of developmental science as involving the swinging of a pendulum. This pendulum moved from conceptions of human development stressing nature to conceptions stressing nurture. At this writing, there is a focus on conceptions stressing that neither extreme is appropriate. Notions such as interactions, relationism, fusion, integration, or dynamic systems are used today to understand how the bases of human development combine to foster systematic change across the life span (Lerner, 2002, 2006).

Nature versus Nurture

Anastasi (1958) explained why split conceptions fail. She noted that the first way that scholars inquired into the nature–nurture problem was to ask, "Which one? Does nature *or* nurture provide the determining source of behavior?" Those who posed the issue in this way were assuming that the independent, isolated action of one *or* the other domain provided the source of a behavior.

However, this split way of posing the problem should be rejected because it is illogical. There would be no one in an environment without heredity, and there would be no place to see the effects of heredity without environment. Genes do not exist in a vacuum. They exert their influence on behavior in an environment. At the same time, if there were no genes or heredity, the environment would not have an organism in it to influence. Accordingly, nature and nurture are inextricably tied together and they never exist independent of the other. As such, Anastasi (1958) argued that *any* theory of development, to be logical and to reflect life situations accurately (to have *ecological validity*), must stress that nature and nurture are always involved in all behavior; both are completely necessary for any organism's existence or for the existence of any behavior.

Some psychologists (e.g., Hebb, 1949; Lehrman, 1953; Schneirla, 1956, 1957) had recognized the inappropriateness of the "which one?" question even before Anastasi (1958). Others had asked another question that Anastasi maintained also was inappropriate because it too led to a conceptual dead end. The question was: "Granted that nature and nurture are always involved in any behavior, *how much* of each is needed for a given behavior?" This question is also fruitless because it too is based on the same split and hence inappropriate underlying assumption. In the case of the "how much?" question, the instantiation of the split assumption may be termed the independent, additive-action assumption. It suggests that the way in which nature and nurture are related to each other is that the contribution of one source is added to the contribution of the other to provide a basis of behavior. However, the "how much?" question leads to separating out (splitting) the independent, isolated effects of nature and nurture, as in the "which one?" question. That is, the "which one?" question is just a special case of the "how much?" question, implying a split between nature and nurture of 100 percent/0 percent (or vice versa).

Thus, a conceptualization of the independent action of either source (in either an isolated or an additive manner) leads to a conceptually vacuous dead end. Two assertions follow directly from the above argument. First, nature and nurture are always completely involved in all behavior. Any method of inquiry into the source of behavioral development that does not take cognizance of this statement and seeks to make artificial distinctions between nature and nurture can lead only to conceptual confusion and an empirical blind alley. Second, because independent-action conceptualizations of the contributions of nature and nurture similarly lead to conceptual dead ends, an alternative conceptualization of their contributions, that of *dynamically interactive* or *fused* action, seems more appropriate.

This alternative indicates that nature and nurture interact dynamically (as components or dimensions of a fused, developmental system) to provide a source of behavioral development. Because both sources are necessarily completely present, and because it is inappropriate to speak of their contributions as adding to each other, then the appropriate questions seem to be: "*How* do nature and nurture dynamically interact to produce behavioral development? *How* do the effects of each multiply (or reciprocally interrelate within a fused developmental system) to provide a source of development?"

This third question, Anastasi argued, is the appropriate way to formulate the issue, because it takes cognizance of the logical necessity of the material existence of both domains for a living organism (or living system; Ford & Lerner, 1992). This question denies a split between nature and nurture or the contention that one domain is real and the other is pseudo-phenomenal (e.g., as in Rowe, 1994). Instead, there exists a relation in which the full presence of each source is completely intertwined with the other. As such, nature never affects behavior directly; it always acts in the context of internal and external environments. Environment never directly influences behavior either; it will show variation in its effects depending on the heredity-related characteristics of the organism on which it acts.

The fused approach to nature and nurture presented by Anastasi (1958) helps frame other key issues involved in understanding the characteristics of human development. One of these is the **continuity–discontinuity issue**.

Continuity–Discontinuity

If behavior seen at one point in the life span can be represented or depicted in the same way as behavior at another point, then descriptive continuity exists. If behavior seen at one point in the life span cannot be represented or depicted in the same way as behavior at another point, then descriptive discontinuity exists. Consider, for instance, recreational behavior studied in adolescence and young adulthood. If the same activity (for instance, bike riding) was the major form of recreational behavior at both points in the life span, then descriptive continuity would exist. If, when as adolescent, the person rode a bike for recreation but, in adulthood, went hiking, then there would be descriptive discontinuity across these portions of ontogeny.

Changes in the description of behavior across a person's life can occur for many reasons. In fact, even the same change, whether continuous or discontinuous, can be explained by many reasons. If the same explanations are used to account for behavior across a person's life, then this means that behavior is interpreted as involving unchanging laws or rules. In this case there is explanatory continuity. If, however, different explanations are used to account for behavior across a person's life, then there is explanatory discontinuity.

Descriptions or explanations of development can involve quantitative or qualitative changes. Descriptively, quantitative changes involve differences in how much (or how many) of something exists. For example, in adolescence quantitative changes occur in such areas as height and weight because there is an adolescent growth spurt and these changes may be interpreted as resulting from quantitative increases in the production of growth stimulating hormone. Descriptive qualitative changes involve differences in what exists, in what sort of phenomenon is present. The emergence in adolescence of a drive-state never before present in life (a reproductively mature sexual drive; Freud, 1969) and the emergence in adolescence of new and abstract thought capabilities not present in younger people (formal operations; Piaget, 1950, 1970) are instances of changes interpreted as arising from qualitative alterations in the person. It is believed that the person is not just "more of the same;" rather the person is seen as having a *new* quality or characteristic.

Explanations of development can also vary in regard to whether one *accounts* for change by positing quantitative changes (for example, increases in the amounts of growth stimulating hormone present in the bloodstream) or by positing a new reason for behaviors (e.g., an infant's interactions in his or her social world are predicated on the need to establish a sense of basic trust in the world, whereas an adolescent's social interactions involve the need to establish a sense of identity, or a self definition). In other words, it is possible to offer an explanatory discontinuous interpretation of development involving *either* quantitative or qualitative change. Figure 1.1 illustrates the various combinations of quantitative and qualitative, descriptive and explanatory, continuity and discontinuity that can occur intra-individually across ontogeny.

Virtually any statement about the character of intraindividual development involves, explicitly or implicitly, taking a position in regard to three dimensions of change: (1) descriptive continuity–discontinuity; (2) explanatory continuity–discontinuity; and (3) the quantitative versus the qualitative character of descriptions and explanations—that is, the quantitative–qualitative dimension pertains to both description and explanation.

The particular couplings that one posits as involved in human life will depend on the substantive domain of development one is studying (e.g., intelligence, motivation, personality, or peer group relations) and primarily on one's theory of development. Any particular description or explanation of intraindividual change is the result of a particular theoretical view of development. Accordingly, commitment to a theory that focuses only on certain variables or processes will restrict one's view of the variety of changes that may characterize

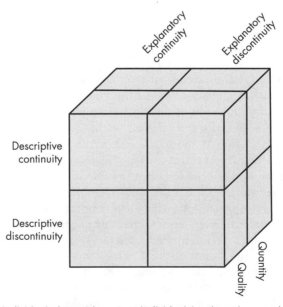

FIGURE 1.1 The intraindividual change box. Intraindividual involves change along three dimensions: descriptive continuity–discontinuity; explanatory continuity–discontinuity; and a quantitative–qualitative dimension (adapted from Lerner, 2002, p. 109).

development. Focusing only on "stages of development" (e.g., Freud, 1954; Piaget, 1950) may lead to an emphasis only on qualitative discontinuity in both descriptions and explanations. Focusing only on stimulus–response connections (e.g., Bijou & Baer, 1961) may result in an emphasis on explanatory continuity and descriptive discontinuity (in regard to the number of connections present in a person's behavioral repertoire). Thus, especially in the case of theories that are based on nature–nurture splits, the range of possible intraindividual changes included in a person's development are split into sets associated with a specific theoretical model. In short, theory, not data, is the major lens through which one "observes" continuity or discontinuity in development.

Stability–Instability

The **stability–instability issue** describes differences that arise between people within groups as a consequence of within-person change. Thus, two types of alterations involving people are occurring simultaneously. People may be changing over time, and because not all people change in the same way or at the same rate, people's locations relative to others may alter as well. Accordingly, to understand all dimensions of a person's alteration over time, both aspects of change (continuity–discontinuity *and* stability–instability) should be considered simultaneously. Only through such a joint, simultaneous focus can development across the life span best be portrayed.

If a person's position relative to his or her reference group changes with development, this is *instability*. If a person's position relative to his or her reference group remains the same with development, this is *stability*. These terms describe a person's ranking relative to some reference group. However, whether stability or instability occurs says nothing whatsoever about whether or not any within-person change took place. A person can change, and this change may still be labeled stability. This could occur if others in the reference group also changed and if the target person remained in the same relative position. By contrast, a person could remain the same from Time 1 to Time 2 and yet his or her position relative to the reference group could be termed unstable. This would occur if others in the group changed while the target person did not. Hence, the terms stability and instability describe relative, not absolute, changes.

Any developmental change may be characterized as being either continuous or discontinuous *and* either stable or instable, and different theories of development proscribe and prescribe the character of the changes that may be involved in human development. Theories that vary in their commitment to nature, to nurture, or to nature–nurture interactional or synthetic ideas may be contrasted in regard to their inclusion of ideas pertinent to qualitative and quantitative, descriptive and explanatory continuity and discontinuity.

Towards the Healing of Conceptual Splits

We have seen that some scholars took split positions in regard to human development, whereas others favored what Overton (1998, 2006) labeled relational conceptions, a set, or "family," of theories labeled developmental systems perspectives. Relational positions aim to "heal" the nature–nurture split (1) by offering categories that describe the biological and the social–cultural as alternative ways of viewing the same whole (e.g., Gottlieb, 1992; Overton, 1973, 2003, 2006; Tobach, 1981) and (2) by suggesting that action constitutes a broad-based mechanism of development that itself differentiates into biological and social–cultural manifestations (e.g., Brandtstädter, 1998, 2006; Overton, 2006).

Prior to Overton's (1998, 2006) discussion of split-versus-relational ideas in philosophy, Overton and Reese (1973, 1981; Reese & Overton, 1970) focused their attention on the import for theory and method in human development of two world views—the mechanistic and the

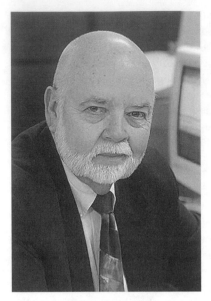

Willis F. Overton.

organismic—which, historically, have been central in influencing theories of development. Although many theories of development associated with mechanism and organicism were similar in adopting split views of nature and nurture, Reese and Overton advanced the understanding of human development significantly by describing the different "families" of theories and methodological traditions associated with mechanistic- and organismic-related theories.

The work of Reese and Overton was seminal in promoting among other developmental scientists an interest in exploring the potential role of other world hypotheses in shaping theories of development. Reese and Overton (Overton, 1984; Overton & Reese, 1981; Reese, 1982) and Lerner (e.g., 1984; Lerner & Kauffman, 1985) discussed the ways in which a "contextual" world hypothesis (Pepper, 1942) could be used to devise a theory of development. In turn, Riegel (1975, 1977) discussed the potential use of a "dialectical" model of development.

Although Pepper (1942) claimed that it was not philosophically permissible to "mix metaphors" and combine mechanistic, organismic, and contextual world views, often scholars believed it was possible to do just this. Arguing on the basis of criteria of usefulness (e.g., in regard to developing statements that, in comparison to those of other positions, account for more variance in developmental data sets, lead to more novel discoveries than do ideas associated with other positions, or integrate a broader range of phenomena pertinent to development than is the case with other positions), Overton (1984) and Lerner and Kauffman (1985) advanced the notion of combining organicism and contextualism to frame a new approach to developmental theory.

The conceptual attractiveness of an integration between contextualism and organicism has resulted within contemporary developmental science in an interest in and elaboration of various instantiations of developmental systems theories.

DEVELOPMENTAL SYSTEMS PERSPECTIVES

The power of a developmental systems perspective is constituted by four interrelated and in fact "fused" (Tobach & Greenberg, 1984) components of such theories: (1) change and relative plasticity; (2) relationism and the integration of levels of organization; (3) historical embeddedness and temporality; and (4) the limits of generalizability, diversity, and individual differences. Although these four conceptual components frame the contemporary set of developmental systems theories within the field of human development (Lerner, 1998), each has a long and rich tradition in the history of the field (Cairns, 1998).

Change and Relative Plasticity

Developmental systems theories stress that the focus of developmental understanding must be on (systematic) change. This focus is required because of the belief that the potential for change exists across (1) the life span and (2) the multiple levels of organization comprising the ecology of human development. Although it is also assumed that systematic change is not limitless (e.g., it is constrained by both past developments and contemporary ecological, or contextual, conditions), developmental systems theories stress that *relative plasticity* exists across life (Lerner, 1984).

There are important implications of relative plasticity for understanding the range of intraindividual variation that can exist over ontogeny (Fisher, Jackson, & Villarruel, 1998) and for the application of development science. For instance, the presence of relative plasticity legitimates a proactive search across the life span for characteristics of people and of their contexts that, together, can influence the design of policies and programs promoting positive development (e.g., Birkel, Lerner, & Smyer, 1989; Kurtines et al., 2008; Lerner & Overton, 2008): for example, the plasticity of intellectual development that is a feature of a systems view of mental functioning, and provides legitimization for educational policies and school- and community-based programs aimed at enhancing cognitive and social cognitive development (Dryfoos, Quinn & Barkin, 2005; Lerner, 2004a, 2007). Such implications for the design of policies and programs stand in marked contrast to those associated with mechanistic, genetic reductionistic theories that suggest that genetic inheritance constrains intellectual development (e.g., Herrnstein & Murray, 1994; Rushton, 2000).

Relationism and the Integration of Levels of Organization

Developmental systems theories stress that the bases for change, and for both plasticity and constraints in development, lie in relations that exist among the multiple levels of organization that comprise the substance of human life (Schneirla, 1957; Tobach, 1981). These levels range from the inner biological, through the individual/psychological and the proximal social relational (e.g., involving dyads, peer groups, and nuclear families), to the sociocultural level (including key macro-institutions such as educational, public policy, governmental, and economic systems) and the natural and designed physical ecologies of human development (Bronfenbrenner, 1979, 2001, 2005; Bronfenbrenner & Morris, 2006; Riegel, 1975). These tiers are structurally and functionally integrated, thus underscoring the utility of a developmental systems view of the levels involved in human life.

A developmental systems perspective promotes a *relational* unit of analysis as requisite for developmental analysis: Variables associated with any level of organization exist (are structured) in relation to variables from other levels; the qualitative and quantitative dimensions of the function of any variable are shaped as well by relations of the variable with ones from other levels. Unilevel units of analysis (or the components of, or elements in, a relation) are not an adequate target of developmental analysis; rather, the relation itself—the interlevel linkage—should be the focus of such analysis (Lerner, Dowling, & Chaudhuri, 2005a; Overton, 2006; Riegel, 1975).

Relationism and integration have a clear implication for unilevel theories of development. At best, such theories are severely limited, and inevitably provide a non-veridical depiction of development, due to their focus on what are essentially main effects embedded in higher-order interactions (e.g., see Walsten, 1990). At worst, such theories are neither valid nor useful. Thus, neither nature nor nurture theories provide adequate conceptual frames for understanding human development (see Hirsch, 1970, 2004; Lewontin, 1992). Moreover, many nature–nurture interaction theories also fall short in this regard because theories of this type still treat nature- and nurture-variables as separable entities, and view their connection in manners analogous to the interaction term in an analysis of variance (e.g., Bijou, 1976; Erikson, 1959; Hartmann, Pelzel, & Abbott, Chapter 3, this volume; Plomin, 2000; cf. Gollin, 1981; Hebb, 1970; Walsten, 1990). Developmental systems theories move beyond the simplistic division of sources of development into nature-related and nurture-related variables or processes; they see the multiple levels of organization that exist within the ecology of human development as part of an inextricably fused developmental system.

Historical Embeddedness and Temporality

The relational units of analysis of concern in developmental systems theories are understood as change units. The change component of these units derives from the ideas that all the levels of organization involved in human development are embedded in the broadest level of the person–context system: history. That is, all other levels of organization within the developmental system are integrated with historical change. History—change over time—is incessant and continuous, and is a level of organization that is fused with all other levels. This linkage means that change is a necessary, an inevitable, feature of variables from all levels of organization. In addition, this linkage means that the structure, as well as the function, of variables changes over time.

Because historical change is continuous and temporality is infused in all levels of organization (Elder, Modell, & Parke, 1993; Elder & Shanahan, 2006), change-sensitive measures of structure and function *and* change-sensitive (i.e., longitudinal) designs are necessitated in contemporary theories of human development (Baltes, Reese, & Nesselroade, 1977; Brim & Kagan, 1980). The key question *vis-à-vis* temporality in such research is not whether change occurs but whether the changes that do occur make a difference for a given developmental outcome (Lerner, Schwartz, & Phelps, 2009; Lerner, Skinner, & Sorell, 1980).

Given that the study of these historical changes will involve appraisal of both quantitative and qualitative features of change, which may occur at multiple levels of organization, there is a need to use both quantitative and qualitative data collection and analysis methods, ones associated with the range of disciplines having specialized expertise at the multiple levels of organization at which either quantitative or qualitative change can occur (Shweder et al., 2006). In essence, the concepts of historical embeddedness and temporality indicate that a program of developmental research adequate to address the relational, integrated, embedded, and temporal changes involved in human life must involve multiple occasions, methods, levels, variables, and cohorts (Baltes, 1987; Baltes, Lindenberger, & Staudinger, 2006; Schaie & Strother, 1968).

A developmental systems perspective, and the implications it suggests for research through concepts such as temporality, may seem descriptively cumbersome; inelegant (if not untestable) in regard to explanations of individual and group behavior and development; and, as a consequence, of little use in formulating interventions aimed at enhancing individual and social life. However, in the face of the several profound historical changes in the lives of children and their families that have occurred across the past century (e.g., see Elder et al., 1993; Elder & Shanahan, 2006; Hernandez, 1993), it would seem, at best, implausible to maintain that the nature of the human life course has been unaffected by this history. Accordingly, it would seem necessary to adopt some sort of developmental systems perspective to incorporate the impact of such historical changes, and of the contemporary diversity they have created, into the matrix of covariation considered in developmental explanations and the interventions that should, at least ideally, be derived from them (Lerner & Miller, 1993).

Yet, it would be traditional in developmental science to assert that the historical variation and contemporary diversity of human (individual and group) development was irrelevant to understanding *basic* processes. Indeed, within developmental science, the conventional view of basic process, whether involving cognition, emotion, personality, or social behavior, is that a developmental process is a function generalizable across time and place. However, data such as those presented by Elder et al. (1993) and Hernandez (1993)—which document the profound impact of historical change on individual and family life over the course of just the past two centuries—constitute a serious challenge to the ontological presuppositions that have grounded this view of basic process and, as such, of developmental psychology's theory and research about people's ontogenies.

The traditional view of basic process found in developmental science (i.e., the prototypic view for much of the past 50 to 60 years) cannot be defended in the face of the historical and contextual variation characterizing American individuals and families across the past century. Indeed, without adequate tests of, and evidence for, its presuppositions about the irrelevance of temporality, context, and diversity for its view of basic process, the field of developmental science fails in even an attempt to represent veridically the course of human life (Cairns, 1998).

By weaving historical change and contextual specificities into the matrix of causal covariation that shapes human developmental trajectories, a developmental systems perspective reconstitutes the core process of human development from a reductionistic and individualistic one to a synthetic, or multilevel integrated, one. Through the seemingly simple step of integrating historical change, contextual variation, and individual developmental change, a developmental systems perspective provides a paradigmatic departure from the psychogenic, biogenic, or reductionistic environmentalist models of causality that have undergirded most theories of human development (Gottlieb, 1992; Lerner, 1991).

The Limits of Generalizability, Diversity, and Individual Differences

The temporality of the changing relations among levels of organization means that changes that are seen within one historical period (or time of measurement), and/or with one set of instances of variables from the multiple levels of the ecology of human development, may not be seen at other points in time (Baltes et al., 1977; Bronfenbrenner, 1979; Bronfenbrenner & Morris, 2006). What is seen in one data set may be only an instance of what does or what could exist. Accordingly, contemporary theories focus on diversity—of people, of relations, of settings, and of times of measurement (Lerner, 2006). Diversity is the exemplary illustration of the presence of relative plasticity in human development (Fisher et al., 1998; Lerner, 1984). Diversity is also the best evidence that exists of the potential for change in the states and conditions of human life (Brim & Kagan, 1980).

In essence, ethnic, cultural, and developmental diversity must be understood systemically to appreciate the nature and variation that exists within and across time in human behavior and development. In other words, individual differences arise inevitably from the action of the development system; in turn, they move the system in manners that elaborate diversity further.

EXAMPLES OF DEVELOPMENTAL SYSTEMS THEORIES

The above four components constitute a developmental systems perspective. This perspective leads us to recognize that, if we are to have an adequate and sufficient science of human development, we must integratively study individual and contextual levels of organization in a relational and temporal manner (Bronfenbrenner, 1974; Zigler, 1998). **Developmental contextualism** is an instance of developmental systems theory. Consistent with the emphases on integrative, or fused, relations between individuals and contexts found in other instances of such systems perspectives, the central idea in developmental contextualism is that changing, reciprocal relations (or dynamic interactions) between individuals and the multiple contexts within which they live comprise the essential process of human development (Lerner & Kauffman, 1985). We consider below this instance of developmental systems theories.

In addition, we briefly review other major examples of such approaches to the understanding of human development.

Richard M. Lerner's Developmental Contextualism

Developmental contextualism is a theoretical approach to the science of, and service to, human development. Building on the integrative ideas found in Schneirla's (1956, 1957; Tobach, 1981) thinking, developmental contextualism represents a model of human life that transcends the dichotomies, or splits (Overton, 2006), found so often in the study of human development.

Developmental contextualism stresses that bidirectional relations exist among the multiple levels of organization involved in human life (e.g., biology, psychology, social groups, and culture) (Bronfenbrenner, 1979; Bronfenbrenner & Morris, 2006; Lerner, 2006). These dynamic relations provide a framework for the structure of human behavior (Ford & Lerner, 1992). In addition, this system is itself dynamically interactive with historical changes. This temporality provides a change component to human life (Dixon, Lerner, & Hultsch, 1991). In other words, within developmental contextualism a changing configuration of relationships constitutes the basis of human life (Ford & Lerner, 1992).

Developmental contextualism reflects the ideas of dynamic interaction, levels of integration, and self-organization associated with other instances of open, living, developmental systems theories of human development. As such, scholarship framed by the model eschews reductionism, unilevel assessments of the individual, and time-insensitive and atemporal analyses of human development. Instead, integrative/holistic, relational, and change-oriented research focused on the individual-in-context is promoted (e.g., Magnusson, 1999a, 1999b; Magnusson & Stattin, 2006). Such research, necessarily embedded in the actual ecology of human development (Bronfenbrenner & Morris, 2006), has another significant feature—its import for actions (e.g., intervention programs and policies) that may enhance human development.

From a developmental contextual perspective, research must be conducted with an appreciation of the individual differences in human development, differences that arise as a consequence of diverse people's development in distinct families, communities, and sociocultural settings. In turn, policies and programs must be similarly attuned to the diversity of people and context to maximize the chances of meeting the specific needs of particular groups of people. Such programs and policies must be derived appropriately from research predicated on an integrative multidisciplinary view of human development. As noted earlier, the evaluation of such applications should provide both societally important information about the success of endeavors aimed at the enhancement of individuals *and* theoretically invaluable data about the validity of the synthetic, multilevel processes posited in developmental contextualism to characterize human development.

Meeting the challenge represented by the need to merge research with policy, and with intervention design, delivery, and evaluation, will bring the study of people and their contexts to the threshold of a new intellectual era. The linkage between research, policy, and intervention will demonstrate to scientists that the basic processes of human behavior are ones involving the development of dynamic, reciprocal relations between individually distinct people and the specific social institutions they encounter in their particular ecological settings. Such demonstrations may then enable developmental scientists to collaborate with communities to use scholarship to promote positive human development and to enhance civil society (Lerner, 2004a; Lerner, Fisher, & Weinberg, 2000). The developmental contextual approach represents an important example of the family of developmental systems theories, but other theories are also quite influential.

We discuss below several other family members that stand out as particularly influential in the creation of the family of developmental systems theories. A brief presentation of these theories will further illustrate the commonality of ideas shared across diverse members of this theoretical family and, at the same time, underscore the unique and important contributions to theory made by each model. Because of its central generative role in the past and present development of developmental systems models in general, and in the other instances of this family of perspectives, the life-span view of human development will be considered first. For more than three decades the work of Baltes and his colleagues has provided the core conceptual and empirical foundation for this theory of human development.

Paul Baltes' Life-Span Developmental Theory

Life-span developmental theory (Baltes, 1987, 1997; Baltes, Reese, & Lipsitt, 1980; Baltes et al., 2006) deals with the study of individual development (ontogenesis) from conception into old age. A core assumption of life-span developmental science is that development is not completed at adulthood (maturity). Rather, the basic premise of life-span developmental science is that ontogenesis extends across the entire life course and that lifelong adaptive processes are involved. In the context of these assumptions, Baltes et al. (2006) note that life-span developmental theory has several scientific goals, ones that span and integrate the basic-to-applied continuum of interest in other members of the developmental systems theory family.

Levels of analysis in life-span developmental scholarship. To pursue the goal of life-span developmental theory, Baltes and his colleagues conduct scholarship at five levels of analysis. Baltes et al. (2006, p. 574) explain that the first level of analysis is the:

> most distal and general one, [and] makes explicit the cornerstones and "norms of reaction" or "potentialities" . . . of life-span ontogenesis. With this approach, which is also consistent with the levels of integration notion of Schneirla or more recently S.-C. Li . . . we obtain information on what we can expect about the general scope and shape of life-span development based on evolutionary, historical, and interdisciplinary views dealing with the interplay between biology and culture during ontogenesis.

They go on to note that:

> Levels 2 and 3 move toward psychological theories of individual development. On these levels of analysis, while keeping the initial overall framework in mind, we shall describe, using an increasingly more fine-grained level of analysis, specific conceptions of life span developmental psychology. On Level 4, we advance one concrete illustration of an overall life span developmental

Margaret M. Baltes and Paul B. Baltes.

theory, a theory that is based on the specification and coordinated orchestration of three processes: Selection, optimization, and compensation. Subsequently, and corresponding to a putative Level 5, we move to more molecular phenomena and functions. Specifically, we characterize life span theory and research in areas of psychological functioning such as cognition, intelligence, personality, and the self (Baltes et al., 2006, p. 574).

In presenting the theoretical ideas associated with life-span developmental theory, Baltes and his colleagues stressed both (1) the commonality of theoretical ideas between life-span developmental theory and other instances of developmental systems theories (e.g., in regard to plasticity and to the embeddedness of development in a dynamic system composed of levels of organization ranging from biology through culture and history) and (2) ideas about human development that are specifically brought to the fore by a life-span perspective (e.g., development as a life-long process, the dynamic between gains and losses, the integration of ontogenetic and historical contextualism, and the functional dynamic between processes of selection, optimization, and compensation that is involved in successful/adaptive development). To illustrate how Baltes and his colleagues conceptualized the five levels of analysis used in the study of development across the life span, consider the interest within Level of Analysis 2 in understanding the structure of gain and loss integrations across ontogeny. To appreciate the character of the developmental process involved across the life span in these integrations, Baltes et al. (1998, p. 1041) saw it as necessary to investigate four dimensions of changing person–context relations: (1) an age-related general reduction in the amount and quality of biology-based resources as individuals move toward old age; (2) the age-correlated increase in the amount and quality of culture needed to generate higher and higher levels of growth; (3) the age-associated biology-based loss in the efficiency with which cultural resources are used; and (4) the relative lack of cultural, "old age-friendly" support structures. This example of the way in which Baltes and his colleagues used the propositions associated with life-span developmental theory to conceptualize and study developmental phenomena associated with the five levels of theoretical analysis they envision illustrates the use by Baltes et al. (1998, 2006) of ideas both common to members of the developmental systems theoretical family (e.g., in regard to life-span changes in plasticity) and specific to life-span theory (e.g., the thorough integration of sociocultural influences across the breadth of the life span).

Given the unique and important role played in life-span developmental theory of propositions specific to this instance of developmental systems theory, it is useful to discuss these features of the conceptual repertoire of this perspective in more detail. In particular, it is useful to review the ideas of Baltes and his colleagues regarding ontogenetic and historical contextualism as paradigm and the concepts of selection, optimization, and compensation. The former instance of the propositions of life-span developmental theory serves as an important conceptual bridge to life-course models of human development, whereas the latter instance is associated closely with action theoretical accounts of human development.

Ontogenetic and historical contextualism as paradigm.   To illustrate the specific theoretical contributions of the life-span developmental perspective, it is useful to discuss how Baltes and his colleagues integrated individual ontogeny and the historical context of human development. Baltes et al. (2006, p. 586) note that:

> individuals exist in contexts that create both special opportunities for, and limitations to, individual developmental pathways. Delineation of these contexts in terms of macrostructural features, like social class, ethnicity, roles, age-based passages and historical periods, is a major goal for the sociological analysis of the life course.

Baltes and his colleagues offered a tripartite model for integrating ontogenetic development with features of historical change, and thus for synthesizing sociological approaches (e.g., Elder & Shanahan, 2006) and individual-psychological ones (Hetherington & Baltes, 1988) to understand the bases of development. The three components of this model involve: (1) normative, age-graded influences; (2) normative, history-graded influences, and (3) nonnormative, life-event influences (Baltes et al., 1980).

Normative, age-graded influences consist of biological and environmental determinants that are correlated with chronological age. They are normative to the extent that their timing, duration, and clustering are similar for many individuals. Examples include maturational events (changes in height, endocrine system function, and central nervous system function) and socialization events (marriage, childbirth, and retirement).

Normative, history-graded influences consist of biological and environmental determinants that are correlated with historical time. They are normative to the extent that they are experienced by most members of a *birth cohort* (that is, a group of people who share a common year of birth or, somewhat more broadly, a group born during a specific historical period). In this sense normative, history-graded events tend to define the developmental context of a given birth cohort. Examples include historic events (wars, epidemics, and periods of economic depression or prosperity) and sociocultural evolution (changes in sex-role expectations, the educational system, and childrearing practices).

Both age-graded and history-graded influences *covary* (change together) with time. Nonnormative, life-event influences are not directly indexed by time because they do not occur for all people, or even for most people. Rather, they are idiosyncratic in development (Baltes et al., 1998, 2006). Thus, when non-normative influences do occur, they are likely to differ significantly in terms of their clustering, timing, and duration. Examples of nonnormative events include illness, divorce, promotion, and death of a spouse.

In short, variables from several sources, or dimensions, influence development. As such, life-span developmental theory stresses that human development is *multidimensional* in character. Variables from many dimensions (ones ranging from biology-related, age-graded events through the normative and the non-normative events constituting history) are involved in developmental change. As we have emphasized, in life-span developmental theory the relationships among the sources of contextual influence—normative, age-graded; normative, history-graded; and non-normative, life-event—are seen as *dynamic*, that is, *reciprocal*. They may continually change, and each influence has an effect on the others and is affected by them.

Baltes et al. (1980) suggested that these three sources of influence exhibit different profiles over the life cycle. Normative, age-graded influences are postulated to be particularly significant in childhood and again in old age, and normative, history-graded influences are thought to be more important in adolescence and the years immediately following it; this is thought to reflect the importance of the sociocultural context as the individual begins adult life. Finally, nonnormative, life-event influences are postulated to be particularly significant during middle adulthood and old age, promoting increasing divergence as individuals experience unique life events. The three sources of time-related influences on development suggested by Baltes reflect a concept of multidirectional development across the life span. The role of the "dynamic collaborations" (Fischer & Bidell, 1998, p. 476) suggested by Baltes et al. (1998, 2006) as a key part of individual development is consistent with dynamic, developmental systems theoretical approaches to development (e.g., Fischer & Bidell, 1998, 2006; Rogoff, 1998).

Conclusions. Life-span developmental theory constitutes a conceptually rich and empirically productive instance of developmental systems theory. The breadth and depth of the sets of ideas of Baltes and his colleagues offer a means to understand the dynamic links between individuals and contexts. These relations underscore the changing character of plasticity across the life span and enable individuals to play an active role throughout their lives in promoting their own positive development.

The conceptual integrations involved in life-span developmental theory span levels of organization ranging from biology through culture and history and, as such, provide a means to achieve another sort of integration, one related to the five levels of analytic work pursued by life-span developmentalists. That is, life-span developmental theory provides a means to synthesize into discussions of the course of human life other instances of developmental systems theories, ones spanning a range of interests from more micro, individual-level psychological interests to more macro, social institutional and historical interests.

For instance, we have seen that the theoretical propositions of life-span developmental theory provide an integration of models associated with historical contextualism and the individual actions taken by people seeking to pursue their immediate and long-term goals within the context of the actual ecologies of their lives. In other words, life-span developmental theory provides a means to see the integrative relevance of individual action, of the institutional/sociological setting of the life course, and of the broad ecology of human development. Accordingly, we turn now to discuss theories associated with these other domains of developmental systems theory.

Jochen Brandtstädter's Action Theories of Human Development

Scholarship pertinent to the nature of human plasticity within developmental systems theories suggests that **developmental regulation**—that is, the processes of dynamic person–context relations—should be a key focus of inquiry in the study of human development. **Action theory** (Brandtstädter, 2006; Brandtstädter & Lerner, 1999) is an exemplar of an approach that is focused on these relational processes (the Baltes and Baltes [1990; Freund, Li, & Baltes, 1999; Gestsdóttir & Lerner, 2008] selection, optimization, and compensation [SOC] model is another). The focus on such self-regulative actions reflects an interest in the ways that the "individual is both the active producer and the product of his or her ontogeny. The central tenet of an action-theoretical perspective thus holds that human ontogeny, including adulthood and later life, cannot be understood adequately without paying heed to the self-reflective and self-regulative loops that link developmental changes to the ways in which individuals, in action and mentation, construe their personal development" (Brandtstädter, 2006, p. 516). Thus, the central feature of action theories is isomorphic with a key idea in the developmental contextual version of developmental systems theory, that of individuals acting as producers of their own development (Gestsdóttir, Lewin-Bizan, von Eye, Lerner, & Lerner, 2009; Lerner, 1982; Lerner & Busch-Rossnagel, 1981; Lerner, Theokas, & Jelicic, 2005b; Lerner & Walls, 1999).

Regulation and plasticity in human development. Across their ontogeny humans actualize a rich potential for cognitive and behavioral plasticity (Lerner, 1984). However, the evolutionary gains in complexity (anagenesis) that underlie human plasticity have come "at a price" that is the ontogenetically protracted development of humans' eventually high-level cognitive and behavioral capacities (Gould, 1977). As discussed by Heckhausen (1999, p. 8),

> the relative dearth of biologically based predetermination of behavior gives rise to a high regulatory requirement on the part of the human individual and the social system. The social and cultural system and the individual have to regulate behavior so that resources are invested in an organized and focused way, and that failure experiences lead to an improvement rather than to a deterioration of behavioral means.

For humans, then, the complexity of their nervous systems and the multiple levels of their contexts mean that there is no one necessarily adaptive relation between context and behavior; what behaviors are requisite for adaptation are uncertain. As a consequence, although plasticity affords vast variation in behavior, the evolutionary status of humans means that the selection of adaptive options from within the array of behaviors available to them constitutes the key challenge in human development. Thus, according to Heckhausen (1999, p. 7):

> Selectivity and proneness to failure as basic challenges both result from the extensive variability and flexibility of human behavior. Other nonprimate species are far more programmed in terms of their repertoire of activities and behavioral responses to the environment, with more instinct-driven behavior and substantially more constrained behavioral options. Humans, in contrast, have evolved with the ability to adapt flexibly to a great range of environmental conditions, and in particular with the ability to generate new systems of behavior.

Similarly, Brandtstädter (1999, p. 46) indicated that:

> a basic evolutionary feature that makes possible—and at the same time enforces—cultural and personal control of ontogeny is the great plasticity and openness of development . . . These features of human ontogeny imply adaptive potentials as well as vulnerabilities, and they have concomitantly evolved with mechanisms to cope with the latter. The capacities to create, maintain, and enact culture, and to plot the "trajectory of . . . life on the societal map" (Berger, Berger, & Kellner, 1967, p. 67), are rooted in this coevolutionary process. Generally, developmental plasticity is already implicated in the notion of culture, as far as this notion connotes the cultivation of some process that is open to modification and optimization.

In essence, the regulation by individuals of their relations with their complex and changing physical, social, cultural, and historical context is the key problem for successful development across life (Baltes et al., 2006). Arguably, the understanding of the system involved in linking individuals and contexts becomes the essential intellectual challenge for developmental science. Indeed, as noted in our earlier discussion in this chapter of the Level 2 analyses that Baltes and his colleagues pursued to understand the cultural embeddedness of gain–loss processes, as the biological underpinnings of human behavior recede in ontogenetic significance as people traverse their post-reproductive years, the need for humans to intentionally draw on either individual-psychological or collective (e.g., cultural) resources (means) to promote their successful development becomes both increasingly salient and the necessary target of life-span developmental analysis (Baltes & Carstensen, 1998; Baltes & Baltes, 1990; Freund & Baltes, 2002).

Accordingly, to understand development as conceived within a dynamic, developmental systems perspective and to appreciate the role of a person's own contributions to this development, focus should be placed on the role of an individual's actions in regulating the course of engagement with the context and in fostering constancy and change (in actualizing plasticity) across life. In the theoretical and empirical scholarship associated with this action theory perspective, the work of Brandtstädter has been the most important in framing and advancing the key conceptual issues in the instance of developmental systems theory. Accordingly, it is useful to continue our discussion of action theory by considering his scholarship.

The contributions of Jochen Brandtstädter. Brandtstädter conceptualized actions as a means through which individuals affect their contexts and, through the feedback resulting from such actions, organize their ideas about their contexts and themselves. As a consequence of this understanding, individuals then develop a set of "guides"—that is, motivations (e.g., intentions, goals), or regulators—for or of future actions. The outcome of this reciprocal, "action–feedback–self-organization–further action" process is, to Brandtstädter (2006), human development. Thus, action constitutes the "engine" of development and, as such, of person–context relations. Indeed, it is the self—the person who reflects on his or her own intentions, goals, and interests and who understands therefore who he or she is at the moment and who he or she would like to be at some future time—that acts to regulate relations with the context.

Thus, akin to other members of the developmental systems theoretical family, action theory as conceptualized by Brandtstädter (1998, 2006) emphasizes the fused, dynamic relations between individuals and their contexts as constituting the core process of human development. However, as is the case with other members of this theoretical family, Brandtstädter's action theory also has attributes specific to it. One key distinctive feature is the central role given to the intentionality of the individual in moderating exchanges occurring between person and context. A second feature is a focus on the changes in development deriving from these intention-based exchanges. That is, as Brandtstädter (2006, p. 535) explained, other instances of developmental systems theory have placed primary emphasis on:

> development as the result of person–environment transactions, rather than as a target area of intentional action; in other words, the relation between action and development has been conceptualized primarily as a functional rather than an intentional one.

Although Brandtstädter (1998, 2006) noted that the functional emphasis is appropriate for the early portions of the life span (e.g., the initial infancy period), by the end of this initial phase of life and certainly thereafter across the life span, intentionality must play a central role in moderating the individual's interactions with his or her physical and social world.

Given this central role of the individual's intentions within the person–context fusions involved in the developmental system, Brandtstädter (2006, pp. 523–524) defined actions as:

> behaviors that (a) can be predicted and explained with reference to intentional states (goals, values, beliefs, volitions); (b) are at least partly under personal control, and have been selected from alternative behavioral options; (c) are constituted and constrained by social rules and conventions or by the subject's representation of these contextual constraints; and (d) aim to transform situations in accordance with personal representations of desired future states.

Contextual and developmental constraints on action. Accordingly, to Brandtstädter, actions link the person dynamically to his or his social context. The plasticity of the individual enables him or her to regulate what he or she does to and in the context and to circumscribe to some extent the influence of the context on him or her.

The developmental capacities of the individual also constrain, or moderate, his or her interactions with the context and, especially in regard to Brandtstädter's emphasis on the centrality of intentions in developmental regulation, the person's changing cognitive capacities are particularly important in respect to possessing the ability to form intentions.

Conclusions. Brandtstädter's action theory placed central emphasis on an individual's intentions in his or her regulatory actions. These actions both reflect and propel development. As such, actions constitute the means through which the active individual, fused with his or her active context, actualizes his or her potential for plasticity in ways that develop, support, and elaborate the self. At the same time, Brandtstädter (1998, 2006) explained that the intentions of the self are limited in the developmental goals that can be actualized due to both individual and contextual constraints on plasticity.

Accordingly, Brandtstädter (1998, 2006) envisioned three dimensions of scholarship that should be pursued to understand the dynamic relations between plasticity and constraints, a relation brought to the fore of conceptual attention by an action theoretical perspective. That is, he recommended that:

> in analyzing the ontogeny of intentional self-development, three basic lines of development should be considered: (1) the development of intentional action in general, and of cognitive and representational processes related to intentionality; (2) the formation of beliefs and competencies related to personal control over development; and (3) the development of the self (or self-concept) as a more or less coherent structure of self-referential values, beliefs, and standards that guides and directs self-regulatory processes. (2006, p. 545)

Other action theorists have pursued theoretical and empirical agendas that correspond to the scholarly vision of Brandtstädter. In particular, Heckhausen (1999) has taken on the challenge of developing a program of work that addresses directly the issue of plasticity and constraints that is of concern in action theory.

Action theory provides a means to understand dynamic relations between individuals and their contexts that exist across the life span. From the point in ontogeny when cognitive development is sufficiently advanced to form intentions and/or to devise strategies for primary control (controlling a goal by acting on it) or secondary control (controlling a goal by thinking differently about it), and then for the rest of the life span, individuals may influence their social world that is influencing them.

Accordingly, to understand the integrations among the levels of the developmental system that comprise the action context for human development we must include a discussion of the social system within which people develop and of the historical/contextual focus used to specify the role of the social world within the developmental system. This social system approach to human development has been termed **life-course theory** and the scholarship of Glen H. Elder, Jr. has been central in understanding the importance of the life course in influencing the character of human development—the transitions in social situations or institutions involved in people's lives and the shaping of the trajectory of human life by its embeddedness in the institutions of society.

Glen H. Elder, Jr.'s Life-Course Theory

As envisioned by Elder (1998, p. 969), this theory is predicated on the following proposition:

> Human lives are socially embedded in specific historical times and places that shape their content, pattern, and direction. As experiments of nature or design, types of historical change are experienced differentially by people of different ages and roles . . . The change itself affects the developmental trajectory of individuals by altering their life course.

Glen H. Elder, Jr.

The life-course theory of human development has emerged over the past 30 years, based on theoretical and empirical contributions derived from three general areas of scholarship. These areas are the study of: (1) social relations, for example, involving scholarship about the study of self (as, for instance, in action theory), social roles, role transitions (for instance, from student to worker), and the linkages among generations (for instance, involving children, parents, and grandparents); (2) **life-span developmental theory**, for instance, as we have discussed earlier in this chapter in regard to the work of Baltes and his colleagues; and (3) age and temporality, for example, involving birth cohort, age, and the role of normative and non-normative historical variation.

Elder (1998; Elder & Shanahan, 2006), in recounting these roots of life-course theory, explained that this perspective emerged, often in collaboration with life-span developmental theory, to meet three interrelated sets of conceptual and empirical challenges to devising an integrated and dynamic view of the entire course of human life. A first challenge was to extend the theoretical frame used to study people from a child-focused one emphasizing only development or growth to one useful across the life span, and thus one encompassing development and aging, growth and decline, or gain and loss. A second challenge was to employ such a frame to develop a set of concepts for depicting the organization of and the changes in humans' lives across their ontogenies and, as well, across different historical events and eras. The third challenge was to use these concepts about ontogeny and history to integrate human lives with the changing social contexts within which each individual and all birth cohorts live across their life spans.

Elder (1998; Elder & Shanahan, 2006) saw life-course theory as enabling scholars to move beyond an additive or simple interactional view of the social system within which development unfolds. Rather, life-course theory synthesizes the social systems into the actual constitution of the structures and functions constituting human development. The means through which this integration is seen to occur in life-course theory is one emphasized as well in life-span developmental theory (Baltes et al., 1998, 2006) and in action theory (Brandtstädter, 1998, 2006); that is, through the selective and intentional regulative actions of individuals, functioning as producers of their own development.

Because of its evolution in intellectual proximity to the also evolving theory of life-span development, the two perspectives have come to rely on very similar ideas about the dynamics of individuals and contexts in the development of the structures and functions constituting the course of human life. Moreover, through this collaboration Elder drew on action theoretical concepts (which of course life-span developmental theory does as well) and emphasized the role of the active individual in the construction of life-course changes. Indeed, as a consequence of these linkages, Elder (1998; Elder & Shanahan, 2006) adopted a theoretical view of developmental process that is completely consistent with life-span developmental theory, with action theory, and with the other instance of developmental systems theory. Elder & Shanahan (2006, p. 679) stated that:

> human development in life course theory represents a process of organism–environment transactions over time, in which the organism plays an active role in shaping its own development. The developing individual is viewed as a dynamic whole, not as separate strands, facets or domains, such as emotion, cognition, and motivation.

Thus, as did Baltes et al. (1998, 2006), Elder saw human development as an interpersonally relational—a dynamically collaborative (Fischer & Bidell, 1998; Rogoff, 1998) social—process. The distinctive features of life-course theory are associated with the link that Elder (1998; Elder & Shanahan, 2006) drew between individual development and the social relationships within which the person's ontogeny is dynamically collaborative.

Constructing the life course. We have noted that Elder (1998; Elder & Shanahan, 2006) specified that the substantive roots of life-course theory lie in the integration of scholarship pertinent to life-span developmental theory, human agency, timing, linked lives, and historical time and place. Elder and Shanahan (2006) presented five principles framing life-course theory. The principles were:

1. the principle of life-span development, which means that human development and aging are life-long processes
2. the principle of human agency, which indicates that individuals construct their own life course through the choices and actions they take within the opportunities and constraints of history and social circumstance
3. the principle of timing, which refers to the fact that the developmental antecedents and consequences of life transitions, events, and behavior patterns vary according to their timing in a person's life
4. the principle of linked lives, which involves the idea that lives are lived interdependently and social–historical influences are expressed through this network of shared relationships
5. the principle of historical time and place, which means that the life course of individuals is embedded in and shaped by the historical times and places they experience over their lifetime.

Accordingly, Elder indicated that the life course is constructed through the *simultaneous* contribution of actions made by individuals dynamically interacting with other individuals while embedded in a context changing along three temporal dimensions: "Life" or "ontogenetic" time (one's age from birth to death), "family" time (one's location within the flow of prior and succeeding generations), and "historical" time (the social and cultural system that exists in the world when one is born and the changing circumstances regarding this system that occur during one's life). That is, Elder (1998, pp. 951–952) pointed out that:

> The life course is age-graded through institutions and social structures, and it is embedded in relationships that constrain and support behavior. In addition, people are located in historical settings through birth cohorts and they are also linked across the generations by kinship and friendship . . . Both the individual life course and a person's developmental trajectory are interconnected with the lives and development of others.

The postulation of a dynamic integration between an individual's regulatory actions and a social system constituted by the people, social institutions, and historical events that vary across these three temporal dimensions provided, for Elder (1998), a means to represent the life course of an individual. As such, Elder's (1998) vision resulted in a theoretical system of singular creativity and enormous value to developmental systems theories of human development. His theory merges within a given person the micro (ontogenetic biological, behavioral, and psychological) and macro (social system) levels of organization that are held to be fused within developmental systems theory.

In short, then, Elder's model constitutes a means to integrate an individual's life into the social system from the moment of his or her birth. Birth provides for his or her immediate membership into (1) a familial flow of generations; and (2) a society that exists at a given point in history with its extant but evolving set of institutions, roles, and socially defined life pathways.

Conclusions. Life-course theory adds a new dimension to the set of concepts associated with developmental systems theories. Building on the ideas associated with other members of this theoretical family—most prominently, life-span developmental theory and, to a somewhat lesser but nevertheless significant extent, action theory—Elder's (1998; Elder & Shanahan, 2006) view of the life course provides a dynamic means to integratively bring the social system into the ontogeny of individuals.

There is always the danger that when scholars whose training or interests are in a discipline more macro than the disciplines having focal units of analysis involving individuals, or even units more molecular than individuals (e.g., genes), the course of an individual life may be interpreted in "sociogenic" terms, that is by exclusive reference to the institutions of society, the rules of culture, or the events of history. Just as we would wish to avoid the alternative conceptual "danger" of a psychogenic or a biogenic interpretation of the life span of a person, such a sociogenic view of human development would not be theoretically desirable (in regard, at least, to the perspective of human development advanced by developmental systems theory) or empirically supportable. Just as Overton (1998, 2006) has cautioned scholars of human development to "avoid all splits," we can offer a similar warning: Avoid all interpretations of human development that are based on the hegemony of one discipline over all others.

The significance of Elder's formulation of life-course theory, then, is that he is able to weave the importance of macro, social system influences into the development of individuals in a manner that is neither disciplinarily "isolationist" (or hegemonist) nor simply additive. Elder's scholarship is an example of the relationism, the multilevel fusions, that define a developmental systems perspective. He brings the social system to human development, not as a context for development but—in the essence of what is sought for in developmental systems theory—as part of the very constitutive fabric of human ontogeny.

There is at least one scholar whom Elder and we would agree integrates person and context seamlessly. Urie Bronfenbrenner has, for a half century, provided a vision for—and a theoretical and empirical literature supportive of—the integration of all levels of organization within the ecology of human development (e.g., see Bronfenbrenner, 2005).

Urie Bronfenbrenner's Bioecological Theory of Developmental Processes

In his 1979 book, *The Ecology of Human Development*, Bronfenbrenner explained the importance for human ontogeny of the interrelated ecological levels, conceived of as nested systems, involved in human development. Bronfenbrenner described the *microsystem* as the setting within which the individual was behaving at a given moment in his or her life and the *mesosystem* as the set of microsystems constituting the individual's developmental niche within a given period of development. In addition, the *exosystem* was composed of contexts that, if not directly involving the developing person (e.g., the work place of a child's parent), had an influence on the person's behavior and development (e.g., as may occur when the parent has had a stressful day at work and as a result has a reduced capacity to provide quality caregiving to the child). Moreover, the *macrosystem* is the superordinate level of the ecology of human development; it is the level involving culture, macro-institutions (such as the federal government), and public policy. The macrosystem influences the nature of interaction within all other levels of the ecology of human development. Finally, time—the *chronosystem*—cuts through all other components of the ecology of human development. As a consequence, change becomes an integral feature of all systems.

Bioecological theory. His 1979 book made an enormous contribution to such a conception of human development, through giving scholars conceptual tools to understand and to study the differentiated but integrated levels of the context of human development. Bronfenbrenner also recognized that his theory would be incomplete until he included in

Urie Bronfenbrenner.

it the levels of individual structure and function (biology, psychology, and behavior) fused dynamically with the ecological systems he described. Accordingly, Bronfenbrenner and his colleagues (e.g., Bronfenbrenner, 2005; Bronfenbrenner & Ceci, 1993; Bronfenbrenner & Morris, 2006) worked to integrate the other levels of the developmental system into the model of human development he was formulating. The span of the levels he seeks to synthesize in his model—biology through the broadest level of the ecology of human development—accounts for the label *bioecological* he attaches to the model.

As Bronfenbrenner described it, the defining properties of the model that has emerged from this scholarship involve four interrelated components: (1) The developmental *process*, involving the fused and dynamic relation of the individual and the context; (2) the *person*, with his or her individual repertoire of biological, cognitive, emotional, and behavioral characteristics; (3) the *context* of human development, conceptualized as the nested levels, or systems, of the ecology of human development he has depicted (Bronfenbrenner, 1979); and (4) *time*, conceptualized as involving the multiple dimensions of temporality that we have noted that Elder and Shanahan (2006) explain are part of life-course theory. Together, these four components of Bronfenbrenner's formulation of **bioecological theory** constituted a process–person–context–time (PPCT) model for conceptualizing the integrated developmental system and for designing research to study the course of human development. Bronfenbrenner believed that just as each of the four components of the PPCT model must be included in any adequate conceptual specification of the dynamic human development system, so too must research appraise all four components of the model to provide data that are adequate for understanding the course of human development.

In turn, in regard to the three remaining defining properties of the model—person (the developing individual), context (the micro-, meso-, exo-, and macro-systems), and time (the chronosystem)—Bronfenbrenner and Morris (2006, p. 795) noted that they give priority in their scholarship to defining the biopsychosocial characteristics of the "Person," because, as noted by Bronfenbrenner in 1989, his earlier formulations of the model (e.g., Bronfenbrenner, 1979) left a gap in regard to this key feature of the theory.

Indeed, Bronfenbrenner redefined the character of the microsystem to link it centrally to what he regarded as the "center of gravity" (Bronfenbrenner & Morris, 2006, p. 814)—the biopsychosocial person—within his theory as it has now been elaborated. That is, although, as in 1979, he saw the ecology of human development as "the ecological environment . . . conceived as a set of nested structures, each inside the other like a set of Russian dolls" (p. 3), he magnified his conception of the innermost, microsystem structure within this ecology by incorporating the activities, relationships, and roles of the developing person into this system. That is, he noted that:

> A microsystem is a pattern of activities, social roles, and interpersonal relations experienced by the developing person in a given face-to-face setting with particular physical, social, and symbolic features that invite, permit, or inhibit, engagement in sustained, progressively more complex interaction with, and activity in, the immediate environment. (Bronfenbrenner, 1994, p. 1645)

What may be particularly significant to Bronfenbrenner in this expanded definition of the microsystem is that he included not only the person's interactions with other people in this level of the ecology but, as well, the interactions the person has with the world of symbols and language (with the semiotic system)—a component of ecological relationships that action theorists also believe is especially important in understanding the formulation of intentions, goals, and actions (cf. Brandtstädter, 1998, 2006). That is, Bronfenbrenner noted that:

> The bioecological model also introduces an even more consequential domain into the structure of the microsystem that emphasizes the distinctive contribution to development of proximal processes involving interaction not with people but with objects and symbols. Even more broadly, concepts and criteria are introduced that differentiate between those features of the environment that foster versus interfere with the development of proximal processes. Particularly significant in the latter sphere is the growing hecticness, instability, and chaos in the principal settings in which human competence and character are shaped—in the family, child-care arrangements, schools, peer groups, and neighborhoods. (Bronfenbrenner & Morris, 2006, p. 796)

Finally, Bronfenbrenner noted that the emphasis on a redefined and expanded concept of the microsystem leads to the last defining property of the current formulation of his theory of human development, i.e., time (the chronosystem). Bronfenbrenner and Morris (2006, p. 796) indicated that:

> the fourth and final defining property of the bioecological model and the one that moves it farthest beyond its predecessor [is] the dimension of Time. The 1979 volume scarcely mentions the term, whereas in the current formulation, it has a prominent place at three successive levels: (1) micro-, (2) meso-, and (3) macro-. *Microtime* refers to continuity versus discontinuity in ongoing episodes of proximal process. *Mesotime* is the periodicity of these episodes across broader time intervals, such as days and weeks. Finally, *Macrotime* focuses on the changing expectations and events in the larger society, both within and across generations, as they affect and are affected by, processes and outcomes of human development over the life course.

Conclusions. Bronfenbrenner's bioecological model is in at least two senses a living system (Ford & Lerner, 1992). First, the theory itself depicts the dynamic, developmental relations between an active individual and his or her complex, integrated and changing ecology. In addition, the theory is itself developing, as Bronfenbrenner (2005) sought to make the features of the theory more precise and, as such, create a more operational guide for PPCT-relevant research about the dynamic character of the human developmental process.

At this writing, then, the bioecological model has developed to include two propositions. Both these sets of ideas promote a dynamic, person–context relational view of the process of human development. As explained by Bronfenbrenner and Morris (2006, p. 797), Proposition 1 of the bioecological model states that:

> Especially in its early phases, but also throughout the life course, human development takes place through processes of progressively more complex reciprocal interaction between an active, evolving biopsychosocial human organism and the persons, objects, and symbols in its immediate external environment. To be effective, the interaction must occur on a fairly regular basis over extended periods of time. Such enduring forms of interaction in the immediate environment are referred to as proximal processes. Examples of enduring patterns of proximal process are found in feeding or comforting a baby, playing with a young child, child–child activities, group or solitary play, reading, learning new skills, athletic activities, problem solving, caring for others in distress, making plans, performing complex tasks, and acquiring new knowledge, and know-how.

Thus, in the first proposition in his theory, Bronfenbrenner emphasized a theme found in the other instances of developmental systems theory—the role of the active individual as an agent in his or her own development. In fact, the idea of the contribution of the individual to the developmental process is present as well in the second proposition of bioecological theory.

> The form, power, content, and direction of the proximal processes effecting development vary systematically as a joint function of the characteristics of the developing person; of the environment —both immediate and more remote—in which the processes are taking place; the nature of the developmental outcomes under consideration; and the social continuities and changes occurring over time through the life course and the historical period during which the person has lived (Bronfenbrenner & Morris, 2006, p. 798).

As is evident from the two propositions, Bronfenbrenner regards proximal processes as the primary sources of development, an assertion that is compatible with the several versions of action theory discussion in this chapter (Baltes & Baltes, 1990; Brandtstädter, 2006; Heckhausen, 1999). That is, in all of the proximal processes described by Bronfenbrenner in the first proposition of the bioecological model, goal selections, intentions, developing means to engage goals, the primacy of primary control, and the importance of compensatory behaviors and/or of secondary control may be involved. In turn, the propositions also point to the fusions across the developmental system described by Bronfenbrenner as providing the dynamism that enables the proximal processes to drive the developmental system.

In addition, the role of the individual, as an active agent in his or her own development, is central in the bioecological model. Indeed, Bronfenbrenner and Morris (2006, p. 798) asked their readers to consider:

> Characteristics of the person actually appear twice in the bioecological model—first as one of the four elements influencing the "*form, power, content, and direction of the proximal process*," and then again as "*developmental outcomes*"—qualities of the developing person that emerge at a later point in time as the result of the joint, interactive, mutually reinforcing effects of the four principal antecedent components of the model. In sum, in the bioecological model, the characteristics of the person function both as an indirect producer and as a product of development. (emphasis in original)

In sum, then, as has been the case in all of the instances of developmental systems theory we have discussed in this chapter, and as emphasized over a half century ago by Schneirla (1957), the active, developing individual was seen by Bronfenbrenner as a central force of his or her own development. This contribution to the process of development is made by a synthesis, an integration, between the active person and his or her active context. We see stress on such individual ↔ context relations in both of the two final instantiations of developmental system theories we discuss.

Esther Thelen and Linda Smith's Dynamic Systems Theory

Thelen and Smith (1998, 2006) noted that their version of developmental systems theory—which they term **dynamic systems theory**—derives from both systems thinking in biology and psychology and the study of complex and nonlinear systems in physics and mathematics. They explained that in its simplest sense the idea of dynamic systems refers to changes over time among elements that are interrelated systemically. Although this idea can be extended more technically or formally, through specific mathematical equations, Thelen and Smith (2006) noted that there are two key features of any physical or biological system: (1) Development can only be understood as the multiple, mutual, and continuous interaction of all levels of the developing system, from the molecular to the cultural. (2) Development can only be understood as nested processes that unfold over many time scales, from milliseconds to years (p. 258). To Thelen and Smith (1998, 2006), dynamic systems theory can be applied to different species, age levels, or domains of development, e.g., from "molecular" patterns of motor functioning involved in walking or reaching to "molar" changes in cognition that may be gained through the integration of humans' actions on their context and the context's actions on them.

The development of novel forms across life.   Thelen and Smith (1994, 1998, 2006) believed that dynamic systems theory affords understanding of what they regard as the defining feature of development: the creation of new forms. That is, Thelen and Smith contended that the essence of those changes termed "developmental"—the property of change that enables one period of life to be designated as involving a distinct point in development—is qualitative discontinuity, emergence, epigenesis, or simply novelty. Once such novelty has been described, however, a central explanatory issue becomes evident: "Where does this novelty come from? How can developing systems create something out of nothing?" (Thelen & Smith, 2006, p. 259).

Answers to these questions have been associated with nature, nurture, and interactionist perspectives. Not surprisingly, Thelen and Smith rejected both nature and nurture explanations and, implicitly, those interactionist positions representative of weak or moderate views of interaction. Instead, consistent with the ideas of developmental systems theorist Gottlieb (1997, 2004; Gottlieb et al., 1998), they noted that:

> The tradition we follow, that of *systems theories of biological organization*, explains the formation of new forms by processes of *self-organization*. By self-organization we mean that *pattern and order emerge from the interactions of the components of a complex system without explicit instructions*, either in the organism itself or from the environment. Self-organization—processes that by their own activities change themselves—is a fundamental property of living things. (Thelen & Smith, 2006, p. 259; emphasis in original)

Other developmental systems theorists agree. For instance, Gottlieb (e.g., 1997), in his view of the coactions that are involved in epigenesis, and Schneirla (1957), in his notion of circular functions and self-stimulation in ontogeny, provided examples of these self-organizational processes.

In turn, Thelen and Smith (1998, 2006) drew on evidence from embryology and morphology that indicates how highly complicated structural patterns arise within dynamic systems *not* from information specifically coded in genes but, instead, from simple initial conditions. For instance, they explained that neither the spots of leopards nor the striped tails of raccoons are derived from genes for these bodily features. Rather, these features are constructed during development when specific chemical and metabolic attributes of these animals—each one mutually facilitating and constraining the others—spontaneously organize themselves into patterns (Thelen & Smith, 2006).

Similarly, behavioral characteristics and patterns can emerge in development without the requirement of specific genetic coding for them, as is held in theories that rely on split concepts of nature and nurture, such as models within the field of behavior genetics (e.g., Plomin, 2000; Rowe, 1994) or as forwarded in concepts such as instinct (e.g., Lorenz, 1937, 1965). The processes that produce such developmental change are again those associated with the probabilistic epigenetic view of organism ↔ context relations associated with the work of Schneirla, Gottlieb, Tobach, Lehrman, and others. Probabilistic epigenetics refers to the view that the changes that occur across the life span are *not* ones performed in the genes and are *not* invariant in regard to norms. Instead, changes *emerge* because of organism ↔ context relations that occur across life and, because the timing of these relations will inevitably vary from one organism to another, the characteristics that emerge are probable, but not certain, in regard to fitting with any norms of development. Simply, because of variation in the timing of organism ↔ context relations, there is diversity in development.

In short, then, Thelen and Smith (1998, 2006) drew on the evidence provided by the scholarship of embryologists, and by comparative psychologists taking a probabilistic epigenetic perspective, to assert that the basis for novelty in development arises from the integrated relation of intra- and extra-organism levels of organization—and not from either genetic or environmental "instructions" for such change.

The dynamics of the developmental system. The probabilistic epigenetic character of the developmental process meant, to Thelen and Smith (1998, 2006), that the duality, or split (Overton, 2006), between individual and context, or between structure and function, should be eliminated from scientific discourse. In their view, then, contextual levels of organizations (e.g., culture) did not just support the course of development, they "are the very stuff of development itself" (Thelen & Smith, 2006, p. 266). They explained that the essential difference between the developmental systems perspective they favor:

> and more individual-centered approaches is that the levels are conceptualized as *more* than just interacting; instead they are seen as integrally fused together. Behavior and its development are melded as ever-changing sets of *relationships* and the history of those relationships over time. (Thelen & Smith, 2006, p. 267; emphasis in original)

Thelen and Smith (1998, 2006) believed that, because of this fusion, we must reject linear systems of causality wherein there is a direct, unidirectional line from an antecedent, "causal" event or structure (e.g., the possession of a gene) to a consequent behavior (e.g., a particular motor behavior, personality attribute, or cognitive capacity, that is where "X" → "Y"). In the place of such linear notions of causality, developmental systems theories suggest a configural view of causality (Ford & Lerner, 1992), wherein bidirectional relations within and across fused levels of organization change interdependently across time.

The causal system presented in this theory coincides with the view of causality conceived of by Thelen and Smith (1998, 2006), wherein the key features of developing individuals—

self-organization, nonlinearity, openness, stability, complexity, wholeness, the emergence of novelty, and change—are produced by the fused, multilevel influences that constitute the developmental system. The outcomes of development—"form"—are products of this process of bidirectional relations (Thelen & Smith, 1998, p. 586).

Thelen and Smith (1998, 2006) indicated that the key feature of dynamic systems is that the many heterogeneous parts of the system (e.g., the different cells, tissues, and organs within the individual and the various individuals, institutions, and physical features of the context of any person) are free to combine in a virtually infinite number of ways. Theoretically at least, there is no limit to the actual number of combinations that might occur. However, in actuality, the patterns of relations that are seen are far less. In regard to the notion of "relative plasticity" discussed earlier in this chapter, the relation among the multiple parts of the system are sources of constraints as well as of variability. Thus, because of this relative plasticity, an order (a pattern) emerges from the complexity of the system as, through the relations within the system, the system organizes itself.

Thelen and Smith (1998, 2006) explained that order emerges from disparate parts because human development is an *open system*; that is, a system wherein energy is taken into the system and is used to increase order within it. Such a system stands in contrast to a *closed system*, wherein there is no infusion of energy into the system. In that an open, human development system increases its organization over time, it exists in "violation" of the second law of thermodynamics (Brent, 1978; Prigogine, 1978). According to this law, a system changes in the direction of greater disorganization, termed *entropy*. However, some systems—open ones—can show *negentropy*; that is, changes in the direction of greater organization.

The Nobel laureate chemist, Prigogine (1978), has shown that negentropic change can occur because an open system draws energy from its context to increase its internal order. Prigogine demonstrated that such use of energy within an open system does result in an overall dissipation in order outside of it; that is, in the universe as a whole; thus, in the broader system there is an increase in entropy, and the second law is actually not violated.

Thelen and Smith (1998, 2006) noted that when the parts involved in an open system interrelate in a nonlinear manner, integration (i.e., a pattern, an organization, structural relations) emerges. Such integration enables the system to be described via reference to fewer dimensions, or parameters, than was the case at the beginning of the development of the system. Heinz Werner's (1948, 1957) concept of orthogenesis is an example of a general principle of systematic change in developing organisms wherein the globality of the individual's organization is reduced through the emergence of hierarchic integration. In turn, Thelen and Smith (1998, 2006) noted that the integrative variables that emerge within an open system to reduce its dispersion and increase its organization, or pattern, may be termed either *collective variables* or *order parameters*.

The emergence of such collective variables not only reduces the theoretically infinite number of combinations within a dynamic (open) system to some much smaller actual subset but, in so doing, the integration reflected by the collective variables provides continuity and stability within the system. As Thelen and Smith (2006, p. 272) explained:

> The system "settles into" or "prefers" only a few modes of behavior. In dynamic terminology, this behavioral mode is an *attractor* state, because the system—under certain conditions—has an affinity for that state. Again in dynamic terms, the system prefers a certain location in its *state*, or *phase space*, and when displaced from that place, it tends to return there ... All the initial conditions leading to a particular fixed point attractor are called *basins of attraction*. (emphasis in original)

Thelen and Smith (1998, 2006) described one type of attractor, the *chaotic* attractor, that seems to be involved in many biological systems (e.g., involving changes in heart rate, the sense of smell, and motor movements during the fetal period). Within dynamic systems, chaos describes a situation wherein the relation among the parts of a system seems random (i.e., lacking any pattern or order). However, when the time period used for viewing a state space is extended over a significantly long time period, non-randomness—order—is evident. In fact, chaotic change is represented by highly elaborate geometric patterns (Gleick, 1987).

Stability and change in dynamic systems. Thelen and Smith (1998, 2006) noted that in the study of human development the most important characteristic of an attractor is its relative stability; that is, the likelihood that the system will exist in a given state (or show a specific behavioral pattern) as compared to other ones. The presence of relative stability means that there is a higher statistical probability of one specific behavioral pattern than another and that if the system is dislodged from its preferred state it will return to it. Moreover, the system will "work" to maintain the preferred state. Thus, in regard to the idea that continuity of behavior can be underlain by dynamic interactions between the individual and the context (Cairns & Hood, 1983), the relative stability of a developmental system does not gainsay the fact that dynamic exchanges are occurring within it.

The relative stability of a system is related to the relative plasticity of the course of development. Although organisms—through their dynamic interactions with their context—maintain the capacity for systematic change across the life span (Baltes et al., 1998; Lerner, 1984), these same organism ↔ context relations constrain the variability in functional change that can be seen; as a consequence, plasticity—although ubiquitous—is relative, not absolute. Similarly, Thelen and Smith (1998, p. 626) observed that "adaptive systems live in quasi-stability; reliable enough to make predictions about what is appropriate in a context, but flexible enough to recruit different solutions if the situation changes."

The ontogenetic changes that exist in plasticity mean that, at advanced developmental levels, when the reserve capacity for plasticity has narrowed (Baltes, 1997; Baltes et al., 1998), change is still possible but a larger than previously necessary level of intervention would be required to produce it (Lerner, 1984; MacDonald, 1985). Similarly, Thelen and Smith (2006) noted that, "Very stable attractors take very large pushes to move them from their preferred positions, but they are dynamic and changeable nonetheless" (p. 274). In other words, the system is not fixed, with hard-wired, immutable connections; rather it is *softly assembled*.

Such soft assembly is the essence of plasticity in human development and, to Thelen and Smith (1998, 2006), the defining feature of a dynamic view of development. The presence of soft assembly means that the concept that human development involves the functioning of permanent, immutable structures is not valid. Rather, developmentalists must view the development of the person as involving a dynamic linkage between (1) the stability of the system, conceived of as the resistance to change existing among the collective states and (2) the fluctuations around the stable states, changes that provide the functional source of novelty within the system.

Transitions in systems. Fluctuations within the system, as well as changes from the context that impinge on the system, can alter the patterns of the system. In either case, the system will change in a manner that increases order, that enhances coherence. The parts of the system will interact, or "cooperate," in the terms of Thelen and Smith (2006, p. 271), in the occurrence of a "phase shift" or, in other terms, a "nonlinear phase shift." To illustrate, Thelen and Smith (2006, p. 275) indicated that:

For example, we can walk up hills of various inclines, but when the steepness of the hill reaches some critical value, we must shift our locomotion to some type of quadrupedal gait—climbing on all fours . . . In dynamic terminology, the slope change acted as a *control parameter* on our gait style. The control parameter does not really "control" the system in traditional terms. Rather, it is a parameter to which the collective behavior of the system is sensitive and that thus moves the system through collective states. (emphasis in original)

For instance, Thelen and Smith (1998) noted that the "disappearance" of the newborn stepping response (i.e., stepping movements made by the newborn when he or she is held upright), which occurs after a few months of life, occurs in relation to the gain in weight, and especially in body fat, during this period. As the infants' legs get heavier across these months there is no corresponding increase in muscle mass. As a consequence, infants have difficulty lifting their legs—not because of a neuronal change within the brain that "suppressed" the reflex, but because they do not have the muscles to do this when in the biomechanically difficult upright position (Thelen & Smith, 1998). Thus, underscoring the coherence of the changing dynamic system, one wherein patterns emerge through self-organization among components, Thelen and Smith (2006, p. 275) noted that, "Body fat deposition is a growth change that is not specific to leg movements, yet it affected the system such that a qualitative shift in behavior resulted."

Times scales within dynamic systems. The time frame for the phase shift involved in the infant stepping response involves several months within the early life of humans. One important temporal parameter of dynamic systems illustrated by this example is that the state of the system in regard to stepping when upright at a later time in ontogeny (e.g., when a lot of body fat had been gained) was related to the system state at the prior time (when the ratio of body fat to muscles afforded stepping while upright). This temporal linkage is an example of the point that the condition of the system at any one point in time provides the basis for the condition of the system at the next immediate point in time.

Thus, as discussed in regard to the notion of successive change as being a core component of the definition of development, Thelen and Smith (1998, 2006) noted that there is always a successive character to change within a dynamic system; that is, the state of the system at Time 1 shapes the state of the system at Time 2, and the state of the system at Time 2 determines the state at Time 3, etc. Thelen and Smith (1998, 2006) noted, then, that dynamic systems are *reiterative*; that is, each state within the system is shaped by the prior state of the system.

Moreover, the time scale dividing the successive influences may vary considerably. Times 1, 2, and 3 may be divided (e.g., along the *x*-axis of a graph) by seconds, days, weeks, months, years, etc. Nevertheless, the same sort of successive interdependency of states, and therefore the same linkages across time, will be evident whether the state-to-state observational interval is months (as in the example of the infant stepping response) or years (as may be seen in regard to changes in IQ scores; Bloom, 1964). Thelen and Smith (1998, 2006) explained that there is, then, a self-similarity of the system across many different levels of temporal observation.

However, because different components of the system have their own developmental course and, as a consequence, because the relations among components change continuously, the time scale used within developmental studies to observe the system, and make judgments about its stability or fluctuation, is critical. For example, in attempting to understand connections between the state of the system in early infancy in regard to the presence and disappearance of the stepping response, appraisal of fat-to-muscle ratios across a monthly time parameter may be useful; however, if the interest is the emergence within the system of the ability to run efficiently, then neither such ratios nor a month-by-month perspective would be useful (Thelen & Smith, 1998, 2006). Instead, different system components (involving, for instance, the development of muscle coordination and lung vital capacity) and different time divisions (e.g., years) may be required to see the reiterative character of the system and the bidirectional influences across levels within it.

Conclusions.   Thelen and Smith (1998, 2006) offered a nuanced conception of the dynamic character of the human developmental system. Their theory underscored the important role of dynamic interactions, fusions, in human development, and the centrality of plasticity—of softly assembled systems—in providing within-person variability across life and between-person differences in such life-span changes. Their theory, and the data they marshal in support of it (Thelen & Smith, 1994, 1998, 2006), thus highlighted the active role of the individual as a central agent in his/her own development and fosters an integrative, holistic understanding of the individual and his/her context. They saw important and singular promise for their dynamic systems theory:

> Only a dynamic account captures the richness and complexity of real-life human behavior. The issue is not just how people learn to think in formal, logical, and abstract terms, but how they can do that *and* all the other things people do in this society: use tools, operate sophisticated machinery, find their way around, play sports and games, create art and music, and engage in complex social interactions. These activities require active perception, precisely timed movements, shifting attention, insightful planning, useful remembering, and the ability to smoothly and rapidly *shift* from one activity to another as the occasion demands. They happen in time and they recruit all the elements in the system. The challenge for developmentalists is to understand the developmental origins of this complexity and flexibility. Only dynamics, we believe, is up to the task. (Thelen & Smith, 1998, p. 626; emphasis in original)

We agree with the appraisal of Thelen and Smith about the challenge that may be met by, and the potential benefits of meeting it through, the dynamic, developmental systems theory they forward. Other developmentalists agree as well and, in addition, have advanced theories consonant with Thelen and Smith (1998, 2006). One instance of such a theory has been formulated by Magnusson who, over the course of more than a quarter century, has contributed to scholarship about developmental systems.

Magnusson's Holistic Person–Context Interaction Theory

Magnusson's theoretical formulations and research programs, including his **holistic person–context interaction theory**, have emphasized the fundamental role of context in human behavior and development (e.g., Magnusson, 1995, 1999a, 1999b; Magnusson & Stattin, 1998, 2006). His intellectual vision includes a compelling conceptual rationale and substantive basis for internationally contextualized, comparative scholarship (e.g., Magnusson, 1995, 1999a, 1999b) and is built on four conceptual pillars: interactionism, holism, interdisciplinarity, and the longitudinal study of the person.

These themes emerge in Magnusson's theory, which stresses the synthesis, or fusion, of the person–environment system. Magnusson sought to understand the structures and processes involved in the operation of this system and the way in which the individual behaves and develops within it. Given this integrative emphasis on person and context, Magnusson (1995) termed his theory a *holistic approach*. He stated that:

> The individual is an active, purposeful part of an integrated, complex, and dynamic person–environment (PE) system . . . Consequently, it is not possible to understand how social systems function without knowledge of individual functioning, just as individual functioning and development cannot be understood without knowledge of the environment. (Magnusson & Stattin, 2006, p. 401)

David Magnusson.

Causality in holistic interactionism. To Magnusson, then, as is seen also in respect to the theories of Schneirla (1957), Kuo (1976), Gottlieb (1997) and Thelen and Smith (1998, 2006), the cause of development—the emergence of novel forms across life—was an outcome of the coactions of the components of the dynamic person–context system. This self-organizational source of developmental change stands in contrast to either the unidirectional, single source (nature or nurture) or the weak or moderate interactional ideas regarding the causes of development.

In what Magnusson termed the modern interactionist perspective, or the holistic interactionist viewpoint, the basis of development lies in two types of interaction: inner interactions, involving bidirectional relationships among biological, psychological, and behavioral characteristics; and outer, person–context interactions, involving continual exchanges between the person and his or her environment. Magnusson explained that holistic interaction builds and extends the ideas of interactionism found in what he terms "classical interactionism" (Magnusson & Stattin, 2006, p. 406).

Holistic interactionism expands on this classic conception of interaction by, first, placing greater emphasis on the dynamic, integrated character of the individual within the overall person–environment system and, second, stressing both biological and behavioral action components of the system. Thus, and drawing on many of the same literature sources relied on by Gottlieb (for example, in regard to neuropsychology and developmental biology, Damasio & Damasio, 1996; Rose, 1995) and by Thelen and Smith (for example, in regard to chaos and general systems theory, e.g., Gleick, 1987; von Bertalanffy, 1968), and buttressed by what Magnusson (1995, 1999a, 1999b) saw as the growing importance of holistically oriented longitudinal studies of human development (e.g., Cairns & Cairns, 1994). Magnusson and Stattin (2006, p. 407) specified the five basic propositions of holistic interaction:

1. The individual is an active, intentional part of a complex, dynamic PE system.
2. The individual functions and develops as a total, integrated organism.
3. Individual functioning in existing psychobiological structures, as well as development change, can best be described [as] an integrated, complex, and dynamic process.
4. Such processes are characterized by continuously ongoing interactions (including interdependence) among mental, behavioral, and biological components of the individual and social, cultural, and physical components of the environment.
5. The environment functions and changes as a continuously ongoing process of interactions and interdependence among social, cultural, and physical factors.

Features of the person–environment system. The holistic interactionist theory has profound implications for the conduct of developmental science. Indeed, the far-reaching character of these implications extends to even the role of the concept of "variable" in developmental research.

Magnusson and Stattin (1998, 2006) noted that in most approaches to developmental science the concept of "variable" is embedded within a theoretically reductionistic model of humans. Within this perspective, the "variable" becomes the unit of analysis in developmental research. However, within the context of what they term *the holistic principle*, Magnusson and Stattin (1998, 2006) forwarded a person-centered view of development and, as such, forward the individual, the whole person, as the core unit of developmental analysis. That is, the holistic principle

> emphasizes an approach to the individual and the person–environment system as organized wholes, functioning as totalities . . . The totality derives its characteristic features and properties from the functional, dynamic interaction of the elements involved, not from each isolated part's effect on the totality. (Magnusson & Stattin, 2006, p. 404)

Accordingly, if the totality, the whole person or, better, the person–environment relation characterizes the essence of developmental change, then developmental analysis that assesses single aspects of the system (single variables, for instance) is necessarily incomplete. Only a distorted view of development can be derived from appraising variables divorced from the context of other, simultaneously acting variables (Magnusson & Stattin, 1998, 2006). It is this integration of variables from across the person–environment system that constitutes the core process of human development and, as such, the necessary focus of developmental science.

Indeed, within holistic interactionist theory, the developmental *process* involves a continual flow of integrated, reciprocally related events. Time becomes a fundamental feature of individual development given that, within the probabilistic epigenetic view taken by Magnusson (1995, 1999a, 1999b) of the interrelation of the constituent events constituting the process of development, the same event occurring at different times in ontogeny will have varying influences on behavior and development. As a consequence, "A change in one aspect affects related parts of the subsystem and, sometimes, the whole organism . . . At a more general level, the restructuring of structures and processes at the individual level is embedded in and is part of the restructuring of the total person–environment system" (Magnusson & Stattin, 2006, p. 433).

Thus, to Magnusson (1995, 1999a, 1999b; Magnusson & Stattin, 1998, 2006), individual development is marked by a continual restructuring of existing patterns and—through the facilitation and constraint of the biological through sociocultural levels of the total person–environment system—the emergence of new structures and processes. In other words, as also specified within the Thelen and Smith (1998, 2006) dynamic systems theory, *novelty* in structures and processes, in forms and patterns, arises through principles of system self-organization. Indeed, *self-organization* is a guiding principle within the developmental systems theory proposed by Magnusson. Thus, development, novelty, arises in the living world because the parts of the organism produce each other and, as such, through their association create the whole (Magnusson & Stattin, 1998, 2006).

Also consistent with the theories of Gottlieb (1997, 2004), Thelen and Smith (1998, 2006), and others (Lerner, 1991, 2002; Schneirla, 1957; Tobach & Greenberg, 1984), was Magnusson's view (1995, 1999a, 1999b; Magnusson & Endler, 1977) of the character of the relation among the components of this system: That is, holistic interaction is synonymous with *dynamic interaction*. Indeed, Magnusson and Stattin (2006, p. 434) noted that, "Functional interaction is a characteristic of the developmental processes of an individual in the life-span perspective; from the interaction that takes place between single cells in the early development of the fetus . . . to the individual's interplay with his or her environment across the lifespan."

Magnusson (1995, 1999a, 1999b; Magnusson & Stattin, 1998, 2006) noted that two key concepts are involved in understanding the character of dynamic interaction: *reciprocity* and *nonlinearity*. Magnusson and Stattin (1998, 2006) pointed to data on the mutual influences of parents and children (e.g., Lerner, Castellino, Terry, Villarruel, & McKinney, 1995) as the best illustration of reciprocity in the person–environment system. Similar to Schneirla's (1957) idea of circular functions, Magnusson and Stattin noted that reciprocity occurs in parent–child interactions. The behaviors of each person in the relationship act as an influence on the behavior of the other person. At the same time, change occurs as a consequence of the influence of the other person's behavior.

As do Thelen and Smith (1998, 2006), Magnusson (1995, 1999a, 1999b; Magnusson & Stattin, 1998, 2006) noted that nonlinearity is the prototypic characteristic of the relationship among constituents of the person–environment system. Non-systems perspectives typically approach scholarship with the perspective that the relation among variables is linear and, as well, that linear relations among variables that are identified by appraising differences between people may be generalized to the relations that exist among variables within a person (Magnusson & Stattin, 1998, 2006). However, increases (or decreases) in one variable are not always accompanied by proportional increases (or decreases) in another variable, either across people or within individuals. That is, rather than finding such linear changes to be ubiquitous, changes in one variable may be accompanied by disproportionate changes in another variable. Such relationships are curvilinear in character and, for instance, may take the form of U- or ∩-shaped functions. For example, low levels of stress may not provide enough impetus to elicit high levels of performance on a given task or skill; high levels of stress may overwhelm the person and produce performance "paralysis" rather than high-level performance; but moderate levels of stress may be associated with the greatest likelihood of high-level performance (Magnusson & Stattin, 1998, 2006; Strauss, 1982).

Together, the notions of reciprocity and nonlinearity associated with dynamic interaction underscore the bidirectional causality involved in the developmental system envisioned by Magnusson (1995, 1999a, 1999b), and return us to the point that his model challenges the key concepts of non-systems approaches to human development, even insofar as fundamental notions, such as the definition of the concept of "variable," are concerned:

> concepts of independent and dependent variables and of predictors and criteria lose the absolute meaning they have in traditional research assuming unidirectional causality. What may function as a criterion or dependent variable in statistical analyses at a certain stage of a process, may at the next stage serve as a predictor or independent variable. (Magnusson & Stattin, 2006, p. 436)

Moreover, Magnusson's theory changed the emphasis in developmental science from one of a search for information that will allow generalizations to be made about how variables function across individuals to one of attempting to understand how variables function within the person. That is, because of the nonlinear relation among variables within the individual, and because the individual's "internal" distinctiveness is both a product and a producer of his or her distinct pattern of exchanges with the other levels of organization within the total person–environment system, individual differences are a fundamental feature of human development. Indeed, to understand the development of the individual, one must identify the particular factors that are pertinent to his or her life and the specific ways these factors are organized and operate within him or her (Magnusson & Stattin, 1998, 2006). In short, "developmental changes do not take place in single aspects isolated from the totality. The total individual changes in a lawful way over time; individuals, not variables, develop" (Magnusson & Stattin, 1998, p. 727).

The complexity of this person-centered analysis is underscored when, as Magnusson (1995, 1999a, 1999b; Magnusson & Stattin, 1998, 2006) explained, one understands that the contextual component of the person–environment system is as multifaceted and individualistic as are the levels of organization having their primary loci within the individual (e.g., biology, cognition, personality, behavior). That is:

> The total, integrated, and organized person–environment system, of which the individual forms a part, consists of a hierarchical system of elements, from the cellular level of the individual to the macro level of environments . . . In actual operation, the role and functioning of each element depends on its context of other, simultaneously working components, horizontally and vertically. (Magnusson & Stattin, 2006, p. 421)

Magnusson and Stattin (1998, 2006) depicted the complexity of these contextual components of the person–environment system by noting that the environment may be differentiated on the basis of its physical and social dimensions, and that a person may be influenced by the actual and/or the perceived features of these two dimensions. Either dimension may serve as a source of stimulation for behavior and/or a resource for information. In addition, environments may differ in the extent to which they provide an optimal context for healthy development, and in regard to the extent to which they serve over time as a basis for developmental change (i.e., as a *formative* environment; Magnusson & Stattin, 1998, 2006) or as a source for a specific behavior at a particular point in time (i.e., as a *triggering* environment; Magnusson & Stattin, 1998, 2006).

In addition, environments may be differentiated on the basis of their proximal or distal relation to the person. For instance, the family or the peer group may constitute proximal contexts for the person, whereas social policies pertinent to family resources (e.g., policies regarding welfare benefits for poor families) may be part of the distal context of human development (Bronfenbrenner & Morris, 1998, 2006).

Conclusions. When the complexity of the environment is coupled with the multiple dimensions of the person (e.g., his or her biology; mental system; subconscious processes; values, norms, motives, and goals; self-structures and self-perceptions; and behavioral characteristics; Magnusson & Stattin, 1998, 2006), the need for a holistic, integrated theory of the developmental system is apparent. This system must be engaged to understand the course of human development and, as well, to enhance or optimize it. Consistent with our earlier discussions of the implications of plasticity for intervention to enhance the course of human life, Magnusson saw the need to involve all levels of the person and the system to not only design a comprehensive scientific research agenda but, as well, to devise strategies to apply developmental science in ways that will integratively promote positive human change:

> The holistic interactionistic view on individual functioning and development, as advocated here, implies that in the development of societal programs for intervention and treatment, the total person–environment system must be considered, not single problems of individual functioning and single risk factors in the social context . . . Multiple agencies, programs, and initiatives must be integrated if the breadth of the person-context system is to be adequately engaged. (Magnusson & Stattin, 1998, p. 740)

Magnusson's ideas about holistic interaction underscore the integral connection between science and application involved in a developmental systems perspective. His views of the scientific and societal utility of such theories, which are consistent with, and buttressed by, the ideas of other developmental systems theorists (e.g., Baltes et al., 1998, 2006), underscore the importance of transcending the basic science–applied science split and of discussing the integral role that application plays in contemporary theory in human developmental science.

Moreover, Magnusson's ideas emphasize that to conduct science that has applicability to policies and programs that can positively impact human development, developmental researchers must enact their science in manners that are sensitive to the diverse developmental trajectories and the participants in their studies, and to the complex and changing ecologies of human development. Only research that is sensitive to such diverse changes of individuals and their settings can hope to be useful for applications that can increase the probability of the positive direction of such time-ordered variation.

Accordingly, as illustrated by the ideas of Magnusson, the theoretical concepts we have discussed have important implications for the methods of developmental science, as well as for the application of such scholarship. As such, we will first discuss briefly the implications of developmental science theory for the methods of developmental science, and then return to the issue of how theory and methods coalesce in developmental science to promote positive human development.

METHODOLOGICAL AND APPLIED IMPLICATIONS OF DEVELOPMENTAL SYSTEMS THEORIES

The integrated levels of organization comprising the developmental system require collaborative analyses by scholars from multiple disciplines. Multidisciplinary knowledge and, ideally, interdisciplinary knowledge is sought. The temporal embeddedness and resulting plasticity of the developmental system requires that research designs, methods of observation and measurement, and procedures for data analysis be change-sensitive and able to integrate trajectories of change at multiple levels of analysis.

Representative Instances of Change-Sensitive Methodologies: Framing the Research Agenda of Human Development

What becomes, then, the key empirical question for developmental scientists interested in describing, explaining, and promoting positive human development? The key question is actually five interrelated "what" questions:

1. What attributes?; of
2. What individuals?; in relation to
3. What contextual/ecological conditions?; at
4. What points in ontogenetic, family or generational, and cohort or historical, time?; may be integrated to promote
5. What instances of positive human development?

Answering these questions requires a non-reductionist approach to methodology. Neither biogenic, psychogenic, nor sociogenic approaches are adequate. Developmental science needs integrative and relational models, measures, and designs (Lerner et al., 2005a). Examples of the use of such methodology within developmental systems-oriented research conducted about adolescent development include the scholarship of Eccles and her colleagues on stage ↔ environment fit (e.g., Eccles, Wigfield, & Byrnes, 2003); of Damon and his colleagues on the community-based youth charter (Damon, 1997, 2004; Damon & Gregory, 2003); of Theokas (2005; Theokas & Lerner, 2006; Urban, Lewin-Bizan, & Lerner, in press) on the role of actual developmental assets associated with families, schools, and neighborhoods on positive youth development; and of Leventhal and Brooks-Gunn (2004), and Sampson, Raudenbush, and Earls (1997) on the role of neighborhood characteristics on adolescent development.

The methodology employed in individual ↔ context integrative research must also include a triangulation among multiple and, ideally, both qualitative and quantitative approaches to understanding and synthesizing variables from the levels of organization within the developmental system. Such triangulation usefully involves the "classic" approach offered by Campbell and Fiske (1959) regarding convergent and discriminant validation through multitrait–multimethod matrix methodology.

Of course, diversity-sensitive measures are needed within such approaches. That is, indices need to be designed to measure change and, at the same time, to possess equivalence across temporal levels of the system (age, generation, history), across differential groups (sex, religion), and across different contexts (family, community, urban–rural setting, or culture). Moreover, to reflect the basic, integrative nature of the developmental system, researchers should seek to use scores derived from relational measures (e.g., person–environment fit scores) as their core units of analysis. Accordingly, trait measures developed with the goal of excluding variance associated with time and context are clearly not optimal choices in such research. In other words, to reflect the richness and strengths of our diverse humanity our repertoire of measures must be sensitive to the diversity of person variables, such as ethnicity, religion, sexual preferences, physical ability status, and developmental status, and to the diversity of contextual variables such as family type, neighborhood, community, culture, physical ecology, and historical moment.

Diversity- and change-sensitive measures must of course be used within the context of change-sensitive designs. Options here include longitudinal or panel designs (Cairns & Cairns, 2006; Lerner et al., 2005a; Magnusson & Stattin, 2006) and the various sequential designs proposed by Schaie (1965; Schaie & Baltes, 1975). Moreover, it is particularly important that our change-sensitive designs and measures be sensitive as well to the different meanings of time. Divisions of the x-axis in our designs—and in the analyses of our data—should be predicated on theoretical understanding or estimation of the nature of the changes prototypic of a given developmental process (Lerner et al., 2009).

For example, are the changes continuous or abrupt? For instance, are there periods of "punctuated equilibria" (e.g., Gould, 1976, 1977) that are preceded or followed by rapid change in the slope of growth? Are changes linear or curvilinear? Moreover, because understanding the developmental process is of paramount importance in such analyses, developmental scientists should consider inverting the x- and the y-axis, and make age the dependent variable in analyses of developmental process (Wohlwill, 1973). That is, if we believe that a process is linked systematically to age, we should be able to specify points along the x-axis that reflect different points in the process and these points should then be associated with distinct ages.

Not unrelated here, of course, is the selection of participants in developmental research. Theory should decide what types of youth are studied at what points in ontogenetic time. In addition, researchers should decide whether it is important theoretically to use age as the selection criterion for participants or whether different statuses along a developmental process should be used as the basis for the selection of youth and for the partitioning of participant variance.

Insightful formulations about the different meanings of time within the dynamic developmental system have been provided by Elder (1998; Elder & Shanahan, 2006), Baltes (Baltes et al., 2006), and Bronfenbrenner (2005; Bronfenbrenner & Morris, 2006). Our methods must appraise age, family, and historical time and must be sensitive to the role of both normative and non-normative historical events in influencing developmental trajectories.

Choices of data analytic procedures should also be predicated on optimizing the ability to understand the form and course of changes involving multiple variables from two or more levels of organization. Accordingly, multivariate analyses of change, involving such procedures as structural equation modeling, hierarchical linear modeling, or growth curve analysis, should be undertaken. It is important to note here that, over the course of the past decade or so, there have been enormous advances in quantitative statistical approaches, arguably especially in regard to the longitudinal methods required to appraise changing relations within the developmental system between the individual and the context (e.g., see Duncan, Magnuson, & Ludwig, 2004; Hartmann, Pelzel, & Abbott, Chapter 3, this volume; Laub & Sampson, 2004; Little, Card, Preacher, & McConnell, 2009; McArdle & Nesselroade, 2003; Molenaar, 2004; Nesselroade & Molenaar, in press; Nesselroade & Ram, 2004; Phelps, Furstenberg, & Colby, 2002; Raudenbush & Bryk, 2002; Singer & Willett, 2003; Skrondal & Rabe-Hesketh, 2004; von Eye, 1990; von Eye & Bergman, 2003; von Eye & Gutiérrez Peña, 2004; Willett, 2004; Young, Savola, & Phelps, 1991). Moreover, there has been an increased appreciation of the importance of qualitative methods, both as valuable tools for the analysis of the life course and as a means to triangulate quantitative appraisals of human development; as such, there has been a growth in the use of traditional qualitative methods, along with the invention of new qualitative techniques (e.g., Burton, Garrett-Peters, & Eaton, 2009; Giele & Elder, 1998; Mishler, 2004).

From Method and Theory to Application

To enhance the ecological validity of developmental scholarship and, as well, to increase the likelihood that the knowledge gained from research will be used in communities and families to improve the lives of young people, our research methods should be informed not only by colleagues from the multiple disciplines with expertise in the scholarly study of human development, but also by the individuals and communities we study (Burton et al., 2009; Lerner, 2002, 2004b; Villarruel, Perkins, Borden, & Keith, 2003). They too are experts about development, a point our colleagues in cultural anthropology, sociology, and community youth development research and practice recognize.

Most certainly, participants in community-based research and applications are experts in regard to the character of development within their families and neighborhoods. Accordingly, research that fails to capitalize on the wisdom of its participants runs the real danger of lacking authenticity, and of erecting unnecessary obstacles to the translation of the scholarship of knowledge generation into the scholarship of knowledge application (Jensen, Hoagwood, & Trickett, 1999).

In short, the possibility of adaptive developmental relations between individuals and their contexts and the potential plasticity of human development that is a defining feature of ontogenetic change within the dynamic, developmental system (Baltes et al., 2006; Gottlieb et al., 2006; Thelen & Smith, 2006) stands as a distinctive feature of the developmental systems approach to human development and, as well, provides a rationale for making a set of methodological choices that differ in design, measurement, sampling, and data analytic techniques from selections made by researchers using split or reductionist approaches to developmental science. Moreover, the emphasis on how the individual acts on the context to contribute to plastic relations with the context that regulate adaptive development (Brandtstädter, 2006) fosters an interest in person-centered (as compared to variable-centered) approaches to the study of human development (Magnusson & Stattin, 2006; Overton, 2006; Rathunde & Csikszentmihalyi, 2006).

Furthermore, given that the array of individual and contextual variables involved in these relations constitute a virtually open set (e.g., there may be as many as 70 trillion potential human genotypes and each of them may be coupled across life with an even larger number of life course trajectories of social experiences; Hirsch, 2004), the diversity of development becomes a prime, substantive focus for developmental science (Lerner, 2004a; Spencer, 2006). The diverse person, conceptualized from a strength-based perspective (in that the potential plasticity of ontogenetic change constitutes a fundamental strength of all humans; Spencer, 2006), and approached with the expectation that positive changes can be promoted across all instances of this diversity as a consequence of health-supportive alignments between people and settings (Benson, Scales, Hamilton, & Semsa, 2006), becomes the necessary subject of developmental science inquiry.

The conduct of such scholarship illuminates the character of the basic relational process of human development and, as well, provides information about how to promote positive human development in real-world settings, in the ecology of everyday life (Bronfenbrenner, 2005). Depending on the levels of analysis involved in the contexts being studied in relation to the developing individuals involved in a given research project, the work of providing information about the promotion of positive development may be termed "intervention research;" such research may be targeted at the level of either community programs or social policies (Lerner, 2004a). Yet, such "applied" work is at the same time the very work that is required to understand the character of (adaptive) developmental regulations. As such, within a developmental systems approach to developmental science, there is no split between theoretically predicated research about basic processes and practically important research elucidating how knowledge may be applied to foster programs or policies better able to promote positive development (Lerner, 1995, 2002, 2004a, 2005).

For instance, Jensen, et al. (1999) described an instance of such research in the arena of community-based programs aimed at enhancing mental health. Termed an "outreach scholarship" model, Jensen et al. (1999) explained how researchers and their universities collaborate with community members to go beyond demonstrating what programs could work in the abstract to identifying what mutually beneficial relations between universities and their community can produce programs that are effective in fostering mental health and, as well, are palatable, feasible, durable, affordable, and hence ultimately sustainable in communities.

The outcome of such synthetic basic ↔ applied scholarship is twofold: positive human development and social justice! At the individual level, we learn how to identify and align the developmental assets of contexts to promote positive human development among diverse individuals. For instance, in regard to youth development we can answer an optimization question such as "What contextual resources, for what youth, at what points in their adolescence, result in what features of positive youth development (PYD)?" In answering this question, we learn at the contextual level the sectors and features of the context that are needed to maximize positive development among diverse youth. For instance, Theokas and Lerner (2006) found that greater access in schools to high-quality teachers (e.g., as operationalized through lower teacher–student ratios) is linked to PYD; however, the opportunity for a youth to be in such a relation with a teacher obviously varies in relation to socioeconomic issues pertaining to a given school or school district (e.g., involving teacher salaries).

Accordingly, given that developmental science is aimed at optimization of developmental changes, as well as at description and explanation of such change (Baltes et al., 1977), theoretically predicated changes in the developmental system need to be evaluated in regard to whether positive human development can be equally promoted among individuals whose socioeconomic circumstances lower the probability of positive development. Identifying means to change the individual ↔ context relation to enhance the probability that all people, no matter their individual characteristics or contextual circumstances, move toward an equivalent chance to experience positive development is scholarship aimed at promoting social justice; that is, the opportunity within a society for all individuals to have the opportunity to maximize their chances to develop in healthy and positive ways.

In short, then, enhancing the presence of social justice in society is a necessary goal of a developmental science that is based on developmental systems theory and relational metatheory; that is concerned, therefore, with learning how to foster adaptive developmental regulations between all individuals and all contexts; and, as such, that is committed to the tripartite scientific mission of description, explanation, and optimization. Consistent with the integration of basic and applied science inherent in the developmental systems perspective, the developmental scientist, through her or his research, needs to be as much an agent of social change in the direction of social justice as a scholar seeking to understand the nomothetic and idiographic laws of human development. Indeed, without theory-predicated tests of how to foster social justice for all youth, our research will be inevitably limited in its potential generalizability and ecological validity. Without the promotion of social justice as a key scholarly goal, developmental science is critically incomplete.

CONCLUSIONS

Contemporary developmental science—predicated on a relational metatheory and focused on the use of developmental systems theories to frame research on dynamic relations between diverse individuals and contexts—constitutes a complex and exciting approach to understanding and promoting positive human development. It offers a means to do good science, informed by philosophically, conceptually, and methodologically useful information from the multiple disciplines with knowledge bases pertinent to the integrated individual ↔ context relations that compose human development. Such science is also more difficult to enact than the ill-framed and methodologically flawed research that followed split and reductionist paths taken during the prior historical era (Cairns & Cairns, 2006; Overton, 2006; Valsiner, 2006). Of course, because developmental science framed by developmental systems theory is so complex, it is also more difficult to explain to the "person in the street" (Horowitz, 2000).

The richness of the science and the applications that derive from developmental systems perspectives, as well as the internal and ecological validity of the work, are reasons for the continuing and arguably still growing attractiveness of this approach. Moreover, this approach underscores the diverse ways in which humans, in dynamic exchanges with their natural and designed ecologies, can create for themselves and others opportunities for health and positive development. As Bronfenbrenner (2005) eloquently put it, it is these relations that make human beings human.

Accordingly, the relational, dynamic, and diversity-sensitive scholarship that now defines excellence in developmental science may both document and extend the power inherent in each person to be an active agent in his or her own successful and positive development (Brandtstädter, 2006; Lerner, 1982; Lerner & Busch-Rossnagel, 1981; Lerner et al., 2005b; Magnusson & Stattin, 1998, 2006; Rathunde & Csikszentmihalyi, 2006). A developmental systems perspective leads us to recognize that, if we are to have an adequate and sufficient science of human development, we must integratively study individual and contextual levels of organization in a relational and temporal manner (Bronfenbrenner, 1974; Zigler, 1998). Anything less will not constitute adequate science. And if we are to serve individuals, families, and communities in the United States and the world through our science, if we are to help develop successful policies and programs through our scholarly efforts, then we must accept nothing less than the integrative temporal and relational model of diverse and active individuals embodied in the developmental systems perspective.

Through such research, developmental science has an opportunity to combine the assets of our scholarly and research traditions with the strengths of our people. We can improve on the often-cited idea of Lewin (1943) that there is nothing as practical as a good theory. We can, through the application of our science to serve our world's citizens, actualize the idea that nothing is of greater value to society than a science that devotes its scholarship to improving the life chances of all people. By understanding and celebrating the strengths of all individuals, and the assets that exist in their families, communities, and cultures to promote those strengths, we can have a developmental science that may, in these challenging times, help us, as a scientific body and as citizens of democratic nations, to finally ensure that there is truly liberty and justice for all.

ACKNOWLEDGMENTS

The preparation of this chapter was supported in part by grants from the National 4-H Council, the John Templeton Foundation, and the Thrive Foundation for Youth.

REFERENCES AND SUGGESTED READINGS (▭)

Anastasi, A. (1958). Heredity, environment, and the question "how"? *Psychological Review, 65*, 197–208.

Baltes, M. M., & Carstensen, L. L. (1998). Social-psychological theories and their applications to aging: From individual to collective. In V. L. Bengtson & K. W. Schaie (Eds.), *Handbook of theories of aging* (pp. 209–226). New York: Springer.

Baltes, P. B. (1987). Theoretical propositions of life-span developmental psychology: On the dynamics between growth and decline. *Developmental Psychology, 23*, 611–626.

Baltes, P. B. (1997). On the incomplete architecture of human ontogeny: Selection, optimization, and compensation as foundations of developmental theory. *American Psychologist, 52*, 366–380.

Baltes, P. B., & Baltes, M. M. (1990). Psychological perspectives on successful aging: The model of selective optimization with compensation. In P. B. Baltes & M. M. Baltes (Eds.), *Successful aging: Perspectives from the behavioral sciences* (pp. 1–34). New York: Cambridge University Press.

▭ Baltes, P. B., Lindenberger, U., & Staudinger, U. M. (1998). Life-span theory in developmental psychology. In W. Damon (Series Ed.) & R. M. Lerner (Volume Ed.), *Handbook of child psychology: Vol. 1. Theoretical models of human development* (5th ed., pp. 1029–1144). New York: Wiley.

Baltes, P. B., Lindenberger, U., & Staudinger, U. M. (2006). Life span theory in developmental psychology. In R. M. Lerner (Ed.), *Handbook of child psychology: Vol. 1. Theoretical models of human development* (6th ed., pp. 569–664). Hoboken, NJ: Wiley.

Baltes, P. B., Reese, H. W., & Lipsitt, L. P. (1980). Life-span developmental psychology. *Annual Review of Psychology, 31*, 65–110.

Baltes, P. B., Reese, H. W., & Nesselroade, J. R. (1977). *Life-span developmental psychology: Introduction to research methods*. Monterey, CA: Brooks/Cole.

Benson, P. L., Scales, P. C., Hamilton, S. F., & Semsa, A., Jr. (2006). Positive youth development: Theory, research, and applications. In R. M. Lerner (Ed.). *Handbook of child psychology: Vol. 1. Theoretical models of human development* (6th ed., pp. 894–941). Hoboken, NJ: Wiley.

Berger, P. L., Berger, B., & Kellner, H. (1967). *The homeless mind: Modernization and consciousness*. New York: Random House.

Bijou, S. W. (1976). *Child development: The basic stage of early childhood*. Englewood Cliffs, NJ: Prentice Hall.

Bijou, S. W., & Baer, D. M. (1961). *Child development: A systematic and empirical theory* (Vol. 1). New York: Appleton-Century-Crofts.

Birkel, R., Lerner, R. M., & Smyer, M. A. (1989). Applied developmental psychology as an implementation of a life-span view of human development. *Journal of Applied Developmental Psychology, 10*, 425–445.

Bloom, B. S. (1964). *Stability and change in human characteristics*. New York: Wiley.

Brandtstädter, J. (1998). Action perspectives on human development. In W. Damon (Series Ed.), & R. M. Lerner (Vol. Ed.), *Handbook of child psychology: Vol. 1. Theoretical models of human development* (5th ed., pp. 807–863). New York: Wiley.

Brandtstädter, J. (1999). The self in action and development: Cultural, biosocial, and ontogenetic bases of intentional self-development. In J. Brandtstädter & R. M. Lerner (Eds.), *Action and self-development: Theory and research through the life-span* (pp. 37–65). Thousand Oaks, CA: Sage.

Brandtstädter, J. (2006). Action perspectives on human development. In R. M. Lerner & W. Damon (Eds.), *Handbook of child psychology: Vol. 1. Theoretical models of human development* (6th ed., pp. 516–568). Hoboken, NJ: Wiley.

Brandtstädter, J., & Lerner, R. M. (Eds.). (1999). *Action and self-development: Theory and research through the life-span.* Thousand Oaks, CA: Sage.

Brent, S. B. (1978). Individual specialization, collective adaptation and rate of environment change. *Human Development, 21,* 21–33.

Brim, O. G., Jr., & Kagan, J. (1980). Constancy and change: A view of the issues. In O. G. Brim, Jr. & J. Kagan (Eds.), *Constancy and change in human development* (pp. 1–25). Cambridge, MA: Harvard University Press.

Bronfenbrenner, U. (1974). Developmental research, public policy, and the ecology of childhood. *Child Development, 45,* 1–5.

Bronfenbrenner, U. (1979). *The ecology of human development.* Cambridge, MA: Harvard University Press.

Bronfenbrenner, U. (1989). Ecological systems theory. In R. Vasta (Ed.), *Six theories of child development: Revised formulations and current issues* (pp. 185–246). Greenwich, CT: JAI Press.

Bronfenbrenner, U. (1994). Ecological models of human development. In T. Husen & T. N. Postletwaite (Eds.), *International encyclopedia of the social and behavioral science.* Oxford, UK: Elsevier.

Bronfenbrenner, U. (2001). The bioecological theory of human development. In N. J. Smelser & P. B. Baltes (Eds.), *International encyclopedia of the social and behavioral sciences* (pp. 6963–6970). Oxford, UK: Elsevier.

Bronfenbrenner, U. (2005). *Making human beings human.* Thousand Oaks, CA: Sage.

Bronfenbrenner, U., & Ceci, S. J. (1993). Heredity, environment, and the question "How?" A new theoretical perspective for the 1990s. In R. Plomin & G. E. McClearn (Eds.), *Nature, nurture, and psychology* (pp. 313–324). Washington, DC: American Psychological Association.

Bronfenbrenner, U., & Morris, P. A. (1998). The ecology of developmental process. In W. Damon (Series Ed.) & R. M. Lerner (Vol. Ed.), *Handbook of child psychology: Vol. 1. Theoretical models of human development* (5th ed., pp. 993–1028). New York: Wiley.

Bronfenbrenner, U., & Morris, P. A. (2006). The bioecological model of human development. In R. M. Lerner & W. Damon (Eds.), *Handbook of child psychology: Vol. 1. Theoretical models of human development* (6th ed., pp. 793–828). Hoboken, NJ: Wiley.

Burton, L. M., Garrett-Peters, R., & Eaton, S. C. (2009). "More than good quotations": How ethnography informs knowledge on adolescent development and contest. In R. M. Lerner & L. Steinberg (Eds.), *Handbook of adolescent psychology: Vol. 1. Individual bases of adolescent development* (3rd ed., pp. 55–91). Hoboken, NJ: Wiley.

Cairns, R. B. (1998). The making of developmental psychology. In W. Damon (Series Ed.) & R. M. Lerner (Vol. Ed.), *Handbook of child psychology: Vol. 1. Theoretical models of human development* (5th ed., pp. 419–448). New York: Wiley.

Cairns, R. B. & Cairns, B. D. (1994). *Lifelines and risks: Pathways of youth in out time.* New York: Cambridge University Press.

Cairns, R. B., & Cairns, B. D. (2006). The making of developmental psychology. In R. M. Lerner (Ed.), *Handbook of child psychology: Vol. 1. Theoretical models of human development* (6th ed., pp. 89–165). Hoboken, NJ: Wiley.

Cairns, R. B., & Hood, K. E. (1983). Continuity in social development: A comparative perspective on individual difference prediction. In P. B. Baltes & O. G. Brim, Jr. (Eds.), *Life-span development and behavior* (Vol. 5, pp. 301–358). New York: Academic Press.

Campbell, D. T., & Fiske, D. W. (1959). Convergent and discriminant validation by the multitrait–multimethod matrix. *Psychological Bulletin, 56*(2), 81–105.

Collins, W. A. (1982). *The concept of development: The Minnesota symposia on child psychology* (Vol. 15). Hillsdale, NJ: Lawrence Erlbaum Associates.

Damasio, A. R. & Damasio, H. (1996). Making images and creating subjectivity. In R. R. Llinas & P. S. Churchland (Eds.), *The mind–brain continuum: Sensory processes* (pp. 19–27). Cambridge, MA: MIT Press.

Damon, W. (1997). *The youth charter: How communities can work together to raise standards for all our children.* New York: The Free Press.

Damon, W. (2004). What is positive youth development? *Annals of the American Academy of Political and Social Science, 591,* 13–24.

Damon, W., & Gregory, A. (2003). Bringing in a new era in the field of youth development. In R. M. Lerner, F. Jacobs, & D. Wertlieb (Eds.), *Applying developmental science for youth and families—Historical and theoretical foundations: Vol. 1. Handbook of applied developmental science—Promoting positive child, adolescent, and family development through research, policies, and programs* (pp. 407–420). Thousand Oaks, CA: Sage.

Dixon, R. A., Lerner, R. M., & Hultsch, D. F. (1991). The concept of development in the study of individual and social change. In P. van Geert & L. P. Mos (Eds.), *Annals of theoretical psychology* (Vol. 7, pp. 279–323). New York: Plenum Press.

Dryfoos, J. G., Quinn, J., & Barkin, C. (Eds.). (2005). *Community schools in action: Lessons from a decade of practice.* New York: Oxford University Press.

Duncan, G. J., Magnuson, K. A., & Ludwig, J. (2004). The endogeneity problem in developmental studies. *Research in Human Development, 1*(1/2), 59–80.

Eccles, J., Wigfield, A., & Byrnes, J. (2003). Cognitive development in adolescence. In I. B. Weiner (Editor-in-Chief) & R. M. Lerner, M. A. Easterbrooks, & J. Mistry (Eds.), *Handbook of psychology: Vol. 6. Developmental psychology* (pp. 325–350). New York: Wiley.

Elder, G. H., Jr. (1998). The life course and human development. In W. Damon (Series Ed.) & R. M. Lerner (Vol. Ed.), *Handbook of child psychology: Vol. 1. Theoretical models of human development* (5th ed., pp. 939–991). New York: Wiley.

Elder, G. H., Modell, J., & Parke, R. D. (1993). Studying children in a changing world. In G. H. Elder, J. Modell, & R. D. Parke (Eds.), *Children in time and place: Developmental and historical insights* (pp. 3–21). New York: Cambridge University Press.

Elder, G. H., Jr., & Shanahan, M. J. (2006). The life course and human development. In R. M. Lerner & W. Damon (Eds.), *Handbook of child psychology: Vol. 1. Theoretical models of human development* (6th ed., pp. 665–715). Hoboken, NJ: Wiley.

Erikson, E. H. (1959). Identity and the life-cycle. *Psychological Issues, 1,* 18–164.

Featherman, D. L. (1985). Individual development and aging as a population process. In J. R. Nesselroade & A. von Eye (Eds.), *Individual development and social change: Explanatory analysis* (pp. 213–241). New York: Academic Press.

Fischer, K. W., & Bidell, T. (1998). Dynamic development of psychological structures in action and thought. In W. Damon (Series Ed.) & R. M. Lerner (Vol. Ed.), *Handbook of child psychology: Vol. 1. Theoretical models of human development* (5th ed., pp. 467–561). New York: Wiley.

Fischer, K. W., & Bidell, T. R. (2006). Dynamic development of action and thought. In W. Damon & R. M. Lerner (Eds.), *Handbook of child psychology: Vol. 1. Theoretical models of human development* (6th ed., pp. 313–399). New York: Wiley.

Fisher, C. B., Jackson, J. F., & Villarruel, F. A. (1998). The study of African American and Latin American children and youth. In W. Damon (Series Ed.) & R. M. Lerner (Vol. Ed.), *Handbook of child psychology: Vol. 1. Theoretical models of human development* (5th ed., pp. 1145–1207). New York: Wiley.

Fisher, C. B., & Lerner, R. M. (1994). Foundations of applied developmental psychology. In C. B. Fisher & R. M. Lerner (Eds.), *Applied developmental psychology* (pp. 3–20). New York: McGraw-Hill.

Ford, D. L., & Lerner, R. M. (1992). *Developmental systems theory: An integrative approach.* Newbury Park, CA: Sage.

Freud, A. (1969). Adolescence as a developmental disturbance. In G. Caplan & S. Lebovic (Eds.), *Adolescence* (pp. 5–10). New York: Basic Books.

Freud, S. (1954). *Collected works, standard edition.* London: Hogarth Press.

Freund, A. M., & Baltes, P. B. (2002). Life-management strategies of selection, optimization and compensation: Measurement by self-report and construct validity. *Journal of Personality and Social Psychology, 82,* 642–662.

Freund, A. M., Li, K. Z., & Baltes, P. B. (1999). The role of selection, optimization, and compensation in successful aging. In J. Brandtstädter & R. M. Lerner (Eds.), *Action and self-development: Theory and research through the life-span* (pp. 401–434). Thousand Oaks, CA: Sage.

Gestsdóttir, G., & Lerner, R. M. (2008). Positive development in adolescence: The development and role of intentional self regulation. *Human Development, 51,* 202–224.

Gestsdóttir, S., Lewin-Bizan, S., von Eye, A., Lerner, R. M., & Lerner, J. V. (2009). The structure and function of selection, optimization, and compensation in middle adolescence: Theoretical and applied implications. *Journal of Applied Developmental Psychology, 30,* 585–600.

Giele, J. Z., & Elder, G. H., Jr. (1998). *Methods of life course research: Qualitative and quantitative approaches.* Thousand Oaks, CA: Sage.

Gleick, J. (1987). *Chaos: Making a new science.* New York: Viking.

Gollin, E. S. (1981). Development and plasticity. In E. S. Gollin (Ed.), *Developmental plasticity: Behavioral and biological aspects of variations in development* (pp. 231–151). New York: Academic Press.

Gottlieb, G. (1992). *Individual development and evolution: The genesis of novel behavior.* New York: Oxford University Press.

Gottlieb, G. (1997). *Synthesizing nature–nurture: Prenatal roots of instinctive behavior.* Mahwah, NJ: Lawrence Erlbaum Associates.

Gottlieb, G. (2004). Normally occurring environmental and behavioral influences on gene activity: From central dogma to probabilistic epigenesis. In C. Garcia Coll, E. Bearer, & R. M. Lerner (Eds.), *Nature and nurture: The complex interplay of genetic and environmental influences on human behavior and development* (pp. 85–106). Mahwah, NJ: Lawrence Erlbaum Associates.

Gottlieb, G., Wahlsten, D., & Lickliter, R. (1998). The significance of biology for human development: A developmental psychobiological systems view. In W. Damon (Series Ed.) & R. M. Lerner (Vol. Ed.), *Handbook of child psychology: Vol. 1. Theoretical models of human development* (5th ed., pp. 233–273). New York: Wiley.

Gottlieb, G., Wahlsten, D., & Lickliter, R. (2006). The significance of biology for human development: A developmental psychobiological systems view. In R. M. Lerner & W. Damon (Eds.), *Handbook of child psychology: Vol. 1. Theoretical models of human development* (6th ed., pp. 210–257). Hoboken, NJ: Wiley.

Gould, S. J. (1976). Grades and clades revisited. In R. B. Masterton, W. Hodos, & H. Jerison (Eds.), *Evolution, brain, and behavior: Persistent problems* (pp. 115–122). New York: Lawrence Erlbaum Associates.

Gould, S. J. (1977). *Ontogeny and phylogeny*. Cambridge, MA: Belknap Press of Harvard.

Harris, D. B. (Ed.). (1957). *The concept of development*. Minneapolis, MN: University of Minnesota Press.

Hebb, D. O. (1949). *The organization of behavior*. New York: Wiley.

Hebb, D. O. (1970). A return to Jensen and his social critics. *American Psychologist*, *25*, 568.

Heckhausen, J. (1999). *Developmental regulation in adulthood: Age-normative and sociocultural constraints as adaptive challenges*. New York: Cambridge University Press.

Hernandez, D. J. (1993). *America's children: Resources for family, government, and the economy*. New York: Russell Sage Foundation.

Herrnstein, R., & Murray, C. (1994). *The bell curve: Intelligence and class structure in American life*. New York: Free Press.

Hetherington, E. M., & Baltes, P. B. (1988). Child psychology and life-span development. In E. M. Hetherington, R. M. Lerner, & M. Perlmutter (Eds.), *Child development in a life-span perspective* (pp. 1–19). Hillsdale, NJ: Lawrence Erlbaum Associates.

Hirsch, J. (1970). Behavior–genetic analysis and its biosocial consequences. *Seminars in Psychiatry*, *2*, 89–105.

Hirsch, J. (2004). Uniqueness, diversity, similarity, repeatability, and heritability. In C. Garcia Coll, E. Bearer, & R. M. Lerner (Eds.), *Nature and nurture: The complex interplay of genetic and environmental influences on human behavior and development* (pp. 127–138). Mahwah, NJ: Lawrence Erlbaum Associates.

Horowitz, F. D. (2000). Child development and the PITS: Simple questions, complex answers, and developmental theory. *Child Development*, *71*, 1–10.

Jensen, P., Hoagwood, K., & Trickett, E. (1999). Ivory towers or earthen trenches?: Community collaborations to foster "real world" research. *Applied Developmental Science*, *3*(4), 206–212.

Kagan, J. (1980). Perspectives on continuity. In O. G. Brim, Jr. & J. Kagan (Eds.), *Constancy and change in human development* (pp. 26–42). Cambridge, MA: Harvard University Press.

Kaplan, B. (1983). A trio of trials. In R. M. Lerner (Ed.), *Developmental psychology: Historical and philosophical perspectives* (pp. 185–228). Hillsdale, NJ: Lawrence Erlbaum Associates.

Kuhn, T. S. (1962). *The structure of scientific revolutions*. Chicago: University of Chicago Press.

Kuo, Z.Y. (1976). *The dynamics of behavior development: An epigenetic view*. New York: Plenum Press.

Kurtines, W. M., Ferrer-Wreder, L., Berman, S. L., Lorente, C. C., Briones, E., Montgomery, M. J., et al. (2008). Promoting positive youth development: The Miami Youth Development Project (YDP). *Journal of Adolescent Research*, *23*(3), 256–267.

Laub, J. H., & Sampson, R. J. (2004). Strategies for bridging the quantitative and qualitative divide: Studying crime over the life course. *Research in Human Development*, *1*(1/2), 81–99.

Lehrman, D. S. (1953). A critique of Konrad Lorenz's theory of instinctive behavior. *Quarterly Review of Biology*, *28*, 337–363.

Lerner, R. M. (1982). Children and adolescents as producers of their own development. *Developmental Review*, *2*, 342–370.

Lerner, R. M. (1984). *On the nature of human plasticity*. New York: Cambridge University Press.

Lerner, R. M. (1991). Changing organism–context relations as the basic process of development: A developmental–contextual perspective. *Developmental Psychology*, *27*, 27–32.

Lerner, R. M. (1995). *America's youth in crisis: Challenges and options for programs and policies*. Thousand Oaks, CA: Sage.

Lerner, R. M. (1998). Theories of human development: Contemporary perspectives. In W. Damon (Series Ed.) & R. M. Lerner (Vol. Ed.), *Handbook of child psychology: Vol. 1. Theoretical models of human development* (pp. 1–24). New York: Wiley.

Lerner, R. M. (2002). *Concepts and theories of human development*. Mahwah, NJ: Lawrence Erlbaum Associates.

Lerner, R. M. (2004a). *Liberty: Thriving and civic engagement among America's youth*. Thousand Oaks, CA: Sage.

Lerner, R. M. (2004b). Innovative methods for studying lives in context: A view of the issues. *Research in Human Development*, *1*(1), 5–7.

Lerner, R. M. (2005, September). *Promoting positive youth development: Theoretical and empirical bases*. White paper prepared for the Workshop on the Science of Adolescent Health and Development, National Research Council/Institute of Medicine. Washington, DC: National Academies of Science.

Lerner, R. M. (2006). Developmental science, developmental systems, and contemporary theories of human development. In R. M. Lerner (Ed.). *Theoretical models of human development: Vol. 1. Handbook of child psychology* (6th ed.) (pp. 1–17). Hoboken, NJ: Wiley.

Lerner, R. M. (2007). *The good teen: Rescuing adolescents from the myths of the storm and stress years*. New York: Crown.

Lerner, R. M., & Busch-Rossnagel, N. A. (1981). *Individuals as producers of their development: A life-span perspective.* New York: Academic Press.

Lerner, R. M., Castellino, D. R., Terry, P. A., Villarruel, F. A., & McKinney, M. H. (1995). A developmental contextual perspective on parenting. In M. H. Bornstein (Ed.), *Handbook of parenting: Biology and ecology of parenting* (Vol. 2, pp. 285–309). Hillsdale, NJ: Lawrence Erlbaum Associates.

Lerner, R. M., Dowling, E., & Chaudhuri, J. (2005a). Methods of contextual assessment and assessing contextual methods: A developmental contextual perspective. In D. M. Teti (Ed.), *Handbook of research methods in developmental science* (pp. 183–209). Cambridge, MA: Blackwell.

Lerner, R. M., Fisher, C. B., & Weinberg, R. A. (2000). Toward a science for and of the people: Promoting civil society through the application of developmental science. *Child Development, 71*, 11–20.

Lerner, R. M., & Kauffman, M. B. (1985). The concept of development in contextualism. *Developmental Review, 5*, 309–333.

Lerner, R. M., & Miller, J. R. (1993). Integrating human development research and intervention for America's children: The Michigan State University Model. *Journal of Applied Developmental Psychology, 14*, 347–364.

Lerner, R. M., & Overton, W. F. (2008). Exemplifying the integrations of the relational developmental system: Synthesizing theory, research, and application to promote positive development and social justice. *Journal of Adolescent Research, 23*(3), 245–255.

Lerner, R. M., Schwartz, S. J., & Phelps, E. (2009). Problematics of time and timing in the longitudinal study of human development: Theoretical and methodological issues. *Human Development, 52*(1), 44–68.

Lerner, R. M., Skinner, E. A., & Sorell, G. T. (1980). Methodological implications of contextual/dialectic theories of development. *Human Development, 23*, 225–235.

Lerner, R. M., Theokas, C., & Jelicic, H. (2005b). Youth as active agents in their own positive development: A developmental systems perspective. In W. Greve, K. Rothermund, & D. Wentura (Eds.). *The adaptive self: Personal continuity and intentional self-development* (pp. 31–47). Göttingen, Germany: Hogrefe & Huber.

Lerner, R. M., & Walls, T. (1999) Revisiting individuals as producers of their development: From dynamic interactions to developmental systems. In J. Brandtstädter & R. M. Lerner (Eds.), *Action and self-development: Theory and research through the life-span* (pp. 3–36). Thousand Oaks, CA: Sage.

Leventhal, T., & Brooks-Gunn, J. (2004). Diversity in developmental trajectories across adolescence: Neighborhood influences. In R. M. Lerner & L. Steinberg (Eds.), *Handbook of adolescent psychology* (pp. 451–486). New York: Wiley.

Lewin, K. (1943). Psychology and the process of group living. *Journal of Social Psychology, 17*, 113–131.

Lewontin, R. C. (1992). Foreword. In R. M. Lerner (Ed.), *Final solutions: Biology, prejudice, and genocide* (pp. vii–viii). University Park, PA: Penn State Press.

Little, T. D., Card, N. A., Preacher, K. J., & McConnell, E. (2009). Modeling longitudinal data from research on adolescence. In R. M. Lerner & L. Steinberg (Eds.), *Handbook of adolescent psychology: Vol. 1. Individual bases of adolescent development* (3rd ed., pp. 15–54). Hoboken, NJ: Wiley.

Lorenz, K. (1937). Ober den begriff der instinkthandlung. *Folia Biotheoretica, 2*, 17–50.

Lorenz, K. (1965). *Evolution and modification of behavior.* Chicago: University of Chicago Press.

MacDonald, K. (1985). Early experience, relative plasticity, and social development. *Developmental Review, 5*, 99–121.

Magnusson, D. (1995). Individual development: A holistic integrated model. In P. Moen, G. H. Elder, & K. Lusher (Eds.), *Linking lives and contexts: Perspectives on the ecology of human development* (pp. 19–60). Washington, DC: APA Books.

Magnusson, D. (1999a). Holistic interactionism: A perspective for research on personality development. In L. A. Pervin & O. P. John (Eds.), *Handbook of personality: Theory and research* (2nd ed., pp. 219–247). New York: Guilford Press.

Magnusson, D. (1999b). On the individual: A person-oriented approach to developmental research. *European Psychologist, 4*, 205–218.

Magnusson, D. & Endler, N. S. (1977). Interactional psychology: Present status and future prospects. In D. Magnusson & N. S. Endler (Eds.), *Personality at the crossroads: Current issues in interactional psychology* (pp. 3–31). Hillsdale, NJ: Lawrence Erlbaum Associates.

Magnusson, D., & Stattin, H. (1998). Person–context interaction theories. In W. Damon (Series Ed.) & R. M. Lerner (Vol. Ed.), *Handbook of child psychology: Vol. 1. Theoretical models of human development* (5th ed., pp. 685–759). New York: Wiley.

Magnusson, D., & Stattin, H. (2006). The person in context: A holistic–interactionistic approach. In R. M. Lerner & W. Damon (Eds.), *Handbook of child psychology: Vol. 1. Theoretical models of human devleopment* (6th ed., pp. 400–464). Hoboken, NJ: Wiley.

McArdle, J. J., & Nesselroade, J. R. (2003). Growth curve analysis in contemporary psychological research. In I. B. Weiner (Editor-in-Chief) & J. A. Schinka & W. F. Velicer (Vol. Eds.), *Handbook of psychology: Vol. 2. Research methods in psychology* (pp. 447–477). Hoboken, NJ: Wiley.

Mishler, E. G. (2004). Historians of the self: Restorying lives, revising identities. *Research in Human Development, 1*(1/2), 101–121.

Molenaar, P. C. M. (2004). A manifesto on psychology as a idiographic science: Bringing the person back into scientific psychology, this time forever. *Measurement, 2*, 201–218.

Nesselroade, J. R. & Molenaar, P. C. M. (in press). Methods—person-centered (intraindividual) & variable-centered (intervariable) approaches. In W. Overton (Vol. Ed.) & R. M. Lerner (Editor-in-Chief), *The handbook of lifespan development: Vol. 1. Cognition, Neuroscience, Methods.* Hoboken, NJ: Wiley.

Nesselroade, J. R., & Ram, N. (2004). Studying intraindividual variability: What we have learned that will help us understand lives in context. *Research in Human Development, 1*(1/2), 9–29.

Overton, W. F. (1973). On the assumptive base of the nature–nurture controversy: Additive versus interactive conceptions. *Human Development, 16*, 74–89.

Overton, W. F. (1984). World views and their influence on psychological theory and research: Kuhn-Kakatos-Lauden. In H. W. Reese (Ed.), *Advances in child development and behavior* (Vol. 18, pp. 191–225). New York: Academic.

Overton, W. F. (1998). Developmental psychology: Philosophy, concepts, and methodology. In W. Damon (Series Ed.) & R. M. Lerner (Vol. Ed.), *Handbook of child psychology: Vol. 1. Theoretical models of human development* (5th ed., pp. 107–187). New York: Wiley.

Overton, W. F. (2003). Development across the life span: Philosophy, concepts, theory. In B. Weiner (Series Ed.) and R. M. Lerner, M. A. Easterbrooks, & J. Mistry (Vol. Eds.), *Handbook of psychology: Vol. 6. Developmental psychology* (pp. 13–42). New York: Wiley.

Overton, W. F. (2006). Developmental psychology: Philosophy, concepts, and methodology. In W. Damon & R. M. Lerner (Eds.), *Handbook of child psychology, Vol. 1. Theoretical models of human development* (6th ed., pp. 18–88). New York: Wiley.

Overton, W. F., & Reese, H. W. (1973). Models of development: Methodological implications. In J. R. Nesselroade & H. W. Reese (Eds.), *Life-span developmental psychology: Methodological issues* (pp. 65–86). New York: Academic.

Overton, W. F., & Reese, H. W. (1981). Conceptual prerequisites for an understanding of stability change and continuity–discontinuity. *International Journal of Behavioral Development, 4*, 99–123.

Pepper, S. C. (1942). *World hypotheses.* Berkeley, CA: University of California.

Phelps, E., Furstenberg, F. F., & Colby, A. (2002). *Looking at lives: American longitudinal studies of the twentieth century.* New York: Russell Sage Foundation.

Piaget, J. (1950). *The psychology of intelligence.* New York: Harcourt Brace.

Piaget, J. (1970). Piaget's theory. In P. H. Mussen (Ed.), *Carmichael's manual of child psychology* (3rd ed., Vol. 1, pp. 703–723). New York: Wiley.

Plomin, R. (2000). Behavioral genetics in the 21st century. *International Journal of Behavioral Development, 24*, 30–34.

Prigogine, I. I. (1978). Time, structure, and fluctuation. *Science, 201*, 777–785.

Rathunde, K., & Csikszentmihalyi, M. (2006). The developing person: An experiential perspective. In R. M. Lerner & W. Damon (Eds.), *Handbook of child psychology: Vol. 1. Theoretical models of human development* (6th ed., pp. 465–515). Hoboken, NJ: Wiley.

Raudenbush, S. W., & Bryk, A. S. (2002). *Hierarchical linear models: Applications and data analysis methods* (2nd ed.). Thousand Oaks, CA: Sage.

Reese, H. W. (1982). Behavior analysis and developmental psychology: Discussant comments. *Human Development, 35*, 352–357.

Reese, H. W., & Overton, W. F. (1970). Models of development and theories of development. In L. R. Goulet & P. B. Baltes (Eds.), *Life-span developmental psychology: Research and theory* (pp. 115–145). New York: Academic.

Riegel, K. F. (1975). Toward a dialectical theory of development. *Human Development, 18*, 50–64.

Riegel, K. F. (1977). The dialectics of time. In N. Datan & H. W. Reese (Eds.), *Life-span developmental psychology: Dialectical perspectives on experimental research* (pp. 4–45). New York: Academic Press.

Rogoff, B. (1998). Cognition as a collaborative process. In W. Damon (Series Ed.) & R. M. Lerner (Vol. Ed.), *Handbook of child psychology: Vol. 1. Theoretical models of human development* (5th ed., pp. 679–744). New York: Wiley.

Rose, S. (1995). The rise of neurogenetic determinism. *Nature, 373*, 380–382.

Rowe, D. C. (1994). *The limits of family influence: Genes, experience, and behavior.* New York: Guilford Press.

Rushton, J. P. (2000). *Race, evolution, and behavior* (2nd special abridged edition). New Brunswick, NJ: Transaction.

Sampson, R., Raudenbush, S. W., & Earls, F. (1997). Neighborhoods and violent crime. A multilevel study of collective efficacy. *Science, 277*, 918–924.

Schaie, K. W. (1965). A general model for the study of developmental problems. *Psychological Bulletin, 64*, 92–107.

Schaie, K. W., & Baltes, P. B. (1975). On sequential strategies in developmental research: Description or explanation? *Human Development, 18*, 384–390.

Schaie, K. W., & Strother, C. R. (1968). A cross-sequential study of age changes in cognitive behavior. *Psychological Bulletin, 70*, 671–680.

Schneirla, T. C. (1956). Interrelationships of the innate and the acquired in instinctive behavior. In P. P. Grasse (Ed.), *L'instinct dans le comportement des animaux et de l'homme* (pp. 387–452). Paris: Masson et Cie.

Schneirla, T. C. (1957). The concept of development in comparative psychology. In D. B. Harris (Ed.), *The concept of development* (pp. 78–108). Minneapolis, MN: University of Minnesota.

Shweder, R. A., Goodnow, J. J., Hatano, G., LeVine, R. A., Markus, H. R., & Miller, P. J. (2006). The cultural psychology of development: One mind, many mentalities. In R. M. Lerner (Ed.), *Handbook of child psychology: Vol. 1. Theoretical models of human development* (6th ed., pp. 716–792). Hoboken, NJ: Wiley.

Singer, D., & Willett, J. B. (2003). *Applied longitudinal data analysis: Modeling change and event occurrence.* New York: Oxford University Press.

Skrondal, A., & Rabe-Hesketh, S. (2004). *Generalized latent variable modeling: Multilevel, longitudinal, and structural equation models.* Boca Raton, FL: Chapman & Hall.

Spencer, M. B. (2006). Phenomenology and ecological systems theory: Development of diverse groups. In R. M. Lerner & W. Damon (Eds.), *Handbook of child psychology, Vol. 1. Theoretical models of human development* (6th ed., 829–893). Hoboken, NJ: Wiley.

Strauss, S. (1982). *U-shaped behavioral growth.* New York: Academic Press.

Thelen, E., & Smith, L. B. (1994). *A dynamic systems approach to the development of cognition and action.* Cambridge, MA: MIT Press.

Thelen, E., & Smith, L. B. (1998). Dynamic systems theories. In W. Damon (Series Editor) & R. M. Lerner (Vol. Ed.), *Handbook of child psychology: Vol. 1. Theoretical models of human development* (5th ed., pp. 563–633). New York: Wiley.

Thelen, E., & Smith, L. B. (2006). Dynamic systems theories. In R. M. Lerner (Ed.). *Theoretical models of human development. Vol. 1. Handbook of child psychology* (6th ed., pp. 258–312). Hoboken, NJ: Wiley.

Theokas, C. (2005). *Promoting positive development in adolescence: Measuring and modeling observed ecological assets.* Unpublished dissertation. Medford, MA: Tufts University.

Theokas, C., & Lerner, R. M. (2006). Observed ecological assets in families, schools, and neighborhoods: Conceptualization, measurement, and relations with positive and negative developmental outcomes. *Applied Developmental Science, 10*(2), 61–74.

Tobach, E. (1981). Evolutionary aspects of the activity of the organism and its development. In R. M. Lerner & N. A. Busch-Rossnagel (Eds.), *Individuals as producers of their development: A life-span perspective* (pp. 37–68). New York: Academic Press.

Tobach, E., & Greenberg, G. (1984). The significance of T. C. Schneirla's contribution to the concept of levels of integration. In G. Greenberg & E. Tobach (Eds.), *Behavioral evolution and integrative levels* (pp. 1–7). Hillsdale, NJ: Lawrence Erlbaum Associates.

Urban, J., Lewin-Bizan, S., & Lerner, R. M. (2009). The role of neighborhood ecological assets and activity involvement in youth developmental outcomes: Differential impacts of asset poor and asset rich neighborhoods. *Journal of Applied Developmental Psychology, 30*(5), 601–614.

Valsiner, J. (2006) The development of the concept of development: Historical and epistemological perspectives. In R. M. Lerner (Ed.). *Handbook of child psychology: Vol. 1. Theoretical models of human development* (6th ed., pp. 166–209). Hoboken, NJ: Wiley.

Villarruel, F. A., Perkins, D. F., Borden, L. M., & Keith, J. G. (Eds.). (2003). *Community youth development: Programs, policies, and practices.* Thousand Oaks, CA: Sage.

von Bertalanffy, L. (1968). *General systems theory.* New York: Braziller.

von Eye, A. (1990). *Statistical methods in longitudinal research: Principles and structuring change.* New York: Academic Press.

von Eye, A., & Bergman, L.R. (2003). Research strategies in developmental psychopathology: Dimensional identity and the person-oriented approach. *Development and Psychopathology, 15*, 553–580.

von Eye, A., & Gutiérrez Peña, E. (2004). Configural frequency analysis—The search for extreme cells. *Journal of Applied Statistics, 31*, 981–997.

Walsten, D. (1990). Insensitivity of the analysis of variance to heredity–environment interaction. *Behavioral and Brain Sciences, 13*, 109–120.

Wapner, S. (1995). Toward integration: Environmental psychology in relation to other subfields of psychology. *Environment and Behavior, 27*, 9–32.

Werner, H. (1948). *Comparative psychology of mental development.* New York: International Universities Press.

Werner, H. (1957). The concept of development from a comparative and organismic point of view. In D. B. Harris (Ed.), *The concept of development* (pp. 125–148). Minneapolis, MN: University of Minnesota.

Willett, J. B. (2004). Investigating individual change and development: The multilevel model for change and the method of latent growth modeling. *Research in Human Development, 1*(1&2), 31–57.

Wohlwill, J. F. (1973). *The study of behavioral development.* New York: Academic Press.

Young, C. H., Savola, K. L., & Phelps, E. (1991). *Inventory of longitudinal studies in the social sciences.* Newbury Park, CA: Sage.

Zigler, E. E. (1998). A place of value for applied and policy studies. *Child Development, 69*, 532–542.

❖ 2 ❖

CULTURE IN DEVELOPMENT

Michael Cole
University of California, San Diego
Martin Packer
Duquesne University and *University of the Andes, Bogotá*

INTRODUCTION

Although it is generally agreed that the need and ability to inhabit a culturally organized environment are among the defining characteristics of human beings, it is a curious fact that until recently the role of **culture** in constituting human nature received relatively little attention in basic textbooks and leading journals, either of general or developmental psychology. This situation seems to be changing at an increasingly rapid pace. Since the early editions of this textbook, specialized handbooks and journals devoted to the topic of culture and psychology, much of it developmentally oriented, have appeared (Bornstein, 2009; Kitayama & Cohen, 2007; Valsiner & Rosa, 2007). Culturally inclusive psychological research has spawned new journals such as *Culture and Cognition* and *Culture and Psychology*, in addition to attracting more attention in major journals, some devoted specifically to development (e.g., *Human Development*) and some not (e.g., *Psychological Review* and *Psychological Bulletin*). Coverage of research featuring cultural themes has now become common in a number of introductory developmental psychology texts.

Culture: Independent Variable or Medium?

Implicit in a good deal of the extant treatment of culture in the psychological literature is the notion that culture is synonymous with cultural *difference*. This assumption is made explicit by Hinde (1987), who argued that culture is "better regarded as a convenient label for many of the diverse ways in which human practices and beliefs differ between groups" (pp. 3–4). This notion has underpinned decades of research exploring the causes and consequences of these differences in the approach known as **cross-cultural psychology**, in which culture is treated as an antecedent or independent variable that acts on psychological processes. In the past decade this emphasis on cross-cultural psychology has been complemented by what is referred to as *cultural psychology*, an approach in which culture is treated as the species-specific medium of human life within which people acquire and share symbolic meanings and practices, so that cultural contributions to psychological processes can be can be fruitfully studied among people within a given cultural group. There is currently a broad discussion about the relation between cultural psychology and cross-cultural psychology (see, e.g., Atran, Medin, & Ross,

TABLE 2.1
Cross-cultural Psychology and Cultural Psychology

Cross-cultural Psychology	Cultural Psychology
Culture as an independent variable	Culture as a medium of human life
Generally compares different cultural groups	Studies people within and between cultural groups
Uses tests and other measures in experimental or quasi-experimental settings	Uses ethnographic methods. If tests are used they are derived from local practices

2005, or Valsiner & Rosa, 2007). Some (e.g., Berry, 2000) identify **cultural psychology** as a sub-field of cross-cultural psychology which, along with indigenous psychologies and the use of the comparative method, defines the "generic field." Others are more likely to see cross-cultural research as a specific method within the toolkit of cultural psychology (Greenfield, 2000; Shweder et al., 2006; see Table 2.1).

The two approaches share a common interest in "the systematic study of relationships between the cultural context of human development and the behaviors that become established in the repertoire of individuals growing up in a particular culture" (Berry, Poortinga, & Pandey, 1997, p. x). However, differences between the two approaches influence how their practitioners go about conducting their research. Greenfield (1997, p. 306) identified the crux of the matter when she wrote that "the ideal in cultural psychology is for problems and procedures to flow from the nature of culture, both in general and specific terms." By contrast, cross-cultural psychology relies more "on the methodological armoire of psychology, rather than on the nature and practice of culture." This difference corresponds to treating culture as a medium, rather than as an independent variable (Cole & Hatano, 2007; Valsiner, 2000). There is growing discussion of the need to view culture in new ways (e.g., Atran et al., 2005).

To cover the diversity of views on this topic we organize this chapter as follows. The next section begins with a summary of alternative conceptions of culture used by psychologists concerned with culture and development. The alternatives generate different approaches to, and conclusions about, the role of culture in development. We then offer a conception of culture in relation to development that appears to be emerging as a kind of consensual meeting ground among various researchers who, however, remain diverse in their particular substantive concerns and preferred domains of research. The third section presents prominent examples of research on how culture enters into the process of development at different periods of the lifespan. This survey draws on both intra-cultural and cross-cultural studies to emphasize several points: (1) that cultural mediation of development is a universal process expressed in historically specific circumstances at different levels of social aggregation; (2) that culture and biology are intertwined in human development; and (3) that there are methodological opportunities and problems associated with the study of cultural constituents of development, both intra-culturally and cross-culturally.[1] This survey is organized in a chronological fashion, with different key issues that apply to all of development highlighted in different periods of life. We end by returning to discuss the general theoretical and methodological challenges that need to be confronted to improve our understanding of the roles of culture in development.

---

[1] For excellent, and still up-to-date, discussions focused on the methodological problems of conducting cross-cultural research on development, see Atran et al. (2005), Bornstein (1980), Greenfield (2009), and Kitayama and Cohen (2007).

CLASSICAL THEORIES OF DEVELOPMENT AND A GENERALIZED CULTURAL ALTERNATIVE

For most of the twentieth century, theories of human development could usefully be summarized by three approaches. The first held that endogenous (phylogenetic) factors dominate development, which passes through a series of invariant stages. Each stage is characterized by a qualitatively distinctive structure of the organism and a qualitatively distinct pattern of interaction between organism and environment. Gesell (1940, p. 13) wrote, for example:

> Environment . . . determines the occasion, the intensity, and the correlation of many aspects of behavior, but it does not engender the basic progressions of behavior development. These are determined by inherent, maturational mechanisms.

The causal relations of development to culture are neatly summarized in Gesell's metaphorical declaration that "Culture accumulates; it does not grow. The glove goes on the hand; the hand determines the glove" (1945, p. 358).

Gesell's ideas went out of fashion in the 1950s, but recent years have witnessed a significant revival of interest in innate biological constraints on development (Grotuss, Bjorklund, & Csinady, 2007; Pinker, 2002). Some of these approaches adopt the view that the role of the environment is restricted to "triggering" the realization of endogenous structures, whereas others emphasize ways in which culture is necessary to complete the process of development and accumulating evidence that the causal relations between culture and development travel in both directions (Li, 2007).

The view that the environment, both cultural and natural, provides the major influence on developmental change provides the traditional opposite to the endogenous view. An extreme version of this exogenous view was put forward by Skinner (1953, p. 91) in the following striking statement:

> Operant conditioning shapes behavior as a sculptor shapes a lump of clay. Although at some point the sculptor seems to have produced an entirely novel object, we can always follow the process back to the original undifferentiated lump, and we can make the successive stages by which we return to this condition as small as we wish. At no point does anything emerge which is very different from what preceded it. The final product seems to have a special unity or integrity of design, but we cannot find a point at which this suddenly appears. In the same sense, an operant is not something which appears full grown in the behavior of the organism. It is the result of a continuous shaping process.

In this view, the environment, the "sculptor," is the active agent in development, not the past coded in the genes; moreover, new forms emerge from this process in a continuous fashion. Contemporary psychologists sympathetic to an environmentalist perspective may consider Skinner's position somewhat exaggerated. The analogy between the organism and a lump of clay is especially unfortunate, because it implies a totally passive organism (contrary to Skinner's own principles!), but his emphasis on the dominant role of the environment in shaping development continues to have many adherents (e.g., Bandura, 2002; Kitayama, Duffy, & Uchida, 2007). Insofar as the "sculptor" is a metaphorical embodiment of society, all of development is engendered by processes of socialization.

Piaget, perhaps the most influential developmental theorist of the twentieth century, argued forcefully for the equal weight of endogenous and exogenous factors in development (Smith, 2002). On one hand, he asserted that "Mental growth is inseparable from physical growth; maturation of the nervous and endocrine systems, in particular, continue until the age of sixteen" (Piaget & Inhelder, 1969, p. viii). At the same time, like those who adopt an environmental shaping perspective, Piaget argued that the role of environmental input goes well beyond determining the occasioning, intensity, and correlation of behavioral aspects:

> The human being is immersed right from birth in a social environment which affects him just as much as his physical environment. Society, even more, in a sense, than the physical environment, changes the very structure of the individual . . . Every relation between individuals (from two onwards) literally modifies them. (Piaget, 1973, p. 156)

Piaget's view is often contrasted with the maturational and environmental shaping views in his emphasis on the crucial role of active organisms, which construct their own development through attempts to adapt to the environment. But culture plays a very limited role in Piaget's theory, restricted in the main to providing differing amounts of raw material for the processes of assimilation and accommodation to "feed upon" in given social circumstances.

Although they differ in the weights that they assign to phylogenetic constraints and ontogenetic experiences as well as to the importance of children's active modifications of their environments, the adherents of all three positions conceive of development as an interaction between *two* juxtaposed forces (nature/nurture, individual/environment, and phylogeny/ontogeny). Gesell, Skinner, Piaget, and their modern followers all implicitly or explicitly suggest that the environmental side of the equation can be partitioned into cultural or social factors versus the physical environment, but these distinctions are not well developed in their writings. Moreover, when culture is identified as a factor in development, it is often conceived of as separate from the organism, merely an influence acting on it (Lucariello, 1995).

A fourth view, which we adopt here, explicitly includes culture as an inseparable constituent of development. According to this cultural-mediational view, the two interacting factors in the previously described approaches do not interact directly. Rather, their interactions occur in the medium of culture—that is, biology and social experience are mediated through a third factor, culture, the accumulation of knowledge, experience, and learning of prior generations that forms the medium for development (Cole & Hatano, 2007; Li, 2007). From this perspective human development is conceived of as an emergent process of **bio-social-cultural change**, in which none of the constituents is reducible to the others.

To develop this fourth perspective, which we will use to guide the exposition of empirical issues in this chapter, it is now necessary to consider the concept of culture as it is used in current academic discourse about development.

CONCEPTIONS OF CULTURE

In its most general sense, the term "culture" refers to patterns of behavior that are passed from one generation to the next through extra-somatic means. It is the socially inherited body of past human behavioral patterns and accomplishments that serves as the resources for the current life of a social group ordinarily thought of as the inhabitants of a country or region (D'Andrade, 1996).[2] When applied to human beings, the notion of culture ordinarily assumes that its creators/bearers/users are capable of symbolic behavior. So, for example, Tylor (1874, p. 1), the titular father of anthropology, defined culture as "that complex whole which includes knowledge, belief, art, morals, law, custom, and any other capabilities and habits

---

[2] Note that when defined in this abstract fashion, many creatures besides human beings exhibit cultural modes of behavior (McGrew, 2002).

acquired by man as a member of society." Tylor's conception is echoed by Herskovitz's (1948, p. 17) widely used definition of culture as "the man made part of the environment."

In trying to specify more carefully the notion of culture as social inheritance, anthropologists have historically tended to emphasize culture either as "something out there," as the term "man made part of the environment" implies, or as "something inside the head," as the terms "knowledge" and "beliefs" imply. As D'Andrade has noted, during the first half of the twentieth century the notion of culture as something "superorganic" and material dominated anthropological thinking. However, as part of the "cognitive revolution" in the social sciences, the pendulum shifted, so that for several decades the "culture-as-knowledge" view has reigned. This view is most closely associated with the work of Goodenough, for whom culture consists of "what one needs to know to participate acceptably as a member in a society's affairs" (Goodenough, 1994, p. 265). This knowledge is acquired through learning and, consequently, is a mental phenomenon. As Goodenough (1976, p. 5) put it:

> in anthropological practice the culture of any society is made of the concepts, beliefs, and principles of action and organization that an ethnographer has found could be attributed successfully to the members of that society in the context of dealing with them.

From this perspective culture is profoundly subjective. It is in people's minds, the mental/symbolic products of the social heritage.

Other anthropologists, as well as psychologists, are seeking to transcend this "ideal versus material culture" dichotomy. In an oft-quoted passage, Geertz (1973, p. 45) wrote that his view of culture begins with the assumption that:

> human thought is basically both social and public—that its natural habitat is the house yard, the market place, and the town square. Thinking consists not of "happenings in the head" (though happenings there and elsewhere are necessary for it to occur) but of trafficking in . . . significant symbols—words for the most part but also gestures, drawings, musical sounds, mechanical devices like clocks.

In recent years it has become common to see efforts to combine the "culture is out there/material" and the "culture is in here/mental" views in definitions of culture. For example, Shweder and his colleagues (2006) define human culture as *both* a symbolic *and* a behavioral inheritance:

> The *symbolic inheritance* of a cultural community consists of its received ideas and understandings . . . about persons, society, nature, and the metaphysical realm of the divine . . . [whereas] the behavioral inheritance of a cultural community consists of its routine or institutionalized family life, social, economic, and political practices. (pp. 719–720; emphasis in original)

Weisner and his colleagues developed a similar perspective. For example, Weisner (1996) argued that the locus for cultural influences on development is to be found in the activities and practices of daily routines that are central to family life. The relation between individuals and activities is not unidirectional, however, because participants take an active role in constructing the activities in which they participate. Consequently, "the subjective and objective are intertwined" in culturally organized activities and practices (Gallimore, Goldenberg, & Weisner, 1993, p. 541).

Our own way of transcending the ideal–material dichotomy with respect to culture is inspired by the work of the Russian "cultural–historical school of psychology" (Vygotsky, 1987). It is to think of the cultural medium as both material and mental. It is a species-specific medium in which human beings live as an environment transformed by the **artifacts** of prior generations, extending back to the beginning of the species (Cole & Hatano, 2007). The basic function of these artifacts is to coordinate human beings with the physical world and each other; in the aggregate, culture is then seen as the species-specific *medium* of human development: as, so to speak, "history in the present." Because artifact mediation was present hundreds of thousands of years prior to the emergence of *Homo sapiens*, it is not appropriate to juxtapose human biology and human culture. The human brain and body co-evolved over a long period of time within our species' increasingly complex cultural environment (Li, 2007; Plotkin, 2002; Quartz & Senjowski, 2002).

As Geertz (1973, p. 68) pointed out, as a result of their tangled relations in the course of human phylogeny culture and biology are equally tangled in the course of human ontogeny, disallowing a superficial view of the role of culture in human nature:

> Rather than culture acting only to supplement, develop, and extend organically based capacities logically and genetically prior to it, it would seem to be ingredient to those capacities themselves. A cultureless human being would probably turn out to be not an intrinsically talented though unfulfilled ape, but a wholly mindless and consequently unworkable monstrosity.

It is important to keep in mind this long-term, phylogenetic perspective when considering the ontogeny of children, for it reminds us that causal influences do not run unidirectionally from biology to culture. Rather, human beings are hybrids of phylogenetic, cultural–historical, and ontogenetic sources (Cole & Hatano, 2007; Li, 2007; Wertsch, 1985).

For this perspective to be useful it is essential to understand how the artifacts that constitute culture-as-medium are combinations of the conceptual/ideal and the material, because it is this combination that makes necessary the linking of phylogeny and cultural history in ontogeny. On one hand, artifacts have a mental/ideal/conceptual aspect in that they embody goal-directed interactions of which they were previously a part and which they mediate in the present (e.g., the structure of a pencil carries within it the history of representing spoken language in a different medium, manufacturing processes, communicative practices, and so forth). On the other hand they are embodied in material form, whether in the morphology of a spoken or written or signed word, or in a solid object such as a pencil. D'Andrade (1986, p. 22) made this point when he said that "Material culture—tables and chairs, buildings and cities—is the reification of human ideas in a solid medium." As a consequence of the dual conceptual–material nature of the systems of artifacts that are the cultural medium of their existence, human beings live in a double world, simultaneously natural and artificial. Hence, the environment into which children are born is more than a material world; both the mental and the material aspects of that world envelop the developing child.

This conception of the relation between culture and the special properties of human nature was expressed in particularly powerful language by the American anthropologist White (1942, p. 372):

> Man differs from the apes, and indeed all other living creatures so far as we know, in that he is capable of symbolic behavior. With words man creates a new world, a world of ideas and philosophies. In this world man lives just as truly as in the physical world of his senses . . . This world comes to have a continuity and a permanence that the external world of the senses can never have . . . Temporally, it is not a succession of disconnected episodes, but a continuum extending to infinity in both directions, from eternity to eternity.[3]

---

[3] It would be an error, in view of decades of work on proto-cultural features among primates, to overstate the discontinuities between *Homo sapiens* and other species (Premack & Hauser, 2006). Hinde (1987) argued that these phenomena do not imply culture in the way in which human beings have culture. We concur, even though we disagree with his identification of culture only with difference.

Among other properties White attributes to culture in this passage, his emphasis on the way it creates an (artificial) continuity between past and future merits special attention, as we show later. It is also significant that both White and Soviet cultural–historical psychologists (e.g., Luria, 1928; Vygotsky, 1987) emphasize that, as mediators of human action, all artifacts can be considered tools. As White (1959, p. 236) expressed the relation:

> An axe has a subjective component; it would be meaningless without a concept and an attitude. On the other hand, a concept or attitude would be meaningless without overt expression, in behavior or speech (which is a form of behavior). Every cultural element, every cultural trait, therefore, has a subjective and an objective aspect.

There are a great many suggestions about the forms taken by the artifacts in terms of which culture operates as a constituent of human activity. One well-known formulation offered by Geertz is that culture should be conceived of by analogy with recipes or computer programs: what he referred to as "control mechanisms." A complementary notion of artifacts constitutive of the medium of culture is offered by D'Andrade, who suggested the term "cultural schemes" to refer to units that mediate entire sets of conceptual–material artifacts. In D'Andrade's (1984, p. 93) terms:

> Typically such schemes portray simplified worlds, making the appropriateness of the terms that are based on them dependent on the degree to which these schemes fit the actual worlds of the objects being categorized. Such schemes portray not only the world of physical objects and events, but also more abstract worlds of social interaction, discourse, and even word meaning.

Finally, psychologists such as Bruner (1990) and Nelson (1981, 2007) identified "event schemas" embodied in narratives as basic organizers of both culture and cognition. Referred to as "scripts" by Nelson, these generalized event schemas specify the people who participate in an event, the social roles that they play, the objects that are used during the event, the sequences of actions required, the goals to be attained, and so on. Nelson's account of scripted activity is similar in many ways to Geertz's and D'Andrade's suggestions for basic units of cultural structure. Her emphasis on the fact that children grow up inside of other people's scripts, which serve as guides to action before the children are ready to understand and execute culturally appropriate actions on their own, leads naturally to her conclusion that "the acquisition of scripts is central to the acquisition of culture" (Nelson, 1981, p. 110).

A Developmentally Relevant Conception of Culture

The properties of culture-as-medium discussed so far—its foundation in artifact-mediated human activities, its co-evolution with the human brain and body, the dual material–conceptual nature of artifacts, the close relation (perhaps identity) of artifact and tool, and (as noted by White in the quotation above) the unique time extension provided by the medium—are all important to understanding the relation between culture and development. Not only the past and present, but the child's future, are present at the child's birth.

In thinking about culture as it relates to development, we have found it useful to begin with the intuitive notion underlying this word, as it has evolved since entering English from Latin many centuries ago (Cole, 1996). As Williams (1973, p. 87) noted, the core features that coalesce in modern conceptions of culture originate in terms that refer to the process of helping things to grow: "Culture, in all of its early uses was a noun of process: the tending of something, basically crops or animals." From earliest times the notion of culture included a general theory of how to promote development: Create an artificial environment in which young organisms could be provided optimal conditions for growth. Such tending required tools, both material (hoes) and knowledge (don't plant until winter is over), perfected over generations and designed for the special tasks to which they were put.

Although it would be foolish to over-interpret the metaphorical parallels between the theory and practice of growing next generations of crops and next generations of children, the exercise has considerable heuristic value. To begin with, the properties that one associates with gardens bear some obvious affinities to classical definitions of culture offered by anthropologists. A garden conceived of as an artificial environment-for-growing-living-things is, as classical definitions of culture emphasize, a "complex whole," and gardening requires both knowledge and beliefs, as well as material tools.

The **garden metaphor of culture** is also useful because it reminds us that gardeners must attend not only to a specialized form of environment created inside the garden but also to the ecological circumstances surrounding the garden. These two classes of concern often seem to be addressable independently of each other, but in reality they are interdependent, as a long tradition of research in ecological psychology has emphasized (Barker, 1968; Heft, 2003; Tudge, 2008; Turvey, 2009). Ecological psychologists' uses of the term "ecological" orient us to the interdependence of each component within a system as well as between the sub-system of interest and its context. Although it is possible to raise any plant anywhere in the world, given the opportunity first to arrange the appropriate set of conditions, it is not always possible to create the right conditions, even for a short while. So, if one is interested in the creation of conditions that not only enhance the needed properties of the artificial (cultural) environment but do so in a sustainable way, then it is essential to attend to how the system in which the garden is embedded shapes the properties of the garden itself.

Inside the garden one must consider the quality of the soil, the best way to till the soil, the right kinds of nutrients to use, the proper amount of moisture, as well as the best time to plant and nurture the seeds, and the need to protect growing plants against predators, disease, and so forth. Each of these tasks has its own material needs, associated tools, beliefs, and knowledge. Consequently, the theory and practice of development require us to focus on finding exactly the right combination of factors to promote development within the garden walls.

With respect to gardens, we can note that, in addition to having a wall separating them from their surroundings, they also have internal organization; different plants are not scattered at random within the garden walls. And so it is with culture. As Super (1987, p. 5) commented:

> Rarely in the developmental sciences . . . does theory acknowledge that environments have their own structure and internal rules of operation, and thus, that what the environment contributes to development is not only isolated, unidimensional pushes and pulls but also structure.

Humanizing the Garden Metaphor

Although the garden metaphor is useful for thinking about culture and development because it emphasizes the fact that human beings live in an artificial environment, and that cultures exist within, are shaped by, and in turn shape their ecological settings, it fails to consider the fact that human beings are not plants; nor does it capture several aspects of modern conceptions of culture that need to be elaborated in the study of development. Fortunately, modern theorizing about culture and development suggests parallels between the metaphor of garden-as-culture and the cultural organization of human development.

For example, Super and Harkness (1997) used the term **developmental niche** to refer to the child's location within the complex set of socio-cultural–ecological relations that form the proximal environment of development. Developmental niches are analyzed in terms of three components: (1) the physical and social settings in which the child lives, (2) the culturally regulated childrearing and socialization practices of the child's society, and (3) the psychological characteristics of the child's parents, especially parental theories about the process of child development and their affective orientation to the tasks of childrearing. Super and Harkness emphasized that these three components of the developmental niche operate in (imperfect) coordination with each other, providing the proximal structured medium through which children experience the world (see Gauvain, 2005, for a similar argument).

As the work of cultural psychologists clearly indicates, a "developmental niche" is roughly synonymous with a "life world." It incorporates many "micro niches" which include not only the circumstances where children are in close proximity to their parents, who might be thought to "mold" their behavior, but also the range of activities that their parents choose for them to experience (Whiting, 1980). Simple examples of such indirect parental influences over enculturation include the differential work roles assigned to boys and girls in agricultural and industrialized societies and decisions about whether and which children attend school, and if so for how long (Tudge, 2008).

Before proceeding to the issue of how culture-as-medium enters into the process of onto-genetic development, we need to address two important issues: First, the question of cultural variability, and especially the issue of **cultural evolution**; and second, the question of the "level" of the social unit to which the term "culture" is applied.

Tylor (1874), whose notion of culture was discussed earlier, believed that cultures could be classified according to their level of development, and characterized by the sophistication of their technology, the complexity of their social organization, and similar criteria, a view referred to in the literature as *cultural evolution*. He assumed in addition that all people are born with the same potential to use culture (an assumption dubbed the *doctrine of psychic unity* in anthropology) but that certain societies developed more fully than others, with industrialized societies at the top of the heap. Combining these two assumptions with the assumption that the cultural traits observed in various cultures were arrived at through a process of independent invention, Tylor believed that he could reconstruct the stages of development of humankind through a comparative analysis of societies at different levels of cultural development.[4]

This line of thinking (discussed at greater length in Cole, 1996; Jahoda, 1993; Laboratory of Comparative Human Cognition, 1983) fit with and gave respectability to the idea that the members of societies judged to be at an earlier stage of cultural evolution were also at an earlier stage of mental development. Captured in the colorful phrase that "primitives think like children," this belief in the mental superiority of people living in industrially advanced countries was held by a vast majority of nineteenth- and early twentieth-century psychologists, anthropologists, and sociologists, and remains a serious issue in the study of culture and development (Hallpike, 1979; Jahoda, 1993).

Despite its modern-sounding claim that there is an intimate relation between culture and thought, this unilinear theory of cultural–mental evolution has long had its critics, starting with Herder (1784/1803), who argued that the history of a culture can only be understood with respect to the specific development of single peoples and communities; general comparisons are deceiving. This idea of the historical specificity of cultures came into modern anthropology largely through the work of Boas (1911), one of the first major figures in

---

[4] Tylor (1874) acknowledged, but did not build on, the fact that "if not only knowledge and art, but at the same time moral and political excellence be taken into consideration, it becomes more difficult to scale societies from lower to higher stages of culture" (p. 29).

anthropology to do fieldwork in societies outside of Europe (see Stocking, 1968, for an interpretive account of Boas' contribution to modern thinking about culture).

Boas conducted research among the peoples of the American and Canadian Northwest with the objective of obtaining first-hand evidence about their technology, language use, art, custom, and myth to determine the empirical validity of evolutionary theorizing. His findings shattered his initial expectations. On the basis of comparative ethnographic data, Boas concluded that borrowing from other groups was a major source of cultural traits among the peoples he studied, undermining the basis for historical reconstruction. Moreover, the within-society heterogeneity of cultural traits contradicted either a simple diffusionist or independent-invention account of cultural change: Tribes with similar languages were found to have quite different customs and beliefs, and tribes with quite different languages were found to have very similar customs and beliefs. Assignment of societies to particular cultural levels was undermined by the great heterogeneity of levels of complexity in different domains of life in a single society. Among the Kwakiutl, for example, the graphic arts revealed a quite abstract way of representing natural forms whereas the technology was relatively unsophisticated.

From these and other observations, Boas concluded that each culture represents a combination of locally developed and borrowed features, the configurations of which are adaptations to the special historical circumstances of the group. Because all societies are characterized by heterogeneous constituent elements with respect to any single criterion of development, and because all societies can be considered equally valid responses to their own historically and ecologically posed problems of survival, there can be no basis for comparisons across societies with respect to *general* levels of development. Such comparisons illegitimately tear aspects of a culture out of context as if these aspects played an equivalent role in the life of the people being compared, when they do not.

Adopting Boas' position has direct implications for how one studies culture and development. It means that if we want to understand a behavior being manifested in any particular cultural context, we need to know the way that this context fits into the pattern of life experiences of the individuals being studied, as well as into the past history of interactions between and within cultures that have shaped the contexts where we make our observations. To fail to consider a behavior in its cultural–historical context is to risk misinterpreting its meaning, and hence its overall psychological significance for the people involved. (See Rogoff, 2003, for an elaboration of this point.)

From this rather truncated discussion of conceptions of culture, we can abstract the following essential points.

1. Culture is the residue in the present of past human activity in which human beings have transformed nature to suit their own ends and passed the cumulated artifacts down to succeeding generations in the form of tools, rituals, beliefs, and ways of conceiving of the world in general. The subjective/ideal and objective/material aspects of culture are inextricably interconnected.
2. Culture is not a random assortment of artifacts; it comes packaged in the form of conceptual systems, social institutions, and a multitude of values—acceptable ways of feeling and behaving in a wide variety of activities. The proximal environment of cultural influences on development consists of activities and practices that can be thought of as a "developmental niche."
3. Culture is a medium. When culture is treated as an independent variable, severe methodological difficulties can arise that compromise the ability of analysts to make clear inferences about causation. Despite these difficulties, varieties of cultural configurations, associated with different historical experiences (where "history" is assumed to

extend back to the first creatures dubbed *Homo sapiens* although we have written records dating back only a few thousand years), make it tempting to treat cultures as independent variables and to privilege observations based on standardized methods instead of making comparisons secondary to locally derived procedures. When cultural variations are studied conceiving of culture as an antecedent, independent variable, the fact that cultures are organized patterns of artifacts means that it will prove difficult or impossible to unpackage them to determine precisely which aspects of culture contribute to the development of particular behavioral outcomes (Whiting, 1976, referred to culture used in this way as a "packaged variable"). In the sections that follow we illustrate these and other psychologically important aspects of culture in development and some of the analytic dilemmas they pose.

The Socially Distributed Nature of Culture

When Mead went to study the people of Samoa and New Guinea in the 1920s and 1930s, it was generally assumed that a culture was widely shared by the adult population. In fact, it was thought to be sufficiently homogeneous that one could talk to a small number of people and generalize to all the people sharing that cultural system. In terms of the garden metaphor, this would be as if all the plants in a garden were the same and all grew at a uniform rate and developed into identical "cultural" clones of each other. Today, it is widely recognized among anthropologists that cultural knowledge is only partially shared, even among members of small face-to-face societies who have lived together over many generations (Romney & Moore, 2001). Within a garden, each plant has its own interaction with its own, intensely local, "micro-climate." Thus, heterogeneity within culturally defined populations ought to be taken into account in any cross-cultural investigation. Only rarely has this been done in developmental research (Medin, Unsworth, & Hirschfeld, 2007).

Level of culture is important, and as a final preliminary consideration concerning the notion of culture in relation to human development, it has long been realized that it is essential to consider what are termed "levels of the environment," ranging from the proximal and local to the distant and global (Bronfenbrenner, 1979; Laboratory of Comparative Human Cognition, 1983). With respect to understanding the role of culture in cognitive development we find it helpful to consider the processes involved in terms of three levels of social groupings: human beings as a mammalian species, societies (thought of as the population of a particular geographical and political region that exhibits common cultural features), and **cultural practices** (thought of as recurrent ways of accomplishing valued social activities in concert with some group of one's proximally circumscribed social unit). These levels are not independent of each other. It is helpful to think of each "smaller" unit of cultural analysis as embedded within the more inclusive levels both spatially (in terms of the number of people involved) and temporally (in terms of time span over which the given cultural feature or formation has existed). Just as geopolitically defined populations can be thought of as branches of a tree of human life extending back to *Australiopithecus*, all of which involve the mediation of experience by culture, so the different cultural practices within a society represent variations in the ways that people organize their everyday lives within the set of possibilities to be found in highly similar ecological circumstances. As a consequence, specifying the linkages among specific cultural practices within more inclusive sociocultural formations, and the linkages of those sociocultural formations within historically formed modes of life, is a major ongoing challenge to the study of culture and development. We will attempt to illustrate how this challenge is currently addressed in the examples of research presented in later sections.

Figure 2.1 (see over) represents the relations in cultural psychology.

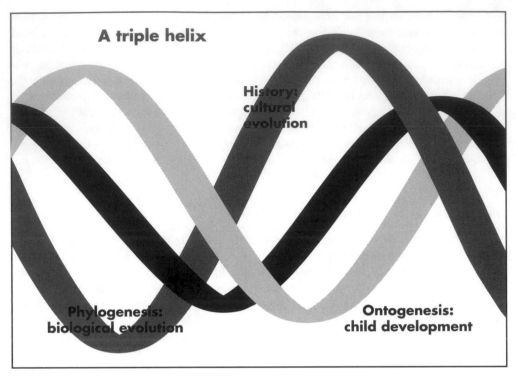

FIGURE 2.1   Cultural psychology studies the interrelations among history (cultural evolution), phylogenesis (biological evolution), and ontogenesis (child development).

TRACKING A DYNAMICAL SYSTEM OVER TIME

One enormous challenge facing students of development in general, and human development in particular, is that they seek to explain the lawful changes in the properties of a complex, interacting system in which different aspects of the system are themselves developing at different rates. As a means of orienting ourselves in attempting to describe this process of growth, we employ a framework proposed by Emde, Gaensbauer and Harmon (1976), who in turn were influenced by what Spitz (1958) called *genetic field theory*. Emde et al.'s basic proposal was to study developmental change as the emergent synthesis of several major factors interacting over time. In the course of their interactions, the dynamic relations among these factors appear to give rise to qualitative rearrangements in the organization of behavior that Emde and his colleagues referred to as *bio-behavioral shifts*. Cole and Cole (1989) expanded on this notion by referring to **bio-social-behavioral shifts** because, as the work of Emde and colleagues shows quite clearly, every bio-behavioral shift involves changes in relations between children and their social world as an integral part of the changing relations between their biological makeup and their behavior. Cole and Cole also emphasized that the interactions out of which development emerges always occur in cultural contexts, thereby implicating all of the basic contributors to development that a cultural approach demands.

In this section, we present a series of examples illustrating how culture is central to the process of development, focusing on major developmental periods and bio-social-behavioral shifts between periods. To keep this chapter within the scope of normal developmental study, we choose examples from broad age periods that, if perhaps not universal stages of development, are very widely recognized in a variety of cultures (Whiting & Edwards, 1988). The examples have been chosen for a variety of reasons. In some cases, our goal is to illustrate one or another universal process through which culture enters into the constitution of developmental stages and the process of change. In other cases, examples are chosen to highlight the impact of particular configurations of cultural mediation. Yet other examples highlight the special difficulties scientists must cope with when they focus on culture in development.

We adopt this strategy because, owing to restrictions on length, we cannot hope to treat all of the relevant issues at every age level. Instead, we have opted to emphasize particular aspects of culture–development relations at different points in the temporal trajectory from conception to adulthood. What is really called for is a life-span perspective in which the manifestations of all of the basic ideas are present, in varied configurations, at all ages.

Prenatal Development: The Cultural Organization of Development

It might seem capricious to begin an examination of cultural influences on development with the prenatal period. After all, the child does not appear to be in contact with the environment until birth. This view is implicit in Leiderman, Tulkin, and Rosenfeld's (1977) introduction to *Culture and Infancy*, which begins with the assertion that "the human environment is inescapably social. From the moment of birth, human infants are dependent on others for biological survival" (p. 1). A little reflection will reveal that the same can be said of prenatal development, with the proviso that the child's experience is, for the most part, mediated by the biological system of the mother. We need the proviso "for the most part" because there is increasing evidence that prenatal humans are sensitive to, and are modified by, culturally organized events occurring in the environment of the mother. The best documented way in which the cultural organization of the mother's experience influences the development of her child is through the selection of food and other substances that she ingests. Current public attention to the devastating effects of alcohol, cigarette smoke, and drug ingestion provides an obvious and painful reminder of cultural effects on prenatal development with long-term consequences (for a summary, see Cole, Cole, & Lightfoot, 2005, pp. 85ff.). At a more mundane level, research in both industrialized and non-industrialized societies demonstrates that beliefs about appropriate foods for expectant mothers are quite variable in ways that are likely to influence such important indicators of development as birth weight and head size. In one of the few intra-cultural studies on this topic, Jeans, Smith, and Stearns (1955) compared the health of babies born to mothers whose diets were judged as either "fair to good" or "poor to very poor." The women were all from a single rural area and did not differ in any indices of social class; it was their choice of foods that differed. The mothers judged as having fair to good diets had markedly healthier babies. When social class does differ, and with it the associated nutritional status of mothers and their offspring, the consequences can be devastating, including death of the infant (Pollitt, Saco-Pollitt, Jahari, Husaini, & Huang, 2000).

There is also reasonably good evidence that pregnant women who inhabit stressful environments have more irritable babies (Chisholm, Burbank, Coall, & Gemmiti, 2005; Leigh & Milgrom, 2008). For example, Chisholm and his colleagues have shown that Navajo women who live within Navajo communities rather than Anglo areas have less irritable babies. Chisholm provided suggestive data implicating high blood pressure resulting from the stress of living in fast-paced and generally unsupportive urban centers dominated by Anglos as the cause of increased infant irritability.

With the advent of modern medical technologies there is an obvious new source of cultural influence on prenatal development through genetic screening techniques, especially the ability to learn the gender of the expected child. In a number of countries selective abortion of females is being reported, where previously female infanticide practices were delayed until the child made its appearance (Sharma, 2003).

More benignly, there is also ample evidence that prenatal humans are sensitive to, and are modified by, the language spoken in the environment of the mother (Kisilevsky et al., 2009; Lecanuet, Graniere-Deferre, Jacquet, & DeCasper, 2000; Mastropieri & Turkewitz, 1999; Mehler, Dupoux, Nazzi, & Dehaene-Lambertz, 1996).

Birth: Evidence for a Universal Mechanism of Cultural Mediation

The realignment of biological, social, and behavioral factors at birth makes it perhaps the most dramatic bio-social-behavioral shift in all development. There is ample evidence of great cultural variation in the organization of the birthing process (Newburn, 2003), but it is also the case that this fundamental transition provides some of the clearest evidence of universal mechanisms relating culture to development (Richardson & Guttmacher, 1967).

When babies emerge from the birth canal and the umbilical cord is cut, their automatic supply of oxygen and nutrients comes to an abrupt halt. Neonates are no longer bound to their environments through a *direct* biological connection. Following birth, even essential biological processes occur *indirectly*—they are mediated by culture and other human beings. The baby's food no longer arrives predigested through the mother's bloodstream, but neither, generally speaking, is it raw. Rather, it is transformed by a preparative process that is neither purely biological nor purely natural, a process that has been shaped as an integral part of the cultural history of the group.

To survive in an environment mediated by culture, the baby must act on the nurturing environment in a qualitatively different way than was true before birth. This is not to say that the baby is ever inactive. With the beginning heartbeat early in embryogenesis, the organism becomes and remains active until it dies. Without such activity during the prenatal period, more complicated neural circuits needed for coordinated movement and thought could not develop adequately. However, the effects of fetal activity on the environment inside and outside its mother's womb are minimal.

Following birth, changes in babies' impact on their environments are no less marked than changes in the way the environment acts on them. They make urgent, vocal demands on their caregivers. They become social actors who reorder the social relationships among the people around them. At birth, *development becomes a co-constructive process* in which *both* the social environment *and* the child are active agents (Valsiner, 2000).

From existing ethnographic evidence, we know that both the mother's and child's experiences at birth vary considerably across societies of the world according to cultural traditions that prescribe the procedures to be followed in preparation for, during, and after the birth. In a few societies, birthing is treated as a natural process that requires no special preparation or care. Shostak (1981) recorded the autobiography of a !Kung-san woman living in the Kalahari desert in the middle of the last century who reported that she observed her mother simply walk a short way out of the village, sit down against a tree, and give birth to her brother. In most societies, however, birthing is treated as dangerous (and in some places as an illness), requiring specialized help (see Cole, Cole, & Lightfoot, 2005, p. 95, for additional examples and references).

Rather than concentrate on the potential consequences of these cultural variations in birthing practices, we focus on the way that birth provides evidence of a universal mechanism of cultural mediation of development—the process through which the ideal side of culture is transformed into material–cultural organization of the child's environment. This example (taken from the work of pediatrician MacFarlane, 1977) also demonstrates in a particularly clear fashion White's point that culture provides a specifically human form of temporal continuity.

Figure 2.2 presents in schematic form five different time scales simultaneously operating at

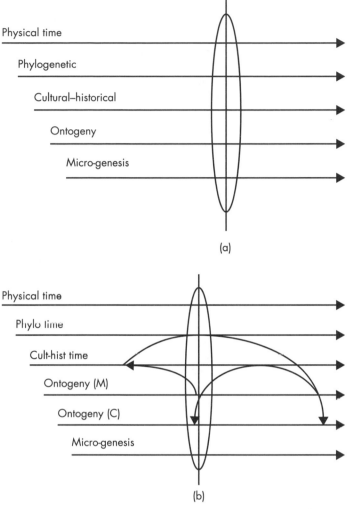

FIGURE 2.2   (a) The kinds of time in effect at the moment a child is born (marked by the vertical line). (b) How culture is converted from an ideational or conceptual property of the mother into a material or interactional organization of the baby's environment. Note that two ontogenies are included, the mother's and the baby's. The curved lines depict the sequence of influences: The mother thinks about what she knows about girls from her (past) cultural experience; she projects that knowledge into the child's future (indicated by remarks such as "It will never be a rugby player"); this ideal or conceptual future is then embodied materially in the way the mother interacts with the child.

the moment at which parents see their newborn for the first time. The vertical ellipse represents the events immediately surrounding birth, which occurs at the point marked by the vertical line. At the top of the figure is what might be called physical time, or the history of the universe that long precedes the appearance of life on earth.

The bottom four time lines correspond to the developmental domains that, according to the cultural psychological framework espoused here, simultaneously serve as major constraints for human development (Cole, 2006). The second line represents phylogenetic time, the history of life on earth, a part of which constitutes the biological history of the newborn individual. The third line represents cultural–historical time, the residue of which is the child's cultural heritage. The fourth line represents ontogeny, the history of a single human being, which is the usual object of psychologists' interest. The fifth line represents the moment-to-moment time of lived human experience, the event called "being born" (from the perspective of the child) or "having a baby" (from the perspective of the parents) in this case. Four kinds of genesis are involved: **phylogenesis**, cultural–historical genesis, **ontogenesis**, and microgenesis, with each lower level embedded in the level above it.

MacFarlane's example reminds us to keep in mind that not one but two ontogenies must be represented in place of the single ontogeny in Figure 2.2a. That is, at a minimum one needs a mother and a child interacting in a social context for the process of birth to occur and for development to proceed. These two ontogenies are coordinated in time by the simultaneous organization provided by phylogeny and culture (Figure 2.2b).

Now consider the behaviors of the adults when they first catch sight of their newborn child and discover if the child is male or female. Typical comments include "I shall be worried to death when she's eighteen," or "She can't play rugby." In each of these examples, the adults interpret the biological characteristics of the child in terms of their own past (cultural) experience. In the experience of English men and women living in the mid-20th century, it could be considered common knowledge that girls do not play rugby and that when they enter adolescence they will be the object of boys' sexual attention, putting them at various kinds of risk. Using this information derived from their cultural past and assuming that the world will be very much for their daughters what it has been for them, parents project probable futures for their children. This process is depicted in Figure 2.2b by following the arrows from the mother to the cultural past of the mother to the cultural future of the baby to the present adult treatment of the baby.

Of crucial importance to understanding the contribution of culture in constituting development is the fact that the parents' (purely ideal) projection of their children's future, derived from their memory of their cultural past, becomes a fundamentally important material constraint organizing the child's life experiences in the present. This rather abstract, nonlinear process is what gives rise to the well-known phenomenon that even adults totally ignorant of the real gender of a newborn will treat the baby quite differently depending on its symbolic or cultural gender. Adults literally create different material forms of interaction based on conceptions of the world provided by their cultural experience when, for example, they bounce boy infants (those wearing blue clothing) and attribute manly virtues to them, while

Social change can invalidate projected ontogenetic trajectories, as illustrated by the rise of women's rugby. Photo source: Selective Focus Photography, www.flickr.com/photos/scottnh/3394339933

they treat girl infants (those wearing pink clothing) in a gentle manner and attribute beauty and sweet temperaments to them (Rubin, Provezano, & Luria, 1974). Similar results are obtained even if the child is viewed *in utero* through ultrasound (Sweeney & Bradbard, 1988). Parental expectations of aspects of infant temperament have been found to anticipate these in time, and so presumably influence them (Pauli-Pott, Mertesacker, Bade, Haverkock, & Beckmann, 2003).

MacFarlane's example also demonstrates that the social and the cultural aspects of the child's environment cannot be reduced to a single "source of development" although the social and the cultural are generally conflated in two-factor theories of development, such as those presented schematically in Figure 2.1. "Culture" in this case refers to remembered forms of activity deemed appropriate to one's gender as an adolescent, whereas "social" refers to the people whose behavior is conforming to the given cultural pattern. This example also motivates the special emphasis placed on the social origins of higher psychological functions by developmental scientists who adopt the notion of culture presented here. As MacFarlane's transcripts clearly demonstrate, human nature is social in a different sense from the sociability of other species. Only a culture-using human being can reach into the cultural past, project it into the (ideal or conceptual) future, and then carry that ideal or conceptual future back into the present to create the (material/ideal) sociocultural environment of the newcomer.

In addition, this example helps us to understand the ways in which culture contributes to both continuity and discontinuity in individual development. In thinking about their babies' futures these parents are assuming that the "way things have always been is the way things will always be," calling to mind White's telling image (see above) that, temporally, the culturally constituted mind "is not a succession of disconnected episodes, but a continuum extending to infinity in both directions, from eternity to eternity." In this manner, culture is the medium that allows people to project the past into the future, providing an essential basis of psychological continuity.

This assumption, of course, is sometimes wrong. The invention of new ways to exploit energy or new media of representation, or simple changes in custom, may sufficiently disrupt the existing cultural order to be a source of significant developmental discontinuity. As an example, in the 1950s American parents who assumed that their daughters would not be soccer players at the age of 16 would have been correct. But by 1990 a great many American girls were playing soccer.

We know of no recordings equivalent to MacFarlane's from very different cultures, but an interesting account of birthing among the Zinacanteco of south-central Mexico appears to show similar processes at work. In their summary of developmental research among the Zinacanteco, Greenfield, Brazelton, and Childs (1989, p. 177) reported a man's account of his son's birth at which the son "was given three chilies to hold so that it would . . . know to buy chili when it grew up. It was given a billhood, a digging stick, an axe, and a [strip of] palm so that it would learn to weave palm." Girls are given weaving sticks, in anticipation of one of their central cultural roles as adults. The future orientation of differential treatment of the babies is not only present in ritual; it is coded in the Zinacantecan saying, "For in the newborn baby is the future of our world."

Infancy: Biology and Culture Working Together

It has long been recognized that there is an intimate link between the relative immaturity of the human newborn, which will require years of nurturing before approaching something akin to self-sufficiency, and the fact that human beings inhabit a culturally mediated environment. Both are distinctive characteristics of our species. Infancy (from a Latin word meaning one who does not speak) is widely, if not universally, considered a distinctive period of development that extends from birth until approximately the age of 2½.

The newborn infant is physically separate from the mother but still completely dependent on others for the basic necessities of life. Parents must wait until social smiling appears at around 2 months for the infant's first acknowledgement of their existence (a change to which they respond with more and more complex speech to the infant, at least in Western middle-class families: Henning, Striano & Lieven, 2005). But the infant is thoroughly embedded in a social situation from the outset, and has an innate "general relational capacity" (Selby & Bradley, 2003). Later we will consider children's acquisition of language, but it is important to recognize that communication between infant and adults occurs from birth in an "intersubjectivity" that at first does not require deliberate or specialized communicative acts on the part of the former (Trevarthen, 2005). Children's later verbal communication will grow out of this preverbal interaction, in which child and adult are best described as a single system rather than as two individuals transmitting coded information.

The system has been characterized as one of "**co-regulation**," "a form of coordinated action between participants that involves a continuous mutual adjustment of actions and intentions" (Fogel & Garvey, 2007). What Bruner (1982) referred to as "formats" and Nelson (1981, 1986) as "scripts" are event-level cultural artifacts, embodied in the vocabulary and habitual actions of adults, which act as structured media within which children can experience the covariation of language and action while remaining coordinated in a general way with culturally organized forms of behavior. In the process of negotiating such events with enculturated caregivers, children discover the vast range of meanings encoded in their culture at the same time as they find new ways to carry out their own intentions.

The cultural orchestration of this communication varies considerably. Cross-cultural research supplements intra-cultural studies by disclosing the incredible diversity of ways in which infants are involved in adult-led activities (de Villiers & de Villiers, 1978). Cross-cultural studies have shown that adults in all societies adopt something akin to a baby-talk mode when speaking to their children, before and while the children are acquiring language, using higher pitch and intonation, simplified vocabulary, grammatically less complex sentences, and utterances designed to highlight important aspects of the situation (Bryant & Barrett, 2007). Cross-cultural data have shown that, although adults everywhere speak to young children differently than they speak to older children and other adults, the particular form of infant-directed speech of middle-class American parents is not universal. Middle-class US parents treat the infant as a social being and as an "addressee" (Schieffelin & Ochs, 1986). Kaluli mothers consider their infants to be "soft" and without understanding, and carry them facing outwards. They talk with other people *about* the child, but rarely *to* the child. In Samoa, talk is directed *at* the infant but not *to* them.

Getting on a schedule.   The neonate's dependence requires that the child participates in a social and cultural system. The earliest, essential condition for continued development following birth is that the child and those who care for him or her must coordinate their conduct in this system. Adults must accumulate enough resources to accommodate the new-comer. They must come to know their child. The newborn must learn how to meet needs through the actions of others, because the child's own behavior is so limited. In this process one sees an intricate interplay between the initial characteristics of children and the cultural environment into which they are born, what Super and Harkness (1986, 2002) refer to as the developmental niche.

A clear illustration of the cultural character of the process of achieving coordination is the contrasting patterns of sleep in the months following birth in American urban dwelling and rural Kenyan (Kipsigis) children (Super & Harkness, 1997). Newborns in the United States show a marked shift toward the adult day/night cycle a few weeks after birth; by the end of the second week, they are averaging about 8½ hours of sleep between the hours of 7 p.m. and 7 a.m. Between 4 and 8 months the longest sleep episode increases from about 4 to 8 hours a night. The pressures toward sleeping through the night are not difficult to identify. American urban dwellers live by the clock. When both parents have jobs the child must be ready when they leave home in the morning. Parents are likely to push as hard as possible for the child to sleep when it is convenient for them.

Among Kipsigis infants, the course of getting on a schedule is very different. At night they sleep with their mothers and are permitted to nurse on demand. During the day they are strapped to their mothers' backs, accompanying them on their daily rounds of farming, household chores, and social activities. They do a lot of napping while their mothers go about their work. At 1 month, the longest period of sleep reported for babies in a Kipsigis sample was 3 hours, and their longest sleep episode increased little during the first 8 months of postnatal life.

This seemingly simple case contains some important lessons. First, the coordination that produces different patterns of sleeping is more than a temporary convenience. Assuming there is little change in Kipsigis life circumstances, the children socialized into a flexible sleep schedule will become more flexible adults than their American counterparts. Second, cultural variations in sleeping arrangements reflect the tacit moral ideals of the community (Shweder, Jensen & Goldstein, 1995), so the pattern the infant comes to participate in is as much ethical as it is practical.

From sucking to nursing. In the 1940s Mead and Macgregor (1951) set out to test Gesell's ideas about the relation between growth (maturation) and learning through cross-cultural research. All biologically normal children are born with a sucking reflex that can be triggered by many different stimuli. But Mead and Macgregor argued that basic principles of the way that cultures interweave learning and maturation can be seen in the way the change from reflex sucking to nursing is organized, and in the long-term behavioral implications of this organization. Some cultures, they noted, take advantage of the sucking reflex by putting the baby to the mother's breast immediately to stimulate the flow of milk, although the baby remains hungry; others provide a wet nurse; others will give the baby a bottle; and so on. In an immediate sense, all of these routes to mature nursing are equally adequate. However, they have different implications in the short, and even the long, run. Mead and Macgregor pointed to one potential short-run effect: Babies who are bottle fed until their mother's milk comes in may elaborate nursing behaviors that interfere with breast-feeding, changing both short-run nutritional and social–interactional experiences. More recent research has shown that mothers who breast feed their children also engage in more touching and gazing at their child than mothers of bottle fed babies, indicating that the choice of feeding method influences interpersonal mother–infant interactions (Lavelli & Poli, 1998).

The future in the present: A cross-cultural example. In the last edition of this text-book an example from work by Bornstein and his colleagues was used to illustrate processes of cultural mediation in infancy similar to those displayed in the conversations of parents greeting their newborns recorded by MacFarlane. That study of the interactions between American and Japanese mothers and their 5-month-old offspring (living in New York and Tokyo, respectively) showed different responses to the infants' orientations to events in the environment or to the mothers themselves (Bornstein, Tal, & Tamis-LeMonda, 1991; Bornstein, Toda, Azuma, Tamis-LeMonda, & Ogino, 1990; Bornstein et al., 1992). Infants in the two cultures behaved in a similar manner, in particular displaying equal levels of orientation to their mothers and to physical objects in the environment, but there was a distinctive

difference in the way their mothers responded to them. American mothers were more responsive when their children oriented to physical objects in the environment; Japanese mothers
were more responsive when their infants oriented to them. Moreover, American mothers
diverted children's attention from themselves to objects, whereas Japanese mothers showed
the opposite pattern. Bornstein et al. proposed that the influence was bidirectional and could
lead to "dramatically divergent ontogenetic paths" (1992, p. 818).

Bornstein's more recent work illustrates another aspect of how development is channeled
by cultural value systems embodied in distinctive cultural practices. Bornstein, Haynes,
Pascual, Painter, & Galperín (1999) compared mothers' play with their 20-month-old infants
in the US (Washington) and Argentina (Buenos Aires). Not surprisingly, at this age of
infants, *both* mothers and infants differed across cultures. Argentine children and their
mothers engaged more in representational play and less in (the presumably less advanced)
exploratory play than US children and their mothers. Bornstein et al. attributed this to an
emphasis in Argentine parenting on control and interdependency, and an emphasis in US
parenting on independence and exploration. When Cote and Bornstein (2009) compared
the play with their 20-month-old infants of South American immigrant mothers to the US
(from Argentina, Colombia, and Peru) and US-born mothers, they found no such differences.
Apparently the immigrant parents quickly adjusted to the value systems of their new sociocultural milieux. In at least some circumstances, "dramatically divergent ontogenetic paths"
exhibit a good deal of plasticity.

A shift in socioemotional and cognitive development at 6 to 9 months.   The period
from 6 to 9 months of age is strategically useful for illustrating several points about culture
and development. First, there is a good deal of evidence pointing to a universal and distinctive reorganization of the overall way in which children interact with their environments at this
time, illustrating the stage-transformation process that we referred to earlier as a bio-social-
behavioral shift (Cole, Cole, & Lightfoot, 2005). Second, there are many cross-cultural data
that allow us to address both general and culture-specific ways in which this change occurs.
The cross-cultural data are as interesting for the general methodological problems of cross-
cultural research that they raise as for their substantive contributions to understanding the
role of culture in development.

The universal changes occurring at 6 to 9 months of age are apparent in all aspects of the
bio-social-behavioral shift. With respect to the biological strand, we find that new patterns
of electrical activity, associated with increased levels of myelinization, arise in several parts
of the brain (Pujol et al., 2006; Richmond & Nelson, 2007). The affected areas include
the frontal lobes (which play a crucial role in deliberate action and planning), the cerebellum
(which is important in controlling movement and balance), and the hippocampus (important
in memory). In addition, the muscles have become stronger and the bones harder than they
were at birth, providing support for increasingly vigorous movement.

Increased motor skills associated with these changes allow children to move around
objects, pick them up, taste them, and attempt to use them for various purposes (Adolph &
Berger, Chapter 5, this volume). This increased exploratory capacity has been shown to have
important psychological consequences because it enables the infant to discover the invariant
properties of objects. Campos and his colleagues (2000), for example, showed that children given
extensive experience moving around in baby walkers before they could locomote on their own
displayed improved social, cognitive, and emotional development, referential gestural communication, wariness of heights, the perception of self-motion, distance perception, spatial
search, and spatial coding strategies.

For these new forms of experience to have a cumulative impact, infants must be able to
remember them. Evidence from a number of sources (Mandler, 2004; Schacter & Moskovitch,

1984) indicates that between 6 and 9 months of age children show a markedly enhanced ability to recall prior events without being reminded of them. Closely related is a shift in the propensity to categorize artificially constructed arrays of objects in terms of conceptual properties (Cohen & Cashon, 2006; Mandler, 1997). Taken together, these enhanced memory and categorizing abilities increase the degree to which children can structure information from past experience, enabling them to deal more effectively with current circumstances. The combination of increased mobility and increased remembering also brings increased awareness of the dangers and discomforts the world has in store. These changes, in turn, are associated with changes in children's social relationships with caregivers, about whom children have begun to build stable expectations.

Once children begin to crawl and walk, caregivers can no longer directly prevent mishaps, no matter how carefully they arrange the environment. Newly mobile babies keep a watchful eye on their caregivers for feedback about how they are doing—called *social referencing* (Tamis-LeMonda & Adolph, 2005). At the same time, children become wary of strangers and become upset when their primary caregivers leave them. This complex of apparently related social behaviors has led a number of psychologists to hypothesize that a new quality of emotional relationship between caregiver and child emerges, called "**attachment**."

Attachment.   Although various aspects of the complex of changes that occur between 6 and 9 months of age have been investigated cross-culturally (e.g., Kagan, 1977, reported data supporting the hypothesis of cross-cultural universals with respect to various aspects of remembering and object permanence), by far the greatest number of data have been collected on cultural contributions to attachment, so it is on this issue that we focus.

After the complete social dependence of the neonate and the diffuse sociality after the first 2 months, infants form their first specific social relationships in the period of 6 to 9 months. The attachment relationship clearly demonstrates biology and culture working together.

Despite the fact that there are competing theories to account for how and why children form special emotional bonds with their caregivers (see Cassidy & Shaver, 2008, for a representative sample of views), current research still takes as its starting point Bowlby's (1969, 1982) attempts to explain why extended periods of separation from parents are upsetting to small children, even though they are maintained in adequate circumstances from a purely physical point of view. His explanation, briefly stated, was that one has to interpret contemporary forms of behavior in terms of the environment in which our species evolved, the "environment of evolutionary adaptedness." In this view, behaviors that might seem irrational today were once crucial to survival, becoming a part of the human biological repertoire through natural selection.

The development of attachment would seem to be a necessary, universal biological requirement to be found in all cultures under normal circumstances because it is a species-specific consequence of our phylogenetic heritage. However, even if the attachment system is a biologically based universal, this in no way contradicts the principle of cultural mediation. Indeed, in the phenomenon of attachment we see clearly the interweaving of biology and culture. Our description of the newborn illustrated that it is overstating the case to say that "cultural learning begins with the attachment relationship" (Grossmann & Grossmann, 2005, p. 208), but certainly "It seems as if nature wanted to make sure that infants begin their lifelong education by first learning about the values of their own people" (p. 207). The biological system of attachment is interwoven with cultural practices because it ensures that the infant relates primarily with kin at the age when he or she is developing important social and cognitive abilities, especially language.

During the past three decades there has been a heated dispute on the implications of cultural variations in the outcomes of this interweaving. The dispute is worth examining in some detail because it is typical of difficulties facing the use of cross-cultural approaches to culture and development. Appropriately, the studies that began the modern debate on culture and attachment arose from comparison of the behaviors of mother–child pairs observed in their homes in the United States and Uganda by Ainsworth (1967; Ainsworth, Blehar, Waters, & Wall, 1978). Ainsworth was struck by the fact that children in both cultural groups exhibited similar patterns of attachment-related behavior (distress during brief, everyday, separation from their mothers, fear of strangers, and use of the mother as a secure base from which to explore). However, the Ugandan children seemed to express these behavior patterns more readily and intensely than did the American children Ainsworth studied. In laboratory studies using the "strange situation," Ainsworth identified three differing patterns of infant response to separation from and reunion with the parent: Type A (anxious–avoidant), Type B (securely attached), and Type C (anxious–resistant). Subsequent work has identified an additional pattern, Type D (disorganized) (Main & Solomon, 1990; Hesse & Main, 2006). Mothers of B babies have been found to typically be sensitively responsive to their infants, mothers of A infants are found rejecting, and mothers of C infants are found inconsistently responsive. Since the 1970s there has been a great deal of research on the behavior produced in the strange situation, its antecedents, and its sequelae (see the articles in Cassidy & Shaver, 2008, for reviews, leading areas of contention, and references to additional primary sources of information).

For at least two decades there has been sharp disagreement among developmentalists concerning how the attachment system is expressed in different cultures. Research initially suggested significant cultural variation in the proportion of infants showing each pattern. For example, several decades ago, children living in some Israeli kibbutzim (collective farms) were reared communally from an early age. Although they saw their parents daily, the adults who looked after them were usually not family members. When at the age of 11 to 14 months such communally reared children were placed in the strange situation with either a parent or a caregiver, many became very upset; half were classified as anxious/resistant, and only 37% appeared to be securely attached (Sagi et al., 1985). Sagi and his colleagues suspected that the high rate of insecure attachment among these children reflected the fact that the communal caregivers could not respond promptly to the individual children in their care, and staffing rotations did not allow the adults to provide individualized attention. To test this hypothesis these researchers compared the attachment behaviors of children reared in traditional kibbutzim, where children slept in a communal dormitory at night, with those of children from kibbutzim where children returned to sleep in their parents' home at night (Sagi et al., 1994). Once again they found a low level of secure attachments among the children who slept in communal dormitories. But those who slept at home displayed a significantly higher level of secure attachments, supporting the idea that cultural differences in the opportunities for sensitive caregiving accounted for differences in attachment quality.

Some have argued that these different proportions of attachment patterns are important cultural variations in attachment and that the very notion of human relatedness which is a part of the concept of attachment is culturally specific (Rothbaum, Weisz, Pott, Miyake, & Morelli, 2000). Others have argued that cultural variations are the result of insufficiently rigorous adherence to the procedures for administering the test, and still others have argued that children display a universal tendency toward secure attachment but insecure attachment is manifest in various ways (van IJzendoorn & Sagi, 1999).

A low percentage of securely attached babies has also been observed among northern (but not southern) German children. Researchers in one study found that 49% of the 1-year-olds tested were anxious–avoidant and only 33% were securely attached (Grossmann, Grossmann, Spangler, Suess, & Unzner, 1985). Having made extensive observations of northern German home life, Grossmann et al. were able to reject the possibility that a large proportion of northern German parents were insensitive or indifferent to their children. Rather, they contended, these parents were adhering to a cultural value that calls for the maintenance of a relatively large interpersonal distance and to a cultural belief that babies should be weaned from parental bodily contact as soon as they become mobile. The researchers suggested that among northern German mothers, "the ideal is an independent, non-clinging infant who does not make demands on the parents but rather unquestioningly obeys their commands" (p. 253).

In Japan, Miyake and his colleagues found a large proportion of anxious–resistant infants among traditional Japanese families, and no anxious–avoidant infants at all (Miyake, Chen, & Campos, 1985; Nakagawa, Lamb, & Miyake, 1992). Miyake and his colleagues explained this pattern by pointing out that traditional Japanese mothers rarely leave their children in the care of anyone else, and they behave toward them in ways that foster a strong sense of dependence. Consequently, the experience of being left alone with a stranger is unusual and upsetting to these children. This interpretation is supported by a study of nontraditional Japanese families in which the mothers were pursuing careers requiring them to leave their children in the care of others (Durrett, Otaki, & Richards, 1984). Among the children of these mothers the distribution of the basic patterns of attachment was similar to that seen in the United States.

The evidence of cultural variation has been brought into question and balanced by evidence that there is a general tendency in all societies for children to become attached to their caregivers. An influential review of research on attachment spanning many cultures conducted by van IJzendoorn and Sagi reported that, although the proportion of children displaying one or another pattern of attachment behaviors may vary in a small number of cases, the overall pattern of results is remarkably consistent with Ainsworth's initial findings and Bowlby's theory (van IJzendoorn & Sagi, 1999, p. 731). The global distribution was found to be 21% type A, 65% type B, and 14% type C, with greater variation within countries than between them.

When Behrens, Hesse, and Main (2007) tried to replicate Miyake's findings with older Japanese children, using the 6th-year parent–child reunion procedure (Main & Cassidy, 1988) and the Adult Attachment Interview (Main, Goldwyn, & Hesse, 2002), they found a distribution of A, B, C categories similar to worldwide norms, but 47% of the children were in category D or unclassifiable. Maternal attachment using their categorization scheme was strongly related to children's attachment in infancy, with securely attached mothers having securely attached children.

One consequence of the view that "sensitive" parenting (especially mothering) is the same for all cultures and all times, however, is that much of human history must then be seen as marked by "epochal derailments" of the attachment system (Grossmann, Grossmann, & Keppler, 2006). According to this view, the history of parental treatment of children is a grim one of "widespread neglect, indifference, maltreatment, sexual abuse and abandonment of infants and children over the ages, particularly during the 18th and early 19th centuries" (Grossmann, 2000, p. 86). It is difficult to reconcile such an account with the notion that attachment has had universal survival value. The possibility should not be ruled out that what seems in hindsight maltreatment of children had functional value in the society of the time. Furthermore, neither the universality of attachment in human relations nor a universal distribution of patterns of attachment behavior excludes the likelihood that attachment develops in specific ways that depend on the cultural niche in which the child has to survive (van IJzendoorn & Sagi, 2001). For example, when attachment researchers offered the "competence hypothesis" that "secure attachment is related to higher competence in dealing with developmental, social, and cultural challenges," they have added that competence has to be defined "in accordance to each specific cultural group" (Grossmann, Grossmann & Kepler, 2006, p. 83). In the US, for example, maternal sensitivity is associated with children's exploratory response to challenging situations; in Japan it is related to cooperativeness. The proposal is that securely attached children "will grow up to value their parents' values" (p. 83).

Associating maternal sensitivity with infant attachment also tends to construe a dyadic interaction as a one-way influence. Evans and Porter (2009) found that patterns of co-regulated interaction (Fogel & Garvey, 2007) were predictive of attachment outcomes, suggesting that both partners play a role.

Attachment researchers grant that "phenotypic attachment behaviors are bound to have specific characteristics," that is, "Attachment behaviors (e.g., actively seeking proximity or only passively crying when left alone, exuberant or subdued greeting behaviors on reunion, more or less expressed separation anxiety) will differ in distinct cultures and in different epochs depending on differences in customs of child care, family or social structure, devastating or benign living conditions and similar environmental circumstances" (Grossmann & Grossmann, 2005, p. 220). But the different categories of attachment—A, B, C, and D—would themselves seem to be phenotypic forms of the common genotypic attachment system, leaving unanswered the question of whether secure attachment can appropriately be considered optimal for all places and times.

Language development.   At around the same time that children form specific attachments, they speak their first words. Although acquisition of language has been one of the major battlefields on which the nature–nurture controversy has been fought (see Bruner, 1983; Elman et al., 1996; Pinker, 1995, for discussions of the contending viewpoints), consensus is emerging that here too we see the intersection of biology and culture. It is evident that the capacity to acquire language is common to all humans and has a biological basis. This places a lower bound on the evolutionary phase at which hominids acquired this ability, because the last common ancestor in the diverse radiation of human beings across the planet was around 100,000 years ago. The upper bound would be the point at which human evolution split from primate evolution, around 160,000 years ago, because language ability is unique to humans: Attempts to teach apes forms of language that compensate for the anatomical limitations of their vocal apparatus (chiefly sign language) have had only limited success (though the case of Kanzi, an "enculturated" bonobo, is a possible exception; Segerdahl, Fields & Savage-Rumbaugh, 2006).

Obviously, children acquire the language of the social group and culture in which they live. Children need interaction with competent adult speakers to acquire a language. What is less obvious is the details of how biology and culture work together in the development of the ability for symbolic communication. The earliest psycholinguistic studies focused on syntax (Brown, 1973), but it is now recognized that the pragmatics of language—how utterances are used in context—is equally or more important.

Furthermore, although learning language has often been considered a specific domain of children's development, a compelling argument can be made that language acquisition and socialization should not be considered two separate processes. Ochs and Schieffelin (1984) pointed out, on the basis of research in several societies, that "the primary concern of caregivers is to ensure that their children are able to display and understand behaviors appropriate to social situations. A major means by which this is accomplished is through language" (p. 276). Learning a language and becoming a member of a community are mutually implicative. It is no accident that the infant's first words can generally be understood only by those who share their current situation and have had a history with them: the members of their family. These competent speakers surround the child with the adult form of language, and the acquisition of oral language is woven in this web of social relations and interactions. Parents provide a "dynamically adjusted frame in which infants' communicative capacities may unfold" (Papousek, 2007, p. 259). Language is a product of adult biology as much as infant biology.

Children's first words are prototypical speech acts (proto-imperatives and proto-declaratives; Bates, 1976) that accomplish social actions. Semantically, the first words are "holophrasic," containing a wealth of meaning packed into a single lexical unit, and adults interpret them with attention to setting, gesture, and facial expression. Although children speak only in one-word phrases, adults talk to them in syntactically complex sentences with a large vocabulary, adjusted to the child's comprehension.

As children move from these holistic utterances to differentiated grammatical sequences, phenomena such as over- and under-extension of reference, simplifying phonological strategies, and overgeneralization of grammatical rules show that they actively construct the language they speak, rather than simply copying adult forms or rules.

Adult talk provides conversational resources—metalinguistic directions—sufficient for children to learn new word meanings, and vocabulary acquisition may be better explained by pragmatic factors than by innate constraints on the mapping of words to meaning (Clark, 2007). In many societies, adults deliberately teach vocabulary, along with styles of address and other linguistic features. There are subcultures within the United States (e.g., working-class people in Baltimore; Miller, 1982) in which it is firmly believed that children must be explicitly taught vocabulary, using quite rigid frames of the sort "How do you call this?" (see Schieffelin & Ochs, 1986, for a wide range of examples). However, although the adults involved in such practices may believe that such special tailoring is helpful to their children's language acquisition, the data indicate that significant benefits associated with deliberate teaching of language are found rather rarely and in restricted domains (Snow, 1995).

As speech becomes more complex, the meaning—the semantic content—of children's words develops. The words of the family language, and the ways in which these words are used in everyday contexts, provide children with ready-made templates for the meanings and distinctions that are important in their community. As Brown (1965) phrased it, words are "invitations to form concepts." The meaning of the word "doggie" is not the same at 12 months as at 3 years, and this suggests an important interaction between language and thought. Words inevitably generalize—even the infant applies the word "doggie" to more than one referent—and generalization serves important cognitive functions. If language were a structurally distinct module there would be no particular relation between language and thought. Insofar as culturally organized experience is essential to the acquisition of language, then language, thought, and development are likely to be intimately connected. This is a topic that requires more extensive treatment than we can give it here.

Studies of deaf children reared with both deaf and hearing parents show a normal pattern of early language acquisition, whether the children are (1) monolingual in sign language, (2) bilingual in oral and sign language, or (3) bilingual in two different sign languages. Hearing children reared to sign by deaf parents show the same pattern (Petitto, 2005). An interesting contrast is children born deaf to hearing parents who do not believe that it is useful for their children to sign, insisting instead that they learn to interact through oral language (Goldin-Meadow, 2007; Goldin-Meadow, Butcher, Mylander, & Dodge, 1994). These children are reared in an environment that is rich in culturally mediated social interactions; they lack only the linguistic behavior that fills the gaps between movements and provides accounts of the rationale and prior history of those actions. Under these circumstances children spontaneously begin to employ *home sign*, a kind of communication through gesture which exhibits a number of properties also found in the early stages of natural language acquisition. Children who start signing in the absence of adult signers begin to make two, three, and longer sign sequences around their second birthdays, at about the same time that hearing children create multiword sentences. Moreover, Goldin-Meadow and Mylander (1996) showed that home sign takes very similar forms in very different cultural/linguistic environments: Chinese and American deaf children showed the same patterns of early gesture sentences. These researchers concluded that the development of these gesture systems is "buffered against large variations in environmental conditions and in this sense can be considered 'innate' " (p. 281).

However, the language development of deaf children born to hearing parents who do not sign comes to a halt at this point. Unless such children are provided access to some form of language as a part of the culturally organized environments they participate in, they will not develop the more subtle features of language on which sustainable cultural formations depend. An illustration of this is the way children joining a new school for the deaf in Nicaragua pooled their different home signs to create their own language, which new arrivals made richer and more complex. In only a few years it became as grammatically structured as any natural language (Senghas, Kita, & Ozyürek, 2004).

Such studies demonstrate that the biological predisposition for language operates at a very general level, and in no way depends on the brain mechanisms of hearing or vocalization. One component appears to be a sensitivity to rhythmical and distributed patterning, whether it be verbal or auditory (Petitto, 2005). They also show that the social environment is crucial. Bruner (1982, p. 15) captured the essence of the view that culture plays an essential role in language development when he wrote that the latter cannot be reduced to:

> either the virtuoso cracking of a linguistic code, or the spinoff of ordinary cognitive development, or the gradual takeover of adults' speech by the child through some impossible inductive tour de force. It is rather, a subtle process by which adults artificially arrange the world so that the child can succeed culturally by doing what comes naturally, and with others similarly inclined.

A similar attempt to overcome the long-standing opposition between nature and nurture in explanations of language acquisition is found in "emergentism," the view that language acquisition is a dynamic process, located not in an individual but in a system, a matter of "simple learning mechanisms, operating in and across the human systems for perception, motor-action, and cognition as they are exposed to language data as part of a communicatively-rich human social environment by an organism eager to exploit the functionality of language" (Ellis, 1998, p. 657; Ke & Holland, 2006, MacWhinney, 2006).

The most secure overall generalization about language acquisition is that culturally organized joint activity which incorporates the child into the scene as a novice participant is one necessary ingredient. Conversely, language plays a central role in the process of children's participation in culturally organized activities (Nelson, 2003; Rogoff, 2003). Language bridges gaps in understanding between people, and allows them to coordinate in shared activities. Language acquisition is a bidirectional process in which biology and culture are equally important. But more than this, in acquiring the capacity to speak effectively (knowing not just what to say, but how and when to say it) children are transformed as cultural participants. The sociocultural niche into which a child is born provides the necessary conditions for language to emerge, but as children struggle to understand objects and social relations to gain control over their environments and themselves, they recreate the culture into which they are born, even as they reinvent the language of their forebears. The consequences of this interplay of language and cultural participation for children's psychological functions have only begun to be explored.

Early Childhood: The Role of Culture in Conceptual Development

In contrast to infancy, which is a good candidate for a universally acknowledged stage of development, there is some uncertainty about how one should specify later parts of the lifespan. Whiting and Edwards (1988), following Mead (1935), divide the period between

2½ and 6 years of age, often designated as early childhood, into two parts: 2- to 3-year-olds are referred to as "knee children," who are kept close at hand but not continuously on the mother's lap or in a crib; 4- to 5-year-olds are referred to as "yard children," because they can leave their mothers' sides but are not allowed to wander far. In many modern, industrialized countries, children between 3 and 5 to 6 years of age spend part of every day in an environment designed to prepare them for school, which has led many to call this time of life the preschool period.

The future in the present in early childhood. With children this age we can find more illustrations of how adults bring the future into the present, shaping children's experiences and future development. Tobin, Hsueh, and Karasawa (2009) conducted a follow-up to their 1985 study of preschool socialization in Hawaii, Japan, and China. They showed recordings of classroom interactions made 20 years ago and today to teachers and other audiences in all three countries, to evoke their interpretations, identify the "informal cultural logic" of preschool education, and consider historical changes in this important institution. In 1985, teachers in Japan, China, and the US had markedly different views about matters such as the appropriate size of a preschool class, the relative importance of character and ability versus effort, when and how a teacher should intervene in conflicts, as well as the degree of acceptable bodily contact among the children and between teacher and child. For instance, where US teachers would intervene in conflicts among children, Japanese teachers considered this inappropriate, for they believed the conflicts provided a valuable opportunity to develop social skills. Twenty years later, the Chinese preschool had changed dramatically. A concern in 1985 with spoiling the child had been replaced by emphasis on promoting independence and creativity, "characteristics needed to succeed in entrepreneurial capitalism" (p. 226). At the same time, concern was growing to ensure that young Chinese do not lack social and moral values. In Japan, after more than a decade of economic difficulties, Tobin and his colleagues found the view that preschools should conserve traditional values, perspectives, and skills. People spoke derisively of modernization. In the US, they found a growing emphasis on academic readiness, accountability, and scientifically based practice. Play-oriented curricula are now out of favor, and there is pressure to credential both teachers and programs. But Tobin, Hsueh, and Karasawa suggest that in each country the implicit cultural logic has not changed, largely because it goes unnoticed. Class size in Japanese preschools remains larger than in the United States, in part because of the implicit cultural value that children need to be socialized to relate to others and their group. In China, the implicit emphasis on mastery and performance is unaltered. In the United States, freedom of choice and individual self-expression are still taken for granted. We can see here again how culture creates an effect conditioned not so much by present necessity as by deep beliefs about "how things work" in adulthood, an effect that may have relatively minor consequences in the present life of the child, but major consequences in the long-term organization of his or her behavior.

The role of biology and culture in children's conceptual development. In early childhood, children's rapidly increasing facility with language gives researchers new and different opportunities to study their knowledge and reasoning. Piaget proposed, in his early writings, that reasoning at this age is "animistic," failing to make a distinction between biological and nonbiological entities (Piaget, 1937). In his later writings he described this form of reasoning as "preoperational" and "precausal," lacking the ability to reason logically and in particular to provide causal explanations (Piaget, 1969). Contemporary work suggests that young children recognize core ontological distinctions, reason about specific causes in distinct knowledge domains, and have interconnected frameworks of knowledge. Frequently, the domain-specificity of young children's conceptual knowledge and reasoning is taken to imply that such knowledge is innate, but logically these are separate matters (Wellman & Gelman, 1992). Whether "core domains" of knowledge are necessarily based on biological "mental modules," innately specified and developing on a species-wide maturational timetable, as some have suggested, is a matter of widespread scholarly dispute.

Chomsky's proposal that there exists a unique and specialized language-learning faculty (the "language acquisition device" or LAD) remains influential in current thinking about early conceptual development as well as in the domain of language. He considered syntax to be of such complexity, and the environmental input so impoverished, that a child must be born with an innate capacity to learn language (Chomsky, 1986). Fodor (1983) coined the term "mental module" to refer to any "specialized, encapsulated mental organ that has evolved to handle specific information types of particular relevance to the species" (Elman et al., 1996, p. 36). Often mental modules are associated with particular regions of the brain: Broca's area, for example, is taken to be the brain locus of the mental module for language.

If domain-specific knowledge were the outcome of maturation of a mental module, the role of culture would presumably be restricted to speeding up or slowing down the fixed course of development (Carey & Spelke, 1994). But just as Chomsky's linguistic nativism has been countered by those who argue that social relations and adult "input" provide sufficient cues for the child to learn language (as we described in the last section), the explanation of domain-specific conceptual knowledge in terms of mental modules has been countered by those who argue that biological constraints provide only "**skeletal principles**" for conceptual development. These principles serve to bias developing children's attention to relevant features of the domain, but they do not determine knowledge completely; on the contrary, concepts *require* the infusion of cultural input to develop past a rudimentary starting point (Chen & Siegler, 2000; Gelman, 2009; Hatano, 1997). This kind of argument has also been made by those neuroscientists focused on the brain bases of development who refer to themselves as "cultural biologists" (e.g., Quartz & Sejnowksi, 2002). They emphasize that, whatever the phylogenetic constraints on development, specific brain areas are neither entirely dedicated to a single function nor unaffected by environment, so, for example, when there is damage to a specific area of the brain early in life the functions ordinarily located in that area often shift to an entirely different area (Battro, 2000; Stiles et al., 2003).

Reviewing the literature on the development of core, or **privileged domains**, Hatano and Inagaki (2002) argued that if innately specified knowledge is only *skeletal* it is essential to study the ways in which cultural groups organize children's experience to enhance and perhaps, in some cases, to modify the knowledge endowed by evolution. Because children everywhere need to understand physical objects, plants and animals, and other people, researchers have focused a great deal of research on children's naive physics, naive biology, and naive psychology. We will review evidence concerning the development of knowledge in the last two of these areas, to provide examples of how biology and culture "co-construct" adult knowledge.

Naive psychology.   The knowledge-specific domain of naive psychology is often referred to as "folk psychology." In this case, during early childhood, children are said to form a "**theory of mind**"—a capacity "to construe people in terms of their mental states and traits" (Lillard & Skibbe, 2004). An important strategy for testing this idea comes from "false-belief" tasks, where a child is asked about a situation in which a person has beliefs that contradict the facts (Liu, Wellman, Tardif, & Sabbagh, 2008). By the end of the first year of life infants show they can distinguish intentional from non-intentional behavior (Gergely, Egyed & Király, 2007). By the time they are 3, children can engage in deception in collaboration with an adult; that is, they can enter into creation of a false belief (Sullivan & Winner, 1993). Three-year-olds can reason about others' desires, but have difficulty reasoning about others' beliefs (Wellman, 2002). Children subsequently master the ability to reason about false belief and mental representations, and their understanding grows to encompass secondary emotions such as surprise and pride. (See Cole, Cole, & Lightfoot, 2005, for more detailed account of these developments.)

Bloom and German (2000) questioned the validity of the false-belief task as a measure of naive psychology, arguing that other tasks show theory of mind is acquired much earlier, and that children show similar difficulties with tasks that don't require theory of mind. But Wellman, Cross, and Watson (2001) concluded from a meta-analysis that the phenomenon is robust.

Primates seem to have some understanding of the intentional character of others' behavior, and some understanding of mental states. The situation is well described by the title of a recent article in these debates, "Chimpanzees have a theory of mind, the question is, which parts" (Tomasello, Call, & Hare, 2003). For example, socially subordinate chimpanzees attend not just to the presence of a dominant but to what they infer the dominant can see (Hauser, 2005; Tomasello & Carpenter, 2007). But there is no doubt that young children's understanding of other people rapidly outpaces primates. The question that interests us is the role of culture in this process.

Cross-cultural research has explored whether or not theory of mind is a universal developmental phenomenon, impervious to cultural variation in timing. Such a result would be somewhat surprising, because cultures around the world show an enormous variety in the extent and ways that mental states and actions are spoken about and presumably how they are conceived (Lillard, 1998; Vinden, 1998). In terms of sheer number, English is at one extreme of the continuum, possessing more than 5000 emotion words alone. By contrast, the Chewong people of Malaysia are reported to have only five terms to cover the entire range of mental processes, translated as *want, want very much, know, forget, miss or remember* (Howell, 1984). Anthropologists have also reported that in many societies there is a positive avoidance of talking about other people's minds (Paul, 1995).

At present, opinion about cultural variation using locally adapted versions of theory of mind tasks is divided (Lillard & Skibbe, 2004; Liu et al., 2008). In an early study, Avis and Harris (1991) reported that children in rural Cameroon developed the ability to make inference on the basis of other's false beliefs, but in other studies, where people were less likely to talk in terms of psychological states in the head, performance on the theory of mind task was absent or partial (Vinden, 1999, 2002). It is unclear whether performance was poor because people lacked the vocabulary or inclination, or because they could not articulate their intuitive understanding in words.

To avoid the confound of a cultural group's mental vocabulary and performance on false belief tasks, Callaghan et al. (2005) conducted a study that used a minimally verbal procedure where it was unnecessary to use difficult-to-translate words such as belief and emotion. They hid a toy under one of three bowls with two experimenters present. Then one experimenter left and the other induced the child to put the toy under a different bowl before asking the child to point to the bowl the first experimenter would pick up when she returned. Notice that the procedure uses language only at the level of behavior (asking the child to point) with no reference to mental terms, so the prediction that the absent experimenter would look where the toy had been when she left would indicate the ability to think about others' beliefs independent of vocabulary.

Under these conditions a large number of children 2½ to 6 years of age were tested in Canada, India, Samoa, Thailand, and Peru. Performance improved over age, with 4½ to 5 years of age being the point where 50% of the children performed correctly, and 5½ to 6 years of age the point at which all the children responded correctly. Here is a case of careful standardization of a precise procedure conducted in such a way that performance did not depend on the ability to communicate using mental language among people who do not use such terms. A common pattern was found (in line with the modularity view). But note that children were asked to demonstrate only the most skeletal core of their understanding of others, devoid of enrichment by the local vocabulary and without needing to reason about beliefs. In contrast, Vinden (1999) found that, whereas children from a variety of small-scale, low-technology groups in Cameroon and New Guinea were able to understand how belief affects behavior, they had difficulty predicting an emotion based on a false belief.

Using a different task, in which children were asked to explain the bad behavior of a story character, Lillard, Skibbe, Zeljo, and Harlan (2001) found culture, regional, and class differences in whether children attributed the behavior to an internal, psychological trait or to external circumstances. Children in all groups gave both kinds of responses, internal and situational, but the frequency and patterns of use differed. Lillard and her colleagues (2001) make the important point that "cultural differences are usually a matter of degrees, of different patterns and frequencies of behaviors in different cultural contexts" (a view put forward early by Cole, Gay, Glick, & Sharp, 1971). They attribute the results to language socialization practices in the different communities, noting, for example, that low-socioeconomic status (SES) children or rural children are more likely to have parents who make situational attributions of behavior and model this form of interpretation for their children, whereas high-SES/urban parents are more likely to use an internal model of interpretation which they embody in their interactions with their children.

So, it seems that when carefully stripped down versions of false-belief tasks are presented to people of widely different cultural backgrounds, they perform the same, but cultural variations appear when language and explanation are made part of the assessment. This pattern of results supports the idea of Hatano and Inagaki (2002) that development is a combination of "skeletal biological constraints" plus "participation in cultural practice." Both phylogeny and cultural history are necessary contributors to the development of an adult mode of thinking about the thoughts and situations of oneself and others.

There is indeed consistent evidence that young children's understanding of false beliefs is related to their language development (Slade & Ruffman, 2005). Deaf children reared by hearing parents show a language delay (as mentioned above) and also a late understanding of false beliefs. This suggests that coming to understand behavior in terms of beliefs and desires—or whatever the local concepts are—depends on participation in a language community (Perner & Ruffman, 2005). Astington and Baird (2005) suggested that this is because language supports the distinction between what is real and what is hypothetical or counterfactual. But the proposal that language makes possible the capacity for representation of propositional attitudes (de Villiers & de Villiers, 2000) has not been supported by comparison of English- and German-speaking children (Perner, Sprung, Zauner, & Haider, 2003). Understanding of desire preceded understanding belief in both cases, even though the grammatical encoding of these processes was the same in German but different in English.

The notion that theory of mind is based on an innate mental module still has its supporters (e.g., Leslie, 2005). But the evidence for specific brain localization is not compelling (Leekam, Perner, Healey, & Sewell, 2008). Moreover, Ruffman and his colleagues have demonstrated the importance of the family context for theory of mind. Children perform better on theory of mind tasks if they have more siblings (Perner, Ruffman, & Leekam, 1994), older siblings (Ruffman, Perner, Naito, Parkin, & Clements, 1998), and mothers who encourage them to reflect on feelings (Ruffman, Perner, & Parkin, 1999) and who talk about mental states (Ruffman, Slade, & Crowe, 2002) and emotions (Taumoepeau & Ruffman, 2008). In contrast, general parenting style (warmth/sensitivity) is not associated with children's performance on theory of mind tasks, although it is associated with children's cooperative conduct (Ruffman, Slade, Devitt, & Crowe, 2006). It has been proposed that mothers' talk helps to make explicit the child's implicit understanding of other minds (Taumoepeau & Ruffman, 2006, p. 478; 2008, p. 297).

But are psychologists explaining children's naive psychology in the correct terms? "Theory of mind" research assumes (1) that mind is a distinct realm and (2) that young children form theories. On the first point, many philosophers have argued that mind–body dualism is inconsistent and should be avoided. If children are dualists, that is an important and interesting fact (Bloom, 2004; Wellman & Johnson, 2008), but if psychologists are dualists theoretical problems ensue, as we noted in the introduction (cf. Costall & Leudar, 2007; Vygotsky also identified the pressing need to overcome dualism in psychology, 2004). Yet theory-of-mind researchers assume the representational character of the mind: that beliefs, and other mental states, refer to a world outside the mind (Gopnik, 2009). Is this more than a metaphor we in the West live by (Lakoff & Johnson, 1980)?

The idea that young children and even infants understand the world around them in terms of abstract entities ("theory theory," see Gopnik & Wellman, 1994) is challenged by those who see infancy and the start of childhood as a period of situated, embodied understanding and tacit comprehension. According to this view, as we proposed in earlier sections, and as Ruffman's work is suggesting, understanding other people emerges in a history of co-regulated interactions with them (e.g., Fogel & Garvey, 2007). Theory-of-mind research effaces the distinction among different developmental forms of knowledge in ontogenesis (Perner, 2008). It also treats understanding other people as a matter of indifferent cognition, whereas evidence shows that deep-seated emotional systems are involved (Trevarthen, 2005). Our own view is that young children understand other people's actions implicitly, emotionally, and pragmatically before they reason explicitly, using the terms of their local language, about mental states.

Naive biology. A second area of research concerning young children's knowledge and reasoning has focused on the domain of plants and animals. Some have argued that children show "rapid conceptual change" in this domain, others that there is merely "knowledge enrichment"—that is to say, the debate is again over qualitative reorganization versus gradual change. Carey (1985) argued for the former idea, proposing that children do not distinguish the biological from the psychological until as late as age 10. This conclusion would suggest that young children should distinguish plants from animals but not animals from humans. They would have no specifically biological kind of explanation, or distinguish psychological from biological phenomena. Data now exist to disprove all three suggestions.

For example, Inagaki and Hatano (1993) showed that 4- and 5-year-olds distinguish psychological and biological causes, and understand vitalism—that living things have a vital energy—as one among several kinds of biological causation. Their understanding is animistic and personifying this is the result not of confusion between the psychological and biological, but of the children applying their greater knowledge of people to reason by analogy—to make "educated guesses"—about plants and animals. Hatano argued that children's biological knowledge contains an innate "skeletal" component but this skeleton is supplemented by a sociocultural component that varies both between and within cultures. Because children in postindustrial societies have little direct experience of plants and animals, they can only reason by analogy to people. But even a city-dwelling child who has direct experience—for example, taking care of a goldfish—will draw analogies to the familiar animal rather than to humans (Inagaki, 1990). Of course, children in different cultures will gain different kinds of direct experience of animals, a point we will return to below (Waxman & Medin, 2007).

Claims to the contrary notwithstanding, young children's reasoning about biology is not like that of a scientist. Researchers have increasingly come to recognize that scientific biology employs various distinct interpretive frameworks, and that scientific reasoning is not the necessary endpoint of conceptual development. For some time it seemed that, in every human society studied, adults tend to think about plants and animals in terms of taxonomic hierarchies, organized around generic species (e.g., oak and robin, rather than tree and bird) which have a common essence, and reason about the features of these species in teleological terms (Atran, Medin, & Ross, 2004). This way of thinking differs significantly from scientific biology, which considers humans to be animals and deals with interrelated genera, rather than species with distinct essences.

But researchers have now discovered significant variation in the forms of adult reasoning about biological kinds in different cultures. Even if there is a universal way of organizing knowledge about biology (a presumption that now has to be doubted), people from different cultures certainly reason from this organization in systematically different ways. Two distinct ways are now distinguished in the literature. Adults in industrialized societies tend to treat the taxonomic hierarchy as a basis for inference about groups and their shared properties. In contrast, the Yukatek Maya, for example, are primarily concerned with "ecological and morpho-behavioral relationships" and they reason in a "systemic" way (a distinction that has relevance for our discussion of **schooling** below) (Atran et al., 2004). In "ecological thinking," two biological kinds would be included in the same category not because of similar biological characteristics but because of their interrelation in the ecology in which they both live.

Researchers increasingly point out that adults in industrial societies lack both scientific knowledge and detailed folk biological knowledge, so their children's reasoning is likely to be limited as a consequence. One result is growing interest in both children and adults in other cultures. For example, research by Atran and colleagues (2001) showed that, in cultures that value ecological reasoning, young children become able to reason in this way. These researchers suggest that the anthropocentric bias of American children results from lack of familiarity with non-human biological kinds. They compared young Yukatek Maya children (aged 4 to 5) with Maya adults. The task (based on Carey's work) was to infer to what degree a property possessed by a base item would be characteristic of a set of target items. For example, they were shown a picture of a wolf and told "Now there is this stuff called *andro* that is found inside some kinds of things. One kind of thing that has *andro* inside is a wolf. Now I will show you other things and you tell me if you think they have *andro* inside like wolves do." This questioning frame was used with a number of inferential "bases" (human, wolf, bee, goldenrod, water) and a larger number of "target objects" from each of the taxonomic categories represented by the bases (for example, raccoon, eagle, rock) to see if the child or adult would reason that "andro" would also be found in the target object. The Maya adults decreased their inductions from humans to other living kinds and then to non-living kinds, following the pattern predicted by standard biological taxonomies. But when "bee" was the base they often inferred that properties would be shared not only with other invertebrates, but also with trees and humans. Atran et al. interpreted this pattern of inference as based on ecological reasoning: Bees build their nests in trees, and bees are sought after by humans for their honey. The participants often explicitly used such ecological justifications in their responses. Most importantly, the young Maya children's responses were very similar to those of the adults. Whatever the base concept, inductive inferences decreased as the target moved from mammals to trees. And, like the adults, the children showed no indication of anthropomorphism: Inferences from humans did not differ from inferences from animals or trees, and the Mayan children did not appear to favor humans as a basis of inference. They did not interpret the biological world anthropocentrically. This evidence highlights the importance of culturally organized experience in the development of inferences in the domain of biology, supporting the conclusion that the anthropocentric bias observed with urban American children reflects their lack of intimate contact with plants and animals.

Citing these and a variety of other studies using historical as well as experimental data, Medin, Ross, and Cox (2006) arrived at the conclusion that over the past 200 years there has been decreased knowledge of, and decreased ability to reason about, the natural world among the increasingly urbanized, schooled populations of the world. In short, with respect to understanding the environment, it is the culturally "less developed" people who are cognitively more sophisticated. Further work by Atran, Ross, Medin, and their colleagues, designed, in their terms, to tease apart the contributions of culture and experience, will be described below when we turn to middle childhood.

In short, neither Piaget's acultural account of reasoning in early childhood nor its explanation in terms of innate mental modules is fully adequate. Young children seem more capable in their reasoning about biological kinds than Piaget recognized. In fact, the research that has been conducted with young children whose culture brings them into close, everyday, practical contact with plants and animals shows that they are capable of sophisticated ecological reasoning. The findings of less advanced reasoning with children in urban, technologically dependent settings seem to reflect their lack of experience, the "devolution" of knowledge (Atran, Medin, & Ross, 2004; Wolff & Medin, 2001), rather than innate or universal abilities (but cf. Ergazaki & Andriotou, 2010). What is innate, if anything, is still unclear.

The studies we have reviewed are informative, but they raise important methodological questions. Frequently, language is used as though it were a transparent medium of communication. For example, Coley (1995) asked young children to name drawings of animals. When the name was "correct" they were told so; when not he provided the "correct label." Then he asked questions ("Can Xs think?") that required only a yes/no answer. Such a procedure offers children little opportunity to articulate their understanding of an animal name, and actually discards useful information about their concepts that is contained in their "incorrect" names.

Consequently, when Medin and Atran (2004, p. 966) suggest that "many different people, observing many different exemplars of dog under varying conditions of exposure to those exemplars, may nonetheless generate more or less the same concept of *dog*" (we have doubts: A child who is familiar with a dog as the family pet is unlikely to form the same concept as one for whom a dog is trained to herd or hunt, or guard the house, or fight).

A further limitation of many studies is that they consider the child largely in isolation, rather than as a participant in cultural practices. Atran, Medin, and colleagues do consider the degree of exposure to animals children have in different societies, but they do not consider the qualitative differences in contact. Children in the United States are likely to have household pets that are spoken to and treated as having personalities, beliefs, and desires. Their other main contact with animals is likely to be in the form of cuts of beef and chicken, purchased at the store. Maya children are likely to be surrounded by domestic animals whose rearing they will participate in, and wild animals which the family may hunt, or venerate. Categorization of animals is a social practice—or system of practices—before it is an individual cognitive scheme.

Middle Childhood: Apprenticeship in Adult Skills

One of the most pervasive changes in the cultural organization of children's lives is the new social arrangements that adults make for their children when they reach 5 to 7 years of age (Rogoff, 2003; Samcroff & Haith, 1996). Across all societies children are expected to stop playing childish games, start learning skills that will be essential to them when they grow up, and to be held accountable if they fail to live up to adult expectations. For example (Read, 1960), among the Ngoni of Malawi in Central Africa (when Read lived there several decades ago), the boys must leave the protection of their home and move into dormitories where they must submit to male authority and begin to engage in at least rudimentary forms of adult work. Read described the effects of this abrupt change by writing that "From having been impudent, well fed, self-confident, and spoiled youngsters among the women many of them quickly became skinny, scruffy, subdued, and had a hunted expression" (1960, p. 49). The Ifaluk of Micronesia identify this age as the time when children acquire "social intelligence," which includes the acquisition of important cultural knowledge and skills, as well as the ability to work, to adhere to social norms, and to demonstrate compassion for others—all valued adult behaviors (Lutz, 1987). In Western Europe and the United States, this same transition has long been considered the advent of the "age of reason" (White, 1996).

This ubiquitous change in parental expectations of, and arrangements for, their children has a corresponding set of changes in biological, behavioral, and social characteristics of children that illustrate clearly the idea of a major bio-social-behavioral shift, specifics of which depend on cultural circumstances. Especially notable in the biological realm are changes in the organization of brain functioning, dexterity and coordination, and physical strength (Bogin, 2009; Janowsky & Carper, 1995; Luria, 1973).

In virtually every country in the modern world, the most striking change in the organization of children's activities is that they begin to attend formal schools. Although schooling has a long history, and its forms have changed over many centuries, the dominant form of schooling adopted currently around the world is based on a European model that evolved in the nineteenth century and followed conquering European armies into other parts of the world. Serpell and Hatano (1997) have dubbed this form of education "institutionalized public basic schooling" (IPBS) (see LeVine, LeVine, & Schnell, 2001; Serpell & Hatano, 1997, for a more extensive treatment of the evolution of formal schooling).

At present, IPBS is an ideal if not a reality all over the world (the Islamic world providing one alternative in favor of adherence to religious/social laws, as written in the Qur'an—a word that means "recitation" in Arabic). This "Western-style" approach operates in the service of the secular state, economic development, the bureaucratic structures through which rationalization of this process is attempted, and exists as a pervasive fact of contemporary life. According to a survey published by UNESCO (2009), there are large disparities among regions in the level of education achieved, varying from almost 100% high school graduation in some industrialized countries to countries in which many children complete few, if any, years of schooling. Nonetheless, experience of IPBS has become a pervasive fact of life the world over.

When we contrast the experiences of children who spend several hours a day, 5 days a week, attending formal schools where literacy and numeracy form the core of the curriculum with comparable children who remain at home helping their mothers with cooking, child care, or gardening, or who accompany their fathers into the fields or forests to assist in farming, hunting, or making mortar bricks with which to build houses, certain prominent characteristics of the classroom experience stand out quite clearly (Cole, 2006; Gaskins, 2000; Serpell & Hatano, 1997).

1. The settings in which schooling occurs are distinctive in that they are removed from contexts of practical activity. Students are trained in the use of mediational means such as writing and provided with dense exposure to the conceptual content of various cultural domains, which are supposed to provide the means to later productive activity.
2. There is a peculiar social structure to formal schooling, in which a single adult interacts with many (often as many as 40 or 50, sometimes as many as 400) children at a

time. Unlike most other settings for socialization, this adult is unlikely to have any familial ties to the learner, rendering the social relationships relatively impersonal. This structure defines abstract positions of "teacher" and "student" to which children must adapt (Packer, 2001a, 2001b).

3. There is a distinctive value system associated with schooling that sets educated people above their peers and that, in secular education, values change and discontinuity over tradition and community. One ubiquitous feature of schooling is the "sorting" of children in terms of this system (Packer, in press; Varenne & McDermott, 1999).

4. There is a special mediational skill, writing, that is essential to the activity of schooling. Writing is used to represent both language and non-verbal systems (e.g., mathematics).

5. On-the-spot assistance is considered inappropriate, in sharp contrast with learning/teaching interactions in many other contexts, and emphasis is placed on learning as an individual achievement (Serpell & Hatano, 1997).

6. All these factors taken together result in a situation in which language is used in distinctive ways. Perhaps the best documented example of this is the pattern of interaction in which teachers ask children to answer questions, the answers to which the teachers already know (Mehan, 1978).

This characterization of the distinctive nature of the activity settings associated with formal schooling does not do justice to all the differences between formal schooling and other socialization settings that might be considered educational in the broad sense. (For more extended discussions see Greenfield & Lave, 1982; Schliemann, Carraher, & Ceci, 1997.) However, it is sufficient to see that cultural discontinuities occurring during middle childhood present an especially attractive proving ground for testing theories about culture and cognitive development (for reviews see Berry, Poortinga, Segall, & Dasen, 2002; Gardiner & Kosmitzki, 2007).

From the many specific developmental phenomena that might be chosen for illustration, we discuss four here: the development of logical operations, memory, the ability to analyze language, and induction based on classification. Each of these psychological processes is the object of a great deal of traditional pedagogical research, and it seems plausible to believe that the many thousands of hours of instruction children experience during middle childhood should be a powerful cultural influence on their development.

Schooling and the development of logical operations.   For purposes of discussion, the logical operations in question are those that form the basis for Piagetian theory, within which it is assumed that concrete operations consist of organized systems (classifications, serial ordering, correspondences) that allow children to think through the consequences of an action (such as pouring water from one pitcher into another) and mentally to reverse that action. However, such operations remain limited in the sense that they proceed from one partial link to the next in a step-by-step fashion, without relating each partial link to all the others, and they must be carried out on actual objects. Formal operations, which Piaget hypothesized to arise in adolescence, differ in that all the possible combinations are considered, they can be carried out without reference to actual objects, and each partial link is grouped in relation to a "structured whole" (Inhelder & Piaget, 1958).

Early in his career, Piaget believed that there would be large cultural differences in cognitive development associated with the difference between primitive and technologically advanced societies (Piaget 1928/1995). However, when he began to address the issue of cultural variations and cognitive development in the 1960s he assumed that the sequence of cognitive changes that he had observed in Geneva was universal, and he restricted his attention to various factors that might modify the rate at which children progressed (Piaget, 1973). The key factor was the amount of operational exercise, the constant interplay of assimilation and accommodation that drives the system to higher, more inclusive, levels of equilibration. Some societies, he speculated, might provide greater opportunities for operational exercise by helping children to confront and think about their environment with greater frequency. However, he was dubious about the extent to which schooling actually accomplished this task because the authority structure of the classroom resulted in accommodation markedly exceeding assimilation, thus hindering equilibration.

Although it would seem that cross-cultural comparisons involving children who had and had not been to school should be well suited to testing Piaget's hypotheses, the history of this line of research has proved as much a cautionary tale about the difficulties of cross-cultural research. The difficulties confronting researchers are well illustrated by studies initiated by Greenfield and Bruner (Greenfield, 1966; Greenfield & Bruner, 1969). Working in rural Senegal, Greenfield and Bruner observed the steady development of conservation among schooled children and its absence among about half of the non-educated adults, leading them to speculate that schooling might actually be necessary for the development of concrete operations. This kind of result was picked up by Hallpike (1979), who claimed that adults in nonliterate societies, as a rule, fail to develop beyond preoperational thought (a conclusion hotly denied by, among others, Jahoda, 1993).

The crucial ambiguity in this research is similar to that which we have already encountered in the work on attachment: When a social context representing a test situation with particular meanings in one cultural system is imported into another, how do we know that the participants have understood the task in the way the experimenter intended so that the results are comparable? For at least some of the research on schooling and the development of concrete operations in which unschooled children fail, results point clearly to the conclusion that the individuals who failed to conserve also failed to enter into the framework of the problem as intended by the experimenter, although they complied in a surface way with instructions. Thus, for example, in the study by Greenfield (1966) among the Wolof of Senegal, it appeared that, unless children attended school, many failed to achieve conservation of volume. However, in a follow-up study, Irvine (1978) asked children to play the role of an informant whose task it was to clarify for the experimenter the meaning of the Wolof terms for equivalence and resemblance. In their role as "participant," these individuals gave non-conserving responses when liquid was poured from one beaker into another. However, in their role as "linguistic informants," they indicated that, although the water in one beaker had increased as a result of pouring, the amounts were the same (using different vocabulary to make the appropriate distinctions). Greenfield's own research also pointed to interpretational factors that interfere with conservation judgments; when she permitted Wolof children to pour water themselves, conservation comprehension improved markedly. Greenfield (2004) currently argues for differential interpretation of the tasks associated with different discourse modes and familiarity with task contents as the explanation of differential performance.

Two additional lines of evidence support the conclusion that problems in interpreting the Piagetian interview situation, not a failure to develop concrete operations, account for cases in which cultures appear to differ. First, Siegal (1991) demonstrated that even 4- to 5-year-old children display an understanding of conservation principles but misunderstand what is being asked of them by the experimenter. Second, in a number of instances no differences between the conservation performance of schooled and unschooled children from developing countries have been observed when the experimenter was a member of the cultural group in question (Kamara & Easley, 1977; Nyiti, 1978). Although some ambiguities remain in this research, it appears most sensible to conclude that concrete operational thinking is not influenced by schooling; what is influenced by schooling is people's ability to understand the language of testing and the presuppositions of the testing situation itself.[5]

Schooling and memory.   The basic expectation underlying research on culture and memory is quite different from that of work on logical operations. At least since the time of Plato, there have been speculations that acquisition of literacy (which, in most circumstances, occurs in school) could actually decrease powers of memory because people could always return to their store of written materials to recall information relevant to the issues at hand (see Cole & Scribner, 1977, for a review of theoretical approaches). Early empirical work was conducted on adults and did not involve schooling as a variable. Nadel (1937), for example, compared recall of a story constructed to be familiar in form and general content to members of two Nigerian groups, the Yoruba and the Nupe. On the basis of prior ethnographic analysis, Nadel predicted that the Yoruba would emphasize the logical structure of the story, whereas the Nupe would emphasize circumstantial facts and details because these two emphases fit their dominant sociocultural tendencies and associated schemes. His results confirmed his expectations, as did a follow-up study many years later by Deregowski (1970).

Research that has contrasted schooled and unschooled people of different ages has found marked effects on performance of the materials to be remembered and specifics of the task used for assessment on memory performance. Clearly, schooling confronts children with specialized information-processing tasks such as committing large amounts of esoteric information to memory in a short time and producing lengthy written discourses on the basis of memorized information. These, and similar tasks that are a routine part of schooling, have few analogies in the lives of people from societies in which there is no formal schooling. Hence, it is only to be expected that, when confronted with such tasks, which carry within them highly specialized histories and associated practices, there would be marked differences in performance—and there are. In line with these expectations, a number of studies show that schooling promotes the ability to remember unrelated materials (Rogoff, 1981; Wagner, 1982). For example, when a list of common items that fall into culturally recognized categories is presented repeatedly to children who are asked to recall as many of them as possible in any order, those children who have completed 6 or more years of schooling remember more and cluster items in recall more than nonschooled comparison groups (Cole et al., 1971; Scribner & Cole, 1981). By contrast, **schooling effects** are generally absent in tests of recall of well-structured stories or when the materials are embedded in a locally meaningful task (Dash & Misthra, 1989; Mandler, Scribner, Cole, & de Forest, 1980; Rogoff & Waddell, 1982).

Thinking about language.   As we pointed out above, schooling involves special ways of using language, both in the forms of oral discourse and in its constant mediation through written language. Several studies that speak to the issue of the consequences of schooling provide evidence that literacy in the context of schooling creates lasting effects on the development of knowledge about spoken language and even of differences in the brain morphology of people who have or have not been to school (Ardila, Roselli, & Rosas, 1989; Bornstein, Arterberry, & Mash, Chapter 6, this volume; Castro-Caldes, 2004; Ostrosky-Solís,

---

[5] The cross-cultural evidence is unclear with respect to the universality of formal operations, which are not expected until adolescence. Generally speaking, when Piagetian tasks have been used to measure formal operations, developing peoples who have not attended school fail, and even those who have attended several years of formal schooling rarely display formal operations (see Berry, Poortinga, Segall, & Dasen, 1992, for a review and additional sources). However, the same result has been claimed for US college students, although the matter is under dispute, and the question of the necessary and sufficient conditions for displaying formal logic remains open (see Cole, Cole, & Lightfoot, 2005, for a review of the issues and relevant data).

Ramirez, & Ardila, 2004). Collectively, these studies have involved a variety of populations ranging from cases of cultural practices in a Portuguese study where older girls were kept at home while second-borns went to school and were tested decades later, to cross-sectional studies of adults who had experienced various of levels of education and come from different parts of the same country. Results of these studies have lead Castro-Caldes to conclude that it is possible to identify brain structures that correspond to the functions of reading and writing, both from functional and anatomical points of view. Note that every one of these effects is specific to analysis of oral language. No evidence of generalized brain changes for problem solving in general or even of different forms of language use associated with schooling have been reported.[6]

Inductions based on classification.   In a well-known series of studies conducted in Central Asia in the early 1930s, Alexander Luria reported an increased likelihood of people (many as young adults) who had attended school categorizing objects taxonomically (given the items hoe, axe, and wood, hoe and axe go together as tools) rather than functionally (axe and wood go together because you cut the wood with an axe). This finding was replicated by Cole and his colleagues, who confirmed that unschooled adults did not lack vocabulary corresponding to the relevant taxonomic categories and that their use of such taxonomic categories was manifested in a variety of experimental conditions, appearing to make Luria's results task-specific (Cole et al., 1971).

That schooling alone could account for differences in experimental categorization tasks has been cast into doubt by Li, Zhang, and Nisbett (2004), who report that college students at Beijing University were most likely to carry out such categorization functionally, like Luria's peasants. Something more, or something else, is involved in the performance changes that Luria attributed to cultural-historical progress and schooling, but it remains unclear what those "somethings" might be.

Other recent cross-cultural research raises further questions about categorization. In a series of studies Ross and his colleagues compared the development of inductive reasoning about biological kinds among rural Menominee Native Americans, Anglo-American children living in a town in the same rural area, and Anglo counterparts living in a large city (Ross, Medin, Coley, & Atran, 2003). They report that, whereas all but the youngest city-dwelling Anglo children showed an appreciation of biological categories and the similarities among them, the rural children, including the Menominee rural children, showed a form of the ecological thinking we described earlier. This ecological thinking was present among the rural Anglo children, although in weaker form, but did not appear even among the oldest urban children.

In summary, school-aged children from indigenous communities, like the younger children we described in the last section, are capable of ecological reasoning. Where Luria considered this a less advanced kind of reasoning that schooling would, and should, replace with taxonomic reasoning, we propose that these are two distinct reasoning styles, each relevant in the appropriate situation. Ecological reasoning, however, is likely to clash with treatments of biology in the classroom, for these tend to start with model species and build gradually to a systems perspective, and often introduce ecosystems without reference to humans (Bang, Medin, & Atran, 2007).

Cross-generational studies of schooling effects.   The most convincing evidence for a generalized impact of schooling on development comes not from cross-sectional experimental

---

[6] It is also relevant that Scribner and Cole (1981) provided evidence of increased ability to analyze language among Vai adults who had become literate without attending school. Their results reinforce the view that cultural influences on the development of particular psychological functions are specific to the practices involved.

studies of cognition, but from studies of the intergenerational effect of schooling on parenting practices of mothers and the effect of these practices on subsequent generations. LeVine and his colleagues have provided convincing evidence of the cognitive and social consequences of schooling. These researchers focused on the ways in which formal schooling changes the behavior of mothers toward their offspring and their interactions with people in modern, bureaucratic institutions, as well as the subsequent impacts on their children (LeVine & LeVine, 2001; LeVine et al., 2001). These researchers propose a set of plausible habits, preferences, and skills that children acquire in school which they retain into adulthood and apply in the course of rearing their own children. These changes in parenting behavior include, in addition to use of rudimentary literacy and numeracy skills:

1. discourse skills that involved using written texts for purposes of understanding and using oral communication that is directly relevant to the negotiation of interactions in health and educational settings involving their children
2. models of teaching and learning based on the scripted activities and authority structures of schooling, such that when in subordinate positions schooled women adopt and employ behaviors appropriate to the student role and, when in superordinate positions adopt behaviors appropriate to the teacher role
3. an ability and willingness to acquire and accept information from the mass media, such as following health prescriptions more obediently.

As a consequence of these changes in the maternal behavior of young women who have attended at least through elementary school, LeVine and his colleagues find that the children of such women experience a lower level of infant mortality, better health during childhood, and greater academic achievement. Hence, if schooling may or may not produce measurable, generalized, cognitive affects at the time, such experience does produce context-specific changes in behavior that have quite general consequences with respect to the task of childrearing, which in turn produces general consequences in the next generation.

Converging evidence of a different kind comes from the work of Correa-Chavez and Rogoff (2009) on changes in children's tendency to learn from closely observing the behavior of their parents carrying out tasks they will be expected to deal with in the future. The tendency to learn effectively by close observation decreased as the level of mother's education increased.

Casting this broader research net indicates that new forms of activity involved in schooling engender not only new, restricted cognitive "tricks of the literate trade" but a more general elaboration of various verbal skills and a "modernist" ideology associated with schooling and modern work that structures the enculturation environment of subsequent generations. It also indicates that some effective ways of learning decrease as an effect of maternal education. In effect, research on the cognitive consequences of education teaches us something about our own cultural practices that should make us more cautious in our claims about the cognitive benefits of schooling, independent of the value we place on the specific abilities that children acquire there and the modes of life made possible and more sensitive to indirect effects associated with generational change.

From Childhood to Adulthood: A Site for Examining the Idea of Developmental Stages

In common parlance, adolescence is so routinely treated as a clearly marked period of development that it is rarely remembered that when Hall (1904) launched the modern study of adolescence over a century ago, he referred to an age period in the life cycle that spanned the ages from 14 to 25 years. At the present time, although it is common to encounter claims of a new period of life that spans all or part of the years that Hall identified as adolescence, there is widespread disagreement on whether those years mark a distinct period of development or a more or less protracted transition to adulthood, which has itself been subjected to extensive changes in definition and periodization in terms of chronological age (Johnson-Hanks, 2002).

For many decades, scholarly interest in the time period identified by Hall as adolescence (a term that came into English from French and Latin, referring to "a youth between childhood and manhood" [*sic*] *Oxford English Dictionary*, Second Electronic Edition, 1989) has focused only on the earlier years in Hall's proposed age period, roughly from 13 to 18, so that "teenager" and "adolescent" became virtually synonymous terms. In 1970, Keniston claimed that new socioeconomic circumstances, at least for the educated elite in advanced industrialized countries, justified the addition of a "new" stage of development, "youth" (ages 18 to 25), between adolescence as it was then understood and adulthood. A decade later the period now accepted as adolescence was further subdivided into early and late "sub-stages" with the inauguration of *The Journal of Early Adolescence*, which focused on the age roughly from 12 to 14 on the grounds that its developmental processes were distinct from those of later adolescence. Later still, the period that Keniston identified as youth was renamed "emerging adulthood," defined by Arnett (1998, p. 312) as "a period of development bridging adolescence and young adulthood, during which young people are no longer adolescents but have not yet attained full adult status." This specification is quite similar to the way that adolescence had been treated as a period bridging childhood and adulthood in earlier eras. Arnett attributed the emergence of this stage to political, economic, and social changes occurring primarily in societies that have undergone a change from industrial to information-based economies, and characterized it as "the age of instability, the self-focused age, the age of feeling in between, the age of possibilities" (Arnett, 2007, p. 208).

During this same period, adulthood, which had traditionally been treated as qualitatively different from both old age and childhood, itself began to be redefined. Social commentators began to talk about a "Third Age" of adulthood, the years from 50 to 74 years:

> Old age is what you make of it. Science has underscored this message by, for example, announcing that grey cells also reproduce themselves in old age, but only if the brain is kept fit. The threat of senility can be countered. Important muscles can, within one or two years, be trained to reach the capacity of those of middle-aged people. In sum, a high quality of life during one's "third age" is not only a gift. It is also one's duty—a duty that consists of exercise, healthy foods, education, and enriching social networks. Those who have neither money nor the motivation to work on themselves, fail. (Greenberg & Muehlbach, 2006, p. 195)

These changing conceptions of "the transition to adulthood" highlight in particularly clear form the interplay of biological and cultural–historical factors in the constitution and interpretation of "stages" of ontogenetic development, because all the proposed stages display cultural and historical variation in the way they are manifested and organized in different societies at different times.

Stages or transitions? Single or multiple?   The stage-versus-transition discussion is important not only because cultural factors are clearly involved in its specification but also because it speaks to the basic question of the existence of, and sources of, discontinuity in development. As ordinarily used by psychologists, the terms "transition" and "stage" are not synonymous. A *stage* is a more or less stable, patterned, and enduring system of interactions between the organism and the environment; a *transition* is a period of flux, when the "ensemble of the whole" that makes up one stage has disintegrated and a new stage is not firmly in place. According to this set of ideas, can adolescence, youth, emerging adulthood,

adulthood and so on be considered stages, even in societies that give them a name and treat them as distinct? Or are they best considered, despite popular understanding, heterogeneous, contingent transitions, whose "stage-like-ness" is itself a cultural construction?

The cultural contingency of adolescence as part of the life cycle. Adolescence is an advantageous point at which to investigate such questions because what is indisputable is that some time near or following the end of a decade of life (the exact onset time depends greatly on nutritional and other factors), a cascade of biochemical events begins that will alter the size, the shape, and the functioning of the human body. The most visible manifestations of these changes are a marked growth spurt and development of the potential for individuals to engage in biological reproduction (Bogin, 2009; Gordon & Laufer, 2005). These biological changes have profound social implications for the simple reason that reproduction cannot be accomplished by a single human being (replaying, in inverted form, the social dependency of infancy). As their reproductive organs reach maturity, boys and girls begin to engage in new forms of social behavior because they begin to find such activity attractive. According to many psychologists, some combination of these biological changes in brain and changes in sociocultural circumstances also gives rise to new cognitive capacities (Nasir, 2005; Tamnes et al., 2010).

The evidence from phylogeny and cultural history. Arguments for the universality of adolescence are sometimes made on the basis of studies of the fossil record in the hominid line, and sometimes on the basis of similarities to non-human primates, often chimpanzees (Bogin, 2009; Leigh, 2004). On the basis of an examination of the fossil record available in the prior edition of this book, Bogin concluded that the emergence of a distinctive stage of life between childhood and adulthood occurred with the evolution of *Homo sapiens* from *Homo erectus*, approximately 125,000 years ago. Bogin argued (1999, p. 216) that "adolescence became a part of human life history because it conferred significant reproductive advantages to our species, in part by allowing the adolescent to learn and practice adult economic, social, and sexual behavior before reproducing." Bogin (2009) now argues that there is no event corresponding to the adolescent growth spurt among chimpanzees, so that adolescence is a peculiarly human part of the life cycle. Others argue that changes associated with sexual maturation and altered social behavior (decreased association of males with their mothers and increased association with older males, decreased play of both sexes with juveniles, and increased aggressive behaviors) point toward the presence of adolescence among chimpanzees (King, Weiss, & Sisco, 2008; Ross, Bloomsmith, Bettinger & Wagner, 2009), so the issue is probably best considered uncertain.

Schlegel and Barry (1991), focusing on variation across human societies, side with those who believe in the presence of adolescence among non-human primates as a starting point for their claim of adolescence as a universal stage of development among humans. They go on to provide data from a sample of 186 societies included in the Human Area Files to substantiate claims that a socially marked period of adolescence is a human universal. Consistent with this line of reasoning, Bloch and Niederhoffer (1958) suggested that one of the universal features shared by the notion of a "transition to adulthood" and "adolescence" is a struggle for adult status. In all societies, the old eventually give way to the young. It is not easy for those in power to give it up, so it is natural to expect that, to some degree, the granting of adult status, and with it adult power, will involve a struggle. A good candidate for a second universal feature of the transition from childhood to adulthood is that it arouses tension because children, who have long identified strongly with members of their own gender while avoiding contact with the opposite gender, must now become attached to a member of the opposite gender (or a member of the same gender, which causes a different set of tensions). But if such evidence is sufficient to indicate a period of transition in which individuals from different generations must readjust their relations with each other, it does not indicate the presence of a distinct stage, as this term is generally used.

Sometimes the argument for the universality of adolescence as a stage of development is based on historical evidence, such as Aristotle's characterization of the young as prone to sexuality, lack of self-restraint, and insolence (cited in Kiell, 1964, pp. 18–19). Combining such historical evidence with similar accounts from various non-industrialized societies around the world today, Schlegel (2008) asserted that the experience of adolescence is universal. However, the data supporting the universality of adolescence as a unified stage are by no means unequivocal.

First, reverting to the primate literature, it is striking that marked shifts in social behavior are reported more frequently for males than for females. The same appears true when we turn to Aristotle's description of adolescents and similar descriptions from other ancient societies (Kiell, 1964): The people being talked about were most often males. Moreover, they were urban males of the moneyed classes who had to undergo a period of extended training, often including formal schooling, which created a delay between puberty and full adult status. Generally speaking, women and most members of the lower classes did not undergo such specialized training, and there is a corresponding lack of evidence that they were included in the category of adolescents. Among the upper classes in Athens, for example, girls were often married and sent to live in their mother-in-law's house before they had gone through puberty, and did not undergo institutionalized formal training to be considered adults.

Moreover, although some of the evidence from other cultures may support the idea that adult status universally brings with it new responsibilities, anxieties, and uncertainty, there is equally strong evidence that adolescence, as the term is used in modern industrialized societies, exists only under particular cultural circumstances, that when it exists it is more a transition accomplished by a variety of means at a variety of ages than a stage, and that it is not necessarily accompanied by the kind of conflict and anxiety said to exist in modern, industrialized societies (Johnson-Hanks, 2002; Whiting, Burbank, & Ratner, 1986). When we consider the actual organization of life in ancient Greece, Europe in the middle ages, and contemporary non-industrialized societies, in terms of the role of culture in development, we are reminded that the process of biological reproduction by itself is insufficient for the continuation of our species. As indicated by Schlegel and others who argue for the universality of adolescence among humans, any biological factors must be complemented by the process of cultural reproduction (education, broadly conceived), which ensures that the designs for living evolved by the group will be inherited by the next generation. Accordingly, in our view, adolescence will exist as a distinctive period of life only under specific cultural or historical circumstances. For example, among the Inuit of the Canadian Arctic in the early twentieth century, special terms were used to refer to boys and girls when they entered puberty, but these terms did not coincide with Western notions of adolescence (Condon, 1987). Young women were considered fully grown (adult) at menarche, a change in status marked by the fact that they were likely to be married and ready to start bearing children within a few years. Young men were not considered fully grown until they were able to build a snow house and hunt large game unassisted. This feat might occur shortly after the onset of puberty, but it was more likely for boys to achieve adult status somewhat later because they had to prove first that they could support themselves and their families. In view of the different life circumstances of these people, it is not surprising that they developed no special concept corresponding to adolescence that applied to boys and girls alike; such a concept did not correspond to their reality.

Closer to the present is the example of the Aka of the rainforests of the Central African Republic and the Northern Congo. The Aka live in bands of 25–35 and engage in hunting which is carried out by entire families. As reported by Bentz (2001), teenagers spend most of their days in the presence of their parents. They are extremely close to their siblings and peers, living in what Bentz refers to as an intense intimacy, closeness, and bonds of tenderness and affection. Aka girls build their own houses when they are 9 to 10 years old, often at the first signs of puberty but well before they are likely to bear children, whereas the boys move into what Bentz refers to as a "bachelor's pad." Girls may begin to engage in sexual activity at this time, but when and who they marry is a matter for them to decide, sometimes earlier, sometimes later. They may or may not take their parents' advice on a suitable husband, as they choose. The result of these arrangements, in which male and female cooperate in both hunting and child care, is, according to Bentz, a pattern that combines characteristics that appear antithetical when viewed from a North American perspective. There is clearly a period of transition between childhood and adulthood, but it results not in conflict between autonomy and closeness to one's parents, nor in alienation between generations, but in additional autonomy within the family unit combined with closeness to peers and minimal levels of conflict. In this society it appears that adolescence is more a process of transition than a stage marked off from those that proceed and follow it.

Societies in which technology and an extended period of formal education are absent may still produce conditions in which adolescence exists as a stage, either for males or for females. Such an example is provided by the Ache, a forest-dwelling, hunter-gatherer group in Paraguay (Hill & Hurtado, 1996). Until they came in contact with modern cultural institutions, the Ache lived in small groups and moved so frequently that they did not set up permanent settlements in the forest. At the age of 9 or 10, before reaching menarche, roughly 85% of Ache females had experienced sexual intercourse with at least one adult male, and many married before puberty. Nevertheless, Hill and Hurtado report that even at such a young age "their behavior would be aggressively flirtatious but sexually coy to the point of causing frustration anxiety among most of their suitors . . . The major activity of girls at this time is walking around in small groups laughing and giggling and carrying on in any manner that will attract attention" (p. 225). Boys, who went through puberty later than girls, exhibited behaviors reminiscent of Western teenage boys: "In particular, males of this age appear extremely insecure and often engage in obnoxious or high-risk behavior in order to gain attention" (Hill & Hurtado, p. 226).

Our conclusion is that although the biological changes associated with the ability to reproduce are universal, there is enormous variability in the extent to which the transition to adulthood can be considered a stage in the accepted sense of that term. Among human beings, the capacities for biological and cultural reproduction are intertwined in ways that continue to defy simple generalizations.

Adolescents/youth in periods of rapid social change.   A related issue of particular contemporary concern is the impact of rapid social change on the specification of developmental periods, particularly under conditions of extensive inter-cultural contact marked by economic and political inequality. Chandler and his colleagues (Chandler, Lalonde, Sokol, & Hallett, 2003; Chandler & Proulx, 2006) documented the cause for such concerns in their study of suicide among 15- to 24-year-old First Nations young people in British Columbia, Canada. For the period from 1987 to 1992 the suicide rate among First Nations adolescents/ youth was five times greater than that for all other ethnic groups combined. Chandler and his colleagues argued that First Nations young people are especially at risk for suicide due to a number of repressive policies pursued by the government, which have deprived them of their land, their fishing rights, their language, their right to self-governance, and control over their own cultural institutions. Combined with poor educational facilities and job discrimination, these conditions could, indeed, produce a sense of hopelessness at a time of life when, according to the normative characterization of adolescence and emerging adulthood in most textbooks, it should be a period of adult identity formation. Chandler and his colleagues hypothesized that the exceedingly high suicide rates among this population were the result, in part, of a failure to solve the problem of self-continuity (the understanding of oneself as the same person through time despite obvious changes in size, appearance, and knowledge). They used comic book renditions of classical stories in which people went through marked changes during their lifetime, such as Scrooge in Dickens' *A Christmas Carol*, and asked their participants to talk about their own sense of self-continuity. They found that European-origin adolescents were likely to explain self-continuity over time as the result of some essential feature such as their fingerprint or DNA. By contrast, First Nations adolescents provided narratives of how various events in their life produced a sequence of changes in them without negating the fact that they were the same person. These First Nations youths' narratives of self-continuity, Chandler and his colleagues argued, are particularly vulnerable to conditions of cultural destruction because the narrative tradition on which such self-construals were based was itself destroyed, leaving adolescents without the resources to form a sense of self-continuity. This study is not alone in providing evidence that cultural discontinuities in a period of rapid social change endanger successful passage from childhood to adulthood, implicating cultural modes of thought in the process of adolescent/youth development (see also Cole & Durham, 2008).

CONCLUSIONS

At the outset of this chapter, we noted the growing attention that psychologists are paying to the role of culture in human development. Our (necessarily abbreviated) review has illustrated, we hope, both the importance of culture in the process of human development and the complexities of studying it. We have argued for an approach that considers culture as a medium rather than a variable while acknowledging the usefulness of cross-cultural research when it is conducted with sufficient care and modesty about the claims made (see Table 2.2).

Culture serves as the specifically human medium in which biological, cognitive, social, and emotional factors are co-occurring throughout development. This change can often be considered "progressive" insofar as the developing individual achieves greater freedom of action in a broader range of relevant activities. But such "progress" must always be evaluated with respect to some, preferably well-specified, set of cultural values and often what appears to be progress in one domain involves losses in others.

We have noted that during certain time periods, different contributing developmental factors converge and become coordinated in particular cultural circumstances such that they mutually amplify each other, giving rise to qualitatively new forms of living, in what

TABLE 2.2
Implications of Considering Culture as a Medium

- The "progress" of development should be evaluated with respect to a set of cultural values; often what appears to be progress in one domain involves losses in others.
- The existence of a specific stage of development may be the consequence of particular cultural–historical circumstances.
- The transition between stages is a phase change in which different developmental factors converge, become coordinated in particular cultural circumstances, mutually amplify each other, and give rise to a qualitatively new form of living.
- This new form of living then becomes embodied in cultural practices and identified as a new stage of development.

amounts to a phase transition that becomes embodied in cultural practices and identified as a "new stage of development." We saw this clearly at 6 to 9 months, where bone and muscle and brain growth make possible locomotion (although the precise timing of onset of motility depends on adult arrangements); locomotion changes the child's practical understanding of space, which transforms the conditions of social interaction with still-essential caregiver attention and the spatial characteristics of joint attention, making new distal forms of communication necessary, and simultaneously introducing a new emotionality into the caregiver–child relation which now becomes specific where before it was diffuse.

Considering culture first and foremost as a medium also has methodological consequences for the study of culture in development. Experimental research in cross-cultural studies is fraught with problems. Although the goal is to provide a neutral set of conditions where "all other things are held equal," experimentation removes participants from their social setting and introduces a new cultural situation with new demands that are rarely neutral with respect to the comparisons being made. When culture is then treated as an independent variable, it can produce the semblance of rigor while masking the fact that the fundamental requirement of true experimentation—the random assignment of participants to treatments—is violated. The very reason for conducting cross-cultural research is to study people who have *not* been assigned to cultures at random!

There is an instructive parallel between the difficulties of conducting convincing cross-cultural research in the late twentieth century and the dispute between Boas and evolutionary anthropologists such as Tylor in the nineteenth century. Recall that Tylor believed he could rank cultures with respect to level of development using a standardized criterion such as "extent of scientific knowledge" or "complexity of social organization." Boas demurred, insisting that the very meaning of these terms shifted with its cultural context and that heterogeneity of functioning depending on the domain studied had to be taken into account. Like Tylor, cross-cultural psychologists who use standardized instruments that they carry from place to place can rank people with respect to developmental level. However, as Boas would have predicted, their conclusions are suspect because the meaning of their criterial instruments changes with its cultural context. Eventually cross-cultural psychologists must engage in local ethnographic work to establish the relation of their testing procedures to the local culture and the kinds of experiences that people undergo over their life spans. It is a giant undertaking, for which there are only a few extended examples on which to draw.

Despite their shortcomings, cross-cultural methods can help us to identify variations in want of deeper analysis and can sometimes help us to understand the contributions of particular kinds of experience to the development of particular kinds of characteristics (as in the cases of the effects of forced change of prolonged sleep episodes in early infancy and modes of explaining self-continuity in adolescence). Cross-cultural research alerts us to the possibility that the very existence of certain stages of development may be the consequence of particular cultural–historical circumstances and not universal, as in the case of adolescence. It also serves the important function of getting us to question the sources of age-related differences observed in our own culture, as indicated by research on the effects of schooling in middle childhood. The fact that we are left wondering about the generality of the resulting changes in many cases (schooling effects being a major case in point) is disappointing, of course, but the good news is that it puts us on our guard against the ever-present danger of overgeneralizing the results of work conducted in our own societies.

When we take seriously the garden metaphor of culture-as-medium (what Valsiner, 1989, referred to as an *organizing variable*), entirely new avenues of research are opened up, and at the same time new challenges. When we take the step from cross-cultural to cultural psychology we stand the usual relation between everyday experience and experimentation on its head. From this viewpoint, experiments themselves need to be considered as social situations. Studies of the child or infant in isolation can tell us little about what they can do in interaction with others—something that we have argued is crucial. Laboratory experiments with children remove them from the particular social networks in which they live and grow. They "limit the subject's freedom to initiate communication inventively" (Trevarthen, 2005) in ways that often destroy the phenomena they seek to investigate, especially with infants. The child's interaction with the researcher, through talk and nonverbal communication, is often not considered an important factor, though it may "prime" the child's responses in ways the researcher does not intend and remains unaware of (Oyserman & Lee, 2008). We need experiments that study children *in their relations* (Selby & Bradley, 2003).

Naturalistic studies become a necessary part of our toolkit. Instead of starting with presumably culture-free measures of psychological process, we begin with observation of everyday activities as part of a culturally organized sequence with its own internal logic and goals. Experiments then become ways to conveniently model existing cultural practices to externalize their inner workings (Scribner, 1975). When we begin in this way, we come across such new (theoretically speaking) phenomena as the revelation of the projection of ideal or mental models of past gender relations onto ideal or mental models of a child's future and the transformation of this ideal model into concrete reality. Or we are led into an analysis of the organization of everyday conversations between mothers and children to understand how their structure is related to the society's world view (Bornstein, 1989; Goodnow, 1984), or school activities to determine how to make instruction developmentally beneficial (Newman, Griffin, & Cole, 1989).

Such analyses are often, from the perspective of experimental psychology, messy and difficult. However, a growing literature on this topic, only a small part of which we have been able to touch on in this chapter (Packer, 2011), suggests that it holds great promise for the future development of the science of human development.

ACKNOWLEDGMENTS

Preparation of this chapter was supported in part by a Grant from the Spencer Foundation. It could not have been completed without the support of colleagues and staff at the Laboratory of Comparative Human Cognition, whose humor and good will are a constant source of inspiration.

REFERENCES AND SUGGESTED READINGS (📖)

Ainsworth, M. D. (1967). *Infancy in Uganda: Infant care and the growth of love*. Baltimore, MD: Johns Hopkins Press.

Ainsworth, M. D., Blehar, M. C., Waters, E., & Wall, S. (1978). *Patterns of attachment*. Hillsdale, NJ: Lawrence Erlbaum Associates.

Ardilla, A. M., Roselli, P., & Rosas, P. (1989). Neuro-psychological assessment in illiterates: Visuospatial and memory abilities. *Brain and Cognition, 11*, 147–166.

Arnett, J. J. (1998). Learning to stand alone: The contemporary American transition to adulthood in cultural and historical context. *Human Development, 41*, 5–6, 295–315.

Arnett, J. J. (2007). Socialization in emerging adulthood: From the family to the wider world, from socialization to self-socialization. In J. E. Grusec & P. D. Hastings (Eds.), *Handbook of socialization: Theory and research.* (pp. 208–231). New York: Guilford Press.

Astington, J. W., & Baird, J. A. (2005). Representational development and false-belief understanding. In J. W. Astington & J. A. Baird (Eds.), *Why language matters for theory of mind* (pp. 163–185). New York: Oxford University Press.

Atran, S., Medin, D., Lynch, E., Vapnarsky, V., Ek, E. U., & Soursa, P. (2001). Folkbiology does not come from Folkpschology: Evidence from Yukatek Maya in cross-cultural perspective. *Journal of Cognition and Culture, 1*(1), 3–41.

Atran, S., Medin, D., & Ross, N. O. (2004). Evolution and devolution of knowledge: A tale of two biologies. *Journal of the Royal Anthropological Institute, 10*(2), 395–421.

Atran, S., Medin, D., & Ross, N. O. (2005). The cultural mind: Environmental decision making and cultural modeling within and across populations. *Psychological Review, 112*(4), 744–776.

Avis, J., & Harris, P. L. (1991). Belief–desire reasoning among Baka children: Evidence for a universal conception of mind. *Child Development, 62*, 460–467.

Bandura, A. (2002). Social cognitive theory in cultural context. *Applied Psychology, 51*(2), 269–290.

Bang, M., Medin, D. L., & Atran, S. (2007). Cultural mosaics and mental models of nature. *Proceedings of the National Academy of Sciences of the United States of America, 104*(35), 13868–13874.

Barker, R. (1968). *Ecological psychology.* Stanford, CA: Stanford University Press.

Bates, E. (1976). *Language and context: The acquisition of pragmatics.* New York: Academic Press.

Battro, A. (2000). *Half a brain is enough: The story of Nico.* New York: Cambridge University Press.

Behrens, K. Y., Hesse, E., & Main, M. (2007). Mothers' attachment status as determined by the adult attachment interview predicts their 6-year-olds' reunion responses: A study conducted in Japan. *Developmental Psychology, 43*(6), 1553–1567.

Bentz, B. (2001). Adolescent culture: An exploration of the socio-emotional development of the Aka adolescents of the Central African Republic. *Oriental Anthropologist, 1*(2), 25–32.

Berry, J. W. (2000). Cross-cultural psychology: A symbiosis of cultural and comparative approaches. *Asian Journal of Social Psychology, 3*(3), 197–205.

Berry, J. W., Poortinga, Y. H., & Pandey, J. (1997). *Handbook of cross-cultural psychology, Vol. 1: Theory and method* (2nd ed.). Boston: Allyn & Bacon.

Berry, J. W., Poortinga, Y. H., Segall, M. H., & Dasen, P. R. (1992). *Cross-cultural psychology: Research and applications.* New York: Cambridge University Press.

Berry, J. W., Poortinga, Y. H., Segall, M. H. & Dasen, P. R. (2002). *Cross-cultural psychology: Research and applications* (2nd ed.). New York: Cambridge University Press.

Bloch, H. A., & Niederhoffer, A. (1958). *The gang: A study in adolescent behavior.* New York: Philosophical Library.

Bloom, P. (2004). *Descartes' baby: How the science of child development explains what makes us human.* New York: Basic Books.

Bloom, P., & German, T. P. (2000). Two reasons to abandon the false belief task as a test of theory of mind. *Cognition, 77*(1), B25–B31.

Boas, F. (1911). *The mind of primitive man.* New York: Macmillan.

Bogin, B. (1999). *Patterns of human growth* (2nd ed.). New York: Cambridge University Press.

Bogin, B. (2009). Childhood, adolescence, and longevity: A multilevel model of the evolution of reserve capacity in human life history. *American Journal of Human Biology, 21*, 567–577.

Bornstein, M. (1980). Cross-cultural developmental psychology. In M. H. Bornstein (Ed.), *Comparative methods in psychology* (pp. 231–281). Hillsdale, NJ: Lawrence Erlbaum Associates.

Bornstein, M. H. (1989). Cross-cultural comparisons: The case of Japanese American infant and mother activities and interactions. What we know, what we need to know, and why we need to know. *Developmental Review, 9,* 171–204.

Bornstein, M. H. (Ed.). (2009). *The handbook of cultural developmental science. Part 1. Domains of development across cultures. Part 2. Development in different places on earth.* New York: Taylor & Francis.

Bornstein, M. H., Haynes, O. M., Pascual, L., Painter, K. M., & Galperín, C. (1999). Play in two societies: Pervasiveness of process, specificity of structure. *Child Development, 70*(2), 317–331.

Bornstein, M. H., Tal, J., & Tamis-LeMonda, C. S. (1991). Parenting in cross-cultural perspective: The United States, France, and Japan. In M. H. Bornstein (Ed.), *Cultural approaches to parenting* (pp. 69–90). Hillsdale, NJ: Lawrence Erlbaum Associates.

Bornstein, M. H., Tamis-LeMonda, C. S., Tal, J., Ludemann, P., Toda, S., Rahn, C. W., et al. (1992). Maternal responsiveness to infants in three societies: The United States, France, and Japan. *Child Development, 63*(4), 808–821.

Bornstein, M. H., Toda, S., Azuma, H., Tamis-LeMonda, C. S., & Ogino, M. (1990). Mother and infant activity and interaction in Japan and in the United States: II. A comparative microanalysis of naturalistic exchanges focused on the organization of infant attention. *International Journal of Behavioral Development, 13,* 289–308.

Bowlby, J. (1969). *Attachment and loss: Vol. 1. Attachment.* New York: Basic Books.

Bowlby, J. (1982). *Attachment and loss: Vol. 1. Attachment* (2nd ed.). New York: Basic Books.

Bretherton, I., & Waters, E. (Eds.). (1985). Growing points in attachment theory. *Monographs of the Society for Research in Child Development, 50*(12), Serial No. 209.

Bronfenbrenner, U. (1979). *The ecology of human development.* Cambridge, MA: Harvard University Press.

Brown, R. (1965). *Social psychology.* New York: Free Press.

Brown, R. (1973). *A first language: The early stages.* Cambridge, MA: Harvard University Press.

Bruner, J. S. (1982). The formats of language acquisition. *American Journal of Semiotics, 1,* 1–16.

Bruner, J. S. (1983). *Child's talk.* New York: Norton.

Bruner, J. S. (1990). *Acts of meaning*. Cambridge, MA: Harvard University Press.

Bryant, G. A. & Barrett, H. C. (2007). Recognizing intentions in infant-directed speech: Evidence for universals. *Psychological Science*, *18*(8), 746–751.

Callaghan, T., Rochat, P., Lillard, A., Claux, M. L., Odden, H., Itakura, S., et al. (2005). Synchrony in the onset of mental-state reasoning: Evidence from five cultures. *Psychological Science*, *16*(5), 378–384.

Campos, J. J., Anderson, D. I., Barbu-Roth, M. A., Hubbard, E. M., Hertenstein, M. J., & Witherington, D. (2000). Travel broadens the mind. *Infancy*, *1*(2), 149–219.

Carey, S. (1985). *Conceptual change in childhood*. Cambridge, MA: MIT Press.

Carey, S., & Spelke, E. (1994). Domain-specific knowledge and conceptual change. In L. A. Hirschfeld & S. A. Gelman (Eds.), *Mapping the mind: Domain specificity in cognition and culture* (pp. 169–200). New York: Cambridge University Press.

Cassidy, J., & Shaver, P. R. (2008). *Handbook of attachment: Theory, research, and clinical applications* (2nd ed.). New York: Guilford Press.

Castro-Caldes, A. (2004). Targeting regions of interest for the study of the illiterate brain. *International Journal of Psychology*, *39*(1), 5–17.

Chandler, M. J., Lalonde, C. E., Sokol, B. W., & Hallett, D. (2003). Personal persistence, identity development, and suicide. *Monographs of the Society for Research in Child Development*, *68*(2), Serial No. 278.

Chandler, M., & Proulx, T. (2006). Changing selves in changing worlds: Youth suicide on the fault-lines of colliding cultures. *Archives of Suicide Research*, *10*(2), 125–140.

Chen, Z., & Siegler, R. S. (2000). Intellectual development in childhood. In R. Sternberg (Ed.), *Handbook of intelligence* (pp. 92–116). New York: Cambridge University Press.

Chisholm, J. S., Burbank, V. K., Coall, D. A., & Gemmiti, F. (2005). Early stress: Perspectives from developmental evolutionary ecology. In B. J. Ellis & D. Bjorklund (Eds.). *Origins of the social mind: Evolutionary psychology and child development* (pp. 76–107). New York: Guilford Press.

Chomsky, N. (1986). *Knowledge of language: Its nature, origin, and use*. London: Praeger.

Clark, A. (2007). A sense of presence. *Pragmatics & Cognition*, *15*(3), 413–433.

Cohen, L., & Cashon, C. H. (2006). Infant cognition. In D. Kuhn, R. S. Siegler, W. Damon, & R. M. Lerner (Eds.), *Handbook of child psychology: Vol. 2. Cognition, perception, and language* (6th ed., pp. 214–251). Hoboken, NJ: Wiley.

Cole, J., & Durham, D. (Eds.). (2008), *Figuring the future: Children, youth, and globalization*. Santa Fe, NM: SAR Press.

Cole, M. (1996). *Cultural psychology: A once and future discipline*. Cambridge, MA: Belknap Harvard.

Cole, M. (2006). Culture and cognitive development in phylogenetic, historical, and ontogenetic perspective. In D. Kuhn & R. S. Siegler (Eds.), *Handbook of child psychology, Vol. 2: Cognition, perception, and language* (6th ed., pp. 636–686). New York: Wiley.

Cole, M., & Cole, S. (1989). *The development of children*. San Francisco: Scientific American.

Cole, M., Cole, S., & Lightfoot, C. (2002). *The development of children* (5th ed.). New York: W. H. Freeman.

Cole, M., Cole, S., & Lightfoot, C. (2005). *The development of children* (5th ed.). New York: Worth.

Cole, M., Gay, J., Glick, J. A., & Sharp, D. W. (1971). *The cultural context of learning and thinking*. New York: Basic Books.

Cole, M., & Hatano, G. (2007). Cultural–historical activity theory: Integrating phylogeny, cultural history, and ontogenesis in cultural psychology. In S. Kitayama & D. Cohen (Eds.), *Handbook of cultural psychology* (pp. 109–135). New York: Guilford Press.

Cole, M., & Scribner, S. (1977). Cross-cultural studies of memory and cognition. In R. V. Kail & J. W. Hagen (Eds.), *Perspectives on the development of memory and cognition* (pp. 239–271). Hillsdale, NJ: Lawrence Erlbaum Associates.

Coley, J. D. (1995). Emerging differentiation of folkbiology and folkpsychology: Attributions of biological and psychological properties to living things. *Child Development*, 1856–1874.

Condon, R. G. (1987). *Inuit youth*. New Brunswick, NJ: Rutgers University Press.

Correa-Chávez, M., & Rogoff, B. (2009). Children's attention to interactions directed to others: Guatemalan Mayan and European-American patterns. *Developmental Psychology*, *45*(3), 630–641.

Costall, A., & Leudar, I. (2007). Getting over "The problem of other minds": Communication in context. *Infant Behavior & Development*, *30*(2), 289–295.

Cote, L. R., & Bornstein, M. H. (2009). Child and mother play in three U.S. cultural groups: Comparisons and associations. *Journal of Family Psychology*, *23*(3), 355–363.

D'Andrade, R. (1984). Cultural meaning systems. In R. A. Shweder & R. A. LeVine (Eds.), *Culture theory: Essays on mind, self, and emotion* (pp. 88–119). New York: Cambridge University Press.

D'Andrade, R. (1986). Three scientific world views and the covering law model. In D. Fiske & R. Shweder (Eds.), *Meta-theory in the social sciences: Pluralisms and subjectivities* (pp. 19–41). Chicago: University of Chicago Press.

D'Andrade, R. (1996). Culture. *Social science encyclopedia* (pp. 161–163). London: Routledge.

Dash, U. N., & Mishra, H. C. (1989). Testing for the effects of schooling on memory in an ecocultural setting. *Psychology and Developing Societies*, *1*(2), 153–163.

Deregowski, J. (1970). Effect of cultural value of time upon recall. *British Journal of Social and Clinical Psychology*, *9*, 37–41.

de Villiers, J. G., & de Villiers, P. A. (1978). *Language acquisition*. Cambridge, MA: Harvard University Press.

de Villiers, J. G., & de Villiers, P. A. (2000). Linguistic determinism and the understanding of false beliefs. In P. Mitchell & K. J. Riggs (Eds.), *Children's reasoning and the mind* (pp. 191–228). Hove, UK: Psychology Press.

Durrett, M. E., Otaki, M., & Richards, P. (1984), Attachment and the mother's perception of support from the father. *International Journal of Behavioral Development*, *7*(2), 167–176.

Ellis, N. C. (1998). Emergentism, connectionism and language learning. *Language Learning*, *48*(4), 631–664.

Elman, J., Bates, E., Johnson, M. H., Karmiloff-Smith, A., Parisi, D., & Plunkett, K. (1996). *Rethinking innateness: A connectionist perspective on development*. Cambridge, MA: MIT Press.

Emde, R. N., Gaensbauer, T. J., & Harmon, R. J. (1976). *Emotional expression in infancy: A behavioral study*. Psychological Issues Monograph Series, *10*(1), Serial No. 37. New York: International Universities Press.

Ergazaki, M., & Andriotou, E. (2010). From "forest fires" and "hunting" to disturbing "habitats" and "food chains": Do young children come up with any ecological interpretations of human interventions within a forest? *Research in Science Education*, *40*, 187–201.

Evans, C. A., & Porter, C. L. (2009). The emergence of mother–infant co-regulation during the first year: Links to infants' developmental status and attachment. *Infant Behavior and Development*, *32*(2), 147–158.

Fodor, J. (1983). *Modularity of mind: An essay on faculty psychology*. Cambridge, MA: MIT Press.

Fogel, A., & Garvey, A. (2007). Alive communication. *Infant Behavior & Development*, *30*(2), 251–257.

Gallimore, R., Goldenberg, C. N., & Weisner, T. S. (1993). The social construction and subjective reality of activity settings: Implications for community psychology. *American Journal of Community Psychology*, *21*(4), 537–559.

Gardiner, H. W., & Kosmitzki, C. (2007). *Lives across cultures. Cross-cultural human development* (4th ed.). Boston: Allyn & Bacon.

Gaskins, S. (2000). Children's daily activities in a Mayan village: A culturally grounded description. *Cross-Cultural Research*, *34*(4), 375–389.

Gauvain, M. (2005). Sociocultural contexts of learning. In A. Maynard & M. I. Martini (Eds.), *Learning in cultural context: Family, peers, and school* (pp. 11–40). New York: Kluwer Academic/Plenum Publishers.

Geertz, C. (1973). *The interpretation of cultures*. New York: Basic Books.

Gelman, R. (2009). Innate learning and beyond. In M. Piattelli-Palmarini, J. Uriagereka, & P. Salaburu (Eds.), *Of minds and language: A dialogue with Noam Chomsky in the Basque country* (pp. 223–238). New York: Oxford University Press.

Gergely, G., Egyed, K., & Király, I. (2007). On pedagogy. *Developmental Science*, *10*(1), 139–46.

Gesell, A. (1940). *The first five years of life* (9th ed.). New York: Harper & Row.

Gesell, A. (1945). *The embryology of behavior*. New York: Harper & Row.

Goldin-Meadow, S. (1985). Language development under atypical learning conditions. In K. E. Nelson (Ed.), *Children's language* (Vol. 5, pp. 197–245). Hillsdale, NJ: Lawrence Erlbaum Associates.

Goldin-Meadow, S. (2007). Pointing sets the stage for learning language—and creating language. *Child Development*, *78*(3), 741–745.

Goldin-Meadow, S., Butcher, C., Mylander, C., & Dodge, M. (1994). Nouns and verbs in a self-styled gesture system: What's in a name? *Cognitive Psychology*, *27*, 259–319.

Goldin-Meadow, S., & Mylander, C. (1996). Spontaneous sign systems created by deaf children in two cultures. *Nature*, *391*, 279–281.

Goodenough, W. H. (1976). Multiculturalism as the normal human experience. *Anthropology & Education Quarterly*, *7*(4), 4–7.

Goodenough, W. H. (1994). Toward a working theory of culture. In R. Borofsky (Ed.), *Assessing cultural anthropology* (pp. 262–273). New York: McGraw-Hill.

Goodnow, J. (1984). Parents' ideas about parenting and development. In A. L. Brown & B. Rogoff (Eds.), *Advances in developmental psychology* (Vol. 3, pp. 193–242). Hillsdale, NJ: Lawrence Erlbaum Associates.

Gopnik, A. (2009). *The philosophical baby: What children's minds tell us about truth, love, and the meaning of life*. New York: Farrar, Straus & Giroux.

Gopnik, A., & Wellman, H. M. (1994). The theory theory. In L. A. Hirschfeld & S. A. Gelman (Eds.) *Mapping the mind: Domain specificity in cognition and culture* (pp. 257–293). New York: Cambridge University Press.

Gordon, C. M., & Laufer, M. R. (2005). Physiology of puberty. In S. J. H. Emans, D. P. Goldstein, & M. R. Laufer (Eds.). *Pediatric and adolescent gynecology* (5th ed.). Philadelphia: Lippincott, Williams & Wilkins.

Greenberg, J., & Muehlebach, A. (2007). The old world and its new economy. In J. Cole & D. L. Durham (Eds.), *Generations and globalization: Youth, age, and family in the new world economy* (pp. 190–214). Bloomington, IN: Indiana University Press.

Greenfield, P. M. (1966). On culture and conservation. In J. S. Bruner, R. P. Olver, & P. M. Greenfield (Eds.), *Studies in cognitive growth* (pp. 225–256). New York: Wiley.

Greenfield, P. M. (1997). Culture as process: Empirical methods for cultural psychology. In J. W. Berry, Y. H. Poortinga, & J. Pandey (Eds.), *Handbook of cross-cultural psychology: Theory and method* (pp. 301–346). Boston: Allyn and Bacon.

Greenfield, P. M. (2000). Three approaches to the psychology of culture: Where do they come from? Where can they go? *Asian Journal of Social Psychology*, *3*(3), 223–240.

Greenfield, P. M. (2004). *Weaving generations together: Evolving creativity in the Maya of Chiapas*. Santa Fe, NM: SAR Press.

Greenfield, P. M. (2009). Linking social change and developmental change: Shifting pathways of human development. *Developmental Psychology*, *45*(2), 401–418.

Greenfield, P. M., Brazelton, T. B., & Childs, C. P. (1989). From birth to maturity in Zinacantan: Ontogenesis in cultural context. In V. Bricker & G. Gossen (Eds.), *Ethnographic encounters in southern Mesoamerica: Celebratory essays in honor of Evon Z. Vogt* (pp. 177–216). Albany, NY: Institute of Mesoamerican Studies, State University of New York.

Greenfield, P. M., & Bruner, J. S. (1969). Culture and cognitive growth. In D. A. Goslin (Ed.), *Handbook of socialization theory and research* (pp. 633–660). New York: Rand McNally.

Greenfield, P. M., & Lave, J. (1982). Cognitive aspects of informal education. In D. A. Wagner & H. E. Stevenson (Eds.), *Cultural perspectives on child development* (pp. 181–207). New York: Freeman.

Grossmann, K. E. (2000). The evolution and history of attachment research and theory. In S. Goldberg, R. Muir, & J. Kerr (Eds.), *Attachment theory: Social developmental, and clinical perspectives* (pp. 85–121). New York: Analytic Press.

Grossmann, K. E., & Grossmann, K. (2005). Universality of human social attachment as an adaptive process. In C. S. Carter, L. Ahnert, K. E. Grossmann, S. B. Hardy, M. E. Lamb, S. W. Porges, et al. (Eds.), *Attachment and bonding: A new synthesis. Dahlem workshop report*. Cambridge, MA: MIT Press.

Grossmann, K. E., Grossmann, K., & Keppler, A. (2006). Universal and culture-specific aspects of human behavior: The case of attachment. In W. Friedlmeier, P. Chakkarath, & B. Schwarz (Eds.), *Culture and human development: The importance of cross-cultural research to the social sciences* (pp. 75–97). New York: Psychology Press.

Grossmann, K., Grossmann, K. E., Spangler, S., Suess, G., & Unzner, L. (1985). Maternal sensitivity and newborn orientation responses as related to quality of attachment in northern Germany. In I. Bretherton & E. Waters (Eds.), Growing points of attachment theory. *Monographs of the Society for Research in Child Development*, *50*(1–2), Serial No. 209.

Grotuss, J., Bjorklund, D. F., & Csinady, A. (2007). Evolutionary developmental psychology: Developing human nature. *Acta Psychologica Sinica*, *39*(3), 439–453.

Hall, G. S. (1904). *Adolescence*. New York: Appleton.

Hallpike, C. R. (1979). *The foundations of primitive thought*. Oxford, UK: Clarendon Press.

Hatano, G. (1997). Commentary: Core domains of thought, innate constraints, and sociocultural contexts. In H. M. Wellman & K. Inagaki (Eds.), *The emergence of core domains of thought: Children's reasoning about physical, psychological, and biological phenomena* (pp. 71–78). San Francisco: Jossey-Bass.

Hatano, G. & Inagaki, K. (2002). In W. W. Hartup & R. K. Silbereisen (Eds.), *Growing points in developmental science: An introduction* (pp. 123–142). Philadelphia: Psychology Press.

Hauser, M. (2005). Our chimpanzee mind. *Nature*, *437*(7055), 60–63.

Heft, H. (2003). Affordances, dynamic experience, and the challenge of reification. *Ecological Psychology*, *15*(2), 149–180.

Henning, A., Striano, T., & Lieven, E. V. M. (2005). Maternal speech to infants at 1 and 3 months of age. *Infant Behavior and Development*, *28*(4), 519–536.

Herder, J. G. V. (1784/1803). *Outlines of a philosophy of the history of man*. London: Luke Hansard.

Herskovitz, M. J. (1948). *Man and his works: The science of cultural anthropology*. New York: Knopf.

Hesse, E., & Main, M. (2006). Frightened, threatening, and dissociative parental behavior in low-risk samples: Description, discussion, and interpretations. *Development and Psychopathology*, *18*, 309–343.

Hill, K., & Hurtado, A. M. (1996). *Ache life history: The ecology and demography of a foraging people*. New York: Aldine de Gruyter.

Hinde, R. A. (1987). *Individuals, relationships and culture: Links between ethology and the social sciences*. New York: Cambridge University Press.

Howell, S. (1984). *Society and cosmos*. Oxford, UK: Oxford University Press.

His, B. L., & Adinolfi, M. (1997). Prenatal sexing of human fetuses and selective abortion [editorial comment]. *Prenatal Diagnosis*, *17*(1), 13.

Inagaki, K. (1990). The effects of raising animals on children's biological knowledge. *British Journal of Developmental Psychology*, *8*(2), 119–129.

Inagaki, K., & Hatano, G. (1993). Young children's understanding of the mind–body distinction. *Child Development*, *64*, 1534–1549.

Ingold, T. (2000). *The perception of the environment: Essays on livelihood, dwelling, and skill*. London: Routledge.

Inhelder, B., & Piaget, J. (1958). *The growth of logical thinking from childhood to adolescence.* New York: Basic Books.

Irvine, J. (1978). Wolof "magical thinking": Culture and conservation revisited. *Journal of Cross-Cultural Psychology, 9,* 38–47.

Jahoda, G. (1993). *Crossroads between culture and mind: Continuities and change in theories of human nature.* Cambridge, MA: Harvard University Press.

Janowsky, J. S., & Carper, R. (1995). A neural basis for cognitive transitions in school-aged children. In M. Haith & A. Sameroff (Eds.), *Reason and responsibility: The passage through childhood.* Chicago: University of Chicago Press.

Jeans, P. C., Smith, M. B., & Stearns, G. (1955). Incidence of prematurity in relation to maternal nutrition. *Journal of the American Dietary Association, 31,* 576–581.

Johnson-Hanks, J. (2002). On the limits of life stages in ethnography: Toward a theory of vital conjunctures. *American Anthropologist, 104*(3), 865–880.

Kagan, J. (1977). The uses of cross-cultural research in early development. In P. H. Liedaman, S. Tulkin, & A. Rosenfeld (Eds.), *Culture and infancy: Variations in the human experience* (pp. 271–286). New York: Academic Press.

Kamara, A. I., & Easley, J. A. (1977). Is the rate of cognitive development uniform across cultures? A methodological critique with new evidence from Themne children. In P. R. Dasen (Ed.), *Piagetian psychology: Cross-cultural contributions* (pp. 26–63). New York: Gardner.

Ke, J., & Holland, J. H. (2006). Language origin from an emergentist perspective. *Applied Linguistics, 27*(4), 691–716.

Keniston, K. (1970). Youth: A "new" stage of life. *American Scholar, 39,* 631–654.

Kiell, N. (1964). *The universal experience of adolescence.* New York: International Universities Press.

King, J. E, Weiss, A., & Sisco, M. M. (2008). Aping humans: Age and sex effects in chimpanzee (*Pan troglodytes*) and human (*Homo sapiens*) personality, *Journal of Comparative Psychology, 122*(4), 418–427.

Kisilevsky, B. S., Hains, S. M., Brown, C. A., Lee, C. T., Cowperthwaite, B., Stutzman, S. S., et al. (2009). Fetal sensitivity to properties of maternal speech and language. *Infant Behavior & Development, 32*(1), 59–71.

Kitayama, S. & Cohen, D. (2007). *Handbook of cultural psychology.* New York: Guilford Press.

Kitayama, S., Duffy, S., & Uchida, Y. (2007). Self as cultural mode of being. *Handbook of cultural psychology* (pp. 136–174). New York: Guilford Press.

Laboratory of Comparative Human Cognition (LCHC). (1983). Culture and development. In P. H. Mussen (Series Ed.) & W. Kessen (Vol. Ed.), *Handbook of child psychology: Vol. 1. History, theory, and methods* (pp. 295–356). New York: Wiley.

Lakoff, G., & Johnson, M. (1980). *Metaphors we live by.* Chicago: University of Chicago Press.

Lavelli, M. & Poli, M. (1998). Early mother–infant interaction during breast- and bottle-feeding. *Infant Behavior & Development, 21*(4), 667–683.

Lecanuet, J. P., Graniere-Deferre, C., Jacquet, A. Y., & DeCasper, A. J. (2000). Fetal discrimination of low-pitched musical notes. *Developmental Psychobiology, 36*(1), 29–39.

Leekam, S., Perner, J., Healey, L., & Sewell, C. (2008). False signs and the non-specificity of theory of mind: Evidence that preschoolers have general difficulties in understanding representations. *British Journal of Developmental Psychology, 26*(4), 485–497.

Leiderman, P. H., Tulkin, S. T., & Rosenfeld, A. (Eds.). (1977). *Culture and infancy: Variations in the human experience.* New York: Academic Press.

Leigh, B., & Milgrom, J. (2008). Risk factors for antenatal depression, postnatal depression and parenting stress. *BMC Psychiatry, 8,* 24.

Leigh, S. R. (2004). Brain growth, life history, and cognition in primate and human evolution. *American Journal of Primatology, 62,* 139–164.

Leslie, A. M. (2005). Developmental parallels in understanding minds and bodies. *Trends in Cognitive Sciences, 9*(10), 459–462.

LeVine, R. A., & LeVine, S. (2001). The schooling of women. *Ethos, 29*(3), 259–270.

LeVine, R. A., LeVine, S. E., & Schnell, B. (2001). "Improve the women": Mass schooling, female literacy, and worldwide social change. *Harvard Educational Review, 71*(1), 1–50.

Li, J., Zhang, Z., & Nisbett, R. (2004). Is it culture or is it language? Examination of language effects in cross-cultural research on categorization. *Journal of Personality and Social Psychology, 87*(1), 57–65.

Li, S.-C. (2007). Biocultural co-construction of developmental plasticity across the lifespan. In S. Kitayama & D. Cohen (Eds.), *Handbook of cultural psychology* (pp. 528–544). New York: Guilford Press.

Lillard, A. (1998). Ethnopsychologies: Cultural variations in theories of mind. *Psychological Bulletin, 123*(1), 3–32.

Lillard, A. & Skibbe, L. (2004). Theory of mind: Conscious attribution and spontaneous trait inference. In R. Hassin, J. S. Uleman, & J. A. Bargh (Eds.), *The new unconscious* (pp. 277–308). Oxford, UK: Oxford University Press.

Lillard, A. S., Skibbe, L., Zeljo, A., & Harlan, D. (2001). *Developing explanations for behavior in different communities and cultures.* Unpublished manuscript, University of Virginia, Charlottesville.

Lindzey, G., & Aronson, E. (Eds.) (1986) *Handbook of social psychology* (Vol. 2, 3rd ed.). New York: Random House.

Liu, D., Wellman, H. M., Tardif, T. & Sabbagh, M. A. (2008). Theory of mind development in Chinese children:

A meta-analysis of false-belief understanding across cultures and languages. *Developmental Psychology*, *44*(2), 523–531.

Lucariello, J. (1995). Mind, culture, person: Elements in a cultural psychology. *Human Development, 38*(1), 2–18.

Luria, A. R. (1928). The problem of the cultural development of the child. *Journal of Genetic Psychology, 35*, 493–506.

Luria, A. R. (1973). *The working brain.* New York: Basic Books.

Lutz, C. (1987). Goals, events and understanding in Ifaluk emotion theory. In D. Holland & N. Quinn (Eds.), *Cultural models in language and thought* (pp. 290–312). New York: Cambridge University Press.

MacFarlane, A. (1977). *The psychology of childbirth.* Cambridge, MA: Harvard University Press.

MacWhinney, B. (2006). Emergentism: Use often and with care. *Applied Linguistics, 27*(4), 729–740.

Main, M., & Cassidy, J. (1988). Categories of response to reunion with the parent at age 6: Predictable from infant attachment classifications and stable over a 1-month period. *Developmental Psychology, 24*, 415–426.

Main, M., Goldwyn, R., & Hesse, E. (2002). *Adult attachment scoring and classification system.* Unpublished manuscript, University of California, Berkeley.

Main, M., & Solomon, J. (1990). Procedures for identifying infants as disorganized/disoriented during the Ainsworth strange situation. In M. T. Greenberg, D. Cicchetti, & E. M. Cummings (Eds.), *Attachment in the preschool years* (pp. 121–160). Chicago: University of Chicago Press.

Mandler, J. M. (1997). Development of categorisation: Perceptual and conceptual categories. In G. Bremner, A. Slater, & G. Butterworth (Eds.). *Infant development: Recent advances* (pp. 163–189). Hove, UK: Taylor & Francis.

Mandler, J. M. (2004). *The foundations of mind.* Oxford, UK: Oxford University Press.

Mandler, J., Scribner, S., Cole, M., & de Forest, M. (1980). Cross-cultural invariance in story recall. *Child Development, 51*, 19–26.

Mastropieri, D., & Turkewitz, G. (1999). Prenatal experience and neonatal responsiveness to vocal expressions of emotion. *Developmental Psychobiology, 35*(3), 204–214.

☐ McGrew, W. C. (2002). The nature of culture: Prospects and pitfalls of cultural primatology. In de Waal, F. B. M. (Ed.), *Tree of origin: What primate behavior can tell us about humans* (pp. 229–254). Cambridge, MA: Harvard University Press.

Mead, M. (1935). *Sex and temperament in three primitive societies.* New York: William Morrow.

Mead, M., & Macgregor, F. C. (1951). *Growth and culture.* New York: Putnam.

Medin, D. L., & Atran, S. (2004). The native mind: Biological categorization, reasoning, and decision making in development and across cultures. *Psychological Review, 111*(4), 960–983.

Medin, D. L., & Atran, S. (Eds.). (1999). *Folkbiology.* Cambridge, MA: MIT Press.

Medin, D., Ross, N., & Cox, D. (2006). *Culture and resource conflict: Why meanings matter.* New York: Russell Sage.

Medin, D., Unsworth, S. J. & Hirschfeld, L. (2007). Culture, categorization, and reasoning. In S. Kitayama & D. Cohen (Eds.), *Handbook of cultural psychology* (pp. 615–644). New York: Guilford Press.

Mehan, H. (1978). *Learning lessons.* Cambridge, MA: Harvard University Press.

Mehler, J., Dupoux, E., Nazzi, T., & Dehaene-Lambertz, G. (1996). Coping with linguistic diversity: The infant's viewpoint. In J. L. Morgan, & K. Demuth (Eds.), *Signal to syntax: Bootstrapping from speech to grammar in early acquisition* (pp. 106–116). Mahwah, NJ: Lawrence Erlbaum Associates.

Miller, P. (1982). *Amy, Wendy and Beth: Learning language in south Baltimore.* Austin, TX: University of Texas Press.

Miyake, K., Chen, S., & Campos, J. J. (1985). Infant temperament, mother's mode of interaction, and attachment in Japan: An interim report. *Monographs of the Society for Research in Child Development, 50*(1–2), 276–297.

Nadel, S. F. (1937). Experiments on culture psychology. *Africa, 10*, 421–435.

Nakagawa, M., Lamb, M. E., & Miyake, K. (1992). Antecedents and correlates of the strange situation behavior of Japanese infants. *Journal of Cross-Cultural Psychology, 23*, 300–310.

Nasir, N. (2005). Individual cognitive structuring and the sociocultural context: Strategy shifts in the game of dominoes. *Journal of the Learning Sciences, 14*(1), 5–34.

Nelson, K. (1981). Social cognition in a script framework. In J. H. Flavell & L. Ross (Eds.), *Social cognitive development.* Cambridge, UK: Cambridge University Press.

☐ Nelson, K. (1986). *Event knowledge: Structure and function in development.* Hillsdale, NJ: Lawrence Erlbaum Associates.

Nelson, K. (2003). Making sense in a world of symbols. In A. Toomela (Ed.), *Cultural guidance in the development of the human mind* (pp. 139–158). Westport, CT: Ablex.

Nelson, K. (2007). *Young minds in social worlds: Experience, meaning, and memory.* Cambridge, MA: Harvard University Press.

Newburn, M. (2003). Culture, control and the birth environment. *Practical Midwife, 6*(8), 20–25.

Newman, D., Griffin, P., & Cole, M. (1989). *The construction zone: Working for cognitive change in the school.* New York: Cambridge University Press.

Nyiti, R. (1978). The development of conservation in the Meru children of Tanzania. *Child Development, 47*(6), 1122–1129.

☐ Ochs, E., & Schieffelin, B. B. (1984). Language acquisition and socialization: Three developmental stories and their implications. In R. Shweder & R. Levine (Eds.), *Culture theory: Essays on mind, self, and emotion* (pp. 276–320). Cambridge, UK: Cambridge University Press.

Ostrosky-Solis, F., Ramirez, M., & Ardila, A. (2004). Effects of culture and education on neuropsychological testing: A preliminary study with indigenous and nonindigenous population. *Applied Neuropsychology, 11*(4), 186–193.

Oyserman, D., & Lee, S. W.-S. (2007). Priming "culture": Culture as situated cognition. In S. Kitayama & D. Cohen (Eds.), *Handbook of cultural psychology* (pp. 255–282). New York: Guilford Press.

Oyserman, D., & Lee, S. W.-S. (2008). Does culture influence what and how we think? Effects of priming individualism and collectivism. *Psychological Bulletin, 134*(2), 311–342.

Packer, M. (2001a). The problem of transfer, and the sociocultural critique of schooling. *Journal of the Learning Sciences, 10*, 493–514.

Packer, M. J. (2001b). *Changing classes: School reform and the new economy.* New York: Cambridge University Press.

Packer, M. (2011). *The science of qualitative research.* New York: Cambridge University Press.

Packer, M. (in press). Schooling: Domestication or ontological construction? In T. Koschmann (Ed.), *Theories of learning and research into instructional practice.* New York: Springer.

Papousek, M. (2007). Communication in early infancy: An arena of intersubjective learning. *Infant Behavior & Development, 30*(2), 258–266.

Paul, R. A. (1995). Act and intention in Sherpa culture and society. In L. Rosen (Ed.), *Other intentions: Cultural contexts and the attribution of inner states* (pp. 15–45). Santa Fe, NM: School of American Research Press.

Pauli-Pott, U., Mertesacker, B., Bade, U., Haverkock, A., & Beckmann, D. (2003). Parental perceptions and infant temperament development. *Infant Behavior and Development, 26*(1), 27–48.

Perner, J. (2008). Who took the cog out of cognitive science? Mentalism in an era of anti-cognitivism. In P. A. Frensch et al. (Eds.), *International Congress of Psychology 2008 Proceedings.* Hove, UK: Psychology Press.

Perner, J., & Ruffman, T. (2005). Psychology. Infants' insight into the mind: How deep? *Science, 308*(5719), 214–216.

Perner, J., Ruffman, T., & Leekam, S. R. (1994). Theory of mind is contagious: You catch it from your sibs. *Child Development, 65*, 1228–1238.

Perner, J., Sprung, M., Zauner, P., & Haider, H. (2003). *Want that* is understood well before *say that, think that,* and false belief: A test of de Villiers's linguistic determinism on German-speaking children. *Child Development, 74*(1), 179–188.

Petitto, L. A. (2005). How the brain begets language. In J. McGilvray (Ed.), *The Cambridge companion to Chomsky* (pp. 84–101). Cambridge, UK: Cambridge University Press.

Piaget, J. (1937). *The construction of reality in the child.* London: Routledge & Kegan Paul.

Piaget, J. (1969). *Judgment and reasoning in the child.* London: Routledge & Kegan Paul.

Piaget, J. (1973). *The psychology of intelligence.* Totowa, NJ: Littlefield & Adams.

Piaget, J. (1995). Genetic logic and sociology. In J. Piaget (Ed.), *Sociological studies* (pp. 184–214). London: Routledge. (Original work published 1928).

Piaget, J., & Inhelder, B. (1969). *The psychology of the child.* New York: Basic Books.

Pinker, S. (1995). *The language instinct.* New York: Norton.

Pinker, S. (2002). *The blank slate: The modern denial of human nature.* New York: Viking.

Plotkin, H. C. (2002). *The imagined world made real: Towards a natural science of culture.* London: Allen Lane.

Pollitt, E., Saco-Pollitt, C., Jahari, A., Husaini, M. A., & Huang, J. (2000). Effects of an energy and micronutrient supplement on mental development and behavior under natural conditions in undernourished children in Indonesia. *European Journal of Clinical Nutrition, 54*, 80–90.

Premack, D., & Hauser, M. (2006). Why animals do not have culture. In S. C. Levinson & J. Pierre (Eds.), *Evolution and culture: A Fyssen Foundation symposium* (pp. 275–278). Cambridge, MA: MIT Press.

Premack, D., & Premack, A. J. (1983). *The mind of an ape.* New York: Norton.

Pujol, J., Soriano-Mas, C., Ortiz, H., Sebastian-Galles, N., Losilla, J. M., & Deus, J. (2006). Myelination of language-related areas in the developing brain. *Neurology, 66*(3), 339–343.

Pusey, A. E. (1990). Behavioural changes at adolescence in chimpanzees. *Behaviour, 115*, 203–246.

Quartz, S. R. & Sejnowski, T. J. (2002). *Liars, lovers, and heroes: What the new brain science reveals about how we become who we are.* New York: Morrow.

Read, M. (1960). *Children of their fathers: Growing up among the Ngoni of Malawi.* New York: Holt, Rinehart & Winston.

Richardson, S. A., & Guttmacher, A. F. (1967). *Childbearing: Its social and psychological aspects.* Baltimore, MD: Williams & Wilkins.

Richman, A. L., Miller, P. M., & LeVine, R. A. (1992). Cultural and educational variations in maternal responsiveness. *Developmental Psychology, 28*(4), 614–621.

Richmond, J., & Nelson, C. A. (2007). Accounting for change in declarative memory: A cognitive neuroscience perspective. *Developmental Review, 27*(3), 349–373.

Rodriguez, C. (2007). Object use, communication, and signs: The triadic basis of early cognitive development. In J. Valsiner & A. Rosa (Eds.), *The Cambridge handbook of sociocultural psychology* (pp. 257–276). Cambridge, UK: Cambridge University Press.

Rogoff, B. (1981). Schooling and the development of cognitive skills. In H. C. Triandis & A. Heron (Eds.), *Handbook of cross-cultural psychology* (Vol. 4, pp. 233–294). Boston: Allyn & Bacon.

Rogoff, B. (2003). *The cultural nature of human development.* New York: Oxford University Press.

Rogoff, B., Gauvain, M., & Ellis, S. (1984). Development viewed in its cultural context. In M. H. Bornstein & M. E. Lamb (Eds.), *Developmental psychology: An advanced textbook* (pp. 139–151). Hillsdale, NJ: Lawrence Erlbaum Associates.

Rogoff, B., Sellers, M. J., Pirrotta, S., Fox, N., & White, S. H. (1975). Age of assignment of roles and responsibilities to children: A cross-cultural survey. *Human Development, 18*, 353–369.

Rogoff, B., & Waddell, K. J. (1982). Memory for information organized in a scene by children from two cultures. *Child Development, 53*(5), 1224–1228.

Romney, A., K., & Moore, C. C. (2001). Systemic culture patterns as basic units of cultural transmission and evolution. *Cross-Cultural Research, 35*(2), 154–178.

Ross, S. R., Bloomsmith, M. A., Bettinger, T. L., & Wagner, K. E. (2009). The influence of captive adolescent male chimpanzees on wounding: Management and welfare implications. *Zoo Biology, 28*, 1–12.

Ross, N., Medin, D., Coley, J. D., & Atran, S. (2003). Cultural and experimental differences in the development of folkbiological induction. *Cognitive Development, 18*(1), 25–47.

Rothbaum, F., Weisz, J., Pott, M., Miyake, K., & Morelli, G. (2000). Attachment and culture: Security in the United States and Japan. *American Psychologist, 55*(10), 1093–1104.

Rowe, M. K., Thapa, B. K., LeVine, R., LeVine, S., & Tuladhar, S. K. (2005). How does schooling influence maternal health practices? Evidence from Nepal. *Comparative Education Review, 49*(4), 512–533.

Rubin, J. Z., Provezano, F. J., & Luria, Z. (1974). The eye of the beholder: Parents' view on sex of newborns. *American Journal of Orthopsychiatry, 44*, 512–519.

Ruffman, T., Perner, J., & Parkin, L. (1999). How parenting style affects false belief understanding. *Social Development, 8*(3), 395–411.

Ruffman, T., Perner, J., Naito, M., Parkin, L., & Clements, W. A. (1998). Older (but not younger) siblings facilitate false belief understanding. *Developmental Psychology, 34*(1), 161–174.

Ruffman, T., Slade, L., & Crowe, E. (2002). The relation between children's and mothers' mental state language and theory-of-mind understanding. *Child Development, 73*(3), 734–751.

Ruffman, T., Slade, L., Devitt, K., & Crowe, E. (2006). What mothers say and what they do: The relation between parenting, theory of mind, language and conflict/cooperation. *British Journal of Developmental Psychology, 24*(1), 105–124.

Sagi, A., Lamb, M. E., Lewkowicz, K. S., Shoham, K. R., Dvir, R., & Estes, D. (1985). Security of infant–mother,– father,–metapelet, attachments among kibbutz-raised Israeli children. In I. Bretherton & K. Watas (Eds.), Growing points of attachment theory. *Monographs of the Society for Research in Child Development, 50* (1–2, Serial No. 209), 257–275.

Sagi, A., van IJzendoorn, M. H., Aviezer, O., Donnell, F., & Mayseless, O. (1994). Sleeping out of home in a kibbutz communal arrangement: It makes a difference for infant–mother attachment. *Child Development, 65*, 992–1004.

Sameroff, A. J. & Haith, M. M. (Eds.) (1996). *The five to seven year shift: The age of reason and responsibility.* Chicago: University of Chicago Press.

Schacter, D. L., & Moscovitch, M. (1984). Infants, amnesics, and dissociable memory systems. In M. Moscovitch (Ed.), *Infant memory* (pp. 173–216). New York: Plenum.

Schieffelin, B., & Ochs, E. (1986). *Language socialization across cultures.* New York: Cambridge University Press.

Schlegel, A. (2008). A cross-cultural approach to adolescence. In D. L. Browning (Ed.). *Adolescent identities: A collection of readings.* (pp. 31–44). New York: Analytic Press/Taylor & Francis.

Schlegel, A., & Barry, H. (1991). *Adolescence: An anthropological inquiry.* New York: Free Press.

Schliemann, A. D., Carraher, D. W., & Ceci, S. J. (1997). Everyday cognition. In J. W. Berry, P. R. Dasen, & T. S. Saraswathi (Eds.), *Handbook of cross-cultural psychology, Vol. 2: Basic processes and human development* (2nd ed., pp. 177–216). Needham Heights, MA: Allyn & Bacon.

Scribner, S. (1975). Situating the experiment in cross-cultural research. In K. F. Riegel & J. A. Meacham (Eds.), *The developing individual in a changing world: Historical and cultural issues.* The Hague, The Netherlands: Mouton.

Scribner, S., & Cole, M. (1973). Cognitive consequences of formal and informal education. *Science, 182*, 553–559.

Scribner, S., & Cole, M. (1981). *The psychology of literacy.* Cambridge, MA: Harvard University Press.

Segerdahl, P., Fields, W., & Savage-Rumbaugh, S. (2006). *Kanzi's primal language: The cultural initiation of primates into language.* Basingstoke, UK: Palgrave Macmillan.

Selby, J. M., & Bradley, B. S. (2003). Infants in groups: A paradigm for the study of early social experience. *Human Development, 46*(4), 197–221.

Senghas, A., Kita, S., & Ozyürek, A. (2004). Children creating core properties of language: Evidence from an emerging sign language in Nicaragua. *Science, 305*(5691), 1779–1782.

Serpell, R., & Hatano, G. (1997). Education, schooling, and literacy. In J. W. Berry, P. R. Dasen, & T. S. Saraswathi

(Eds.), *Handbook of cross-cultural psychology, Vol. 2: Basic processes and human development* (2nd ed., pp. 339–376). Needham Heights, MA: Allyn & Bacon.

Sharma, D. C. (2003). Widespread concern over India's missing girls. Selective abortion and female infanticide cause girl-to-boy ratios to plummet. *Lancet, 363*(9395), 1553.

Shostak, M. (1981). *Nissa: The life and words of a !Kung woman.* Cambridge, MA: Harvard University Press.

Shweder, R. A., Jensen, L. A., & Goldstein, W. M. (1995). Who sleeps by whom revisited: A method for extracting the moral goods implicit in practice. *New Directions for Child Development, 67,* 21–39.

Shweder, R. A., Goodnow, J. J., Hatano, G., LeVine, R. A., Markus, H. R., & Miller, P. J. (2006). The cultural psychology of development: One mind, many mentalities. In R. M. Lerner & W. Damon, London (Eds.). *Handbook of child psychology (6th ed.): Vol. 1, Theoretical models of human development* (pp. 716–792). Hoboken, NJ: Wiley.

Siegal, M. (1991). A clash of conversational worlds: Interpreting cognitive development through communication. In J. M. Levine & L. B. Resnick (Eds.), *Socially shared cognition.* Washington, DC: American Psychological Association.

Skinner, B. F. (1953). *Science and human behavior.* New York: Appleton, Century, Crofts.

Slade, L., & Ruffman, T. (2005). How language does (and does not) relate to theory of mind: A longitudinal study of syntax, semantics, working memory and false belief. *British Journal of Developmental Psychology, 23*(1), 117–142.

Smith, L. (2002). Piaget's model. In U. Goswami (Ed.), *Blackwell handbook of cognitive development* (pp. 515–537). Malden, MA. Blackwood.

Snow, C. (1995). Issues in the study of input: Finetuning, universality, individual and developmental differences, and necessary causes. In P. Fletcher & B. MacWhinney (Eds.), *The handbook of child language* (pp. 180–193). Oxford, UK: Blackwell.

Snow, C. E., & Ferguson, C. A. (Eds.). (1977). *Talking to children.* Cambridge, UK: Cambridge University Press.

Spitz, R. (1958). *A genetic field theory of ego development.* New York: International Universities Press.

Stiles, J., Moses, P., Roe, K., Akshoomoff, N., Trauner, D., Hesselink, J., et al. (2003). Alternative brain organization after prenatal cerebral injury: Convergent fMRI and cognitive data. *Journal of the International Neuropsychological Society, 9*(4), 604–622.

Stocking, G. (1968). *Race, culture, and evolution.* New York: Free Press.

Sullivan, K., & Winner, E. (1993). Three-year-olds' understanding of mental states: The influence of trickery. *Journal of Experimental Child Psychology, 56*(2), 135–148.

Super, C. (1987). The role of culture in developmental disorder. In C. Super (Ed.), *The role of culture in developmental disorder* (pp. 1–8). New York: Academic Press.

Super, C. M., & Harkness, S. (1982). The infant's niche in rural Kenya and metropolitan America. In L. Adler (Ed.), *Issues in cross-cultural research* (pp. 47–56). New York: Academic Press.

Super, C. M., & Harkness, S. (1986). The developmental niche: A conceptualization at the interface of child and culture. *International Journal of Behavioral Development, 9,* 545–569.

Super, C. M., & Harkness, S. (1997) The cultural structuring of child development. In J. W. Berry, P. S. Dasen, & T. S. Saraswathi (Eds.), *Handbook of cross-cultural psychology, Vol. 2: Basic processes and human development* (2nd ed., pp. 1–40). Needham Heights, MA: Allyn & Bacon.

Super, C. M., & Harkness, S. (2002). Culture structures the environment for development. *Human Development, 45*(4), 270–274.

Sweeney, J., & Bradbard, M. R. (1988). Mothers' and fathers' changing perception of their male and female infants over the course of pregnancy. *Journal of Genetic Psychology, 149*(3), 393–404.

Tamis-LeMonda, C. S., & Adolph, K. (2005). Social referencing in infant motor action. In B. D. Homer & C. S. Tamis-LeMonda (Eds.), *The development of social cognition and communication* (pp. 145–164). Mahwah, NJ: Lawrence Erlbaum Associates.

Tamnes, C. K., Østby, Y., Fjell, A. M., Westlye, L. T., Due-Tønnessen, P., & Walhovd, K. B. (2010). Brain maturation in adolescence and young adulthood: Regional age-related changes in cortical thickness and white matter volume and microstructure. *Cerebral Cortex, 20,* 534–548.

Taumoepeau, M., & Ruffman, T. (2006). Mother and infant talk about mental states relates to desire language and emotion understanding. *Child Development, 77,* 465–481.

Taumoepeau, M., & Ruffman, T. (2008). Stepping stones to others' minds: Maternal talk relates to child mental state language and emotion understanding at 15, 24, and 33 months. *Child Development, 79*(2), 284–302.

Tobin, J., Hsueh, Y., & Karasawa, M. (2009). *Preschool in three cultures revisited: China, Japan, and the United States.* Chicago: University of Chicago Press.

Tomasello, M., Call, J., & Hare, B. (2003). Chimpanzees understand psychological states—The question is which ones and to what extent? *Trends in Cognitive Sciences, 7*(4), 153–156.

Tomasello, M., & Carpenter, M. (2007). Shared intentionality. *Developmental Science, 10,* 121–125.

Trevarthen, C. (2005). Stepping away from the mirror: Pride and shame in adventures of companionship. Reflections on the nature and emotional needs of infant intersubjectivity. In C. S. Carter et al. (Eds.). *Attachment and bonding: A new synthesis. Dahlem Workshop Report 92* (pp. 55–84). Cambridge, MA: MIT Press.

Tudge, J. (2008). *The everyday lives of young children: Culture, class, and child rearing in diverse societies*. New York: Cambridge University Press.

Turvey, M. (2009). On the notion and implications of organism–environment interaction. *Ecological Psychology, 21*(2), 97–111.

Tylor, E. B. (1874). *Primitive culture: Researches into the development of mythology, philosophy, religion, language, art, and custom*. London: J. Murray.

UNESCO Institute for Statistics (2009). Global education digest 2009: Comparing education statistics across the world. New York: UNESCO.

Valsiner, J. (1989). From group comparisons to knowledge: Lessons from cross-cultural psychology. In J. P. Forgas & J. M. Innes (Eds.), *Recent advances in social psychology: An international perspective* (pp. 69–106). Boston: Allyn & Bacon.

Valsiner, J. (2000). *Culture and human development*. Thousand Oaks, CA: Sage.

Valsiner, J. & Rosa, A. (2007). *The Cambridge handbook of sociocultural psychology*. New York: Cambridge University Press.

van IJzendoorn, M. H., & Sagi, A. (1999). Cross-cultural patterns of attachment: Universal and contextual dimensions. In J. Cassidy & P. R. Shaver (Eds.), *Handbook of attachment: Theory, research, and clinical applications* (pp. 713–734). New York: Guilford Press.

van IJzendoorn, M. H., & Sagi, A., (2001). Cultural blindness or selective inattention? *American Psychologist, 56*(10), 824–825.

Varenne, H., & McDermott, R. (1999). *Successful failure: The school America builds*. Boulder, CO: Westview Press.

Vinden, P. G. (1998). Imagination and true belief: A cross-cultural perspective. In J. de Rivera & T. R. Sarbin (Eds.), *Believed-in imaginings: The narrative construction of reality* (pp. 73–85). Washington, DC: American Psychological Association.

Vinden, P. G. (1999). Children's understanding of mind and emotion: A multi-culture study. *Cognition & Emotion, 13*(1), 19–48.

Vinden, P. G. (2002). Understanding minds and evidence for belief: A study of Mofu children in Cameroon. *International Journal of Behavioral Development, 26*(5), 445–452.

Vygotsky, L. S. (1987). Thinking and speech. In N. Minick (Ed. & Trans.), *The collected works of L. S. Vygotsky: Vol. 1. Problems of general psychology* (pp. 39–285). New York: Plenum.

Vygotsky, L. S. (2004). The historical meaning of the crisis in psychology: A methodological investigation. In R. W. Rieber & D. K. Robinson (Eds.), *The essential Vygotsky* (pp. 227–357). New York: Kluwer Academic/Plenum Publishers.

Wagner, D. A. (1982). Ontogeny in the study of culture and cognition. In D. A. Wagner & H. W. Stevenson (Eds.), *Cultural perspectives on child development* (pp. 105–123). San Francisco: Freeman.

Wagner, D. A., (1993). *Literacy, culture, and development: Becoming literate in Morocco*. New York: Cambridge University Press.

Waxman, S. R., & Medin, D. (2007). Experience and cultural models matter: Placing firm limits on childhood anthropocentrism. *Human Development, 50*, 23–30.

Weisner, T. S. (1996). The 5 to 7 transition as an ecocultural project. In A. Sameroff & M. M. Haith (Eds.), *The five to seven year shift: The age of reason and responsibility* (pp. 295–326). Chicago: University of Chicago Press.

Weisner, T. (2002). Ecocultural understanding of children's developmental pathways. *Human Development, 45*(4), 275–281.

Wellman, H. C. (2002). Understanding the psychological world: Developing a theory of mind. In U. Goswami (Ed.), *Blackwell handbook of childhood cognitive development* (pp. 167–187). Malden, MA: Blackwell.

Wellman, H. M., Cross, D., & Watson, J. (2001). Meta-analysis of theory-of-mind development: The truth about false belief. *Child Development, 72*(3), 655–684.

Wellman, H. M., & Gelman, S. A. (1992). Cognitive development: Foundational theories of core domains. *Annual Review of Psychology, 43*, 337–375.

Wellman, H. M., & Johnson, C. N. (2008). Developing dualism: From intuitive understanding to transcendental ideas. In A. Antonietti, A. Corradini, & E. J. Lowe (Eds.), *Psycho-physical dualism today: An interdisciplinary approach* (pp. 3–36). Plymouth, UK: Lexington Books.

Wertsch, J. (1985). *Vygotsky and the social formation of mind*. Cambridge, MA: Harvard University Press.

White, L. (1942). On the use of tools by primates. *Journal of Comparative Psychology, 34*, 369–374.

White, L. (1959). The concept of culture. *American Anthropologist, 61*, 227–251.

White, S. H. (1996). The child's entry into the "age of reason". In A. J. Sameroff & M. M. Haith (Eds.), *The five to seven year shift: The age of reason and responsibility* (pp. 17–30). Chicago: University of Chicago Press.

Whiting, B. B. (1976). The problem of the packaged variable. In K. F. Riegel & J. A. Meacham (Eds.), *The developing individual in a changing world* (Vol. 1). Chicago: Aldine.

Whiting, B. B. (1980). Culture and social behavior: A model for development of social behaviors. *Ethos*, *8*, 95–116.

Whiting, B. B., & Edwards, C. P. (1988). *Children of different worlds: The formation of social behavior*. Cambridge, MA: Harvard University Press.

Whiting, J. W. M., Burbank, V. K., & Ratner, M. S. (1986). The duration of maidenhood. In J. W. M. Whiting, V. K. Burbank, & M. S. Ratner (Eds.), *School-age pregnancy: Biosocial dimensions* (pp. 273–302). New York: Aldine de Gruyer.

Williams, R. (1973). *Keywords*. New York: Oxford University Press.

Wolff, P., & Medin, D. L. (2001). Measuring the evolution and devolution of folkbiological knowledge. In L. Maffi (Ed.), *On biocultural diversity: Linking language knowledge and the environment* (pp. 212–27). Washington, DC: Smithsonian Institution.

❖ 3 ❖

DESIGN, MEASUREMENT, AND ANALYSIS IN DEVELOPMENTAL RESEARCH

Donald P. Hartmann
University of Utah

Kelly E. Pelzel
University of Iowa

Craig B. Abbott
National Institute of Child Health and Human Development

INTRODUCTION

This chapter is concerned with technical aspects of traditional developmental research, including the following topics: the **design** of studies, the **measurement** of variables, the analysis of data, and ethical considerations. To the neophyte who has attempted to read the method and results sections of developmental papers, these largely "methodological" aspects of research appear to be bewildering, and infinitely varied in type, form, and perhaps function.

However complex the technical aspects of research may be, it is important to emphasize from the start the dependence of research technology on the *theoretically based* questions motivating empirical investigations. The question to be answered should determine the most effective design, the most appropriate measures, and the most informative forms of analysis applied to the resulting scores. When the technical tail wags the substantive dog, research questions tend to be unsystematic, atheoretical, and of dubious use in advancing the science of development. The dependence of research technology on the substance of experimental questions places an additional burden on investigators: They must find or develop *the* design, *the* measurement operations, and *the* methods of analysis that are uniquely suited to their research questions.

The aspects of design, measurement, and analysis presented in this chapter are not intended to qualify individuals to select their own design, measurement, and analysis procedures. Instead, this chapter shows how design, measurement, and analysis function by specifying commonly used methods, indicating major issues, noting more serious pitfalls, and suggesting where additional information might be obtained.

The section on *design* focuses on four classes of threats to validity and on how non-experimental, quasi-experimental, and true experimental designs meet, or fail to meet, the challenges represented by these threats. Special attention is paid to design difficulties that plague developmental investigators, and to the traditional as well as newer designs developed in response to these difficulties.

The section on *measurement* addresses the purposes of measurement, the types of scores generated by developmental investigators, and the criteria used for judging the worth of these scores. **Standardization**, **reliability**, and validity criteria emerge as uniquely important for assessing the quality of scores. Many aspects of measurement—including the nature of the underlying constructs, accessible characteristics of target responses, relevant comparison standards for deciphering the meaning of scores, and available sources of information—determine how scores are operationalized as well as judged.

The section on *analysis* begins with a presentation of the distinctions between **categorical** and **quantitative** approaches to data. We focus on quantitative procedures, beginning with preliminary data analysis: methods of appropriately laundering data and developing an intimate familiarity with them. Formal statistical analysis is viewed as serving two interrelated functions: describing data by means of various indices of typical performance, variability, and relation; and testing whether the value of these indices is consistent with theoretical expectations or differs from null values—that is, whether the data are statistically significant.[1] A substantial number of techniques for serving these functions are described, with brief mention made of pitfalls and problems in their use and of the sources for learning more about them. These techniques of analysis accommodate the two major purposes of developmental research: assessing average performance across time (e.g., the developmental function; Wohlwill, 1973) as well as variation about the average, or individual, differences (e.g., Baltes & Nesselroade, 1979). Univariate and multivariate analytic techniques for categorical and quantitative data are described, and three increasingly popular techniques (hierarchical linear modeling, structural modeling, and meta-analysis) are singled out for special attention. The analysis section ends with a brief discussion of statistical significance, **effect size**, importance, and their interrelations.

The chapter's penultimate section is a brief discussion of *qualitative methods*, which are assuming an increasingly important role in the methodological armamentarium of developmentalists.

The chapter ends with a short discussion of *ethical issues* in developmental research. The discussion is aimed primarily at those issues that directly affect child research participants, including justifiable risk, invasion of privacy, and informed consent.

DESIGN

Traditional science has three main purposes: the prediction of important criteria, the control of relevant outcomes, and the search for causal relations between independent variables (IVs) and dependent variables (DVs). The substantive area of investigation determines the most important of these goals and the variables investigated. Once an investigator chooses the research question—and thereby defines the purposes of the research—a design must be constructed so that that question can be answered in as unambiguous a manner as is

---

[1] The long history of controversy over null hypothesis testing (e.g., Nickerson, 2000) has entered a new level of intensity (e.g., Harlow, Mulaik, & Steiger, 1997). Even the often staid American Psychological Association established a study group to determine whether null hypothesis testing should be discouraged from its journals (see Wilkinson & the Task Force on Statistical Inference, 1999). Abelson (1997a, p. 13) typified the dilemma confronting investigators this way: "Whatever else is done about null-hypothesis tests, let us stop viewing statistical analysis as a sanctification process. We are awash in a sea of uncertainty, caused by a flood tide of sampling and measurement errors, and there are no objective procedures that avoid human judgment and guarantee correct interpretations of results." A variety of approaches has been recommended as adjuncts to, or even substitutes for, null hypothesis testing. These procedures include, foremost, a model-comparison approach to data analysis that emphasizes the use of goodness of fit indices; critical thinking and sound judgment; confidence intervals and effect-size estimates; Bayesian statistics, and appropriate consideration of power (see, e.g., Harlow, 1997; Judd, McClelland, & Culhane, 1995; Wilkinson & the Task Force on Statistical Inference, 1999). These issues are examined in more detail in the analysis section.

reasonable given the ethical, technological, and practical constraints under which we function. Design involves the structure of investigations, the extent and means by which investigators exercise control over their independent, as well as other, variables that might be operating in the investigative context, so that appropriate conclusions can be drawn from the research.

Experimental design is intended to guard against alternative or competing plausible interpretations of the phenomena under study. These competing interpretations have been construed as *threats* to the validity of the investigation. This section describes the most common of these validity threats, with attention directed to problems common to the research experiences of developmentalists. The solutions to these problems afforded by a variety of design variations, including true experimental, quasi-experimental, and **nonexperimental designs**, are described. Special attention is paid to the designs defined by the developmental variables of age, cohort, and time of assessment, both in their traditional combination and in their more complex combination in sequential designs. The section ends with a listing of suggested readings for readers who may want additional information on these issues.

Validity Threats

Campbell and his associates (Campbell & Stanley, 1963; Cook & Campbell, 1979; Shadish, Cook, & Campbell, 2002) distinguished four classes of threats to the validity of investigations that developmental, as well as other researchers, must confront. These four classes, their definitions, and specific examples are given in Tables 3.1–3.4 (also see Huck & Sandler, 1979, for illustrations of many of the frequently discussed validity threats).

Statistical conclusion validity. Threats to **statistical conclusion validity**—or to the validity of the inferences we make from statistical tests—are easier to understand with at least some acquaintance with traditional statistical decision theory. Table 3.1 illustrates a simple decision matrix that describes the decisions that might be made as a result of **null hypothesis testing**. Two decisions and two states of nature are shown: The decisions are to accept or to reject the null hypothesis; the states of nature are that the null hypothesis is either true or false. The resulting decision matrix shows two types of correct and two types of incorrect decisions. The incorrect decisions are referred to as *Type I* and *Type II errors.*

Type I errors occur when a true null hypothesis is rejected mistakenly. True null hypotheses are incorrectly rejected with a probability equal to α, where α is the critical value required for rejection of the null hypothesis, traditionally set at either $p = .05$ or $p = .01$.

TABLE 3.1
A Matrix Illustrating Statistical Decision Theory

| | | State of Nature: H_o | |
		True	*False*
	Reject H_o	Type Error (α)	Correct Rejection (Power)
Investigator's Decision			
	Accept H_o	Correct Acceptance	Type II Error (β)

Note. H_o refers to the null hypothesis.

Type II errors occur when a false null hypothesis is accepted wrongly. Rejection of a false null hypothesis occurs when we fail to detect a real effect that exists in nature. The probability of a real effect not being detected is equal to β, where $[1 - \beta] =$ **power**.

Threats to statistical conclusion validity represented by Type I errors occur as a result of conducting one of the many kinds of fishing expeditions that investigators are known to perform on their data. One of the more egregious forms of fishing occurs when a data analyst performs numerous statistical tests on the same set of data, such as comparing each of $k = 6$ means to every other mean, resulting in $k(k - 1)/2 = 15$ comparisons. Unless the analyst makes adjustments for the number of statistical tests conducted (e.g., the Bonferroni correction, where α is set for the entire collection of tests), Type I error mushrooms for the entire *set* of tests, and clearly exceeds α. Additional threats represented by distortions of Type I error occur when certain kinds of statistical assumptions are violated (e.g., Judd et al., 1995; Kenny & Judd, 1986; Kirk, 1995). Failure to meet the assumptions of statistical tests can be particularly lethal when the assumptions of independence are violated and when testing causal models (see the discussion of nesting and structural equation modeling).

Threats represented by Type II errors also can occur when statistical assumptions are violated; however, they primarily occur when *power*—the probability of rejecting a false null hypothesis—is low. The notion of power is so critical in research that we digress here to amplify its implications. To the extent that our theory directs us to important phenomena that produce real, nontrivial effects, the likelihood that we will detect (in a statistical sense) these effects is given by the power of our investigation. Power depends on the size of the effect we are attempting to detect—a factor that ordinarily may not be under our control—plus a variety of factors that are controllable (see Table 3.2 and Shadish et al., 2002, pp. 46–47). These factors deserve our careful attention because our success as investigators hinges critically on the power of our investigations. This occurs in part because the value of manuscripts reporting "failure to find significant effects" is severely limited. Thus, we strongly recommend

TABLE 3.2
Statistical Conclusion Validity Threats: Definition and Examples[a]

Are the results of the statistical tests—acceptance or rejection of each of the null hypotheses—valid? OR Is statistical conclusion validity threatened by design or analytic weaknesses or errors?

Fishing Expeditions: Have Type I errors been inflated—sometimes referred to as probability pyramiding (Neher, 1967)—as a result of excessive, overlapping analysis of the data?

Violation of the Assumptions of the Statistical Tests: Has an incorrect conclusion been drawn—either an incorrect rejection (Type I error) or an incorrect acceptance of the null hypothesis (Type II error)—because an important assumption of the statistical test has been violated?

Low Power or Power Incorrectly Estimated: Is failure to reject a null hypothesis ascribable to the fact that the null hypothesis was true and there was no effect to be detected or to low power (a Type II error)? Low power might occur as a result of

(1) inadequate sample size
(2) measures that are lacking in construct validity or reliability (the latter perhaps due to too few waves or panels in a longitudinal study or too few or too short data collection sessions in an observational investigation)
(3) weak or inconsistent manipulation of the independent variable
(4) poor experimental control (random irrelevancies present in the investigative setting)
(5) excessive respondent heterogeneity
(6) weak statistics
(7) excessively small alpha levels.

[a] Strictly speaking, no null hypothesis may be precisely true. Trivial differences may even be found for the null hypothesis such as that involving the equivalence in IQ of people living east of the Mississippi in comparison to those living west of the Mississippi (see Morrison & Henkel, 1970). The relevant difference to be detected is not *any* difference, but any difference large enough to be interesting to the investigator.

conducting power analyses (Cohen, 1988; Maxwell, Kelley, & Rausch, 2008) prior to implementing any investigation.

Internal validity.   Threats to **internal validity** (Table 3.3) represent mistaken inferences about the causal connectedness between independent variable and dependent variable in a particular investigation. These threats, called confounds, are, with few exceptions, easily understood. One of the more knotty confounds is regression to the mean. Regression occurs when participants (poor readers, highly aggressive children, or insensitive mothers) are selected on the basis of the extremity of their scores. If the measures used to select these extremely performing individuals are less than perfectly reliable—which is almost always true in our study of the empirical world—the individuals can be expected to score less deviantly when they are reassessed. Thus, as a group, poor readers appear to be less deviant in their reading performance on a second reading assessment—even one that occurs immediately following the first assessment! Why? Because the poor readers were deviant in part because chance factors contributed to the extremity of their scores, and these chance components are unlikely to reoccur.

A second seemingly opaque class of confounds involves ambiguity about the direction of causal influence. However, this threat to internal validity is recognizable as the old adage that "correlation does not imply causation." Even if all potential third variable causes can be excluded (the troublesome variable Z, when variables X and Y are investigated), it is still possible, particularly in nonexperimental investigations, that X (the putative IV) is caused by Y (the ostensible DV), rather than the other way around.

TABLE 3.3
Internal Validity Threats: Definition and Examples

Can the observed findings be attributed to the independent variable? OR Is internal validity threatened by some methodological confound?

History: Did some event intervene, say, between the pretest and the posttest that produced an effect that might be confused with an effect produced by the independent variable (IV)?

Maturation: Are the observed findings ascribable to the growth or other internal changes in the participant rather than to the IV?

Testing: Did the participant's familiarity with the assessment device produce the observed changes in the dependent variable (DV)?

Instrumentation: Did the measurement instrument itself change over the course of the study so that differences are a result of changes in the calibration of the instrument and not to changes produced by the IV?

Regression: Are observed changes due to the selection of deviant respondents based on their performance on an unreliable assessment device, and their scores moving toward the mean on repeated testing as a function of the combination of selection and unreliability, rather than as a result of changes produced by the IV?

Selection: Are observed differences attributable to preexisting differences in the individuals assigned to the groups compared, rather than to effects produced by differences in exposure to the IV?

Mortality: Are observed differences due to differential dropouts or attrition in the groups compared?

Interactions with Selection: Are the observed findings ascribable to the interaction of selection with, say, maturation (because of selection factors, groups of participants are maturing at different rates) rather than to the effects of the IV?

Ambiguity about the Direction of Causal Influence: Is the causal connection from the presumed DV to the IV rather than the other way around?

Diffusion of Treatments, Compensatory Equalization of Treatments, or Compensatory Rivalry: Is the *lack of* observed differences a result of the fact that the non-treated participants were inadvertently exposed to the treatment, provided with compensatory treatments, or "worked harder" because they did not receive the favored treatment?

Resentful Demoralization: Was the effect observed attributable to the demoralized responding of participants who thought that they received a less desirable treatment?

Most threats to internal validity can be avoided by random assignment of participants to conditions, a critical method of control in psychological research and a characteristic of **true experiments**. However, even randomization may not rule out some threats to internal validity, such as those represented in the last two paragraphs of Table 3.3 (e.g., diffusion of treatments and resentful demoralization).

Construct validity. In general, threats to **construct validity** occur when the variables, as operationalized, either underrepresent the intended constructs or include surplus components. For example, the construct "anxiety" that did not include physiological, ideational, and behavioral components might be faulted for construct underrepresentation. However, a paper-and-pencil measure of anxiety that correlated highly with verbal IQ might be criticized for including surplus irrelevancies.

Construct validity threats can be sustained by either the IV or the DV. Consider, for example, the use of a single male and a single female model (an example of mono-operation bias—see Table 3.4) in a study of the effects of model gender on the imitation of aggression. In this example, mono-operationalization of the IV might result in a unique characteristic of one of the models, such as attractiveness, producing an effect that is confused with a gender effect. A construct validity threat to DVs might occur when all of the outcome variables are assessed using a single method, such as self-report. In such cases of monomethod bias, relations found between the outcome variables might be produced by the self-report method that they share (Campbell & Fiske, 1959), rather than by actual interdependence of the constructs.

Campbell and Fiske's (1959) notion that a score is a joint function of the construct, trait, or

TABLE 3.4
Construct Validity Threats: Definition and Examples

Do the critical variables in the study (the independent and dependent variables) measure the intended constructs? OR Is construct validity threatened by one or more methodological artifacts?

Inadequate Preoperational Explication of Constructs: Does the meaning of the construct as used in the investigation match (include neither more nor less than) the ordinary meaning of the construct as used in this area of study?

Mono-operational Bias: Have the critical variables in the study been operationalized in only one way, so that the results are a function of the particular operationalization employed?

Mono-method Bias: Have the operationalizations of a construct or constructs all used the same method, so that the results might be ascribable to overlapping method variance rather than overlapping construct variance?

Hypothesis Guessing: Are the results attributable to participants acting consistently with their hypotheses about the study, or how they believe the experimenter wants them to behave (the Hawthorne effect)?

Evaluation Apprehension: Is some "subject effect" (Webber & Cook, 1972) such as fear of evaluation responsible for the observed changes in performance, rather than the IV?

Experimenter Expectancies: Are the results a function of the expectancies of the experimenter—a treatment-correlated irrelevancy—which are somehow transmitted to the participant?

Confounding Constructs and Levels of Constructs: Is it the particular level of the IV that produced (or failed to produce) the observed effect, rather than the entire range of levels of the IV?

Interaction of Different Treatments: Is the effect observed a result of the particular combination or sequence of IVs employed, rather than to the pivotal treatment variable?

Interaction of Testing and Treatment: Does the putative effect of treatment require the use of pretesting—where participants may be primed to respond in a particular manner?

Restricted Generalizability across Constructs: Does the IV affect a range of outcome constructs, or instead, just the more or less narrow range of outcome constructs employed in the investigation?

Treatment-Sensitive Factorial and Reactive Self-Report Changes: Do the treatments or the selection process (e.g., being assigned to the control versus the treatment condition) interact with the assessment method so that the resulting scores have different meaning for the groups compared (see Shadish et al., 2002, p. 77)?

---

characteristic it is intended to assess *and* the method used to produce it has profound implications. The wise investigator uses multiple measures (or indicators, as they are sometimes called) when assessing constructs to minimize the irrelevant components of each measure and produce more construct-valid assessments (e.g., Pedhazur & Schmelkin, 1991).

Construct validity threats include not only measurement artifacts, but other artifacts as well that distort the meaning of either the IV or DV. Among these are:

1. "subject effects" (e.g., evaluation apprehension and the distrusting participant) that produce atypical responding
2. experimenter effects such as expectancies that influence participants in irrelevant ways
3. pretest assessments that sensitize the participants to the treatments
4. a particular sequence or combination of treatments that modifies the effect of the target treatment.

External validity. Issues of **external validity** are sometimes labeled as issues of ecological validity, generalizability, or representativeness. Whatever label is attached, the primary concern is the extent to which the results of studies are applicable to individuals, settings, treatments, and times different from those existing during the conduct of the study (see Table 3.5). Generalizability is one of psychology's seminal issues and requires continued vigilance. Are the results of research performed on rural European American adolescents applicable to African American adolescents living in urban settings? Are the findings of research conducted in the 1930s on the effects of nursery school applicable to nursery school experiences in the twenty-first century, when the nature of nursery schools and the parents who enroll their children in them differ? Shadish et al. (2002) presented a grounded theory of generalized causal inference based on the practices that scientists have used to generalize in a variety of investigative areas. Their analysis broadened the issue of generalizabilty from the context of participant sampling,[2] where it largely had resided for many years, to encompass other important facets of generalizability, including settings, treatments, and measurements. The principles developed by Shadish et al. (2002) for assessing the likelihood of generalizing an experimental finding include:

TABLE 3.5
External Validity Threats: Definition and Examples

Can the results of the investigation be generalized broadly? OR Is external validity threatened by contrived settings, unusual participants, or other factors that limit the generality of the results of the study?

Interaction of Selection and Treatment: Are the results limited to the particular sample investigated, or can they be generalized to a broader range of participants?

Interaction of Setting and Treatment: Are the effects produced applicable to other settings than the specific settings employed in the present investigation?

Interaction of History and Treatment: Can the results be generalized to other time periods, or are they limited to the particular historical circumstances in which the study was conducted?

Context-Dependent Mediation: Is the mediator or process operating to produce the effect limited to the particular investigative context?

---

[2] Even the more tractable issue of generalization across participants has been treated in a rather cavalier manner by many investigators—as if any sampling method would do, whether it be convenience or accidental sampling, or involves snowballing (one subject recommends a second, and so on), coercion, or bribery. Unless it is implausible that participant variables could modify important conclusions drawn from the research, such an attitude seems scientifically perilous.

1. *surface similarity*—judging the apparent similarities between the relevant characteristics of the present investigation and the target of generalization
2. *ruling out irrelevancies*—identifying those attributes that seem irrelevant because they do not change a generalization (e.g., parental eye color and the effectiveness of induction procedures)
3. *making discriminations*—making discriminations that limit generalization, such as the effect of ethnicity on parental punishment
4. *interpolation and extrapolation*—for example, parent training demonstrated to be effective in laboratory and home settings would probably also be effective when applied in a clinician's office
5. *causal explanation*—generalization based on developing and testing theories about explanatory mechanisms, for example, that the beneficial effects on children in interaction with both parents and teachers are mediated by warmth and reasonable expectations (e.g., Baumrind, 1991).

No investigator can thwart all of these common validity threats, as some requirements conflict with others. For example, the uniform application of treatments may increase statistical conclusion validity, but at the cost of external validity. No study has been, nor will any ever be, perfect. Basic researchers, those studying basic processes of development, may tend to emphasize internal, construct, and statistical conclusion validity to the detriment of external validity, whereas applied researchers studying social policy issues may emphasize internal, external, and statistical conclusion validity at the cost of construct validity. Investigators must consider the risks of the various validity threats with the potential uses of the research outcomes.

Seminal Design Issues for Developmental Investigators

All investigators, whatever their focus or interest, must confront these four classes of validity threats. In addition to these generic threats to the validity of research findings, there are other design concerns that are more or less the province of developmental investigators. These special issues, not surprisingly, concern the modifiability of the variables studied by developmentalists; the changing form of the phenomena they study; their participants' limited abilities to perceive or describe their experiences; the complexity out of which the behavior they study develops; the dangerous causal biases held by them, as well as by many students of development; and attrition—the loss of data because a participant fails to answer one or more questions in a questionnaire or interview or because the participant is unavailable on one or more occasions of measurement.

Intractable variables.   Many of the important variables investigated by developmental researchers are relatively intractable. For example, a pivotal question to the field is the means by which heredity and environment conspire to produce behavior. But heredity cannot be manipulated, except in studies of non-human species, and environments are likewise generally not modifiable over broad sweeps or for extensive periods of an individual's life. Even that most popular of all developmental variables, age, has clear limitations as a causal variable. Age cannot be modified or manipulated, although individuals of various ages can be chosen for investigation. And although it is unquestionably useful to find that a phenomenon covaries with age, neither age nor the related variable time is a causal variable; changes occur *in time*, but not as a result of time. Instead, time or age is part of a context in which causal processes operate. At best, age may serve as a *proxy* for variables that are causally potent for development. Thus, in an important sense, the most studied developmental variable (see Miller, 2007) is causally impotent (Wohlwill, 1970).

Change. The study of development is foremost the study of change. Historically, the study of change has associated with it a variety of thorny technical problems (Gottman, 1995; Rogosa, 1988) including the reliability of change scores and the negative correlation of change scores with initial scores. However, some of the "seminal" problems associated with the assessment of change literally disappeared as a result largely of a simple improvement in methodology: employing multiwave, instead of the traditional two-wave (e.g., pre- and post-test), **longitudinal designs**. Collecting multiwave data dramatically increases the precision and reliability of the growth measurement—an extra wave of data may double or triple the reliability of the growth rate. Additionally, multiwave data tell us about the shape of change— does change occur immediately after the first assessment or is it steady or delayed?—and may permit a more sophisticated individual model of growth to be adopted (Singer & Willett, 2003; Willet, 1989, 1994). However, not all of the problems associated with change partici- pated in this disappearing act. A construct may itself change in topography or other import- ant characteristics with development, for example, such that a measure of emotional control appropriate for an early developmental level may be inappropriate for assessing emotional control during a later phase of development. When measures do not assess the same construct across occasions (or groups), interpretation of score comparisons is at best muddied, and may result in inferences that are "potentially artifactual and . . . substantively misleading" (Wida- man & Reise, 1997, p. 282). This vexing and technically complex issue of "measurement equivalence" is variously discussed by Hartmann (2005) and by Knight and Hill (1998).

Change may be incremental (i.e., gradual and linear) or transformational (e.g., sudden, nonlinear reorganization of system-wide processes). The parameters of change may also vary: For some individuals, change may occur briefly and comparatively late; for others, change may occur early and over more protracted periods of time. A lack of sensitivity to these temporal parameters of change may mean that the time period when a process is most open to inspection will be missed, and that measurements may occur either with insufficient frequency to "resolve" the underlying process or over shorter duration than is necessary to capture the entire process.

Limited availability of self-reports. Unlike the sophisticated college student often stud- ied by cognitive and social psychologists, the participants in many developmental investiga- tions are unable to aid the investigator by describing their experiences—because either they are unaware of the relevant behaviors or processes or they do not have a communicative system that can be accessed readily. Other complex methods must be used to address even limited aspects of the young child's mental and emotional experiences: Sophisticated technology, participant observers, such as parents and teachers, or independent raters must be relied on to gain access to even the more obvious manifestations of these experiences (Bornstein, Arterberry, & Mash, Chapter 6, this volume).

Complexity of causal networks. Most developmental phenomena are embedded intri- cately in a complex, interacting network of environmental and genetic–constitutional forces that defies simple analysis or study. And in many cases, the factors of presumed importance— such as severe environmental deprivation—cannot be reproduced with humans because of obvious ethical concerns. As a result, investigators are forced to the laboratory where analogs of naturally occurring phenomena are created, and where complex, naturalistic conditions are greatly simplified. The consequences of these actions are that external and construct validity may be substantially strained.

Directional causal biases. Developmentalists traditionally have attributed causal agency to adults rather than children, to families rather than cultural factors, and to environmental rather than complexly interacting biological and environmental determinants. The reasons for these biases are undoubtedly complex and are not widely discussed—although the research by Bell (1968) on the direction of effects in the socialization literature is cited widely and appears to have an important impact on developmental research. Nonetheless, we must be cautious in imputing direction of causation, particularly for findings that are produced by passive observational (*ex post facto*) studies, because requirements for inferring causality are difficult to meet (Shonkoff & Phillips, 2000, Chapter 4). Not only does correlation not imply causation in these designs, but a lack of correlation does not disprove causation (Bollen, 1989, p. 52). Furthermore, we must exercise constraint in not overemphasizing the causal importance of proximal variables (such as parents), while underplaying the role of more distal variables, such as unemployment or inequitable distribution of wealth. And we must be wary of overstating the causal importance of currently "politically correct" causes to the detriment of equally important but unpopular causes. We may, for example, be prone to attribute children's aggressive behavior to violence in TV programming rather than to competitive learning environments in our educational institutions, when both factors are equally plausible and potent determinants of aggression. Finally, we must be wary of making simple dichotomous causal judgments (e.g., heredity *or* environment is the cause of a behavior) when the answer is almost certainly setting-specific, and causal processes involve complex interacting systems (e.g., Anastasi, 1958; Fischer & Bidell, 1998; also see Hoffman, 1991).

Attrition. Attrition and its consequence, unplanned missing scores,[3] are problems that developmental researchers will surely grapple with, especially those doing longitudinal research. "Scientists engaged in longitudinal research deal with unplanned missing data constantly; in fact, it is difficult to imagine a longitudinal study without at least some unplanned missing data" (Collins, 2006, p. 521). Attrition threatens statistical conclusion validity by decreasing statistical power and internal validity when dropouts in different study conditions differ in ways related to the outcome (Shadish & Cook, 2009). Dealing with attrition starts in the planning stages of the study, should be monitored during the course of the study, and must be considered when analyzing and interpreting the data. To minimize attrition, developmental researchers plan for and carefully implement strategies that help prevent it, such as recording complete demographic information of the participants and their family, friends, and coworkers; training research staff to build rapport with the participants; and offering appropriate financial or other incentives for continued participation. Excellent and thorough summaries for retaining and tracking participants are found in Cauce, Ryan, and Grove (1998) and in Ribisl et al. (1996); see also Hartmann (2005) and Shadish et al. (2002). Despite our best preventive efforts, however, attrition will occur, and researchers need to know how to deal with missing scores. Procedures that are based on statistical theory, such as multiple imputation and maximum likelihood, are recommended over *ad hoc* procedures such as casewise deletion and mean substitution (Collins, 2006; Graham, 2009; see also footnote 7 in "preliminary analysis" section).

Design Variations

Developmental investigators have employed a variety of design variations in response to the validity threats and problems already discussed. Many of the common variations are

---

[3] "Unplanned missing data" refers to data loss that is out of the control of the investigator. Some designs however include "planned missing data" for reasons of economy and reduction in the response burden on participants. Known as efficiency designs, their value depends on the investigator's ability to use analysis procedures for handling missing data (Graham, Taylor, Olchowski, & Cumsille, 2006).

summarized in Table 3.6. As the footnote to that table suggests, a design chosen to control one type of validity threat may promote another. For example, contrived settings have allowed investigators to exercise experimental control over unwanted sources of variation—but at the expense of external validity. The study of natural treatments promotes external validity, but the complexity and "noise" associated with these treatments often blurs their meaning or construct validity. The intensive study of a few individuals may allow investigators to capture the complexity of their target phenomena, but may raise questions of generalizability.

TABLE 3.6
The Advantages of Design Variations Intended to Solve Validity Threats and Other Design Concerns

Versus	
Experimental Control:	*Statistical Control:*
Nuisance variables are precluded from occurring by isolation or selection.	Nuisance factors are removed by statistical means (e.g., using partial correlation techniques).
Improves internal validity by avoiding error variance.	Promotes internal validity by reducing error variance.
	Preserves external validity by not tampering with the setting.
Contrived Setting:	*Field Setting:*
Modifies settings so that target behaviors occur and extraneous variables are controlled (e.g., laboratories).	Employs untampered settings for investigations.
	Facilitates external validity by providing a natural context.
Promotes internal validity by exercising tight control over nuisance variables.	Provides estimates of naturally occurring rates of behaviors.
Saves investigative time by decreasing dross rate.	
Artificial Treatments:	*Natural Treatments:*
Introduces ideal or prototypical forms of treatments.	Examines naturally occurring treatments.
Improves construct validity of causes by control over the nature of the DV.	Promotes external validity by studying natural variation in treatment implementation.
Crossed Designs:	*Nested Designs:*
Designs in which each level of every factor is paired with each level of every other factor (e.g., in an Age × Gender design, girls and boys are represented for each age group).	Designs in which each level of every factor is *not* paired with each level of every other factor.
	Improves efficiency by omitting treatment conditions of little interest.
Allows for the assessments of interactions.	Facilitates construct validity by precluding certain forms of multiple-treatment interference.
Within-Subjects Designs:	*Between-Subjects Designs:*
Uses each respondent as own control.	Control provided by random assignment of participants to condition.
Promotes statistical conclusion validity by controlling error variance.	May foster construct validity by avoiding multiple treatment interference.
	Uses investigative time efficiently by allowing simultaneous study of many treatments.
Intensive (Idiographic) Designs:	*Extensive (Nomothetic) Designs:*
Designs in which one or a few participants are intensively assessed, usually across time as in a longitudinal or time-series study.	Many participants are assessed, but typically only once.
Furthers the study of performance across time (e.g., the study of trends).	Makes efficient use of investigative time.
Accommodates the complexity of performance changes across time.	
Provides access to where the laws of behavior reside—in the individual.	

Note. The advantages of one alternative typically, though not always, are the limitations of the parallel alternative.

Perhaps the most important differences between families of designs are those based on the nature of the causal statement allowed by the designs. Campbell and his associates (Campbell & Stanley, 1963; Cook & Campbell, 1979; Shadish et al., 2002) distinguished three levels of investigation based on the design's allowable causal implications: true experiments, **quasi-experiments**, and nonexperiments.

True experiments.   True experiments include manipulation of the independent variable by the investigator and control of extraneous variables by random assignment of participants to conditions. Random assignment of participants has a number of truly astounding consequences (Shadish et al., 2002, p. 248).

1. It ensures that alternative causes are not confounded with treatment conditions.
2. It reduces the plausibility of a variety of validity threats by distributing them randomly over conditions.
3. It equates groups on the expected value of all variables at pretest—whether or not they are measured.
4. It allows the investigator to know and model the selection process correctly.
5. It allows computation of a valid estimate of error variance that is independent or orthogonal to treatment.

Not surprising, true experimental designs, if conducted properly, allow investigators to make strong inferences regarding the causal effect exerted by the IV over the DV. Table 3.7 illustrates two true experimental designs: the simplest of all true experimental designs—and from which all other true experimental designs are derived—the experimental–control group design with posttests only; and the more complex, Solomon four-group design (Solomon & Lessac, 1968). The Solomon four-group and other true experimental designs are discussed in most design texts, including those by Campbell and his associates (e.g., Campbell & Stanley, 1963).

Quasi-experiments.   Quasi-experiments are investigations in which control procedures are instigated, but assignment to conditions is not random. In such cases, the thread connecting cause and effect is less susceptible to clear delineation, although some causal inferences often are possible.[4] Panel A of Table 3.8 illustrates two quasi-experimental designs frequently used by applied behavior analysts, the ABA and multiple baseline designs (e.g., Gelfand & Hartmann, 1984). With the ABA or interrupted time-series design, a single case (e.g., an individual, family, or classroom) is observed repeatedly under a control series (the repeated Os at the beginning of the series); then a treatment is imposed and observation continues during that treatment phase (the repeated X_1O linkages). The initial observation phase is reinstituted (the second set of Os), and in many cases, a second phase of treatment–observations (X_1Os) is also reinstated. (The reintroduction of the second treatment phase formally makes this an ABAB design.)

With the multiple baseline design, treatment is introduced successively into each of two or more units (behaviors, participants, or contexts) following a series of control observations. These and other quasi-experimental designs can, with the addition of special features (e.g.,

---

[4] An underutilized but promising quasi-experimental design for estimating causal effects is the regression discontinuity design (RDD). The design assigns participants to conditions based on a cutoff score on an ordered assignment variable. A regression is fit to predict outcome from the assignment variable and dummy-coded treatment variable. Treatment effects are estimated from the discontinuity (change in slope or intercept) at the cutoff between treatment and control (Cook & Wong, 2008; Shadish & Cook, 2009).

TABLE 3.7
Illustrations of True Experimental Designs

Experimental-Control Group Design Employing Posttest-Only Assessments:
Group

Experimental	R:	X	O
Control	R:		O

Solomon Four-Group Design:
Group

Experimental	R:	O	X	O
	R:		X	O
Control	R:	O		O
	R:			O

Note. By convention, R indicates random assignment of participants to groups, O indicates an assessment, and X indicates a treatment.

TABLE 3.8
Illustrations of Quasi-Experimental and Nonexperimental Design

Panel A: Quasi-experimental Designs

Interrupted Time-Series (ABA) Design:

Group (or Participant)

Unit 1:   O. .O. .O. .X_1O. .X_1O. .X_1O. .O. .O. .O

Interrupted Time-Series (Multiple Baseline) Design

Group (or Participant)

Unit 1[a]	O. .O. .O. .X_1O. .X_1O. .X_1O. .
Unit 2	O. .O. .O. .O. .X_1O. .X_1O. .X_1O
Unit 3	O. .O. .O. .O. .O. .X_1O. .X_1O. .X_1O

Panel B: Nonexperimental Designs
One-Group, Pretest and Posttest Design

Group
Experimental: O   X   O

Note. The separation of events by . . indicates that the event may be repeated one or more times.
[a] Units can represent individuals or treatment settings or behaviors for an individual. Individuals may be either a single individual or an aggregate of individuals such as a classroom of students (e.g., Gelfand & Hartmann, 1984).

the random assignment of treatment order to units in the multiple baseline design), exclude many or even all plausible alternative interpretations, and allow strong causal inferences.

Nonexperimental designs.   Nonexperimental designs employ neither randomization nor adequate control conditions. Designs in this class provide a product that does not allow investigators to reach conclusions about causality. Included in this group are case studies, one-group pretest and posttest designs (see Panel B of Table 3.8), and similar designs that are used primarily for hypothesis generation. *Ex post facto* or passive observational designs also are members of the nonexperimental design family. (In the past, these designs were sometimes referred to as *correlational designs*. However, that is an unfortunate term, as correlations are statistical measures of association, not designs, and can be applied to the data from any of the three types of designs just described.)

The lack of clarity regarding causal connections between the variables investigated in nonexperimental designs is generally well known. Nonetheless, they serve the important role of *probing* (in contrast to *testing*) potential causal models. Certainly a causal model relating X and Y is probed if X and Y are found to be uncorrelated. But even then, one could argue that the relation was too complex to be revealed by the design, or that the investigator made a poor decision in choosing the time delay between putative cause and effect (e.g., hunger is undoubtedly causally related to food intake, but self-reported hunger and observed food ingestion might only be correlated if eating was assessed for the meal immediately following the assessment of hunger). Unfortunately, many traditional developmental designs are closer to nonexperimental designs than to true experimental designs in the level of causal inference allowed.

Developmental Design

Developmentalists have been concerned traditionally with two issues: the normative changes that occur in developing individuals and individual differences in these developmental changes. The pursuit of these goals involves generally the variable of age, and age typically has been investigated using either cross-sectional or longitudinal designs.

Before discussing these and other developmental designs, it is useful to examine three variables that distinguish the various developmental designs: cohort, age, and time of assessment (Schaie & Caskie, 2005). *Cohorts* are groups of participants who are born—or experience some other common event—in the same time period. Thus, we speak of the 1979 cohort and of the cohort of baby boomers. Age has its usual meaning, as does time of assessment.

The design-defining variables of cohort, age, and time of assessment are not independent. This lack of independence can be seen by specifying a cohort and a time of assessment in the matrix shown in Table 3.9. Once the values for these two variables are specified, age—the variable indicated in the body of the matrix—is not free to vary, but instead is fixed or determined. Herein lies one of the major problems with the designs derived from this matrix: The variables of cohort, age, and time of assessment in these designs are inherently confounded. Consider the cross-sectional design (shown in Panel A of Table 3.10).

Cross-sectional designs are those in which at least two cohorts are assessed at the same time of assessment. As a result, the cohorts differ in age. If DV performance in a cross-sectional study differed across the age groups, one would be tempted to attribute the performance difference to age or development. However, note that the same variation in performance on the DV also can be attributed to cohort differences! Cohort differences might be produced by genetic variation resulting from changes in migration patterns or exposure to radiation, or they might stem from environmental variation (such as educational reform associated with living during a somewhat different historical epoch). Each of the simple developmental designs diagrammed in Tables 3.9 and 3.10 shares an analogous confound. These elementary developmental designs

TABLE 3.9
Cohort × Time of Assessment Matrix Illustrating Simple
Developmental Designs

Cohort	Time of Assessment		
	1975	*1980*	*1985*
1960	15[bc]	20[ab]	25[b]
1965	10	15[ac]	20
1970	5	10[a]	15[c]

Note. Age is given in the body of the table
[a] Cross-sectional design; [b] Longitudinal design; [c] Time-lagged design.

TABLE 3.10
Simple Developmental Designs

Panel A

Cross-Sectional Design:	*Cohort*	
	1965	*1970*
Time of Assessment: 1980	15	10

Panel B

Longitudinal Design:	*Age*	
	15	*20*
Cohort: 1960	1975	1980

Panel C

Time-lagged Design:	*Time of Assessment*	
	1980	*1985*
Age: 15	1965	1970

Note. Age is given in the body of the table in Panel A; Time of Assessment is given in the body of the table in Panel B; Cohort is given in the body of the table in Panel C.

also share two other interpretive difficulties. First, the variables of cohort and time of assessment are *not* causally active—a status that has already been noted for age. At best, the variables of cohort, age, and time of assessment are *proxy* variables for the real causal processes that operate in time or are associated with cohort or time of assessment. Second, the variables of cohort, age, and time of assessment are not manipulated in these designs, nor are participants assigned randomly to cohorts or ages, although they can be assigned randomly to times of assessment—but not after age and cohort are assigned. Thus, the aspects of these developmental designs involving cohort, age, and time of assessment are not truly experimental. Indeed, the designs are nonexperimental (*ex post facto*), and the resulting data do not lend themselves to strong causal inferences regarding the effects of age, cohort, or time of assessment.

A prototypic longitudinal design is illustrated in Panel B of Table 3.10. Longitudinal designs have been described as "the lifeblood of developmental psychology" (McCall, 1977, p. 341). Nonetheless, they confound age and time of assessment and are nonexperimental with respect to these two variables. In addition, age and time of assessment are only proxies for active causal variables. We have already considered some of the causally active variables for which age could serve as a proxy; in the case of time of assessment, the causal variables may be events such as a turndown in the economy, the death of a prominent official, or a natural disaster.

A time-lagged design, the last of the simple designs (but not a true developmental design), is illustrated in Panel C of Table 3.10. Time-lagged designs confound the variables of cohort and time of assessment and are nonexperimental with respect to these two variables as well. Although these simple designs suffer from a variety of interpretive problems, they provide valuable information to developmentalists as to whether standing on important DVs varies as a function of age, cohort, or time of assessment. Once such a discovery has been made, the search for the explanation—the underlying process responsible for the finding—can begin.

In an attempt to remedy some of the problems associated with these simple developmental designs, more complex developmental designs—called *sequential designs*—have been developed (Schaie, 1965; Schaie & Caskie, 2005). These designs are illustrated in Tables 3.11 and 3.12. Table 3.11 displays a *Cohort × Time of Assessment* matrix similar to the one shown in Panel A of Table 3.10. In this case, however, the designs that are derived from the matrix are more complex than those derived from the matrix in Table 3.9. Each of the sequential designs

TABLE 3.11
Cohort × Time of Assessment Matrix Illustrating Complex (Sequential)
Developmental Designs

	Time of Assessment		
Cohort	1975	1980	1985
1960	15[b]	20[bc]	25
1965	10	15[abc]	20[abc]
1970	5	10[a]	15[ac]

Note. Age is given in the body of the table.
[a] Cohort × Time of Assessment (cross-sequential) design; [b] Age × Cohort (cohort-sequential) design; [c] Time of Assessment × Age (time-sequential) design.

TABLE 3.12
Sequential Developmental Designs

Panel A
Cohort × Time of Assessment Design

	Cohort	
	1965	1970
Time of Assessment: 1980	15	10
1985	20	15

Panel B
Age × Cohort Design

	Age	
	15	20
Cohort: 1960	1975	1980
1965	1980	1985

Panel C
Time of Assessment × Age Design

	Time of Assessment	
	1980	1985
Age: 15	1965	1970
20	1960	1965

Note. Age is given in the body of the table in Panel A; Time of Assessment is given in the body of the table in Panel B; and Cohort is given in the body of the table in Panel C.

(Panels A–C in Table 3.12) represents the crossing (see Table 3.6 for the definition of crossing) of two of the three definitional variables of cohort, age, and time of assessment.

Consider the cross-sequential design (Panel A of Table 3.12) and note how the design is generated and how its findings might be interpreted. The cross-sequential design—renamed the *Cohort × Time of Assessment* design—represents the crossing of the two variables, cohort and time of assessment. That is, each level of the cohort variable is combined with each level of the time of assessment variable to generate the conditions included in the design. (In many design books, the × symbol represents the operation of crossing.) The *Cohort × Time of Assessment* design depicted in Panel A of Table 3.12 can be compared to the cross-sectional design illustrated in Panel A of Table 3.10, which compared 10- and 15-year-olds when they were assessed in 1980. The presence of a second group of l5-year-olds (from the 1970 cohort assessed in 1985) assists in determining whether the performance of the l5-year-olds from the 1980 cohort is ascribable to age or to cohort differences. Furthermore, if the two cohorts of l5-year-olds respond similarly (*converge*), the data might be treated analogously to the data obtained from a longitudinal design with age ranging from 10 through 20 years—but instead of requiring 10 years to conduct, the study would take only 5 years (Anderson, 1995)!

One must be wary in interpreting the data from even these more complex sequential designs, however. Figure 3.1 displays data from a *Cohort × Time of Assessment* design such as the one shown in Panel B of Table 3.10. Exactly the same data are graphed as a function of age (Panel A of Figure 3.1) and as a function of time of assessment (Panel B of Figure 3.1). Are the results a linear function of age (Panel A) or joint main effects of cohort and of time of assessment (Panel B)?

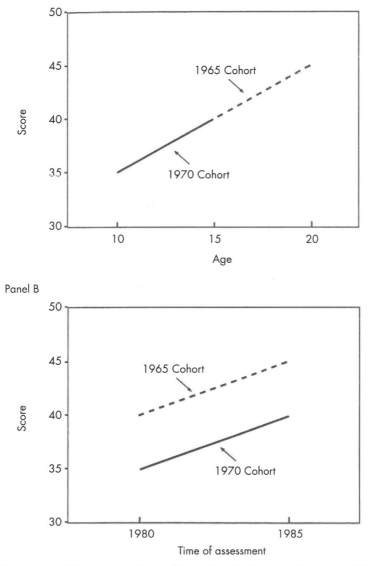

FIGURE 3.1 The same set of data graphed by age (Panel A) and by the time of assessment (Panel B).

The two remaining sequential designs, renamed the *Age × Cohort* design and the *Time of Assessment × Age* design (as the two designs represent the crossing of the two variables included in their names) are shown in Panels B and C of Table 3.12. The interpretation of the data from these designs is analogous to that made for the *Cohort × Time of Assessment* design.

Sample Size for Power and Accuracy

A key aspect of research design is sample size planning. It is important both for the individual researcher who wants a reasonable probability of finding statistically significant results and for a research domain striving to build a cumulative knowledge base. With respect to the latter goal, one of the consequences of low-powered studies is an abundance of apparent contradictions in the published literature (Kelley & Maxwell, 2008). A sample size that is too small or too large for the objectives of the study can have negative economic consequences and—because it misleads and needlessly exposes participants to risk—may be unethical (Lenth, 2001).

Before sample size planning can occur, investigators must clearly identify their goals for the study. A first step is to assess what is known about the subject of inquiry and where the study fits along the continuum of scientific understanding. Formal sample size analyses may not be necessary for exploratory or pilot studies, but well-reasoned sample size analyses are required for studies designed to reach confirmatory or confident conclusions (O'Brien & Castelloe, 2007). Study goals can be conceptualized in a 2 × 2 table (see Table 3.13) with the level of effect, an omnibus or targeted effect, along one dimension, and either power or accuracy along the second dimension (Kelley & Maxwell, 2008). For example, for multiple **regression analysis**, the investigator may be interested in the overall fit of the model, R^2 (omnibus effect), or in the regression coefficients of specific predictor variables, β (focused effect), or both. With respect to the second dimension, the goal may be to reject the null hypothesis and establish the direction of an effect (power), or to estimate the magnitude of the effect accurately (accuracy), or both. Accuracy in estimating the parameter effect (AIPE; Maxwell et al., 2008) involves estimating the **confidence interval** of an effect, where a narrower confidence interval implies greater accuracy or certainty that the observed parameter closely approximates its population parameter. Other things being equal, an appropriate sample size will vary depending on the desired objective. Often larger sample sizes are required for accurately estimating parameters than for detecting even small effects.

A second, and often the most troublesome (Lipsey, 1990), step in sample size planning is specifying an expected effect size. A commonly used approach is to use Cohen's (1988) suggested guidelines for "small," "medium," or "large" standardized effect sizes (see chapter section "interpreting the results of statistical tests"), but this approach has been criticized by Lenth (2001). Other options include basing effect sizes on those obtained in published studies, meta-analyses, and pilot studies (Kelley & Maxwell, 2008). If these options are not available, Lenth describes questions that can be asked about what differences are expected or would be of scientific or clinical interest (see also Bloom, 2008). In some instances, an unknown effect

TABLE 3.13

Conceptualization for Sample Size Planning for Multiple Regression Parameters Given the Investigator's Study Goals and Desired Effect

| | | Effect | |
		Omnibus	Targeted
Goal	Power	Power of R^2	Power of β
	Accuracy	Accuracy of R^2	Accuracy of β

size is not a major problem for sample size planning for accuracy because the formulas for computing narrow confidence intervals are not dependent on the value of the effect size (Maxwell et al., 2008).

Additional Concerns and References

Experimental design issues do not end with our brief discussion of generic and special developmental validity threats and problems, and design variations that have been developed to address these concerns. Additional topics, such as philosophy of science considerations underlying the choice of design, participant selection, and single-subject design strategies, also are major aspects of design that are given short shrift in this chapter. Interested readers are referred to the following references.

1. *General design issues:* Alasuutari, Bickman, & Brannen (2008), Appelbaum and McCall (1983), Baltes, Reese, & Nesselroad (1988), Cairns, Bergman, & Kagan (1998), Meehl (1978), Miller (2007), Pedhazur and Schmelkin (1991), Rosenthal and Rosnow (1969), and Teti (2005).
2. *Implications of the philosophy of science for design:* Braybrooke (1987), Cook and Campbell (1979, Chapter 1), Kuhn (1970), the volume edited by Lerner (1998)—but particularly the chapter by Overton (1998)—and Popper (1959).
3. *Selecting, assigning, recruiting, and maintaining participants:* Cauce et al. (1998), Hartmann (2005), Pedhazur and Schmelkin (1991, Chapter 15), Ribisl et al. (1996); Shadish et al. (2002, pp. 323–340), and Suen and Ary (1989, Chapter 3).
4. *General and special issues when doing internet-based research:* Kraut et al. (2004) and Skitka & Sargis (2006).
5. *Change and growth:* Among many others, see Cohen and Reese (1994), Collins and Horn (1991), Gottman (1995), and Willett (1988).
6. *Power and its analysis:* Cohen (1988, 1990) and sources for power analysis software: Lenth (2001) and Thomas and Krebs (1997).
7. *Single-subject designs*: Franklin, Allison, and Gorman (1997), Iwata et al. (1989), Kratochwill and Levin (1992), and—for a somewhat different look—Valsiner (1986).

MEASUREMENT

Measurement includes the operations that are used to obtain scores. In developmental research, the scores provided by measurement operations assess DV performance, evaluate participants' IV status, and also determine their standing on other dimensions used to describe the research sample or to control for differences among individuals or groups. These research-related decision-making functions of measurement, or *scaling* as it is sometimes called, require that the resulting scores be both relevant and of high quality.

Issues of measurement quality are particularly acute in developmental investigations because of the vicissitudes of assessing participants occupying the ends of the developmental spectrum. Youngsters in particular present problems "of establishing rapport and motivation; of ensuring that instructions are well understood; of maintaining attention; and, of coping with boredom, distraction, and fatigue" (Messick, 1983, p. 479). In addition, because of children's rapid changes in many cognitively based activities, it may be difficult to capture their transient performance levels. Furthermore, the meaning of test scores may change in concert with changes in the children's development, as we previously noted (see also Patterson's, 1993, discussion of this issue—which he terms a "chimera" in the context of antisocial behavior).

As a result of these problems in measuring children's performance, developmental investigators have an added responsibility to demonstrate that their measures are of high quality.

The assessment of measurement quality, not surprisingly, depends on the nature of the research and the specific questions put forward for investigation. Nevertheless, certain criteria are generally relevant to judgments of quality: They include whether or not the measurement device is applied in a standard fashion; and whether or not the resulting scores are replicable (reliable) and measure what they are supposed to measure—a notion that bears very close resemblance to the notion of construct validity. Still other criteria, such as the presence of a meaningful zero point for the measurement scale, may be required by the nature of the statistical methods that are to be applied to the resulting scores.

Precisely how these criteria or standards are applied, and which are relevant, may also depend on various technical or theoretical considerations—sometimes referred to as measurement *facets* and *sources* (Messick, 1983; see also Baltes, Lindenberger, & Staudinger, 1998). The facets include the nature of the characteristics assessed—whether they are stable traits or changing states, structures or functions, and competence or typical performance. Other facets involve whether the scores are used for interindividual (normative) or intraindividual (ipsative) comparisons, and depend for their interpretation on norms (norm-referenced) or on objective performance standards (criterion-referenced).

The sources of measurement include whether the assessment responses are based on self-reports, constitute test responses, or are reports of performance in naturalistic settings by participant or independent observers. We briefly discuss scores—which are the products of measurement—and then the criteria for evaluating scores, measurement facets, and sources of data. The section on measurement ends with a listing of recommended sources for additional study.

Types of Scores

Scores come in a bewildering assortment of types. Most scores obtained from participants in developmental research will be straightforward and understandable either from reading the description of the study's procedures or from examining the study's tables or figures. Examples include scores that are expressed in basic units of measurement such as extension, frequency, and duration (see Johnston & Pennypacker, 1993) as well as aggregate scores resulting from the addition of item scores obtained on questionnaires and tests. These scores need not concern us further.

Other scores pose slight interpretive problems because they are constructions of the original scores—percentiles and "alphabet scores" (T and z scores)—which come with additional interpretive baggage. These scores are often designed to meet the assumptions of statistical tests or to remedy some perturbation, such as skewness, in the original distribution of scores. Such scores are described in Table 3.14, as are the defects they are intended to remedy and the interpretive warnings with which they are associated.

Still other scores represent more complicated transformations of the original data—difference or change scores, scores obtained from Q-sorts, and age- or grade-equivalent scores; they must be treated with some caution.

Difference scores.   Perhaps the most troublesome of these prudence-demanding scores are simple difference scores, X_2 (posttreatment or Time 2) − X_1 (pretreatment or Time 1), popularly used in the past to index change over some period of development or as a result of treatment. Difference scores were often employed to assess change or growth, but are widely regarded as multiply flawed—for example, Cronbach and Furby (1970), Harris (1963); but compare with Rogosa (1988) and Willett (1988). Difference scores suffer from problems of

TABLE 3.14
Transformed Scores, Their Purposes and Qualifications to Their Interpretation

Transformation	Purpose	Interpretive Qualifications
$[X + 1]^{1/2}$, log X, arc sin X	Regularize (e.g., normalize) distributions for data analytic purposes	Interpretation must be applied to transformed scores
Proportion of X_1, X_2, etc.	Control for variation in respondent productivity	All participants have the same total score (across all variables)[a]
Standard score: $z = (X - M)/SD$	Control for disparate Ms and SDs for variables	All variables have Ms = 0 and SDs = 1.0[b]
Percentile rank of X	Reduce the disparity of extreme scores	All variables are given identical ranges (i.e., 1 to 99)

Note. X is the symbol for the original raw scores, M for the mean, and SD for the standard deviation.
[a] See discussion of ipsative scores.
[b] Distributions of standardized scores can be generated with any convenient mean and standard deviation. For example, if the transformed score distribution has a mean of 50 and a standard deviation of 10, the scores are referred to as T scores. T scores are generated by the following equation: $T = 50 + z(10)$.

unreliability—although the scores that are differenced may themselves be reliable! This is so because (1) the non-error variance in the two measures that are differenced is largely used up by the correlation between the two measures, so the precision of the difference scores is low, or (2) the variation in the difference scores is low, thus precluding high reliability because of restriction in range. Difference scores are not base free as is sometimes believed, but are frequently negatively correlated with initial or prescores because individuals who score low on the initial assessment are likely to have larger change scores than individuals who score higher. Additional problems occur when the characteristic that is assessed changes across the period of assessment. Many, although not all, of these problems are substantially reduced or eliminated when multiwave data are employed to assess *growth*, rather than two-wave data to assess *change*—as pointed out previously.

Q-sorts. A Q-sort is a forced-choice method of assessment. The method requires participants to order or sort a set of items (e.g., trait descriptors or behaviors) from least characteristic to most characteristic of some target person. The sort may be restricted to a specific number of categories or follow a prescribed distribution (e.g., a normal distribution); scores are assigned to items based on the category into which they are sorted: Often the resulting scores are used in ipsative, rather than normative comparisons; that is, an item score is compared only to other item scores for the target individual. However, a common use of the Q-sort compares an individual's sort to some criterion or prototypic sort, such as a consensual sort by experts (Strayer, Verissimo, Vaughn, & Howes, 1995). Such a comparison might be summarized by a correlation coefficient, the correlation reflecting the degree to which the individual's sort corresponds to or matches the criterion. Like all correlations, these Q-sort-based scores range from +1.0 (perfect correspondence) through 0.0 (no relation) to −1.0 (perfect inverse correspondence) with the criterion sort. And because correlations are not isomorphic with our ordinary number system, an $r = .40$ is not twice as similar to the criterion as an $r = .20$.

Age-(grade-)adjusted scores. Other problematic scores are age- or grade-equivalent (e.g., "mental age" or MA) and age-adjusted scores (e.g., IQ). Age-equivalent scores are, of course, only as good as the normative groups on which they are based. In addition, they may vary in meaning at different locations on the measurement scale. For example, during periods when skills and abilities are improving dramatically, the performance differences between adjacent age or grade groups may be appreciable; yet during periods of sluggish growth, performance differences between adjacent groups may be minimal. Consider the differences in mental ability between 2- and 5- year-old children and between 22- and 25-year-old adults. In the former case the differences are substantial; in the latter case they are trivial. Thus, developmental researchers need to exercise caution in interpreting differences expressed in age equivalents.

Age-adjusted scores such as IQ scores are not only encumbered by the surplus meanings attributed to them (e.g., that IQ scores are fixed in the way eye color is fixed—see Hunt, 1961; Neisser et al., 1996), but also by the special measurement properties shared by all such age-adjusted scores. Equal scores for children of different ages do not indicate equal skill or ability, but instead indicate equivalent statuses for the children in their respective age groups. Thus, groups of 8-year-olds and 10-year-olds with equal mean IQs of 115 do not have equivalent cognitive skills. Indeed, the 10-year-olds clearly are the more skillful. What the two groups of children do have in common is that they are both one standard deviation above their age-group means with respect to IQ. Age-adjusted scores, similar to age-equivalent scores, must be interpreted with care.

Criteria for Evaluating Scores

The quality of scores usually is judged by their conformity to standard psychometric criteria. These criteria include the standardization of administration and scoring procedures and the demonstration of acceptable levels of reliability and validity (American Educational Research Association, 1999). Some of these criteria require modification as a result of the nature of the variable under investigation. For example, because many performance variables, such as children's social skills, are assumed to be consistent over at least a few weeks, scores that assess these variables must demonstrate temporal reliability or stability over that time period. However, a measure of some transient characteristic, such as mood, would be suspect if it produced scores displaying temporal stability over a 2-week period.

Standardization. Standardization is intended to ensure that procedurally comparable scores are obtained for all participants assessed. Thus, standardization requires the use of equivalent administrative procedures, materials (such as items for tests or questionnaires and the timing and setting for observations), and methods of recording responses and of arriving at scores. In addition, it may be necessary to provide directions on how to develop and maintain rapport, whether to modify instructions for disabled participants (e.g., allow more time), when to present assessment materials and social commentary, and how to ensure that participants understand necessary instructions (Miller, 2007). Even slight variation from standardized procedures can introduce substantial noise into data and ambiguity into the interpretation of individual studies or even groups of studies as has occurred, for example, in the literature on the assessment of children's fears using behavioral avoidance tests (Barrios & Hartmann, 1988).

Reliability. Reliability concerns the dependability, consistency, or generalizability of scores (e.g., Cronbach, Gleser, Nanda, & Rajaratnam, 1972). Theoretical treatises on reliability decompose obtained scores (X) into at least two generic components: true or universe scores (X_t) and error scores (e_x).

$$X = X_t + e_x$$

The true score portion of one's obtained score ordinarily is the part that remains constant across time. This component is sometimes defined as the mean of an infinite number of measurements, or across all parallel forms of an instrument, or across all relevant measurement conditions (also sometimes referred to as *facets*), such as occasions, scorers, and the like. The error component is the portion of one's score that changes across time and results in inconsistent performance. Inconsistent performance might be produced by any number of factors, including chance events such as breaking a pencil during a timed test of mathematical problem solving, temporary states of the assessment setting (e.g., a crowded, noisy room) or of the participant (e.g., being ill, elated, or angry), or idiosyncratic aspects of the measurement instrument such as inconsistent observer behavior or scorer error. Unfortunately, the factors that produce consistent and inconsistent responding on measurement instruments vary depending on how reliability is assessed. For example, an illness might affect a child's playground aggression consistently across an observation session broken into temporal parts; aggression would thus be consistent or reliable across these parts. However, aggression would be inconsistent across observation sessions separated by longer intervals during which the child's health status changed.

As this discussion suggests, reliability may be assessed in a number of ways that differently divide obtained scores into true and error scores, including the following.

1. *Internal consistency* measures assess the consistency of performance across a measure's internal or constituent parts. Internal consistency reliability is one of the only forms of reliability that does not require repeated administration or scoring of an instrument. The Spearman-Brown prophesy formula (e.g., Nunnally & Bernstein, 1994) allows estimation of the internal consistency of an instrument from information about its items. Consider a test containing $k = 20$ items that have average intercorrelations ($\bar{r}_{ij}$) equal to .20. Absolutely speaking, these are low intercorrelations, but they would not be considered particularly low for test items. The internal consistency reliability, (r_{kk}) of the test $= k\bar{r}_{ij}/[1 + (k - 1)\bar{r}_{ij}] = .83$, a very respectable value.

2. *Interobserver* (or *interscorer*) *reliability* assesses the extent to which observers or scorers obtain equivalent scores when assessing the same individual. Interobserver reliability is assessed or measured with agreement statistics (e.g., percent agreement or kappa) or with traditional reliability statistics (e.g., correlation coefficients).

3. *Parallel-form reliability* determines the degree to which alternate (parallel) forms of an instrument provide equivalent scores. Parallel form reliability is to tests as interobserver reliability is to direct observations.

4. *Situational consistency* (generalizability) indexes the extent to which scores from an instrument are consistent across settings. For example, is the punctuality of children in the completion of their mathematics assignments consistent with their punctuality in the completion of their writing assignments? This form of reliability is analogous to the concept of the external validity of investigations.

5. *Temporal reliability* (stability) measures the degree to which an instrument provides equivalent scores across time. Test–retest correlations frequently are used to assess stability.

Two types of reliability, internal consistency and interobserver agreement, are required for most uses of assessment instruments. The scores obtained from an instrument composed of internally consistent parts assess a single characteristic or a set of highly interrelated characteristics. In contrast, assessment procedures containing internally inconsistent items, time periods, or analogous constituent parts measure a hodgepodge; as a result, scores obtained from them will not be comparable. For example, two children who obtain identical total scores on an internally inconsistent measure may perform quite differently from one another on the instrument's parts.

Interobserver reliability likewise is requisite for the minimal interpretability of scores. Without adequate agreement between observers, the very nature of the phenomenon under study is unclear (e.g., Hartmann & Wood, 1990). Interobserver reliability is sometimes surprisingly low even when the phenomenon of interest is clearly defined and easily observed. When this occurs, it may be that differences between observers are confounded with setting differences. For example, parents and teachers may disagree about an easily observed behavior because the teacher observes the child in school and the parents observe their child at home. In addition, if the same teacher rates all children but each child is rated by a different parent, disagreements may occur because parents use the rating scale in an idiosyncratic manner.

The remaining forms of reliability, situational consistency and temporal stability, are required when an investigator wishes to generalize, respectively, across settings and time. Such would be the case if, for example, infants' attachment to their mothers assessed in the laboratory at age 10 months were used to infer their attachment in the home at age 10 months (situational consistency or setting generalizability) or their attachment in the laboratory at age 24 months (temporal stability). Temporal stability is found to be negatively correlated consistently with the length of time between assessments. Indeed, the decreasing stability with increasing interassessment time (sometimes described as *simplex* in structure) has been observed so commonly in investigations of stability that it has assumed the character of a basic law of behavior. Over a standard time interval, temporal consistency increases typically with age during childhood. Brief temporal consistency often exceeds situational consistency (Mischel & Peake, 1983), although this finding is open to some dispute (Epstein & Brady, 1985).

It is important to note that test–retest statistics are sometimes used mistakenly. One frequent error is to describe stability without providing the interval over which it is assessed. A second common error occurs when developmental researchers interpret low stability as evidence against measurement equivalence. The latter interpretation can be dangerous as test–retest correlations "confound issues of construct validity, instrument equitability over time, and interindividual differences in growth" (Willett, 1988, p. 362).

Despite the quite different meanings of the various forms of reliability, they are often assessed in much the same manner—by correlating pairs of participants' scores. The scores may be paired across items, observers, time, or settings, depending on the type of reliability assessed. The statistics commonly used to summarize reliability data are noted in Table 3.15. The advantages and disadvantages of various statistics for summarizing reliability analyses are described by Hartmann (1982a) and Suen and Ary (1989).

Reliability gains general importance because it places a very specific limit on an instrument's empirical validity. If validity is indexed by an instrument's correlation with a criterion (r_{xy}), and the instrument's reliability is expressed as r_{xx}, the upper limit of r_{xy} is $r_{xx}^{1/2}$. That is, $|r_{xy}| \leq r_{xx}^{1/2}$—which is a form of the well-known correction for attenuation formula (e.g., Nunnally & Bernstein, 1994). Thus, a measuring instrument with $r_{xx} = .50$ could not expect to correlate $> .707$ with any criteria.

Measurement validity. Although all of the abovementioned psychometric criteria involve the interpretation or meaning of scores, validity is the psychometric criterion most directly relevant to their meaning. Instruments, and the scores that they produce, may have various forms of validity.

1. *Face validity* refers to whether the instrument *appears* to be a valid measure of some construct, as would a measure of altruism that asked children about the amount of money they donated to charity. Except for its public relations value, face validity is the least important form of **measurement validity**.

TABLE 3.15
Commonly Used Statistical Techniques for Summarizing Reliability Data

Statistical Technique	Primary Use
Coefficient Alpha (α)[a]	Describes internal consistency reliability. Ranges from .0 to +1.0.
Intraclass Correlation (*ICC*)	General method of summarizing reliability data. *ICC* indicates the ratio of subject variance to total variance. Typically ranges from .0 to +1.0
Kappa (κ)	Summarizes the reliability of categorical data. Recommended because it corrects for chance agreement. κ ranges from <.0 to +1.0.
Kuder-Richardson-20 and -21	Assesses the internal consistency reliability of a device composed of dichotomous items, such as true–false achievement test items.
Product Moment Correlation (r_{xx})	General method of summarizing reliability data. r_{xx} indicates the ratio of true score to total variance; $1 - r_{xx}$ indicates the proportion of error variance. Typically ranges from .0 to +1.0.
Raw (Percent) Agreement	Method of summarizing interobserver reliability data; criticized for its failure to correct for chance agreement.
Spearman-Brown Prophesy Formula	Used for estimating the internal consistency reliability of lengthened or shortened assessment devices.

Note. For more extended lists of statistics used for summarizing reliability data, see Berk (1979), Fleiss (1975), and House, House, and Campbell (1981).
[a] Not to be confused with α, the level of significance chosen for testing a null hypothesis.

2. *Content validity* assesses the degree to which the content of the instrument constitutes a representative sample of some substantive domain (e.g., do the items on an exam represent the material taught in the course adequately?). This form of validity is particularly important for achievement tests and observational coding systems.

3. *Factorial validity* indexes the extent to which an instrument taps some substantive construct or factor, and is most often determined for instruments developed using factor analysis. Factorial validity is closely related to the notion of internal consistency.

4. *Predictive validity* indicates the degree to which the scores from an assessment device are useful for predicting certain future criteria, such as academic success. This form of validity is similar to concurrent validity. Indeed, predictive and concurrent validity are sometimes referred to as various forms of "criterion-related validity." Criterion-related validity is typically assessed with a correlation coefficient. A correlation of $r = .50$ between predictor and criterion measures indicates that the percentage of variance that overlaps between the two is 25%. Percent overlap equals $100 \times r^2$ (McNemar, 1969, pp. 152–153; also see Ozer, 1985, and Steiger & Ward, 1987).

5. *Concurrent validity* indicates an instrument's correspondence with an important, currently assessed criterion. A test with substantial concurrent validity may be preferred over the device against which it is validated, if it is more efficient or less expensive than the criterion measure.

6. *Construct validity* indicates the extent to which an instrument assesses some theoretical construct, such as concrete operational reasoning, anxiety, or self-efficacy. Construct validity is perhaps the most basic, and at the same time most inclusive form of validity. Indeed, some have argued that validity is basically unitary, and the various types of validity are merely subclasses of construct validity (e.g., Messick, 1994).

Silva (1993, p. 69) nicely summarized current notions of validity as well as highlighting the inadequacies of earlier formulations, as follows:

- Validity is associated with each inference made from assessment information.
- It is not the instrument that is validated but rather the interpretation of scores obtained from the instrument.
- Validity is an integrative judgment, reached after considering all of the information—both empirical evidence and theoretical rationales. It is not reducible to a coefficient or set of coefficients.
- Types and classes of validity are misnomers for types and classes of *arguments*. The concept of validity is essentially unitary.
- There is no limit to the range of data used to estimate validity. Any information may be relevant in the validation process—which is simply the process of hypothesis construction and testing.

Traditionally, construct validity depends on the congruence between the pattern of results an instrument provides and the theoretical superstructure for the construct it presumably measures. The demonstration of congruence usually involves numerous sources of information. For example, the scores obtained from a construct-valid measure of children's interpersonal self-efficacy expectations (Bandura, 1997) presumably would distinguish socially successful from less successful children; show reasonable temporal stability except when following treatments intended to improve children's self-efficacy expectations; and correlate modestly with traditional measures of intelligence and moderately with peer-based measures of popularity and self-perceived competence. The more extensive and collaborative the interconnections between theory and measure, the stronger is the evidence of the validity of the measure for assessing the construct.

Wise investigators provide evidence for the construct validity of their measures: evidence that is independent of the results of the study that uses the measures to answer substantive questions. Failure to do so may result in a serious interpretive dilemma, particularly if the investigation does not work out as predicted. Critics may ask: Did the assessment instrument assess the construct inadequately? Was the theory supporting the construct faulty? Or did the study itself contain fatal validity threats? Without independent support for the construct validity of the measures, it may not be possible to decide among these three vastly different alternative interpretations.

Other criteria.   With some interpretations of scores, the standard psychometric criteria must be supplemented with additional quantitative requirements. These requirements may include that (1) the scores have a meaningful zero point, (2) the differences between scores have direction, and (3) the differences between scores are scaled (Nunnally & Bernstein, 1994). For example, if the differences between popularity scores are scaled, interpretations such as "Suzy is as different from Chen in popularity as Sigerdur is from Abdul" are possible. If, in addition, the popularity scale has a meaningful zero point, interpretations such as "Ling is twice as popular as Danielle" also are possible. Whichever of these criteria is met establishes the *level* of measurement obtained by the instrument's scores. The level of measurement relates not only to the interpretations that can be applied to the scores, but also to the statistics that are most commonly used with them. The typically distinguished levels of measurement, along with illustrations, interpretations, and statistics typically applied to them, are summarized in Table 3.16.

Data Facets

Measurement specialists and personality theoreticians have described an array of conceptualizations or facets of measurement that concern developmental investigators. The

TABLE 3.16
Typically Distinguished Levels of Measurement

Level	Example	Interpretation	Typical Statistics
Nominal	Gender	= or ≠	Counts; chi-square
Ordinal	Friendship rankings	< or >	Centiles and rank-order correlations
Interval	Grade equivalent	differences are =, <, or >	Ms, SDs, rs, and ANOVAs; t and F
Ratio	Height	ratios	Geometric and harmonic means; coefficient of variation

Note. The interpretations and typical statistics appropriate for more primitive levels of measurement also are applicable to higher levels of measurement.

more important of these facets concern the organization, stability, and content of the constructs assessed, the characteristic or property of the response that is targeted for assessment, and the standards against which scores are compared. These facets are generally noteworthy because they influence the planning, execution, analysis, and interpretation of developmental investigations. More specifically, they determine which of the psychometric standards are relevant to judging the adequacy of scores.

Nature of the measurements. The variables that developmentalists assess in their empirical investigations invariably represent classes or categories. These categories may be narrow and seemingly simple, such as smiles or sitting at desk; or they may be broad and encompassing, such as dominance, achievement orientation, or aggression. These response categories may be conceptualized as *traits* (relatively enduring, internally organized patterns of responding), *as response classes* (sets of responses that are elicited and/or maintained by similar environmental contingencies), or as *states* (relatively transient conditions of the organism).

Whichever of these conceptualizations is adopted has implications for the internal consistency and the temporal stability of the scores used in an investigation. For example, behaviors composing a trait should display substantial internal consistency, temporal stability, and perhaps situational consistency as well, but only internal consistency would be expected of behaviors constituting a response class or state.

The responses assessed can also be considered as *samples* of behavior of interest or as *signs* of some substrate not directly accessible. Children's eye contact, for example, might be a sample of an important aspect of social skill, or a sign of the trait of introversion. In the former case, the investigator must be concerned about the representativeness of the sample of eye contact obtained, and in the latter case about the extent to which eye contact correlates with other measures of introversion.

The substrate assessed need not be some relatively enduring, organized *structure*, such as a trait, but could instead be a *process* or function, such as social problem solving. And either children's *competence* (i.e., their capability or capacity) or their current level of *performance* on these structures or processes could be targeted for assessment. According to Messick (1983, p. 484), "Competence embraces the structure of knowledge and abilities, whereas performance subsumes as well the processes of accessing and utilizing those structures and a host of affective, motivational, attentional, and stylistic factors that influence the ultimate responses." The distinction between competence and performance is particularly important for developmental researchers, as it is tempting to imply that children are incompetent based on their inadequate performance. However, it may be erroneous to imply, for example, that young children do not have the concept of conservation because they fail to solve Piaget's water-glass problem, or that they do not have a particular linguistic structure because they do not use the structure in their spontaneous verbalizations. Instead, the failure may belong to the investigator, who did not elicit competent responses because of faulty selection of test stimuli or setting, or because of the use of inadequately motivating instructions.

Responses can also be conceptualized in terms of whether they assess behavior, attitudes and images, or physiological responding. This triple response *mode* distinction has been particularly useful for the assessment of the constructs of fear and anxiety, for example, which are construed as being represented in varying degrees by different individuals through the three modes (Barrios & Hartmann, 1988).

Response characteristics.   There are many properties of responses that could form the basis for scoring systems. Some of these properties, such as number, duration, and amplitude, are simple and easy to measure. Other characteristics of responses are more complex, and must be inferred or judged by some standard that exists beyond the response, such as the correctness or the goodness of the response. In assessing correctness, scoring of responses usually occurs by comparing the responses to a list of acceptable alternatives, and a total score is obtained by accumulating all correct or partially correct responses. This is the procedure that is followed typically in scoring achievement and ability tests. Response goodness may be substantially more difficult to judge and to summarize. To illustrate this difficulty, consider the situation in which children's block play is scored for the uniqueness of their constructions. The children may use quite different building strategies, with some of them generating a few, highly elaborated constructions, others generating many simple ones, and still others some mixture of these two strategies. Thus, a summary response score may need to be based on some weighting of response number, complexity, and uniqueness, although the last of these is of primary interest.

This example illustrates a ubiquitous characteristic of performance—that responses differ not only in substance, but also in style. The stylistic aspects of responding initially captured the attention of measurement specialists because they were a nuisance; differences in style were targets of control as they colored judgments of substance. Later, when the ugly duckling had turned into the Prince Charming, so to speak (McGuire, 1969, p. 20), and style became the focus of investigation, measurement specialists were faced with the opposite task—of assessing style untainted by substance! This latter focus on the manner or style of responding led to the creation of a number of major style constructs, including social desirability, cognitive tempo, and field dependence.

Comparison standards.   Because most scores are not meaningful in themselves, they must be compared to some standard in order to achieve meaning. Traditionally, scores have acquired meaning by comparison with the average performance of some relevant comparison group, called a *norm group*. Such scores, not surprisingly, are called *normative* scores. Typical standard scores and percentile ranks are normative scores. *Ipsative* scores, in contrast, are obtained by comparing the scores to other scores obtained by the same individual (Cattell, 1944).[5] Proportion scores obtained from observational measures of children's social behavior are ipsative scores; they indicate, for example, how the individual's total behaviors were

---

[5] A somewhat related distinction is made between whether the methods and procedures of investigation are designed to discover general laws (the *nomothetic* approach) or to discover laws that may be unique to the individual (the *idiographic* approach); see, for example, Allport (1937) and West (1983). This distinction is one of those that separate behavioral assessment from more traditional branches of assessment (Hartmann, Roper, & Bradford, 1979).

apportioned to the observational categories. Ipsative scores can be perplexing and sometimes troublesome, first, because they have unusual statistical properties. For example, the mean of a set of k ipsative subscales is $1/k$, their average intercorrelation is $-1/(k-1)$, and their average correlation with a criterion is exactly zero. Second, ipsative scores pose knotty problems of interpretation when investigators use both normative and ipsative comparisons. For example, one could be in the difficult position of having to explain how a child who scores consistently below par (normatively) on an IQ test could score higher (ipsatively) on the vocabulary subscale than another child scoring consistently above average (normatively) on the very same test.

Another possible method of inducing meaning in scores is to compare them with a criterion or a behavioral referent. Using this *criterion-referenced* approach, a child might be said to have mastered the ability to add two-digit numbers or to have mastered 80% of the tasks necessary to replace the rear wheel of a bicycle. Instruments that are constructed with the intent of using criterion-referenced scoring have substantially different statistical properties than have instruments developed with the intent of employing normative scoring. The primary statistical differences between these two approaches to test construction are summarized in Table 3.17.

Sources of Data

Assessment data in developmental studies come from a number of sources: from self-/ other-reports, from objective tests, and from observations in more or less natural settings. These three sources can be further subdivided. For example, self-/other-reports can be open-ended or provided in response to standard questions, their content can be narrowly focused or far-ranging, and they can be intuitively judged or formally scored.

Each of the sources of assessment information is associated with a relatively unique set of distortions. The presence of these method-specific distortions (called method variance) prompted Campbell and Fiske (1959) to propose that the construct assessed and the method of measurement contribute to the resulting scores. As a consequence, total score variation is sometimes decomposed into two variance components: construct variance and method variance. To avoid research results that are limited in generality by method variance, investigators assess their major constructs with multiple measures that differ in method-specific variation (see threats to construct validity in the design section).

The primary distortions (contributors to method variance) associated with the three sources of assessment information are summarized in Table 3.18. It is important to note in interpreting this table that the distortions lose their unique associations with the sources if, for

TABLE 3.17
Distinguishing Features of Criterion-referenced and Norm-referenced Assessment Instruments

Method	Purpose	Statistical Characteristics
Criterion-referenced	Determining what a child can do, or what a child knows	Truncated, sometimes dichotomous score distributions. Items have variable intercorrelations; many easy or difficult items.
Norm-referenced	Determining how a child compares to other children	Highly variable, often normal score distributions. Items are moderately intercorrelated. No very easy or very difficult items.

TABLE 3.18
Sources of Method Variance for Self-report, Objective-test, and Observational Sources of
Assessment Data

Sources of Data	Distortions
Self- or Other-Report	Misinterpretations; atypical use of descriptors (differing "anchor points")
	Degree of relevant knowledge; observational skills; memory; verbal skills
	Reactive effects such as deception, defensiveness, and impression management
Objective-Test	Cognitive styles such as impulsivity and field dependence
	Response styles such as acquiescence or position preferences (e.g., prefer first alternative)
	Instrumentation effects such as differential familiarity with various item formats and content selection biases
Observations	Observer biases and expectancies
	Observer distortions including memory loss and leveling (Campbell, 1958)
	Instrumentation effects such as halo error, leniency error, and central tendency errors (Guilford, 1954)
	Reactivity effects, such as avoidance of the observational setting

example, the participant is aware of the purpose of an objective-test assessment, or is even aware that an observational assessment is under way. In these two cases, the distortions produced by deception, defensiveness, and impression management are shared by all three sources.

It is not uncommon in assessment research to confound mode (behavior, images or thoughts, and physiological responses) with source in examining the consistency of responding in the three modes. For example, fearful behavior measured observationally might be compared with fearful images and physiological responses assessed by means of self-report. It would not be surprising in these comparisons to find greater correspondence between self-reports of fearful images and physiological responses than between either of these two and observed fearful behavior. This pattern of responding may not reflect greater agreement or synchrony between imaginal and physiological response systems. Instead, it may be attributable to the self-report method variance shared by the imaginal and physiological response measures.

Additional References

More specific information on the development of observational procedures may be found in Bakeman and Gottman (1987), Hartmann (1982b), and Haynes and O'Brien (2000). General information on measurement and scaling is available in Anastasi (1988), Cohen, Montague, Nathanson, and Swerdlik (1988), Crocker and Algina (1986), and especially Nunnally and Bernstein (1994); on measurement considerations in developmental research, in Baltes et al. (1998); on multimethod measurement Eid and Diener (2006); and on reliability statistics in behavioral observations, in Hartmann and Wood (1990) and Suen and Ary (1989). Information on measurement using the internet and web-based methods may be found in Birnbaum (2004) and Reips (2006).

ANALYSIS

Analysis refers to those procedures, largely although not exclusively statistical in nature, that are applied to the products of measurement (scores) to describe them and assess their meaning. Methods of analysis, because they are equated with sometimes difficult and obscure aspects of mathematics, are sometimes more distressing than any other aspect of scientific inquiry. This section discusses some of the technical aspects of statistical analysis as well as more friendly graphic methods.

Once scores have been obtained, preliminary operations are performed so that the scores will be suitable for formal analysis. These operations include adjusting the data for missing scores and outliers (extreme scores that indicate either errors in handling data or atypical participant responding). These preliminary operations also include any additional measurement manipulations that need to be completed such as the construction of composite scores—difference scores, ratio scores, or total scores—and transformations of the scores in cases where they fail to meet the assumptions of the statistical tests that will be performed on them. With intractable or otherwise troublesome data sets, these adjustments—sometimes referred to as "cleaning" or "laundering" the data—may occur repeatedly and at various points during the data analysis process.

Another important goal of preliminary analysis is to become familiar with the data through hands-on experience. This familiarization process often occurs as part of, preceding, or following adjustments of the data. It may involve careful study of frequency distributions and scrutiny of descriptive statistics calculated on the scores, such as measures of central tendency, variability, and correlation.

Once the data's general meaning is understood, the investigator conducts formal inferential tests. These tests function as decision aids that supplement the "binocular" tests conducted during the familiarization stage. The statistical tests determine which of the effects—hypothesized or not—are unlikely to be a function of chance variation in the data; that is, are statistically significant or reliable.

The statistical analysis, whether intended to describe the data or to test hypotheses relevant to them, differs depending primarily on the research question, and secondarily on the nature of the data. Most research questions can be conceived as belonging to one or two analytic classes. In one class are research questions that involve either the correlates of individual differences or the consistency of individual differences across time, settings, or behaviors. The data from these studies require some form of correlational, that is **Pearsonian, analysis**. Correlation analysis includes simple, part, partial, and multiple regression analysis, factor analysis, and structural equation modeling. In the other class are questions about longitudinal changes or cross-sectional differences in average performance. The data from these studies often are subjected to some form of **Fisherian analysis**, such as the **analysis of variance (ANOVA)**. Both Pearsonian and Fisherian approaches to data analysis are based on the general linear model (e.g., Kirk, 1995). However, the distinction between these approaches has been associated with design, subject matter, and other aspects of research strategy (Cronbach, 1957).

As has already been indicated, scores differ in a variety of ways. Two of these dimensions have particular relevance for the selection of statistical tests. The first dimension is whether the scores are categorical or quantitative in nature. Categorical scores include binary (e.g., yes–no) and other few-categorized discrete scores, such as "like–neutral–dislike" scales. Quantitative scores are continuous and multipointed, and include ratio, interval, and near-interval scores such as ratings on 5-point Likert scales. Categorical scores often require some form of contingency table analysis, not unlike common chi-square analyses, whereas quantitative scores usually are analyzed using some form of the analysis of variance or traditional regression analysis.

The second dimension concerns the number and type of scores contributed by each sampling unit (sampling units usually are composed of individual participants, but sometimes are composed of dyads or larger groups such as a family or a classroom). If each sampling unit contributes one score, then a **univariate analysis** is performed; if one score is repeatedly assessed over time or setting, then a repeated-measures univariate analysis may be conducted; or for multiple scores, ordinarily obtained during the same time period, a multivariate analysis is conducted.

These analyses require a wide variety of specific statistical tests, each of which has its assumptions, advantages, and pitfalls. Whatever the form of analysis, the ubiquitous $p < .05$ or $p < .01$ resulting from the analysis has a specific technical meaning that is critical to an understanding of hypothesis testing as it is currently practiced. Unfortunately, that meaning is widely misunderstood. These, and related issues, are addressed in the following section.

Preliminary Analyses

Adjusting scores.   Scores, like toddlers, require constant vigilance and repeated intervention if they are to stay out of trouble. Some participants have missing scores, and we must decide whether estimated scores should be derived for them, or whether those individuals should be omitted from some or all of the analyses.[6] Other scores may be transcribed incorrectly on data sheets or entered mistakenly into the computer. Most of these errors can be avoided if investigators emphasize accuracy in their scientific work, provide instructions in how to attain error-free data, institute frequent accuracy checks, and provide incentives for accurate results (Hartmann & Wood, 1990).

Still other data inaccuracies may reflect respondents' misunderstandings of instructions, their incorrect use of answer sheets, or even faking or cheating on their part. If these and other errors cannot be avoided by suitable instructions or by performance monitoring, they might be detected—and either corrected or eliminated—if the erroneous data are sufficiently atypical. Unusual scores are detectable if they are substantially different in value from those of neighboring scores. For example, a child who scored 2 *SD* either above or below his or her nearest scoring classmate on an observational assessment of aggression would certainly be a candidate for further investigation, and for possible removal from the data set. Incorrect scores also may be detectable because they represent an improbable *pattern* of responding. Examples include responding to the same question differently when it is asked twice; missing three very easy problems but answering correctly four more difficult problems; and admitting to taking birth control pills by someone who indicates being a 10-year-old boy. Sieves for the detection of errors of this sort require close scrutiny of the data by members of the research team, perhaps supplemented by computer programs developed to detect unusual responses or patterns of responses (see Tabachnick & Fidell, 2007, Chapter 4).

Still other adjustments may have to be made to the data before they are suitable for analyses. For example, it is not uncommon for scores to be combined or aggregated prior to major data analysis. The item, or other subpart, scores may be combined based on purely theoretical considerations—all items measure the same construct, and so the item scores are simply summed to generate a composite total score. Instead, the item scores may be combined

---

[6] The advent of modern computers facilitated a revolution in statistical procedures for handling missing data. Referred to as methods of data imputation, these procedures have had a major impact on longitudinal studies. According to Shadish et al. (2002), imputation methods enable investigators "to make use of all the data that are present and to eliminate much of the bias associated with nonrandom attrition" (p. 482). These procedures are reviewed and described in, for example, Graham (2009), Little and Rubin (1987), Schafer and Graham (2002), and Shadish et al. (2002).

on empirical bases, including the item intercorrelations, their reliability, or their correlations with a criterion (see Nunnally, 1978, for a not entirely dispassionate discussion of these alternative empirical strategies for combining assessment information).[7] Finally, and most often, scores are combined with an eye to theoretical and empirical considerations. Simultaneously serving more than one criterion need not be troublesome, unless of course the criteria suggest opposite courses of action, as may happen when theoretically appropriate items are inconsistently correlated with one other. In that case, after suitable digging into the data in an effort to make sense of the inconsistencies, investigators must rely on their good judgment and perhaps the good judgment of colleagues.

Another common preliminary manipulation of the data involves equating scores for differences in overall rates of behavior. For example, children may be evaluated on the number and kinds of errors they make in solving mathematics problems, but may differ in the number of problems attempted. In such cases, investigators adjust scores by prorating, by shifting to proportion or percentage scores, or by employing other ratios such as rate per unit of time. Still other transformations of scores, such as square root, log, and arc sin transformations (see Table 3.14) may be required because the original scores violate the assumptions of statistical tests that will be performed on them. These transformations and their effects were outlined earlier in the section on measurement. Following, as part of, or sometimes interspersed between such laundering operations, investigators are wise to construct graphs of their data and calculate descriptive statistics on them.

Becoming familiar with data. Informal or **exploratory data analysis**—consisting of constructing graphs, charts, and plots, and calculating simple descriptive statistics—is critically important to understanding the meaning of data. Indeed, some investigators argue that these procedures, particularly the scrutiny of graphic displays, should constitute the primary method of judging the outcomes of experiments (Baer, 1977; also see Shadish, 1986).

Whether these methods are primary, or merely contributory for judging the outcomes of experiments, there is little doubt of their importance. Unfortunately, it seems that novice investigators omit all, or the greater portion of, the preliminary stages of data analysis: The excitement of having completed data collection is quickly followed by the need to know if the data contain anything "statistically significant." And so the data are prematurely formally analyzed, perhaps using only standard or "canned" computer programs, with results that unnecessarily support the adage "garbage in, garbage out." This misplaced enthusiasm deprives investigators of the opportunity to experience a sense of intimacy with their data— the kinds of hands-on experiences from which serendipitous findings and otherwise new perspectives are discovered. Unfortunately, there is not a large literature on the procedures useful for gaining familiarity with data, and so the procedures tend to be idiosyncratic and somewhat artistic in nature. Generally, however, they involve constructing graphic displays and calculating standard as well as "quick and dirty" descriptive statistics (Tukey, 1977).

Graphing data. Useful graphic displays range from freehand sketches of univariate and bivariate frequency distributions to computer-crafted, publication-ready, three-dimensional drawings of multiple time series (see Parsonson & Baer, 1978). The concern during preliminary data analysis is not with beauty, however, but with utility. For example, when groups

---

[7] One of the alternative strategies discussed by Nunnally (1978) is item response theory (IRT) or item characteristic curve (ICC) theory. IRT is a well-established alternative to classical measurement theory for the model of measurement error. It is popular in educational testing, but it has not achieved widespread use in developmental science, although it is potentially very relevant. Explanations and applications to developmental science of IRT are available in Boivard and Embretson (2008), Bornstein, Hahn, Haynes, Manian, & Tamis-LeMonda (2005), and Embretson & Reise (2000).

are being compared, simple bar graphs (Figures 3.2–3.4) of each group's performance can readily be drawn.

Each display might be checked for atypical performances (Figure 3.2) if this has not already been done in some other way, and a decision might be made concerning the treatment of unusual respondents—sometimes termed outliers (see Tabachnick & Fidell, 2007, for a discussion of outliers and their detection, including tests of significance). Other aspects of the data also might be noted, such as the modality or peakedness *(kurtosis)* of the distribution of scores (see the bimodal distribution in Figure 3.2), their symmetry (see the positively skewed distribution in Figure 3.3), and whether floor and ceiling effects (also see Figure 3.2) are present. Bimodal distributions are found when a sample is composed of scores for two different types of respondents, such as a distribution of birth weights for a sample composed of term and preterm infants. *Skewness*, or lack of symmetry in the scores, might occur for a variety of reasons, including the presence of floor or ceiling effects. These latter forms of asymmetry are observed when a substantial proportion of participants receives the lowest scores (floor effect) or the highest scores (ceiling effect) on the assessment instrument. In ability testing, the presence of a floor effect suggests that the test was too difficult, and a ceiling effect suggests that the test was too easy. The statistical significance of skewness and kurtosis can also be analyzed more formally (e.g., Fidell & Tabachnick, 2003).

If the data are approximately normal in their distribution, both the mean and standard deviation can be readily estimated from graphic displays. The mean will lie approximately in the center of the distribution, and the ratio of the group's range to its standard deviation varies from approximately 3 ($N \approx 10$), to 4 ($N \approx 30$), to 5 ($N \approx 100$), and to 6 ($N \approx 450$); see Guilford (1965, p. 81) and the data shown in Figure 3.4.

FIGURE 3.2 Univariate bimodal frequency distribution containing an outlier (indicated by arrow). With the outlier, $M = 34.3$, $SD = 9.56$, and $N = 35$; without the outlier, $M = 33.5$, $SD = 8.57$ and $N = 34$.

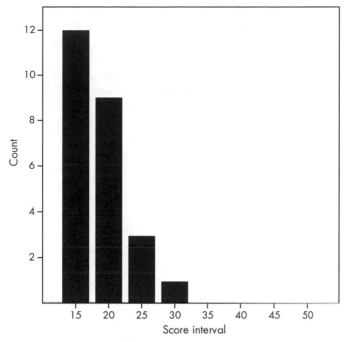

FIGURE 3.3 Illustration of a positively skewed frequency distribution with a distinct floor effect. For this distribution, $M = 18.6$, $SD = 4.21$, skewness = 1.049, and $N = 25$.

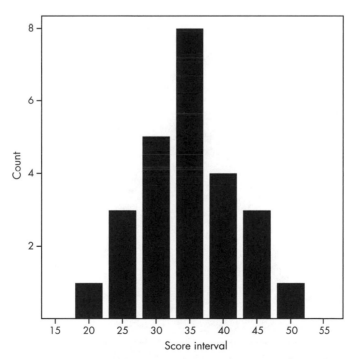

FIGURE 3.4 Illustration of an approximately normal frequency distribution for which rules of thumb provide close approximations to the M and SD of the distribution. $M = 34.8$ (estimated $M = 35$). $SD = 7.29$ (estimated $SD = $ range/3.8 = 35/3.8 = 7.89); $N = 23$.

When investigations employ more than one DV, it often proves useful to cross-tabulate the scores or to sketch their bivariate frequency distribution (Figure 3.5). The resulting displays—sometimes referred to as *scatter diagrams*—can be examined for a number of disturbances, including the presence of outliers. When outliers are present, they can change dramatically the magnitude of the correlation between the variables. (Compare the value of *r* for the data in Figure 3.5 when the outlier is included and when the outlier is excluded.)

Scatter diagrams also can be checked for the extent to which the regression between the variables is linear. Nonlinear regression is illustrated in Figure 3.6. Because the product moment correlation (*r*) assesses the linear part of the relation between variables, *r* will under-estimate the relations between variables that are nonlinearly related. Compare, for example, the value of *r* and of η (eta, the curvilinear correlation coefficient) for the data shown in Figure 3.6.

In addition to disclosing the presence of outliers and nonlinear regressions, scatter diagrams can indicate *heteroscedasticity* (unequal dispersion of scores about the regression line). Heteroscedasticity indicates that errors of predictions vary depending on the value of the predictor score. With the data displayed in Figure 3.7, *Y* scores are less accurately predicted for individuals with high *X* scores than for individuals with low *X* scores. Scatter diagrams and other graphic plots serve both as important detection devices and as judgmental aids in the hands of experienced investigators.

More on descriptive statistics.   Means, standard deviations, and correlation coefficients are the most commonly used descriptive statistics. In addition, a number of other statistics are sufficiently common to deserve brief mention. First we consider a number of the many

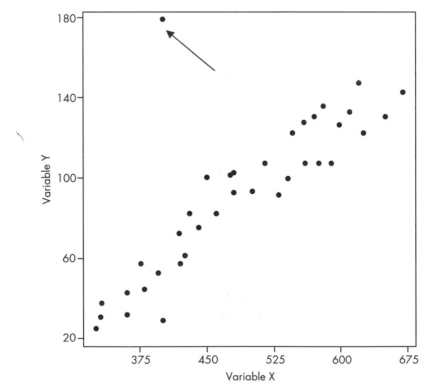

FIGURE 3.5   Illustration of a positive linear relation between variables *X* and *Y*. Outlier indicated by arrow. With the outlier included, *r* = +.81; with the outlier omitted, *r* = +.95. The dispersion of scores with each *X*-array is approximately normal (homoscedasticity). *N* = 37 with outlier included.

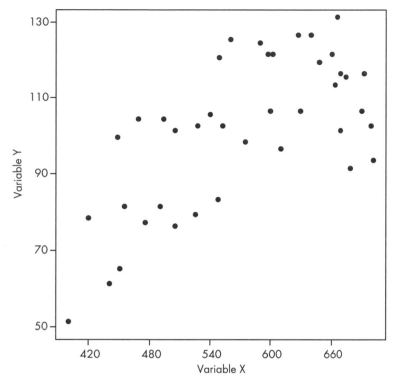

FIGURE 3.6   Illustration of curvilinear relation between X and Y. The value of the linear correlation is +.66, whereas the value of eta, the curvilinear correlation, for predicting Y from X is .99 and for predicting X from Y is +.94. The dispersion of scores within X-arrays is approximately equal (homoscedasticity). N = 40.

descriptive statistics related to r, the correlation coefficient: part and partial correlation, kappa (see Table 3.15), and conditional probability.

Part and *partial correlations* are ordinary product-moment correlations that deserve special names because of the nature of the scores to which they are applied. Using the three variables of age, height, and weight, the distinctions between simple correlations and part and partial correlations are illustrated by the Venn diagrams shown in Figure 3.8. Either one (part) or both (partial) of the scores correlated are corrected for uncontrolled variation in a third variable. For example, in a three-variable regression problem involving height, weight, and age, the correlation between height and weight, with age corrected, is called the partial correlation and is symbolized $r_{hw.a}$ (see Figure 3.8, Panel B). The partial correlation between height and weight is equal to the correlation between these two variables when calculated for participants who all are at the mean age of the group. Partial correlation is used when the effects of a third variable, such as age in the abovementioned example, cannot be experimentally controlled. If age were partialed out of weight, but not out of height, the resulting correlation would be the part correlation between height and weight (see Figure 3.8, Panel A). This part correlation is symbolized $r_{h(w.a)}$. Part correlations play an important role in multiple regression, as they indicate the overlap of the criterion with the unique portion of each of the predictors.

Kappa is an agreement statistic that is used to summarize interjudge reliability data, particularly for observational data. Assume that two observers each classified independently the same 200 10-s observation intervals into whether a target child interacted with her peers, interacted with her teacher, or failed to interact. The resulting data might resemble those given in Figure 3.9. A typical, older, and flawed method of summarizing these data is simply

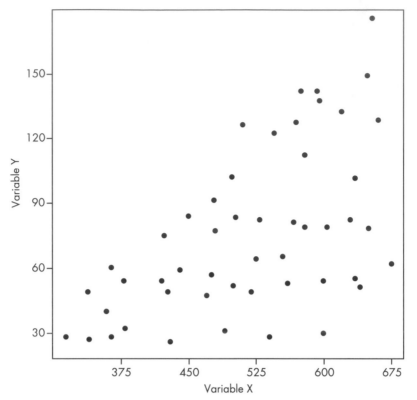

FIGURE 3.7   Illustration of heteroscedasticity (unequal dispersion of scores within each *X*-array). $r = +.56$ and $N = 50$.

to tabulate the proportion of intervals for which the two observers agreed. For the data in Figure 3.9, the observers agreed on 95 intervals scored as "interacted with peers," 25 intervals rated as "interacted with teacher," and 40 intervals classified as "alone." These 160 intervals, when divided by 200 (the total number of intervals during which observations were taken), gives a proportion of agreement of .80. When kappa is calculated on these same data, a somewhat lower estimate of agreement is obtained, as kappa corrects for agreements that might have occurred by chance. Kappa is equal to

$$(p_o - p_c)/(1 - p_c)$$

where p_o is the proportion of observed agreements and p_c is the proportion of chance agreements.

For the data in Figure 3.9, p_o is .80, as we have already determined in the calculation of the simple agreement statistic, and p_c is equal to the sum of the expected values for each of the agreement cells in Figure 3.9 divided by the total number of observation intervals ($p_c = .4275$).[8] Kappa is then equal to

$$(.80 - .4275)/(1 - .4275) = .65.$$

---

[8] The expected values are determined in exactly the same manner as they typically are for chi-square tables, that is by summing the products of corresponding marginal values and dividing by N. For the data given in Figure 3.9, the expected value for the agreement cell for "interacts with peers" is $(120 \times 110)/200 = 66$; for the agreement cell "interacts with teacher" the expected value is $(30 \times 30)/200 = 4.5$; and for the agreement cell "alone," the expected value is $(50 \times 60)/200 = 15$. Summing these values and dividing by N yields $p_c = (66 + 4.5 + 15)/200 = .4275$.

Figure A

Figure B

Figure C

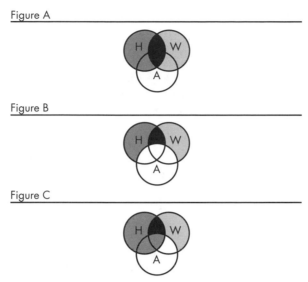

FIGURE 3.8   Venn diagrams illustrating the distinctions between simple correlations, and partial- and part-correlations. In general, the lightly shaded areas indicate the independent portions of the two variables correlated, and the darkly shaded portion indicates the overlapping or nonindependent portions of the variables. For the simple correlation between height and weight (r_{hw})—shown in Panel A—the darkly shaded area that overlaps portions of the entirety of H and W indicates the degree of correlation. For the partial correlation ($r_{hw.a}$)—shown in Panel B—the darkly shaded area overlapping the *remaining* portions of H and W indicates the degree of correlation. Finally, for the part correlation, $r_{h(w.a)}$—shown in Panel C—the darkly shaded area that overlaps portions of the entirety of H and portions of the *remaining* of W indicates the degree of correlation.

| | | Observer 1
Child interacts with | | | |
		Peer	Teacher	No one	Totals
Observer 2	Peer	95	05	10	110
Child interacts with	Teacher	05	25	00	30
	No one	20	00	40	60
	Totals	120	30	50	200 = N

FIGURE 3.9   Joint, but independent, observations of a child's interactions by Observer 1 and Observer 2 used to illustrate the calculation of interobserver reliability using Cohen's kappa. N = the number of observation intervals, not the number of participants. The values in the principal diagonal cells—the cells for which like categories intersect for the two observers and extending from upper left to lower right—represent observation intervals for which the observers agreed. The values in the off-diagonal cells represent disagreements between the two observers (e.g., the 10 entries in the cell defined by the first row and third column are those for which Observer 2 indicated that the child was interacting with her peers, but Observer 1 stated that she was alone).

Conditional probabilities play an important role in analysis of fine-grained interactional data, sometimes called micro-analytic analysis (Bakeman & Gottman, 1997; Kerig & Lindahl, 2001). These probabilities perhaps can best be understood by examining 2×2 table data, such as those shown in Figure 3.10. The data in Figure 3.10 describe the temporal patterning of talking by a mother and her child. These data can be summarized in various ways: by a correlation statistic such as the phi coefficient or by means of a conditional probability. The conditional probability of the child talking given that her mother talked in the prior interval is equal to the joint probability that the child talked and the mother talked in the previous interval divided by the probability that the mother talked in the previous interval. For the example given in Figure 3.10, the conditional probability of the child talking at time $t + 1$ given that her mother talked in the previous interval is equal to

$$(B/N)/[(A + B)/N] = B/(A + B) = 40/(10 + 40) = .80$$

The conditional probability is often compared with its unconditional probability. The unconditional probability of the child talking is $(B + D)/(N) = (40 + 20)/(100) = .60$. Thus, the mother's talking in the previous interval increases the likelihood that the child will talk in the following interval from .60 to .80.

The final descriptive statistic, one similar to an ordinary variance, is the characteristic root or the eigen value of a matrix. *Eigen values* are to matrices what the variance is to a distribution of numbers. Not surprisingly, then, eigen values (symbolized as γ) are frequently encountered in **multivariate analysis**, where one deals with matrices of scores. For example, in principal component analysis, a factoring technique, the eigen value for each principal component may be thought of as the amount of variance in the original standardized variables associated with that principal component. In multivariate ANOVAs, the eigen value can be thought of as the variance between the group centroids. (A centroid is to multiple dependent variables what a mean is to a single dependent variable.)

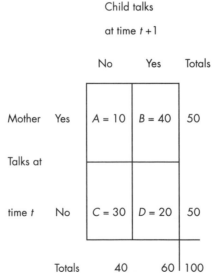

FIGURE 3.10   Temporal sequence of mother and child talking (mother talking at time t and child talking at time $t + 1$) used to illustrate the calculation of conditional probabilities. N = the number of observation intervals, not the number of participants.

Null Hypothesis Testing

Following the calculation of descriptive statistics, several methods are available to judge the significance of the statistics. Significance in this context refers to whether or not the effects of interest, which are presumably reflected in the data and in the summary descriptive statistics applied to the data, could have arisen by chance. The primary method that developmentalists use to judge the statistical significance of their results is null hypothesis testing. Preference for this method of assessing statistical significance exists despite the very substantial criticism directed at null hypothesis testing procedures (see Harlow et al., 1997; Meehl, 1978; Morrison & Henkel, 1970, Nickerson, 2000).

Null hypothesis testing, as currently employed, is a multistep process (see Table 3.19) that begins with the development of two models or hypotheses about the data. One model, sometimes called the *experimental model*, contains the putative effect of interest to the investigator, such as treatment, age, or gender. The other model, often called the *null* or *restricted model*, does not contain this effect or states that the effect of interest equals zero. Null models or hypotheses often are stated in one of two forms. In one form of the null hypothesis, some effect or parameter is assumed to equal zero in the population under investigation. The parameter, for example, may be a simple correlation coefficient or a beta weight in a multiple regression analysis (e.g., $\beta = 0$). In another form of the null hypothesis, the values of the parameter of interest for two or more populations are assumed to be equal. The parameters to be compared most often include population means or variances (e.g., $\sigma_w^2 = \sigma_b^2$).

In the second step of null hypothesis testing, the investigator decides how unlikely the obtained results must be before concluding that the null hypothesis is probably false. The logic implied here is that if the sample data are unlikely to have occurred under the null model, then that model must not be true. This step is sometimes referred to as "selecting an α level." α levels (or probabilities) of .05 or .01 are the conventional ones used in deciding whether to reject null models or hypotheses. However, it is important to add that the selection of α should be based

TABLE 3.19
Illustration of Null Hypothesis Testing

Step 1. An investigator explores the relation between the number of observed positive social requests and sociometric status in a group of 6-year-old children. The null hypothesis states the following about the population correlation, ρ (rho):

$\rho = .00$. This null hypothesis is contrasted with an alternative hypothesis that states that $(\rho) \neq .00$

Step 2. α, the probability associated with rejection of the null hypothesis, is set at $p = .05$. Therefore, the obtained finding must have a probability of occurrence $\leq .05$ before the null hypothesis will be rejected and the alternative hypothesis accepted.

Step 3. The obtained correlation is tested with the z test for the significance of r using Fisher's r to z_r transformation.

$z = (z_r - 0)/\sigma_{z_r}$, and $\sigma_{z_r} = 1/(N-3)^{\frac{1}{2}}$

With $r = .50$, and $N = 19$, $z_r = .549$ and $\sigma_{z_r} = 1/(19-3)^{\frac{1}{2}} = .25$, so

$z = (.549 - 0)/.25 = 2.20$

Step 4. The two-sided probability value associated with $z = 2.20$, according to the normal curve table, is approximately $p = .028$.

Step 5. Because $p = .028$ meets the criterion established in Step 2 where α was set at $p = .05$, the null hypothesis is rejected. Therefore, it is concluded that positive social requests and sociometric status are significantly correlated in 6-year-old children.

Note. This traditional approach described in Step 5 has been replaced with simply providing the obtained p-value associated with the value of the inferential statistic.

on the consequences of rejecting a true null hypothesis (a Type I error) versus the consequences of accepting a false null hypothesis (a Type II error), and not by convention. If the consequences of rejecting a true null hypothesis are substantial—say, millions of dollars may be spent in changing an existing social policy—and the consequences of accepting a false null hypothesis are minor, a very, very small α level, such as .0001, might be employed.

In the third step, the investigator uses the sample data to compute the value of a test or inferential statistic. This test statistic measures the extent of the deviation of the sample data from those expected on the basis of the null hypothesis. Traditional univariate test statistics are the z (normal curve) test, the t test, the F test, and the chi-square (χ^2) test.

In the fourth step, the investigator determines the probability associated with the test statistic, often by reference to statistical tables or computer output. In order for these sources to provide appropriate probability values, the sample data must be consistent with a set of assumptions required by the statistical test. Although each statistical test has its own set of assumptions, some assumptions are common to many inferential tests. Typical among these shared assumptions are that scores (usually error or residual scores) must be distributed normally, homogeneously, and independently. Violation of these assumptions—particularly that of independence and to a lesser degree that of homogeneity—can result in highly erroneous probability values (Judd et al., 1995; Kirk, 1995). To help insure the correctness of probability values that result from the major statistical analyses, the tenability of critical assumptions should be tested formally (e.g., Kirk, 1995; Tabachnik & Fidell, 2007).

In the final step of null hypothesis testing, it was traditional to compare the probability value associated with the statistical test with the value of α selected by the investigator. As a result of this comparison, the null hypothesis and the model on which it is based were either rejected or not rejected. However, standards recommended by the American Psychological Association (Wilkinson & the Task Force on Statistical Inference, 1999, p. 599) state that "It is hard to imagine a situation in which a dichotomous accept–reject decision is better than reporting an actual p value . . . [and] never use the unfortunate expression 'accept the null hypothesis.' "

It is also important to understand just what a reported p value means, as they are often misinterpreted. Consider a study reporting that $p = .05$. What is the appropriate interpretation of this probability value? It is clearly incorrect to conclude that the result is important, that the probability of this result being replicated is .05, that the probability is .95 (1 − .05) of the obtained result having occurred, or that the probability is .05 that the obtained result is 0. If you chose any of these interpretations you were incorrect, but you are also in good company, as even statisticians frequently err in interpreting the probability values from experiments (Tversky & Kahneman, 1971). Instead, the p value provides the likelihood of the obtained or more extreme result given that the null hypothesis model is correct (see Gigerenzer, Krauss, & Vitouch, 2004; Hartmann & George, 1999).

The statistical testing procedures just outlined differ in detail depending on a variety of considerations. These considerations include the descriptive statistic that answers the investigator's question. For example, questions answered by examining means may require different testing procedures than do questions concerned with variability or correlation. Another consideration involves whether each independent experimental unit[9] receives a

---

[9] The number of independent experimental units (called *units of analysis*) usually, although not always, is equal to the number of participants. Exceptions occur when the sampling units are themselves aggregates, such as dyads, families, or classrooms. In these exceptional cases, the responses of individual respondents may be linked (dependent), and the independent experimental units are given by the number of dyads, families, or classrooms, respectively. When the number of units of analysis exceeds the number of sampling units, one is often in imminent danger of lethally threatening statistical conclusion validity. See, for example, the discussion of dependency by Kenny and Judd (1986) and of "nested" subjects by Anderson and Anger (1978) and by Cairns (1983).

score on a single dependent variable (univariate analysis), more than one score on a single dependent variable (**repeated-measures analysis**), or one or more scores on more than one dependent variable (multivariate analysis). Still another consideration is whether categorical or quantitative data are tested for significance. The following sections address significance testing in these various circumstances—which, as we shall find out a bit later, are all examples of the **generalized linear model**. Because of the large number of combinations of circumstances involved, however, only those commonly occurring are discussed.

Analysis of Categorical Data

Categorical data are those that are typically obtained from nominal scales (see Table 3.16). Sometimes, however, quantitative scores are split artificially, say, at the median, and treated as if they were categorical. Such a strategy is almost always foolhardy, as degrading scores in this way is equivalent to throwing away information, and results in lowered power.

Chi-square analysis. The analysis of categorical data typically has involved some form of chi-square or closely related analysis. Less frequently used are other nonparametric tests, such as Fisher's Exact Test and parametric tests that are more appropriate for quantitative data. Chi-square tests have a variety of uses in the statistical testing of categorical data. For example, they are used to determine whether proportions or frequencies differ from one another, whether categorical variables are correlated, and whether distributional assumptions, such as normality, hold. These uses of chi-square and of other traditional nonparametric testing procedures have been ably described in a large number of books, including those by Conover (1999), Fleiss, Levin, and Paik (2003), and Hollander (1999), and are not cataloged here. Instead, some common errors made in these analyses are noted, and then a number of relatively new methods for analyzing complex categorical data are described.

Perhaps not surprising in view of their general utility, chi-square tests have long been a favorite for abuse. The sources of this abuse are clearly spelled out in a sequence of critical papers, including Lewis and Burke (1949, 1950) and Delucchi (1983). Perhaps the most serious of the many errors made in the use of chi-square is violation of the independence assumption. This error occurs when investigators shift experimental units from participants to the events in which they engage. Consider a set of fictitious data gathered to assess a prediction derived from a theory of moral development: that 4-year-olds would cheat more frequently in turn-taking than would 6-year-olds. The data gathered to test this hypothesis might take the form of the number of violations of turn-taking observed during 10-min samples of free play for 15 4-year-old and 15 6-year-old children. If the number of cheating incidents totaled 40, and individual scores ranged from 0 to 3, some investigators might be tempted to conduct the chi-square analysis summarized in Panel A of Figure 3.11 (also see the data display in Panel A). It is apparent from inspection of this figure that the investigator has shifted experimental units from children ($N = 30$) to some combination of children and cheating incidents ($N = 40$). The 19 entries in cell A represent the number of incidents of cheating engaged in by nine 4-year-old children. It is difficult to argue that these cheating incidents were independent, as individual children contributed as many as three entries to this cell.

The correct display of the data is shown in Panel B of Figure 3.11, maintaining children as the unit of analysis. The proper analysis of these data is given in the Panel B description. As can be seen from this latter analysis, the two age groups do not differ significantly in the proportion of children who are observed cheating; that is, age and cheating are not

	PANEL A		
	AGE OF CHILD		
CHEATING	4	6	
Occurrences	$A = 19$	$B = 6$	25
Nonoccurrences	$C = 6$	$D = 9$	15
Totals	25	15	40

	PANEL B		
	AGE OF CHILD		
CHEATER	4	6	
Yes	$A = 9$	$B = 6$	15
No	$C = 6$	$D = 9$	15
Totals	15	15	30

Panel A. Chi square (χ^2) calculations based on $A = 19$ (see Panel A).

$$\chi^2 = \Sigma\Sigma[(o_{ij} - e_{ij})^2 / e_{ij}],$$

where o_{ij} is the observed frequency in the ith row and jth column, e_{ij} is the expected frequency in the ith row and jth column and is equal to the product of the ith row frequency and the jth column frequency divided by N.

$$\chi^2 = [(19 - (25 \times 25/40))^2 / (25 \times 25/40)] + 2 \times [(6 - (25 \times 15/40))^2 / (25 \times 15/40)]$$
$$+ [(9 - (15 \times 15/40))^2 / (15 \times 15/40)] = 5.184.$$

which, with 1 degree of freedom is associated with $p < .05$.

Panel B. Chi square calculations based on $A = 19$ (see Panel B).

$$\chi^2 = 2 \times [(9 - (15 \times 15/30))^2 / (15 \times 15/30)] + 2 \times [(6 - (15 \times 15/30))^2 / (15 \times 15/30)] = 1.20,$$

which, with 1 degree of freedom is associated with $p > .20$.

FIGURE 3.11 Incorrect (Panel A) and correct (Panel B) data displays for cheating during turn-taking in 15 4-year-old and 15 6-year-old children, and incorrect (Part A) and correct (Part B) applications of chi-square analyses to these data. Note that even though some of the cells in the correct (Part B) analysis included small expected values, no correction for continuity was included. Simulation research indicates that the correction usually is unnecessary as long as N exceeds 20; indeed, use of the correction produces overly conservative probabilities (Delucchi, 1983).

significantly correlated in these data.[10] Comparing the results of the appropriate and inappropriate analyses illustrates that violating the independence assumption can produce serious distortions in chi-square probabilities. Similar distortions of chi-square probabilities have been noted by Gardner, Hartmann, and Mitchell (1982) in the analysis of dyadic time series data when an interacting dyad provides all of the data entries (see Figure 3.10 for an example of data of this type).

Log-linear analysis. The newer methods of analyzing categorical data are variously called *log-linear analysis* and (multidimensional) *contingency table analysis*. These approaches allow investigators to analyze complicated cross-classified categorical data, such as the data presented in Figures 3.10 and 3.11 made more complex with the inclusion of additional variables. The analytic approach is similar to that used in an ANOVA. As in ANOVA, a linear model is developed that expresses a table entry (a frequency) as a function of main and interaction effects. Multidimensional contingency table analysis differs from ANOVA in that in the former case the *logarithms* of the putative effects are summed. Because the equation is linear in its log form, the approach is referred to as log-linear. In addition, testing procedures

---

[10] The analysis given in Figure 3.11 is a test of the difference between independent proportions. That is, is the proportion of 4-year-olds who engage in cheating different from the proportion of 6-year-olds who engage in cheating? As such, the analysis is one of the differences between independent means (as the two group proportions in this problem are really group means). The analyses can also be viewed as one of the correlation between group status (age) and cheating. Thus, in an important sense, differences between means and correlations are but two alternative ways of viewing data analysis.

resemble those used with data from unbalanced ANOVA designs. That is, a hierarchical model testing procedure is followed in which each lower-level model might be tested until a model that adequately fits the data is encountered. A set of hierarchical models for the data shown in Figure 3.10 would look like this:

(1) $m_{ij} = \mu$

(2) $m_{ij} = \mu + \lambda^M$

(3) $m_{ij} = \mu + \lambda^M + \lambda^I$

(4) $m_{ij} = \mu + \lambda^M + \lambda^I + \lambda^{MI}$ (the saturated model, including all effects)

where m_{ij} = the log expected frequency in the ith row and jth column; μ = the log of N/rc, or the average cell frequency; and λ^M, λ^I, and λ^{MI} = the log expected row (mother), column (infant), and interaction (Mother × Infant) effects, respectively.

A large value of the test statistic for a model (say, model 2) indicates that additional parameters must be included in the model—as in models 3 and 4—whereas a small value of the test statistic indicates that the model adequately fits the data. This *model comparison* approach to statistical testing is popular (see structural equation modeling; Judd et al., 1995).

The test statistic used for multidimensional contingency table analysis is either the ordinary chi-square statistic or the likelihood ratio statistic, G^2. G^2 involves the logarithm of the ratio of observed and expected frequencies, rather than the squared discrepancy between observed and expected frequencies that the ordinary chi-square test involves.

These techniques for analyzing multidimensional table data have the advantages of the ANOVA: They provide omnibus (overall) tests of main and interaction effects in factorial investigations, allow for subsequent contrast tests, and control for Type I error rates. These advantages come with some cost, however. According to Appelbaum and McCall (1983), multidimensional contingency analysis requires large numbers of participants, particularly when repeated-measures versions of this approach are used.

When these as well as other methods of statistical analysis are used for the first time, the computer program as well as the user should be tested by replicating a textbook example. After an example from any of the standard texts—such as Fleiss et al. (2003), Kennedy (1992), or Wickens (1989)—is analyzed successfully, the new data are ready for analysis. Additional useful material on multidimensional table analysis can be found in Knoke and Burke (1980) and Landis and Koch (1979).

Loglinear analysis is used to test the association between multiple categorical factors that are all regarded as response variables. However, when one of the factors is regarded as a response variable and the other factors are regarded as explanatory variables, *logistic regression analysis* is appropriate (Agresti, 1996).

Logistic regression. Logistic regression can be applied when the response variable is binary (binomial logistic regression) or polytomous (multinomial logistic regression). The explanatory variables are used to model the probability, $\hat{p}$, of the response. Whereas log-linear analysis models the natural log of the expected cell counts of a contingency table, logistic regression models the natural log of the odds of the response variable (Christensen, 1997). The natural log of the odds, $\ln\left(\dfrac{\hat{p}}{1-\hat{p}}\right)$, is called the logit or logistic unit, hence the name logistic regression. The logit form of the logistic regression equation is

$$\ln \left(\frac{\hat{p}}{1 - \hat{p}} \right) = \beta_0 + \beta_1 X_1 + \beta_2 X_2 + \ldots + \beta_k X_k$$

The regression coefficient, β_k, indicates the amount of linear change in the logit for a one-unit change in the predictor. Because logits are difficult to interpret, regression coefficients are typically transformed into odds ratios or probabilities for interpretation. For example, using the contingency table in Figure 3.11, Panel B, the logistic regression equation for predicting cheating from age is logit(Cheating) = .41 − .811(Age). Transforming −.811 by taking the inverse of the natural log, $e^{-.811}$, gives .44, which is an odds ratio. It indicates that cheating by 6-year-old children is .44 times less likely than cheating by 4-year-old children. Logistic regression is a very flexible analytic technique. It accommodates multiple explanatory variables that can be a mix of all types (continuous, discrete, and dichotomous), and that can represent interactions between predictors and polynomials. Detailed presentations and worked examples of logistic regression are found in Agresti (2007), Cohen, Cohen, West, & Aiken (2003), Pampel (2000), and Tabachnick and Fidell (2007).[11]

Quantitative Analysis[12]

Often data are multipoint and ordered, such as Likert scale data,[13] and can be analyzed with one or other of the general methods of quantitative analysis. The more common of these are the ANOVAs and regression/correlation analysis. Both methods are based on the general linear model, in which a score is conceived of as a linear combination of main and interaction effects, plus error. Although in many respects ANOVA and regression analysis can be thought of as alternative approaches to the analysis of quantitative data, certain problems are more closely tied to one approach than to the other. Consequently, the following material discusses the two approaches separately. However, it is important to recognize that the problems discussed under one or the other approach do not disappear when one shifts from regression analysis to the ANOVA, or vice versa. The problems, such as lack of independence of the predictor variables (referred to as *nonorthogonality* in the analysis of variance), inflating Type I error by conducting many tests of significance on the same set of data, and the like must be dealt with whatever the form of analysis.

Regression analysis. Regression analysis is the most general approach for the analysis of quantitative data. It accommodates data aimed at answering the two general types of question asked by developmentalists: questions regarding group trends and those involving individual differences. Most readers will be familiar with the latter use of regression analysis, for example, to explore the correlates of popularity in a group of 8-year-old children. That regression analysis also can evaluate group trends may be less familiar—but review the discussion of the data on cheating in 4- and 6-year-olds.

---

[11] Two other methods for analyzing categorical data that are growing in use are survival or time-event occurrence analysis (Bornstein et al., 2005; Singer & Willett, 2003; Willett & Singer, 2004) and latent class analysis (LCA; Collins, 2006; Magidson & Vermunt, 2004). Rindskopf (2004, p. 106) described LCA as the "categorical variable analog of factor analysis."

[12] For clarity of exposition, we have omitted an intermediate category: ranked data. Statistical procedures appropriate for ranked data typically are found in books on order, ranking, or nonparametric statistical procedures (e.g., Maritz, 1995; Reiss, 1989).

[13] Likert, or summated rating, scales typically ask the participant to respond to items using a 5-point scale with anchors ranging from *strongly agree* (perhaps scored 4) to *strongly disagree* (then scored 0). Total scores are obtained by summing scores on the individual items composing the scale.

A special use that regression analysis serves is as a test of mediation effects (MacKinnon, Fairchild, & Fritz, 2007). A mediator variable is one through which another variable operates to produce its effect on some outcome. For example, the effect of parental SES on children's social skills might be mediated by child IQ (also see Figure 3.15). Baron and Kenny (1986) distinguish mediator variables from moderator variables—the latter change the direction or strength of the relation between IV and DV. Gender, for example, may moderate the relation between popularity and intimacy. It clearly does not mediate the relation between these two variables.

In all its applications, regression analysis is plagued with difficulties for the unwary. Many of these difficulties are primarily interpretive in nature, rather than involving problems in statistical testing. Nevertheless, they seem worthy of note, and the conditions responsible for these difficulties are summarized in Table 3.20. Additional information on the foibles associated with the interpretation of regression/correlation analysis can be found in Darlington (1990, Chapters 8 and 9), McNemar (1969, Chapter 10) and Cohen et al. (2003).

The effects tested in regression/correlation analysis involve either correlation coefficients (bivariate rs or multiple Rs) or statistics such as path coefficients and beta weights that are a function of correlation coefficients. Tests of these statistics most often employ the F distribution (after Fisher), but in certain simple or unusual cases the t test or the normal curve (or z) test may be used (see the analysis conducted in Table 3.19).

As in many uses of statistical testing, problems occur when investigators are insufficiently sensitive to violations of independence assumptions when conducting statistical tests in conjunction with regression/correlation analysis. Nonindependence (dependence) affects statistical tests in regression analysis in at least two ways. First, tests may be conducted on nonindependent statistics from a regression analysis, but the testing procedure may only be appropriate for independent statistics. This may occur whenever investigators attempt to answer the generic question, "Is X more highly correlated with Y than S is correlated with Z?" and both r_{xy} and r_{sz} are obtained from the same individuals. Because they are obtained from the same respondents, such correlation coefficients are likely to be correlated, and their testing requires adjustments to accommodate the dependency between the coefficients (Meng, Rosenthal, & Rubin, 1992).

The second dependency problem occurs when the pairs of scores on which the correlation coefficient is calculated are not independent. (A similar problem was discussed with

TABLE 3.20
Disturbance Factors in Regression and Correlation Analysis

Disturbance factors	Consequences
Unreliable measurement	Correlation is underestimated.
Restricted score range	Correlation typically underestimated.
Non-normal distributions	Maximum value $\lvert r \rvert < 1.0$ unless the variables correlated are identically non-normal.
Small N to IV ratio	R overestimated; R regresses toward zero when cross-validated.
Correlated IVs	$r^2_{(x,y)}$ does not give the proportion of variance in Y (the DV) uniquely associated with X_i; $\Sigma r^2_{(x,y)}$ does not equal R^2.
Highly correlated IVs[a] (multicollinearity)	Beta weights (βs) unstable.

[a] Correlated IVs (called nonorthogonal IVs) also produce complicated issues of statistical testing when data are analyzed via ANOVA. The problem of correlated independent variables in the analysis of variance is discussed by Kahneman (1965) and by Cohen (1968). Appelbaum and his associates (Appelbaum & Cramer, 1974; Appelbaum & McCall, 1983) have presented methods of analyzing these data.

respect to the cheating data shown in Figure 3.11.) This dependency problem occurs, for example, when more than one member of a family contributes pairs of scores to the correlation analysis, or when the same individual contributes all of the scores entering into the analysis.

A final problem in testing correlational statistics occurs when a large number of variables are intercorrelated, and the correlation between each pair of variables is tested for significance in the usual manner. When this is done, the probability of making one or more Type I errors (see Table 3.1) may approach 1.0. To avoid the problem of inflating Type I errors with a large matrix of intercorrelations, the entire matrix is first tested to ensure that some significant covariation exists in the matrix as a whole.[14] If that test proves to be significant, then statistical tests are conducted on the individual correlations with α adjusted so as to hold the probability of a Type I error for the entire collection of tests to some specified level (Larzelere & Mulaik, 1977). This procedure has the effect of using a much more conservative alpha for tests of the significance conducted on the individual correlations.

ANOVA.   ANOVA is the approach most often used to assess differences in means for the variables investigated in developmental research, such as age and time of measurement. ANOVA, like regression, is a general approach to data analysis that can accommodate the data from a wide variety of experimental designs. ANOVA can be used when all design facets involve between-subject effects (i.e., completely randomized designs), within-subject effects (randomized block or repeated-measures designs), or within- and between-subject effects (mixed or split-plot designs). ANOVA procedures also can be applied when additional measured variables are included to statistically control unwanted sources of variation (analysis of covariance, ANCOVA), and when the design employs multiple dependent variables (multivariate analysis of variance, MANOVA and multivariate analysis of covariance, MANCOVA).

An ANOVA is illustrated with a 4 (age) × 2 (gender) × 3 (time of measurement) split-plot factorial design in Part A of Table 3.21. The ANOVA of the data from that design might be used to test whether the means for the groups defined by age, gender, and time of testing, alone and in combinations, vary significantly. The latter tests of combinations of variables are referred to as tests of interactions. The tests performed require that the scores used in the analysis meet certain assumptions, including those of normality, homogeneity (equivalence) of variance, and "homogeneity" of covariance or correlation between the repeated measures. ANOVA is relatively robust (insensitive) to violations of the former assumptions as long as each group contains approximately the same number of participants and sample sizes are not very small (Glass, Peckham, & Sanders, 1972; but see Judd et al., 1995). It is not robust, however, to violations of the requirement concerning the correlation between the repeated measures (Kirk, 1995). This requirement is often violated whenever more than two times of testing are employed. This is because the essence of the assumption is that all of the repeated measures are equally correlated. However, scores almost always correlate more highly with measures that are adjacent in time, and less highly with temporally more remote measures. Hence, with even three repeated measures, the correlations between Time 1 and Time 2 scores,

---

[14] The simultaneous test for a sample correlation matrix, **R**, is accomplished by testing the multivariate hypothesis that the population correlation matrix is an identity matrix, H_0: **P** = **I**, which means that all correlations between variables are simultaneously equal to zero, against the alternative H_1: **P** ≠ **I**. The test statistic is, $\chi^2 = -[(N-1) - (2p+5)/6]\ln|\mathbf{R}|$, where N is the sample size, p is the number of variables in **R**, and $\ln|\mathbf{R}|$ is the natural logarithm of the determinant of the sample correlation matrix. H_0 is rejected if χ^2 exceeds the critical value at the $100(1-\alpha)$ percentile point of the chi-square distribution with $p(p-1)/2$ degrees if freedom (Larzelere & Mulaik, 1977, p. 560; Morrison, 2000, pp. 116–118).

TABLE 3.21
Schematic Design and ANOVA Summary Table for an Age by Sex by Time of Testing Factorial Design

Part A. Design Schematic		Testing Period		
Age	Gender	1	2	3
4	Girl ($n = 5$)			
	Boy ($n = 5$)			
6	Girl ($n = 5$)			
	Boy ($n = 5$)			
8	Girl ($n = 5$)			
	Boy ($n = 5$)			
10	Girl ($n = 5$)			
	Boy ($n = 5$)			

Part B. ANOVA Summary Table

Source	Degrees of Freedom (df)	MS	F	p
Between Subjects				
Age (A)	(a 1) = 4 1 = 3	25.0	5.00	<.01
Gender (B)	(b − 1) = 2 − 1 = 1	5.5	1.10	>.25
A × B	(a − 1)(b − 1) − 3	10.0	2.00	<.25
Error (S/A × B)	ab(n − 1) = 32	5.0		
Within Subjects				
Assessments (D)	(d − 1) = 3 − 1 = 2	8.4	3.36	<.05 (<.10[a])
D × A	(d − 1)(a − 1) = 6	10.0	4.00	<.01 (<.05[b])
D × B	(d 1)(b 1) = 2	2.8	1.12	>.25 (>.25[a])
D × A × B	(d − 1)(a − 1)(b − 1) = 6	3.1	1.24	>.25 (>.25[b])
Error (D × S/A × B)	ab(n − 1)(d − 1) = 64	2.5		

Note. MS indicates "mean square." The lower case letters in the summary table equal the number of levels for the source indicated in the corresponding upper case letter. For example, there are 4 ages, so the source age (A) has four levels (a = 4). In generating F-tests, age, gender, and time of testing are considered fixed so that all between-subjects and within-subjects effects are tested with their respective subject—S/A × B or D × S/A × B—error terms (Kirk, 1995).
[a] Tested with 1 and 32 degrees of freedom (Geisser-Greenhouse correction).
[b] Tested with 3 and 32 degrees of freedom (Geisser-Greenhouse correction).

and between Time 2 and Time 3 scores, are likely to exceed the correlation between Time 1 and Time 3 scores. When the assumption of "homogeneity" of covariance is violated, the probability values obtained from ordinary statistical testing are too small (i.e., the effects appear to be "more significant" than they are). A number of procedures have been developed to remedy the biasing of probability values when this assumption may be violated, the most popular of which is the procedure developed by Geisser and Greenhouse (1958). The Geisser-Greenhouse adjustment was applied to all of the within-subject tests conducted in Part B of Table 3.21. That is, the degrees of freedom used in determining the probability values for the tests were reduced by dividing the usual degrees of freedom by the degrees of freedom associated with the repeated measure ($d - 1$). The resulting statistical tests indicate that the main effect of age and the interaction between age and time of assessment significantly "determine" performance. The interaction between age and time of assessment is shown in Figure 3.12. From an inspection of this figure, it can be discerned that the interaction, revealed by a lack of parallelism of the four data lines, is due largely to the performance of the

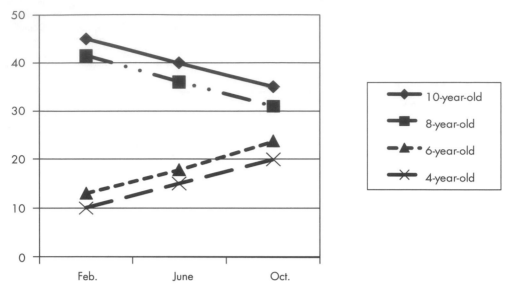

FIGURE 3.12   Illustration of the interaction between age and time of assessment for the design shown in Table 3.20.

two older age groups of children in comparison with that of the two younger age groups of children. That is, the 8- and 10-year-olds slightly deteriorate in performance across time, whereas the 4- and 6-year-olds improve somewhat with each repetition of the assessment procedures. Note that the presence of a significant interaction requires qualification of the lower-level effects of which the interaction is composed; that is, interactions take precedence interpretively over their component effects. In our example, we would interpret the significant D × A (assessments *by* age) interaction rather than the two component main effects (assessments *and* age)—even if these component main effects were significant. The significant D × A interaction requires us to recognize that the effect of age varies depending on which time of assessment one focuses on, or alternatively that the differences between assessment times vary depending on which age group one focuses on.

The standard tests conducted by ANOVA can be supplemented (and sometimes replaced) by other statistical tests under at least two sets of circumstances. First, additional tests usually are conducted to determine exactly what level(s) of a factor differ from which other level(s) following a significant ANOVA test involving more than one degree of freedom. (More than one degree of freedom means that more than one contrast—e.g., two groups—are being compared.) The procedures used for these follow-up tests involve some form of trend test, test of simple main effects, or other comparisons between combinations of means. Generically, these tests are referred to as *multiple comparison tests*. Their intent is to determine which specific levels of the IVs included in the omnibus test are significantly different, while maintaining some control of Type I error rate produced by conducting multiple tests of significance on a set of data. (See the related discussion in the regression analysis section.) Of course, neither these nor any other form of significance testing are appropriate for "test hopping"—that is, hopping from one inferential testing procedure to another until "significant" results are found.[15]

---

[15] A subtle and common, but nonetheless illegitimate, variant of test hopping involves switching the form of the data as well as the method of analysis. For example, an investigator interested in differences in prosocial behavior between children of different ages may initially analyze rate of donation with a *t* test, and finding the test nonsignificant, switch to a chi-square analysis conducted on the transformed data of whether or not each child donated.

Many multiple comparison tests are available. Table 3.22 summarizes the characteristics of 30 multiple comparison tests, most of which are available in major statistical software packages such as SAS and SPSS. The selection among tests is based on a number of considerations, including the experimental model, what statistical assumptions are met (e.g., homogeneity of variance), whether confidence intervals are required, the level of control of the Type I error rate, whether the comparisons were planned prior to data analysis (*a priori* comparisons) or are selected after examining the data (*a posteriori* comparisons or fishing expeditions), and the types of comparisons to be conducted (e.g., all pairwise or more complex comparisons among means, or all condition means contrasted with a control group mean). In addition to the procedures listed in Table 3.22, simulation methods are available for complex designs such as repeated measures ANOVA, or ANCOVA (see Westfall, Tobias, Rom, Wolfinger, & Hochberg, 1999). Recent developments have extended the application of multiple comparison procedures to a broad class of parametric and semi-parametric statistical models, including generalized linear models, mixed models, models for censored data (survival analysis) and more (Hothorn, Bretz, & Westfall, 2008). Detailed explanations of multiple comparison tests and recommendations for their use are available in Hochberg and Tamhane (1987), Hsu (1996), Kirk (1995), Tamhane (2009), Toothaker (1991), and Westfall et al. (1999).

The second basis for not relying solely on omnibus tests from ANOVA relates to a central tenet of statistical application: The analysis should suit the question, and the standard tests performed by ANOVA may not adequately evaluate the comparisons that are involved in an *a priori* hypothesis. Consider the interaction illustrated in Figure 3.13 among the four levels from a 2×2 completely randomized factorial design. (In a completely randomized design, all effects involve between-subjects comparisons.) Using standard ANOVA tests, the variation associated with this interaction would be split between the main effects of age and of gender, and the Age $\times$ Gender interaction. All of the tests of these effects may be nonsignificant, yet a contrast written specifically for this expected pattern of interaction[16] might be highly significant. And of course, this is exactly the approach that should be taken with a typical *a priori* hypothesis: The contrast for the expected effect should be constructed and then tested. These *a priori* contrast tests may be conducted prior to, or even instead of, the traditional omnibus ANOVA tests (see Rosenthal & Rosnow, 1985).

In addition to these general issues associated with the use of ANOVAs, specific concerns accrue with the use of special, commonly used ANOVA designs. Two of these designs are hierarchical analysis of variance and the analysis of covariance.

Hierarchical designs. Formally, hierarchical designs are those in which the levels of one factor are nested within the levels of another factor. The design would be hierarchical, for example, if both second- and fourth-grade girls and boys were taught spelling using mnemonic devices, but different procedures were used for the second graders and for the fourth graders. Such obvious examples of nesting (think of the grades as nests, and the mnemonic devices as eggs within the nests) are unlikely to be analyzed mistakenly. Mistakes do occur, however, when a nuisance variable such as classroom, play group, or family is nested within an experimental factor. Consider the case in which child aggression comprised the DV, the design factor concerned whether aggression was disregarded or interpreted, and children were assessed and treated within play groups. In this example, a particularly aggressive group member might instigate counteraggression from other group members. As a result, the scores for all or most members of this play group would be elevated, scores for members within the

---

[16] In this case, we might write the numerator of contrast as the mean for 10-year-old girls minus the average of the three remaining means: $\mu_{\female 10} - .33(\mu_{\male 16} + \mu_{\female 16} + \mu_{\male 10})$.

TABLE 3.22

Characteristics of Multiple Comparison Tests

	Pairwise Only	Pairwise or Non-pairwise	Equal ns Only	Equal ns or Unequal ns	Homogeneous Variances	Heterogeneous Variances	Confidence Intervals[a]	Error Rate
A Priori Orthogonal Comparisons								
Student t^{bc}		X		X	X		X	PC
Student t with Welch df		X		X		X	X	PC
$k^d - 1$ a Priori Nonorthogonal Comparisons Involving a Control Group Mean								
Dunnett^{bc}	X		X[e]	X[e]	X	X[e]	X	FW
C^f *a Priori Nonorthogonal Comparisons*								
Dunn (Bonferroni)^{bc}		X		X	X		X	FW
Dunn with Welch df		X		X		X	X	FW
Dunn-Sidak^{bc}		X		X	X		X	FW
Dunn-Sidak with Welch df		X		X		X	X	FW
Holm^c		X		X	X			FW
Holm with Welch df		X		X		X		FW
All Pairwise Comparisons (a Posteriori)								
Fisher LSD^{bc}	X			X	X		X	PC
Fisher-Hayter	X			X	X		X	FW
Tukey HSD^{bc}	X		X		X		X	FW
Tukey-Kraemer^{bc}	X			X	X		X	FW
Hockberg GT2^{bc}	X			X	X		X	FW
Gabriel^{bc}	X			X	X		X	FW
Games-Howel^b	X			X		X	X	FW
Dunnett T3^b	X			X		X	X	FW
Dunnett C^b	X			X		X	X	FW
Tamhane T2^b	X			X		X	X	FW
REGW Q^{bc}	X		X		X			FW
REGW F^b	X			X	X			FW
Shaffer-Ryan	X		X		X			FW
Peritz Q	X		X		X			FW
Peritz F	X			X	X			FW
Peritz Shaffer-Ryan	X		X		X			FW

Procedure		All Comparisons Including Non-pairwise Comparisons (a Posteriori)	Table Note
Newman-Keuls[b,c]	X	X	FW[g]
Duncan[b,c]	X	X	PC[g]
Waller-Duncan[b,c]	X	X	
Scheffe[b,c]	X	X	FW
Brown-Forsythe	X	X	FW

Note. **FW** (familywise error rate)—Type I error rate (rejecting a true null hypothesis) is controlled at α for the family of comparisons. A set of contextually related comparisons is a family (e.g., the six pairwise comparisons for comparing the means of a treatment with four levels). **PC** (per comparison error rate)—Type I error rate is controlled at α for each comparison. Procedures that control α at the PC rate will generally exceed α at the FW rate and are generally not recommended; however, contemporary practice favors adopting the PC error rate for a priori orthogonal comparisons. The Waller-Duncan test minimizes risk based on a Bayesian approach instead of controlling for Type I error. [a] Single-step multiple comparison procedures (procedures that use the same critical value for all tests compared; e.g., Dunn, Tukey) yield $100(1 - \alpha)$% confidence intervals and are generally preferred because they provide the greatest level of inference. Confidence intervals can be computed for Students t and Fisher's *LSD* but are not simultaneous confidence intervals since they are not adjusted for multiplicity. Multiple-step procedures (procedures [d] that adjust the critical value at each step of the hypothesis; e.g., Holm, REGW Q) do not yield confidence intervals but are generally more powerful and are recommended when confidence intervals are not needed. [b] Supported by SAS. k = number of groups or levels of the independent variable. [e] With modification. [f] C is the number of comparisons. [g] Although supported in major statistical packages, the Newman-Keuls and Duncan procedures are not recommended because they fail to control FW error rates when the number of groups is $k > 2$ for the Duncan and $k > 3$ for the Newman Keuls; the REGW, Shafer-Ryan, and Peritz methods are recommended instead.

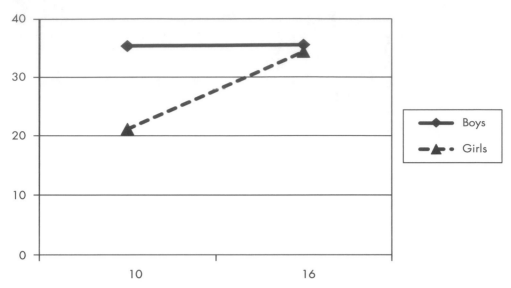

FIGURE 3.13   Illustration of a predicted interaction between gender and age not adequately assessed using standard omnibus ANOVA tests.

group likely would be *interdependent*, and play group membership may be a substantial source of nuisance variation. Thus, the dependency between scores for members of a group and the effect of the group itself must be accommodated in the data analysis—or else serious inferential errors may be made (Kenny & Judd, 1986). Various methods for integrating nested variables into the statistical analysis are discussed by Anderson and Anger (1978), Kraemer and Jacklin (1979), Raudenbush and Bryk (2002), and Kirk (1995).

   ANCOVA.   ANCOVA is involved when one or more measured variables are used to control unwanted sources of variance through statistical means in any of the standard ANOVA designs. (This is not unlike the method of statistical control served by partial correlations.) For example, in an experiment on methods of teaching reading, children's IQ scores might be used as a covariate to reduce naturally occurring differences in "reading potential" for the children participating in the experiment. Because unwanted sources of variability can be reduced statistically when they cannot be controlled experimentally, ANCOVA is a popular means of increasing statistical power or sensitivity. However, its use requires strict attention to a rigorous set of requirements. These include the usual assumptions of ANOVA of having errors due to treatment that are normally and independently distributed and equal variance across experimental conditions (homogeneity of variance). Additional requirements include homogeneity of the within-group regression slopes, independence between treatment scores and the covariate, covariate values measured without error, a linear relationship between outcome and the covariate, and errors due to the covariate (regression) that are normally and independently distributed with equal variance across the levels of the covariate (Huitema, 1980; Kirk, 1995; Tabachnick & Fidell, 2007).

   Two particularly serious problems can occur as a result of using ANCOVA incorrectly: One problem results from violating the ANCOVA assumptions; the other occurs when ANCOVA is asked to perform roles for which it is ill-suited. The ANCOVA assumption that can be particularly problematic when violated is the assumption of independence between treatment and scores on the covariate. In the reading example mentioned earlier, the IQ scores must be independent of treatment, perhaps requiring that we obtain them prior to implementation of the treatment for reading—when it is impossible for the treatment to have affected the IQ scores. The second problem occurs when investigators employ ANCOVA to adjust for initial differences between preexisting groups, such as classrooms. Selecting preexisting *groups*, and then focusing the analysis on the performance of *individuals*, is a clear violation of random assignment procedures. Furthermore, initial biases typically cannot be undone by ANCOVA procedures (e.g., Overall & Woodward, 1977).

Multivariate extensions. Various multivariate extensions of ANOVA and regression analysis are used by developmental investigators. There follow—in alphabetical order—brief descriptions of the more popular of these extensions, their primary functions or uses, their most common problems, and where interested readers can find out more about them. Beforehand, it is important to note a few similarities among the various multivariate techniques. Most importantly, all of the multivariate procedures apply weights to the participants' scores on the original set of measured variables to form one or more new composite variables; the weights are selected to optimize some function. For example, if the newly constructed composite variable is Y, and the original variables are X_a through X_e with optimum weights a through e, then the composite score for the ith individual is given by

$$Y_i = aX_{ai} + bX_{bi} + cX_{ci} + dX_{di} + eX_{ei}$$

where, for example, X_{ai} is the ith individual's score on variable X_a.

This process is similar to forming the composite variable, total score, for a classroom achievement test. The total score is based on a linear combination of weighted item scores. The item scores may be weighted to maximize individual differences in performance on the test—or an approximation to this, weighting each item 1.0, is more likely used. In multivariate analysis, the weights may be selected, for example, to maximize the correlation between two sets of variables (canonical correlation), to minimize the number of independent dimensions necessary to characterize a set of variables (factor analysis), or to maximize the differences between two or more groups (discriminant analysis).

All multivariate techniques also share a number of common weaknesses. Foremost among these is that they eschew perfectly, or near perfectly, correlated variables. Perfectly correlated variables pose a problem to multivariate analysis called *linear dependency*. Highly correlated variables pose a slightly different problem called *multicollinearity*. Both conditions are undesirable for all forms of multivariate analysis. Second, multivariate procedures require substantial numbers of participants. As the ratio of variables to participants approaches 1.0, the optimizing algorithm used to generate weights increasingly exploits chance relations in the data. As a consequence, the results of the study will not replicate.

Canonical correlation. The aim of canonical correlation is to explore the interrelations between two sets of variables. It is the multivariate analog of bivariate correlation. Instead of single predictor and criterion variables, canonical correlation is used when sets of predictor and criterion variables are obtained. The technique generates composite scores from a weighted linear combination of the set of predictor variables and of the set of criterion variables; the weights are selected to maximize the correlation between the two composite scores. The linear combinations of variables generated by this procedure are called *canonical variates*; hence, the correlation between canonical variates is called a *canonical correlation*. Following the construction or extraction of the first canonical variate from the predictor and criterion sets of variables and the calculation of their correlation, additional canonical variates may be extracted and correlated. The weights used in forming these subsequent canonical variates are chosen with an additional criterion: The new variates must be independent of the canonical variates already constructed.

Canonical correlation is used when an investigator intends to explore the relations between sets of variables in separate domains; for example, between nursery school children's social interactional behaviors and their performance on cognitive tasks. Unless the ratio of participants to variables in such an investigation is quite large, say 10 to 1, the specific optimum weights used are unlikely to cross-validate in subsequent investigations. Additional information on canonical correlation can be found in Thompson (1984), and in multivariate textbooks by Tabachnick and Fidell (2007) and Stevens (1992).

Discriminant analysis.[17]   The purpose of discriminant analysis is to assign individuals to the appropriate group. Assignments are based on the individual's standing on one or more weighted linear composites of their scores on a set of predictor variables. The weights are selected so that the predictor variables maximize differences between the groups. For example, a discriminant analysis might be used to assign children to popular, neglected, or rejected groups based on composite scores formed by weighting their scores on the scales of the Child Behavior Checklist (CBCL; e.g., Achenbach & Dumenci, 2001). This problem, involving as it does classification into one of three groups, requires the construction of two (one less than the number of groups) composite variables. The composite variables formed in discriminant analysis are called *discriminant functions*. Typical discriminant analysis output provides the weights for the predictor variables that are used in constructing the discriminant functions, that is the weights for the variables that aid in the prediction of group membership. The output also includes information on which category individual children are assigned based on their scores on the discriminant functions, as well as the proportion of children correctly classified. (See standard multivariate texts previously mentioned as well as manuals for standard computer data analysis software such as SPSS; Bryman & Cramer, 2001.)

Factor analysis.   Factor analysis and related techniques such as principal component analysis have as their purpose the discovery of the minimum dimensions underlying a set of variables. Investigators may be interested, for example, in the number of dimensions underlying performance on the subtests of the WISC-R or underlying endorsement of the items included in the CBCL. These dimensions, referred to as factors or components, are constructed by forming weighted linear composites of the original variables (e.g., subtest or item scores). The weights applied to the variables in the construction of each factor vary depending on the factoring technique used. In general, however, the weights are chosen to "explain" the maximum variation in the entire set of variables. Thus, the weights assigned to the variables in the construction of the first factor are chosen so as to maximize the correlations of that factor with the original variables. The weights for the variables in the construction of the second factor are chosen so that factor has the highest correlations with those parts of the original variables not accounted for by the first factor, and so forth.

After factors are extracted, they often are rotated. *Rotation* refers to the transformation of factors by modifying the weights for the variables from which they were constructed. The purpose of rotation is to facilitate description, and hence understanding of the factors

---

[17] Statisticians recommend using logistic regression analysis instead of discriminant function analysis when doing two-group classification (e.g., depressed or not depressed). Discriminant analysis makes two strong assumptions for inference—(1) multivariate normality among the set of predictors for each group on the dependent variable and (2) homogeneity of the within-group covariance matrices—that are rarely met in practice and that are not made in logistic regression (Cohen et al., 2003; Press & Wilson, 1978).

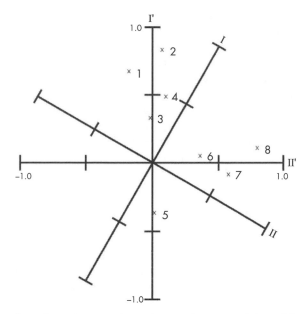

FIGURE 3.14 Illustration of rotation to achieve improved interpretability of factors. The correlations between the original eight variables and the factors, I and II, are indicated by finding the coordinates used to represent the eight variables. For example, Variable 1 (see x associated with 1) has correlations of about +.5 with factor I and −.5 with factor II. The original factors were rotated approximately 30° counterclockwise to form the new factors, I' and II'. As a result, the five verbal tests (numbered 1 through 5) defined the first rotated factor (I') and the three quantitative tests (numbered 6 through 8) defined the second rotated factor (II'). Rotation has no effect on the correlations between the variables, but it does change the loadings (correlations) of the variables with the factors. For example, Variable 1 now correlates in excess of .6 with Factor I', and slightly negatively with factor II'.

extracted from a set of data. In Figure 3.14, the two original factors extracted (I and II) from eight verbal and quantitative tests were rotated (counterclockwise) some 30° to promote understanding of the factors. The original factors (labeled I and II) are hodgepodges of verbal and quantitative abilities; the new factors (labeled I' and II') appear to be relatively pure measures of verbal and quantitative skills, respectively. Readers interested in learning more about factor analysis and related techniques can consult the articles by Comrey (1978) and by Rummel (1967), texts by Gorsuch (1983) and McDonald (1985), as well as the multi-variate textbooks already noted.

MANOVA. MANOVA is a straightforward generalization of ANOVA to investigations employing more than one dependent variable. For example, if the Age × Gender × Repeated Assessment problem described in Table 3.21 included two or more DVs, rather than just one DV, MANOVA would be the appropriate method of analysis of the data. Furthermore, the MANOVA summary table would closely resemble in form Part B of Table 3.21, the ANOVA summary table. The primary difference between ANOVA and MANOVA is that the latter forms one or more weighted composites of the DVs that maximize the differences between the levels of the IVs. It is these composite scores, called *discriminant function scores*, that are tested for significance. If two or more discriminant functions are formed, each subsequent discriminant function is orthogonal to (independent of) the previous discriminant functions.

MANOVA has a number of advantages when compared with conducting separate ANOVAs on each dependent variable.

1. MANOVA provides better control over Type I error. Subsequent statistical tests (e.g., ANOVAs) are only conducted if MANOVA indicates that at least one independent variable produces an effect on some linear combination of the dependent variables. (This rule is relaxed when *a priori* predictions are advanced.)
2. MANOVA may detect differences—when a weak effect is distributed over each of a number of correlated dependent variables—that would not be found if a separate ANOVA was conducted on each dependent variable. Thus, in some circumstances, MANOVA may be a more powerful method of analysis than are separate ANOVAs. (However, if the effect is carried by just one DV, MANOVA may be more conservative.)
3. MANOVA has less restrictive assumptions than does the comparable repeated measures ANOVA (Tabachnick & Fidell, 2007).

Other Statistical Techniques

A number of other, newer forms of analysis are available to developmental researchers. Three of these—hierarchical linear modeling (HLM) or multilevel models, structural equation modeling (SEM), and meta-analysis—are sufficiently common and important to deserve mention. A brief explanation of nonlinear regression is also given.

HLM. HLM, also known as multilevel analysis, is a set of regression-like analytic techniques that is particularly well adapted for multistage analysis. Multistage analysis is called for when two or more analytic approaches are combined to address a problem, and two situations encountered by developmental investigators that are likely to require multistage analysis are the analysis of growth and situations in which the number of units of analysis exceeds the number of sampling units.

In the analysis of growth, which prior to multilevel analysis was plagued by problems (see the "Change" subsection under "Seminal Design Issues for Developmental Investigators" and the "Difference scores" subsection under "Types of Scores" above), the first stage in the analysis involves determining a growth function for each participant (see Burchinal & Appelbaum, 1991). These growth functions are based on multiwave assessments, but need not require that each participant be measured on every occasion or on fixed occasions (Hoeksma & Koomen, 1992). In the second stage, the individual growth functions are examined to identify their correlates (e.g., causes or consequences). According to Bryk and Raudenbush (1987), HLM enables investigators to study the structure of individual growth (identify and describe individual growth trajectories), discover the correlates of growth, and also test hypotheses about the effects of experimental treatment on growth curves.

Units of analysis commonly exceed independent sampling units in developmental studies. Consider, for example, an investigation of the relation between friendship status and academic performance when schools are selected that vary, say, in the proximity of classmates' homes to one another and in socioeconomic status (SES). As a result of selection at the level of schools, classrooms are *nested* within schools and children are *nested* within classrooms. This nesting may cause linkages (lack of independence) between respondents' scores, both within schools and within classrooms. HLM (1) provides improved estimates of the relation of friendship status to academic performance by borrowing strength from the fact that similar estimates exist for other schools; (2) allows the testing of how schools varying in the average proximity of classmates' homes to one another and in SES might affect the relation between friendship and academic achievement; and (3) provides partitioning of the relation between friendship and achievement into within- and between-school components.

Although HLM is a powerful general approach for dealing with what have been thorny analytic problems for developmentalists, the technique comes with a set of daunting assumptions regarding the distribution of variables, the structure of the relations between variables, and the metric in which the outcome variables are measured (Bryk & Raudenbush, 1987). According to Raudenbush and Bryk (2002, p. 253), skillful data analysts pay close attention to the assumptions required by their models. They investigate the tenability of assumptions in light of the available data; they consider how sensitive their conclusions are likely to be to violations of these assumptions; and they seek ameliorative strategies when significant violations are discovered. In this regard, a caveat is in order. Hierarchical linear models are relatively new and there are few in-depth studies of the consequences of violating model assumptions. Excellent explanations and tutorials of HLM analysis are available in Cohen et al. (2003), Fitzmaurice, Laird, & Ware (2004), Kristjansson, Kircher, and Webb (2007), Raudenbush and Bryk (2002), Singer and Willett (2003), and Tabachnick and Fidell (2007).

SEM. SEM, structural modeling, linear structural equations, or covariance structural modeling is a multiple regression-like statistical methodology for probing causal models. In contrast to more typical descriptive interpretations of, say, the regression coefficients in a multiple regression analysis, SEM hypothesizes that the coefficients indicate the rate with which the IVs *cause* changes in the DVs. SEM is perhaps most closely associated with the computer program LISREL (linear structural relations), developed by Jöreskog and Sörbom (1983) for estimating the parameters of structural models. However, other approaches to structural model testing are available (e.g., Arbuckle, 1997; Heise, 1975; Kenny, 1979; Ullman & Bentler, 2003).

Structural modeling is particularly attractive to developmentalists. The reasons for this popularity are easily understood. The technique is well adapted for use with nonexperimental data, and it makes its strongest case with multiwave longitudinal data—the kind of data associated traditionally with developmental investigations.[18] In fact, manuscripts using as well as misusing structural modeling increased at such a dramatic rate that a prominent developmental journal, *Child Development*, devoted much of an entire issue "to illuminate the nature and possible applications of this statistical technique to developmental data" (Bronson, 1987). Lists of woes over the misuse of SEM are given by Freedman (1991) and MacCallum (2003).

Structural modeling employs a somewhat different vocabulary than do more traditional forms of design and analysis. In SEM, the variable set is divided into two classes, *exogenous* variables and *endogenous* variables. Exogenous variables are those variables that are hypothesized to produce changes in other (endogenous) variables in the model, but the causes for the exogenous variables themselves are not included in the model. Endogenous variables, in contrast, are presumably changed as a result of other variables in the model. Thus, exogenous variables are always IVs, whereas endogenous variables are DVs, but also can serve as IVs. A variable serving both IV and DV status is sometimes referred to as a mediator variable.

Variables included in some structural models also may be classified as *measured variables* or as *latent variables*. Measured variables (also known as manifest variables), as the name suggests, are variables that are directly assessed; latent variables are estimated—usually by more than one measured variable. As this vocabulary exercise suggests, a structural model (the multiple regression-like part of structural modeling) is often joined with a measurement model (the factor analytic-like part of SEM). When these two models are joined, as in LISREL, a good part of the Greek and English alphabets are required to symbolize the components of the model and their interconnecting equations. Fortunately, models typically

---

[18] SEM and HLM are but two of a number of different approaches to modeling longitudinal (growth) data. See Collins and Sayer (2000) and Raudenbush (2000) for discussions of various approaches to the analysis of growth.

are expressed pictorially, in the form of path diagrams, in addition to being expressed as a series of equations.

A *path diagram* illustrating the structural relations among four variables is displayed in Panel A of Figure 3.15. In path diagrams such as this one, exogenous variables are placed on the far left of the diagram, intervening variables in the middle, and other endogenous variables at the far right. Once the data have been obtained, the path coefficients (correlations and regression coefficients) often are placed on the arrows; the values of the residuals—$(1 - R^2)$ or the proportion of variance in each variable not explained by the model—are included in the ellipses (see McDonald & Ho, 2002). Panel B of Figure 3.15 illustrates the measurement submodel for the Panel A latent variable of child social skills. This latent variable is indexed with three measurement operations: independent observations of the child, teacher ratings, and peer sociometrics. Multiple indexing is a critical aspect of SEM and, in general, is a good research practice.

Each variable in path diagrams that is touched by a single-headed arrow is included as the DV in a structural equation. Each variable attached to the DV by the end of an arrow is included on the right-hand side of the same structural equation as an IV. For example, in the rudimentary model described in Figure 3.15, child social skills would be expressed as a

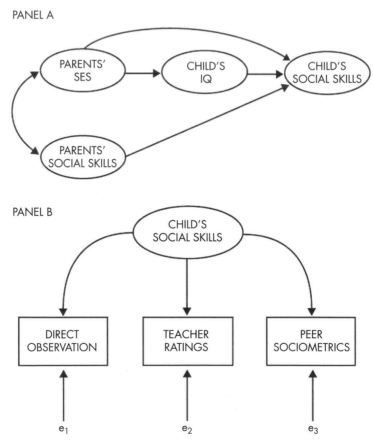

FIGURE 3.15 Path diagrams. Panel A illustrates the structural relations between the exogenous variables, parental SES and social skills, and the endogenous variables of child's IQ (an intervening variable) and social skills. Disturbance components are not included. Panel B illustrates a measurement model for the latent variable, child social skills. e_1, e_2, e_3 indicate error in assessing the latent construct, "child social skill," by means of each of the three measurement operations.

function of child IQ and parental SES and social skills (Panel A), whereas the observational measure of social skill would comprise the DV in an equation including the latent variable of child social skill and error (Panel B).

SEM testing requires a number of reasonably complicated steps or phases. The first step involves formulation of the structural model, in which the hypothesized causal relations between sets of variables are formulated. The second step involves operationalization of the variables and gathering data relevant to the test of the model. Because causes require time to produce their effects, longitudinal data involving a time lag suitable for "capturing" the causal connections stipulated in the model typically are required. After the data have been gathered—and structural modeling requires substantial data, as do all multivariate statistical techniques—they are summarized in a form appropriate for testing the goodness of fit of the model. The summary statistics are then operated on, often with rather complex statistical programs such as LISREL, to produce estimates of the model parameters and tests of statistical significance. One or more of these tests of significance are conducted on the model as a whole. A statistically nonsignificant (typically, chi-square) test indicates that the model adequately *fits* the data, whereas a statistically significant test suggests that the model requires revision—that significant amounts of variability in the data are not accounted for by the model. Statistical tests also are conducted on the individual model components, such as the regression weights relating putative effects to their causes and indicators to their latent variables. For these statistical tests of predicted relations, a nonsignificant test indicates that the subpart of the model tested has been *disconfirmed*—that the expected relation is not reliably different from zero.

It is important to recognize the nature of the causal inferences that can be drawn from confirmation of a structural model. As anyone who has survived an elementary course in statistics has repeatedly heard, correlation does not prove causation. (Nor, it might be added, does any other statistic. The determination of causality is a function of design—and perhaps philosophy of science.) Thus, finding that the predicted correlations between the variables included in the model fit the data increases the credibility of the causal model and the theory on which it was based. This increased credibility resulting from model confirmation assumes, of course, that the model was potentially disconfirmable by the data gathered.

Following testing of the model to determine whether it can be confirmed, or must be disconfirmed, further *exploratory* analyses may be conducted on the model. These analyses are controversial, and are performed to assess how the model might be revised to better fit the empirical results (Overton, 1998, p. 165). The revised model produced as a result of this exploratory work requires additional empirical testing with a fresh sample of data—as does all exploratory model building, no matter which statistical technique provided the means of exploration—to determine whether it will pass a reasonable test of disconfirmation.

SEM is a powerful approach for the analysis of nonexperimental data, but the power comes at some cost. The model requires a careful balance of variables to respondents (some, but by no means all experts suggest not more than $[N]10 - 2$ variables, where N is the number of participants), multiple measures or indicators for its latent variables, appropriate lags between the waves of the longitudinal data that are gathered, and assurance that certain statistical assumptions, including that of linear relations among the variables, are upheld (Freedman, 1991; Hoyle, 2008). Very readable accounts of structural modeling can be found in the special issue of *Child Development* (Bronson, 1987) devoted to that topic (see also McArdle, 2009) and in textbooks (e.g., Bohrnstedt & Knoke, 1994; Pedhazur & Schmelkin, 1991; Ullman, 2007). More technical presentations are available in Ullman and Bentler (2003), Jöreskog and Sörbom (1983), and Kelloway (1998).

Nonlinear regression.   Longitudinal studies frequently give rise to nonlinear patterns of change. These nonlinear changes can be seen in situations when change is faster in some periods and slower in others. For example, learning of many skills can be characterized by an *s*-shaped curve: slow initial gain, followed by rapid improvement, and then small gains again until maximum learning is reached (Cudeck & Harring, 2007). A common approach to analyzing nonlinear relations between independent and dependent variables is to linearize the relation by transforming either the independent or dependent variables, or both, and then applying OLS regression. However, this approach is appropriate only when the relation is intrinsically linear (Cohen et al., 2003). When the relation is intrinsically nonlinear, a suitable transformation is not available and nonlinear regression is the most appropriate method of analysis. Logistic regression is one example of nonlinear regression when change or growth is characterized as an *s*-shaped curve. Additional examples of behavioral processes that show nonlinear change and explanations of suitable nonlinear analytic approaches, including hierarchical nonlinear models, are found in Cohen et al. (2003, Chapter 6), Cudeck and Harring (2007), and Fitzmaurice, Davidian, Verbeke, and Molenberghs (2009).

Meta-analysis. Meta-analysis is a systematic, quantitative method of summarizing the results of studies composing a research literature (Curran, 2009; Strube & Hartmann, 1983; Sutton & Higgins, 2008). In the 1970s and 1980s concerns were raised about literature review methods that were less rigorous, systematic, and transparent than the studies they summarized, especially when the research area was characterized by disparate results (Cooper & Hedges, 1994). Unsystematic literature reviews were criticized for their subjectivity, imprecision, and neglect of important information contained in primary studies (Jackson, 1980). These concerns, coupled with the relative explosion of scientific information, suggested the need for better methods of summarizing research literatures.[19]

Meta-analytic techniques serve a variety of functions involved in reviewing a research literature. From the very beginning of operationalizing the review, the techniques include methods for collecting the studies composing the literature systematically to ensure that the "raw data" for the analysis will not be biased (e.g., Hunter, Schmidt, & Jackson, 1982, Chapter 7). The heart of meta-analysis, however, contains the statistical methods for summarizing the results of the primary studies composing the literature. Foremost among these statistical methods are techniques for combining probabilities across studies (Becker, 1994; Rosenthal, 1980b). A number of probability-combining techniques are available, and they all have as their principal purpose determining whether the set of results composing a literature could have arisen by chance. The combination of effect sizes represents another major approach to summarizing results across studies. The methods of determining average effect size assist the reviewer in determining the importance or strength of effect of the findings in a literature. A number of effect size indicators are available for accomplishing this goal (Tatsuoka, 1993), but the correlation coefficient and Cohen's *d* statistic, a standard score variant, are most commonly used for this purpose (Smith, Glass, & Miller, 1980).[20]

---

[19] Cooper and Patall (2009) describe two forms of meta-analysis. The first and more common form analyzes the pooled summary statistics from multiple individual studies and has been called aggregated data (AD) meta-analysis. The second, newer form analyzes the pooled raw data from multiple individual studies or samples and has been variously called individual participant data (IPD) meta-analysis (Cooper & Patall, 2009), integrative data analysis (Curran & Hussong, 2009), and mega-analysis (Sternberg, Baradaran, Abbott, Lamb, & Guterman, 2006). The use of this second form of meta-analysis has grown out of the need for increased collaboration among researchers to share limited resources and may be especially beneficial for developmental science, where long-term longitudinal studies are relatively rare and require years to complete (Curran, 2009; Hoffer & Piccinin, 2009).

[20] The odds ratio (OR) is a third effect size estimate commonly used for meta-analyses of medical treatments and education interventions (Patall & Cooper, 2008). It is the effect size measure of choice for categorical outcomes (Fleiss, 1994).

Beyond the computation of a combined probability and of an average effect size, meta-analysis also provides methods of determining the stability of results. Stability is often assessed using Rosenthal's (1979) fail-safe or file-drawer method. This method estimates the number of unpublished studies with zero effect size that would have to be filed away in the desks of investigators to "wash out" the results of the available studies included in the review.

Finally, because the probability values and effect sizes of the individual studies composing a literature are likely to vary substantially, a number of procedures and strategies have been proposed for identifying those factors associated with variation in outcomes across studies. Potential factors include any number of primary study characteristics that might be coded during the review such as the nature of the sample of participants studied, the methods of operationalizing IVs and DVs, as well as how adequately validity threats were handled in the study. These factors are then treated as IVs (the p-values and effect sizes serve as DVs) in analyses using regression, HLM, or ANOVA techniques, or methods of analysis especially developed for meta-analysis (Hedges & Olkin, 1985; Raudenbush & Bryk, 2002).

Meta-analytic procedures have been reviewed (Bangert-Drowns, 1986)—although, perhaps ironically, using traditional review techniques—and have grown in variety as to require a handbook (Cooper & Hedges, 1994); software for conducting meta-analysis is also available (e.g., Rosenberg, Adams, & Gurevitch, 1997; Sutton & Higgins, 2008). Understandable, technical presentations of meta-analysis are given in a variety of sources, including Cooper (1989), Glass, McGaw, and Smith (1981), Hunter et al. (1982), and Rosenthal (1980a).

Generalized Linear Models

All of the statistical approaches that we have described are special cases of a broad class of regression models collectively known as *generalized linear models*. Generalized linear model theory was developed to bring the analytic techniques applied to quantitative (continuous) and categorical response variables under one general framework (McCullagh & Nelder, 1989; Nelder & Wedderburn, 1972). The models extend the basic concepts of standard regression (ordinary least squares, OLS) and ANOVA to settings where the response variables are discrete and are not assumed to have a normal distribution.

All generalized linear models consist of three components: a random component, a systematic component, and a link function. The random component specifies the type of response variable and its assumed probability distribution. For example, for continuous responses, a normal distribution is assumed; for dichotomous outcomes, such as success/failure or the number of successes out of a fixed number of trials, a binomial distribution is assumed; and for nonnegative counts, such as a cell count in a contingency table, a Poisson distribution is assumed (Agresti, 2007). The systematic component specifies the predictor variables, (e.g., $\beta_0 + \beta_1 X_1$). The link function, $g(\mu)$, specifies a function or transformation that linearly relates the expected value of the response variable, μ, to the predictor variables. The link function also ensures that the values of the predicted scores are within the possible range of observed scores. For example, for count data, the link function is the natural log of the mean, and the form of the generalized linear model is

$$\ln(\hat{\mu}) = \beta_0 + \beta_1 X_1 + \beta_2 X_2 + \ldots + \beta_k X_k$$

This model, the *log-linear model*, specifies that the natural log of the mean, rather than the mean itself, changes linearly with changes in the predictor variables.

Generalized linear models use the method of maximum likelihood, which is not restricted to normality, to fit the model. Maximum likelihood (ML) uses an iterative process that estimates coefficients (and their standard errors) and provides methods for constructing confidence intervals, testing hypotheses, and assessing model fit. All generalized models use the same algorithm for estimating ML parameters (Agresti, 2007). Maximum likelihood and OLS methods yield equivalent estimates when applied to normally distributed continuous data with uncorrelated errors (Fitzmaurice et al., 2004).

Generalized linear models assume that observations are independent. Longitudinal studies, however, violate that critical assumption. Special extensions of generalized linear models, including the method of *generalized estimating equations (GEE)*, have been developed to handle longitudinal and other designs that have nonindependent data (see Agresti, 2007, Chapters 9 & 10; Fitzmaurice et al., 2004, Chapters 10 to 13; Moskowitz & Hershberger, 2002; and Raudenbush & Bryk, 2002, Chapter 10).

Interpreting the Results of Statistical Tests

Developmentalists want to answer three basic questions from their hypothesis-testing research (Kirk, 2003, p. 88): "(1) Is an observed effect real or should it be attributed to chance? (2) If the effect is real, how large is it? And (3) is the effect large enough to be useful?" Unfortunately *only* the first question is answered by a test of statistical significance, but the number of zeros following the decimal in such tests apparently is often used to answer the second and third questions as well. Indeed, as stated by Kirk, null hypothesis statistical testing "distracts us from our real goals: deciding whether data support our scientific hypothesis and are practically significant" (p. 100). For less critical commentaries on null hypothesis statistical testing, see Mulaik, Raju, and Harshman (1997) and Abelson (1997b).

How Large Is It?

Because tests of significance are importantly a function both of the magnitude of the effect and of the sample size—as well as a number of other factors related to power—a statistically significance test cannot be directly interpreted as addressing the question of the size of the effect. Fortunately, however, a substantial number of ancillary statistics have been developed to answer the size question (see, for example, Fleiss, 1994; Rosenthal, 1994). These statistics can be divided into two relatively homogeneous families and one wastebasket "other" category. The homogeneous—and familiar—families are those statistics loosely based on the standardized mean difference statistic (z) and those resembling the correlation coefficient (r). The final wastebasket category contains a variety of types of size estimators—"you name your inferential statistic and we'll provide a size statistic"—and will not be further discussed (see, for example, Kirk, 2003, Table 5.1).

Standardized mean difference-like measures. You will recall from our earlier discussion of z scores that the standardized mean difference describes the signed difference between two means using the standard deviation as the unit of measurement. Consider a two-group design in which the groups have means of 15.2 and 16.4 and the average standard deviation for the two groups is 1.6. The two means differ by .8 (16.4 − 15.2), or by one-half standard deviation units (.8/1.6 = .5). This value of .5 is essentially equal to Cohen's effect-size measure, delta (δ), calculated on these values (Cohen, 1988; Kirk, 2003). Other measures from this effect size family take basically similar form, but differ in detail, such as the method of estimating σ (the population standard deviation) or whether or not corrections for bias are included in the formula.

Cohen provides a set of widely accepted guidelines for interpreting δ, with a value of .2 indicating a small effect, .5 a medium effect, and .8 a large effect (e.g., Cohen, 1992). These guidelines are also useful for determining sample size for a study in the planning stage. If one knows the smallest effect size that is desirable to detect (e.g., medium), the desired likelihood of detecting it (power), and such things as the α-level (e.g., $\alpha = .05$), one can then readily—at least with fairly simple designs—determine how many participants must be recruited to meet those requirements (see, for example, Cohen, 1988; but see Lenth, 2001 for a criticism of this approach).

Correlational measures.   Correlational measures of effect size assess the degree of relation between the independent and dependent variables. Moreover, these correlational measures are often presented in their squared form, yielding a proportional overlap between the IV and DV, as in the square of the bivariate (r^2) or multivariate correlation coefficient (R^2). The specific correlational statistic used to assess effect size importantly depends on whether the IV and DV are continuous or categorical, and on the nature of the investigative design and whether it is considered fixed or random. Kirk (2003) suggests that for situations for which fixed-effect ANOVA is employed, omega squared (ω^2) is a commonly used statistic for assessing the strength of association, whereas for random effects designs, rho squared (ρ^2) is more commonly—and appropriately—employed. Both of these squared statistics—as we earlier stated—indicate the proportion of the DV variance that can be attributed to the particular IV. Cohen (1988) also has provided guidelines for interpreting the measures of association: $r^2 = .01$ is a small effect size, $r^2 = .06$ is a medium effect size, and $r^2 = .14$ is a large effect size. Not surprisingly, a number of individuals have provided equations for translating effect size statistics into measures of association and vice versa (e.g., Kirk, 2003).

In interpreting effect size measures it is important to note that a number of critics have discussed their limitations and perturbing factors (e.g., Mitchell & Hartmann, 1981; O'Grady, 1982). These concerns—involving such issues as the effect of restriction of range and unreliability of measures on the interpretation of effect size statistics—are based largely on McNemar's (1969) classic discussion of factors that affect the interpretation of the correlation coefficient.

Confidence intervals.   Confidence intervals (CIs) are very useful for evaluating both whether an effect is real and how large it is. Reporting CIs is strongly encouraged because of their superiority to reporting the results of null hypothesis testing alone (e.g, Cumming & Finch, 2005; Kirk, 2003; Nickerson, 2000; Smithson, 2001). Cumming and Finch (2001) list four general ways that CIs are valuable: (1) they give point and interval estimation that is easily understood and facilitate interpretation; (2) they have a link with null hypothesis testing; (3) they support meta-analysis and meta-analytic thinking; (4) they give width information that may be more useful and accessible than statistical power values. The fifth edition of the APA publication manual recommended the following:

> The reporting of confidence intervals . . . can be an extremely effective way of reporting results. Because confidence intervals combine information on location and precision and can often be directly used to infer significance levels, they are, in general, the best reporting strategy. The use of confidence intervals is therefore strongly recommended. (American Psychological Association, 2001, p. 22)

The sixth edition of the publication manual (American Psychological Association, 2010) gave additional guidelines: "whenever possible, provide a confidence interval for each effect size reported to indicate the precision of estimation of the effect size" (p. 34); and "When a table includes point estimates, for example, means, correlations, or regression slopes, it should also, where possible, include confidence intervals" (p. 138).

A CI (e.g., 95% CI) is a calculated interval estimate that surrounds a point estimate and indicates the precision, or likely accuracy, of the point estimate. Whereas a point estimate, such as a mean or effect size, is a single value estimate of a parameter, an interval estimate is a range or band, bounded by an upper and lower end point, within which the parameter is said to lie. The CI is centered on the point estimate and extends a distance, or width, on either side. The width, known as the margin of error, is computed by multiplying the standard error, SE, of the point estimate by the critical values that cut off $\alpha/2$ of the upper and lower tails of a distribution such as the z or t distribution[21] (e.g., $M \pm 1.96 \times SE$, or alternatively $M - 1.96 \times SE < \mu < M + 1.96 \times SE$ for a 95% CI using the z distribution).

Associated with the CI is a confidence level that typically is expressed as a percentage, $100(1 - \alpha)\%$. The confidence level is the probability that an interval estimate, randomly selected from a large number of similarly constructed intervals from independent samples of the same population, includes the population parameter (Fidler & Thompson, 2001).[22] Using a probability statement to interpret a CI can be confusing, however (Nickerson, 2002; see Fidler & Thompson, 2001 for examples of common versus accurate definitions of CIs). Cumming and Finch (2005) recommend that probability statements about individual CIs be avoided since they can be easily misinterpreted. They suggest four alternative interpretations, their top recommendation being "CI is a range of plausible values for μ. Values outside the CI are relatively implausible" (p. 174).

Though investigators may choose any level of confidence, by convention a 95% confidence level, which corresponds with the .05 p-level used in null hypothesis testing, is typically used. All things being equal, the higher the confidence level (e.g., 99%), the wider the CI; the larger the sample size, the narrower the CI and the more precise or accurate the estimate (Kelley & Rausch, 2006).

Additional discussion and instruction on constructing CIs for a variety of models and parameters are given by Cumming and Finch (2001), Fidler and Thompson (2001), and Smithson (2001, 2003). Cumming and Finch (2005) discuss seven rules of inference by eye for interpreting figures with confidence intervals.

---

[21] Confidence intervals for effect sizes expressed in their original units (e.g., $M_1 - M_2$) are constructed as explained above. In contrast, standardized effect sizes, such as Cohen's d, R^2, and η^2, require the critical values from noncentral distributions to construct an accurate CI. CIs constructed using noncentral distributions may not be symmetric around the point estimate and nearly always require iterative estimations that are best done by a computer (Cumming & Finch, 2001; Smithson, 2001).

[22] We can illustrate the correct interpretation of the probability of a CI by deriving the 95% CI for a sample mean in terms of the sampling distribution of the mean from a known population (e.g., Steiger & Fouladi, 1997; see Cumming & Finch, 2001, for an example of deriving a 95% CI for the one-sample t-test). If we take a large number of independent random samples of size N from a normal population with mean μ and standard deviation σ, we will generate a normal distribution of sample means with mean μ and standard deviation (standard error) $\sigma_M = \sigma/\sqrt{N}$. We know that 95% of all possible sample means of size N from the population will fall between -1.96 and 1.96 standard errors of the population mean μ. This fact can be stated as a probability: We know that for all samples of size N from the population the $\Pr(-1.96\sigma_M \le M - \mu \le 1.96\sigma_M) = .95$. We can algebraically manipulate this inequality without changing the correctness of the statement by subtracting M from each of the terms, then multiplying each term by -1, and reversing the inequalities. This gives $\Pr(M - 1.96\sigma_M \le \mu \le M + 1.96\sigma_M) = .95$. That is, over all possible samples, the range between $M - 1.96\sigma_M$ and $M + 1.96\sigma_M$ will include the true mean, μ, 95% of the time. The range of values constitutes the 95% CI for μ. The two end points of the interval are called the 95% confidence limits. It is important to note that the probability statement is not about μ, but about samples. The actual range of numbers making up the CI for a given sample will depend on the sample mean, M. For 95% of the samples, the CI actually will include or "capture" the value of μ; for 5% of the samples, it will not.

Is It Important?

When answered affirmatively, the question of importance in most cases will be accompanied by a significant p value and by a large measure of effect size. But even these two criteria have exceptions: Nonsignificant findings may be suggestively important if they were obtained under particularly adverse conditions of power (e.g., weak design, unreliable measures, shaky manipulations, and few participants); even small effect sizes may be important because they are associated with important theoretical issues. A number of other considerations may determine the importance of an effect, as follows.

1. The relative cost of producing the effect. Even a small effect produced cheaply may be practically important.
2. The minimalist nature of the manipulation. If the manipulation that produced even a small effect was extremely minor (or weak) in nature, it may be important. Prentice and Miller (1992) give numerous illustrations of important effects that were produced from minimalist manipulations in the social psychological literature, including those involving ethnocentrism and mere exposure.
3. The availability of competing treatment. If alternative treatments are not available, even a small effect may be practically important.
4. The intractableness of the DV. Consider a seemingly intractable DV such as the speed with which corpses are pronounced dead. Prentice and Miller (1992) argue that if we found that outcome was influenced by the attractiveness of the corpse—even if only slightly—this would truly be an important illustration of the psychosocial importance of physical attractiveness.

Also see Abelson (1985), Mook (1983), Rosenthal and Rubin (1983), and Yeaton and Sechrest (1981) for additional discussions of the importance issue.

QUALITATIVE RESEARCH METHODS

In this section, we will describe how the qualitative approaches to research differ from the quantitative approach just presented, discuss when the qualitative approaches may be useful, and describe one popular qualitative approach, narrative analysis, as an example. In addition, we will consider how to evaluate the rigor of qualitative studies and entertain the question of whether one should use qualitative methods in combination with quantitative methods.

Qualitative research methods encompass a variety of general approaches. Some of the better known include grounded theory (e.g., Charmaz, 2003; Corbin & Strauss, 2008; Henwood & Pigeon, 2003), narrative analysis (e.g., Murray, 2003), case study (e.g., Lancy, 2001), discourse analysis (e.g., Antaki, 2008; Potter, 2003; Willig, 2003), and action research (e.g., Fine et al., 2003; Kemmis & McTaggart, 2008). What is common among these approaches is an emphasis on capturing the qualities of a phenomenon through verbal and visual description rather than through statistical analyses (Morrow & Smith, 2000). A variety of data gathering methods is used singly or in combination in qualitative research, including observing and interviewing participants as well as collecting documents and artifacts from or about them (Berg, 2003; Esterberg, 2002). Finally, there are specific strategies for analyzing data gathered, such as grounded theory analysis (e.g., Charmaz, 2003) and narrative analysis (e.g., Murray, 2003). The various approaches, methods, and strategies have unique elements, and unfortunately, a full examination of each is beyond the scope of this chapter. Thus, our present discussion of qualitative research pertains to broader issues common among them. Because narrative analysis is familiar to many developmental scientists, we present it in more detail as an example of a qualitative approach to research.

At the heart of qualitative research lies rich description of the phenomena of interest. Camic, Rhodes, and Yardley (2003b, p. 10) describe the difference between quantitative and qualitative approaches as being akin to the difference between a map and a video:

> A map is extremely useful; it conveys with economy and precision the location of a place and its relationship to other places in terms of proximity and direction. However, even the most detailed map is unable to convey an understanding of what it is like to be at that place. In contrast, a video conveys in vivid detail the constantly changing perspective of the observer. Although this perspective is selective and could not easily be used for navigation, it is able to communicate something of the subjective experience of being there.

Although developmental scientists tend to work with "maps," many appreciate the rich descriptions of "videos." Consider the value of Piaget's interviews with and observations of children (Piaget, 1932/1965; Piaget, Weaver, & Inhelder, 1972/2000). Recall Bowlby's, Mahler's, or Stern's accounts of how relational behavior unfolds between mother and child during the first years of life, and try to imagine their developmental theories without these rich descriptions (Bowlby, 1969/1982; Mahler, Pine, & Bergman, 1975/2000; Stern, 1985). It is no doubt a difficult or impossible task; qualitative information often seems necessary for full comprehension of how individuals change over time.

Given that one acknowledges the epistemological importance of rich description, it is somewhat curious that developmentalists as well as other psychologists tend to favor quantitative methodological and analytic approaches over qualitative approaches (Camic et al., 2003b). It is uncommon to see an exclusively qualitative study presented as the final product in a peer-reviewed developmental science journal. What accounts for this favoritism? Eisner (2003) speculated that psychology's strong positivistic roots continue to shape thinking about what "counts" as science and thus limits what questions psychologists ask and how they go about answering the questions they do ask. Way and Pahl (1999) noted that developmental scientists generally see quantification as a more objective, and thus, a more acceptable means of providing evidence for or against a theory. Overall, psychologists tend to assign qualitative research secondary status by considering it beneficial for obtaining an initial understanding of a topic, theory development, or for illustrative purposes, but not as a finished work (Sciarra, 1999). Also contributing to the bias, training in qualitative research methods is typically not required of undergraduate or graduate students in North American psychology programs (Camic et al., 2003b).

Individuals favoring a qualitative approach reject the tenets of positivism and instead subscribe to idealism, or one of its modern day progenies (e.g., constructivism, interpretivism, hermeneutics). Idealists argue that reality cannot be objectively known, individuals construct their own versions of reality based on their experiences and meanings assigned to those experiences, and investigators' constructions of reality are inseparable from those being investigated (Sciarra, 1999, see also Denzin & Lincoln, 2000). These assumptions lead to different methods of data collection and analysis as well as different ideas about how to evaluate the methodological rigor of research.

When might one consider using qualitative methods?   Some research questions and goals lend themselves particularly well to qualitative methodologies. Camic et al. (2003b) described six reasons for using the qualitative approach.

1. A qualitative approach is often valuable when exploring a topic that few have previously researched. This is probably the most acceptable use for those trained in the positivistic tradition. Qualitative methods allow for theory building and discovery of what is most important about participants' experiences (in contrast to hypothesis testing). For example, Baker and Carson (1999) began interviewing women in substance abuse treatment not anticipating the importance the women would place on their roles as mothers. Upon discovery, however, interview questions about mothering became paramount to their study. Along similar lines, Shadish et al. (2002) stated that qualitative methods are often useful tools for discovering and exploring causal mechanisms prior to designing experimental or quasi-experimental studies of a hypothesis-testing sort.

2. Qualitative methods may be appropriate if one is particularly interested in establishing ecological validity (e.g., Bronfenbrenner, 1979). Qualitative investigators are encouraged to learn about and become part of the real-world context in which their phenomenon occurs to understand it better. For example, Hey (1997) examined adolescent girls' friendships by conducting ethnographic work in schools. Her descriptions primarily come from girls' notes, discourse, and journals gathered in the school setting rather than from rating scales and structured interviews.

3. The qualitative approach tends to emphasize a holistic picture; "microanalysis of parts is always undertaken in the context of a larger whole" (Camic et al., 2003b, p. 9). Qualitative investigators commonly analyze complex relations and inconsistencies to relate the data to larger contexts, such as culture, in ways that are vastly more difficult when one must meet statistical assumptions. For example, a quantitative analyst may treat inconsistent responding by a participant as measurement error, but a qualitative analyst may use those inconsistencies to build a more complex picture of the phenomenon of interest.

4. Qualitative research is quite useful if one is interested in analyzing the subjective meaning participants assign to their experiences. A well-known example in developmental science is Gilligan and colleagues' examination of participants' "voices" as a way to understand identity development (e.g., Gilligan, 1982; see also Gilligan, Spencer, Weinberg, & Bertsch, 2003).

5. Qualitative research allows for an examination of the "aesthetic dimension of human experience" as well as giving the investigator some artistic freedom (Camic et al., 2003b, p. 10). For example, Esterberg (2002) described a study (Becker, 1999) in which the investigator transcribed an individual's narrative into poem-like stanzas so that its circular and repetitive qualities were clearer (see also Gee, 1991, and Gilligan et al., 2003, for similar examples). Artwork was the data in an ethnography focusing on the experience of adolescent pregnancy; Luttrell (2002) collected and analyzed pregnant adolescents' collages as well as theatrical reenactments of their social interactions with peers and parents.

6. Qualitative research may have utility if one is interested in the relationships among participants, participants' relations to their larger society, or the participants' relationship to the researcher and research process. Participatory action research is one example of a qualitative approach that has focused on participants' role in collaborating on or creating research agenda (Fine et al., 2003).

An example of the qualitative approach: Narrative interviews and narrative analysis. Examining the stories individuals tell about themselves is a popular method for understanding development, particularly the processes of identity development and adjustments to life events—see McAdams, Josselson, and Lieblich (2001) for examples. Qualitative investigators refer to these stories as "narratives" (Murray, 2003) or "accounts" (Harvey,

Orbuch, & Weber, 1992). According to Bruner (1990), individuals tell stories to understand their life experiences and to illuminate relations between these experiences. In addition to the stories' content, narrative psychologists are often interested in the stories' structure and function (Murray, 2003).

A narrative is defined by its story-like features. Like stories, narratives have a beginning, middle, and end as well as some type of action. In these ways, they are different from non-narrative answers to questions in structured or unstructured interviews (Esterberg, 2002). Biographical interviews are often the primary method of gathering narratives, although investigators also find individuals' stories in other forms of data, such as observational field notes and personal journals (Esterberg, 2002). Murray (2003) recommended building relationships with participants before collecting their narratives. Participants are less likely to provide good narratives if they do not trust or feel valued.

Biographical interviews tend to be fairly unstructured and participant-driven, but researchers often have some general questions to guide the overall interview process. For example, when gathering the life stories of generative and non-generative African American adults McAdams and Bowman (2001) divided their interview protocol into eight components (life chapters, significant scenes, life challenge, characters, favorite stories, future plot, personal ideology, and life theme). Likewise, Murray (2003) described collecting both life story narratives and more specific, episodic narratives from individuals who experience chronic pain. Murray and colleagues instructed participants to recount specific chronic pain experiences and to provide a more general life history narrative so they could understand participants' chronic pain experiences within the context of their overall life history.

Once narratives are collected, one can analyze different aspects of the stories, including content, structure, and function. Consider the following episodic narrative written by the second author's father:

> In the late 1950s and early 1960s there were hundreds of corner grocery stores and no quick trips [convenience stores]. One of their staple items was candy and small toys for kids. The toys changed with the season—kites in the spring, baseballs in the summer, and Duncan Yo Yo's made of Maple and Birch in the spring. To hype the sales the Duncan company employed Hawaiian, Filipino, and Japanese men about 40 years old who drove from store to store to stock the yo-yo displays. They were in all of the downtown dime stores too. Each week in the spring on a certain day, after school, which was across the street, Gus the Yo-Yo Man would show up. All of the local kids with yo-yos would practice a while and Gus would give them a free, new string. Then they would line up on the curb by the store and he would go down the line announcing each trick he wanted you to do. If you missed the trick, it was quick and simple, Gus shouted, "You're out," and you stepped back. This was a rapid, single elimination process. Towards the end of the school year those of us who had won contests regularly and received patches and yo-yos for our effort were invited to Woolworth's dime store downtown for the "City Championship." Gus showed up, everybody was ushered out into the delivery alley where we lined up against the wall. The elimination began and before long it was down to me and another kid. He went first and missed the "Three-Leaf Clover." I hit it without a problem and the trophy with the yo-yo-headed man was mine. Gus showed me the toughest trick he knew, called "Spider in a Cage," I got on my Schwinn bike and rode home. I lost competitive interest in the yo-yo after that, and yet when some 12- and 13-year-old Scouts had a couple [yo-yos] at the "Order of the Arrow Fall Conclave" in September, I couldn't resist, got one from one of them, and reprised all of the old standards: "Walk the Dog," "Eating Spaghetti," "Around the World," "Rock the Baby," "Over the Falls," and, of course, "Three-Leaf Clover." (narrative taken from Smith, 1996)

Depending on the goals of a study, different aspects of this narrative (and any other narratives collected) can be analyzed. For instance, examining the actual *content* of the story would be appropriate if an investigator is interested in the types of competitive events individuals recall from preadolescence. In general, investigators analyzing narrative content want to know about an individual's experience in the individual's own words. Many times investigators analyze narratives' content with a specific *social context* in mind (Esterberg, 2002). For example, the second author originally framed the story of the yo-yo championship in the context of what it was like to grow up during the 1960s in a working class, Midwestern family.

However, what if an investigator was uninterested in the story of the yo-yo championship itself, but rather interested in how the participant told this story? Then, analyzing the *structure* of the narrative would be appropriate. For example, an investigator might be interested in examining what accounts for a shift in perspective, such as the shift from third-person to first-person perspective in the story above. Alternatively, one might be interested in how the storyteller ends his story by making a connection to a more recent event in his life.[23] Similar to content analysis, one may make connections between the individual's social context (e.g., from a Western culture, being female, being an ethnic minority) and structural elements present in their stories (Murray, 2003).

Finally, rather than focusing on content or structure, qualitative investigators may ask questions about the *function* of the story being told. For example, in the beginning of the yo-yo championship story, the storyteller, now an adult with children of his own, seemingly wants to convey how the world has changed across time ("there were hundreds of corner grocery stores and no quick trips"). In an interesting parallel, at the end of the story the storyteller seemingly wants to convey how a part of him has stayed the same across time ("I couldn't resist, got one from one of them, and reprised all of the old standards"). The storyteller's audience is important to consider when analyzing function; the purpose of the story may change significantly depending on who is listening (Esterberg, 2002). For example, how might the yo-yo championship story be different when told to a stranger rather than to a family member?

Regardless of whether one analyzes content, structure, or function, narrative analysis is a time-consuming process. For this reason, narrative studies typically do not involve large samples (see Kuzel, 1999, for recommendations on sampling). After collecting narratives, qualitative examiners typically transcribe them and read them repeatedly, making decisions about which portions of the narratives to analyze. Sometimes investigators re-transcribe segments into a format that will ease analysis, such as the poetic stanzas described earlier. Once the narratives are in a manageable format, a qualitative investigator can begin formally analyzing the data. Murray (2003) described four analytic approaches for understanding narratives: linguistic (breaking narratives down into their story-like components), literary (examining narratives in terms of their genre or plots), grounded (inductively examining the themes present in narratives), and social contextual (considering the role of context in how narratives are constructed). For the purposes of illustration, we will discuss the steps involved when one uses a linguistic approach.

As first described by Labov (1978) and summarized by Esterberg (2002), one linguistic approach involves segmenting the narratives into six basic parts: abstract, orientation, complicating action, evaluation, results, and coda. The complicating action is essential for a narrative (i.e., something has to happen), but the other elements may or may not be present in any one particular narrative. We will describe each of these elements and use the yo-yo championship narrative to illustrate them. The *abstract* lets the audience know a narrative is about to start. Individuals often signal the beginning of a narrative with something like "You won't believe what just happened." The yo-yo story does not contain an abstract, perhaps

---

[23] In developmental psychology literature, McAdams and Bowman (2001) provided another example of structural analysis when examining redemption and contamination sequences in individuals' life stories.

because the narrative was in response to a very specific question rather than an open-ended question. The *orientation* gives the audience background information so that they know the "setting" and main "characters" in the story. For example, in the yo-yo championship narrative, the storyteller describes Gus, the yo-yo man, the basic way in which the yo-yo contests worked, and the context in which they occurred. After the orientation comes the *complicating action*. The complicating action is the main event that happens in the story. In the yo-yo championship narrative, the complicating action is city championship competition. Typically, narratives also contain some sort of *evaluation* component that lets the reader know why they should be interested in what happened. The evaluation component is difficult to pick out in the example of the yo-yo championship story. However, the narrator describes getting a special trophy and learning a difficult yo-yo trick as rewards for winning, relaying to the audience that this is a success story, rather than, for example, a cautionary tale or a conversion story (Esterberg, 2002). The *results* serve as sort of a punch line at the end of the story. Esterberg relates that having a twist at the end of the story is a common practice. This appears to be the case in the yo-yo story; it first appears that the narrator has "retired" from yo-yo tricks, but then the audience finds out he actually has not. Finally, the *coda* lets the audience know the story is finished. In the yo-yo championship story, the storyteller ends by bringing the audience back to his winning yo-yo trick. As Murray (2003, p. 105) related, the linguistic approach "enables the researcher to grasp not only the action core of the narrative account but also the interpretive orientation the participant adopts and the issues that the participant chooses to emphasize and to ignore."

Some qualitative investigators use computer software programs to assist in analyzing qualitative data, such as the narrative data above. More information about computer software options is available in most introductory qualitative methods texts (see also Kelle, 1996). These programs may aid in organizing, segmenting, and coding data. However, be forewarned that much like statistical programs used by quantitative researchers, the software used by qualitative researchers does not replace the investigator's role in data analysis and interpretation (Morrow & Smith, 2000).

Assessing the quality of qualitative studies.   There is a longstanding debate among qualitative investigators about how to assess the rigor of qualitative studies (Hammersley, 2008; Merrick, 1999; Willig, 2001). Concepts used in quantitative work, such as reliability and validity, may not be directly applicable when determining the methodological rigor of qualitative work (Merrick, 1999; see Kidder, 1981, for an opposing viewpoint). As stated by Willig (2001), the way in which one evaluates qualitative research needs to be compatible with one's epistemological framework (post-positivist, post-modernist, etc.). For example, if one acknowledges subjectivity in the research process and the construction of knowledge (as the epistemological frameworks above do), assessing inter-rater reliability may be a questionable strategy for determining methodological rigor.

With a post-positivist view in mind, Merrick (1999) described three concepts important to the evaluation of qualitative research: trustworthiness, reflexivity, and representation. *Trustworthiness* is somewhat akin to internal validity in that it is meant to establish the credibility of the qualitative findings. As noted by Merrick (1999), Stiles (1993) described several ways in which qualitative investigators establish trustworthy data. First, they disclose their theoretical orientation so research consumers can better understand their methodological choices and analytic interpretations. Of course, not all consumers will agree with this orientation; however, having it will aid in understanding the investigator's decisions. Elliott, Fischer, and Rennie (1999) called this process "owning one's perspective," whereas Henwood and Pidgeon (1992) considered it a part of "reflexivity" (see the following). Next, investigators should discuss with their readers how they engaged with the research participants and data. Investigators typically need to immerse themselves in their data in intense and prolonged ways, often coming back to the data multiple times, to exhaust the iterative relation between data and interpretation. In addition, qualitative investigators should consider the advantages of triangulating findings with multiple data sources to build a stronger case for their interpretation of the data. Triangulation may increase the likelihood of the data being inconsistent, but these inconsistencies or contradictions sometimes ultimately make sense when a more holistic interpretive approach is employed (Lancy, 2001). Finally, qualitative investigators need to get continual feedback from peers about the research process, their interpretations of data, and their findings. Some may choose to work in peer research teams to ensure they get this feedback (Deutsch, Luttrell, & Dorner, 2004). Debriefing sessions among peer research team members (or just among colleagues) in which the research process and data are discussed provide valuable information to investigators on how they are conceptualizing and representing their phenomenon of interest.

Expanding on concept of *reflexivity*, Merrick (1999) argued that investigators doing good qualitative research contemplate and evaluate their decisions concerning research topic, design, and process as well as introspecting on their personal experiences carrying out the study. The reflective process should ideally occur throughout the life of the study. Reflexivity can be further broken down into three types: personal, functional, and disciplinary (Wilkinson, 1988, as cited in Merrick, 1999). Qualitative investigators demonstrate personal reflexivity when they acknowledge their own background and what effect their experiences might have on the study and its findings. For example, depending on the focus of the study, investigators might consider their age, ethnicity, or marital status as important factors. Functional reflexivity deals with examining the choices made during the research process, such as the decisions on what type of data to gather or from whom to gather it. Finally, disciplinary reflexivity has to do with examiners reflecting on larger issues, such as their assumptions about research methods and science.

Representation, the third concept Merrick (1999) discussed, deals with how investigators share their findings with others (see also Fine, 1994). Investigators need to be sensitive to how they influence what others learn about those whom they have studied. Participants' data, particularly by the time an investigator presents them to the public, contains not only the participants' voices but also the investigator's voice. Acknowledging and explaining possible ways in which the co-construction of data has taken place is encouraged by many qualitative investigators (Merrick, 1999).

A few additional noteworthy concepts are important to assessing rigor in qualitative studies: transferability, independent audit, and negative case analysis. Qualitative investigators often do not discuss external validity or generalizability, but rather the related concept of *transferability* (Merrick, 1999; Henwood & Pidgeon, 1992). Emphasizing the importance of context at all levels (from the specific relation developed between researcher and participants to the relation between these particular participants and culture at large), many using qualitative methods would not expect their results to generalize to a larger population of individuals. However, this does not make their findings useless or meaningless to investigators working in other contexts. Investigators should disclose detailed information about the participants, their participants' background, and the context in which they gathered the data so their audience can make informed decisions about the findings' applicability to other individuals in other contexts (Henwood & Pidgeon, 1992).[24] The principles of the grounded theory of causal inference (Shadish et al., 2002), discussed in the earlier section on quantitative analysis, may help consumers decide on the transferability of qualitative findings.

---

[24] However, this is not to say that two researchers studying the same phenomena in the same context will necessarily arrive at the same results (Eisner, 2003).

Qualitative investigators also discuss the idea of the *independent audit* (Yardley, 2000). Independent audits involve investigators filing all their data, analyses, and other study items in such a way that someone else would see their final product as credible and justified if they were to look through all the materials (regardless of whether it is the only possible product that could have resulted). Evidence of internal consistency, coherence, and documentation of systematic decision-making are key to establishing credibility in an independent audit.[25]

Finally, an understanding of how qualitative investigators conduct their *negative case analysis* is also important to determining the quality of their work. Negative case analysis is the way in which one explores data not fitting with preexisting theory or conceptualizations. Often an inductive process occurs; investigators modify the theory or conceptualization in such a way that all cases fit (McGrath & Johnson, 2003). Qualitative analysts need to describe negative cases and their relation to theory when reporting their findings so consumers understand which parts of theory existed prior to data collection and which emerged through negative case analysis. Hypertypification, the tendency to only see data that fit with preexisting theory or conceptualizations, often results from insufficient immersion with the data and a lack of negative case analysis (Erickson, 1992). When analysts describe how they identified negative cases and subsequently modified theory, they inform consumers of their sensitivity to hypertypification.

Combining qualitative and quantitative methods.[26]   Should qualitative and quantitative methods be used together? Opinions are mixed (see Marecek, 2003, for a good discussion). With their contrasting strengths and weaknesses, it is easy to think the two approaches could potentially complement each other quite nicely and assist in triangulating the phenomenon of interest. However, using the two methods concurrently in the same study or same program of research may be difficult. As articulated earlier, the qualitative approach involves more than just different data collection methods; it has a different epistemological orientation with its own set of assumptions. For example, consider the inherent tensions between objectivity and subjectivity as well as those between the deductive process of hypothesis-testing and the inductive process of negative case analysis.

However, it may be possible for investigators to have multiple epistemologies, acknowledge the strengths and weaknesses of each, and use each without relegating one to secondary status. Lavelli, Pantoja, Hsu, Messinger, and Fogel (2005) provided one example of how to combine quantitative and qualitative approaches harmoniously. Their microgenetic design incorporated both inferential statistics and narrative analysis, resulting in a more extensive understanding of change processes than either methodology could provide independently. Clarke (2003) furnished another illustration of how to use qualitative and quantitative methods in a single study. She statistically demonstrated how social support and education moderate the negative relation between physical disability (due to stroke) and well-being. Then Clarke described the themes present in individuals' accounts of their experiences after having a stroke to elucidate the actual processes by which social support and education moderate the relation. Fine and Elsbach (2000) used six classic social psychological studies as examples to illustrate specific tactics for combining qualitative and quantitative research methods.

Summary.   Qualitative research methods offer investigators not only alternative methods to data collection and analyses, but also alternative epistemological paradigms. With

---

[25] An individual unassociated with the research study may literally carry out an independent audit.

[26] "Mixed method studies" and "mixed model studies" are terms used for studies that combine qualitative and quantitative research methods (Tashakkori & Teddlie, 1998).

qualitative methods, the goal is to illuminate the subjective qualities of a psychological phenomenon rather than trying to quantify it. Investigators accomplish this goal using a wide variety of general approaches, data collection methods, and analytic strategies and evaluate the quality of their studies using alternative criteria, such as trustworthiness, reflexivity, and representation. Readers interested in learning more about qualitative research methods may find the following books useful: Berg (2003), Camic, Rhodes, and Yardley (2003a), Denzin and Lincoln (2000), Esterberg (2002), Flick (2007), Gibbs (2007), Kopala and Suzuki (1999), Lancy (2001), Luttrell (2009), Smith (2003), and Willig (2001). For information about internet-based qualitative and mixed-methods research see Hewson (2008).

ETHICS

Ethics, the field involving the study of right and wrong conduct, seems at first glance to have little relevance to a chapter on the technical aspects of research. However, ethics relates to the conduct of research in the same way as the various aspects of methodology and analysis previously discussed. Every investigator must make a variety of decisions based on ethics during the course of a developmental investigation. Ethical decisions both interact with and determine the methodology and other technical aspects of the research.

International guidelines base research ethics on three general ethical principles:

* *beneficience*—the obligation to maximize research benefits and minimize research harms
* *respect*—the responsibility to ensure that research participation is informed, rational, and voluntary
* *justice*—the obligation to ensure the fair distribution of research benefits and burdens across populations (Fisher & Anushko, 2008).

Perhaps the most general ethical question that every investigator must ask is the following: Should I conduct this research, given its likely contributions in comparison to the risk, discomfort, and inconvenience inflicted or potentially inflicted on those participating in the study? In addition to this overarching ethical question, the investigator must confront numerous other ethical issues concerning participants, their guardians, and research personnel (American Psychological Association, 1982, 1987, 2002a, 2002b).

This section focuses on the ethical issues pertaining to children and their guardians. We describe special ethical problems associated with using children as participants, and the ethical principles for the conduct of research promulgated by the Society for Research in Child Development (SRCD).

Protection of Child Subjects

Commonly, children are participants in developmental research, and their legal status as minors, their level of cognitive development, and their limited experiences may present special ethical problems. Based on these considerations, the SRCD developed a set of principles regarding the conduct of research with children. SRCD first published Principles 1 to 14 in 1990 and added Principles 15 and 16 in 1991. They are located in the Society's annual *Directory of Members* (e.g., SRCD, 2003) and on its website (SRCD, 2007); the annotations below are paraphrases from the standards as well as interpretation of them by the authors.

1. *Non-harmful procedures:* Investigators should not use research procedures that may harm the child, and are obligated to use the least stressful research operation whenever possible. Thompson (1990) reminded investigators to use their knowledge of child development when designing studies; procedures that may be stressful at one age may be less stressful at other ages (e.g., separation from caregivers is probably stressful for young children, but not for adolescents). If investigators introduce stress with their procedures, the anticipated benefits of the study must clearly exceed any risk to the children. If a study is carried out so negligently that nothing can be learned from the results, there is no justification for putting participants though unpleasant experiences (Aronson et al., 1990). Whenever investigators are in doubt as to the harmful properties of their procedures, they should seek consultation from others. When harmful procedures are proposed, it is important to have careful deliberation by an institutional review board (IRB).

2. *Informed consent and assent:* Investigators working with toddlers and preschool children should make efforts to at least tell the children what will be done, where it will be done, who will be involved, how long their participation will last, whether other children have participated and how they reacted to the research, and whether an incentive will be offered. Then, the children can decide to say "yes" or "no" regarding participation (Miller, 2007). Investigators working with infants and young children should use special effort to explain the research procedures to parents, and should be especially sensitive to any indicators of participants' discomfort because young children are less likely to possess full comprehension of what they are doing or why they are doing it (Abramovitch, Freedman, Thoden, & Nikolich, 1991). Investigators should try to tailor the information they provide based on participants' developmental level. They should also work to minimize coercion because young children sometimes make decisions based on what they think authority figures want them to do (Abramovitch et al., 1991). Investigators should obtain assent from children 7 years of age and older (National Commission for the Protection of Human Subjects, 1977) and possibly for younger children, if they can understand what they will be doing in the study (Bell-Dolan & Wessler, 1994). Informed consent may not be required with certain kinds of observational research conducted in contexts such as supermarkets and playgrounds. Generally, consent need not be obtained if the behaviors studied are naturally occurring ones that are unaffected by the decision to study them; the behaviors are innocuous and are neither revealing nor embarrassing; and the participants are anonymous and certain to remain so (e.g., Miller, 2007, p. 179).

3. *Parental consent:* Investigators should obtain written informed consent from parents or children's legal guardians. Not only should investigators recognize the right of parents and guardians to refuse, but they should also remind them of their right to withdraw permission at any time without penalty.

4. *Additional consent:* Investigators should afford the same rights just mentioned for parents to those who act *in loco parentis*, such as teachers or camp counselors, particularly if their interaction with the child is the focus of study.

5. *Incentives:* Incentives to participate must be fair and must not exceed the range of incentives that the child normally experiences. In particular, incentives should not serve to coerce the child to participate.

6. *Deception:* Some psychologists take the position that deception is never justified with children (e.g., Ferguson, 1978), but this is not a generally accepted position. If deception is used, investigators should satisfy their colleagues that such procedures are warranted. If investigators believe that the deception they employ has the potential to harm, they should apprise participants of the need for deception in a sensitive

and developmentally appropriate manner. Debriefing, which is so critical in research with adults and older children and adolescents, with young children may largely involve providing the children with good feelings about their research participation (Smith, 1967).

7. *Anonymity:* If investigators collect data from institutional records, they should obtain permission from responsible individuals and take precautions to preserve the anonymity of the information contained in these records.

8. *Mutual responsibilities:* Investigators should clarify the responsibilities of all participants in the research enterprise—children, parents, teachers, administrators, and research assistants—at the inception of the study. Investigators should also honor all promises made to parties involved in the research.

9. *Jeopardy:* If an investigator learns of information that jeopardizes a child's well-being during the conduct of a study, he or she has a responsibility to discuss the information with the parents and with experts in the field who may arrange the necessary assistance for the child.

10. *Unforeseen consequences:* If research procedures result in unforeseen negative consequences for child participants, the investigator should take immediate action to ameliorate the untoward effects and should modify the procedures for subsequent participants. If, for example, the procedures instigate negative affect in the child, investigators should institute procedures to reinstate positive feelings immediately.

11. *Confidentiality:* Procedures insuring the confidentiality of participants' responses must be in place. When a possibility exists that others may gain access to research responses, investigators should explain this possibility (along with plans for protecting confidentiality) to participants as part of the procedure of obtaining informed consent.

12. *Informing participants:* The investigator recognizes a duty to inform participants of any misunderstandings, and to report general findings to them in terms appropriate to their understanding. If investigators must withhold information, they should make efforts to ensure that the participants are not damaged by the withheld information.

13. *Reporting results:* Because investigators' comments may carry undue weight, they should exercise caution in reporting results, making evaluative statements, or giving advice to parents, teachers, and the like.

14. *Implications of findings:* Investigators should be particularly mindful of the social, political, and human implications of their research.

15. *Scientific misconduct:* Investigators must refrain from scientific misconduct, including such practices as plagiarism. Plagiarism is the failure to appropriately credit the contributions of others—ranging from "stealing" the studies and research ideas of colleagues and assistants to lesser ethical indiscretions involving the order of authorship and the inclusion of assistants in acknowledgments. The fabrication or falsification of data also constitutes scientific misconduct. This may include fraud or other forms of "scientific embezzlement" (Broad & Wade, 1982; Mahoney, 1976). The Society does not consider unintentional errors or differences in opinion on how to interpret data scientific misconduct. SCRD members guilty of scientific misconduct may be expelled from the Society as well as face other consequences (see APA, 2002a).

16. *Personal misconduct:* Committing a criminal felony may be grounds for expulsion from SRCD. As with scientific misconduct, voting members of the Society's Governing Council make this decision.

It is important to recognize that these principles apply not only to the principal investigator but also to all assistants and technical personnel.

Ethical Issues Not Addressed by SRCD Principles

Investigators' relationships with other researchers, funding agencies, and various special interest groups also involve ethical issues, concerns, and potential conflicts (Dooley, 1990). For example, conflicts of interest may arise when a drug or cigarette company hires researchers to investigate the benefits of the company's products. Clear guidelines are provided for action in these and other related situations, but far fewer safeguards are available—perhaps because breaches of ethics in these areas are thought less likely to produce the shocking moral tragedies of those involving human participants and perhaps because the relevant behaviors are less accessible to public scrutiny. Whatever the case, science is much more dependent on each individual investigator's conscience to move him or her in the direction of ethically correct behavior in these instances. In general, investigators are tasked with "doing good science well" (Fisher & Anushko, 2008, p. 106). The conduct of responsible developmental science depends on investigators' commitment and efforts to act ethically, accompanied by familiarity with national and international regulations, ethics codes, and laws. Doing good science well requires flexibility and sensibility to the research context, the investigator's fiduciary responsibilities, and participant expectations unique to each study (Fisher & Anushko, 2008).

CONCLUSIONS

The advancement of science depends on the quality of substantive questions asked by investigators as well as by the adequacy of the technical means that they employ to answer these questions. This chapter has focused on this technical side of research, including design, measurement, and analysis—as well as ethics. Readers should not expect to be qualified to meet the challenges represented by these technicalities merely as a result of studying this chapter. However, it should have increased their appreciation for this aspect of the research armamentarium and increased their ability to secure the expertness required to become sophisticated consumers and producers of developmental research.

REFERENCES AND SUGGESTED READINGS (▢)

Abelson, R. P. (1985). A variance explanation paradox: When a little is a lot. *Psychological Bulletin, 97*, 128–132.

Abelson, R. P. (1997a). On the surprising longevity of flogged horses: Why there is a case for the significance test. *Psychological Science, 8*, 12–15.

Abelson, R. P. (1997b). A retrospective on the significance test ban of 1999 (If there were no significance tests, they would be invented). In L. L. Harlow, S. A. Mulaik, & J. H. Steiger (Eds.), *What if there were no significance tests?* (pp. 117–141). Mahwah, NJ: Lawrence Erlbaum Associates.

Abramovitch, R., Freedman, J. L., Thoden, K., & Nikolich, C. (1991). Children's capacity to consent to participation in psychological research: Empirical findings. *Child Development, 62*, 1100–1109.

Achenbach, T. M. (1978). *Research in developmental psychology: Concepts, strategies, methods.* New York: Free Press.

Achenbach, T. M., & Dumenci, L. (2001). Advances in empirically based assessment: Revised cross-informant syndromes and new DSM-oriented scales for the CBCL, YSR, and TRF. *Journal of Consulting & Clinical Psychology, 69*, 699–702.

Agresti, A. (1996). *An introduction to categorical data analysis.* New York: Wiley.

▢ Agresti, A. (2007). *An introduction to categorical data analysis* (2nd ed.). Hoboken, NJ: Wiley.

▢ Alasuutari, P., Bickman, L., & Brannen, J. (Eds.). (2008). *The Sage handbook of social research methods.* London: Sage.

Allport, G. W. (1937). *Personality: A psychological interpretation.* New York: Holt.

American Educational Research Association. (1999). *Standard for educational and psychological testing.* Washington, DC: AERA.

American Psychological Association. (1982). *Ethical principles in the conduct of research with human participants.* Washington, DC: APA.

American Psychological Association. (1987). *Casebook on ethical principles of psychologists.* Washington, DC: APA.

American Psychological Association. (2001). *Publication manual of The American Psychological Association* (5th ed.). Washington, DC: APA.

American Psychological Association. (2002a). Ethical principles of psychologists and code of conduct. *American Psychologist, 57,* 1060–1073.

American Psychological Association. (2002b). Ethical principles of psychologists and code of conduct. Retrieved August 1, 2009, from www.apa.org/ethics/code2002.pdf

American Psychological Association (2010). *Publication manual of the American Psychological Association* (6th ed.). Washington, DC: American Psychological Association.

Anastasi, A. (1958). Heredity, environment, and the question "how"? *Psychological Review, 65,* 197–208.

Anastasi, A. (1988). *Psychological testing* (6th ed.). New York: Macmillan.

Anderson, E. R. (1995). Accelerating and maximizing information from short-term longitudinal research. In J. M. Gottman (Ed.), *The analysis of change* (pp. 139–163). Mahwah, NJ: Lawrence Erlbaum Associates.

Anderson, L. R., & Anger, J. W. (1978). Analysis of variance in small group research. *Personality and Social Psychology Bulletin, 4,* 341–345.

Antaki, C. (2008). Discourse analysis and conversation analysis. In P. Alasuutari, L. Bickman, & J. Brannen (Eds.), *The Sage handbook of social research methods* (pp. 431–446). London: Sage.

Appelbaum, M. I., & Cramer, E. M. (1974). Some problems in the nonorthogonal analysis of variance. *Psychological Bulletin, 81,* 335–343.

Appelbaum, M. I., & McCall, R. B. (1983). Design and analysis in developmental psychology. In P. H. Mussen (Ed.), *Handbook of child psychology: Vol. I. History, theory, and methods* (4th ed., pp. 415–476). New York: Wiley.

Arbuckle, J. L. (1997). *Amos user's guide, Version 3.6.* Chicago: SmallWaters Corporation.

Aronson, E., Ellsworth, P. C., Carlsmith, J. M., & Gonzales, M. H. (1990). *Methods of research in social psychology* (2nd ed.). New York: McGraw-Hill.

Baer, D. M. (1977). Reviewer's comment: Just because it's reliable doesn't mean that you can use it. *Journal of Applied Behavior Analysis, 10,* 117–119.

Bakeman, R., & Gottman, J. M. (1987). Applying observational methods: A systematic view. In J. D. Osofsky (Ed.), *Handbook of infant development* (2nd ed., pp. 818–854). New York: Wiley.

Bakeman, R., & Gottman, J. M. (1997). Observing interaction: An introduction to sequential analysis (2nd ed.). New York: Cambridge University Press.

Baker, P. L., & Carson, A. (1999). I take care of my kids: Mothering practices of substance-abusing women. *Gender and Society, 13,* 347–363.

Baltes, P. B., Lindenberger, U., & Staudinger, U. M. (1998). Life-span theory in developmental psychology. In W. Damon (Series Ed.) & R. M. Lerner (Vol. Ed.), *Handbook of child psychology. Volume 1: Theoretical models of human development* (5th ed., pp. 1029–1143). New York: Wiley.

Baltes, P. B., & Nesselroade, J. R. (1979). History and rationale of longitudinal research. In J. R. Nesselroade & P. B. Baltes (Eds.), *Longitudinal research in the study of behavior and development* (pp. 1–39). New York: Academic Press.

Baltes, P. B., Reese, H. W., & Nesselroade, J. (1988). *Life-span developmental psychology: Introduction to research methods.* Hillsdale, NJ: Lawrence Erlbaum Associates.

Bandura, A. (1997). *Self-efficacy: The exercise of control.* New York: Freeman.

Bangert-Drowns, R. L. (1986). Review of developments in meta-analytic method. *Psychological Bulletin, 99,* 388–399.

Barber, T. X. (1976). *Pitfalls in human research: Ten pivotal points.* New York: Pergamon Press.

Baron, R. M., & Kenny, D. A. (1986). The moderator–mediator distinction in social psychological research: Conceptual, strategic, and statistical considerations. *Journal of Personality and Social Psychology, 51,* 1173–1182.

Barrios, B., & Hartmann, D. P. (1988). Fears and anxieties. In E. J. Mash & L. G. Terdal (Eds.), *Behavioral assessment of childhood disorders* (2nd ed.). New York: Guilford Press.

Baumrind, D. (1991). Effective parenting during the early adolescent transition. In P. A. Cowan & E. M. Hetherington (Eds.), *Advances in family research* (Vol. 2). Hillsdale, NJ: Lawrence Erlbaum Associates.

Becker, B. J. (1994). Combining significance levels. In H. Cooper & L. V. Hedges (Eds.), *The handbook of research synthesis* (pp. 215–230). New York: Sage.

Becker, B. (1999). Narratives of pain in later life and conventions of storytelling. *Journal of Aging Studies, 13,* 73–87.

Bell, R. Q. (1968). A reinterpretation of the direction of effects of socialization. *Psychological Review, 75,* 81–95.

Bell-Dolan, D., & Wessler, A. E. (1994). Ethical administration of sociometric measures: Procedures in use and suggestions for improvement. *Professional Psychology: Research and Practice, 25,* 23–32.

Berg, B. L. (2003). *Qualitative research methods for the social sciences* (5th ed.). Boston: Pearson Allyn & Bacon.

Berk, R. A. (1979). Generalizability of behavioral observations: A clarification of interobserver agreement and interobserver reliability. *American Journal of Mental Deficiency, 83,* 460–472.

Birnbaum, M. H. (2004). Human research and data collection via the internet. *Annual Review of Psychology*, *55*, 803–822.

Bloom, H. S. (2008). The core analytics of randomized experiments for social research. In P. Alasuutari, L. Bickman, & J. Brannen (Eds.), *The Sage handbook of social research methods* (pp. 115–133). London: Sage.

Bohrnstedt, G. W., & Knoke, D. (1994). *Statistics for social data analysis* (3rd ed.). Itasca, IL: F.E. Peacock.

Boivard, J. A., & Embretson, S. E. (2008). Modern measurement in the social sciences. In P. Alasuutari, L. Bickman, & J. Brannen (Eds.), *The Sage handbook of social research methods* (pp. 269–289). London: Sage.

Bollen, K. A. (1989). *Structural equations with latent variable*. New York: Wiley.

Bornstein, M. H., Hahn, C.-S., Haynes, M., Manian, N., & Tamis-LeMonda, C. S. (2005). New research methods in developmental science: Applications and illustrations. In D. M. Teti (Ed.), *Handbook of research methods in developmental science* (pp. 509–533). Malden, MA: Blackwell.

Bowlby, J. (1969/1982). *Attachment and loss: Vol. 1. Attachment*. New York: Basic Books.

Braybrooke, D. (1987). *Philosophy of the social sciences*. New York: Prentice Hall.

Broad, W. J., & Wade, N. (1982). *Betrayers of the truth*. New York: Simon & Schuster.

Bronfenbrenner, U. (1979). *The ecology of human development*. Cambridge, MA.: Harvard University Press.

Bronson, W. C. (1987). Special section on structural equation modeling: Introduction. *Child Development*, *58*, 1.

Bruner, J. (1990). *Acts of meaning*. Cambridge, MA: Harvard University Press.

Bryk, A. S., & Raudenbush, S. W. (1987). Application of hierarchical linear models to assessing change. *Psychological Bulletin*, *101*, 147–158.

Bryman, A., & Cramer, D. (2001). *Quantitative data analysis with SPSS release 10 for Windows: A guide for social scientists*. New York: Routledge.

Burchinal, M., & Appelbaum, M. I. (1991). Estimating individual developmental functions: Methods and their assumptions. *Child Development*, *62*, 23–43.

Cairns, R. B. (1983). Sociometry, psychometry, and social structure: A commentary on six recent studies of popular, rejected, and neglected children. *Merrill-Palmer Quarterly*, *29*, 429–438.

Cairns, R. B., Bergman, L. R., & Kagan, J. (Eds.). (1998). *Methods and models for studying the individual: Essays in honor of Marian Radke-Yarrow*. Thousand Oaks, CA: Sage.

Camic, P. M., Rhodes, J. E., & Yardley, L. (Eds.). (2003a). *Qualitative research in psychology: Expanding perspectives in methodology and design*. Washington, DC: American Psychological Association.

Camic, P. M., Rhodes, J. E., & Yardley, L. (2003b). Naming the stars: Integrating qualitative methods into psychological research. In P. M. Camic, J. E. Rhodes, & L. Yardley (Eds.), *Qualitative research in psychology: Expanding perspectives in methodology and design* (pp. 3–15). Washington, DC: American Psychological Association.

Campbell, D. T. (1958). Systematic error on the part of human links in communication systems. *Information and Control*, *1*, 297–312.

Campbell, D. T., & Fiske, D. W. (1959). Convergent and discriminant validation by the multitrait–multimethod matrix. *Psychological Bulletin*, *56*, 81–105.

Campbell, D. T., & Stanley, J. C. (1963). *Experimental and quasi-experimental designs for research*. Chicago: Rand McNally.

Cattell, R. B. (1944). Psychological measurement: Normative, ipsative, interactive. *Psychological Review*, *51*, 292–303.

Cauce, A. M., Ryan, K. D., & Grove, K. (1998). Children and adolescents of color, where are you? Participation, selection, recruitment, and retention in developmental research. In V. C. McLoyd & L. Steinberg (Eds.), *Studying minority adolescents: Conceptual, methodological, and theoretical issues* (pp. 147–166). Mahwah, MJ: Lawrence Erlbaum Associates.

Charmaz, K. (2003). Grounded theory. In J. A. Smith (Ed.), *Qualitative psychology: A practical guide to research methods* (pp. 81–110). Thousand Oaks, CA: Sage.

Christensen, R. (1997). *Log-linear models and logistic regression* (2nd ed.). New York: Springer-Verlag.

Clarke, P. (2003). Towards a greater understanding of the experience of stroke: Integrating quantitative and qualitative methods. *Journal of Aging Studies*, *17*, 171–187.

Cohen, J. (1968). Multiple regression as a general data-analytic system. *Psychological Bulletin*, *70*, 426–443.

Cohen, J. (1988). *Statistical power analysis for the behavioral sciences* (2nd ed.). Hillsdale, NJ: Lawrence Erlbaum Associates.

Cohen, J. (1990). Things I have learned (so far). *American Psychologist*, *45*, 1304–1312.

Cohen, J. (1992). A power primer. *Psychological Bulletin*, *112*, 155–159.

Cohen, J., Cohen, P., West, S. S., & Aiken, L. S. (2003). *Applied multiple/correlation analysis for the behavioral sciences* (3rd ed.). Mahwah, NJ: Lawrence Erlbaum Associates.

Cohen, R. J., Montague, P., Nathanson, L. S., & Swerdlik, M. E. (1988). *Psychological testing: An introduction to tests & measurement*. Mountain View, CA: Mayfield.

Cohen, S. H. & Reese, H. W. (Eds.) (1994). *Life-span developmental psychology: Methodological contributions*. Hillsdale, NJ: Lawrence Erlbaum Associates.

Collins, L. M. (2006). Analysis of longitudinal data: The integration of theoretical model, temporal design, and statistical model. *Annual Review of Psychology*, *57*, 505–528.

Collins, L. M., & Sayer, A. G. (2000). Modeling growth and change processes: Design, measurement, and analysis for research in social psychology. In H. M. Reis & C. M. Judd (Eds.), *Handbook of research methods in social and personality psychology* (pp. 478–495). New York: Cambridge University Press.

Collins, L. M., & Horn, J. L. (Eds.). (1991). *Best methods for the analysis of change: Recent advances, unanswered questions, future directions*. Washington, DC: American Psychological Association.

Comrey, A. L. (1978). Common methodological problems in factor analytic studies. *Journal of Consulting and Clinical Psychology*, *46*, 648–659.

Conover, W. J. (1999). *Practical nonparametric statistics* (3rd ed.). New York: Wiley.

Cook, T. D., & Campbell, D. T. (1979). *Quasi-experimentation: Design and analysis issues for field settings*. Chicago: Rand McNally.

Cook, T. D., & Wong, V. C. (2008). Better quasi-experimental practice. In P. Alasuutari, L. Bickman, & J. Brannen (Eds.), *The Sage handbook of social research methods* (pp. 134–165). London: Sage.

Cooper, H. M. (1989). *Integrating research: A guide for literature reviews*. Newbury Park, CA: Sage.

Cooper, H., & Hedges, L. V. (Eds.). (1994). *The handbook of research synthesis*. New York: Russell Sage Foundation.

Cooper, H., & Patall, E. A. (2009). The relative benefits of meta-analysis conducted with individual participant data versus aggregated data. *Psychology Methods*, *14*, 165–176.

Corbin, J., & Strauss, A. (2008). *Basics of qualitative research: Techniques and procedures for developing grounded theory* (3rd ed.). Thousand Oaks, CA: Sage.

Crocker, L., & Algina, A. (1986). *Introduction to classical & modern test theory*. New York: Holt, Rinehart, & Winston.

Cronbach, L. J. (1957). The two disciplines of scientific psychology. *American Psychologist*, *12*, 671–684.

Cronbach, L. J., & Furby, L. (1970). How should we measure change—Or should we? *Psychological Bulletin*, *74*, 68–80. (Also see Errata, ibid., 1970, *74*, 218.)

Cronbach, L. J., Gleser, G. C., Nanda, H., & Rajaratnam, N. (1972). *The dependability of behavioral measurements*. New York: Wiley.

Cudeck, R., & Harring, J. R. (2007). Analysis of nonlinear patterns of change with random coefficient models. *Annual Review of Psychology*, *58*, 615–637.

Cumming, G., & Finch, S. (2001). A primer on the understanding, use, and calculation of confidence intervals that are based on central and noncentral distributions. *Educational and Psychological Measurement*, *61*, 532–574.

Cumming, G., & Finch, S. (2005). Inference by eye: Confidence intervals and how to read pictures of data. *American Psychologist*, *60*, 170–180.

Curran, P. J. (2009). The seemingly quixotic pursuit of a cumulative psychological science. Introduction to the special issue. *Psychological Methods*, *14*, 77–80.

Curran, P. J., & Hussong, A. M. (2009). Integrative data analysis: The simultaneous analysis of multiple data sets. *Psychology Methods*, *14*, 81–100.

Darlington, R. B. (1990). *Regression and linear models*. New York: McGraw-Hill.

Delucchi, K. L. (1983). The use and misuse of chi-square: Lewis and Burke revisited. *Psychological Bulletin*, *94*, 166–176.

Denzin, N. K., & Lincoln, Y. S. (1994). Introduction: Entering the field of qualitative research. In N. K. Denzin & Y. S. Lincoln (Eds.), *Handbook of qualitative research* (pp. 1–17). Thousand Oaks, CA: Sage.

Denzin, N. K., & Lincoln, Y. S. (2000). *Handbook of qualitative research* (2nd ed.). Thousand Oaks, CA: Sage.

Deutsch, N. L., Luttrell, W., & Dorner, L. M. (2004, March). *Engaging with adolescents: The rewards and challenges of qualitative methods and feminist methodology*. Discussion hour presented at the biennial meeting of the Society for Research on Adolescence, Baltimore.

Dooley, D. (1990). *Social research methods* (2nd ed.). Englewood Cliffs, NJ: Prentice Hall.

Eid, M., & Diener, E. (Eds.) (2006). *Handbook of multimethod measurement in psychology*. Washington, DC: American Psychological Association.

Eisner, E. W. (2003). On the art and science of qualitative research in psychology. In P. M. Camic, J. E. Rhodes, & L. Yardley (Eds.), *Qualitative research in psychology: Expanding perspectives in methodology and design* (pp. 17–29). Washington, DC: American Psychological Association.

Elliott, R., Fischer, C. T., & Rennie, D. L. (1999). Evolving guidelines for publication of qualitative research studies in psychology and related fields. *British Journal for Clinical Psychology*, *38*, 215–229.

Embretson, S. E., & Reise, S. P. (2000). *Item response theory for psychologists*. Mahwah, NJ: Lawrence Erlbaum Associates.

Epstein, S., & Brady, E. J. (1985). The person–situation debate in historical and current perspective. *Psychological Bulletin*, *98*, 513–537.

Erickson, F. (1992). Ethnographic microanalysis of interaction. In M. D. LeCompte, L. W. Millroy, & J. Preissle (Eds.), *The handbook of qualitative research in education* (pp. 201–225). San Diego, CA: Academic Press.

Esterberg, K. G. (2002). *Qualitative methods in social research*. New York: McGraw-Hill.

Ferguson, L. R. (1978). The competence and freedom of children to make choices regarding participation in research: A statement. *Journal of Social Issues, 34*, 114–121.

Fidell, L. S., & Tabachnick, B. G. (2003). Preparatory data analysis. In J. A. Schinka (Series Ed.) and W. F. Velicer (Vol. Ed.), *Handbook of psychology: Research methods in psychology* (Vol. 2, pp. 115–141). New York: Wiley.

Fidler, F., & Thompson, B. (2001). Computing correct confidence intervals for anova fixed- and random-effects effect sizes. *Educational and Psychological Measurement, 61*, 575–604.

Fine, M. (1994). Working the hyphens: Reinventing self and other in qualitative research. In N. K. Denzin & Y. S. Lincoln (Eds.), *Handbook of qualitative research* (pp. 70–82). Thousand Oaks, CA: Sage.

Fine, M., Torre, M. E., Boudin, K., Bowen, I., Clark, J., Hylton, D., et al. (2003). Participatory action research: From within and beyond prison bars. In P. M. Camic, J. E. Rhodes, & L. Yardley (Eds.), *Qualitative research in psychology: Expanding perspectives in methodology and design* (pp. 173–198). Washington, DC: American Psychological Association.

Fine, G. A., & Elsbach, K. D. (2000). Ethnography and experiment in social psychological theory building: Tactics for integrating qualitative field data with quantitative lab data. *Journal of Experimental Social Psychology, 36*, 51–76.

Fischer, K. W., & Bidell, T. (1998). Dynamic development of psychological structures in action and thought. In W. Damon (Series Ed.) & R. M. Lerner (Vol. Ed.) *Handbook of child psychology. Volume 1: Theoretical models of human development* (5th ed., pp. 467–561). New York: Wiley.

Fisher, C. B., & Anushko, A. E. (2008). Research ethics in social science. In P. Alasuutari, L. Bickman, & J. Brannen (Eds.), *The Sage handbook of social research methods* (pp. 95–109). London: Sage.

Fitzmaurice, G., Davidian, M., Verbeke, G., & Molenberghs, G. (Eds.) (2009). *Longitudinal data analysis*. Boca Raton, FL: Chapman & Hall/CRC.

Fitzmaurice, G. M., Laird, N. M., & Ware, J. H. (2004). *Applied longitudinal analysis*. Hoboken, NJ: Wiley.

Fleiss, J. L. (1975). Measuring agreement between two judges on the presence or absence of a trait. *Biometrics, 31*, 651–659.

Fleiss, J. L. (1994). Measures of effect size for categorical data. In H. Cooper & L. V. Hedges (Eds.), *The handbook of research synthesis* (pp. 245–260). New York: Sage.

Fleiss, J. L., Levin, B., & Paik, M. C. (2003). *Statistical methods for rates and proportions* (3rd ed.). New York: Wiley.

Flick, U. (2007). *Designing qualitative research*. London: Sage.

Franklin, R. D., Allison, D. B., & Gorman, B. S. (Eds.). (1997). *Design and analysis of single-case research*. Mahwah, NJ: Lawrence Erlbaum Associates.

Freedman, D. A. (1991). Statistical models and shoe leather. In P. V. Marsden (Ed.), *Sociological methodology, 1991* (pp. 291–313). Washington, DC: American Sociological Association.

Gardner, W., Hartmann, D. P., & Mitchell, C. (1982). The effects of serial dependency on the use of χ^2 for analyzing sequential data. *Behavioral Assessment, 4*, 75–82.

Gee, J. (1991). A linguistic approach to narrative. *Journal of Narrative and Life History, 1*, 15–39.

Geisser, S., & Greenhouse, S. W. (1958). An extension of Box's results on the use of the F distribution in multivariate analysis. *Annals of Mathematical Statistics, 29*, 885–891.

Gelfand, D. M., & Hartmann, D. P. (1984). *Child behavior analysis and therapy* (2nd ed.). New York: Pergamon.

Gibbs, G. (2007). *Analyzing qualitative data*. London: Sage.

Gigerenzer, G., Krauss, S. & Vitouch, O. (2004). The null ritual: What you always wanted to know about significance testing but were afraid to ask. In D. Kaplan (Ed.), *The Sage handbook of quantitative methodology for the social sciences* (pp. 391–408). Thousand Oaks, CA: Sage.

Gilligan, C. (1982). *In a different voice: Psychological theory and women's development*. Cambridge, MA: Harvard University Press.

Gilligan, C., Spencer, R., Weinberg, M. K., & Bertsch, T. (2003). On the listening guide: A voice-centered relational model. In P. M. Camic, J. E. Rhodes, & L. Yardley (Eds.), *Qualitative research in psychology: Expanding perspectives in methodology and design* (pp. 157–172). Washington, DC: American Psychological Association.

Glass, G. V., McGaw, B., & Smith, M. L. (1981). *Meta-analysis in social research*. Beverly Hills, CA: Sage.

Glass, G. V., Peckham, P. D., & Sanders, J. R. (1972). Consequences of failure to meet assumptions underlying the analysis of variance and covariance. *Review of Education Research, 42*, 237–288.

Gorsuch, R. L. (1983). *Factor analysis* (2nd ed.). Hillsdale, NJ: Lawrence Erlbaum Associates.

Gottman, J. M. (Ed.). (1995). *The analysis of change*. Mahwah, NJ: Lawrence Erlbaum Associates.

Graham, J. W. (2009). Missing data analysis: Making it work in the real world. *Annual Review of Psychology, 60*, 549–576.

Graham, J. W., Taylor, B. J., Olchowski, A. E., & Cumsille, P. E. (2006). Planned missing data designs in psychological research. *Psychological Methods, 11*, 323–343.

Guilford, J. P. (1954). *Psychometric methods* (2nd ed.). New York: McGraw-Hill.

Guilford, J. P. (1965). *Fundamental statistics in psychology and education*. New York: McGraw-Hill.

Hammersley, M (2008). Assessing validity in social research. In P. Alasuutari, L. Bickman, & J. Brannen (Eds.), *The Sage handbook of social research methods* (pp. 42–53). London: Sage.

Harlow, L. L. (1997). Significance testing introduction and overview. In L. L. Harlow, S. A. Mulaik, & J. H. Steiger (Eds.), *What if there were no significance tests?* (pp. 1–17) Mahwah, NJ: Lawrence Erlbaum Associates.

Harlow, L. L., Mulaik, S. A., & Steiger, J. H. (Eds.). (1997). *What if there were no significance tests?* Mahwah, NJ: Lawrence Erlbaum Associates.

Harris, C. W. (Ed.) (1963). *Problems in measuring change*. Madison, WI: University of Wisconsin Press.

Hartmann, D. P. (1982a). Assessing the dependability of observational data. In D. P. Hartmann (Ed.), *Using observers to study behavior: New directions for methodology of social and behavioral science* (pp. 51–65). San Francisco: Jossey-Bass.

Hartmann, D. P. (Ed.). (1982b). *Using observers to study behavior: New directions for methodology of behavioral science*. San Francisco: Jossey-Bass.

Hartmann, D. P. (2005). Assessing growth in longitudinal investigations: Selected measurement and design issues. In D. Teti (Ed.), *Handbook of research methods in developmental psychology* (pp. 319–339). Malden, MA: Blackwell.

Hartmann, D. P., & George, T. P. (1999). Design, measurement, and analysis in developmental research. In M. H. Bornstein & M. E. Lamb (Eds.), *Developmental psychology: An advanced textbook* (4th ed., pp. 125–195). Mahwah, NJ: Lawrence Erlbaum Associates.

Hartmann, D. P., & Pelzel, K. (2005). Design, measurement, and analysis in developmental research. In M. H. Bornstein & M. E. Lamb (Eds.), Developmental science: An advanced textbook (5th ed., pp. 103–184). Mahwah, NJ: Lawrence Erlbaum Associates.

Hartmann, D. P., Roper, B. L., & Bradford, D. C. (1979). Some relationships between behavioral and traditional assessment. *Journal of Behavioral Assessment, 1*, 3–21.

Hartmann, D. P., & Wood, D. D. (1990). Observational methods. In A. S. Bellack, M. Hersen, & A. E. Kazdin (Eds.), *International handbook of behavior modification and therapy* (2nd ed., pp. 107–138). New York: Plenum.

Harvey, J. H., Orbuch, T. L., & Weber, A. L. (Eds.). (1992). *Attributions, accounts, and close relationships*. New York: Springer-Verlag.

Hays, W. L. (1988). *Statistics* (4th ed.). Fort Worth, TX: Holt, Rinehart and Winston.

Haynes, S. N., & O'Brien, W. H. (2000). *Principles and practice of behavioral assessment*. New York: Kluwer Academic/Plenum.

Hedges, L. V., & Olkin, I. (1985). *Statistical methods for meta-analysis*. New York: Academic Press.

Heise, D. R. (1975). *Causal analysis*. New York: Wiley.

Henwood, K., & Pidgeon, N. F. (1992). Qualitative research and psychology theorising. *British Journal of Psychology, 83*, 97–112.

Henwood, K., & Pidgeon, N. (2003). Grounded theory in psychological research. In P. M. Camic, J. E. Rhodes, & L. Yardley (Eds.), *Qualitative research in psychology: Expanding perspectives in methodology and design* (pp. 131–155). Washington, DC: American Psychological Association.

Hewson, C. (2008). Internet-mediated research as an emergent method and its potential role in facilitating mixed methods research. In S. N. Hesse-Biber & P. Leavy (Eds.), *Handbook of emergent methods* (pp. 543–570). New York: Guilford.

Hey, V. (1997). *The company she keeps: An ethnography of girls' friendship*. Philadelphia: Open University Press.

Hicks, L. E. (1970). Some properties of ipsative, normative, and forced-choice normative measures. *Psychological Bulletin, 74*, 167–184.

Hochberg, Y. & Tamhane, A. C. (1987). *Multiple comparison procedures*. New York: Wiley.

Hoeksma, J. B., & Koomen, H. M. Y. (1992). Multilevel models in developmental psychological research: Rationales and applications. *Early Development and Parenting, 1*(3), 157–167.

Hoffer, S. M., & Piccinin, A. M. (2009). Integrative data analysis through coordination of measurement and analysis protocol across independent longitudinal studies. *Psychology Methods, 14*, 150–164.

Hoffman, L. W. (1991). The influence of the family environment on personality: Accounting for sibling differences. *Psychological Bulletin, 1991*, 187–203.

Hollander, M. (1999). *Nonparametric statistical methods* (2nd ed.). New York: Wiley.

House, A. E., House, B. J., & Campbell, M. B. (1981). Measures of interobserver agreement: Calculation formulas and distribution effects. *Journal of Behavioral Assessment, 3*, 37–57.

Hothorn, T., Bretz, F., & Westfall, P. (2008). Simultaneous inference in general parametric models. *Biometrical Journal, 50*, 346–363.

Hoyle, R. H. (2008). Latent variable models of social research data. In P. Alasuutari, L. Bickman, & J. Brannen (Eds.), *The Sage handbook of social research methods* (pp. 395–413). London: Sage.

Hsu, J. C. (1996). *Multiple comparisons: Theory and methods*. London: Chapman & Hall.

Huck, S. W., & Sandler, H. M. (1979). *Rival hypotheses: Alternative interpretations of data based conclusions.* New York: Harper & Row.

Huitema, B. E. (1980). *The analysis of covariance and alternatives.* New York: Wiley.

Hunt, J. M. (1961). *Intelligence and experience.* New York: Ronald Press.

Hunter, J. E., Schmidt, F. L., & Jackson, G. B. (1982). *Meta-analysis: Cumulating research findings across studies.* Beverly Hills, CA: Sage.

Iwata, B. A., Bailey, J. S., Fuqua, R. W., Neef, N. A., Page, T. J., & Reid, D. H (Eds.) (1989). *Methodological and conceptual issues in applied behavior analysis: 1968–1988.* Lawrence, KS: Society for the Experimental Analysis of Behavior.

Jackson, G. B. (1980). Methods for integrative reviews. *Review of Educational Research, 50,* 438–460.

Johnston, J. M., & Pennypacker, H. S. (1993). *Strategies and tactics of behavioral research* (2nd ed.). Hillsdale, NJ: Lawrence Erlbaum Associates.

Jöreskog, K. G., & Sörbom, D. (1983). *Lisrel V and Lisrel VI: Analysis of linear structural relationships by maximum likelihood and least squares methods* (2nd ed.). Uppsala, Sweden: University of Uppsala Department of Statistics.

Judd, C. M., & McClelland, G. H. (1989). *Data analysis: A model-comparison approach.* New York: Harcourt Brace Jovanovich.

Judd, C. M., McClelland, G. H., & Culhane, S. E. (1995). Data analysis: Continuing issues in the everyday analysis of psychological data. *Annual Review of Psychology, 46,* 433–465.

Kahneman, D. (1965). Control of spurious association and the reliability of the controlled variable. *Psychological Bulletin, 64,* 326–329.

Kazdin, A. E. (1980). *Research design in clinical psychology.* New York: Harper & Row.

Kelle, U. (Ed.). (1996). *Computer-aided qualitative data analysis: Theory, methods and practice.* Thousand Oaks, CA: Sage.

Kelley, K., & Maxwell, S. (2008). Sample size planning with applications to multiple regression: Power and accuracy for omnibus and targeted effects. In P. Alasuutari, L. Bickman, & J. Brannen (Eds.), *The Sage handbook of social research methods* (pp. 166–192). London: Sage.

Kelloway, E. K. (1998). *Using LISREL for structural equation modeling: A researcher's guide.* Thousand Oaks, CA: Sage Publications.

Kelley, K., & Rausch, J. R. (2006). Sample size planning for the standardized mean difference: Accuracy in parameter estimation via narrow confidence intervals. *Psychological Methods, 11,* 363–385.

Kemmis, S., & McTaggart, R. (2008). Participatory action research. Communicative action and the public sphere. In N. K. Denzin & Y. S. Lincoln (Eds.), *Strategies of qualitative inquiry* (3rd ed., pp. 271–330). Thousand Oaks, CA: Sage.

Kennedy, J. J. (1992). *Analyzing qualitative data: Log-linear analysis for behavioral research* (2nd ed.). New York: Praeger.

Kenny, D. A. (1979). *Correlation and causality.* New York: Wiley.

Kenny, D. A., & Judd, C. M. (1986). Consequences of violating the independence assumption in analysis of variance. *Psychological Bulletin, 99,* 422–431.

Kerig, P. K., & Lindahl, K. M. (Eds.). (2001). *Family observational coding systems: Resources for systemic research.* Mahwah, NJ: Lawrence Erlbaum Associates.

Kidder, L. H. (1981). Qualitative research and quasi-experimental frameworks. In M. B. Brewer & B. E. Collins (Eds.), *Scientific inquiry and the social sciences* (pp. 226–256). San Francisco: Jossey-Bass.

Kirk, R. E. (1995). *Experimental design: Procedures for the behavioral sciences* (3rd ed.). Pacific Grove, CA: Brooks/Cole.

Kirk, R. E. (2003). The importance of effect magnitude. In S. F. Davis (Ed.), *Handbook of research methods in experimental psychology* (pp. 83–105). Malden, MA: Blackwell.

Knight, G. P., & Hill, N. E. (1998). Measurement equivalence in research involving minority adolescents. In V. C. McLoyd & L. Steinberg (Eds.), *Studying minority adolescents: Conceptual, methodological, and theoretical issues* (pp. 183–210). Mahwah, NJ: Lawrence Erlbaum Associates.

Knoke, D., & Burke, P. J. (1980). *Log-linear models.* Beverly Hills, CA: Sage.

Kopala, M., & Suzuki, L. A. (Eds.). (1999). *Using qualitative methods in psychology.* Thousand Oaks, CA: Sage.

Kraemer, H. C., & Jacklin, C. N. (1979). Statistical analysis of dyadic social behavior. *Psychological Bulletin, 86,* 217–224.

Kratochwill, T. R., & Levin, J. R. (Eds.). (1992). *Single-case research design and analysis: New directions for psychology and education.* Hillsdale, NJ: Lawrence Erlbaum Associates.

Kraut, R., Olson, J., Banaji, M., Bruckman, A., Cohen, J., & Couper, M. (2004). Psychological research online: Report of board of scientific affairs' advisory group on the conduct of research on the internet. *American Psychologist, 59,* 105–117.

Kristjansson, S. D., Kircher, J. C., & Webb, A. K. (2007). Multilevel models for repeated measures research designs in psychophysiology: An introduction to growth curve modeling. *Psychophysiology, 44,* 728–736.

Kuhn, T. S. (1970). *The structure of scientific revolutions* (2nd ed.). Chicago: University of Chicago Press.

Kuzel, A. J. (1999). Sampling in qualitative inquiry. In B. F. Crabtree & W. L. Miller (Eds.), *Doing qualitative research* (2nd ed., pp. 33–46). Thousand Oaks, CA: Sage.

Labov, W. (1978). Crossing the gulf between sociology and linguistics. *American Sociologist, 13*, 93–103.

Lancy, D. F. (2001). *Studying children and schools: Qualitative research traditions.* Prospect Heights, IL: Waveland.

Landis, J. R., & Koch, G. G. (1979). The analysis of categorical data in longitudinal studies of development. In J. R. Nesselroade & P. B. Baltes (Eds.), *Longitudinal research in the study of behavior and development* (pp. 233–261). New York: Academic Press.

Larzelere, R. E., & Mulaik, S. A. (1977). Single-sample tests for many correlations. *Psychological Bulletin, 84*, 557–569.

Lavelli, M., Pantoja, A. P. F., Hsu, H.-C., Messinger, D., & Fogel, A. (2005). Using microgenetic designs to study developmental change processes. In D. M. Teti (Ed.), *Handbook of research methods in developmental science* (pp. 40–65). Malden, MA: Blackwell.

Lenth, R. V. (2001). Some practical guidelines for effective sample size determination. *American Statistician, 55*, 187–193.

Lerner, R. M. (1998). The life course and human development. In W. Damon (Series Ed.) and R. M. Lerner (Vol. Ed.), *Handbook of child psychology. Volume 1: Theoretical models of human development* (5th ed., pp. 1–24). New York: Wiley.

Lewis, D., & Burke, C. J. (1949). The use and misuse of the chi-square test. *Psychological Bulletin, 46*, 433–489.

Lewis, D., & Burke, C. J. (1950). Further discussion of the use and misuse of the chi-square test. *Psychological Bulletin, 47*, 347–355.

Lipsey, M. W. (1990). *Design sensitivity: Statistical power for experimental research.* Newbury Park, CA: Sage

Little, R. J., & Rubin, D. B. (1987). *Statistical analysis with missing data.* New York: Wiley.

Luttrell, W. (2002). *Pregnant bodies, fertile minds: Gender, race, and the schooling of pregnant teens.* London: Routledge.

Luttrell, W. (Ed.). (2009). *Qualitative educational research: Readings in reflexive methodology and transformative practice.* London: Routledge.

MacCallum, R. C. (2003). 2001 presidential address: Working with imperfect models. *Multivariate Behavioral Research, 38*, 113–139.

MacKinnon, D. P., Fairchild, A. J., & Fritz, M. S. (2007). Mediation analysis. *Annual Review of Psychology, 58*, 593–614.

Magidson, J., & Vermunt, J. K. (2004). Latent class models. In D. Kaplan (Ed.) *The Sage handbook of quantitative methodology for the social sciences* (pp. 175–198). Thousand Oaks, CA: Sage.

Mahler, M. S., Pine, F., & Bergman, A. (1975/2000). *The psychological birth of the human infant: Symbiosis and individuation.* New York: Basic Books.

Mahoney, M. J. (1976). *Scientist as subject: The psychological imperative.* Cambridge, MA: Ballinger Publication Company.

Marecek, J. (2003). Dancing through minefields: Toward a qualitative stance in psychology. In P. M. Camic, J. E. Rhodes, & L. Yardley (Eds.), *Qualitative research in psychology: Expanding perspectives in methodology and design* (pp. 49–69). Washington, DC: American Psychological Association.

Maritz, J. S. (1995). *Distribution-free statistical methods* (2nd ed.). New York: Chapman & Hall.

Maxwell, S. E., Kelley, K., & Rausch, J. R. (2008). Sample size planning for statistical power and accuracy in parameter estimation. *Annual Review of Psychology, 59*, 537–563.

McAdams, D. P., & Bowman, P. J. (2001). Narrating life's turning points: Redemption and contamination. In D. P. McAdams, R. Josselson, & A. Lieblich (Eds.), *Turns in the road: Narrative studies of lives in transition* (pp. 3–34). Washington, DC: American Psychological Association.

McAdams, D. P., Josselson, R., & Lieblich, A. (Eds.). (2001). *Turns in the road: Narrative studies of lives in transition.* Washington, DC: American Psychological Association.

McArdle, J. J. (2009). Latent variable modeling of difference and changes with longitudinal data. *Annual Review of Psychology, 60*, 577–605.

McCall, R. B. (1977). Challenges to a science of developmental psychology. *Child Development, 48*, 333–344.

McCullagh, P., & Nelder, J. A. (1989). *Generalized linear models* (2nd ed.). London: Chapman & Hall.

McDonald, R. P. (1985). *Factor analysis and related methods.* Hillsdale, NJ: Lawrence Erlbaum Associates.

McDonald, R. P., & Ho, M. H. R. (2002). Principles and practice in reporting structural equation analyses. *Psychological Methods, 7*, 64–82.

McGrath, J. E., & Johnson, B. A. (2003). Methodology makes meaning: How both qualitative and quantitative paradigms shape evidence and its interpretation. In P. M. Camic, J. E. Rhodes, & L. Yardley (Eds.), *Qualitative research in psychology: Expanding perspectives in methodology and design* (pp. 31–48). Washington, DC: American Psychological Association.

McGuire, W. J. (1969). Suspiciousness of experimenter's intent. In R. Rosenthal & R. L. Rosnow (Eds.), *Artifact in behavioral research* (pp. 13–57). New York: Academic Press.

McNemar, Q. (1969). *Psychological statistics* (4th ed.). New York: Wiley.

Meehl, P. E. (1978). Theoretical risks and tabular asterisks: Sir Karl, Sir Ronald, and the slow progress of soft psychology. *Journal of Consulting and Clinical Psychology, 46*, 806–834.

Meng, X., Rosenthal, R., & Rubin, D. B. (1992). Comparing correlated correlation coefficients. *Psychological Bulletin, 111*, 172–175.

Merrick, E. (1999). An exploration of quality in qualitative research: Are "reliability" and "validity" relevant? In M. Kopala & L. A. Suzuki (Eds.), *Using qualitative methods in psychology* (pp. 25–36). Thousand Oaks, CA: Sage.

Messick, S. (1983). Assessment of children. In P. Mussen (Ed.), *Handbook of child psychology: Vol. 1. History, theory, and methods* (4th ed., pp. 477–526). New York: Wiley.

Messick, S. (1994). Foundations of validity: Meaning and consequences in psychological assessment. *European Journal of Psychological Assessment, 10*, 1–9.

Miller, S. A. (2007). *Developmental research methods* (3rd ed.). Thousand Oaks, CA: Sage.

Mischel, W., & Peake, P. K. (1983). Analyzing the construction of consistency in personality. In M. M. Page (Ed.), *Personality—Current theory & research: 1982 Nebraska symposium on motivation* (pp. 233–262). Lincoln, NE: University of Nebraska Press.

Mitchell, C., & Hartmann, D. P. (1981). A cautionary note on the use of omega squared to evaluate the effectiveness of behavioral treatments. *Behavioral Assessment, 3*, 93–100.

Mook, D. G. (1983). In defense of external invalidity. *American Psychologist, 38*, 379–387.

Morrison, D. F. (2000). *Multivariate statistical methods* (3rd ed.). New York: McGraw-Hill.

Morrison, D. E., & Henkel, R. E. (Eds.). (1970). *The significance test controversy*. Chicago: Aldine.

Morrow, S. L., & Smith, M. L. (2000). Qualitative research for counseling psychology. In S. D. Brown & R. W. Lent (Eds.), *Handbook of counseling psychology* (3rd ed., pp. 119–230). New York: Wiley.

Moskowitz, D. S. & Hershberger, S. L. (Eds.). (2002). *Modeling intraindividual variability with repeated measures data: Methods and applications*. Mahwah, NJ: Lawrence Erlbaum Associates.

Mulaik, S. A., Raju, N. S., & Harshman, R. A. (1997). There is a time and place for significance testing. In L. L. Harlow, S. A. Mulaik, & J. H. Steiger (Eds.), *What if there were no significance tests?* (pp. 65–115). Mahwah, NJ: Lawrence Erlbaum Associates.

Murray, M. (2003). Narrative psychology and narrative analysis. In P. M. Camic, J. E. Rhodes, & L. Yardley (Eds.), *Qualitative research in psychology: Expanding perspectives in methodology and design* (pp. 95–112). Washington, DC: American Psychological Association.

National Commission for the Protection of Human Subjects. (1977). *Report and recommendations: Research involving children*. Washington, DC: U.S. Government Printing Office.

Neher, A. (1967). Probability pyramiding, research error and the need for independent replication. *Psychological Record, 17*, 257–262.

Neisser, U., Boodoo, G., Bouchard, T. J., Jr., Boykin, A. W., Brody, N., Ceci, S. J., et al. (1996). Intelligence: Knowns and unknowns. *American Psychologist, 51*, 77–101.

Nelder, J. A., & Wedderburn, R. W. M. (1972). Generalized linear models. *Journal of the Royal Statistical Society: Series A (General), 135*, 370–384.

Nesselroade, J. R., & Baltes, P. B. (Eds.). (1979). *Longitudinal research in the study of behavior and development*. New York: Academic Press.

□ Nickerson, R. S. (2000). Null hypothesis significance testing: A review of an old and continuing controversy. *Psychological Methods, 5*, 241–301.

Nunnally, J. C. (1978). *Psychometric theory* (2nd ed.). New York: McGraw-Hill.

□ Nunnally, J. C., & Bernstein, I. H. (1994). *Psychometric theory* (3rd ed.). New York: McGraw-Hill.

O'Brien, R. G., & Castelloe, J. (2007). Sample-size analysis for traditional hypothesis testing: Concepts and issues. In A. Dmitrienko, C. Chuang-Stein, & R. D'Agostino (Eds.), *Pharmaceutical statistics using SAS: A practical guide* (pp. 237–271). Cary, NC: SAS.

O'Grady, K. E. (1982). Measures of explained variance: Cautions and limitations. *Psychological Bulletin, 92*, 766–777.

Overall, J. E., & Woodward, J. A. (1977). Nonrandom assignment and the analysis of covariance. *Psychological Bulletin, 84*, 588–594.

Overton, W. F. (1998). Developmental psychology: Philosophy, concepts, and methodology. In W. Damon (Series Ed.) & R. M. Lerner (Vol. Ed.), *Handbook of child psychology. Volume 1: Theoretical models of human development* (5th ed., pp. 107–188). New York: Wiley.

Ozer, D. J. (1985). Correlation and the coefficient of determination. *Psychological Bulletin, 97*, 307–315.

Pampel, F. C. (2000). *Logistic regression: A primer*. Thousand Oaks, CA: Sage.

Parsonson, B. S., & Baer, D. M. (1978). The analysis and presentation of graphic data. In T. R. Kratochwill (Ed.), *Single subject research: Strategies for evaluating change* (pp. 101–165). New York: Academic Press.

Patall, E. A., & Cooper, H. (2008). Conducting a meta-analysis. In P. Alasuutari, L. Bickman, & J. Brannen (Eds.), *The Sage handbook of social research methods* (pp. 536–554). London: Sage.

Patterson, G. R. (1993). Orderly change in a stable world: The antisocial trait as a chimera. *Journal of Consulting and Clinical Psychology*, *61*, 911–919.

Pedhazur, E. J., & Schmelkin, L. P. (1991). *Measurement, design, and analysis: An integrated approach*. Hillsdale, NJ: Lawrence Erlbaum Associates.

Piaget, J. (1932/1965). *The moral judgment of the child*. New York: Free Press.

Piaget, J., Inhelder, B., & Weaver, H. (1972/2000). *The psychology of the child*. New York: Basic Books.

Popper, K. (1959). *The logic of scientific discovery*. New York: Basic Books.

Potter, J. (2003). Discourse analysis and discursive psychology. In P. M. Camic, J. E. Rhodes, & L. Yardley (Eds.), *Qualitative research in psychology: Expanding perspectives in methodology and design* (pp. 73–94). Washington, DC: American Psychological Association.

Prentice, D. A., & Miller, D. T. (1992). When small effects are impressive. *Psychological Bulletin*, *12*, 160–164.

Press, S. J., & Wilson, S. (1978). Choosing between logistic regression and discriminant analysis. *Journal of the American Statistical Association*, *73*, 699–705.

Raudenbush, S. W. (2000). Comparing personal trajectories and drawing causal inferences from longitudinal data. *Annual Review of Psychology*, *52*, 501–525.

Raudenbush, S. W. & Bryk, A. S. (2002). Hierarchical linear models: Applications and data analysis methods (2nd ed.). Thousand Oaks, CA: Sage.

Reips, U.-D. (2006). Web-based methods. In M. Eid & E. Diener (Eds.), *Handbook of multimethod measurement in psychology* (pp. 73–85). Washington, DC: American Psychological Association.

Reiss, R. D. (1989). *Approximate distributions of order statistics: With applications to nonparametric statistics*. New York: Springer-Verlag.

Ribisl, K. M., Walton, M., Mowbray, C. T., Luke, D. A., Davidson, W. S., & Bootsmiller, B. J. (1996). Minimizing participant attrition in panel studies through the use of effective retention and tracking strategies: Review and recommendations. *Evaluation and Program Planning*, *19*, 1–25.

Rindskopf, D. (2004). Trends in categorical data analysis: New, semi-new, and recycled ideas. In D. Kaplan (Ed.) *The Sage handbook of quantitative methodology for the social sciences* (pp. 137–149). Thousand Oaks, CA: Sage.

Rogosa, D. (1988). Myths about longitudinal research. In K. W. Schaie, R. T. Campbell, W. Meredith, & S. C. Rawlings (Eds.), *Methodological issues in aging research* (pp. 171–209). New York: Springer.

Rosenberg, M. S., Adams, D. C., & Gurevitch, J. (1997). *Metawin: Statistical software for meta-analysis with resampling tests*. Sunderland, MA: Sinauer.

Rosenthal, R. (1979). The "file-drawer problem" and tolerance for null results. *Psychological Bulletin*, *85*, 185–193.

Rosenthal, R. (Ed.). (1980a). *Quantitative assessment of research domains*. San Francisco: Jossey-Bass.

Rosenthal, R. (1980b). Summarizing significance levels. In R. Rosenthal (Ed.), *Quantitative assessment of research domains* (pp. 33–46). San Francisco: Jossey-Bass.

Rosenthal, R. (1994). Parametric measures of effect size. In H. Cooper & L. V. Hedges (Eds.), *The handbook of research synthesis* (pp. 231–244). New York: Sage.

Rosenthal, R., & Rosnow, R. L. (Ed.). (1969). *Artifact in behavioral research*. New York: Academic Press.

Rosenthal, R., & Rosnow, R. (1985). *Contrast analysis: Focused comparisons in the analysis of variance*. New York: Cambridge University Press.

Rosenthal, R., & Rubin, D. (1983). A note on percent of variance explained as a measure of the importance of effects. *Journal of Applied Social Psychology*, *9*, 395–396.

Rummel, R. J. (1967). Understanding factor analysis. *Journal of Conflict Resolution*, *XI*, 444–480.

Schafer, J. L., & Graham, J. W. (2002). Missing data: Our view of the state of the art. *Psychological Methods*, *7*, 147–177.

Schaie, K. W. (1965). A general model for the study of developmental problems. *Psychological Bulletin*, *64*, 92–107.

Schaie, K. W., & Caskie, G. I. L (2005). Methodological issues in aging research. In D. M. Teti (Ed.), *Handbook of research methods in developmental science* (pp. 21–39). Malden, MA: Blackwell.

Sciarra, D. (1999). The role of the qualitative researcher. In M. Kopala & L. A. Suzuki (Eds.), Using qualitative methods in psychology (pp. 37–48). Thousand Oaks, CA: Sage.

Shadish, W. R. (1986). Planned critical multiplism: Some elaborations. *Behavioral Assessment*, *8*, 75–103.

Shadish, W. R., & Cook, T. D. (2009). The renaissance of field experimentation in evaluation interventions. *Annual Review of Psychology*, *60*, 607–629.

Shadish, W. R., Cook, T. D., & Campbell, D. T. (2002). *Experimental and quasi-experimental designs for generalized causal inference*. Boston: Houghton Mifflin.

Shonkoff, J. P., & Phillips, D. A. (Eds.). (2000). *From neurons to neighborhoods: The science of early childhood development*. Washington, DC: National Academy Press.

Silva, F. (1993). *Psychometric foundations and behavioral assessment*. Newbury Park, CA: Sage.

Singer, J. D., & Willett, J. B. (2003). *Applied longitudinal data analysis: Modeling change and event occurrence*. New York: Oxford University Press.

Skitka, L. J., & Sargis, E. G. (2006). The internet as psychological laboratory. *Annual Review of Psychology*, *57*, 529–555.

Smith, J. A. (Ed.). (2003). *Qualitative psychology: A practical guide to research methods*. Thousand Oaks, CA: Sage.

Smith, K. E. (1996). *Changing times: My father's life from 1960 to 1970*. Unpublished manuscript, University of Idaho, Moscow, ID.

Smith, M. B. (1967). Conflicting values affecting behavioral research with children. *American Psychologist*, *22*, 377–382.

Smith, M. L., Glass, G. V., & Miller, T. I. (1980). *The benefits of psychotherapy*. Baltimore: Johns Hopkins University Press.

Smithson, M. (2001). Correct confidence intervals for various regression effect sizes and parameters: The importance of noncentral distributions in computing intervals. *Educational and Psychological Measurement*, *61*, 605–632.

☐ Smithson, M. (2003). *Confidence intervals*. Thousand Oaks, CA: Sage.

Society for Research in Child Development. (2003). *Directory of members*. Chicago: SRCD.

Society for Research in Child Development. (2007). SRCD ethical standards for research with children: Updated by the SRCD Governing Council, March 2007. Retrieved July 9, 2009, from www.srcd.org/index2.php?option=com_content&do_pdf=1&id=68

Solomon, R. L., & Lessac, M. S. (1968). A control group design for experimental studies of developmental processes. *Psychological Bulletin*, *70*, 145–150.

Steiger, J. H., & Fouladi, R. T. (1997). Noncentrality interval estimation and the evaluation of statistical models. In L. L. Harlow, S. A. Mulaik, & J. H. Steiger (Eds.), *What if there were no significance tests?* (pp. 221–257). Mahwah, NJ: Lawrence Erlbaum Associates.

Steiger, J. H., & Ward, L. M. (1987). Factor analysis and the coefficient of determination. *Psychological Bulletin*, *101*, 471–474.

Stern, D. N. (1985). *The interpersonal world of the infant*. New York: Basic Books.

Sternberg, K. J., Baradaran, L. P., Abbott, C. B., Lamb, M. E., & Guterman, E. (2006). Type of violence, age, and gender differences in the effects of family violence on children's behavior problems: A mega-analysis. *Developmental Review*, *26*, 89–112.

Stevens, J. (1992). *Applied multivariate statistics for the social sciences* (2nd ed.). Hillsdale, NJ: Lawrence Erlbaum Associates.

Stiles, W. B. (1993). Quality control in qualitative research. *Clinical Psychology Review*, *13*, 593–618.

Strayer, F. F., Verissimo, M., Vaughn, B. E., & Howes, C. (1995). A quantitative approach to the description and classification of primary social relationships. In E. Waters, B. E. Vaughn, G. Posada, & K. Kondo-Ikemura (Eds.), Caregiving, cultural, and cognitive perspectives on secure-base behavior and working models: New growing points of attachment theory and research. *Monographs of the Society for Research in Child Development*, *60*, 49–70.

Strube, M. J., & Hartmann, D. P. (1983). Meta-analysis: Techniques, applications, and functions. *Journal of Consulting and Clinical Psychology*, *51*, 14–27.

Suen, H. K., & Ary, D. (1989). *Analyzing quantitative behavioral observation data*. Hillsdale, NJ: Lawrence Erlbaum Associates.

Sutton, A. J., & Higgins, J. P. T. (2008). Recent developments in meta-analysis. *Statistics in Medicine*, *27*, 625–650.

Tabachnick, B. G., and Fidell, L. S. (2007). *Using multivariate statistics* (5th ed.). Boston: Pearson.

Tamhane, A. C. (2009). *Statistical analysis of designed experiments: Theory and applications*. Hoboken, NJ: Wiley.

Tashakkori, A., & Teddlie, C. (1998). *Mixed methodology: Combining qualitative and quantitative approaches*. Thousand Oaks, CA: Sage.

Tatsuoka, M. (1993). Effect size. In G. Keren & C. Lewis (Eds.), *A handbook for data analysis in the behavioral sciences: Methodological issues* (pp. 461–479). Hillsdale, NJ: Lawrence Erlbaum Associates.

☐ Teti, D. (Ed.). (2005). *Handbook of research methods in developmental science*. Malden, MA: Blackwell.

Thomas, L., & Krebs, C. J. (1997). A review of statistical power analysis software. *Bulletin of the Ecological Society of America*, *78*, 128–139.

Thompson, B. (1984). *Canonical correlation analysis: Uses and interpretation*. Beverly Hills, CA: Sage.

Thompson, R. A. (1990). Vulnerability in research: A developmental perspective on research risk. *Child Development*, *61*, 1–16.

Toothaker, L. E. (1991). *Multiple comparisons for researchers*. Newbury Park, CA: Sage.

Tukey, J. W. (1977). *Exploratory data analysis*. Reading, MA: Addison-Wesley.

Tversky, A., & Kahneman, D. (1971). Belief in the law of small numbers. *Psychological Bulletin*, *76*, 105–110.

Ullman, J. B. (2007). Structural equation modeling. In B. G. Tabachnick & L. S. Fidell, *Using multivariate statistics* (5th ed., pp. 676–780). New York: Pearson.

Ullman, J. B., & Bentler, P. M. (2003). Structural equation modeling. In J. A. Schinka (Series Ed.) & W. F. Velicer (Vol. Ed.), *Handbook of psychology: Research methods in psychology* (Vol. 2, pp. 607–634). New York: Wiley.

Valsiner, J. (Ed.). (1986). *The individual subject and scientific psychology*. New York: Plenum Press.

Way, N., & Pahl, K. (1999). Friendship patterns among urban adolescent boys: A qualitative account. In M. Kopala & L. A. Suzuki (Eds.), *Using qualitative methods in psychology* (pp. 145–161). Thousand Oaks, CA: Sage.

Webber, S. J., & Cook, T. D. (1972). Subject effects in laboratory research: An examination of subject roles, demand characteristics, and valid inference. *Psychological Bulletin, 77*, 273–295.

West, S. (Ed.). (1983). Personality and prediction: Nomothetic and idiographic approaches. *Journal of Personality, 51* (No. 3, whole).

Westfall, P. H., Tobias, R. D., Rom, D., Wolfinger, R. D., & Hochberg, Y. (1999). *Multiple comparisons and multiple tests using SAS*. Cary, NC: SAS.

Wickens, T. D. (1989). *Multiway contingency tables analysis for the social sciences*. Hillsdale, NJ: Lawrence Erlbaum Associates.

Widaman, K. F., & Reise, S. P. (1997). Exploring the measurement invariance of psychological instruments: Applications in the substance use domain. In K. J. Bryant, M. Windle, & S. G. West (Eds.), *The science of prevention: Methodological advances from alcohol and substance abuse research* (pp. 281–324). Washington, DC: American Psychological Association.

Wilkinson, L., & the Task Force on Statistical Inference. (1999). Statistical methods in psychology journals: Guidelines and explanations. *American Psychologist, 54*, 594–604.

Wilkinson, S. (1988). The role of reflexivity in feminist psychology. *Women's Studies International Forum, 11*, 493–502.

Willett, J. B. (1988). Questions and answers in the measurement of change. In E. Z. Rothkopf (Ed.), *Review of research in education 15: 1988–89* (pp. 345–422). Washington, DC: American Educational Research Association.

Willett, J. B. (1989). Some results on reliability for the longitudinal measurement of change: Implications for the design of studies of individual growth. *Educational and Psychological Measurement, 49*, 587–602.

Willett, J. B. (1994). Measurement of change. In T. Husen and T. N. Postlewaite (Eds.), The international encyclopedia of education (2nd ed., pp. 671–678). Oxford, UK: Pergamon Press. Retrieved October 19, 2009, from http://gseacademic.harvard.edu/~willetjo/pdffiles/Willett1994.pdf

Willett, J. B., & Singer, J. D. (2004). Discrete-time survival analysis. In D. Kaplan (Ed.), *The Sage handbook of quantitative methodology for the social sciences* (pp. 199–211). Thousand Oaks, CA: Sage.

Willig, C. (2001). *Introducing qualitative research in psychology: Adventures in theory and method*. Philadelphia: Open University Press.

Willig, C. (2003). Discourse analysis. In J. A. Smith (Ed.), *Qualitative psychology: A practical guide to research methods* (pp. 159–183). Thousand Oaks, CA: Sage.

Wohlwill, J. F. (1970). The age variable in psychological research. *Psychological Review, 77*, 49–64.

Wohlwill, J. F. (1973). *The study of behavioral development*. New York: Academic Press.

Yardley, L. (2000). Dilemmas in qualitative health research. *Psychology and Health, 15*, 215–228.

Yeaton, W., & Sechrest, L. (1981). Meaningful measures of effect. *Journal of Consulting and Clinical Psychology, 49*, 766–767.

NEUROSCIENCE, PERCEPTUAL, COGNITIVE, AND LANGUAGE DEVELOPMENT

The focus shifts in the five chapters that compose the second section of *Developmental Science: An Advanced Textbook* from the discipline's foundations, perspectives, and methods to substantive issues of developmental science. In Chapter 4, Mark H. Johnson introduces the new and exciting developments that connect contemporary neuroscience and genetics with developmental science. Johnson first describes the major features of brain development (from prenatal to postnatal) and then relates them to developments in action, perception, cognition, language, and behavior. In so doing, Johnson describes the methods and fundamental assumptions of developmental neuroscience using examples drawn from several domains of study to elucidate the underlying neural systems.

Karen E. Adolph and Sarah E. Berger begin Chapter 5 on physical and motor development by addressing the question "why study movement?" They then take the balance of their chapter to demonstrate just how integral physical and motor development is to the unfolding of the psychology of the individual. Adolph and Berger take us on a tour as they carefully trace growth and development from fetus to newborn to infant to toddler to child. They recount how contact with the environment makes possible multifaceted discoveries for the developing human.

In Chapter 6, Marc H. Bornstein, Martha E. Arterberry, and Clay Mash review the controversies and issues that continue to make the study of perceptual functioning central to our understanding of psychological development. Perceptual development has long been the forum for debates between nativists and empiricists—the fundamental battle that began with philosophical assertion and continues as the driving force behind much research in perceptual development, particularly in infancy. Now, however, sophisticated experimental techniques have supplanted introspection and speculation, enabling researchers to address questions concerning the origins, status, and development of perception empirically rather than theoretically. Bornstein and colleagues embed a review of methodology while explaining the ontogeny of perception via the five senses.

In Chapter 7, Damian P. Birney and Robert J. Sternberg shift the reader's focus from the registration and initial evaluation of sensory information to its interpretation and use. Birney and Sternberg summarize a succession of scholarly attempts to explain the transformation of information into understanding, emphasizing prominent perspectives on cognitive development—notably those of Piaget, neo-Piagetians, and recent cognitive theorists. Such theories emphasize developmental changes in the modes of understanding reality, rather than the gradual accretion of information. Several alternative perspectives on cognitive development and mental functioning currently coexist and compete for prominence. Birney and Sternberg discuss information-processing theories of cognitive development and conclude with an overview of intelligence and more traditional psychometric concerns regarding individual differences in cognitive abilities, including wisdom.

In Chapter 8, the last of this section, Brian MacWhinney describes the acquisition of language. Of all the hurdles faced by the young child, cracking the linguistic code is perhaps the most impressive in the eyes of parents and other observers. One cannot help but marvel at the speed and seeming ease with which preverbal infants learn how to articulate meaningful statements and understand the speech of others. Because language is purely symbolic, its acquisition serves as the basis for advanced and abstract problem solving and cognition. MacWhinney reviews and integrates developmental research on both the production and comprehension of language, moving over six major components of language, beginning with auditory and articulatory development, then turning to lexical and grammatical issues, and culminating with communication and literacy.

❖ **4** ❖

DEVELOPMENTAL NEUROSCIENCE, PSYCHOPHYSIOLOGY, AND GENETICS

Mark H. Johnson
Birkbeck College, University of London

INTRODUCTION

Ontogenetic development involves the construction of increasingly complex levels of biological organization, including the brain and the cognitive processes it supports. As more complex forms are generated, different groups of scientists use different methods and approaches appropriate for that level (see Johnson, in 2011). Thus, as distinct from most other areas of psychological science, a complete account of developmental change specifically requires an interdisciplinary approach. Although these considerations suggest that the study of development requires collaboration and exchange of information between scientists with different methodological expertise, until the past decade the study of development has been conducted largely independently of consideration of the brain. This relative neglect of biological factors in the study of behavioral development from the 1970s until the past decade is somewhat surprising when one considers that the origins of developmental science can be traced to biologists such as Charles Darwin and Jean Piaget. Darwin (1872/1965) was one of the first to take a scientific approach to human behavioral development and to speculate on relations between phylogenetic and ontogenetic change. Piaget imported current theories of embryological development, mainly due to the developmental biologist C. H. Waddington, to generate his accounts of human cognitive development (see Waddington, 1975). However, a curious aspect of Piaget's biological approach to human cognitive development was his relative neglect of the importance of brain development, which Segalowitz (1994) attributed to a lack of information about brain development and function at the time Piaget was developing his theories.

In contrast to Piaget, some early developmental psychologists in America, such as McGraw and Gesell, did try to integrate brain development with what was known of behavioral ontogeny. Although they focused on motor development, they also extended their conclusions to mental and social development (e.g., Gesell, 1929; McGraw, 1943). They described stages in the development of motor abilities from prone positions to walking and stair climbing, and McGraw proposed that the transition between these stages could be accounted in terms of the maturation of motor cortex and its inhibition of subcortical pathways, a notion that still provides a basis for some research today. Although both McGraw and Gesell developed sophisticated informal theories that attempted to capture nonlinear and dynamic approaches to development, their efforts to relate brain development to behavioral change remained largely speculative. In Europe, Konrad Lorenz and Niko Tinbergen, contemporaries of McGraw, Gesell, and Piaget, originated the field of ethology, and were particularly concerned with causal factors in the development of the natural behavior of animals. Due to the more direct interventions possible with animals, they addressed issues about the relative contribution of "**innate**" as opposed to "experiential" contributions to behavior. The results of their experiments, in which early environmental conditions were manipulated, quickly led to the realization that the dissociation of behavior into innate and acquired components was inadequate to account for the complexities of behavioral development. However, the notion that some brain and cognitive systems are more impervious to experience during development than others remains important today. Furthermore, the notion that theories of behavioral development should take into account both the whole organism and the natural environment (social and physical) within which it develops is currently regaining popularity (e.g., Gottlieb, 2007; Mareschal et al., 2007; Thelen & Smith, 1994).

From the mid-1960s to the past decade biological approaches to human behavioral development fell out of favor for a variety of reasons, including the widely held belief among cognitive psychologists in the 1970s and 1980s that the "software" of the mind is best studied without reference to the "hardware" of the brain. However, the recent explosion of knowledge on brain development and genetics makes the task of relating them to behavioral changes considerably more viable than previously. In parallel, new molecular, genetic, and cellular methods, along with theories of self-organizing dynamic networks, have led to great advances in our understanding of how vertebrate brains are constructed during ontogeny. These advances, along with those in functional neuroimaging, have led to the recent emergence of the interdisciplinary science of developmental cognitive neuroscience (Johnson, 2011).

In this chapter I provide an overview of current knowledge on brain development and its relation to behavioral development, and I begin by describing some of the basic assumptions and methods that underlie recent research programs. Following this there is a summary review of prenatal and postnatal brain development, with a particular emphasis on the primate cerebral neocortex. Considerable evidence supports the importance of activity-dependent processes in the differentiation of cortical areas. Most of the chapter is devoted to a selective review of attempts to relate the postnatal development of the human brain to changes in aspects of perception, cognition, and behavior. In all the domains reviewed, questions about the process of specialization of regions of cortex, and their emergent function, are addressed by discussion of particular extended examples. It will be seen that in some domains purely psychological accounts of behavioral development often fail to take account of multiple underlying neural systems with overlapping functions. In even the simplest behavioral tasks multiple neural pathways and structures are likely to be active. I end the chapter with some general conclusions and prospects for future research.

SOME BASICS OF BRAIN STRUCTURE

The brains of all mammals follow a basic vertebrate brain plan that is found even in species such as salamanders, frogs, and birds. The major differences between these species and higher primates is in the dramatic expansion of the overlying cerebral cortex, together with associated structures such as the basal ganglia. The cerebral cortex of all mammals, including humans, is basically a thin (about 3–4 mm) flat sheet. Although complex, its general layered structure is relatively constant throughout its extent. The rapid expansion in the overall size of the cortex during evolution has resulted in it becoming increasingly intricately folded with various indentations (sulci) and lobes (gyri). The extra cortex possessed by primates, and especially humans, is presumably related to the higher cognitive functions they possess.

Most areas of the cerebral cortex (in all mammals) are made up of six layers of cells. Although this basic laminar structure holds throughout most of the neocortex, there are some regional variations. For example, sensory cortex has a particularly thick input layer (layer 4) and motor cortex a well output (projection) layer. In addition to the slightly different properties of different layers, regions of cortex also vary in their patterns of connectivity to other parts of the cortex, the prevalence of particular neurotransmitters, and the relative balance of **excitatory** and **inhibitory** activity. Finally, as we will see later, different cortical regions vary in the timing of key developmental events, such as the postnatal reduction in the number of synapses (Huttenlocher, 1990), and these differences have been proposed to be linked to changes in cognition and behaviour during postnatal development.

BASIC ASSUMPTIONS ABOUT BRAIN DEVELOPMENT AND BEHAVIORAL CHANGE

A number of assumptions are commonly made about relations between brain development and behavioral change which stem from the beliefs that brain development involves a process of unfolding of a genetic plan and that such development in particular regions of the brain causes or allows specific advances in cognitive, perceptual, or motor abilities in the infant or child. This overly static view of brain development fails to capture the importance of activity-dependent processes. Brain development is not just a genetic process, but is an epigenetic one heavily dependent on complex interactions at the molecular, cellular, and behavioral levels.

A contentious topic in behavioral development concerns the nature of **plasticity**. When brain development is commonly viewed simply as the unfolding of a genetic "plan," recovery of function after early brain damage is then attributed to specialized mechanisms of plasticity that are only activated in such cases. In fact, plasticity is probably better viewed as an inherent property of developmental processes. Like any aspect of biological development, brain growth involves a process of increasing specialization (or "restriction of fate") in the sense that tissue or cells become more specialized in their morphology and functioning during the process. Plasticity simply represents the state of not yet having achieved specialization at some level. For example, a piece of tissue from the cerebral cortex may not yet have developed functional specialization for processing a certain category of information when a neighboring region is damaged. The same developmental mechanisms that would have ensured specialization for one type of processing may now bias the tissue toward the type of processing normally subserved by its unfortunate neighbor. Thus, in many instances abnormal patterns of brain specialization may reflect the action of normal developmental processes following some earlier perturbation from the normal case. Identifying and understanding the mechanisms underlying specialization, particularly in postnatal life, remain the major challenges of developmental cognitive neuroscience for the future.

METHODS FOR STUDYING FUNCTIONAL BRAIN DEVELOPMENT

Part of the reason for the recently renewed interest in relating brain development to cognitive, social, and emotional change comes from advances in methodology that allow hypotheses to be generated and tested more readily than previously (Casey & de Haan, 2002). One set of tools relates to brain imaging—the generation of "functional" maps of brain activity based on changes in cerebral metabolism, blood flow, or electrical activity. Some of these imaging methods, such as positron emission tomography (PET), are of limited utility for studying transitions in behavioral development in normal infants and children due to their invasive nature (requiring the intravenous injection of radioactively labeled substances) and their relatively coarse temporal resolution (on the order of minutes). Three brain imaging techniques are currently being applied to development in normal children—**event-related potentials (ERPs)**, **functional magnetic resonance imaging (fMRI)**, and near infrared spectroscopy (NIRS).

ERPs involve measuring the electrical activity of the brain generated as groups of neurons fire synchronously by means of sensitive electrodes that rest on the scalp surface. These recordings can be of either the spontaneous natural rhythms of the brain (electroencephalography, EEG) or the electrical activity induced by the presentation of a stimulus (ERP). Normally the ERP from many trials is averaged, resulting in the spontaneous natural rhythms of the brain that are unrelated to the stimulus presentation averaging to zero. With a high density of electrodes on the scalp, algorithms can be employed that infer the position and orientation of the brain sources of electrical activity (dipoles) for the particular pattern of scalp surface electrical activity. In some recent studies bursts of high frequency EEG have been observed and analyzed in infants. These "event-related oscillations" appear to mark important stages of information processing in the infant brain (e.g., Csibra & Johnson, 2007; Csibra, Tucker, & Johnson, 2001).

FMRI allows the non-invasive measurement of cerebral blood flow, with the prospect of millimeter spatial resolution and temporal resolution on the order of seconds. Although this technique has been applied to children (Thomas & Tseng, 2008), the distracting noise and vibration make its usefulness for healthy awake infants unclear. However, studies on drowsy or sleeping infants are feasible when auditory processing is the focus of interest.

The most recent method developed for studying brain function in healthy infants, NIRS, involves placing a number of light emitters and detectors on the scalp and measuring the bending or scattering of light resulting from changes in blood flow and oxygenation in the underlying cortex. To date, only a handful of studies have been published with this method, but it promises much for the future (see Grossmann et al., 2008).

Developmental psychobiological research on animals has contributed greatly to our understanding of the relation between developing brain and behavior, and recent techniques in molecular genetics open up new possibilities. For example, it is now possible to "knock out" specific genes from the genome of an animal and study effects on subsequent development. An example of this approach was the deletion of the alpha-calcium calmodulin kinase II gene, which results in rats being unable to perform certain learning tasks when adults (Silva, Paylor, Wehner, & Tonegawa, 1992; Silva, Stevens, Tonegawa, & Wang, 1992). This method may open new vistas in the analysis of genetic contributions to perceptual and cognitive change in animals. However, it should be noted that lesioning a single gene during development is likely to have a cascade of effects caused by the abnormal, or absent, interactions with other genes and thus may be more complex to interpret than it initially appears. In human infants and children it is now possible to study individual differences in cognitive and brain function by combining these techniques with genetic analyses (Viding, Williamson, Forbes, & Hariri, 2008). Furthermore, the study of cognitive and neural atypicalities in developmental disorders of genetic origin has begun to help build bridges between genes and cognition through development (Karmiloff-Smith, 1998). In the near horizon, the possibility of gene expression studies of cognitive development in human and animal models offers much promise.

Another useful approach for linking brain development to behavior is the "marker task." This method involves the use of specific behavioral tasks that have been linked to a brain region or pathway in adult primates and humans by neurophysiological, neuropsychological, or brain imaging studies. By testing infants or children with versions of such a task at different ages, the researcher can use the success or otherwise of individuals as indicating the functional development of the relevant regions of the brain. Later in this chapter, several lines of inquiry that illustrate the marker task approach are discussed.

Finally, connectionist neural network modeling offers the possibility of assessing the information-processing consequences of developmental changes in the neuroanatomy and neurochemistry of the brain (see Mareschal et al., 2007, for review). For example, O'Reilly and Johnson (1994) demonstrated how the micro-circuitry of a region of vertebrate forebrain could lead to certain self-terminating sensitive period effects. Such models promise to provide a bridge between our observations of development at the neural level and behavioral change in childhood.

BUILDING A BRAIN

Brain development may be divided into that which occurs prior to birth (prenatal) and that which takes place after birth (postnatal). Although some of the same developmental processes can be traced from prenatal to postnatal life, in postnatal development there is obviously more scope for influence from the world outside the infant. A striking feature of human brain development is the comparatively long phase of postnatal development, and therefore the increased extent to which the later stages of brain development can be influenced by the environment of the child. Some degree of plasticity is retained into adulthood, but this may decline with age.

Prenatal Brain Development

The major stages of prenatal brain development in humans correspond closely to those of other mammals. Shortly after conception a fertilized cell undergoes a rapid process of cell division, resulting in a cluster of proliferating cells (called the blastocyst) that somewhat resembles a bunch of grapes. Within a few days, the blastocyst differentiates into a three-layered structure, with each of these layers subsequently differentiating into major parts of the body. The outer layer (ectoderm) gives rise to the skin surface and the nervous system (including the eyes). The nervous system continues its development with a process known as neurolation. A portion of the ectoderm begins to fold in on itself to form a hollow cylinder called the neural tube.

The neural tube differentiates along three dimensions: the length, the circumference, and the radius. The length dimension gives rise to the major subdivisions of the central nervous system, with the forebrain and midbrain arising at one end and the spinal cord at the other. The end that will become the spinal cord differentiates into a series of repeated units or segments, and the front end of the neural tube organizes in a different way with a series of bulges and convolutions emerging. By around 5 weeks after conception these bulges can be identified as protoforms for major components of the mammalian brain. Within these bulges cells are born, travel from one place to another, and develop into particular types. The vast majority of the cells that will compose the brain are born in the so-called proliferative zones. These zones are close to the hollow of the neural tube (which subsequently become the ventricles of the brain).

Division of cells within the proliferative zone produces clones (a group of cells that are produced by division of a single precursor cell). Neuroblasts produce neurons, and glioblasts produce glial cells. Although glial cells are not thought to play a major role in information processing in the brain, they are important for a variety of support functions in the brain. Each of the neuroblasts gives rise to a definite and limited number of neurons. In some cases particular neuroblasts also give rise to particular types of neuron, although in other cases the distinctive morphology of the type of neuron arises as a product of its developmental inter-actions (e.g., Marin-Padilla, 1990). After young neurons are born, they have to travel or migrate from the proliferative zone to the particular region where they will be employed in the mature brain. Two forms of migration are observed during brain development. The first, and more common, is passive cell displacement. This occurs when cells that have been generated are simply pushed further away from the proliferative zone by more recently born cells. This form of migration gives rise to an outside-to-inside spatiotemporal gradient in which the oldest cells are pushed toward the surface of the brain, while the most recently produced cells are toward the inside. Passive migration gives rise to brain structures such as the thalamus, the dentate gyrus of the hippocampus, and many regions of the brain stem. The second form of migration is more active and involves the young cell moving past previously generated cells to create an "inside-out" gradient. This pattern is found in the cerebral cortex and in some subcortical areas that have a laminar (divided into parallel layers) structure.

The prenatal development of the cerebral cortex, the region of the brain implicated in many cognitive, perceptual, and motor functions, has been studied in some detail. In particu-lar Rakic (1988) proposed a "radial unit model" in which the laminar organization of the cerebral cortex (Figure 4.1) is determined by the fact that each cortical neuroblast gives rise to about 100 neurons. The progeny from each neuroblast all migrate up the same one of many radial glial fibers, with the latest to be born traveling past their older relatives. A radial glial fiber is a long process that stretches from top to bottom of the cortex and originates from a glial cell. These radial glial fibers act like a climbing rope to ensure that cells produced by a single neuroblast all contribute to one radial column of neurons within the cortex. Rakic's proposed method of migration is illustrated in Figure 4.2.

In the human brain by around the time of birth the vast majority of cells are in their appropriate adult locations (although there may be some limited generation of new neurons in some regions—Tanapat, Hastings, & Gould, 2001), and all the major landmarks of the brain, such as the most distinctive patterns of folding of the cerebral cortex, are in place. However, this does not mean that brain development is complete. Furthermore, it is important to stress that prenatal brain development does not consist simply of the unfolding of a rigid "genetic plan" (see Nelson, Thomas & de Haan, 2006). For example, the detailed folding patterns of the cerebral cortex can vary considerably, even between identical twins (Bartley et al., 1997).

Postnatal Brain Development

A number of lines of evidence indicate that substantive changes take place during postnatal development of the human brain. At the most gross level of analysis, the volume of the brain quadruples between birth and adulthood. This increase comes from a number of sources such as more extensive fiber bundles, and nerve fibers becoming covered in a fatty myelin sheath which helps conduct electrical signals (**myelinization**). But perhaps the most obvious mani-festation of postnatal neural development as viewed through a standard microscope is the increase in size and complexity of the dendritic tree of many neurons. This is illustrated in Figure 4.3, which shows drawings from microscope views of the human visual cortex from birth to six months of age. The extent and reach of a cell's dendritic tree may increase dramatically, and it often becomes more specific and specialized. Less apparent through standard microscopes, but more evident with electron microscopy, is a corresponding increase in density of functional contacts between neurons and synapses.

Huttenlocher (1990) and colleagues reported a steady increase in the density of synapses in several regions of the human cerebral cortex. For example, in parts of the visual cortex, the

FIGURE 4.1 A simplified schematic diagram illustrating that, despite its convoluted surface appearance (top), the cerebral cortex is a thin sheet (middle) composed of six layers (bottom). The convolutions in the cortex arise from a combination of growth patterns and the restricted space inside the skull. In general, differences between mammals involve the total area of the cortical sheet, and not its layered structure. Each of the layers possesses certain neuron types and characteristic input and projection patterns.

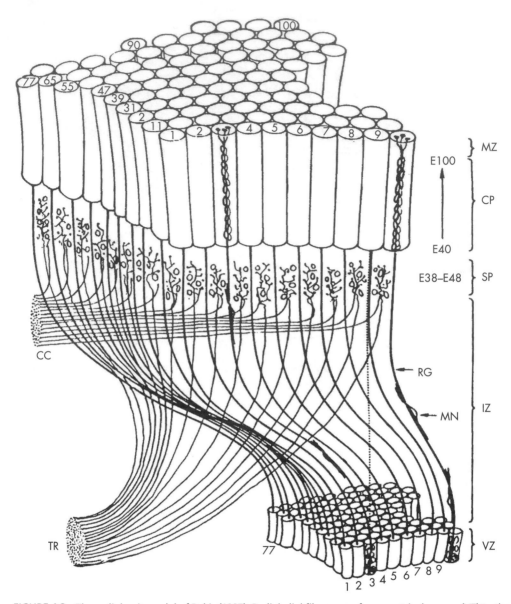

FIGURE 4.2   The radial unit model of Rakic (1987). Radial glial fibers span from ventricular zone (VZ) to the cortical plate (CP). Migrating neurons (MN) travel up the radial glial fibers (RG) to reach the cortical plate. From *Neurobiology of Neocortex*, P. Rakic and W. Singer (Eds.). Copyright 1987 John Wiley & Sons Limited. Reproduced with permission.

generation of synapses (synaptogenesis) begins around the time of birth and reaches a peak around 150% of adult levels toward the end of the first year. In the frontal cortex (the anterior portion of cortex, considered by most investigators to be critical for many higher cognitive abilities), the peak of synaptic density occurs later, at around 24 months of age (but see Goldman-Rakic, Bourgeois, & Rakic, 1997). Although there may be variation in the time-table, in all regions of cortex studied so far, synaptogenesis begins around the time of birth and increases to a peak level well above that observed in adults.

Somewhat surprisingly, regressive events are commonly observed during the development of nerve cells and their connections in the brain. For example, in the primary visual cortex the

FIGURE 4.3 Drawings of the cellular structure of the human visual cortex based on Golgi stain preparations from Conel (1939–1967). Reprinted by permission of the publisher from *Postnatal Development of Human Cerebral Cortex*, Vols. 1–8 by J. L. Conel, Cambridge, MA: Harvard University Press, Copyright 1939–1967 by the President and Fellows of Harvard College.

mean density of synapses per neuron starts to decrease at the end of the first year of life (e.g., Huttenlocher, 1990). In humans, most cortical regions and pathways appear to undergo this "rise and fall" in synaptic density, with the density stabilizing to adult levels during later childhood. The postnatal rise and fall developmental sequence can also be seen in other measures of brain physiology and anatomy. For example, PET studies of children can measure the glucose uptake of regions of the brain. Glucose uptake is necessary in regions of the brain that are active, and because it is transported by the blood is also a measure of blood flow. Using this method, Chugani, Phelps, & Mazziotta (1987) observed an adult-like distribution of resting brain activity within and across brain regions by the end of the first year. However, the overall level of glucose uptake reaches a peak during early childhood that is much higher than that observed in adults. These rates returned to adult levels after about 9 years of age for some cortical regions. The extent to which these changes relate to those in synaptic density is currently the topic of further investigation.

Recently, magnetic resonance imaging (MRI) has been used to study the postnatal development of brain structure. Specifically, the increased lipid content of brain structures caused by myelinization provides a clear gray–white matter contrast that allows quantitative volume measurements of brain regions in infancy and childhood. Using this method, the consensus is that brain structures have the overall appearance of those in the adult by 2 years of age, and that all the major fiber tracts can be observed by 3 years of age (Matsuzawa et al., 2001; Paus et al., 2001). Some reports suggest that after a rapid increase in gray matter up to 4 years of age, there is then a prolonged period of slight decline that extends into the adult years (Pfefferbaum et al., 1994). Whether this decline is due to the dendritic and synaptic pruning described above remains unknown (Matsuzawa et al., 2001). Building on the evidence for individual variability in the rise and fall in the developmental trajectory of gray matter, Shaw and colleagues (2006) demonstrated from MRI images that it is the trajectory of change in cortical thickness, and not the thickness itself, that best predicts a measure of intelligence (IQ). In this study, more intelligent children (as assessed by IQ) went through a larger and clearer pattern of rise and fall in their cortical thickness between 7 and 19 years of age than did those with more average intelligence scores. This groundbreaking study suggests that differences in the dynamic changes that occur during development are critical for our understanding of individual differences in intelligence and cognition in adults.

Changes in the extent of white matter are of interest because they reflect inter-regional communication in the developing brain. Although increases in white matter continue through adolescence into adulthood, particularly in frontal brain regions (Giedd et al., 1999), the most rapid changes occur during the first two years. For example, at around 8–12 months of age the white matter associated with the frontal, parietal, and occipital lobes becomes apparent (Paus et al., 2001).

DIFFERENTIATION OF THE CEREBRAL CORTEX

A controversial issue in developmental neuroscience concerns the extent to which the differentiation of the cerebral cortex into areas or regions with particular cognitive, perceptual, or motor functions can be shaped by postnatal interactions with the external world. This issue reflects the debate in cognitive development about whether infants are born with domain-specific "modules" for particular cognitive functions such as language, or whether the formation of such modules is an experience-dependent process (see Elman et al., 1996; Karmiloff-Smith, 1992, Mareschal et al., 2007). Brodmann (1912) was one of the first to propose a scheme for the division of cortex into structural areas assumed to have differing functional properties. A century of neuropsychology has taught us that the majority of normal adults tend to have similar functions within approximately the same regions of cortex, but we cannot necessarily infer from this that this pattern of differentiation is intrinsically prespecified ("pre-wired"), because most humans share very similar prenatal and postnatal environments. In developmental neurobiology this issue has focused on the relative importance of neural activity for cortical differentiation, as opposed to intrinsic molecular and genetic specification of cortical areas. Supporting the importance of the latter processes,

Rakic (1988) proposed that the differentiation of the cortex into areas is due to a protomap. The hypothesized protomap involves either prespecification of the proliferative zone or intrinsic molecular markers that guide the division of cortex into particular areas. One mechanism for this would be through the radial glial fiber path from the proliferative zone to the cortex discussed earlier. By this view the differentiation of cortex is mainly due to the unfolding of a genetic plan implemented by molecular markers. The alternative viewpoint, advanced by O'Leary (1989) among others, is that genetic and molecular factors build an initially undifferentiated protocortex, but that the cortex subsequently becomes divided into specialized areas as a result of activity within neural circuits. This activity within neural circuits need not be the result of input from the external world, but may result from intrinsic, spontaneous patterns of firing within sensory organs or subcortical structures that feed into cortex, or from activity within the cortex itself (e.g., Katz & Shatz, 1996).

This debate in developmental neurobiology has elicited a very large number of empirical studies. Reviews of this literature have agreed on a middle ground in view in which gradients of gene expression across the developing cortex define large-scale regions (Kingsbury & Finlay, 2001; Pallas, 2001; Ragsdale & Grove, 2001). However, with a few exceptions, these large-scale regions generally do not map onto the detailed functional areas observed in the adult mammal. Specifically, Kingsbury and Finlay (2001) suggested that multiple dimensions of cell structure relevant to stimulus processing are laid out such that "regions" arise combinatorially as a result of particular sensory thalamic input overlaid by large-scale gradients in patterns of neurotransmitter expression, axon extension, and neuromodulator production. For example, a region might emerge that has visual input, high levels of certain **neurotransmitters**, and short-range connections. Such a region may initially be ill-defined and lack specialization, but will be better at performing some types of computation than neighboring regions. Sub-parts of this region may become "recruited" for certain computational functions (Elman et al., 1996; Johnson, 2000; Mareschal et al., 2007). This process could result in the cortical region fragmenting into a series of functionally distinct areas. However, it is important to note that the genes concerned are not usually expressed within the clearly defined boundaries of particular *functional* areas, but define larger-scale areas and gradients across areas of cortex. Thus, mutated genes that are expressed during development of cortex are unlikely to be confined to specific cortical functional areas, and are even less likely to show clear mappings onto precise cognitive functions. Consistent with this, mouse models of genetic disorders have shown that there is rarely a simple neat mapping between a single gene mutation and a single phenotypic outcome (Cattanach, Peters, Ball, & Rasberry, 2000; Crabbe, Wahlsten, & Dudek, 1999; Homanics et al., 1997; Keverne, 1997).

In summary, while the general sequence of human prenatal and postnatal brain development follows closely that of other mammals, the prolonged time course of development in humans reveals a differential time course for different cortical areas. In addition, the greatly extended period of postnatal development in humans allows greater scope for functional and structural development to be influenced by the environment than in most other species.

POSTNATAL DEVELOPMENT AND BEHAVIORAL CHANGE

The following review of relations between postnatal brain specialization and cognitive development is necessarily selective (see Johnson, 2011, for a more detailed review). These specific lines of research illustrate broader principles about interactions between brain and behavioral development. As discussed earlier, the activity-dependent specialization of the cerebral cortex begins prenatally, but extends well into postnatal life in humans. We may expect that both for different domains of cognition and for different areas of cortex, there will be different timetables of specialization. Cerebral cortical connections to other regions of the brain that become specified earlier, such as the hippocampus and thalamus, may serve to further shape the emerging specificity of regions of cerebral cortex.

Vision

A variety of lines of evidence indicate that the primary visual cortex is processing input from birth in primates. In recent years investigators have begun to use functional imaging to see what visual pathways and structures can be activated at different ages. Due to the difficulties of keeping young infants still for long enough, fMRI studies with this population typically involve sedated infants being scanned for clinical reasons. Nevertheless, the studies have demonstrated that sedated and sleeping infants respond to visual stimulation in some of the same visual cortical regions as adults (Born, Rostrup, Leth, Peitersen, & Lou, 1996; Born, Rostrup, Miranda, Larsson, & Lou, 2002; Yamada et al., 1997, 2000). These findings have been confirmed in healthy awake infants using the new technique of optical imaging (NIRS). Following on from an earlier study with a single site (Meek et al., 1998), Taga, Asakawa, Maki, Konishi, and Koizumi (2003) used a multi-channel optical system to study blood oxygenation in occipital and frontal sites while 2- to 4-month-olds viewed dynamic schematic face-like patterns. The results demonstrated that a localized area of the occipital cortex responded to brief changes in luminance contrasts in the form of event-related changes in blood oxygenation similar to those seen in adults. More importantly, this study helped establish that this technique can be used in the near future to explore visual function during early infancy.

Ocular dominance columns are functional and anatomical structures observed in layer IV of the primary visual cortex. These columns arise from the segregation of inputs from the two eyes. In other words, neurons in a single ocular dominance column are dominated by input from one eye in adult mammals. Ocular dominance columns are thought to be the stage of processing necessary to achieve binocular vision. Held (1985) reviewed converging evidence that binocular vision develops at approximately the end of the fourth month of life in human infants. One of the abilities associated with binocular vision, stereoacuity, increases very rapidly from the onset of stereopsis, such that it reaches adult levels within a few weeks. This is in contrast to other measures of acuity, such as grating acuity, which are thought to increase much more gradually. Held suggested that this very rapid spurt in stereoacuity requires some equally rapid change in the neural substrate supporting it. On the basis of evidence from animal studies, he proposed that this substrate is the development of ocular dominance columns found in layer IV of the primary visual cortex. Although Held's proposal was initially based on a simple causal association between the formation of ocular dominance columns and the onset of binocularity, more recent research has provided a closer link between the processes of change at the two levels.

As mentioned earlier, processes of selective loss commonly contribute to the sculpting of specific pathways in the cortex. Neurophysiological evidence indicates that the geniculocortical afferents from the two eyes are initially mixed so that they synapse on common cortical neurons in layer IV. These layer IV cells project to disparity selective cells (possibly in cortical layers II and III). During ontogeny, geniculate axons originating from one eye withdraw from the region leaving behind axons from the other eye. Held suggested that it is these events at the neural level that give rise to the sudden increase in stereoacuity observed by behavioral measures at around 4 months of age in the human infant.

This process of selective loss has the consequence that information from the two eyes that was previously combined in layer IV of the primary visual cortex becomes segregated (Held, 1993). Specifically, there will be a certain degree of integration between the eyes that will decline once each neuron receives innervation from only one eye. Held and colleagues (see Held, 1993) tested this hypothesis by showing that younger infants (under 4 months) can perform certain types of integration between the two eyes that older infants cannot.

The loss of these connections is probably due to the refinement of synapses by selective loss. The refinement of synapses probably occurs through activity-dependent neural mechanisms because the formation of ocular dominance columns can be experimentally blocked by reducing neuronal activity (Stryker & Harris, 1986). Monocular deprivation (Wiesel & Hubel, 1965) also results in abnormal ocular dominance columns; in this case, the eye that is preserved takes over more than its normal share of cortical area. Based on these experimental findings, Miller and colleagues (Miller, 1990; Miller, Keller, & Stryker, 1989) developed a neural network model of ocular dominance column development that depends on correlated neuronal firing within an eye and the comparatively uncorrelated firing between the two eyes. Whether these patterns of firing originate from spontaneous intrinsic firing or from visual experience may not matter so long as there is greater correlation within an eye than between the eyes.

In summary, while at least some visual cortical areas can be activated from birth in humans, there is clearly considerable functional refinement of these areas over the first year. One example of this refinement is the emergence of brain areas responsive to integrated binocular input around 4 months of age. While visual cortical areas can be activated from early on, the question remains whether this activation actually influences the behavior of the infant. This question is addressed in the next section.

Attention and Visually Guided Action

Over the first few months of life infants' main way of interacting with their physical environment is through shifts of eye gaze and attention. This is why most of what we have learned about the mental life of infants has come from tasks in which some measure of looking behavior is utilized (Aslin, 2007). In one of the first attempts to relate changes in behavior to brain development in infants, Bronson (1974, 1982) argued that visually guided action in the newborn human infant is controlled primarily by the subcortical retino-collicular visual pathway, and that it is only by 2 or 3 months of age that the control over visually guided behavior switches to cortical pathways.

As discussed above, it has become evident that there is some, albeit limited, cortical visual activity in newborns, and that the onset of cortical functioning probably proceeds by a series of graded steps, rather than in an all-or-none manner. Correspondingly, neurophysiological research on monkeys and neuropsychological research with human adults has revealed multiple pathways involved in eye movement control and attention shifts in the primate brain. For brevity, only three of these pathways will be discussed here: (1) the pathway from the eye to the superior colliculus (this subcortical pathway has heavy input from the temporal visual field, and is thought to be important for rapid reflexive eye movements to easily discriminable stimuli); (2) a pathway from the primary visual cortex (V1) on to temporal lobe areas, such as area MT (believed to play an important role in the detection of motion and smooth tracking); and (3) a pathway from V1 to other visual cortical regions, and then on to the parietal cortex and the frontal eye fields (FEFs). Structures on this third pathway are thought to be involved in more complex aspects of eye movement planning and attention, such as "anticipatory" **saccades** (which predict the location of a visual target) and learning sequences of scanning patterns. One challenge in developmental neuroscience has been to relate the development of these various pathways to the competencies of the infant at different ages. Until recently, this has mainly involved two complementary approaches: predictions about the sequence of development of the pathways based on developmental neuroanatomy (Atkinson, 1984; Johnson, 1990), and the use of behavioral marker tasks to ascertain the functional development of particular structures or pathways.

Johnson (1990) proposed a hypothesis about the sequence of development of the above pathways, and used this neural level prediction to generate further hypotheses about changes in visually guided behavior in infants. Specifically, Johnson argued that the developmental state of the primary visual cortex determines which of the pathways receives structured input. By using information about the developmental neuroanatomy of the primary visual cortex, Johnson (1990) hypothesized a particular sequence of postnatal development of the pathways underlying oculomotor control.

Specifically, he speculated that the best functioning pathway in the newborn infant was the subcortical pathway from the eye directly to the superior colliculus, and possibly also some cortical projections from the deeper layers of V1 to superior colliculus. Evidence from newborn infants that supported this hypothesis included that the visual tracking of a moving stimulus in the first few months of life is not smooth but saccadic, and that these eye movements always lag behind the movement of the stimulus, rather than predicting its trajectory (Aslin, 1981). A second characteristic of newborn visually guided behavior consistent with the largely subcortical control is that newborns orient more readily toward stimuli in the temporal, as opposed to the nasal, visual field (e.g., Lewis, Maurer & Milewski, 1979). Posner and Rothbart (1980) suggested that midbrain structures such as the superior colliculus can be driven most readily by temporal field input. Finally, infants in the first few months of life do not attend to stationary pattern elements within a larger frame or pattern (e.g., Maurer, 1983) unless these elements are moving (Bushnell, 1979). One important question that remained unresolved is whether the subcortical visual pathway, in isolation of the cortical pathways, can drive saccades on its own in infants. This issue was addressed by Braddick et al. (1992), who studied two infants who had undergone complete hemispherectomy (removal of the cortex on one side) to alleviate severe epilepsy. They established that these infants were able to make directed eye movements to targets that appeared in their "cortically blind" visual field, indicating that the subcortical (collicular) pathway is capable of supporting saccades in the absence of the cortex in human infants. Johnson (1990) argued that by 2 months of age further development of middle layers in V1 would allow output to the pathway involving structure(s) MT/MST (sometimes known as V5). In accord with this prediction, at this age infants should begin to show periods of smooth visual tracking and become sensitive to coherent motion in visual input. Both of these predictions are consistent with the available behavioral data (Johnson, 1990; Wattam-Bell, 1991).

Johnson suggested that further growth of dendrites within the upper layers of the primary visual cortex could strengthen projections to other cortical areas around 3 months of age, thus allowing pathways to the frontal eye fields to become functional. This neuroanatomical development may allow infants to make anticipatory eye movements and learn sequences of looking patterns, both functions associated with the frontal eye fields. With regard to the visual tracking of a moving object, at 3 months infants not only show smooth tracking, but their eye movements often predict the movement of the stimulus in an anticipatory manner.

Consistent with Johnson's model, behavioral marker tasks for the parietal cortex, frontal eye fields, and dorsolateral prefrontal cortex (DLPFC) all show rapid development of abilities between 2 and 6 months of age. However, data recently collected from functional imaging suggest that the original model requires some modification. Specifically, a more direct assessment of the hypotheses advanced in the Johnson model can be provided by ERP measures (time-locked to the initiation of the eye-movements; Balaban & Weinstein, 1985; Csibra, Tucker, & Johnson, 1997). By time-locking to the onset of eye movements we can examine the brain events that precede the production of this simple action. In adults such experiments reveal characteristic pre-saccadic components recorded over the parietal cortex prior to the execution of saccades. The clearest of these components is the pre-saccadic "spike potential" (SP), a sharp positive-going deflection that precedes the saccade by 8–20 ms (Csibra et al.,

1997). The spike potential is observed in most saccade tasks in adults, and is therefore thought to represent an important stage of cortical processing required to generate a saccade. Csibra, Tucker, and Johnson (1998) investigated whether there are pre-saccadic potentials recordable over parietal leads in 6-month-old infants. Given the prediction that by this age infants have essentially the same pathways active for saccade planning as do adults, we were surprised to find no evidence of this component (Figure 4.4) in our infants (see also Kurtzberg & Vaughan, 1982; Richards, 2008). This finding suggests that the target-driven saccades performed by 6-month-olds were controlled largely by subcortical routes for visually guided responses mediated by the superior colliculus.

Because this result was surprising, we conducted two follow-up studies. In one of these we tested 12-month-olds with the same procedure. These older infants did show a spike potential like that observed in adults, though somewhat smaller in amplitude (Figure 4.4). The other study explored whether the dorsal pathway could be activated in very young infants through a more demanding saccade task. Specifically, we compared ERPs before reactive (target-elicited) and anticipatory (endogenous) saccades in 4-month-old infants (Csibra et al., 2001). We were not able to record any reliable posterior activity prior to either reactive or anticipatory eye-movements. Thus, even when the saccade is generated by cortical computation of the likely location of the next stimulus, as in the case of anticipatory eye-movements, posterior cortical structures do not seem to be involved in the planning of this action.

In all these infant ERP studies, although there was a lack of evidence for posterior structure control over eye movements in our experiments with 6-month-olds, we observed effects recorded over frontal leads. These saccade-related effects were consistent with the frontal eye field disinhibition of subcortical (collicular) circuits when a central foveated stimulus is removed (Csibra et al., 1998, 2001). In brief, we interpreted these findings in terms of the frontal eye fields helping to maintain fixation on to foveated stimuli by inhibiting collicular circuits. This is consistent with the predictions of the Johnson (1990) model. However, when saccades to peripheral stimuli are made, the ERP evidence indicated that these are largely initiated by collicular circuits, sometimes as a consequence of inhibition being released by the frontal eye fields.

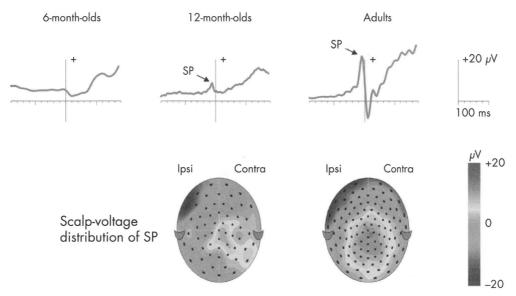

FIGURE 4.4 Presaccadic potentials recorded over a parietal site in adults, 12-month-olds, and 6-month-old infants. Only the adults and 12-month-olds show clear spike potentials.

In a converging line of thinking, Canfield and colleagues argued on the basis of behavioral and further neuroanatomical evidence that the FEF pathway would precede the more posterior pathways developmentally (Canfield et al., 1997). This early involvement of the FEF pathway could be consistent with a skill-learning hypothesis in which more anterior structures get activated earlier than posterior circuits. By this interpretation, there is greater involvement of frontal cortex circuitry in infants because they are still acquiring the skill of planning and executing eye movements.

The discussion so far has concerned overt shifts of attention due to eye and head movements, but it is evident that adults are also capable of shifting their attention covertly (without moving the receptors). Research on the neural basis of the development of covert attention in childhood has only just begun, and has been based on three topics: (1) ERP studies, (2) effects of early cortical damage, and (3) developmental disorders of genetic origin. Richards (2003) describes several experiments in which he has used the spatial cueing procedure while recording ERPs from infants in order to detect neural signatures of covert attention. In one study he examined the "P1 validity effect" in young infants. The P1 is a large positive ERP component that occurs around 100 ms after stimulus presentation. Studies with adult participants have shown that the P1 is enhanced in scale in valid trials (where the cue correctly predicts the target) (Hillyard, Mangun, Woldorff, & Luck, 1995). This is of interest because this short-latency component reflects early stages of visual processing, demonstrating that shifts of covert attention modulate early sensory processing of the target. Richards (2003) reported that, although there was little ERP evidence for covert attention shifts in 3-month-old infants, by 5 months the pattern of ERP data resembled that in adults indicating that infants at this age were shifting attention to the cued location covertly.

Another way to examine the neural basis of covert orienting in development has been to assess the consequences of perinatal damage to the cerebral cortex. We examined spatial cueing in infants who had unfortunately suffered perinatal damage to one of four quadrants of the cortex (Johnson, Tucker, Stiles, & Trauner, 1998). The results were somewhat surprising in that the posterior lesions that would normally cause deficits in adults had no effect on the infants. In contrast, frontal damage had a measurable effect on spatial cueing. Although surprising, these results fit well with work from other laboratories. For example, Craft, Shatz, and colleagues have studied the consequences of perinatal brain injury (sometime associated with sickle cell anemia) on performance in spatial cueing tasks during childhood. In several studies deficits were observed following anterior (frontal) damage, and not (or less) with posterior damage (Craft, White, Park, & Figiel, 1994; Schatz, Craft, Koby, & DeBaun, 2000; Schatz, Craft, White, Park, & Figiel, 2001).

A third way to address the neurodevelopment of covert attention is to study disorders of this process in groups of atypically developing children. ADHD (attention deficit/hyperactivity disorder) is characterized by inattention, hyperactivity, and impulsivity beginning before 7 years of age (Karatekin, 2001). Estimates for its prevalence run as high as 3–5% of school children in the USA, although this figure varies enormously across cultures. Despite its title, there is no general agreement about specific deficits in components of attention in these children. Rather, they appear to have mild difficulties in some tests of sustained and selective attention that may reflect difficulties in processing attended stimuli and/or in maintaining attention in tasks that make demands on cognitive resources (see Karetekin, 2001, for review).

Another manifestation of the endogenous control of attention concerns so-called "sustained" attention. Sustained attention refers to the ability to maintain the direction of attention toward a stimulus even in the presence of distracters. Richards (2008) discovered characteristic decreases in heart rate that can serve as a marker for sustained attention in infants. These heart rate defined periods of sustained attention usually last for between 5 and 15 s after the onset of a complex stimulus, and during these periods it takes around twice as long for infants to shift their gaze toward a stimulus presented in the periphery as compared to when heart rate has returned to pre-stimulus presentation levels. Furthermore, those saccades that are made to a peripheral stimulus during sustained attention are less accurate than normal and involve multiple hypometric (shorter than necessary to reach the target) saccades, characteristics of superior colliculus generated saccades (Richards, 2008). Thus, the lack of distractibility during periods of sustained attention is likely to be due to cortically mediated pathways inhibiting collicular mechanisms.

To summarize, even a form of action as apparently simple as shifting the eyes involves multiple cortical and subcortical pathways. This observation illustrates the point that most psychological accounts of behavioral development that do not take account of brain systems are likely to grossly underestimate the complexity of the underlying computations. Even if multiple pathways involved in oculomotor control are likely to have some unique functions, behavioral responses in most real-world situations are likely to engage several pathways. To some extent, these pathways may have a hierarchical organization, with the latest developing pathways (commonly frontal) providing the basis of endogenous voluntary action. Pathways present in the newborn have less cortical involvement and tend to be more reflexive in nature.

The Development of the Social Brain

One of the major characteristics of the human brain is its social nature. As adults, we have areas of the brain specialized for processing and integrating sensory information about the appearance, behavior, and intentions of other humans. A variety of cortical areas have been implicated in the "social brain," including the superior temporal sulcus (STS), the fusiform "face area" (FFA), and orbitofrontal cortex (for reviews, see Adolphs, 2003 and Grossmann & Johnson, 2007). One of the major debates in cognitive neuroscience concerns the origins of the "social brain" in humans, and theoretical arguments abound about the extent to which this is acquired through experience.

The ability to detect and recognize faces is commonly considered to be a good example of human perceptual abilities, as well as being the basis of our adaptation as social animals. There is a long history of research on the development of face recognition in young infants extending back to the studies of Fantz more than 45 years ago (e.g., Fantz, 1964). Over the past decade numerous papers have addressed the cortical basis of face processing in adults, including identifying areas that may be specifically dedicated to this purpose (de Haan, 2008). Despite these bodies of data, surprisingly little is known about the developmental cognitive neuroscience of face processing.

De Schonen and Mathivet (1989) and Johnson and Morton (1991; Morton & Johnson, 1991) speculated that the preferential responding to faces observed in newborn infants may be largely mediated by the **subcortical** visuo-motor pathway (see previous section), whereas later developing abilities to recognize individual faces (on the basis of internal features) are mediated by the ventral stream of visual cortical processing. Although cortical regions such as the parietal cortex (discussed in the previous section) are part of the so-called dorsal ("how") pathway for visual processing, the ventral pathway extends from visual cortex to regions of the temporal lobe involved in object and face recognition, and is sometimes termed the "what" pathway (see Milner & Goodale, 1995).

Much research has focused on the two systems postulated by Johnson and Morton (1991). With regard to newborns' responses to faces, the majority of behavioral studies to date have found some evidence for sensitivity to face-like patterns (see Johnson, 2011). Although views still vary as to the specificity of this newborn bias, we have speculated that the face bias ("Conspec") was mediated largely, but not necessarily exclusively, by subcortical visuo-motor pathways. This proposal was originally made for several reasons: (1) that the newborn preference declined at the same age as other newborn reflexes assumed to be under subcortical control, (2) evidence from the maturation of the visual system indicating later development of cortical visual pathways, and (3) evidence from another species (the domestic chick). Due to the continuing difficulty in successfully using functional imaging with healthy awake newborns, this hypothesis has, as yet, only been indirectly addressed. First, de Schonen and colleagues examined face preferences in a number of infants with perinatal damage to regions of cortex. Even in cases of damage to the visual cortex, the bias to orient to faces remained (Mancini et al., 1998). The second line of evidence used the fact that the nasal and temporal visual fields feed differentially into the cortical and subcortical visual pathways. Specifically, Simion and colleagues predicted that the face bias would be found in the temporal visual field, but not the nasal visual field. This prediction was confirmed (Simion, Valenza, Umilta, & Dalla Barba, 1998). A third line of evidence comes from a large number of adult neuropsychological and neuroimaging studies showing evidence for a subcortical "quick and dirty" route for face processing (see Johnson, 2005 for review). Analysis of these studies reveals that the adult subcortical route rapidly processes low spatial frequency "coarse" information about faces, and then modulates activity in the face-sensitive cortical areas that process fine detailed information about faces. The visual stimuli that maximally elicit activity in the adult subcortical route are strikingly similar to those to which newborns preferentially orient, strongly suggesting that this route is the basis for newborn behavior (Johnson, 2005).

Although Johnson and Morton (1991) identified the superior colliculus as a major visuomotor structure that could be involved in determining Conspec preferences, the pulvinar and the amygdala are also known to be involved in the adult subcortical route (Johnson, 2005). Our knowledge of the pulvinar has increased dramatically over the past decade, and the description of its function makes it now a candidate for involvement in newborn visual preferences. Specifically, portions of pulvinar receive input directly from the superior colliculus (as well as from the retina and, at least in adults, striate and extrastriate visual cortex). Additionally, in adults there are reciprocal connections to frontal, temporal, and parietal regions and to anterior cingulate and amygdala. The advent of new technology suitable for studying the neural correlates of behavior in newborns may allow further investigation of this issue.

I now turn to the neurodevelopment of face processing during infancy and childhood. Several laboratories have examined changes in ERPs as adults view faces. In particular, interest has focused on an ERP component termed the "N170" (because it is a negative-going deflection that occurs after around 170 ms) that has been strongly associated with face processing in a number of studies on adults (see de Haan, 2008 for review). Specifically, the amplitude and latency of this component vary according to whether or not faces are present in the visual field of the adult volunteer under study. An important aspect of the N170 in adults is that its response is highly selective. For example, the N170 shows a different response to human upright faces than to very closely related stimuli such as inverted human faces and upright monkey faces (de Haan, 2008). Although the exact underlying neural generators of the N170 are currently still debated, the specificity of response of the N170 can be taken as an index of the degree of specialization of cortical processing for human upright faces. For this reason de Haan and colleagues undertook a series of studies on the development of the N170 over the first weeks and months of postnatal life.

The first issue we addressed in these developmental ERP studies was when does the face-sensitive N170 emerge? In a series of experiments we have identified a component in the infant ERP that has many of the properties associated with the adult N170, but that is of a slightly longer latency (240–290 ms; de Haan, Humphrey, & Johnson, 2002; Halit, Csibra, Volein, & Johnson, 2004; Halit, de Haan, & Johnson, 2003). In studying the response properties of this potential at 3, 6, and 12 months of age we have discovered that (1) the component is present from at least 3 months of age (although its development continues into middle childhood) and (2) the component becomes more specifically tuned to human upright faces with increasing age. To expand on the second point, we found that while 12-month-olds and adults show different ERP responses to upright and inverted faces, 3- and 6-month-olds do not (de Haan et al., 2002; Halit et al., 2003). Thus, the study of this face-sensitive ERP component is consistent with the idea of increased specialization of cortical processing with age, a result also consistent with some behavioral results (see below).

Recently, a number of fMRI studies of the neurodevelopment of face processing in children have been published (for review see Johnson, Grossmann, & Cohen-Kadosh 2009). These studies can potentially inform us about changes in the degree of localization and functional specialization of the cortical face network. All of the studies conducted to date were able to show that certain regions of the cortex show reliable activation to faces from at least mid-childhood. Most studies found evidence for dynamic changes in the extent of cortical tissue activated between children and adults (including activation of additional areas that are not typically found in the mature adult brain), and some also provided evidence for increasing functional specialization (degree of face specificity) with age or experience. For example, Scherf, Behrmann, Humphreys, & Luna (2007) used naturalistic movies of faces, objects, buildings, and navigation scenes in a passive viewing task with children (5–8 years), adolescents (11–14 years), and adults. They found that the children exhibited similar patterns of activation of the face processing areas commonly reported in adults (such as the fusiform face area). However, this activation was not selective for the category of face stimuli; the regions were equally strongly activated by objects and landscapes. Moreover, this lack of fine-tuning of classical face processing areas stood in contrast to distinct preferential activation patterns for other object categories (occipital object areas and the parahippocampal place area). In a similar study, Golarai et al. (2007) tested children (7–11 years), adolescents (12–16 years), and adults with static object categories (faces, objects, places, and scrambled abstract patterns). They found substantially larger right FFA and left parahippocampal volumes of selective activation in adults than in children. Although this increase in functionally defined areas with development may initially appear to contradict predictions of the IS (interactive specialization) view, it is important to note that the contrasts employed defined the increase as an expansion of the area of category-specific activation of FFA. The developmental changes observed in these fMRI studies thus provide strong support for the gradual emergence of specifically tuned functions within the cerebral cortex (Johnson, 2001).

Converging evidence about the increasing specialization of face processing during development comes from a behavioral study that set out to test the intriguing idea that, as processing "narrows" (Nelson, 2001) to human faces, infants will lose their ability to discriminate non-human faces (Pascalis, de Haan, & Nelson, 2002). Pascalis and colleagues demonstrated that, if 6-month-olds could discriminate between individual monkey faces as well as human faces, 9-month-olds and adults could only discriminate the human faces. These results are particularly compelling because they demonstrate a predicted competence in young infants that is not evident in adults.

Before leaving the topic of face and individual face recognition, I should note that there is some evidence that infants in the first week of life are able to identify their mother (e.g., Pascalis, de Schonen, Morton, Fabre-Grenet, & Deruelle, 1995). At first sight this evidence seems to conflict with the view that cortical face processing does not emerge until at least the second month. However, this discriminative ability in newborns is based only on the general shape of the head and hair, and not on facial configuration or features. De Schonen, Mancini, and Leigeois (1998) argued that this "third system" is a non-specific visual pattern learning ability which has also been evident from studies with visual patterns of many other kinds. Johnson and de Haan have modified the original Johnson and Morton two-process theory to take account of early hippocampal based learning (see de Haan, Johnson, Maurer, & Perrett, 2001).

Moving beyond the relatively simple perception of faces, a more complex attribute of the adult social brain is processing information about the eyes of other humans. There are two important aspects of processing information about the eyes. The first of these is being able to detect the direction of another's gaze in order to direct your own attention to the same object or spatial location. Perception of averted gaze can elicit an automatic shift of attention in the same direction in adults (Driver et al., 1999), allowing the establishment of "joint attention" (Butterworth & Jarrett, 1991). Joint attention to objects is thought to be crucial for a number of aspects of cognitive and social development, including word learning. The second critical aspect of gaze perception is the detection of direct gaze, enabling mutual gaze with the viewer. Mutual gaze (eye contact) provides the main mode of establishing a communicative context between humans and is believed to be important for normal social development (e.g., Kleinke, 1986; Symons, Hains, & Muir, 1998). It is commonly agreed that eye gaze perception is important for mother–infant interaction and that it provides a vital foundation for social development (e.g., Jaffe, Stern, & Peery, 1973; Stern, 1977).

In a series of experiments with 4-month-old infants using a simple eye gaze cueing paradigm, Farroni, Mansfield, Lai, and Johnson (2003) established that it is only following a period of mutual gaze with an upright face that cueing effects are observed. In other words, mutual gaze with an upright face may engage mechanisms of attention such that the viewing infant is more likely to be cued by subsequent motion. In summary, the critical features for eye gaze cueing in young infants are (1) lateral motion of elements and (2) a brief preceding period of eye contact with an upright face.

Following the surprising observation that a period of direct gaze is required before cueing can be effective in infants, we investigated the earliest developmental roots of eye contact detection. It is already known that human newborns have a bias to orient toward face-like stimuli (see earlier), prefer faces with eyes opened (Batki, Baron-Cohen, Wheelwright, Connellan, & Ahluwalia, 2000), and tend to imitate certain facial gestures (Meltzoff & Moore, 1977). Preferential attention to faces with direct gaze would provide the most compelling evidence to date that human newborns are born prepared to detect socially relevant information. For this reason we investigated eye gaze detection in humans from birth. Farroni, Csibra, and Johnson (2002) tested healthy human newborn infants by presenting them with a pair of stimuli, one a face with eye gaze directed straight at the newborns and the other with averted gaze. Results showed that the fixation times were significantly longer for the face with the direct gaze. Furthermore, the number of orientations was higher with the straight gaze than with the averted gaze.

In a second experiment, we attempted to gain converging evidence for the differential processing of direct gaze in infants, by recording ERPs from the scalp as infants viewed faces. We studied 4-month-old babies with the same stimuli as those used in the previous experiment with newborns, and found a difference between the two gaze directions at the time and scalp location at the previously identified face-sensitive component of the infant ERP discussed earlier. Our conclusion from these studies is that direct eye contact enhances the perceptual processing of faces in 4-month-old infants. This conclusion was reinforced by recent experiments analyzing high-frequency EEG bursting in the gamma (40 Hz) range (Grossman, Johnson, Farroni, & Csibra, 2007). Gamma oscillations are of interest partly because they correlate with the blood-oxygen-level-dependent (BOLD) response used in fMRI. Grossmann, Johnson, Farroni, and Csibra (2007) predicted a burst of gamma oscillation over prefrontal sites to direct gaze if gamma oscillations are indeed related to detecting eye contact/communicative intent as suggested by adult fMRI work (Schilbach et al., 2006). The data revealed that gamma oscillations varied as a function of gaze direction only in the context of an upright face, which extended the previous ERP results. As predicted, direct gaze within an upright face also elicited a late (300 ms) induced gamma burst over right prefrontal channels. A similar result was also obtained with a different imaging method, NIRS, and we observed convergence between the two methods in individual infants (Grossmann et al., 2008).

Eye contact serves as an important ostensive signal in face-to-face interactions that helps in establishing a communicative link between two people. Successful communication between two people may well depend crucially on the ability to detect the intention to communicate conveyed by signals directed at the self such as making eye contact. On a neural level, the medial prefrontal cortex (MPFC) is consistently activated when gaze is directed at, but not when gaze is averted away from, the self (Schilbach et al., 2006). Because gamma oscillations measured with EEG are correlated with the BOLD response used in fMRI (Fiebach et al., 2006; Foucher, Otzenberger, & Gounot, 2003), eye contact detection in 4-month-old infants may well recruit some of the same brain regions as in adults. However, the gamma burst distributed over right frontal cortex in infants might reflect less localized functional activity than in adults, suggesting a more diffuse to a more focal pattern of cortical activity with age.

In summary, the human brain is adapted to develop within an intensely social environment, and the adult social brain network is the inevitable result of cortical and subcortical biases ensuring that the infant's brain attends toward and processes information about this social world. Beyond face processing and eye gaze detection, there are many more complex aspects of the social brain such as the coherent perception of human action and the appropriate attribution of intentions and goals to conspecifics. Investigating the cognitive neuroscience of these abilities in infants and children will be a challenge for the next decade (see Grossmann & Johnson, 2007).

Memory

Although learning is clearly important in psychological development, it is sometimes difficult to tease apart specific memory processes from general developmental plasticity. One of the first specific hypotheses advanced about the neurodevelopment of memory was that the brain mechanisms necessary for the long-term storage of information, most probably in the limbic system, are not functional for the first year or two of life (Bachevalier & Mishkin, 1984; Schacter & Moscovitch, 1984). These authors pointed to similarities between the amnesic syndrome (in which limbic system damage in adults results in deficits in recognition memory but relative sparing of learning stimulus-response "habits") and the behavioral profile of memory abilities in infants. Mishkin and colleagues had earlier demonstrated that a similar pattern of deficits to that observed in human amnesic syndrome patients could be seen in adult monkeys following surgical lesions to portions of the limbic system. These observations led to the proposal that the profile of infant memory abilities reflected the relatively delayed postnatal maturation of limbic circuitry.

To test the hypothesis that "cognitive memory" and "habit" systems show a different ontogenetic timetable, Bachevalier and Mishkin (1984) examined the performance of infant monkeys on two types of tasks. The first task was a visual recognition task involving learning to identify the novel object of a pair (delayed non-match to sample, DNMS). This task was hypothesized to require a "cognitive memory" system. In the second visual discrimination habit task, the infant monkey was sequentially exposed to 20 pairs of objects every day. Every day the same object of each pair was baited with a food reward, even though their relative positions were varied. The monkeys had to learn to displace the correct object in each pair.

Although infant monkeys failed to learn the "cognitive memory" task until they were over 4 months (and did not reach adult levels of proficiency even by the end of the first year),

3-month-old monkeys were able to learn the visual "habit" as easily as adults. Bachevalier and Mishkin suggested that this dissociation in memory abilities in infant monkeys is due to the prolonged postnatal development of the limbic system delaying the ability of recognition and "cognitive" memory relative to sensory-motor habit formation (see also Bachevalier, 2008). This explanation was extended to human infants because they are also unable to acquire the delayed non-match to sample task in early infancy (until around 15 months), and still have not reached adult levels of performance in this task at 6 years old (Overman, Bachevalier, Turner, & Peuster, 1992).

Evidence from both cognitive and neuroscience studies has cast some doubt on this initial view of the ontogeny of memory. The cognitive evidence comes from studies indicating that human infants can recall experiences from the first year of life several years later (Rovee-Collier, 1993), suggesting some continuity of memory mechanisms from early infancy to later life, and no marked transition from one form of memory to another during development. However, perhaps more damaging for Bachevalier and Mishkin's original hypothesis is evidence that lesions to the limbic system impair recognition memory abilities in infant monkeys in the first month of life (Bachevalier, Brickson, & Hagger, 1993), indicating that even from this early age the limbic system plays some role in memory processes.

Nelson (1995) proposed that there are more than two types of memory system that develop from infancy: explicit, pre-explicit, working memory, and habit memory. Specifically, he suggested that between 8 and 18 months of age infants become able to perform DNMS and other tasks that depend on explicit or cognitive memory. This form of memory requires adequate development of the hippocampus, but also related cortical areas such as area TE. However, apparently successful performance can be elicited from infants younger than 8 months in tasks that depend solely on them showing a novelty preference, and that do not require them to determine how often events were presented or do not involve a delay before the response is required. Nelson (1995) hypothesized that this form of "pre-explicit" memory requires only the functioning of the hippocampus, and not the related temporal cortex structures. Around 8 months of age in the human infant, the development of temporal cortical areas, or their integration with the hippocampus, correlates with a transition from pre-explicit to explicit memory. Explicit memory continues to develop into the teenage years associated with prefrontal cortical development, and may be further divided into semantic memory (e.g., remembering one's name) and episodic memory (remembering the first time one went to the beach) (Drummey & Newcombe, 2002; Tulving, 1983).

One form of explicit memory that has recently become a topic for investigation in developmental cognitive neuroscience is source or "autobiographical" memory. Source memory refers to recall of the context (place, time, etc.) for a remembered event (Johnson, Hashtroudi, & Lindsay, 1993). Autobiographical memories relate an experience to one's own personal past, including any emotions or perceptual details (Tulving, 1983). Drummey and Newcombe (2002) tested children of 4, 6, and 8 years in a source memory paradigm adapted from those previously used with adults. In this task the children were first presented with 10 facts (on a variety of topics) by either an experimenter or a puppet. After a delay of one week, the children were asked questions on the facts, and also asked to identify the source of the fact (experimenter, puppet, teacher, or parent). Children showed a steady improvement with age in their ability to remember the facts, but showed an abrupt improvement between 4 and 6 years in their ability to monitor the source of those facts. In particular, the 4-year-olds made many errors in identifying the source of the facts. Because this kind of "source amnesia" is characteristic of adult populations with frontal cortex disruption, it was intriguing that the changes in the children were in some cases related to behavioral measures of prefrontal cortex (PFC) function.

Another memory system that develops around the same age and shows protracted development is working memory. Nelson (1995) suggests that the DLPFC is a critical component of the neural substrate for this form of memory. Nelson's proposal corresponds with the observation that 6-month-olds can successfully perform a marker task for the DLPFC, the oculomotor delayed response task (Gilmore & Johnson, 1995). Although such behavioral measures are useful as marker tasks, it is even better to use functional imaging while children perform tasks likely to engage prefrontal cortical regions. Several fMRI studies by Klingberg and colleagues (Klingberg, 2006) document that the DLPFC is involved in working memory in both children and adults, but also show that it is activated as part of a network that also involves the intraparietal cortex. These studies show that stronger activation of the fronto-parietal network is related to greater working memory capacity, and that activation of the network also increases with age independent of performance (Klingberg, Forssberg, & Westerberg, 2002). Development of white matter tracts connecting the frontal and parietal regions seems to play a role in this process: Maturation of these tracts relates to working memory performance and to the degree of cortical activation in the frontal and parietal gray matter (Olesen, Nagy, Westerberg, & Klingberg, 2003). Recent evidence suggests that working memory can also be trained during development, and thus may make a good target for early intervention. For example, Holmes, Gathercole, and Dunning (2009) used an adaptive training program to tax working memory to its limits in children with poor working memory. The training was associated with substantial and sustained gains in working memory in these children, and also extended to other domains such as mathematics. This and other training studies suggest that experience using working memory during childhood might drive changes in the brain network underlying this ability.

Finally, another source of evidence on the development of memory systems comes from rare cases of children who, as infants, suffer damage to the hippocampus. Vargha-Khadem and colleagues reported that such children, termed "developmental amnesiacs," grow up with persisting deficits in episodic memory, but show relative sparing of semantic memory (Gadian et al., 2000; Vargha-Khadem et al., 1997). In general, however, these children are surprisingly typical in their cognitive abilities, including near-normal language ability. One reason for the relative sparing of aspects of explicit memory in these children might be that the entorhinal cortex is relatively spared (and functionally active—Maguire, Vargha-Khadem, & Mishkin, 2001). However, it is also likely that other regions and pathways involved in learning and memory adjust their functionality in an activity-dependent way to compensate for the missing components.

From the evidence discussed in this section it is evident that most memory tasks likely engage multiple memory systems, in a similar way to the partially independent brain pathways that are engaged in eye movement control and attention shifts. Thus, a lack of maturity in one or other pathway may be masked in some tasks due to compensatory activity in other pathways. Possibly it is the extent of integration between different memory pathways that is the most significant change with postnatal development. If this is the case, we will not be able to make sense of the developmental data until we have a more integrative account of relations between different brain memory pathways.

Language Acquisition and Speech Recognition

Is language biologically special? This motivating question refers to the extent to which the human infant is predisposed to process and learn about language, and the extent to which the underlying neural circuits are "pre-wired" to process language input. Two cognitive neuroscience approaches to this question have been taken. The first approach addresses the issue of whether particular parts of the cortex are critical for primary language acquisition, or whether a variety of cortical areas can support this function. The second strategy has been to attempt to identify neural correlates of speech processing abilities present from very early in life, before experience is thought to have shaped cortical specialization.

Language acquisition has become a focal point for studies designed to investigate the extent to which particular cortical areas, such as Broca's and Wernicke's areas, are "pre-wired" to support specific functions. Two main lines of research have been pursued, with one set of studies examining the extent to which language functions can be subserved by other regions of the cortex, and another line of research concerned with whether other functions can "occupy" regions that normally support language. The first of these approaches has been pursued through investigations of whether children suffering from perinatal lesions to the classical "language areas" of cortex can still acquire language. The second approach has involved the testing of congenitally deaf children to see what, if any, functions are present in regions of cortex that are normally (spoken) language areas.

If particular cortical regions are uniquely pre-wired to support language, then it is reasonable to assume that damage to such regions will impair the acquisition of language regardless of when the insult occurs. This implicit hypothesis has motivated a good deal of research, the conclusions of which remain somewhat controversial. Lenneberg (1967) argued that if localized left hemisphere damage occurred early in life, it had little effect on subsequent language acquisition. This view contrasted with the effect of similar lesions in adults or older children, and with many congenital abnormalities in which language is delayed or never emerges. Lenneberg's view lost adherents in the 1970s, as evidence accumulated from studies of children with hemispherectomies suggesting that left hemisphere removal commonly leads to selective subtle deficits in language, especially for syntactic and phonological tasks (Dennis & Whitaker, 1976). Similar results have also been reported for children with early focal brain injury due to strokes (Vargha-Khadem, Isaacs, & Muter, 1994). These findings were compatible with studies of normal infants showing a left hemisphere bias at birth in processing speech and other complex sounds (Molfese, 1989), and led some researchers to the conclusion that functional asymmetries for language in the human brain are established at birth, and cannot be reversed. This view was reinforced by a number of neuroanatomical studies that have shown differences between parts of left and right cerebral cortex in adults. For example, Geschwind and Levitsky (1968) reported that the left planum temporale (an area associated with language processing) was larger than the right in 65% of adult brains studied. A number of groups have looked for similar differences in infant brains as evidence for prespecified language abilities. As early as the 29th week of gestation, the left planum temporale is usually larger on the left than on the right in human infants (Teszner, Tzavaras, Gruner & Hecaen, 1972; Wada, Clarke & Hamm, 1975; Witelson & Pallie, 1973). It is important to remember, however, that (1) this asymmetry is probably not specific to humans (Gannon, Holloway, Broadfield, & Braun, 1998) and (2) gyral and sucal measures only tell us about the quantity of cortical tissue within a region, and cannot therefore be used to argue for the detailed specific pre-wiring assumed by some to be necessary for language specific processing (Pinker, 1994). In addition to these reservations about the neuroanatomical evidence, many of the secondary sources that summarized the work on hemispherectomies and/or early focal injury failed to note that the deficits shown by these children are very subtle—far more subtle in fact than the frank aphasias displayed by adults with homologous forms of brain damage (see Bishop, 1983, for a critique of the Dennis & Whitaker, 1976 study). Significantly, most of the children with left hemisphere injury who have been studied to date fall within the normal range, attend public schools (Stiles, Bates, Thal, Trauner, & Reilly, 2002), and certainly do better than adults with equivalent damage.

The other approach to studying the extent to which the cortical areas supporting language-related functions are prespecified is to see whether other functions can occupy such regions. This issue has been investigated in an fMRI study in which hearing and deaf participants were scanned while reading sentences in either English or American Sign Language (ASL) (see Neville & Bavelier, 2002; Neville et al., 1998). When hearing adults read English, there was robust activation within some classical left hemisphere language areas, such as Broca's area. No such activation was observed in the right hemisphere. When deaf people viewed sentences in their native ASL, they showed activation of most of the left hemisphere regions identified for the hearing participants. Because ASL is not sound-based, but does have all of the other characteristics of language including a complex grammar (Klima & Bellugi, 1979), these data suggest that some of the neural systems that mediate language can do so regardless of the modality and structure of the language acquired. Having said this, there were also some clear differences between the hearing and deaf activations, with the deaf group activating some similar regions in the right hemisphere. One interpretation of the right hemisphere activation is that it is evoked by the biological motion inherent in sign, but not spoken, language. A third condition addressed the issue of whether there is a sensitive period for the establishment of left-hemisphere language. In this condition, deaf people read English (their second language, learned late) and did not show activation of the classical left hemisphere language regions, suggesting that, if a language is not acquired within the appropriate developmental time window, the typical pattern of adult activation does not occur.

A number of developmental disorders that affect cognition, such as autism (South, Ozonoff, & Schultz, 2008) and Williams syndrome (Karmiloff-Smith, 2008), may also provide ways to examine the neural basis of language acquisition. For example, autistic individuals commonly have severe deficits in social cognition (such as aspects of language, face recognition, and "theory of mind"; see Frith, 1989), but they can be at, or above, normal levels of performance in other domains. In contrast, Williams syndrome individuals suffer from severe deficits in many aspects of cognition, but are often relatively spared in face recognition and language capabilities (Bellugi, Wang & Jernigan, 1994; Karmiloff-Smith, 2008).

The other general approach to investigating the extent to which language is biologically special involves attempting to identify language-relevant processes in the brains of very young infants. One example of this concerns the ability to discriminate speech-relevant sounds such as phonemes (see Bornstein, Arterberry, & Mash, Chapter 6, this volume). Behavioral experiments have demonstrated that young infants show enhanced (categorical) discrimination at phonetic boundaries used in speech such as /ba/—/pa/. That is, like adults, a graded phonetic transition from /ba/ to /pa/ is perceived as a sudden categorical shift by infants. This observation was initially taken as evidence for a language-specific detection mechanism present from birth. However, it has since become clear that other species, such as chinchillas, show similar acoustical discrimination abilities, indicating that this ability may merely reflect general characteristics of the mammalian auditory processing system, and not an initial spoken language specific mechanism (see Kuhl, 2007, for review).

In a further line of behavioral experiments, Werker and Polka (1993) reported that, although young infants discriminate a wide range of phonetic contrasts including those not found in the native language (e.g., Japanese infants, but not Japanese adults, can discriminate between "r" and "l" sounds), this ability becomes restricted to the phonetic constructs of the native language around 12 months of age. If brain correlates of this process could be identified, it may be possible to study the mechanisms underlying this language-specific selective loss of sensitivity. Dehaene-Lambertz and Dehaene (1994) presented infants with trials in which a series of four identical syllables (the standard) was followed by a fifth that was either identical or phonetically different (deviant). They recorded high-density ERPs time-locked to the onset of the syllable and observed two voltage peaks with different scalp locations. The first peak occurred around 220 ms after stimulus onset and did not habituate to repeated presentations (except after the first presentation) or dishabituate to the novel syllable. Thus, the generators of this peak, probably primary and secondary auditory areas in the temporal lobe, did not appear to be sensitive to the subtle acoustical differences that encoded phonetic information. The second peak reached its maximum around 390 ms after stimulus onset and again did not habituate to repetitions of the same syllable, except after the first presentation. However, when the deviant syllable was introduced the peak recovered to at least its original level. Thus, the neural generators of the second peak, also in the temporal lobe but in a distinct and more posterior location, are sensitive to phonetic information. Further studies need to be done to see if the recovery of the second peak is due to the categorical perception of phonemes, or whether it would be elicited by any acoustical change.

Researchers have used functional imaging methods with greater spatial resolution to investigate early correlates of speech perception. Dehaene-Lambertz, Dehaene, and Hertz-Pannier (2002) measured brain activation with fMRI in awake and sleeping healthy 3-month-olds while they listened to forward and backward speech in their native tongue (French). The authors assumed that forward speech would elicit stronger activation than backward speech in areas related to the segmental and suprasegmental processing of language, while both stimuli will activate mechanisms for processing fast temporal auditory transitions (Werker & Vouloumanos, 2001 discuss the appropriate control stimuli for human speech). Compared to silence, both forward and backward speech activated widespread areas of the left temporal lobe, which was greater than the equivalent activation on the right for some areas (planum temporale). These results provide converging evidence for the ERP data discussed earlier. Forward speech activated some areas that backward speech did not, including the angular gyrus and mesial parietal lobe (precuneus) in the left hemisphere. The authors suggest that these findings demonstrate an early functional asymmetry between the two hemispheres. However, they acknowledge that their results cannot discriminate between an early bias for speech perception and a greater responsivity of the left temporal lobe for processing auditory stimuli with rapid temporal changes.

Developmental disorders involving language can also be informative about the neurodevelopmental basis of these abilities. Some authors have argued that developmental disorders in which language is relatively impaired, despite a lack of impairment in other domains, constitute evidence for an innate language module. Conversely, cases where language is supposedly intact despite impairment in other domains could provide powerful converging evidence. An example of the former kind that has attracted much attention concerns three generations of the KE family and the "FOXP2" gene. Initial reports suggested that about half of the members of this unfortunate family had an inherited specific impairment in grammar (Gopnik, 1990), and excitement surrounded the identification of a specific gene, "FOXP2," associated with this disorder (Lai Fisher, Hurst, Vargha-Khadem, & Monaco, 2001). However, claims for a "grammar gene" have been diluted by the finding that the deficits in the affected family members are much broader than grammar alone. Vargha-Khadem, Watkins, Alcock, Fletcher, and Passingham (1995) conducted extensive work on the family and found deficits in coordinating complex mouth movements (orofacial dyspraxia), various aspects of language outside grammar (e.g., lexical decision), and IQ scores 18–19 points below unaffected members of the same family. Nevertheless, the relatively simple single gene basis of the condition, and its association with language, make it worthy of further study (see Marcus & Fisher, 2003, for further discussion). One such study has involved fMRI during verb generation and repetition tasks (Liégeois et al., 2003). This study demonstrated that affected members of the family showed significant underactivation mainly in two regions: Broca's area and the putamen. However, the affected members also showed greater activation than controls in a variety of other cortical regions, suggesting widespread adjustment of cortical networks in response to the aberrant gene.

Although the KE family may not have turned out to have the specific deficits initially hypothesized, similar claims about the specificity of language deficits have been made for so-called "specific-language impairment" (SLI). Although there is much controversy about the behavioral specificity or otherwise of this condition (see Bishop, 1998), most neuro-anatomical studies have tended to focus on the particular regions thought to be important for language. Thus, it is difficult to know whether or not regions outside the adult classical language regions are abnormal also. However, Herbert et al. (2003) set out to examine with MRI the whole brain of SLI participants. Compared to controls these children showed a substantial increase (more than 10%) in cerebral white matter throughout the brain. This atypical pattern was no more severe in the classical language areas than anywhere else in the brain, suggesting that the studied population had a "generalized systems impairment" that differentially affected language.

In summary, therefore, a reasonable working hypothesis is that regions of the left temporal lobe are most suitable for supporting speech recognition. This suitability likely comes from a combination of spatial and temporal factors that may predispose this region to the processing of rapid temporal stimuli. Other regions of cortex are probably also important for the acquisition of language, and can substitute for the left temporal region if required. Language is only "biologically special" in the broadest sense in which the human species' typical environment interacts with the architecture of cortex and its developmental dynamics to generate representations appropriate for the domain.

Frontal Cortex Development, Object Permanence, and Planning

The region of the frontal lobe anterior to the primary motor and premotor cortex, the PFC, accounts for almost one-third of the total cortical surface in humans (Brodmann, 1909) and is considered by most investigators to be critical for many higher cognitive abilities (Fuster, 1989; Goldman-Rakic, 1987; Milner, 1982). In adults, types of cognitive processing that have been associated with frontal cortex concern the planning and execution of sequences of action, the maintenance of information "online" during short temporal delays, and the ability to inhibit a set of responses that are appropriate in one context but not another. The frontal cortex shows the most prolonged period of postnatal development of any region of the human brain, with changes in synaptic density detectable even into the teenage years (Kostovic, Judas, & Petanjek, 2008), and for this reason it has been the region most frequently associated with developments in cognitive abilities.

Two approaches to the relation between frontal cortex structural development and advances in cognitive ability in childhood have been taken. One of these is the attempt to relate structural developments in the frontal cortex at a particular age to changes in certain cognitive abilities. A refinement of this approach is that the frontal lobes are composed of a number of regions that subserve different functions and show a different timetable of maturation (e.g., Diamond, 1991). The alternative approach is based on the assumption that the frontal cortex is involved in acquisition of new skills and knowledge from very early in life and that it may also play a key role in organizing other parts of cortex (e.g., Thatcher, 1992). According to this latter view, regions of frontal cortex are important in many cognitive transitions primarily because of the regions' involvement in the acquisition of any new skill or knowledge. A corollary of this is that frontal cortex involvement in a particular task or situation may decrease with increased experience or skill in the domain. There is currently evidence consistent with both of these approaches.

One of the most comprehensive attempts to relate a cognitive change to underlying brain developments has concerned marked behavioral changes around 8 to 10 months of age. In particular, Diamond, Goldman-Rakic, and colleagues (Diamond & Goldman-Rakic, 1986, 1989; Goldman-Rakic, 1987) argued that the maturation of PFC during the second half of the human infant's first year of life accounts for a number of transitions observed in the behavior of infants in object permanence and object retrieval tasks. One of the behavioral tasks they used to support this argument comes from Piaget (1954), who observed that infants younger than 8 months often fail to accurately retrieve a hidden object after a short delay period if the object's location is changed from one where it was previously and successfully retrieved. Infants often made a particular preservative error in which they reached to the hiding location where the object was found on the immediately preceding trial. This characteristic pattern of error was cited by Piaget (1954) as evidence for the failure to understand that objects retain their existence or permanence when moved from view. By around 9 months, infants begin to succeed in the task at successively longer delays of 1 to 5 s (Diamond, 1985), although their performance remains unreliable up to about 12 months if the delay between hiding and retrieval is incremented as the infants age (Diamond, 1985).

Diamond and Goldman-Rakic (1989) tested monkeys in a modification of the above object permanence task. Consistent with the observations on human infants, infant monkeys failed to retrieve the hidden object. Furthermore, adult monkeys with lesions to the DLPFC were also impaired in this task. Lesions to some other parts of the brain (parietal cortex or hippocampal formation) did not significantly impair performance, suggesting that the DLPFC plays a central role in tasks that require the maintenance of spatial or object information over temporal delays.

Further evidence linking success in the object permanence task to frontal cortex maturation in the human infant comes from two sources. The first of these is a series of EEG studies with normal human infants (Bell & Fox, 1992; Fox & Bell, 1990), in which increases in frontal EEG responses correlate with the ability to respond successfully over longer delays in delayed response tasks. The second source is work on cognitive deficits in children with a neurochemical deficit in the PFC resulting from phenylketonuria (PKU). Even when treated, this inborn error of metabolism can have the specific consequence of reducing the levels of a neurotransmitter, dopamine, in the DLPFC, resulting in infants and children being impaired on tasks thought to involve parts of the PFC such as the object permanence task and object retrieval tasks, and being relatively normal in tasks thought to depend on other regions of cortex such as the DNMS task mentioned earlier (Welsh, Pennington, Ozonoff, Rouse, & McCabe, 1990).

Having established a link between PFC maturation and behavioral change in a number of tasks, Diamond (1991) speculated on the computational consequence of this aspect of postnatal brain development. Specifically, she suggested that the DLPFC is critical for performance when (1) information has to be retained or related over time or space and (2) a prepotent response has to be inhibited. Only tasks that require both of these aspects of neural computation are likely to engage the DLPFC. In the case of the object permanence task, a spatial location has to be retained over time and the prepotent previously rewarded response inhibited. One experiment suggests that the PFC maturation hypothesis is not the whole story, however, and that some modification or elaboration of the original account is required. Gilmore and Johnson (1995) observed that infants succeed on a task that requires temporal spatial integration over a delay at a much younger age than is indicated by the object permanence tasks. In addition, studies by Baillargeon (1987, 1993) and others entailing infants viewing "possible" and "impossible" events involving occluded objects have found that infants as young as 3.5 months look longer at impossible events, indicating that they have an internal representation of the occluded object. To account for the apparent discrepancy between these results and those with the reaching measures, some have provided "means–ends" explanations, arguing that infants are unable to coordinate the necessary sequence of motor behaviors to retrieve a hidden object (Baillergeon, 1993; Diamond, 1991). To test this hypothesis, Munakata, McClelland, Johnson, and Siegler (1997) trained 7-month-olds to retrieve objects placed at a distance from them by means of pulling on a towel or pressing a button.

Infants retrieved the objects when a transparent screen was interposed between them and the toy, but not if the screen was sufficiently opaque to make the object invisible. Because the same means–ends planning is required whether the screen is transparent or opaque, it was concluded that "means–ends" explanations cannot account for the discrepancy between the looking and the reaching tasks. Munakata et al. (1997) proposed an alternative "graded" view of the discrepancy implemented as a connectionist model.

The maturational approach to PFC development has also been extended to later childhood and adolescence. The results from a variety of behavioral tasks designed to tap into advanced PFC functions have demonstrated that adult levels of performance are not reached until adolescence or later (see Olson & Luciana, 2008). For example, participants from 3 to 25 years old were tested on the CANTAB (Cambridge Neuropsychological Testing Automated Battery), a well established and validated battery of tests previously used on adult human and animal lesion populations (Fray, Robbins, & Sahakian, 1996). This battery assesses several measures including working memory skills, self-guided visual search, and planning. Importantly for developmental studies, the battery is administered with touchscreen computer technology and does not require any verbal or complex manual responses. Using the CANTAB, Luciana and Nelson (1998, 2000; Luciana, 2003) found that, although measures that depend on posterior brain regions (such as recognition memory) were stable by 8 years, measure of planning and working memory had not yet reached adult levels by age 12.

Although such behavioral measures are useful as marker tasks, it is even better to use functional imaging while children perform tasks likely to engage PFC regions. This strategy was adopted by Casey and colleagues, who used fMRI to compare children and adults in working memory and inhibition tasks. In one experiment they used event-related fMRI while children and adults were engaged in a "go–no-go" task (Durston et al., 2002). In this task, participants had to suppress their response when presented with a particular visual item within an ongoing sequence of stimulus presentations (e.g., one Pokemon character within a sequence of other Pokemon characters). The difficulty of the task was increased by increasing the number of "go" items that preceded the "no-go" character. Successful response inhibition was associated with stronger activation of prefrontal regions for children than for adults. Also, although in adults the activation of some prefrontal regions increased with increasing numbers of preceding "go" trials (consistent with increasing need for inhibition), in children the circuit appeared to be maximally active for all trial types. Along with the poorer behavioral performance of children in this and other inhibitory tasks, these findings suggest that the functional development of some PFC regions is important for the mature ability to inhibit prepotent tendencies. The greater activation seen in children will be discussed further below.

An alternative approach to understanding the role of the PFC in cognitive development has been advanced by several authors who have suggested that the region plays a critical role in the *acquisition* of new information and tasks. By this account the PFC involvement in the object retrieval tasks is only one of many manifestations of PFC involvement in cognitive change. From this perspective, the challenge to the infant brain in, for example, learning to reach for an object is equivalent in some respects to that of the adult brain when facing complex motor skills such as learning to drive a car. A concomitant of this general view is that the cortical regions crucial for a particular task will change with the stage of acquisition. Three lines of evidence indicating the importance of PFC activation early in infancy have given further credence to this view: (1) fMRI and PET studies, (2) psychophysiological evidence, and (3) the long-term effects of perinatal damage to PFC.

The limited number of fMRI and PET studies that have been done with infants have often surprisingly revealed functional activation in PFC, even when this would not be predicted from adult studies. For example, in an fMRI study of speech perception in 3-month-olds, Dehaene-Lambertz et al. (2002) observed a right DLPFC activation that discriminated (forward) speech in awake, but not sleeping, infants. Similar activation of DLPFC was found in response to faces at the same age (Tzourio-Mazoyer et al., 2002). Although this is evidence for activation of at least some of the PFC in the first few months, it remains possible that this activation is passive as does not play any role in directing the behavior of the infant. Two other recent lines of evidence, however, suggest that this is not the case.

Although developmental ERP studies have often recorded activity changes over frontal leads in infants, some recent experiments suggest that this activity has important consequences for behavioral output. These experiments involve examining patterns of activation that precede the onset of a saccade. In one example, Csibra, Tucker, and Johnson (1998) observed that pre-saccadic potentials that are usually recorded over more posterior scalp sites in adults are observed in frontal channels in 6-month-old infants (Figure 4.5). Because these potentials are time-locked to the onset of an action, it is reasonable to infer that they are the consequence of computations necessary for the planning or execution of the action.

Further evidence for the developmental importance of the PFC from early infancy comes from studies of the long-term and widespread effects of perinatal damage to PFC. In contrast to some other regions of cortex, perinatal damage to frontal and PFC regions often results in both immediate and long-term difficulties. For example, Johnson et al. (1998) studied infants with perinatal focal lesions to parts of cortex in a visual attention task. Damage to parietal cortical regions would be expected to produce deficits in this task in adults, but only infants

FIGURE 4.5   A diagram illustrating activation over frontal cortical regions during a visual fixation and orienting task with 6-month-old infants. From "Neural correlates of saccade planning in infants" by G. Csibra, L. A. Tucker, and M. H. Johnson (1998), *International Journal of Psychophysiology*, *29*, 201–215. Reprinted with permission from Elsevier.

with perinatal lesions to the anterior (frontal) regions of cortex were impaired, suggesting that these regions were involved to a greater extent in the task in infants than in adults.

Another area of behavioral development that has been related to changes in frontal cortical function has been emotional development. For example, Dawson (1994; see also Davidson, 1994) reviewed a number of studies on the relation between frontal EEG measures and measures of emotional expression in infants and children. She concluded that while the type of emotional expression (e.g., joy, anger, distress, fear) was associated with asymmetries between the right and left frontal cortex, the intensity of the expression is associated with generalized activation of both right and left frontal regions, regardless of the type of emotion. These two dimensions of emotional expression also show other differential properties. The degree of asymmetry in frontal EEG is a better predictor of individual differences in the tendency to express emotions, whereas generalized measures of frontal activity are better predictors of overall emotional reactivity and intensity. Dawson (1994) also suggested that generalized measures of frontal EEG may reflect the diffuse influence of subcortical structures on the cortex, and general arousal levels. Because these influences do not require development of frontal cortex, they may be observable very early in infancy and represent stable individual differences throughout the life course. In contrast, functions that require frontal cortical development, such as the ability to inhibit prepotent responses mentioned earlier, develop more gradually and may be more sensitive to experience. Thus, it is possible that the specialization of the left and right frontal regions, and the asymmetric EEG patterns observed, may be sensitive to early experience such as rearing with a depressed mother. Evidence for this prediction was found by Dawson, Grofer Klinger, Panagiotides, Hill, & Spieker (1992).

CONCLUSIONS

The specialization of cortical regions for particular functions may be largely an activity-dependent process extending from prenatal into postnatal life. Questions that have been posed during the course of this chapter include what is the state of the newborn infants' brain in terms of the transition from plasticity to specificity, and is this the same for different brain regions and all domains of cognition? Addressing the first question, it is clear that in at least some domains of cognition, such as language, there is considerable plasticity in the first few months of life in the sense that different cortical regions can potentially support this function following focal perinatal brain damage. In contrast, other domains more closely tied to sensory input, such as aspects of spatial cognition, may be less plastic. Such differences lead us to address the other two questions.

The cerebral neocortex appears to be on a slower developmental pathway than other regions of the brain in terms of both prenatal and postnatal development (Finlay & Darlington, 1995). Subcortical regions such as the cerebellum, hippocampus, and thalamus clearly undergo some postnatal changes, and these may at least be partially a response to changes in their interconnectivity with the cortex. As a whole, the human cerebral cortex has not reached adult levels of specificity at birth, but it appears that some regions of cortex may be relatively delayed compared to others. This leads us to the further question of whether all domains of cognition follow the same timetable of cortical specialization.

Some domains of cognition, such as language, appear plastic in the sense that regions of cortex are not exclusively dedicated to them from birth, but other domains, such as face processing, may have fewer options. Less extensive plasticity does not necessarily imply strict genetic determinism, however, because functions more closely tied to sensory input or motor output are likely to be more restricted to the cortical regions that have the appropriate information in their input. For example, face recognition is necessarily restricted to structures on the visual "what" (ventral) pathway because it requires both visual analysis and encoding of particular items within a category. Language may be less constrained in the sense that it is less restricted to particular information processing routes within the cortex. Thus, a key point about the emergence of localization of functions within the cortex is that the restrictions on localization may be more related to which cortical routes of information processing are viable for supporting the functions, rather than being due to pre-wired intrinsic circuitry within regions of cortex.

During prenatal development spontaneous activity in sensory systems appears to play an important role in contributing to the differentiation of cortical regions. In early postnatal life infants contribute further to the specialization of their brain by preferentially orienting and attending to certain types of stimuli, such as faces. Later, social experience and interaction with caregivers may contribute further to the specialization of late developing parts of the cerebral cortex. Indeed, de Haan, Luciana, Malone, Matheny, and Richards (1994, p. 169) speculated that "experience, in this case psychosocial experience, may affect the synaptic structure of PFC in much the same way as it does sensory cortices." Much of later postnatal brain development, therefore, can be viewed as an active process to which both children and their caregivers contribute. Thus, studying the postnatal emergence of cortical specialization for different cognitive functions offers the possibility of new perspectives not only on the study of perceptual and cognitive development in healthy human infants, but also for social development, education, and atypical developmental pathways. The new theoretical and methodological advances of developmental neuroscience will allow these advances.

ACKNOWLEDGMENTS

Sections of text in this chapter are adapted from Johnson (2011), and I am grateful to my various colleagues and collaborators who commented on that work for their indirect contribution to the present chapter. Marc H. Bornstein and Michael Lamb provided useful feedback on earlier versions of this chapter. The writing of this chapter was primarily funded by the UK Medical Research Council (G0701484) and Birkbeck College, University of London.

REFERENCES AND SUGGESTED READINGS (📖)

Adolphs, R. (2003). Cognitive neuroscience of human social behaviour. *Nature Reviews Neuroscience*, *4*, 165–178.

Aslin, R. N. (1981). Development of smooth pursuit in human infants. In D. F. Fisher, R. A. Monty, & J. W. Senders (Eds.), *Eye movements: Cognition and visual perception* (pp. 31–51). Hillsdale, NJ: Lawrence Erlbaum Associates.

Aslin, R. N. (2007). What's in a look? *Developmental Science*, *10*, 48–53.

Atkinson, J. (1984). Human visual development over the first six months of life: A review and a hypothesis. *Human Neurobiology*, *3*, 61–74.

📖 Bachevalier, J. (2008) Nonhuman primate models of memory development. In C. A. Nelson & M. Luciana (Eds.), *The handbook of developmental cognitive neuroscience* (2nd ed., pp. 499–508). Cambridge, MA: MIT Press.

Bachevalier, J., Brickson, M., & Hagger, C. (1993). Limbic-dependent recognition memory in monkeys develops early in infancy. *NeuroReport*, *4*, 77–80.

Bachevalier, J., & Mishkin, M. (1984). An early and a late developing system for learning and retention in infant monkeys. *Behavioral Neuroscience*, *98*, 770–778.

Baillargeon, R. (1987). Object permanence in very young infants. *Cognition*, *20*, 191–208.

Baillargeon, R. (1993). The object concept revisited: New directions in the investigation of infant's physical knowledge. In C. E. Granrud (Ed.), *Visual perception and cognition in infancy* (pp. 265–315). Hillsdale, NJ: Lawrence Erlbaum Associates.

Balaban, C. D., & Weinstein, J. M. (1985). The human pre-saccadic spike potential: Influences of a visual target, saccade direction, electrode laterality and instruction to perform saccades. *Brain Research*, *347*, 49–57.

Bartley, A. J., Jones, D. W., & Weinberger, D. R. (1997). Genetic variability of human brain size and cortical gyral patterns. *Brain, 120*, 257–269.

Batki, A., Baron-Cohen, S., Wheelwright, S., Connellan, J., & Ahluwalia, J. (2000). Is there an innate gaze module? Evidence from human neonates. *Infant Behavior and Development, 23*(2), 223–229.

Bell, M. A., & Fox, N. A. (1992). The relations between frontal brain electrical activity and cognitive development during infancy. *Child Development, 63*, 1142–1163.

Bellugi, U., Wang, P. P., & Jernigan, T. L. (1994). Williams syndrome: An unusual neuropsychological profile. In S. Broman & J. Grafman (Eds.), *Atypical cognitive deficits in developmental disorders: Implications for brain function* (pp. 23–56). Hillsdale, NJ: Lawrence Erlbaum Associates.

Bishop, D. V. M. (1983). Linguistic impairment after hemidecortication for infantile hemiplegia? A reappraisal. *Quarterly Journal of Experimental Psychology, 35A*, 199–207.

Bishop, D. V. M. (1998). Development of the Children's Communication Checklist (CCC): A method for assessing qualitative aspects of communicative impairment in children. *Journal of Child Psychology and Psychiatry and Allied Disciplines, 39*, 879–891.

Born, P., Rostrup, E., Leth, H., Peitersen, B., & Lou, H. C. (1996). Change of visually induced cortical activation patterns during development. *Lancet, 347*, 543.

Born, A. P., Rostrup, E., Miranda, M. J., Larsson, H. B. W., & Lou, H. C. (2002). Visual cortex reactivity in sedated children examined with perfusion MRI (FAIR). *Magnetic Resonance Imaging, 20*(2), 199–205.

Braddick, O. J., Atkinson, J., Hood, B., Harkness, W., Jackson, G., & Vargha-Khadem, F. (1992). Possible blindsight in infants lacking one cerebral hemisphere. *Nature, 360*, 461–463.

Brodmann, K. (1909). *Vergleichende Lokalisationslehre der Grosshirnrinde in ihren Prinzipien dargestellt auf Grund des Zellenbaues*. Leipzig, Germany: Barth.

Brodmann, K. (1912). Neue Ergebnisse über die vergleichende histologische Lokalisation der Grosshirnrinde mit besonderer Berücksichtigung des Stirnhirns. *Anatomischer Anzeiger (Suppl.), 41*, 157–216.

Bronson, G. W. (1974). The postnatal growth of visual capacity. *Child Development, 45*, 873–890.

Bronson, G. W. (1982). *The scanning patterns of human infants: Implications for visual learning*. Norwood, NJ: Ablex.

Bushnell, I. W. R. (1979). Modification of the externality effect in young infants. *Journal of Experimental Child Psychology, 28*, 211–229.

Butterworth, G., & Jarrett, N. (1991). What minds have in common is space: Spatial mechanisms serving joint visual attention in infancy. *British Journal of Developmental Psychology, 9*, 55–72.

Canfield, R. L., Smith, E. G., Brezsnyak, M. P., & Snow, K. L. (1997). Information processing through the first year of life: A longitudinal study using the Visual Expectation Paradigm. *Monographs of the Society for Research in Child Development, 62*, v–vi, 1–145.

Casey, B. J., & de Haan, M. (2002). Imaging techniques and their application in developmental science. *Developmental Science* (Special Issue), *5*, 265–396.

Cattanach, B. M., Peters, J., Ball, S., & Rasberry, C. (2000). Two imprinted gene mutations: Three phenotypes. *Human Molecular Genetics, 9*(15), 2263–2273.

Chugani, H. T., Phelps, M. E., & Mazziotta, J. C. (1987). Positron emission tomography study of human brain functional development. *Annals of Neurology, 22*, 487–497.

Conel, J. L. (1939–1967). *The postnatal development of the human cerebral cortex* (Vols. I–VI). Cambridge, MA: Harvard University Press.

Crabbe, J., Wahlsten, D., & Dudek, B. C. (1999). Genetics of mouse behavior: Interactions with laboratory environment. *Science, 284*, 1670–1672.

Craft, S., White, D. A., Park, T. S., & Figiel, G. (1994). Visual attention in children with perinatal brain injury: Asymmetric effects of bilateral lesions. *Journal of Cognitive Neuroscience, 6*, 165–173.

Csibra, G. and Johnson, M. H. (2007) Investigating event-related oscillations in infancy. In M. De Haan (Ed.), *Infant EEG and event-related potentials* (pp. 289–304). Hove, UK: Psychology Press.

Csibra, G., Tucker, L. A., & Johnson, M. H.(1997). Attention and oculomotor control: A high-density ERP study of the gap effect. *Neuropsychologica, 35*, 855–865.

Csibra, G., Tucker, L. A., & Johnson, M. H. (1998). Neural correlates of saccade planning in infants: A high-density ERP study. *International Journal of Psychophysiology, 29*, 201–215.

Csibra, G., Tucker, L. A., & Johnson, M. H. (2001). Differential frontal cortex activation before anticipatory and reactive saccades in infants. *Infancy, 2*, 159–174.

Darwin, C. R. (1965). *The expression of emotions in man and animals*. Chicago: University of Chicago Press. (Original work published in 1872.)

Davidson, R. J. (1994). Temperament, affective style, and frontal lobe asymmetry. In G. Dawson & K. W. Fischer (Eds.), *Human behavior and the developing brain* (pp. 518–536). New York: Guilford Press.

Dawson, G. (1994). Development of emotional expression and emotion regulation in infancy. In G. Dawson & K. W. Fischer (Eds.), *Human behavior and the developing brain* (pp. 346–379). New York: Guilford Press.

Dawson, G., Grofer Klinger, L., Panagiotides, H., Hill, D., & Spieker, S. (1992). Frontal lobe activity and affective behavior of infants of mothers with depressive symptoms. *Child Development, 63,* 725–737.

de Haan, M. (2008). Neurocognitive mechanisms for the development of face processing. In C. A. Nelson & M. Luciana (Eds.), *Handbook of developmental cognitive neuroscience* (2nd ed., pp. 509–520). Cambridge, MA: MIT Press.

de Haan, M., Humphrey, K., & Johnson, M. H. (2002). Developing a brain specialized for face perception: A converging methods approach. *Developmental Psychobiology, 40,* 200–212.

de Haan, M., Johnson, M., Maurer, D., Perrett, D. I. (2001). Recognition of individual faces and average face prototypes by 1- and 3-month-old infants. *Cognitive Development, 16,* 659–678.

de Haan, M., Luciana, M., Malone, S., Matheny, L., & Richards, M. L. M. (1994). Development, plasticity and risk. In C. A. Nelson (Ed.), *Threats to optimal development* (pp. 161–178). New York: Lawrence Erlbaum Associates.

Dehaene-Lambertz, G., & Dehaene, S. (1994). Speed and cerebral correlates of syllable discrimination in infants. *Nature, 370,* 292–295.

Dehaene-Lambertz, G., Dehaene, S., & Hertz-Pannier, L. (2002). Functional neuroimaging of speech perception in infants. *Science, 298,* 2013–2015.

Dennis, M., & Whitaker, H. A. (1976). Language acquisition following hemidecortication: Linguistic superiority of the left over the right hemisphere. *Brain and Language, 3,* 404–433.

de Schonen, S., Mancini, J., & Leigeois, F. (1998). About functional cortical specialisation: The development of face recognition. In F. Simion & G. Butterworth (Eds.), *The development of sensory, motor and cognitive capacities in early infancy: From perception to cognition* (pp. 103–120). Hove, UK: Psychology Press.

de Schonen, S., & Mathivet, E. (1989). First come, first served: A scenario about the development of hemispheric specialisation in face recognition during infancy. *Current Psychology of Cognition, 9,* 3–44.

Diamond, A. (1985). Development of the ability to use recall to guide action, as indicated by infants' performance on AB. *Child Development, 56,* 868–883.

Diamond, A. (1991). Neuropsychological insights into the meaning of object concept development. In S. Carey & R. Gelman (Eds.), *The epigenesis of mind: Essays on biology and cognition* (pp. 67–110). Hillsdale, NJ: Lawrence Erlbaum Associates.

Diamond, A., & Goldman-Rakic, P. S. (1986). Comparative development of human infants and infant rhesus monkeys of cognitive functions that depend on prefrontal cortex. *Neuroscience Abstracts, 12,* 274.

Diamond, A., & Goldman-Rakic, P. S. (1989). Comparison of human infants and infant rhesus monkeys on Piaget's AB task: Evidence for dependence on dorsolateral prefrontal cortex. *Experimental Brain Research, 74,* 24–40.

Driver, J., Davis, G., Ricciardelli, P., Kidd, P., Maxwell, E., & Baron-Cohen, S. (1999). Gaze perception triggers reflexive visuo-spatial orienting. *Visual Cognition, 6,* 509–540.

Drummey, A. B., & Newcombe, N. S. (2002). Developmental changes in source memory. *Developmental Science, 5,* 502–513.

Durston, S., Thomas, K., Yang, Y., Ulug, A., Zimmerman, R., & Casey, B. J. (2002). A neural basis for the development of inhibitory control. *Developmental Science, 5,* F9–F16.

Elman, J., Bates, E., Johnson, M. H., Karmiloff-Smith, A., Parisi, D., & Plunkett, K. (1996). *Rethinking innateness: A connectionist perspective on development.* Cambridge, MA: MIT Press.

Fantz, R. L. (1964). Visual experience in infants: Decreased attention to familiar patterns relative to novel ones. *Science, 46,* 668–670.

Farroni, T., Csibra, G., Simion, F., & Johnson, M. H. (2002). Eye contact detection in humans from birth. *Proceedings of the National Academy of Sciences of the United States of America, 99,* 9602–9605.

Farroni, T., Mansfield, E. M., Lai, C., & Johnson, M. H. (2003). Infants perceiving and acting on the eyes: Tests of an evolutionary hypothesis. *Journal of Experimental Child Psychology, 85,* 199–212.

Fiebach, C., Rissman, J., & D'Esposito, M. (2006). Modulation of inferotemporal cortex activation during verbal working memory maintenance. *Neuron, 51*(2), 251–261.

Finlay, B. L., & Darlington, R. B. (1995). Linked regularities in the development and evolution of mammalian brains. *Science, 268,* 1578–1584.

Finlay, B. L., Darlington, R. B., & Nicastro, N. (2001). Developmental structure in brain evolution. *Behavioral and Brain Sciences, 24,* 263–308.

Foucher, J. R., Otzenberger, H., & Gounot, D. (2003). The BOLD response and the gamma oscillations respond differently than evoked potentials: An interleaved EEG–fMRI study. *BMC Neuroscience, 4,* 22.

Fox, N. A., & Bell, M. A. (1990). Electrophysiological indices of frontal lobe development. In A. Diamond (Ed.), *The development and neural bases of higher cognitive functions* (pp. 677–698). New York: New York Academy of Sciences.

Fray, P. J., Robbins, T. W., & Sahakian, B. J. (1996). Neuropsychiatric applications of CANTAB. *International Journal of Geriatric Psychiatry, 11,* 329–336.

Frith, U. (1989). *Autism: Explaining the enigma.* Oxford, UK: Basil Blackwell.

Fuster, J. M. (1989). *The prefrontal cortex* (2nd ed.). New York: Raven Press.

Gadian, D. G., Aicardi, J., Watkins, K. E., Porter, D. A., Mishkin, M., & Vargha-Khadem, F. (2000). Developmental amnesia associated with early hypoxic–ischaemic injury. *Brain,* 499–507.

Gannon, P. J., Holloway, R. L., Broadfield, D. C., & Braun, A. R. (1998). Asymmetry of chimpanzee planum temporale: Humanlike pattern of Wernicke's brain language area homolog. *Science, 279*, 220–222.

Geschwind, N., & Levitsky, W. (1968). Human brain: Left–right asymmetries in temporal speech region. *Science, 161*(837), 186–187.

Gesell, A. (1929). *Infancy and human growth.* New York: Macmillan.

Giedd, J. N., Blumenthal, J., Jeffries, N. O., Castellanos, F. X., Lui, H. Z., A., Paus, T., et al. (1999). Brain development during childhood and adolescence: A longitudinal MRI study. *Nature Neuroscience, 2*, 861–863.

Gilmore, R. O., & Johnson, M. H. (1995). Working memory in infancy: Six-month-olds' performance on two versions of the oculomotor delayed response task. *Journal of Experimental Child Psychology, 59*, 397–418.

Golarai, G., Ghahremani, D. G., Whitfield-Gabrieli, S., Reiss, A., Eberhardt, J. L., Gabrieli, J. D. E, et al. (2007). Differential development of high-level visual cortex correlates with category-specific recognition memory. *Nature Neuroscience, 10*(4), 512–522.

Goldman-Rakic, P. S. (1987). Development of cortical circuitry and cognitive function. *Child Development, 58*, 601–622.

Goldman-Rakic, P. S., Bourgeois, J., & Rakic, P. (1997). Synaptic substrate of cognitive development: Life-span analysis of synaptogenesis in the prefrontal cortex of the nonhuman primate. In N. A. Krasnegor, G. Reid Lyon, & P. S. Goldman-Rakic (Eds.), *Development of the prefrontal cortex: Evolution, neurobiology and behaviour* (pp. 27–48). Baltimore: Paul H. Brookes.

Gopnik, M. (1990). Feature-blind grammar and dysphasia. *Nature, 344*(6268), 715.

Gottlieb, G. (2007). Probabilistic epigenisis. *Developmental Science, 10*, 1–11.

Grossmann, T., & Johnson, M. H. (2007). The development of the social brain in human infancy. *European Journal of Neuroscience, 25*, 909–919.

Grossmann, T., Johnson, M. H., Lloyd-Fox, S., Blasi, A., Deligianni, F., Elwell, C., et al. (2008). Early cortical specialization for face-to-face communication in human infants. *Proceedings of the Royal Society, B: Biological Sciences, 275*(1653), 2803–2811.

Grossmann, T., Johnson, M. H., Farroni, T. & Csibra, G. (2007). Social perception in the infant brain: Gamma oscillatory activity in response to eye gaze. *Social Cognitive and Affective Neuroscience, 2*(4), 284–291.

Halit, H., Csibra, G., Volein, Á., & Johnson, M. H. (2004). Face-sensitive cortical processing in early infancy. *Journal of Child Psychology and Psychiatry, 45*, 1228–1234.

Halit, H., de Haan, M., & Johnson, M. H. (2003). Cortical specialisation for face processing: Face-sensitive event-related potential components in 3 and 12 month-old infants. *NeuroImage, 19*, 1180–1193.

Held, R. (1985). Binocular vision: Behavioral and neuronal development. In J. Mehler & R. Fox (Eds.), *Neonate cognition: Beyond the blooming, buzzing confusion.* Hillsdale, NJ: Lawrence Erlbaum Associates.

Held, R. (1993). Development of binocular vision revisited. In M. H. Johnson (Ed.), *Brain development and cognition: A reader* (pp. 159–166). Oxford, UK: Blackwell.

Herbert, M. R., Ziegler, D. A., Makris, N. B., Dakardjiev, A., Hodgson, J., Adrien, K. T., et al. (2003). Larger brain and white matter volumes in children with developmental language disorder. *Developmental Science, 6*(4), F11–F22.

Hillyard, S. A., Mangun, G. R., Woldorff, M. G., & Luck, S. J. (1995). Neural systems mediating selective attention. In M. S. Gazzaniga (Ed.), *The cognitive neurosciences* (pp. 665–681). Cambridge, MA: MIT Press.

Holmes, J., Gathercole, S. E., & Dunning, D. L. (2009). Adapative training leads to sustained enhancement of poor working memory in children. *Developmental Science, 12*, F9–F15.

Homanics, G. E., DeLorey, T. M., Firestone, L. L., Quinlan, J. J., Handforth, A., Harrison, N. L., et al. (1997). Mice devoid of γ-aminobutyrate type A receptor$^\beta$ 3 subunit have epilepsy, cleft palate, and hypersensitive behavior. *Proceedings of the National Academy of Sciences of the United States of America, 94*, 4143–4148.

Huttenlocher, P. R. (1990). Morphometric study of human cerebral cortex development. *Neuropsychologia, 28*, 517–527.

Jaffe, J., Stern, D. N., & Peery, J. C. (1973). "Conversational" coupling of gaze behavior in prelinguistic human development. *Journal of Psycholinguistic Research, 2*, 321–329.

Johnson, M. H. (1990). Cortical maturation and the development of visual attention in early infancy. *Journal of Cognitive Neuroscience, 2*, 81–95.

Johnson, M. H. (2000). Functional brain development in infants: Elements of an interactive specialization framework. *Child Development, 71*, 75–81.

Johnson, M. H. (2001). Functional brain development in humans. *Nature Reviews Neuroscience, 2*, 475–483.

Johnson, M. H. (2005). Sub-cortical face processing. *Nature Reviews Neuroscience, 6*, 766–774.

Johnson, M. H. (2011). *Developmental cognitive neuroscience* (3rd ed.). Oxford, UK: Wiley-Blackwell.

Johnson, M. H., Grossmann, T., and Cohen-Kadosh, K. (2009). Mapping functional brain development: Building a social brain through interactive specialization. *Developmental Psychology, 45*, 151–159.

Johnson, M. H., & Morton, J. (1991). *Biology and cognitive development: The case of face recognition.* Oxford, UK: Blackwell.

Johnson, M. H., Tucker, L. A., Stiles, J., & Trauner, D. (1998). Visual attention in infants with perinatal brain damage: Evidence of the importance of left anterior lesions. *Developmental Science*, *1*, 53–58.

Johnson, M. K., Hashtroudi, S., & Lindsay, D. S. (1993). Source monitoring. *Psychological Bulletin*, *114*, 3–28.

Karatekin, C. (2001). Developmental disorders of attention. In C. A. Nelson & M. Luciana (Eds.), *Handbook of developmental cognitive neuroscience* (pp. 561–576). Cambridge, MA: MIT Press.

Karmiloff-Smith, A. (1992). *Beyond modularity: A developmental perspective on cognitive science*. Cambridge, MA: MIT Press/Bradford Books.

Karmiloff-Smith, A. (1998). Development itself is the key to understanding developmental disorders. *Trends in Cognitive Sciences*, *2*, 389–398.

Karmiloff-Smith, A. (2008). Research into Williams syndrome: The state of the art. In C. A. Nelson & M. Luciana (Eds.), *The handbook of developmental cognitive neuroscience* (2nd ed., pp. 691–700). Cambridge, MA: MIT Press.

Katz, L. C., & Shatz, C. J. (1996). Synaptic activity and the construction of cortical circuits. *Science*, *274*, 1133.

Keverne, E. B. (1997). Genomic imprinting in the brain. *Current Opinion in Neurobiology*, *7*(4), 463–468.

Kingsbury, M. A., & Finlay, B. L. (2001). The cortex in multidimensional space: Where do cortical areas come from? *Developmental Science*, *4*, 125–142.

Kleinke, C. L. (1986). Gaze and eye contact; a research review. *Psychological Bullatin*, *100*, 78–100.

Klima, E., & Bellugi, U. (1979). *The signs of language*. Cambridge, MA: Harvard University Press.

Klingberg, T. (2006) Development of a superior frontal–intraparietal network for visuo-spatial working memory. *Neuropsychologia*, *44*(11), 2171–2177.

Klingberg, T., Forssberg, H., & Westerberg, H. (2002) Increased brain activity in frontal and parietal cortex underlies the development of visuospatial working memory capacity during childhood. *Journal of Cognitive Neuroscience*, *14*(1), 1–10.

Kostovic, I., Judas, M., & Petanjek, Z. (2008). Structural development of the human prefrontal cortex. In C. A. Nelson & M. Luciana (Eds.), *The handbook of developmental cognitive neuroscience* (2nd ed., pp. 213–236). Cambridge, MA: MIT Press.

Kuhl, P. K. (2007). Is speech learning gated by the social brain? *Developmental Science*, *10*, 110–120.

Kurtzberg, D., & Vaughan, J. (1982). Topographic analysis of human cortical potentials preceding self-initiated and visually triggered saccades. *Brain Research*, *243*(1), 1–9.

Lai, C. S. L., Fisher, S. E., Hurst, J. A., Vargha-Khadem, F., & & Monaco, A. P. (2001). A forkhead-domain gene is mutated in a severe speech and language disorder. *Nature*, *413*(6855), 519–523.

Lenneberg, E. (1967). *Biological foundations of language*. New York: Wiley.

Lewis, T. L., Maurer, D., & Milewski, A. (1979). The development of nasal detection in young infants. *Investigative Ophthalmology and Visual Science Supplement*, *18*, 271.

Liégeois, F., Baldeweg, T., Connelly, A., Gadian, D. G., Mishkin, M., & Vargha-Khadem, F. (2003). Language fMRI abnormalities associated with FOXP2 gene mutation. *Nature Neuroscience*, *6*(11), 1230–1237.

Luciana, M. (2003). The neural and functional development of human prefrontal cortex. In M. de Haan & M. H. Johnson (Eds.), *The cognitive neuroscience of development* (pp. 157–174). Hove, UK: Psychology Press.

Luciana, M., & Nelson, C. A. (1998). The functional emergence of prefrontally-guided working memory systems in four-to-eight year-old children. *Neuropsychologia*, *36*(3), 273–293.

Luciana, M., & Nelson, C. A. (2000). Neurodevelopmental assessment of cognitive function using the Cambridge Neuropsychological Testing Automated Battery (CANTAB): Validation and future goals. In M. Ernst and J. M. Rumsey (Eds.), *Functional neuroimaging in child psychiatry*. Cambridge: Cambridge University Press.

Maguire, E. A., Vargha-Khadem, F., & Mishkin, M. (2001). The effects of bilateral hippocampal damage on fMRI regional activations and interactions during memory retrieval. *Brain*, *124*, 1156–1170.

Mancini, J., Casse-Perrot, C., Giusiano, B., Girard, N., Camps, R., Deruelle, C., et al. (1998). *Face processing development after a perinatal unilateral brain lesion*. Human Frontiers Science Foundation Developmental Cognitive Neuroscience Technical Report Series 98.6.

Marcus, G. F., & Fisher, S. E. (2003). FOXP2 in focus: What can genes tell us about speech and language? *Trends in Cognitive Sciences*, *7*(6), 257–262.

Mareschal, D., Johnson, M. H., Sirois, S., Spratling, M., Thomas, M., & Westermann, G. (2007). *Neuroconstructivism: How the brain constructs cognition*. Oxford, UK: Oxford University Press.

Marin-Padilla, M. (1990). The pyramidal cell and its local-circuit interneurons: A hypothetical unit of the mammalian cerebral cortex. *Journal of Cognitive Neuroscience*, *2*, 180–194.

Matsuzawa, J., Matsui, M., Konishi, T., Noguchi, K., Gur, R. C., Bilker, W., et al. (2001). Age-related volumetric changes of brain gray and white matter in healthy infants and children. *Cerebral Cortex*, *11*(4), 335–342.

Maurer, D. (1983). The scanning of compound figures by young infants. *Journal of Experimental Child Psychology*, *35*, 437–448.

McCabe, B. J., Cipolla-Neto, J., Horn, G., & Bateson, P. P. G. (1982). Amnesic effects of bilateral lesions placed in the hyperstriatum ventrale of the chick after imprinting. *Experimental Brain Research*, *48*, 13–21.

McGraw, M. B. (1943). *The neuromuscular maturation of the human infant*. New York: Columbia University Press.

Meek, J. H., Firbank, M., Elwell, C. E., Atkinson, J., Braddick, O., & Wyatt, J. S. (1998). Regional hemodynamic responses to visual stimulation in awake infants. *Peadiatric Research*, *43*, 840–843.

Meltzoff, A. N., & Moore, M. K. (1977). Imitation of facial and manual gestures by human neonates. *Science*, *198*, 74–78.

Miller, K. D. (1990). Correlation-based models of neural development. In M. A. Gluck & D. E. Rumelhart (Eds.), *Neuroscience and connectionist theory* (pp. 267–353). Hillsdale, NJ: Lawrence Erlbaum Associates.

Miller, K. D., Keller, J. B., & Stryker, M. P. (1989). Ocular dominance column development: Analysis and simulation. *Science*, *245*, 605–615.

Milner, A. D., & Goodale, M. A. (1995). *The visual brain in action*. Oxford, UK: Oxford University Press.

Milner, B. (1982). Some cognitive effects of frontal-lobe lesions in man. *Philosophical Transactions of the Royal Society of London B: Biological Sciences*, *298*, 211–226.

Molfese, D. (1989). Electrophysiological correlates of word meanings in 14-month-old human infants. *Developmental Neuropsychology*, *5*, 70–103.

Morton, J., & Johnson, M. H. (1991). CONSPEC and CONLERN: A two-process theory of infant face recognition. *Psychological Review*, *98*(2), 164–181.

Munakata, Y., McClelland, J. L., Johnson, M. H., & Siegler, R. S. (1997). Rethinking infant knowledge: Toward an adaptive process account of successes and failures in object permanence tasks. *Psychological Review*, *104*(4), 686–713.

Nelson, C. A. (1995). The ontogeny of human memory: A cognitive neuroscience perspective. *Developmental Psychology*, *31*(5), 723–738.

Nelson, C. A. (2001). The development and neural bases of face recognition. *Infant and Child Development*, *10*, 3–18.

Nelson, C. A., Thomas, K. M., & de Haan, M. (2006). Neural bases of cognitive development. In D. Kuhn & R. S. Siegler (Eds.), W. Damon (Series Ed.), *Handbook of child psychology: Vol. 2. Cognition, Perception, and language* (6th ed., pp. 3–57). Hoboken, NJ: Wiley.

Neville, H. J. (1991). Neurobiology of cognitive and language processing: Effects of early experience. In K. R. Gibson & A. C. Petersen (Eds.), *Brain maturation and cognitive development: Comparative and cross-cultural perspectives* (pp. 355–380). New York: Aldine de Gruyter.

Neville, H., & Bavelier, D. (2002). Specificity and plasticity in neurocognitive development in humans. In *Brain development and cognition: A reader* (2nd ed., pp. 251–270). Oxford, UK: Blackwell.

Neville, H., Bavelier, D., Corina, D., Rauschecker, J. P., Karni, A., Lalwani, A., et al. (1998). Cerebral organization for language in deaf and hearing subjects: Biological constraints and effects of experience. *Proceedings of the National Academy of Sciences of the United States of America*, *95*, 922–929.

O'Leary, D. D. M. (1989). Do cortical areas emerge from a protocortex? *Trends in Neuroscience*, *12*, 400–406.

Olesen, P. J., Nagy, Z., Westerberg, H., & Klingberg, T. (2003). Combined analysis of DTI and fMRI data reveals a joint maturation of white and grey matter in a fronto-parietal network. *Cognitive Brain Research*, *18*(1), 48–57.

Olson, E. A. & Luciana, M. (2008). The development of prefrontal cortex functions in adolescence. In C. A. Nelson & M. Luciana (Eds.), *Handbook of developmental cognitive neuroscience* (2nd ed., pp. 575–590). Cambridge, MA: MIT Press.

O'Reilly, R., & Johnson, M. II. (1994). Object recognition and sensitive periods: A computational analysis of visual imprinting. *Neural Computation*, *6*, 357–390.

Overman, W., Bachevalier, J., Turner, M., & Peuster, A. (1992). Object recognition versus object discrimination: Comparison between human infants and infant monkeys. *Behavioral Neuroscience*, *106*, 15–29.

Pallas, S. L. (2001). Intrinsic and extrinsic factors shaping cortical identity. *Neurosciences*, *24*, 417–423.

Pascalis, O., de Schonen, S., Morton, J., Fabre-Grenet, M., & Deruelle, C. (1995). Mother's face recognition by neonates: A replication and an extension. *Infant Behavior and Development*, *18*, 79–85.

Pascalis, O., de Haan, M., & Nelson, C. A. (2002). Is face processing species-specific during the first year of life? *Science*, *296*(5571), 1321–1323.

Paus, T., Collins, D. L., Evans, A. C., Leonard, G., Pike, B., & Zijdenbos, A. (2001). Maturation of white matter in the human brain: A review of magnetic-resonance studies. *Brain Research Bulletin*, *54*, 255–266.

Pfefferbaum, A., Mathalon, D. H., Sullivan, E. V., Rawles, J. M., Zipursky, R. B., & Lim, K. O. (1994). A quantitative magnetic resonance imaging study of changes in brain morphology from infancy to late adulthood. *Archives of Neurology*, *51*(9), 874–887.

Piaget, J. (1954). *The construction of reality in the child* (M. Cook, Trans.). New York: Basic Books.

Pinker, S. (1994). *The language instinct*. New York: William Morrow.

Posner, M. I., & Rothbart, M. K. (1980). The development of attentional mechanisms. In J. H. Flower (Ed.), *Nebraska Symposium on Motivation*. Lincoln, NE: University of Nebraska Press.

Ragsdale, C. W., & Grove, E. A. (2001). Patterning in the mammalian cerebral cortex. *Current Opinion in Neurobiology*, *11*, 50–58.

Rakic, P. (1987). Intrinsic and extrinsic determinants of neocortical parcellation: A radial unit model. In P. Rakic & W. Singer (Eds.), *Neurobiology of neocortex* (pp. 5–27). New York: Wiley.

Rakic, P. (1988). Specification of cerebral cortical areas. *Science, 241*, 170–176.

Richards, J. E. (2003). The development of visual attention and the brain. In M. de Haan & M. H. Johnson (Eds.), *The cognitive neuroscience of development* (pp. 73–93). Hove, UK: Psychology Press.

Richards, J. E. (2008). Attention in young infants: A developmental psychophysiological perspective. In C. A. Nelson & M. Luciana (Eds.), *The handbook of developmental cognitive neuroscience* (2nd ed., pp. 479–498). Cambridge, MA: MIT Press.

Rovee-Collier, C. K. (1993). The capacity for long-term memory in infancy. *Current Directions in Psychological Science, 2*(4), 130–135.

Schacter, D., & Moscovitch, M. (1984). Infants, amnesia and dissociable memory systems. In M. Moscovitch (Ed.), *Infant memory* (pp. 173–216). New York: Plenum Press.

Schatz, J., Craft, S., Koby, M., & DeBaun, M. (2000). A lesion analysis of visual orienting performance in children with cerebral vascular injury. *Developmental Neuropsychology, 17*, 49–61.

Schatz, J., Craft, S., White, D., Park, T. S., & Figiel, G. (2001). Inhibition of return in children with perinatal brain injury. *Journal of the International Neuropsychological Society, 7*, 275–284.

Scherf, K. S., Behrmann, M., Humphreys, K. & Luna, B. (2007). Visual category-selectivity for faces, places and objects emerges along different developmental trajectories. *Developmental Science, 10*(4), F15–F30.

Schilbach, L., Wohlschlaeger, A. M., Kraemer, N. C., Newen, A., Shah, N. J., Fink, G. R., et al. (2006). Being with virtual others: Neural correlates of social interaction. *Neuropsychologia, 44*(5), 718–730.

Segalowitz, S. J. (1994). Developmental psychology and brain development: A historical perspective. In G. Dawson & K. W. Fischer (Eds.), *Human behavior and the developing brain* (pp. 67–92). New York: Guilford Press.

Shaw, P., Greenstein, D., Lerch, J., Clasen, L., Lenroot, R., Gogtay, N., et al. (2006). Intellectual ability and cortical development in children and adolescents. *Nature, 440*, 676–679.

Silva, A. J., Paylor, R., Wehner, J. M., & Tonegawa, S. (1992). Impaired spatial learning in alpha-calcium–calmodulin kinase II mutant mice. *Science, 257*, 206–211.

Silva, A. J., Stevens, C. F., Tonegawa, S., & Wang, Y. (1992). Deficient hippocampal long-term potentiation in a-calcium–calmodulin kinase II mutant mice. *Science, 257*, 201–206.

Simion, F., Valenza, E., Umilta, C., & Dalla Barba, B. (1998). Preferential orienting to faces in newborns: A temporal–nasal asymmetry. *Journal of Experimental Psychology: Human Perception and Performance, 24*(5), 1399–1405.

South, M., Ozonoff, S., & Schultz, R. T. (2008). Neurocognitive development in autism. In C. A. Nelson & M. Luciana (Eds.), *The handbook of developmental cognitive neuroscience* (2nd ed., pp. 701–716). Cambridge, MA: MIT Press.

Stern, D. N. (1977). *The first relationship: Infant and mother*. Cambridge, MA: Harvard University Press.

Stiles, J., Bates, E., Thal, D., Trauner, D., & Reilly, J. (2002). Linguistic and spatial cognitive development in children with pre- and perinatal focal brain injury: A ten-year overview from the San Diego Longitudinal Project. In M. H. Johnson, Y. Munakata, & R. O. Gilmore (Eds.), *Brain development and cognition: A reader* (2nd ed., pp. 272–291). Oxford, UK: Blackwell.

Stryker, M. P., & Harris, W. (1986). Binocular impulse blockade prevents the formation of ocular dominance columns in cat visual cortex. *Journal of Neuroscience, 6*, 2117–2133.

Symons, L. A., Hains, S. M. J., & Muir, D. W. (1998). Look at me: Five-months-old infants' sensitivity to very small deviations in eye-gaze during social interactions. *Infant Behavior and Development, 21*, 531–536.

Taga, G., Asakawa, K., Maki, A., Konishi, Y., & Koizumi, H. (2003). Brain imaging in awake infants by near-infrared optical topography. *Proceedings of the National Academy of Sciences of the United States of America, 100*, 10722–10727.

Tanapat, P., Hastings, N. B., & Gould, E. (2001). Adult neurogenesis in the hippocampal formation. In C. A. Nelson & M. Luciana (Eds.), *The handbook of developmental cognitive neuroscience* (pp. 93–106). Cambridge, MA: MIT Press.

Teszner, D., Tzavaras, A., Gruner, J., & Hecaen, H. (1972). Right–left asymmetry of the planum temporale; apropos of the anatomical study of 100 brains. *Review-Neurologique-Paris, 126*(6), 444–449.

Thatcher, R. W. (1992). Cyclic cortical reorganization during early childhood. *Brain and Cognition, 20*(1), 24–50.

Thelen, E., & Smith, L. B. (1994). *A dynamic systems approach to the development of cognition and action*. Cambridge, MA: MIT Press.

Thomas, K. M. & Tseng, A. (2008). Functional MRI methods in developmental cognitive neuroscience. In C. A. Nelson & M. Luciana (Eds.), *The handbook of developmental cognitive neuroscience* (2nd ed., pp. 311–324). Cambridge, MA: MIT Press.

Tulving, E. (1983). *Elements of episodic memory*. Oxford, UK: Clarendon Press.

Tzourio-Mazoyer, N., de Schonen, S., Crivello, F., Reutter, B., Aujard, Y., & Mazoyer, B. (2002). Neural correlates of woman face processing by 2-month-old infants. *NeuroImage, 15*, 454–461.

Vargha-Khadem, F., Gadian, D. G., Watkins, K. E., Connelly, A., Van Paesschen, W., & Mishkin, M. (1997). Differential effects of early hippocampal pathology on episodic and semantic memory. *Science, 277*, 376–380.

Vargha-Khadem, F., Isaacs, E., & Muter, V. (1994). A review of cognitive outcome after unilateral lesions sustained during childhood. *Journal of Child Neurology, 9* (suppl. 2), 67–73.

Vargha-Khadem, F., Watkins, K., Alcock, K. J., Fletcher, P., & Passingham, R. E. (1995). Praxic and nonverbal cognitive deficits in a large family with a genetically transmitted speech and language disorder. *Proceedings of the National Academy of Sciences of the United States of America, 92*, 930–933.

Viding, E., Williamson, D. E., Forbes, E. E., & Hariri, A. R. (2008). The integration of neuroimaging and molecular genetics in the study of developmental cognitive neuroscience. In C. A. Nelson & M. Luciana (Eds.), *The handbook of developmental cognitive neuroscience* (2nd ed., pp. 351–366). Cambridge, MA: MIT Press.

Wada, J. A., Clarke, R., & Hamm, A. (1975). Cerebral hemispheric asymmetry in humans. *Archives of Neurology, 32*, 239.

Waddington, C. H. (1975). *The evolution of an evolutionist.* Edinburgh, UK: Edinburgh University Press.

Wattam-Bell, J. (1991). Development of motion-specific cortical responses in infants. *Vision Research, 31*, 287–297.

Welsh, M. C., Pennington, B. F., Ozonoff, S., Rouse, B., & McCabe, E. R. B. (1990). Neuropsychology of early-treated phenylketonuria: Specific executive function deficits. *Child Development, 61*, 1697–1713.

Werker, J. F., & Polka, L. (1993). The ontogeny and developmental significance of language-specific phonetic perception. In B. de Boysson-Bardies et al. (Eds.), *Developmental neurocognition: Speech and face processing in the first year of life* (pp. 275–288). Dordrecht, The Netherlands: Kluwer Academic.

Werker, J. F., & Vouloumanos, A. (2001). Speech and language processing in infancy: A neurocognitive approach. In C. A. Nelson & M. Luciana (Eds.), *Handbook of developmental cognitive neuroscience* (2nd ed., pp. 269–280). Cambridge, MA: MIT Press.

Wiesel, T. N., & Hubel, D. H. (1965). Comparison of the effects of unilateral and bilateral eye closure on cortical unit responses in kittens. *Journal of Neurophysiology, 28*, 1029–1040.

Witelson, S. F., & Pallie, W. (1973). Left hemisphere specialization for language in the newborn: Neuroanatomical evidence of asymmetry. *Brain, 94*, 641.

Yamada, H., Sadato, N., Konishi, M., Muramoto, S., Kimura, K., Tanaka, M., et al. (2000). A milestone for normal development of the infantile brain detected by functional MRI. *Neurology, 55*, 218–223.

Yamada, H., Sadato, N., Konishi, Y., Kimura, K., Tanaka, M., Yonekura, Y., et al. (1997). A rapid brain metabolic change in infants detected by fMRI. *NeuroReport, 8*, 3775–3778.

❖ 5 ❖

PHYSICAL AND MOTOR DEVELOPMENT

Karen E. Adolph
New York University
Sarah E. Berger
The College of Staten Island, and
the Graduate Center of the City University of New York

INTRODUCTION

Why Study Movement?

When parents brag about their children's accomplishments to friends and family or document important events with camcorders and baby books for posterity, they tend to focus on infants' physical and motor development. Parents view physical growth and motor skills as important milestones, because getting bigger and stronger and rolling over, sitting up, and the like are dramatic, easily observable signs that children are developing normally. Psychologists, like parents, have a long tradition of using physical and motor development as a yardstick for verifying that infants are developing on schedule.

But why include a chapter about physical and motor development in a book about psychological development? What is psychological about the growing body in action (Adolph, 2008)? The answer is threefold. First, physical and motor development involve more than lists of developmental norms on growth charts or screening inventories. Motor behavior is integral to psychology. For those psychologists who believe that psychology is the study of behavior, movement is the stuff of the science (Adolph & Berger, 2006). Behavior is movement. Infants' visual exploration of events, smiles and babbles to caregivers, manipulation of objects, and navigation of the environment involve movements of the eyes, mouth, arms, and legs. Alternatively, for those psychologists who believe that psychology is the study of mind, infants' movements are the medium for making inferences about thoughts, perceptions, and intentions that are not directly observable. Researchers rely on movements to study infants who cannot understand verbal questions or respond with spoken answers. Eye movements, smiles and cries, reaching, kicking, and walking are essential tools for studying infants' perception, cognition, emotion, and social interaction (Adolph & Joh, 2007).

Second, motor actions are fundamental to other domains of psychology and their development. Adaptive control of movement is a psychological problem in itself. Motor action is inextricably coupled with perception. Every movement gives rise to perceptual information (Gibson, 1979), and perception in turn guides action adaptively (Bornstein, Arterberry, & Mash, Chapter 6, this volume; von Hofsten, 1993). Perceptual information allows children to modify movements in accordance with their growing bodies, changing skill level, and expanding environments, and provides them with the means to exploit new **affordances** for action (Adolph & Berger, 2006; Bertenthal & Clifton, 1998; Gibson, 1988). Moreover, motor development is implicated in the development of perception, cognition, and emotion. Burgeoning motor skills provide infants with new opportunities for learning. As Piaget (1954) pointed out, sensorimotor behavior is the fodder for cognition, and cognitive problem-solving skills enable infants to plan and select motor strategies more adaptively. Infants' developing bodies and motor competencies are linked with changes in emotional and social development (Campos et al., 2000). Every parent knows that social pressures help to spur new skills and that infants delight in their own motor achievements.

A third reason why our chapter belongs in a textbook on developmental science is that motor actions and all the accompanying percepts, thoughts, plans, and emotions are **embodied** (Adolph, 2008; Thelen, 1995). Movements depend on and exploit the physical properties and biomechanical constraints of the body. The intimate relations between the propensity for movement and infants' body characteristics affect the real-time control of motor action (how these fingers move to type these words) and changes in the control of action over development (aiming the finger to depress a key depends on finger size, strength, agility, and so on).

Chapter Overview

This chapter focuses on the development of motor action in the fetal and infancy periods because it is during these early periods that the foundation for skilled action is laid down. More of the important motor milestones appear during the first 2 years of life than during any other developmental period. Consequently, most of the research literature focuses on the infancy period. Fetal growth and motility is an exciting new research frontier, the study of which has been recently made possible due to technological and procedural innovations.

The chapter is loosely organized in chronological order. We begin by detailing spontaneous fetal movements and motor responses to external stimuli that reach the fetus in the womb. Fetal movements are essential for normal body growth, and fetal growth has remarkable effects on possibilities for movement. In the second section, we describe rudimentary motor abilities in newborns. Although newborns' movements are hampered by gravity rather than facilitated by the buoyant uterine environment, we show how they are developmentally continuous with those performed in the womb. The next section focuses on movements of the face. Although most people do not think of sucking, swallowing, chewing, talking, and facial expressions as in the province of motor development, everyone would agree that these motor actions are critical for infants' entrée in the social world. We continue with infants' triumph over gravity as they gain the muscle strength and balance control to lift their heads and sit without support. We introduce the crucial role of perceptual information in keeping balance. In subsequent sections, we describe the biomechanical and perceptual processes involved in interacting with objects—reaching, grasping, object exploration, and the use of hand-held objects as tools. Elegant new studies challenge several common-sense assumptions about the development of goal-directed arm movements. The section on independent mobility describes infants' first success at moving their whole bodies from place to place. Although most people assume that infants first navigate the world on hands and knees, in fact infants devise a variety of unique locomotor strategies including scooting on their bottoms and shimmying on their bellies. This section also highlights specificity in motor learning. Infants have to learn about each motor milestone separately. What they knew about keeping balance in an experienced sitting **posture** does not help them to keep balance after they begin **crawling**; practice with sitting and crawling does not help infants to keep balance upright.

The section on upright posture describes how infants drag themselves to a stand, cruise along furniture, and eventually walk. We focus on why babies walk when they do and what factors make walking skill improve. Changes in body proportions and exposure to risky ground surfaces impose new challenges for perceptual control of locomotion. Finally, we describe complex forms of locomotion that require cognitive skills for planning and constructing movement strategies to descend stairs and pedestals, and cross narrow bridges.

Throughout the chapter, we debunk several long-standing myths of physical and motor development. Recent breakthroughs in research have provided new insights into the role of maturation versus experience, the integrity of neonatal reflexes, the universality of motor milestones, the head-to-toe direction of growth, and the smooth continuous changes in body growth depicted on standard growth charts.

MOVING BEFORE BIRTH: FETAL GROWTH AND BEHAVIOR

Access to the Fetus

Everyone knows that fetuses grow from microscopic eggs to baby-sized newborns. Most of us, however, have only a murky understanding of the remarkable changes in fetuses' shape and size over the 40 weeks of normal gestation. Part of the mystery stems from the difficulty in gaining visual access to fetal development. Like a thick blackout curtain, fetal development occurs behind the barrier of mothers' abdominal wall.

Early researchers were restricted to educated guesswork about fetal growth and behavior because the existing technology precluded direct observation in the womb. To describe fetal development in the first weeks of gestation, researchers conducted quick and simple tests on aborted and miscarried fetuses kept alive in a warm bath for a few minutes (Prechtl, 1986). For example, Hooker (1952) elicited neck flexion and arm movement in 8- to 9-week-old abortuses in response to light stroking with a stiff hair. Knowledge was similarly limited about the later weeks of gestation because researchers could only observe infants born prematurely or infer fetal growth and behavior from palpating mothers' abdomens and documenting mothers' reports of fetal movement. The knowledge gained was sub-optimal because miscarried, aborted, and preterm infants may be misrepresentative of healthy development, and mothers' reports and palpation through the abdominal wall lead to interpretive problems such as distinguishing a fetal kick from a mother's rumbling stomach (Munn, 1965).

The advent of ultrasound in the 1950s opened a new frontier of fetal research (see Prechtl, 1985, for historical review). With ultrasound, high-frequency sound waves are bounced off the fetus to create a live-action black-and-white video image (sonogram). Modern three- and four-dimensional ultrasound techniques provide such high-resolution images that fetuses' face, sex organs (many parents learn their infants' sex at an 18-week ultrasound), parts of the brain and internal organs, fingers and toes, and so on are clearly visible. Fetal movements appear in such fine detail, from the kick of a leg to a hiccup or flutter of an eyelid, that laypersons can distinguish them on the ultrasound monitor. Prenatal magnetic resonance imaging reveals structural developments in the fetal brain (Perkins et al., 2007; Salomon & Garel, 2007), and Doppler scanning links fetal cerebral blood flow velocities to early indications of brain lateralization (Feng, Raynor, Fiano, & Emory, 1997). Although microphotography through an endoscope is also possible, ironically, famed photographer Nilsson's (Nilsson & Hamberger, 1990) iconic and widely reprinted images of a fetus sucking its thumb and spinning like a space man in the constellation of the chorion are actually staged displays of aborted fetuses.

Animal models provide an additional exciting avenue for research on fetal development because fetuses can be observed directly using various external preparations for bridging the barrier of the abdominal wall (Alberts & Ronca, 1993). For example, researchers remove the uterus from anesthetized rat dams and maintain the fetal environment by keeping it in a temperature-controlled bath. Late in gestation, the growing fetuses stretch the uterine wall to transparency so that fetal movements can be directly observed. Alternatively, researchers exteriorize fetuses and keep them alive in a temperature-controlled bath while still connected to the dam by the umbilical cord and placenta. By preserving their life-support systems, researchers can observe and test healthy, living fetuses for sessions lasting several hours (Smotherman & Robinson, 1996).

Fetal Growth

Based on the combination of available techniques, researchers have compiled a detailed trajectory of fetal growth and physical development. The structural changes in the shape of fetuses' body are more radical and dramatic than at any other period of development. At 4 weeks after fertilization, human embryos still look like tadpoles, with a huge head region, tiny limb buds from which the arms and legs will grow, and a pointed tail that curls up toward the face region (Nilsson & Hamberger, 1990). The face is still undifferentiated. Layers of specialized, thickened tissue cover the parts of the face from which the ears, eyes, nose, and mouth will form.

Nine weeks after fertilization marks the official end of the embryonic period and the start of the fetal period of development. Fetuses' bodies are more human looking; they have lost their tails, and their facial features are sketched in. The body and limbs are girded with rudimentary muscles and bones. Arms and legs are tipped with the beginnings of fingers and toes. Elbows appear like little bumps. By 12 weeks, fetuses have a neck. Limbs look long and thin, and fingers and toes are well developed. The genitalia are differentiated. At 16 weeks, fetuses' skin is virtually transparent like a capillary map. The lungs are developing, bones have strengthened, and more muscle tissue covers the bones (Moore & Persaud, 1993; Ratner, 2002). By 20 weeks, nails appear on fingers and toes, and fetuses' heartbeat can be heard through a stethoscope on mothers' abdomens. Between 24 and 28 weeks, eyelids open and close, fingerprints and footprints appear, air sacs develop in the lungs, and the cerebral cortex develops. Between 28 and 38 weeks, a layer of body fat appears beneath the skin. The lungs are capable of breathing air and are almost fully mature, and the central nervous system has increasing control over bodily functions (Moore & Persaud, 1993; Ratner, 2002).

As shown in Figure 5.1, the change in fetuses' body size and proportions are as dramatic as the structural changes in the shape of their bodies. The rate of fetal growth is far more astronomical than the view from outside mothers' bulging abdomens might suggest. At 4 weeks after conception, the average embryo is 4 mm long from crown to rump, about the size of a pea (Moore & Persaud, 1993). The head comprises one-half of the body length. At 8 weeks, fetuses measure 3.18 cm from crown to rump, one half of which is still composed of head. By the twelfth week, fetuses measure 8.5 cm. By the sixteenth week, fetuses are 15.24 cm long from head to toe and weigh 200 g (less than half a can of soda). Between weeks 16 and 24, fetuses have nearly doubled in size. Their length is 28.45 cm and their weight is 820 g. The head grows more slowly so that now it is only one-third the length of the fetus. By 32 weeks, fetuses are 38.1 cm long and weigh 2100 g. By 36 weeks, they are 44.45 cm long and weigh 2900 g (Moore & Persaud, 1993; Ratner, 2002). The head continues to grow more slowly relative to the rest of the body so that its relative length shrinks to one-quarter of total body length. Overall, from pea-sized embryo to term newborn, fetuses increase their length by approximately 8000% and their weight by 42,500%. By the time gestation nears completion at 38 to 40 weeks, fetuses fill the entire uterine space.

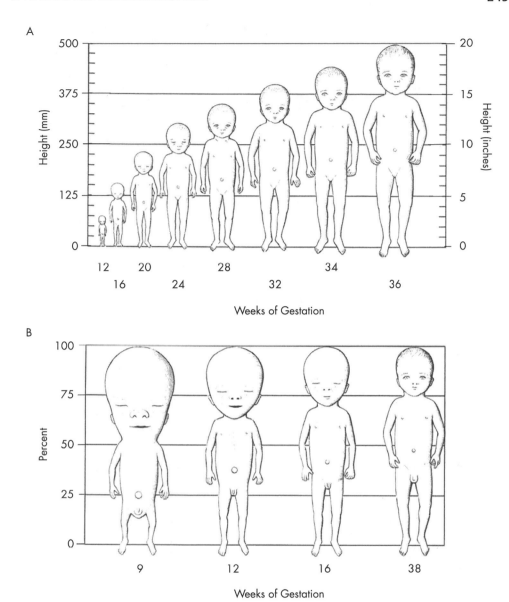

FIGURE 5.1 Dramatic changes in fetal (A) body size and (B) body proportions from 9 weeks of gestation to birth. From *The Developing Human* by K. L. Moore & T. V. N. Persaud (1993). Copyright © 1993 by Elsevier. Reprinted with permission.

Stimulation from Outside

The popular notion of returning to the peaceful quiet of the mother's womb is only a myth. The uterus is not like a sterile incubator for housing the developing fetus. "Carrying" a fetus during pregnancy is not like transporting a bubble-wrapped glass egg. Who would design an incubator that is infused with the taste and smell of mothers' last meal or their half-digested stomach contents? Or an incubator that jostles with mothers' every step, tips over when mothers lean forward, and deforms when mothers tighten their belts?

Research suggests that, in fact, the womb is an environment rich with potential stimulation

(Alberts & Ronca, 1993; Smotherman & Robinson, 1996). Sounds, smells, tastes, pressure, movement—even light—come through the abdominal wall. Stimulation is most keen toward the end of gestation when there is less amniotic fluid to buffer fetuses from the outside world. Moreover, fetuses are equipped to experience the rich stimulation of the uterine world. In humans, all of the sensory systems come on line prior to birth (Robinson & Kleven, 2005). The ears, formed at 9 weeks, detect sounds such as mothers' heartbeat by 26 weeks of gestation (Smith, Gerhardt, Griffiths, Huang, & Abrams, 2003). The eyes, structurally formed at 6 weeks, detect light by 20 weeks. The olfactory and chemosensory apparatus detect smells and tastes by 26–28 weeks. Mechanoreceptors in the muscles, joints, and skin are sensitive to the pressure of a touch by 10 weeks. The vestibular system detects movement after 13 weeks (Moore & Persaud, 1993; Robinson & Kleven, 2005).

Animal models show most dramatically the wide variety and frequency of stimulation that permeates the uterine environment and the remarkable ability of the fetus to detect and respond to stimulation. Time-lapse video recordings show that pregnant rat dams run back and forth in their cages, rear onto their hind legs, turn in tight circles prior to lying down, lick their abdomens, and scratch their abdomens with a hindlimb as frequently as do virgin dams (Ronca & Alberts, 1995). By replacing rat fetuses with saline-filled balloons connected to pressure transducers, researchers demonstrated that mothers' activity is transmitted into the uterine world. In the last days of gestation, the "peaceful quiet" of the rat womb is disturbed by 150 linear accelerations and 600 angular accelerations from mothers' locomotor movements, 10 min of mechanical pressure from mothers' grooming, and 125 episodes of vibration from mothers' hindlimb scratching (Ronca & Alberts, 1995). When fetuses are exteriorized into a temperature-controlled bath and stimulated by simulated maternal activity (researchers moved the tray to simulate the average linear and angular accelerations, pressed the fetuses with rubber balloons to simulate pressure from mothers' hindlimb scratching, and so forth), fetal rats respond with changes in heart rate and motor behaviors (Ronca & Alberts, 1994).

Fetal Movements

Human fetuses begin moving from the instant that they have rudimentary muscles to activate their body parts and the primitive neural circuitry to activate their muscles (Humphrey, 1944). At 8 to 9 weeks of gestation, fetuses display quick startles that start in their limbs and radiate to the trunk and neck (Prechtl & Hopkins, 1986). They writhe in slow indeterminate sequences of arm, leg, neck, and trunk movements. Their hiccups are strong enough to cause their whole bodies to jump up and down in the amniotic fluid. By 10 weeks, fetuses display a variety of arm and leg movements, sometimes alternating between one arm and the other or one leg and the other, and sometimes moving their limbs in conjunction with whole-body activation. In addition, fetuses perform isolated limb and digit movements, keeping the rest of their body still while flailing an arm or leg, wiggling their fingers, or forming a fist (Prechtl, 1985, 1986).

Many hand movements are not random (see Figure 5.2). Rather, starting at 14 weeks, fetuses direct approximately 66% of their hand movements toward objects in the uterus—their own faces and bodies, the wall of the uterus, and the umbilical cord (Sparling, van Tol, & Chescheir, 1999). Many hand-to-body and hand-to-object movements occur in brief bouts of activity (Sparling et al., 1999), like fetal versions of Piaget's primary and secondary circular reactions (see Birney, in this textbook).

Between 10 and 11 weeks, fetuses turn their heads to the side and nod them up and down. They open and close their jaws and begin making breathing movements from contractions of the diaphragm. Beginning in the 11th and 12th weeks, fetuses make more movements with their mouths—they yawn, suck, and swallow the amniotic fluid (De Vries, Visser, & Prechtl, 1982). By week 20, fetuses produce movements with all the parts of their face. They wrinkle

FIGURE 5.2 Fetal hand movements after 14 weeks of gestation. Note that the majority of fetal hand movements are directed toward objects in the uterus, like the fetus's own body, the umbilical cord, and the uterine wall. Adapted from J. W. Sparling, J. van Tol, & N. C. Chescheir (1999). Fetal and neonatal hand movement. *Physical Therapy, 79*, 24–39.

their foreheads, move their lips and tongue, and raise their eyebrows (Nilsson & Hamberger, 1990). After 25 weeks, fetuses' eyes are no longer fused shut; they open and close their eyes.

Ironically, "quickening" (mothers' awareness of fetal movement) occurs between 16 and 20 weeks of gestation (Kuno et al., 2001), at about the same time as fetal movements begin to decrease because of decreased space in the amniotic sac (Sparling et al., 1999). Mothers feel more fetal movements despite the smaller joint excursions and lower frequency because now the limbs make contact with the uterine wall. What mothers call "kicking" at this point is most often partial leg extensions and arm flexions (Sparling et al., 1999). At 15 to 16 weeks' gestation, fetal movements are reduced to approximately 60% of the time when fetuses are awake or in active sleep (Kuno et al., 2001). Fetuses' arms move most often and mouths least often. As shown in Figure 5.2, fetal hand movements directed toward their mouths, face, and head decrease linearly from week 14; fetal hand movements directed toward the uterine wall increase in the same time period (Sparling et al., 1999). The increasingly confining space of the womb continues to dampen fetal movements until fetuses are restricted to head, face, and breathing movements and to partial movements of the extremities. By week 38, fetal movements are reduced to 10% or less of the time during awake periods or active sleep (de Vries, Visser, & Prechtl, 1988; Roodenburg, Wladimiroff, van Es, & Prechtl, 1991; Ten Hof et al., 2002).

The Meaning and Function of Fetal Movements

The evidence indicates that fetal movements serve important developmental functions. The common fetal behavior of swallowing amniotic fluid, for example, contributes to the normal development of the oropharyngeal cavity, the lungs, and the digestive system (Moore & Persaud, 1993). Body movements function to facilitate the normal development of muscles, bones, joints, and skin. Rat fetuses deprived of movement by curare during the last 3 days of gestation show system-wide effects in their bodies' morphology. Their joints are frozen and fused, bone growth is altered, hind limbs are underdeveloped, mouths are small, skin is thin and tight, lung development is retarded, and the umbilical cord is too short (Moessinger, 1983). Movement disabilities are long-term, continuing after birth. Similarly, alcohol is typically viewed as teratogenic because of effects at the cellular level. However, because alcohol suppresses fetal motility for several hours, repeated fetal alcohol exposure may be detrimental for infants' physical and motor development due to the reduction of normal movement (Moessinger, 1983).

But why do fetuses move? They cannot possibly "know" that their movements will serve important functions in the long run. Clearly, some movements are in response to external stimulation. For example, fetuses moved their hand to cover their eyes when microphotographer Nilsson flashed his tiny strobe (Nova, 1996). Fetuses increase overall motility and blink their eyes in response to a loud sound. Some movements are in response to self-stimulation. For example, perceptual feedback from touching the face with a hand might elicit a head movement just as Hooker's (1952) stiff hair swipe might elicit a fetal head movement. Some movements, however, are just spontaneous bursts of motor activity without any proximal elicitor or goal. A primary reason why fetuses move is that they can.

On a traditional interpretation, fetal movements are reflexive, hard-wired programs controlled by the central nervous system (McGraw, 1945). This interpretation is problematic, however. A rigid program would mean that the central nervous system controls movements by dictating the timing and amplitude of fetuses' muscle contractions. For example, some researchers have proposed that a central pattern generator in the spinal cord is responsible for fetuses' step-like leg movements (see Selverston, 1980, for a review). A rigid program like a central pattern generator for stepping is not responsive to changing biomechanics due to body growth. Likewise, a rigid "trunk, arm, hand, head, or face generator" for programming twisting, reaching, grasping, and nodding movements should not be sensitive to fetuses' changing body dimensions.

Contrary to the traditional view, the dramatic changes in the shape and size of fetuses' bodies mean that the central nervous system would need to change the timing and magnitude of muscle activations to produce the same external movement. An example is fetal hand-to-mouth behavior (Robinson & Kleven, 2005). Young human fetuses' arms are so short that they can only get their hands to their face by extending their arms. The central nervous system must activate the triceps brachi muscles on the backs of the upper arms. Older fetuses' arms are much longer. Toward the end of gestation, fetuses need to flex their arms at the elbows to bring their hands to their mouth. A completely different set of muscles is involved. The central nervous system must activate the biceps brachi muscles on the front of the upper arms. Thus, ongoing developmental changes in fetuses' bodies argue against the traditional interpretation of rigidly programmed movements.

NEWBORN MOVEMENTS: SPONTANEOUS, REFLEXIVE, AND INTENTIONAL

Newborns' Bodies

Newborns are beautiful in their parents' eyes, but to more objective observers, they look alien—red, lumpy-headed creatures with tiny thin limbs. Newborns' heads are often misshapen because the soft sutures between their skull bones allow their heads to compress as they squeeze through the birth canal. Their skin is coated with a white cheesy vernix that acts like a greasy moisturizing cream to protect it from chapping during the long immersion in a saline, watery environment. Some newborns are covered with a temporary coat of downy hair over their entire bodies.

On average, newborn infants weigh 3.3 kg (Wang, Dorer, Fleming & Catlin, 2004), about the weight of a standard laptop computer. They measure 57 cm from crown to heel (Ounsted & Moar, 1986). Minus the head and legs, newborns' bodies are the approximate size of a football or the length of an adult's forearm. In fact, many new mothers breastfeed their newborns in the so-called "football position", holding their babies' bodies along their forearm with their legs draping down. Like fetuses, newborns' body dimensions are extremely top-heavy. Their heads are huge relative to their torsos and limbs. Their head circumference (35 cm) is actually larger (106%) than their chest circumference (Ounsted & Moar, 1986). Their head length is 1/4 of their total height. In comparison, adults' head circumference is only 72% of their chest circumference (minus women's bust) and adults' head length is 1/8 of their total body height (Palmer, 1944).

Newborns' limbs are tightly flexed in the so-called "fetal position" from being crunched into the tight confines of the uterus (Amiel-Tison & Grenier, 1986; Bly, 1994). As fetuses fill the uterine space in the final weeks of gestation, their arms bend at the elbow and their knees draw up to their chests. The flexor muscles that bend the arms and legs become increasingly strong, whereas the extensor muscles that straighten babies' limbs become increasingly weak. Newborns' physiological flexion is so powerful that adults must apply strong pressure to fully extend babies' arms and legs and when the limbs are released they spring back into their bent position.

Newborns' Abilities

Environmental conditions constrain possibilities for action (Bernstein, 1967; Gibson, 1979). Like fetuses, newborns possess a rich repository of potential movements. Performing the movements in their repertoire, however, requires the appropriate biomechanical context. Radical differences in the fetal and newborn environments result in different constraints on movement and consequently differences in the quality and quantity of movements produced. The buoyancy of the amniotic fluid in the womb supports fetuses' limbs and dampens inertial forces, resulting in the balletic movements displayed by 14- to 20-week-old fetuses. In comparison, newborns must cope with the new constraints of moving their limbs against gravity and controlling the inertial forces generated by their own movements. Lifting an arm or raising the head must be powered completely by muscle strength. Likewise, muscle activations, not water, must dampen the inertial forces caused by an arm flail or a head turn. The limited gross motor repertoire of late-gestation fetuses is a consequence of their confinement within the shrinking uterine space, not due to a lack of underlying ability. In contrast to fetuses, newborns have abundant space in which to move.

Spontaneous movements. Many parents believe that newborns' motor abilities are limited to a handful of physiological responses, state changes, and crude uncontrolled movements of the head, face, and limbs. Researchers, however, have shown that most parents greatly underestimate newborns' abilities. Newborns, like fetuses, display a wide variety of movements using all of their body parts in various combinations (Cioni, Ferrari, & Prechtl, 1989; Hadders-Algra & Prechtl, 1992; Prechtl & Hopkins, 1986). They blink their eyes and turn them to track sounds and moving objects. They rotate their heads from side to side, protrude their tongues, open and close their mouths, and purse their lips (Green & Wilson, 2006). They arch their backs, turn their torsos, flail their arms, kick their legs, open and close their hands, and wiggle their fingers and toes. Like fetuses, newborns' flexed limb posture and loose muscles and joints allow them to bring their hands and feet up to their mouths to suck on their fingers, hands, and toes (Brazelton, 1956).

Many of infants' spontaneous movements are cyclical: They repeatedly move a body part in short bouts of activity (Thelen, 1979, 1981a, 1981b). For example, infants kick their legs in alternation (Figure 5.3A), whack a foot over and over against the floor, or flex and extend both legs simultaneously. They bang their arms and hands against surfaces, flap their arms up and down, bend and straighten their elbows, and rotate their hands in circles. They pulse their tongues in and out of their mouths and make rhythmic sucking movements. Researchers

A   B

C   D

FIGURE 5.3   (A) supine kicking. (B) Upright stepping. (C) Stick figure diagrams of kicking and stepping in a 2-week-old infant. The lines chart the movements of one of the infant's legs at toe, ankle, knee, and hip every 33 ms. Reprinted from *Developmental Psychology, 18*, E. Thelen and D. M. Fisher, Newborn stepping: An explanation for a disappearing reflex, pp. 765–766. Copyright © 1982 with permission from the American Psychological Association.

termed such cyclical movements "**stereotypies**" to denote rhythmic behaviors that appear stereotyped in form and timing (Thelen, 1979, 1981b). Ironically, the same movements that appear repetitive and stereotyped while viewing them at 30 fps on video may turn out to be variable and unique when measured with high-speed motion tracking devices: So-called "stereotypies" may not be stereotyped at all. In fact, infants' first banging movements are extremely variable, carving unique paths through the air (although they occur in rhythmical bouts of activity). Months later, infants' motor control improves and bouts of spontaneous banging are far more uniform and trace the same path through the air over and over (Kahrs & Lockman, 2010).

In addition to their seemingly rigid patterning, stereotypies are performed for their own sake, without an eliciting cause or a desired goal. The accepted view from ethologists, psychoanalysts, and physicians was that stereotypies are rare in primates and that their presence should be considered a sign of pathology (e.g., Spitz, 1965). Autistic rocking, head banging, and the like were thought to arise only in abnormal populations or in infants reared under impoverished conditions (e.g., Harlow & Harlow, 1961). But the early pioneers in motor development observed spontaneous cyclical movement in healthy, typically developing infants (Preyer, 1905). McGraw (1945) and Gesell (1946), for example, described rhythmic rocking on hands and knees as a typical developmental stage prior to crawling. Piaget (1954) highlighted "circular reactions" such as kicking and arm waving as a normal and necessary part of cognitive development. In fact, spontaneous, rhythmic movements make up a surprisingly large portion of healthy infants' waking activity. Spontaneous cyclical movements begin in the newborn period and continue over infants' entire first year of life (Thelen, 1979). Infants exhibit 47 different kinds of spontaneous cyclical movements involving the legs, arms, torso, head, and face, averaging 33 bouts of cyclical movements per hour. By the time infants are 12 months old, they have likely experienced over 110,000 bouts of wiggles, waves, kicks, and flaps in their legs, arms, heads, and trunks.

Newborn reflexes. In contrast to spontaneous movements that infants perform without a clear cause or goal, some of newborns' movements appear to be reflexive responses to particular eliciting stimuli (Bly, 1994; Capute, Accardo, Vining, Rubenstein, & Harryman, 1978; McGraw, 1932). A host of "oral reflexes" involves the mouth (Sheppard & Mysak, 1984): A touch on the cheek, lip, or tongue elicits mouth opening and a head turn toward the touch—the "rooting," "lip," and "tongue reflexes." A touch on the gums in the back of infants' mouths elicits the "biting reflex." Pressure on the palms of infants' hands elicits mouth opening in the fascinating and mysterious "Babkin reflex." And in response to a nipple or finger in their mouths, newborns exhibit the "sucking reflex." Other responses involve coordination among limbs, head, and torso. In response to feeling their heads turned to one side, newborns exhibit the fencing posture characteristic of the "asymmetric tonic neck reflex" in which the arm on the side of infants' face extends and the arm on the back of infants' skull bends. When infants feel themselves begin to fall or in response to a sudden vibration or noise, they demonstrate the "Moro reflex" by flinging their arms out to the sides and then bringing them back toward their chests. Infants display the "grasping reflex" when an object or adult's finger is placed into their palms, sometimes gripping so tightly that they can support their own weight dangling above the examination table. When babies are held by the thighs and squeezed inwards, the pressure elicits the "sitting reflex" (Katona, 1989; N. A. Zelazo, Zelazo, Cohen, & Zelazo, 1993). And when newborns are held upright with their feet touching a hard surface, they respond with the "stepping reflex"—alternating leg movements that look like exaggerated marching (Figure 5.3B).

Unlike the eye blink response to a puff of air or the leg kick in response to a hammer on the patellar tendon that are displayed over the life span, the so-called "**newborn reflexes**" disappear after a few months. However, many of the newborn reflexes also reappear after the newborn period in a different, more intentional guise. Some researchers' accounts (e.g., McGraw, 1945; Peiper, 1963; Zelazo, 1976) of the function of newborn reflexes and their continuity with later intentional actions have a teleological aspect. The oral reflexes function to facilitate nursing and later become intentional drinking from the breast or bottle. The asymmetric tonic neck reflex functions to orient infants' visual attention toward their hands and is later coopted for intentional object exploration. The Moro and grasping reflexes are residual behaviors from when non-human primates clung to their mothers swinging through the trees. The grasping reflex later becomes intentional grasping. The sitting reflex becomes intentional sitting. The stepping reflex serves to turn fetuses head-down in the womb and later becomes intentional walking. But, are these just-so stories really the reason for reflexes?

Are Reflexes Really Reflexive?

Traditionally, researchers have considered newborn reflexes to be unintentional movements over which infants have no control. That is, newborns suck, sit, step, and so on for the same reason that we withdraw our hand from a flame: Reflexes are unmodifiable, hard-wired, automatic, low-level responses to particular eliciting stimuli. However, modern research calls every assumption about newborn reflexes into question. Eliciting stimuli, for example, are not required: Newborns make stepping movements without feeling a surface under their feet; they "air step" when held with their feet in the air (Peiper, 1963; Thelen & Fisher, 1982). Perhaps the feeling of being upright is the elicitor? No, because newborns make alternating leg movements to "walk" up a vertical wall, up or down slopes, and upside-down on the ceiling (Peiper, 1963). Newborns also make alternating kicking movements when they lie on their backs (Thelen, 1979). Infants' supine kicking movements have the same pattern of muscle activations and the same time-space trajectories as the legs move up and down as upright stepping movements (Thelen & Fisher, 1982). In fact, modern motion analysis techniques allow researchers to plot recordings of leg movements as overlayed stick figures. As illustrated in Figure 5.3C, if you turn the kicking movements 90°, they look like stepping movements.

The meaning of the eliciting stimulus matters and the form of the responses is not rigid or obligatory: Newborns do not root when their own hand touches their cheek, only when the touch is external (Rochat & Hespos, 1997). The normal fencing pose of the asymmetric tonic neck reflex may reflect neonates' visual exploration of their outstretched arm, not an obligatory pose (van der Meer, 1997; van der Meer, van der Weel, & Lee, 1995, 1996). Even with weights tied to their wrists, newborns moved their hands when they could see them. Most important, babies moved their hands regardless of *how* they saw them. As shown in Figure 5.4, some infants saw their ipsilateral hand as usual, but others who saw their contralateral hand via a video monitor moved it more frequently than the occluded ipsilateral hand.

Most tellingly, responses can be produced and modified intentionally to bring about a desired consequence (DeCasper & Fifer, 1980; Kalnins & Bruner, 1973). Newborns increase or decrease their rate of sucking to hear a preferred sound (their mother's voice, their parents' native language, a familiar Dr Seuss story) or to view a preferred scene (e.g., bring a film into focus). Researchers monitor suck rate using non-nutritive pacifiers connected to pressure-sensitive transducers. Similarly, newborns can produce alternating leg movements intentionally. Piaget (1954), Rovee-Collier and colleagues (e.g., Hitchcock & Rovee-Collier, 1996; Rovee-Collier, 1999; Rovee-Collier & Gekoski, 1979) and many other researchers have demonstrated operant conditioning of supine leg kicks in 2- to 6-month-old infants. In a typical paradigm, the researchers tie one end of a ribbon to one of infants' ankles and attach the other end to an overhead mobile. Within a few minutes, infants' spontaneous kicking becomes exploratory in nature as they test the contingency between their leg movements and the jiggling of the mobile elements. After only a few minutes of exploration, infants' kicks become deliberate. They increase the frequency of kicking compared with baseline measures (before the ribbon activated the mobile), and they kick the contingent leg faster than the noncontingent leg (Thelen & Fisher, 1983). Moreover, newborns can change their pattern of interlimb coordination to activate the mobile. When infants' ankles were yoked together with an elastic tether, babies shifted from alternating leg movements to simultaneous double-leg kicks (Thelen, 1994). Infants can even discover subtle constraints on the contingency such as particular joint angles to activate the mobile (Angulo-Kinzler, 2001; Angulo-Kinzler & Horn, 2001; Angulo-Kinzler, Ulrich, & Thelen, 2002; Chen, Fetters, Holt, & Saltzman, 2002).

Disappearing Reflexes?

Part of the lore of newborn reflexes is that the movements show a U-shaped developmental trajectory (e.g., McGraw, 1935; Zelazo, 1998; Zelazo, Zelazo, & Kolb, 1972): high frequency in the first few months after birth, low or zero frequency in the next several months of life, then reappearance of the movement in contexts involving intentional, goal-directed actions.

FIGURE 5.4   Neonate turning head to the right to see left hand displayed on television monitor. Note the hand is lifted to keep it in sight, despite the weight attached to the wrist. Infants did not lift their unweighted hands if they could not see them. Reprinted from *Science, 267*, A. L. H. Van der Meer, F. R. van der Weel, & D. N. Lee, The functional significance of arm movements in neonates, p. 694. Copyright 1995 with permission from AAAS.

Newborn stepping is the most studied example of a "disappearing reflex." Upright stepping usually disappears by 8 weeks of age and reappears at around 8 months when infants begin to walk with caregivers holding their hands to provide balance. The traditional explanation is that neural maturation underlies the U-shaped trajectory. On this account, cortical maturation suppresses the reflexive movements at 8 weeks so that infants stand "as if glued to the floor" (McGraw, 1940, p. 751). With increasing myelinization of the cortical-spinal tract, the stepping movements reappear under cortical control at 8 months. Finally, maturation of neural structures and circuitry increases information-processing speed and efficiency so that infants walk independently at approximately 12 months of age (Zelazo, 1998; Zelazo, Weiss, & Leonard, 1989).

However, Thelen and colleagues showed that alternating leg movements are only masked, not disappeared (e.g., Thelen, Fisher, & Ridley-Johnson, 1984; Thelen, Fisher, Ridley-Johnson, & Griffin, 1982). Given that upright stepping and supine kicking are similar, Thelen puzzled over why upright stepping disappears, but supine kicking does not. Kicking is a high-frequency behavior throughout infants' first year of life. What kind of maturational "brain switch" would turn off the movements in one posture but not in another?

Thelen et al. (1982) noticed that infants with thinner legs continued to display upright stepping movements at the same ages when infants with fatter legs had stopped stepping. Experimental studies confirmed the relation between leg fat and upright stepping (Thelen et al., 1984). When 4-week-olds who were normally exhibiting the stepping movements had their legs weighted to simulate gains in leg fat over the first few months of life, the babies stopped stepping. When 4-week-olds, who were normally not displaying upright stepping, had their legs lightened by submerging them chest-deep into a tank of water, the babies stepped. When non-stepping 7-month-olds were supported over a motorized treadmill, their hidden stepping movements were unmasked (Thelen & Ulrich, 1991; Thelen, Ulrich, & Niles, 1987; Vereijken & Thelen, 1997). The moving treadmill belt pulled the legs backward, supplying the requisite leg strength, and the experimenter holding infants under the arms provided the necessary balance control. The legs sprang back on their own due to the visco-elastic springiness of the hip and knee joints. In principle, infants might hop along with both legs simultaneously moving backward then springing forward. In fact, the alternating pattern emerges, and infants appear to "walk" on the treadmill.

Thelen (et al., 1984; Thelen & Smith, 1994) proposed an alternative explanation that was agnostic with regard to changes in the central nervous system. Just as fetal movements are facilitated and constrained by factors outside the province of the central nervous system (the buoyancy of the amniotic fluid and the confines of the womb), so might newborns' movements be facilitated and constrained by developmental changes in non-neural biomechanical factors. Infants might stop stepping because the normal gains in leg fat over the first few months of life typically outstrip gains in muscle strength. Babies have to lift heavier limbs with less leg strength. In the upright position, infants must use muscle actions to flex their legs at the hip against the pull of gravity (like marching in place). In the supine position, gravity assists hip flexion by pulling the bent thigh toward the chest. Gravity, inertia, and the spring-like quality of the muscles and tendons help to extend the hip and spring the leg straight again. By 8 months of age, infants have built sufficient muscle strength to lift their legs in an upright position.

In line with Thelen's account, exercise moving the legs in an upright position causes upright stepping to persist beyond the usual 8-week cut-off. When parents provided their newborns with a few minutes of upright stepping exercise per day, infants did not show the typical decline in stepping movements (Zelazo et al., 1972). Only overload training appeared to build the requisite leg strength. When parents passively exercised their newborns' legs in the supine position (by pumping them up and down), upright stepping showed the typical disappearing trajectory.

MOVING THE FACE: EATING, SPEAKING, EMOTING

Facial movements are both life-sustaining and life-enriching. Eating—controlling the head and neck muscles required to suck, chew, and swallow—is necessary for life. And vocal and facial expressions—controlling the 80-some muscles from the top of the scalp to the bottom of the throat that allow us to make speech sounds and communicate our feelings—form the basis for the social connections that make life worth living. Ironically given the centrality of facial movements for normal functions, psychological research on motor development has largely ignored movement in every part of the face except for the eyes. Facial movements are entirely missing from most reviews of motor development (e.g., Adolph & Berger, 2006; Bertenthal & Clifton, 1998). Moreover, with the exception of automated remote eye trackers, until recently, technologies and procedures for precise time-based analyses of facial movements have lagged far behind those for recording limb movements (Wilson & Green, 2009). The current state of the art involves painstaking video coding of various parts of the face (Oster, 2005; Sheppard & Mysak, 1984), tiny facial markers for use with high-speed motion tracking (Green, Moore, & Reilly, 2002; Wilson & Green, 2009), and electromyography to measure activation of facial muscles (Green et al., 1997; Steeve, Moore, Green, Reilly, & McMurtry, 2008).

As with the rest of the body, some of infants' facial movements are produced spontaneously without any apparent reason. Infants silently and spontaneously move their mouths by opening and closing their jaws and puckering and spreading their lips (Green &

Wilson, 2006). With age, such movements use more parts of the face in unison and increase in frequency and speed, but remain highly variable, not cyclical and stereotypic. Some task-oriented and exploratory movements occur in bouts (sucking, chewing, and repetitive babbling), but these repetitive movements are still variable and modifiable rather than rigidly patterned. Like adults who frequently talk and chew at the same time, infants can produce various types of facial movements simultaneously. For example, producing vocalizations while mouthing objects to explore them is common in 6- to 9-month-olds (Fagan & Iverson, 2007).

Sucking, Swallowing, and Chewing

The image of a healthy newborn nursing at the mother's breast makes sucking and swallowing look deceptively simple. In fact, these actions are complex and involve different patterns of coordination with tongue, jaws, and lips. To suck, the tongue moves up and down with the jaws to create negative pressure and draw liquid into the mouth (Wilson, Green, Yunusova, & Moore, 2008). The lips must create a seal against the nipple (Geddes, Kent, Mitoulas, & Hartmann, 2008). To swallow, the tongue moves in a wave-like manner from the pointed tip across the top surface to transport the liquid through the mouth to the pharynx (Wilson & Green, 2006). When breathing is added to the mix, all three sets of movements must be coordinated with each other. Although sucking is possible while breathing, initially milk and air share the same passage as they enter the body through the pharynx, but milk must divert to the esophagus and air to the trachea. The trick is for neonates to time the various movements so that they do not get gas pains from ingesting air, choke from aspirating milk, or wait too long between breaths. The optimal coordination of suck–swallow–respiration appears to be a ratio of 1:1:1 or 2:2:1 (Barlow, 2009; van der Meer, Holden, & van der Weel, 2005), wherein sucking pressure occurs while breathing out, and swallowing takes place just before the onset of the next suck and between breathing out and breathing in. Before birth, fetuses exercise the muscles and body parts used for swallowing, sucking, and breathing, but fetuses do not breathe air and the movements do not need to be coordinated (Miller, Sonies, & Macedonia, 2003; Humphrey, 1970).

Chewing solid food adds complexity (Wilson et al., 2008). In mature chewing, the tongue moves the bolus (bite of food or swig of liquid) to the appropriate place in the mouth. The jaws move up and down, back and forth, and in rotary motions to create shearing and grinding forces to break up the bolus. The underlying muscle actions are finely attuned to each task constraint (Green et al., 1997). The muscles fire to open the jaws, but due to elastic recoil, the jaws begin to close without additional muscle power. A quick muscle jolt completes the closure without banging the teeth together. The tongue forms the food into a tight ball in preparation to swallow. The lips make a seal and the tongue pushes the bolus to the throat.

Infants can chew—more or less—even before they've got teeth or begin eating solid food. Some of the components of chewing are present in the first week of life: Neonates can mush around a banana cube placed in their mouth (Sheppard & Mysak, 1984). They move the bolus to the middle, and move their jaws up and down and their tongues from side to side. By 12 months of age, infants can chew well enough to break down food and swallow it, and they display the basic pattern of reciprocal muscle activation in the jaw (Green et al., 1997). But infants' crude strategies for mushing up food are not as distributed, organized, flexible, and automatized as mature chewing. They rely on lateral jaw movements to do most of the work of chewing (Wilson & Green, 2009). It takes years before the lips and tongue are involved and cooperating in a planful and deliberate way and before rotary movements are incorporated into the chewing action. The muscle activation patterns in infants' jaws are poorly organized, and refinements continue for several years (Steeve et al., 2008). Moreover, infants chew the same way for every kind of food, whereas older children flexibly adapt their jaw movements and chew forces to the food consistency (Wilson & Green, 2009) and to the emergence of teeth and molars. Even habitual automatized actions such as moving the bolus to a consistent "working" side of the mouth take years to develop (Wilson et al., 2008).

Speech

The speech sounds of infancy—cooing, babbling, and real words—are the product of motor actions in the face and throat. Air is forced through the oral and/or nasal cavities, and the sound is shaped by the position of the jaws, lips, and tongue. In fact, the motor skills required to produce speech are among the most sophisticated learned by humans (Green & Nip, 2010).

Speech movements require only a fraction of the force produced during chewing, but they must be extremely fast and accurate to make the appropriate sounds (Wilson et al., 2008): Adults produce 180 words per minute or 15 sounds per second (Green & Nip, 2010). Although researchers now agree that speech and chewing are developmentally distinct behaviors, they share some common developmental features. As with chewing, infants discover functional strategies that get the job done, but the details of the movements are not adult-like. For example, adults use quick simultaneous movements of the jaws and lips to make babbling sounds (baba, mama, dada), but infants rely primarily on their jaws to do the work and as a consequence they are prone to speech errors and distortions (Green, Moore, Higashikawa, & Steeve, 2000; Green et al., 2002). Why do children initially use simpler strategies that rely on the jaw? Presumably, the jaw is easier to control. The mandible is a single bone with a network of symmetrical musculature that lifts and drops the jaw. The lips and tongue are harder to control because they are highly deformable with layers of muscles. Between 2 and 6 years of age, children get better control over their lips and then incorporate those movements into the well-established jaw movements. As a consequence they can produce a greater range of sounds (Wilson et al., 2008).

Facial Gestures

Infants produce a rich and varied array of easily recognizable facial expressions including interest, surprise, joy, and distress, and they do so right from birth (Field, Woodson, Greenberg & Cohen, 1982). Neonates wrinkle their noses, raise their upper lips, and furrow their brows in reaction to strong, unfamiliar scents or flavors. In contrast, neonates who experience the flavor via their mother's amniotic fluid during the last weeks of gestation respond with positive facial gestures, such as sucking, licking, and mouthing (Mennella, Griffin, & Beauchamp, 2004; Schaal, Marlier, & Soussignan, 2000).

Organization of facial expressions continues to develop over the first year. At 4 months of age, infants' facial expressions across a variety of situations are primarily joy and interest, but expressions become more differentiated and context-specific by 12 months. For example, 12-month-olds showed more disgust expressions in response to a sour taste and more anger expressions in response to an arm being restrained than they did several months earlier (Bennett, Bendersky, & Lewis, 2005).

Infants' facial movements are highly patterned. For example, a simple smile involves only one primary muscle to raise the corners of the lips. But more complex smiles with mouth opening and other facial actions may involve a variety of muscles. Duchenne smiles raise the cheeks and crinkle the skin below the eyes. Newborns occasionally display Duchenne smiles while they sleep, but they appear at around 2 months during social interactions (Oster, 2005). Ten independent muscle actions may co-occur in infants' faces when they cry (Oster, 2005).

The old saying that it takes more muscles to frown than to smile isn't really a fair comparison because facial expressions—frowns, smiles, and all the rest—typically involve many muscles moving many parts of the face in a highly redundant way. As illustrated in Figure 5.5, redundancy ensures multiple pathways to emotional expression—so much so that even untrained, undergraduate judges could reliably identify the facial expressions (smiling, crying, interest) of infants with severe craniofacial anomalies like Goldenhar's syndrome (Figure 5.5A), cleft lip and palate (Figure 5.5B), and hemangiomas (Figure 5.5C) (Oster, 2003). Regardless of the developmental pathway, variability in infants' movements and redundancy in musculature ensure effective emotional expression, vocalization, and chewing even when one mechanism is impaired or missing.

TRIUMPH OVER GRAVITY: CONTROLLING THE HEAD AND TORSO

First, the Head

For decades, psychologists have operated under the general rule of thumb that physical and motor development occur in a cephalocaudal (downward from the head to the feet) and proximodistal (outward from the torso to the hands and feet) direction (Assaiante,

FIGURE 5.5 Examples of slides used in the observer judgment study of facial expressions in infants with craniofacial anomalies. (A) Goldenhar's syndrome; (B) bilateral cleft lip; (C) hemangioma; (D) typically developing infant. Reprinted from *Annals of the New York Academy of Sciences, 1000*, H. Oster, Emotion in the infant's face: Insights from the study of infants with facial anomalies, p. 200. Copyright 2003 with permission from Wiley-Blackwell.

Thomachot, Aurently, & Amblard, 1998; Gesell, 1946; Shirley, 1931; Woollacott, Debu, & Mowatt, 1987). As described earlier, fetuses grow from head to tail. Their arms and legs form before their fingers and toes. Fetuses twist and bend their torsos before flexing and extending their limbs. They punch and kick their arms and legs before wiggling their fingers and toes.

Similarly, infants' growth and motor development follows a general cephalocaudal and proximodistal trend. At first, infants' heads and torsos are relatively large compared with their spindly arms and legs. The extremities grow faster than the head and trunk so that, in effect, babies grow into their big heads. Infants' big heads pose a difficult problem for resisting gravity. For example, when young infants are pulled to a sitting position, their heads flop backward with their face toward the ceiling. When held in a sitting position, their heads flop forward with their chins on their chests (Bly, 1994).

In the developmental triumph over gravity, head and torso take the lead. To pry their bodies from the floor, infants must first lift up their heads. In a prone position, newborns can quickly turn their heads from side to side to facilitate breathing, but they cannot hold their heads off the floor for sustained periods of time. By 2 to 3 weeks of age, babies can briefly hold their chins off the floor. By 5 to 10 weeks of age, infants can lift their heads and chest in a prone position (Bly, 1994; Shirley, 1931). By 3 months, they have sufficient control to prop themselves up on their forearms. Balance is still so precarious, however, that infants cannot shift their weight from one arm to the other or use their hands. McGraw (1945, p. 67) noted that, except for the fact that some of her participants were boys, one might be tempted to call the prone-prop position the "mermaid posture" because the legs extend inertly back from the body like a mermaid's tail. By 5 months, infants can shift their weight from one arm to the other thereby freeing their hands to reach for and manipulate toys (Soska & Adolph, in preparation).

Now, the Body

The cephalocaudal progression is especially striking in the development of sitting, as if infants gain control of the sitting posture one vertebra at a time (Woollacott, 2009). At first, infants' heads flop when they are supported at the shoulders. Then, after babies can balance their heads between their shoulders, their backs crumple when they are supported at the hips. After infants can keep a straight back, they still topple, chest to knees, without hip support. To sit alone, infants must have muscular control over the entire trunk.

Infants require months of preparation before they can sit on chairs with the legs hanging freely (the adult version of sitting). Initially, infants rely on external support (parents' arms or couch cushions) to stay upright in a sitting position. Their neck, torso, and hip muscles are so weak and uncoordinated, and their hamstring muscles are so loose, that infants can fall over with their chests resting flat on their outstretched legs. At approximately 5 months, before infants can keep balance solely on their bottoms, they sit in a "tripod" position and prop themselves on their arms with their hands resting on the floor between their outstretched legs. By 6 months, they can sit for extended periods with their hands free, but they still cannot turn to the side without losing balance. Most new sitters sit in the "ring position" (legs outstretched, knees to the sides, and bottoms of the feet close together) to provide extra stability for the pelvis (Bly, 1994). By 7 months, infants finally acquire sufficient trunk and hip control to turn and reach while sitting. Also at 7 to 9 months, infants can push themselves backward from hands and knees into a sitting position and can transition themselves out of sitting into kneeling or crawling without an intermediate belly flop between postures (Adolph, Vereijken, & Denny, 1998).

Because the trunk is well developed at 9 months and infants' hamstrings are loose, in addition to the stable "v" and ring positions, infants can arrange their legs into positions that would rival a yoga instructor. For example, many infants "w-sit" with both legs rotated internally with knees in front and feet pointing backward. Some "side sit" with one leg rotated externally with the foot in front and the other leg rotated internally with the foot behind.

Sitting may appear to be a stationary static posture. But in a sitting position (or any posture that defies gravity), the body is always continually in motion. If infants sit on a force plate, the apparatus reveals that the body is always swaying backward and forward and from side to side (Deffeyes et al., 2009). To keep balance, a body sway in one direction must be followed by a compensatory sway response in the opposite direction. New sitters fall because their body moves too far in one direction without sufficient strength and coordination to generate the appropriate compensatory response. New sitters try to keep their bodies rigidly upright because leaning to one side or even turning their heads or extending an arm can overtax their ability to maintain balance.

REACHING FOR OBJECTS

The problem of learning to reach is partly biomechanical (getting the arms up) and partly perceptual (guiding the hand to the target). Getting the arms up is primarily a balance problem. Infants require sufficient muscle strength in their torso to keep their bodies in balance when their arms move. However, what distinguishes mere arm waves and flaps from goal-directed reaching is deliberate contact with the target object. Goal-directed reaching requires perceptual information about the location of the object relative to the location of the hand. Accordingly, much of the work on reaching has focused on developmental changes in infants' ability to use visual information to guide their reaching movements.

Stabilizing the Body in Preparation to Reach

The developmental impediment to reaching is not arm strength; even neonates have sufficient strength to lift their arms against gravity. The problem is sufficient strength to stabilize the rest of the body. Arm movements disrupt balance by displacing the location of the body's center of mass. For example, sitting infants must activate muscles in their trunk before extending their arms to prepare for the forward displacement of their center of mass caused by their extended arms (von Hofsten, 1993). Neonates cannot get their arms up to reach for an object while their heads flop and torsos collapse (Amiel-Tison & Grenier, 1986; von Hofsten, 1993; Spencer, Vereijken, Diedrich, & Thelen, 2000).

Because reaching is a "whole-body engagement" (Rochat & Goubet, 1995, p. 65), the development of reaching is protracted and has different trajectories for sitting, supine, and prone postures (Bly, 1994; Carvalho, Tudella, & Savelsbergh, 2007; Carvalho, Tudella, Caljouw, & Savelsbergh, 2008). At 4 months of age, infants can contact a toy when strapped into a reclined sitting position, and they can bring their arms up toward a toy dangling in front of them when they are lying on their backs, but they are not yet good at reaching. They often flail their arms upward and miss the target. When 4-month-olds are lying flat on their stomachs, they cannot reach at all because they can't prop themselves up on one arm to reach with the other. By 5 months, infants strapped in a sitting position or lying supine are more skillful at making contact with the object of their reach, but they do so by extending both arms simultaneously and clapping them together in a dual swipe (Rochat, 1992). In a prone position, they can now reach for toys with one arm while leaning on the other arm (Bly, 1994). At 6 months, supine infants begin to reach forward with just one arm. By 7 months, prone and sitting infants can reach with one arm in all directions. By 8 months, infants do not like being restricted to a supine or prone position, so almost all of their reaching occurs in a sitting position.

Keeping balance in a sitting position is integral to the development of reaching (Rochat & Goubet, 1995). When sitting skill is poor, infants are limited to one-handed reaching because they have to hold themselves up with the other hand. Accordingly, 5- to 6-month-old tripod-sitters who attempted bimanual reaches in a sitting position toppled forward and completely missed the target (Rochat, 1992). However, in prone, supine, and strapped-in sitting positions, tripod-sitters reached with both hands simultaneously. Bimanual reaching increases the likelihood of contacting the target object in young infants whose reaching precision is poor (Corbetta, Thelen, & Johnson, 2000).

Between 5 and 7 months of age, infants use a variety of visual depth cues—binocular depth cues, pictorial depth cues, and kinetic information—to gauge the closer of two objects and to determine whether objects are within arm's reach (Bornstein Arterberry, & Mash, Chapter 6, this volume; Yonas & Granrud, 1985). Many 5-month-olds even judged reaching distance in terms of their arm length along with the additional distance gained by leaning forward (Yonas & Hartman, 1993). However, some leaning infants overshot their ability to reach the target by leaning so far forward that only the seat belt prevented them from tumbling out of their car seat (McKenzie, Skouteris, Day, Hartman, & Yonas, 1993). With increase in postural stability in a sitting position, infants gain the flexibility to use their hands independently of each other. By 8 months, sitters reach for small objects unimanually regardless of postural position.

Normally, postural control in sitting emerges as a result of increased muscle strength, but higher levels of postural control can be facilitated with the help of experimental manipulations that mimic the kinds of support that infants will eventually generate for themselves. Rochat and Goubet (1995), for example, simulated increased levels of postural control in 5- to 6-month-old pre-sitters by supporting their hips with inflated cushions. Hopkins and Ronnqvist (2001) supported pre-sitters with a specially built infant seat with wells where they could rest their thighs. With the additional support, non-sitters' reaching movements were as coordinated as those of sitting infants. Normally, new sitters lean toward and reach for an object as separate actions, and their reaches are made up of several jerky arm and trunk movements (Hopkins & Ronnqvist, 2001; McKenzie et al., 1993; Rochat & Goubet, 1995). However, extra trunk stabilization, hip support, and a supportive sitting surface helped pre-sitters to coordinate reaching with forward leaning, thereby creating smoother, more mature reaches by reducing the number of arm and head movements (Hopkins & Ronnqvist, 2001; Rochat & Goubet, 1995). To summarize, postural development facilitates reaching regardless of whether balance improves naturally or with the help of an experimenter.

Contact! The Development of Visually Guided Reaching

Pre-reaching in neonates.   Using clever means to augment infants' balance, researchers have found the developmental origins of visually guided reaching in neonates' spontaneous arm movements. In studies with neonates, researchers securely strap the babies across the upper chest and hips against a slightly reclined cradle board and prop their heads up between two padded cushions (e.g., von Hofsten, 1982). Another method is to gently suspend neonates from the head in the grip of the experimenter's hand to liberate the arms and shoulders (Amiel-Tison & Grenier, 1986). Both methods are illustrated in Figure 5.6. With their heads and torsos freed from balance constraints, neonates flap their arms to the sides and to the front of their bodies, both with and without a target object in their view (von Hofsten, 1982). However, the flapping movements can be related to the presence of an object. At 5 to 9 days of age, neonates extend their arms in a forward direction more frequently when a

FIGURE 5.6 Two methods to provide neonates with sufficient postural support to facilitate their arm extensions and reaches toward objects. (A) Strapping newborns into a reclining seat. Adapted with permission from *Developmental Psychology, 18*, C. von Hofsten, Eye–hand coordination in the newborn, p. 452. Copyright © 1982 by the American Psychological Association. (B, C) Gently suspending neonates by holding their heads. Reprinted with permission from *Neurological assessment during the first year of life*, C. Amiel-Tison and G. Albert, pp. 139–140. Copyright 1986 by Oxford University Press, Inc.

target object (colorful dangling fuzz ball) is in view than when no object is present (von Hofsten, 1982).

Researchers do not suppose that 1-week-old infants intend to grasp the toy. Rather, neonatal arm extensions function to orient infants' attention to the goal. As such, the data on neonatal arm extensions point to a tight link between arm/hand activity and looking behaviors, providing a perceptual basis for visual–manual exploration of objects and for visually guided reaching. Indeed, about a month before infants execute their first successful reaches, they increase the number of arm movements in the presence of a toy, and raise their shoulders and arms in an approximation of a reach (Bhat, Heathcock, & Galloway, 2005; Lee, Bhat, Scholz, & Galloway, 2008).

Supported reaching and catching.   Like neonates, 3- to 5-month-olds demonstrate visually guided reaching (and even catching) before they can sit independently when they are freed from balance constraints. Researchers provide infants with the requisite postural support by strapping them to a reclined board or propping them in a reclined infant seat. Alternatively, parents may provide stability to babies' heads and torsos by supporting them in their laps and holding them under the arms or along their sides.

In supported reaching, most infants' first successful contact with stationary objects occurs between 12 and 18 weeks of age (Bhat et al., 2005; Clifton, Muir, Ashmead, & Clarkson, 1993). However, even with balance accounted for, infants solve the reaching problem in different ways. Some "constructivist" infants build their reaches up from scratch, and other "selectionist" infants carve goal-directed reaching from spontaneous arm "flaps." In a longitudinal study, Thelen and colleagues (Thelen et al., 1993; Thelen, Corbetta, & Spencer, 1996) tracked infants' weekly progress in supported reaching, obtaining detailed kinematics of infants' arm movements at each session. One infant, Hannah, exemplified the constructivist approach to reaching. Prior to first contact with the target toy, Hannah displayed few spontaneous arm movements. Those movements that she did produce were slow, small, and quiet. Hannah could barely lift her arms. Her first successful reaches occurred between 20 and 22 weeks and involved mustering the energy to lift her arm. The movements at wrist, elbow, and shoulder were slow and small; the hand wavered back and forth and frequently overshot the target toy. Over weeks of observations, Hannah's reaching movements became faster, straighter, and more forceful.

In contrast, a second infant, Gabriel, exemplified the selectionist approach to reaching, appearing to carve his first reaches out of ongoing flapping movements. Prior to first toy contact, Gabriel displayed a high frequency of spontaneous arm movements. The movements that he produced were so wild and energetic that they were too uncontrolled to contact the target toy. Gabriel's first success at reaching occurred at 15 weeks and involved dampening the inertial forces caused by his ongoing flapping. He stiffened his shoulder, elbow, and wrist to gain control over his flailing arm. Over weeks of observations, Gabriel's reaching movements became slower, straighter, and less forceful.

As infants become more experienced at reaching, they can adapt to weight changes in their arms, as when we place an object that we're holding in our hand onto a surface. In the laboratory, weight changes were induced by strapping loads (10% of arm mass) onto 4- to 6-month-old infants' arms. Infants reached, grasped, and showed the same proportion of one- and two-handed reaches with their arms weighted as they did without the weights (Rochaa, da Costa, Savelsbergh, & Tudella, 2009).

At approximately the same age as infants contact stationary objects in supported reaching, they also begin to show evidence of supported catching (von Hofsten, 1980, 1983; von Hofsten & Lindhagen, 1979). Starting at about 12 weeks of age, infants extend their arms toward a moving object that sweeps across their field of view on a semicircular path (an attractive fuzzy ball dangling from a rotating lever). By 15 weeks, infants' arm extensions are so accurate that they can intercept the object as it moves past. They adjust the timing of their arm movements so that their hand arrives at the same location as the object at the same time, and they adjust their aim so that they reach directly toward the location where the object will be, rather than where it was at the start of the reach. But there is room for improvement. Grasping the moving lure does not usually occur until infants are 18 weeks old. Six- to 7-month-olds can catch moving balls at twice the velocity of 3- to 5-month-olds, and infants do not cross midline with both hands to catch until they are 10 months old (Fagard, Spelke, & von Hofsten, 2009; van Hof, van der Kamp, & Savelsbergh, 2008).

Visually guided reaching.   Despite the differences in the speed and size of their first reaching movements, Hannah, Gabriel, and most other infants share a common pattern of development. Detailed motion analysis indicates that infants' first reaches are less controlled and direct than more practiced reaches (e.g., Berthier, Clifton, McCall, & Robin, 1999; Berthier & Keen, 2006; Thelen et al., 1993, 1996; von Hofsten, 1980, 1983, 1991). Early reaches are composed of several arm movements, termed "movement units" (von Hofsten, 1979). Each movement unit represents an acceleration followed by a deceleration, usually accompanied by a change in direction. Immature infant reaches contain, on average, four movement units. In contrast, mature adult reaches contain two movement units, an initial large movement that brings the hand in the near vicinity of the object, then a smaller movement that prepares the hand to grasp the object. With practice, infants' reaches became straighter and smoother with fewer start-and-stop corrections and fewer deviations from a bee-line path. By the time they are 30 weeks old, the majority of infants' reaches consist of only two movement units (von Hofsten, 1993; von Hofsten & Ronnqvist, 1993).

For many years, researchers assumed that multiple movement units reflect online corrections to the arm's trajectory. That is, newly reaching infants are unable to program the initial movement unit with sufficient accuracy to bring their hand close to the toy. To compensate, they continually track the location of their hand relative to the toy in a series of corrections and over-corrections (McDonnell, 1974; Piaget, 1952; White, Castle, & Held, 1964). Studies of reaching in the dark challenge the view that newly reaching infants must continually monitor the trajectory of their hands. To study the necessity of visual corrections in reaching, an experimenter offers infants a toy. But before infants can retrieve it, the lights go out so that babies can no longer see their own hands. The target toy either glows in the dark or emits a noise to help infants to locate it.

Longitudinal data show that infants begin reaching in the light and in the dark at the same age (Clifton et al., 1993), meaning that new reachers do not need to see their hand to contact an object. Moreover, over weeks of reaching, infants are equally successful (or not) at contacting a glowing object in the dark as they are at contacting a visible object in the light (Clifton et al., 1993; Perris & Clifton, 1988). The detailed kinematics of infants' reaches are the same for objects in the light and for glowing objects in the dark (Clifton, Rochat, Robin, & Berthier, 1994). In both cases, reaches are jerky and composed of three or four movement units. In other words, multiple movement units do not necessarily mean that infants are visually tracking their hand because infants display multiple movement units when they cannot see their hand.

The plot thickens. The same infants who reach successfully for objects in the light and dark are likely to completely miss an invisible but sounding target (Clifton et al., 1994). However, with only a noise to guide them to the object's location, infants' reaches were *faster* in the dark to a sounding object than in the dark to a glowing object or in the light to a visible object. In addition, reaches to sounding objects were *smoother* and more ballistic, consisting of two movement units (Clifton et al., 1994; Perris & Clifton, 1988). Thus, infants have the ability to generate adult-like reaching movements, albeit unsuccessful ones.

So, as Clifton et al. (1993) ask: "Is visually guided reaching just a myth?" Clearly, visual information is important for reaching. Blind infants reach at later ages than do sighted infants, presumably because seeing attractive objects motivates infants to reach (Fraiberg, 1977). And by 15 months of age, sighted infants rely on vision for precision reaching toward small objects—Cheerios perched on a light-emitting diode (Berthier & Keen, 2006). Precise manual actions require vision: threading a needle, or "taking deliberately from one hand into the other a long hair . . . found on the carpet" as Preyer (1905, p. 253) observed in his 10-month-old. However, for reaching that does not require a high level of precision, studies of infants reaching in the dark show that sight of the hand and the object is not necessary. Possibly, vision, like audition and **proprioception**, is merely a potential source of information that can specify the location of an object or surface relative to one's body or hand (Clifton et al., 1993, 1994). Infants use visual information when it is available because the sight of the object and the hand is the easiest way to monitor the situation. But, when infants are denied visual information in the dark, they can rely on proprioceptive and auditory information to monitor their arm during a reach (Clifton, Perris, & McCall, 1999).

Feet reaching.   We normally think of reaching as a manual activity, but more than 100 years ago, researchers documented instances of infants using their legs for reaching and their toes for grasping. For example, Trettien (1900) described a 7-month-old who used her foot to drag over a distant object until it was close enough to reach with her hands. Feet reaching may actually be easier for infants than manual reaching because the legs are stronger than the arms and the direction of leg movements is more constrained by the relatively narrow range of motion in the hip joint.

Modern researchers have confirmed Trettien's observations experimentally (Galloway & Thelen, 2004). Infants' balance was stabilized by strapping them to a slightly reclined board. An experimenter presented them with toys at chest level and at hip level (Figure 5.7). Infants contacted the toys with their feet at 2 to 3 months of age—a full month before they contacted the toys with their hands (3 to 4 months of age). Apparently, the general cephalocaudal (head-to-toe) direction of development is a handy rule of thumb, not a law of nature.

Grasping.   Whereas accurate reaching requires guiding the trajectory of the hand (or foot) to the object's location, grasping entails preparing the hand to hold the object according to its size and orientation (McCarty, Clifton, Ashmead, Lee, & Goubet, 2001). Before 4 months of age, infants have minimal hand control. Their attempts to grasp look like clumsy swipes, and the object drops as often as it is captured. When adults put an object into babies' hands, they either drop the toys or hold them without adjusting their grip (Bly, 1994; Rochat, 1989). After 10 months of age, infants have such fine modulated control of their hands that they can grasp a small pellet using a precise pincer grip between index finger and thumb (Gesell, 1952).

One critical aspect of preparing to grasp is positioning the hand with regard to object properties. By 5 months, infants can differentiate their grip according to object size and shape (Newell, Scully, McDonald, & Baillargeon, 1989). They use one hand to grasp small objects and two hands to grasp large ones. They use only their thumb, index, and middle fingers to grasp small objects or objects with edges, like cups, and they use the entire hand to grasp large objects.

Five-month-olds can even prepare their grasp in anticipation of the properties of the object they are reaching for (Barrett, Traupman, & Needham, 2008). However, there is a discrepancy between planning and execution and 5-month-olds have trouble following through with the grasp (Lockman, Ashmead, & Bushnell, 1984; von Hofsten & Fazel-Zandy, 1984; Witherington, 2005). For example, when presented with dowels oriented horizontally or vertically, either fully visible (Lockman, 1984) or in a dark room (McCarty et al., 2001), infants managed to grasp the object only after their hand banged into it, and they subsequently corrected their hand position. In contrast, by 7.5 months of age, infants pre-orient their hands to the orientations of the target objects prior to grasping. Infants positioned their hands prospectively in the light, and more impressively, they shaped their hand prior to object contact when the room was darkened in the midst of the reach (McCarty et al., 2001). In the latter case, infants completed their reach and grasp in complete darkness. By 9 months of age, infants did not even need to see their hands at the beginning of the reach to pre-orient their grasp appropriately. They were shown the target object, the room was darkened, and then they were allowed to reach for it. Instead of visually monitoring their hands during the reach, they used the feel of the hand and moving arm to gauge their hand position and trajectory in relation to the target object.

FIGURE 5.7   Three-month-old infant making foot contact with a toy. Infants are strapped into a reclining seat for stability. Note that feet-reaching occurs a full month earlier than reaching with the hand. (Courtesy of Cole Galloway and Jill Heathcock, Infant Behavior Lab, Department of Physical Therapy, University of Delaware. Drawn by Samira Iravani.)

FROM OBJECT EXPLORATION TO HAND-HELD TOOL USE

Object Exploration

Reaching and grasping provide infants with new ways to gather information about object properties and new ways to use objects to enact change on the environment. As Gibson (1988, p. 7) noted, "exploratory development during the first year of life . . . build[s] the infant's knowledge of the permanent features of the world, of the predictable relations between events, and of its own capacities for acting on objects and intervening in events." Reaching and grasping are milestones in the development of exploratory behaviors. An object in an infant's hand can be explored visually, manually, and orally, and the hand facilitates the optimal vantage point by bringing the object to the eyes, other hand, and mouth. As noted in one of the first baby biographies (Preyer, 1905), the object can even be the infant's own foot: "In the thirty-second week, as he lies on his back, he likes to stretch his legs up vertically, and observes the feet attentively as he does other objects held before him. Then he grasps with the hands at his own feet, and often carries his toes to his mouth with his hand" (p. 249).

Before 4 or 5 months of age, infants have poor manual control over objects, so the primary role of the hands in object exploration is to carry objects up to the face to look at them or to bring objects to the mouth to explore them orally (Rochat & Senders, 1991). At this age, mouthing is composed primarily of licking, sucking (Bly, 1994; Rochat, 1989), and occasional biting (Norris & Smith, 2002). As infants' grasp becomes stronger and more modifiable, babies rely less on their mouths to support the objects during a bout of mouthing, and hand-to-mouth behaviors appear in alternation with taking the object out of the mouth and holding it up to the face for visual inspection (Eppler, 1995). Between 12 and 24 months, infants stop bringing objects to their mouths and instead explore object properties using only their eyes and their hands.

After 4 or 5 months, burgeoning manual skills provide augmented means for exploring objects with the hands and eyes (Bly, 1994; Palmer, 1989; Rochat, 1989). **Bimanual coordination** is a first step. Now infants can intentionally release their grip on an object, allowing them to transfer an object from hand to hand and to rotate an object in front of the eyes (Soska, Adolph, & Johnson, 2010). A real milestone in bimanual object exploration is the complementary differentiation of hand function (Kotwica, Ferre, & Michel, 2008; Thelen & Corbetta, 1994). One hand serves a supporting function by grasping the object and keeping it in view. The other hand generates information about object properties by rubbing and pressing against the object's surface or following its contours. The fingering and palpating motions of the exploring hand require new levels of control so as to lightly scan the surface with the tips of the fingers or to hold the fleshy part of the hand in place while squeezing. By the end of the first year, infants can transfer an object from one hand to the other to obtain a second object without giving up the first. By 6 to 8 months of age, infants' manual exploratory behaviors relate properties of the object in hand to relevant properties of surfaces, such as banging a toy on a solid surface to make a noise (Bourgeois, Khawar, Neal & Lockman, 2005; Fontenelle, Kahrs, Neal, Newton, & Lockman, 2007).

As in reaching, manual exploration also depends on postural development. Sitting infants display more sophisticated **object manipulation** skills—more coordinated looking, rotating, transferring, and fingering—than in supine or prone positions (Soska & Adolph, in preparation). On their backs, infants' arms drop downward against the pull of gravity and the object ends up in their mouths instead of in front of their faces. On their stomachs, one arm is engaged in balance, so transferring objects from hand to hand and holding an object with one hand while fingering it with the other are more difficult. The new forms of manual exploration engendered by sitting have important ramifications for perceptual learning. Transferring, rotating, and fingering give infants opportunities to learn about the normally hidden, back sides of objects. As a consequence, infants who actively looked at objects while fingering, rotating, and transferring them between hands were more likely to demonstrate 3-D form perception by looking longer at displays of objects with surprising concave back sides than at expected 3-D forms (Soska et al., 2010). These findings indicate that developing motor skills drive changes in exploration, learning, and object knowledge.

From Exploration to Tools

How might infants' growing manual skills lead to expanded knowledge of the world via object exploration? Gibson (1988) proposed that new skills generate new sorts of perceptual information and, thereby, shift infants' attention to new aspects of objects and events. For example, increased object manipulation skills facilitate infants' understanding about events involving objects. Five-and-a-half-month-olds who were skilled at manipulating objects, such as holding objects with both hands, transferring objects from hand to hand, and banging two objects together were more likely to understand the properties of objects (i.e., matching the appropriate sounds with images of object events) than were infants of the same age who were less skilled at manipulating objects (Eppler, 1995).

When 3-month-olds who normally lack the motor skill to handle objects manually were provided with a tool to allow them to manipulate objects, the infants performed similarly to 5-month-olds who acquired their manual skills naturally (Needham, Barrett, & Peterman, 2002). Infants wore mittens with Velcro-covered palms as they played with Velcro-edged toys that stuck to the mittens. As a result, infants could pick up the toys and explore them visually and orally, even though they could not have done so without the mittens. After 2 weeks of practice with the "sticky mittens," infants showed enhanced object manipulation skills, and, more critical for Gibson's argument, enhanced understanding of object properties. Trained infants outperformed untrained babies in object segregation tasks. After just a few minutes of practice with the mittens, infants demonstrated greater understanding of others' intentions towards objects (Sommerville, Woodward, & Needham, 2005).

Manual Tool Use

Bona fide **tool use**, of course, requires more than an adult augmenting infants' abilities by putting sticky mittens on their hands. Infants must generate the critical steps by themselves. Infants must (1) perceive a gap between their own motor abilities and a desired goal, (2) find an alternative means to bridge the gap, and (3) implement the tool successfully (Berger & Adolph, 2003). Although most researchers focus on the cognitive skills required by the second step (Piaget, 1954), several investigators have noted that perceptual-motor skills are central to the first and third steps (Lockman, 2000; Cox & Smitsman, 2006; Smitsman & Cox, 2008). The first step involves perceiving (lack of) affordances for action, and the third step involves the biomechanics of tool use (Berger, Adolph, & Lobo, 2005).

Perception of a gap between the self and a goal requires infants to detect the limits of their abilities—that a desired object is too far out of reach or that there is an obstacle between themselves and a goal (Berger, Adolph & Kavookjian, in press; McKenzie et al., 1993; Yonas & Hartman, 1993). A tool can make the otherwise unobtainable goal obtainable. By 10 months of age, infants can extend their reaching abilities using sticks, hooks, rakes, or rings to drag over distant objects if the goal and the tool are located near each other (Bates, Carlson-Luden, & Bretherton, 1980; Brown, 1990; Chen & Seigler, 2000; van Leeuwen, Smitsman, & van Leeuwen, 1994).

Beyond knowing that a tool is necessary for task completion and that certain items make appropriate tools, infants must perceive how to use the tool. Before 1 year of age, infants have difficulty planning appropriate motor strategies for tool use in advance. Instead, they end up making corrections after they have already begun to use the tool. For example, 9-month-olds sometimes grab a spoon by the bowl-end instead of by the handle or hold it with the bowl pointing away from their mouths (Figure 5.8). They then have to awkwardly rotate their hands or switch hands to eat the food. They recognize that the spoon can be used as a tool for transporting food, but cannot implement the tool efficiently. Ironically, infants' experiences with spoons instill a kind of functional fixedness so that they rigidly grasp the handle, even when grasping the other end would be more appropriate for the task (Barrett, Davis, & Needham, 2007). By 18 months of age, infants know which end of a tool to grasp, how to grasp it, and how to plan their motor actions in advance (McCarty, Clifton, & Collard, 1999, 2001), but they are still inefficient when using a tool to act on another object rather than performing an action centered on their own body (Claxton, McCarty, Keen, 2009). It is not until 24 months of age that infants can adjust their typical strategies to use tools in a novel way, such as gripping a spoon with a bent handle to scoop food from a bowl (Steenbergen, van der Kamp, Smitsman, & Carson, 1997).

FIGURE 5.8   Using a (A) goal-end grip to grab a spoon by the bowl end, (B) an ulnar grip with the bowl pointing away from the mouth, and (C) a radial grip to grasp the spoon appropriately. Adapted from "Problem-solving in infancy: The emergence of an action plan," by M. E. McCarty, R. K. Clifton, and R. Collard, 1999, *Developmental Psychology, 35*, pp. 1091–1101. Copyright © 1999 by the American Psychological Association.

INDEPENDENT MOBILITY!

Mobility is a landmark developmental achievement, involving new constraints on movement and offering new opportunities for learning. Whereas sitting and reaching facilitate visual and manual exploration of objects, independent mobility facilitates visual, tactile, and whole-body exploration of surfaces and places (Gibson, 1988). Locomotion allows infants to leave their caregivers and to seek their proximity; they can engage with distal objects and visit familiar places.

Moving in Place

The simplest ways to move the whole body in space—rolling and pivoting—change the body's position and orientation, but keep the body in the same geographic location. In rolling, infants flip from their stomachs to their backs and vice versa with their bodies outstretched like logs. In pivoting, babies rotate their whole body in circles. The goal seems to be improving body orientation and vantage point with respect to nearby objects and events, rather than transport. For example, 6- to 9-month-olds used the sound of their mother's voice to decide in which direction and how quickly to pivot around to see her. They took the shortest path and they moved more quickly when they had more distance to cover (van der Meer, Ramstad, & van der Weel, 2008).

At first, rolling is random, and pivoting is tediously incremental. Parents return to infants' cribs in the morning to find their babies flipped onto their stomachs or with their heads where their feet once were. However, in the real-time moment, infants are stuck mid-roll and their slow-motion pivot requires time lapse videography to record. At approximately 5 months, infants begin to display accidental rolling from prone to supine (stomach to back). Typically, the flip is prompted serendipitously by the effort to reach for an object. Over 100 years ago, Trettien (1900) described infants' "extreme surprise" at rolling over as they lost their balance in the midst of a reach. Five-month-olds have sufficient shoulder control to push themselves onto their sides from their stomachs, but they have trouble maintaining the position. Thus, infants either flop back onto their stomachs or roll serendipitously onto their backs.

Crawling: Historical and Cultural Differences

Researchers have been formally documenting infants' route to mobility for more than a century (Ames, 1937; Burnside, 1927; Preyer, 1905; Trettien, 1900). But no one had the stamina of Gesell. With a tenacity unrivalled before or after his time, Gesell (1939; Gesell &

Ames, 1940; Gesell, 1946) identified 23 ordered stages in prone progression. Stage 1 was "passive kneeling" at 1 week of age; stage 5 was "swimming" at 4 months of age; stage 7 was "frogging" at 5.5 months; and so on, until belly crawling at 7 months in stage 11, rocking on hands and knees at 8 months in stage 16, crawling on hands and knees at 10 months in stage 19, and walking at 14 months in the final stage 23. According to more recent norms, infants begin belly crawling around 7 months, crawling on hands and knees at 8 months, and walking at 12 months (Capute, Shapiro, Palmer, Ross, & Wachtel, 1985; Frankenburg et al., 1992). Gesell (1933, 1939, 1946) argued that the stages were necessary, appeared in invariant order, reflected the underlying maturity of infants' neuromotor system, and that apparent back-sliding was illusory in an ever-upward spiral of growth.

Thanks largely to Gesell's influence, motor development and body growth have typically been presented as a universal, maturational sequence. However, before, during, and after Gesell's heyday, researchers noted cultural and historical differences in motor development. For example, at the turn of the twentieth century, 30 years before Gesell popularized the practice of collecting developmental norms, Trettien (1900) and G. Stanley Hall sent around a "circular" asking for parents' observations of infants' early mobility. Every infant found some solution to independent mobility prior to upright walking: 42% were reported to crawl on their hands and knees, 10% dragged their bellies along the floor, 5.5% crept on hands and feet, and 2.5% launched from hands and knees onto their bellies like inchworms. Other infants bypassed prone progression: 30% moved in a sitting position by hitching with one leg, 3% crabbed along on their backs "wearing a bald spot onto the back of their heads" (p. 33), and 7% log-rolled. Trettien attributed the large percentage of hitching to infants' long dresses that hampered their movements in a prone position. When infants tried to crawl, their knees caught at the edge of their long gowns pinning them in place. Moreover, modern American infants display loco-motor skills such as rolling, sitting, crawling, **cruising**, walking, and stair ascent and descent in a staggering variety of orders, rather than in the invariant sequence suggested by ordering average onset ages in normative data (Berger, Theuring, & Adolph, 2007).

While Gesell was documenting age norms in white, American middle-class infants in the 1930s, researchers began to compare infants' age at onset in various cultural and ethnic groups. Initially, reports of "African infant precocity"—findings that black African infants achieved gross motor milestones at earlier ages than did white babies in Western cultures—were explained in terms of ethnic differences (Geber & Dean, 1957; Jensen, 1973, cited in Super, 1976). In reaction to the racial implications of such claims, several modern psychologists challenged the validity of the earlier work (e.g., Hopkins & Westra, 1988). In addition to documenting the ages at which infants attained their motor milestones, the modern researchers interviewed mothers about their theories of motor development, asked mothers about the ages at which they expected infants to achieve their milestones, and observed mothers' daily childrearing routines (Bril & Sabatier, 1986; Hopkins & Westra, 1988, 1989, 1990; Super, 1976). Mothers showed cultural differences on all measures. For example, mothers in Western cultures shared Gesell's theory that maturation drives motor develop-ment without special impetus from the environment (Hopkins & Westra, 1989). They believed that crawling is an important necessary stage in motor development. They expected infants to begin crawling at approximately 8 months, after the onset of sitting and before the onset of walking. During baths and carrying, they handled their newborns like a fragile carton of eggs, always supporting babies' heads as if their weak necks would snap. In contrast, Jamaican mothers espoused a naive theory that training and exercise provide the impetus for motor development (Hopkins & Westra, 1988). They expected their infants to sit and walk at earlier ages than did the Western mothers. As illustrated in Figure 5.9, they performed daily massage and exercise routines, stretching, shaking, and stroking their infants. They grasped newborns by a limb and expected them to support their own heads against gravity. To train infants to sit, they propped 3- to 4-month-old infants up with pillows or set them in a special hole in the ground designed to provide back support. In accordance with mothers' theories, expectations, and childrearing routines, researchers found cultural differences for the age at which motor milestones were achieved. Jamaican infants sat and walked at earlier ages than did Western infants (Hopkins & Westra, 1988, 1989). Most strikingly, 29% of Jamaican infants never crawled at all. And infants who crawled did so at the same time that they began walking. Thus, naive theories, parents' expectations, and everyday childrearing routines—all aspects of the physical and social environments that Gesell had dismissed—can affect motor development (for review see Adolph, Karasik, & Tamis-LeMonda, 2009).

Even within a culture, daily childrearing practices affect the schedule of motor development. For decades, pediatricians in America recommended that parents put infants to sleep

FIGURE 5.9 African, Caribbean, and West Indian mothers engage in elaborate handling routines to massage (A–C), stretch (D–F), and exercise (G–I) their infants. These special handling routines may contribute to the cultural differences in the ages at which motor milestones are achieved. Images for Figure 9A–F and H–I were redrawn by Lana Karasik from "Maternal handing and motor development: An intra-cultural study" by B. Hopkins and T. Westra, 1988, *Genetic, Social and General Psychology Monographs, 114*, pp. 379–408. Reprinted with permission of the Helen Dwight Reid Educational Foundation. Published by Heldref Publications, 1319 Eighteenth St., NW, Washington, DC 20036-1802. Copyright © 1988. Image for Figure 9G was adapted from R. Siegler, J. DeLoache, and N. Eisenberg, (2003). How Children Develop, 1st ed., New York: Worth Publishers.

on their stomachs to prevent babies from aspirating regurgitated milk. In 1994, the American Academy of Pediatrics launched a "Back to Sleep" campaign recommending that infants sleep on their backs to reduce the incidence of sudden infant death syndrome (SIDS) (Carolan, Moore, & Luxenberg, 1995). Within 2 years of the media campaign, the proportion of parents who put their infants to sleep on their backs doubled (Gibson, Dembofsky, Rubin, & Greenspan, 2000; Willinger, Ko, Hoffman, Kessler, & Corwin, 2000). Although doctors advise parents to give their waking infants "tummy time," back-sleepers tend to fuss when they have to fight gravity to pull their face out of the carpet. Among back-sleepers, tummy time is related to earlier onset ages for sitting, crawling, and pulling to a stand (Davis, Moon, Sachs, & Ottolini, 1998; Majnemer & Barr, 2006), presumably because the prone position facilitates muscle strength in the arms and shoulders. Moreover, back-sleepers sit, crawl, and pull to stand at later ages and score lower on measures of gross motor skill than do infants who sleep on their stomachs (Davis et al., 1998; Dewey, Fleming, Golding, & Team, 1998).

Most people's vision of "crawling" is a quadrupedal gait on hands and knees. However, the lay person's emphasis on hands and knees ignores the variety of idiosyncratic forms of mobility that infants exhibit *en route* to crawling on hands and knees. In McGraw's words (1945, p. 50), "No other neuromuscular function of the growing infant exhibits greater individual variations in pattern" than prone progression.

Prior to crawling on hands and knees, infants practice pivoting, rocking, swimming in place, and other prone skills that do not move them across the room (Adolph et al., 1998; Freedland & Bertenthal, 1994; Goldfield, 1989). Approximately half of infants also exhibit a period of belly crawling before they crawl on hands and knees (Adolph et al., 1998; Freedland & Bertenthal, 1994). Because these infants rest on their bellies during each crawling cycle, locomotion is not constrained by balance requirements. Babies use their arms, legs, and bellies in various combinations, sometimes pushing with only one limb in a girdle and dragging the lame arm or leg behind and sometimes launching themselves from knees or feet onto belly during each cycle (Figure 5.10). Infants move arms and legs on alternate sides of the body together like a trot, arms and legs on the same side of the body together, lift front then back limbs into the air like a bunny hop, and so on. Belly crawlers simply power up their limbs and allow whatever idiosyncratic and arduous patterns to emerge.

The other half of infants skip belly crawling entirely. When these babies are ready to move, they proceed directly to hands-and-knees crawling. In contrast to the variability endemic in belly crawling, the timing of hands-and-knees gaits is nearly uniform (Adolph et al., 1998; Freedland & Bertenthal, 1994). Within the first week or two, timing in inter-limb coordination conforms to an alternating near-trot. Clearly, many patterns of inter-limb coordination are available in infants' repertoires. The abrupt developmental shift in inter-limb timing from belly crawling to hands-and-knees crawling suggests that infants respond to the increased biomechanical constraints of keeping balance with the belly raised.

For infants who first achieved mobility by dragging their bellies along the ground, their struggles pay off in terms of function (Adolph et al., 1998). Former belly crawlers took larger, faster steps from their very first week on hands and knees than non-belly crawlers. The non-belly crawlers required several weeks to catch up. In addition, the duration of infants' experience with any of the prone skills—even pivoting, rocking, and skills that did not involve traveling somewhere—predicted their initial proficiency at crawling on hands and knees. The findings indicate that practice executing the variety of movements involved in various prone positions has beneficial effects on movements that use different parts of infants' bodies in different temporal patterns once they have sufficient strength to move on hands and knees.

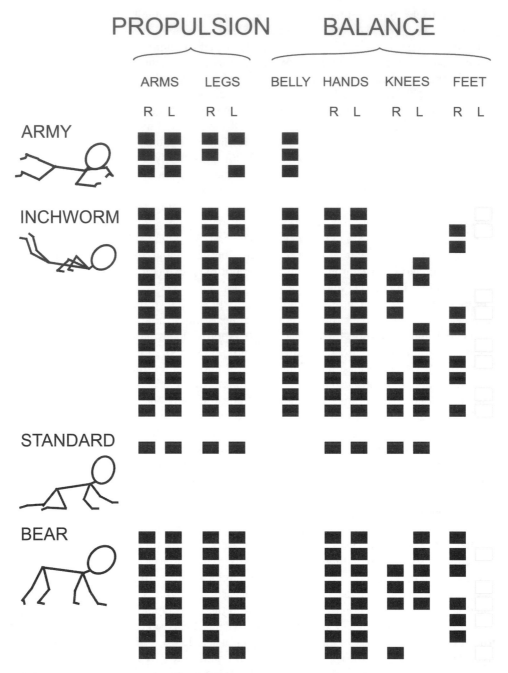

FIGURE 5.10 Some of the many individual variations in infants' crawling patterns. Left column illustrates four types of increasingly erect crawling postures: "army" belly crawls, "inchworm" belly crawls, standard hands-and-knees crawling, and "bear" crawls on hands and feet. Columns represent combinations of arms, legs, and belly used for propulsion and balance. Each row represents a unique crawling pattern displayed by at least one infant. Reprinted with permission from *Child Development, 69*, K. E. Adolph, B. Vereijken and M. A. Denny, Learning to Crawl, p. 1305. Copyright (1998) by the Society for Research in Child Development. Reproduced with permission from John Wiley & Sons, Inc.

Perceptual Control of Crawling

Crawling, like any locomotor action, involves perceptual control of balance. The most famous paradigm to study locomotor development is the "**visual cliff**" (e.g., Bertenthal & Campos, 1984; Campos, Bertenthal, & Kermoian, 1992; Rader, Bausano, & Richards, 1980; Richards & Rader, 1981, 1983; Witherington, 2005). The paradigm, first invented by Gibson and Walk (1960; Walk, 1966; Walk & Gibson, 1961), is designed to test a basic tenet of balance control: To prevent falling, infants must ensure that there is a sturdy floor to support their bodies. The apparatus is a 4-ft drop-off covered by an invisible glass tabletop—hence, the "visual-only" ascription (see Figure 5.11A).

Although depth cues specify the height of the drop-off, behavioral measures provide conflicting evidence about whether infants recognize that balance is impossible beyond the brink (Campos et al., 1992). Pre-crawlers show decelerated heart rates when they are lowered toward the drop-off, suggesting interest, and infants with 2 weeks of crawling experience display accelerated heart rates, suggesting that locomotor experience leads to wariness of depth. But the 2 weeks of crawling experience does not ensure an appropriate avoidance response, and fear of heights is not evidenced in infants' facial expressions or vocalizations. After 2 weeks of crawling experience, most infants crawl straight over the apparent drop-off. They do not avoid going until they have acquired 6 weeks of crawling experience. Regardless of whether they plunge or avoid, infants' facial expressions and vocalizations are generally positive, not negative (Richards & Rader, 1983; Sorce, Emde, Campos, & Klinnert, 1985).

In a modern twist on the classic visual cliff experiment, recent work has examined what infants know about keeping balance at the edge of a *real* cliff (Adolph, 2000; Kretch, Karasik, & Adolph, 2009). As illustrated in Figure 5.11B–D, the visual cliff and real cliff paradigms differ in important ways. In contrast to the visual cliff, real cliffs have no safety glass. Instead, an experimenter follows alongside infants to rescue them if they begin to fall. On the visual cliff, visual and haptic information are in conflict; the drop-off looks risky but feels safe. On a real cliff, visual and haptic information are in concert; the drop-off looks risky and feels risky. Moreover, because of the safety glass, the visual cliff is forgiving of errors: Infants can venture slightly onto the glass and then retreat to the starting platform. A real cliff does not allow such mistakes: If infants put their weight over the edge, they fall. The visual cliff has fixed dimensions, but the real cliff apparatuses are adjustable in 1- or 2-cm increments either in the size of the gap (Figure 5.11B–C) or the height of the drop-off (Figure 5.11D). Finally, on the visual cliff, each infant can be tested in only one trial because they quickly learn the trick (Campos, Hiatt, Ramsay, Henderson, & Svejda, 1978). In contrast, by using an adjustable cliff without safety glass, it is possible to test each infant over dozens of trials.

As in studies with the visual cliff, avoidance of a real cliff is related to infants' experience with balance and locomotion. But experience does not transfer from earlier developing skills to later developing ones. When 9-month-old infants were tested at the edge of an adjustable gap in the surface of support (Figure 5.11B) in an experienced sitting posture (average sitting experience was 3 months), they perceived precisely how far forward they could lean without falling into the precipice (Adolph, 2000). When the same infants faced the same gaps as novice crawlers (average crawling experience was 1 month), they fell into impossibly risky gaps on trial after trial (Figure 5.11C). Nearly half of the sample in each of two experiments attempted to crawl over the brink of the largest 90-cm gap. Infants show the same kind of specificity of learning between crawling and walking. Experienced 12-month-old crawlers precisely perceive the limits of their ability to crawl down an adjustable drop-off (Figure 5.11D), but novice 12-month-old walkers march cheerfully over the edge—even the largest 90-cm drop-off (Kretch et al., 2009).

FIGURE 5.11   Testing paradigms for observing infants at the edge of a precipice. (A) Crawling infants are coaxed to cross a 3-in or 3-ft Plexiglas-covered drop-off on the "visual cliff." Drawn by Karen Adolph with permission from *Psychological Monographs: General and Applied, 75*, R. W. Walk and E. J. Gibson, A comparative and analytical study of visual depth perception, p. 8. (1963). (B) Sitting and (C) crawling infants are coaxed to lean and reach over a real drop-off on the "veritable cliff." Adapted with permission from *Psychological Science, 11*, K. E. Adolph, Specificity of Learning: Why infants fall over a veritable cliff, p. 242. Reprinted by permission of SAGE Publications (drawn by Karen Adolph). (D) Crawling infant at the edge of an actual, adjustable cliff (drawn by Samira Iravani).

What infants know about keeping balance while sitting does not help them to keep balance when learning to crawl, and what they've learned as crawlers does not transfer to walking. In short, infants' knowledge about balance control is specific to the postures with which they have extended experience. Specificity of learning may seem surprising (how could the same infants display both accurate and erroneous behaviors on the same dangerous cliff?), but specificity makes good sense in terms of biomechanics. Sitting, crawling, and walking are different balance control systems. They involve different key pivots about which the body rotates (hips for sitting, wrists for crawling, ankles for walking), different muscle groups for generating compensatory sways, different vantage points for viewing the ground ahead, and different correlations between **optic flow** and vestibular stimulation. Thus, when infants acquire the strength and coordination for a new posture in development, they must identify the new parameters for this new balance control system and then learn to recalibrate the settings of each parameter as they approach novel ground surfaces (Adolph, 2002, 2008; Adolph & Joh, 2008).

UPRIGHT BALANCE: STANDING, CRUISING, AND WALKING

Walking upright is unique from infants' other motor milestones. It is a developmental rite of passage marking the transition from infant to toddler. Like infants' first words, walking is emblematic of human culture. Walking also shares important similarities with other motor milestones. As with sitting, reaching, and crawling, keeping balance is a central problem for walking. To conquer balance on two feet, infants must cope with rapid changes in body proportions and newly relevant aspects of the ground surface.

Changing Body Proportions

After the fetal growth explosion, the two most rapid and dramatic periods of growth are infancy and adolescence. The left panels in Figure 5.12A and B show **growth curves** for height and weight from birth to adulthood based on national norms collected by the United States National Center for Health Statistics and updated by the Center for Disease Control in 2000. The right panels in Figure 5.12A and B show a magnified view of children's growth from birth to 2 years. Figure 5.12C shows head circumference (measured around the head at eyebrow line). Body mass index (BMI; Figure 5.12D) is a measure of overall chubbiness that combines children's weight and height (weight in kilograms/[height in meters]^2).

The thick curves on each graph represent the 50th percentile, meaning that a 12-month-old girl whose weight is at the 50th percentile for her age group weighs at least as much as 50% of the 12-month-old girls in the reference population. The thin curves below and above the 50th percentiles represent the 5th and 95th percentiles, respectively. Children show a wide range in height, weight, head circumference, and BMI at each age. By 2 years of age, children's height may vary by 12 cm between the 5th and 95th percentiles. The size of the normal range increases with age so that children's height may vary by 22 cm at 10 years of age between the 5th and 95th percentiles.

Growth is especially rapid during infancy, as portrayed by the steep upward trajectory on the growth charts illustrated in Figure 5.12A and B. Infants become taller and heavier, of course, but they get bigger at different rates for the different parts of their bodies. For example, in the first 12 months of life, infants' height increases by 44% (25 cm) but their head circumference increases by only 29% (10 cm). Lengthening is faster than fattening, so that infants' proportions undergo a general slimming. Newborns' top-heavy bodies become increasingly cylindrical and the center of mass moves from the sternum to below the belly

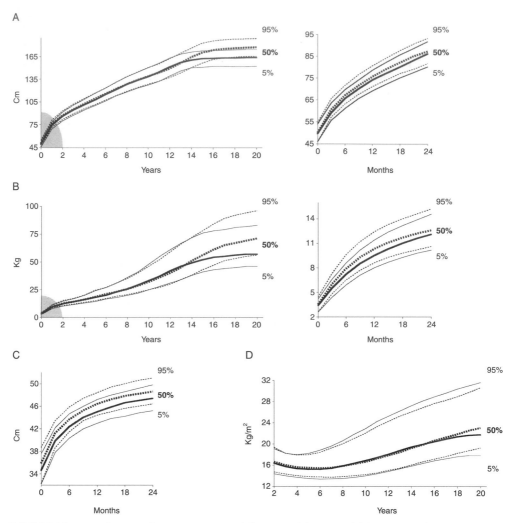

FIGURE 5.12 Growth curves from 0 to 20 years. (A) Height, (B) weight, (C) head circumference, (D) body mass index. Solid lines = girls. Dashed lines = boys. Thick lines = 50th percentile. Thin lines = 5th and 95th percentiles. Gray shaded regions in (A) and (B) are depicted in greater detail to the right to illustrate rapid growth in infancy. Adapted from growth charts developed by the National Center for Health Statistics in collaboration with the National Center for Chronic Disease Prevention and Health Promotion (2000).

button. The typically fat-bellied toddlers become slender kindergarteners. Accordingly, the growth chart illustrating BMI shows a dip from birth to 5 years of age. Subsequent increase in the BMI reflects a shift to more fattening and increased muscle mass relative to lengthening of the limbs and body. After 2 years of age, children's rate of growth slows down as shown by a shallower upward trajectory on the growth charts for height, weight, and head circumference.

From birth, boys are consistently taller and heavier than girls. Thus, the United States National Center for Health Statistics and the Centers for Disease Control (CDC) issue separate growth charts for girls and boys. However, sex differences are relatively small before puberty (e.g., 1 or 2 cm for height at the same percentile). At around 10 to 12 years of age, girls begin their adolescent growth spurt, and they frequently tower over same-aged boys. At around 14 years of age, boys begin their adolescent growth spurt, and they once again become taller and heavier than girls. By adulthood, the sex gap is huge: 12 to 15 cm for height at the same percentile.

In 2000, the United States National Center for Health Statistics published new growth charts for children younger than 24 months of age. The previously published growth charts from 1977 included primarily babies who had breast-fed for less than 3 months, then switched to formula milk. Recent studies show that babies who drink breast milk throughout their first year grow rapidly in their first 2 to 3 months of life but more slowly from 3 to 12 months. However, the formula-fed sample in the 1977 growth charts did not portray infants' growth as slowing after 3 months. Thus, when clinicians compared breast-fed babies to the norms on the old growth chart, infants were often misdiagnosed as "faltering." To circumvent this problem, the newer 2000 growth charts are based on a more representative sample including more infants who were breast-fed for longer durations.

Typically, growth researchers measure children in cross-sectional samples or observe them longitudinally at monthly or wider spaced intervals and then interpolate between observations to yield smooth growth curves like the ones illustrated in Figure 5.12. Pediatricians do likewise when they document children's growth at their monthly and yearly check-ups. However, CDC growth charts are only designed to show the relative size of individuals—not to show change in growth of individual infants (Lampl & Thompson, 2007). Smaller sampling intervals reveal a very different picture of growth. Smooth growth curves are a statistical average, not a true description of children's growth trajectories. Daily observations reveal that infants' growth is **episodic,** not continuous (Johnson, Veldhuis, & Lampl, 1996; Lampl, 1993; Lampl & Johnson, 1993; Lampl, Johnson, & Frongillo, 2001; Lampl & Veldhuis, 1992). That is, dramatic growth spurts in the course of a single day alternate with long periods of stasis in which no growth occurs for days or weeks on end (Figure 5.12D). During 1-day growth spurts, infants' height can increase by 0.5 cm to 1.65 cm! The long plateaus with no growth are not related to stress or illness. Rather, normal, healthy babies grow in fits and starts. Infants must cope with changing constraints on balance because they begin a new day with a new set of body proportions.

Pediatricians use growth charts as crude diagnostic instruments. Parents have cause for worry if children are smaller than the 5th percentile for height, weight, or head circumference, above the 95th percentile on the BMI charts, or if children's continuing progress "falls" off their current growth curve, suggesting failure to thrive. The body mass chubbiness index has become increasingly important because more children are overweight at younger ages. Overweight shows up in the asymmetry between the 95th and 5th percentiles on the weight-for-age growth charts and on the BMI charts. The range in weight and in chubbiness is wider on the heavy side of the 50th percentile than on the light side.

Some researchers cite "epidemic proportions" of obesity and overweight in children and adolescents (Jolliffe, 2004; Reilly & Dorosty, 1999). Surprisingly, the increase in obesity may not result from overeating. Instead, modern children are less active than previous generations. They spend more time in sedentary activities such as watching television, and they get only 20 of the recommended 60 minutes of physical activity per day (Reilly et al., 2004; Trost, Sirard, Dowda, Pfeiffer, & Pate, 2003; Vandewater, Shim, & Caplovitz, 2004).

One physical effect associated with higher rates of obesity in children is earlier pubertal onset compared to children with a normal BMI, particularly in white girls (Kaplowitz, Slora, Wasserman, Pedlow, & Herman-Giddens, 2001; Rosenfield, Lipton, & Drum, 2009). A critical "fat mass" may trigger hormone secretion that initiates the onset of puberty (Ahmed, Ong, & Dunger, 2009). As a result, some studies have found a secular trend towards early puberty, with girls experiencing earlier breast development onset and menarche over the decades from 1940 to 1994 (Euling et al., 2008a; Euling, Selevan, Pescovitz, & Skakkebaek, 2008b; but see Ahmed et al., 2009).

Getting Upright

The job of getting their bodies upright for stance and locomotion takes infants several months. On average, the typical sequence of milestones begins at 7 to 10 months of age and ends at 11 to 15 months. The protracted acquisition of upright posture reflects a combination of increasing leg strength and balance control. Between 4 and 7 months of age, infants' legs are so weak that if parents hold them upright, babies pop their legs straight and lock them in place in the so-called "positive supporting reflex" (Capute, Accardo, Vining, Rubenstein, & Harryman, 1978). As infants' muscles tire, they bend and straighten their knees simultaneously as if jumping. By 7 months or so, most infants have acquired sufficient leg strength to hold their body weight on both legs, but they still cannot cope with balance. If parents prop babies against the couch or coffee table, the babies stand by controlling balance with their arms. At first, infants may stand on their toes or with their feet turned inward or outward along the lateral edges. Later, they stand flat-footed, bearing their weight squarely over the feet.

When infants have sufficient strength to hold part of their body weight on one leg, they begin to "cruise" along furniture by moving sideways, lifting the legs and arms one at a time (Vereijken & Adolph, 1998). They also display supported walking, facing frontward while parents hold their hands to provide the missing balance and leg strength. In early stages of supported walking, infants may be tilted 45° forward or backward as exhausted parents tramp around the house bent double at the waist. As infants' own strength and balance gradually begin to replace the supports provided by furniture and parents, infants begin to exert less force on their hands, bear more weight on their legs, and keep their bodies more perpendicular to the floor (Haehl, Vardaxis, & Ulrich, 2000; Vereijken & Adolph, 1998; Vereijken & Waardenburg, 1996). Eventually, they may require only one hand during cruising and supported walking, or hold only one of their parents' fingers for support.

At some point, the furniture or parents' finger may provide more moral support than balance. Many infants accidentally remove their hands from the furniture to manipulate a toy or watch an event. Upon realizing that they are standing independently, they immediately sit down or re-grip the furniture. Some babies take their first independent steps with one hand in the air, as if they were holding their parents' finger. Trettien (1900, pp. 41–42) provides a wonderful description of how G. Stanley Hall's daughter found the emotional impetus to walk:

> One day the father came home to dinner and placed his cuffs upon a table . . . The child, seeing the cuffs, crept to the table, pulled herself up by the leg of the table, took the cuffs . . . and slipped them over her wrists, standing unsupported while doing it . . . Then, to the great surprise of the father, she walked with great confidence with a pleased expression on her face . . . Without the cuffs, however, she could not be induced to take a single step. She was given an old pair of cuffs and she seemed greatly delighted; she walked and ran as before. She used the cuffs for two days, after which she walked without them and did not revert to crawling.

Getting upright is not the same problem as moving in an upright position. Infants first hoist themselves upright by pulling up on furniture at around 9 months of age (Frankenburg et al., 1992). From a crawling position, infants lift their torsos to kneel, then heave themselves erect using their arms to pull up or push down on the furniture (Bly, 1994). From a sitting position, the same babies may be stymied by the requirements of first transitioning onto their knees to pull up to a stand. Standing up from a squat without holding onto furniture requires more coordination and strength than simply standing (imagine doing leg squats in an exercise class) and thus appears shortly before or even several weeks after independent walking (Bly, 1994; Frankenburg et al., 1992).

Walking

First steps. Typically, infants take their first independent walking steps around their first birthday (Frankenburg et al., 1992). However, like the onset of most motor skills, walking onset has a wide age range: 9 to 17 months in Western cultures. Although some babies, like Hall's daughter, may be reticent to begin walking, most infants are highly motivated to walk and delight in their first steps. Bolstered by cultural norms, parents' expectations, and daily childrearing routines, walking is an eagerly awaited and highly valued achievement. Amid cheers and praise, toddlers launch themselves into parents' open arms.

Why might infants walk when they do? There is widespread agreement among researchers that infants' first independent walking steps await sufficient muscle strength and balance control to hold the body on one leg while the other leg swings forward (e.g., McGraw, 1945; Thelen et al., 1984; Zelazo et al., 1989). But what factors give infants sufficient muscle strength and balance control to take independent steps?

On a brain-based account of walking onset, maturational changes in neural structures and circuitry facilitate strength and balance by increasing information-processing speed and efficiency (Zelazo, 1998; Zelazo et al., 1989). The maturing cortex allows intentional control of alternating leg movements by regenerating the primitive stepping pattern (Forssberg, 1985; McGraw, 1932, 1935, 1945) and by sequencing movements with the advent of combinatorial behaviors (Zelazo, 1998). Indeed, correlational evidence is consistent with a brain-based account. Infants' brains grow from 30% to 70% of adult weight over the first 2 years of life (Thatcher, Lyon, Rumsey, & Krasnegor, 1996). Neural fibers become increasingly myelinated in the corticospinal tract (Johnson, Chapter 4, this volume).

On a body-based account of walking onset, changes in infants' body proportions facilitate improvements in strength and balance. Toward the end of the cruising and supported walking periods, an increased muscle-to-fat ratio in the legs and stronger hip, back, and abdominal muscles allow infants to bear weight on one leg while simultaneously stabilizing the torso. The slimming of infants' overall body proportions and the lowering of center of mass decrease the size of destabilizing torque. Correlational evidence is also consistent with body-based accounts. Chubbier, more top-heavy infants tend to begin walking at later ages than slimmer, more maturely proportioned babies (Adolph, 1997; McGraw, 1945; Shirley, 1931). Experimental simulations of more babyish body proportions by loading infants with weights causes them to fall more frequently. When they manage to stay upright, weight-loaded infants display less advanced walking patterns (Adolph & Avolio, 2000; Garciaguirre, Adolph, & Shrout, 2007; Schmuckler, 1993; Vereijken, Pedersen, & Storksen, 2009).

On an experience-based account, practice moving in an upright position facilitates strength and balance. Lifting their legs in cruising and supported walking provides infants with rigorous strength training in their leg muscles. Infants must pull the legs upward against gravity during the entire flexion segment of the step cycle. Along the same lines, practice with upright movements in infants' first months of life retains newborn stepping movements and induces earlier walking onset. For example, in a classic study, Zelazo et al. (1972) showed that 2-month-olds who were provided with daily stepping practice retained newborn stepping movements longer and began walking earlier than infants whose legs were passively exercised with supine leg kicks.

Natural experiments also support an experience-based account of walking onset. Parents in some cultures provide infants with daily strength training in a real-life version of Zelazo et al.'s experiment. For example, Jamaican mothers and Kipsigis mothers in Western Kenya exercise their infants' stepping movements (Hopkins & Westra, 1988, 1989, 1990; Super, 1976), as shown in Figure 5.9H. The Kipsigis mothers also engage in *kitwalse* (meaning "to make jump"), exercising infants' positive supporting responses and jumping movements. Like the infants in Zelazo's upright exercise group, Jamaican and Kipsigis infants walk several weeks earlier than do their non-exercised counterparts. In addition to building muscle strength, practice might facilitate balance control by giving infants the opportunity to learn about compensatory sway responses that maintain the body's position. Infants with more experience standing display more efficient compensatory responses when their balance is disrupted (Metcalfe et al., 2004; Woollacott, Shumway-Cook, & Williams, 1989).

Historically, brain-based explanations are maturational accounts, experience-based explanations are learning accounts, and body-based explanations are agnostic regarding the respective roles of nature and nurture. However, the historical compartmentalization of theories does not reflect researchers' sensitivity to the bidirectional nature of development. Both early pioneers and modern researchers in motor development agree that brain, body, and practice are likely to be interrelated (e.g., Adolph, Vereijken, & Shrout, 2003; Gesell, 1939; McGraw, 1945; Thelen & Ulrich, 1991). For example, maturation of the central nervous system and of infants' various body parts might spur infants to engage in more practice. Alternatively, practice might hone the neural circuitry and slenderize infants' bodies.

Walking proficiency.   Since the 1930s, researchers have devised elegant and innovative methods to capture changes in infants' walking patterns. Shirley (1931) sprinkled oil and graphite on the bottoms of infants' feet and scored footfall measures such as step length from the trails left behind on rolls of paper. McGraw (1935, 1945) recorded infants' walking movements using high-speed film and analyzed limb positions by projecting each movie frame onto a surface and tracing the outline of the babies' bodies. Modern researchers attach inked tabs to the bottoms of infants' shoes (Adolph et al., 2003) or use mechanized gait carpets (Garciaguirre et al., 2007) to document changes in patterns of foot placement. They use video (Thelen, Bril, & Breniere, 1992) and high-speed film (Clark, Whitall, & Phillips, 1988) to measure the timing and variability of infants' steps. High-resolution force platforms measure changes in the location of infants' center of gravity in three dimensions (Breniere, Bril, & Fontaine, 1989; Bril & Breniere, 1992), and marker-tracking motion analyses systems record infants' limb trajectories and joint angles (Assaiante et al., 1998).

Regardless of the method used, laboratory findings about infant walking are remarkably consistent (e.g., Adolph et al., 2003; Bril & Breniere, 1989, 1992, 1993; Clark et al., 1988; McGraw, 1935, 1945; Shirley, 1931; Thelen et al., 1992). In their first weeks of independent walking, infants' steps are shaky and inconsistent. Babies typically point their toes out to the sides, take tiny forward steps, and plant their feet so wide apart from side to side that their step width may be larger than their step length. They travel distances slowly but slam each foot down quickly, resulting in short periods with one leg in the air and long periods with both feet on the floor. Their legs bend and straighten with inconsistent, jerky motions at hip, knee, and ankle, and their feet contact the ground on toes or flat-footed. Their arms are flexed at the elbow in a frozen "jazz-hands" position (Corbetta & Bojczyk, 2002; Ledebt, 2000; McGraw, 1945).

In contrast, after 4 to 6 months of independent walking, infants' walking patterns are more adult-like. Rather than stumbling along, responding *ad hoc* to the outcome of their last step, infants' movements are uniform and consistent over the whole path of progression. Their steps are longer, their feet are closer together laterally, and their toes point forward. They walk at higher velocities and spend more time with each foot in the air and less time with both feet on the ground. Their joint angles are smooth and consistent and their feet contact the floor with a heel-toe progression. Their hands are down at their sides and their arms swing in unison with the leg on the opposite side of the body. Improvements are fastest in the first few months of independent walking, as if infants are figuring out the critical parameters of this new action system. Then the rate of improvements slows, suggesting that they are learning to tweak the settings of the various parameters (Adolph et al., 2003; Ledebt & Bril, 2000).

The early pioneers and the modern researchers agree that the list of deficiencies in infants' early walking patterns stems from the same problem that stalled walking onset: Sufficient strength and balance control to hold the body on one leg while the other leg swings forward (e.g., Adolph et al., 2003; Bril & Breniere, 1993; McGraw, 1945). New walkers are, in fact, falling downward into each step; the vertical acceleration of their center of mass is negative when their foot contacts the floor. In contrast, experienced walkers and adults are propelling upward at each step; the vertical acceleration of their center of mass is positive at foot contact (Breniere et al., 1989; Bril & Breniere, 1993). In essence, new walkers sacrifice balance to solve forward propulsion. They allow their bodies to fall forward while they stand on their stationary foot and then catch themselves mid-fall with their moving foot. More experienced walkers and adults control balance during forward propulsion by pushing upward with the stationary foot supporting their body.

What, then, might explain the improvements in strength and balance that could spur improvements in walking proficiency? The same putative factors that researchers proposed to explain walking onset could also explain improvements in walking skill—brain, body, and experience. The independent contributions of these factors can be compared statistically, with infants' chronological age as a crude stand-in for brain development, the duration of their locomotor experience a stand-in for practice, and body dimensions measured directly. The findings are very robust. Experience is the strongest predictor of improvements in walking skill (step length, step width, foot rotation, and dynamic base of support), accounting for statistical effects above and beyond those exerted by age and body dimensions (Adolph et al., 2003). In contrast, the other two factors are poor predictors of improvements in walking skill. Neither age nor body dimensions exerted statistical effects above and beyond those produced by experience.

Although the statistical power of experience is impressive, the construct is conceptually weak. The standard way to quantify locomotor experience is to count the number of days between walking onset and test day. Hence, some researchers refer to experience as "walking age" (Clark et al., 1988; Metcalfe & Clark, 2000). Like chronological age, walking age does not speak to underlying mechanisms: How many steps do babies take, how far do they travel, and what is the nature of their experiences?

To describe the content of infants' locomotor experiences, Adolph and colleagues designed a diary procedure for parents to track infants' whereabouts, a video-based procedure to document infants' steps, falls, and paths, and a step-counter device for infants to wear in their shoes (Adolph, 2002; Adolph, Garciaguirre, Badaly, & Sotsky, 2010; Adolph, Robinson, Young, & Gill-Alvarez, 2008a; Sotsky, Garciaguirre, & Adolph, 2004). At 14 months of age, walkers are on the floor engaged in balance and locomotion for 50% of their waking day (approximately 6 hours of floor time). Over the course of a day they log an average of 15,000 steps and travel the distance of 49 football fields. During this time, they are likely to walk through every room in their home and traverse 5 to 12 different surfaces.

Perceptual Control of Balance and Navigation

When standing stationary, infants typically keep balance by controlling the sway around their ankles. The body has multiple segments so infants can also generate compensatory swaying motions at their hips or regain balance by bending their knees or grasping onto a support (Stoffregen, Adolph, Thelen, Gorday, & Sheng, 1997). Multiple sources of perceptual information specify the body's position as it sways within the base of support: stretching and deformation of the skin on the feet, stimulation of the muscles and joints in the legs, accelerations detected by the vestibular system, and optic flow available to the visual system. Even the subtle deformation of the skin on the fingers can specify the body's swaying motions: Infants are so sensitive to perceptual information for body sway that they can minimize backward and forward swaying movement with merely a light touch of their hand on a support surface (Barela, Jeka, & Clark, 1999; Metcalfe & Clark, 2000; Metcalfe et al., 2004, 2005).

Vision for action. Visual motion information from optic flow is especially important for balance control in standing and walking. The structure of optic flow differs at the center of the optic array and at the periphery (Gibson, 1979). At the center of expansion, flow structure is radial and is especially useful for steering. Optic texture elements stream outward like the reflective markers on highway guardrails while driving in the dark. At the periphery of the optic array, the flow has a layered, almost parallel structure and is especially useful for maintaining balance. Optic texture elements stream in parallel like the scene whizzing past a side window. A series of "moving room" experiments demonstrates that infants can see as well as feel themselves swaying (e.g., Bertenthal, Boker, & Xu, 2000; Bertenthal, Rose, & Bai, 1997; Butterworth & Hicks, 1977; Stoffregen, Schmuckler, & Gibson, 1987). In fact, visual information is so important for keeping balance that infants give it more weight than proprioceptive information from the muscles and joints.

The moving room gives the visual illusion of body sway, comparable to what passengers might feel as the train on the next track leaves the station, even though their own train is not moving. As shown in Figure 5.13, children stand on the stationary floor, but the walls around them oscillate forward and backward (the arrangement is rigged by swinging temporary walls along the ceiling or rolling walls along the floor). The movements of the front wall create radial flow structure and the movements of the side walls create lamellar flow structure. Forward movement of the walls simulates the optic flow resulting from a backward body sway; backward movement of the walls simulates the optic flow resulting from a forward sway. Although visual and muscle-joint information are in conflict (infants see that they are moving but feel that they are stationary), the sensation of induced sway is very compelling. Some seated adults fall off their chairs (Poore, Campos, Anderson, Anderson, & Uchiyama, 2004), some standing adults stagger, and some become nauseous (Smart, James, Stoffregen, & Bardy, 2002). Adult walkers use radial flow information for steering and lamellar flow information for keeping balance. Thus, while standing in a moving room, they generate compensatory sways only in response to movement of the side walls (Stoffregen, 1985). As the side walls roll forward and backward, adults shift their weight backward and forward, entrained like puppets to the simulated lamellar flow.

Children's age and locomotor experience are related to their ability to differentiate radial from lamellar flow (Woollacott et al., 1989). For example, neonates increase stepping movements of their legs if they are held in the path of simulated flow (Barbu-Roth, Anderson, Despres, Provasi, & Campos, 2009). Neonates (Jouen, Lepecq, Gapene, & Bertenthal, 2000), and 2-month-olds (Butterworth & Pope, 1983) move their heads in accordance with the speed and direction of the simulated visual flow. Seated in slings or car seats, infants respond to forward wall movement by leaning forward as if compensating for a backward sway and to backward wall movement by straining backward as if compensating for a forward body sway. With increased sitting experience, infants more accurately scale the force and timing of their compensatory sway responses to the optic flow in the moving room. By 8 months of age, infants show different looking behaviors in response to forward and backward optic flow (Gilmore, Baker, & Grobman, 2004) and different patterns of electrical activity in their brains in response to patterned optic flow versus random dots (van der Meer, Fallet, & van der Weel, 2008). However, while seated in the moving room, pre-crawling infants sway equally

FIGURE 5.13 Infant standing in a "moving room." The movement of the walls creates the visual illusion that infants' bodies are swaying, even when they are standing still. Infants sway, stagger, or fall in response to the room movement, demonstrating that they use visual information to keep their balance. Reprinted with permission from *Developmental Psychology, 25*, B. I. Bertenthal and D. L. Bai, Infant's sensitivity to optical flow for controlling posture, p. 939. Copyright © 1989 by the American Psychological Association.

vigorously to front and side movement of the walls (Higgins, Campos, & Kermoian, 1996). In contrast, 8-month-old crawlers and infants who have experience wheeling themselves around in mechanical "walkers" or mobility devices self-powered via a joystick produce more compensatory sway responses to movements of the side walls (Uchiyama et al., 2008).

When infants first begin walking, they respond so strongly to simulated optic flow that they stagger and frequently fall while standing in a moving room (Bertenthal et al., 1997; Butterworth & Hicks, 1977; Lee & Aronson, 1974) and their balance in a sitting position is temporarily disrupted (Chen, Metcalfe, Jeka, & Clark, 2007). New walkers' upright balance is disrupted by movement of both the front and side walls, but they stagger and fall more frequently after movement of the side walls, suggesting that they are beginning to functionally differentiate radial from lamellar flow (Bertenthal et al., 1997; Schmuckler & Gibson, 1989; Stoffregen et al., 1987). Older, more experienced preschool-age children stagger only after movement of the side walls, and they rarely fall (Schmuckler & Gibson, 1989; Stoffregen et al., 1987). However, force plates and motion analysis systems that can detect swaying movements that are invisible to the naked eye show that preschoolers display subtle compensatory sway responses after movement of the front wall and that postural control is not adult-like until 12 years of age (Godoi & Barela, 2008; Peterson, Christou, & Rosengren, 2006; Schmuckler, 1997). In contrast, force plate recordings show that adults are nearly impervious to front wall movement.

The moving room elicits more staggers and falls when infants are standing stationary than when they are walking (Stoffregen et al., 1987). But walking in an empty moving room is a poor analog of walking in everyday locomotion. Normally, steering and balance are inseparable as babies navigate around couches, tables, and chairs *en route* to their destination. To assess infants' ability to use lamellar flow information selectively for balance, babies were tested in a sort of slalom course in a "moving hallway" (Schmuckler & Gibson, 1989). Their task was to navigate around traffic cones to reach their mothers cheering them from the end of the hallway. Infants staggered and fell more frequently while walking down the moving hallway when they had the additional task of steering around obstacles compared with an uncluttered path. Preschoolers, in contrast, weaved through the obstacles as easily as through the uncluttered hallway.

Obstacle navigation requires visual information for steering and—in the case of changes in elevation—for gait modifications such as slowing down and lifting a leg to clear a stair. Development of a new, state-of-the-art, wireless, head-mounted eye-tracker has provided a way to know where walkers direct their visual attention while navigating obstacles. Recordings of visual fixations—the center of gaze on the fovea of the retina—show a developmental progression in the use of visual information for navigating through a room cluttered with changes in elevation (Franchak & Adolph, 2009; Franchak, Kretch, Soska, & Adolph, 2009): Adults primarily use visual information from the periphery of their eyes to control gait modifications. Children navigate using information from fixations a little over half the time. And infants fixate most obstacles before they step up, down, or over them. Occasionally, infants retain their gaze on the obstacle as their foot clears it.

Gauging risky ground.   Reactive control of balance in the moving room demonstrates that infants are sensitive to perceptual information for balance and can respond adaptively. However, reactive responding is always the strategy of last resort. Ideally, infants (and adults) must act on information prospectively before they begin to fall (von Hofsten, 1993, 2004). **Prospective control** of balance requires infants to gauge variations in the ground relative to their own body proportions and propensities.

To test prospective control of locomotion, Adolph and colleagues (e.g., Adolph, 1995, 1997; Adolph & Avolio, 2000; Adolph, Eppler, & Gibson, 1993) tested walking infants on a mechanized sloping walkway (Figure 5.14A). Flat starting and landing platforms flanked an adjustable sloping section (0° to 90°). Parents stood at the bottom of the slope and encouraged their infants to descend. An experimenter followed alongside infants to ensure their safety.

Experienced walkers display exquisitely fine-tuned prospective control of balance. Based on exploratory looking and touching from the flat starting platform, experienced toddlers determined which slopes were safe for walking and which were risky within a few degrees of accuracy (e.g., Adolph, 1995; Adolph et al., 1993). Experienced walkers can even update their assessment of their own abilities. For example, Adolph and Avolio (2000) loaded infants with lead-weight shoulder-packs to make their body proportions more top-heavy. As a consequence, infants could not walk down slopes as steep as those they could manage when they wore featherweight shoulder-packs. Infants recalibrated their judgments of risky slopes to their diminished, lead-weighted abilities. They correctly treated the same degrees of slope as risky while wearing the lead-weight shoulder-packs but as safe while wearing the featherweight packs.

Gauging threats to balance is not innate or automatic. Instead, longitudinal observations show that infants require a protracted period of learning. Infants were tested every three weeks on the adjustable sloping walkway, from their first week of crawling until several weeks after they began walking (Adolph, 1997). Each week brought about naturally occurring changes in infants' bodies and skills. A risky slope one week might be perfectly safe the next week when crawling skill improved. A safe slope for crawling might be impossibly risky when infants first began walking. Thus, prospective guidance over potentially risky ground requires continual updating.

Just as learning to gauge the limits of postural sway in a sitting posture does not transfer to crawling, learning to keep balance in a crawling posture does not transfer to walking. In their first weeks of crawling, infants plunged headlong down steep slopes, requiring rescue by the experimenter. With each week of crawling experience, infants responded more adaptively.

FIGURE 5.14 (A) Mechanized sloping walkway. Middle section varied from 0° to 90° via a push-button remote. Reprinted from *Advances in Child Development and Behavior*, Vol. 30, K. E. Adolph, Learning to keep balance, pp. 18–19, Copyright 2002 with permission from Elsevier (drawn by Karen Adolph). (B) Typical cruising infant correctly judging his ability to keep balance over a gap in the handrail, where he can rely on information relevant to maintaining balance with the arms and (C) incorrectly judging constraints on balance with an impossibly large gap in the floor, where he must take into account information relevant to maintaining balance with the legs. (Courtesy of Karen E. Adolph, New York University. Drawn by Samira Iravani.) In all illustrations, an experimenter (shown) ensured infants' safety. Caregivers (not shown) encouraged their infants from the end of the landing platform.

However, when infants faced the same risky slopes the next week as walkers, they walked blithely over the brink and fell. The urge to walk was so strong that when infants were placed on the starting platform in their old familiar crawling posture, half of them stood themselves up, walked over the brink of a 36° slope, and fell. When infants remained in their experienced crawling posture, they slid down the 36° slope or avoided going. Finally, over weeks of walking experience, infants' responses became increasingly adaptive. Despite months of testing and hundreds of trials on slopes, infants showed no evidence of transfer between crawling and walking (Adolph, 1997). Errors were just as high in infants' first week of walking as in their first week of crawling, and learning was no faster the second time around. Moreover, infants in a control group who were tested only in their first and tenth weeks of crawling and in their first week of walking were indistinguishable from infants who had experienced hundreds of trials on slopes. Apparently, infants learn to gauge threats to balance from a protracted period of everyday locomotor experience. Slope experience was not required.

A final experiment provides corroborating evidence that sophisticated recalibration of balance is learned and relearned with the acquisition of each postural milestone in the course of motor development (Adolph, Berger, & Leo, in press). Although cruising and walking share a common upright posture, the shift from keeping balance with the arms in cruising to keeping balance with the legs in walking might constitute distinct postural milestones. Thus, 11-month-old cruising infants were tested in two postural conditions on an adjustable gap apparatus (Figure 5.14B–C). The "handrail" condition was relevant for keeping balance in the arms: There was a continuous floor and an adjustable gap in the handrail that infants clung onto for support. The "floor" condition was relevant for keeping balance with the legs: There was a continuous handrail and an adjustable gap in the floor. In both conditions, an assistant drew infants' attention to the gap. Then the experimenter released babies on the starting platform.

Cruisers accurately gauged threats to balance in the handrail condition. Infants cruised over safe gaps within their arm span, and avoided or crawled past risky gaps wider than their arm span. In contrast, infants stepped into impossibly wide gaps and fell in the floor condition. A handful of infants had begun taking independent steps by the day of the test session. These infants attempted to walk over risky gaps in both conditions, seemingly unaware of how many steps they could manage between gaps in the handrail and equally oblivious to the impossibility of keeping balance without a floor to support their bodies. The cruisers' and new walkers' errors in the floor condition indicate that practice cruising does not teach infants to attend to variations in the ground surface that are relevant for keeping balance using the legs to support the body. In other words, prospective control of balance does not transfer from cruising to walking because cruisers fail to learn that they need a floor to support their body. Instead, cruising infants have learned to use information at their arms—the utility of the handrail or furniture—for keeping balance.

Social information.   As in many arenas of developmental science, motor development is typically portrayed as a lonely enterprise, as if infants learn to keep balance and navigate all on their own. This is not true. Caregivers in every culture serve as both lifeguards and cheerleaders in infants' motor development (Adolph, Karasik, & Tamis-LeMonda, 2009c). They safeguard infants from accidents by carrying them in slings and packs and by "baby proofing" the house with gates across the stairs; they scaffold infants' achievements with special sand pits to promote sitting and "activity centers" to encourage gross motor play.

Caregivers also provide infants with social information about how to respond to potential motor challenges (Karasik, Tamis-LeMonda, Adolph, & Dimitropoulou, 2008; Tamis-Lemonda, Adolph, Dimitropoulou, & Zack, 2007). Mothers' words, facial expressions, manual gestures, and body position can provide powerful social messages for guiding action. However, infants' use of social information depends on their age (a stand-in for language knowledge and social cognition) and the duration of their locomotor experience. At 12 months of age, experienced crawlers refused to descend risky slopes regardless of mothers' messages, but became slightly more cautious on safe slopes when their mothers discouraged them. Novice 12-month-old walkers marched straight over the edge of both safe and risky slopes, but became slightly more cautious at the steepest increments when their mothers discouraged them (Adolph, Tamis-LeMonda, Ishak, Karasik, & Lobo, 2008). By 18 months of age, when infants are both sophisticated consumers of social information and experienced walkers, they only deferred to mothers' advice when risk level was uncertain: On slopes at the limits of their abilities, infants walked when mothers said go and avoided when mothers said no. Otherwise, infants ignored their mothers' advice by avoiding steep slopes and crossing safe ones regardless of the social message (Tamis-LeMonda et al., 2008). However, when 18-month-olds were outfitted with slippery Teflon-soled shoes that diminished their walking skill, they relied on mothers' social messages to decide whether formerly safe slopes were safe or risky (Adolph, Tamis-LeMonda, Karasik, & Lobo, 2009). Clearly, when social information is available—as it is in the everyday lives of infants and caregivers—infants weigh and integrate social messages with the perceptual information generated by their own exploratory activities in making decisions about action.

FROM STAIR CLIMBING TO LOCOMOTOR TOOL USE

Up and Down

Once infants can use their arms and legs for balance and propulsion, new opportunities for locomotion become available in the third dimension. Given the appropriate environmental supports, infants can climb up and slide down. The world in three dimensions is a playground handily equipped with countless objects that serve as infants' "jungle gym." The literature is filled with rich descriptions of children climbing and descending slopes, fences, gates, ladders, trees, troughs, animal cages, and other outdoor obstacles and going up and down stairs, window sills, crib rails, people, toy boxes, overturned buckets, bathtubs, furniture, and other indoor obstacles (Adolph, 1997; McGraw, 1935; Trettien, 1900; Valsiner & Mackie, 1985).

Toddlers appear to climb for the sheer love of doing so, as if irresistibly challenged to surmount three-dimensional obstacles (Harlow & Mears, 1979; McGraw, 1935; Trettien, 1900). For example, infants frequently respond more to stairs as an opportunity for gross motor play than as a path toward a goal at the landing. Even in an experimental arrangement with toys offered as attractive lures at the top landings, infants meandered between adjacent staircases, crawled up and down repeatedly, and turned in circles midway up rather than take a direct route to the top (Ulrich, Thelen, & Niles, 1990). For human infants, going up is easier than going down (Adolph, 1997; McGraw, 1935). Climbing up slopes, stairs, and ladders is energetically costly but relatively easy to control (Dean, 1965). Upward motions are tiring because infants must hoist their bodies against the pull of gravity. However, gravity makes upward motions easier to control by slowing forward momentum and giving infants more time to place their limbs into the appropriate positions. Crawling infants support more of their body weight on their legs, relieving their weaker, spindly arms from their usual contribution to support. In fact, infants who cannot push their bellies off the floor while horizontal can push themselves onto hands and knees or hands and feet while climbing up slopes or stairs. Walking infants' supporting leg and crawlers' supporting arm are typically extended so that muscles contract to produce force. The moving leg or arm traces a smaller arc than it does during locomotion on flat ground. It contacts the slope, riser, and rung while still in a flexed position. In the event that they fall, infants' hands are well positioned to protect their face and head.

In contrast, going down slopes, stairs, and ladders is less tiring but extremely difficult to control (Adolph, 1995, 1997; Dean, 1965; Nelson & Osterhoudt, 1971). Moving the body in the direction of gravity is energetically efficient, but forward momentum can make infants' downward motions spin out of control. In face-first descent of slopes, crawlers must support more body weight on their weak arms than they would on flat ground, exacerbating the problem of keeping balance. Beginning walkers may also lack sufficient strength to descend slopes and stairs face-first in an upright position because to bear weight on the bent support leg, their muscles must lengthen rather than contract, requiring more strength to produce force.

Infants' success at climbing reflects the different biomechanics of going up versus going down. For example, after an intense regimen of daily practice climbing up and down slopes, one infant climbed up an incredible 70° slope using his hands to grip and his toes to propel, but the steepest slope that he crawled down face-first was 40° (McGraw, 1935). After daily practice on stairs, one infant clambered up a staircase on hands and knees in 26 s and another sprinted up in 10 s, but neither infant could crawl down independently (Gesell & Thompson, 1929). Without special training, most infants' success is more modest. Crawling and walking infants scaled slopes in the 2° to 36° range and nearly all babies managed to climb up steeper slopes than they could crawl or walk down (Adolph, 1995, 1997; Adolph et al., 1993).

Stair-climbing follows a predictable sequence (Bayley, 1993; Berger et al., 2007). Infants can crawl up a step or two shortly after they can crawl on flat ground (Berger et al., 2007; Gesell & Thompson, 1934; Trettien, 1900). Soon, they master an entire flight of stairs, but appear to solve the problem of climbing one step at a time. They put both knees onto one riser or rest momentarily in a sitting position before turning back to the staircase. Over weeks of crawling, infants' stair-climbing posture becomes increasingly erect. Instead of balancing on their knees, they push up onto their feet. Eventually, crawlers can climb up on hands and feet using an alternating gait pattern with only one limb on a step at one time.

Most infants cannot walk up or down stairs until several weeks after they begin walking on flat ground (Bayley, 1993; Berger et al., 2007). At first, infants can only manage a riser or two and they need to hold onto the wall or turn sideways to hold a banister with both hands for support (Berger et al., 2007; Trettien, 1900). Eventually, they can manage a flight of stairs while holding the wall or banister with one hand. As in crawling, they "mark time" by putting both feet onto each riser before moving to the next. For descent, their method of choice is to crawl backward with their heads pointing away from the bottom landing. They walk down a riser or two holding the wall or banister several weeks after mastering the same skill for ascent. Typically, children cannot walk up stairs without holding a support or marking time until they are 30 to 36 months of age, and they meet the same milestone for walking down stairs between 3 and 4 years of age. The typical stair-climbing sequence may be disrupted if infants do not have regular access to stairs. For example, children with stairs in their homes learn to ascend stairs earlier than children without daily access (Berger et al., 2007).

Cognition in Locomotion

Travel may broaden the mind (Campos et al., 2000), but, reciprocally, infants' minds can enrich their travels. Effective strategies for coping with challenging locomotor tasks may involve higher-level problem-solving skills. Means–ends exploration can allow infants to discover alternative locomotor strategies for descending slopes and stairs. Whole-body problem solving can present a stool or a banister in a new light.

Means-ends problem solving in locomotion.   When experienced crawlers or walkers face a staircase or steep slope for the first time, they correctly recognize that crawling or walking head-first is impossible, but they cannot find an alternative strategy to get down (Adolph, 1997). Infants are stuck in an approach–avoidance conflict (Lewin, 1946). Babies alternate between approaching and backing away from the brink, typically calling to their mothers, peering over the edge, touching the offending surface, becoming more and more frustrated until thankfully the trial ends and rescue is provided (Adolph et al., 2008b; Tamis-LeMonda et al., 2008). Toward the end of their first year of life, infants begin to demonstrate means–ends exploration at the edge of a slope (Adolph, 1997). They shift from one position to another as if testing the efficacy of alternative locomotor strategies as means for descent—from hands and knees to sitting with their feet dangling over the brink, to pivoting around with their backs to the slope or stairs, and so on. At first they figure out how to slide down face-first with their arms extended forward and their legs extended backward like Superman (Adolph, 1997; Adolph et al., 1993). Next they figure out how to slide down in a sitting position. Although most adults view sitting as the prototypical sliding position, for infants, the possibility of locomoting in a sitting posture appears to be a real discovery. Although sitting is also a viable strategy for descending stairs, it is difficult to execute for an entire staircase and infants tend to attack each step individually, regaining their balance between risers (Berger, 2004).

The last descent strategy to enter infants' repertoires is a backing position (Adolph, 1995, 1997; Adolph & Avolio, 2000; Adolph et al., 1993a). On stairs, most parents teach their infants the backing strategy with hands-on assistance by turning infants' bodies at the top landing and moving babies' arms and legs down each riser (Berger et al., 2007). The backing strategy is optimal in terms of safety and balance control across a wide range of descent situations including slopes, stairs, furniture, and drop-offs (Berger, 2004; McGraw, 1935). However, backing is also cognitively demanding: Infants must put themselves into a prone position, execute a detour by pivoting 180° so that their heads point away from the brink, and finally move backward toward a goal, either peering over one shoulder or facing away from the direction of travel.

None of the component actions for the backing strategy is motorically difficult (infants have been pivoting, keeping balance on their bellies, and unintentionally pushing backward for months). However, each component is cognitively difficult and sequencing the components creates an additional challenge. Even though reaching and locomotor detours are often the safest or most effective means for achieving a goal, they are notoriously difficult for infants because they involve counterintuitively turning away from the desired goal (Diamond, 1990; Lockman, 1984; Lockman & Adams, 2001; McGraw, 1935). Intentional backward movements appear several months after their forward counterparts; for example, backward walking appears at 18.5 months (Frankenburg et al., 1992). Locomotion with reversed visual guidance is difficult for adults (imagine walking backward without peering over your shoulder or driving in reverse without looking in the rear-view mirror). In addition, unless a caregiver stands at the bottom landing shouting encouragement, infants must represent the goal destination in memory.

Whole-body problem solving. The pinnacle of means–ends problem solving is tool use. Traditionally, researchers think of tools in terms of hand-held implements found in a toolbox. A classic example is Köhler's (1925) chimps raking in a distant banana by piecing together several interlocking sticks. However, tool use can involve the whole body, rather than merely the arms (Berger & Adolph, 2003; Berger et al., 2005; Berger et al., in press). Equally salient but less famous examples of means–ends problem solving are Köhler's (1925) chimps retrieving a distant banana hung from the ceiling by vaulting themselves through the air on the end of a pole or by stacking boxes large to small and then climbing to the top. In these cases of whole-body problem solving, the pole or the boxes share many of the features of hand-held tools.

In a daily training regimen, McGraw (1935) replicated with human infants versions of Köhler's box-stacking experiment with chimps. Lured by a toy hung from the ceiling, one task was to seriate a set of pedestals from shortest to tallest so as to climb from low to high. The pedestals ranged in height from 19 cm to 161 cm (more than twice infants' height) and weighed 4 kg to 28 kg (more than infants' body weight). Another task was to stack a set of boxes from largest on the bottom to smallest on the top. Infants' initial attempts to solve the problem did not take into account the utility of the pedestals or boxes as a means to reach the goal. Instead, they reached futilely toward the distant lure. Over weeks of practice, infants gradually made the connection between the moveable objects as means and the lure. They dragged a box a few feet or pushed a pedestal but on the way to positioning it, they seemed to forget why they were moving it. Eventually, they figured out that the small pedestals and boxes were too short to use alone but could be arranged with the larger objects to climb to the lure.

Berger and colleagues tested whole–body, means–ends problem solving by observing infants' use of a handrail to augment their balance (Berger & Adolph, 2003; Berger, 2005; Berger et al., in press). Sixteen-month-old walking infants were encouraged to cross wide and narrow bridges (12–72 cm) spanning a deep, wide precipice. On some trials, a handrail spanned the precipice along the bridge (Figure 5.15A). On other trials, the handrail was removed (Figure 5.15B). Parents stood at the far side of the precipice offering toys as a lure. As expected, infants recognized that narrow bridges posed a threat to balance. More important, they also recognized that the handrail could serve as a tool for augmenting their balance. Infants ran straight over the widest bridges and ignored the handrail. They avoided the narrowest bridges, regardless of whether the handrail was available. However, on intermediate bridges, infants attempted to walk when the handrail was available but avoided when the handrail was removed. When the substance of the handrail was varied, infants walked over challenging bridges with a sturdy wooden handrail to hold onto, and they avoided when the handrail was made of wobbly foam (Figure 5.15C). When the distance between the handrail and bridge was varied, infants attempted to walk when the handrail was within reach but not when it was too far away (Figure 5.15D).

CONCLUSIONS

A central theme of this chapter is the entwined nature of physical and motor development. Movement is embodied (Adolph & Berger, 2006; Gibson & Pick, 2000). From the first writhing motions of an 8-week-old embryo, the shape and proportions of the body, the distribution

FIGURE 5.15   Illustrations of variations of the bridge–handrail apparatus used for testing walking infants' whole-body problem-solving: (A) using a handrail to augment balance on a narrow bridge, (B) exploring a bridge over a precipice (reprinted with permission from *Developmental Psychology, 39*, S. E. Berger and K. E. Adolph, Infants use handrails as tools in a locomotor task, pp. 594–605. Copyright © 2003 by the American Psychological Association, drawn by Karen Adolph), (C) exploring a wobbly handrail made from foam or latex (reprinted with permission from *Child Development, 76*, S. E. Berger, K. E. Adolph & S. A. Lobo, Out of the toolbox: Toddlers differentiate wobbly and wooden handrails, pp. 1294–1307. Copyright © 2005 by the Society for Research in Child Development, drawn by Karen Adolph), reproduced with permission from John Wiley and Sons, (D) crossing a narrow bridge when the handrail is just within reach. (Courtesy of Sarah E. Berger, City University of New York. Drawn by Samira Iravani.)

of muscle mass and fat, the springiness of the joints and the links among muscle synergies affect the possibilities and function of movements. Infants' brains control only muscle actions. Movements, however, are the net result of muscle forces and passive forces arising from both the pull of gravity on the body and the consequences of ongoing movements (Bernstein, 1967; Thelen et al., 1993). Amazing robot legs that "walk" due only to passive forces attest to the importance of the body for controlling movement (Ruina, 2005). The dramatic changes in infants' bodies from the prenatal to preschool periods spur important changes in the biomechanical constraints on action that researchers are only beginning to understand.

A second theme in the chapter is the inseparability of action and perception (Bertenthal & Clifton, 1998). Researchers have long recognized that perceptual information is requisite for guiding the hand's trajectory during a reach to a target object and for guiding the body's path during locomotion to a destination. However, perceptual information is also requisite for balance control. Quiet stance in a sitting or upright posture must be continually monitored to keep the body in balance. Infants must use perceptual information to stabilize their bodies prior to a deliberate movement of their various body parts. In short, perceptual control of balance provides the very basis for movements of the head, trunk, and limbs during reaching, locomotion, and any other intentional action (Reed, 1982).

A final theme that we stressed is the contextualized nature of physical and motor development (Adolph et al., 2009). Traditionally, textbooks portray infants' motor development with simple line drawings on a milestone chart. However, infants do not lift their heads, roll over, or walk simply because of their age. The old-fashioned view that growth and motor development reflect merely the age-related output of maturation is, at best, incomplete. Rather, infants acquire new skills with the help of their caregivers in a real-world environment of objects, surfaces, and places. The structure of that environment, infants' access to its features, and their interactions with caregivers depend on the cultural and historical context.

We began by asking why a chapter on infants' physical and motor development belongs in a textbook on developmental science. We conclude by suggesting that psychological functions are integral for controlling movements adaptively. Perception, cognition, and emotion give infants the wherewithal to cope with changes in their bodies, to explore new affordances for action, and to make their way through a complex social and physical environment. New motor skills, in turn, provide infants with new opportunities for learning and enhance cognitive and social development.

ACKNOWLEDGMENTS

This work was funded by Grant # R37-HD33486 from the National Institute of Child Health and Human Development to KEA. We thank Lana Karasik and Samira Iravani for their beautiful line drawings for figures.

REFERENCES AND SUGGESTED READINGS (▢)

Adolph, K. E. (1995). A psychophysical assessment of toddlers' ability to cope with slopes. *Journal of Experimental Psychology: Human Perception and Performance, 21*, 734–750.

Adolph, K. E. (1997). Learning in the development of infant locomotion. *Monographs of the Society for Research in Child Development, 62*(3, Serial No. 251).

▢ Adolph, K. E. (2000). Specificity of learning: Why infants fall over a veritable cliff. *Psychological Science, 11*, 290–295.

Adolph, K. E. (2002). Learning to keep balance. In R. Kail (Ed.), *Advances in child development and behavior* (Vol. 30, pp. 1–40). New York: Elsevier.

Adolph, K. E. (2008). The growing body in action: What infant locomotion tells us about perceptually guided action. In R. Klatzky, M. Behrmann, & B. MacWhinney (Eds.), *Embodiment, ego-space, and action* (pp. 275–321). Mahwah, NJ: Lawrence Erlbaum Associates.

Adolph, K. E. (2008). Learning to move. *Current Directions in Psychological Science, 17,* 213–218.

Adolph, K. E., & Avolio, A. M. (2000). Walking infants adapt locomotion to changing body dimensions. *Journal of Experimental Psychology: Human Perception and Performance, 26,* 1148–1166.

📖 Adolph, K. E. & Berger, S. E. (2006). Motor development. In W. Damon & R. Lerner (Series Eds.) and D. Kuhn & R. S. Siegler (Vol. Eds.), *Handbook of child psychology: Vol. 2: Cognition, Perception and Language* (6th ed., pp. 161–213). New York: Wiley.

Adolph, K. E., Berger, S. E., & Leo, A. J. (in press). Developmental continuity? Crawling, cruising, and walking. *Developmental Science.*

Adolph, K. E., Eppler, M. A., & Gibson, E. J. (1993). Crawling versus walking infants' perception of affordances for locomotion over sloping surfaces. *Child Development, 64,* 1158–1174.

Adolph, K. E., Garciaguirre, J. S., Badaly, D., and Sotsky, R. B. (2010). How infants learn to walk: 15,000 steps and 100 falls per day. Manuscript under review.

Adolph, K. E. & Joh, A. S. (2007). Motor development: How infants get into the act. In A. Slater & M. Lewis (Eds.), *Introduction to infant development* (2nd ed., pp. 63–80). New York: Oxford University Press.

Adolph, K. E., & Joh, A. S. (2008). Multiple learning mechanisms in the development of action. In A. Woodward & A. Needham (Eds.), *Learning and the infant mind* (pp. 172–207). New York: Oxford University Press.

📖 Adolph, K. E., Karasik, L., & Tamis-LeMonda, C. S. (2009). Motor skills. In M. Bornstein (Ed.), *Handbook of cross-cultural developmental science, Vol. 1, Domains of development across cultures* (pp. 61–88). Mahwah, NJ: Lawrence Erlbaum Associates.

Adolph, K. E., Robinson, S. R., Young, J. W., & Gill-Alvarez, F. (2008a). What is the shape of developmental change? *Psychological Review, 115,* 527–543.

Adolph, K. E., Tamis-LeMonda, C. S., Ishak, S., Karasik, L. B., & Lobo, S. A. (2008). Locomotor experience and use of social information are posture specific. *Developmental Psychology, 44,* 1705–1714.

Adolph, K. E., Tamis-LeMonda, C. S., Karasik, L. B., & Lobo, S. A. (2009). *Multiple sources of information for guiding locomotion over slippery slopes.* Manuscript in preparation.

Adolph, K. E., Vereijken, B., & Denny, M. A. (1998). Learning to crawl. *Child Development, 69,* 1299–1312.

Adolph, K. E., Vereijken, B., & Shrout, P. E. (2003). What changes in infant walking and why. *Child Development, 74,* 475–497.

Ahmed, M. L., Ong, K. K., & Dunger, D. B. (2009). Childhood obesity and the timing of puberty. *Trends in Endocrinology and Metabolism, 20,* 237–242.

Alberts, J. R., & Ronca, A. E. (1993). Fetal experience revealed by rats: Psychobiological insights. *Early Human Development, 35,* 153–166.

Ames, L. B. (1937). The sequential patterning of prone progression in the human infant. *Genetic Psychology Monographs: Child Behavior, Animal Behavior, and Comparative Psychology, 19,* 409–460.

Amiel-Tison, C., & Grenier, A. (1986). *Neurological assessment during the first year of life.* New York: Oxford University Press.

Anderson, D. I., Campos, J., & Barbu-Roth, M. (2004). A developmental perspective on visual proprioception. In G. Bremner & A. Slater (Eds.), *Theories of infant development* (pp. 30–69). Malden, MA: Blackwell.

Angulo-Kinzler, R. M. (2001). Exploration and selection of intralimb coordination patterns in three-month-old infants. *Journal of Motor Behavior, 33,* 363–376.

Angulo-Kinzler, R. M., & Horn, C. L. (2001). Selection and memory of a lower limb motor-perceptual task in 3-month-old infants. *Infant Behavior & Development, 24,* 239–257.

Angulo-Kinzler, R. M., Ulrich, B., & Thelen, E. (2002). Three-month-old infants can select specific leg motor solutions. *Motor Control, 6,* 52–68.

Assaiante, C., Thomachot, B., Aurently, R., & Amblard, B. (1998). Organization of lateral balance control in toddlers during the first year of independent walking. *Journal of Motor Behavior, 30,* 114–129.

Barbu-Roth, M., Anderson, D. I., Despres, A., Provasi, J., & Campos, J. J. (2009). Neonatal stepping in relation to terrestrial optic flow. *Child Development, 80,* 8–14.

Barela, J. A., Jeka, J. J., & Clark, J. E. (1999). The use of somatosensory information during the acquisition of independent upright stance. *Infant Behavior and Development, 22,* 87–102.

Barlow, S. M. (2009). Oral and respiratory control for preterm feeding. *Current Opinion in Otolaryngology & Head and Neck Surgery, 17,* 179–186.

Barrett, T. M., Davis, E. F., & Needham, A. (2007). Learning about tools in infancy. *Developmental Psychology, 43,* 352–368.

Barrett, T. M., Traupman, E., & Needham, A. (2008). Infants' visual anticipation of object structure in grasp planning. *Infant Behavior and Development*, *31*, 1–9.

Bates, E., Carlson-Luden, V., & Bretherton, I. (1980). Perceptual aspects of tool using in infancy. *Infant Behavior and Development*, *3*, 127–140.

Bayley, N. (1993). *Bayley scales of infant development* (2nd ed.). New York: Psychological Corporation.

Bennett, D. S., Bendersky, M., & Lewis, M. (2005). Does the organization of emotional expression change over time? Facial expressivity from 4 to 12 months. *Infancy*, *8*, 167–187.

Berger, S. E. (2004). Demands on finite cognitive capacity cause infants' perseverative errors. *Infancy*, *5*, 217–238.

Berger, S. E., & Adolph, K. E. (2003). Infants use handrails as tools in a locomotor task. *Developmental Psychology*, *39*, 594–605.

Berger, S. E., Adolph, K. E., & Kavookjian, A. E. (in press). Bridging the gap: Solving spatial means–ends relations in a locomotor task. *Child Development*.

Berger, S. E., Adolph, K. E., & Lobo, S. A. (2005). Out of the toolbox: Toddlers differentiate wobbly and wooden handrails. *Child Development*, *76*, 1294–1307.

Berger, S. E., Theuring, C. F., & Adolph, K. E. (2007). How and when infants learn to climb stairs. *Infant Behavior and Development*, *30*, 36–49.

Bernstein, N. (1967). *The coordination and regulation of movements*. Oxford, UK: Pergamon Press.

Bertenthal, B. I., Boker, S. M., & Xu, M. (2000). Analysis of the perception–action cycle for visually induced postural sway in 9-month-old sitting infants. *Infant Behavior and Development*, *23*, 299–315.

Bertenthal, B. I., & Campos, J. J. (1984). A reexamination of fear and its determinants on the visual cliff. *Psychophysiology*, *21*, 413–417.

Bertenthal, B. I., & Clifton, R. K. (1998). Perception and action. In D. Kuhn & R. S. Siegler (Eds.), *Handbook of child psychology* (Vol. 2: *Cognition, Perception, and Language*, pp. 51–102). New York: Wiley.

Bertenthal, B. I., Rose, J. L., & Bai, D. L. (1997). Perception–action coupling in the development of visual control of posture. *Journal of Experimental Psychology: Human Perception and Performance*, *23*, 1631–1643.

Berthier, N. E., Clifton, R. K., McCall, D. D., & Robin, D. J. (1999). Proximodistal structure of early reaching in human infants. *Experimental Brain Research*, *127*, 259–269.

Berthier, N. E., & Keen, R. E. (2006). Development of reaching in infancy. *Experimental Brain Research*, *169*, 507–518.

Bhat, A., Heathcock, J., & Galloway, J. C. (2005). Toy-oriented changes in hand and joint kinematics during the emergence of purposeful reaching. *Infant Behavior and Development*, *28*, 445–465.

Bly, L. (1994). *Motor skills acquisition in the first year*. San Antonio, TX: Therapy Skill Builders.

Bourgeois, K. S., Khawar, A. W., Neal, S. A., & Lockman, J. J. (2005). Infant manual exploration of objects, surfaces and their interrelations. *Infancy*, *8*, 233–252.

Brazelton, T. B. (1956). Sucking in infancy. *Pediatrics*, *17*, 404.

Brenicre, Y., Bril, B., & Fontaine, R. (1989). Analysis of the transition from upright stance to steady state locomotion in children with under 200 days of autonomous walking. *Journal of Motor Behavior*, *21*, 20–37.

Bril, B., & Breniere, Y. (1989). Steady-state velocity and temporal structure of gait during the first six months of autonomous walking. *Human Movement Science*, *8*, 99–122.

Bril, B., & Breniere, Y. (1992). Postural requirements and progression velocity in young walkers. *Journal of Motor Behavior*, *24*, 105–116.

Bril, B., & Breniere, Y. (1993). Posture and independent locomotion in early childhood: Learning to walk or learning dynamic postural control? In G. J. P. Savelsbergh (Ed.), *The development of coordination in infancy* (pp. 337–358). Amsterdam: Elsevier.

Bril, B., & Sabatier, C. (1986). The cultural context of motor development: Postural manipulations in the daily life of Bambara babies (Mali). *International Journal of Behavioral Development*, *9*, 439–453.

Brown, A. (1990). Domain specific principles affect learning and transfer in children. *Cognitive Science*, *14*, 107–133.

Burnside, L. H. (1927). Coordination in the locomotion of infants. *Genetic Psychology Monographs: Child Behavior, Differential and Genetic Psychology*, *2*, 283–372.

Butterworth, G., & Hicks, L. (1977). Visual proprioception and postural stability in infancy: A developmental study. *Perception*, *7*, 513–525.

Butterworth, G., & Pope, M. (1983). Origine et fonction de la proprioception visuelle chez l'enfant. In S. de Schonen (Ed.), *Le développement dans la prèmiere année* (pp. 107–128). Paris: Presses Universitaires de Frances.

Campos, J. J., Anderson, D. I., Barbu-Roth, M. A., Hubbard, E. M., Hertenstein, M. J., & Witherington, D. C. (2000). Travel broadens the mind. *Infancy*, *1*, 149–219.

Campos, J. J., Bertenthal, B. I., & Kermoian, R. (1992). Early experience and emotional development: The emergence of wariness of heights. *Psychological Science*, *3*, 61–64.

Campos, J. J., Hiatt, S., Ramsay, D., Henderson, C., & Svejda, M. (1978). The emergence of fear on the visual cliff. In M. Lewis & L. Rosenblum (Eds.), *The development of affect* (pp. 149–182). New York: Plenum.

Capute, A. J., Accardo, P. J., Vining, E. P. G., Rubenstein, J. E., & Harryman, S. (1978). *Primitive reflex profile*. Baltimore: University Park Press.

Capute, A. J., Shapiro, B. K., Palmer, F. B., Ross, A., & Wachtel, R. C. (1985). Normal gross motor development: The influences of race, sex and socio-economic status. *Developmental Medicine and Child Neurology*, *27*, 635–643.

Carolan, P. L., Moore, J. R., & Luxenberg, M. G. (1995). Infant sleep position and the sudden infant death syndrome: A survey of pediatric recommendations. *Clinical Pediatrics*, *34*, 402–409.

Carvalho, R. P., Tudella, E., & Savelsbergh, G. J. P. (2007). Spatio-temporal parameters in infants' reaching movements are influenced by body orientation. *Infant Behavior and Development*, *30*, 26–35.

Carvalho, R. P., Tudella, E., Caljouw, S. R., & Savelsbergh, G. J. P. (2008). Early control of reaching: Effects of experience and body orientation. *Infant Behavior and Development*, *31*, 23–33.

Chen, L.-C., Metcalfe, J. S., Jeka, J. J., & Clark, J. E. (2007). Two steps forward and one back: Learning to walk affects infants' sitting posture. *Infant Behavior and Development*, *30*, 16–25.

Chen, Y.-P., Fetters, L., Holt, K. G., & Saltzman, E. (2002). Making the mobile move: Constraining task and environment. *Infant Behavior and Development*, *25*, 195–220.

Chen, Z., & Seigler, R. S. (2000). Across the great divide: Bridging the gap between understanding of toddlers' and older children's thinking. *Monographs of the Society for Research in Child Development*, *65*(2, Serial No. 261).

Cioni, G., Ferrari, F., & Prechtl, H. F. R. (1989). Posture and spontaneous motility in fullterm infants. *Early Human Development*, *18*, 247–262.

Clark, J. E., Whitall, J., & Phillips, S. J. (1988). Human interlimb coordination: The first 6 months of independent walking. *Developmental Psychobiology*, *21*, 445–456.

Claxton, L. J., McCarty, M. E., & Keen, R. (2009). Self-directed action affects planning in tool-use tasks with toddlers. *Infant Behavior and Development*, *32*, 230–233.

Clifton, R. K., Muir, D. W., Ashmead, D. H., & Clarkson, M. G. (1993). Is visually guided reaching in early infancy a myth? *Child Development*, *64*, 1099–1110.

Clifton, R. K., Perris, E. E., & McCall, D. D. (1999). Does reaching in the dark for unseen objects reflect representation in infants? *Infant Behavior and Development*, *22*, 297–302.

Clifton, R. K., Rochat, P., Robin, D. J., & Berthier, N. E. (1994). Multimodal perception in the control of infant reaching. *Journal of Experimental Psychology: Human Perception and Performance*, *20*, 876–886.

Corbetta, D., & Bojczyk, K. E. (2002). Infants return to two-handed reaching when they are learning to walk. *Journal of Motor Behavior*, *34*, 83–95.

Corbetta, D., Thelen, E., & Johnson, K. (2000). Motor constraints on the development of perception–action matching in infant reaching. *Infant Behavior and Development*, *23*, 351–374.

Cox, R. F. A., & Smitsman, A. W. (2006). The planning of tool-to-object relations in young children. *Developmental Psychobiology*, *48*, 178–186.

Davis, B. E., Moon, R. Y., Sachs, H. C., & Ottolini, M. C. (1998). Effects of sleep position on infant motor development. *Pediatrics*, *102*, 1135–1140.

Dean, G. A. (1965). An analysis of the energy expenditure in level and grade walking. *Ergonomics*, *8*, 31–47.

DeCasper, A. J., & Fifer, W. P. (1980). Of human bonding: Newborns prefer their mother's voices. *Science*, *208*, 174–176.

DeCasper, A. J., Lecanuet, J.-P., Busnel, M. C., & Granier-Deferre, C. (1994). Fetal reactions to recurrent maternal speech. *Infant Behavior and Development*, *17*, 159–164.

Deffeyes, J. E., Harbourne, R. T., DeJong, S. L., Kyvelidou, A., Stuberg, W. A., & Stergiou, N. (2009). Use of information entropy measures of sitting postural sway to quantify developmental delay in infants. *Journal of NeuroEngineering and Rehabilitation*, *6*, 34–47.

de Vries, J. I. P., Visser, G. H. A., & Prechtl, H. F. R. (1982). The emergence of fetal behaviour. I. Qualitative aspects. *Early Human Development*, *7*, 301–322.

de Vries, J. I. P., Visser, G. H. A., & Prechtl, H. F. R. (1988). The emergence of fetal behavior. III. Individual differences and consistencies. *Early Human Development*, *16*, 85–103.

Dewey, C., Fleming, P., Golding, J., & Team, A. S. (1998). Does the supine sleeping position have any adverse effects on the child? II. Development in the first 18 months. *Pediatrics*, *101*, e5.

Diamond, A. (1990). Developmental time course in human infants and infant monkeys, and the neural bases of inhibitory control in reaching. In A. Diamond (Ed.), *The development and neural bases of higher cognitive functions* (pp. 637–676). New York: New York Academy of Sciences.

Eppler, M. A. (1995). Development of manipulatory skills and the deployment of attention. *Infant Behavior and Development*, *18*, 391–405.

Euling, S. Y., Herman-Giddens, M. E., Lee, P. A., Selevan, S. G., Juul, A., Sorensen, T. I. A., et al. (2008a). Examination of U puberty-timing data from 1940 to 1994 for secular trends: Panel findings. *Pediatrics*, *121*, S172–S191.

Euling, S. Y., Selevan, S. G., Pescovitz, O. H., & Skakkebaek, N. E. (2008b). Role of environmental factors in the timing of puberty. *Pediatrics*, *121*, S167–S171.

Fagard, J., Spelke, E., & von Hofsten, C. (2009). Reaching and grasping a moving object in 6-, 8-, and 10-month-old infants: Laterality and performance. *Infant Behavior & Development, 32,* 137–146.

Fagan, M. K. & Iverson, J. M. (2007). The influence of mouthing on infant vocalization. *Infancy, 11,* 191–202.

Feng, T. I., Raynor, B. D., Fiano, K., & Emory, E. K. (1997). Doppler velocimetry of the fetal Circle of Willis: A longitudinal study. *Journal of Maternal–Fetal Investigation, 7,* 133–138.

Field, T. M., Woodson, R., Greenberg, R., & Cohen, D. (1982). Discrimination and imitation of facial expressions by neonates. *Science, 218,* 179–181.

Forssberg, H. (1985). Ontogeny of human locomotor control. I. Infant stepping, supported locomotion, and transition to independent locomotion. *Experimental Brain Research, 57,* 480–493.

Fontenelle, S. A., Kahrs, B. A., Neal, S. A., Newton, A. T., & Lockman, J. J. (2007). Infant manual exploration of composite substrates. *Journal of Experimental Child Psychology, 98,* 153–167.

Fraiberg, S. (1977). *Insights from the blind: Comparative studies of blind and sighted infants.* New York: Meridian Books.

Fraisse, F. E., Couet, A. M., Bellanca, K. J., & Adolph, K. E. (2001). Infants' response to potential risk: Social interaction and perceptual exploration. In G. A. Burton & R. C. Schmidt (Eds.), *Studies in perception and action VI.* Mahwah, NJ: Lawrence Erlbaum Associates.

Franchak, J. M., & Adolph, K. E. (2010). *Navigation from the corner of the eye: Head-mounted eye-tracking of natural locomotion in children and adults.* Manuscript under review.

Franchak, J. M., Kretch, K. S., Soska, K. C., Babcock, J. S., & Adolph, K. E. (2010). *Head-mounted eye-tracking in infants' natural interactions: A new method.* Proceedings of the 2010 Symposium on Eye Tracking Research and Applications, Austin, TX.

Frankenburg, W. K., Dodds, J. B., Archer, P., Bresnick, B., Maschka, P., Edelman, N., et al. (1992). *Denver II screening manual.* Denver, CO: Denver Developmental Materials.

Freedland, R. L., & Bertenthal, B. I. (1994). Developmental changes in interlimb coordination: Transition to hands-and-knees crawling. *Psychological Science, 5,* 26–32.

Galloway, J. C., & Thelen, E. (2004). Feet first: Object exploration in young infants. *Infant Behavior and Development, 27,* 107–112.

Garciaguirre, J. S., Adolph, K. E., & Shrout, P. E. (2007). Baby carriage: Infants walking with loads. *Child Development, 78,* 664–680.

Geber, M., & Dean, R. (1957). The state of development of newborn African children. *Lancet,* 1216–1219.

Geddes, D. T., Kent, J. C., Mitoulas, L. R., & Hartmann, P. E. (2008). Tongue movement and intra-oral vacuum in breastfeeding infants. *Early Human Development, 84,* 471–477.

Gesell, A. (1933). Maturation and the patterning of behavior. In C. Murchison (Ed.), *A handbook of child psychology* (2nd ed., pp. 209–235). Worcester, MA: Clark University Press.

Gesell, A. (1939). Reciprocal interweaving in neuromotor development. *Journal of Comparative Neurology, 70,* 161–180.

Gesell, A. (1946). The ontogenesis of infant behavior. In L. Carmichael (Ed.), *Manual of child psychology* (pp. 295–331). New York: Wiley.

Gesell, A. (1952). *Infant development: The embryology of early human behavior.* New York: Harper & Brothers.

Gesell, A., & Ames, L. B. (1940). The ontogenetic organization of prone behavior in human infancy. *Journal of Genetic Psychology, 56,* 247–263.

Gesell, A., & Thompson, H. (1929). Learning and growth in identical infant twins: An experimental study by the method of co-twin control. *Genetic Psychology Monographs, 6,* 11–124.

Gesell, A., & Thompson, H. (1934). *Infant behavior: Its genesis and growth.* New York: Greenwood Press.

Gibson, E., Dembofsky, C. A., Rubin, S., & Greenspan, J. S. (2000). Infant sleep position practices 2 years into the "Back to Sleep" campaign. *Clinical Pediatrics, 39,* 285–289.

Gibson, E. J. (1988). Exploratory behavior in the development of perceiving, acting, and the acquisition of knowledge. *Annual Review of Psychology, 39,* 1–41.

Gibson, E. J., & Pick, A. D. (2000). *An ecological approach to perceptual learning and development.* New York: Oxford University Press.

Gibson, E. J., & Walk, R. D. (1960). The "visual cliff". *Scientific American, 202,* 64–71.

Gibson, J. J. (1979). *The ecological approach to visual perception.* Boston: Houghton Mifflin.

Gilmore, R. O., Baker, T. J., & Grobman, K. H. (2004). Stability in young infants' discrimination of optic flow. *Developmental Psychology, 40,* 259–270.

Godoi, D., & Barela, J. A. (2008). Body sway and sensory motor coupling adaptation in children: Effects of distance manipulation. *Developmental Psychobiology, 50,* 77–87.

Goldfield, E. C. (1989). Transition from rocking to crawling: Postural constraints on infant movement. *Developmental Psychology, 25,* 913–919.

Green, J. R., Moore, C. A., Higashikawa, M., & Steeve, R. W. (2000). The physiologic development of speech motor control: Lip and jaw coordination. *Journal of Speech, Language, and Hearing Research, 43,* 239–255.

Green, J. R., Moore, C. A., & Reilly, K. J. (2002). The sequential development of jaw and lip control for speech. *Journal of Speech, Language, and Hearing Research, 45,* 66–79.

Green, J. R., Moore, C. A., Ruark, J. L., Rodda, P. R., Morvée, W. T., & VanWitzenburg, M. J. (1997). Development of chewing in children from 12 to 48 months: Longitudinal study of EMG patterns. *Journal of Neurophysiology, 77*, 2704–2716.

Green, J. R., & Nip, I. S. B. (2010). Organization principles in the development of early speech: Catalysts, constraints, and synergy. In B. Maaseen & P. H. H. M. van Lieshout (Eds.), *Speech motor control: New developments in basic and applied research*. New York: Oxford University Press.

Green, J. R., & Wilson, E. M. (2006). Spontaneous facial motility in infancy: A 3D kinematic analysis. *Developmental Psychobiology, 48*, 16–28.

Hadders-Algra, M., & Prechtl, H. F. R. (1992). Developmental course of general movements in early infancy. I. Descriptive analysis of change in form. *Early Human Development, 28*, 201–213.

Haehl, V., Vardaxis, V., & Ulrich, B. (2000). Learning to cruise: Bernstein's theory applied to skill acquisition during infancy. *Human Movement Science, 19*, 685–715.

Harlow, H. F., & Harlow, M. K. (1961). Effects of various mother–infant relationships on rhesus monkey behaviors. In B. M. Foss (Ed.), *Determinants of infant behavior IV*. New York: Wiley.

Harlow, H. F., & Mears, C. (1979). *The human model: Primate perspectives*. New York: Wiley.

Higgins, C. I., Campos, J. J., & Kermoian, R. (1996). Effect of self-produced locomotion on infant postural compensation to optic flow. *Developmental Psychology, 32*, 836–841.

Hitchcock, D. F., & Rovee-Collier, C. (1996). The effect of repeated reactivations on memory specificity in infancy. *Journal of Experimental Child Psychology, 62*, 378–400.

Hooker, D. (1952). *The prenatal origins of behavior*. Lawrence, KS: University of Kansas Press.

Hopkins, B., & Ronnqvist, L. (2001). Facilitating postural control: Effects on the reaching behavior of 6-month-old infants. *Developmental Psychobiology, 40*, 168–182.

Hopkins, B., & Westra, T. (1988). Maternal handling and motor development: An intracultural study. *Genetic, Social and General Psychology Monographs, 114*, 379–408.

Hopkins, B., & Westra, T. (1989). Maternal expectations of their infants' development: Some cultural differences. *Developmental Medicine and Child Neurology, 31*, 384–390.

Hopkins, B., & Westra, T. (1990). Motor development, maternal expectations, and the role of handling. *Infant Behavior and Development, 13*, 117–122.

Humphrey, T. (1944). Primitive neurons in the embryonic human central nervous system. *Journal of Comparative Neurology and Psychology, 81*, 1–45.

Humphrey, T. (1970). Reflex activity in the oral and facial area of the human fetus. In J. F. Bosma (Ed.), *Second symposium on oral sensation and perception* (pp. 195–233). Springfield, IL: Thomas.

Johnson, M. H. (1998). The neural basis of cognitive development. In D. Kuhn & R. Siegler (Eds.), *Handbook of child psychology: Vol. 2. Cognition, perception, and language* (pp. 1–49). New York: Wiley.

Johnson, M. L., Veldhuis, J. D., & Lampl, M. (1996). Is growth saltatory? The usefulness and limitations of frequency distributions in analyzing pusatile data. *Endocrinology, 137*, 5197–5204.

Jolliffe, D. (2004). Extent of overweight among US children and adolescents from 1971 to 2000. *Pediatric Focus, 28*, 4–9.

Jouen, F., Lepecq, J. C., Gapene, O., & Bertenthal, B. I. (2000). Optic flow sensitivity in neonates. *Infant Behavior and Development, 23*, 271–284.

Kahrs, B. A. & Lockman, J. J. (2010). *Are manual stereotypies stereotypic?* Manuscript in preparation.

Kalnins, I. V., & Bruner, J. S. (1973). The coordination of visual observation and instrumental behavior in early infancy. *Perception, 2*, 307–314.

Kaplowitz, P. B., Slora, E. J., Wasserman, R. C., Pedlow, S. E., & Herman-Giddens, M. E. (2001). Earlier onset of puberty in girls: Relation to increased body mass index and race. *Pediatrics, 108*, 347–353.

Karasik, L. B., Tamis-LeMonda, C. S., & Adolph, K. E. (in press). Relations between infant walking and interactions with objects and people. *Child Development*.

Karasik, L. B., Tamis-LeMonda, C. S., Adolph, K. E., & Dimitropoulou, K. A. (2008). How mothers encourage and discourage infants' motor actions. *Infancy, 13*, 366–392.

Katona, F. (1989). Clinical neuro-developmental diagnosis and treatment. In P. R. Zelazo & R. G. Barr (Eds.), *Challenges to developmental paradigms: Implications for theory, assessment and treatment*. Hillsdale, NJ: Lawrence Erlbaum Associates.

Kipling, R. (1952). *Just so stories*. Garden City, NY: Garden City Books.

Köhler, W. (1925). *The mentality of apes*. London: Kegan.

Kotwica, K. A., Ferre, C. L., & Michel, G. F. (2008). Relation of stable hand-use preferences to the development of skill for managing multiple objects from 7 to 13 months of age. *Developmental Psychobiology, 50*, 519–529.

Kretch, K. S., Karasik, L. B., & Adolph, K. E. (2009, October). *Cliff or step? Posture-specific learning at the edge of a drop-off*. Paper presented to the International Society for Developmental Psychobiology, Chicago, IL.

Kuno, A., Akiyama, M., Yamashiro, C., Tanaka, H., Yanagihara, T., & Hata, T. (2001). Three-dimensional sonographic assessment of fetal behavior in the early second trimester of pregnancy. *Journal of Ultrasound Medicine, 20*, 1271–1275.

Lampl, M. (1993). Saltatory growth in infancy. *American Journal of Human Biology*, *5*, 641–652.

Lampl, M., & Johnson, M. L. (1993). A case study in daily growth during adolescence: A single spurt or changes in the dynamics of saltatory growth? *Annals of Human Biology*, *20*, 595–603.

Lampl, M., Johnson, M. L., & Frongillo, E. A. (2001). Mixed distribution analysis identifies saltation and stasis growth. *Annals of Human Biology*, *28*, 403–411.

Lampl, M., & Thompson, A. L. (2007). Growth chart curves do not describe individual growth biology. *American Journal of Human Biology*, *19*, 643–653.

Lampl, M., & Veldhuis, J. D. (1992). Saltation and stasis: A model of human growth. *Science*, *258*, 801–803.

Ledebt, A. (2000). Changes in arm posture during the early acquisition of walking. *Infant Behavior and Development*, *23*, 79–89.

Ledebt, A., & Bril, B. (2000). Acquisition of upper body stability during walking in toddlers. *Developmental Psychobiology*, *36*, 311–324.

Lee, D. N., & Aronson, E. (1974). Visual proprioceptive control of standing in human infants. *Perception and Psychophysics*, *15*, 529–532.

Lee, H. M., Bhat, A., Scholz, J. P., & Galloway, J. C. (2008). Toy-oriented changes during early arm movements IV: Shoulder–elbow coordination. *Infant Behavior and Development*, *31*, 447–469.

Leo, A. J., Chiu, J., & Adolph, K. E. (2000, July). *Temporal and functional relationships of crawling, cruising, and walking*. Poster presented at the International Conference on Infant Studies, Brighton, England.

Lewin, K. (1946). Behavior and development as a function of the total situation. In L. Carmichael (Ed.), *Manual of Child Psychology* (pp. 791–844). New York: Wiley & Sons.

Lockman, J. J. (1984). The development of detour ability during infancy. *Child Development*, *55*, 482–491.

Lockman, J. J. (2000). A perception–action perspective on tool use development. *Child Development*, *71*, 137–144.

Lockman, J. J., & Adams, C. D. (2001). Going around transparent and grid-like barriers: Detour ability as a perception–action skill. *Developmental Science*, *4*, 463–471.

Lockman, J. J., Ashmead, D. H., & Bushnell, E. W. (1984). The development of anticipatory hand orientation during infancy. *Journal of Experimental Child Psychology*, *37*, 176–186.

Majnemer, A., & Barr, R. G. (2006). Association between sleep position and early motor development. *Journal of Pediatrics*, *149*, 623–629.

McCarty, M. E., Clifton, R. K., Ashmead, D. H., Lee, P., & Goubet, N. (2001). How infants use vision for grasping objects. *Child Development*, *72*, 973–987.

McCarty, M. E., Clifton, R. K., & Collard, R. (1999). Problem solving in infancy: The emergence of an action plan. *Developmental Psychology*, *35*, 1091–1101.

McCarty, M. E., Clifton, R. K., & Collard, R. (2001). The beginnings of tool use by infants and toddlers. *Infancy*, *2*, 885–893.

McDonnell, P. (1974). The development of visually guided reaching. *Perception and Psychophysics*, *19*, 181–185.

McGraw, M. B. (1932). From reflex to muscular control in the assumption of an erect posture and ambulation in the human infant. *Child Development*, *3*, 291–297.

McGraw, M. B. (1935). *Growth: A study of Johnny and Jimmy*. New York: Appleton-Century.

McGraw, M. B. (1940). Neuromuscular development of the human infant as exemplified in the achievement of erect locomotion. *Journal of Pediatrics*, *17*, 747–771.

McGraw, M. B. (1945). *The neuromuscular maturation of the human infant*. New York: Hafner.

McKenzie, B. E., Skouteris, H., Day, R. H., Hartman, B., & Yonas, A. (1993). Effective action by infants to contact objects by reaching and leaning. *Child Development*, *64*, 415–429.

Mennella, J. A., Griffin, C. E., & Beauchamp, G. K. (2004). Flavor programming during infancy. *Pediatrics*, *113*, 840–845.

Metcalfe, J. S., McDowell, K., Chang, T.-Y., Chen, L.-C., Jeka, J. J., & Clark, J. E. (2004). Development of somato-sensory–motor integration: An event-related analysis of infant posture in the first year of independent walking. *Developmental Psychobiology*, *46*, 19–35.

Metcalfe, J. S., Chen, L.-C., Chang, T.-Y., McDowell, K., Jeka, J. J., & Clark, J. E. (2005). The temporal organization of posture changes during the first year of independent walking. *Experimental Brain Research*, *161*, 405–416.

Metcalfe, J. S., & Clark, J. E. (2000). Sensory information affords exploration of posture in newly walking infants and toddlers. *Infant Behavior and Development*, *23*, 391–405.

Miller, J. L., Sonies, B. C., & Macedonia, C. (2003). Emergence of oropharyngeal, laryngeal and swallowing activity in the developing fetal upper aerodigestive tract: An ultrasound evaluation. *Early Human Development*, *71*, 61–87.

Moessinger, A. C. (1983). Fetal akinesia deformation sequence: An animal model. *Pediatrics*, *72*, 857–863.

Moore, K. L., & Persaud, K. L. (1993). *The developing human: Clinically oriented embryology*. Philadelphia: W. B. Saunders.

Munn, N. L. (1965). *The evolution and growth of human behavior*. Boston: Houghton Mifflin Company.

Needham, A., Barrett, T., & Peterman, K. (2002). A pick me up for infants' exploratory skills: Early simulated experiences reaching for objects using "sticky" mittens enhances young infants' object exploration skills. *Infant Behavior and Development, 25*, 279–295.

Nelson, R. C., & Osterhoudt, R. G. (1971). Effects of altered sloped and speed on the biomechanics of running. *Medicine and Sport, 6*, 220–224.

Newell, K. M., Scully, D. M., McDonald, P. V., & Baillargeon, R. (1989). Task constraints and infant grip configurations. *Developmental Psychobiology, 22*, 817–832.

Nilsson, L., & Hamberger, L. (1990). *A child is born*. New York: Delacorte Press.

Norris, B., & Smith, S. (2002). *Research into the mouthing behaviour of children up to 5 years old*. London: Consumer and Competition Policy Directorate.

Nova (1996). *Behind the lens: An interview with Lennart Nilsson*. Retrieved June 1, 2004 from www.pbs.org/wgbh/nova/odyssey/nilsson.html

Oster, H. (2003). Emotion in the infant's face: Insights from the study of infants with facial anomalies. *Annals of the New York Academy of Sciences, 1000*, 197–204.

Oster, H. (2005). The repertoire of infant facial expressions: An ontogenetic perspective. In J. Nadel & D. Muir (Eds.), *Emotional development: Recent research advances* (pp. 261–292). New York: Oxford University Press.

Ounsted, M., & Moar, V. A. (1986). Proportionality changes in the first year of life: The influence of weight for gestational age at birth. *Acta Paediatrica Scandinavica, 75*, 811–818.

Palmer, C. E. (1944). Studies of the center of gravity in the human body. *Child Development, 15*, 99–163.

Palmer, C. F. (1989). The discriminating nature of infants' exploratory actions. *Developmental Psychology, 25*, 885–893.

Peiper, A. (1963). *Cerebral function in infancy and childhood*. New York: Consultants Bureau.

Perkins, L., Hughes, E., Srinivasan, L., Allsop, J., Glover, A., Kumar, S., et al. (2007). Exploring cortical subplate evolution using magnetic resonance imaging of the fetal brain. *Developmental Neuroscience, 30*(1–3), 211–220.

Perris, E. E., & Clifton, R. K. (1988). Reaching in the dark toward sound as a measure of auditory localization in infants. *Infant Behavior and Development, 11*, 473–491.

Peterson, M. L., Christou, E., & Rosengren, K. S. (2006), Children achieve adult-like sensory integration during stance at 12-years-old. *Gait & Posture, 23*, 455–463.

Piaget, J. (1952). *The origins of intelligence in children*. New York: Norton.

Piaget, J. (1954). *The construction of reality in the child*. New York: Free Press.

Poore, T., Campos, J. J., Anderson, D. I., Anderson, D., & Uchiyama, I. (2004, May). *Does the moving room elicit emotional responses in locomotor-experienced infants?* Paper presented at the International Conference on Infant Studies, Chicago.

Prechtl, H. F. R. (1985). Ultrasound studies of human fetal behaviour. *Early Human Development, 12*, 91–98.

Prechtl, H. F. R. (1986). Prenatal motor development. In M. G. Wade & H. T. A. Whiting (Eds.), *Motor development in children: Aspects of coordination and control* (pp. 53–64). Dordrecht, The Netherlands: Nijhoff.

Prechtl, H. F. R., & Hopkins, B. (1986). Developmental transformations of spontaneous movements in early infancy. *Early Human Development, 14*, 233–238.

Preyer, W. (1905). *The mind of the child: Part I*. (H. W. Brown, Trans.). New York: D. Appleton & Company.

Rader, N., Bausano, M., & Richards, J. E. (1980). On the nature of the visual-cliff-avoidance response in human infants. *Child Development, 51*, 61–68.

Ratner, A. (2002). *Fetal development*, from www.nlm.nih.gov/medlineplus/ency/article/002398.htm

Reed, E. S. (1982). An outline of a theory of action systems. *Journal of Motor Behavior, 14*, 98–134.

Reilly, J. J., & Dorosty, A. R. (1999). Epidemic of obesity in UK children. *The Lancet, 354*, 1874–1875.

Reilly, J. J., Jackson, D. M., Montgomery, C., Kelly, L. A., Slater, C., Grant, S., et al. (2004). Total energy expenditure and physical activity in young Scottish children: Mixed longitudinal study. *The Lancet, 363*, 211–212.

Richards, J. E., & Rader, N. (1981). Crawling-onset age predicts visual cliff avoidance in infants. *Journal of Experimental Psychology: Human Perception and Performance, 7*, 382–387.

Richards, J. E., & Rader, N. (1983). Affective, behavioral, and avoidance responses on the visual cliff: Effects of crawling onset age, crawling experience, and testing age. *Psychophysiology, 20*, 633–642.

Robertson, S. S. (1990). Temporal organization in fetal and newborn movement. In H. Bloch & B. I. Bertenthal (Eds.), *Sensory-motor organizations and development in infancy and early childhood* (pp. 105–122). Dordrecht, The Netherlands: Kluwer.

Robinson, S. R., & Kleven, G. A. (2005). Learning to move before birth. In B. Hopkins & S. Johnson (Eds.), *Prenatal development of postnatal functions (Advances in Infancy Research series)* (Vol. 2, pp. 131–175). Westport, CT: Praeger.

Rochaa, N. A. C. F., da Costa, C. S. N., Savelsbergh, G., & Tudella, E. (2009). The effect of additional weight load on infant reaching. *Infant Behavior and Development, 32*, 234–237.

Rochat, P. (1989). Object manipulation and exploration in 2- to 5-month-old infants. *Developmental Psychology, 25*, 871–884.

Rochat, P. (1992). Self-sitting and reaching in 5- to 8-month-old infants: The impact of posture and its development on early eye–hand coordination. *Journal of Motor Behavior*, *24*, 210–220.

Rochat, P., & Goubet, N. (1995). Development of sitting and reaching in 5- to 6-month-old infants. *Infant Behavior and Development*, *18*, 53–68.

Rochat, P. & Hespos, S. J. (1997). Differential rooting response by neonates: Evidence for an early sense of self. *Early Development and Parenting*, *6*, 105–112.

Rochat, P., & Senders, S. J. (1991). Active touch in infancy: Action systems in development. In M. J. S. Weiss & P. R. Zelazo (Eds.), *Newborn attention: Biological constraints and the influence of experience* (pp. 412–442). Norwood, NJ: Ablex.

Ronca, A. E., & Alberts, J. R. (1994). Sensory stimuli associated with gestation and parturition evoke cardiac and behavioral responses in fetal rats. *Psychobiology*, *22*, 270–282.

Ronca, A. E., & Alberts, J. R. (1995). Maternal contributions to fetal experience and the transition from prenatal to postnatal life. In J.-P. Lecanuet et al. (Eds.), *Fetal development: A psychobiological perspective*. Hillsdale, NJ: Lawrence Erlbaum Associates.

Roodenburg, P. J., Wladimiroff, J. W., van Es, A., & Prechtl, H. F. R. (1991). Classification and quantitative aspects of fetal movements during the second half of normal pregnancy. *Early Human Development*, *25*, 19–35.

Rosenfield, R. L., Lipton, R. B., & Drum, M. L. (2009). Thelarche, pubarche, and menarche attainment in children with normal and elevated body mass index. *Pediatrics*, *123*, 84–88.

Rovee-Collier, C. (1999). The development of infant memory. *Current Directions in Psychological Science*, *8*, 80–85.

Rovee-Collier, C. K., & Gekoski, M. (1979). The economics of infancy: A review of conjugate reinforcement. In H. W. Reese & L. P. Lipsitt (Eds.), *Advances in child development and behavior* (Vol. 13, pp. 195–255). New York: Academic Press.

Ruina, A. (2005). *Passive dynamic walking*, from http://ruina.tam.cornell.edu/hplab/pdw.html

Salomon, L. J., & Garel, C. (2007). Magnetic resonance imaging examination of the fetal brain. *Ultrasound in Obstetrics & Gynecology*, *30*, 1019–1032.

Schaal, B., Marlier, L., & Soussignan, R. (2000). Human foetuses learn odours from their pregnant mother's diet. *Chemical Senses*, *25*, 729–737.

Schmuckler, M. A. (1993). Perception–action coupling in infancy. In G. J. P. Savelsburgh (Ed.), *The development of coordination in infancy* (pp. 137–173). Amsterdam: Elsevier.

Schmuckler, M. A. (1997). Children's postural sway in response to low- and high-frequency visual information for oscillation. *Journal of Experimental Psychology: Human Perception and Performance*, *23*, 528–545.

Schmuckler, M. A., & Gibson, E. J. (1989). The effect of imposed optical flow on guided locomotion in young walkers. *British Journal of Developmental Psychology*, *7*, 193–206.

Selverston, A. I. (1980). Are central pattern generators understandable? *Behavioral and Brain Sciences*, *3*, 535–571.

Sheppard, J. J. & Mysak, E. D. (1984). Ontogeny of infantile oral reflexes and emerging chewing. *Child Development*, *55*, 831–853.

Shirley, M. M. (1931). *The first two years: A study of twenty-five babies*. Westport, CT: Greenwood Press.

Smart, L., James, J. R., Stoffregen, T. A., & Bardy, B. G. (2002). Visually induced motion sickness predicted by postural instability. *Human Factors*, *44*, 451–465.

Smith, S. L., Gerhardt, K. J., Griffiths, S. K., Huang, X., & Abrams, R. M. (2003). Intelligibility of sentences recorded from the uterus of a pregnant ewe and from the fetal inner ear. *Audiology and Neuro-Otology*, *8*, 347–353.

Smitsman, A. D., & Cox, R. F. A. (2008). Perseveration in tool use: A window for understanding the dynamics of the action-selection process. *Infancy*, *13*, 249–269.

Smotherman, W. P., & Robinson, S. R. (1991). Accessibility of the rat fetus for psychobiological investigation. In H. Shair, G. A. Barr, & M. A. Hofer (Eds.), *Developmental psychobiology: New methods and changing concepts* (pp. 148–166). New York: Oxford University Press.

Smotherman, W. P., & Robinson, S. R. (1996). The development of behavior before birth. *Developmental Psychology*, *32*, 425–434.

Sommerville, J. A., Woodward, A. L., & Needham, A. (2005). Action experience alters 3-month-old infants' perception of others' actions. *Cognition*, *96*, B1–B11.

Sorce, J. F., Emde, R. N., Campos, J. J., & Klinnert, M. D. (1985). Maternal emotional signaling: Its effects on the visual cliff behavior of 1-year-olds. *Developmental Psychology*, *21*, 195–200.

Soska, K. C., & Adolph, K. E. (2010). *Posture changes infants' visual, oral, and manual exploration of object properties*. Manuscript under review.

Soska, K. C., Adolph, K. E., & Johnson, S. P. (2010). Systems in development: Motor skill acquisition facilitates 3D object completion. *Developmental Psychology*, *46*, 129–138.

Sotsky, R. B., Garciaguirre, J. S., & Adolph, K. E. (2004, May). *New York infant walking tours*. Poster presented at the International Conference on Infant Studies, Chicago.

Sparling, J. W., van Tol, J., & Chescheir, N. C. (1999). Fetal and neonatal hand movement. *Physical Therapy*, *79*, 24–39.

Spencer, J. P., Vereijken, B., Diedrich, F. J., & Thelen, E. (2000). Posture and the emergence of manual skills. *Developmental Science, 3*, 216–233.

Spitz, R. (1965). *The first year of life*. New York: International Universities Press.

Steenbergen, B., van der Kamp, J., Smitsman, A., & Carson, R. G. (1997). Spoon-handling in two- to four-year-old children. *Ecological Psychology, 9*, 113–129.

Steeve, R. W., Moore, C. A., Green, J. R., Reilly, K. J., & McMurtry, J. R. (2008). Babbling, chewing, and sucking: Oromandibular coordination at 9 months. *Journal of Speech, Language, and Hearing Research, 51*, 1390–1404.

Stoffregen, T. A. (1985). Flow structure versus retinal location in the optical control of stance. *Journal of Experimental Psychology: Human Perception and performance, 11*, 554–565.

Stoffregen, T. A., Adolph, K. E., Thelen, E., Gorday, K. M., & Sheng, Y. (1997). Toddlers' postural adaptations to different support surfaces. *Motor Control, 1*, 119–137.

Stoffregen, T. A., Schmuckler, M. A., & Gibson, E. J. (1987). Use of central and peripheral optical flow in stance and locomotion in young walkers. *Perception, 16*, 113–119.

Super, C. M. (1976). Environmental effects on motor development: The case of "African infant precocity". *Developmental Medicine and Child Neurology, 18*, 561–567.

Tamis-LeMonda, C. S., Adolph, K. E., Dimitropoulou, K. A., & Zack, E. A. (2007). "No! Don't! Stop!": Mothers' words for impending danger. *Parenting: Science & Practice, 7*, 1–25.

Tamis-LeMonda, C. S., Adolph, K. E., Lobo, S. A., Karasik, L. B., Dimitropoulou, K. A., & Ishak, S. (2008). When infants take mothers' advice: 18-month-olds integrate perceptual and social information for guiding motor action. *Developmental Psychology, 44*, 734–746.

Ten Hof, J., Nijhuis, I. J., Mulder, E. J., Nijuis, J. G., Narayan, H., Taylor, D. J., et al. (2002). Longitudinal study of fetal body movements: Nomograms, intrafetal consistency, and relationship with episodes of heart rate patterns A and B. *Pediatric Research, 52*, 568–575.

Thatcher, R. W., Lyon, G. R., Rumsey, J., & Krasnegor, J. (1996). *Developmental neuro-imaging*. San Diego, CA: Academic Press.

Thelen, E. (1979). Rhythmical stereotypies in normal human infants. *Animal Behavior, 27*, 699–715.

Thelen, E. (1981a). Kicking, rocking, and waving: Contextual analysis of rhythmical stereotypies in normal human infants. *Animal Behavior, 29*, 3–11.

Thelen, E. (1981b). Rhythmical behavior in infancy: An ethological perspective. *Developmental Psychology, 17*, 237–257.

Thelen, E. (1994). Three-month-old infants can learn task-specific patterns of interlimb coordination. *Psychological Science, 5*, 280–285.

Thelen, E. (1995). Motor development: A new synthesis. *American Psychologist, 50*, 79–95.

Thelen, E., Bril, B., & Breniere, Y. (1992). The emergence of heel strike in newly walking infants: A dynamic interpretation. In M. Woollacott & F. Horak (Eds.), *Posture and gait: Control mechanisms* (Vol. 2, pp. 334–337). Eugene, OR: University of Oregon.

Thelen, E., & Corbetta, D. (1994). Exploration and selection in the early acquisition of skill. *International Review of Neurobiology, 37*, 75–102.

Thelen, E., Corbetta, D., Kamm, K., Spencer, J. P., Schneider, K., & Zernicke, R. F. (1993). The transition to reaching: Mapping intention and intrinsic dynamics. *Child Development, 64*, 1058–1098.

Thelen, E., Corbetta, D., & Spencer, J. P. (1996). Development of reaching during the first year: Role of movement speed. *Journal of Experimental Psychology: Human Perception and Performance, 22*, 1059–1076.

Thelen, E., & Fisher, D. M. (1982). Newborn stepping: An explanation for a "disappearing reflex". *Developmental Psychology, 18*, 760–775.

Thelen, E., & Fisher, D. M. (1983). From spontaneous to instrumental behavior: Kinematic analysis of movement changes during very early learning. *Child Development, 54*, 129–140.

Thelen, E., Fisher, D. M., & Ridley-Johnson, R. (1984). The relationship between physical growth and a newborn reflex. *Infant Behavior and Development, 7*, 479–493.

Thelen, E., Fisher, D. M., Ridley-Johnson, R., & Griffin, N. J. (1982). Effects of body build and arousal on newborn infant stepping. *Developmental Psychobiology, 15*, 447–453.

Thelen, E., & Smith, L. B. (1994). *A dynamic systems approach to the development of cognition and action*. Cambridge, MA: MIT Press.

Thelen, E., & Ulrich, B. D. (1991). Hidden skills: A dynamic systems analysis of treadmill stepping during the first year. *Monographs of the Society for Research in Child Development, 56*(1, Serial No. 223).

Thelen, E., Ulrich, B. D., & Niles, D. (1987). Bilateral coordination in human infants: Stepping on a split-belt treadmill. *Journal of Experimental Psychology: Human Perception and Performance, 13*, 405–410.

Trettien, A. W. (1900). Creeping and walking. *American Journal of Psychology, 12*, 1–57.

Trost, S. G., Sirard, J. R., Dowda, M., Pfeiffer, K. A., & Pate, R. R. (2003). Physical activity in overweight and nonoverweight preschool children. *International Journal of Obesity, 27*, 834–839.

Uchiyama, I., Anderson, D. I., Campos, J. J., Witherington, D., Frankel, C. B., Lejeune, L., & Barbu-Roth, M. (2008). Locomotor experience affects self and emotion. *Developmental Psychology, 44*, 1225–1231.

Ulrich, B., Thelen, E., & Niles, D. (1990). Perceptual determinants of action: Stair-climbing choices of infants and toddlers. In J. E. Clark & J. H. Humphrey (Eds.), *Advances in motor development research* (Vol. 3, pp. 1–15). New York: AMS Publishers.

Valsiner, J., & Mackie, C. (1985). Toddlers at home: Canalization of climbing skills through culturally organized physical environments. In T. Garling & J. Valsiner (Eds.), *Children within environments: Toward a psychology of accident prevention.* New York: Plenum.

van der Meer, A. L. H. (1997). Keeping the arm in the limelight: Advanced visual control of arm movements in neonates. *European Journal of Paediatric Neurology, 4,* 103–108.

van der Meer, A. L. H., Holden, G., & van der Weel, F. R. (2005). Coordination of sucking, swallowing, and breathing in healthy newborns. *Journal of Pediatric Neonatology, 2,* NT1–NT4.

van der Meer, A. L. H., Fallet, G., & van der Weel, F. R. (2008). Perception of structured optic flow and random visual motion in infants and adults: A high-density EEG study. *Experimental Brain Research, 186,* 493–502.

van der Meer, A. L. H. Ramstad, M., van der Weel, F. R. (2008). Choosing the shortest way to mum: Auditory guided rotation in 6- to 9-month-old infants. *Infant Behavior and Development, 31,* 207–216.

van der Meer, A. L. H., van der Weel, F. R., & Lee, D. N. (1995). The functional significance of arm movements in neonates. *Science, 267,* 693–695.

van der Meer, A. L. H., van der Weel, F. R., & Lee, D. N. (1996). Lifting weights in neonates: Developing visual control of reaching. *Scandinavian Journal of Psychology, 37,* 424–436.

Vandewater, E. A., Shim, M., & Caplovitz, A. G. (2004). Linking obesity and activity level with children's television and video game use. *Journal of Adolescence, 27,* 71–85.

van Hof, P., van der Kamp, J., & Savelsbergh, G. J. P. (2008). The relation between infants' perception of catchableness and the control of catching. *Developmental Psychology, 44,* 182–194.

van Leeuwen, L., Smitsman, A., & van Leeuwen, C. (1994). Affordances, perceptual complexity, and the development of tool use. *Journal of Experimental Psychology: Human Perception and Performance, 20,* 174–191.

Vereijken, B., & Adolph, K. E. (1998). Transitions in the development of locomotion. In G. J. P. Savelsbergh, H. L. J. van der Maas & P. C. L. van Geert (Eds.), *Non-linear analyses of developmental processes* (pp. 137–149). Amsterdam: Elsevier.

Vereijken, B., Pedersen, A. V., & Storksen, J. H. (2009). Learning to walk: Postural control and muscular strength in early independent walking. *Developmental Psychobiology, 51,* 374–383.

Vereijken, B., & Thelen, E. (1997). Training infant treadmill stepping: The role of individual pattern stability. *Journal of Developmental Psychobiology, 30,* 89–102.

Vereijken, B., & Waardenburg, M. (1996, April). *Changing patterns of interlimb coordination from supported to independent walking.* Poster presented at the International Conference on Infant Studies, Providence, RI.

von Hofsten, C. (1979). Development of visually directed reaching: The approach phase. *Journal of Human Movement Studies, 30,* 369–382.

von Hofsten, C. (1980). Predictive reaching for moving objects by human infants. *Journal of Experimental Child Psychology, 30,* 369–382.

von Hofsten, C. (1982). Eye–hand coordination in the newborn. *Developmental Psychology, 18,* 450–461.

von Hofsten, C. (1983). Catching skills in infancy. *Journal of Experimental Psychology: Human Perception and Performance, 9,* 75–85.

von Hofsten, C. (1991). Structuring of early reaching movements: A longitudinal study. *Journal of Motor Behavior, 23,* 280–292.

von Hofsten, C. (1993). Prospective control: A basic aspect of action development. *Human Development, 36,* 253–270.

von Hofsten, C. (2004). An action perspective on motor development. *Trends in Cognitive Sciences, 8,* 266–272.

von Hofsten, C., & Fazel-Zandy, S. (1984). Development of visually guided hand orientation in reaching. *Journal of Experimental Child Psychology, 38,* 208–219.

von Hofsten, C., & Lindhagen, K. (1979). Observations on the development of reaching for moving objects. *Journal of Experimental Child Psychology, 28,* 158–173.

von Hofsten, C., & Ronnqvist, L. (1993). The structuring of neonatal arm movements. *Child Development, 64,* 1046–1057.

Walk, R. D. (1966). The development of depth perception in animals and human infants. *Monographs of the Society for Research in Child Development, 31*(5, Serial No. 107), 82–108.

Walk, R. D., & Gibson, E. J. (1961). A comparative and analytical study of visual depth perception. *Psychological Monographs, 75*(15, Whole No. 519).

Wang, M. L., Dorer, D. J., Fleming, M. P., & Catlin, E. A. (2004). Clinical outcomes of near-term infants. *Pediatrics, 114,* 372–376.

White, B., Castle, P., & Held, R. (1964). Observations on the development of visually directed reaching. *Child Development, 35,* 349–364.

Willinger, M., Ko, C.-W., Hoffman, H. J., Kessler, R. C., & Corwin, M. J. (2000). Factors associated with caregivers' choice of infant sleep position, 1994–1998. *Journal of the American Medical Association, 283*, 2135–2142.

Wilson, E. M. & Green, J. R. (2006). Coordinative organization of lingual propulsion during the normal adult swallow. *Dysphagia, 21*, 226–236.

Wilson, E. M. & Green, J. R. (2009). The development of jaw motion for mastication. *Early Human Development, 85*, 303–311.

Wilson, E. M., Green, J. R., Yunusova, Y. Y., & Moore, C. A. (2008). Task specificity in early oral motor development. *Seminars in Speech and Language, 29*, 257–266.

Witherington, D. C. (2005). The development of prospective grasping control between 5 and 7 months: A longitudinal study. *Infancy, 7*, 143–161.

Witherington, D. C., Campos, J. J., Anderson, D. I., Lejeune, L., & Seah, E. (2005). Avoidance of heights on the visual cliff in newly walking infants. *Infancy, 7*, 3.

Woollacott, M. H. (2009). Personal communication.

Woollacott, M. H., Debu, B., & Mowatt, M. (1987). Neuromuscular control of posture in the infant and child: Is vision dominant? *Journal of Motor Behavior, 19*, 167–186.

Woollacott, M. H., Shumway-Cook, A., & Williams, H. G. (1989). The development of posture and balance control in children. In M. H. Woollacott & A. Shumway-Cook (Eds.), *Development of posture and gait across the life span* (pp. 77–96). Columbia, SC: University of South Carolina Press.

Yonas, A., & Granrud, C. E. (1985). Reaching as a measure of infants' spatial perception. In G. Gottlieb & N. A. Krasnegor (Eds.), *Measurement of audition and vision in the first year of postnatal life* (pp. 301–322). Norwood, NJ: Ablex.

Yonas, A., & Hartman, B. (1993). Perceiving the affordance of contact in four- and five-month-old infants. *Child Development, 64*, 298–308.

Zelazo, N. A., Zelazo, P. R., Cohen, K. M., & Zelazo, P. D. (1993). Specificity of practice effects on elementary neuromotor patterns. *Developmental Psychology, 29*, 686–691.

Zelazo, P. R. (1976). From reflexive to instrumental behavior. In L. P. Lipsitt (Ed.), *Developmental psychobiology: The significance of infancy*. Hillsdale, NJ: Lawrence Erlbaum Associates.

Zelazo, P. R. (1998). McGraw and the development of unaided walking. *Developmental Review, 18*, 449–471.

Zelazo, P. R., Weiss, M. J., & Leonard, E. (1989). The development of unaided walking: The acquisition of higher order control. In P. R. Zelazo & R. G. Barr (Eds.), *Challenges to developmental paradigms*. Hillsdale, NJ: Lawrence Erlbaum Associates.

Zelazo, P. R., Zelazo, N. A., & Kolb, S. (1972). "Walking" in the newborn. *Science, 176*, 314–315.

-------------------------------------- ❖ **6** ❖ --------------------------------------

PERCEPTUAL DEVELOPMENT

Marc H. Bornstein
Editor, *Parenting: Science and Practice*
Eunice Kennedy Shriver, National Institute of Child Health and Human Development
Martha E. Arterberry
Gettysburg College
Clay Mash
Eunice Kennedy Shriver, National Institute of Child Health and Human Development

All that a mammal does is fundamentally dependent on perception, past or present.

(D. O. Hebb, 1953, p. 44)

INTRODUCTION

Perception begins our experience and interpretation of the world, and so is crucial to the growth of thought, to the regulation of emotions, to interaction in social relationships, and indeed to most aspects of our development. The input, translation, and encoding of sensory information in perception are essential to thought and action. Even very young children recognize the fundamental position of perception in life (Pillow, 1989): Three-year-olds will attribute knowledge about an object only to people who have viewed the object, and not to people who have not viewed the object (Gopnik, Slaughter, & Meltzoff, 1994). For all these reasons, philosophers, physicists, physiologists, and psychologists have been strongly motivated to study perception and especially its development.

Our everyday experiences raise many challenging questions about perception. How faithful are our perceptions of properties, objects, people, and events in the world? How is a stable world perceived in the midst of continuous environmental variation and biological fluctuation? How are perceptual aspects of the world invested with meaning? How and why do perceptual qualities differ across modalities? How do we apprehend individual features of things and simultaneously know their synthesized whole?

Philosophy provided major initial impetus to study perceptual development: Epistemology asks questions about the origins and nature of human knowledge. Extreme views on epistemology were proposed by empiricists, who asserted that all perceptual knowledge derives from the senses and grows by way of experience, and by nativists, who reasoned that some kinds of knowledge cannot possibly rely on experience and thus that human beings enter the world with a sensory apparatus equipped (at the very least) to order and organize their percepts. Philosophical speculation also focused attention on the early ontogenesis of perception, a period during which epistemologically meaningful issues related to the origins of knowledge are most directly addressed. Thus, the study of perceptual development initially captured the philosopher's imagination as it promised to speak to questions about inborn knowledge versus knowledge acquired through experience.

Developmental research in perception has since provided many and varied kinds of information including, for example, normative data concerning the quality, limits, and capacities of perceptual systems across the life span. For example, the sensory systems are brain matter, and they do not lie dormant until suddenly "switched on" at birth; rather, they begin to function before birth. Determining how and approximately when the senses begin to function normally is important for several reasons. One reason is that knowing about development of the sensory systems enlarges our understanding of the general relation between structure and function. A second reason is that it is theoretically and practically important to learn how early brain development is influenced by stimulation. Preterm babies, born before their expected due date, are exposed to environmental stimulation from which they would normally be shielded. If the sensory systems are not functional prenatally, preterms would be protected; if the sensory systems function, however, then preterm babies might be adversely affected by the stimulating environment of the Neonatal Intensive Care Unit. Third, the human infant is recognized today as "perceptually competent"; determining just how perception functions in infancy helps to specify the effective perceptual world of babies. If a substance tastes sweet to adults, they may readily suppose that it tastes that way to infants, and even that infants will like it; in fact, however, taste receptors for sweetness may not even be present in infants or, if present, may not function or signal the same perception or quality to infants as to adults. Defining normative perceptual capacity in early life also permits developmental comparisons of mature versus immature perceptual functions, and studies of perception in childhood provide baseline data against which the normal course of maturation as well as the effects of experience into adulthood can be assessed.

All these reasons motivate studies of perceptual development, and given their nature and prominence it is not surprising that studies of perceptual development have focused most intensively on infancy.[1] However, perception is a lifelong developmental process, and this chapter discusses perception and its development in infancy, childhood, adulthood, and old age. We begin the chapter with a discussion of prominent theories of perception and then turn to some central issues in perceptual development, namely, status and origins, and stability and continuity in perceiving. In the next section we describe methodologies commonly employed to study perception across the life span. The third section surveys representatively our current knowledge of perceptual abilities—at the beginning and end of life and at points in between. In the fourth section, we consider the roles of experience in perceptual development.

PERSPECTIVES ON PERCEPTUAL DEVELOPMENT

Perception has historically been tied intimately to nature–nurture questions. What do we know before we have any experience in the world? What knowledge requires such experience? The two main outlooks (as just described) were **empiricist** and **nativist**: *Empiricists* asserted that there is no endowed knowledge at birth, that all knowledge comes through the senses, and that perceptual development proceeds through experience and associations. Empiricists

---

[1] The story of the ontogeny of perception begs the question of the evolution of perception. Organisms and their environments "co-construct" perceptual structure and function. In the terms of Levins and Lewontin (1985), in and through their interactions with the environment organisms determine which aspects of the ambient physical environment constitute the effective environment, they alter the world external to them as they interact with it, and they transduce the physical signals that reach them (and so the significance of those signals depends on the structure of the organism), just as environments select sensory-motor capacities in animals and thereby constrain perceptual development and activity.

argue that stimuli in the world naturally provoke bodily sensations that, occurring close together in space or in time, give rise to more global "ideas" and thereby invest the perceptual world with meaning. It is through association, empiricism further explains, that separate raw sensations aggregate into meaningful perceptions. The empiricist's view of the nature of the mind early in life was fostered by two separate, though conceptually related, schools of thought. One derived from John Locke (1632–1704), who in *An Essay Concerning Human Understanding* (1959, Book II, Chapter 1.2) described the mind at birth as a "white paper": Mental life begins "without any ideas," and understanding the world depends wholly on the accumulation of experiences. A slightly different empiricist view can be attributed to William James (1842–1910), who in *Some Problems of Philosophy* (1924, p. 50) described the "immediate sensible life" as a big "blooming buzzing confusion" out of which experience organizes and creates knowledge and order. According to empiricist beliefs, the naive child does not share the same perceptual world of the experienced adult. Empiricism is inherently developmental because, by whatever mechanism is postulated, human beings grow from perceptually immature to perceptually mature.

The belief that human beings begin life "empty headed" has been conceived by many to be both philosophically intolerable and logically indefensible. Extreme *nativists* postulate that human beings are not "created" mindless and that the knowledge that humans possess cannot be achieved by learning alone in so short a span of time as childhood. As a consequence, philosophers such as René Descartes (1596–1650) and Immanuel Kant (1724–1804) conceived of humans as endowed from birth with "ideas" or "categories" of knowledge that undergird perceptual functions. They postulated innate perceptual ideas for size, form, position, and motion, as well as more abstract conceptions for space and time. The nativist argument, contra the empiricist, holds that the human mind naturally and from the beginning of life imposes order on sensory input, thereby transforming raw sensations into meaningful perceptions. According to the nativist account, the child and adult may share many perceptual capacities, and the two perceive the world in much the same way. For those abilities that are congenital, nativism is not a developmental view; for those abilities that mature, however, nativism is developmental in outlook.

Today we see vestiges of this debate in contemporary theories of perception and perceptual development. Some argue that meaningful perceptual structure exists in the environment independently of the way we perceive the world: "The world is real and this reality includes such things as structure. But the organism also interacts with reality to seek and select structure. Rarely, however, does the organism create structure. There is no need. Structure is everywhere to be found and the information processing organism need only look, find, and select" (Garner, 1974, p. 186). The developmental corollary of this view is that perceptual growth consists of the perceiver's increasing sophistication to "pick up" relevant available information (E. J. Gibson, 1982; J. J. Gibson, 1979). So-called direct perception theories maintain that meanings of events in the world are automatically perceived ("afforded") in relations among higher-order variables to which the sensory systems have specifically evolved; they are not constructed from individual sensations. Thus, we directly perceive a support surface when looking at the floor below, and directly use it as such to control our walking.

Alternative views explain our interpretations of the physical world based on information in the world in conjunction with the evolutionary and developmental history of the organism and whatever the contemporary neural, sensory, and cognitive constraints of the organism may be. In this account, structure and information in the external environment are to a certain extent created through ongoing interactions between the organism and the environment (Hebb, 1949; Piaget, 1969). So-called constructivist theories may admit that a few rudimentary perceptual abilities—such as the capacity to distinguish figure from ground—are inborn, but beyond these the bulk of perceptual development is founded in the interplay of action and experience in the world. In seeing a form, we develop an internal representation of the form that is related to the movements of our eyes as well as to the activity of our brains. Interactive experiences thus promote perceptual organization and help to construct our understanding of the world, space, time, and so forth.

Status and Origins of Development

Perhaps the first question the perceptual developmentalist poses is, what the current *status* of the perceptual structure or function of interest is in the organism. This is a proper and logical starting point. For many, the answer to this question is also the end point. Not so for the developmentalist, who will pose (at least) two additional questions: What are the *origins* of the perceptual structure or function? How does the *development* of the perceptual structure or function unfold? In essence, nativism and empiricism constitute two (major) opinions about origins and assign differential weights to the roles that biology and experience play in development. Traditionally, theory and research in perceptual development are designed to characterize when a structure or function emerges, the course of its development (i.e., whether and how it changes over time), and what factors influence its developmental trajectory.

Development

Perception begins with the reception and transduction of physical information arriving at the sensory surface. Perceptual representations reflect the quality of this sensory transduction and information transmission. Developmental study broadly, and perceptual development specifically, are interested not only in manifestations and quality of ability and performance but also in the expression of two metrics of development, individual **stability** and group *continuity* of ability and performance (Bornstein & Bornstein, 2008). If a perception showed continuity in development, children as a group would perceive at the same average level at one point in time and at a second point later in time. A discontinuity in perception would be indicated by group improvement or deterioration. If a perception showed stability, individual children who displayed relatively high levels of perception at one point in time would display relatively high levels at a second point later in time. Instability in perception would be indicated by children's changing in their relative positions through time. Continuity and stability—central constructs in developmental science—describe related, but conceptually and statistically independent, realms of development (Bornstein & Suess, 2000; Hartmann, Pelzel, & Abbott, Chapter 3, this volume; McCall, 1981; Roberts, Walton, & Viechtbauer, 2006; Wohlwill, 1973). Developmentalists are concerned, moreover, with the question of *why* development has occurred. Developmental changes in perception could be attributable to (a) neural, anatomical, or sensory maturation; (b) changes in attention; (c) alterations in motivation or improved task performance; (d) learning and experience; or (e) combinations and interactions of all of these. Despite the fact that they are sometimes conceived as either–or contributors to developmental theories, nature and nurture inevitably and invariably interact through time. That is, perceptual development is influenced by organismic maturation in conjunction with specific effects of experience.

   The potential ways in which the forces of nature and nurture possibly interact to influence the course of development can be conceptualized in a simple but comprehensive manner. Figure 6.1 shows different possible courses of development of a perceptual structure or function before the onset of experience and the few possible ways experience may influence eventual perceptual outcome afterwards (Gottlieb, 1981). Experience operates through modification, enrichment, or deprivation. How does experience (or the lack thereof) interact with

Possible developmental outcomes

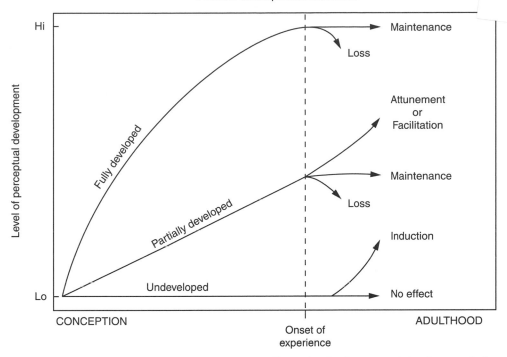

FIGURE 6.1 Possible developmental outcomes given different levels of perceptual development before the onset of experience and different experiences afterward. From Aslin (1981) after Gottlieb (1981). Copyright © 1981 by Academic Press. Reprinted with permission from Elsevier and the author. From *Development of Perception: Psychobiological Perspectives. Vol. 2: The Visual System*, by R. N. Aslin (after Gottlieb, 1981), 1981, New York: Academic Press. Copyright 1981 by Academic Press.

biology to affect the course of perceptual development? First, there is the possibility that a perceptual structure or function is undeveloped at the onset of experience, but can be induced or suppressed by relevant experience; without such experience, the structure or function is presumed never to emerge (see Figure 6.1). Second, a perceptual structure or function may develop partially before the onset of experience, after which experience could operate in one of three ways: Relevant experience could facilitate further development or attune the structure or function; experience could maintain the structure or function at the partial level of development attained before the onset of experience; or, in the absence of relevant experience or the presence of experience that suppresses the structure or function may be lost. (Of course, experience *per se* may not be altogether necessary where the perceptual structure or function would continue to mature as a reflection of the genetic blueprint.) Third, a perceptual structure or function could develop fully before the onset of experience, after which it requires experience only to be maintained; without relevant experience or with suppressing experience, the structure or function may be lost.

The topics in perceptual development to which scientists have historically devoted their attention are those that require answers to descriptive as well as to theoretical questions. The degree to which similarities among human beings are guided by biological or structural identities is difficult to specify, as is the degree to which differences among human beings reflect anatomy or ecology or tuition. Cultural studies of perception (which we review later) reveal clear developmental differences as well as similarities. For this reason perceptual studies often serve as models for other developmental and psychological processes.

METHODOLOGY IN PERCEPTUAL DEVELOPMENT

From a developmental point of view, the study of perception from young adulthood through old age poses relatively few methodological challenges because mature individuals can readily be instructed to report about or to behave in ways that communicate validly about their perceptions. In childhood and especially in infancy, however, the communication barrier throws up a fundamental impediment to perceptual study. Moreover, infants are motorically incompetent, and infants and young children are subject to state fluctuations and are inherently unreliable reporters. As a consequence, our knowledge of early perception must be inferred from reports and behaviors of varying, and usually impoverished, fidelity and credibility. Studies of perceptual development in the early part of the life span are therefore especially challenging. Moreover, perceptual research must be especially vigilant. We see the world—literally and figuratively—through adult eyes. Children do not. They see the world through child eyes. What looks like one thing to us may look quite different to a child, and it can be a gaffe to misattribute our perceptions to the child.

Two main paths to studying perceptual development, *neuroscience* and *behavior*, and several techniques within each, have been utilized. For purposes of comparison, the methodologies we review are ordered along a hypothetical continuum roughly in terms of the strength, from low to high, of **inference** about perception that they permit.

Despite important differences among methodologies, virtually all techniques developed to study perception have been engineered to address a surprisingly small number of perceptual questions. One question has to do with whether the observer detects the presence of a stimulus—in the psychophysicist's terms, whether the stimulus surpasses an **absolute threshold**. A second question has to do with whether the observer detects differences between perceptible stimuli—whether the stimuli surpass a **difference threshold**. Physically nonidentical stimuli that are still not discriminated give evidence of being treated similarly or categorized. Furthermore, some investigators elect to study naturally occurring, usually complex stimulation, whereas others elect to study stripped down stimulus variation along isolated dimensions. As usual, the scientific questions that motivate the research best dictate the nature of the stimuli used as well as the methodology chosen to study them.

The Neurosciences Path

Investigations of perceptual development that have adopted the techniques of contemporary neuroscience approach their subject of study via assessments of the central and autonomic nervous systems (Johnson, Chapter 4, this volume).

Central nervous system. Research efforts related to perceptual development focused on the **central nervous system** (CNS) have adopted four general techniques—neurological anatomy, single-cell and intercellular physiology, and aggregated cortical electrical activation as well as central function. Questions asked at the level of anatomical investigation concern the structural ontogeny of the perceptual apparatus, with a view to defining its relation to function. A presumption of this research strategy is that structure (anatomy) is necessary for function (perception), and so understanding function is, in a sense, enriched by a knowledge of underlying structure. On occasion, perceptual theorists turn this argument on its head and postulate the existence of structures based on observed functions; for example, the ability of newborns to discriminate shapes, orientations, and colors implies that some part or parts of the geniculostriate pathway of the brain must be developed at birth. Note, however, that structure is necessary but not sufficient for function: Babies have legs but do not walk. Thus, insofar as inference about perception is concerned, evidence based on anatomical structure alone is very weak.

The second technique of neuroscience investigation has focused more narrowly on the development and specificity of individual neurons and interneuronal connectivity in different sensory systems. Neurophysiological recordings of the brain reveal that individual cells code diverse specific characteristics of the environment. Some so-called "trigger features" of environmental stimulation to which individual neurons in the visual system, for example, have been found to be sensitive include wavelength of light, orientation of form, and direction of movement (Livingstone & Hubel, 1988). Neurons at higher regions of the brain show sensitivity to more complex stimuli. Barlow (1953) first used the term *bug detectors* based on his work in the frog, and Lettvin, Maturana, McCulloch, and Pitts (1959) proposed the term *grandmother cell* (Gross, 2002) to describe neurons that respond best to hypercomplex stimuli such as faces and hands (Gross, Bender, & Rocha-Miranda, 1969; Gross, Rocha-Miranda, & Bender, 1972). Although it is exciting and provocative, several questions render this area of research of limited value and suggest that these findings need to be viewed with caution when used to explicate perceptual development. For example, although single neurons show sensitivity to individual properties of environmental stimulation, their actual role (if any) in perception is still largely undefined. Furthermore, as virtually all studies of single units have been conducted in infrahuman species (e.g., cat or monkey), the direct relevance or applicability of single-unit studies to human perception remains open to question. Finally, an intriguing challenge to perceptual development is whether single neurons are innately sensitive to their trigger features, their sensitivity reflects experience, or (as is probable) the developmental interaction of the two.

The third and fourth research techniques into CNS contributions to perceptual development most directly address intact human beings and derive from aggregation and neuroimaging, tools that permit simultaneous examination of structure and function of the brain (Johnson, Chapter 4, this volume; Nelson, Thomas, & De Haan, 2006). They include the electroencephalogram (EEG) and event-related potential (ERP) and magnetic source imaging that taps electrical activity at the scalp that is a byproduct of underlying neuronal activity. The geodesic sensor net, for example, applies as many as 128 electrodes to the scalp surface (Tucker, 1993) for the purpose of identifying patterns of neural activity that may be time-locked to a stimulus (Figure 6.2A). For example, responsiveness to speech sounds has been studied in infants still in the first year of life using ERPs (Rivera-Gaxiola, Silva-Pereyra, & Kuhl, 2005). Reynolds and Richards (2005) made a close examination of ERPs in relation to underlying brain structure in infants 4.5, 6, and 7.5 months of age. They identified different underlying neural mechanisms for different aspects of information processing. Spatial independent components analysis of the electroencephalogram and "equivalent current dipole" analysis revealed putative cortical sources of the ERP components in areas of prefrontal cortex and anterior cingulate cortex (as in Figure 6.2B).

The fourth kind of neuroscience technique includes positron emission tomography (PET) and functional magnetic resonance imaging (fMRI; Figure 6.3). These two approaches provide spatial indications of brain metabolism and activity. Studies using fMRI with infants as young as 2 months reveal the involvement of different neural systems in response to speech (Dehaene-Lambertz, Dehaene, & Hertz-Pannier, 2002).

Widespread use of imaging techniques can lead not only to a greater basic science understanding of structure–function relations in perception, but also to more accurate diagnoses of problem states and enhanced efficiency in assessment and treatment. For example, a neuroscience approach has proved valuable for the light it sheds on atypical development. Electrical responses have been used to diagnose deafness at birth (Figure 6.4): If the newborn does not respond to sound, such responses can indicate whether or not brain pathways are intact.

Autonomic nervous system. A second set of neuroscience techniques widely applied to

A   B

FIGURE 6.2   (A) An infant wearing a high-density EEG sensor array (the geodesic sensor net). The elastic net contains 128 individual sensors for recording scalp EEG and ERP signals. Photo courtesy of Electrical Geodesics, Inc. (B) A source localization solution for ERPs that were collected when participants were hearing the speech sound /ba/ (Brain Electrical Source Analysis, MEGIS Software GmbH). The markers represent modeled locations of signal generators and their corresponding axes of charge polarity. Courtesy of S. Key.

FIGURE 6.3   A 10-year-old normal, healthy child about to be tested in a study of working memory involving fMRI. An overhead projector (not seen) projects visual images onto a screen at the foot of the table. A mirror directly above the child's head allows him to see these images. The child has a button box (containing nonmagnetic material) in his hand, and during the study (when the child will be in the scanner itself), he will push buttons that correspond to task demands (e.g., push a button that corresponds to a position of a light on the screen). Courtesy of C. Nelson.

FIGURE 6.4   A newborn being tested for hearing. Photo courtesy of T. Hellbrügge.

gaining information about perception has followed a path through monitoring **autonomic nervous system** (ANS) reactions in perceptual tasks. Cardiac and cardiorespiratory measures, such as heart rate, heart rate variability, and respiratory sinus arrhythmia (RSA), reflect orienting, sustained attention, and state changes in infants and children (Bornstein & Colombo, 2010).

These measures have proved to be particularly useful in research in perception because they are sensitive to changes in attentional state. They are also important indices of individual differences in children's capacity to regulate state of arousal and respond appropriately to environmental demand (Bornstein & Suess, 2000; Porges, 1995, 2001, 2003). For example, heart rate has been not only used as a measure of orienting but also to distinguish phases of attention in information processing (Colombo, 2001; Colombo, Richman, Shaddy, Greenhoot, & Maikranz, 2001; Richards, 2003, 2004). In this research, heart rate is measured during stimulus presentation. According to Richards (2004), heart rate changes systematically as an infant looks at a stimulus, and these changes correspond to different phases of attentional engagement. An infant's heart rate decelerates during orienting, shows sustained deceleration during sustained attention, and increases at the end of sustained attention. There is evidence that infants' information processing occurs primarily during phases of sustained attention (Frick & Richards, 2001; Richards, 1987, 2003).

Despite these several virtues, the contributions of neuroscience to understanding perception proper are limited, factors other than those under experimental scrutiny can influence responses, and perceptual understanding based on these techniques requires high degrees of inference. As noted, that a cortex exists or that a stimulus presented to the sensory system creates an identifiable and even consistent pattern of electrical activity at the cortex does not guarantee that the stimulus registers in a perceptually meaningful way for the observer. Some ANS measures fare somewhat better in this regard, but they still do not provide convincing evidence of conscious perception as the body may respond in the absence of stimulation giving rise to psychological awareness. Moreover, a basic principle of this approach is that many factors influence these kinds of responses, and thus there is almost never an exact one-to-one correspondence between a physiological index and a psychological state (Kandel, 2007). Access to conscious perceptual function is achieved only through behavioral report.

The Behavioral Path

To assess perceptual life in infancy, in childhood, or in maturity on surer footing, developmental scientists have invented or adapted a wide variety of behavioral techniques. The first of these methods, historically, relied on naturally occurring behaviors, such as looking patterns and facial expressions. Other methods involve infants' preferences and learning.

Naturally occurring behaviors—looking patterns and actions. Kessen, Haith, and Salapatek (1970) argued that it ought to be possible to assess visual function at birth simply by "looking at infant looking." These investigators photographed the reflection of a stimulus in the cornea of the baby's eye and tracked eye movements. They assumed that perceiving is in some degree implied in fixating a stimulus—voluntary visual orienting so as to bring a stimulus into the line of visual regard—and that where a baby looks indicates visual selectivity and, hence, visual perception. Until their studies, basic questions, such as whether or not newborn babies even see, went unanswered. In the decades since, many experimenters (e.g., Haith, 2004) have advanced on the logic of their inquiry and its methodology (Figure 6.5).

With advances in motor development, infants become increasingly capable of intentional action, and researchers use these actions to assess perception. For example, Ruff (1990) observed that infants' mouthing objects decreased over the second half of the first year,

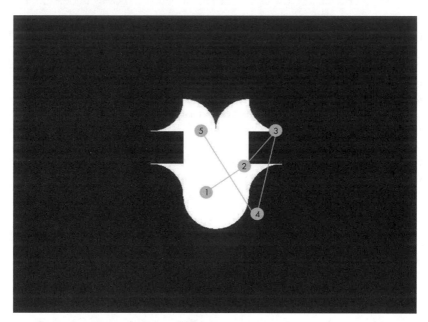

FIGURE 6.5   The photo shows an infant participating in an eyetracking study. An eye camera situated beneath the stimulus monitor measures and records the location of infants' fixations. Also shown is an example of fixation data plotted on a stimulus image.

whereas their fingering and more precise forms of manipulation both increased (accompanying the further development of fine motor coordination). Infants also vary their exploratory activities to match the object being explored. When Ruff systematically changed the nature of an object (once the infant had the chance to explore the object in some detail), the infant in turn changed patterns of tactual exploration so as to maximize acquisition of information about the new object. For example, infants responded to a change in shape by rotating and fingering the object more and transferring it more often from one hand to the other, but they responded to a change in texture only by fingering the new object more.

Other actions used to study perception are reaching (see Figure 6.6; e.g., Yonas & Hartman, 1993) and crawling and walking (see Figure 6.7). For example, infants will reach to the closer of two objects, indicating that they see the difference in depth between the two, and infants will crawl rather than walk down a steep incline or across a waterbed, indicating that they perceive the characteristics of the surface they are walking on and so adjust their actions accordingly (Adolph & Berger, Chapter 5, this volume).

Preference.　Fantz (1958, 1964) argued that, if an observer looked preferentially at one stimulus over another in a choice situation, irrespective of the spatial location of the two stimuli, the observer's **preference** could be taken to indicate detection and discrimination. Today Fantz's argument is the bedrock of the many popular and productive developmental research techniques. Consider the study of visual acuity as an example.

Studies of visual scanning indicate at a minimum that young observers see something when they look at patterns, but do not reveal how well they see. To study visual acuity, Fantz, Ordy, and Udelf (1962) capitalized on the observation that infants prefer to look at heterogeneous over homogeneous patterns. They posted pairs of patterns for infants to look at, in which one member of the pair was always gray and the other an alternation of black and white stripes that varied systematically in width. (The two stimuli were always matched in overall brightness.) As pattern is consistently preferred, the stripe width that fails to evoke a preference is the one that marks the limit of the observer's ability to tell stripes from the solid gray. (At some point, stripe width becomes so fine as to fade into homogeneity.) Preferential looking has been used to investigate a wide variety of perceptual abilities in infancy, especially in pattern vision and in color vision (Bornstein, 2006, 2007; Ruff & Rothbart, 1996). This technique has also been adapted to explore smell and taste (e.g., Steiner, 1977).

Demonstrable preferences provide evidence for absolute and discriminative thresholds; unfortunately, the preference paradigm suffers from a major shortcoming. The failure to observe a preference is ambiguous with respect to the observer's ability to detect or to discriminate stimuli. This is a nontrivial methodological drawback, and for this reason many investigators have turned to paradigms that draw even more actively on demonstrative behavioral acts of infants and children to study absolute and difference thresholds in perception. Among the most widely used paradigms are conditioned head rotation and habituation–recovery.

Conditioned head rotation.　An experimental paradigm that successfully taps into perceptual development is conditioned head rotation (Werker et al., 1998). In this form of learning, the reinforcement of a voluntarily controlled motor activity results in its being repeated. The child sits on the mother's lap, otherwise unencumbered, and with a loudspeaker to one side. When a sound (e.g., tone or speech syllable) is played through the speaker and the child responds by orienting to it, the child is rewarded by activation of cartoons or a colorful mechanical toy co-located with the speaker. Using this procedure developmental psycho-acousticians have charted the growth of basic sound perception capabilities—detection of sounds of different frequencies, discrimination among frequencies—as well as the growth of responsiveness to complex sounds that specify speech (Saffran, Werker, & Werner, 2006).

Habituation–recovery.　Conditioned head rotation provides reasonably reliable data about perception because infant observers actively, voluntarily, and definitely respond and thereby directly "communicate" their perceptions to the experimenter. An equally clear and reliable technique, and one that has been adopted widely in experimental studies of perception in the first years of life, is habituation–recovery (Bornstein, 1985; Bornstein & Colombo, 2010). This procedure has the advantages that it draws minimally on motor ability and that it

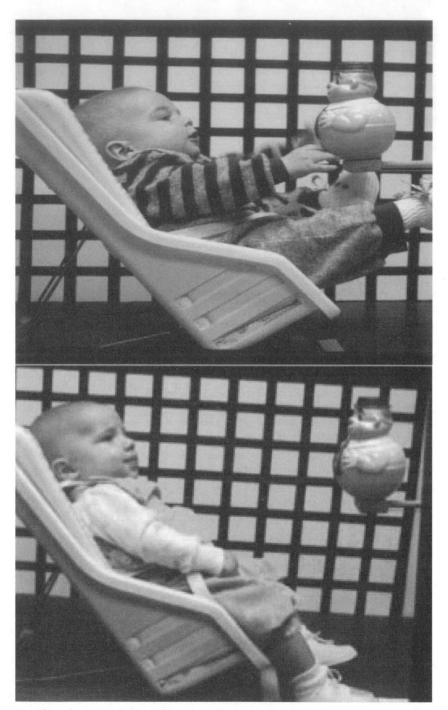

Out of reach.

FIGURE 6.6   The fine-tuned nature of infants' ability to link perception and action. Top: The infant reaches for an object that is within reach. Bottom: The same infant leans forward to make contact with a more distant object. After Yonas and Hartman, 1993.

FIGURE 6.7 Infants' locomotion decisions (whether to crawl or to walk) and how they explore the surface (e.g., pat it and rock over their ankles) provide insight into their perception of surface features. Courtesy of K. Adolph.

can and has been used to investigate perception in every modality; for purposes of this exposition, vision serves as an example.

In habituation, an infant is shown a stimulus, and the infant's visual attention to the stimulus is monitored. Typically, when placed in an otherwise homogeneous environment, an infant will orient and attend to a stimulus on its initial presentation. If the stimulus is available to the infant's view continuously or if it is presented repeatedly, the infant's attention to the stimulus will diminish. This decrement in attention, called *habituation*, presumably reflects two component processes: the infant's developing a mental representation of the stimulus and the infant's continuing comparison of whatever stimulation is present with that internal representation. If external stimulus and mental representation match, and the infant knows the stimulus, there is little reason to continue to look; mismatches, however, maintain or even evoke the infant's attention. A novel (and discriminable) stimulus, introduced in a test after habituation to a now familiar stimulus, typically reexcites infant attention to "recover" to the infant's initial level of looking. Habituation to familiarity and recovery to novelty have proved to be versatile and fruitful testing methods in developmental studies, permitting investigators the possibility of assessing many aspects of early perception. In vision, developmental researchers have used habituation–recovery to address classic questions about the perception of form, orientation, location, movement, color, and more complex events such as the appearance and disappearance of objects.

Conclusions

Our understanding of perception, its bases, and its development has been enhanced considerably by studies of the central and autonomic nervous systems and by active behavioral choice and learning. Techniques from neuroscience are valuable as objective and sensitive measures of perception, but the inferences we can make about perception from behavioral methods are stronger. In the next sections we illustrate the wealth of information about perceptual development gleaned from these methodologies.

PERCEPTUAL DEVELOPMENT IN INFANCY, CHILDHOOD, ADULTHOOD, AND OLD AGE

Prolegomena

As noted above, the study of perceptual development has largely focused on infancy and early childhood. This is so for several reasons. First, as we learned, perceptual study as a whole was motivated by philosophical debate. To study perception was to address epistemological controversies, and so to study perception effectively was to do so near the beginning of life before much experience had accrued. Second, by early childhood perception of the world (although certainly not interpretation) was thought to be reasonably mature and stable. Thus, most of the "action" in perceptual development was believed to take place very early in life. The sensory systems function and provide us with highly sophisticated information, systematically and forever eradicating the myth of the perceptually incompetent infant. The exciting and sometimes startling observations about infant perception made in the second half of the twentieth century do not mean that newborn perceptual capacities are fully developed, however; even if rudimentary function is present, qualitative sophistication is often still lacking. Third, after infancy, cognitive factors (including language mediation) play increasingly integrated roles in perception, and so distinguishing perceptual processes *per se* from other associated mental acts becomes problematic. On this account, the "perceptual plateau" of adulthood was often excluded from studies of perceptual development, with two important exceptions: One is when ontogenetic comparisons were called for; and the other is studies of aging. Today, the picture of perceptual development is changing for two main reasons. First, continuing research into cognitive neuroscience shows that the brain after birth is not a static organ (as once believed), but is plastic to new experiences throughout the life course. Second, demographic changes in the population associated with the increasing longevity of the "baby boom" generation have drawn more attention to aging in general and specifically to perceptual factors in aging. In the life-span view we adopt here, we address perception in infancy and childhood as well as in adulthood and old age.

Anatomical Beginnings

The course of anatomical development of the sensory systems has received more than modest attention, leading to the conclusion that human beings are reasonably well prepared to perceive in many modalities once extrauterine life begins. By the second trimester of prenatal life, the eye and the visual system, the ear and the auditory system, the nose and the olfactory system, and the tongue and the gustatory system are well on their way to being structurally and functionally mature. In general, two principles of development appear to characterize sensory system development. Within systems, maturation tends to proceed from the periphery to the central parts of the brain, so that, for example, the eye differentiates structurally and reaches functional maturity before the visual cortex (Conel, 1939/1959; Nelson, Thomas, & De Haan, 2006), and the electroretinogram before the cortical event-related potential (Barnet, Lodge, & Armington, 1965; Lodge, Armington, Barnet, Shanks, & Newcomb, 1969). Across systems, different senses tend to achieve functional development in sequence (Gottlieb, 1981): cutaneous, gustatory, olfactory, auditory, and finally visual. Turkewitz and Kenny (1982, 1985) argued that this staggered program of development has biopsychological advantages for reducing mutual competition among systems for ambient stimulation, and thereby allowing for eventual heightened sensory organization and integration.

Perhaps the two most important developments at the intercellular level involve biochemical neurotransmission and reorganization among neurons. In the first 2 years of life, proliferation of synapses—the connections across neurons—proceeds to the point at which there are up to 10,000 connections per cell (Kandel, 2007). This over-proliferation results in a chaotic and immature pattern of multiple intercellular connections (Huttenlocher, 2002). A second wave of overproduction occurs just prior to puberty. Synaptic "pruning" or elimination begins around 1 year of age and again around 13 years of age. At both times, initial chaotic patterns are gradually replaced by more efficient and streamlined systems of central nervous information transmission (Bergström, 1969). Thus, in infancy a discrete stimulus that excites the immature system is likely to result in a diffuse tonic or global response, whereas in maturity interconnections are orderly, and the same discrete stimulus produces a phasic response that is exact in time and parallel in space. Consider how children respond to a loud clap of the hands. Early in life, such auditory stimulation elicits a whole body shudder, for example. Later, the same clap will produce a quick and efficient turn of the head. CNS development at the intercellular level is characterized generally by differentiation and growth of specificity (Purves & Lichtman, 1980).

The Five Senses in Early Life: Touch, Taste, Smell, Hearing, and Sight

Touch. We know from everyday experience that soothing pats can quiet a fussy infant, whereas the DPT shot invariably causes an infant distress. Infants are sensitive to the location of a touch and may also feel pain when the tactile stimulus is severe. Alert newborns will turn toward a stimulus that touches near their mouth or a puff of air on their cheek (Kisilevsky, Stach, & Muir, 1991). Newborns also show differential responses to invasive and noninvasive procedures soon after birth; infants react to invasive procedures with a common facial expression composed of lowered brows, tightly shut eyes, nasolabial furrow, open lips, and a cupped taut tongue suggesting that they feel pain from invasive procedures (Craig, Whitfield, Grunau, Linton, & Hadjistavropoulos, 1993; Grunau, Johnston, & Craig, 1990).

Taste. Taste is a primitive sensory system that is developed early and of significance to survival. Psychophysical research has led to broad conclusions that four basic qualities (and their combinations) together compose taste experience: sweet, salt, sour, and bitter. Tastes are very powerful stimuli in learning: As most people know, a single experience of nausea associated with a particular taste is sufficient to cause a long-lasting or even life-long aversion to that taste (Garcia & Koelling, 1966). Newborn babies, even those who have tasted nothing but amniotic fluid, appear to discriminate among sensory qualities that signify different tastes and give evidence that they prefer certain tastes to others (Ganchrow & Steiner, 1984; Ganchrow, Steiner, & Daher, 1983). Taste discrimination is organized at a primitive level of the brain; it appears in anencephalic babies (those born without a cortex). Thus, it comes as no surprise that newborn babies show differential reactions to different tastes. Steiner (1977) gave newborn infants sweet, sour, or bitter substances to taste, and he photographed their gustofacial reactions—all prior to the very first time any of the babies ate. Figure 6.8A shows the results. A sweet stimulus evoked an expression of satisfaction, often accompanied by a slight smile and sucking movements. A sour stimulus evoked lip-pursing, often accompanied or followed by wrinkling the nose and blinking the eyes. A bitter stimulus evoked an expression of dislike and disgust or rejection, often followed by spitting or even movements preparatory to vomiting. Oster (2005) observed that 2-hour-old neonates produce different facial responses to sweet versus non-sweet tastes as well as to salty, sour, and bitter tastes. Infants discriminate within, as well as between, these taste categories: Sweeter sucrose solutions elicit fewer and longer bursts of sucking separated by longer pauses than do less sweet solutions (Crook, 1987).

FIGURE 6.8   Gustatory and olfactory sensitivity in newborn babies. (A) Infants' gustofacial response to the taste of sweet (left column), sour (middle column), and bitter (right column). Infants' nasofacial response to the smell of (B) vanilla and (C) raw fish. After Steiner, 1977.

Smell.   Odor is another primitive sensory system that develops early. Newborns possess a keen ability to detect and discriminate odors (Engen, 1982; Porter, Balogh, & Makin, 1988), perhaps approaching mature levels (Schaal, 1988). Steiner (1977, 1979) documented neonates' nasofacial reactions to odors placed on cotton swabs held beneath the nose: Butter and banana elicited positive expressions; vanilla, either positive or indifferent expressions; a fishy odor, some rejection; and the odor of rotten eggs, unanimous rejection (see Figure 6.8B and C). Breast-fed and bottle-fed infants only 12 to 18 days of age were systematically compared for their olfactory recognition of mother, father, and stranger. Babies were photographed while exposed to pairs of gauze pads worn in the underarm area by an adult on the night previous to the test, and the duration of infant preferential orienting to one or another of the gauze pads was recorded. Only breast-feeding infants oriented preferentially and exclusively to their own mothers' scents, thereby giving evidence that they discriminate among odors and prefer that of mother. (Infants did not recognize their fathers preferentially; nor did bottle-fed infants recognize their mothers.) This pattern of results suggests that, while they are breast-feeding, infants are exposed to, and apparently learn, unique olfactory signatures (Porter & Levy, 1995). Goubet and her colleagues (2002; Goubet, Rattaz, Pierrat, Bullinger, & Lequien, 2003) showed that learning odors, such as vanilla, occurs rapidly in both preterm and term infants, and the presence of a familiar odor during a medical procedure has a calming effect.

Femandez and Bahrick (1994) assessed whether 4-month-olds could learn an arbitrary object–odor pairing. Girls (but not boys) increased their looking to a target object that had previously been paired with a cherry odor when the object was presented in the presence of the cherry odor but not in the absence of the odor. These findings point to memory for odors and the potential for a prior experience with an odor to influence infants' later responses. In another study, 3-month-olds learned to kick to control the movement of an overhead mobile in the presence of an ambient odor. Infant retention was assessed 1, 3, or 5 days later. During the retention test, the olfactory context was either the same odor, a different odor, or "no odor." At 1 day, infants exhibited retention when tested in the presence of the same odor; infants in the no odor condition exhibited partial retention, whereas memory retrieval was completely disrupted for infants tested in the presence of the different odor. After the 3- and 5-day intervals, all groups showed forgetting (Rubin, Fagen, & Carroll, 1998).

Hearing. We have a fairly good understanding of early auditory perception, i.e., hearing (Saffran et al., 2006). How loud does a sound have to be to be heard? For adults, the amount of energy defining the auditory absolute threshold varies with the frequency of the sound: The least energy is required around 1,000 Hz, and more energy is required at both lower and higher frequencies. Virtually the entire audible frequency spectrum (from 200 to 19,000 Hz) has been mapped in children of various ages and compared with that of adults (Trehub & Schneider, 1985). Infant thresholds for noise (as opposed to pure tones) vary substantially with frequency; they are higher than those of adults for low frequencies (200 Hz), approach adult levels for middle frequencies (1,000 Hz), and are again higher than those of adults at very high frequencies (10,000 Hz). Furthermore, hearing at low and high frequencies nearly continuously improves during the first 20 years of life, with sensitivity to high frequency maturing first (Schneider, Trehub, Morrongiello, & Thorpe, 1986; Trehub, Schneider, Morrongiello, & Thorpe, 1988, 1989). Changes in ear structure, nervous system maturation, and experience could account for increasing developmental sensitivity.

Young children also clearly discriminate among sounds of different frequencies. Five- to 8-month-old babies tell apart tones differing by only about 2% in frequency in the 1,000- to 3,000-Hz range (where adult frequency discrimination is about 1%); infant thresholds are twice those of adults at lower frequencies (250–1,000 Hz), whereas they are virtually the same as those of adults at higher frequencies (3,000–8,000 Hz; Werner & Bargones, 1992). Fagen et al. (1997) investigated the role of a complex auditory context (music) on retrieval. They trained 3-month-olds in the presence of a musical sequence (either a classical or jazz piano piece) and then tested infants for retention 1 or 7 days later in the presence of either the same or a different musical pattern. Infants displayed 1-day retention regardless of which music was played during the 1-day test. At 7 days, however, retention was seen only when the music being played during the retention test matched what the infant had heard during training.

A vital function of hearing for the young infant involves perceiving speech. Newborn babies prefer speech that has been filtered to mimic what they heard *in utero* over matched complex non-speech sounds, and babies will even work (by sucking more frequently and harder) to present themselves with speech sounds but will not do so for complex non-speech (Vouloumanos & Werker, 2007a, 2007b). Cortical imaging techniques show more activity in left-hemisphere "language" areas when babies are exposed to regular speech but activity in both the left and right hemispheres when babies are exposed to the same speech played backwards (Pena et al., 2003). By the middle of the first year infants discriminate most acoustic differences that signal phonologically relevant speech contrasts in language. In addition, infants perceive phonemes (units of meaningful speech) as equivalent when they are spoken by male and female talkers and, thus, differ in fundamental frequency; and within the first year infants are able to parse the speech stream into smaller units—phrases, words, and syllables. For example, infants prefer pauses placed between clauses rather than pauses placed within clauses; they rely on stress patterns and sequential regularities (the ordering of phonemic segments) to separate phrases into words; they divide words into syllables; and they detect statistical relations between neighboring speech sounds after relatively little experience with new sound combinations (Saffran et al., 2006).

Sight.   Eye scan patterns signify that infants from the first days of life actively orient to visual information in the environment, and not only do such patterns reveal what babies look at, but looking patterns develop and are distributed differently over different visual forms. Even in the first hours after birth, infants tend to scan the parts of faces or geometric forms that contain information (usually high-contrast features such as along the contours of figures) in lieu of scanning randomly about the background or over the central part of a figure (Haith, 2004). Generally speaking, visual scanning relates systematically to the content and structure of scenes examined (Figure 6.5). It is likely that these patterns of attentional bias limit some aspects of visual scenes that younger infants actually detect. For instance, one investigation of feature learning and discrimination revealed a failure among young infants to process elements appearing inside a salient outer boundary even though they were able to discriminate patterns on the basis of those external contours. It is possible that such constraints serve a functionally beneficial role in reducing the amount of sensory information that younger infants must process with their more limited cognitive resources.

Color is an intellectually impressive and aesthetically attractive kind of information. Infants see colors and seem to do so pretty well. Darwin (1877) speculated on his own children's color vision in the 1870s, but real progress toward understanding the development of color vision only began in the 1970s. Studying color vision is particularly formidable technically (Bornstein, 2006, 2007): For example, hue, brightness, and saturation, the major components of color, covary so that whenever a color changes, its hue, brightness, and saturation are normally changing. To distinguish hue alone, which is proof of color vision, it is necessary to match hues in brightness and saturation or make brightness and saturation differences between the hues unrelated. With adults, this is relatively easy, as there exist formulae to relate the amount of change or difference in hue to the amount of change or difference in brightness and saturation; alternatively, adults can match colored stimuli for brightness and saturation directly. In babies, however, the precise relation between brightness or saturation and hue was for a long time unknown, and babies cannot be asked to match brightnesses or saturations. As a consequence, an understanding of early color vision begins with proper controls, and then proceeds to test discrimination, preference, and organization of hue. The development of color vision right after birth has not been studied extensively. Yet infants 3 months of age and older are acknowledged to possess basically normal color vision (Teller, 1998). Moreover, by 4 months of age infants perceive the color spectrum as organized qualitatively into categories of hue (Figure 6.9; Bornstein, Kessen, & Weiskopf, 1976; see also Franklin & Davies, 2004). Preverbal infants categorize the visible spectrum into relatively discrete basic hues of blue, green, yellow, and red, which are similar to those of adults, even though infants, like adults, can also discriminate among colors within a given category (Bornstein, 2006, 2007).

If newborn gustatory and olfactory acuities are highly developed, visual acuity—the level of detail that can be distinguished in a visual scene—is rather poor at birth. Infants begin life "legally blind," around 20/400. Improvement is linear and quick, however, reaching adult levels by about 8 months of age (Norcia & Tyler, 1985). Nonetheless, young infants' acuity does not severely limit their perception. They may not be able to read a book, but they can discern objects in their environment and most properties of those objects.

Infants' perception of form is relevant in this connection. The fact that an observer scans

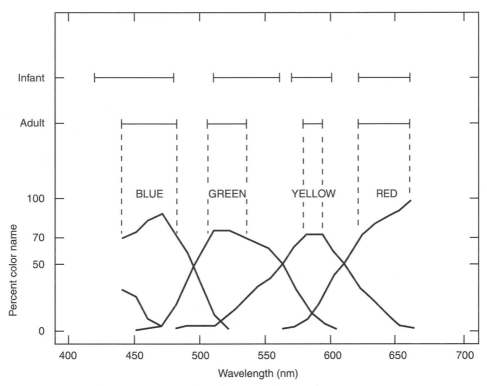

FIGURE 6.9 Wavelength groupings (i.e., hue categories) for 4-month-old infants and for adults. Bottom: Percentage of color name use as a function of wavelength for the color names blue, green, yellow, and red (after Boynton & Gordon, 1965). The rising function at very short wavelengths is for red. Top: Summary results for hue categories for infants and adults. The infant summary is derived from Bornstein, Kessen, and Weiskopf (1976). The adult summary reflects a projection from the color-naming data at a psychophysical criterion of 70%. Infant and adult grouping patterns are highly similar, suggesting that by 4 months of age infants' hue categories are similar to those of adults.

an angle of a triangle, and even resolves contour well, does not mean that the observer perceives the triangle as a "triangle." For some time, the problem of form perception in early life proved remarkably resistant to resolution because almost any discrimination between two forms (a triangle from a circle) could be explained as discrimination on some simpler, featural basis (as between an angle and an arc) without whole-form perception being implicated. Because visual object recognition requires form perception, infants' recognition performance offers clues to their perception of form. In one such study, 5-month-olds were familiarized to a simple, novel object by either a series of images depicting a single view of the object or a series depicting different views around its vertical axis (Mash, Arterberry, & Bornstein, 2007). Infants in the single-view group failed to recognize the same object when inverted, but infants seeing multiple views did recognize the object when inverted. A control experiment confirmed that infants were capable of discriminating subtle shape differences in the stimulus objects. Because such performance requires an initial extraction of 3D form, these findings indicate that infants are capable of combining discrepant static views into a cohesive representation of an object's 3D visual form. This kind of research provides converging evidence that babies, still only in the first year of life, can perceive form *qua* whole form.

Objects are specified not only by their form but also by their coordination in space, that is, by their orientation, location, and movement. Physical space extends outward from the central ego equally in all directions, yet perceived orientation is not uniform: For adults, vertical holds a higher psychological status than does horizontal, and horizontal is generally higher in status than is oblique (Bornstein, 1982; Essock, 1980). For instance, we accept the statement that "5° is almost vertical" as truer than the statement that "vertical is almost 5°." Vertical is the reference point for orientation (Wertheimer, 1938). Studies of detection, discrimination, and preference suggest that this hierarchy among orientations exists in early life for artificial geometric forms as well as for more meaningful patterns like the human face, and for static as well as for dynamic forms (Bornstein, Ferdinandsen, & Gross, 1981; Held, 1989; Leehey, Moskowitz-Cook, Brill, & Held, 1975). Young babies also seem able to discriminate orientation, not only in telling vertical and horizontal apart: They can resolve finer differences involving only obliques (Bornstein et al., 1981; Bornstein, Gross, & Wolf, 1978; Slater, Morison, & Somers, 1988).

Location in depth is also an important spatial dimension, and there are numerous cues available for depth perception. Three types of stimulus information specify depth—binocular, kinetic, and static–monocular cues—and infants appear to develop sensitivity to these types of information at different times. Binocular information is available by virtue of the fact that human beings have two eyes. This information consists of the convergence angle of the two eyes and stereopsis (the disparity between the two slightly different images of the visual world each eye receives). Binocular convergence yields information about close-up distances and serves as a reliable source of information about depth by 5 months (von Hofsten, 1974) or possibly earlier (Granrud, 1987; Slater, Mattock, & Brown, 1990). The onset of sensitivity to binocular disparity emerges around 4 months of age (Fox, Aslin, Shea, & Dumais, 1980; Held, Birch, & Gwiazda, 1980), and infants who show disparity sensitivity demonstrate improved spatial perception (Yonas, Arterberry, & Granrud, 1987a).

Young infants' depth perception is also supported by sensitivity to kinetic information. There are several kinetic cues. When an object comes directly toward us on a "hit path," we normally move out of the way to avoid the impending collision, and babies as young as 1 month of age consistently show a defensive response (e.g., they blink) to approaching objects (Nanez & Yonas, 1994). Another kinetic cue occurs during movement when closer surfaces are perceived to occlude more distant ones, called accretion and deletion of texture: Sitting in a moving car, we notice that the nearby billboard "moves" in front of and partially covers the more distant hill. Five-month-old babies use this kind of information to perceive the relative ordering of surfaces in depth (Granrud et al., 1984).

Sensitivity to a third type of depth information, static–monocular depth pictorial cues, appears to develop after sensitivity to binocular and kinetic information. When normal conditions of viewing are degraded, as in the case when distances are great or a single eye is looking at a nonmoving single point of observation, we may still perceive depth. Seven-month-olds, but not 5-month-olds, respond to a number of static–monocular depth cues, such as shading, interposition, familiar size, relative size, texture gradient, and linear perspective (Yonas, Arterberry, & Granrud, 1987b; Yonas & Granrud, 2006). Height-in-the-picture-plane may be the only type of static monocular depth information used by infants at 5 months of age (Arterberry, 2008).

Movement of objects also contributes information about their position, shape, and integrity (Kellman & Arterberry, 2006). Perception of objects naturally occurs in the context of their movement, and from such perceptions observers appear to pick up information about movement as well as about objects (Butterworth, 1989). This information "pickup" permits recognition of the same object regardless of its motion, and recognition of a particular movement regardless of the object that is moving (Gibson, 1979). On this account, object and movement perception are separate abilities but closely intertwined. Motion perception is cued by several types of information, including retinal image motion, retinal image displacement, and observer motion; even young infants show sensitivity to motion (Aslin & Shea, 1990;

Dannemiller & Freedland, 1991). They will look more at moving versus stationary versions of the same stimulus (Slater, Morison, Town, & Rose, 1985), locking on to moving heads and blinking eyes (Samuels, 1985). Ruff (1985) habituated babies to a series of objects, each one of which moved the same way (say, from side to side), and then tested them with a novel object moving in the familiar (side to side) motion and with a novel object moving in a novel way (say, from side to side and rotating). Infants at 3½ months discriminated side to side from side to side plus rotation, and by 5 months infants discriminated side to side from rotation alone, rotation from oscillation around the vertical, and left versus right rotation.

In addition to their form and spatial dimensions, patterns and objects in the environment are also specified, identified, and distinguished by surface features. Which features do infants attend to in determining the identity of objects? Wilcox (1999) examined infants' use of specific object properties in an object individuation task. She measured infants' looking time to hiding events in which objects' visual features were switched when briefly hidden (say, a change in the color of a ball from red to blue), assuming that longer looking indicates detection of the switch. Failure to detect switches in particular features would suggest that infants do not focally attend to those features when tracking individual objects through such events. Wilcox found that 4-month-olds attended to both the shape and the size of objects when identifying them after the event had begun, but only after 11 months did they attend to the objects' surface features of pattern and color. Mash (2007) observed individuation by color in infants as young as 9 months when they were also provided with correlated haptic cues to object identity, a finding that provides clues to infants' emerging ability to combine information from different senses into coherent representations of distinct objects.

By now it is clear that infants discern the patterns, forms, and objects that they see around them. What is less clear is how they extract coherent, organized forms from an otherwise crowded environment. This question has guided perceptual research across all age groups, and some of the most enduring solutions are found among the Gestalt laws of organization. Gestaltists argued for innate, systematic constraints on the grouping of image primitives in the perception of visual scenes (Wertheimer, 1958), but only more recently have these principles been tested in infants. Quinn and colleagues examined whether manipulating the similarity of contiguous elements in stimulus arrays affected the perceptual organization of those arrays for infants. They found that infants at 3 months could organize arrays by lightness similarity (light vs. dark elements; Quinn, Burke, & Rush, 1993), but that the ability to do so on the basis of form similarity (x elements vs. o elements) did not emerge until closer to 7 months of age (Quinn, Bhatt, Brush, Grimes, & Sharpnack, 2002). These and related studies are consistent with the notion that at least some basic organizational principles guide the extraction of form information very early in life, but not necessarily with the Gestaltist position that these principles are present at birth.

Conclusions. The emerging picture of the beginnings of perception is one of substantial, if incomplete, competency relatively early in life. Young infants start life with a repertoire of abilities that are refined as they grow older. This refinement may result from further maturation of the perceptual systems and development of complementary systems (such as motor skills), experience, or their interaction. The infant perceptual system is by no means simply a small version of that of the adult. Even though quite functional, infants experience limitations that most adults do not. Yet, even infants' stripped-down version of perception consists of sensitivities that lead to veridical perceptions that are useful to the immature organism. Infants are sensitive to motion-carried information before other types of depth information; acuity is best at distances where important information is usually located (12 inches away where parents' faces are most likely to be found); likely encountered tastes (sweetness) are discriminated earlier than less likely encountered tastes (bitterness); sounds at decibel levels around the average speaking voice are detected more easily than are whispers. Infants are adapted to take advantage of the most useful information in their environment, and it is possible that further perceptual and related developments build on this initial high-quality information (Kellman & Arterberry, 2006).

Perception in Childhood

The study of perceptual development after infancy is less motivated by age-old questions, such as the nature–nurture debate, and substitutes a practical emphasis. Many applied investigators have expressed interest in perceptual development in childhood for its relation to children's performance in school, for example. The significance of developmental questions in perception is brought home when children begin to learn how to read. Visual and auditory abilities (beyond verbal capacities) are persistently implicated in reading performance (e.g., Fisher, Bornstein, & Gross, 1985; Johnston, Anderson, Perrett, & Holligan, 1990; Kavale, 1982; Rayner, 1998; Solan & Ficarra, 1990; van Kleeck, 2003) as are other individual differences in young children such as temperament (Pellegrini & Galda, 2003). For example, individual differences in children's attention affects the quality of picture book reading (Karrass, VanDeventer, & Braungart-Rieker, 2003; Ortiz, Stowe, & Arnold, 2001; Sénéchal, Cornell, & Broda, 1995). Picture book reading between an adult and a child involves "an attentional state during which the child and partner share a site of interest, such as an object or an event, in their immediate surroundings" (Adamson & Chance, 1998, p. 16). The ability to produce and comprehend rapid speech has been supported by nearly 10,000 generations of natural selection. However, writing and reading have arisen in just the past 5,000 years, and adaptation to these tasks is supported by only 250 generations of natural selection. Thus, it is not surprising to find that so many children have trouble learning to read and are diagnosed as "dyslexic" (Booth, Perfetti, MacWhinney, & Hunt, 2000). Another applied topic is the perceptual developmentalist's perennial interest in children's artistic abilities (Golomb, 2004) and perceptual substrates of children's musical skills (Deliège & Sloboda, 1996; Lynch, Eilers, & Bornstein, 1992; Wilson, Wales, & Pattison, 1997). A further practical side to the study of perceptual abilities is children's attention to and awareness of dangers posed by the environment (Lis, Venuti, & de Zordo, 1990; Plumert, Kearney, & Cremer, 2007), and the potential influences of entertainment technology (e.g., TV and video games) on children's perceptual proclivities and abilities (Green & Bavelier, 2003). In American homes, the television is on approximately 6 hours a day on average. Rideout, Vandewater, and Wartella (2003; Vandewater et al., 2005) examined the impact of "heavy-television" households on reading in 756 children aged 0 to 6 drawn from a nationally representative sample. Two-thirds of 0- to 6-year-olds (65%) live in homes where the TV is on half the time or more, even if no one is watching, and one-third (36%) live in "heavy" TV households, where the television is left on "most of the time" or "always." As a whole, 0- to 6-year-olds average about an hour a day of TV watching (1:05), plus another 38 minutes a day watching videos. Regardless of their age, children from heavy-television households watched more television and were less likely to read.

Perceptual development in childhood generally involves increasing efficiency, as in the abstraction of invariants (constant stimulus features) from the ever-changing environmental array. Both speech and color perception in children give evidence of tuning, which refers to the broadening of categories and reciprocal sharpening of boundaries between them: Zlatin and Koenigsknecht (1975) found that boundaries between speech categories sharpened between 2 and 6 years of age, and Raskin, Maital, and Bornstein (1983) found that boundaries between color categories sharpened between 3 and 4 years of age. The Gibsons (E. J. Gibson, 1969, 1982; J. J. Gibson, 1979) asserted that perceptual life begins as diffuse, and through experience differentiates, becoming ever more selective and acute. They demonstrated increasing perceptual differentiation of form in children aged 6 to 11 years (Gibson & Gibson, 1955). Other work shows that as children age, they become better able to deploy visual information as, for example, in maintaining postural stability (Schmuckler, 1997) or navigating through space (Newcombe & Huttenlocher, 2000). In childhood, we learn to look for what is distinctive and helpful versus what is irrelevant to perception.

One aspect of perception that changes over the course of childhood, and that is linked to growth in selective attention, is the nature of dimensions that underlie perception of complex stimuli. Objects and patterns can typically be described with distinct visual dimensions such as size, color, and texture. Although adults readily select and attend to the individual dimensions that compose visual objects—say, the shape of an apple as opposed to its color—young children tend to perceive objects and patterns more holistically. This trend in development reveals itself in studies of visual classification in which participants of different ages are asked to classify patterns that vary in only two different dimensions. Whereas children younger than 5 tend to classify such patterns on the basis of their overall similarity, older children and adults are much more likely to classify patterns on the basis of either one dimension or the other (Smith & Kemler, 1977). Using similar task conditions, Mash (2006) examined children's visual classification of object images instead of the simpler patterns used previously. With object stimuli, 5-year-olds directed their perceptual analysis to local parts, whereas 8-year-olds and adults integrated visual object elements more holistically with development. Together, such findings suggest that as children get older, they gain increasing control over the distribution of their attention to perceptual attributes.

Studies of perception in childhood offer special challenges because, for example, considerations of perceptual development after infancy are often bound up with the growth of language and cognition. From infancy to adulthood, children acquire ever-greater cognitive skill, in domains ranging from reasoning to mathematics to wayfinding. Many theorists believe that a small number of general processing mechanisms are implicated in children's performance across a wide range of tasks (e.g., Case, 1998; Demetriou & Valanides, 1998). Such global mechanisms are not specific to particular tasks or domains but are, instead, fundamental characteristics of the developing information-processing system; good candidates include processing speed (or efficiency) and working memory. Like the speed of a computer's central processing unit, processing speed denotes the amount of time required for a person to execute fundamental cognitive processes. As children process information more rapidly, they use working memory more effectively, which in turn allows them to solve problems and reason more successfully. Processing speed therefore influences cognitive development directly (by allowing processes to be performed more rapidly) and indirectly (by increasing the functional capacity of working memory). As children's general processing mechanisms develop, it becomes increasingly difficult to separate how children perceive the world from how they act on it and what they know about it. Although sensory abilities may mature by puberty, more comprehensive perceptual functioning has not; young children grow continually in integrating perceptions with verbal descriptions and conceptions of the world (Pitchford & Mullen, 2003; Smith, 2003). Selective attention, visual integration of shape, and speed of visual information processing vary among children, but all nevertheless generally increase across childhood, reaching whatever their adult asymptote will be around the onset of adolescence (Gerhardstein, Kraebel, Gillis, & Lassiter, 2002; Kail, 2003).

Even seemingly straightforward studies of perceptual development often involve cognitive processes. An illustration is Lee (1989), who asked 4- to 14-year-olds simply to copy line drawings of tables. It turned out that children's copying errors related to their knowledge that lines "represent" a table rather than to any difficulty in "drawing" lines *per se*. Children made few errors when copying lines when they did not know what the lines represented, but they made more errors when copying lines that were component parts of drawings of a table. In other words, even in a simple copying task children's cognitions influenced their perceptions. Language is likewise inextricably entangled with perception. It could be that perception precedes language developmentally and forms a basis on which language is built; or, it could be that perception depends on understanding the world, itself intimately involved with language categories and social interactions (Smith, 2003). Marks, Hammeal, and Bornstein (1987) investigated the development of cross-modal correspondences between perceptual dimensions of pitch and brightness, loudness and brightness, and pitch and size using purely perceptual and purely verbal stimuli in children aged 3½ to 13½ years. The youngest children easily matched pitch and brightness, and loudness and brightness, showing that perceptual similarities between hearing and vision are evident even to very young children, and they did so in the perceptual realm (with actual lights and tones) earlier than they did in the verbal realm (rating the word "sunlight" brighter but not louder than the word "moonlight"). Only older children, however, consistently recognized similarity between pitch and size. This difference in developmental timetables accords with the view that some similarities (e.g., pitch–brightness and loudness–brightness) are intrinsic characteristics of perception (characteristics based, perhaps, on common sensory codes), whereas others (e.g., pitch–size similarity) may be learned (perhaps through association of size with acoustic resonance properties). Consistent time lags across tasks pointed to a developmental priority of the perceptual over the linguistic system.

Alongside what appear to be biological changes that underlie perceptual development, unique experiences that children have also influence the early development of perceptual abilities. For example, off the west coast of Thailand, the island preserves of Ko Surin, Ko Poda, and Ko Phi Phi in the Andaman Sea are home to a tribe of so-called "sea gypsies," the Moken. These people dive to harvest clams, sea cucumbers, and other marine foods. Without goggles or other aids, sea gypsy children routinely spot even the smallest shellfish. Swimming normally presents a problem for human vision because water has essentially the same density as does the fluid inside the eye, so underwater light bends as it enters the eye, resulting in the blurry vision known to all swimmers. Moken children and European children have the same visual acuity on land, but Moken children have better than twice the underwater resolving power of European children—a level of underwater acuity previously thought to be impossible in humans. Mokens shrink the size of their pupils, the round black aperture through which light enters the eye, 22% smaller than the minimum seen in Europeans. Moken apparently learn this adaptive skill in childhood and do not simply inherit it as an inborn reflex (Gislen, Dacke, Kroger, Abrahamsson, Nilsson, & Warrant, 2003).

The importance of perception to children—even older children in school—however underresearched, cannot be overestimated. Consider children's sometimes surprising level of comprehension and interpretation of basic drawings. Constable, Campbell, and Brown (1988) investigated secondary schoolers' understanding of biological illustrations in textbooks. Both the features of objects depicted and the number and type of conventions used posed significant difficulties for children through their adolescence. Similarly, children demonstrate significant difficulties reading maps, which has implications for wayfinding and spatial representation (Liben, Kastens, & Stevenson, 2002).

Perceptual Stability and Change in Adulthood

Perception is often thought of as stable from later childhood through adulthood, until the pesky effects of aging begin to make themselves felt. In fact, cross-sectional studies of perception show developmental **continuity** in some spheres, but discontinuities in others. In perceiving symmetry, for example, Bornstein (1982; Bornstein et al., 1981) found that young infants preferred and processed vertical better than horizontal better than oblique, Bornstein and

Stiles-Davis (1984) found that among 4- to 6-year-olds vertical symmetry possesses the highest perceptual advantage (e.g., in discrimination and memory), then horizontal, and then oblique, and Fisher and Bornstein (1982) also found vertical and horizontal to be special *vis-à-vis* oblique in adults.

The window of modifiability in perceptual adaptation appears to open early in life, so that organisms can prepare quickly, efficiently, and optimally for the particular ecology in which they develop. This is not to say that structural or functional change in maturity does not occur; special experiences can effect both structural and functional changes pertinent to perception. Gould, Reeves, Graziano, and Gross (1999; Gould, Vail, Wagers, & Gross, 2001) demonstrated hippocampal neurogenesis in the adult macaque but noted that new cortical neurons, like all new neurons, tend to have a transitory existence, perhaps related to a role in learning (Gould, 2007; Gross, 2000; Leuner, Gould, & Shors, 2006). The human brain adapts to moment-to-moment changes in experience even in adulthood and with unsuspected speed. The brain may have networks of silent connections that underlie its plasticity, and rapid reorganized responses to sensory information reflect rewiring in the brain or the growth of new connections through short-term plasticity mechanisms. The visual cortex changes its response almost immediately to sensory deprivation and to new input (Dilks, Baker, Liu, & Kanwisher, 2009). The capacity to change is a fundamental characteristic of the nervous system and can be seen in even the simplest of organisms, such as the tiny worm *Caenorhabditis elegans* that has only 302 cells.

One of the most intriguing questions in neuroscience concerns the ways in which the nervous system modifies its organization and ultimately its psychological function throughout an individual's lifetime. Adults who speak tone languages (such as Mandarin Chinese) process pitch with greater accuracy than do adults who speak non-tone languages (such as English): They can repeat a word on the same note or begin a song on the same note (Deutsch, Henthorn, & Dolson, 2004), and they are more likely to possess absolute pitch (Deutsch et al., 2004). The Eguchi method is used around Japan to teach perfect pitch to very young children (claiming a success rate of almost 100 percent for those who start before they are 4 years old). At home, the parent instructs by playing the C chord a few times every day, and the child, sitting where he or she cannot see the keyboard, raises the red flag. After some weeks, a second chord and flag are added. Now the child has to raise a yellow flag for an F major chord, and the red for a C. Eventually all the white-key chords are associated with colored flags, then all black keys. The child names the chord only by its color. Training is not effective after 8. (There is a test of perfect pitch at www.acoustics.org/press/157th/deutsch3.htm.) Furthermore, language experience and early musical training appear to interact: Early trained musicians with absolute pitch are more common among speakers of tone than non-tone languages (Deutsch, Henthorn, Marvin, & Xu, 2006). Behavioral changes in function are often associated with maturation, learning, and memory; however, behavioral changes also imply changes in properties or organization of neural circuitry that underlies the behavior (Kandel, 2007). Conversely, nervous system changes induced by experience imply corresponding change in function. In order to drive a traditional black cab in London, drivers have to gain what is colloquially referred to as "the knowledge"—an intimate acquaintance with the myriad streets in a 6-mile radius of Charing Cross. Mastery can take up to 3 years of hard training, and three-quarters of those who embark on the course drop out. Taxi drivers given MRIs by Maguire et al. (2000) had a larger hippocampus compared to controls. The hippocampus is a part of the brain associated with navigation in birds and animals. Moreover, the hippocampus was larger in taxi drivers who spent more time on the job. Another example of such structural change was provided by Elbert, Pantev, Weinbruch, Rockstroh, and Taub (1995), who used magnetic encephalography (MEG) to map the somatosensory cortex of adults with and without experience of playing a stringed instrument (e.g., guitar or violin).

The area of the somatosensory cortex in musicians that represented the fingers of the left hand (the hand requiring greater fine motor learning, as it is used on the finger board) was larger than the area represented by the right hand (which is used to bow), and larger than the left-hand area in nonmusicians. Adult human brains appear to reorganize themselves based on particular experiences, in these cases musical training and taxi driving. Thus, the healthy adult human brain has the capacity for local plastic changes in structure in response to environmental experiences and demands.

Moving from purely structural change to structure–function relations that reflect specific or unique experience, Tsunoda (1985) developed a behavioral method to evaluate cerebral dominance: He asked adults to tap out a rhythm fed to one ear as he provided the other ear with a half-second-delayed variable-intensity feedback. At some intensity level, the feedback disrupts perception, and the person can no longer tap out the correct rhythm. When the two ears are compared, a performance advantage emerges for the ear with greater resistance to disruption, and ear advantage indicates contralateral hemispheric dominance. Tsunoda examined laterality for all sorts of stimuli, including many basic parameters of language. He showed that predominantly right-handed individuals possess the expected left-hemisphere processing advantage for language stimuli (e.g., consonant–vowel and consonant–vowel– consonant combinations) and the expected right-hemisphere advantage for processing steady-state vowels. With Japanese adults, however, Tsunoda found a left-hemisphere processing advantage for steady-state vowels; that is, Japanese process vowels as verbal sounds in the left hemisphere. Tsunoda also used independent electrophysiological confirmation of this hemispheric difference between Japanese and Western people. Japanese is a vowel-rich language: Like English, Japanese has five major vowels, but vowels alone and in combinations can uniquely constitute words in Japanese. For example, *e* means "picture," *o* means "tail," *ii* means "good," and *ao* means "bluish"; vowels can be used as phrases and whole sentences, too: *oi o ooi* means "concealing old age," *ai o ou* means "he seeks love," and *ooo, oooo, oo ooo* means "the courageous king conceals his tail when he goes out." Simply put, these vowels are not pure sounds in Japanese, but signify meaning, and they are processed in the language-dominant hemisphere in Japanese people. Notably, second- and third-generation Japanese speakers of foreign languages, as well as Asians of other nationalities, consistently give Western right-hemisphere patterns of responses. Thus, experience with language rewires brain dominance patterns and influences function.

In overview, changes in the cortex likely reflect the differential sensitivity and plasticity of the brain to experience, and changed cortical structures pave the way for enhanced perceptual performance in related and relevant tasks. Although the brain was once regarded as a rather static organ, it is now clear that the organization of brain circuitry is constantly changing as a function of experience. Brain structure and behavior can be influenced by myriad factors, including an unexpectedly wide range of prenatal and postnatal experiences.

Perception in Old Age

Many structures and functions in the body deteriorate from their peak performance in early adulthood, although not all do (Birren & Schaie, 1990; Schneider & Rowe, 1990; Stevens, Cruz, Marks, & Lakatos, 1998). Corso (1987) noted that many anatomical and physiological characteristics of the visual system decline with age; for example, the size of the useful visual field, distance acuity, dynamic and static sensitivity, color perception of blue and green, and depth perception (Fozard, 1990; Greene & Madden, 1987; Knoblauch, Vital-Durand, & Barbur, 2001; Matjucha & Katz, 1993; Sekuler & Ball, 1986). Hearing thresholds change, and in old age there is considerable hearing loss at frequencies that result in speech hearing difficulties (Strouse, Ashmead, Ohde, & Grantham, 1998; Wallace, Hayes, & Jerger, 1993).

Less than 1% of individuals 17 to 20 years of age fail to discriminate odor qualities, whereas nearly 50% of individuals 65 to 88 years of age fail to do so, and, even among the half of elderly who discriminate odors, performance in odor identification is worse than that of younger people (Doty, 1993; Schemper, Voss, & Cain, 1981). Happily, deterioration is not a rule of aging. Taste, which like smell plays an important part in enhancing the quality of life as well as in alerting us to danger, constitutes a telling contrast. Taste receptor cells have relatively short life spans and are constantly replaced; we happily retain our sense of taste in aging.

When perceptual function is observed to decline in old age, the significant question turns on cause: Is nervous system degeneration and organ impairment or diminished psychological judgment involved? Some types of poor performance in old age seem clearly to reflect underlying neural or sensory change. For example, conduction velocity of nerve fibers slows approximately 15% between 20 and 90 years of age, and simple reaction time to lights and sounds concomitantly lengthens 50% over the same period (Bromley, 1974). Some changes reflect anatomical factors. The lens of the eye grows like an onion over the course of the life span, adding layer upon layer. Each layer is pigmented, and so as the lens grows, light must traverse more and more absorptive material before it reaches the retina to be effective in vision. Lens pigment selectively absorbs short-wavelength light, causing perception of blue to systematically attenuate in old age (Bornstein, 2006, 2007). Finally, attention continues to play an important role in perception in later life. Attention is prerequisite to cognition and central to the continued success of many important kinds of behavior. Detailed studies of divided, switching, sustained, and selective attention have (with exceptions of more complex tasks) failed to support popular beliefs that older adults undergo a "global reduction in attentional resources" and that, in consequence, perceptual efficiency and cognitive processes are broadly compromised (Salthouse, Rogan, & Prill, 1984; Somberg & Salthouse, 1982). Some performance declines in old age may reflect a combination of CNS or anatomical deterioration along with adverse changes in judgment.

The question of cause leads to a caveat. Before ascribing differences in perceptual performance to aging processes *per se*, researchers need to take alternative factors into consideration, such as distracters and context. Moreover, beliefs about perceptual and cognitive limitations in older adults may undermine performance (Chasteen, Bhattacharyya, Horhota, Tam, & Hasher, 2005). In studying perceptual processes in the aged, investigators must always also show sensitivity to broader effects associated with age *per se* versus effects of specific neural or sensory disorders.

A survey of adults 18 to 100 years of age revealed that five dimensions of visual function become increasingly problematic in aging: visual processing speed, light sensitivity, dynamic vision, near vision, and visual search (Kosnik, Winslow, Kline, Rasinsiki, & Sekuler, 1988), and 50 years is the average age at which these visual functions begin to change noticeably (Johnson & Choy, 1987). Whatever their cause, changes in perception with aging have implications for everyday life. For example, postural stability depends on visual and auditory information processing (Tanaka, Kojima, Takeda, Ino, & Ifukube, 2001), and falls are a common hazard among the aged. Driving is another example. At night, drivers over age 60 need to be more than 75% closer to highway signs before correctly identifying them than drivers under age 25 (Sivak, Olson, & Pastalan, 1981), and older drivers are less accurate in estimating vehicular motion (Schiff, Oldak, & Shah, 1992), two of many perceptual impairments that doubtlessly factor into the rates of vehicular accidents in older drivers (Marottoli et al., 1998; Owsley, Ball, Sloane, Roenker, & Bruni, 1991). More than 20 states require drivers 70 years or older to pass vision and road tests before they can renew their licenses. Happily, Fozard (1990) pointed out that many perceptual failings of old age are amenable to remediation (with eyeglasses, training, and so forth).

The Life Span Approach to Perception

Insofar as life-span study, as a comprehensive approach to development, entails its own theories and methods, life-span approaches of perceptual development do the same. Some (nurture) theories propose that perceptual development reflects primarily changes in knowledge and experience over the life course (Roth, 1983), whereas other (nature) theories point to life-span changes in biological mechanisms (Kail & Salthouse, 1994; Salthouse, 1991). In addition, both these theories of life-span perceptions point to ∩-shaped efficiency and performance functions, development being most active early and late in the life cycle (Brodeur, Trick, & Enns, 1997). However, one can reasonably expect that specific perceptual structures and functions will follow a diversity of developmental trajectories over the life course.

The questions often asked after infancy are also normally specific to a target age group such as school-age children or teens. As a result, a cohesive story of perceptual development across the entire life span is often difficult to piece together. One notable exception is face perception, a topic that has been investigated in infants, children, and adults alike. From the earliest moments of life, infants respond to face-like stimuli differently from other stimuli (Johnson & Morton, 1991). For example, newborns will follow a schematic face farther than a scrambled face (Johnson, Dziurawiec, Ellis, & Morton, 1991), suggesting that there is something special about facial structure. By 3 days of age, infants recognize the face of their mothers based on visual cues alone, even if they have seen the mother for as little as 5.5 hours during those 3 days (Bushnell, 2001), and newborns show a preference for attractive faces (Quinn & Slater, 2003). As human babies grow (and improve in their acuity), the internal features of faces become more prominent (Turati, Macchi Cassia, Simion, & Leo, 2006). Five-month-old infants can discriminate between a face with typical spacing of the eyes and the eyes and mouth from a face with exaggerated spacing between features (Bhatt, Bertin, Hayden, & Reed, 2005). The privilege for face-like stimuli continues throughout development, and specific deficits in face processing, but not in the processing of other objects, are linked to damage in specific neurological regions (Hadjikhani & de Gelder, 2002). This pattern across the life span has led some to suggest that face processing is in some way different from the processing of other objects due to either an innate mechanism or quickly learned expertise (e.g., Farah, Rabinowitz, Quinn, & Liu, 2000; Gauthier & Nelson, 2001; Johnson, Chapter 4, this volume). The ability to recognize facial identity is critical to culturally appropriate responses to kin, same-gender versus opposite-gender strangers, and so forth (Werker, Maurer, & Yoshida, 2009). At the same time, we need to be skilled at recognizing and discriminating facial expressions, which even young infants are (Bornstein & Arterberry, 2003), as well as other changeable aspects of the face, such as direction of gaze and sounds being spoken that transmit socially relevant information such as threat and acceptance (Johnson, Chapter 4, this volume; Werker et al., 2009).

The study of face perception across the life span has revealed both developmental continuities and discontinuities. One example of continuity has to do with configural face perception. When we look at a face we process many features in relation to each other, called configural or holistic processing (e.g., the nose in relation to the brow), rather than each feature in isolation (e.g., just the nose). One way to test whether a stimulus is perceived configurally or featurally is to present the stimulus upside down. Inverted presentation has all the same features but disrupts configural processing. For example, adults' reaction time and accuracy suffer when they must recognize upside-down faces, and these are much larger differences than are seen for upside-down objects (Freire, Lee, & Symons, 2000; Malcolm, Leung, & Barton, 2005; Mondloch, Geldart, Maurer, & Le Grand, 2003; Mondloch, LeGrand, & Maurer, 2003). Infants, children, and adults process faces configurally rather than featurally: Even if there are slight differences among children and adults in the degree to which a face is processed configurally, when familiarized to upright faces all age groups show better recognition when tested with upright faces than with inverted faces (Mondloch, LeGrand, & Maurer, 2002; Cashon & Cohen, 2004). Configural face processing appears to be tuned by peoples' experience with upright faces. Adults are more sensitive to spacing differences in human than in monkey faces even when the physical differences are identical (Mondloch, Maurer, & Aloha, 2006).

An example of discontinuity in development pertains to perceptions of gender and ethnicity in faces (Kelly et al., 2007; Leinbach & Fagot, 1993). Infants and young children have difficulty perceiving the gender of faces when superficial cues such as hair, makeup, and clothing are removed or covered (Leinbach & Fagot, 1993; Poulin-Dubois, Serbin, Kenyon, & Derbyshire, 1994). Adults, in contrast, are quite good at determining gender (or other facial indicators) relying only on subtle differences in the structure of the face (Bruce et al., 1993), and the most useful cue appears to be the distance between the eye and the eyebrow (Campbell, Benson, Wallace, Doesbergh, & Coleman, 1999). It is not surprising that young children may not home in on this cue for determining gender because they may not yet have achieved gender constancy, which depends on the irrelevancy of superficial features (e.g., you are still female if you have short hair). Development of gender perception may also require a certain level of experience once gender constancy is achieved. Children do not reach adult levels of expertise in recognizing individual faces until adolescence (Bruce et al., 2000; Mondloch et al., 2002, 2003). For example, up to at least 10 years, children are not as good as adults at recognizing a face previously seen from a different point of view (Mondloch et al., 2003). Moreover, even adolescents differ from adults in how they read emotional expressions on a face as well as in the parts of the brain underlying that reading. Yurgelun-Todd (2002) scanned teens and adults using fMRI at the same time as she asked them to report about the emotion on a series of faces. Adults identified one emotion as fear, but many teenagers saw something different, such as shock or anger. Adults also used a recently evolved brain system, the prefrontal cortex, which plays a role in self-regulation. Teenagers use a different part of their brain when reading the images. Teens activated the amygdala, a brain center that mediates fear and other "gut" reactions, more than the frontal lobe. (Among older and older teens, brain activity during this task shifted to the frontal lobe.)

Next, we consider the roles of biology and experience in perceptual development more broadly.

THE ROLES OF BIOLOGY AND EXPERIENCE IN PERCEPTUAL DEVELOPMENT

All human beings are believed to be endowed with roughly the same perceptual anatomy and physiology, so it is reasonable to expect that most perceptual structures or functions are essentially universal and that all human beings begin life on much the same perceptual footing. How do varying experiences, say rearing circumstances, influence perceptual development? In many ways our perceptual systems appear to be unperturbed by normal (if large) variation in environmental stimulation. For example, children and adults from rural villages in New Guinea (Kennedy & Ross, 1975), Ethiopia (Deregowski, 1977), and Ghana (Jahoda, Deregowski, Ampene, & Williams, 1977), where representational arts were unknown, reportedly identify or recognize immediately two-dimensional realistic representations of three-dimensional objects. Infant studies support this nativist view (Dirks & Gibson, 1977), as does a study of a 19-month-old Western child whose parents exposed him to and named a wide variety of toys and other solid objects, but who was never told the name or meaning of any picture or depicted object and was generally deprived of seeing pictures (Hochberg & Brooks, 1962). When first tested at almost 2, the child could recognize objects portrayed by two-dimensional line drawings and photographs. In addition, some functions are stable across the life span (such as visual search; Plude, Enns, & Brodeur, 1994), and perceptual features might universally affect other cognitive processes: For example, Malt (1995, p. 117) reviewed evidence to show that many cultures spontaneously categorize entities into recognizable life-form groups (e.g., mammals, fish, and birds) on the basis of their "universal, perceptual features."

As noted earlier, spatial processing is a core component of visual perception, and researchers have documented numerous age-related improvements in the spatial processing of visual information (e.g., Newcombe & Huttlenlocher, 2000; Piaget, 1954). The most explicit accounts of development in this domain have come in the form of neural field models that specify how spatial accuracy in visual processing varies with interactions among layers of neural fields (e.g., Simmering, Schutte, & Spencer, 2008). Consistent with some of the same core assumptions, Mash, Quinn, Dobson, and Narter (1998) found that physical maturation of the visual system accounted for group differences in infants' perceptual organization of spatial relations, while group differences in postnatal visuospatial experience did not convey a measurable effect on performance. Other discussions of maturational effects on visual perception have been motivated by the neurophysiological finding that cortical visual streams segregate in processing an object's identity versus its affordances for action (e.g., Milner & Goodale, 1995). If different pathways process different aspects of the visual environment, different processing capacities may differ in developmental status (Bertenthal, 1996; Mareschal & Johnson, 2003).

There can be little doubt, however, that experience, or a lack thereof, also plays important roles in maintaining, facilitating and attuning, and inducing sight, hearing, smell, taste, and touch. Some perceptions are plastic to experience, and we consider several examples.

Individual Experience: Binocular Disparity Sensitivity, Configural Processing, and Categorization

Binocular disparity sensitivity underlies binocular depth perception, as described earlier. The onset of sensitivity to binocular disparity in children in the United States occurs on average between 14 and 16 weeks of age (Fox et al., 1980; Held et al., 1980). To more clearly understand the development of binocular disparity, Held and his colleagues (Birch, Gwiazda, & Held, 1982; Held et al., 1980) measured disparity sensitivity in infants each week between 10 and 30 weeks of age. The onset of disparity sensitivity is shown in Figure 6.10 for 16 children. Several patterns emerge in these individual graphs: (a) onset of sensitivity is typically rapid, (b) onset occurs at different times for different infants, and (c) at least one infant (see JG) does not begin by 30 weeks. Combining this work with knowledge of development of anatomical structures, the development of disparity sensitivity appears to be a biologically programmed process that is reliant on a specific type of experience, namely, fusion of the two eyes. Without this type of experience within a particular time period, the neural structures for binocular vision do not develop and binocular sensitivity is compromised (e.g., Banks, Aslin & Letson, 1975; Gwiazda & Birch, 2001). A similar longitudinal assessment of sensitivity to pictorial depth cues was conducted by Yonas, Elieff, and Arterberry (2002). Their results revealed variation in the age of onset of depth perception specified by texture gradients and linear perspective, which also suggests a role for experience in the onset of this type of depth information.

Maurer, Lewis, Brent, and Levin (1999) examined the time course of experience in the development of visual acuity by studying infants who were deprived of patterned visual input because they were born with a dense cataract in one or both eyes. Following an average of 3.7 months of visual deprivation, these infants were surgically treated by removal of the affected

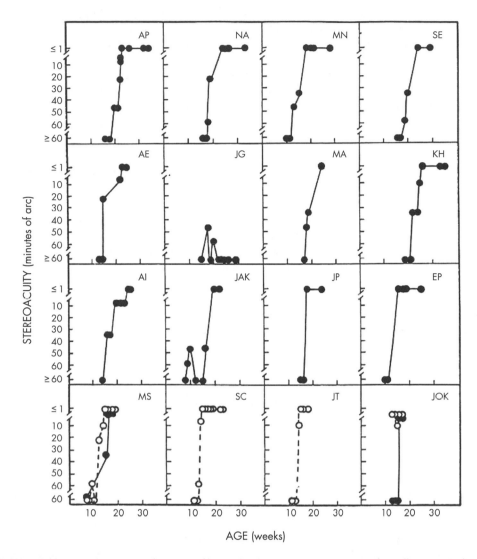

FIGURE 6.10 A study assessing the onset of binocular disparity sensitivity in 16 infants illustrates individual differences in achieving sensitivity, which occurs on average by 16 weeks of age. Smaller numbers indicate finer stereoacuity. From R. Held, E. Birch, & J. Gwiazda. (1980). Stereoacuity in human infants. *Proceedings of the National Academy of Sciences of the United States of America, 77*, 5572–5574. Reprinted with permission.

lenses and by insertion of contact lenses that enabled them for the first time to focus images on their retinas. Tests of visual acuity that were administered within 10 minutes of initial insertion of the new lenses revealed newborn-like acuity among all infants regardless of age. Remarkably, follow-up tests revealed modest but very reliable improvement in visual acuity after just 1 hour of focused visual input. Children who were finally treated after years of delayed visual input could recognize facial expression, follow direction of eye gaze, and identify faces; these tasks all relied on featural processing (Geldart, Mondloch, Maurer, de Schonen, & Brent, 2002; Le Grand, Mondloch, Maurer, & Brent, 2001). However, children treated for bilateral congenital cataracts did not develop configural face processing (Le Grand, Mondloch, Maurer, & Brent, 2004), and they were poor at detecting differences between faces in the spacing of features and recognizing the identity of a face across changes in orientation (Geldart et al., 2002; Le Grand et al., 2001; Le Grand, Mondloch, Maurer, & Brent, 2003). Early visual experience appears to be required for the later development of configural face processing. A final example of the effects of individual experience on face processing illustrates an enhancement rather than a degradation in perception. Children who have been abused and live in homes with high levels of anger and physical violence are faster in recognizing anger than those who have not been abused. Moreover, the speed of recognizing anger is correlated with the level of anger or hostility in the child's environment (Pollak, Messner, Kistler, & Cohn, 2009).

In addition to its sustaining effects in basic sensory processes, infants must also utilize visual experience to form stable representations of the objects and object kinds that they encounter in routine daily life. A large number of studies have demonstrated infants' ability to perceptually categorize exemplars of familiar classes, but very few have controlled infants' actual experience with exemplars prior to their participation in laboratory tasks. Bornstein and Mash (in press) used novel stimulus objects comprising two shape/color categories in a study of 5-month-olds' perceptual **categorization**. One group of infants was shown images of the objects from one category or the other every day at home for 2 months prior to participating in a laboratory categorization task with the same objects. Another group of infants participated in the laboratory task without the prior stimulus experience at home. Although infants in both groups categorized the stimuli, only those in the second group demonstrated any category learning during the task. Infants in the first group categorically organized the experience they had acquired at home, and utilized it systematically in a novel context outside their home.

Cultural Experience: Audition and Speech Perception

Some of the most interesting examples of cross-cultural research informing us of nature–nurture influences on perception come from the auditory and speech perception literatures. We consider two examples, one focusing on hearing loss in the elderly and one on speech perception early in life.

Audition and aging.   Auditory sensitivity (as we learned earlier) is measured by assessing absolute thresholds for sounds of different frequencies. In aging, deterioration in auditory sensitivity is common: In essence, elderly people require more energy to hear certain frequencies than do younger people. As Figure 6.11A shows, among Americans hearing loss in aging is more pronounced at higher frequencies. One prominent and straightforward explanation for this finding has been that aging entails the natural and regular deterioration of anatomical and neural mechanisms that subserve hearing. An alternative hypothesis is that exposure to noise over the course of the life span cumulates and deleteriously affects perception of high frequencies. How can these nature and nurture explanations be adjudicated?

Additional data help; first, from individuals in cultures with other noise histories and, second, from individuals in American society who have contrasting life histories of exposure to noise. As Figure 6.11B shows, older American women experience less hearing loss than do older American men; and Sudanese Africans, who show no gender differences in hearing with age, sustain less hearing deterioration than do Americans of either gender. It could be, however unlikely, that genders and races differ biologically in the integrity or susceptibility of their auditory apparatuses to aging. However, contrary to the initial biological deterioration hypothesis, gender and culture data suggest that physiological aging alone is probably not the sole factor in hearing loss. The data on elderly American men exposed to different amounts of noise over the course of their lifetimes further support an interpretation rooted in experience.

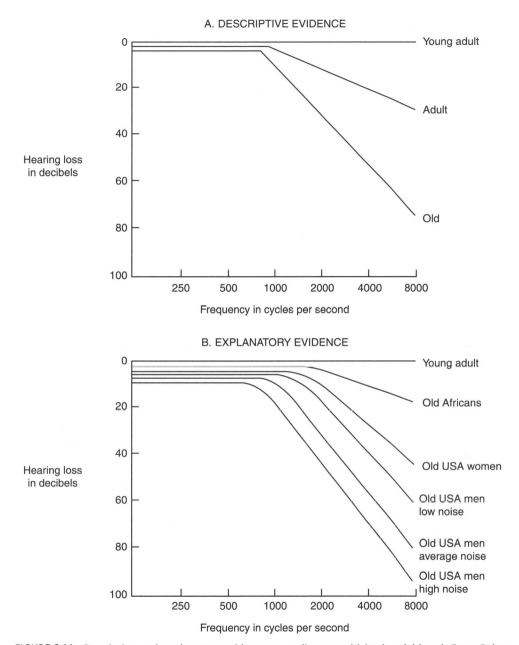

FIGURE 6.11 Descriptive and explanatory evidence on auditory sensitivity in adulthood. From Baltes, Reese, and Nesselroade (1977). Reprinted with permission from the authors.

Findings from this third research source—effects of noise history—reinforce the view that hearing loss in old age perhaps relates more to level of exposure to noise and less to natural physiological deterioration, just as cultural experience affects perception by improving processing of faces from one's own ethnic group than those from other groups. The three research programs together supplement the original descriptive evidence with explanatory evidence and invest greater credence in nurture. Of course, the fact that noise history selectively affects high frequencies indicates that nature and nurture interact. Indeed, Tokyo police have availed themselves of this fact to fight crime. In Kitashikahama Park in Adachi Ward, neighborhood teenagers, probably from a local junior high school, were defacing property. Authorities rented a British-made Mosquito MK4 Anti-Vandal System and screwed it into a wall not far from park toilets. The device emits a high-pitched, highly irritating whine that has a frequency above 17,000 Hz. Most adults cannot hear it, but teens can. Seven days a week, the whining begins at 11 p.m. and continues until 4 a.m. Video surveillance cameras that monitor park buildings attest that Kitashikahama Park empties out.

Infant speech perception.   Another illustration of the ways nature and nurture interact in perceptual development is provided by a single perceptual domain in which multiple pathways of development have been explored. This domain is a narrow but important one in speech perception (Saffran et al., 2006).

Sounds are essentially different sine-wave frequencies produced simultaneously, and speech is the complex array of different frequencies produced at different intensities over time. Spoken language abstracts particular subsets from the universe of all possible speech sounds (phonetics) and invests some with meaning (phonemics). One dimension along which certain phonemes in many languages are distinguished is their voicing. Differences in voicing are perceived when a speaker produces different frequencies of sound waves at slightly different times. In voicing, a sound like /b/ (pronounced "ba") is produced by vibrating the vocal cords and producing higher frequencies before or at the same time the lips are opened and low-frequency energy is released—/b/ is a voiced phoneme. By contrast, for sounds like /p/ (pronounced "pa") the vocal cords do not begin to vibrate higher frequencies until some time after the lips release lower frequencies—/p/ is a voiceless phoneme. Thus, high-frequency components of a sound may precede low-frequency components, low- and high-frequency components may begin simultaneously, or high-frequency may follow low-frequency. The relative onset times of low and high frequencies cue phonemic perceptions. Physically, the relative onsets of low- and high-frequency components of a sound vary continuously with time; however, adults perceive differences in voicing more or less categorically. That is, although we can distinguish many differences in relative onset times of low- and high-frequency sounds, we classify some different sounds as equivalent while discriminating others. English distinguishes voiced–voiceless /b/–/p/. Of course, different people say /b/ and /p/ in different ways; yet adult listeners seldom misidentify particular speech sounds, as they employ implicit category definitions to allot a given sound to either the /b/ or the /p/ category. Cross-language research has revealed that adults hear one, two, or at most three categories of voicing: prevoiced, voiced, and voiceless. Categorical perception means that, across a nearly infinite spectrum of minute discriminable possibilities, only a small number are functionally distinguished, and they are distinguished by nearly all peoples despite wide language differences.

Many researchers speculate that phenomena so ubiquitous, consistent, circumscribed, and significant in human behavior as perceptual categories of speech sounds might have a biological foundation. To test this assumption, Eimas, Siqueland, Jusczyk, and Vigorito (1971) sought to discover whether preverbal human infants perceive acoustic changes in voicing categorically, that is, in a manner parallel to adult phonemic perception. These investigators arranged to ask infants some simple same–different questions about their auditory perceptions using the habituation–recovery paradigm. They found that 1- and 4-month-olds behaved as though they perceived speech sounds in the adult-like categorical manner: Babies distinguished examples of /b/ from /p/, but not examples of two different /b/s. That is, babies categorize variations of sounds as either voiced or voiceless long before they use language or presumably have extensive experience in hearing language. This result seemed to suggest that categorical perception is innate. Returning to Figure 6.1, it would seem that categorical perception of phonemes closely fits the topmost developmental function: It is fully developed at the onset of experience and might require language experience for maintenance purposes only.

However, the experiment does not conclusively rule out roles for maturation or experience in perceptual development. After all, the infants who participated in the Eimas experiment were born into monolingual English-speaking families in which the voiced–voiceless distinction they discriminated is common (as in *baby* vs. *papa*), and fetuses hear and process sounds from outside the womb (e.g., DeCasper & Spence, 1986) so that even 1-month-old babies have months of experience with the language. In a follow-up study, monolingual English or Spanish newborns were examined using a procedure in which their sucking controlled how long English or Spanish language was played to them (Moon, Cooper, & Fifer, 1993): During the last 6 minutes (of 18 minutes), the infants sucked more to hear their native language than the nonnative language. This is evidence for an experience-specific newborn preference. Newborns (up to 4 days old) also prefer to hear their mother's voice (Decasper & Fifer, 1980), a preference that likely reflects prenatal exposure and learning because it is selective to the mother's, not the father's or a stranger's, voice (Kisilevsky et al., 2003). It could be that categorical perception is partially developed at the onset of experience and then its continuing development is facilitated or attuned by early experience. This is the middle course in Figure 6.1. It could even be that categorical perception is undeveloped until the onset of experience, and that experience in hearing language over several months of prenatal development and months of postnatal development quickly induces these sophisticated auditory perceptions, following the bottom course in Figure 6.1.

Although surveys of the world's languages show that only three categories of voicing are common, not all languages use all categories. Eimas et al. (1971) tested only an English-language category in their babies. Several researchers have since provided data indicating that infants born in different places possess some or all of the same categories, although the adults in their cultures do not. Lasky, Syrdal-Lasky, and Klein (1975) found that 4- and 6-month-olds in Spanish-speaking (Guatemalan) monolingual families discriminated the English voice–voiceless sound contrast that is close to, but not the same as, the Spanish one. Likewise, Streeter (1976) found that Kenyan 2-month-olds from families that speak Kikuyu categorized the English voicing contrast that is not present in Kikuyu as well as a Kikuyu prevoiced–voiced contrast that is not present in English. Spanish- and Kikuyu-speaking adults perceive (although they do not use) the universal English voicing contrast, but they perceive it only weakly. The phoneme inventory shows other differences among languages. Young Japanese-learning infants can discriminate contrasts that are used in English but not in Japanese; young English-learning infants can discriminate consonant contrasts that are used in Czech, Hindi, Nthlakampx, Spanish, and Zulu (Werker et al., 2009).

The rise or persistence of perceptions, even in the absence of relevant experience, probably reflects their foundation in the natural, resilient psychoacoustic properties of the auditory system. Perhaps general experience with the wide range of sounds produced in the natural environment is sufficient to maintain sensitivities that are native to the perceptual apparatus. By the end of the first year of life, long before many infants have even acquired their first word, speech perception capacities have been modified to match the properties of the sound structure of the native language. Nor are these kinds of effects unique to speech. Infants and adults are noticeably better at recognizing a face if the face is from their own ethnic group than from another ethnic group (e.g., Kelly et al., 2007; Meissner & Brigham, 2001), and this effect obtains for Africans, Japanese, Koreans, Chinese, East Indians as well as European Americans and African Americans. The effect appears to be the product of experience with faces from other ethnic groups, and its strength depends on the level of exposure to people of other ethnicities (Hancock & Rhodes, 2008).

Conclusions.   The influences of nature and nurture are integrally entwined. Yet assessment of their differential contributions is critical to understanding the life-span ontogeny of perceptual processes. An additional benefit of developmental investigations derives from information they afford regarding prevention: In the auditory illustration, whereas descriptive evidence alone strongly implicates biological deterioration, alleviation might best be achieved, for example, through specialized hearing aids for the elderly; the explanatory evidence, which derives from diverse biological and experiential comparisons in development, points to more productive intervention strategies that would effectively obviate sensory deterioration and hearing loss in the first place.

Such research also will determine the limits of a specific ability's plasticity as well as which experiences are most influential in its expression. Overall, our physical and perceptual experiences appear sufficiently common to render our perceptions more or less similar. When contingencies vary sufficiently, however, perceptions are sure to follow (Cole & Packer, Chapter 2, this volume).

Differential cultural experience has even been found to affect children's and adults' understanding of perception itself (Lillard, 1998). In the European American *weltanschauung*, people are believed to possess five senses (sight, hearing, smell, taste, and touch), each sense providing a different kind of information about the world. Even European American children know this by age 3, asserting, for example, that to know a toy dinosaur is red they would have to see it (Pillow, 1989). Not all cultures subscribe to this European American view: The Hausa (Nigeria) linguistically mark only two senses: *Gani* refers to sight only and is not used to denote knowing or understanding, and *Ji* refers to hearing, smelling, tasting, and feeling in the sense of knowing (Ritchie, 1991). These must be cultural differences in emphasis because Hausa certainly distinguish the smell of cooking from hearing an airplane overhead. Cultures also vary in terms of how they rank the senses: Vision predominates among European Americans, but for the Ongee (South Pacific) olfaction predominates (Pandya, 1987, as cited in Lillard, 1998), for the Hausa taste is the most important sense (Ritchie, 1991), and for the Suya (Brazil) hearing is: European Americans say "I see" to mean "I know" or "I understand," whereas the Suya say "I hear" (Seeger, 1981). Again, the different preferences are likely a matter of different cultural emphasis, rather than perceptual ability or acumen (although they might be), and this cultural variability moves us away from biological determinism.

CONCLUSIONS

We take in information from the world through our senses, and we begin to make sense of the world through our perceptual systems. Perception is among the oldest and most venerable fields of study in psychology and among the most closely tied to psychology's origins in philosophy. Studies of infancy constitute the bulk of research in perceptual development, and studies of perceptual development have in the past constituted the bulk of research on infancy. However, perceptual development is a lifelong process, even if much of perceptual development in childhood and after is bound up with more comprehensive and overarching developments in cognition. Human beings begin life with perceptual capacities primed to acquire information and knowledge that is requisite to survive in their ecology. Specific experiences interact with developing sensitivities to induce, maintain, or attune perception to optimally match those ecological requirements.

In recent years, the perceptual secrets of infants and young children—formidable and intractable as they once seemed—have given way to a variety of ingenious procedural techniques. Research shows that even the very young of our own species perceive beyond simply sensing. But several traditional and important questions about perceptual development are still open, left unanswered even by the wealth of research amassed in recent decades. Moreover, many startling revelations that spring to mind even from our simplest introspections continue to spark curiosity about perceptual development. How do we move so effortlessly from sensing patterns received and transduced at the surface of the body to perceiving objects and events in the real world? How is a world that is constantly in flux perceived as stable? As context is so influential in perception, how does selective attention to signal and figure develop in coordination with selective elimination of noise and ground? How do perceived objects come to be invested with meaning?

The development of perceptual capabilities should not be viewed as isolated events. The study of perceptual development naturally spills over into studies of neural, motor, cognitive, language, emotional, and social development, as chapters in other parts of this textbook attest. Perception needs to be understood in terms of a systems model, that is, a unifying conception of different components mutually influencing one another (Thelen & Smith, 1994). Development in this perspective is dynamic in the sense that the organization of the system as a whole changes with maturity and the acquisition of new experiences. Moreover, as one subsystem emerges, the change brings with it a host of new experiences that influence and are influenced by changes in related systems. Thus, change is not only dynamic but also thoroughgoing, taking place at many levels in the system and affecting many other levels of the system at the same time.

The study of perception across the life span has widely acknowledged practical implications, in its relevance to social and emotional development and to education and medicine. Physical and social stimulation are perceptual stimulation, and many aspects of emotional and social development depend initially on perceptual capacity. Specific examples abound— from the neonate's perception and consequent ability to read facial expressions (Bornstein & Arterberry, 2003) to the toddler's acceptance of photographs to mediate separation stress from parents (Passman & Longeway, 1982) to the role of attention and perceptual interpretation in normal personality (Achenbach, 1992; Enns & Burak, 1997).

In the past, experimental traditionalists have expressed reluctance at adding a developmental perspective to the formal study of sensation and perception, psychophysics, and the like—developmental science often being treated as a different field—and the experimental study of sensation and perception was confined largely to adults and to infrahuman animals. Today, research progress with infant, child, and aged populations demonstrates the broadly informative contribution of the developmental view. Knowledge of the developmental perspective is now regarded as essential by all enlightened students of perception.

Perceptual development could serve as a model of developmental studies, one as good as that of any field described in this textbook. It encompasses important questions of philosophy and methodology, and it confronts all of the overarching theoretical and empirical issues in developmental study. Some perceptual capacities are given congenitally and function stably with growth, whereas other perceptual capacities develop and change from infancy through maturity. This ontogenesis, in turn, has several possible sources: Development may be genetically motivated and transpire largely on the *élan* of maturational forces, or it may be experiential and in the main respond to the influences of the environment and of particular life events. At one time or another, the éclat of each of these possibilities has been championed. Modern studies have informed a modern view, however, that perceptual development doubtlessly reflects the complex transaction of a diversity of biological and experiential forces. Through their systematic efforts at studying perception from infancy through maturity, developmental scientists have determined that basic mechanisms help to impose perceptual structure, but that perceptual development is also determined and guided by a transaction of these structural endowments with self-constructed or environment-provided experience.

Thus, neither nativism nor empiricism holds sway in contemporary views of life-span perceptual development; rather, biology and experience co-determine how we first come—and continue—to perceive the world as we do.

REFERENCES AND SUGGESTED READINGS (⌓)

Achenbach, T. A. (1992). Developmental psychopathology. In M. H. Bornstein & M. E. Lamb (Eds.), *Developmental psychology: An advanced textbook* (3rd ed.). Hillsdale, NJ: Lawrence Erlbaum Associates.

Adamson, L. B., & Chance, S. E. (1998). Coordinating attention to people, objects, and language. In A. M. Wetherby, S. F. Warren & J. Reichle (Eds.), *Transition in prelinguistic communication: Preintentional to intentional and presymbolic to symbolic* (pp. 15–37). Baltimore: Brookes.

Adolph, K. E., Eppler, M. A., & Gibson, E. J. (1993). Crawling versus walking in infants' perception of affordances for locomotion over sloping surfaces. *Child Development, 64*, 1158–1174.

Arterberry, M. E. (2008). Infants' sensitivity to the depth cue of height-in-the-picture-plane. *Infancy, 13*, 544–555.

Arterberry, M. E., & Yonas, A. (1988). Infants' sensitivity to kinetic information for three-dimensional object shape. *Perception & Psychophysics, 44*, 1–6.

Arterberry, M. E., & Yonas, A. (2000). Perception of structure from motion by 8-week-old infants. *Perception and Psychophysics, 62*, 550–556.

Aslin, R. N. (1981). Experiential influences and sensitive periods in perceptual development: A unified model. In R. N. Aslin, J. R. Alberts, & M. R. Peterson (Eds.), *Development of perception: Psychobiological perspectives. Vol. 2: The visual system.* New York: Academic Press.

Aslin, R. N., Pisoni, D. B., Hennessy, B. L., & Perey, A. J. (1981). Discrimination of voice onset time by human infants: New findings and implications for the effect of early experience. *Child Development, 51*, 1135–1145.

Aslin, R. N., & Shea, S. L. (1990). Velocity thresholds in human infants: Implications for the perception of motion. *Developmental Psychology, 26*, 589–598.

Baltes, P. B., Reese, H. W., & Nesselroade, J. R. (1977). *Life-span developmental psychology: Introduction to research methods.* Monterey, CA: Brooks/Cole.

Banks, M. S., Aslin, R. N., & Letson, R. D. (1975). Sensitive period for the development of human binocular vision. *Science, 190*, 675–677.

Barlow, H.B. (1953). Summation and inhibition in the frog's retina. *Journal of Physiology, 119*, 69–88.

Barnet, A. B., Lodge, A., & Armington, J. C. (1965). Electroretinogram in newborn human infants. *Science, 148*, 651–654.

Bartlett, J. C. & Searcy, J. (1993). Inversion and configuration of faces. *Cognitive Psychology, 25*, 281–316.

Beauchamp, G. K., Cowart, B. J., Mennella, J. A., & Marsh, R. R. (1994). Infant salt taste: Developmental, methodological, and contextual factors. *Developmental Psychobiology, 27*, 353–365.

Bergström, R. M. (1969). Electrical parameters of the brain during ontogeny. In R. J. Robinson (Ed.), *Brain and early behavior: Development in the fetus and infant.* New York: Academic Press.

Berntson, G. G., & Boysen, S. T. (1990). Cardiac indices of cognition in infants, children, and chimpanzees. In C. Rovee-Collier & L. P. Lipsitt (Eds.), *Advances in infancy research* (Vol. 6). Norwood, NJ: Ablex.

Bertenthal, B. I. (1996) Origins and early development of perception, action, and representation. *Annual Review of Psychology, 47*, 431–459.

Bertenthal, B., Campos, J., & Haith, M. M. (1980). Development of visual organization: Perception of subjective contours. *Child Development, 51*, 1072–1080.

Best, C. T., & McRoberts, G. W. (2003). Infant perception of non-native consonant contrasts that adults assimilate in different ways. *Language & Speech, 46*, 183–216.

Best, C. T., McRoberts, G. W., LaFleur, R. & Silver-Isenstadt, J. (1995). Divergent developmental patterns for infants' perception of two nonnative consonant contrasts. *Infant Behavior and Development, 18*, 339–350.

Best, C. T., McRoberts, G. W., & Sithole, N. N. (1988). The phonological basis of perceptual loss for non-native contrasts: Maintenance of discrimination among Zulu clocks by English-speaking adults and infants. *Journal of Experimental Psychology: Human Perception and Performance, 14*, 345–360.

Bhatt, R. S., Bertin, E., Hayden, A., and Reed, A. (2005). Face processing in infancy: Developmental changes in the use of different kinds of relational information. *Child Development, 76*, 169–181.

Birch, E. E., Gwiazda, J., & Held, R. (1982). Stereoacuity development for crossed and uncrossed disparities in human infants. *Vision Research, 22*, 507–513.

⌓ Birren, J. E., & Schaie, K. W. (Eds.). (1990). *Handbook of the psychology of aging.* San Diego, CA: Academic Press.

Booth, J., Perfetti, C., MacWhinney, B., & Hunt, S. (2000). The association of rapid temporal perception with orthographic and phonological processing in children and adults with reading impairment. *Scientific Studies of Reading, 4*, 101–132.

Bornstein, M. H. (1982). Perceptual anisotropies in infancy: Ontogenetic origins and implications of inequality in spatial vision. In H. W. Reese & L. P. Lipsitt (Eds.), *Advances in child development and behavior* (Vol. 16). New York: Academic Press.

Bornstein, M. H. (1985). Habituation of attention as a measure of visual information processing in human infants: Summary, systematization, and synthesis. In G. Gottlieb & N. A. Krasnegor (Eds.), *Measurement of audition and vision in the first year of postnatal life: A methodological overview*. Norwood, NJ: Ablex.

Bornstein, M. H. (1987). Perceptual categories in vision and in audition. In S. Harnad (Ed.), *Categorical perception*. New York: Cambridge University Press.

Bornstein, M. H. (2006). Hue categorization and color naming: Physics to sensation to perception. In N. J. Pitchford & C. P. Biggam (Eds.), *Progress in colour studies, Volume II. Psychological aspects* (pp. 35–68). Amsterdam/Philadelphia: John Benjamins.

Bornstein, M. H. (2007). Hue categorization and color naming: Cognition to language to culture. In R. E. MacLaury, G. V. Paramei, & D. Dedrick (Eds.), *Anthropology of color: Interdisciplinary multilevel modeling* (pp. 3–27). Amsterdam/Philadelphia: John Benjamins.

Bornstein, M. H., & Arterberry, M. E. (2003). Recognition, discrimination, and categorization of smiling by 5-month-old infants. *Developmental Science, 6*, 585–599.

Bornstein, M. H., & Bornstein, L. (2008). Psychological stability. In W. A. Darity, Jr. (Ed.), *International encyclopedia of social sciences* (2nd ed., Vol. 8, pp. 74–75). Detroit, MI: Macmillan Reference USA.

Bornstein, M. H., & Colombo, J. (2010). Infant cognitive functioning and child mental development. In S. Pauen & M. H. Bornstein (Eds.), *Early childhood development and later achievement*. New York: Cambridge University Press.

Bornstein, M. H., Ferdinandsen, K., & Gross, C. G. (1981). Perception of symmetry in infancy. *Developmental Psychology, 17*, 82–86.

Bornstein, M. H., Gross, J., & Wolf, J. (1978). Perceptual similarity of mirror images in infancy. *Cognition, 6*, 89–116.

Bornstein, M. H., Kessen, W., & Weiskopf, S. (1976). The categories of hue in infancy. *Science, 191*, 201–202.

Bornstein, M. H., & Mash, C. (in press). Experience-based and on-line categorization of objects in early infancy. *Child Development*.

Bornstein, M. H., & Stiles-Davis, J. (1984). Discrimination and memory for symmetry in young children. *Developmental Psychology, 20*, 639–649.

Bornstein, M. H., & Suess, P. E. (2000). Child and mother cardiac vagal tone: Continuity, stability, and concordance across the first 5 years. *Developmental Psychology, 36*, 54–65.

Boynton, R. M., & Gordon, J. (1965). Bezold-Brüke hue shift measured by color-naming technique. *Journal of the Optical Society of America, 55*, 78–86.

Brodeur, D. A., Trick, L. M., & Enns, J. T. (1997). Selective attention over the lifespan. In J. A. Burack & J. T. Enns (Eds.), *Attention, development, and psychopathology*. New York: Guilford.

Bromley, D. B. (1974). *The psychology of human aging*. Harmondsworth, UK: Penguin.

Brown, M. A., & Smelka, R. C. (1995). *MRI: Basic principles and applications*. New York: Wiley-Liss.

Bruce, V., Campbell, R. N., Doherty-Sneddon, G., Import, A., Langton, S., McAuley, S., et al. (2000). Testing face processing skills in children. *British Journal of Developmental Psychology, 18*, 319–333.

Bruce, V., & Humphreys, G. W. (Eds.). (1994). *Object and face recognition* [Special issue of *Visual cognition*]. Hove, UK: Lawrence Erlbaum Associates.

Bruce, V., Burton, A. M., Hanna, E., Healey, P., Mason, O., Coombes, A., et al. (1993). Sex discrimination: How do we tell the difference between male and female faces? *Perception, 22*, 131–152.

Burns, T. C. Yoshida, K. A., Hill, K., Werker, J. F. (2007). Bilingual and monolingual infant phonetic development. *Applied Psycholinguistics, 28*, 455–474.

Bushnell, I. W. R. (2001). Mother's face recognition in newborn infants: Learning and memory. *Infant and Child Development, 10*, 67–74.

Bushnell, I. W. R., Sai, F. & Mullin, J. T. (1989). Neonatal recognition of the mother's face. *British Journal of Developmental Psychology, 7*, 3–15.

Butterworth, G. E. (1989). Events and encounters in infancy. In A. Slater & J. G. Bremner (Eds.), *Infant development*. Hove, UK: Lawrence Erlbaum Associates.

Campbell, R., Benson, P. J., Wallace, S. B., Doesbergh, S., & Coleman, M. (1999). More about brows: How poses that change brow position affect perceptions of gender. *Perception, 28*, 489–504.

Carey, S. (1982). Semantic development: The state of the art. In G. Wanner & L. R. Gleitman (Eds.), *Language acquisition: The state of the art*. New York: Cambridge University Press.

Carey, S., & Diamond, R. (1994). Are faces perceived as configurations more by adults than by children? In V. Bruce & G. W. Humphreys (Eds.), *Object and face recognition* [Special issue of *Visual Cognition*] (pp. 253–274). Hove, UK: Lawrence Erlbaum Associates.

Carey, S., Diamond, R., & Woods, B. (1980). Development of face recognition: A maturational component? *Developmental Psychology*, *16*, 257–269.

Carroo, A. (1986). Other race recognition: A comparison of black American and African subjects. *Perceptual and Motor Skills*, *62*, 135–138.

Case, R. (1998). The development of conceptual structures. In W. Damon (Ed.), *Handbook of child psychology* (Vol. 2, pp. 745–800). New York: Wiley.

Cashon, C. H., & Cohen, L. B. (2004). Beyond U-shaped development in infants' processing of faces: An information-processing account. *Journal of Cognition and Development*, *5*, 59–80.

Chance, J., Goldstein, A., & McBride, L. (1975). Differential experience and recognition memory for faces. *Journal of Social Psychology*, *97*, 243–253.

Chasteen, A. L., Bhattacharyya, S., Horhota, M., Tam, R., & Hasher, L. (2005). How feelings of stereotype threat influence older adults' memory performance. *Experimental Aging Research*, *31*, 235–260.

Cheour, M., Ceponiene, R., Lehtokoski, A., Luuk, A., Allik, J., Alho, K., et al. (1998). Development of language-specific phoneme representations in the infant brain. *Nature Neuroscience*, *1*, 351–353.

Chugani, H. T. (1994). Development or regional brain glucose metabolism in relation to behavior and plasticity. In G. Dawson & K. Fischer (Eds.), *Human behavior and the developing brain*. New York: Guilford.

Cohen, L. B., & Cashon, C. H. (2001). Do 7-month-old infants process independent features or facial configurations? *Infant and Child Development*, *10*, 83–92.

Coles, M. G. H., & Rugg, M. D. (1995). Event-related brain potentials: An introduction. In M. D. Rugg & M. G. H. Coles (Eds.), *Electrophysiology of mind: Event-related brain potentials and cognition*. Oxford, UK: Oxford University Press.

Colombo, J. (2001). The development of visual attention in infancy. *Annual Review of Psychology*, *52*, 337–367.

Colombo, J., Richman, W. A., Shaddy, D. J., Greenhoot, A. F., & Maikranz, J. M. (2001). Heart rate-defined phases of attention, look duration, and infant performance in the paired-comparison paradigm. *Child Development*, *72*, 1605–1616.

Conel, J. L. (1959). *The postnatal development of the human cerebral cortex* (Vols. 1–6). Cambridge, MA: Harvard University Press. (Original work published 1939.)

Constable, H., Campbell, B., & Brown, R. (1988). Sectional drawings from science textbooks: An experimental investigation into pupils' understanding. *British Journal of Educational Psychology*, *58*, 89–102.

Corso, J. F. (1987). Sensory-perceptual processes and aging. *Annual Review of Gerontology and Geriatrics*, *7*, 29–55.

Cowart, B. J. (1981). Development of taste perception in humans: Sensitivity and preference throughout the life span. *Psychological Bulletin*, *90*, 43–73.

Craig, K. D., Whitfield, M. F., Grunau, R. V., Linton, J., & Hadjistavropoulos, H. D. (1993). Pain in the preterm neonate: Behavioural and physiological indices. *Pain*, *52*, 287–299.

Crook, C. K. (1987). Taste and olfaction. In P. Salapatek & L. B. Cohen (Eds.), *Handbook of infant perception* (Vol. 1). New York: Academic Press.

Dannemiller, J. L., & Freedland, R. L. (1991). Detection of relative motion by human infants. *Developmental Psychology*, *27*, 67–78.

Darwin, C. (1877). A biographical sketch of an infant. *Mind*, *2*, 286–294.

de Heering, A., Houthuys, S., & Rossion, B. (2007). Holistic face processing is mature at 4 years of age: Evidence from the composite face effect. *Journal of Experimental Child Psychology*, *96*, 57–70.

DeCasper, A. J., & Fifer, W. P. (1980). Of human bonding: Newborns prefer their mothers' voices. *Science*, *280*, 1174–1176.

DeCasper, A. J., & Spence, M. J. (1986). Prenatal maternal speech influences newborns' perception of speech sounds. *Infant Behavior and Development*, *9*, 133–150.

Dehaene-Lambertz, G., Dehaene, S., & Hertz-Pannier, L. (2002). Functional neuroimaging of speech perception in infants. *Science*, *298*, 2013–2015.

Deliège, I., & Sloboda, J. (Eds.). (1996). *Musical beginnings: Origins and development of musical competence*. New York: Oxford University Press.

DeLoache, J. S., Miller, K. F., & Pierroutsakos, S. L. (1998). Reasoning and problem solving. In W. Damon (Ed.), *Handbook of child psychology* (Vol. 2, pp. 801–850). New York: Wiley.

Demetriou, A., & Valanides, N. (1998). A three-level theory of the developing mind: Basic principles and implications for instruction and assessment. In R. J. Sternberg & W. M. Williams (Eds.), *Intelligence, instruction, and assessment: Theory in practice* (pp. 149–199). Mahwah, NJ: Lawrence Erlbaum Associates.

Deregowski, J. B. (1977). An aspect of perceptual organization: Some cross-cultural studies. In H. McGurk (Ed.), *Ecological factors in human development*. Amsterdam: North-Holland.

Descartes, R. (1824). La dioptrique (M. D. Boring, Trans). In V. Coursin (Ed.), *Oeuvres de Descartes*. Paris: np. (Original work published 1638.)

Deutsch, D., Henthorn, T., & Dolson, M. (2004). Speech patterns heard early in life influence later perception of the tritone paradox. *Music Perception*, *21*, 357–372.

Deutsch, D., Henthorn, T., Marvin, E., & Xu, H.-S. (2006). Absolute pitch among American and Chinese conservatory students: Prevalence differences, and evidence for a speech-related critical period. *Journal of the Acoustical Society of America*, *119*, 719–722.

Diamond, R., & Carey, S. (1986). Why faces are and are not special: An effect of expertise. *Journal of Experimental Psychology: General*, *115*, 107–117.

Dilks, D. D., Baker, C. I., Liu, Y., & Kanwisher, N. (2009). "Referred visual sensations": Rapid perceptual elongation after visual cortical deprivation. *Journal of Neuroscience*, *29*, 8960–8964.

Dirks, J., & Gibson, E. (1977). Infants' perception of similarity between live people and their photographs. *Child Development*, *48*, 124–130.

Doty, R. L. (1993). Smell and taste in the elderly. In M. L. Albert & J. E. Knoefel (Eds.), *Clinical neurology of aging*. New York: Oxford University Press.

Dukette, D., & Stiles, J. (1996). Children's analysis of hierarchical patterns: Evidence from a similarity judgment task. *Journal of Experimental Child Psychology*, *63*, 103–140.

Eimas, P. D., Siqueland, E. R., Jusczyk, P., & Vigorito, J. (1971). Speech perception in infants. *Science*, *171*, 303–306.

Elbert, T., Pantev, C., Wienbruch, C., Rockstroh, B., & Taub, E. (1995). Increased cortical representation of the fingers of the left hand in string players. *Science*, *270*, 305–307.

Engen, T. (1982). *The perception of odors*. Toronto, Canada: Academic Press.

Enns, J. T., & Burack, J. A. (1997). Attention, development, and psychopathology: Bridging disciplines. In J. A. Burack & J. T. Enns (Eds.), *Attention, development, and psychopathology*. New York: Guilford.

Enns, J. T., & Girgus, J. S. (1985). Developmental changes in selective and integrative visual attention. *Journal of Experimental Child Psychology*, *40*, 319–337.

Enns, J. T., & Girgus, J. S. (1986). A developmental study of shape integration over space and time. *Developmental Psychology*, *22*, 491–499.

Enns, J. T., & King, K. A. (1990). Components of line-drawing interpretation: A developmental study. *Developmental Psychology*, *26*, 469–479.

Essock, E. A. (1980). The oblique effect of stimulus identification considered with respect to two classes oblique effects. *Perception*, *9*, 37–46.

Fagen, J., Prigot, J., Carroll, M., Pioli, L., Stein, A., & France, A. (1997). Auditory context and memory retrieval in young infants. *Child Development*, *68*, 1057–1066.

Fantz, R. L. (1958). Pattern vision in young infants. *Psychological Record*, *8*, 43–47.

Fantz, R. L. (1964). Visual experience in infants: Decreased attention to familiar patterns relative to novel ones. *Science*, *146*, 668–670.

Fantz, R. L., Ordy, J. M., & Udelf, M. S. (1962). Maturation of pattern vision in infants during the first six months. *Journal of Comparative and Physiological Psychology*, *55*, 907–917.

Farah, M. J., Rabinowitz, C., Quinn, G. E., & Liu, G. T. (2000). Early commitment of neural substrates for face recognition. *Cognitive Neuropsychology*, *17*, 117–123.

Fernandez, M., & Bahrick, L. E. (1994). Infants' sensitivity to arbitrary object–odor pairings. *Infant Behavior and Development*, *17*, 471–474.

Fisher, C. B., & Bornstein, M. H. (1982). Identification of symmetry: Effects of stimulus orientation and head position. *Perception and Psychophysics*, *32*, 443–448.

Fisher, C. B., Bornstein, M. H., & Gross, G. G. (1985). Left–right coding skills related to beginning reading. *Journal of Developmental and Behavioral Pediatrics*, *6*, 279–283.

Fletcher, K. L., & Reese, E. (2005). Picture book reading with young children: A conceptual framework. *Developmental Review*, *25*, 64–103.

Fox, R., Aslin, R., Shea, S. L., & Dumais, S. (1980). Stereopsis in human infants. *Science*, *207*, 323–324.

Fozard, J. L. (1990). Vision and hearing in aging. In J. E. Birren & K. W. Schaie (Eds.), *Handbook of the psychology of aging*. San Diego, CA: Academic Press.

Franklin, A., & Davies, I. R. L. (2004). New evidence for infant colour categories. *British Journal of Developmental Psychology*, *22*, 349–377.

Freire, A., Lee, K., & Symons, L. A. (2000). The face-inversion effect as a deficit in the encoding of configural information: Direct evidence. *Perception*, *29*, 159–170.

Frick, J. E. & Richards, J. E. (2001). Individual differences in infants' recognition of briefly presented visual stimuli. *Infancy*, *2*, 331–352.

Ganchrow, J. R., & Steiner, J. E. (1984). Classical conditioning in newborn humans 2–48 hours of age. *Infant Behavior and Development*, *7*, 223–235.

Ganchrow, J. R., Steiner, J. E., & Daher, M. (1983). Neonatal facial expressions in response to different qualities and intensities of gustatory stimuli. *Infant Behavior and Development*, *6*, 189–200.

Garcia, J., & Koelling, R. (1966). Relation of cue to consequence in avoidance learning. *Psychonomic Science*, *4*, 123–124.

Garner, W. R. (1974). *The processing of information and structure*. Potomac, MD: Lawrence Erlbaum Associates.

Gauthier, I., & Nelson, C. A. (2001). The development of face expertise. *Current Opinion in Neurobiology, 11*, 219–224.

Geldart, S., Mondloch, C. J., Maurer, D., de Schonen, S., & Brent, H. P. (2002). The effect of early visual deprivation on the development of face processing. *Developmental Science, 5*, 490–501.

Gerhardstein, P., Kraebel, K. S., Gillis, J., & Lassiter, S. (2002). Visual search for high-level configural differences as well as low-level critical features is highly efficient early in childhood. *Developmental Psychobiology, 41*, 241–252.

Gibson, E. J. (1969). *Principles of perceptual learning and development.* New York: Appleton, Century, Crofts.

Gibson, E. J. (1982). The concept of affordances in development: The renascence of functionalism. In W. A. Collins (Ed.), *The Minnesota symposia on child psychology* (Vol. 15). Hillsdale, NJ: Lawrence Erlbaum Associates.

Gibson, J. J. (1979). *The ecological approach to visual perception.* Boston: Houghton Mifflin.

Gibson, J. J., & Gibson, E. J. (1955). Perceptual learning: Differentiation or enrichment? *Psychological Review, 62*, 32–41.

Gislen, A., Dacke, M., Kroger, R. H. H., Abrahamsson, M., Nilsson, D. E., & Warrant, E. J. (2003). Superior underwater vision in a human population of sea gypsies. *Current Biology, 13*, 833–836.

Golomb, C. (2004). *The child's creation of a pictorial world* (2nd ed.). Mahwah, NJ: Lawrence Erlbaum Associates.

Gopnik, A., Slaughter, V., & Meltzoff, A. N. (1994). Changing your views: How understanding visual perception can lead to a new theory of the mind. In C. Lewis & P. Mitchell (Eds.), *Origins of a theory of mind* (pp. 157–181). Hillsdale, NJ: Lawrence Erlbaum Associates.

Gottlieb, G. (1981). Roles of early experience in species-specific perceptual development. In R. N. Aslin, J. R. Alberts, & M. R. Peterson (Eds.), *Development of perception* (Vol. 1). New York: Academic Press.

Goubet, N., Rattaz, C., Pierrat, V., Allemann, E., Bullinger, A., & Lequien, P. (2002). Olfactory familiarization and discrimination in preterm and full-term newborns. *Infancy, 3*, 53–76.

Goubet, N., Rattaz, C., Pierrat, V., Bullinger, A., & Lequien, P. (2003). Olfactory experience mediates response to pain in preterm newborns. *Developmental Psychobiology, 42*, 171–180.

Gould, E. (2007). How widespread is adult neurogenesis in mammals? *Nature Reviews Neuroscience, 8*, 481–488.

Gould, E., Reeves, A. J., Graziano, M. S. A., & Gross, C. G. (1999). Neurogenesis in the neocortex of adult primates. *Science, 286*, 548–552.

Gould, E., Vail, N., Wagers, M., & Gross, C. G. (2001). Adult-generated hippocampal and neocortical neurons in macaques have a transient existence. *Proceedings of the National Academy of Sciences of the United States of America, 98*, 10910–10917.

Granrud, C. E. (1986). Binocular vision and spatial perception in 4- and 5-month-old infants. *Journal of Experimental Psychology: Human Perception and Performance, 12*, 36–49.

Granrud, C. E. (1987). Size constancy in newborn human infants. *Investigative Ophthalmology and Visual Science, 28* (Suppl.), 5.

Granrud, C. E., Yonas, A., Smith, I. M., Arterberry, M. E., Glicksman, M. L., & Sorkness, A. C. (1984). Infants' sensitivity to accretion and deletion of texture and information for depth at an edge. *Child Development, 55*, 1630–1636.

Green, C. S., & Bavelier, D. (2003). Action video game modifies visual selective attention. *Nature, 423*, 534–537.

Greene, H. A., & Madden, D. J. (1987). Adult age differences in visual acuity, stereopsis, and contrast sensitivity. *American Journal of Optometry and Physiological Optics, 64*, 749–753.

Greenfield, P. M. (Ed.). (1994). Special issue: Effects of interactive entertainment technologies on development. *Journal of Applied Developmental Psychology, 15*, 1–140.

Gross, C. G. (2000). Neurogenesis in the adult brain: Death of a dogma. *Nature Reviews Neuroscience, 1*, 67–73.

Gross, C. G. (2002). The genealogy of the "grandmother cell". *The Neuroscientist, 8*, 512–518.

Gross, C. G., Bender, D. B., & Rocha-Miranda, C. E. (1969). Visual receptive fields of neurons in inferotemporal cortex of the monkey. *Science, 166*, 1303–1306.

Gross, C. G., Rocha-Miranda, C. E., and Bender, D. B. (1972). Visual properties of cells in inferotemporal cortex of the macaque. *Journal of Neurophysiology, 35*, 96–111.

Grunau, R. V., Johnston, C. C., & Craig, K. D. (1990). Neonatal facial and cry responses to invasive and non-invasive procedures. *Pain, 42*, 295–305.

Gwiazda, J., & Birch, E. E. (2001). Perceptual development: Vision. In E. B. Goldstein (Ed.), *Blackwell handbook of perception* (pp. 636–668). Malden, MA: Blackwell.

Hadjikhani, N., & de Gelder, B. (2002). Neural basis of prosopagnosia: An fMRI study. *Human Brain Mapping, 16*, 176–182.

Haith, M. M. (2004). Progress and standardization in eye movement work with human infants. *Infancy, 6*, 257–265.

Hancock, K. J., & Rhodes, G. (2008). Contact, configural coding and the other-race effect in face recognition. *British Journal of Psychology, 99*, 45–56.

Hebb, D. O. (1949). *The organization of behavior: A neuropsychological theory.* New York: Wiley.

Hebb, D. O. (1953). Heredity and environment in mammalian behaviour. *British Journal of Animal Behaviour, 1*, 43–47.

Held, R. (1989). Perception and its neuronal mechanisms. *Cognition, 33*, 139–154.

Held, R., Birch, E., & Gwiazda, J. (1980). Stereoacuity in human infants. *Proceedings of the National Academy of Sciences of the United States of America*, 77, 5572–5574.

Hirsh-Pasek, K., Nelson, D. K., Jusczyk, P. W., Cassidy, K. W., Druss, B., & Kennedy, L. (1987). Clauses are perceptual units for young infants. *Cognition*, 26, 269–286.

Hochberg, J., & Brooks, V. (1962). Pictorial recognition as an unlearned ability: A study of one child's performance. *American Journal of Psychology*, 75, 624–628.

Huttenlocher, P. R. (2002). *Neural plasticity: The effects of the environment on the development of the cerebral cortex.* Cambridge, MA: Harvard University Press.

Jacobs, B., Schall, M., & Scheibel, A. B. (1993). A quantitative dendritic analysis of Wernicke's area in humans. II. Gender, hemispheric, and environmental factors. *Journal of Comparative Neurology*, 327, 97–111.

Jacobs, B., & Scheibel, A. B. (1993). A quantitative dendritic analysis of Wernicke's area in humans. I. Lifespan changes. *Journal of Comparative Neurology*, 32, 83–96.

Jahoda, G., Deregowski, J. B., Ampene, E., & Williams, N. (1977). Pictorial recognition as unlearned ability: A replication with children from pictorially deprived environments. In G. Butterworth (Ed.), *The child's representation of the world*. New York: Plenum Press.

James, W. (1924). *Some problems of philosophy*. New York: Longmans, Green.

Johnson, M. A., & Choy, D. (1987). On the definition of age-related norms for visual function testing. *Applied Optics*, 26, 1449–1454.

Johnson, M. H., Dziurawiec, S., Ellis, H., & Morton, J. (1991). Newborn's preferential tracking of face-like stimuli and its subsequent decline. *Cognition*, 40, 1–19.

Johnson, M. H., & Morton, J. (1991). *Biology and cognitive development*. Oxford, UK: Blackwell.

Johnston, J. R. (1985). Cognitive prerequisites: Cross linguistic study of language acquisition. In D. Slobin (Ed.), *Universals of language acquisition: Theoretical issues* (Vol. 2). Hillsdale, NJ: Lawrence Erlbaum Associates.

Johnston, R. S., Anderson, M., Perrett, D. I., & Holligan, C. (1990). Perceptual dysfunction in poor readers: Evidence for visual and auditory segmentation problems in a sub-group of poor readers. *British Journal of Educational Psychology*, 60, 212–219.

Kail, R. V. (2003). Information processing and memory. In M. H. Bornstein ct al. (Eds.), *Well-being: Positive development across the life course* (pp. 269–279). Mahwah, NJ: Lawrence Erlbaum Associates.

Kail, R., & Salthouse, T. A. (1994). Processing speed as a mental capacity. *Acta Psychologica*, 86, 199–225.

Kandel, E. C. (2007). *In search of memory: The emergence of a new science of mind*. New York: W. W. Norton.

Kant, I. (1924). *Critique of pure reason* (F. M. Miller, Trans.). New York: Macmillan. (Original work published 1781.)

Karrass, J., VanDeventer, M. C., & Braungart-Rieker, J. M. (2003). Predictors of shared parent–child book reading in infancy. *Journal of Family Psychology*, 17, 134–146.

Kavale, K. (1982). Meta-analysis of the relationship between visual perceptual skills and reading achievement. *Journal of Learning Disabilities*, 15, 42–51.

Kellman, P. J., & Arterberry, M. E. (2006). Infant visual perception. In D. Kuhn & R. S. Siegler (Eds.), W. Damon (Series Ed.), *Handbook of child psychology: Vol. 2. Cognition, perception, and language* (6th ed., pp. 109–160). Hoboken, NJ: Wiley.

Kelly, D. J., Quinn, P. C., Slater, A. M., Lee, K., Ge, L., & Pascalis, O. (2007). The other-race effect develops during infancy: Evidence of perceptual narrowing. *Psychological Science*, 8, 1084–1089.

Kemler Nelson, D. G., Hirsh-Pasek, K., Jusczyk, P. W., & Cassidy, K. W. (1989). How the prosodic cues in motherese might assist language learning. *Journal of Child Language*, 16, 55–68.

Kennedy, J. M., & Ross, A. S. (1975). Outline picture perception by the Songe of Papua. *Perception*, 4, 391–406.

Kessen, W., Haith, M. M., & Salapatek, P. H. (1970). Human infancy: A bibliography and guide. In P. Mussen (Ed.), *Carmichael's manual of child psychology*. New York: Wiley.

Kisilevsky, B. S., Hains, S. M. J., Lee, K., Xie, X., Huang, H., Ye, H.-H., et al. (2003). Effects of experience on fetal voice recognition. *Psychological Science*, 14, 220–224.

Kisilevsky, B. S., Stach, D. M., & Muir, D. W. (1991). Fetal and infant response to tactile stimulation. In M. J. S. Weiss & P. R. Zelazo (Eds.), *Newborn attention: Biological constraints and the influence of experience* (pp. 63–98). Norwood, NJ: Ablex.

Knoblauch, K., Vital-Durand, F., & Barbur, J. L. (2001). Variation in chromatic sensitivity across the life span. *Vision Research*, 41, 23–36.

Kosnik, W., Winslow, L., Kline, D., Rasinski, K., & Sekuler, R. (1988). Visual changes in daily life throughout adulthood. *Journal of Gerontology*, 43, P63–P70.

Kuhl, P. K., Stevens, E., Hayashi, A., Degushi, T., Kiritani, S., & Iverson, P. (2006). Infants show a facilitation effect for native language phonetic perception between 6 and 12 months. *Developmental Science*, 9, F13–F21.

Kuhl, P. K., Williams, K. A., Lacerda, F., Stevens, K. N. & Lindblom, B. (1992). Linguistic experience alters phonetic perception in infants by 6 months of age. *Science*, 255, 606–608.

Lasky, R. E., Syrdal-Lasky, A., & Klein, R. E. (1975). VOT discrimination by four- to six-and-a-half-month-old infants from Spanish environments. *Journal of Experimental Child Psychology*, 20, 215–225.

Le Grand, R., Mondloch, C. J., Maurer, D., & Brent, H. (2001). Early visual experience and face processing. *Nature* *410*, 890. Correction, *412*, 786.

Le Grand, R., Mondloch, C. J., Maurer, D., & Brent, H. P. (2003). Expert face processing requires visual input to the right hemisphere during infancy. *Nature Neuroscience*, *6*, 1108–1112. Erratum, *8*, 1329.

Le Grand, R., Mondloch, C. J., Maurer, D., & Brent, H. P. (2004). Impairment in holistic face processing following early visual deprivation. *Psychological Science*, *15*, 762–768.

Leder, H., & Bruce, V. (1998). Local and relational aspects of face distinctiveness. *Quarterly Journal of Experimental Psychology A: Human Experimental Psychology*, *51A*, 449–473.

Lee, M. (1989). When is an object not an object? The effect of "meaning" upon the copying of line drawing. *British Journal of Psychology*, *80*, 15–37.

Leehey, S. C., Moskowitz-Cook, A., Brill, S., & Held, R. (1975). Orientational anisotropy in infant vision. *Science*, *190*, 900–901.

Leinbach, M. D., & Fagot, B. I. (1993). Categorical habituation to male and female faces: Gender schematic processing in infancy. *Infant Behavior & Development*, *16*, 317–332.

Lettvin, J. Y., Maturana, H. R., McCulloch, W. S., & Pitts, W. H. (1959). What the frog's eye tells the frog's brain. *Proceedings of the Institute of Radio Engineers*, *47*, 1940–1951.

Leuner, B., Gould, E., & Shors, T. J. (2006). Is there a link between adult neurogenesis and learning? *Hippocampus*, *16*, 216–224.

Levins, R., & Lewontin, R. (1985). *The dialectical biologist*. Cambridge, MA: Harvard University Press.

Liben, L. S., Kastens, K. A., & Stevenson, L. M. (2002). Real-world knowledge through real-world maps: A developmental guide for navigating the educational terrain. *Developmental Review*, *22*, 267–322.

Lillard, A. (1998). Ethnopsychologies: Cultural variations in theories of mind. *Psychological Bulletin*, *123*, 3–32.

Lis, A., Venuti, P., & de Zordo, M. R. (1990). [Representation and acquisition of the awareness of danger: A theoretical contribution.] *Etá Evolutiva*, *35*, 103–112.

Livingstone, M. S., & Hubel, D. H. (1988). Segregation of color, movement, and depth: Anatomy, physiology, and perception. *Science*, *240*, 740–749.

Locke, J. (1959). *An essay concerning human understanding*. New York: Dover. (Original work published 1689.)

Lodge, A., Armington, J. C., Barnet, A. B., Shanks, B. L., & Newcomb, C. N. (1969). Newborn electroretinograms and evoked electroencephalographic responses to orange and white light. *Child Development*, *40*, 267–273.

Lynch, M., Eilers, R., & Bornstein, M. H. (1992). Speech, vision, and music perception: Windows on the ontogeny of mind. *Psychology of Music*, *20*, 3–14.

MacWhinney, B., & Bornstein, M. H. (2003). Language and literacy. In M. H. Bornstein et al. (Eds.), *Well-being: Positive development across the life course* (pp. 331–339). Mahwah, NJ: Lawrence Erlbaum Associates.

Maguire, E. A., Gadian, D. G., Johnsrude, I. S., Good, C. D. Ashburner, J., Frackowiak, R. S. J., et al. (2000). Navigation-related structural change in the hippocampi of taxi drivers. *Proceedings of the National Academy of Sciences of the United States of America*, *97*, 4398–4403.

Malcolm, G., Leung, C., & Barton, J. J. S. (2005). Regional variations in the inversion effect for faces: Differential effects for feature shape, spatial relations, and external contour. *Perception*, *33*, 1221–1231.

Malt, B. C. (1995). Category coherence in cross-cultural perspective. *Cognitive Psychology*, *29*, 85–148.

Mareschal, D., & Johnson, M. H. (2003). The "what" and "where" of object representations in infancy. *Cognition*, *88*, 259–276.

Marks, L. E., Hammeal, R. J., & Bornstein, M. H. (1987). Perceiving similarity and comprehending metaphor. *Monographs of the Society for Research in Child Development*, *52*(1, No. 215).

Marottoli, R. A., Richardson, E. D., Stowe, M. H., Miller, E. G., Brass, L., Cooney, L. M., et al. (1998). Development of a test battery to identify older drivers at risk for self-reported adverse driving events. *Journal of the American Geriatric Society*, *46*, 562–568.

Mash, C. (2006). Multidimensional shape similarity in the development of visual object classification. *Journal of Experimental Child Psychology*, *95*, 128–152.

Mash, C. (2007). Object representation in infants' coordination of manipulative force. *Infancy*, *12*, 329–341.

Mash, C., Arterberry, M. E., & Bornstein, M. H. (2007). Mechanisms of object recognition in 5-month-old infants. *Infancy*, *12*, 31–43.

Mash, C., Quinn, P. C., Dobson, V., & Narter, D. B. (1998). Global influences on the development of spatial and object perceptual categorization abilities: Evidence from preterm infants. *Developmental Science*, *1*, 85–102.

Matjucha, I. C. A., & Katz, B. (1993). Neuro-ophthalmology of aging. In M. L. Albert & J. E. Knoefel (Eds.), *Clinical neurology of aging*. New York: Oxford University Press.

Maurer, D., Lewis, T. L., Brent, H. P., & Levin, A. V. (1999). Rapid improvement in the acuity of infants after visual input. *Science*, *286*, 108–110.

Maurer, D., & Salapatek, P. (1976). Developmental changes in the scanning of faces by young infants. *Child Development*, *47*, 523–527.

McCall, R. B. (1981). Nature–nurture and the two realms of development: A proposed integration with respect to mental development. *Child Development, 52*, 1–12.

Meissner, C., & Brigham, J. (2001). Thirty years of investigating the own-race bias in memory for faces. *Psychology, Public Policy, and Law, 7*, 3–35.

Milewski, A. E. (1976). Infants' discrimination of internal and external pattern elements. *Journal of Experimental Child Psychology, 22*, 229–246.

Milner, A. D., & Goodale, M. A. (1995). *The Visual Brain in Action.* Oxford: Oxford University Press.

Mondloch, C. J., Dobson, K. S., Parsons, J., & Maurer, D. (2004). Why 8-year-olds cannot tell the differences between Steve Martin and Paul Newman: factors contributing to the slow development of sensitivity to the spacing of facial features. *Journal of Experimental Child Psychology, 89*, 159–181.

Mondloch, C. J., Geldart, S., Maurer, D., & Le Grand, R. (2003). Developmental changes in face processing skills. *Journal of Experimental Child Psychology, 86*, 67–84.

Mondloch, C. J., Le Grand, R., & Maurer, D. (2002). Configural face processing develops more slowly than feature face processing. *Perception, 31*, 553–566.

Mondloch, C., Maurer, D., & Ahola, S. (2006). Becoming a face expert. *Psychological Science, 17*, 930–934.

Mondloch, C., Pathman, T., Maurer, D., Le Grand, R., & de Schonen, S. (2007). The composite face effect in six-year-old children: Evidence of adultlike holistic face processing. *Visual Cogntion, 15*, 564–577.

Moon, C., Cooper, R. P., & Fifer, W. P. (1993). Two-day-olds prefer their native language. *Infant Behavior & Development, 16*, 495–500.

Muir, D. W., & Nadel, J. (1998). Infant social perception. In A. Slater (Ed.), *Perceptual development: Visual, auditory and speech perception in infancy.* Hove, UK: Psychology Press.

Nanez, J., Sr. (1988). Perception of impending collision in 3- to 6-week-old infants. *Infant Behavior and Development, 11*, 447–463.

Nanez, J. E., & Yonas, A. (1994). Effects of luminance and texture motion on infant defensive reactions to optical collision. *Infant Behavior and Development, 17*, 165–174.

Narayan, C. (2006). *Acoustic-perceptual salience and developmental speech perception.* Unpublished doctoral dissertation, University of Michigan.

Narayan, C., Werker, J. F., & Beddor, P. (under review). *Acoustic salience effects speech perception in infancy: Evidence from nasal place discrimination.*

Nelson, C. A., & Bloom, F. E. (1997). Child development and neuroscience. *Child Development, 68*, 970–987.

Nelson, C. A., III, Thomas, K. M., & De Haan, M. (2006). Neural bases of cognitive development. In D. Kuhn & R. S. Siegler (Eds.), W. Damon (Series Ed.), *Handbook of child psychology: Vol. 2. Cognition, perception, and language* (6th ed., pp. 3–57). Hoboken, NJ: Wiley.

Nettlebeck, T., & Wilson, C. (1985). A cross-sequential analysis of developmental differences in speed of visual information processing. *Journal of Experimental Child Psychology, 40*, 1–22.

Newcombe, N. S., & Huttenlocher, J. (2000). *Making space: The development of spatial representation and reasoning.* Cambridge, MA: MIT Press.

Norcia, A. M., & Tyler, C. W. (1985). Spatial frequency sweep VEP: Visual acuity during the first year of life. *Vision Research, 25*, 1399–1408.

Nunez, P. L. (1990). Physical principles and neurophysiological mechanisms underlying event-related potentials. In J. W. Rohrbach, R. Parasurman, & R. Johnson (Eds.), *Event-related brain potentials: Basic issues and applications* (pp. 19–36). New York: Oxford University Press.

Ortiz, C., Stowe, R. M. & Arnold, D. H. (2001). Parental influence on child interest in shared picture book reading. *Early Childhood Research Quarterly, 16*, 263–281.

Oster, H. (2005). The repertoire of infant facial expressions: An ontogenetic perspective. In J. Nadel & D. Muir (Eds), *Emotional development* (pp. 261–292). New York: Oxford University Press.

Owsley, C., Ball, K., Sloane, M. E., Roenker, D. L., & Bruni, J. R. (1991). Visual/cognitive correlates of vehicle accidents in older drivers. *Psychology and Aging, 6*, 403–415.

Parmelee, A. H., & Sigman, M. D. (1983). Perinatal brain development and behavior. In P. H. Mussen (Series Ed.), M. M. Haith & J. J. Campos (Eds.), *Handbook of child psychology, Vol. 2. Infancy and developmental psychophysiology.* New York: Wiley.

Pascalis, O., & de Schonen, S. (1994). Recognition memory in 3- to 4-day-old human neonates. *NeuroReport, 5*, 1721–1724.

Passman, R. H., & Longeway, K. P. (1982). The role of vision in maternal attachment: Giving 2-year-old a photograph of their mother during separation. *Developmental Psychology, 18*, 530–533.

Pegg, J. E. & Werker, J. F. (1997). Adult and infant perception of two English phones. *Journal of the Acoustical Society of America, 102*, 3742–3753.

Pellegrini, A. D., & Galda, L. (2003). Joint reading as a context: Explicating the ways context is created by participants. In A. van Kleeck, S. A. Stahl, & E. B. Bauer (Eds.), *On reading books to children: Parents and teachers* (pp. 321–335). Mahwah, NJ: Lawrence Erlbaum Associates.

Pellicano, E., & Rhodes, G. (2003). Holistic processing of faces in preschool children and adults. *Psychological Science, 14*, 618–622.

Peña, M., Maki, A., Kovacic, D., Dehaene-Lambertz, G., Bouquet, F., Koizumi, H., et al. (2003). Sounds and silence: An optical topography study of language recognition at birth. *Proceedings of the National Academy of Sciences of the United States of America, 10*, 11702–11705.

Piaget, J. (1954). *The construction of reality in the child.* New York: Basic Books.

Piaget, J. (1969). *The mechanisms of perception* (G. N. Seagrim, Trans.). London: Routledge & Kegan Paul.

Pillow, B. H. (1989). Early understanding of perception as a source of knowledge. *Journal of Experimental Child Psychology, 47*, 116–129.

Pitchford, N. J., & Mullen, K. T. (2003). The development of conceptual colour categories in pre-school children: Influence of perceptual categorization. *Visual Cognition, 10*, 51–77.

Plude, D., Enns, J. T., & Brodeur, D. A. (1994). The development of selective attention: A lifespan overview. *Acta Psychologica, 86*, 227–272.

Plumert, J. M., Kearney, J. K., & Cremer, J. F. (2007). Children's road crossing: A window into perceptual-motor development. *Current Directions in Psychological Science, 16*, 255–258.

Polka, L., & Werker, J. F. (1994). Developmental changes in perception of non-native vowel contrasts. *Journal of Experimental Psychology: Human Perception and Performance, 20*, 421–435.

Pollak, S. D., Messner, M., Kistler, D. J., & Cohn, J. F. (2009). Development of perceptual expertise in emotion recognition. *Cognition, 110*, 242–247.

Porges, S. W. (1995). Orienting in a defensive world: Mammalian modifications of our evolutionary heritage. A polyvagal theory. *Psychophysiology, 32*, 301–318.

Porges, S. W. (2001). The polyvagal theory: Phylogenetic substrates of a social nervous system. *International Journal of Physiology, 42*, 123–146.

Porges, S. W. (2003). The polyvagal theory: Phylogenetic contribution to social behavior. *Physiology and Behavior, 79*, 503–513.

Porter, R. H., Balogh, R. D., & Makin, J. W. (1988). Olfactory influences on mother–infant interactions. In C. Rovee-Collier & L. P. Lipsitt (Eds.), *Advances in infancy research* (Vol. 5, pp. 39–68). Norwood, NJ: Ablex.

Porter, R. H., & Levy, F. (1995). Olfactory mediation of mother–infant interactions in selected mammalian species. In R. Wong (Ed.), *Biological perspectives on motivated activities* (pp. 77–110). Westport, CT: Ablex Publishing.

Poulin-Dubois, D., Serbin, L. A., Kenyon, B., & Derbyshire, A. (1994). Infants' intermodal knowledge about gender. *Developmental Psychology, 30*, 436–442.

Price-Williams, D. R., Gordon, W., & Ramirez, M., III. (1969). Skill and conservation: A study of pottery-making children. *Developmental Psychology, 1*, 769.

Purpura, D. P. (1975). Morphogenesis of visual cortex in the preterm infant. In M. A. B. Brazier (Ed.), *Growth and development of the brain.* New York: Raven.

Purves, D., & Lichtman, J. W. (1980). Elimination of synapses in the developing nervous system. *Science, 210*, 153–157.

Quinn, P. C., Bhatt, R. S., Brush, D., Grimes, A., & Sharpnack, H. (2002). Development of form similarity as a Gestalt grouping principle in infancy. *Psychological Science, 13*, 320–328.

Quinn, P. C., Burke, S., & Rush, A. (1993). Part–whole perception in early infancy: Evidence for perceptual grouping produced by lightness similarity. *Infant Behavior and Development, 16*, 19–42.

Quinn, P. C., & Slater, A. (2003). Face perception at birth and beyond. In Pascalis, O., & Slater, A. (Eds.), *The development of face processing in infancy and early childhood: Current perspectives* (pp. 3–11). Hauppauge, NY: Nova Science Publishers.

Raskin, L. A., Maital, S., & Bornstein, M. H. (1983). Perceptual categorization of color: A life-span study. *Psychological Research, 45*, 639–649.

Rayner, K. (1998). Eye movements in reading and information processing: 20 years of research. *Psychological Bulletin, 124*, 372–422.

Reynolds, G. D., & Richards, J. E. (2005). Familiarization, attention, and recognition memory in infancy: An event-related potential and cortical source localization study. *Developmental Psychology, 41*, 598–615.

Richards, J. E. (1987). Infant visual sustained attention and respiratory sinus arrhythmia. *Child Development, 58*, 488–496.

Richards, J. E. (2003). The development of visual attention and the brain. In M. de Haan & M. H. Johnson (Eds.), *The cognitive neuroscience of development* (pp. 73–98). Hove, UK: Psychology Press.

Richards, J. E. (2004). The development of sustained attention in infants. In M. I. Posner (Ed.), *Cognitive neuroscience of attention* (pp. 342–356). New York: Guilford Press.

Rideout, V. J., Vandewater, E. A., & Wartella, E. A. (2003). *Zero to six: Electronic media in the lives of infants, toddlers, and preschoolers.* Menlo Park, CA: The Henry J. Kaiser Family Foundation.

Ritchie, I. (1991). Fusion of the faculties: A study of the language of the sense in Hausaland. In D. Howes (Ed.), *The varieties of sensory experience.* Toronto, Canada: University of Toronto Press.

Rivera-Gaxiola, M., Silva-Pereyra, J., & Kuhl, P. K. (2005). Brain potentials to native and non-native speech contrasts in 7- and 11-month-old American infants. *Developmental Science, 8*, 162–172.

Roberts, B. W., Walton, K. E., & Viechtbauer, W. (2006). Patterns of mean-level change in personality traits across the life course: A metaanalysis of longitudinal studies. *Psychological Bulletin, 132*, 3–27.

Roth, C. (1983). Factors affective developmental changes in the speed of processing. *Journal of Experimental Child Psychology, 35*, 509–528.

Rubin, G. B., Fagen, J. W., & Carroll, M. H. (1998). Olfactory context and memory retrieval in 3-month-old infants. *Infant Behavior & Development, 21*, 641–658.

Ruff, H. A. (1985). Detection of information specifying the motion of objects by 3- and 5-month-old infants. *Developmental Psychology, 21*, 295–305.

Ruff, H. A. (1990). Individual differences in sustained attention during infancy. In J. Colombo & J. Fagen (Eds.), *Individual differences in infancy: Reliability, stability, prediction.* Hillsdale, NJ: Lawrence Erlbaum Associates.

Ruff, H. A., & Rothbart, M. K. (1996). *Attention in early development: Themes and variations.* New York: Oxford University Press.

Saffran, J. R., Werker, J. F., & Werner, L. A. (2006). The infant's auditory world: Hearing, speech, and the beginnings of language. In D. Kuhn & R. S. Siegler (Eds.), W. Damon (Series Ed.), *Handbook of child psychology: Vol. 2. Cognition, perception, and language* (6th ed., pp. 58–108). Hoboken, NJ: Wiley.

Salapatek, P., & Kessen, W. (1973). Prolonged investigation of a plane geometric triangle by the human newborn. *Journal of Experimental Child Psychology, 15*, 22–29.

Salthouse, T. (1991). *Theoretical perspectives on cognitive aging.* Hillsdale, NJ: Lawrence Erlbaum Associates.

Salthouse, T. A., Rogan, J. D., & Prill, K. (1984). Division of attention: Age differences on a visually presented memory task. *Memory and Cognition, 12*, 613–620.

Samuels, C. A. (1985). Attention to eye contact opportunity and facial motion by three-month-old infants. *Journal of Experimental Child Psychology, 40*, 105–114.

Schaal, B. (1988). Olfaction in infants and children: Developmental and functional perspectives. *Chemical Senses, 13*, 145–190.

Schaie, K. W. (1989). Perceptual speed in adulthood: Cross-sectional and longitudinal studies. *Psychology and Aging, 4*, 443–453.

Schaie, K. W. (1990). "Perceptual speed in adulthood: Cross-sectional and longitudinal studies": Correction. *Psychology and Aging, 5*, 171.

Schemper, T., Voss, S., & Cain, W. S. (1981). Odor identification in young and elderly persons: Sensory and cognitive limitations. *Journal of Gerontology, 36*, 452–466.

Schiff, W., Oldak, R., & Shah, V. (1992). Aging persons' estimates of vehicular motion. *Psychology and Aging, 7*, 518–525.

Schmuckler, M. (1997). Children's postural sway in response to low- and high-frequency visual information for oscillation. *Journal of Experimental Psychology: Human Perception and Performance, 23*, 582–545.

Schneider, B. A., Trehub, S. E., Morrongiello, B. A., & Thorpe, L. A. (1986). Auditory sensitivity in preschool children. *Journal of the Acoustic Society of America, 79*, 447–452.

Schneider, E. L., & Rowe, J. W. (Eds.). (1990). *Handbook of the biology of aging.* San Diego, CA: Academic Press.

Seeger, A. (1981). *Nature and society in central Brazil: The Suya indians of Mato Grosso.* Cambridge, MA: Harvard University Press.

Sekuler, R., & Ball, K. (1986). Visual localization: Age and practice. *Journal of the Optical Society of American (Section A), 3*, 864–867.

Sénéchal, M., Cornell, E. H. & Broda, L. S. (1995). Age-related differences in the organization of parent–infant interactions during picture-book reading. *Early Childhood Research Quarterly, 10*, 317–337.

Shaw, P., Greenstein, D. Lerch, J., Clasen, L., Lenroot, R., Gogtay, N., et al. (2006). Intellectual ability and cortical development in children and adolescents. *Nature, 440*, 676–679.

Simmering, V. R., Schutte, A. R., & Spencer, J. P. (2008). Generalizing the dynamic field theory of spatial working memory across real and developmental time scales. In S. Becker (Ed.), *Computational Cognitive Neuroscience* [special issue]. *Brain Research, 1202*, 68–86.

Sivak, M., Olson, P. L., & Pastalan, L. A. (1981). Effect of driver's age on nighttime legibility of highway signs. *Human Factors, 23*, 59–64.

Slater, A. M. (1989). Visual memory and perception in early infancy. In A. Slater & J. G. Bremner (Eds.), *Infant development.* Hove, UK: Lawrence Erlbaum Associates.

Slater, A., Mattock, A., & Brown, E. (1990). Size constancy at birth: Newborn infants' responses to retinal and real size. *Journal of Experimental Child Psychology, 49*, 314–322.

Slater, A., Morison, V., & Somers, M. (1988). Orientation discrimination and cortical function in the human newborn. *Perception, 17*, 597–602.

Slater, A., Morison, V., Town, C., & Rose, D. (1985). Movement perception and identity constancy in the new-born baby. *British Journal of Developmental Psychology, 3*, 211–220.

Smith, L. B. (1989). From global similarities to kinds of similarities: The construction of dimensions in develop-ment. In S. Vosniadou & A. Ortony (Eds.), *Similarity and analogy*. Cambridge, MA: Cambridge University Press.

Smith, L. B. (2003). Learning to recognize objects. *Psychological Science, 14*, 244–250.

Smith, L. B., & Kemler, D. G. (1977). Developmental trends in free classification: Evidence for a new conceptualiza-tion of perceptual development. *Journal of Experimental Child Psychology, 24*, 279–298.

Solan, H. A., & Ficarra, A. P. (1990). A study of perceptual and verbal skills of disabled readers in grades 4, 5 and 6. *Journal of the American Optometric Association, 61*, 628–634.

Somberg, B. L., & Salthouse, T. A. (1982). Divided attention abilities in young and old adults. *Journal of Experimental Psychology: Human Perception and Performance, 8*, 651–663.

Stankov, L. (1988). Aging, attention and intelligence. *Psychology and Aging, 3*, 59–74.

Steiner, J. E. (1977). Facial expressions of the neonate infant indicating the hedonics of food-related chemical stimuli. In J. M. Weiffenbach (Ed.), *Taste and development*. Bethesda, MD: Department of Health, Education, and Welfare.

Steiner, J. E. (1979). Human facial expressions in response to taste and smell stimulation. In H. Reese & L. Lipsitt (Eds.), *Advances in child development and behavior* (Vol. 13). New York: Academic Press.

Stevens, J. C., Cruz, S. L. A., Marks, L. E., & Lakatos, S. (1998). A multimodal assessment of sensory thresholds in aging. *Journal of Gerontology: Psychological Sciences, 53B*, 263–272.

Strange, W., & Jenkins, J. (1978). Role of linguistic experience in the perception of speech. In R. D. Walk & H. L. Pick (Eds.), *Perception and experience*. New York: Plenum Press.

Streeter, L. A. (1976). Language perception of 2-month-old infants shows effects of both innate mechanisms and experience. *Nature, 259*, 39–41.

Strouse, A., Ashmead, D. H., Ohde, R. N., & Grantham, D. W. (1998). Temporal processing in the aging auditory system. *Journal of Acoustical Society of America, 104*, 2385–2399.

Tanaka, J. W., & Farah, M. J. (1993). Parts and wholes in face recognition. *Quarterly Journal of Experimental Psychology, Human Experimental Psychology, 46*, 225–245.

Tanaka, J. W., Kay, J. B., Grinnell, E., Stansfield, B., & Szechter, T. (1998). Face recognition in young children: When the whole is greater than the sum of its parts. *Visual Cognition, 5*, 479–496.

Tanaka, T., Kojima, S., Takeda, H., Ino, S., & Ifukube, T. (2001). The influence of moving auditory stimuli on standing balance in healthy young adults and the elderly. *Ergonomics, 44*, 1403–1412.

Teller, D. Y. (1998). Spatial and temporal aspects of infant color vision. *Vision Research, 38*, 3275–3282.

Thelen, E., & Smith, L. B. (1994). *A dynamic systems approach to the development of cognition and action*. Cambridge, MA: MIT Press.

Trehub, S. D. (1976). The discrimination of foreign speech contrasts by infants and adults. *Child Development, 47*, 466–472.

Trehub, S. E., & Schneider, B. A. (1985). *Auditory development in infancy*. New York: Plenum.

Trehub, S. E., Schneider, B. A., Morrongiello, B. A., & Thorpe, L. A. (1988). Auditory sensitivity in school-age children. *Journal of Experimental Child Psychology, 46*, 273–285.

Trehub, S. E., Schneider, B. A., Morrongiello, B. A., & Thorpe, L. A. (1989). Developmental changes in high-frequency sensitivity. *Audiology, 28*, 241–249.

Tsao, F., Liu, H., Kuhl, P. K., & Tseng, C. (2000, July). *Perceptual discrimination of a Mandarin fricative–affricate contrast by English-learning and Mandarin-learning infants*. Poster presented at the meeting of the International Society on Infant Studies, Brighton, UK.

Tsunoda, T. (1985). *The Japanese brain: Uniqueness and universality* (Y. Oiwa, Trans.). Tokyo: Taishukan Publishing Co.

Tucker, D. (1993). Spatial sampling of head electrical fields: The geodesic sensor net. *Electroencephalography and Clinical Neurophysiology, 87*, 154–163.

Turati, C., Macchi Cassia, V., Simion, F., & Leo, I. (2006). Newborns' face recognition: Role of inner and outer facial features. *Child Development, 77*, 297–311.

Turkewitz, G., & Kenny, P. A. (1982). Limitations on input as a basis for neural organization and perceptual development: A preliminary theoretical statement. *Developmental Psychology, 15*, 357–368.

Turkewitz, G., & Kenny, P. A. (1985). The role of developmental limitations of sensory input on sensory/perceptual organization. *Journal of Developmental and Behavioral Pediatrics, 6*, 302–306.

Vandewater, E. A., Bickham, D. S., Lee, J. H., Cummings, H. M., Wartella, E. A., & Rideout, V. J. (2005). When the television is always on: Heavy television exposure and young children's development. *American Behavioral Scientist, 48*, 562–577.

van Kleeck, A. (2003). Research on book sharing: Another critical look. In A. van Kleek, S. A. Stahl, & E. B. Bauer (Eds.), *On reading books to children* (pp. 272–320). Mahwah, NJ: Lawrence Erlbaum Associates.

von Hofsten, C. (1974). Proximal velocity change as a determinant of space perception. *Perception & Psychophysics, 15*(3), 488–494.

Vouloumanos, A., & Werker, J. F. (2007a). Listening to language at birth: Evidence for a bias for speech in neonates. *Developmental Science, 10*, 159–164.

Vouloumanos, A., & Werker, J. F. (2007b). Why voice melody alone cannot explain neonates' preference for speech. *Developmental Science, 10,* 170–172.

Wallace, E., Hayes, D., & Jerger, J. (1993). Neurology of aging: The auditory system. In M. L. Albert & J. E. Knoefel (Eds.), *Clinical neurology of aging.* New York: Oxford University Press.

Weikum, W. Vouloumanos, A., Navarro, J., Soto-Faraco, S., Sebastián-Gallés, N., & Werker, J. F. (2007). Visual language discrimination in infancy. *Science, 316,* 1159.

Werker, J. F. (1990). Cross-language speech perception: Developmental change does not involve loss. In H. Nusbaum & J. Goodman (Eds.), *The transition from speech sounds to spoken words: The development of speech perception.* Cambridge, MA: MIT Press.

Werker, J. F., Maurer, D. M., & Yoshida, K. A. (2009). Perception. In M. H. Bornstein (Ed.), *The handbook of cultural developmental science. Part 1. Domains of development across cultures* (pp. 89–125). New York: Taylor & Francis Group.

Werker, J. F., Gilbert, J. H. V., Humphrey, K., & Tees, R. C. (1981). Developmental aspects of cross-language speech perception. *Child Development, 52,* 349–353.

Werker, J. F. & Lalonde, C. E. (1988). Cross-language speech perception: Initial capabilities and developmental change. *Developmental Psychology, 24,* 672–683.

Werker, J. F., Shi, R., Desjardins, R., Pegg, J. E., Polka, L., & Patterson, M. (1998). Three methods for testing infant speech perception. In A. Slater (Ed.), *Perceptual development: Visual, auditory and speech perception in infancy.* Hove, UK: Psychology Press.

Werker, J. F., & Tees, R. C. (1984). Phonemic and phonetic factors in adult cross-language speech perception. *Journal of the Acoustical Society of America, 75,* 1866–1878.

Werker, J. F., & Tees, R. C. (1984). Cross-language speech perception: Evidence for perceptual reorganization during the first year of life. *Infant Behavior and Development, 7,* 49–63.

Werner, L. A., & Bargones, J. Y. (1992). Psychoacoustic development of human infants. In C. Rovee-Collier & L. Lipsitt (Eds.), *Advances in infancy research* (Vol. 7, pp. 103–145). Norwood, NJ: Ablex.

Wertheimer, M. (1938). Numbers and numerical concepts in primitive peoples. In W. D. Ellis (Ed.), *A source book of Gestalt psychology.* New York: Harcourt.

Wertheimer, M. (1958). Principles of perceptual organization. In D. C. Beardslee & M. Wertheimer (Eds.), *Readings in perception* (pp. 115–135). Princeton, NJ: Van Nostrand.

Wilcox, T. (1999). Object individuation: Infants' use of shape, size, pattern, and color. *Cognition, 72,* 125–166.

Wilson, S. J., Wales, R. J., & Pattison, P. (1997). The representation of tonality and meter in children aged 7 and 9. *Journal of Experimental Child Psychology, 64,* 42–66.

Wohlwill, J. F. (1973). *The study of behavioral development.* New York: Academic Press.

Yakovlev, P. I., & Lecours, A. R. (1967). The myelogenetic cycles of regional maturation of the brain. In A. Minkowski (Ed.), *Regional development of the brain in early life.* Oxford, UK: Blackwell.

Yin, R. K. (1969). Looking at upside down faces. *Journal of Experimental Psychology, 81,* 141–145.

Yonas, A. (1981). Infants' responses to optical information for collision. In R. N. Aslin, J. R. Alberts, & M. R. Peterson (Eds.), *Development of perception: Psychobiological perspectives* (Vol. 2). New York: Academic Press.

Yonas, A., Arterberry, M. E., & Granrud, C. E. (1987a). Four-month-old infants' sensitivity to binocular and kinetic information for three-dimensional object shape. *Child Development, 58,* 910–971.

Yonas, A., Arterberry, M. E., & Granrud, C. E. (1987b). Space perception in infancy. In R. Vasta (Ed.), *Annals of child development* (pp. 1–34). Greenwich, CT: JAI Press.

Yonas, A., Elieff, C. A., & Arterberry, M. E. (2002). Emergence of sensitivity to pictorial depth cues: Charting development in individual infants. *Infant Behavior and Development, 25,* 495–514.

Yonas, A., & Granrud, C. E. (2006). Infants' perception of depth from cast shadows. *Perception & Psychophysics, 68,* 154–160.

Yonas, A., & Hartman, B. (1993). Perceiving the affordance of contact in four- and five-month-old infants. *Child Development, 64,* 298–308.

Young, A. W., Hellawell, D., & Hay, D. C. (1987). Configurational information in face perception. *Perception, 16,* 747–759.

Yurgelun-Todd, D. (2002). Frontline interview, "Inside the Teen Brain." Retrieved September 24, 2009 from www.pbs.org/wgbh/pages/frontline/shows/teenbrain/interviews/todd.html

Zlatin, M. A., & Koenigsknecht, R. A. (1975). Development of the voicing contrast: Perception of stop consonants. *Journal of Speech and Hearing Research, 18,* 541–553.

THE DEVELOPMENT OF COGNITIVE ABILITIES

Damian P. Birney
University of New South Wales
Robert J. Sternberg
Yale University

INTRODUCTION

Although the study of cognitive and intellectual development is often seen as quite separate and distinct from, say, social development, emotional development, and moral development, few researchers would disagree that development draws from a multitude of cognitive, non-cognitive, and situational facets—that together, the processes involved in social, emotional, moral, as well as cognitive development determine at least to some extent how closely an individual's global potential is realized (Neisser et al., 1996). Even within the group of researchers who study cognitive and intellectual abilities and their development, different approaches and methodological paradigms have been used. These approaches have at times been thought to be so distinct that they have been considered as separate domains of investigation. Whereas it might be convenient and expedient to parcel the study of cognition and its development into manageable pieces, it is also important to recognize that these pieces are often just part of the full cognitive development story. There have been various calls over the years to try to integrate the findings from the different approaches to conceptualizing cognition (e.g., Ackerman, 1987; Cronbach, 1957; Hunt, 1980; Sternberg, 1977). When attempting this, one is pressed to recognize the large dependency of many factors in the developmental process. This dependency is unlikely to emerge clearly when only a single methodological approach is used. In this chapter, we attempt to review a selection of theories, findings, and issues that span methodologies which we believe are significantly related to the development of cognitive abilities. Some of the theories and findings we discuss have a long history of investigation within traditional developmental psychology (i.e., Piagetian theories). Other theories are more contemporary (i.e., development of wisdom), tend to be less explicitly associated with chronological—maturational development (i.e., theories of knowledge-acquisition), or are only tangentially related to traditional Piagetian-like conceptualizations of development (i.e., the relation between concept formation and creativity). We feel this breadth provides for a deeper appreciation of the multifaceted issues that influence cognitive development.

We have separated the chapter into five sections. The first section reviews briefly what is considered the traditional developmental perspective of cognitive abilities. The second section considers some of the theorizing and findings in cognitive development from the information-processing tradition. These types of theories were built on a metaphor of the mind as a computer (Sternberg, 1990) and emerged following a general dissatisfaction with the ability of the behaviorist movement of the 1960s to sufficiently account for variability in learning. Over time the "computing mind" analogy was extended to try to model the massive parallel processing believed to take place in the human brain (e.g., McClelland, Rumelhart & Hinton, 1986; Rumelhart, 1990), while at the same time reflecting known psychological limitations in working memory (e.g., Halford & Wilson, 1980; Halford, Wilson & Phillips, 1998) and knowledge-acquisition processes (Anderson, 1982). Research in this area has seen considerable growth, in large part due to the active involvement of multidisciplinary teams of researchers that have included psychologists, linguists, neuroscientists, statisticians, mathematicians, computer scientists and engineers, and philosophers. The great advances and espoused potentials also attracted traditional developmental scientists. As we hope to show, cognitive science now subsumes much of the infrastructure of what was once considered Piagetian and then neo-Piagetian theories of cognitive development.

The third section explores some of the findings from psychometric studies of cognitive and intellectual development using correlational methodologies that attempt to identify and map out the constellation of cognitive abilities. Much of what is known about intelligence and cognitive abilities is due to psychometric studies. This is due in part to the immense importance placed on the outcomes of psychometric testing by its stakeholders. Because the correlational methodology of psychometric studies focuses on prediction (partly for construct validation, and partly as an end in itself), this area of research has been of applied interest for selection decisions in education, military institutions, and training in corporate and other government organizations. The psychometric approach has been and continues to be influential in expanding our view of intelligence and cognitive development and in modeling relations with other non-cognitive factors such as personality, motivation, and knowledge (e.g., Ackerman, 1996; Ackerman & Beier, 2003). Whereas psychometric theories have been instrumental in mapping the range of different abilities, the differential approach underlying these theories has been less useful in eliciting an understanding of the intellectual processes involved (Deary, 2001; Lohman & Ippel, 1993).

In the fourth section, we explore systems theories of cognitive development. We look at two theories, those of Sternberg (1997) and of Gardner (1993). These theories integrate aspects of cognitive information-processing and psychometric approaches.

In the fifth and final section, we explore some relatively recent findings from approaches to the development of wisdom. Intuitively, wisdom is seen as the culmination of development on various fronts. It is the intersection of highly developed knowledge, advanced cognitive processing, creativity, and a well-developed capacity for social, emotional, and moral reasoning.

CLASSIC DEVELOPMENTAL APPROACHES TO COGNITIVE DEVELOPMENT

Piaget

Jean Piaget (1896–1980) is arguably the most influential researcher of all time within the area of cognitive–developmental psychology (Bidell & Fischer, 1992). He began his work in cognitive development as a graduate student working in Alfred Binet's psychometric laboratory. There he became interested in children's answers to intelligence-test items. Piaget asserted that researchers could learn as much about children's intellectual development by examining their incorrect answers to test items as by examining their correct answers. By observing children's errors in reasoning, Piaget determined that coherent logical systems underlie children's thinking. These systems differ from the systems adults use. To understand development, these systems and their distinctive characteristics must be identified. With this interest, Piaget proceeded to write about his observations of children, especially his own.

Specific and General Heredity

Piaget conceived of intelligence as a form of biological adaptation to the environment. Development of knowledge and abilities was, according to the Piagetian account, the result of the individual constantly interacting with the environment in an attempt to maintain a balance between his or her current needs and understandings, on one hand, and the demands of the environment on the other. Piaget's theory embraces two biological antecedents of cognitive development, *specific heredity* and *general heredity*. Specific heredity takes several forms. One aspect of specific heredity is the automatic behavioral reaction, or reflex. All members of a species, with the exception of those with defects, inherit the same physical mechanism that creates the reflex. The presence of a stimulus activates this mechanism which, in turn, causes the reflex. For example, the sucking reflex in human infants is necessary for infants' survival. An infant does not need to be taught how to suck, and the response will enable the infant to eat. If an object (the stimulus) touches the infant's lips, the infant will automatically respond with sucking (the reflex). These reflexes are significant in the first few days of an infant's life. After that initial period, the infant's interactions with the environment (i.e., experience) modify the reflexes (Ginsburg & Opper, 1979).

Another form of specific heredity is physical maturation, whereby members of a species follow a genetically determined course for the growth of physical structures. This physical maturation is frequently correlated with psychological activities. As these physical structures mature, various activities are able to emerge. For example, as children age, their brains grow and their muscles become stronger. Children's ability to speak emerges as their brains grow (MacWhinney, Chapter 8, this volume). Also, as their leg muscles strengthen, they gain the ability to walk, which allows them to explore the world (Adolph & Berger, Chapter 5, this volume). According to Piaget, physical maturation, coupled with experience and other factors, is necessary for development. Although contemporary developmental scientists acknowledge the dual role of maturation and experience (e.g., Halford, 1993), the extent to which the effects of maturation and experience are dissociable has been an issue of continued debate. This is epitomized in the identification of precocity—the case in which a child's level of performance is beyond what would be expected given his or her developmental level. Precocity is contentious because the relative distribution of maturation versus experience has many applied implications, particularly for early education (e.g., at what age will the cognitive architecture be in place to enable a given concept to be understood and mastered). Precocity, as we will show below, has also been the primary piece of evidence used to dispute Piaget's theory.

The second biological factor in Piaget's theory is general heredity. General heredity comprises two basic inherited tendencies, or invariant functions that govern interactions of the individual with the environment: organization and adaptation. The first process, *organization*, is effectively a tendency toward generalization. When two or more representations of a concept exist, there is a tendency toward combining these representations into a higher-order, integrated scheme. Schemes are structures of knowledge and, in the Piagetian account, are the building blocks of development and cognition.

The second process, **adaptation**, consists of two sub-processes: assimilation and accommodation. *Assimilation* is the process of fitting information from new experiences into existing concepts. *Accommodation* is the process of changing existing knowledge structures to take account of new information. Although assimilation and accommodation occur at the same time, the balance of each is determined by the specific situation. Cognitive structures and hence abilities are seen as a result of the child's (and later adult's) attempts to organize experience in a coherent way (Bidell & Fischer, 1992; Case, 1992b; Piaget, 1950; Sattler, 1992).

Schemes and Stages of Development

As individuals organize their behavior and adapt to the environment, certain psychological structures result. These structures, called *schemes*, change as a child matures. Some schemes are innate, but most are not and are based largely on experience. For example, Piaget refers to the sucking reflex as the "sucking scheme." However, thumb sucking is not innate because, although sucking is a reflex, the act of moving the thumb to the mouth is learned.

When children do not change very much, they assimilate more than they accommodate. Piaget referred to this steady period as a state of cognitive equilibrium. During periods of rapid cognitive change, however, children are in a state of disequilibrium, in which they accommodate more than they assimilate. They find that they frequently have to modify their current schemes due to an influx of new information. Piaget referred to this back-and-forth movement from equilibrium to disequilibrium as **equilibration**. Equilibration ultimately produces efficient schemes (Piaget, 1985). Schemes that are similar and occur in the same developmental time period cluster together to form stages (Tanner & Inhelder, 1956). In terms of intellectual development, the Piagetian theory proposes four major developmental stages (or periods) through which the child progresses. These are the: (1) sensorimotor period, (2) preoperational period, (3) concrete-operations period, and (4) formal-operations period. These stages reflect the gradual reorganization of basic cognitive processes and operations that facilitate (or at least coincide with) certain important developmental milestones.

Sensorimotor development (birth to 2 years). The first stage, the sensorimotor period, is divided into six sub-stages because so much change occurs in children's first 2 years of life. Piaget believed that children are born with little knowledge about the world and a limited capacity to explore it. Because they need an effective way to modify their early schemes, Piaget asserted that infants use a circular reaction. Such reactions originate when infants accidentally generate a new experience because of their own motor activity. Through a process of trial and error, infants try to repeat the occurrence over and over. The circular reaction strengthens into a scheme for the child. Two other abilities that Piaget cited as occurring in the sensorimotor period are play and imitation. They have important roles in consolidating old schemes and developing new ones. Piaget viewed play as a form of assimilation. Through play, children rehearse current schemes simply for pleasure. Piaget also associated imitation and accommodation. By imitating others, children copy and learn behaviors that are not in their inventory of schemes.

In *Sub-stage 1: Reflexive Schemes* (birth to 1 month), the various reflexes with which the infant is born are the initial sensorimotor schemes, and therefore, the building blocks for later and more complex schemes. For example, a newborn will suck when presented with a nipple, but the newborn may also appear to suck when no stimuli are present.

Sub-stage 2: Primary Circular Reactions (1 to 4 months) is characterized by the infant's ability to gain simple motor control through primary circular reactions. In this stage, infants also experience some anticipation (e.g., sucking behavior is displayed, in anticipation of being fed, as soon as the child is placed in the mother's arms), and play and imitation make their first appearances—infants appear to enjoy practicing simple motor actions.

Sub-stage 3: Secondary Circular Reactions (4 to 8 months) are responses on the part of the infant that produce responses from objects or people. Children begin to display diverse motor skills, learning to manipulate objects, sit up, and crawl. These skills direct their attention away from themselves and toward the environment. When children at this age discover an exciting behavior, such as banging a toy against a table, they will repeat this action. They also have a better formation of object concept, or object permanence. In contrast to Sub-stage 2 children, 4- to 8-month-old children are able to retrieve objects that are partially but not completely hidden. Children at this age can also anticipate where to look for an object. For example, if an infant drops a toy, the infant will anticipate where it will land, even if the descent of the toy was too fast to see.

In *Sub-stage 4: Coordination of Secondary Circular Reactions* (8 to 12 months), infants begin to coordinate their schemes to build more complex action sequences. As a consequence, infants become more skilled at two cognitive abilities—object permanence and goal-directed behavior. Infants are more skilled at understanding that objects truly continue to exist when they are not in view. Therefore, when an object is completely covered by a cloth, the infant will lift the cloth off and grasp the object. However, if the object is moved under a different cloth (B), the infant will continue to look under the original cloth (A). Piaget concluded that 8- to 12-month-olds make this AB (or A not B) search error because they cannot sustain a clear image of the object after the object is removed from their sight. In Substage 4, a child will engage in goal-directed behaviors. At this point, infants have had a great deal of experience with various schemes and are therefore able to coordinate several schemes using an overarching goal to solve a variety of problems. Piaget considered this coordination to be the first real intelligent behavior and the basis for future problem solving.

By *Sub-stage 5: Tertiary Circular Reactions* (12 to 18 months), children are no longer concerned only with themselves; they now have true interest in their surroundings. As a result, they have circular reactions—tertiary ones—that are novel, creative, and experimental, and that allow them to explore the world. Children now deliberately vary their repetitions to produce different outcomes. For example, infants will devote time to experimenting with a block and a hole, varying the orientation of the block until it fits the hole.

This experimentation with different types of objects provides a child at this substage with a better understanding of object permanence. The child will no longer make the AB search error because the child will search in several places until he or she finds the hidden object. Furthermore, children's ability to experiment and systematically to control their movements enables them to imitate a variety of unfamiliar behaviors in the presence of a model.

In *Sub-stage 6: Mental Representation* (18 to 24 months), children reach the ability to create mental representations, which includes the ability to use mental terms, symbols, and images to refer back to previously experienced events and objects. Children can now solve problems using mental representations instead of using circular reactions. For instance, suppose a child gets a toy stuck in the slats of a crib. A child younger than 18 months would move and pull the toy in a random manner until the toy came loose. A child in Sub-stage 6 would study the situation and find a systematic way of loosening the toy, as if the child were mentally representing various solutions to the problem.

With the ability to represent objects and events mentally comes deferred imitation—the ability to repeat the behavior of a model who is no longer present. Children at this age are able to imitate new behaviors without the numerous trials of a Sub-stage 5 child. When the model is absent, the child can reenact the previously learned behavior. It is assumed here that mental representation is required to remember and reproduce an event successfully. Mental representation also ushers in the beginnings of pretend play. Shortly before their second birthday, children start to pretend to act out familiar activities, such as eating and sleeping.

Preoperational period (2 to 7 years). The most noticeable change that children undergo from the sensorimotor stage to the preoperational stage is their tremendous increase in representational activity. Piaget recognized that language is an individual's most flexible means of representation. By thinking in words, individuals can deal with the past, present, and future at the same time and create powerful images of reality (Miller, 1993). However, Piaget did not consider language as creating higher forms of cognition. Instead, although the details were never clearly explained, Piaget believed that experience with sensorimotor activity leads to mental images, which children in turn label with words.

The ability to understand that objects can be represented in pictures is an aspect of *symbolic-representational ability*, which blossoms in the preoperational stage. Parents would generally agree that toddlers understand that pictures stand for real objects. In fact, even young infants can recognize the similarities between pictures and their represented objects (e.g., DeLoache, Strauss, & Maynard, 1979) and their differences (e.g., Slater, Rose, & Morrison, 1984).

Young children do, however, run into some confusion with more difficult problems. For instance, suppose a child is watching a television show containing a helium balloon and then is asked, "If I take the top off the TV and then I shake it, would a real balloon come floating out into the room?" The majority of 3-year-olds would say "yes." However, when explicitly taught about the differences between photos of objects, videos of objects, and real objects, many more of them would answer correctly (Flavell, Flavell, Green, & Korfmacher, 1990).

Pretend play is another example of symbolic representation in the preoperational period, which emerges around the age of 2 years. Its development has been written about extensively by researchers, including Bretherton (1984), Fein (1979), Garvey (1990), and Vygotsky (1978). Piaget (1951) viewed pretend play as an opportunity for a child to exercise symbolic schemes. This view is now considered too narrow because research shows that pretend play also contributes to a child's social and cognitive skills (Singer & Singer, 1990). Children who spend a great deal of time in sociodramatic play—pretend play with others—tend to be more socially competent (Burns & Brainerd, 1979; Connally & Doyle, 1984) and more imaginative and creative (Dansky, 1980; Pepler & Ross, 1981). Pretend play comes from separating behaviors and objects from their actual use and using these behaviors and objects for play. For instance, a child eats dinner at dinnertime, in the kitchen, and usually when hungry. However, when pretending to eat dinner, a child can do so at another time, in another place, and in another physiological or psychological state. Piaget (1950) considered children in this stage to be *egocentric* with respect to their symbolic viewpoints. They believe that everyone else's thoughts, feelings, desires, and perceptions are the same as theirs (Piaget & Inhelder, 1956). Piaget claimed that egocentrism is also responsible for children's erroneous and inflexible thinking. Because they are unable to consider other people's points of view, they do not always accommodate in response to feedback from their environment.

Concrete-operational period (7 to 11 years).   When children reach the concrete-operational stage, their thought resembles adult thought more than the thought of a sensorimotor or a preoperational child, because their reasoning becomes more flexible, logical, and organized, and thus more powerful (Piaget & Inhelder, 1969). This period is marked by the acquisition of operations. Prior development has placed the groundwork for this achievement. Children in the sensorimotor stage learned to interact physically with the world; preoperational children learned to represent states mentally. Concrete-operational children learn as well to manipulate their mental representations internally. Operations are characterized by their ability to be reversed and to be organized with other operations into greater systems. Children acquire logico-arithmetical operations, including concepts such as class-inclusion, conservation, perspective taking; and spatial operations, including comprehension of distance, time, velocity, and space. However, concrete-operational children can think only about concrete information. Their operations fail when applied to abstract ideas. Although their problem-solving ability mushrooms, they cannot do certain types of abstract reasoning. This ability is acquired in the formal-operations stage.

Formal-operational period (11 years onward).   This stage is characterized by the ability to "operate on operations" because adolescents and near-adolescents can now think abstractly (Inhelder & Piaget, 1958). Three main capabilities arise: reasoning with abstract possibilities, hypothetico-deductive reasoning, and propositional thought. Concrete-operational children tend to look for the solution to conceptual problems by manipulating the data with their logical concrete-operational skills. They seek the one real answer. By contrast, formal-operational adolescents and adults tend to work in the opposite direction: They start with possible solutions and progress to determine which is the real solution, called *reasoning with abstract possibilities* (Flavell, Miller, & Millar, 1993).

Formal-operational thinkers inspect the given data, form some hypothesis about what possibly could be the correct explanation, deduce whether it logically can occur in reality, and then test their theories to see whether their predictions hold. This is called *hypothetico-deductive reasoning*. If any of these steps fall short, the process is reiterated. These theories are conceptual entities constructed by abstract thinkers after careful analyses of the problem situations. These are not representations of the perceived situation (Flavell et al., 1993).

There is a difference between the way concrete-operational thinkers and formal-operational thinkers handle propositions. Concrete-operational thinking, termed *intrapropositional thinking* by Piaget, involves considering propositions as single entities and testing each one individually against reality. Concrete-operational thinkers look only for a factual relation between a single proposition and reality. A formal-operational thinker goes one step further and reasons about the logical relations that exist between two or more propositions. Piaget dubbed this more abstract form of reasoning *interpropositional* (Flavell et al., 1993).

Cross-cultural studies of Piagetian tasks in the 1960s and 1970s showed that people in many cultures do not seem to achieve formal operations without schooling (e.g., Ashton, 1975; Goodnow, 1962; Laurendeau-Bendavid, 1977). In response to this finding, Piaget (1972) repealed the claim that his stages are universal, because achieving formal operations is dependent on experience with the specific scientific thinking found in science classes and is thereby not domain- and culture-free.

Evaluation of Piaget's Theory

Piaget's theory of cognitive development involves development through a series of stages. To Piaget, stages occur at roughly the same ages for different children, and each stage builds on the preceding stage. Stages occur in a fixed order and are irreversible: Once a child enters a new stage, the child thinks in ways that characterize that stage, regardless of the task domain, the specific task, or even the context in which the task is presented. Other theorists (e.g., Beilin, 1971; Gelman, 1969), including some neo-Piagetians (e.g., Case, 1992a), would disagree with this view, suggesting that there may be greater flexibility in the cognitive-developmental progression across tasks and task domains than Piaget suggested. Much of the criticism of Piaget's theory has to do with the inflexibility of his proposed stages and uses of evidence of precocity as support.

For example, Piaget asserted that object permanence develops from manipulating objects, a skill he believed emerges in Sub-stage 4. Yet all his tests of object permanence involve infants' reaching for objects. Using reaching tests may underestimate infants' conceptual abilities because the infants' failure to respond correctly may be due simply to their immature motor systems (Baillargeon, 1993; Diamond, 1990; Mandler, 1988). In Piaget's tests, the infant has a difficult task of removing the cover before grasping the object. Regardless, Piaget concluded from these tests that young infants are lacking the ability to represent objects mentally. Later developed tests seem to show otherwise. In a collection of studies by Baillargeon (1987; Baillargeon & DeVos, 1991), which used a method to study object permanence that did not require the infant to reach for an object (habituation/dishabituation task), infants as young as 3½ months showed indications of object permanence. This finding, combined with the findings of Spelke (1991; Spelke, Breinlinger, Macomber, & Jacobson, 1992), lends credence to the hypothesis that young infants fail Piaget's original tests because the tests require behaviors of which the infants are not yet capable (e.g., reaching). Research suggests that infants probably have some understanding that hidden objects continue to exist, and that this understanding comes months earlier than Piaget had thought, and may even be present from birth. Similar evidence of apparent precocity that questions the immutability of other stages and operations such as mental representation and problem solving has also been presented (see Lutz & Sternberg, 1999, for more detailed discussion).

Fundamental Criticisms

Piaget's fundamental assertion—that the changes in children's cognition occur chiefly as an outcome of maturational processes—has been questioned. Although Piaget observed that developmental processes result from children's adaptations to their environment, he held that internal maturational processes, rather than environmental contexts or events, determine the sequence of cognitive-developmental progression. Evidence of environmental influences on children's perception of the environment, of the child's prior experiences with the task and the task materials, and even of the experimenter's presentation of the task itself may lead to apparent unevenness in cognitive development. Although Piaget allowed for some differences across task domains through a construct he called *horizontal décalage*, the mechanism underlying this construct was never clearly explained, and in the context of the theory, it seemed to be an after-the-fact explanation rather than a motivated part of the entire picture.

Consistent with this fact, theorists and researchers have questioned Piaget's interpretation regarding what causes difficulty for children in certain Piagetian tasks. Piaget's theory emphasizes the development of deductive and inductive reasoning, and Piaget held that limitations on children's ability to reason cause their difficulties in solving particular cognitive tasks. Different theorists have suggested that other kinds of limitations may at least partly influence children's performance on Piagetian tasks. Such limitations include children's motor coordination, as well as working memory capacity (e.g., Bryant & Trabasso, 1971; Kail, 1984; Kail & Park, 1994), memory strategies (Siegler, 1991), or verbal understanding of questions (e.g., Sternberg, 1985).

The evidence cited against Piaget's theory often refers to children's inconsistent abilities to perform well on tasks believed to be beyond their stage of development. However, Thelen and Smith (1994) presented an approach to development that assuages many of the apparent problems for Piaget's theory. In particular, Thelen and Smith's dynamic-systems approach, in which discontinuities occur as part of the natural interaction of nonlinear dynamic systems (systems with highly complex physical properties—in this case, children and their environment), predicts the very kinds of conflicting performance seen in children on the verge of stage transition. Indeed, Thelen and Smith pointed out that instability is necessary for new abilities to develop—a system must contain variability in its behavior for new behaviors to be selected. Furthermore, this disequilibrium is part of the natural interaction of the nonlinear dynamic systems involved in children's interactions with their environment. Thus, the dynamic systems approach to development encompasses conflicting evidence into a new framework—children do progress through stages, but not strictly via maturation. Research on the nonlinear development of mathematical skills supports such a dynamic view of development (Rittle-Johnson, Siegler, & Alibali, 2001).

These ideas notwithstanding, even adolescents and adults do not show formal-operational thinking under many circumstances (Neimark, 1975). They often seem to think associatively rather than logically (Sloman, 1996). In 1972, Piaget modified his own theory to acknowledge that the stage of formal operations may be a product more of an individual's domain-specific expertise, based on experience, than of the maturational processes of cognitive development.

In sum, Piaget's descriptions of infant development and the research methods he used are commendable and historically important, but the theory he originally posed has not endured. Although substantial biological maturation occurs at each of Piaget's stages, maturation is seen primarily as a necessary but not sufficient condition for the development of many cognitive skills. Learning experiences derived from optimal interactions with the environment help to determine the full extent of the development of cognitive abilities (Bidell & Fischer, 1992; Halford, 1999; Piaget, 1950). In fact, learning experiences, particularly those in which the complexity of the environment is mediated by a "teacher," are considered by many to be not only advantageous, but crucial to cognitive development (e.g., Feuerstein, 1979; Lidz, 2000; Vygotsky, 1962).

Beyond Piaget: Development of Working Memory

Limitations of Piaget's theory as described above (see also Lutz & Sternberg, 1999; Sternberg & Powell, 1983) led to subsequent extensions and advances on many of Piaget's original conceptualizations (e.g., Carey, 1985; Case, 1985, 1992b; Halford, 1993; Pascual-Leone, 1970). In general, *neo-Piagetian* researchers acknowledge the existence of stage-like maturation but focus more within a framework of working memory development. We review two related but somewhat quite distinct approaches as espoused by Case and by Halford, and then consider the possible role of knowledge in the assessment of working memory development.

Case. Case (1985, 1992a), like Piaget, proposed that children move through four developmental stages. The types of mental representations children can form and the types of responses they give characterize these stages. In the first stage, sensorimotor operations, children's representations consist of sensory input, and their responses to this input are physical movements. In the second stage, representational operations, children's representations involve concrete mental images, and their responses can produce additional mental representations. In the next stage, logical operations, children have the abilities to represent stimuli abstractly and to respond to them with simple transformations. The final stage, formal operations, differs from the previous stage in that children continue to represent stimuli abstractly, but they can now execute complex transformations of the information.

An interesting aspect of Case's theory of cognitive development is his view of cognitive change. In one of Case's demonstrations of the existence of this ability, he placed children of different ages at one end of a balance beam. Case showed the child that if the balance beam were pushed down, it would ring a bell. A young infant would only be able to follow visually the beam's movements. Older infants between 4 and 8 months would be able to push down the beam and ring the bell, thereby coordinating two actions (visual tracking and hand movements) instead of one isolated activity as before (visual tracking). An even older child, between 8 and 12 months, would be able to incorporate another property in a modified version of this problem, when the bell was moved out of the child's sight and placed on a different part of the beam. Finally, 12- to 18-month-old children were able to succeed when the problem required the child to push the beam up instead of down. Younger children were

Piagetian Tasks: The Balance Beam

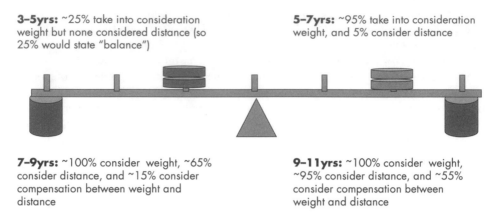

3–5yrs: ~25% take into consideration weight but none considered distance (so 25% would state "balance")

5–7yrs: ~95% take into consideration weight, and 5% consider distance

7–9yrs: ~100% consider weight, ~65% consider distance, and ~15% consider compensation between weight and distance

9–11yrs: ~100% consider weight, ~95% consider distance, and ~55% consider compensation between weight and distance

FIGURE 7.1   The balance beam task is an example of a task used by Piaget to study the development of cognitive abilities (Inhelder & Piaget, 1958). The development of reasoning in this task has been investigated by many researchers since. Halford et al. (2002a) argued that increases in performance with age, as reported in this figure, is concomitant with the development of the capacity to deal with increasingly complex relations.

not able to reverse the learned action, as they consistently pushed the beam down and became upset when the bell would not ring as it had in the past (Figure 7.1).

Case's explanation for older children's success on the final problem was that the problem contains two units, the pushing of the beam and the ringing of the bell, which are separate enough for older children to be able to see their reversible relation. The children are able to see that, when one end of the beam goes down, the other end goes up, and vice versa. Within Case's theory of development, the execution of this behavior shows that a child has the ability to form subgoals (pushing beam) to reach a final goal (ringing bell). The behaviors that lead up to a child's success on a given problem illustrate cognitive change. To reach a goal, a child must either draw on learned strategies or formulate new ones. Children's collections of strategies expand as they mature. They gain mental capacity and the ability to deal with more and more information. In this respect his theory is similar to Halford's theory of **relational complexity**. We consider this theory next.

Halford et al.: relational complexity theory.   Similar to Case, Halford and his associates (Halford, 1993; Halford & Andrews, 2004; Halford, Baker, McCredden, & Bain, 2005; Halford, et al., 1998) view cognitive development as the result of the differentiation of working memory that facilitates the capacity to deal with tasks of increasing complexity. In their account, complexity is formalized theoretically and mathematically, and is seen as the defining characteristic of both development and working memory-capacity limitations. Halford et al. (1998) argued that capacity limitations are not best conceptualized simply as a count of the pieces of information that can be stored and manipulated in working memory, but that the complexity of relations between these pieces of information is crucial. Hence, the theory has been referred to as *relational complexity* theory. In terms of development, the capacity to represent increasingly complex relations is said to increase with age (Figure 7.2).

What does a relation look like? Consider for example the comparison of size. Halford (1993) argued that size comparison requires a *binary* relation between "has *two* pieces of information" (or *arguments*, in the author's parlance), as might be represented by: LARGER-THAN (elephant, mouse). This is read as, "elephant is larger than mouse," where "elephant"

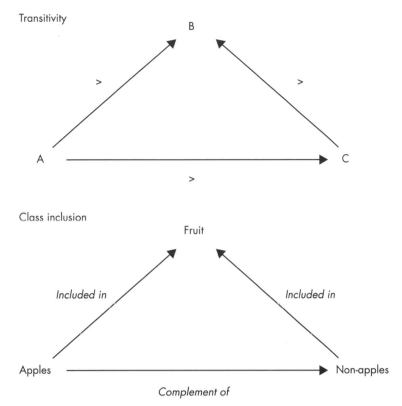

FIGURE 7.2 Underlying structure of transitive inference and class inclusion tasks. According to relational complexity theory, these tasks have the same degree of structural complexity despite surface dissimilarities. As such, class equivalence across tasks, in terms of the age of attainment of better than chance levels of performance, is predicted and observed. Reprinted from Andrews, G., & Halford, G. S. (2002). A cognitive complexity metric applied to cognitive development. *Cognitive Psychology, 45*, 153–219 with permission from Elsevier.

and "mouse" are the two arguments that form the relation, LARGER-THAN. Ternary relations have three arguments as in ADDITION(2, 3, 5). Quaternary relations have four interacting components. The more arguments or pieces of information that are required to instantiate a relation, the greater the cognitive complexity of the task and the greater the demand placed on working memory (Halford et al., 1998).

At least four types of evidence have been used to provide support for the conceptualization of cognitive development and working memory capacity limitations using relational complexity theory. These are: (1) age-of-attainment evidence—the finding that tasks of similar relational complexity have similar median ages at which levels of performance become better than chance (Andrews & Halford, 2002; Bunch, Andrews, & Halford, 2007; Halford, Andrews, Dalton, Boag, & Zielinski, 2002a; Halford, Bunch, & McCredden, 2007); (2) dual-task studies—the finding that secondary (dual) task deficits increase as relational complexity in the primary task increases (e.g., Foley, 1997; Foley & Berch, 1997; Halford, Maybery, & Bain, 1986; Maybery, Bain, & Halford, 1986); (3) neurological correlates of relational reasoning—the finding that increasing relational complexity of tasks is associated with increased activation in regions of the brain associated with executive function, the main processing component of working memory (e.g., Kroger et al., 2002; Waltz et al., 1999); and (4) perceived or subjective workload ratings—the finding that increases in relational complexity are associated with perceived increases in cognitive demand (Andrews & Halford, 1995;

Boag, Neal, Halford, & Goodwin, 2000). The age-of-attainment evidence is particularly relevant in terms of cognitive development, and it is appropriate to consider the context in which this evidence is acquired in more detail.

Andrews and Halford (2002, p. 161) argued that a conceptual complexity metric, such as provided by relational complexity theory, has much to offer the investigation of cognitive development across task domains:

> Attempts to define cognitive performances operationally by the tasks used to measure them appear to have the advantage of simplicity, but they provide no way of comparing tasks for their conceptual complexity. Thus superficially dissimilar tasks, such as transitivity, class inclusion, and interpretation of object-relative clause sentences, may turn out to be equivalent in conceptual complexity. Apparently similar tasks may be very different in complexity. A complexity metric can help to resolve this issue by identifying tasks that are at the same levels of complexity and separating them from lower and higher levels of complexity.

To investigate their claim, Andrews and Halford (2002) considered the performance of children on a number of superficially dissimilar tasks that have similar levels of complexity. We consider two of their tasks as examples, transitivity and class inclusion. Their transitive inference task required children to order colored-squares (e.g., red, green, blue, yellow, pink) so that they were consistent with separately presented premises that described the correct order of the squares (e.g., red is above green; green is above blue; blue is above yellow; yellow is above pink). The binary version of the task required children to construct a five-square tower in which the order of the squares was consistent with the premises. The ternary version required children to determine which of two non-adjacent squares (i.e., green and yellow) would be higher up the tower. This second version of the task required the integration of two separate premises in working memory (green is above blue; blue is above yellow), and this type of reasoning has been shown to entail greater cognitive demand than simple (binary) ordering of adjacent elements (Maybery et al., 1986).

The class-inclusion task requires recognition of the fact that the relation between a superordinate class (e.g., fruit) and two or more subordinate classes (e.g., apples and non-apples) is asymmetrical. That is, while all members of a sub-class (apples) can be included in and share the properties or attributes of the superordinate class (fruit), the reverse does not necessarily hold—all fruit do not have the same properties as apples. Andrews and Halford (2002) argued that a capacity to process ternary relations is required to understand this type of asymmetry. Therefore, although a task requiring this reasoning is clearly different from, say, the ternary version of the transitive inference task, they are similar in the complexity of the relations that are entailed. Consistent with the relational complexity theory, the authors showed that the median age at which the superficially dissimilar ternary tasks were mastered is in fact similar. Furthermore, in terms of cognitive development, the average proportion of participants succeeding on the ternary tasks at each age-level were approximately 15.5% of 3- and 4-year olds, 48.3% of 5-year olds, 70.2% of 6-year olds, and 77.8% of 7- and 8-year olds. Thus it was concluded that the capacity to process ternary relations develops gradually between 3 and 8 years.

Halford et al. (1998) argued that relational-complexity theory is not a stage theory in the way other neo-Piagetian theories might be considered to be (Case, 1985; Pascual-Leone, 1970). However, as we have just described, mastering a particular level of relational processing has been aligned with ages of attainment that are similar to Piagetian stages (Halford, 1993) on what are often called Piagetian tasks. This finding has been cited as evidence to support relational complexity theory. The crucial difference, it would seem, is at least twofold. First, development is conceptualized by relational complexity theorists as being more gradual and less explicitly "stage-like." Second, development is conceptualized more as an increase in the general capacity for relational processing that coincides with age than as the development of specific skills or operations *per se*. This is not to say that specific skills and knowledge are not important in relational complexity theory; they are. Differences in strategies can result in marked differences in the complexity of the processing. It is therefore very important to ensure that an appropriate methodology is in place to take knowledge into consideration (see Andrews & Halford, 2002, for a discussion of this issue).

Knowledge and the development of working memory capacity. The types of errors made in Piagetian tasks can be diagnostic of a variety of misunderstandings in knowledge. These have implications for cognitive theory testing (e.g., Lohman & Ippel, 1993; Roberts, 1993). For instance, various modifications of Piaget's balance-beam task have been useful in exploring the interplay between knowledge and cognitive capacity in complex reasoning. In another version of the balance-beam task (we have already considered one version as used by Case, 1985, 1992a), individuals are required to indicate whether a beam with various weights at certain distances on each side of a fulcrum will balance (see for example, Halford et al., 2002a; Siegler & Chen, 2002). An algorithmic approach to determining whether the beam will balance is to calculate the product of weight and distance on one side of the beam and to compare this with the product of weight and distance on the other side. Such a strategy is demanding of working memory resources. Young children (<7 years) typically resort to considering fewer dimensions. Is this difficulty a result of lack of knowledge or limited cognitive capacity? The answer is probably "both." Although it is clear that relations among weight, distance, and balance can be discovered with experience, there also appears to be a maturational component to performance.

Halford et al. (2002) argued that more complex relations (among weight, distance, and balance) can be represented as age and working memory capacity increase, consistent with the predictions of relational complexity theory (Halford, 1993). However, adults have also been observed to have difficulty with the balance-beam task (even though capacity is presumably less of an issue). This difficulty tends to indicate that knowledge and experience are also important factors influencing performance (for a discussion of methodological limitations in the balance-beam task see Turner & Thomas, 2002).

Although neo-Piagetian research has provided many insights into the sequential development of children's long-term understanding of basic logical reasoning (e.g., Carey, 1985; Case, 1985, 1992b; Halford, 1993; Pascual-Leone, 1970; Schliemann & Carraher, 2002), it is not always clear that development is as regular and sequential as these theories might imply. Research in mathematical abilities, for instance, has shown that skill development can be quite chaotic and nonlinear (Rittle-Johnson et al., 2001). The theories we have discussed so far have been predominantly concerned with describing and explaining cognitive development. An area of cognitive science research that is less frequently aligned with traditional conceptualizations of development focuses on the process of knowledge acquisition and information processing, rather than development *per se*. The fact that development can be quite chaotic and nonlinear may be partly due to differences in available knowledge and experience that lead to both different strategies for information processing and further knowledge acquisition. We consider some of the theorizing in these areas next, and argue that this work has indirect but important implications for developmental theorizing.

COGNITIVE INFORMATION-PROCESSING THEORIES

Cognitive-processing theories tend to focus on task and person characteristics that relate to learning and lead to differences in performance (e.g., novices versus expertise; Chi, Glaser &

Rees, 1982; Shafto & Coley, 2003). They are not necessarily explicitly linked to cognitive maturation through childhood (although some are). They have often been developed using adult populations. Knowledge acquisition and information-processing theories are often characterized by what are referred to as **computational models**. These models attempt to formalize cognitive theories using advanced mathematics and statistics (e.g., Braine, 1990; Johnson-Laird, 2001; Johnson-Laird, Byrne, & Schaeken, 1992; Rips, 1983, 1994; Simon & Halford, 1995). There are important differences between the models in terms of the level and type of formalization as well as the psychological theory on which they are based. What is common to each is an attempt to model the effect of task characteristics on reasoning and problem solving while taking into consideration plausible psychological limitations, such as working memory capacity or available knowledge. That is, there is a concerted attempt to specify a theory of reasoning sufficiently detailed to be able to identify and methodologically differentiate the specific task characteristics that mediate performance (Embretson, 1995, 1998; Embretson & Gorin, 2001).

The impact of these complex theories is far reaching. Taken to their extreme (i.e., with the psychological limitations removed), computational information-processing models are all but indistinguishable from the artificial intelligence models that are the basis of many computer-based "intelligent systems," such as speech-recognition software and economic models of financial markets. They all try to characterize the often complex interactions between components of the environment—such as the phonology of an utterance or the subtle fluctuations in stock-exchange trade—so as to be able to predict some outcome (recognition of a word or financial success).

One of the earlier examples of an information-processing model was proposed by Sternberg (1977), who decomposed the classical analogy task (A:B::C:?) into elementary performance components. The types of components or process that have been investigated in this task include the encoding of problem details, inference making processes, mapping of inferred relations, and processes related to the application, comparison, and justification of the final response. The general strategy of this research was to specify an information-processing model of task performance and to propose a parameterization of this model so that each information-processing component (encoding, inference, mapping, and so forth) is assigned a mathematical parameter corresponding to its latency (Figure 7.3).

Halford et al. (1998) also proposed an advanced computational model of relational reasoning based on the theoretical specification of relational complexity, which we described in a previous section. In fact, Case's model of development also has information-processing characteristics. Recall that Case regarded cognitive change as the ability to deal with more and more elements of a problem. The change in ability was seen as a change in the efficiency of processing. That is, reminiscent of classic working memory models in which separate storage and processing components are proposed (Baddeley & Hitch, 1974) and consistent with *resource theory* (Kahneman, 1973; Norman & Bobrow, 1975), Case proposed that total processing space (TPS) was a resource that could be flexibly allocated to either processing (i.e., operating space, OS) or storage (short-term storage-space, STSS)—that is, TPS = OS + STSS. After infancy, total processing space was considered to be relatively constant over age. Case argued that the demands for operating space actually declined with age because of the increase in processing efficiency. Given the closed nature of the proposed system, this served to free short-term storage-space. Hence the empirical research that demonstrated an increase in short-term memory span with age was attributed to more efficient processing. This was considered the main factor responsible for cognitive development (Case, Kurland, & Goldberg, 1982; Halford, 2002).

It is important to comment on the unitary nature of the processing system that *resource theory* might be assumed to propose, given what is presented in the previous paragraph. First,

Sternberg's (1977) Componential Analysis Of Analogical Reasoning

Processing components:

- encoding
- inferring
- mapping
- application
- comparison
- justification
- response

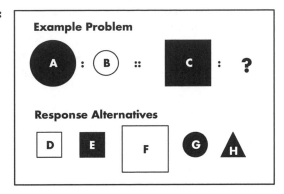

Potential Solution

1. *Encode* attributes of stimuli

2. *Infer* A:B relationship

3. *Map* elements from A to C

4. *Apply* A:B relationship to C:? transformation

5. *Compare* alternatives with extrapolated ideal

6. *Justify* chosen alternative as preferred even if not ideal

7. *Respond* as format requires

FIGURE 7.3   Componential analysis of analogical reasoning. Proposed processing components and potential solution (Sternberg, 1977).

most researchers now accept the existence of multiple resources, rather than a single resource (e.g., Wickens, 1991). Second, even though resource theory has served as the dominant metaphor for limited capacity theories such as those proposed by Case and by Halford, its utility has been questioned. Navon (1984) argued that resource theory should be considered only as a *metaphor* for information-processing because it cannot differentiate between the effects of processes that compete for a common resource and the effect of output interference generated elsewhere in the system. That is, differentiation of the cognitive architecture is often identified by the characteristics of tasks that interfere with each other and those that do not. For instance, the finding that certain visual processing tasks did not interfere (in terms of accuracy and response times) with phonological processing tasks leads to the postulation of separate visual- and auditory-processing systems (Baddeley, 1986). Tasks that interfere with each other are assumed to require a common system of resources, and, hence, freeing up resources in one task should result in better performance in the other. Navon argued that **dual-task deficit**, as this interference is known, can be accounted for without imposing the additional baggage of resource theory (such as the need to postulate additional resources when interference is not complete). Oberauer and Kliegl (2001) suggested that decay (temporal loss of information in working memory) and interference are sufficient to account for limits in working memory without additional constructs like limited resource pools.

Concurrent development of knowledge and increased experiences provide an additional factor that impacts on the assessment of a developing cognitive system. The evidence that working memory develops with age does not necessarily mean that development entails a quantitative change of a single entity, such as resources. Fry and Hale (2000, p. 6) described "some evidence [that] suggests that there may be *qualitative changes* in working memory function prior to entering the first grade. In particular, under some circumstances younger children prefer to use different mnemonic strategies than older children" (emphasis added). Part of this qualitative change is seen to be a function of pre-school children's preference for visual processing rather than phonological processing. This preference changes as the focus of experience at school becomes more verbally based. The potential role of knowledge and experience are once again implicated in the relation between development and capacity and the apparent increase in efficiency of the cognitive system. Research therefore tends to support a multi-component perspective of working memory, not only in terms of the differentiation of the storage systems, but also in terms of the differentiation of the central executive and its relation with long-term memory (or knowledge) (Baddeley & Logie, 1999).

Representations of Knowledge and Processing

Many formalized information-processing theories of knowledge acquisition are probably best epitomized by the early work of Newell and Simon (1972) and that of Anderson and his associates in their conceptualization of the adaptive control of thought (ACT) framework (Anderson, 1982, 1983, 1990; Anderson & Lebiere, 1998; Anderson & Schunn, 2000; Rumelhart & Norman, 1981). ACT is *adaptive* because it attempts to formalize knowledge-acquisition, learning, and problem-solving processes in the same network. Learning is conceptualized to entail the assimilation of new information into the network as a series of declarative facts or productions. During the early stages of skill acquisition, this **declarative information** can be used with general problem-solving procedures (e.g., means–ends analyses) in an interpretative fashion to facilitate successful problem solving without the need to access (or possess) context-specific strategies. With each successful application of the information, links between appropriate nodes are strengthened. Unsuccessful applications result in the links between nodes being weakened. Together, these experiences can be brought to bear on new information and new problems to facilitate a more automatized set of procedures that can be implemented with increasing efficiency to acquire new information and to solve problems (Schunn & Reder, 2001)—this is procedural knowledge. For instance, a child learning a new mathematical rule relating the area of a rectangle to the product of its length and breadth will store this information in the semantic network as a declarative fact. Links from this fact to other personally relevant types of information are likely to be developed at the same time— for instance, "*the table is a rectangle*," "*squares are like rectangles*," and "*the area of a square is length × length*." With experience, appropriate links will be reinforced and inappropriate ones weakened. Within the ACT framework, **procedural knowledge** is represented by a large number of rule-like units that are referred to as *productions* (Anderson & Schunn, 2000). Production rules are condition–action units (i.e., IF . . . THEN rules) that specify the cognitive actions that are the responses to certain problem-solving conditions.

For instance:

IF area of rectangle is needed,
THEN multiply breadth by length.

A production can trigger the implementation of a series of additional productions and thereby facilitate subgoaling (e.g., IF multiply, THEN . . ., and so on). The centrality of productions in this theorizing has meant that the framework is sometimes referred to as a production-system.

An extended conceptualization of the organization and development of knowledge can be found in the concept of a schema. *Schematic knowledge* is highly context-specific (Quilici & Mayer, 2002). It contains declarative knowledge (also referred to as conceptual knowledge; de Jong & Ferguson-Hessler, 1996; Rittle-Johnson et al., 2001) and procedural knowledge, in addition to what has been referred to as *situational* knowledge, which provide cues to when knowledge should be used (Cheng & Holyoak, 1985; de Jong & Ferguson-Hessler, 1996).

Contextualized schematic knowledge reflects the development of a deep structural under-standing of the domain, but this high contextualization can come at a cost. It may place constraints on the availability of certain information and in some cases can produce near-transfer failure—the unexpected failure to transfer knowledge from one context to a similar one in the *same* domain (Woltz, Gardner, & Gyll, 2000). That is, situation cues can become so entrenched with task performance that even slight changes in the nature of the task can produce failure because the appropriateness of a known response is overlooked.

Information-processing theorists argue that empirical evidence of individual differences in intelligent behavior is the result of variations in system efficiency and flexibility in selecting and applying appropriate rules to problem solving (Just & Carpenter, 1992). For instance, in the simulated air-traffic control task described by Kanfer and Ackerman (1989) and an appli-cation of the ACT framework, Schunn and Reder (2001) showed that although people may appear to possess similar strategies for allocation of task resources, there are individual differences in the ability to appropriately select from the available strategies in response to feedback from the environment (i.e., success or failure in landing aircraft). Schunn and Reder argued that these differences in "strategy adaptivity" are associated with differences in reasoning ability and working memory capacity.

Concept Development and Creativity

Many of the theories so far discussed have been criticized as being too reductionistic and as being incapable of accounting for individual differences in strategy use (e.g., Roberts, 1993). Although this criticism is acknowledged by cognitive scientists who attempt to incorporate a role for individual differences in information-processing theories (e.g., Schroyens, Schaeken, & d'Ydewalle, 1999; Schunn & Reder, 2001), others have arguably pursued an even greater degree of reductionism in attempts to identify the very basic and implicit processes of cogni-tion. One such area where considerable research has been invested explores how categories and concepts form and develop (e.g., Markman & Gentner, 1993; Murphy & Medin, 1985; Posner & Keele, 1968). For instance, what are the processes involved in the development of an understanding that a Doberman, say, is a member of the dog family, that dogs are part of an even larger superordinate category of mammals, and so on? In general, the research questions how different branches and nodes within and between trees of knowledge become related to each other, and how they are modified with experience.

Early research in category/concept formation was concerned with the development of prototypes (Posner & Keele, 1968). **Prototypes** are defined as a generalized conceptualization of an entity that consists of the typical attributes associated with the most commonly found instances of the entity (prototypical entities are, in effect, averages, and—like statistical averages—they may not actually occur in practice). Given the shared experiences of most people through mass education and popular media, prototypes tend to be relatively consistent from one individual to another, although not completely so, particularly within a given cul-ture. A prototype of a dog, say, may be a medium-sized animal that has four legs, is brownish in color, has a wagging tail, and do forth (Chi, 1997). The ease in classifying a new previously unseen instance of the dog category will be determined partly by how typical the attributes of the "new dog" are. That is, "the likelihood of assigning some example to a category depends on the similarity of the example to the category representation" (Medin, Goldstone, & Gentner, 1993, p. 254). For instance, a Labrador is likely to be more readily recognized and classified as dog than a toy poodle because many of the attributes of a Labrador are more similar to the common conceptualization of "dog." In much the same way, a whale might be more readily, although incorrectly, identified as a fish rather than as a mammal, because certain attributes of whales are not typically associated with mammals (e.g., they live in the ocean and swim). Furthermore, beliefs about whether one entity of a category (e.g., tuna) has a certain property (e.g., disease X), given that another entity of the category (e.g., goldfish) has the same property (disease X), vary as a function of how similar the two entities (tuna and goldfish) are perceived to be (Medin et al., 1993; Shafto & Coley, 2003).

Much of the research in this area has been conducted under the experimental/cognitive paradigm. The focus is predominantly on knowledge-acquisition processes and sometimes on the direct effect of experience and expertise (Shafto & Coley, 2003), although not exclusively so. As children learn and experience more, their knowledge base expands and new or unseen instances (entities) are not only classified into one or more categories, but the categories themselves may continually be modified by experience. This is not unlike the processes of accommodation and assimilation proposed by Piaget. In other words, category definitions and concepts expand and narrow to accommodate new information and new attributes. This process is ongoing and continues into adulthood. For instance, the list of attributes of mammals might be expanded to include some qualifications stating that *whales* are in fact mammals that breathe air and have live young, even though they live in the ocean.

This line of research has focused on identifying the processes and nature of knowledge acquisition. However, the findings also have direct implications for the investigation of more complex reasoning (Coley, Hayes, Lawson, & Moloney, 2004) and cognitive development. For example, the analogical reasoning involved in the classic A:B::C: ? type-problem (where ? is D, E, F, or G) relies on individuals being able to identify relations between attributes of the components (A, B, C, D, E, F, and G). These relations and attributes often belong to overlapping categories that sometimes differ in hierarchical levels. This knowledge may be necessary for efficient solution. Consider the following analogy problem:

HORSE is to STABLE as CHICKEN is to . . . *HOME, STY, COOP*, or *FARM*?

There are numerous factors that need to be considered to determine the correct response (*coop*). The relation between *horse* and *stable* will need to be considered. So will the different categorical (hierarchical) levels between the response options (e.g., *sty, coop*, and *stable* are subordinate to *farm*). Successful performance will require retrieval of previously acquired knowledge about the relations and categories, and of course, individuals will need to have had the opportunity to acquire this knowledge. This opportunity can vary quite substantially both between and within cultures.

Over and above the opportunity to learn, individuals differ in their basic capacity to acquire and represent knowledge and then to draw on this knowledge for future reasoning (Just & Carpenter, 1992; Schunn & Reder, 2001). There is also recognition of the role of individual differences from within cognitive research in concept formation. Chi (1997), for instance, argued that one component of creativity entails flexible movement between branches and nodes of categorical trees of knowledge. Moving within levels of one tree tends to be reasonably straightforward. For instance, reclassifying a whale as a mammal rather than as a fish can be accomplished gradually over time with experience, or through direct mediated instruction from a respected and more knowledgeable other (e.g., teacher, peer, or parent). However, re-representing entities from one tree to another tends to be more difficult because different trees, especially those that are fundamentally different, are considered to be different ontologically (in their fundamental conceptualization), and therefore have different **ontological attributes**. In philosophical terms, ontologies (or ontological trees) are structures of knowledge that have an entire hierarchy of categories that are fundamentally different from each other. The attributes of such trees are referred to as *ontological attributes* (Figure 7.4; see Chi, 1997, for further discussion of the distinction between various types of attributes).

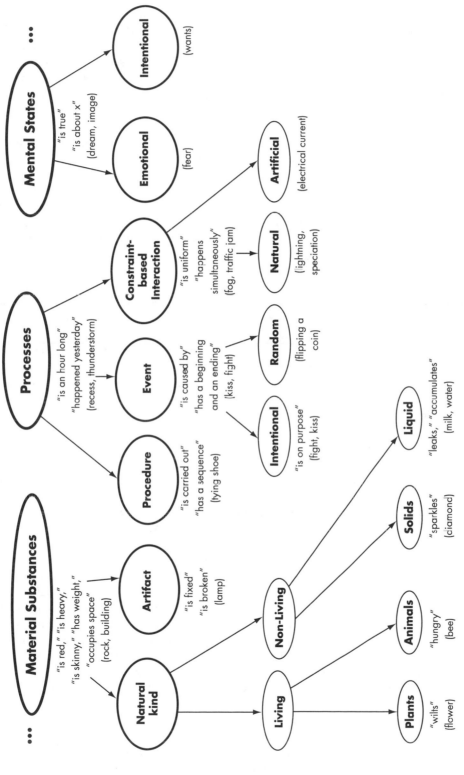

FIGURE 7.4 An example of a plausible organization of ontological trees (taken from Chi, 1997). Reproduced with permission from the American Psychological Association.

The distinction between ontological trees is philosophically defined. It is a complex but important distinction. Chi (1992) argued that ontological attributes are not modifiable, either physically or mentally. Yet other types of attributes that are not fundamental may be modified. That is, once an entity is classified into a particular categorical tree—into a particular framework of knowledge—it inherits all the ontological attributes associated with that tree or framework. Moving from one tree to another is difficult because all the basic ontological attributes associated with the entity need to be modified to move between trees (Chi, 1997). The typical outcome of an attempt to reconceptualize entities across ontological boundaries is, for all intents and purposes, nonsensical. Chi (1997, p. 218) argued that one can move between branches of a tree that have a common ontology and be able to conceptualize a statement such as, "*A dog is purple.*" One attribute of the category *dog* is color. Although purple may be a false instantiation of the color of dogs (at least as far as we currently know), the statement makes sense. With sufficient factual support, it could result in a minor restructuring of the concept/category of *dog* without changing the ontological attributes associated with dogs in general (and other entities within the tree). However, if, as suggested by Chi (1997), we cross over between trees and try to conceive of a statement such as, "*A dog is an hour-long,*" we are in a fundamentally different situation. We cannot make sense of this statement without reconceptualizing many of the fundamental (ontological) attributes associated with both dogs and time.

As a practical example of ontological restructuring, imagine the difficulty experienced by citizens in the late 1800s, when evolutionary theorists began to argue that humans are not as distinct from non-human primates and other animals as was once believed. That is, rather than being conceived of as two distinct categorical trees (humans vs. others) consisting of distinct and separate ontological paths and attributes, humans and other animals began to be considered as inhabiting different levels of the *same* ontological category. Similarly, one can imagine the difficulty of people at the time when Galileo and others shook the religious and scientific thinking of the day and argued that the Earth was not the center of the universe and that it, in fact, revolved around the sun, rather than vice versa. Arguably, both these conceptual changes had massive rippling effects throughout science and society, as the full implications of changing ontological categories became more and more evident and the cognitive dissonance generated by new information and previously held (and conflicting) beliefs was reconciled (e.g., the implications of evolutionary theory on religious beliefs still cause concern in many parts of the world today).

Crossing these types of ontological barriers so as to re-represent entities is considered by Chi (1997) to be a candidate for a core component of creativity. It is a difficult and cognitively demanding process that entails a certain degree of knowledge and experience, but it is also a process that requires the flexibility to appreciate and apprehend the full implications of changing the underlying associations with ontological attributes. To the extent that there are individual differences in flexibility, or creativity, one might also expect individual differences in at least two areas. First, there may be individual differences in the knowledge required to modify the representation of the entity (e.g., when new information becomes available that refutes the original classification of an entity). Second, there may be individual differences in the cognitive capacity or flexibility of individuals in seeing how new and disparate pieces of information can be combined in novel ways to generate a new and insightful solution to an old problem (e.g., information that conflicted with the view that the sun revolves around the Earth).

This latter requirement, the capacity for flexible thinking, is probably the most psychologically demanding on a number of levels. First, there is a distinct cognitive demand in the analytical skill necessary to assimilate multiple perspectives. Traditional ability theories (e.g, working memory theories) are in a good position to account for some of this difficulty. For instance, the process theories described earlier, such as relational complexity theory (Halford et al., 1998), may be useful in the analysis of the difficulty or complexity of different types of ontological shifts and reclassification (e.g., Halford, Andrews, & Jensen, 2002b, using the relational complexity theory, account for the difficulty of cognitive processing in class inclusion tasks and hierarchical classification tasks that exploit the products of concept-category formation processes). However, as the above examples also demonstrate, there are other demands (social, cultural, motivational) that can also influence the likelihood of creative ideas being supported and further developed. Sternberg's (1997) theory of **successful intelligence**, particularly that part of the theory related to creative intelligence, has been used to account not only for the analytical demands of the creative process, but also for the practical skills required to sell and develop the creative idea.

Both Darwin and Galileo were under intense pressures of the time not to report their creative ideas. Defying this pressure required considerable courage, as well as practical intelligence to know when and how best to sell their ideas. The theory of successful intelligence (Sternberg, 1997) formalizes an explicit role for creativity that, with further development and research, may provide an individual-differences framework for exploring the type of flexibility–creativity processes proposed by Chi (1997).

It is reasonably clear that many issues in cognitive development can be addressed by viewing processes at different levels of focus. Although it is true that, alone, much of the basic research described in this section is probably too reductionistic and ecologically weak to be of any use in directly predicting successful cognitive development (and success in life), it is invaluable in providing insights into future applied research. Traditionally, there have been only limited links between developmental/information-processing research, which we have reviewed above, and what are referred to as individual-differences or psychometric theories of intelligence. Psychometric theories attempt to identify the full constellation of cognitive abilities and to map the interrelations between them. Given this focus, psychometric theories have typically tended to be somewhat agnostic to the underlying processes of the abilities that have been identified (Deary, 2001; Lohman & Ippel, 1993). However, much is being done to link process theories of abilities (e.g., working memory theories) and development with psychometric theories (e.g., Cowan et al., 2005; Unsworth & Engle, 2007). We turn now to the area of psychometric intelligence to consider how differential psychologists model and conceptualize cognitive development.

THE PSYCHOMETRIC APPROACH: INDIVIDUAL DIFFERENCES IN COGNITIVE ABILITIES

Many different definitions of intelligence have been proposed over the years (see, e.g., "Intelligence and its measurement: A symposium", 1921; Sternberg & Detterman, 1986). The conventional notion of intelligence is built around a loosely consensual definition of intelligence in terms of generalized adaptation to the environment. Psychometric theories of intelligence tend to extend this definition by suggesting that there is a general factor of intelligence, often labeled g, that underlies all adaptive behavior (Brand, 1996; Jensen, 1998; see essays in Sternberg & Grigorenko, 2002). As we describe briefly below, the consensual notion of intelligence as one's ability to adapt to one's current situation or environment has been formalized by Sternberg (1997) in his theory of successful intelligence, and in particular in the conceptualization of practical intelligence (Sternberg et al., 2000). This has been done in a way that is quite distinct from typical conceptualizations of psychometric intelligence.

In many psychometric theories, including those most widely accepted today (e.g., Carroll, 1993; Gustafson, 1994; Horn, 1994), a number of differentiable but variously related mental abilities are proposed. The positive interrelation between these abilities—that people strong in one area also tend to be strong in others—is used as evidence to support the proposed hierarchical nesting of these abilities under one or more general cognitive ability factors at successively greater levels of specificity. In fact, most psychometric theories, described in more detail elsewhere (Brody, 2000; Carroll, 1993; Embretson & McCollam, 2000; Herrnstein & Murray, 1994; Jensen, 1998; Sternberg, 2000), use evidence from correlational research to support their view.

As an example of how correlational evidence is used for construct validation and theory building, consider the common distinction that has been empirically identified between verbal and visual–spatial abilities. Different verbal measures (e.g., vocabulary, sentence comprehension) tend to be more correlated with each other than with visual-spatial measures (e.g., paper folding, mental rotation). The converse is also true—different visual–spatial measures tend to be more highly correlated with each other than with verbal ability measures. In factor analysis, an advanced statistical technique based on correlations (Hartmann, Pelzel, & Abbott, Chapter 3, this volume), this would result in the identification of two separate factors, a verbal and a visual–spatial factor. The separation of factors is used as evidence that the measures tap distinct constructs. However, research has also shown that even though verbal and visual-spatial abilities are separable, the correlation between the measures of each ability is not exactly zero. This pattern of varying but positive correlation persists across many cognitive measures (i.e., the so-called "positive manifold"). This manifold has been cited as evidence that there is something real and common driving performance on many, if not all, cognitive tasks.

Exactly how the common variation in cognitive performance is partitioned is one major way in which psychometric theories are differentiated. Some argue that a higher-order general ability construct ("g") that variously determines performance in each of the specific lower-order abilities is the most parsimonious account for this commonality (e.g., Herrnstein & Murray, 1994; Jensen, 1998). Carroll (1993) suggested that three levels (narrow, broad, and general) are needed to capture the hierarchy of abilities, whereas Cattell (1971) suggested that two levels were especially important. In the case of Cattell, nested under general intelligence are what he referred to as fluid intelligence (Gf) and crystallized intelligence (Gc). Fluid intelligence is skill in reasoning in novel ways. Typical tests of Gf, such as Raven's progressive matrices, entail the ability to induce relations and deal with various levels of abstraction. Crystallized intelligence is "a type of broad mental ability that develops through the 'investment' of general intelligence into learning through education and experience" (Carroll, 1993, p. 599). Crystallized abilities are therefore of the kind considered to be the main manifestation of education, experience, and acculturation. Extensions of the Gf–Gc theory include a range of other broad and specific abilities, including those associated with memory, visuo-spatial abilities, and speed of processing (e.g., Roberts & Stankov, 1999; Stankov, 2000).

Some psychometric theorists believe that, relative to one's peers, intelligence is fixed relatively early in life—between 5 and 10 years of age—after which it tends to remain stable (see Bjorklund, 1995; Neisser et al., 1996). The stability beyond this period is seen by some as an epiphenomenon (Cattell, 1987; McArdle, Ferrer-Caja, Hamagami, & Woodcock, 2002). Cattell (1987), for instance, argued that the apparent stability of intelligence is the necessary outcome of aggregating across multiple abilities that have different developmental trajectories. That is, Cattell, and also Horn (1988), argued that, whereas both Gf and Gc rise through youth until early adulthood, Gf reaches its peak relatively early (15–20 years) and later declines at a relatively rapid rate. Gc, in contrast, tends to continue increasing well into the 60s and 70s. This research has been extended. For instance, McArdle et al. (2002) showed a range of differences in the developmental trajectories of the various cognitive abilities and

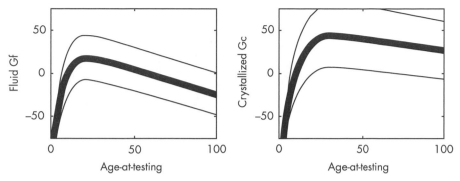

FIGURE 7.5 Differences in idealized average developmental trajectories of *Gf* and *Gc*. Taken from McArdle, J. J., Ferrer-Caja, E., Hamagami, F., & Woodcock, R. W. (2002). Comparative longitudinal structural analyses of the growth and decline of multiple intellectual abilities over the life span. *Developmental Psychology, 38*, 115–142 by the American Psychological Association. Reproduced with permission.

academic knowledge assessed by the Woodcock-Johnson tests (Woodcock & Johnson, 1989) (see Figure 7.5). Different developmental trajectories are also cited as evidence for separable factors and the diminutive importance of "*g*."

Psychometric test scores administered after about 5 years of age tend to be reasonably predictive of later abilities and achievement (Bjorklund, 1995; Sattler, 1992). At younger ages, the stability and predictive utility of ability estimates is substantially weaker, particularly for individuals in the average or superior levels (Chen & Siegler, 2000; Sattler, 1992). For infants, sensory-oriented measures, such as of rapidity of habituation–dishabituation and encoding, are better predictors of future abilities than are reasoning measures, although the correlations are typically modest (Bornstein & Colombo, 2010). One explanation for the lack of predictive power of early performance on psychometric tests is that cognitive abilities become increasingly differentiated with age and experience (Carroll, 1993; Halford, 1993). Generally, after this period, psychometric test scores become stable and follow the trajectory described above. The question remains, do psychometric test scores sufficiently represent the abilities needed to adapt successfully to one's environment—the consensual definition of intelligence reported earlier?

Sternberg (1985, 1998a, 1999a) and an increasing group of others (e.g., Ackerman & Beier, 2003; Ericsson, Krampe, & Tesch-Römer, 1993; Gardner, 1993) have argued that the psychometric definition of intelligence has become (or always was) too narrow to provide a reasonable account of performance in real-world settings: the settings within which many of the measures were originally designed to assess. The restriction, we believe, is due partly to the theoretical narrowness of the common operationalization of intelligence (in looking at only "analytical" abilities) and partly to the inadequacies of available methodologies to fully accommodate multidimensional and complex traits (Birney & Sternberg, 2006; see Figure 7.6). Research on practical and creative intelligence (Sternberg, 2003c; Sternberg et al., 2000), social intelligence (Cantor & Kihlstrom, 1987; Kihlstrom & Cantor, 2000; Sternberg & Smith, 1985), and emotional intelligence (Goleman, 1995; Mayer & Salovey, 1993; Salovey & Mayer, 1990) is expanding the theoretical foundations of intelligence. Promising methodological work on latent trait theories (e.g., Borsboom, Mellenbergh, & van Heerden, 2003) and measurement (e.g., Linacre, 1989; Michell, 1999; Wright, 1999) will further strengthen the methodological foundations to accommodate even more refined empirical research into these complex traits. Already, considerable work has been invested to demonstrate that it is possible not only to assess creative and practical intelligence (e.g., Birney, Grigorenko, & Sternberg, 2004) but also to develop effective educational interventions that exploit students' range of

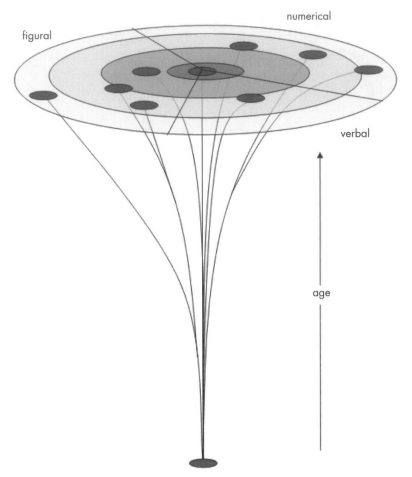

FIGURE 7.6   Concept of differentiation of cognitive abilities with age, as represented by the psychometric approach. The series of concentric circles represents a canvas on which distinct abilities (dark disks) are mapped. The closer the disks are to each other, the higher the correlation between abilities. At the center are abilities tapped by complex reasoning tasks. Toward the outer circles, tasks tend to be less complex and more content-specific. Differentiation as it occurs over age is represented by the branching of abilities over time starting from a generalized cognitive resource. From Birney & Sternberg, 2006, by permission of Oxford University Press, Inc.

creative, practical, analytical, and memory abilities (e.g., Grigorenko, Jarvin, & Sternberg, 2002; Sternberg, Torff, & Grigorenko, 1998; Williams et al., 2002). Much of this thinking forms the foundation for the theory of developing expertise.

SYSTEMS THEORIES OF COGNITIVE DEVELOPMENT

Abilities as Developing Expertise

The theoretical basis for the developing expertise model is Sternberg's (1985, 1997, 2003c) triarchic theory of successful intelligence (Figure 7.7). According to this theory, intelligence is, in part, the ability to achieve success in life through a balance of analytical, creative, and practical skills. Success is conceptualized as adaptation to, shaping of, and selection of environments as a function of the ability to recognize and capitalize on one's strengths and

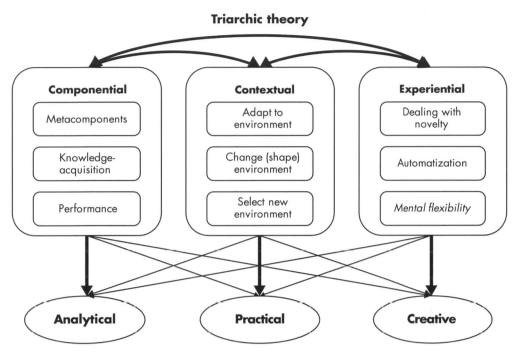

FIGURE 7.7   The components of the triarchic theory of successful intelligence.

to correct or compensate for one's weaknesses. Fitting in with this view is the broad conceptualization of intelligence and intellectual achievements as forms of developing expertise—they can be developed, just like any other forms of expertise. The theory of developing expertise conceptualizes abilities as a set of at least five cognitive competencies in varying stages of development (Sternberg, 1998a, 1999a, 2003a).

1. *Metacognitive skills* are related to skills required for recognizing, defining, and representing the problem; for formulating strategies and resource allocation; and for planning, monitoring, and evaluating success of a chosen strategy.
2. *Learning skills or knowledge-acquisition skills* are the skills that are necessary to know which information in a problem to attend to (i.e., to encode); to know which existing information to select for comparison with the new information; and to know how to combine new and old understandings to solve the problem at hand.
3. *Thinking skills* are related to performance. A context-appropriate balance of analytical, creative, and practical thinking skills is necessary to optimize success (Sternberg, 1997).
4. *Knowledge* is not only an outcome of development, but is also necessary for future development. Knowledge in both declarative and procedural forms is necessary.
5. The determining element is having sufficient *motivation* to bring these skills to bear on problem solving. Without sufficient motivation, abilities remain inert. Hence motivation is the driving force behind the developing-expertise model (Sternberg, 1998a, 1999a, 2003a).

Past experiences and differences in personality will influence levels of motivation in any given context and ultimately determine the opportunities that children (and then adults) have to develop certain abilities and expertise (Ackerman, 1996; Ackerman & Beier, 2003). Parents and teachers are significant determinants of the experiences of young children (Ceci, Ramey, & Ramey, 1990). They are also likely to have some impact on whether the child perceives

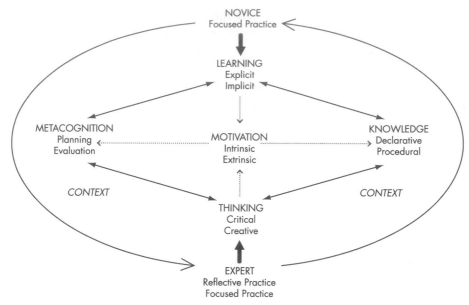

FIGURE 7.8 The developing expertise model (taken from Sternberg, 1998a). Reprinted by permission of SAGE Publications.

these experiences as successful or not. This perception is likely to influence future levels of motivation. Over time, the developing child has increasingly more choice in the types of experiences he or she engages in, and a more complex array of factors starts to play on levels of motivation (e.g., developing interests, peer pressure, financial and romantic rewards). The five components of the developing expertise theory (Figure 7.8) all interact fully in context as the novice works toward expertise through deliberate practice (see Ericsson et al., 1993, for a discussion on the role of deliberate practice). For instance, motivation drives the application of metacognitive skills. These skills in turn facilitate learning, which enables not only one's level of expertise to increase, but also the efficiency with which these skills will be implemented in the future.

Multiple Intelligences

Gardner (1993, 1999) does not view intelligence as a single construct. Instead of speaking of multiple abilities that together constitute intelligence, like some other theorists, Gardner proposed a theory of multiple intelligences, in which eight distinct intelligences function somewhat independently but may interact to produce intelligent behavior. The types of intelligence are linguistic, logical–mathematical, spatial, musical, bodily–kinesthetic, interpersonal, intrapersonal, and naturalist. Gardner (1999) also speculated on the possible existence of existential and spiritual intelligences. Each intelligence is a separate system of functioning. Nevertheless, these systems can interact to produce intelligent performance. For example, novelists rely heavily on linguistic intelligence but might use logical–mathematical intelligence in plotting story lines or checking for logical inconsistencies. Measuring intelligences separately may produce a profile of skills that is broader than would be obtained from, say, measuring verbal and mathematical abilities alone. This profile could then be used to facilitate educational and career decisions.

To identify particular intelligences, Gardner used converging operations, gathering evidence from multiple sources and types of data. The evidence includes (but is not limited to) the distinctive effects of localized brain damage on specific kinds of intelligences, distinctive patterns of development in each kind of intelligence across the life span, exceptional individuals (from both ends of the spectrum), and evolutionary history.

Gardner's view of the mind is *modular*. Modularity theorists believe that different abilities can be isolated as they emanate from distinct portions or modules of the brain. Thus, a major task of existing and future research on intelligence is to isolate the portions of the brain responsible for each of the intelligences. Gardner has speculated about some of these relevant portions, but hard evidence for the existence of separate intelligences has yet to be produced.

One might argue that the culmination of the skills and abilities we have so far reviewed in this chapter leads not only to the development of effective analytical, critical, creative, and practical thinking, but also to some sense of wisdom. It is to this concept that we turn in the final section.

WISDOM AS A COGNITIVE ABILITY

Wisdom has, among other things, been defined as the power of judging rightly based on knowledge, experience, and understanding. Reaching a wise decision involves a balancing act of intrapersonal, interpersonal, and extrapersonal interests. In turn, short- and long-term interests must be considered to achieve a balance among adaptation to existing environments, shaping of existing environments, and/or the selection of a new environments (Sternberg, 1998b). Intelligence and creativity are necessary but not sufficient skills for wisdom. Furthermore, wisdom is not simply the application of intelligence in creative ways, but rather the more highly evolved form of successful intelligence. It is not enough to have an understanding of the situation at hand, but rather it is necessary to have the ability to dynamically consider different perspectives to the mutual benefit of all those involved. This balancing act requires the application of values with the intent of achieving a common good (Figure 7.9; Sternberg, 1998b). In this section we explore the relation of wisdom to other cognitive abilities.

Wisdom's Relation to Other Cognitive Abilities

Wisdom is related to other cognitive abilities, but is also unique. In particular, it is related to knowledge, as well as to the analytical, creative, and practical aspects of intelligence (Sternberg, 2003c, 2007). Indeed, Baltes built his widely accepted theory of wisdom around the concept of knowledge about the pragmatics of life (Baltes & Staudinger, 2000; Baltes, Staudinger, Maercker, & Smith, 1995). We consider five characteristics of wisdom: knowledge, **metacognition**, creativity, practical intelligence, and social intelligence, and then consider some of the developmental implications.

First, wise thinking requires knowledge, but a major part of wisdom is tacit, informal knowledge of the kind learned from hands-on experience, not the kind of explicit formal knowledge taught in schools. One could possess "book smarts" or excel in the classroom, yet show little or no wisdom because the kind of knowledge one needs to be wise is typically not found in books or in the type of teaching found in most schools. That is, wisdom requires not simply the kind of knowledge and analytical thinking emphasized in schools or measured on tests of academic achievement. Rather, wisdom requires the analysis of real-world dilemmas where clean and neat abstractions often give way to messy, disorderly, and conflicting concrete interests.

Second, although metacognition is an important part of analytical thinking and developing expertise, wisdom also seems related to metacognition because the metacomponents involved in wisdom are similar or identical to those that follow from other accounts of

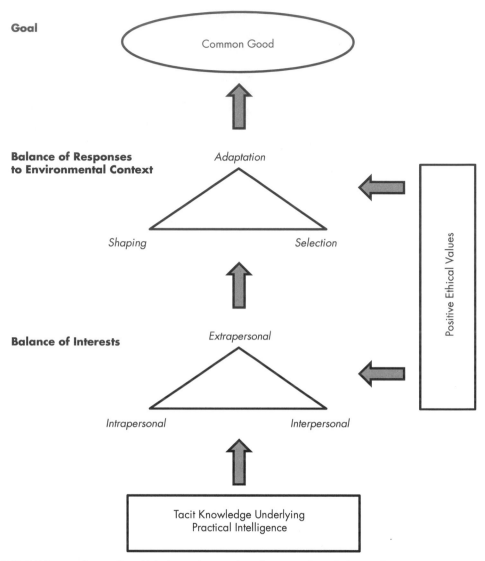

Goal

**Balance of Responses
to Environmental Context**

Balance of Interests

FIGURE 7.9 Sternberg's (1998b) balance theory of wisdom. Tacit knowledge underlying practical intelligence is applied to balance intrapersonal, interpersonal, and extrapersonal interests to achieve a balance of the responses to the environmental context in order to achieve a common good.

metacognition (Campione, Brown, & Ferrara, 1982; Nelson, 1999; Sternberg, 1985). In wisdom, as in other types of thinking, one especially needs to be aware of one's own thought processes. This awareness requires identifying problems, formulating solutions to solve problems, allocating resources to the solution of these problems, and so forth. These skills are used in wisdom, as they are in other types of thinking, but in wisdom they are especially important in achieving a balance of different interests to seek a common good.

Third, wisdom is related to creativity. Creative people often tend toward extremes, although their later contribution may be more integrative (Gardner, 1993). Creative thinking can often be brash, whereas wise thinking is balanced. This is not to say that the same people cannot be both creative and wise. It is to say, however, that the kinds of thinking required to be creative and wise are different and thus will not necessarily be found in the same person. As Gardner (1993) suggested, creative people may not be wise, and they may even be foolish in their dealings with other people. Moreover, teaching people to think creatively (see Sternberg & Williams, 1986) will not necessarily teach them to think wisely.

Wisdom shares with creativity, insightfulness. According to Sternberg (2003c), intuition can offer alternative solutions by allowing the individual to read between the lines, as well as the ability to understand and interpret their environment. Creativity allows the wise thinker to generate novel solutions in situations that cannot be resolved by defined and pre-existing heuristics. Wise thinking must be creative to generate a novel and task-relevant high-quality solution involved in the balancing of interests. Novelty, task-appropriateness, and quality are hallmarks of creativity (Sternberg, 1999b). A solution can be creative—as in solving a mathematical proof—but have no particular characteristics of wisdom. The proof does not require the balancing of interests or pursuit of a common good. It is an intellectual problem involving creative thinking (Sternberg, 2003b).

Fourth, although practical thinking is closer to wisdom than are analytical and creative thinking, it is also not the same as wisdom. Wisdom is a particular kind of practical thinking. It (1) balances competing intrapersonal (one's own), interpersonal (others'), and extrapersonal (larger) interests, (2) over the short and long terms, (3) balances adaptation to, shaping of, and selection of environments, in (4) the service of a common good. People can be good practical thinkers without being wise, but they cannot be wise without being good practical thinkers. Good practical thinking is necessary but not sufficient for the manifestation of wisdom (Sternberg, 2003c).

Fifth, wisdom also seems to be related to constructs such as social intelligence (Cantor & Kihlstrom, 1987; Kihlstrom & Cantor, 2000; Sternberg & Smith, 1985), emotional intelligence (Goleman, 1995; Mayer & Salovey, 1993; Salovey & Mayer, 1990), and interpersonal and intrapersonal intelligences (Gardner, 1993, 1999). Again, there are also differences. Social intelligence can be applied to understanding and getting along with others to any ends for any purposes. Wisdom seeks a good outcome through a balancing of interests. Thus, a sales person who figures out how to sell a worthless product to a customer might do so through using social intelligence to understand the customer's wants, but has not done so to achieve a mutually beneficial end.

Social and emotional skills are important parts of wisdom. But making wise judgments requires going beyond the understanding, regulation, or judgment of emotions. It requires processing the information to achieve a balance of interests and the formulation of a judgment that make effective use of available information to achieve a common good. Moreover, wisdom may require a balance of interpersonal and intrapersonal intelligences, but it also requires an understanding of extrapersonal factors, and a balance of these three (often conflicting) factors to attain a common good. Thus wisdom seems to go somewhat beyond these theoretically distinct kinds of intelligences as well. Perhaps the most salient differences among constructs is that wisdom is applied toward the achievement of ends that are perceived as yielding a common good, whereas the various kinds of intelligence we have mentioned may be applied deliberately toward achieving either good ends or bad ones, at least for some of the parties involved. It is interesting that the conception of wisdom proposed here is substantially closer to Chinese than to American conceptions of intelligence (Yang & Sternberg, 1997a, 1997b). One of the words used in Chinese to characterize intelligence is the same word used to characterize wisdom.

To a large extent, the development and display of the attributes described in this section is a decision over which one has substantial control, not merely some kind of innate set of predispositions. That is, wisdom is in large part an active decision to use one's intelligence, creativity, and knowledge for a common good (Sternberg, 2007). Thus, the development of wisdom entails the application of many of the attributes that have been discussed in this chapter. It entails the application of cognitive abilities; it entails the application of knowledge;

and it entails the application of creativity. But most importantly, wisdom entails the development of a mindset or habit to be motivated to understand things from diverse points of view across time and space (Sternberg, 2004).

CONCLUSIONS

In this chapter we have considered just a small selection of the many theories that have been proposed to describe and account for the development of a range of cognitive and intellectual abilities. We have attempted to broaden our view beyond the areas that are typically considered central to cognitive development in the hope that we can demonstrate the complexity of the issues that are involved, and provide evidence for an increased emphasis on integration. We have emphasized traditional developmental approaches (Piagetian and neo-Piagetian) as well as cognitive, psychometric, and systems approaches.

We believe that each approach invariably draws more heavily on the others than has often been recognized. Psychometric theories model individual differences in a broad range of abilities and have indeed provided much of what is currently known about intelligence. However, even though the psychometric approach has continued to be immensely influential in various educational, military, and commercial applications, it is not currently well equipped for modeling the processes of cognitive development. In terms of development, psychometric theories are typically restricted to describing the changing constellation of abilities over time (e.g, differentiation of abilities with age and changing developmental trajectories), with little direct explanation of the causes of these changes.

Information-processing theories are much better equipped to provide an explanatory account of development and have been particularly successful in identifying knowledge acquisition processes and the development of such constructs as working memory capacity. This approach is subsuming much of the traditional Piagetian notions of development. However, there is still considerable work to be done to clarify relations among knowledge, working-memory capacity, and psychometric constructs such as fluid and crystallized intelligence, as well as the role of creative and practical abilities. This is particularly true given that many information-processing theories have traditionally conceptualized development as a function of quantitative changes in the cognitive system (e.g., increase in available resources), and that such change may turn out to be more chaotic, nonlinear (recursive), and based on qualitatively different uses of knowledge and experience than have thus far been modeled.

Even though the traditional individual differences and information-processing approaches could be considered the middle ground on cognitive development, we believe that a complete understanding of the cognitive developmental process will not be obtainable from these approaches or in fact from any other single approach in isolation from other research. As such, we have presented research on such enigmatic constructs as concept development, creativity, and wisdom. We believe that future theorists of cognitive development may wish to take these constructs into account more than they have.

ACKNOWLEDGMENTS

An earlier version of this chapter (Birney, Citron-Pousty, Sternberg, & Lutz, 2005) was co-authored by Donna Lutz; we acknowledge her sections on Piaget from the previous edition that have been maintained in the current chapter.

REFERENCES AND SUGGESTED READINGS (📖)

Ackerman, P. (1987). Individual differences in skill learning: An integration of psychometric and information processing perspectives. *Psychological Bulletin, 102*, 3–27.

Ackerman, P. (1996). A theory of adult intellectual development: Process, personality, interests, and knowledge. *Intelligence, 22*, 227–257.

Ackerman, P., & Beier, M. E. (2003). Trait complexes, cognitive investment, and domain knowledge. In R. J. Sternberg & E. L. Grigorenko (Eds.), *The psychology of abilities, competencies, and expertise* (pp. 1–30). Cambridge, UK: Cambridge University Press.

Anderson, J. R. (1982). Acquisition of cognitive skill. *Psychological Review, 89*, 369–406.

Anderson, J. R. (1983). *The architecture of cognition*. Cambridge, MA: Harvard University Press.

Anderson, J. R. (1990). *The adaptive character of thought* (Vol. 1). Hillsdale, NJ: Lawrence Erlbaum Associates.

📖 Anderson, J. R., & Lebiere, C. (1998). *The atomic components of thought*. Mahwah, NJ: Lawrence Erlbaum Associates.

Anderson, J. R., & Schunn, C. D. (2000). Implications of the ACT-R learning theory: No magic bullets. In R. Glaser (Ed.), *Advances in instructional psychology* (Vol. 5, pp. 1–33). Mahwah, NJ: Lawrence Erlbaum Associates.

Andrews, G., & Halford, G. S. (1995). *Working memory capacity and the comprehension of relative clause sentences*. Paper presented at the 3rd Conference of the Australasian Cognitive Science Society, Brisbane.

Andrews, G., & Halford, G. S. (2002). A cognitive complexity metric applied to cognitive development. *Cognitive Psychology, 45*, 153–219.

Ashton, P. T. (1975). Cross-cultural Piagetian research: An experimental perspective. *Harvard Educational Review, 45*, 475–506.

Baddeley, A. D. (1986). *Working memory*. Oxford, UK: Clarendon Press.

Baddeley, A. D., & Hitch, G. J. (1974). Working memory. In G. H. Bower (Ed.), *The psychology of learning and motivation: Advances in research and theory* (Vol. 8, pp. 47–89). New York: Academic Press.

📖 Baddeley, A. D., & Logie, R. H. (1999). Working memory: The multiple-component model. In A. Miyake & P. Shah (Eds.), *Models of working memory: Mechanisms of active maintenance and executive control* (pp. 28–61). New York: Cambridge University Press.

Baillargeon, R. (1987). Object permanence in 3½- and 4½-month-old infants. *Developmental Psychology, 23*, 655–664.

Baillargeon, R. (1993). The object concept revisited: New directions in the investigation of infants' physical knowledge. In C. E. Granrud (Ed.), *Visual perception and cognition in infancy* (pp. 265–315). Hillsdale, NJ: Lawrence Erlbaum Associates.

Baillargeon, R., & DeVos, J. (1991). Object permanence in young infants: Further evidence. *Child Development, 62*, 1227–1246.

📖 Baltes, P. B., & Staudinger, U. M. (2000). Wisdom: A metaheuristic (pragmatic) to orchestrate mind and virtue toward excellence. *American Psychologist, 55*, 122–135.

Baltes, P. B., Staudinger, U. M., Maercker, A., & Smith, J. (1995). People nominated as wise: A comparative study of wisdom-related knowledge. *Psychology and Aging, 10*, 155–166.

Beilin, H. (1971). Developmental stages and developmental processes. In D. R. Green, M. P. Ford & G. B. Flamer (Eds.), *Measurement and Piaget* (pp. 172–196). New York: McGraw-Hill.

Bidell, T. R., & Fischer, K. W. (1992). Beyond the stage debate: Action, structure, and variability in Piagetian theory and research. In R. J. Sternberg & C. A. Berg (Eds.), *Intellectual development* (pp. 100–140). New York: Cambridge University Press.

Birney, D. P., Citron-Pousty, J. H., Sternberg, R. J., & Lutz, D. J. (2005). The development of cognitive and intellectual abilities. In M. E. Lamb & M. H. Bornstein (Eds.), *Developmental science: An advanced textbook* (5th ed., pp. 327–358). Mahwah, NJ: Lawrence Erlbaum Associates.

Birney, D. P., Grigorenko, E. L., & Sternberg, R. J. (2004). *An application of the many-facet Rasch measurement approach to the evaluation of triarchic instruction*. Paper presented at the annual meeting of the American Educational Research Association, San Diego, CA.

📖 Birney, D. P., & Sternberg, R. J. (2006). Intelligence and cognitive abilities as competencies in development. In E. Bialystok & G. Craik (Eds.), *Lifespan cognition: Mechanisms of change* (pp. 315–330). New York: Oxford University Press.

Bjorklund, D. F. (1995). *Children's thinking: Developmental function and individual difference*. Pacific Grove, CA: Brooks/Cole Publishing Company.

Boag, C. C., Neal, A., Halford, G. S., & Goodwin, G. (2000). *Comparing measures of cognitive complexity: Cognitive psychology applied to air traffic control*. Paper presented at the British Psychological Society Cognitive Section Conference, University of Essex, Colchester, UK.

Bornstein, M. H., & Colombo, J. (2010). Infant cognitive functioning and child mental development. In S. Pauen & M. H. Bornstein (Eds.), *Early childhood development and later achievement*. New York: Cambridge University Press.

Borsboom, D., Mellenbergh, G. J., & van Heerden, J. (2003). The theoretical status of latent variables. *Psychological Review*, *110*, 203–219.

Braine, M. D. S. (1990). The "natural logic" approach to reasoning. In W. F. Overton (Ed.), *Reasoning, necessity, and logic: Developmental perspectives* (pp. 133–157). Hillsdale, NJ: Lawrence Erlbaum Associates.

Brand, C. (1996). *The g factor: General intelligence and its implications*. Chichester, UK: Wiley.

Bretherton, I. (Ed.). (1984). *Symbolic play*. New York: Academic Press.

Brody, N. (2000). History of theories and measurements of intelligence. In R. J. Sternberg (Ed.), *Handbook of intelligence* (pp. 16–33). New York: Cambridge University Press.

Bryant, P. E., & Trabasso, T. (1971). Transitive inference and memory in young children. *Nature*, *232*, 456–458.

Bunch, K. M., Andrews, G., & Halford, G. S. (2007). Complexity effects on the children's gambling task. *Cognitive Development*, *22*, 376–383.

Burns, S. M., & Brainerd, C. J. (1979). Effects of constructive and dramatic play on perspective taking in very young children. *Developmental Psychology*, *15*, 512–521.

Campione, J. C., Brown, A. L., & Ferrara, R. (1982). Mental retardation and intelligence. In R. J. Sternberg (Ed.), *Handbook of human intelligence* (pp. 393–490). New York: Cambridge University Press.

Cantor, N., & Kihlstrom, J. F. (1987). *Personality and social intelligence*. Englewood Cliffs, NJ: Prentice Hall.

Carey, S. (1985). *Conceptual change in childhood*. Cambridge, MA: MIT Press.

Carroll, J. B. (1993). *Human cognitive abilities: A survey of factor-analytic studies*. New York: Cambridge University Press.

Case, R. (1985). *Intellectual development: Birth to adulthood*. London: Academic Press.

Case, R. (1992a). *The mind's staircase: Exploring the conceptual underpinnings of children's thought and knowledge*. Hillsdale, NJ: Lawrence Erlbaum Associates.

Case, R. (1992b). Neo-Piagetian theories of child development. In R. J. Sternberg & C. A. Berg (Eds.), *Intellectual development* (pp. 161–196). New York: Cambridge University Press.

Case, R., Kurland, M., & Goldberg, J. (1982). Operational efficiency and the growth of short-term memory span. *Journal of Experimental Child Psychology*, *33*, 386–404.

Cattell, R. B. (1971). *Abilities: Their structure, growth and action*. Boston: Houghton Miffin.

Cattell, R. B. (1987). *Intelligence: Its structure, growth and action*. Amsterdam: Elsevier Science Publishers.

Ceci, S. J., Ramey, S. L., & Ramey, C. T. (1990). Framing intellectual assessment in terms of person–process–context model. *Educational Psychologist*, *25*, 269–291.

Chen, Z., & Siegler, R. S. (2000). Intellectual development in childhood. In R. J. Sternberg (Ed.), *Handbook of intelligence*. New York: Cambridge University Press.

Cheng, P. W., & Holyoak, K. J. (1985). Pragmatic reasoning schemas. *Cognitive Psychology*, *17*, 391–416.

Chi, M. T. (1992). Conceptual change within and across ontological categories: Examples from learning and discovery in science. In R. Giere (Ed.), *Cognitive models of science: Minnesota studies in the philosophy of science* (pp. 129–186). Minneapolis, MN: University of Minnesota Press.

Chi, M. T. (1997). Creativity: Shifting across ontological categories flexibly. In T. B. Ward, S. M. Smith & J. Vaid (Eds.), *Creative thought: An investigation of conceptual structures and processes* (pp. 209–234). Washington, DC: American Psychological Association.

Chi, M. T., Glaser, R., & Rees, E. (1982). Expertise in problem solving. In R. J. Sternberg (Ed.), *Advances in the psychology of human intelligence* (Vol. 1, pp. 7–75). Hillsdale, NJ: Lawrence Erlbaum Associates.

Coley, J. D., Hayes, B. K., Lawson, C., & Moloney, M. (2004). Knowledge, expectations, and inductive reasoning within conceptual hierarchies. *Cognition*, *90*, 217–253.

Connally, J. A., & Doyle, A. B. (1984). Relations of social fantasy play to social competence in preschoolers. *Developmental Psychology*, *20*, 797–806.

Cowan, N., Elliott, E. M., Saults, J. S., Morey, C. C., Mattox, S., Hismjatullina, A., et al. (2005). On the capacity of attention: Its estimation and its role in working memory and cognitive aptitudes. *Cognitive Psychology*, *51*, 42–100.

Cronbach, L. J. (1957). The two disciplines of scientific psychology. *American Psychologist*, *12*, 671–684.

Dansky, J. L. (1980). Make-believe: A mediator of the relationship between play and associative fluency. *Child Development*, *51*, 576–579.

Deary, I. J. (2001). Human intelligence differences: Towards a combined experimental–differential approach. *Trends in Cognitive Sciences*, *5*, 164–170.

de Jong, T., & Ferguson-Hessler, M. (1996). Types and qualities of knowledge. *Educational Psychologist*, *31*, 105–113.

DeLoache, J. S., Strauss, M. S., & Maynard, J. (1979). Picture perception in infancy. *Infant Behavior and Development*, *2*, 77–89.

Diamond, A. (1990). Developmental time course in human infants and infant monkeys, and the neural bases of inhibitory control in reaching. In A. Diamond (Ed.), *The development and neural bases of higher cognitive functions* (pp. 637–669). New York: New York Academy of Sciences.

Embretson, S. E. (1995). The role of working memory capacity and general control processes in intelligence. *Intelligence, 20*, 169–189.

Embretson, S. E. (1998). A cognitive design system approach to generating valid tests: Application to abstract reasoning. *Psychological Methods, 3*, 380–396.

Embretson, S. E., & Gorin, J. (2001). Improving construct validity with cognitive psychology principles. *Journal of Educational Measurement, 38*, 343–368.

Embretson, S. E., & McCollam, K. (2000). Psychometric approaches to the understanding and measurement of intelligence. In R. J. Sternberg (Ed.), *Handbook of intelligence* (pp. 423–444). New York: Cambridge University Press.

Ericsson, K. A., Krampe, R. T., & Tesch-Römer, C. (1993). The role of deliberate practice in the acquisition of expert performance. *Psychological Review, 100*, 363–406.

Fein, G. G. (1979). Pretend play: New perspectives. *Young Children, 34*, 61–66.

Feuerstein, R. (1979). *The dynamic assessment of retarded performers: The learning potential assessment device theory, instruments, and techniques.* Baltimore: University Park Press.

Flavell, J. H., Flavell, E. R., Green, F. L., & Korfmacher, J. E. (1990). Do young children think of television images as pictures or real objects? *Journal of Broadcasting and Electronic Media, 34*, 399–417.

Flavell, J. H., Miller, P. H., & Millar, S. A. (1993). *Cognitive development* (3rd ed.). Englewood Cliffs, NJ: Prentice Hall.

Foley, E. J. (1997). *Assessing conceptual complexity in hierarchical reasoning: A dual-task approach.* Unpublished dissertation, University of Cincinnati.

Foley, E. J., & Berch, D. B. (1997). Capacity limitations of a classical M-Power measure: A modified dual-task approach. *Journal of Experimental Child Psychology, 66*, 129–143.

Fry, A. F., & Hale, S. (2000). Relationships among processing speed, working memory, and fluid intelligence in children. *Biological Psychology, 54*, 1–34.

Gardner, H. (1993). *Frames of mind: The theory of multiple intelligences.* New York: Basic Books.

Gardner, H. (1999). *Intelligence reframed: Multiple intelligences for the 21st century.* New York: Basic Books.

Garvey, C. (1990). *Play.* Cambridge, MA: Harvard University Press.

Gelman, R. (1969). Conservation acquisition: A problem of learning to attend to relevant attributes. *Journal of Experimental Child Psychology, 7*, 167–187.

Ginsburg, H., & Opper, S. (1979). *Piaget's theory of intellectual development.* Englewood Cliffs, NJ: Prentice Hall.

Goleman, D. (1995). *Emotional intelligence.* New York: Bantam Books.

Goodnow, J. J. (1962). A test of milieu effects with some of Piaget's tasks. *Psychological Monographs, 76* (Whole No. 555).

Grigorenko, E. L., Jarvin, L., & Sternberg, R. J. (2002). School-based tests of the triarchic theory of intelligence: Three settings, three samples, three syllabi. *Contemporary Educational Psychology, 27*, 167–208.

Gustafson, J. E. (1994). Hierarchical models of intelligence and educational achievement. In A. Demetriou & A. Efklides (Eds.), *Intelligence, mind, and reasoning: Structure and developments. Advances in psychology* (pp. 45–73). Amsterdam: North-Holland/Elsevier.

Halford, G. S. (1993). *Children's understanding: The development of mental models.* Hillsdale, NJ: Lawrence Erlbaum Associates.

Halford, G. S. (1999). The development of intelligence includes capacity to process relations of greater complexity. In M. Anderson (Ed.), *The development of intelligence* (pp. 193–213). Hove, UK: Psychology Press.

Halford, G. S. (2002). Information-processing models of cognitive development. In U. Goswami (Ed.), *Blackwell handook of childhood cognitive development* (pp. 555–574). Oxford, UK: Blackwell.

Halford, G. S., & Andrews, G. (2004). The development of deductive reasoning: How important is complexity? *Thinking and Reasoning, 10*, 123–145.

Halford, G. S., Andrews, G., Dalton, C., Boag, C. C., & Zielinski, T. (2002a). Young children's performance on the balance scale: The influence of relational complexity. *Journal of Experimental Child Psychology, 81*, 383–416.

Halford, G. S., Andrews, G., & Jensen, I. (2002b). Integration of category induction and hierarchical classification: One paradigm at two levels of complexity. *Journal of Cognition and Development, 3*, 143–177.

Halford, G. S., Baker, R., McCredden, J. E., & Bain, J. D. (2005). How many variables can humans process? *Psychological Science, 16*, 70–76.

Halford, G. S., Bunch, K. M., & McCredden, J. E. (2007). Problem decomposability as a factor in complexity of the dimensional change card sort task. *Cognitive Development, 22*, 348–391.

Halford, G. S., Maybery, M. T., & Bain, J. D. (1986). Capacity limitations in children's reasoning: A dual-task approach. *Child Development, 57*, 616–627.

Halford, G. S., & Wilson, W. H. (1980). A category theory approach to cognitive development. *Cognitive Psychology, 12*, 356–411.

Halford, G. S., Wilson, W. H., & Phillips, S. (1998). Processing capacity defined by relational complexity: Implications for comparative, developmental, and cognitive psychology. *Behavioral and Brain Sciences, 21*, 803–831.

Herrnstein, R. J., & Murray, C. (1994). *The bell curve*. New York: Free Press.

Horn, J. L. (1988). Thinking about human abilities. In J. R. Nesselroade (Ed.), *Handbook of multivariate psychology* (2nd ed., pp. 645–685). New York: Plenum Press.

Horn, J. L. (1994). Theory of fluid and crystallized intelligence. In R. J. Sternberg (Ed.), *The encyclopedia of human intelligence* (Vol. 1, pp. 443–451). New York: Macmillan.

Hunt, E. B. (1980). Intelligence as an information-processing concept. *British Journal of Psychology*, *71*, 449–474.

Inhelder, B., & Piaget, J. (1958). *The growth of logical thinking from childhood to adolescence: An essay on the construction of formal operational structures*. New York: Basic Books.

"Intelligence and its measurement: A symposium" (1921). *Journal of Educational Psychology*, *12*, 123–147, 195–216, 271–275.

Jensen, A. (1998). *The g factor: The science of mental ability*. Westport, CT: Praeger/Greenwood.

Johnson-Laird, P. N. (2001). Mental models and deduction. *Trends in Cognitive Sciences*, *5*, 434–442.

Johnson-Laird, P. N., Byrne, R. M., & Schaeken, W. (1992). Propositional reasoning by model. *Psychological Review*, *99*, 418–439.

Just, M. A., & Carpenter, P. A. (1992). A capacity theory of comprehension: Individual differences in working memory. *Psychological Review*, *99*, 122–149.

Kahneman, D. (1973). *Attention and effort*. Englewood Cliffs, NJ: Prentice Hall.

Kail, R. (1984). *The development of memory in children* (2nd ed.). New York: Freeman.

Kail, R., & Park, Y. (1994). Processing time, articulation time, and memory span. *Journal of Experimental Child Psychology*, *57*, 281–291.

Kanfer, R., & Ackerman, P. (1989). Motivation and cognitive abilities: An integrative/aptitude–treatment interaction approach to skill acquisition. *Journal of Applied Psychology*, *74*, 657–690.

Kihlstrom, J. F., & Cantor, N. (2000). Social intelligence. In R. J. Sternberg (Ed.), *Handbook of intelligence* (2nd ed.). Cambridge, UK: Cambridge University Press.

Kroger, J., Sabb, F. W., Fales, C., Bookheimer, S. Y., Cohen, M. S., & Holyoak, K. (2002). Recruitment of anterior dorsolateral prefrontal cortex in human reasoning: A parametric study of relational complexity. *Cerebral Cortex*, *12*, 477–485.

Laurendeau-Bendavid, M. (1977). Culture, schooling, and cognitive development: A comparative study of children in French Canada and Rwanda. In P. R. Dasen (Ed.), *Piagetian psychology: Cross-cultural contributions* (pp. 123–168). New York: Gardner Press.

Lidz, C. S. (2000). Theme and some variations on the concepts of mediated learning experience and dynamic assessment. In A. Kozulin & Y. Rand (Eds.), *Experience of mediated learning: An impact of Feuerstein's theory in education and psychology* (pp. 166–174). Oxford, UK: Elsevier Science.

Linacre, J. M. (1989). *Many-facet Rasch measurement*. Chicago: MESA Press.

Lohman, D. F., & Ippel, M. J. (1993). Cognitive diagnosis: From statistically based assessment toward theory-based assessment. In N. Frederiksen, R. J. Mislevy, & I. I. Bejar (Eds.), *Test theory for a new generation of tests* (pp. 41–70). Hillsdale, NJ: Lawrence Erlbaum Associates.

Lutz, D. J., & Sternberg, R. J. (1999). Cognitive development. In M. H. Bornstein & M. E. Lamb (Eds.), *Developmental psychology: An advanced textbook (4th ed.)*. Mahwah, NJ: Lawrence Erlbaum Associates.

Mandler, J. M. (1988). How to build a baby: On the development of an accessible representational system. *Cognitive Development*, *3*, 113–136.

Markman, A. B., & Gentner, D. (1993). Structural alignment during similarity comparisons. *Cognitive Psychology*, *25*, 431–467.

Maybery, M. T., Bain, J. D., & Halford, G. S. (1986). Information-processing demands of transitive inference. *Journal of Experimental Psychology: Learning, Memory, and Cognition*, *12*, 600–613.

Mayer, J. D., & Salovey, P. (1993). The intelligence of emotional intelligence. *Intelligence*, *17*, 433–442.

McArdle, J. J., Ferrer-Caja, E., Hamagami, F., & Woodcock, R. W. (2002). Comparative longitudinal structural analyses of the growth and decline of multiple intellectual abilities over the life span. *Developmental Psychology*, *38*, 115–142.

McClelland, J. L., Rumelhart, D. E., & Hinton, G. E. (1986). The appeal of parallel distributed processing. In D. E. Rumelhart & J. L. McClelland (Eds.), *Parallel distributed processing* (Vol. 1, pp. 3–44). Cambridge, MA: MIT Press.

Medin, D., Goldstone, R. L., & Gentner, D. (1993). Respects for similarity. *Psychological Review*, *100*, 254–278.

Michell, J. (1999). *Measurement in psychology: Critical history of a methodological concept*. New York: Cambridge University Press.

Miller, P. H. (1993). *Theories of developmental psychology* (3rd ed.). New York: Freeman.

Murphy, G. L., & Medin, D. (1985). The role of theories in conceptual coherence. *Psychological Review*, *92*, 289–316.

Navon, D. (1984). Resources: A theoretical soup stone? *Psychological Review*, *91*, 216–234.

Neimark, E. D. (1975). Intellectual development during adolescence. In F. D. Horowitz (Ed.), *Review of child development research* (Vol. 4, pp. 541–594). Chicago: University of Chicago Press.

Neisser, U., Boodo, G., Bouchard, T. J., Jr., Boykin, A. W., Brody, N., Ceci, S. J., et al. (1996). Intelligence: Knowns and unknowns. *American Psychologist, 51*, 77–101.

Nelson, T. O. (1999). Cognition versus metacognition. In R. J. Sternberg (Ed.), *The nature of cognition*. Cambridge, MA: MIT Press.

Newell, A., & Simon, H. A. (1972). *Human problem solving*. Englewood Cliffs, NJ: Prentice-Hall.

Norman, D. A., & Bobrow, D. G. (1975). On data-limited and resource-limited processes. *Cognitive Psychology, 7*, 44–64.

Oberauer, K., & Kliegl, R. (2001). Beyond resources: Formal models of complexity effects and age differences in working memory. *European Journal of Cognitive Psychology, 13*, 187–215.

Pascual-Leone, J. (1970). A mathematical model for the transition rule in Piaget's developmental stages. *Acta Psychologica, 32*, 301–345.

Pepler, D. J., & Ross, H. S. (1981). The effects of play on convergent and divergent problem solving. *Child Development, 52*, 1202–1210.

Piaget, J. (1950). *The psychology of intelligence* (M. Piercy & D. E. Berlyne, Trans.). London: Routledge & Kegan Paul.

Piaget, J. (1951). *Play, dreams, and imitation in childhood*. New York: Norton.

Piaget, J. (1972). Intellectual evolution from adolescence to adulthood. *Human Development, 15*, 1–12.

Piaget, J. (1985). *The equilibration of cognitive structures: The central problem of intellectual development*. Chicago: University of Chicago Press.

Piaget, J., & Inhelder, B. (1956). *The child's conception of space*. London: Routledge & Kegan Paul.

Piaget, J., & Inhelder, B. (1969). *The psychology of the child*. London: Routledge & Kegan Paul.

Posner, M. I., & Keele, S. W. (1968). On the genesis of abstract ideas. *Journal of Experimental Psychology, 77*, 353–363.

Quilici, J. L., & Mayer, R. E. (2002). Teaching students to recognize structural similarities between statistics word problems. *Applied Cognitive Psychology, 16*, 325–342.

Rips, L. (1983). Cognitive processes in propositional reasoning. *Psychological Review, 90*, 38–71.

Rips, L. (1994). *The psychology of proof: Deductive reasoning in human thinking*. Cambridge, MA: MIT Press.

Rittle-Johnson, B., Siegler, R. S., & Alibali, M. W. (2001). Developing conceptual understanding and procedural skill in mathematics: An iterative process. *Journal of Educational Psychology, 93*, 346–362.

Roberts, M. J. (1993). Human reasoning: Deduction rules or mental models, or both? *Quarterly Journal of Experimental Psychology, 46A*, 569–589.

Roberts, R. D., & Stankov, L. (1999). Individual differences in speed of mental processing and human cognitive abilities: Toward a taxonomic model. *Learning and Individual Differences, 11*, 1–120.

Rumelhart, D. E. (1990). Brain style computation: Learning and generalisation. In S. F. Zornetzer, J. L. Davis, & C. Lau (Eds.), *An introduction to neural and electronic networks* (pp. 405–420). Cambridge, MA: MIT Press.

Rumelhart, D. E., & Norman, D. A. (1981). Analogical processes in learning. In J. R. Anderson (Ed.), *Cognitive skills and their acquisition* (pp. 335–359). Hillsdale, NJ: Lawrence Erlbaum Associates.

Salovey, P., & Mayer, J. D. (1990). Emotional intelligence. *Imagination, Cognition, and Personality, 9*, 185–211.

Sattler, J. M. (1992). *Assessment of children* (3rd ed.). San Diego, CA: Jerome M. Sattler.

Schliemann, A. D., & Carraher, D. W. (2002). The evolution of mathematical reasoning: Everyday versus idealized understandings. *Developmental Review, 22*, 242–266.

Schroyens, W., Schaeken, W., & d'Ydewalle, G. (1999). Error and bias in meta-propositional reasoning: A case of the mental model theory. *Thinking and Reasoning, 5*, 29–65.

Schunn, C. D., & Reder, L. M. (2001). Another source of individual differences: Strategy adaptivity to changing rates of success. *Journal of Experimental Psychology: General, 130*, 59–76.

Shafto, P., & Coley, J. D. (2003). Development of categorization and reasoning in the natural world: Novices to experts, naive similarity to ecological knowledge. *Journal of Experimental Psychology: Learning, Memory, and Cognition, 29*, 641–649.

Siegler, R. S. (1991). *Children's thinking*. Englewood Cliffs, NJ: Prentice Hall.

Siegler, R. S., & Chen, Z. (2002). Development of rules and strategies: Balancing the old and the new. *Journal of Experimental Child Psychology, 81*, 446–457.

Simon, T., & Halford, G. S. (Eds.). (1995). *Developing cognitive competence: New approaches to cognitive modelling*. Hillsdale, NJ: Lawrence Erlbaum Associates.

Singer, D. G., & Singer, J. L. (1990). *The house of make-believe*. Cambridge, MA: Harvard University Press.

Slater, A., Rose, D., & Morrison, V. (1984). Newborn infants' perception of similarities and differences between two- and three- dimensional stimuli. *British Journal of Developmental Psychology, 2*, 287–294.

Sloman, S. A. (1996). The empirical case for two systems of reasoning. *Psychological Bulletin, 2*, 287–294.

Spelke, E. S. (1991). Physical knowledge in infancy: Reflections on Piaget's theory. In S. Carey & R. Gelman (Eds.), *The epigenesis of mind: Essays in biology and cognition* (pp. 133–169). Hillsdale, NJ: Lawrence Erlbaum Associates.

Spelke, E. S., Breinlinger, K., Macomber, J., & Jacobson, K. (1992). Origins of knowledge. *Psychological Review, 99*, 605–632.

Stankov, L. (2000). The theory of fluid and crystallized intelligence: New findings and recent developments. *Learning and Individual Differences, 12*, 1–3.

Sternberg, R. J. (1977). *Intelligence, information processing, and analogical reasoning: The componential analysis of human abilities*. Hillsdale, NJ: Lawrence Erlbaum Associates.

Sternberg, R. J. (1985). *Beyond IQ: A triarchic theory of human intelligence*. Cambridge, UK: Cambridge University Press.

Sternberg, R. J. (1990). *Metaphors of mind: Conceptions of the nature of intelligence*. New York: Cambridge University Press.

Sternberg, R. J. (1997). *Successful intelligence*. New York: Plume.

Sternberg, R. J. (1998a). Abilities are forms of developing expertise. *Educational Researcher, 27*, 11–20.

Sternberg, R. J. (1998b). A balance theory of wisdom. *Review of General Psychology, 2*, 347–365.

Sternberg, R. J. (1999a). Intelligence as developing expertise. *Contemporary Educational Psychology, 24*, 359–375.

Sternberg, R. J. (Ed.). (1999b). *Handbook of creativity*. New York: Cambridge University Press.

Sternberg, R. J. (Ed.). (2000). *Handbook of intelligence*. New York: Cambridge University Press.

Sternberg, R. J. (2003a). What is an expert student? *Educational Researcher, 32*, 5–9.

Sternberg, R. J. (2003b). *WICS: A theory of wisdom, intelligence, and creativity synthesized*. New York: Cambridge University Press.

Sternberg, R. J. (2003c). *Wisdom, intelligence, and creativity synthesized*. New York: Cambridge University Press.

Sternberg, R. J. (2004). Four alternative futures for education in the United States: It's our choice. *School Psychology Review, 33*, 67–77.

Sternberg, R. J. (2007). A systems model of leadership: WICS. *American Psychologist, 62*, 34–42.

Sternberg, R. J., & Detterman, D. K. (1986). *What is intelligence?* Norwood, NJ: Ablex.

Sternberg, R. J., Forsythe, G. B., Hedlund, J., Horvath, J., Snook, S., Williams, W. M., et al. (2000). *Practical intelligence in everyday life*. New York: Cambridge University Press.

Sternberg, R. J., & Grigorenko, E. L. (Eds.). (2002). *The general factor of intelligence: How general is it?* Mahwah, NJ: Lawrence Erlbaum Associates.

Sternberg, R. J., & Powell, J. S. (1983). The development of intelligence. In J. Flavell & E. Markman (Eds.), *Handbook of child psychology* (3rd ed., Vol. 3, pp. 341–419). New York: Wiley.

Sternberg, R. J., & Smith, C. (1985). Social intelligence and decoding skills in nonverbal communication. *Social Cognition, 2*, 168–192.

Sternberg, R. J., Torff, B., & Grigorenko, E. L. (1998). Teaching triarchically improves school achievement. *Journal of Educational Psychology, 90*, 374–384.

Sternberg, R. J., & Williams, W. M. (1986). *How to develop student creativity*. Alexandria, VA: Association for Supervision and Curriculum Development.

Tanner, J. M., & Inhelder, B. (Eds.). (1956). *Discussions on child development* (Vol. 1). London: Tavistock.

Thelen, E., & Smith, L. B. (1994). *A dynamic systems approach to the development of cognition and action*. Cambridge, MA: MIT Press/Bradford Books.

Turner, G., & Thomas, H. (2002). Bridging the gap between theory and model: A reflection in the balance scale task. *Journal of Experimental Child Psychology, 81*, 466–481.

Unsworth, N., & Engle, R. W. (2007). On the division of short-term and working memory: An examination of simple and complex span and their relation to higher order abilities. *Psychological Bulletin, 133*, 1038–1066.

Vygotsky, L. (1962). *Thought and language*. Cambridge, MA: MIT Press (Original work published 1934.)

Vygotsky, L. (1978). *Mind in society: The development of higher psychological processes*. Cambridge, MA: Harvard University Press.

Waltz, J. A., Knowlton, B. J., Holyoak, K. J., Boone, K. B., Mishkin, F. S., de Menezes Santos, M., et al. (1999). A system for relational reasoning in human prefrontal cortex. *Psychological Science, 10*, 119–125.

Wickens, C. D. (1991). Processing resources and attention. In D. L. Damos (Ed.), *Multiple-task performance* (pp. 3–34). London: Taylor & Francis.

Williams, W. M., Blythe, T., White, N., Li, J., Gardner, H., & Sternberg, R. J. (2002). Practical intelligence for schools: Developing metacognitive sources of achievement in adolescence. *Mensa Research Journal, 33*, 14–94.

Woltz, D. J., Gardner, M. K., & Gyll, S. P. (2000). The role of attention processes in near transfer of cognitive skills. *Learning and Individual Differences, 12*, 209–251.

Woodcock, R. W., & Johnson, M. B. (1989). *Woodcock-Johnson psycho-educational battery—revised*. Allen, TX: DLM Teaching Resources.

Wright, B. D. (1999). Fundamental measurement for psychology. In S. E. Embretson & S. L. Hershberger (Eds.), *The new rules of measurement: What every psychologist and educator should know* (pp. 65–104). Mahwah, NJ: Lawrence Erlbaum Associates.

Yang, S., & Sternberg, R. J. (1997a). Conceptions of intelligence in ancient Chinese philosophy. *Journal of Theoretical and Philosophical Psychology, 17*, 101–119.

Yang, S., & Sternberg, R. J. (1997b). Taiwanese Chinese people's conceptions of intelligence. *Intelligence, 25*, 21–36.

❖ 8 ❖

LANGUAGE DEVELOPMENT

Brian MacWhinney
Carnegie Mellon University

INTRODUCTION

Every normal human child succeeds at learning language. As a result, people often tend to take the process of language learning for granted. To many, language seems like a basic instinct, as simple as breathing or blinking. But, in fact, language is the most complex skill that a human being will ever master. We come to realize the complexity of language when, as adults, we try to learn a very different foreign language, such as an English-speaker learning Chinese or Arabic. Suddenly, we are confronted with a vastly different set of articulations and sounds, a new orthography, radically different word meanings, and new rules of grammar and word formation. The fact that all people succeed in learning to use language, whereas not all people learn to swim or sing very well, demonstrates how fully language conforms to our human nature. Languages avoid sounds that people cannot produce, words they cannot learn, or sentence patterns they cannot parse. Moreover, the things we choose to talk about and the expressions we select provide a full compendium of the scope of human life and society. It is the complexity of our nature and our society that leads directly to the complexity of language. Language learning seems like an effortless process because all this structure emerges so directly from the shape of human nature, the human body, and human society.

Unlike the communication systems of other species, language allows humans to create complete and open-ended descriptions of all manner of objects and activities outside of the here and now. These obvious differences between human language and animal communication have led philosophers from Plato to Descartes to think of language as a species-specific ability, something like a "Special Gift." But this gift does not depend on some single ability that arose suddenly in modern *Homo sapiens*. Instead, growing evidence from the study of **language development**, language evolution, and neurophysiology paints a complex and increasingly dynamic view of the emergence of this Special Gift. We now know that language learning depends on the acquisition of abilities across the six dimensions given in Table 8.1, namely audition, articulation, words, grammar, communication, and literacy. In this chapter, we will examine recent models and accounts of each of these six dimensions of language learning with an eye toward understanding what they have to tell us about the modern notion of a Special Gift for language development. As indicated in Table 8.1, the functioning of each of these dimensions depends on processing in particular brain areas. However, each of these

TABLE 8.1
Levels of Linguistic Processing

Dimension	Brain area	Theory
1. Audition	Auditory cortex	Statistical learning
2. Articulation	IFG, motor cortex	Resonance, gating
3. Words	Wernicke's area	Self-organizing maps
4. Grammar	Inferior frontal gyrus	Item-based patterns
5. Communication	Dorsolateral prefrontal cortex	Turn-taking, perspective
6. Literacy	Dorsal cortex	Schema theory

brain areas functions in synchrony with many other areas, so we cannot think in terms of a simple set of modules for language processing. Researchers have proposed theories that account for the learning of skills on these six dimensions. Some of the relevant theories, which we will examine later, are indicated in the third column of Table 8.1.

Before beginning, let us take a brief look at the contents of these six dimensions, beginning with auditory and articulatory learning. Auditory development involves learning how to distinguish the basic sounds of the language and using them to chop up or segment the flow of speech into distinguishable words. This learning involves the receptive or perceptual side of language use. In contrast, children's articulatory development involves learning to control the mouth, tongue, and larynx to produce sounds that imitate those produced by adults. This learning involves the productive or expressive use of language. Auditory learning and articulatory learning are the two sides of phonological development. We cannot acquire control over articulation until we have learned the correct auditory contrasts. Thus, audition logically precedes articulation.

The third dimension of language development is lexical development, or the learning of words. In order to serve as a means of communication between people, words must have a shared or conventional meaning. Picking out the correct meaning for each new word is a major learning task for the child. But it is not enough for children just to recognize words produced by their parents. To express their own intentions, they have to be able to recall the names for things on their own and convert these forms into actual articulations. Thus, lexical development, like phonological development, includes both receptive and expressive components.

Having acquired a collection of words, children can then put them into combinations. Grammar—the fourth dimension of language—is the system of rules by which words and phrases are arranged to make meaningful statements. Children need to learn how to use the ordering of words to mark grammatical functions such as subject or direct object.

The fifth dimension of language is pragmatics. This is the system of patterns that determines how we can use language in particular social settings for particular communicative purposes. Because pragmatics refers primarily to the skills needed to maintain conversation and communication, child language researchers find it easiest to refer to pragmatic development as the acquisition of communicative competence and conversational competence (Ochs & Schieffelin, 1983). A major component of communicative competence involves knowing that conversations customarily begin with a greeting, require turn-taking, and concern a shared topic. Children must also learn that they need to adjust the content of their communications to match their listener's interests, knowledge, and language ability. Finally, children need to acquire literate control of language to use printed material and formal spoken dialog to express increasingly complex social, cognitive, and linguistic structures or schemas. Literacy is the sixth and final dimension of the language acquired by the child.

As we progress through our study of the learning of these six dimensions of language, we will find three recurring themes. First, to study each dimension, researchers have devised a unique set of methods that we will want to understand. Second, for each dimension, we can present a set of standard age-linked milestones in acquisition for normal development, as long as we understand that, even within normal children, there is immense variation in the age of attainment of these milestones. Third, for each dimension, we can examine specific mental and physical processes that the child can use to acquire systematic control of language. If we can specify in detail the exact steps that produce a particular increase in the child's linguistic abilities, then we can say that we have provided a mechanistic account for this aspect of language development. In the best of all cases, we would be able to link this type of detailed mechanistic account to actual changes in the brain structures that support language. In practice, explanations at this detailed neurological level are still largely outside our grasp (MacWhinney, 2009).

AUDITORY DEVELOPMENT

William James (1890) described the world of the newborn as a "blooming, buzzing confusion." However, we now know that, at the auditory level at least, the newborn's world is remarkably well structured (Bornstein, Arterberry, & Mash, Chapter 6, this volume). The cochlea and auditory nerve provide extensive preprocessing of signals for frequency and intensity. By the time the signal reaches the auditory cortex, it has already been processed and categorized. In the 1970s, researchers (Eimas, Siqueland, Jusczyk, & Vigorito, 1971) discovered that human infants were specifically adapted at birth to perceive contrasts such as that between /b/ and /p/, as in *bit* and *pit*, in a categorical fashion. Figure 8.1 illustrates that listeners make a sharp crossover from perceiving /b/ to perceiving /p/ when voicing begins at about 20 ms after the release of the labial closure. Remarkably, we then learned (Kuhl & Miller, 1978) that even chinchillas were capable of making this distinction. This result indicates that the basic structure of the infant's auditory world arises from fundamental processes in the mammalian ear and cochlear nucleus, rather than from some specifically human adaptation. Beyond this basic level of auditory processing, it appears that infants have a remarkable capacity to record and store sequences of auditory events. It is as if the infant's auditory cortex has a tape recorder that stores and replays input sounds. In this way, the ear accustoms itself to the general sound patterns of the language, as well as the specific forms of some highly frequent words, long before learning the actual meanings of particular words.

FIGURE 8.1   Perception of a VOT continuum (from Wikipedia).

One method (Aslin, Saffran, & Newport, 1999) for studying early audition relies on the fact that babies tend to habituate to repeated stimuli from the same perceptual class. If the perceptual class of the stimulus suddenly changes, the baby will brighten up and turn to look at the new stimulus. To take advantage of this, experimenters can play back auditory stimuli through speakers placed either to the left or to the right of the baby. If the experimenter constructs a set of words that share a certain property and then shifts to words that have a different property, the infant may demonstrate awareness of the distinction by turning away from the old stimulus and orienting to the more interesting, new stimulus. For example, when the sequence /badigudibagadigudigagidu/ is repeated many times, the parts that are repeated come to stand out perceptually and in the infant's memory. In this example, the repeated string is /digudi/. If 6-month-olds are trained on this string, they will grow tired of the repeated sound and will come to prefer to listen to new sound strings, rather than to one with the old /digudi/ string. This habituation effect is strongest for stressed syllables and syllables immediately following stressed syllables (Jusczyk, 1997). This memory for sequences of syllables suggests that we are born with an ability to store and recall the sounds of human language. During the first year, the child is exposed to several thousand hours of human language. By continually attending to the auditory patterns of the language, the child builds up a rich repertoire of expectations about the forms of words. However, during this early period, the child still has no idea about the link between sounds and meanings.

In addition to demonstrating early abilities to store sequences of sounds, babies also demonstrate preferences for the language that resembles the speech of their mothers. Thus, a French infant will prefer to listen to French, whereas a Polish infant will prefer to listen to Polish (Jusczyk, 1997). In addition, babies demonstrate a preference for their own mother's voice, as opposed to that of other women. Together, these abilities and preferences suggest that, during the first 8 months, the child is remarkably attentive to language. In fact, this learning seems to begin even before birth. DeCasper and Fifer (1980) tape-recorded mothers reading a Dr Seuss book and then played back these tapes to babies before they were 3 days old. Making the playback of the tapes contingent on the sucking of a pacifier, they found that babies sucked harder for recordings from their own mothers than for those from other mothers. Moreover, newborns preferred stories their mothers had read out loud even before they were born over stories that were new (DeCasper, Lecanuet, & Busnel, 1994). Thus, it appears that their prenatal auditory experience shaped their postnatal preferences.

Although infants are not yet learning words, they are acquiring the basic auditory and intonational patterns of their native language. As they sharpen their ability to hear the contrasts of their native language, they begin to lose the ability to hear contrasts not represented in their native language (Kuhl, Conboy, Padden, Nelson, & Pruitt, 2005; Werker, 1995). If the infant is growing up in a bilingual world, full perceptual flexibility is maintained. Moreover, within the first year, bilingual children become increasingly able to distinguish the two different languages they are learning (Bosch & Sebastián-Galles, 1997). However, if the infant is growing up monolingual, flexibility in processing is gradually traded off for quickness and automaticity. As adults, bilinguals continue this trade-off of flexibility for automaticity, showing slightly slower reaction times in speeded lexical decision tasks than monolinguals (Kilborn, 1989).

ARTICULATORY DEVELOPMENT

Running in parallel with these growths in auditory ability, children display continual advances in vocal production. At birth, or shortly thereafter, the child is capable of four distinct types of cries (Wäsz-Hockert, Lind, Vuorenkoski, Partanen, & Valanne, 1968): the birth cry, the pain cry, the hunger cry, and the pleasure cry. The birth cry occurs only at birth and involves the infant trying to clear out the embryonic fluid that has accumulated in the lungs and trachea. The pain cry can be elicited by pricking the baby with a pin. The hunger cry is a reliable indicator of the infant's need to be fed. The pleasure cry, which is softer and not too frequent at first, seems to be the cry from which later language develops. Moreover, using spectrographic analysis, one can distinguish children with genetic abnormalities such as *cri du chat* or Lesch-Nyan syndrome at this age through their cries (Wäsz-Hockert, et al., 1968).

Infant cry patterns can be understood from the framework of the study of animal behavior or ethology (Tinbergen, 1951). In that framework, animals are viewed as capable of producing certain fixed action patterns. For example, bucks have fixed action patterns for locking horns in combat. Birds have fixed action patterns for seed pecking and flying. In humans, fixed action patterns include sucking, crying, eye fixation, and crawling. These various fixed action patterns are typically elicited by what ethologists call innate releasing mechanisms. For example, the sight of the nipple of the mother's breast elicits sucking. Mothers respond to an infant's hunger cry by lactating. If baby feels like it is falling, it will throw its arm outwards with the fingers out. A pinprick on a baby's foot elicits the pain cry, and parents respond to this cry by picking up and cuddling the child. On this level, we can think of the origins of language as relatively phylogenetically ancient and stable.

Articulatory development progresses through a fairly clear set of milestones, although with much individual variation. During the first 3 months, a baby's vocalizations involve nothing more than cries and vegetative adaptations, such as sucking, chewing, and coughing. However, just before 3 months (Lewis, 1936; McCarthy, 1954), at the time of the first social smiles, babies begin to make the delightful little sounds that we call "cooing." These sounds have no particular linguistic structure, but their well-integrated intonation makes them sure parent pleasers. During this time, the number and variety of vowel-like sounds the infant produces shows a marked increase. Unlike the vowels of crying, these vowels are produced from pleasure. Irwin (1936) noted that, up to 6 months, the infant's sounds are 90% consonants produced with closures in the back of the mouth like /g/ and /k/ and mid-vowels like /ʌ/ and /ə/.

Babbling

At around 6 months there is shift from back consonants, such as /g/ and /k/, to front consonants, such as /p/ and /t/. This shift in consonants is accompanied by an increase in front vowels like /e/ and /i/. This shift may be a result of the shift from the dominance of spinal control of grosser synergisms such as swallowing to cortical control of finer movements (Berry & Eisenson, 1956; Tucker, 2002). This shift allows the baby to produce structured vocalizations, including a larger diversity of individual vowels and consonants, mostly in the shape of the consonant–vowel (CV) syllables like /ta/ or /pe/. As the frequency of these structured syllable-like vocalizations increases, we begin to say that the infant is **babbling**. Neural control of early babbling is built on top of patterns of noisy lip-smacking that are present in many primates (MacNeilage, 1998). These CV vocal gestures (Hoyer & Hoyer, 1924) have two pieces. The first part is a consonantal vocal closure that allows for a build-up of subglottalic pressure. Once this consonantal closure is released, the second part of the CV gestures begins. During this part, the vocal cords can vibrate freely, producing the resonant sound of the following vowel.

Until the sixth month, deaf infants babble much like hearing children (Oller & Eilers, 1988). However, well before 9 months, deaf infants lose their interest in vocal babbling, diverging more and more from the normal pathway (Mavilya, 1970; Wallace, Menn, & Yoshinaga-Itano, 1998). This suggests that their earlier babbling is sustained largely through proprioceptive and somaesthetic feedback, as babies explore the various ways in which they can play with their mouth. After 6 months, babbling relies increasingly on auditory feedback.

During this period, the infant tries to produce specific sounds to match up with specific auditory impressions. It is at this point that the deaf child no longer finds babbling entertaining, because it is not linked to auditory feedback. Instead, deaf children begin at this time to engage in forms of manual babbling. These facts suggest that, from the infant's point of view, babbling is essentially a process of exploring the coordinated use of the mouth, lungs, and larynx (Oller, 2000; Thelen & Smith, 1994).

In the heyday of behaviorism (Lerner, Lewin-Bizan, & Warren, Chapter 1, this volume), researchers viewed the development of babbling in terms of reinforcement theory. For example, Mowrer (1960) thought that babbling was driven by the infant's attempt to create sounds like those made by their mothers. In behaviorist terms, this involves secondary goal reinforcement. Other behaviorists thought that parents differentially reinforce or shape babbling through smiles or other rewards. They thought that these reinforcements would lead a Chinese baby to babble the sounds of Chinese, whereas a Quechua baby would babble the sounds of Quechua. This was the theory of "babbling drift." However, closer observation has indicated that this drift toward the native language does not occur clearly until after 10 months (Boysson-Bardies & Vihman, 1991). After 12 months, we see a strong drift in the direction of the native language, as the infant begins to acquire the **first words**. Opponents of behaviorism (Jakobson, 1968) stressed the universal nature of babbling, suggesting that, during babbling, all children produce all the sounds of all the world's language. However, this position also seems to be too strong. Although it is certainly true that some English-learning infants will produce Bantu clicks and Quechua implosives, not all children produce all of these sounds (Cruttenden, 1970).

Although vowels can be acquired directly as whole stable units in production, consonants can only be articulated in combinations with vowels, as pieces of whole syllables. The information regarding the place of articulation for all consonants except fricatives, such as /s/ or /z/, is concentrated in the transition that occurs between the release of the consonant and the steady state of the vowel (Cole & Scott, 1974). During this transition between the consonant and the vowel, the identity of the preceding consonant can be detected in a sound spectrograph by looking at deflections in the bands of energy that are unique to each vowel. Each vowel has three such formants or bands of sound energy concentrated at certain frequencies. In CV syllables like /pa/ or /ko/, each different consonant will be marked by different patterns of transitions in these formants before and after different vowels. Thus, in /di/, the second format rises in frequency before the steady state of the vowel, whereas in /du/ the second formant falls before the vowel. Massaro (1975) argued that this blending makes the syllable the natural unit of perception, as well as the likely initial unit of acquisition. By learning syllables as complete packages, the child avoids the problem of finding acoustic invariance for specific phonemes. If the syllable is, in fact, the basic unit of perception, we would expect to find that auditory storage would last at least 200 ms, or about as long as the syllable. In fact, it appears that auditory storage lasts about 250 ms (Massaro, 1975), indicating that it may be designed to encode and process syllables.

Ongoing practice with whole syllables occurs throughout the babbling period that extends from around 4 months to the end of the first year. In languages like Japanese, which has only 77 syllable types, this learning may allow the child to control some significant part of adult phonology. In English, with over 7,000 possible syllables, learning of the language through the acquisition of syllables seems to be a less realistic goal.

Infants commonly produce syllables sounding like /ba/ and /di/, but are relatively less likely to produce /bi/, probably because making a /b/ results in a tongue position well suited to following with /a/ but not /i/ (Massaro, 1975). Vihman (1996) studied infants and toddlers learning Japanese, French, Swedish, and English. A very small number of syllables accounted for half of those produced in all the groups, and the two most frequent syllables, /da/ and /ba/, were used by all language groups. These patterns suggest that infants use a basic motor template to produce syllables. These same constraints also affect the composition of the first words (Oller, 2000). For example, instead of pronouncing *mother* as /mʌðər/, the child will produce it as /mada/ or /mama/.

Between 6 and 10 months, there seems to be a tight linkage between babbling and general motoric arousal. The child will move arms, head, and legs while babbling, as if babbling is just another way of getting exercise while aroused. During the last months of the first year, the structure of babbling becomes clearer, more controlled, and more organized. Some children produce repetitive syllable strings, such as */badibadibadibadigu/*; others seem to be playing around with intonation and the features of particular articulations.

Piaget's (1952) theory of sensorimotor learning provides an interesting account of many of these developments. Piaget viewed much of early learning as based on circular reactions in which the child learned to coordinate the movements of one process with another. In the case of babbling, the child is coordinating the movements of the mouth with their proprioceptive and auditory effects. In these circular reactions, the child functions as a "little scientist" who is observing and retracing the relations between one schema and another. For example, in the first month the infant will assimilate the schema of hand motion to the sucking schema. In babbling, the child assimilates the schema of mouth motions to the perceptual schema of audition, proprioception, and oral somaesthesia. There is much to support this view. It seems to be particularly on the mark for those periods of late babbling when the child is experimenting with sounds that are found in other languages. Also, the fact that deaf babies continue to babble normally until about 6 months tends to support this view.

Phonological Processes

The child's first words can be viewed as renditions or imitations of adult forms that have gone through a series of simplifications and transformations. Some of these simplifications lead to the dropping of difficult sounds. For example, the word *stone* is produced as *tone*. In other cases, the simplifications involve making one sound similar to those around it. For example, *top* may be produced as *pop* through regressive assimilation. Assimilation is a process that results in the features of one sound being adapted or assimilated to resemble those of another sound. In this case, the labial quality of the final /p/ is assimilated backwards to the initial /t/, replacing its dental articulation with a labial articulation. We can refer to these various types of assimilations and simplifications as "phonological processes" (Menn & Stoel-Gammon, 1995; Stampe, 1973). Many of these processes or predispositions seem to be based on something like the principle of "least effort" (Ponori, 1871). A proper theory of least effort has to be grounded on an independent phonetic account of effort expenditure. Ohala (1974, 1981, 1994) explored many of the components of this theory. However, most child phonologists have not yet made use of phonetically grounded principles, preferring to construct more abstract descriptive accounts (Bernhardt & Stemberger, 1998; Kager, 1999).

The child's problems with phonological form are very much focused on production rather than on perception. An illustration of this comes from the anecdote in which a father and his son are watching boats in the harbor. The child says, *look at the big sip*. Echoing his son's pronunciation, the father says, *yes, it's quite a big sip*. To this, the child protests, saying *no, Daddy say "sip," not "sip."* Such anecdotes underscore the extent to which the child's auditory forms for words line up with the adult standard, even if their actual productions are far from perfect. Table 8.2 presents some of the common types of phonological processes.

It is important to realize that many of these processes are also operative in adult language. For example, in Spanish, the dental /n/ in the word combination *digan paja* "say nice" becomes assimilated in normal speech to the labial sound /m/ under the influence of the

TABLE 8.2
Examples of Phonological Processes

Process	Target	Actual
final devoicing	bed	bet
final deletion	home	hoe
depalatalization	show	so
consonant harmony	dog	gog
syllable deletion	telephone	teffone
cluster reduction	bracket	backet
gliding	real	weal
stopping	funny	punny
stopping /z/	zoo	do
stopping /th/	them	dem
deaffrication	chip	ship
affrication	some	thumb
spirantization	thumb	fun
reduplication	baby	baybay
place assimilation	mad	mab

following labial sound. Assimilations and changes of this type are fundamental to the changes that languages undergo over the centuries.

Detailed observations of the course of phonological development have shown that the development of individual word forms does not follow a simple course toward the correct adult standard. Sometimes there are detours and regressions from the standard. For example, a child may start by producing *step* accurately. Later, under the influence of pressures for simplification of the initial consonant cluster, the child will regress to production of *step* as *tep*. Finally, *step* will reassert itself. This pattern of good performance, followed by poorer performance, and then finally good performance again is known as "U-shaped learning," because a graph of changes in accuracy across time resembles the letter "U." The same forces that induce U-shaped learning can also lead to patterns in which a word is systematically pronounced incorrectly, even though the child is capable of the correct pronunciation. For example, Smith (1973) reported that his son systematically produced the word *puddle* as *puggle*. However, he was also able to produce *puzzle* as *puddle*. Smith's account of this pattern assumes that the production of *puggle* for *puddle* is based on a consistent and deterministic rule. Another possible interpretation is that the child produces *puggle* in an attempt to distinguish it from *puddle* as the pronunciation of *puzzle*. Here, as elsewhere in language development, the child's desire to mark clear linguistic contrasts may occasionally lead to errors.

THE FIRST WORDS

The emergence of the first word is based on three earlier developments. The first is the infant's growing ability to record the sounds of words. The second is the development of an ability to control vocal productions, which occurs in the late stages of babbling. The third is the general growth of the symbolic function, as represented in play, imitation, and object manipulation. Piaget (1954) characterized the infant's cognitive development in terms of the growth of representation or the "object concept." In the first 6 months of life, the child is unable to think about objects that are not physically present. However, a 12-month-old will see a dog's tail sticking out from behind a chair and realize that the rest of the dog is hiding behind the chair. This understanding of how parts relate to wholes supports the child's first major use of the symbolic function. When playing with toys, the 12-month-old will begin to produce sounds such as *vroom* or *bam-bam* that represent properties of these toys and actions. Often these phonologically consistent forms appear before the first real words. Because they have no clear conventional status, parents may tend to ignore these first symbolic attempts as nothing more than spurious productions or babbling.

Even before producing the first conventional word, the 12-month-old has already acquired an ability to comprehend as many as 10 conventional forms. The infant learns these forms through frequent associations among actions, objects, and words. Parents often realize that prelinguistic infants are beginning to understand what they say. However, it is difficult for parents to provide evidence that demonstrates this ability convincingly. Researchers deal with this problem by bringing infants into the laboratory, placing them into comfortable high-chairs, and asking them to look at pictures, using the technique of visually reinforced preferential looking. A word such as *dog* is broadcast across loudspeakers. Pictures of two objects or actions are then displayed in two computer monitors, as illustrated in Figure 8.2. For example, a dog may be on the screen to the right of the baby and a car may be on the screen to the left. If the child looks at the picture that matches the word, a toy bunny pops up and does an amusing drum roll. This convinces babies that they have chosen correctly, and they then do the best they can to look at the correct picture on each trial. Some children get fussy after only a few trials, but others last for 10 trials or more at one sitting and provide reliable evidence that they know a few basic words. Many children show this level of understanding by the 10th month—2 or 3 months before the child has produced a recognizable first word (Oviatt, 1980).

Given the fact that the 10-month-old is already able to comprehend several words, why is the first recognizable conventional word not produced until several months later? Undoubtedly, many of the child's first attempts to match an articulation with an auditory target fall on deaf ears. Many are so far away from the correct target that even the most supportive parent cannot divine the relation. Eventually, the child produces a clear articulation that makes clear sense in context. The parent is amazed and smiles. The child is reinforced and the first word is officially christened.

But all is still not smooth sailing. The child still has no systematic method for going from auditory forms for words to the corresponding articulatory forms. Earlier experience with

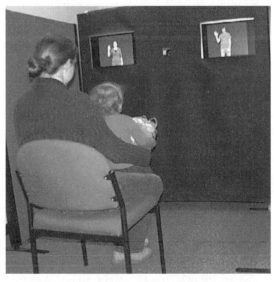

FIGURE 8.2 The preferential looking paradigm.

babbling provides some guide, but now the linkage requires increased precision and control over difficult articulators such as the tongue and the lips. The many simplifications that the 1-year-old introduces to adult phonology are well known to students of phonological development. Children tend to drop unstressed syllables, producing *Cinderella* as *rella*. They repeat consonants, producing *water* as *wawa*. And they simplify and reduce consonant clusters, producing *tree* as *pee*. All of these phonological processes echo similar processes found in the historical development and dialectal variation of adult languages (Stampe, 1973). What is different in child language is the fact that so many simplifications occur at once, making so many words difficult to recognize. Rather than repeating this experience, children may spend a month or two consolidating their conceptual and phonological systems in preparation for an attack on the adult target. However, most children do not go through this silent period. Instead, late babbling tends to coexist with the first words in most cases.

One way of understanding the challenge presented by the first words looks at the problem from the viewpoint of the infant. When babbling, the only constraints infants face are those arising from their own playfulness and interest. There are no socially defined constraints on the range of variation of those sounds. Some babies may try to get each sound "just right," but they do this to match their own goals and not ones imposed from outside.

It is easy to assume that children have some innate knowledge that tells them that words will always involve some spoken verbal form. However, an innate constraint of this type would severely limit the learning of sign language by deaf children. It would also inhibit gestural learning by hearing children. Rather than obeying some narrow view of the possible shape of a word, children are willing to learn all sorts of meaningful relations between signs and the objects that they represent. For example, Namy and Waxman (1998) found that normal 18-month-olds were happy to learn gestures as object labels. Similarly, Woodward and Hoyne (1999) found that 13-month-olds were happy to pick up a sound, such as clapping or banging, as if it was the name of an object.

Word Meanings

From Plato to Quine, philosophers have considered the task of figuring out word meaning to be a core intellectual challenge. Quine (1960) illustrated the problem by imagining a scenario in which a hunter is out on safari with a native guide. Suddenly, the guide shouts *Gavagai* and the hunter, who does not know the native language, has to quickly infer the meaning of the word. Does it mean *shoot now!* or *there's a rhino* or *it got away*, or maybe something else? If the word refers to the rhino, does it point to the horn, the hooves, the skin, or the whole animal? Worse still, the word could refer to the horn of a rhino if it is before noon and the tail of a jackal after noon. Without some additional cues regarding the likely meaning of the word, how can the poor hunter figure this out?

Fortunately, the toddler has more cues to rely on than does the hunter. The first person to recognize the importance of these additional cues was Augustine, the great Church Father, who wrote this in his *Confessions* (Augustine, 1952):

> This I remember; and have since observed how I learned to speak. It was not that my elders taught me words (as, soon after, other learning) in any set method; but I, longing by cries and broken accents and various motions of my limbs to express my thoughts, that so I might have my will, and yet unable to express all I willed or to whom I willed, did myself, by the understanding which Thou, my God, gavest me, practice the sounds in my memory. When they named anything, and as they spoke turned towards it, I saw and remembered that they called what they would point out by the name they uttered. And that they meant this thing, and no other, was plain from the motion of their body, the natural language, as it were, of all nations, expressed by the countenance, glances

of the eye, gestures of the limbs, and tones of the voice, indicating the affections of the mind as it pursues, possesses, rejects, or shuns. And thus by constantly hearing words, as they occurred in various sentences, I collected gradually for what they stood; and, having broken in my mouth to these signs, I thereby gave utterance to my will. Thus I exchanged with those about me these current signs of our wills, and so launched deeper into the stormy intercourse of human life, yet depending on parental authority and the beck of elders.

The important point here is not whether Augustine could actually recall these memories, but rather how he conceptualized language learning. In this regard, his observations are remarkably astute. First, he emphasized the natural, emergent nature of word learning situated directly in situational contexts. Second, he understood the importance of a preliminary period of auditory learning, as discussed earlier. Third, he characterized the learning of words as occurring in the direct presence of the referent. Fourth, he understood the guiding role of eye gaze in establishing shared attention. Fifth, he recognized the importance of gestural and postural cues from the child's elders. Sixth, he recognized the difficulties involved in word production, as children have to "break in" their mouths to the pronunciation of words. Finally, he understood the central role of imitation in word learning.

Recent research has supported and elaborated Augustine's intuitions. One group of studies has supported the importance of gesture as a cue to meaning assignment. For example, Bates, Benigni, Bretherton, Camaioni, and Volterra (1979) showed how 10-month-olds would reliably follow eye gazes, pointing, and gesturing. More recent studies (Baldwin, 1993; Tomasello & Haberl, 2003) have further clarified the role of the cues of gesture, posture, intonation, and gaze (Pelphrey, Morris, & McCarthy, 2005) in establishing shared attention for word learning. For example, Gogate, Bahrick, and Watson (2000) showed that mothers, when they teach infants a name for a novel toy, tend to move the toy as they name it, much as Augustine suggested.

One hardly needs to conduct studies to demonstrate the role of gaze, intonation, and pointing, because these cues are so obvious to all of us. However, another aspect of Augustine's analysis is subtler and less fully appreciated. This is the extent to which children seek to divine the intention of the adult as a way of understanding a word's meaning (Bloom, 2000; Tomasello, 2003). They want to make sure that the adult is directly attending to an object before they decide to learn a new word (Baldwin et al., 1996). If the adult is speaking from behind a screen, children are uncertain about the adult's intentions and fail to learn the new word. Tomasello and Akhtar (1995) illustrated this by teaching 2-year-olds a new verb such as *hoisting*. In some of the trials, the toy character would inadvertently swing away and the experimenter would say "whoops." In those trials, the children would not associate *hoisting* with the failed demonstration. Autistic children have problems picking up on both gestural and intentional cues, possibly because of the fact that they have incompletely constructed models of the goals and intentions of other people (Baron-Cohen, Baldwin, & Crowson, 1997; Frith & Frith, 1999).

Augustine briefly alludes to one further way in which adults often simplify the word-learning task. This is by deciding to present words in a simplified, bare form outside of a complex sentential context. Corpus studies of adult input to children who are learning their first words have shown that as much as 20% of early utterances involve single words (Cartwright & Brent, 1997; Huttenlocher, 1974). By presenting single words in isolation, adults remove the problem of word segmentation, thereby further simplifying and facilitating the learning of the first words. This presentation of words in isolation occurs not only for common nouns, but also for words linked to social activities and games such as *bath*, *byebye*, *hi*, *uppie*, *no*, *yes*, *peekaboo*, and *yummy* (Ninio & Snow, 1988). It appears that some children focus learning on social rituals, whereas others are more oriented toward learning the names of objects (Ninio & Snow, 1988). However, in both cases, the initial referent for the word is a very rich encoding that is highly specific to the initial context of exposure.

Undergeneralization and Overgeneralization

The fact that words are picked up in specific contexts suggests that meanings may begin with a great deal of detail, much of it eventually irrelevant, which is then pruned off over time. These activities of refinement and pruning are reflected in the twin developmental patterns of **undergeneralization** and **overgeneralization** of early word meanings (see Figure 8.3).

Because they are initially acquired in very concrete situations, early word meanings are often highly *undergeneralized* (Dromi, 1987; Kay & Anglin, 1982). For example, a child may think that *dog* is the name for the family pet or that *car* refers only to vehicles parked at a specific point outside a particular balcony (Bloom, 1973). It is sometimes difficult to detect undergeneralization because it never leads to errors. Instead, it simply leads to a pattern of idiosyncratic limitations on word usage. Early undergeneralizations are gradually corrected as the child hears the words used in a variety of contexts. Each new context is compared with the current meaning. Those features that match are strengthened (MacWhinney, 1989), and those that do not match are weakened. When a feature becomes sufficiently weak, it drops out altogether.

This process of generalization is guided by the same cues that led to initial attention to the word. For example, it could be the case that every time the child hears the word *apple*, some light is on in the room. However, in none of these cases do the adults focus their attention on the light. Thus, the presence or absence of a light is not a central element of the meaning of *apple*. The child may also occasionally hear the word *apple* used even when the object is not present. If, at that time, attention is focused on some other object that was accidentally associated with *apple*, the process of generalization could derail. However, cases of this type are rare. The more common case involves use of *apple* in a context that totally mismatches the earlier uses. In that case, the child simply assumes nothing and ignores the new exemplar (Stager & Werker, 1997).

This process of initial undergeneralization and gradual generalization is the primary stream of semantic development. However, often children need to go outside this primary stream to find ways of expressing meanings that they do not yet fully control. When they do this, they produce *overgeneralizations*. For example, children may overgeneralize (and alarm their parents) by referring to tigers as *kitties*. Although overgeneralizations are not as frequent as undergeneralizations, they are easier to spot because they always produce errors. Overgeneralization errors arise because children have not yet learned the words they need to

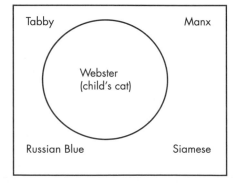

FIGURE 8.3   Overextension of CAT; underextension of CAT.

express their intentions. It is not that the child actually thinks that the tiger is a kitty. It is just that the child has not yet learned the word *tiger* and would still like to be able to draw the parent's attention to this interesting catlike animal.

The smaller the child's vocabulary, the more impressionistic and global will be the nature of these overgeneralizations. For example, Ament (1899) reported that his son learned the word "duck" when seeing some birds on a lake. Later he used the word to refer to other ponds and streams, other birds, and coins with birds on them. Bowerman (1978b) reported that her daughter Eve used "moon" to talk about a lemon slice, the moon, the dial of a dishwasher, pieces of toenail on a rug, and a bright street light. But this does not necessarily mean that the child actually thinks that *duck* refers to both lakes and birds or that *moon* refers to both lemon slices and hangnails. Rather, the child is using one of the few words available to describe features of new objects. As the child's vocabulary grows in size, overgeneralization patterns of this type disappear, although more restricted forms of overgeneralization continue throughout childhood.

This model of overgeneralization assumes that the child understands the difference between a *confirmed core* of features for a word and the area of potential further generalization. The confirmed core (see Figure 8.4) extends to referents that have been repeatedly named with the relevant word. The area of extension is an area outside this core where no other word directly competes and where extension is at least a possibility.

Constraints

The Augustinian vision of attunement between children and their parents provides a set of clear solutions to Quine's *Gavagai* problem. However, researchers have also explored a second major class of solutions to Quine's problem. This is the idea that children may come pre-programmed with fixed ideas that sharply limit the possible hypotheses for the meanings of words. In the 1980s, this approach to the challenge of word learning was characterized as constraint-based learning. The task of the developmental theorist was conceived in terms of discovering the shapes of these various **constraints**. One prominent proposal regarding a major constraint on word learning was the principle of mutual exclusivity formulated by Markman (1989). This principle held that a child would assume that a given referent could be named by one and only one word. However, it was soon noted that bilingual children are not constrained by this principle (Au & Glusman, 1990) and that monolingual children violate the principle when naming plurals, classes, and collections. To deal with these problems and additional experimental evidence, the principle was revised to emphasize the idea that alternative names for the same object tend to compete with each other. The revised constraint was

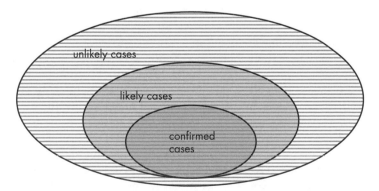

FIGURE 8.4 The confirmed core and its periphery.

characterized in terms of the competition (MacWhinney, 1991; Merriman, 1999), contrast (Clark, 1987), or the tendency to associate a new name with a novel object (Golinkoff, Hirsh-Pasek, & Hollich, 1999).

In addition to the principle of mutual exclusivity and its reformulations in terms of competition and contrast, researchers have proposed several other constraints or principles as partial solutions to Quine's *Gavagai* problem. As the child begins to learn new words, the process of learning itself produces new generalizations (Smith, 1999). For example, children soon come to realize that new words almost always refer to whole objects. There is no reason to think that this is some genetically determined, species-specific constraint. Within the first three months, children have come to realize that objects typically function as perceptual wholes (Bower, 1974). However, a cautious child will also realize that this assumption can sometimes be wrong. For example, one evening, I was sitting on a Victorian couch in our living room with my son Ross, aged 2, when he pointed to the arm of the couch, asking "couch?" He then pointed at the back and then the legs, again asking if they were also "couch." Each time, I assured him that the part to which he was attending was indeed a part of a *couch*. After verifying each component, he seemed satisfied. In retrospect, it is possible that he was asking me to provide names for the subparts of the couch. However, like most parents, I tried to focus his attention on the whole object, rather than on the parts. Perhaps I should have first taught him that all of the parts were pieces of couch and then gone on to provide additional names for the subparts, such as *arm*, *seat*, *back*, and *edge*, ending with a reaffirmation of the fact that all of these parts composed a *couch*.

It is clear that nature does not need to build in any language-specific machinery to enforce the whole object constraint. Rather, this constraint emerges from earlier developments in perception and cognition. However, there are other plausible constraints that one could frame in more purely linguistic terms. One such constraint is against the idea that words meanings can never include the notion of a disjunction. Consider the hypothetical example of the word *grue* that would mean "green in the morning, but blue at night." If the possible search space for word meanings included disjunctive concepts of this type, then the *Gavagai* problem might indeed be nearly impossible to solve. The unlikeliness of this constraint indicates that the view of word learning as unsituated hypothesis testing is itself a bit wide of the mark. It is true that children form hypotheses or guesses about word meanings, but these guesses are rooted deeply in the current situation. Thus, the constraint against disjunctives could be reformulated in terms of the observations that concrete situations themselves never involve disjunctions.

Flexible Learning

A third general approach to *Gavagai* problem focuses not just on the recharacterization of constraints, but rather on the idea that children are flexible word learners. One important aspect of this view is the idea that children can use their experiences with the meanings of the first few words they learn to sharpen their ideas about word meanings in general. As we noted earlier, Woodward and Hoyne (1998) found that 13-month-olds were happy to pick up a sound, such as clapping or banging, as if it were the name of an object. At this early point, children seem to be quite catholic in their views of what might be a word. We also noted the report from Ament (1899) showing that some of the meanings of early words take on rather unconventional shapes. However, as MacWhinney (1989) has argued, these various unconventional ideas are quickly rejected because they are not supported by later word learning. Children soon come to realize that clapping and banging are not used as the names for things. Similarly, they soon come to learn that words are most likely to refer to whole objects, rather than their parts.

Learning to learn can also induce the child to treat early word meanings in terms of common object functions. For example, Brown (1958) noted that parents typically label objects at the level of their most common function. Thus, parents will refer to *chairs*, but avoid *furniture* or *stool*, because *chair* best captures the level of prototypical usage of a class of objects (Adams & Bullock, 1986). As a result, children also come to realize that the names for artificial objects refer to their functions and not to their shape, texture, or size.

Children are also quick to pick up on a variety of other obvious correlations. They learn that the color of artificial objects such as cars and dresses can vary widely, but that many animals have unique colorings and patterns. They learn that any new word for an object can also refer to a toy characterizing that object or a picture of the object. They learn that people can have multiple names, including titles and nicknames. They learn that actions are mapped onto the human perspective (MacWhinney, 2008b), that objects can vary in qualities such as size, color, and texture, and that objects also produce a wide variety of pleasurable experiences through their qualities. Eventually, they use these facts and other data to govern their learning of nouns, verbs, adjectives, and other words. Generally speaking, children must adopt a highly flexible, bottom-up approach to the learning of word meanings (Maratsos & Deak, 1995), attending to all available cues, because words themselves are such flexible things.

This flexibility also shows up in the child's handling of cues to object word naming. Because shape is a powerful defining characteristic for so many objects, children learn to attend closely to this attribute. However, children can easily be induced to attend instead to substance, size, or texture, rather than to shape. For example, Smith (1999) was able to show how children could be induced, through repeated experiences with substance, to classify new words not in terms of their shape, but in terms of their substance.

Children's Agenda

The view of the child as a flexible word learner has to be balanced against the view of the child as having some definite personal agenda. Like Augustine, children often see language as a way of expressing their own desires, interests, and opinions. This then suggests a fourth major type of solution to Quine's problem. If the child's agenda aligned well with the words that adults are presenting to the child, then there would be little need for the child to confront the *Gavagai* problem. It is likely that this type of close alignment does occur for some words, but it is unlikely that it occurs for all words. Moreover, there is a danger inherent in sticking too closely to a self-determined agenda for learning word. In the extreme case, children might adopt the position espoused by Humpty Dumpty in *Alice in Wonderland*, when he chastises Alice for failing to take charge over the meanings of words. As Humpty Dumpty (see Figure 8.5) puts it, "When I use a word, it means just what I choose it to mean—neither more nor less." Unfortunately, the word meanings that Humpty Dumpty had selected failed to align properly with those that Alice had expected, confusing her badly.

In other cases, the ideas that children seek to express through early words match up closely with what their parents expect them to express. During the months before the first words, the child may use certain gestures and intonational patterns to express core agenda items such as desire, question, and attention focusing (Halliday, 1975). These non-conventional patterns may still possess a certain iconic basis that allows parents to guess at the meanings their children intend. Later, children seem to seek out words for talking about fingers, hands, balls, animals, bottles, parents, siblings, and food. Many of these early agenda items appear to focus on nouns, rather than on verbs or other parts of speech. Gentner (1982) argues that this is because it is easier to map a noun to a constant referent. Gentner referred to this tendency as the nominal bias, arguing that this bias is a cognitive universal. A variant of Gentner's position holds that nouns are learned more readily because it is easier for children to figure

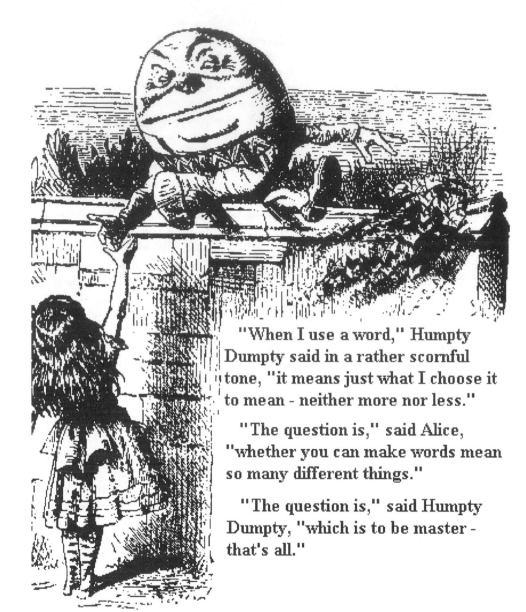

FIGURE 8.5 Humpty Dumpty's theory of word meaning. Illustration by John Tenniel from *Through the Looking Glass*, 1871.

out what people are talking about when they use nouns than when they use verbs. Moreover, nouns tend to be used in the same categorical and taxonomic ways (Sandhofer, Smith, & Luo, 2000), whereas verbs refer to a wider range of conceptual structures, include wishes, movements, states, transitions, and beliefs.

Input factors play a role as well. Studies of languages other than English show that sometimes children do not produce more nouns than verbs, at least during the first stages. For example, children learning Korean (Gopnik & Choi, 1995) and Mandarin Chinese (Tardif, 1996) may produce more verbs than nouns under certain conditions of elicitation. Two plausible explanations for this phenomenon have been offered. First, in both Korean and Mandarin verbs are much more likely to appear at the ends of utterances than in English, where the last word in input sentences tends to be a noun (Nicoladis, 2001). Perceptual studies (Jusczyk, 1997) have shown that it is easier for children to recognize familiar words at the ends of sentences, suggesting that this structural feature of languages influences rates of word learning as well. Second, Korean and Mandarin mothers tend to talk about actions more than do English-speaking mothers, who tend to focus on labeling things. Goldfield (1993) showed that American mothers who used more nouns tended to have infants with a higher proportion of nouns in their vocabularies.

The study of part of speech distribution within and between languages is probably highly sensitive to variations in the mode of data collection. In this regard, Sugárné (1970) showed that, in Hungarian preschoolers, verbs exceeded nouns when recordings were taken during playground interactions, but that nouns exceeded verbs under all other conditions of elicitation. Using comparable parental report measures in Spanish, Dutch, French, Hebrew, Italian, Korean, and American English, Bornstein et al. (2004) found that nouns dominated consistently over the other parts of speech by 20 months. These results seem to lend strong support to the idea that the nominal bias is universal. However, to fully evaluate this issue, we will eventually need actual child speech samples from across a wider variety of languages and activity types using maximally comparable data collection and analysis methods.

Whorf versus Humpty Dumpty

As learning progresses, the child's agenda become less important than the shape of the resources provided by the language. For example, languages like Salish or Navajo expect the child to learn verbs instead of nouns. Moreover, the verbs children will learn focus more on position, shape, and containment than do verbs in English. For example, the verb *áhéénishtiih* in Navajo refers to "carrying around in a circle any long straight object such as a gun." The presence of obligatory grammatical markings in languages for concepts such as tense, aspect, number, gender, and definiteness can orient the child's thinking in certain paths at the expense of others. Whorf (1967) proposed that the forms of language end up shaping the structure of thought. Such effects are directly opposed to the Humpty Dumpty agenda-based approach to language. Probably the truth involves a dynamic interaction between Whorf and Humpty Dumpty. Important though language-specific effects may be, all children end up being able to express basic ideas equally well, no matter what language they learn.

Learning from Syntactic Contexts

Shared reference is not the only cue toddlers can use to delineate the meanings of words. They can also use the form of utterances to pick out the correct referents for new words. Consider these contexts:

Here is a pum. – count noun
Here is Pum. – proper noun
I am pumming. – intransitive verb
I pummed the duck. – transitive (causative) verb
I need some pum. – mass noun
This is the pum one. – adjective

Each of these sentential contexts provides clear evidence that *pum* is a particular part of speech. Other sentential frames can give an even more precise meaning. If the child hears, *this is not green, it is pum*, it is clear that *pum* is a color. If the child hears, *please don't cover it, just pum it lightly*, then the child knows that *pum* is a verb of the same general class as *cover*. The use of cues of this type leads to a fast, but shallow, mapping of new words to new meanings. Learning of this type was first identified in 3-year-olds by Brown (1957, 1973) and later in children younger than 2 by Katz, Baker, and Macnamara (1974). Carey (1978) later used the term *fast mapping* to refer to this induction of word meaning from syntactic context. The idea here is that the child can quickly pick up a general idea of the meaning of a new word in this way, although it may take additional time to acquire the fuller meaning of the word. Fast learning has also been identified in much younger children (Schafer & Plunkett, 1998). However, before age 2, fast mapping depends only on memory for the referent itself and not on induction from syntactic frames.

Words as Invitations

In a very real sense, words function as invitations for the construction of new categories. The child soon realizes that each new word is a pointer into a whole set of related objects or events that share some discoverable similarity. The more words the child learns, the clearer this effect becomes. New words for animals, like *hedgehog* and *dolphin*, invite an exploration of the habits, shapes, colors, and activities of that animal. New words for physical actions, like *gallop* and *knit*, invite an exploration of the ways in which the body can use these motions to act on other objects. Research has shown that the mere presence of a word can induce sharper and more consistent concept formation. For example, Waxman and Kosowski (1990) gave children two stories. In the first, they used the word *dobutsu* as a label, saying, "There's a being from another planet who wants some dobutsus. I don't know what dobutsus means, but he likes things like a dog, a duck, or a horse. Can you find him something he wants?" In the second story, they provided no label, saying, "This puppet only likes things like dogs, ducks, and horses. Can you find him something he likes?" Children were much more likely to point to another animal when the label *dobutsu* was used than when no label was provided. This effect has also been demonstrated for infants (Waxman & Markow, 1995) and echoed in several further studies, all of which emphasize the role that words play as invitations to categorization and cognition (Gentner, 2005; Lupyan, Rakison, & McClelland, 2007).

Competition and Mutual Exclusivity

Even the most complete set of syntactic cues and the fullest level of shared attention cannot completely preclude the occasional confusion about word meanings. Some of the most difficult conflicts among words involve the use of multiple words for the same object. For example, a child may know the word *hippo* and hear a hippopotamus toy referred to as a *toy*. But this does not lead the child to stop calling the toy a *hippo* and start calling it a *toy*. Some have suggested that children are prevented from making this type of error by the presence of a universal constraint called *mutual exclusivity*. This constraint holds that each object can only have one name. If children hear a second name for the old object, they can either reject the new name as wrong or else find some distinction that disambiguates the new name from the old. If mutual exclusivity were an important constraint on word meaning, we would expect children to show a strong tendency toward the first solution—rejection. However, few children illustrate such a preference. The fact is that objects almost always have more than one name. For example, a *fork* is also *silverware*, and a *dog* is also an *animal*. Linguistic structures expressing a wide variety of taxonomic and metonymic relations represent a fundamental and principled violation of the proposed mutual exclusivity constraint. The most consistent violations occur for bilingual children, who learn that everything in their world must, by necessity, have at least two names. Mutual exclusivity is clearly not a basic property of natural language.

One reason why researchers have devoted so much attention to mutual exclusivity stems from the shape of the laboratory situation in which word learning is studied. The child is presented with a series of objects, some old and some new, given a word that is either old or new, and then asked to match up the word with an object. For example, the child may be given a teacup, a glass, and a demitasse. She already knows the words *cup* and *glass*. The experimenter asks her to *give me the demitasse*. She will then correctly infer that *demitasse* refers to the object for which she does not have a well-established name. In this context, it makes sense to use the new name as the label for some new object.

Instead of thinking in terms of mutual exclusivity, the child appears to be thinking in terms of competition among words, with each word vying for a particular semantic niche. At the same time, the child is thinking in terms of the pragmatics of mutual cooperation (Clark, 1987). When two words are in head-on conflict and no additional disambiguating cues are provided, it makes sense for the child to assume that the adult is being reasonable and using the new name for the new object (Golinkoff, et al., 1999). The child assumes that the cooperative experimenter knows that the child has words for cups and glasses, so it only makes sense that the new word is for the new object.

In the real world, competition forces the child to move meanings around so that they occupy the correct semantic niche. When the parent calls the toy hippo a *toy*, the child searches for something to disambiguate the two words. For example, the parent may say, "Can you give me another toy?" or even "Please clean up your toys." In each case, *toy* refers not only to the hippo but also potentially to many other toys. This allows the child to shift perspective and to understand the word *toy* in the framework of the shifted perspective. Consider the case of a rocking horse. This object may be called *toy*, *horsie*, or even *chair* depending on how it is being used at the moment (Clark, 1997). This flexible use of labeling is an important ingredient in language learning. By learning how to shift perspectives, children develop powerful tools for dealing with the competitions among words. In this way conflicts among meanings give rise to complex structures and cognitive flexibility.

Building Theories

As children learn more and more words, they begin to develop clearer ideas about the ways in which words can refer to objects, properties, and events. The meanings of organized groups of words come to represent many aspects of the cognitive structure of the child's world. Children begin to realize that certain properties of objects are more fundamental and inherent than others. For example, Keil and Batterman (1984) talked to children about a cat that had been given a skunk's tail, nose, and fur. Before the age of 5, children believed that this animal would now actually be a skunk. After age 5, children began to realize that mere addition of these features would not change the fact that the animal was still inherently a cat. In effect, children are beginning to develop belief in a scientific theory that holds that animals cannot change their genetic status through simple transformations. Theories also provide children with conceptual structures they can use to infer the properties of new words. For example, if children are told that a *dobro* is a fish, then they can also infer that the *dobro* swims and has gills (Gelman, 1998).

Milestones in Vocabulary Growth

Typically, the child demonstrates new language abilities first in comprehension and only later in production. For example, children comprehend their first words by 9 months or even earlier, but only produce the first word after 12 months. Children are able to comprehend 50 words by about 15 months, but do not produce 50 words in their own speech until about

20 months. More generally, children acquire words into their receptive vocabulary more than twice as fast as into their productive vocabulary.

Children tend to produce their first words sometime between 9 and 12 months. One-year-olds have about 5 words in their vocabulary on average, although individual children may have none or as many as 30; by 2 years, average vocabulary size is more than 150 words, with a range among individual children from as few as 10 to as many as 450 words. Children possess a vocabulary of about 14,000 words by 6 years of age (Templin, 1957); adults have an estimated average of 40,000 words in their working vocabulary at age 40 (McCarthy, 1954). In order to achieve such a vocabulary, a child must learn to say at least three new words each day from birth.

GRAMMATICAL DEVELOPMENT

In terms of **grammatical development**, the transition from the first words to the first sentences is nearly imperceptible. After learning the first words, children begin to produce more and more single-word utterances. As their vocabulary grows, children begin saying words in close approximation, separated only by short pauses (Branigan, 1979). For example, they may say *wanna*, followed by a short pause and then *cookie*. If the intonational contour of *wanna* is not closely integrated with that of *cookie*, adults tend to perceive this as two successive single-word utterances. However, the child may already have in mind a clear syntactic relation between the two words.

As the clarity of the relations between single words strengthens, the temporal gap between the words will decrease. However, the transition from successive single-word utterances to true word combinations requires more than just faster timing. Two other achievements must occur. First, the child has to figure out how to join words together into a single intonational package or breath group. Second, the child also has to figure out which words can meaningfully be combined and in what order.

The level of successive single-word utterances is one that chimpanzees also reach when they learn signed language. Domesticated chimps like Sarah, Washoe, or Kanzi can learn about 100 conventional signs or tokens. They can then combine these words to produce meaningful communication. However, the combinations that chimpanzees produce never really get beyond the stage of successive single-word utterances. For example, the chimpanzee Washoe, who was raised by the Gardners (Allen & Gardner, 1969), produced strings such as "Open, now, me, now, open, door, please, open, please, me" to express the request to have a door opened. In a sequence like this, the chimp is basically using every item in her lexicon that might apply to the current scene without paying much attention to particular binary combinations of items (Terrace, Petitto, Sanders, & Bever, 1980). Human children take a very different approach to word combination.

When looking at children's first clumsy attempts to combine words, it is important to realize that they have already spent several months listening to words in combination during comprehension. Consider the case of the child's first use of the word *want* in combination with a noun like *cup* at 18 months. Before using the operator *want* for the first time, the child may well have heard it in combination dozens of times. During these exposures, the child comes to expect that certain words will follow directly after *want*. MacWhinney (1982) called such combinations **item-based patterns** because they specify the ways in which particular lexical items can combine with other words. In an item-based grammar of this type, lexical items produce syntactic combinations by combining with words that complete their argument structure (Bresnan, 1982; Tesniére, 1959).

In the case of the item-based pattern for *want* there are two terms that can complete its argument structure. First, there must be a nominal that serves as a direct object, as in *want cookie*. Second, there must be a nominal that serves as the subject, as in *I want cookie*. Because *want* expects these two additional words, we call it a two-argument predicate. Other predicates, such as *under* or *my*, take only one argument, and a few such as *give* take three *(John gave Bill a dollar)*. The only words that take no obligatory additional arguments are nouns. Unlike verbs, adjectives, prepositions, and other words that require additional arguments, nouns can express a full meaning without attaching additional arguments. Nouns that are derived from verbs, such as *destruction* or *remission*, can take optional arguments *(the destruction of the city* or *a decline in the dollar)*, but basic nouns such as *chair* and *goat* do not even have these expectations.

During the period of the first words, children are able to listen to speech and occasionally pick out verbs, adjectives, adverbs, and prepositions that they are starting to learn. However, to make sense of these words, they must link them to item-based patterns. Thus, some use of item-based patterns must be present in comprehension, well before we see it in production. Unfortunately, it is difficult to derive solid evidence regarding the exact shape of children's early abilities to comprehend syntactic patterns. As in the case of studies of early word comprehension, we have to assess children's early syntactic comprehension by controlled experiments in the laboratory. To do this, researchers have often relied on the preferential looking paradigm (Golinkoff, Hirsh-Pasek, Cauley, & Gordon, 1987). To the right of the child, there is a TV monitor with a movie of Big Bird tickling Cookie Monster. To the child's left, there is a TV monitor with a movie of Cookie Monster tickling Big Bird. The experimenter produces the sentence "Big Bird is tickling Cookie Monster." If the child looks at the matching TV monitor on the right, a toy makes a "success" noise and a correct look is scored. Using this technique, researchers have found that 17-month-olds already have a good idea about the correct word order for English sentences. This is about 3 months before they begin to use word order systematically in production.

Item-Based Patterns

Braine (1976) and Schlesinger (1974, 1975) made a close study of the exact semantic composition of early word combinations in several languages. These positional patterns involved combinations of predicates such as *want*, *more*, or *go* with arguments such as *cookie* or *flower*. Braine found that a small set of semantic combination types could be used to account for nearly all of the early sentences in the fairly small corpora that he studied. In some cases, the positional occurrence of the words involved was quite fixed. For example, children always said *my + X* and never *X + my* to express the possession relation. However, in other cases, the order was more variable. When the order became variable and applied inconsistently to various predicates, Braine referred to the ordering as indicating a "groping pattern." Braine thought that patterns of this type expressed high-level semantic relational features such as recurrence *(another doll)*, possession *(my doll)*, agency *(doll runs)*, or object *(want doll)*.

MacWhinney (1975) took a related, but somewhat different, approach to early word combination. Instead of assuming descriptions based on feature-based rules, he emphasized children's learning of low-level, item-based rules. Rather than viewing the combination of *more* and *milk* as expressing a pattern such as *recurrence + object*, MacWhinney interpreted the combination as evidence of the pattern *more + X*, where the italicization of the word *more* indicates that it is a particular lexical item and not a general concept. This analysis stresses the extent to which the item-based pattern first emerges as a highly limited construction based on the single lexical item *more*.

In MacWhinney's (1975) account, the grammar of the child's first word combinations is extremely concrete. The child learns that each predicate should appear in a constant position with respect to the arguments it requires. For example, in English, the word *more* appears before the noun it modifies, and the verb *run* appears after the subject with which it combines. The combination is based on a slot-filler relation. Consider the combination *more milk* which is generated from the item-based pattern *more + X*. In this combination, *milk* is a filler of the slot represented by the *X*.

Later, the child may generalize above the level of *more* and *milk* to acquire the higher-level pattern *want + object desired*. Once this pattern is learned, the child can then treat the whole unit or cluster *more milk* as an argument to the verb *want* producing *want more milk*. Finally, the child can express the second argument of the verb *want*, and the result is *I want more milk*. Thus, the child gradually builds up longer sentences and a more complex grammar. This recursive operation of item-based patterns uses basic mammalian cognitive mechanisms for structure building that have been further elaborated in the human species (Hauser, Chomsky, & Fitch, 2002; MacWhinney, 2008a).

Item-based patterns can be used equally well to characterize the positioning of affixes or inflections in words. For example, English marks the plural with the suffix *–s*, using the pattern: *object + s* to express the plural. Because affix-based patterns are so frequent and consistent, children find them very easy to learn. We know that in English (Braine, 1963), Garo (Burling, 1959), Hungarian (MacWhinney, 1976), Japanese (Clancy, 1985), and Turkish (Slobin, 1973), the ordering of affixes in words is almost always correct, even at the youngest ages. Together, item-based patterns coded on affixes like *–s* and stems like *wanna* can be used to describe and generate all of the basic aspects of grammar (MacWhinney, 1987; Sagae, Davis, Lavie, MacWhinney, & Wintner, 2007).

Applying the notion of item-based patterns to a corpus of Hungarian, MacWhinney (1975) examined the word order of 11,077 utterances produced by two Hungarian children between the ages of 17 and 29 months. He found that between 85% and 100% of the utterances in these samples could be generated by a set of 42 item-based patterns. Some examples of these patterns in English translation are: *X + too*, *no + X*, *where + X*, *dirty + X*, and *see + X*. The item-based pattern model was able to achieve a remarkably close match to the child's output, because it postulates an extremely concrete set of abilities that are directly evidenced in the child's output.

Children learn item-based patterns by listening to sentences. For example, if the child's older sister says *this is my dollie*, the child may only store the last two words as *my dollie*. Within this sequence, the child will then recognize the word *dollie* from previous experience and associate that word with the actual doll. This then leaves the segment *my* as uninterpreted (MacWhinney, 1978). At this point, the child can compare the phrase *my dollie* with the single word *dollie*, noticing the differences. The first difference is the presence of *my* before *dollie*. At this point, the child can establish a new lexical entry for *my* and associate it with the meaning of being possessed by the speaker (the older sister). While setting up this new form, the child also extracts the item-based positional pattern *my + X*. In this case, the older sister may be asserting her control over the doll and wresting it from the younger sister's possession. Thus, the younger child can pick up not only the meaning of *my* and the positional pattern but also the notion of a relation of possession and control between the two words. Thus, it is more accurate to speak of this item-based pattern as combining *my + object possessed*, rather than just *my + X*. By specifying a particular semantic role for the filler, we are emphasizing the fact that the pattern encodes both syntax and semantics.

Initially, this pattern is restricted to the words *my* and *dollie* and the relation of possession that occurs between them. However, if the older sister then says "and this is my horsie," the child can begin to realize that the open slot for the item-based pattern linked to *my* refers potentially to any manner of toy. Subsequent input will teach the child that any object can fill the slot opened up by the operator *my*. Each item-based pattern goes through this type of generalization (MacWhinney, 1975; Tomasello, Akhtar, Dodson, & Rekau, 1997).

Early child syntax is replete with examples of errors produced by the simple application of item-based patterns (Brown, Cazden, & Bellugi, 1968; Klima & Bellugi, 1966; Menyuk, 1969). Examples include *where Mama boot, no Rusty hat*, and *that no fish school*. These combinations arise from the application of item-based patterns such as *where + object located*, or *no + object denied*. In these patterns, the open slot can hold single nouns, noun phrases, or simple sentences. Errors arise because children are omitting articles and auxiliaries, but over time they will learn to add these through additional item-based patterns. Soon, children learn to use *where's* rather than *where* for interrogatives, producing correct combinations, such as *where's the wheel?* Some children form an overgeneralized *no + X* negation pattern in which X is not restricted to an object. Errors illustrating this incorrect overextension include *no do this, no wipe finger, no sit there, no play that, he no bite you*, and *I no taste them*. Parallel interrogative combination errors include *where go, what happen, where put him on a chair, what happen me*, and *why need them more*. Interrogative errors with missing auxiliaries of the shape *what they are doing* and *where he's going* are extremely common. There are also errors, such as *where the wheel do go* and *what you did eat*, in which the auxiliary is misplaced after the subject. These errors are further evidence for patterns such as *where + S*. Later, children replace *where + S* with *where + tense*. However, they fail to restrict the *where + tense* pattern to exclude main verbs. Overgeneralization errors attesting to the productivity of this later pattern include *where goes the wheel, where could be the shopping place, where's going to be the school*. After the first few months of word combination, there are no reports of errors that go against the basic item-based interrogative patterns. For example, there are no reports of errors such as *he can't do it why* (Labov & Labov, 1978).

The fact that grammatical patterns are often acquired word by word provides further evidence for the operation of item-based patterns. For example, Kuczaj and Brannick (1979) showed that children are quicker to show placement of the tensed auxiliary after the interrogatives *what* and *where* than after *how long* or *when*. Thus, children will produce *what is he doing?* at the same time they produce *when he coming?* Similarly, Bowerman (1978a) noted that, at 17 months, her daughter Eva used the patterns *want + X* and *more + X* productively. However, these patterns did not generalize to other words like *open, close, bite, no more*, or *all gone*.

One could argue that sentences of the type I have discussed are produced not through word combination but through **analogy**. Accounts based on analogy can be used to account for virtually any particular form. However, accounts based on analogy also typically predict many error types that never occur. For example, Kuczaj and Brannick (1979) noted that questions like *gonna he go?* have never been reported, although children say *he's gonna go, he will go*, and *will he go?* If analogy were operating here, we would expect to find *gonna he go?* on analogy with *will he go?* However, item-based patterns account for these data correctly. The auxiliary *will* is combined with *he go* using the item-based pattern *will + action*. This pattern does not generalize to *gonna*, because, by definition, the item-based pattern *will + action* is restricted to the auxiliary *will*. The item *gonna* never appears in initial position without a preceding nominal, so there is no evidence or form in support of an error such as *gonna he go?*.

Consider another example of how lexical classes help the child avoid overgeneralization. Children may notice that *big* and *red* pattern together in forms such as *big barn* and *red barn*. This might induce them to produce forms such as *I painted the barn big* on analogy with *I painted the barn red*. A conservative learner would stick close to facts about the verb *paint* and the arguments that it permits. If the child has heard a form like *I painted the barn white*, it would make sense to extend this frame to include the resultative predicate *red*. However, to extend from the word *white* to semantically unrelated words like *happy* or *difficult* would be to go far beyond the attested construction. As a result, this type of category-leaping overgeneralization is extremely infrequent.

Item-based patterns support gradual, but conservative productivity. We can also demonstrate the productivity of item-based patterns by teaching children novel words that serve as slot fillers. For example, we can show a child a picture of a birdlike creature that we call a *wug*. The positioning of the nonce word *wug* after the article *the* induces the child to treat the word as a common noun. We can show the child two pictures of the strange creature and ask them, "What are these?" By responding with the answer *wugs*, children show productivity of the item-based pattern based on the plural suffix. Similarly, we can set up a game in which each person names some toys. This will lead the child to produce the combination *my wug*, thereby showing the productivity of the pattern *my + object possessed*. Similarly, a German-speaking child can be taught the nonce name *der Gann* (nominative, masculine, and singular) for a toy. The experimenter can then pick up the toy and ask the child what he is holding. By the age of 3, children will correctly produce the accusative form *den Gann* (accusative, masculine, and singular).

Although it is easy to convince children to accept new slot fillers, it is far more difficult to teach them to accept new operators. This is because new operators must establish their own new item-based patterns. As a result, it is difficult to convince children to use novel verbs in a fully productive fashion. Instead, children tend to be conservative and unsure about how to use verbs productively until about age 5 (Tomasello, 2000). By then, they start to show productive use of constructions such as the double object, the passive, or the causative (Bowerman, 1988). For example, an experimenter can introduce a new verb like *griff* in the frame *Tim griffed the ball to Frank*, and the child will productively generalize to *Tim griffed Frank the ball*.

Combining Patterns

To understand how children learn complex syntactic structures, we need to see how a syntactic processor can combine words using item-based and feature-based patterns operating in real time. Most current accounts of real-time syntactic processors use the logic of the competition model of MacWhinney (1987). That model specifies a series of steps for the competition between constructions.

1. Sounds are processed as they are heard in speech.
2. Competition during sound processing controls activation of a current word.
3. Each new word activates its own item-based patterns along with related feature-based patterns (see following).
4. Item-based patterns then initiate tightly specified searches for slot fillers.
5. Slots may be filled either by single words or by whole phrases. In the latter case, the attachment is made to the head of the phrase.
6. To fill a slot, a word or phrase must receive support from cues for word order, prosody, affixes, or lexical class.
7. If several words compete for a slot, the one with the most cue support wins.

The details of the operation of this parser are controlled by the competitions between specific lexical items and the cues that support alternative assignments. Consider the case of prepositional phrase attachment. Prepositions such as *on* take two arguments: The first argument is the object of the preposition; the second argument is the head of the prepositional phrase (i.e., the word or phrase to which the prepositional phrase attaches). We can refer to argument 1 as the local head or endohead and argument 2 as the external head or exohead. Consider the sentence *the man positioned the coat on the rack*. Here, the endohead of *on* is *rack* and its exohead (the head of the whole prepositional phrase) could be either *positioned* or *the coat*. These two alternative attachment sites for the prepositional phrase are in competition with each other.

Competition also governs the interpretation of verbs as either transitive or intransitive. Verbs like *jog* that have transitive and causative and intransitive readings can be represented by two competing lexical entries. When we hear the phrase, *since John always jogs a mile*, we activate the transitive reading. However, if the full sentence then continues as *since John always jogs a mile seems like a short distance*, then the intransitive reading takes over from the transitive one. Consider these two illustrations of the results of a few attachment competitions:

> *Mary likes a young soldier:*
> Mary – likes – (a – (young – soldier))
> *The cat the dog chased ate the cheese:*
> ((the – dog) – chased – (the – cat)) – ate – (the – cheese)

For detailed examples of the step-by-step operations of this type of processor consult MacWhinney (1987) or O'Grady (2005).

Feature-Based Patterns

Although item-based patterns can be used to generate nearly all word combinations, there is good evidence that children soon go beyond item-based patterns to learn more general combinatorial rules. Consider the learning of the pattern that places the adjective before the noun in English. At first, children pick up a few item-based patterns such as *nice + object, good + object*, and *pretty + object*. They acquire these patterns during the learning of new adjectives from the input. For example, children may hear the form *nice kitty*, from which they create the pattern *nice + X*. At first, the slot filler is limited to the original noun *kitty*, but it is then quickly generalized to all possible objects. When the child then begins to learn the parallel patterns for *good* and *pretty*, the process of slot generalization becomes quicker, as the child begins to realize that words like *nice, good*, and *pretty* that describe characteristics of objects all accept a related object in the following syntactic position. This linking of item-based patterns then gives rise to a feature-based pattern that specifies the combination *modifier + object described* for English. Other early feature-based patterns include *possessor + possession (John's computer)* and *locative + location (behind the tree)*. Once children have learned these more general patterns, they apply immediately to newly learned words.

Feature-based patterns can also apply to the positioning of nouns as topics in languages like Hungarian or Chinese. These languages encourage the formation of sentences that place nominal topics in initial position, according to the feature-based pattern *topic + comment*. At first, children may pick this up as an item-based pattern. For example, they might hear a Hungarian sentence of the shape *the glass # empty* with the # sign indicating an intonational break between the topic and the comment. They first encode this as a pattern linked to *glass*. However, after hearing a few more parallel patterns for other nouns, they then extract a general feature-based pattern, just as they do for the *modifier + object described* pattern for adjectives. Studies such as MacWhinney (1975) and Lee (1999) have demonstrated that children use these patterns productively by age 2.

Grammatical Markers

The account of grammatical acquisition presented previously is highly anglocentric. English is rather unique in terms of the extent to which it relies on strict word order patterns, rather than on grammatical markers for case and agreement. English does have a few grammatical markers, such as the final /s/ that can mark plurality, possession, or subject–verb agreement in the present tense when the subject is third person singular. But English only marks case in the pronoun through distinctions such as *he* vs. *him*. Other languages, such as Japanese, Hungarian, Navajo, or Russian, permit a far wider variation in the order of words, because the roles and links between words are marked by a rich system of grammatical morphemes, including both prefixes and suffixes. For example, it is always possible to spot the direct object in Hungarian, because it ends with a final /t/ on the noun, as in the contrast between the nominative form *kabát* (coat) and the accusative *kabátot*.

At first, children seem blissfully unaware of the presence of these grammatical markings, treating complex multimorphemic words as if they were single units. For example, a child might use the word *cookies* even before learning the singular *cookie*. At this point, we can refer to the unanalyzed two-morpheme combination *cookies* as an *amalgam* (MacWhinney, 1978). The child language literature is replete with examples of uses of inflected amalgams before the child has learned the stems. For example, Brown et al. (1968) reported use of *can't, won't*, and *don't* at a time when *can, will*, and *do* were absent. Similarly, Leopold (1949, p. 8) reported use of *sandbox* at a time when *sand* was still absent. Children also use inflected forms before they have acquired the inflections. Kenyeres (1926) reported that his daughter used the inflected Hungarian word *kenyeret* (bread + accusative) at 16 months, when there was no other evidence for productive use of the accusative "-et." Moreover, Hungarian children often use *kalapáccsal* (hammer—with) before demonstrating productive use of either the stem *kalapács* (hammer) or the instrumental suffix *-val*. Of course, for the child, the main interest value of a hammer involves its use as an instrument, just as a child may be particularly interested in having more than just one cookie.

One can also argue that precocious usage of a string indicates underanalysis. Peters (1977) noted that, when her 14-month-old child controlled only 6 to 10 words, he said quite clearly *open the door*. Similarly, my son Ross produced *no, Mommy, I don't want to go bed* and *I like it; I love it* at a time when the first two-word combinations were just emerging. The use of amalgams can also produce grammatical errors. For example, if children learn *like it* and *want some* as amalgams, they can produce errors such as *I like it the ball* or *I want some a banana*. Clark (1977) reported the utterance *hat on gone now* in which *hat on* is acting as a unit with *on* as an unanalyzed suffix.

A fairly strong type of evidence for the nonproductivity of early affixes or word endings is the fact that, when they first appear, affixes are seldom overgeneralized (Ervin, 1964). Children begin by saying *went* and *saw*, and overregularizations such as *goed* or *sawed* typically do not occur before correct irregular forms are produced. Later, when errors like *goed* and *sawed* begin to appear, they serve as evidence of the productivity of the past-tense suffix as well as evidence of its earlier nonproductivity. After a few weeks, the child corrects these errors and returns to correct use of *went* and *saw*. This pattern of correct performance with an intermediate period of overgeneralization produces a U-shaped curve that has a different developmental profile for each verb.

It is possible to track the rise of affix productivy by teaching children new, nonce words. For example, Berko (1958) showed children pictures of an imaginary creature called a "wug" and then asked them how you would call two of them, as illustrated in Figure 8.6. This method can be extended quite generally to study the productivity of all sorts of affixes, compounds, and other word formation devices. In general, children make fewer morphophonological errors on common irregular words than on rare irregular words (MacWhinney, 1978). This effect indicates that children rely on rote to produce at least some inflected forms. Frequent forms can be acquired as chunks or amalgams because they are heard so often.

This is a WUG

Now there is another one.
There are two of them.
There are two_____ .

FIGURE 8.6   The "wugs" test of Berko (1958).

The absence of productivity for a suffix should not be taken as absence of the underlying concept. For example, Brown and Bellugi (1964) found that children would refer to *many shoe* and *two shoe* at a time when there is still no clear evidence for the productivity of the plural suffix. However, the words *many* and *two* by themselves show that the child not only thinks in terms of the concept of plurality, but also has succeeded in finding two ways of expressing this concept. At this point, acquisition of the plural is driven not by the child's need to express concepts, but by the need to match the formal structures of the adult language.

COMMUNICATIVE DEVELOPMENT

Babies and their parents engage in conversations even before the child has begun to produce words. These conversations may share smiles, gazes, coos, and grunts (Snow, 1977). Parents of young children will speak to them as if they were full conversational participants. For examples, one can browse the transcripts linked to audio at http:/childes.psy.cmu.edu/browser such as those in the Eng-USA/Brent corpus. These early dialogs demonstrate the extent to which children acquire language not only to solve problems or express themselves, but also to participate fully in conversational interactions. Even these early conversations allow us to engage socially as members of dyads and groups. To the degree that there is a fundamental urge to produce language, it is in large part an urge not to talk, but to converse.

This urge to socialize affects mothers as well as infants. Papoušek and Papoušek (1991) showed that mothers use rising pitch contours to engage infant attention and elicit responses, falling contours to soothe their babies, and bell-shaped contours to maintain their attention. In general, these patterns are useful not only for directing attention to new words (Thiessen, Hill, & Saffran, 2005; Thiessen & Saffran, 2007), but also for involving babies in the "melody" of conversation (Locke, 1995), even before they have learned "the words."

Conversations between mothers and their infants involve a variety of alternating activities. Infants tend to produce positive vocalization when gazing into their parents' eyes (Keller, Poortinga, & Schomerich, 2002). When infants produce negative vocalizations, parents often respond by touching and cuddling them. However, infants will produce more vocalizations when parents vocalize to them, rather than merely respond with touch or gesture (Bloom, Russell, & Wassenberg, 1987). A longitudinal study of naturalistic talk (Snow, Pan, Imbens-Bailey, & Herman, 1996) found a continuing increase in child speech during 10-min segments from 4 at 14 months to 7 at 20 months and 11 at 32 months. This ongoing growth of participation in conversations emphasizes the extent to which infants are being mainstreamed into a world of continual conversational turn-taking.

The logic of parent–child conversational turn-taking is not fundamentally different from that used between adults. The basic rule underlying all forms of turn-taking (Sacks, Schegloff, & Jefferson, 1974) is that, at any given moment, one of the participants is deemed to "have the floor." While that participant holds the floor, the other participants are supposed to pay attention to the conversational contribution. At some point the speaker begins to yield the floor and thereby invites a new conversational contribution. Signals that invite a new contribution include pauses, questions, and drops in intonation. Of course, conversations are not controlled as carefully as the flow of traffic through signal lights. Often there are collisions between speakers resulting in overlaps. At other times, there are complete breaks in the interaction. All of these features can be detected in vocal–visual interactions between mothers and children as young as 12 months. What distinguishes parent–child dialogs from adult–adult dialogs is the extent to which the parent uses specific devices to interpret children's ill-formed actions as conversational actions and the extent to which the parent attempts to maintain and guide the interaction, both verbally and physically.

Toward the end of the first year, children develop increasing ability to control conversations through specific routines. The most well-developed routine is pointing. Children show reliable responding to pointing by about 10 months. They are able to look at their parents' faces and use their gaze and pointing to locate objects. Soon after this, by about 12 months, children begin to produce their own communicative pointing (Lempers, 1979). In the period between 12 and 15 months, just before the first words, children also develop a set of intonational patterns and body postures intended to communicate other detailed meanings (Halliday, 1975).

Parents provide interpretive scaffolds for many of the child's early communicative behaviors (Bruner, 1992). After the child produces a smile, the parent may then respond with a fully fledged verbal interpretation of the meaning implicit in the smile, as in, "Is David having fun?" If the child shakes a spoon, the mother will attempt to interpret this gesture too, suggesting, "Ready for dinner?" Beginning around 9 months, this sequence of child action and maternal interpretation takes on a choral quality involving alternating, rather than overlapping, contributions (Jasnow & Feldstein, 1986). By combining verbal responses with the child's gestures, mothers are able to produce a scaffold on which children can construct a vision of communicative interactions. The transcripts with videos available from http://childes.psy.cmu.edu provide many illustrations of choral sequences of this type.

Snow (1999) argued that early participation in conversational interactions is the primary support for the initial stages of language acquisition. She emphasized the extent to which early words serve social functions in games and routines, rather than serving merely to request objects. Crucially, language learning depends on the construction of a shared intersubjective understanding of the intentions of the parent. Conversational sequencing is the scaffold on which this understanding develops. Sequencing receives support from the processes of identification (Rizzolatti, Fadiga, Gallese, & Fogassi, 1996), embodiment (MacWhinney, 2008b), and imitation (Meltzoff, 1995). Together, these processes allow us to construct a complete image of the other person as a complete conversational partner who is participating and acting in ways that are parallel to the ways we ourselves act.

The growth of children's vocabulary is heavily dependent on specific conversational input. The more input the child receives, the larger the vocabulary (Huttenlocher, Haight, Bryk, Seltzer, & Lyons, 1991). Children from higher socioeconomic status (SES) groups tend to have more input and a more advanced vocabulary (Arriaga, Fenson, Cronan, & Pethick, 1998). More educated families provide as much as three times more input than less educated families (Hart & Risley, 1995). Social interaction (quality of attachment, parent responsiveness, involvement, sensitivity, and control style) and general intellectual climate (providing enriching toys, reading books, and encouraging attention to surroundings) predict developing language competence in children as well (van IJzendoorn, Dijkstra, & Bus, 1995). Children with verbally responsive mothers achieve the vocabulary spurt and combine words into simple sentences sooner than do children with less verbally responsive mothers (Tamis-LeMonda &

Bornstein, 2002). These facts have led educators to suspect that basic and pervasive differences in the level of social support for language learning lie at the root of many learning problems in the later school years.

THE DEVELOPMENT OF LITERACY

Increased input during early childhood leads to increases in vocabulary growth and other aspects of language structure. These differences in input quantity and quality continue to widen as children get older, with children from higher SES and more educated families receiving more instruction both in the home and in the school in language forms, reading, literature, and composition (Dickinson & Moreton, 1993).

As children move on to higher stages of language development and the acquisition of literacy, they depend increasingly on wider social institutions. They may rely on Sunday school teachers as their source of knowledge about Biblical language, prophets, and the geography of the Holy Land. They will rely on science teachers to gain vocabulary and understandings about friction, molecular structures, the circulatory system, and DNA (Keil, 1989). The vocabulary demands placed by such materials can be enormous, with a typical textbook in biology requiring the learning of as many as 1,000 technical terms.

Students will rely on peers to introduce them to the language of the streets, verbal dueling, and the use of language for courtship. They will rely on the media for exposure to the verbal expressions of other ethnic groups and religions. When they enter the workplace, they will rely on their coworkers to develop a literate understanding of work procedures, union rules, and methods for furthering their status. By reading to their children, by telling stories, and by engaging in supportive dialogs, parents set the stage for their child's entry into the world of literature and schooling (Snow, 1999). Here, again, the parent and teacher must teach by displaying examples of the execution and generation of a wide variety of detailed literate practices, ranging from learning to write through outlines to taking notes in lectures (Connors & Epstein, 1995).

It is important to recognize that the literate practices used in today's schools are specific adaptations to the requirements of our current educational system. In the past, a great deal of emphasis was placed on the learning of Greek, Latin, and Hebrew. Currently, we see a relatively greater emphasis on the acquisition of technical vocabulary, including programming languages. If foreign languages are taught, they are no longer the classics, but rather major living languages such as Spanish or Chinese.

Educators and parents are likely to attribute a general decrease in young people's abilities to the advent of tools for Web searching: Students have access to an encyclopedia of knowledge far greater than that of their parents. In many ways, our concept of literate practices is undergoing continual transformation as technological advances in video, telecommunications, and computers allow us to explore new modes of communication (McLuhan & Fiore, 1967). However, to maintain cultural continuity, students will still need to be able to appreciate the structure of a Greek drama, the rules of formal debate, and the allegorical features in the *Divine Comedy*.

CONCLUSIONS

This discussion of language learning has examined the various cognitive and social processes that move the child into the verbal interplay of what Augustine called the "stormy intercourse of human life." These forces involve dynamic and emergent processes that link core language learning abilities with social input and general learning mechanisms. Many of the auditory and cognitive abilities underlying language are available to other primates; but only humans possess the full set of articulatory, cognitive, and social abilities that are required for human language. Although there is no single special gift underlying language and no genetically encoded knowledge about languages, language acquisition is supported by a rich collection of abilities that have accumulated through 6 million years of human evolution. Together, these abilities represent a unique capacity for learning and using language.

There is clear individual variation in many of these abilities. For example, we know that, overall, girls are faster than boys in their learning of both vocabulary and grammar (Bornstein, Hahn, & Haynes, 2004). Children with specific language impairment (SLI) (Bishop, 1997) show marked deviation from the normal pattern of language development. Despite these many individual differences, and despite wide variation in language input and linguistic structures, all children eventually succeed in learning their native language. This is because learning to speak is such a fundamental part of becoming human.

REFERENCES AND SUGGESTED READINGS (▯)

Adams, A., & Bullock, D. (1986). Apprenticeship in word use: Social convergence processes in learning categorically related nouns. In S. Kuczaj & M. Barrett (Eds.), *The development of word meaning* (pp. 155–197). New York: Springer.

Allen, R., & Gardner, B. (1969). Teaching sign language to a chimpanzee. *Science*, *165*, 664–672.

Ament, W. (1899). *Die Entwicklung von Sprechen und Denken beim Kinder*. Leipzig, Gemany: Ernst Wunderlich.

Arriaga, R., Fenson, L., Cronan, T., & Pethick, S. (1998). Scores on the MacArthur communicative development inventory of children from low and middle income families. *Applied Psycholinguistics*, *19*, 209–223.

▯ Aslin, R. N., Saffran, J. R., & Newport, E. L. (1999). Statistical learning in linguistic and nonlinguistic domains. In B. MacWhinney (Ed.), *The emergence of language* (pp. 359–380). Mahwah, NJ: Lawrence Erlbaum Associates.

Au, T. K., & Glusman, M. (1990). The principle of mutual exclusivity in word learning: To honor or not to honor? *Child Development*, *61*, 1474–1490.

Augustine, S. (1952). *The Confessions* (Vol. 18). Chicago: Encyclopedia Britannica.

Baldwin, D. A. (1993). Early referential understanding: Infants' ability to recognize referential acts for what they are. *Developmental Psychology*, *29*, 832–843.

Baldwin, D. A., Markman, E. M., Bill, B., Desjardins, R. N., Irwin, J. M., & Tidball, G. (1996). Infants' reliance on a social criterion for establishing word–object relations. *Child Development*, *67*, 3135–3153.

Baron-Cohen, S., Baldwin, D. A., & Crowson, M. (1997). Do children with autism use the speaker's direction of gaze strategy to crack the code of language? *Child Development*, *68*, 48–57.

Bates, E., Benigni, L., Bretherton, I., Camaioni, L., & Volterra, V. (1979). *The emergence of symbols: Cognition and communication in infancy*. New York: Academic Press.

Berko, J. (1958). The child's learning of English morphology. *Word*, *14*, 150–177.

Bernhardt, B. H., & Stemberger, J. P. (1998). *Handbook of phonological development from the perspective of constraint-based nonlinear phonology*. San Diego, CA: Academic Press.

Berry, M., & Eisenson, J. (1956). *Speech disorders: Principles and practices of therapy*. New York: Appleton-Century-Crofts.

▯ Bishop, D. (1997). *Uncommon understanding*. Hove, UK: Psychology Press.

Bloom, K., Russell, A., & Wassenberg, K. (1987). Turntaking affects the quality of infant vocalizations. *Journal of Child Language*, *14*, 211–227.

Bloom, L. (1973). *One word at a time: The use of single word utterances*. The Hague, The Netherlands: Mouton.

▯ Bloom, P. (2000). *How children learn the meanings of words*. Cambridge, MA: MIT Press.

Bornstein, M., Cote, L., Maital, S., Painter, K., Park, S.-Y., Pascual, L., et al. (2004). Cross-linguistic analysis of vocabulary in young children: Spanish, Dutch, French, Hebrew, Italian, Korean, and American English. *Child Development*, *75*, 1115–1139.

Bornstein, M., Hahn, C., & Haynes, M. (2004). Specific and general language performance across early childhood: Stability and gender considerations. *First Language*, *24*, 267–304.

Bosch, L., & Sebastián-Galles, N. (1997). Native-language recognition abilities in four-month-old infants from bilingual environments. *Cognition*, *65*, 33–69.

Bower, T. G. R. (1974). *Development in infancy*. San Francisco: Freeman.

Bowerman, M. (1978a). The acquisition of word meaning: An investigation into some current conflicts. In N. Waterson & C. Snow (Eds.), *The development of communication*. New York: Wiley.

Bowerman, M. (1978b). Systematizing semantic knowledge: Changes over time in the child's organization of word meaning. *Child Development, 49*, 977–987.

Bowerman, M. (1988). The "no negative evidence" problem. In J. Hawkins (Ed.), *Explaining language universals* (pp. 73–104). London: Blackwell.

Boysson-Bardies, B., & Vihman, M. M. (1991). Adaption to language: Evidence from babbling and first words in four languages. *Language, 67*, 297–320.

Braine, M. D. S. (1963). The ontogeny of English structure: The first phase. *Language, 39*, 1–13.

Braine, M. D. S. (1976). Children's first word combinations. *Monographs of the Society for Research in Child Development, 41* (Whole No. 1).

Branigan, G. (1979). Some reasons why successive single word utterances are not. *Journal of Child Language, 6*, 411–421.

Bresnan, J. (Ed.). (1982). *The mental representation of grammatical relations*. Cambridge, MA: MIT Press.

Brown, R. (1957). Linguistic determinism and the part of speech. *Journal of Abnormal and Social Psychology, 55*, 1–5.

Brown, R. (1958). How shall a thing be called? *Psychological Review, 65*, 14–21.

Brown, R. (1973). *A first language: The early stages*. Cambridge, MA: Harvard University Press.

Brown, R., & Bellugi, U. (1964). Three processes in the child's acquisition of syntax. In E. H. Lenneberg (Ed.), *New directions in the study of language*. Cambridge, MA: MIT Press.

Brown, R., Cazden, C., & Bellugi, U. (1968). The child's grammar from I to III. In J. P. Hill (Ed.), *Minnesota symposia on child development*. Minneapolis, MN: University of Minnesota Press.

Bruner, J. (1992). *Acts of meaning*. Cambridge, MA: Harvard University Press.

Burling, R. (1959). Language development of a Garo and English speaking child. *Word, 15*, 45–68.

Carey, S. (1978). The child as word learner. In M. Halle, J. Bresnan, & G. Miller (Eds.), *Linguistic theory and psychological reality* (pp. 264–293). Cambridge, MA: MIT Press.

Cartwright, T. A., & Brent, M. R. (1997). Syntactic categorization in early language acquisition: Formalizing the role of distributional analysis. *Cognition, 61*, 121–170.

Clancy, P. M. (1985). The acquisition of Japanese. In D. I. Slobin (Ed.), *The crosslinguistic study of language acquisition: Volume 1. The data*. Hillsdale, NJ: Lawrence Erlbaum Associates.

Clark, E. (1987). The principle of contrast: A constraint on language acquisition. In B. MacWhinney (Ed.), *Mechanisms of language acquisition* (pp. 1–34). Hillsdale, NJ: Lawrence Erlbaum Associates.

Clark, E. (1997). Conceptual perspective and lexical choice in acquisition. *Cognition, 64*, 1–37.

Clark, R. (1977). What's the use of imitation? *Journal of Child Language, 4*, 341–358.

Cole, R. A., & Scott, B. (1974). Toward a theory of speech perception. *Psychological Review, 81*(4), 358–374.

Connors, L. J., & Epstein, J. L. (1995). Parent and school partnerships. In M. H. Bornstein (Ed.), *Handbook of parenting* (Vol. 4, pp. 437–457). Mahwah, NJ: Lawrence Erlbaum Associates.

Cruttenden, A. (1970). A phonetic study of babbling. *British Journal of Disorders of Communication, 5*, 110–117.

DeCasper, A. J., & Fifer, W. P. (1980). Of human bonding: Newborns prefer their mothers' voices. *Science, 208*, 1174–1176.

DeCasper, A. J., Lecanuet, J., & Busnel, M. (1994). Fetal reactions to recurrent mother speech. *Infant Behavior and Development, 17*, 159–164.

Dickinson, D. K., & Moreton, J. (1993). Preschool classrooms as settings for the acquisition of emergent literacy and literacy-related language skills. *Merrill-Palmer Quarterly*.

Dromi, E. (1987). *Early lexical development*. New York: Cambridge University Press.

Eimas, P. D., Siqueland, E. R., Jusczyk, P., & Vigorito, J. (1971). Speech perception in infants. *Science, 171*, 303–306.

Ervin, S. (1964). Imitation and structural change in children's language. In E. H. Lenneberg (Ed.), *New directions in the study of language*. Cambridge, MA: MIT Press.

Frith, C. D., & Frith, U. (1999). Interacting minds: A biological basis. *Science, 286*, 1692–1695.

Gelman, S. A. (1998). Categories in young children's thinking. *Young Children, 53*, 20–26.

Gentner, D. (1982). Why nouns are learned before verbs: Linguistic relativity versus natural partitioning. In S. Kuczaj (Ed.), *Language development: Language, culture, and cognition* (pp. 301–334). Hillsdale, NJ: Lawrence Erlbaum Associates.

Gentner, D. (2005). The development of relational category knowledge. In L. Gershkoff-Stowe & D. Rakison (Eds.), *Building object categories in developmental time* (pp. 245–276). Mahwah, NJ: Lawrence Erlbaum Associates.

Gogate, L. J., Bahrick, L. E., & Watson, J. D. (2000). A study of multimodal motherese: The role of temporal synchrony between verbal labels and gestures. *Child Development, 71*, 878–894.

Goldfield, B. (1993). Noun bias in maternal speech to one-year-olds. *Journal of Child Language, 13*, 455–476.

Golinkoff, R., Hirsh-Pasek, K., Cauley, K., & Gordon, L. (1987). The eyes have it: Lexical and syntactic comprehension in a new paradigm. *Journal of Child Language, 14*, 23–46.

Golinkoff, R., Hirsh-Pasek, K., & Hollich, G. (1999). Emergent cues for early word learning. In B. MacWhinney (Ed.), *The emergence of language* (pp. 305–330). Mahwah, NJ: Lawrence Erlbaum Associates.

Gopnik, A., & Choi, S. (1995). Names, relational words, and cognitive development in English and Korean speakers: Nouns are not always learned before verbs. In M. Tomasello & M. Merriman (Eds.), *Beyond names for things* (pp. 63–80). Hillsdale, NJ: Lawrence Erlbaum Associates.

Halliday, M. (1975). *Learning to mean: Explorations in the development of language*. London: Edward Arnold.

Hart, B., & Risley, T. R. (1995). *Meaningful differences in the everyday experience of young American children*. Baltimore: Paul H. Brookes.

Hauser, M., Chomsky, N., & Fitch, T. (2002). The faculty of language: What is it, who has it, and how did it evolve? *Science, 298*, 1569–1579.

Hoyer, A., & Hoyer, G. (1924). Über die Lallsprache eines Kindes. *Zeitschrift für angewandte Psychologie, 24*, 363–384.

Huttenlocher, J. (1974). The origins of language comprehension. In R. Solso (Ed.), *Theories in cognitive psychology: The Loyola symposium* (pp. 331–388). Potomac, MD: Lawrence Erlbaum Associates.

Huttenlocher, J., Haight, W., Bryk, A., Seltzer, M., & Lyons, T. (1991). Early vocabulary growth: Relation to language input and gender. *Developmental Psychology, 27*(2), 236–248.

Irwin, O. C. (1936). *Infant speech*. New York: Harcourt, Brace.

Jakobson, R. (1968). *Child language, aphasia and phonological universals*. The Hague, The Netherlands: Mouton.

James, W. (1890). *The principles of psychology*. New York: Holt, Rinehart, and Winston.

Jasnow, M., & Feldstein, S. (1986). Adult-like temporal characteristics of mother–infant vocal interactions. *Child Development, 57*, 754–761.

Jusczyk, P. W. (1997). *The discovery of spoken language*. Cambridge, MA: MIT Press.

Kager, R. (1999). *Optimality theory*. New York: Cambridge University Press.

Katz, N., Baker, E., & Macnamara, J. (1974). What's in a name? A study of how children learn common and proper names. *Child Development, 45*, 469–473.

Kay, D. A., & Anglin, J. M. (1982). Overextension and underextension in the child's expressive and receptive speech. *Journal of Child Language, 9*, 83–98.

Keil, F. C. (1989). *Concepts, kinds, and cognitive development*. Cambridge, MA: MIT Press.

Keil, F. C., & Batterman, N. (1984). A characteristic-to-defining shift in the development of word meaning. *Journal of Verbal Learning and Verbal Behavior, 23*, 221–236.

Keller, H., Poortinga, Y., & Schomerich, A. (2002). *Between culture and biology: Perspectives on ontogenetic development*. New York: Cambridge University Press.

Kenyeres, E. (1926). *A gyermek elsö szavai es a szófajók föllépése*. Budapest: Kisdednevelés.

Kilborn, K. (1989). Sentence processing in a second language: The timing of transfer. *Language and Speech, 32*, 1–23.

Klima, E., & Bellugi, U. (1966). Syntactic regularities in the speech of children. In J. Lyons & R. J. Wales (Eds.), *Psycholinguistics papers*. Edinburgh, UK: Edinburgh University Press.

Kuczaj, S., & Brannick, N. (1979). Children's use of the Wh question modal auxiliary placement rule. *Journal of Experimental Child Psychology, 28*, 43–67.

Kuhl, P. K., Conboy, B., Padden, D., Nelson, T., & Pruitt, J. (2005). Early speech perception and later language development: Implications for the "critical period". *Language Learning and Development, 1*, 237–264.

Kuhl, P. K., & Miller, J. D. (1978). Speech perception by the chinchilla: Identification functions for synthetic VOT stimuli. *Journal of the Acoustical Society of America, 63*, 905–917.

Labov, T., & Labov, W. (1978). The phonetics of cat and mama. *Language, 54*, 816–852.

Lee, T. H. (1999). Finiteness and null arguments in child Cantonese. *Tsinghua Journal of Chinese Studies, 33*, 1–16.

Lempers, J. (1979). Young children's production and comprehension of nonverbal deictic behaviors. *Journal of Genetic Psychology, 135*, 93–102.

Leopold, W. (1949). *Speech development of a bilingual child: A linguist's record: Vol. 3. Grammar and general problems in the first two years*. Evanston, IL: Northwestern University Press.

Lewis, M. M. (1936). *Infant speech: A study of the beginnings of language*. New York: Harcourt, Brace.

Locke, J. (1995). Development of the capacity for spoken language. In P. Fletcher & B. MacWhinney (Eds.), *The handbook of child language* (pp. 278–302). Oxford, UK: Basil Blackwell.

Lupyan, G., Rakison, D. H., & McClelland, J. L. (2007). Language is not just for talking: Redundant labels facilitate learning of novel categories. *Psychological Science, 18*, 1077–1083.

MacNeilage, P. (1998). The frame/content theory of evolution of speech production. *Behavioral and Brain Sciences, 21*, 499–546.

MacWhinney, B. (1975). Pragmatic patterns in child syntax. *Stanford Papers and Reports on Child Language Development, 10*, 153–165.

MacWhinney, B. (1976). Hungarian research on the acquisition of morphology and syntax. *Journal of Child Language, 3*, 397–410.

MacWhinney, B. (1978). The acquisition of morphophonology. *Monographs of the Society for Research in Child Development, 43*, Whole no. 1, pp. 1–123.

MacWhinney, B. (1982). Basic syntactic processes. In S. Kuczaj (Ed.), *Language acquisition: Vol. 1. Syntax and semantics* (pp. 73–136). Hillsdale, NJ: Lawrence Erlbaum Associates.

MacWhinney, B. (1987). The competition model. In B. MacWhinney (Ed.), *Mechanisms of language acquisition* (pp. 249–308). Hillsdale, NJ: Lawrence Erlbaum Associates.

MacWhinney, B. (1989). Competition in language and thought. In J. Montangero (Ed.), *Language and cognition. Cahiers Jean Piaget 10*. Geneva, Switzerland: Fondation Archives Jean Piaget.

MacWhinney, B. (1991). Reply to Woodward and Markman. *Developmental Review, 11*, 192–194.

MacWhinney, B. (2008a). Cognitive precursors to language. In K. Oller & U. Griebel (Eds.), *The evolution of communicative flexibility* (pp. 193–214). Cambridge, MA: MIT Press.

MacWhinney, B. (2008b). How mental models encode embodied linguistic perspectives. In R. Klatzky, B. MacWhinney, & M. Behrmann (Eds.), *Embodiment, ego-space, and action* (pp. 369–410). Mahwah, NJ: Lawrence Erlbaum Associates.

MacWhinney, B. (2009). The emergence of linguistic complexity. In T. Givon (Ed.), *Linguistic complexity* (pp. 405–432). New York: Benjamins.

Maratsos, M., & Deak, G. (1995). Hedgehogs, foxes, and the acquisition of verb meaning. In M. Tomasello & M. Merriman (Eds.), *Beyond names for things* (pp. 377–404). Hillsdale, NJ: Lawrence Erlbaum Associates.

Markman, E. (1989). *Categorization and naming in children: Problems of induction*. Cambridge, MA: MIT Press.

Massaro, D. (Ed.). (1975). *Understanding language: An introduction-processing analysis of speech perception, reading, and psycholinguistics*. New York: Academic Press.

Mavilya, M. (1970). Spontaneous vocalication and babbling in hearing impaired infants. In G. Fant (Ed.), *International symposium on speech communication abilities and profound deafness*. Washington, DC: Alexander Graham Bell Association for the Deaf.

McCarthy, D. (1954). Language development in children. In L. Carmichael (Ed.), *Handbook of child psychology*. New York: Wiley.

McLuhan, M., & Fiore, Q. (1967). *The medium is the massage*. New York: Bantam Books.

Meltzoff, A. N. (1995). Understanding the intentions of others: Re-enactment of intended acts by 18-month-old children. *Developmental Psychology, 31*, 838–850.

Menn, L., & Stoel-Gammon, C. (1995). Phonological development. In P. Fletcher & B. MacWhinney (Eds.), *The handbook of child language* (pp. 335–360). Oxford, UK: Blackwell.

Menyuk, P. (1969). *Sentences children use*. Cambridge, MA: MIT Press.

Merriman, W. (1999). Competition, attention, and young children's lexical processing. In B. MacWhinney (Ed.), *The emergence of language* (pp. 331–358). Mahwah, NJ: Lawrence Erlbaum Associates.

Mowrer, O. (1960). *Learning theory and the symbolic processes*. New York: Wiley.

Namy, L., & Waxman, S. (1998). Words and gestures: Infants' interpretations of different forms of symbolic reference. *Child Development, 69*, 295–308.

Nicoladis, E. (2001). Finding first words in the input. In J. Cenoz & F. Genesee (Eds.), *Trends in bilingual acquisition* (pp. 131–148). New York: Benjamins.

Ninio, A., & Snow, C. (1988). Language acquisition through language use: The functional sources of children's early utterances. In Y. Levy, I. Schlesinger, & M. Braine (Eds.), *Categories and processes in language acquisition* (pp. 11–30). Hillsdale, NJ: Lawrence Erlbaum Associates.

Ochs, E., & Schieffelin, B. B. (1983). *Acquiring conversational competence*. London: Routledge & Kegan Paul.

O'Grady, W. (2005). *Syntactic carpentry*. Mahwah, NJ: Lawrence Erlbaum Associates.

Ohala, J. J. (1974). Phonetic explanation in phonology. In A. Bruck, R. Fox, & M. La Galy (Eds.), *Papers from the parassession on natural phonology* (pp. 251–274). Chicago: Chicago Linguistic Society.

Ohala, J. J. (1981). The listener as a source of sound change. In R. H. C. Masek & M. Miller (Eds.), *Papers from the Parasession on Language and Behavior*. Chicago: Chicago Linguistic Society.

Ohala, J. J. (1994). The frequency codes underlying the symbolic use of voice pitch. In L. Hinton, J. Nichols, & J. Ohala (Eds.), *Sound symbolism* (pp. 325–347). New York: Cambridge University Press.

Oller, D. K. (2000). *The emergence of the speech capacity*. Mahwah, NJ: Lawrence Erlbaum Associates.

Oller, D. K., & Eilers, R. E. (1988). The role of audition in infant babbling. *Child Development, 59*, 441–449.

Oviatt, S. (1980). The emerging ability to comprehend language: An experimental approach. *Child Development, 51*, 97–106.

Papoušek, M., & Papoušek, H. (1991). The meanings of melodies in motherese in tone and stress languages. *Infant Behavior and Development, 14*, 415–440.

Pelphrey, K. A., Morris, J. P., & McCarthy, G. (2005). Neural basis of eye gaze processing deficits in autism. *Brain, 128*, 1038–1048.

Peters, A. M. (1977). Language learning strategies: Does the whole equal the sum of the parts? *Language, 53*, 560–573.

Piaget, J. (1952). *The origins of intelligence in children*. New York: International Universities Press.

Piaget, J. (1954). *The construction of reality in the child*. New York: Basic Books.

Ponori, T. E. (1871). A gyermeknyelvról. *Természettudományi Közlöny, 3*, 117–125.

Quine, W. (1960). *Word and object*. Cambridge, MA: MIT Press.

Rizzolatti, G., Fadiga, L., Gallese, V., & Fogassi, L. (1996). Premotor cortex and the recognition of motor actions. *Cognitive Brain Research*, *3*, 131–141.

Sacks, H., Schegloff, E., & Jefferson, G. (1974). A simplest systematics for the organization of turn-taking for conversation. *Language*, *50*, 696–735.

Sagae, K., Davis, E., Lavie, E., MacWhinney, B., & Wintner, S. (2007). High–accuracy annotation and parsing of CHILDES transcripts *Proceedings of the 45th Meeting of the Association for Computational Linguistics*. Prague, Czech Republic: ACL.

Sandhofer, C., Smith, L., & Luo, J. (2000). Counting nouns and verbs in the input: Differential frequencies, different kinds of learning? *Journal of Child Language*, *27*, 561–585.

Schafer, G., & Plunkett, K. (1998). Rapid word learning by 15-month-olds under tightly controlled conditions. *Child Development*, *69*, 309–320.

Schlesinger, I. M. (1974). Relational concepts underlying language. In R. L. Schiefelbusch & L. L. Lloyd (Eds.), *Language perspectives: Acquisition, retardation, and intervention*. Baltimore: University Park Press.

Schlesinger, I. M. (1975). Grammatical development—the first steps. In E. H. Lenneberg & E. Lenneberg (Eds.), *Foundations of language development: A multidisciplinary approach* (Vol. 1). New York: Academic Press.

Slobin, D. I. (1973). Cognitive prerequisites for the development of grammar. In C. A. Ferguson & D. I. Slobin (Eds.), *Studies of child language development*. New York: Holt, Rinehart and Winston.

☐ Smith, L. (1999). Children's noun learning: How general processes make specialized learning mechanisms. In B. MacWhinney (Ed.), *The emergence of language* (pp. 277–304). Mahwah, NJ: Lawrence Erlbaum Associates.

Smith, N. V. (1973). *The acquisition of phonology: A case study*. Cambridge, UK: Cambridge University Press.

Snow, C. E. (1977). The development of conversation between mothers and babies. *Journal of Child Language*, *4*, 1–22.

☐ Snow, C. E. (1999). Social perspectives on the emergence of language. In B. MacWhinney (Ed.), *The emergence of language* (pp. 257–276). Mahwah, NJ: Lawrence Erlbaum Associates.

Snow, C. E., Pan, B., Imbens-Bailey, A., & Herman, J. (1996). Learning how to say what one means: A longitudinal study of children's speech act use. *Social Development*, *5*, 56–84.

Stager, C. L., & Werker, J. F. (1997). Infants listen for more phonetic detail in speech perception than in word learning tasks. *Nature*, *388*, 381–382.

Stampe, D. (1973). *A dissertation on natural phonology*. Chicago: University of Chicago.

Sugárné, K. J. (1970). A szokincs és a szófajok gyakoriságának alakulása 3–6 éves gyermekek beszédének feladatmegoldás, illetőleg kommunikáció során. *Altalános Nyelvészeti Tanulmányok*, *7*, 149–159.

Tamis-LeMonda, C., & Bornstein, M. H. (2002). Maternal responsiveness and early language acquisition. In R. Kail & J. Reese (Eds.), *Advances in child development and behavior* (Vol. 29, pp. 89–127). San Diego, CA: Academic Press.

Tardif, T. (1996). Nouns are not always learned before verbs: Evidence from Mandarin speakers' early vocabularies. *Developmental Psychology*, *32*, 492–504.

Templin, M. (1957). *Certain language skills in children*. Minneapolis, MN: University of Minnesota Press.

Terrace, H. S., Petitto, L. A., Sanders, R. J., & Bever, T. G. (1980). On the grammatical capacity of apes. In K. Nelson (Ed.), *Children's language: Vol. 2*. New York: Gardner.

Tesniére, L. (1959). *Elements de syntaxe structurale*. Paris: Klincksieck.

Thelen, E., & Smith, L. (1994). *A dynamic systems approach to the development of cognition and action*. Cambridge, MA: MIT Press.

Thiessen, E. D., Hill, E., & Saffran, J. R. (2005). Infant directed speech facilitates word segmentation. *Infancy*, *7*, 53–71.

Thiessen, E. D., & Saffran, J. R. (2007). Learning to learn: Acquisition of stress-based strategies for word segmentation. *Language Learning and Development*, *3*, 75–102.

Tinbergen, N. (1951). *The study of instinct*. New York: Clarendon Press.

☐ Tomasello, M. (2000). The item-based nature of children's early syntactic development. *Trends in Cognitive Sciences*, *4*, 156–163.

Tomasello, M. (2003). *Constructing a first language: A usage-based theory of language acquisition*. Cambridge, MA: Harvard University Press.

Tomasello, M., & Akhtar, N. (1995). Two-year-olds use pragmatic cues to differentiate reference to objects and actions. *Cognitive Development*, *10*, 201–224.

Tomasello, M., Akhtar, N., Dodson, K., & Rekau, L. (1997). Differential productivity in young children's use of nouns and verbs. *Journal of Child Language*, *24*, 373–387.

Tomasello, M., & Haberl, K. (2003). Understanding attention: 12- and 18-month-olds know what is new for other persons. *Developmental Psychology*, *39*, 906–912.

Tucker, D. (2002). Embodied meaning. In T. Givon & B. Malle (Eds.), *The evolution of language out of pre-language* (pp. 51–82). Amsterdam: Benjamins.

van IJzendoorn, M. H., Dijkstra, J., & Bus, A. G. (1995). Attachment, intelligence, and language: A meta-analysis. *Social Development*, *4*, 115–128.

Vihman, M. (1996). *Phonological development: The origins of language in the child*. Cambridge, MA: Blackwell.

Wallace, V., Menn, L., & Yoshinaga-Itano, C. (1998). Is babble the gateway to speech for all children? A longitudinal study of children who are deaf or hard of hearing. *Volta Review*, *100*, 121–148.

Wäsz-Hockert, O., Lind, J., Vuorenkoski, V., Partanen, T., & Valanne, E. (1968). *The infant cry: A spectrographic and auditory analysis* (Vol. 29). Lavenham, UK: Lavenham Press.

Waxman, S., & Kosowski, T. (1990). Nouns mark category relations: Toddlers' and preschoolers' word-learning biases. *Child Development*, *61*, 1461–1473.

Waxman, S., & Markow, D. (1995). Words as invitations to form categories: Evidence from 12- to 13-month-old infants. *Cognitive Psychology*, *29*, 257–302.

Werker, J. F. (1995). Exploring developmental changes in cross-language speech perception. In L. Gleitman & M. Liberman (Eds.), *An Invitation to Cognitive Science: Vol. 1. Language* (pp. 87–106). Cambridge, MA: MIT Press.

Whorf, B. (1967). *Language, thought, and reality*. Cambridge, MA: MIT Press.

Woodward, A. L., & Hoyne, R. (1999). Infants' learning about words and sounds in relation to objects. *Child Development*, *70*, 65–77.

PERSONALITY AND THE SOCIAL CONTEXTS OF DEVELOPMENT

Language permits abstract thought; it also allows interpersonal communication, a primary medium for social interaction that lies at the heart of personality and social development. Chapters in the last section of *Developmental Science: An Advanced Textbook* examine personality and social development in the context of the various relationships and situations in which developing individuals function and by which they are shaped. Chapter 9 focuses on temperament, emotions, and self in the individual child as they evolve into personality. As Ross A. Thompson, Abby C. Winer, and Rebecca Goodvin show, personality as we understand it integrates over the development of temperament, emotion, and self. The authors set themselves and the reader the goal of understanding what each is, how each develops, and the ways in which each contributes to the psychological make-up of the individual. The self unfolds in close relation to temperament, emotions, and personality in the course of early psychological development.

However, the self emerges in social contexts. One primary social context for developing individuals is represented by the family. In Chapter 10, Michael E. Lamb and Charlie Lewis recount the development of social relationships within the family during the first years of life. They describe normative developmental progressions in the emergence of these relationships as well as factors that account for individual differences in relationships, creating some that foster healthy adjustment and development and others that subvert developmental processes and lead to the emergence of behavioral pathology.

In Chapter 11, Kenneth H. Rubin, Robert Coplan, Xinyin Chen, Julie Bowker, and Kristina L. McDonald shift the developing child's focus to relationships established with children outside the family, notably with peers. As Rubin and his coauthors point out, relationships with peers play a central and formative role in children's development. These authors document how, with increasing age, peers in various kinds of groups account for a growing proportion of children's social experiences, creating an increasingly important context within which children manifest their distinctive personality and social styles and by which these styles are modified and honed. How peer influences are measured, why individual children are so influenced by peers, how children essentially negotiate their relationships with friends, and the consequences of good and poor peer relationships in children's lives are topics of keen interest in contemporary developmental science.

As most children grow, self and social relationships are increasingly organized within

425

institutional contexts such as school and community. These social institutions serve as environments in which children are expected to perform and by which their tendencies, preferences, and abilities are shaped. School and community are, therefore, as Jacquelynne S. Eccles and Robert W. Roeser show in Chapter 12, pervasive and powerful developmental ecologies for children. Although psychologists have often viewed the family as the primary context within which children are reared, and peers as a close runner-up, the authors of this chapter make clear that children are profoundly influenced by relationships and experiences outside the family in schools and communities where they are most often found.

As noted in many of the preceding chapters, developmental science is not only a subdiscipline in which scientists seek basic knowledge of developmental processes. The individuals at the center of developmental research face real problems and challenges, and the results of that research often have implications for the design of intervention programs and for the initiation of social policy. An increasing portion of attention in developmental science today is paid to applied as well as basic research issues. In Chapter 13, Lindsay C. Malloy, Michael E. Lamb, and Carmit Katz illustrate the ways in which developmental thinking and research affect and are affected by practice and social policy. Their chapter is a guide to the student of the discipline who would see her or his work impact the society at large.

THE INDIVIDUAL CHILD: TEMPERAMENT, EMOTION, SELF, AND PERSONALITY

Ross A. Thompson and Abby C. Winer
University of California, Davis
Rebecca Goodvin
Western Washington University

INTRODUCTION

This chapter is concerned with the unique qualities that develop to distinguish the individual child from others, the qualities that contribute to the growth of personality. The goal is to understand what the child brings to the social world from the very beginning that marks developing individuality. It is important to note, however, that "the individual child" does not really exist except in the mind of the theorist. From the moment of conception throughout life, a person's growth is constituted by the influences of others, beginning with the quality of prenatal care and continuing in the variety of social influences that guide developing thoughts, emotions, and personality throughout adulthood. Nor do developing people come as empty entities to these interactions. They bring with them temperamental predispositions, unfolding emotional capacities, and developing self-awareness that individualize each transaction with the social world. In this regard, considering "the individual child" involves asking what developing people bring to their encounters with family members, peers, the school, and community.

Why focus on developing temperament, emotion, and self in the construction of personality? One reason is that these three early-emerging attributes establish young children's individuality to others—and to themselves. Temperament forms the initial bedrock of personality development through the dispositions by which young infants first exert a unique influence on others around them, and become recognized by others as distinct individuals. Emotion is an important way that individuality is developmentally broadened and deepened as emerging capacities for emotional expression, understanding, and regulation contribute to the growth of personality. Self is important for how it organizes emergent personality processes around a changing, yet consistent, core of self-perceived personhood. This trio of emerging capacities helps to define individuality from the beginning of life. Another reason is that temperament, emotion, and self each reflects an interaction between emergent intrinsic capacities and the influences of the social world. In this ongoing dynamic between nature and nurture, personality takes shape, and each developing child becomes a unique actor in a complex social world.

The development of temperament is considered first, in the next section. We address the defining features that distinguish temperament from moods or emotions, and then consider the core dimensions of temperamental individuality. Then we summarize research findings concerning the stability of temperament over time and its relation to personality features, especially in relation to new research in **molecular genetics** on the biological foundations of temperament. This leads to a broader discussion of how temperament develops, and the influence of temperament in the growth of behavior and personality. Emotional development is profiled in the section that follows. Definitional issues are again considered first. Because emotions are so complex, our discussion then turns to the question, "what is emotional development the development of?" In answering this question, the psychobiological foundations of emotion; the growth of emotion perception and understanding; empathy; emotion and the growth of self-understanding; emotional **display rules**; and **emotion regulation** are each profiled, along with the growth of emotion in close relationships. The last major section considers the development of self. Not surprisingly, we first consider "what is 'self'?" and the various dimensions of self-awareness and self-understanding that emerge developmentally. We then offer a developmental outline of how the self emerges in infancy, early childhood, middle childhood, adolescence, and adulthood. In a concluding section, we relate the developmental processes discussed in this chapter to the growth of personality. Throughout this chapter, we consider for each topic the importance of culture, emerging new research questions, and methods of study.

TEMPERAMENT

Beginning shortly after birth, a child's individuality is manifested primarily in temperament. The child's dominant mood, adaptability, activity level, persistence, threshold for distress (or happiness), self-regulation, and other characteristics are important because of the influence they have on others, and because they constitute the foundations of personality growth. Parents and other caregivers devote considerable effort to identifying, accommodating to, and sometimes modifying the temperamental features of young children. Parents also understand that, to the extent that we can see in the baby the person-to-be, we see in temperament the personality-to-be. Most parents are fascinated by their child's temperamental individuality because it distinguishes their child in ways that foreshadow, they believe, the growth of personality dispositions. Developmental research into temperament has been motivated by the same interests. What is temperament and its core features? How consistent over time are temperamental characteristics, and do they constitute the basis for personality development? How does temperament influence development—and how does temperament itself develop over time?

Defining Temperament

Temperament concerns the early emerging, stable individuality in a person's behavior, and this is what distinguishes temperamental individuality from more transient moods, emotions, or other influences on the developing child. More specifically, temperament is defined as constitutionally based individual differences in behavioral characteristics, especially those reflecting reactivity and self-regulation, that are relatively consistent across situations and over time (Goldsmith et al., 1987; Rothbart & Bates, 2006). Encompassed within this definition are several important points.

First, temperamental characteristics are *constitutional* in nature. Temperament is biologically based and derives from the interaction of genetic predispositions, maturation, and experience. The biological foundations of temperament are multifaceted. Individual differences in temperamental qualities associated with emotionality, activity, and other characteristics are strongly heritable (Caspi & Shiner, 2006; Goldsmith, 2002; Plomin, DeFries,

Craig, & McGuffin, 2003). Molecular genetics research has implicated several common genetic polymorphisms with temperament and personality characteristics. These include polymorphisms in the dopamine D4 receptor (DRD4), which is associated with novelty seeking and impulsivity, and the serotonin transporter promoter region (5HTTLPR), which is associated with negative emotionality and harm avoidance (Ebstein, Benjamin, & Belmaker, 2000). Genetic individuality is, in turn, expressed in many physiological systems, including individual differences in the reactivity of subcortical and sympathetic nervous system structures (Kagan & Fox, 2006), neuroendocrine functioning (Gunnar & Davis, 2003; Gunnar & Vasquez, 2006), cerebral asymmetry (Fox, Schmidt, & Henderson, 2000), parasympathetic regulation (Porges, 2007; Porges, Doussard-Roosevelt, & Maiti, 1994), attentional processes in the central nervous system (Rothbart, 2007; Rothbart, Posner, & Kieras, 2006), and many other psychobiological processes (see Martin & Fox, 2006, and Rothbart & Bates, 2006 for reviews).

Many of these features of biological individuality emerge very early in life, and thus influence developing social, emotional, and other dispositional qualities in the child. Although it is common to assume that the biological foundations of temperament account for the stability of temperamental attributes over time, it is important to remember that these biological foundations are also developing systems whose maturation may change the nature or organization of temperament. The early months and years of life witness not only the budding of behavioral individuality, in other words, but also the rapid growth and consolidation of neurological, neuroendocrine, neocortical, and other biological systems on which temperament is based. As a consequence, the 3-year-old is biologically much different from the newborn, and these biological differences contribute to developmental changes in temperamental qualities. Emotional reactivity, for example, is manifested within the context of far more organized behavioral capabilities in the older child, and the self-control of a 3-year-old is greater than it is just after birth—but less than it will be at age 6—which further alters emotional reactivity (Eisenberg & Morris, 2002; Rothbart et al., 2006).

Furthermore, experiences can also modify biological functioning in ways that influence temperament. This is seen most clearly in how early experiences of social adversity heighten biological stress reactivity in young children, such as how neglectful or abusive care can alter cortisol levels and other aspects of biological stress responding, causing children to become more temperamentally wary and irritable (Ashman & Dawson, 2002; Wiik & Gunnar, 2009). Supportive relationships can buffer stress reactivity, however, as when children who are temperamentally reactive to threat or danger are able to respond in a physiologically more adaptive manner in the presence of a sensitive caregiver (Nachmias, Gunnar, Mangelsdorf, Parritz, & Buss, 1996). These examples illustrate the fundamental interaction of biology and experience in the growth of temperament and its developmental influences.

A second defining feature is that temperament is expected to be *relatively stable* over time. That is, individual differences in temperamental characteristics are stable: A child who is dispositionally more cheerful than peers in infancy should, as a preschooler, still be more cheerful than age-mates. We should not expect temperamental characteristics to be rigidly stable in developing persons, but they should show greater stability than do other behavioral attributes. Studying the stability of temperament over time poses theoretical as well as methodological challenges, however. Theoretically, under what circumstances are temperamental attributes likely to be stable over time, and when is discontinuity more likely? Are there developmental phases when temperament is more likely to be modifiable, for instance, and does the quality of an individual's transactions with the social environment, such as parent–child relationships, influence the stability of temperament? Are some individuals more susceptible to changes in temperament than others? We shall consider later in greater detail these theoretical issues.

Methodologically, temperamental characteristics are inferred from behavior, but a person's behavior changes substantially with development. Growth of this kind makes the study of stability or change in temperament a difficult task. An infant with a high activity level manifests this attribute quite differently from a comparable preschooler or adolescent, for example, and high activity level is also likely to mean different things to other people in that child's world (it may be an amusing characteristic to the parents of an infant, but an irritating attribute to a preschool teacher seeking to manage a group of children). Using developmentally appropriate indicators, it is tricky to assess the same temperamental characteristic in an individual over time, but the failure to do so can contribute to a misestimation of the stability of temperament.

Third, temperament *interacts with the environment* as an influence on development. Although it is common to think of temperament as having a direct and specific influence on developing capacities such as attachment, sociability, and adjustment, it is more often true that its influence is mediated by environmental characteristics, such as the demands and stresses of the child's home, the sensitivity and adaptability of social partners, and the manner in which temperament guides the child's choices of activities in the environment as well as interpretations of those experiences. Several studies have shown, for example, that the quality of parental care interacts with early temperament to shape later physiological and behavioral outcomes associated with temperament (Crockenberg, Leerkes, & Lekka, 2007; Porter, Wouden-Miller, Silva, & Porter, 2003; Sheese, Voelker, Rothbart, & Posner, 2007). This is true even for children with "difficult" temperaments, because the consequences of temperamental difficulty are mediated by the ways in which temperament can be expressed in social contexts (in constructive or inappropriate ways), the reactions of other people, and the values of the culture concerning normative behavior. The fact that temperament interacts with environmental influences should not be surprising because development is complex and is rarely guided by one or a few primary influences. Any temperamental attribute can yield diverse developmental trajectories depending on the context in which temperament is perceived and interpreted, and other influences on the same trajectories.

Temperament also interacts with the environment because of how temperament is construed in light of cultural values and beliefs (Bornstein, 1995). Differences in how children's characteristics are conceptualized arise from cultural variation in how particular temperamental characteristics are valued (Cole & Dennis, 1998; Cole & Packer, Chapter 2, this volume; Harwood, Miller, & Irizarry, 1995). Shy and inhibited behavior is viewed much differently, and is associated with different parenting practices, in North American and Chinese families, for example, with inhibition associated with warm, accepting parenting in traditional areas of China but with punitiveness in Canada (Chen et al., 1998). Likewise, Japanese mothers are reported to value levels of proximity-seeking and fussiness in their infants that US mothers find problematic or indicative of developmental problems (Rothbaum, Weisz, Pott, Miyake, & Morelli, 2000).

Dimensions of Temperament

Another way of answering the question "what is temperament?" is to identify the primary dimensions of temperament. In what ways is temperamental individuality typically expressed? Temperament theorists vary somewhat in their answers to this question (Goldsmith et al., 1987; Rothbart & Bates, 2006). To Thomas, Chess, and their colleagues—who emphasized that temperament defines the stylistic component (the "how") of behavior rather than the content (the "what") of behavior—temperament is expressed in characteristics such as the *rhythmicity* of biological functions, *approach* to or *withdrawal* from new stimuli, *adaptability, distractability, activity level, quality of mood, persistence* or *attention span, intensity of reaction,* and *sensory threshold of responsiveness* (Chess & Thomas, 1986; Thomas & Chess, 1977; Thomas, Chess, & Birch, 1968). To Rothbart and her colleagues, temperamental individuality includes broad dimensions such as *negative affectivity, surgency/extraversion*, and **effortful control** as well as specific temperament features such as *soothability* and *activity* (see Rothbart & Bates, 2006). Buss and Plomin (1984) portrayed temperament in terms of variability in three dimensions: *activity level, emotionality*, and *sociability*.

There are some common themes in these alternative conceptualizations of temperament (see Table 9.1). Each regards activity level as a distinctive temperamental quality (to Rothbart, as a component of surgency), primarily owing to its salience and its broad influence on behavior. Each views self-regulation as important to temperamental variability because of how differences in regulatory capacities influence behavior, attention, impulsivity, and emotional expression. In addition, variations in positive and negative emotionality figure prominently in each formulation. Indeed, Goldsmith and Campos (1982) defined temperament as individual differences in the expression of the primary emotions, such as happiness, sadness, distress, fear, and anger. It is interesting that emotionality is such an important part of how temperament is conceptualized because this feature of temperament reflects the centrality of emotion to the behavioral variability that we can observe in infants and young children, whose proneness to distress, soothability, and smiling and laughter are extremely important to caregivers. Of course, temperament is different from emotion because it is more multidimensional and more enduring than are transient emotional states, but it is unmistakable that both immediate

TABLE 9.1
Temperament Dimensions as Described by Developmental Temperament Researchers

Common Dimensions	Rothbart & Bates[1]	Thomas & Chess[2]	Buss & Plomin
Emotion[3]	*Negative affectivity* Frustration Fear Discomfort Sadness Soothability	*Quality of mood*	*Emotionality*
Self-regulation[4]	*Effortful control* Attentional control Inhibitory control Perceptual sensitivity Low-intensity pleasure	*Rhythmicity* Approach/Withdrawal Adaptability Distractability Persistence–Attention span Sensory threshold of responsiveness	
Activity level	*Extraversion/surgency* Activity Shyness (low) High-intensity pleasure Smiling & laughter Impulsivity Positive anticipation Affiliation	*Activity level* Intensity of reaction	*Activity level* Sociability

[1] Rothbart and Bates identify three broad temperament dimensions, along with specific features of temperament reflecting variability in each dimension.
[2] Thomas, Chess, and their colleagues believed that these specific dimensions of temperament could be integrated into three broad temperament types: "easy," "slow to warm up," and "difficult."
[3] Goldsmith and Campos (1982) proposed a theory of temperament that defined temperament as individual differences in the arousal and expression of the primary emotions.
[4] Kagan (2002) focuses on behavioral inhibition as a core temperament dimension, which reflects the self-regulatory features of temperament.

emotional expressions and the more enduring emotion-related features of temperament are salient features of early behavior.

Moreover, early temperamental distress proneness, soothability, and positive emotionality are also salient as developmental precursors to later personality features such as extraversion, agreeableness, neuroticism, conscientiousness, shyness, and aggressiveness. Indeed, the emotional features of early temperament make it easy to see the conceptual overlap between infancy/childhood temperament and the structure of adult personality, and this connection adds credence to the view that temperament constitutes an important foundation for personality development (Caspi & Shiner, 2006).

Emotional dispositions are also central to the conceptualization of temperamental "*difficulty*." Temperamental difficulty is a profile that includes predominantly negative mood, frequent and intense negative emotional behavior, irregularity, poor adaptability, and demandingness (Bates, 1980, 1987; Chess & Thomas, 1986; Thomas et al., 1968). (Its counterpart, *easy* temperament, is characterized by generally positive mood, soothability, regularity, and adaptability.) The concept of difficult temperament implies that particular constellations or profiles of temperamental attributes may be "greater than the sum of their parts" because they have a more significant impact on social relationships and behavioral adjustment than do individual dimensions taken alone. Consistent with the characteristics of difficultness, several researchers have found that infants with a difficult temperamental profile are more likely than others later in development to exhibit externalizing difficulties (such as aggression and conduct problems) and internalizing difficulties (such as anxiety) (Bates, Bayles, Bennett, Ridge, & Brown, 1991; Keily, Bates, Dodge, & Pettit, 2001; see Rothbart & Bates, 2006). These associations may occur because difficult temperament renders a child more vulnerable to later behavior problems, but they may also occur because temperamental difficulty influences the social relationships that also shape personality growth and the emergence of externalizing and internalizing difficulties.

A very different approach to temperamental difficulty, however, has been proposed by Belsky (Belsky, 2005; Belsky, Bakermans-Kranenburg, & van IJzendoorn, 2007), who argues that negative temperamental characteristics render children more susceptible to positive as well as negative environmental influences. This **differential susceptibility hypothesis** argues that the association of difficult temperament with later behavioral problems is not owing to continuity in intrinsic vulnerability, but because difficult children are more likely to be affected by negative environmental influences around them (such as frustrated parenting). However, research suggests that children with difficult temperament are also more susceptible to positive parenting influences than are children with easier temperamental qualities, suggesting that temperament may influence how much children are affected by the social environment (Gallagher, 2002). These processes require further study.

Another way of understanding temperamental profiles is to conceptualize temperament as revealing fundamental variability in *reactivity* and *self-regulation* (Rothbart & Bates, 2006; Rothbart, Ellis, & Posner, 2004). Reactive features of temperament reflect how easily a person becomes aroused to respond to events, and can be observed in the rate of onset, speed of escalation, persistence, and intensity of emotional reactions, as well as variability in activity level, attention span, and sensory threshold. Self-regulatory features of temperament are revealed in how reactivity is modulated, and can be observed in effortful control, inhibition of responding (as in soothability), orienting, and adaptability. One advantage of the conceptualization of temperament in terms of reactivity and self-regulation is that it mirrors the dynamic interaction between excitatory and inhibitory nervous system processes, and thus better enables researchers to map the psychobiological components of temperamental individuality (Kagan & Fox, 2006; Rothbart & Bates, 2006; Rothbart et al., 2004). This approach also enables theorists to see the range of temperamental attributes in terms of two broad aspects of behavioral responding that characterize people throughout life, because individual differences in reactivity and self-regulation remain important throughout the life course.

Different theoretical views of the dimensions of temperament have methodological implications, of course. Temperament can be measured in various ways, but each approach has interpretive problems as well as advantages (Bates, 1987; Rothbart & Goldsmith, 1985). Parents are likely to have considerable insight into the temperamental attributes of offspring because of their long-term knowledge of the child's behavior in many different circumstances, and parent-report temperament questionnaires are inexpensive and convenient to use. But parents may be biased informants in various ways: Their relationships with offspring, their personality characteristics, and their efforts to present their children (and themselves) in a positive light can each skew temperament reports. There is currently vigorous debate concerning the suitability of using parent-report temperament questionnaires and the extent to which these measures can be made more valid (compare Kagan & Fox, 2006, with Rothbart & Bates, 2006).

Laboratory and naturalistic observations of temperament-related behavior in children have their own strengths and weaknesses. Direct observations by unacquainted observers are more objective, and laboratory studies enable researchers to control more precisely the conditions in which children are studied. But observational approaches are expensive and time-consuming, are limited (by practical and ethical considerations) in the range of circumstances in which children are studied, and cannot easily enable repeated assessments in different situations of the same temperamental attributes (comparable to how parent-report measures index temperamental variability over a range of situations). The result may be a comparatively distorted or incomplete portrayal of temperament. Consequently, some researchers recommend a multimethod strategy in which parent-report and observational assessments of temperament are used convergently and in which the unique and shared variance of each measure can be studied (see Bornstein, Gaughran, & Segui, 1991, and Kochanska, 1995, for illustrations of such a strategy).

Stability of Temperamental Qualities, and Prediction of Later Behavior

Is it true that we see in temperament the foundations of later personality? Or are temperamental attributes observed early in life rather pliable and changing over time? Embedded within these superficially straightforward questions are more difficult queries (see Bornstein, 1998, for a thoughtful discussion of different meanings of stability and continuity in behavior). Can the same temperamental attribute be measured at different ages using age-appropriate measures? If so, is there a strong association between comparable measures of temperament at each age (i.e., does a child rank similarly among peers on the same temperamental quality at different ages)? Does temperament at an earlier age predict other relevant later behavior, such as personality attributes, in the same person? If so, does the strength of prediction depend on the age at which temperament is initially assessed?

The answers to these questions depend, not surprisingly, on the specific temperament dimensions of interest, along with other developmental considerations (see Caspi & Shiner, 2006, Rothbart & Bates, 2006, and Shiner & Caspi, 2003, for reviews of this research in which the following account is based). Several general conclusions seem warranted.

First, measures of temperament obtained neonatally or in the initial months of life are only weakly or inconsistently associated with later assessments of the same temperament dimensions. This is true, for example, of distress proneness, activity level, and attention. The instability of individual differences in these dimensions of temperament should not be surprising in view of how significantly the infant is changing during the first year as psychobiological systems progressively mature. The generalized distress response of the newborn gradually becomes more differentiated to distinguish anger/frustration and fear, for example, as the infant's appraisal capacities and neurophysiological systems mature (Buss & Goldsmith, 1998). Later in the first year, inhibition begins to appear (illustrated in the wariness that 9-month-olds often show to a stranger) that further alters the child's negative reactivity, and may also affect activity level (Thompson & Limber, 1990). At the same time, neocortical maturation underlies changes in attentional processes that result in greater voluntary control over visual attention and changes in temperamental qualities such as attention span (Rothbart et al., 2004). Taken together, the rapid pace of developmental change in the first year means that the biological systems that express temperament are themselves changing, and these changes likely contribute to the instability of individual differences in temperament during this period. A temperamental characteristic such as attention span is a psychobiologically more mature behavior in a 3-year-old than in a 6-month-old, and the developing neuro-biological, perceptual, and cognitive systems associated with temperament likely reorganize developing individuality.

Second, greater short-term stability in certain temperament dimensions begins to be observed after the first year, and sometimes earlier. Characteristics such as **behavioral inhibition**, positive emotionality, effortful control, and even activity level show moderate stability in repeated assessments over periods of several months or sometimes years when they are carefully measured in age-appropriate ways (or based on parent reports using developmentally appropriate questions). Moreover, these early assessments of temperament sometimes predict later personality characteristics. Kagan, Snidman, Kahn, and Townsley (2007) found, for example, that groups of infants who were distinguished by their emotional reactions to novelty were also different in adolescence: Infants who were highly reactive, for example, were found to be dour and anxious about the future as adolescents. In another study, Bosquet and Egeland (2006) provided a description of how these kinds of long-term influences may occur through the ways that early temperament contributes to a developmental cascade of intervening influences leading to adolescent anxious symptomatology. In their study, early differences in reactivity and regulation predicted emotion regulation problems in preschool that foreshadowed, in turn, childhood anxiety problems in a cumulation of emotional risks over time. However, associations between temperament assessments and long-term behavioral outcomes are weaker or inconsistent in most other studies, suggesting that aspects of developing individuality remain fairly pliable across childhood. In many respects, developing individuality has not yet become consolidated.

Third, there is increasing evidence for longer-term associations between temperament and later behavior after the second year of life. Sometimes these long-term associations are quite impressive. In a sample of over 800 children in New Zealand studied every 2 years from early childhood to young adulthood, Caspi and his colleagues have found significant associations between temperamental qualities at age 3 and personality traits at ages 21 and 26 (Caspi et al., 2003; Newman, Caspi, Silva, & Moffitt, 1997; see also Caspi & Silva, 1995). Young children who were temperamentally "undercontrolled" (impulsive, irritable, distractable) were more likely to show externalizing behavioral problems in adolescence and lower levels of adjustment and greater interpersonal conflict in early adulthood. By contrast, young children who were temperamentally inhibited were, as young adults, more likely to be rated as cautious and restrained but showed adequate adjustment. These impressive consistencies in individual characteristics indicate that childhood temperament can have long-term correlates in later personality growth. Not all studies show such strong continuities, however, and such findings are not apparent for all children (see, e.g., Pfeifer, Goldsmith, Davidson, & Rickman, 2002). Considerably more research is required to discover why these continuities between temperament and later personality exist for some children, but not for others. Some theoretical proposals are presented in the next section.

Why does temperament have greater predictive power after infancy? One reason may be that some of the psychobiological foundations of temperament have become consolidated (although many continue to mature throughout childhood) and are having enduring influences on personality development. Once many of the core neurobehavioral bases of temperament have become organized during the early years, in other words, temperamental individuality is expressed more consistently. Another reason may be that other concurrent developmental processes help to consolidate temperamental individuality after infancy. As we shall see, the preschooler is an increasingly self-aware, intentional child who is developing a more complex self-image and whose choices of friends, activities, and settings are guided, in part, by an emerging sense of self. That sense of self is likely to be grounded in temperamental individuality. For instance, young children who begin to perceive themselves as more shy will choose friends with similar characteristics, participate in certain activities (such as dyadic play) in which they feel comfortable in preference to other activities requiring leadership or public performance, and become increasingly perceived by others in ways that are consistent with their self-perception as shy or inhibited. Because this sense of self is influenced by temperamental characteristics, it may contribute to the integration of temperamental characteristics with the development of personality and the consolidation of behavioral individuality in the years to come. Finally, the perceptions of others are also important contributors to the consolidation of temperamental individuality. By the time a young child reaches the toddler and preschool years, caregivers, childcare teachers, peers, siblings, and others have likely developed stable perceptions of what the child is like that influence how they respond to her or him. In doing so, they help to reinforce and consolidate the behavioral characteristics they perceive.

Taken together, temperament research shows that the stability of temperament, and its prediction to later behavioral attributes, is contingent. Some researchers believe that temperament is more likely to be stable within, but not between, major periods of developmental change and reorganization, such as the transition from infancy to early childhood (Goldsmith et al., 1987). Others argue that temperament will become increasingly stable, and predictive, with increasing age because of the ways that developing self-understanding, social awareness, intentionality, social comparison, and other changes make children increasingly aware of their individual characteristics and capable of acting on this realization (Caspi & Silva, 1995; Shiner & Caspi, 2003). These two views are not, of course, inconsistent approaches, and each helps to explain why early temperament is sometimes not very predictive of later individuality. Despite this, theorists concur, temperament becomes a foundation for personality as temperamental attributes become developmentally consolidated and incorporated into a stable personality structure.

Temperament and Development

Temperamental dispositions do not always foreshadow later personality. Sometimes change rather than continuity over time is more apparent. Understanding why this is so requires appreciating the dynamic interaction of temperamental characteristics with other developmental influences in personality growth, particularly from the social environment, and how this interaction shapes behavioral individuality. Temperament researchers have several ways of portraying this developmentally interactive process.

First, a child's temperamental profile may mesh well, or poorly, with the requirements and opportunities of the child's social setting. Consequently, the influence of temperament on personality or adjustment depends on the "goodness of fit" between temperament and environmental demands. Chess and Thomas (1986; Thomas & Chess, 1977) originated this concept in describing the developmental outcomes of difficult temperament. As they argued, temperamental difficulty need not contribute to later behavior problems if the social and physical environment is accommodated to the child's needs and characteristics. When parents are tolerant and understanding, for example, and opportunities for constructively channeling temperamental qualities are provided (e.g., frequent flexible self-chosen options rather than no choices in activities), difficult temperament can lead to more positive, adaptive personality attributes. By contrast, even children who are temperamentally easy will likely develop behavioral problems if they live in settings where demands are excessive and developmentally inappropriate, and partners are cold and insensitive. The same process of environmental "match" or "mismatch" applies to other temperamental attributes, such as activity level, negative or positive emotionality, or attention span. In each case, the accommodation of the environment to the child's unique characteristics foreshadows better adjustment than the failure of social partners to recognize and adapt to the child's temperamentally based needs. This is one of the reasons why sensitive, responsive parenting is such an important predictor of positive personality outcomes in children and a buffer of the negative effects of early poor adjustment (Thompson, 2006a).

It is important to remember, however, that a child's environment changes significantly over time in ways that can also influence temperament–environment goodness-of-fit. As children mature, for example, parents, teachers, and other adults increasingly expect more competent, self-controlled behavior, children enter into settings (such as preschool and school) that require compliance, initiative, and cooperation, and children increasingly participate with adults in circumstances (such as church, concerts, and other events) in which they must understand and enact socially appropriate behavior. Environmental expectations thus become less flexible and less amenable to some children's temperamental profiles over time, consistently with the normative expectations of the culture (Bornstein, 1995). These changes in social expectations may also include divergent expectations for gender-appropriate conduct, such that boys and girls find environmental demands differentially amenable to their behavioral styles. As a consequence, a particular temperamental profile may fit well with environmental demands and opportunities at one age (e.g., low persistence or attention span in infancy), but provide a poor fit later (e.g., the same characteristics during the school years). In this way, the temperament–environment match is a developmentally dynamic one, and this dynamic is likely to influence the stability of temperamental attributes over time as well as their relations to later personality.

Second, a child's temperamental profile may influence how the child interacts with people and settings. This can occur in several ways (Scarr & McCartney, 1983; Shiner & Caspi, 2003). For one, a child's behavioral style may *evoke* certain reactions from others, such as how a child with a temperamentally sunny disposition naturally elicits smiles and interest from peers and adults. These positive social reactions are likely, in turn, to influence the child's development and the growth of personality attributes (such as sociability) much differently from the reactions evoked by a child with a more negative temperamental profile. For another, a child's behavioral style may guide that person's *preferences* for partners, settings, and activities. For example, someone with a high activity level is more likely to participate in sports with other active people than a person with a low activity level for whom more sedentary activities and partners are more comfortable. These choices also influence development because they channel the range of opportunities and challenges that children are likely to encounter to those that accord with their dispositional characteristics. Furthermore, children's behavioral styles may influence how they *alter* their social environments. For example, a child with a difficult temperamental profile may have a stronger influence on other people than a child with a more inhibited or adaptable style.

Over time, of course, children and youth become progressively more capable of choosing their partners and settings to harmonize with their personal preferences. By the time of adulthood they can often create lifestyles that are consistent with their personality styles in the choices they have made of marital partner, occupation, residence, hobbies, and other activities. This is one reason, therefore, that temperamental and personality dispositions tend to become more consolidated over time: People increasingly choose partners and create lifestyles with characteristics that are compatible with their own. However, many people are incapable of exercising this kind of choice, especially when they encounter unexpected misfortune or have limited resources or options (such as in poverty) with which to exercise choice. In these circumstances, especially when the environmental demands are out of sync with temperamental attributes, we might expect poorer adjustment (and less stability in personality attributes) because of the difficulties presented by a mismatched, unaccommodating, or unexpectedly changing environment.

Third, a child's temperamental profile may influence how that person perceives, experiences, interprets, and thinks about life events (Rothbart & Bates, 2006; Shiner & Caspi, 2003; Wachs & Gandour, 1983). This can begin quite early. A 1-year-old with a positive, outgoing disposition is likely to regard the approach of an unfamiliar but friendly adult much differently than a temperamentally inhibited infant, and will feel greater interest and curiosity (rather than fear) when encountering a new setting (such as a peer's playroom). Children's different responses in these and similar circumstances may have broader consequences for the growth of social skills, the emergence of peer relationships, and intellectual development. Temperament may also be an important influence on how a child interprets and responds to the parent. Kochanska (1993, 1995) argues, for example, that **conscience** develops differently for young children who differ in temperamental fearfulness. Conscience develops best for temperamentally fearful children when their mothers use gentle, nonassertive discipline practices in a manner that avoids overstressing their offspring. By contrast, for temperamentally nonfearful children conscience is best predicted by a secure attachment to the mother and the positive, shared partnership it helps to create between them. Temperamental qualities cause the two types of young children to perceive and respond to their mothers' discipline practices in different ways. It is also possible that temperament influences thinking and information processing more broadly, especially in light of the importance of emotion and attentional persistence to an individual's capacities to concentrate, remember, and reason competently at all ages.

Temperament is likely to interact with environmental influences in other ways as well. Temperamental qualities may enhance a person's vulnerability to intrinsic or extrinsic stressors and, in doing so, contribute to the development of maladjustment or dysfunction. Alternatively, temperamental attributes may provide buffers against the stressors that might occur by strengthening resiliency, such as that provided by positive mood, adaptability, and greater self-regulation (Rothbart & Bates, 2006). Or temperament may enhance or diminish a person's sensitivity to all kinds of environmental influences, whether positive or negative (Belsky, 2005; Belsky et al., 2007). In each of these profiles of temperament–environment interactions, it is clear that the developmental trajectories yielded by a particular temperamental profile depend not only on temperamental attributes, but also on the nature of environmental demands and opportunities. In a sense, these formulations converge on the conclusion that temperament causes people to experience the world in distinct ways (Wachs, 1992).

Temperament: Conclusion and Future Directions

Contemporary research on temperament offers conclusions that differ markedly from traditional portrayals. By contrast with traditional formulations that temperament emerges early, is highly consistent across situations and over time because of its psychobiological origins, and is directly tied to the growth of personality, current research underscores that temperament is a biologically based but developmentally evolving feature of behavior. For this reason, temperamental attributes become increasingly more consistent over time as temperamental individuality is enveloped into the network of self-perceptions, behavioral preferences, and social experiences that together shape developing personality. Moreover, contemporary research shows that, although temperament may have direct effects on behavior and development, temperament more commonly interacts with environmental influences to shape development in complex ways.

These conclusions remind us of the complexity of human development and of the multi-faceted ways that temperament influences emergent individuality. They also help to explain why we commonly consider infant or child temperament, but rarely conceive of adult temperament. By adulthood, personality has fully developed to include many features of self-understanding, social dispositions, behavioral style, attributional processes, and other facets that incorporate, elaborate, and extend initial temperamental dispositions.

Future directions in temperamental research will be enlivened by methodological advances, particularly in the field of molecular genetics, which enables researchers to identify specific gene polymorphisms and study how their behavioral correlates interact with environmental characteristics. Just as temperamental research has underscored the importance of temperament–environment transactions in behavioral development, molecular genetics is highlighting the pervasiveness of gene–environment interactions. As a practical illustration, researchers found that a program designed to improve maternal sensitivity to young children with behavioral problems worked best for children with a gene polymorphism (DRD4 7-repeat) that is associated with problem behavior, aggression, and hyperactivity (Bakermans-Kranenburg, van IJzendoorn, Pijilman, Mesman, & Juffer, 2008). Genetic vulnerability in the child interacted with the environmental intervention to alter behavioral outcomes for young children (see Figure 9.1). Molecular genetics research will also play a role in studying the effects of gene–gene interactions on behavioral development, which are likely to be especially important for complex behaviors such as temperament. The influence of one gene may depend on the presence or absence of another gene or genes (Ebstein et al., 2000; see Lakatos et al., 2003, for an example), and better understanding of these interactions will contribute to understanding genetic and environmental risk processes.

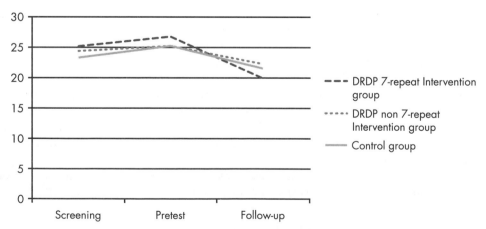

FIGURE 9.1   Summary of findings from Bakermans-Kranenburg et al. (2008), illustrating the interaction of genes (i.e., the DRD4 7-repeat gene polymorphism, associated with problem behavior and hyperactivity) and environment (i.e., a program designed to improve maternal sensitivity) in children's behavior (represented by arbitrary units on the y-axis) at the follow-up assessment. Children with the DRD4 7-repeat polymorphism responded more positively to the program than did children without the polymorphism, or children in the control group.

Current researchers are also devoting considerable attention to the interactive and mediated influences of temperamental processes on development. For example, early temperamental vulnerability interacts with harsh parenting in the development of conduct disorders in young children (see Owens & Shaw, 2003; Shaw, Miles, Ingoldsby, & Nagin, 2003). This highlights one of the important applications of temperamental theory and research to the field of developmental psychopathology as researchers are better understanding how temperamental individuality confers unique vulnerabilities, and strengths, on children in their encounters with supportive or stressful social environments. In all, this means that one can no longer append a parent-report temperament measure to a research design and, by doing so, create a temperament study. Instead, contemporary developmental research on temperament is examining theoretically sophisticated questions based on temperament theory using multiple methods that are well suited to the developmental samples and questions under study.

EMOTION

Emotions also shape our experience of the world, and they exercise a pervasive influence throughout the life span. By contrast with temperamental variability, however, the effects of emotional reactions can be enduring or brief, transcontextual or situationally specific. Moreover, emotional experience changes considerably with development and includes a rich variety of basic and complex feelings that far surpass the range of temperamental variability in mood. Emotions are also complexly tied to other developmental processes. Emotional development is associated with psychobiological maturation, self-understanding and the understanding of others, the child's growing capacities to appraise people and environments, social interaction and self-control, and the awareness of social rules and social conventions.

We take for granted that emotions are part of everyday life. But consider how much emotional experience changes over the life course. It is easy to see in infancy the extremes of emotional arousal, from raucous crying to exuberant delight, that are minimally regulated by the child and sometimes uncontrollable except through the sensitive intervention of caregivers. In infants the raw, basic experience of emotion is readily apparent, but the infant is also sensitive to the emotions of others and strives to comprehend their meaning. For the preschooler, basic emotions that have been present from early in life have become supplemented by self-conscious emotions, such as pride, guilt, shame, and embarrassment, that reflect evaluations of the self (see Table 9.2). Emotional experiences are also thought about, discussed with parents and peers, and frequently enacted in sociodramatic play. The preschooler is more self-aware emotionally and has begun to understand the causes and consequences of emotional experiences and the influence of emotions on social interaction.

By middle childhood, children have become more reflective and strategic in their emotional lives. Emotions can be more effectively regulated through cognitive means (such as using distracting thoughts) as well as behavioral strategies (such as fleeing a distressing situation), and emotions can be intentionally hidden through display rules that dissemble genuine feelings. But children of this age are also capable of genuine empathy and greater emotional understanding than ever before. In adolescence, it appears as if the emotional swings of infancy have reappeared, but the emoter is now a psychologically more complex individual who reflects on the unique origins of personal emotional experience, is acutely sensitive to the psychological bases of emotion in others (especially peers), and can feel strongly in response to symbolic (c.g., music, narrative) as well as direct elicitors of emotion.

Does emotional development continue into adulthood? Yes, but the character of its development changes. Rather than witnessing the unfolding of new, psychologically more complex emotional experiences, adults often seek to create personal lifestyles that are emotionally

TABLE 9.2
Basic and Self-Conscious Emotions in Development

	Basic Emotions	Self-conscious Emotions
Examples	• Happiness • Sadness • Fear • Interest • Anger • Disgust • Surprise	• Pride • Guilt • Shame • Embarrassment
Origins	Biologically deeply rooted in the human species	Arousal depends on social values and expectations
Universal?	Strongest evidence that these are universal for humans	Unclear whether self-conscious emotions are all culturally universal
Development	Appear at birth or early in infancy	Develop late in the second and the third year of life

Sources: Izard (1991), Izard & Ackerman (2000), Lewis & Michalson (1983).

satisfying, predictable, and manageable through their choices of occupation, partners, and other activities. In other words, adults strive to construct their lives to incorporate emotional experiences that are personally desirable, and this strategy may include career choices that promise the satisfactions and challenges of productive labor, personal choices such as making (and breaking) marital ties and the pleasures (and turmoil) of childrearing, and leisure choices that offer the excitement of musical, artistic, athletic, or other creative pursuits. Of course, not all succeed in doing so, especially when their economic conditions do not permit much choice in life decisions. Adults also become skillful at managing the expression of their personal feelings to accord with their social circumstances and personal goals. Although new capacities for emotion may emerge (e.g., poignancy), the theme of emotional development in adulthood is the adaptive integration of emotional experience into satisfying daily life and successful relationships with others. This is one reason why adults seem emotionally more stable and predictable—and, sometimes, less animated—than children or adolescents.

This developmental survey not only underscores the changing tapestry of emotional experience, but also highlights the relation between emotional development and the growth of personality. At each stage of life, new capacities for emotional experience, expression, and understanding contribute to personality development as they help to organize and express developing individuality. In this respect, emotional growth is an important part of the growth of personality from infancy through later life. Furthermore, in tracing the influence of emotion in development, it is increasingly clear that emotional development is shaped by cultural beliefs about emotion. From parents' reactions to their infants' emotional displays to everyday views of what constitutes mature emotionality in adulthood, cultural values influence the salience of particular emotions, the significance accorded emotional life, and the specific ways that emotion influences personality development.

Defining Emotion

But what is emotion? The question almost begs an answer because of the ubiquity of emotion in everyday experience. Each person is intimately acquainted with the visceral reactions (rapid heart rate, sweaty palms), subjective experience (inability to concentrate, infusion or depletion of energy), cognitive appraisals (of threat, the unexpected, goal achievement), facial expressions, and other familiar constituents of emotions that we linguistically demarcate as fear, anger, joy, distress, guilt, or other feelings.

Our common-sense view is that emotions are organized categorically because our subjective, physiological, and cognitive experiences of emotions, such as sadness, anger, disgust, and joy, are so different. This view has deep roots within developmental emotions research (see, for example, Izard, 1991; Izard & Ackerman, 2000; Lewis & Michalson, 1983). But this view has been increasingly questioned. Researchers examining emotion in different cultures point out that the manner in which we commonly conceptualize different emotions reflects the linguistic distinctions of English-speaking people and are different for people from different cultural and linguistic systems (Lutz, 1988). Others argue that our emotional lives are constituted not by a succession of qualitatively distinct emotions but rather by subtly nuanced blends of a broad variety of emotional states that range in dynamic and intensive qualities according to our interactions with the surrounding world (Thompson, 1990).

As a result, most emotion theorists have adopted a **functionalist approach** (Saarni, Campos, Camras, & Witherington, 2006) that emphasizes the role of emotion in goal attainment in everyday experience, as reflected in the following definition: "Emotion is thus the person's attempt or readiness to establish, maintain, or change the relation between the person and his or her changing circumstances, on matters of significance to that person" (Saarni et al., 2006, p. 227). By defining emotion in very broad terms of person–environment transactions that matter to the person, emotion is associated with goal-attainment, as well as with social relationships, situational appraisals, action tendencies, self-understanding, self-regulation, and a variety of other developmentally changing processes. The range of emotion is not confined to a specific set of categories defined by their linguistic delineation (although functionalist theorists talk of "emotion families" that share common characteristics), but is considerably broader because of how emotion is conceptualized in different social and cultural groups based on the nature of typical person–environment transactions. The definition of emotion is thus more open-ended in functionalist accounts. To be sure, the openness in how emotion is regarded from a functionalist perspective introduces considerably greater ambiguity into theory and research on emotional growth (e.g., are hunger, effort, arrogance, and indifference also emotions?), and it is unclear what (if any) features distinguish emotion from other motivational states or from personality processes. But by linking emotion to an individual's goals, developmental researchers have found the functionalist perspective valuable for understanding emotional development in the context of the increasingly complex, sophisticated interactions of the child with a changing social world.

What is Emotional Development the Development of?

We can easily observe the changes that occur in emotion with increasing age. A toddler rages at the collapse of a block tower while an adult purses his lips while figuring out alternative ways around a blocked goal. But what accounts for growth in emotionality? Emotional development incorporates many features of psychological growth, making this topic an especially integrative field of study (Denham, 1998). These include the psychobiological foundations of emotion, developing capacities for perceiving emotion in others, emotional understanding, the development of empathy, the growth of self-understanding, mastery of emotional display rules, and developing capacities for emotion regulation. The story of emotional development is how these different features of emotion mature and become integrated in shaping emotional experience and its expression.

Neurobiological foundations. In light of the preceding discussion of the psychobiological foundations of temperament, it is unsurprising that emotional development is also based on neurophysiological, neuroendocrine, and other biological processes that change rapidly in infancy and childhood (LeDoux, 2000; Panksepp, 1998). As a biologically ancient feature of human functioning, emotion is rooted in primitive regions of the brain such as the limbic system, especially the amygdale, which is often regarded as the "emotion center" of the brain (Johnson, Chapter 4, this volume). But because it is involved in the most complex aspects of human behavior, emotion is also guided by some of the most sophisticated regions of the cerebral cortex, especially the evolutionarily newer prefrontal cortex (Davidson, Fox, & Kalin, 2007). Moreover, emotional reactions are also influenced by hormones and **neurotransmitters** regulated by a variety of brain areas (Gunnar & Vasquez, 2006). This makes an apparently simple emotional reaction a surprisingly complex psychobiological event, and there are significant developmental changes in these neurobiological processes that affect emotional behavior. For example, the unpredictable swings of arousal of the neonate become progressively more modulated and controllable in infancy as maturational advances occur in adrenocortical activation and in parasympathetic regulation (Gunnar & Davis, 2003; Porges et al., 1994). With later developing functional connections between subcortical and frontal systems regulating emotion, furthermore, enhanced capacities for emotion regulation emerge in the childhood years (Lewis & Todd, 2007; Ochsner & Gross, 2007).

Emotion perception.   Another important facet of emotional development is the capacity to accurately perceive emotion in others. This is an early emerging phenomenon: Even 5-month-olds can discriminate and categorize facial expressions of smiling (Bornstein & Arterberry, 2003). By the end of the first year and early in the second, infants have become capable of discerning the emotional meaning underlying many adult facial and vocal expressions and of incorporating this meaning into their interpretation of the adult's behavior in a phenomenon called "social referencing" (Saarni et al., 2006). When an infant encounters an unfamiliar person or object, for instance, the sight of the adult's reassuring smile or terrified look (especially if it is accompanied by appropriate vocalizations and other behavior) influences the child's tendency to approach or withdraw. The baby appropriately "reads" the meaning of the adult's emotional expression and its relevance to the unfamiliar event. In later months, this basic capacity for accurate perception of emotional signals is supplemented by a more acute awareness of the meaning of the emotional signal. By the end of the second year, for example, toddlers seem to be more consciously aware of the subjectivity of emotional experience: Another person can feel differently than oneself (Repacholi & Gopnik, 1997). As a consequence, parents begin to witness their toddlers intervening in the emotions of others by comforting a distressed peer or teasing a sibling.

Emotional understanding.   With further conceptual growth, understanding of emotion becomes incorporated into young children's broader knowledge about the psychological states of others. Consistent with the expansion of their naive "theory of mind," for example, 2- to 3-year-olds understand that emotion is associated with the fulfillment of desires, and 4- to 5-year-olds appreciate the more complex linkages between emotions and thoughts, beliefs, and expectations (Bartsch & Wellman, 1995; Thompson & Lagattuta, 2006; Wellman, 2002). This broadening psychological understanding richly expands children's conceptualization of emotion because it enables young children to appreciate how emotion is linked to the satisfaction or frustration of desires (which vary in different people) and to beliefs (which may be incorrect, such as the child who mistakenly thinks that her lunch bag contains a delectable dessert when in fact her father forgot to include it).

In middle childhood, children begin to conceive of emotional processes, such as how emotional intensity gradually dissipates over time, how specific emotions are related to antecedent causes, and how personal background, experiences, and personality can yield unique emotional reactions (see review by Thompson, 1990). Somewhat later, by about age 9 or 10, children begin to understand how multiple emotions can be simultaneously evoked by the same event, such as feeling happy and scared when performing before a group (Donaldson & Westerman, 1986). Later, adolescents better appreciate the complex psychological causes of emotion in relational experience, self-reflection, and existential concerns (Harter, 2006; Harter & Monsour, 1992). It is easy to see how these advances in emotional understanding are relevant to children's growing self-awareness and to the growth of personality because of how they offer insight into experiences of ambivalence, emotional self-control (and lacking emotional control), relationships, and psychological conflict.

The development of emotion understanding also reflects the influences of cultural beliefs about emotion. Because of how emotions are perceived and interpreted to young children by parents and others, children from different cultures derive different understandings of the antecedent causes of emotion and the appropriate emotions to experience and express in different social situations. Cole and her colleagues, for example, have identified cultural differences in children's understanding of appropriate emotional responses to difficult inter-personal situations, such as whether negative emotions should be revealed and whether shame or anger is an acceptable response, consistent with broader differences in interpersonal beliefs between individualist and collectivist cultures (Cole & Tamang, 1998; Cole & Tan, 2007). Emotion understanding is thus shaped by both the local (e.g., familial) and the broader (e.g., cultural) contexts in which children live.

By what processes do children acquire this expanding understanding of emotion? Along with the influences of developing intellectual capacities and social experience (especially with peers), researchers note that everyday conversations between young children and their parents provide potent opportunities to learn about emotion (Lagattuta & Wellman, 2002; Thompson, 2006b; Thompson, Laible, & Ontai, 2003). This is especially so in cultures that accord significance to discussing emotional experiences. As children begin to share their experiences and observations with caregivers in simple accounts (beginning almost from the time they can talk), parents elaborate, inquire, interpret, and otherwise clarify the child's accounts in ways that contribute to the growth of emotional understanding (Denham, 1998; Dunn, 1994; Thompson, 2006b). Thus when a young preschooler observes his older sister arriving home from school in tears, his inquiry about why this was so can provide a conversational forum for learning about emotion and its causes. In acting thus, of course, adults not only clarify but also socialize emotional knowledge, conveying expectations about appropriate emotional behavior and the causes and consequences of emotional displays (Thompson et al., 2003; Thompson & Meyer, 2007).

In this way, norms and expectations concerning emotion are explicitly communicated to children through conversation. However, the messages that children receive about the causes of emotion, the consequences of emotional displays, and the value of particular emotions depend on both cultural context and the personal characteristics of the child. For example, Fivush's (1994, 1998) research indicates that lessons about emotion differ based on the gender of the child. With girls, parents discuss more sadness than anger, attribute emotions to social-relational causes (e.g., sadness is caused when someone else is hurt), and resolve negative emotions through reassurance and reconciliation. Parents conversing with boys discuss anger more often than sadness, attribute emotions to autonomous causes (e.g., sadness is caused by losing a toy), and are less likely to discuss resolution of negative emotions. Cultural differences also exist in emotion-related beliefs and in parents' inclusion of emotion in con-versation, which alters the opportunities for children to learn about emotion in this manner. Mullen and Yi (1995), for example, found that in conversation about past events with their 3-year-old children, US mothers referred to their child's and others' thoughts and feelings nearly twice as often as Korean mothers.

Empathy and emotional contagion.   The growth of emotion perception and emotional understanding also enhances the child's vicarious sensitivity to the emotions of others. Young infants often respond resonantly to the emotions they perceive in others—fussing when they hear another person crying, for instance (Sagi & Hoffman, 1976)—but these early episodes of emotional contagion are not truly empathic because the baby has no real comprehension of the circumstances provoking another's feelings. With the rapid growth in emotional understanding that occurs in early childhood, however, young children can respond with genuine empathy (as well as a variety of other emotional reactions) to another's anguish. In everyday circumstances as well as in experimental contexts, toddlers are observed to react with concerned attention to the sight and sound of the mother's distress (Zahn-Waxler, 2000; Zahn-Waxler & Radke-Yarrow, 1990), and empathic responses increase in sophistication and scope in the years that follow. Early empathic responding is sometimes (although not consistently) accompanied by prosocial initiatives, such as efforts to comfort the distressed person, but with increasing age empathy becomes somewhat more reliably associated with helping behavior as well as with other prosocial initiatives, although empathy remains motivationally complex (Eisenberg, Spinrad, & Sadovsky, 2006). Taken together, the growth of empathy reflects children's developing affective as well as cognitive awareness of the emotional experiences of others, as well as the changing role of interpersonal emotion in social relationships.

Emotion and the growth of self-understanding.   Emotional growth is also closely tied to the development of self-understanding, which we consider in greater detail in the section that follows. A major advance in emotional growth occurs during the late second and third years of life, when young children become more physically and psychologically self-aware (reflected in verbal self-references and efforts to "do it myself") and, at the same time, show emerging reactions of pride, guilt, shame, embarrassment, and other self-conscious emotions (Lagattuta & Thompson, 2007; Thompson, 2006a). Thus, the simple joy of success becomes accompanied by looking and smiling to an adult and calling attention to the feat (pride), and in response to conspicuous attention toddlers increasingly respond with smiling, gaze aversion, and self-touching (embarrassment). These responses reflect new emotional capacities built on new forms of self-awareness.

The emergence of self-conscious evaluative emotions such as pride and shame during the third year depends not only on the growth of self-awareness, however, but also on young children's appreciation of standards of conduct and the ability to apply those standards to an evaluation of their own behavior (Thompson, Meyer, & McGinley, 2006). Feelings of pride derive from the realization of an accomplishment that is personally meaningful, and likewise guilt is elicited when one violates a significant standard of conduct. The capacities to understand behavioral standards and apply them personally are slowly developing, and young children initially rely on parental evaluations as the basis for their feelings of pride, guilt, or shame in their behavior (Stipek, 1995). Indeed, it is common to find young preschoolers checking back regularly with the parent as they work on a challenging task or are engaged in misbehavior, and the adult's subsequent emotional response—combined with verbal comments underscoring the evaluative standard ("You worked hard at that puzzle!")—significantly shapes the child's own.

In this regard, therefore, the development of self-conscious emotions such as pride, shame, and guilt has a complex connection to the growth of self-understanding. These emotional capacities depend on a young child's self-awareness, but the circumstances in which they are elicited provide important cues to the child concerning self-worth and its association with the child's fidelity to specific standards of achievement or morality. Furthermore, the importance of these evaluative standards to the child, and the feelings associated with compliance or misbehavior, are also tied to the warmth and security of the parent–child relationship (Thompson, 2006a, 2008). These themes are considered in greater detail below.

Understanding and use of display rules.   Emotions are intrinsically social, and one aspect of emotional development is understanding and applying social rules for the display of emotion in social settings (see Table 9.3). A person is supposed to show delight when opening a gift, even if it is undesirable (especially in the presence of the gift-giver), and one is not supposed to laugh at a defeated opponent or at someone who takes an unexpected spill on a slippery sidewalk. People use emotional "display rules" to mask the expression of true feelings with a more appropriate emotional expression to protect self-esteem, avoid hurting others' feelings, and preserve relationships. Young children clearly do not fully share this awareness, which is why they commonly reject undesirable gifts and act in other socially inappropriate ways. Although they begin to manage their emotional expressions to protect the feelings of others as young as age 4 (Banerjee, 1997; Cole, 1986), it is not until they reach middle childhood that they can conceptualize the meaning of emotional display rules and their purposes (Jones, Abbey, & Cumberland, 1998; Saarni, 1999). Their grasp of the meaning, application, and importance of display rules for emotional behavior increases significantly in the years that follow. As it does so, children make a remarkable discovery: Emotional appearance is not necessarily emotional reality. What others show is not necessarily what they feel. People may deliberately seek to deceive concerning their true feelings. And most important, one can disguise one's own true feelings and thus retain the privacy of emotional experience.

As a social phenomenon, display rules are susceptible to the same cultural and contextual variability as other features of emotional development. Thus, cultural values differ significantly concerning the importance of dissembling one's emotions to others. Cole's work in Nepal suggests that there are important conventions, different from those of the United States, for displaying both positive and negative emotions, and these are recognized by children as young as age 6 (Cole & Tamang, 1998; Cole & Tan, 2007). Even within Western cultures the display rules conveyed to boys and girls differ. It is more appropriate for girls than for boys, for example, to display feelings of sadness or fear (Fivush, 1994).

TABLE 9.3
Display Rules for Emotional Expressions

Rule	Definition	Application
MAXIMIZE	Enhancing the expression of an emotion that you actually feel	• A young child cries more loudly after a fall when a caregiver is present • An adult expresses far more delight at a pleasant gift than he or she actually feels
MINIMIZE	Reducing the expression of an emotion that you actually feel	• A child or adolescent seems not to care very much after losing a competitive game • An adult shows mild dismay when receiving disappointing news in the presence of others
NEUTRALIZE	Showing no emotional expression at all even though you are feeling aroused	• A child puts on a "poker face" despite being teased by a sibling • An adult has an immobile, expressionless face when being reprimanded by an authority
MASK	Replacing the expression of emotion that you feel with the opposite emotional expression	• A child expresses delight when opening a disappointing gift in the presence of the gift-giver • An adult smiles and congratulates a coworker who has achieved recognition that the adult envies

Source: Ekman, 2003; Ekman & Friesen, 1975.

Emotion regulation. Emotion regulation concerns the management of emotional experience. In contrast to display rules, which regulate emotional expressions, strategies of emotion regulation influence emotion itself (Cole, Martin, & Dennis, 2004; Eisenberg & Morris 2002; Thompson, 1990, 1994). There are many reasons why people of all ages seek to change their emotional experience. People seek to regulate their emotions to feel better under stress (managing negative emotions and increasing feelings of happiness or well-being), think better (managing any kind of strong emotion), act courageously (curtailing feelings of fear or anxiety), enhance motivation (sometimes by accentuating guilt), elicit support (by focusing on personal distress or anxiety), affirm relationships (by enhancing sympathetic or empathetic feelings for another), and for other reasons. Understanding emotion regulation thus requires appreciating the diverse personal goals underlying regulatory efforts. Sometimes these goals are self-evident: Children and adults manage emotions when striving to cope with difficult circumstances. But these goals are also shaped by the social context: Competent emotion regulation may be best observed, for example, when a young child loudly protests a bully's provocations when adults are nearby, but quietly tolerates this abuse when adults are absent (Thompson, 1994). In this regard, processes of emotion regulation—such as the use of display rules—are social and cultural, and it is unsurprising that skills in emotion regulation are related to social competence in children (e.g., Gilliom, Shaw, Beck, Schonberg, & Lukon, 2002).

Emotion regulation is social also because the earliest forms of emotion regulation are the efforts of caregivers to manage the emotions of their young offspring. Parents do so by directly intervening to soothe or pacify the child, and also do so in other ways, such as by regulating the emotional demands of familiar settings such as home and daycare (often in accord with their perceptions of the child's temperamental strengths and vulnerabilities), altering the child's construal of emotionally arousing experiences (acting enthusiastically while going on a Ferris wheel or taking a trip to the dentist), and coaching children on expectations or strategies for emotional management (Garner & Spears, 2000; Spinrad, Stifter, Donelan-McCall, & Turner, 2004). With growing maturity, however, emotions become internally managed in increasingly sophisticated ways (Thompson, 1990, 1994). Whereas the newborn infant may cry uncontrollably, the toddler can seek assistance from others, the preschooler can talk about her feelings and their causes, the school-age child can redirect attention, reconceptualize the situation, and use other deliberate cognitive strategies to manage feelings, the adolescent can use personally effective means of regulating emotion (such as playing meaningful music or talking to a close friend), and the adult can alter schedule, responsibilities, and activities to change emotional demands. The growth of these intrinsic capacities for emotion regulation is thus built on advances in emotional understanding (discussed earlier) and self-understanding (discussed later) that enable developing persons to better understand the personal causes and consequences of emotional arousal, and devise increasingly sophisticated and effective means of managing emotion.

This portrayal of the growth of emotion regulation suggests that skills of emotion management increase with age as the result of brain maturation, greater emotion understanding, and enhanced experience. But the developmental story is more complex (Thompson, Lewis, & Calkins, 2008). One reason is that neurobiologically there is a continuing interaction between lower emotion centers (such as the amygdala) and higher regulatory centers (such as the prefrontal cortex) such that they are mutually influential (Lewis & Todd, 2007; Ochsner & Gross, 2007; Quirk, 2007). The prefrontal cortex exerts inhibitory influence over the amygdala, for example, but the amygdala also constrains cortical processing in the prefrontal cortex according to emotional meanings that have been previously established. As a practical matter, this means that emotion regulation at any age is colored by emotional biases that have become incorporated into nervous system processes through genetic influences (e.g., Ebstein et al., 2000), experience (such as early chronic exposure to stress), or their interaction. In one study, for example, 2-year-olds who were behaviorally identified as emotionally inhibited or uninhibited were later studied as adults, and neuroimaging analyses were conducted as they viewed novel faces. The findings revealed heightened amygdala activation in the inhibited group of adults when viewing novel (vs. familiar) faces, but no differences in the uninhibited group (Schwartz, Wright, Shin, Kagan, & Rauch, 2003; see also Kagan et al., 2007). Although more longitudinal research is needed, these findings suggest that a strong biological bias toward fearful reactions to unfamiliar events based in limbic system thresholds may color emotional processes to maturity, despite the growth of higher cortical inhibitory systems. The same may be true when early experiences (such as physical abuse) introduce similar biases into the brain's emotional processing. Pollak and his colleagues have found, for example, that children with a history of maltreatment showed lower perceptual thresholds for identifying angry facial and vocal expressions in adults that were complemented by lower activational thresholds in brain regions governing focused attention when viewing these faces (Pollak, 2008; Pollak & Kistler, 2002; Pollak, Klorman, Thatcher, & Cicchetti, 2001). Experiences of abuse had altered brain functioning with respect to alertness to cues of interpersonal threat.

The growth of emotion regulation is important because it reflects both the significance of developing self-control over basic emotional reactions and also the complexity of the processes underlying emotional arousal. For this reason, and also because of its practical and therapeutic implications (see Luby & Belden, 2006; Thompson, 2000), study of the growth of emotion regulation remains one of the most vigorous areas of developmental emotions research.

Emotion and Relationships

Contemporary research on emotional development shows that emotions are not just internal experiences with outward expression, but are deeply influenced by the social contexts in which they occur. As functionalist emotion theorists note, the person–environment transactions of significance to an individual are usually social, and relationships influence not only emotion elicitation but also strategies for managing emotional experience and its expression. The social context is also crucial to the growth of emotion perception and emotional understanding by which children develop an appreciation of the meaning of emotion to themselves and others, and emotional development is further enlivened by the vicarious experiences of empathy and emotional contagion. A child's skills in emotion perception, understanding, and self-regulation are, in turn, significant influences on the child's social acceptance and social competence (Denham et al., 2003). In one study, multiple measures of preschoolers' emotional competence predicted their social competence with peers a year later, and also partially mediated the influence on social competence of a secure attachment (Denham, Blair, Schmidt, & DeMulder, 2002; see Figure 9.2). Emotional competence was measured, in this study, as individual differences in emotion regulation and emotion understanding. It is, in short, impossible to conceptualize emotional development except with reference to the social conditions that add meaning to emotional behavior throughout life.

The most important feature of the social context is, of course, the close relationships on which people depend for support. This is especially true during the early years of life, when a child's attachment to caregivers provides an emotional context of security and reassurance, or insecurity and uncertainty, that colors self-perception and understanding of others (Thompson, 2006a). Close relationships influence emotional development because they shape many of the conditions in which young children experience, understand, and interpret emotion in the context of everyday social interaction, shared conversations, coping support, instruction and modeling, and a variety of other social influences on emotional development

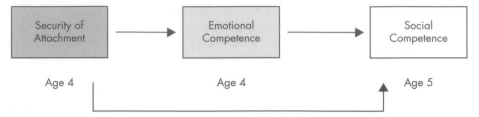

FIGURE 9.2 Summary of findings from Denham et al. (2002), showing the importance of emotional competence to the development of social competence in preschoolers. Multiple measures of emotional competence directly predicted social competence a year later, and also partially mediated the influence of a secure parent–child attachment.

(Gottman, Katz, & Hooven, 1997; Laible & Thompson, 2007). Even more fundamentally, parent–child relationships color emotional development through children's developing expectations of support and sensitivity (or lack of it), the construals of emotionally relevant situations that are shaped by the adult's attributional style, and the emotional demands of these relationships on the developing person (see Figure 9.3).

Unfortunately, these relational influences are sometimes most clearly apparent in disturbed parent–child relationships when the consequences of emotional turmoil in the home for early emotional development are evident (Thompson & Calkins, 1996; Thompson, Flood, & Goodvin, 2006; Thompson & Goodman, 2010). Young offspring of parents with affective disorders such as depression are at heightened risk of problems with emotion and emotional regulation, for example, because of the caregiver's limited accessibility as a source of emotional support, and the adult's parenting practices that enhance the child's feelings of responsibility and helplessness (Goodman & Gotlib, 1999). As a result, the offspring of a depressed caregiver become overinvolved in the parent's affective problems, unduly obligated to buttress the parent's emotional state, and feeling inappropriately guilty when their efforts inevitably fail. Children from homes characterized by marital conflict show a heightened sensitivity to distress and anger that is manifested in insecurity and diminished coping

You didn't like that he was bouncing your guy off the game, and that made you really mad.

It's hard when you feel so angry. You're going "AAAH, he's bouncing my guy off there!" Right?

It makes you sad thinking about it, doesn't it?

You know, after you stopped the game, the other guys said, "You know, Joey wasn't really doing so bad." You thought you were losing, but you weren't.

FIGURE 9.3 Excerpt from a mother's conversation with her 5-year-old about a recent emotional experience, illustrating one of the ways that experience of close relationships contributes to emotion understanding.

capacities when adults argue between themselves (Cummings & Davies, 1996; Davies & Woitach, 2008). From the preschool years onward, these children also become overinvolved in their parents' emotional conflicts and have difficulty managing the strong emotions these conflicts arouse in them (Sturge-Apple, Davies, Winter, Cummings, & Schermerhorn, 2008). Maltreating mothers are less aware of their children's feelings and less competent at helping their children cope with emotionally arousing situations, which contributes to the emotional difficulties of their offspring (Shipman & Zeman, 2001). At times, the quality of parenting interacts with young children's genetic vulnerability to either enhance children's risk of developing self-regulatory problems or buffer them against these difficulties (Kochanska, Philibert, & Barry, 2009). The sensitivity and support provided by close relationships are required for children to develop in an emotionally healthy manner. Unfortunately, these studies also illustrate how emotional processes in the home can contribute to the intergenerational transmission of emotional problems from parent to offspring.

Emotion: Conclusion and Future Directions

Understanding how significantly social relationships influence emotional experience underscores the complexity of emotion and its development, and constitutes an important direction for future research. Contrary to the view that emotion is the outward expression of an internal subjectivity, research highlights that the elicitors of emotion, the meaning of emotional arousal, and the understanding of emotional experience and its expression are each deeply social processes. This research is important also for understanding the role of emotion in personality development. Because the emotions with which infants and young children begin to understand themselves and others and communicate with partners are socially instigated and construed, personality is founded on the shared meanings associated with emotion in a particular culture.

As is true in the study of temperament, developmental emotions research is also advancing through genetically informed research designs that enable scientists to understand the hereditary foundations to emotional responding, and by neurobiological research that permits greater insight into the areas of the brain relevant to emotion activation and emotion regulation. It is easy to read these research literatures and conclude that these represent the "nature" of emotional development whereas studies of social influences reflect its "nurture." But as research on temperament has also shown, dichotomizing biological and social influences on developing individuality is scientifically obsolete as research, earlier reviewed, increasingly demonstrates that gene–environment interactions are important, as are the influences of experiences on brain development. In each case, emotional growth is the result of the dynamic interaction over time of biology and experience.

This conclusion is also true of the development of emotion regulation, which will also continue to provoke future research in this field. It is not difficult to understand why, in light of the importance of emotion regulation to the development of social competence and emotional well-being, and the relevance of emotion regulation to understanding problems in developmental psychopathology—such as conduct disorders, depression, and aggressive behavior—and their remediation. But research increasingly shows that emotion regulation is a more complicated developmental process than is often assumed, involving a deeper interaction between the "activational" and the "regulatory" features of emotion. As this interaction is further studied, it will likely lead to more insightful ways of understanding the origins of affective psychopathology in childhood as well as promising treatment interventions.

SELF

As mature people, it is almost impossible to conceive of life without a sense of self. The integrated perception of "me" at the center of all of life experience seems natural and inevitable. But if we stop to consider all that "self" encompasses, it is apparent that this concept is considerably more complex than our intuitive experience suggests, and that the development of self is a multifaceted process that extends throughout life. Moreover, because the sense of self organizes and integrates our experience of who we are in the context of changing life events, it provides an essential foundation to personality development. Studying the growth of self is thus an essential developmental task, and (as we shall see) requires methods that are as diverse as are the different facets of "self."

What is "Self"?

At the core of "self" is, of course, the sense of *subjective self-awareness*. This is the perception of self as an actor, perceiver, emoter, thinker, and experiencer in the midst of all of which one is consciously aware. It is the "I-self" that, to William James (1890) and his followers (Harter, 2006), denotes the uniquely personal experience of life, in contrast to the "me-self" that constitutes the various characteristics that can be objectively known about a person by others. Subjective self-awareness develops very early in life and provides a foundation for the growth of self.

But there is more. Self also includes *self-representation*: who you think you are. This includes physical self-recognition, assigning categorical labels to the self (for gender, racial or ethnic identity, age, and the like), attributing characterological qualities to self (such as shy, friendly, bright, or strong-willed), and understanding how self-relevant processes function (such as thinking, feeling, and motivation). These forms of physical and psychological self-definition provide the basis for perceiving similarities and differences between self and other people, applying social constructions of psychological attributes (such as gender) to the self, gaining insight into the causes and motives underlying one's behavior, making ingroup–outgroup differentiations, self-management, and creating a self-concept. Although self-representation expands and is refined considerably throughout life as self-awareness assumes progressively more complex and differentiated features, the development of self-representation also begins quite early. Long before the second birthday, for example, toddlers are capable of recognizing their physical mirror image (Lewis & Brooks-Gunn, 1979), have begun to use language for simple self-description (Stern, 1985), and can identify basic emotional states in themselves (Bretherton, Fritz, Zahn-Waxler, & Ridgeway, 1986). By contrast, it is not until later childhood and adolescence that children begin to perceive themselves as members of societal groups and can evaluate ingroup–outgroup distinctions (Killen, Lee-Kim, McGlothlin, & Stangor, 2002).

Another feature of self is *autobiographical personal narrative* by which the recollections of specific events in the past are integrated because of their personal meaning and relation to the self (Nelson & Fivush, 2004). Although young children are fairly proficient at recalling general events in the immediate past, it is not until after age 3 that **autobiographical memory** emerges, and most adults cannot recall events of their lives prior to this age (Howe & Courage, 1993; Welch-Ross, 1995). Autobiographical memory differs from general event recall because of the sense of self that is central to the narrative account, organizing and giving meaning to the events that are remembered. One reason for the relatively late emergence of autobiographical personal narrative, therefore, is that the kind of self-knowledge required to instill past events with personal meaning does not begin to emerge until after the third birthday (Howe & Courage, 1993, 1997; Nelson & Fivush, 2004).

A fourth aspect of self consists of the variety of *self-evaluations* that color self-representations and become integrated into the self-concept and self-image (Cole et al., 2001; Harter, 2006). Self-evaluations often derive from the internalization of others' evaluations, but they also arise from the quality of personal self-regard and developing capacities for self-understanding (Stipek, 1995). A temperamentally shy child living in a society that values assertion and extraversion may increasingly view this characteristic as a liability, for example, as she becomes more aware of the difficulties posed by shyness in socializing with others. These self-evaluations guide how personal characteristics (or the self as a whole) come to be colored as strengths or weaknesses, benefits or liabilities, desirable or undesirable. As we shall see, it is likely that rudimentary ways of perceiving the self as good or bad develop in a nonlinguistic form in the initial 2 years of life, but these self-evaluations become considerably more multifaceted, incisive, nuanced, and differentiated in the years to come.

Finally, another emergent aspect of self is the *social self*—that is, the self primarily regarded in a social context. Although the sense of self is continuously influenced by social interactions and relationships (especially with parents), it is not until around the second birthday that young children begin to be interested and concerned with how their behavior is perceived by caregivers (Lagattuta & Thompson, 2007; Stipek, 1995). This is the beginning of more complex processes by which the self is oriented to its social context. In the years that follow, for example, social comparison processes will become an important facet of self-evaluation (Frey & Ruble, 1990), children and adolescents will be concerned with managing their self presentation through self-monitoring strategies (Snyder, 1987), and adolescents will realize that they have "multiple selves" that are suited to the expectations and demands of different social situations—and they will sometimes wonder which is their "true self" (Harter & Monsour, 1992).

Although these different facets of the "self" are not independent, conceptually disentangling them allows insight into two features of the development of self that might otherwise remain unrecognized. First, the growth of self begins surprisingly early but is an extraordinarily complex, and therefore extended, developmental process. Although some sense of self exists from very early in the first year, self-awareness is qualitatively different for infants, young children, adolescents, young adults, and older people because of the changes in self-representation, autobiographical personal narrative, and self-evaluative processes that occur over time. Asking when "the self" develops is, in this sense, a meaningless question.

Second, the developing self is the core of developing individuality and of the growth of personality. The sense of self provides coherence and organization to personal experience through the feeling of subjective self-awareness and the self-representations through which experience is interpreted (Sroufe, 1996; Stern, 1985). It offers the realization of temporal continuity between personal past, present experience, and expectations for the future through autobiographical narrative and a continuing self-concept (Moore & Lemmon, 2001). It provides a means of self-understanding and thus contributes also to understanding other people through the recognition of how one is similar to, as well as different from, others (Harter, 2006). In these ways, the developing self, like temperament and emotional growth, provides an essential scaffold to the developing personality.

These features of the self develop within the context of cultural beliefs about the nature of self. Thus, although children universally distinguish themselves from others and assign categorical labels to who they are, the nature and characteristics of self that children identify, and what children value (or devalue) about themselves depend on the culture context in which they live. These cultural views of the self are developed quite early. Mothers from the United States emphasize their preschool offspring's autonomy much more in conversation and social interaction than do Japanese mothers, for example, although there are also social class differences in maternal behavior within the US (Dennis, Cole, Zahn-Waxler, & Mizuta, 2002;

Wiley, Rose, Burger, & Miller, 1998). These socialization differences are already reflected in the autobiographical narratives of children from Western and non-Western cultures (Han, Leichtman, & Wang, 1998; Wang, 2004). Such cultural differences in conceptions of the self are important because Western ideas are inherent in how self-development is conceptualized and studied in contemporary psychology, and offer a reminder that the self is socially constructed in somewhat different ways throughout the world (Thompson & Virmani, 2009).

Methods of Developmental Study

As this discussion of the multifaceted features of the self suggests, researchers rarely strive to study the developing "self" in a comprehensive fashion. Rather, they study the growth of elements of self: self-descriptive statements, autobiographical memory, self-esteem, and other self-system processes. This means that research methods must be carefully developed to index the specific self-related processes of interest, as well as being suitable to the ages of the children under study. Researchers use different empirical tools for studying the growth of autobiographical memory (involving, for example, guided recall of events in the recent or distant past in conversation with the mother, with particular attention to the child's self-referential statements) than they use to investigate developmental changes in self-esteem (in which affective self-regard is assessed, often in response to carefully designed interview questions) or young children's self-descriptions. Each is a component of the developing "self," but each must be evaluated using methods that are specific to the particular domain of the self that is of special interest.

Studying the developing "self" is challenging also because the focus of empirical inquiry is on a young person's self-perceptions, and thus research methods often depend on self-report. The development of appropriate self-report measures for children of different ages can be challenging. Developmental scientists have long known, for example, that the conceptual capabilities of toddlers and preschoolers can be underestimated because of their limited capacities to verbalize their own thoughts and understanding, so researchers in this field have had to be creative in developing procedures to assess developing self-awareness in very young children who may not yet have the words to express what they think or feel. This can involve ingenious strategies of story construction (Emde, Wolfe, & Oppenheim, 2003), puppets (Measelle, Ablow, Cowan, & Cowan, 1998), or other procedures to elucidate what young children know and think about themselves. Researchers' success in doing so has helped to reveal that young children think of themselves more complexly and with greater psychological insight than was earlier believed. Even more striking is research on infants' self-recognition enlisting nonverbal methods that require babies to discriminate the effects of their own actions from those of others (Rochat & Striano, 2002). Creative methods are, in short, necessary in this field.

A Developmental Outline of the Self

There is considerable interest in the growth of the self because of the insights it affords into the emergence of personality. Moreover, because the experience of self provides a window into what a person finds rewarding or unpleasant, how he or she is motivated, and how personal experiences are construed, understanding the growth of self offers insights into individual differences in many other developmental processes.

Infancy.   In traditional formulations, the newborn enters the world in a state of psychological disorganization or in a condition of psychological undifferentiation from the caregiver. In either case, the newborn was believed to be poorly prepared for the development of a sense of self. Current views emphasize, by contrast, that young infants have surprising capabilities for assembling, from isolated everyday experiences, the consistent frame of reference that eventually develops into subjective self-awareness (Gergely, 2007; Meltzoff, 2007). As they are physically handled, move and touch things, respond to social interaction, and experience assorted visceral sensations, young infants progressively acquire a sense of physical self-awareness related to the functioning of their bodies. As they act on social and nonsocial objects (especially those that respond contingently), the experience of agency contributes to a dawning awareness of volition and its consequences. As they experience varieties of emotion, especially in response to social interaction, the sense of subjectivity is enriched and further consolidated. These experiences contribute to the development of a basic experience of the subjective self within the first 6 to 8 months of life.

After this, the self grows dramatically. By the end of the first year, self-awareness in relation to interpersonal (or intersubjective) events has emerged with the infant's dawning realization that others are also subjective entities who have viewpoints that are different from, and potentially can be shared with, the self (Tomasello & Rakoczy, 2003). Self-awareness is revealed in behavior as diverse as protocommunicative acts (sounds to others that signal intention or desire), efforts to achieve **joint attention** (when the baby reaches from a high chair to a desired toy, for example, while making urgent sounds and maintaining eye contact with the caregiver), striving to reengage social interaction after a period of inattention, and social referencing (Rochat & Striano, 2002; Tomasello & Rakoczy, 2003). In these and other ways, young infants reveal an implicit awareness that others have subjective states (such as attention and emotion) that can be altered by the child's efforts. Well before the second birthday, infants also become capable of physical self-recognition when presented with their mirror images (Lewis & Brooks-Gunn, 1979). They touch self-referentially when looking at themselves in the mirror (see Figure 9.4).

Late in the second year and early in the third, toddlers show indications of early self-representation in their verbal self-reference, such as using their names or referring to "me" (Bates, 1990) and in their use of simple emotion terms to describe their internal experiences (Bretherton et al., 1986). Other indications of emerging self-representation are assertions of competence, such as insisting on "do it myself" (Bullock & Lutkenhaus, 1988; Stipek, Gralinski, & Kopp, 1990), identifying the self by gender and in other ways (Ruble, Martin, & Berenbaum 2006), and the emergence of self-conscious emotions such as pride, embarrassment, and guilt (Lagattuta & Thompson, 2007). During this time, toddlers are also acquiring a sensitivity to standards and their applications to the self (Kochanska, Aksan, Prisco, & Adams, 2008), showing early signs of conscience (Thompson et al., 2006), and beginning to exercise self-control (Kopp & Wyer, 1994). Young children in the second and third years are, in short, experiencing rapidly expanding self-awareness and self-representation.

FIGURE 9.4   In infancy, playful responding to one's mirror image evolves, by the end of the second year, to self-referential touching that reflects the child's self-recognition in the mirror image.

The growth of self occurs because of changes within the child, and also because of relational influences. The organization and continuity of early experience provide the basis for emerging self-awareness. This organization derives from how parents structure the baby's experience around routines that are manageable, repetitive, and predictable, so that the baby becomes capable of anticipating events that will occur. Caregivers also offer social interactive experiences that are emotionally salient and reciprocal, so that the baby's social initiatives and responses have meaningful and contingent consequences (Thompson, 2006a). In providing experiences with these characteristics, sensitive caregivers offer the structure and consistency that enable a sense of self to become organized. Caregivers also provide opportunities in social interaction for infants to learn about the different subjective viewpoints that people possess, and to practice the skills for gaining access to these alternative subjectivities (through gestural and vocal communication, social referencing, and in other ways) (Tomasello & Rakoczy, 2003). Later, as self-representations begin to take shape, social interactions with caregivers shape the conditions in which toddlers feel proud or shameful, the competencies that they seek to exercise independently or with assistance, and the ways that they begin to identify and represent themselves as well as other people (Lagattuta & Thompson, 2007; Stipek, 1995). In this respect, consistent with classic theories of the self (e.g., Mead, 1934), young children begin to regard themselves through the lens of others' regard for them (i.e., the "looking glass self").

Unfortunately, not all caregivers provide a sensitive relational context for the development of positive or healthy self-regard. As self-representations begin to take shape in the second and third years of life, a parent's inappropriate expectations, belittling judgments, or impatience can contribute to negative self-regard, expressed in young children's shame or avoidance, even before a young child has mastered the linguistic capabilities for expressing self-regard (Kelley & Brownell, 2000). Indeed, it is possible that the roots of negative self-representations begin even earlier, in the manner in which infants learn to expect either positive and supportive assistance or more abrupt or negative interactions with their care-givers during everyday episodes of social play, caregiving routines, and the relief of distress. In one study, the mother's report of parenting stress and depressive symptomatology was associated with young children's negative self-concept, but a secure mother–child attachment was associated with positive self-concept in the same children (Goodvin, Meyer, Thompson, & Hayes, 2008). It is for this reason that many developmental researchers regard a secure parent–infant attachment as a crucial foundation for the growth of healthy self-regard because of its influence on the young child's developing self-representations or, in the words of some attachment theorists, **internal working models** of the self (Thompson, 2006a).

Early childhood. These "working models" become further elaborated and consolidated in the relational experiences of early childhood. This occurs because of significant growth in young children's self-representations during the preschool years. During this period, children acquire an expanded appreciation of psychological states in themselves and others, incorporating an increasing understanding of people's intentions, goals, emotions and desires, and later of thoughts, beliefs, and expectations, into their rudimentary "theory of mind" (Wellman, 2002). An expanding comprehension of internal psychological states not only assists young children in comprehending the thoughts and emotions of others, but also in understanding themselves and their own feelings and thinking. This development is reflected in how they describe themselves. Young children rely primarily on concrete, observable features in their spontaneous self-descriptions (e.g., "I am big, I can run fast, and can count to 100"), but they can also use psychological trait terms ("I am naughty sometimes, but good with adults") when describing themselves (Eder, 1989, 1990; Measelle et al., 1998). Although young children's use of trait terms such as "good" and "naughty" lacks the rich meaning inherent in how older people use these concepts, these self-descriptions are like personality traits in that they show stability over time and are similar to how others (such as their mothers) describe them (Brown, Mangelsdorf, Agathen, & Ho, 2008; Eder & Mangelsdorf, 1997). Even a preschooler's use of a concrete feature, such as describing herself/himself as a girl or boy, is accompanied by a basic understanding of the psychological attributes and stereotypes associated with being male or female (Ruble et al., 2006). Preschoolers are, in short, beginning to acquire increasingly complex and multidimensional self-representations based on how they perceive their physical (including temperamental qualities) and psychological characteristics (Brown et al., 2008; Marsh, Ellis, & Craven, 2002; Measelle, John, Ablow, Cowan, & Cowan, 2005) (see Table 9.4).

These self-representations are strongly influenced by how children believe they are regarded by others. Indeed, one of the hallmarks of early childhood is preschoolers' growing concern with how they are seen by the significant people in their lives (Lagattuta & Thompson, 2007; Stipek, 1995; Thompson et al., 2006). When they are engaged in misbehavior or tackling challenging tasks, for instance, young children are sensitive to the implicit or explicit standards of conduct that are reflected in parental evaluations of their behavior. They often anticipate positive parental responses (and seek to avoid negative reactions) before they occur, and incorporate parental standards into their own self-evaluations. Parental values, expectations, and beliefs are transmitted in many other contexts also. As noted earlier, for instance, everyday conversations between young children and their parents are a forum for meaningful lessons about behavioral expectations, emotional reactions, causal attributions, and the self in the context of the shared recall of the day's events. Consider, for example, the following brief conversation between a young child and his mother about an event earlier in the morning (Dunn & Brown, 1991, p. 97):

Child: Eat my Weetabix. Eat my Weetabix. Crying.
Mother: Crying, weren't you? We had quite a battle. "One more mouthful, Michael." And what did you do? You spat it out!
Child: *(Pretends to cry)*

Embedded within this short, shared recollection about a breakfast dispute are significant messages from the mother about the causal sequence of events, the reason for Michael's distress, and culpability for perceived misbehavior. These messages to the child are also

TABLE 9.4
Early Psychological Self-Representations in Preschoolers

4½- to 7½-year-olds[1]	4- and 5-year-olds[2]	5½-year-olds[3]	4- and 5-year-olds[4]
Academic competence	Timidity	Self-control	Self-concept in
Achievement motivation	Agreeableness	Self-acceptance via achievement	terms of:
Social competence	Negative affect	Self-acceptance via affiliation	• physical
Peer acceptance	Positive self-concept		appearance
Depression–anxiety			• peers
Aggression–hostility			• parents
			• verbal
			• math

[1] Measelle et al. (1998).
[2] Brown et al. (2008); Goodvin et al. (2008) (each research group used the same dimensions, although Goodvin and colleagues also identified positive self-concept).
[3] Eder (1990).
[4] Marsh et al. (2002).

lessons about the self, of course. By the mother's account, Michael's crying resulted from uncooperative behavior (by contrast with good boys, who cooperate) that resulted in his crying, whereas Michael's initial representation of the morning's confrontation likely focused instead on his mother's insistence about eating unpleasant breakfast cereal. In discussing everyday events like these with young children, similar lessons about the self are implicitly transmitted by caregivers in how they structure, elaborate, and clarify the child's simple representations of daily experience.

Furthermore, many developmental researchers believe that early, shared recountings of daily experiences with an adult also provide the basis for autobiographical personal narrative (Miller, 1994; Nelson & Fivush, 2004; Welch-Ross, 1995). It is easy to see why. By instilling an interpretive framework organized with reference to the child, caregivers structure the shared recounting of personal experiences in a manner that reinstantiates and consolidates recall, and also underscores the personal significance of events for the child. This makes events more memorable and helps to integrate them into a network of representations of events that are knit together because of their relevance to self. Indeed, parents' use of rich emotional language for highlighting the personal significance of events in conversations with their young children is associated with children's early self-concept development (Bird & Reese, 2006; Welch-Ross, Fasig, & Farrar, 1999).

Autobiographical memory does not begin to emerge until after the third birthday because prior to this time, young children have limited self-knowledge, are insufficiently self-aware psychologically to represent events autobiographically, and also have minimal capabilities for conversing meaningfully with parents (Nelson & Fivush, 2004; Reese, 2002; Welch-Ross, 1995). Furthermore, children's capacity to conceptualize the self as enduring over time may not develop until early in the fourth year (Povinelli & Simon, 1998). Once these abilities have developed, shared conversations with caregivers provide an important foundation to the growth of autobiographical memory. This means that children's autobiographical personal narratives—or, put differently, their emergent "working model" of the self—are likely to incorporate the moral values, causal attributions, emotional inferences, and perceptions of the child that caregivers incorporate into their shared recollections of the child's experiences (Thompson, 2006a). A parent who regards the young child as mischievous, rambunctious, cautious, or moody is likely to instill these perceptions into the shared recounting of the day's events, and these characteristics are likely, in turn, to be incorporated into the child's self-representations. At later ages, as children become mnemonically more skilled, they are less reliant on shared conversations with parents to retain autobiographical events, but for younger children the influence of these conversations is powerful. It is unsurprising, therefore, that young children's psychological self-representations are similar to how their mothers regard them (Brown et al., 2008; Eder & Mangelsdorf, 1997). But as a consequence, some young children are vulnerable to incorporating the negative or demeaning judgments of their caregivers.

In general, most young children have a positive view of their competencies (Wigfield, Eccles, Schiefele, Roeser, & Davis-Kean, 2006). Young children perceive themselves as capable in many things, confidently predicting success even when they have failed, and maintaining sunny expectations for the future (Harter & Pike, 1984). One reason is that young children have difficulty distinguishing between their desired and their actual performance and, believing that ability can be changed with increased effort, do not easily recognize the limits in their capabilities (Stipek, 1984). Another reason is that preschoolers do not spontaneously enlist social comparison to evaluate their performance against the behavior of others, but instead evaluate their skills against what they were capable of accomplishing at an earlier age (Frey & Ruble, 1990). By the standard of temporal comparison, of course, most young children can feel positive and optimistic about their capabilities. However, when social comparison information is made salient to them, even children as young as 4½ may knowingly use this information to evaluate their own competence (Butler, 1998). Their sunny self-regard does not last long, however. There is a progressive decline in children's judgments of their own competencies as they proceed through the primary grades (Wigfield et al., 2006).

Middle childhood. Self-understanding changes considerably in the school years as children develop more differentiated, realistic, and sophisticated forms of self-representation and self-evaluation. One reason this occurs is the growth of spontaneous social comparison enlisted into self-evaluation. In middle childhood, children spontaneously and more thoughtfully compare their capabilities and attributes with those of their peers to determine how well they "measure up" (Frey & Ruble, 1990; Pomerantz, Ruble, Frey, & Greulich, 1995). Because few children excel in all aspects, social comparison fosters a more differentiated awareness of personal strengths and weaknesses—the realization, for example, that someone may be skilled at sports, have difficulty with math, but be average in social popularity (Cole et al., 2001). Social comparison processes are fostered by the intellectual competencies that emerge during this period of life (Case, 1991), and also by the social conditions of middle childhood. Schools increasingly use comparative performance-based evaluations (in contrast with the rewards in preschool for simply trying), and in clubs, athletic groups, and other gatherings children are organized into age-stratified groups that better enable them to compare their capabilities with those of their peers (Wigfield et al., 2006).

Social and temporal comparison processes, together with expanding cognitive capabilities, have important consequences for children's developing self-understanding in middle childhood. They contribute to more complex and sophisticated self-evaluations. In contrast to the comparatively general positive self-regard of preschoolers, older children's self-descriptions include a more balanced assessment of personal strengths and weaknesses. Distinguishing among various domains of competency—such as academic achievement, athletic prowess, peer popularity, physical appearance, behavioral conduct, and, somewhat later, romantic appeal and job competence—children view themselves as having desirable and/or undesirable qualities in each of many different domains (Cole et al., 2001; Harter, 2006). Children also see themselves in the context of the multiple roles they assume in middle childhood as family member, student, teammate, club member, and other roles, and in relation to the various identities they assume as Asian, Jewish, female, middle-class, and so forth (Harter, 2006). In middle childhood, children also become increasingly aware that differences in ability are not easily changed, and can constrain potential achievement (Dweck, 2002; Pomerantz & Saxon, 2001). They are thus better able to use past performance and personal self-awareness as a guide to more accurately predicting how well they will perform.

Self-esteem in certain domains begins to decline during the school years because of children's more realistic and self-critical self-assessments and the influence of social comparison. Children's perceptions of their physical and intellectual competencies, for example, decline progressively throughout the school years (Eccles, Wigfield, Harold, & Blumenfeld, 1993; Wigfield et al., 2006; but see Cole et al., 2001, for different conclusions). These declines are for both boys and girls, although depending on the domain, rates of decline vary somewhat by gender (Jacobs, Lanza, Osgood, Eccles, & Wigfield, 2002). A decline in academic self-esteem is perhaps inevitable in light of the unrealistic optimism of the preschool years, but it helps to explain why individual differences in self-confidence and their motivational implications become so important in middle childhood (Dweck, 2002). By contrast, other facets of self-esteem, such as children's perceptions of their social competence, rise rather than decline throughout middle childhood (Cole et al., 2001). As these diverse changes in self-concept reflect, older children have a better understanding of personality traits as internal dispositions that are manifested in diverse behavior, and begin to perceive themselves as persons with complex personalities.

The emergence of social comparison and other social influences on developing self-understanding reveals also the growth of the social self, as children increasingly perceive themselves in terms of a complex social context. In middle childhood, children become more adept at self-presentation: managing how they appear before others. With respect to emotions, for example, children acquire considerably greater understanding and apply this insight to developing skills of emotion regulation and in using emotional display rules to dissemble their true feelings in the presence of others (Saarni, 1999). Children know how to act appropriately in different social situations and have the self-control to do so, whether remaining quiet at a concert, looking attentively in class, or adopting an easy-going demeanor with friends. The increasingly self-conscious enactment of socially appropriate behaviors on the stage of public regard reflects the greater insight of older children into their social selves, and provides a foundation for further advances in self-understanding of adolescence.

Adolescence and beyond.   The intellectual capacity for abstract thought flourishes during adolescence, and abstract thought enables teenagers to think of themselves and others much differently than before (Collins & Steinberg, 2006). They can reflect on discrepancies as well as consistencies within their profile of personality characteristics, and ponder what these discrepancies mean for the integrity of who they are (Harter, 2006). They can appreciate the different personae they appear to be in different social situations, and wonder which (if any) reveals their "true self" (Harter & Monsour, 1992). They can contrast their personal characteristics with the attributes of an idealized self, and worry over whether the gap will ever be narrowed (Markus & Nurius, 1986). As one teenager put it, "I'd like to be friendly and tolerant all of the time. That's the kind of person I want to be, and I'm disappointed when I'm not" (Harter, 1990).

Adolescents can also reflect on the life experiences that have contributed to their unique personalities, and believe that nobody else has the same personal outlook that they do. They can ponder how others regard them and experience considerable self-consciousness that derives from assuming that others view them with the same critical scrutiny with which they regard themselves. They can also begin wondering about the roles and responsibilities they will assume as adults, and in doing so begin the process of forging an occupational, religious, political, and sexual identity (Erikson, 1968; Kroger, 1993). Gender identity intensifies, along with teenagers' self-segregation into gender-typed activities and interests (Ruble et al., 2006). The burgeoning capacities for abstract thought, together with the social circumstances of adolescence and the psychobiological changes associated with puberty, can foster significant changes in self-understanding, self-evaluation, and the social self (Collins & Steinberg, 2006). They can also make adolescence a period of introspection, disturbing self-criticism, and pain as well as pleasure at the new forms of self-awareness that emerge. These challenges can invite anxious self-reflection, bold experimentation, or both. Indeed, two reasons that adolescents report for engaging in "false self" behavior, besides the effort to ensure acceptable self-presentation to significant others, are that others devalue who they truly are and to experiment with different roles and different possible selves (Harter, Marold, Whitesell, & Cobbs, 1996).

The effort to "discover" or "find" oneself in adolescence derives not necessarily from deficiencies in prior self-understanding but rather from the new questions about the self that are raised by new forms of self-awareness, as well as new social roles and circumstances. The psychobiological changes of puberty mean that teenagers are perceiving themselves, and are being perceived by others, less as children and more like young adults, and these changes in how they are regarded by others can introduce welcomed as well as confusing revisions in self-perception depending on the timing of puberty and its meaning to the teenager. At the same time, adolescents are departing from childhood roles (their schools are larger, classes more impersonal, expectations more stringent, teachers more authoritarian; see Wigfield et al., 2006) and are beginning to enter into adult roles and activities (in an after-school job, in classes that teach job skills or prepare for college, and in exploring romantic and sexual relationships). Given how much one's physical appearance and social context are bedrocks to personal identity at any stage of life, it is unsurprising that these rather dramatic pubertal and role-related changes can provoke significant questions about the self in adolescence.

It might be expected that with the onset of these psychobiological, cognitive, and contextual changes in early adolescence, self-esteem declines. But the story of adolescence is similar to middle childhood: Self-esteem changes in various ways for different domains of self-perceived competence, such as academic, social, and athletic (Cole et al., 2001). Consistent with their experience at earlier ages, adolescents can benefit from positive, supportive parenting that incorporates acceptance and approval, permitted self-expression, and behavioral guidelines that are rationally discussed (Collins & Steinberg, 2006; Grolnick, 2003). Indeed, contrary to popular stereotypes about the teenage years, parents remain important to adolescents' self-esteem even as peers also become important, partly because of parents' centrality to the teenager's life experience.

As many of the psychological, psychobiological, and social transitions of early adolescence are consolidated and accommodated, teenagers increasingly look to young adulthood with goals and plans that they are working to achieve. To be sure, the "who am I?" questions that are inaugurated in adolescence are rarely answered with any certainty or completeness by the close of the teenage years. Issues of identity, multiple selves, and the dissonance between actual and ideal selves continue to be explored in early adulthood, and may be reevoked much later in life as the result of significant life changes (e.g., divorce, job loss, personal injury). By contrast with the adolescent's initial encounter with these questions about self, however, the adult can approach these issues as familiar if nagging concerns, having crystallized a sense of self in the choices of occupation, marital partner, and lifestyle that both reflect and help to define who you are, and in the other life circumstances that provide stability and consistency to daily experience. In this respect, the sense of self is more reliable in adulthood because, having engaged in the explorations of the teenage years, the adult has made choices and commitments that (to a greater or lesser extent) are satisfactory, and that provide a foundation for occupation, family, and other pursuits of life.

Self: Conclusion and Future Directions

A sense of self is such a familiar part of individuality and self-regard that it is easy to forget how painstakingly self-understanding is constructed through infancy, childhood, and adolescence. Moreover, a sense of self is such a central frame of reference for personal experience that it is easy to neglect how much it is a product of social influences. These influences begin with the quality of care an infant receives, continue with how autobiographical self-awareness is constructed through conversation, and extend even to the discovery of self in the context of adolescent peer relationships. This is important especially when we appreciate that a sense of self is a core feature of personality development. Personality derives, in part, from how people create a sense of themselves from personal self-reflection and self-awareness, and also by looking in the mirror of others' regard for them.

Cultural practices provide an envelope within which the self develops from birth throughout life, and future research will devote greater attention to the intersection between cultural values, family practices, and the development of self (Thompson & Virmani, 2009). All of the social influences on the development of self discussed above are culturally colored, and this begins early in the different experiences of contingent social play that help to create a sense of subjective self-awareness in infancy, to the different opportunities afforded for mirror self-recognition, to the incentives and support for developing skills in self-management, to parents' expressed and implied evaluations of children's conduct (see Keller, 2007; Rogoff, 2003). Cultural practices further influence the development of self in how parents converse with their children about everyday experiences, emphasizing the child's feelings, the lessons of experience, or responsible conduct depending on the cultural context (Wang & Fivush, 2005; Wang, Leichtman, & Davies, 2000). To the extent that the development of self is socially constructed, culture will receive increased attention as an important part of that constructive context.

The importance of culture is also reflected in the cultural diversity of children growing up in the United States. In light of the remarkable increase in racial and ethnic diversity, attention to the development of self, ethnic and racial identity, cultural identity development, and acculturation processes as part of the development of self will require increased research attention (Quintana, 2007, 2008). Research findings suggest that for children of immigrants, for example, the manner in which children fit into the broader community—and the community, in turn, fits into the dominant American society—can significantly determine the extent of acculturative stress they experience, including stress related to self-understanding and identity (Zhou, 1997). Attention to cross-cultural and within-culture diversity in the development of self will contribute to a broader appreciation of the social determinants of how children come to understand who they are, and the influence of developing self-awareness on personality growth.

CONCLUSIONS

Although the newborn enters the world as a biologically unique individual, temperamental individuality provides only the most basic core of personality development. As capacities for emotional responding and understanding subsequently unfold, temperamental qualities become elaborated and integrated into a broader network of capabilities. And as a nascent sense of self and self-understanding also develop, temperament becomes incorporated into how the child experiences the self, how others perceive the child, and how self-understanding emerges from the interaction of these processes.

Personality development encompasses, of course, a broader range of influences than just temperament, emotion, and self-awareness. This discussion has touched on many of these additional contributors to personality growth. Personality is shaped by significant relationships, especially those with the mother, father, and other primary caregivers, who provide an emotional context of security and support (or, alternatively, insecure uncertainty) in which confidence, self-esteem, sociability, and empathy (or their opposites) can emerge (Thompson, 2006a). Personality is also forged by broader social experiences, such as with peers in the school and neighborhood, the socioeconomic conditions of the family that shape life challenges and opportunities, and the cultural norms and beliefs that envelop all of these processes, which remind us that the development of "the individual child" is a theoretical abstraction. Personality development is also shaped by the emergence of conscience and moral understanding, social cognition and its influence on social behavior, and the emergence of gender identity that also infuse the growth of emotion and of self. In a sense, personality development is an inclusive construct that incorporates the variety of psychobiological, conceptual, social, and contextual influences that self-organize to constitute developing individuality through the life course.

In focusing on temperament, emotion, and self, however, we have considered three of the earliest foundations to developing individuality that provide a basis for personality growth and the elaboration of personality in the years following infancy (Caspi & Shiner, 2006). With the foundation in place in the initial years of life, personality unfolds and becomes individually refined, consolidated, and strengthened in many ways (Caspi & Shiner, 2006; Thompson, 1988). Personality influences how experiences are construed and interpreted by people, and thus how they respond to social and nonsocial events, and the reciprocal effects they have on future development. Personality influences the choices of social partners, activities, and environmental settings, and the opportunities and challenges these choices pose for further growth. Personality influences the resiliency and vulnerabilities that all individuals experience in their encounters with stressful and everyday life events, as well as the resources people have for coping. Personality influences self-construction and the multifaceted ways that individuals perceive themselves in their current life circumstances in light of how they understand their personal past, their current dispositions, and their needs and desires. In these and many other ways, therefore, personality develops but also mediates between the individual and the social and nonsocial world, and the interaction between personality and the social context affects growth in many developmental domains, and shapes the further growth of personality.

Developing individuality is thus both exceedingly personal—touching at the heart of our sense of self—and socially constituted. This is true at the beginning of life, and throughout the life course. It is in this manner that we experience ourselves as unique actors in the social world, but sharing much in common with those with whom we live life.

REFERENCES AND SUGGESTED READINGS (📖)

Ashman, S. B., & Dawson, G. (2002). Maternal depression, infant psychobiological development, and risk for depression. In S. H. Goodman & I. H. Gotlib (Eds.), *Children of depressed parents* (pp. 37–58). Washington, DC: American Psychological Association.

Bakermans-Kranenburg, M. J., van IJzendoorn, M. H., Pijlman, F. T. A., Mesman, J., & Juffer, F. (2008). Experimental evidence for differential susceptibility: Dopamine D4 receptor polymorphism (DRD4 VNTR) moderates intervention effects on toddlers' externalizing behavior in a randomized controlled trial. *Developmental Psychology, 44*, 293–300.

Banerjee, M. (1997). Hidden emotions: Preschoolers' knowledge of appearance–reality and emotion display rules. *Social Cognition, 15*, 107–132.

Bartsch, K., & Wellman, H. M. (1995). *Children talk about the mind*. New York: Oxford University Press.

Bates, E. (1990). Language about me and you: Pronomial reference and the emerging concept of self. In D. Cicchetti & M. Beeghly (Eds.), *The self in transition* (pp. 165–182). Chicago: University of Chicago Press.

Bates, J. E. (1980). The concept of difficult temperament. *Merrill-Palmer Quarterly, 29*, 299–319.

Bates, J. E. (1987). Temperament in infancy. In J. D. Osofsky (Ed.), *Handbook of infant development* (2nd ed., pp. 1101–1149). New York: Wiley.

Bates, J. E., Bayles, K., Bennett, D. S., Ridge, B., & Brown, M. M. (1991). Origins of externalizing behavior problems at eight years of age. In D. Pepler & K. Rubin (Eds.), *Development and treatment of childhood aggression* (pp. 93–120). Hillsdale, NJ: Lawrence Erlbaum Associates.

Belsky, J. (2005). Differential susceptibility to rearing influences: An evolutionary hypothesis and some evidence. In B. Ellis & D. Bjorklund (Eds.), *Origins of the social mind: Evolutionary psychology and child development* (pp. 139–163). New York: Guilford.

Belsky, J., Bakermans-Kranenburg, M. J., & van IJzendoorn, M. H. (2007). For better and for worse: Differential susceptibility to environmental influences. *Current Directions for Psychological Science, 16*, 300–304.

Bird, A., & Reese, E. (2006). Emotional reminiscing and the development of an autobiographical self. *Developmental Psychology, 42*, 613–626.

Bornstein, M. H. (1995). Form and function: Implications for studies of culture and human development. *Culture & Psychology, 1*, 123–137.

Bornstein, M. H. (1998). Stability in mental development from early life: Methods, measures, models, meanings and myths. In F. Simion & G. Butterworth (Eds.), *The development of sensory, motor and cognitive capacities in early infancy: From perception to cognition* (pp. 301–332). Hove, UK: Psychology Press.

Bornstein, M. H., & Arterberry, M. E. (2003). Recognition, discrimination, and categorization of smiling by 5-month-old infants. *Developmental Science*, *6*, 585–599.

Bornstein, M. H., Gaughran, J. M., & Segui, I. (1991). Multimethod assessment of infant temperament: Mother questionnaire and mother and observer reports evaluated and compared at five months using the Infant Temperament Measure. *International Journal of Behavioral Development*, *14*, 131–151.

Bosquet, M., & Egeland, B. (2006). The development and maintenance of anxiety symptoms from infancy through adolescence in a longitudinal sample. *Development and Psychopathology*, *18*, 517–550.

Bretherton, I., Fritz, J., Zahn-Waxler, C., & Ridgeway, D. (1986). Learning to talk about emotions: A functionalist perspective. *Child Development*, *57*, 529–548.

Brown, G. L., Mangelsdorf, S. C., Agathen, J. M., & Ho, M. (2008). Young children's psychological selves: Convergence with maternal reports of child personality. *Social Development*, *17*, 161–182.

Bullock, M., & Lutkenhaus, P. (1988). The development of volitional behavior in the toddler years. *Child Development*, *59*, 664–674.

Buss, A. H., & Plomin, R. (1984). *Temperament: Early developing personality traits*. Hillsdale, NJ: Lawrence Erlbaum Associates.

Buss, K. A., & Goldsmith, H. H. (1998). Fear and anger regulation in infancy: Effects on the temporal dynamics of affective expression. *Child Development*, *69*, 359–374.

Butler, R. (1998). Age trends in the use of social and temporal comparison for self-evaluation: Examination of a novel developmental hypothesis. *Child Development*, *69*, 1054–1073.

Camras, L. A. (2000). Surprise! Facial expressions can be coordinative motor structures. In M. Lewis & I. Granic (Eds.), *Emotion, development, and self-organization* (pp. 100–124). New York: Cambridge University Press.

Case, R. (1991). Stages in the development of the young child's first sense of self. *Developmental Review*, *11*, 210–230.

Caspi, A., Harrington, H., Milne, B., Amell, J. W., Theodore, R. F., & Moffitt, T. E. (2003). Children's behavioral styles at age 3 are linked to their adult personality traits at age 26. *Journal of Personality*, *71*, 495–513.

📖 Caspi, A., & Shiner, R. L. (2006). Personality development. In W. Damon & R. M. Lerner (Eds.), N. Eisenberg (Vol. Ed.), *Handbook of child psychology, Vol. 3: Social, emotional and personality development* (6th ed., pp. 300–365). New York: Wiley.

Caspi, A., & Silva, P. A. (1995). Temperamental qualities at age three predict personality traits in young adulthood: Longitudinal evidence from a birth cohort. *Child Development*, *66*, 486–498.

Chen, X., Hastings, P. D. Rubin, K. H., Chen, H., Cen, G., & Stewart, S. L. (1998). Child-rearing attitudes and behavioral inhibition in Chinese and Canadian toddlers: A cross-cultural study. *Developmental Psychology*, *34*, 677–686.

Chess, S., & Thomas, A. (1986). *Temperament in clinical practice*. New York: Guilford.

Cole, D. A., Maxwell, S. E., Martin, J. M., Peeke, L. G., Seroczynski, A. D., Tram, J. M., et al. (2001). The development of multiple domains of child and adolescent self-concept: A cohort sequential longitudinal design. *Child Development*, *72*, 1723–1746.

Cole, P. (1986). Children's spontaneous control of facial expression. *Child Development*, *57*, 1309–1321.

Cole, P. M., & Dennis, T. A. (1998). Variations on a theme: Culture and the meaning of socialization practices and child competence. *Psychological Inquiry*, *9*, 276–278.

Cole, P. M., Martin, S. E., & Dennis, T. A. (2004). Emotion regulation as a scientific construct: Methodological challenges and directions for child development research. *Child Development*, *75*, 317–333.

Cole, P. M., & Tamang, B. L. (1998). Nepali children's ideas about emotional displays in hypothetical challenges. *Developmental Psychology*, *34*, 640–646.

📖 Cole, P. M., & Tan, P. Z. (2007). Emotion socialization from a cultural perspective. In J. E. Grusec & P. D. Hastings (Eds.), *Handbook of socialization: Theory and research* (pp. 516–542). New York: Guilford.

Collins, W. A., & Steinberg. L. (2006). Adolescent development in interpersonal context. In W. Damon & R. M. Lerner (Eds.), N. Eisenberg (Vol. Ed.), *Handbook of child psychology, Vol. 3: Social, emotional, and personality development* (6th ed., pp. 1003–1067). New York: Wiley.

Crockenberg, S. C., Leerkes, E. M., & Lekka, S. K. (2007). Pathways from marital aggression to infant emotion regulation: The development of withdrawal in infancy. *Infant Behavior & Development*, *30*, 97–113.

Cummings, E. M., & Davies, P. (1996). *Children and marital conflict*. New York: Guilford.

Davidson, R. J., Fox, A., & Kalin, N. H. (2007). Neural bases of emotion regulation in nonhuman primates and humans. In J. J. Gross (Ed.), *Handbook of emotion regulation* (pp. 47–68). New York: Guilford.

Davies, P. T., & Woitach, M. J. (2008). Children's emotional security in the interparental relationship. *Current Directions in Psychological Science*, *17*, 269–274.

📖 Denham, S. (1998). *Emotional development in young children*. New York: Guilford.

Denham, S. A., Blair, K. A., DeMulder, E., Levitas, J., Sawyer, K., Auerbach-Major, S., et al. (2003). Preschool emotional competence: Pathway to social competence. *Child Development*, *74*, 238–256.

Denham, S., Blair, K., Schmidt, M., & DeMulder, E. (2002). Compromised emotional competence: Seeds of violence sown early? *American Journal of Orthopsychiatry*, *72*, 70–82.

Dennis, T. A., Cole, P. M., Zahn-Waxler, C., & Mizuta, I. (2002). Self in context: Autonomy and relatedness in Japanese and U.S. mother–preschool dyads. *Child Development*, *73*, 1803–1817.

Donaldson, S. K., & Westerman, M. A. (1986). Development of children's understanding of ambivalence and causal theories of emotion. *Developmental Psychology*, *22*, 655–662.

Dunn, J. (1994). Changing minds and changing relationships. In C. Lewis & P. Mitchell (Eds.), *Children's early understanding of mind* (pp. 297–310). Hove, UK: Lawrence Erlbaum Associates.

Dunn, J., & Brown, J. (1991). Relationships, talk about feelings, and the development of affect regulation in early childhood. In J. Garber & K. A. Dodge (Eds.), *The development of emotion regulation and dysregulation* (pp. 89–108). New York: Cambridge University Press.

Dweck, C. S. (2002). The development of ability conceptions. In A. Wigfield & J. S. Eccles (Eds.), *Development of achievement motivation* (pp. 57–88). San Diego, CA: Academic.

Ebstein, R. P., Benjamin, J., & Belmaker, R. H. (2000). Personality and polymorphism of genes involved in aminergic neurotransmission. *European Journal of Pharmacology*, *410*, 205–214.

Eccles, J. S., Midgley, C., Wigfield, A., Buchanan, C. M., Reuman, D., Flanagan, C., et al. (1993). Development during adolescence: The impact of stage–environment fit on young adolescents' experiences in schools and in families. *American Psychologist*, *48*, 90–101.

Eccles, J. S., Wigfield, A., Harold, R. D., & Blumenfeld, P. (1993). Age and gender differences in children's self- and task perceptions during elementary school. *Child Development*, *64*, 830–847.

Eder, R. A. (1989). The emergent personologist: The structure and content of 3½-, 5½-, and 7½-year-olds' concepts of themselves and other persons. *Child Development*, *60*, 1218–1228.

Eder, R. A. (1990). Uncovering children's psychological selves: Individual and developmental differences. *Child Development*, *61*, 849–863.

Eder, R. A., & Mangelsdorf, S. C. (1997). The emotional basis of early personality development: Implications for the emergent self-concept. In R. Hogan & S. Briggs (Eds.), *Handbook of personality psychology* (pp. 209–240). Orlando, FL: Academic Press.

Eisenberg, N. & Morris, A. S. (2002). Children's emotion-related regulation. In R. Kail (Ed.), *Advances in child development and behavior* (Vol. 30, pp. 190–229). San Diego, CA: Academic.

Eisenberg, N., Spinrad, T. L., & Sadovsky, A. (2006). Empathy-related responding in children. In M. Killen & J. Smetana (Eds.), *Handbook of moral development* (pp. 517–549). Mahwah, NJ: Lawrence Erlbaum Associates.

Ekman, P. (2003). *Emotions revealed*. New York: Times Books.

Ekman, P., & Friesen, W. (1975). *Unmasking the face*. Englewood Cliffs, NJ: Prentice Hall.

Emde, R. N., Wolfe, D. P., & Oppenheim, D. (2003). *Revealing the inner worlds of young children: The MacArthur Story Stem Battery and parent–child narratives*. New York: Oxford University Press.

Erikson, E. H. (1968). *Identity, youth, and crisis*. New York: Norton.

Fivush, R. (1994). Constructing narrative, emotion, and self in parent–child conversations about the past. In U. Neisser & R. Fivush (Eds.), *The remembering self* (pp. 136–157). Cambridge, UK: Cambridge University Press.

Fivush, R. (1998). Gendered narratives: Elaboration, structure, and emotion in parent–child reminiscing across the preschool years. In C. P. Thompson & D. J. Herrmann (Eds.), *Autobiographical memory: Theoretical and applied perspectives* (pp. 79–103). Mahwah, NJ: Lawrence Erlbaum Associates.

Fox, N. A., Schmidt, L. A., & Henderson, H. A. (2000). Developmental psychophysiology: Conceptual and methodological perspectives. In J. T. Cacioppo, L. G. Tassinary, & G. G. Berntson (Eds.), *Handbook of psychophysiology* (2nd ed., pp. 665–686). New York: Cambridge University Press.

Frey, K. S., & Ruble, D. N. (1990). Strategies for comparative evaluation: Maintaining a sense of competence across the life span. In R. J. Sternberg & J. Kolligian, Jr. (Eds.), *Competence considered* (pp. 167–189). New Haven, CT: Yale University Press.

Gallagher, K. C. (2002). Does child temperament moderate the influence of parenting on adjustment? *Developmental Review*, *22*, 623–643.

Garner, P. W., & Spears, F. M. (2000). Emotion regulation in low-income preschoolers. *Social Development*, *9*, 246–264.

Gergely, G. (2007). The social construction of the subjective self: The role of affect-mirroring, markedness, and ostensive communication in self-development. In L. Mayes, P. Fonagy, & M. Target (Eds.), *Developmental science and psychoanalysis: Integration and innovation* (pp. 45–88). London: Karnac Books.

Gilliom, M., Shaw, D. S., Beck, J. E., Schonberg, M. A., & Lukon, J. L. (2002). Anger regulation in disadvantaged preschool boys: Strategies, antecedents, and the development of self-control. *Developmental Psychology*, *38*, 222–235.

Goldsmith, H. H. (2002). Genetics of emotional development. In R. J. Davidson, K. R. Scherer, & H. H. Goldsmith (Eds.), *Handbook of affective sciences*. New York: Oxford University Press.

Goldsmith, H. H., Buss, A. H., Plomin, R., Rothbart, M. K., Thomas, A., Chess, S., et al. (1987). Roundtable: What is temperament? Four approaches. *Child Development*, *58*, 505–529.

Goldsmith, H. H., & Campos, J. J. (1982). Toward a theory of infant temperament. In R. N. Emde & R. J. Harmon (Eds.), *The development of attachment and affiliative systems* (pp. 161–193). New York: Plenum.

Goodman, S. H., & Gotlib, I. H. (1999). Risk for psychopathology in the children of depressed mothers: A developmental model for understanding mechanisms of transmission. *Psychologial Review*, *106*, 458–490.

Goodvin, R., Meyer, S., Thompson, R. A., & Hayes, R. (2008). Self-understanding in early childhood: Associations with attachment security, maternal perceptions of the child, and maternal emotional risk. *Attachment & Human Development*, *10*(4), 433–450.

Gottman, J. M., & Katz, L. F., & Hooven, C. (1997). *Meta-emotion: How families communicate emotionally*. Mahwah, NJ: Lawrence Erlbaum Associates.

Grolnick, W. S. (2003). *The psychology of parental control*. Mahwah, NJ: Lawrence Erlbaum Associates.

Gunnar, M. R., & Davis, E. P. (2003). Stress and emotion in early childhood. In R. M. Lerner & M. A. Easterbrooks (Eds.), *Handbook of psychology, Vol. 6: Developmental Psychology* (pp. 113–134). New York: Wiley.

Gunnar, M. R., & Vasquez, D. (2006). Stress neurobiology and developmental psychopathology. In D. Cicchetti & D. Cohen (Eds.), *Developmental psychopathology, Vol. 1: Developmental neuroscience* (2nd ed., pp. 533–577). New York: Wiley.

Han, J. J., Leichtman, M. D., & Wang, Q. (1998). Autobiographical memory in Korean, Chinese, and American children. *Developmental Psychology*, *34*, 701–713.

Harter, S. (1990). Causes, correlates and the functional role of global self-worth: A life-span perspective. In R. J. Sternberg & J. Kolligian, Jr. (Eds.), *Competence considered* (pp. 67–98). New Haven, CT: Yale University Press.

Harter, S. (2006). The self. In W. Damon & R. M. Lerner (Eds.), *Handbook of child psychology, Vol. 3: Social, emotional and personality development* (6th ed., pp. 505–570). New York: Wiley.

Harter, S., Marold, D. B., Whitesell, N. R., & Cobbs, G. (1996). A model of the effects of parent and peer support on adolescent false self behavior. *Child Development*, *67*, 360–374.

Harter, S., & Monsour, A. (1992). Developmental analysis of conflict caused by opposing attributes in the adolescent self-portrait. *Developmental Psychology*, *28*, 251–260.

Harter, S. & Pike, R. (1984). The pictorial scale of perceived competence and social acceptance for young children. *Child Development*, *55*, 1969–1982.

Harwood, R. L., Miller, J. G., & Irizarry, N. L. (1995). *Culture and attachment*. New York: Guilford.

Howe, M. L., & Courage, M. L. (1993). On resolving the enigma of infantile amnesia. *Psychological Bulletin*, *113*, 305–326.

Howe, M. L., & Courage, M. L. (1997). The emergence and early development of autobiographical memory. *Psychological Review*, *104*, 499–523.

Izard, C. E. (1991). *The psychology of emotions*. New York: Plenum.

Izard, C. E., & Ackerman, B. (2000). Motivational, organizational, and regulatory functions of discrete emotions. In M. E. Lewis & J. M. Haviland-Jones (Eds.), *Handbook of emotions* (2nd ed.). New York: Guilford.

Jacobs, J. E., Lanza, S., Osgood, D. W., Eccles, J. S., & Wigfield, A. (2002). Changes in children's self-competence and values: Gender and domain differences across grades one through twelve. *Child Development*, *73*, 509–527.

James, W. (1890). *The principles of psychology*. New York: Henry Holt.

Jones, D. C., Abbey, B. B., & Cumberland, A. (1998). The development of display rule knowledge: Linkages with family expressiveness and social competence. *Child Development*, *69*, 1209–1222.

Kagan, J. (2002). Behavioral inhibition as a temperamental category. In R. J. Davidson, K. R. Scherer, & H. H. Goldsmith (eds.), *Handbook of affective sciences* (pp. 320–331). New York: Oxford University Press.

Kagan, J., & Fox, N. A. (2006). Biology, culture, and temperamental biases. In W. Damon & R. M. Lerner (Eds.), *Handbook of child psychology, Vol. 3: Social, emotional and personality development* (6th ed., pp. 167–225). New York: Wiley.

Kagan, J., Snidman, N., Kahn, V., & Townsley, S. (2007). The preservation of two infant temperaments into adolescence. *Monographs of the Society for Research in Child Development*, *72*, 1–75.

Keily, M. K., Bates, J. E., Dodge, K. A., & Pettit, G. S. (2001). Effects of temperament on the development of externalizing and internalizing behaviors over 9 years. In F. Columbus (Ed.), *Advances in psychology research* (Vol. 6, pp. 255–288). Hauppauge, NY: Nova Science Publishers.

Keller, H. (2007). *Cultures of infancy*. Mahwah, NJ: Lawrence Erlbaum Associates.

Kelley, S. A., & Brownell, C. (2000). Mastery motivation and self-evaluative affect in toddlers: Longitudinal relations with maternal behavior. *Child Development*, *71*, 1061–1071.

Killen, M., Lee-Kim, J., McGlothlin, H., & Stangor, C. (2002). How children and adolescents evaluate gender and racial exclusion. *Monographs of the Society for Research in Child Development*, *67*.

Kochanska, G. (1993). Toward a synthesis of parental socialization and child temperament in early development of conscience. *Child Development*, *64*, 325–347.

Kochanska, G. (1995). Children's temperament, mothers' discipline, and security of attachment: Multiple pathways to emerging internalization. *Child Development*, *66*, 597–615.

Kochanska, G., Aksan, N., Prisco, T. R., & Adams, E. E. (2008). Mother–child and father–child mutually responsive orientation in the first 2 years and children's outcomes at preschool age: Mechanisms of influence. *Child Development*, *79*, 30–44.

Kochanska, G., Philibert, R. A., & Barry, R. A. (2009). Interplay of genes and early mother–child relationship in the development of self-regulation from toddler to preschool age. *Journal of Child Psychology and Psychiatry*, *50*, 1331–1338.

Kopp, C. B., & Wyer, N. (1994). Self-regulation in normal and atypical development. In D. Cicchetti & S. L. Toth (Eds.), *Disorders and dysfunctions of the self. Rochester Symposium on Developmental Psychopathology* (Vol. 5, pp. 31–56). Rochester, NY: University of Rochester Press.

Kroger, J. (1993). Ego identity: An overview. In J. Kroger (Ed.), *Discussions on ego identity* (pp. 3–20). Hillsdale, NJ: Lawrence Erlbaum Associates.

Lagattuta, K., & Thompson, R. A. (2007). The development of self-conscious emotions: Cognitive processes and social influences. In R. W. Robins & J. Tracy (Eds.), *Self-conscious emotions* (2nd ed., pp. 91–113). New York: Guilford.

Lagattuta, K. H., & Wellman, H. M. (2002). Differences in early parent–child conversations about negative versus positive emotions: Implications for the development of emotion understanding. *Developmental Psychology*, *38*, 564–550.

Laible, D. J., & Thompson, R. A. (2007). Early socialization: A relational perspective. In J. Grusec & P. Hastings (Eds.), *Handbook of socialization* (pp. 181–207). New York: Guilford.

Lakatos, K., Nemoda, Z., Birkas, E., Ronai, Z., Kovacs, E., Ney, K., et al. (2003). Association of D4 dopamine receptor gene and serotonin transporter promoter polymorphisms with infants' response to novelty. *Molecular Psychiatry*, *8*, 90–97.

LeDoux, J. E. (2000). Emotion circuits in the brain. *Annual Review of Neuroscience*, *23*, 155–184.

Lewis, M. D. (1997). Personality self-organization: Cascading constraints on cognition–emotion interaction. In A. Fogel, M. C. Lyra & J. Valsiner (Eds.), *Dynamics and indeterminism in developmental and social processes* (pp. 193–216). Mahwah, NJ: Lawrence Erlbaum Associates.

Lewis, M., & Brooks-Gunn, J. (1979). *Social cognition and the acquisition of self*. New York: Plenum.

Lewis, M., & Michalson, L. (1983). *Children's emotions and moods*. New York: Plenum.

Lewis, M. D., & Todd, R. M. (2007). The self-regulating brain: Cortical–subcortical feedback and the development of intelligent action. *Cognitive Development*, *22*, 406–430.

Luby, J. L., & Belden, A. C. (2006). Mood disorders: Phenomenology and a developmental emotional reactivity model. In J. L. Luby (Ed.), *Handbook of preschool mental health* (pp. 209–230). New York: Guilford.

Lutz, C. (1988). *Unnatural emotions: Everyday sentiments on a Micronesian atoll and their challenge to Western theory*. Chicago: University of Chicago Press.

Markus, H., & Nurius, P. (1986). Possible selves. *American Psychologist*, *41*, 954–969.

Marsh, H. W., Ellis, L. A., & Craven, R. G. (2002). How do preschool children feel about themselves? Unraveling measurement and multidimensional self-concept structure. *Developmental Psychology*, *38*, 376–393.

Martin, J. N., & Fox, N. A. (2006). Temperament. In K. McCartney & D. Phillips (Eds.), *Blackwell handbook of early childhood development* (pp. 126–146). Oxford, UK: Blackwell.

Mead, G. H. (1934). *Mind, self, and society*. Chicago: University of Chicago Press.

Measelle, J. R., Ablow, J. C., Cowan, P. A., & Cowan, C. P. (1998). Assessing young children's views of their academic, social, and emotional lives: An evaluation of the self-perception scales of the Berkeley Puppet Interview. *Child Development*, *69*, 1556–1576.

Measelle, J. R., John. O. P., Ablow, J. C., Cowan, P. A., & Cowan, C. P. (2005). Can children provide coherent, stable, and valid self-reports on the Big Five dimensions? A longitudinal study from ages 5 to 7. *Journal of Personality and Social Psychology*, *89*, 90–106.

Meltzoff, A. (2007). "Like me": A foundation for social cognition. *Developmental Science*, *10*, 126–134.

Miller, P. J. (1994). Narrative practices: Their role in socialization and self-construction. In U. Neisser & R. Fivush (Eds.), *The remembering self: Construction and accuracy in the self-narrative* (pp. 158–179). New York: Cambridge University Press.

Moore, C., & Lemmon, K. (2001). *The self in time: Developmental perspectives*. Mahwah, NJ: Lawrence Erlbaum Associates.

Mullen, M. K., & Yi, S. (1995). The cultural context of talk about the past: Implications for the development of autobiographical memory. *Cognitive Development*, *10*, 407–419.

Nachmias, M., Gunnar, M., Mangelsdorf, S., Parritz, R., & Buss, K. (1996). Behavioral inhibition and stress reactivity: The moderating role of attachment security. *Child Development*, *67*, 508–522.

Nelson, K., & Fivush, R. (2004). The emergence of autobiographical memory: A social cultural developmental theory. *Psychological Review*, *111*, 486–511.

Newman, D. L., Caspi, A., Silva, P. A., & Moffitt, T. E. (1997). Antecedents of adult interpersonal functioning: Effects of individual differences in age 3 temperament. *Developmental Psychology*, *33*, 206–217.

Ochsner, K. N., & Gross, J. J. (2007). The neural architecture of emotion regulation. In J. J. Gross (Ed.), *Handbook of emotion regulation* (pp. 87–109). New York: Guilford.

Ontai, L. L., & Thompson, R. A. (2002). Patterns of attachment and maternal discourse effects on children's emotion understanding from 3- to 5-years of age. *Social Development*, *11*, 433–450.

Owens, E. B., & Shaw, D. S. (2003). Predicting growth curves of externalizing behavior across the preschool years. *Journal of Abnormal Child Psychology*, *31*, 575–590.

Panksepp, J. (1998). *Affective neuroscience*. London: Oxford University Press.

Pfeifer, M., Goldsmith, H. H., Davidson, R. J., & Rickman, M. (2002). Continuity and change in inhibited and uninhibited children. *Child Development*, *73*, 1474–1485.

Plomin, R., DeFries, J. C., Craig, I. W., & McGuffin, P. (Eds.) (2003). *Behavioral genetics in the postgenomic era*. Washington, DC: American Psychological Association.

Pollak, S. D. (2008). Mechanisms linking early experience and the emergence of emotions: Illustrations from the study of maltreated children. *Current Directions in Psychological Science*, *17*, 370–375.

Pollak, S. D., & Kistler, D. J. (2002). Early experience is associated with the development of categorical representations for facial expressions of emotion. *Proceedings of the National Academy of Sciences of the United States of America*, *99*, 9072–9076.

Pollak, S. D., Klorman, R., Thatcher, J. E., & Cicchetti, D. (2001). P3b reflects maltreated children's reactions to facial displays of emotion. *Psychophysiology*, *38*, 267–274.

Pomerantz, E. M., Ruble, D. N., Frey, K. S., & Greulich, F. (1995). Meeting goals and confronting conflict: Children's changing perceptions of social comparison. *Child Development*, *66*, 723–738.

Pomerantz, E. M., & Saxon, J. L. (2001). Conceptions of ability as stable and self-evaluative processes: A longitudinal examination. *Child Development*, *72*, 152–173.

Porges, S. W. (2007). The polyvagal perspective. *Biological Psychology*, *74*, 116–143.

Porges, S. W., Doussard-Roosevelt, J. A., & Maiti, A. K. (1994). Vagal tone and the physiological regulation of emotion. In N. A. Fox (Ed.), Emotion regulation: Behavioral and biological considerations. *Monographs of the Society for Research in Child Development*, *59* (Serial no. 240), 167–186.

Porter, C. L., Wouden-Miller, M., Silva, S. S., & Porter, A. E. (2003). Marital harmony and conflict: Linked to infants' emotional regulation and cardiac vagal tone. *Infancy*, *4*, 297–307.

Povinelli, D. J., & Simon, B. B. (1998). Young children's understanding of briefly versus extremely delayed images of self: Emergence of the autobiographical stance. *Developmental Psychology*, *34*, 188–194.

Quintana, S. M. (2007). Racial and ethnic identity: Developmental perspectives and research. *Journal of Counseling Psychology*, *54*, 259–270.

Quintana, S. M. (2008). Racial perspective taking ability: Developmental, theoretical, and empirical trends. In S. M. Quintana and C. McKown (Eds.), *Handbook of race, racism, and the developing child* (pp. 16–36). New York: Wiley.

Quirk, G. J. (2007). Prefrontal–amygdala interactions in the regulation of fear. In J. J. Gross (Ed.), *Handbook of emotion regulation* (pp. 27–46). New York: Guilford.

Reese, E. (2002). Social factors in the development of autobiographical memory: The state of the art. *Social Development*, *11*, 124–142.

Repacholi, B., & Gopnik, A. (1997). Early reasoning about desires: Evidence from 14- and 18-month-olds. *Developmental Psychology*, *33*, 12–21.

Rochat, P., & Striano, T. (2002). Who's in the mirror? Self–other discrimination in specular images by four- and nine-month-old infants. *Child Development*, *73*, 35–46.

Rogoff, B. (2003). *The cultural nature of human development*. New York: Oxford University Press.

Rothbart, M. K. (2007). Temperament, development, and personality. *Current Directions in Psychological Science*, *16*, 207–212.

Rothbart, M. K., & Bates, J. E. (2006). Temperament. In W. Damon & R. M. Lerner (Eds.), *Handbook of child psychology, Vol. 3: Social, emotional and personality development* (6th ed., pp. 99–166). New York: Wiley.

Rothbart, M. K., Ellis, L. K., & Posner, M. I. (2004). Temperament and self-regulation. In R. F. Baumeister & K. D. Vohs (Eds.), *Handbook of self-regulation* (pp. 357–370). New York: Guilford.

Rothbart, M. K., & Goldsmith, H. H. (1985). Three approaches to the study of infant temperament. *Developmental Review*, *5*, 237–260.

Rothbart, M. K., Posner, M. I., & Kieras, J. (2006). Temperament, attention, and the development of self-regulation. In K. McCartney & D. Phillips (Eds.), *The Blackwell handbook of early childhood development* (pp. 328–357). London: Blackwell.

Rothbaum, F., Weisz, J., Pott, M., Miyake, K., & Morelli, G. (2000). Attachment and culture: Security in the United States and Japan. *American Psychologist*, *55*, 1093–1104.

Ruble, D. N., Martin, D. L., & Berenbaum, S. A. (2006). Gender development. In W. Damon & R. M. Lerner (Eds.), *Handbook of child psychology, Vol. 3: Social, emotional and personality development* (6th ed., pp. 858–932). New York: Wiley.

Saarni, C. (1999). *The development of emotional competence*. New York: Guilford.

Saarni, C., Campos, J. J., Camras, L., & Witherington, D. (2006). Emotional development: Action, communication, and understanding. In W. Damon & R. M. Lerner (Eds.), *Handbook of child psychology, Vol. 3: Social, emotional and personality development* (6th ed., pp. 226–299). New York: Wiley.

Sagi, A., & Hoffman, M. L. (1976). Empathic distress in the newborn. *Developmental Psychology*, *12*, 175–176.

Scarr, S., & McCartney, K. (1983). How people make their own environments: A theory of genotype–environment effects. *Child Development*, *54*, 424–435.

Schwartz, C., Wright, C., Shin, L., Kagan, J., & Rauch, S. (2003). Inhibited and uninhibited infants "grown up": Adult amygdalar response to novelty. *Science*, *300*, 1952–1953.

Shaw, D. S., Miles, G., Ingoldsby, E. M., & Nagin, D. S. (2003). Trajectories leading to school-age conduct problems. *Developmental Psychology*, *39*, 189–200.

Sheese, B. E., Voelker, P. M., Rothbart, M. K., & Posner, M. I. (2007). Parenting quality interacts with genetic variation in dopamine receptor D4 to influence temperament in early childhood. *Development and Psychopathology*, *19*, 1039–1046.

Shiner, R., & Caspi, A. (2003). Personality differences in childhood and adolescent: Measurement, development, and consequences. *Journal of Child Psychology and Psychiatry*, *44*, 2–32.

Shipman, K. L., & Zeman, J. (2001). Socialization of children's emotion regulation in mother–child dyads: A developmental psychopathology perspective. *Development and Psychopathology*, *13*, 317–336.

Snyder, M. (1987). *Public appearances, private realities: The psychology of self-monitoring*. New York: Freeman.

Spinrad, T. L., Stifter, C. A., Donelan-McCall, N., & Turner, L. (2004). Mothers' regulation strategies in response to toddlers' affect: Links to later emotion self-regulation. *Social Development*, *13*, 40–55.

Sroufe, L. A. (1996). *Emotional development*. New York: Cambridge University Press.

Stern, D. N. (1985). *The interpersonal world of the infant*. New York: Basic Books.

Stipek, D. (1984). Young children's performance expectations: Logical analysis or wishful thinking? In J. Nicholls (Ed), *The development of achievement motivation* (pp. 33–56). Greenwich, CT: JAI Press.

Stipek, D. (1995). The development of pride and shame in toddlers. In J. P. Tangney & K. W. Fischer (Eds.), *Self-conscious emotions* (pp. 237–252). New York: Guilford.

Stipek, D., Gralinski, J. H., & Kopp, C. B. (1990). Self-concept development in the toddler years. *Developmental Psychology*, *26*, 972–977.

Sturge-Apple, M. L., Davies, P. T., Winter, M. A., Cummings, E. M., & Schermerhorn, A. (2008). Interparental conflict and children's school adjustment: The explanatory role of children's internal representations of interparental and parent–child relationships. *Developmental Psychology*, *44*, 1678–1690.

Thomas, A., & Chess, S. (1977). *Temperament and development*. New York: Brunner/Mazel.

Thomas, A., Chess, S., & Birch, H. G. (1968). *Temperament and behavior disorders in children*. New York: New York University Press.

Thompson, R. A. (1988). Early development in life-span perspective. In P. B. Baltes, D. L. Featherman, & R. M. Lerner (Eds.), *Life-span development and behavior*, Vol. 9 (pp. 129–172). Hillsdale, NJ: Lawrence Erlbaum Associates.

Thompson, R. A. (1989). Causal attributions and children's emotional understanding. In C. Saarni & P. Harris (Eds.), *Children's understanding of emotion* (pp. 117–150). New York: Cambridge University Press.

Thompson, R. A. (1990). Emotion and self-regulation. In R. A. Thompson (Ed.), *Socioemotional development. Nebraska Symposium on Motivation* (Vol. 36, pp. 367–469). Lincoln, NE: University of Nebraska Press.

Thompson, R. A. (1994). Emotion regulation: A theme in search of definition. In N. A. Fox (Ed.), The development of emotion regulation and dysregulation: Biological and behavioral aspects. *Monographs of the Society for Research in Child Development*, *59*, 25–52.

Thompson, R. A. (1998). Empathy and its origins in early development. In S. Braten (Ed.), *Intersubjective communication and emotion in early ontogeny* (pp. 144–157). New York: Cambridge University Press.

Thompson, R. A. (2000). Childhood anxiety disorders from the perspective of emotion regulation and attachment. In M. W. Vasey & M. R. Dadds (Eds.), *The developmental psychopathology of anxiety* (pp. 160–182). Oxford, UK: Oxford University Press.

Thompson, R. A. (2006a). The development of the person: Social understanding, relationships, conscience, self. In W. Damon & R. M. Lerner (Eds.), *Handbook of child psychology, Vol. 3: Social, emotional and personality development* (6th ed., pp. 24–98). New York: Wiley.

Thompson, R. A. (2006b). Conversation and developing understanding: Introduction to the special issue. *Merrill-Palmer Quarterly*, *52*(1), 1–16.

Thompson, R. A. (2008). Early attachment and later development: Familiar questions, new answers. In J. Cassidy & P. R. Shaver (Eds.), *Handbook of attachment* (2nd ed., pp. 348–365). New York: Guilford.

Thompson, R. A., & Calkins, S. (1996). The double-edged sword: Emotional regulation for children at risk. *Development and Psychopathology*, *8*, 163–182.

Thompson, R. A., Flood, M. F., & Goodvin, R. (2006). Social support and developmental psychopathology. In D. Cicchetti & D. Cohen (Eds.), *Developmental psychopathology, Vol. III: Risk, disorder, and adaptation* (2nd ed., pp. 1–37). New York: Wiley.

Thompson, R. A., & Goodman, M. (2010). Development of emotion regulation: More than meets the eye. In A. Kring & D. Sloan (Eds.), *Emotion regulation and psychopathology* (pp. 38–58). New York: Guilford Press.

Thompson, R. A., & Lagattuta, K. (2006). Feeling and understanding: Early emotional development. In K. McCartney & D. Phillips (Eds.), *The Blackwell handbook of early childhood development* (pp. 317–337). Oxford, UK: Blackwell.

Thompson, R. A., Laible, D. J., & Ontai, L. L. (2003). Early understanding of emotion, morality, and the self: Developing a working model. In R. V. Kail (Ed.), *Advances in child development and behavior* (Vol. 31, pp. 137–171). San Diego, CA: Academic.

Thompson, R. A., Lewis, M., & Calkins, S. D. (2008). Reassessing emotion regulation. *Child Development Perspectives*, 2(3), 124–131.

Thompson, R. A., & Limber, S. (1990). "Social anxiety" in infancy: Stranger wariness and separation distress. In H. Leitenberg (Ed.), *Handbook of social and evaluation anxiety* (pp. 85–137). New York: Plenum.

Thompson, R. A. & Meyer, S. (2007). The socialization of emotion regulation in the family. In J. Gross (Ed.), *Handbook of emotion regulation* (pp. 249–268). New York: Guilford.

Thompson, R. A., Meyer, S., & McGinley, M. (2006). Understanding values in relationship: The development of conscience. In M. Killen & J. Smetana (Eds.), *Handbook of moral development* (pp. 267–297). Mahwah, NJ: Lawrence Erlbaum Associates.

Thompson, R. A. & Virmani, E. A. (2009). Self and personality. In M. H. Bornstein (Ed.), *Handbook of cultural developmental science* (pp. 175–187). Mahwah, NJ: Lawrence Erlbaum Associates.

Tomasello, M., & Rakoczy, H. (2003). What makes human cognition unique? From individual to shared to collective intentionality. *Mind & Language*, 18, 121–147.

Wachs, T. D. (1992). *The nature of nurture*. Newbury Park, CA: Sage.

Wachs, T. D., & Gandour, M. J. (1983). Temperament, environment, and six-month cognitive–intellectual development: A test of the organismic specificity hypothesis. *International Journal of Behavioral Development*, 6, 135–152.

Wang, Q. (2004). The emergence of cultural self-constructs: Autobiographical memory and self-description in European American and Chinese Children. *Developmental Psychology*, 40, 3–15.

Wang, Q., and Fivush, R. (2005). Mother–child conversations of emotionally salient events: Exploring the functions of emotional reminiscing in European-American and Chinese families. *Social Development*, 14, 473–495.

Wang, Q., Leichtman, M., and Davies, K. (2000). Sharing memories and telling stories: American and Chinese mothers and their 3-year-olds. *Memory*, 8, 159–178.

Welch-Ross, M. K. (1995). An integrative model of the development of autobiographical memory. *Developmental Review*, 15, 338–365.

Welch-Ross, M. K., Fasig, L. G., & Farrar, M. J. (1999). Predictors of preschoolers' self-knowledge: Reference to emotion and mental states in mother–child conversation about past events. *Cognitive Development*, 14, 401–422.

Wellman, H. M. (2002). Understanding the psychological world: Developing a theory of mind. In U. Goswami (Ed.), *Blackwell handbook of childhood cognitive development* (pp. 167–187). Oxford, UK: Blackwell.

Wigfield, A., Eccles, J. S., Schiefele, U., Roeser, R. W., & Davis-Kean, P. (2006). Development of achievement motivation. In W. Damon & R. M. Lerner (Eds.), *Handbook of child psychology, Vol. 3: Social, emotional and personality development* (6th ed., pp. 933–1002). New York: Wiley.

Wiik, K. L., & Gunnar, M. R. (2009). Development and social regulation of stress neurobiology in human development: Implications for the study of traumatic memories. In J. Quas & R. Fivush (Eds.), *Stress and memory development: Biological, social and emotional considerations* (pp. 256–277). New York: Oxford University Press.

Wiley, A. R., Rose, A. J., Burger, L. K., & Miller, P. J. (1998). Constructing autonomous selves through narrative practices: A comparative study of working-class and middle class families. *Child Development*, 69, 833–847.

Zahn-Waxler, C. (2000). The development of empathy, guilt, and internalization of distress: Implications for gender differences in internalizing and externalizing problems. In R. J. Davidson (Ed.), *Anxiety, depression, and emotion* (pp. 222–265). New York: Oxford University Press.

Zahn-Waxler, C., & Radke-Yarrow, M. (1990). The origins of empathic concern. *Motivation and Emotion*, 14, 107–130.

Zhou, M. (1997). Growing up American: The challenge confronting immigrant children and children of immigrants. *Annual Review of Sociology*, 23, 63–95.

10

THE ROLE OF PARENT–CHILD RELATIONSHIPS IN CHILD DEVELOPMENT

Michael E. Lamb
Cambridge University
Charlie Lewis
Lancaster University

INTRODUCTION

Within accounts of personality development and **socialization** over the past century, the central role of parent–child relationships has been emphasized with great consistency. Freud's (e.g., 1940) emphasis on the importance of early parent–child relationships and his conclusion that children's experiences in early life can have lasting influences on later life have been especially influential, with a focus on the infant–mother relationship especially prominent in his later work. In many respects, these concerns resonated in the theoretical debates that characterized the second half of the twentieth century. During this period, many scholars switched their allegiance from psychoanalytic theory to a perspective based on **attachment theory**, which itself reflected the integration of psychoanalytic, cybernetic, and ethological theory and therefore nicely exemplified the forces that have helped shape the emergence of developmental science. Within the broader debate between perspectives inspired by psycho-analysis and learning theory, which stressed the primacy of observable patterns of interaction (for a history, see Maccoby, 1992), attachment theory has become the dominant perspective on parent–child relationships, in part because it has accommodated the emerging cognitivist paradigm (the assumption that psychology should focus on mental processes) that has become popular (Carpendale & Lewis, 2006).

The concept of attachment is essentially relational, however, and thus contrasts with con-temporary drives to locate human cognition solely within the individual (Overton, 2006). The theory holds that attachments develop out of interactions within dynamic relationships, with individuals' experiences of different relationships making up their grasp of the social world. Three related issues have also drawn increasing attention from developmental psychologists over the past 40 years or so. First, there has been increasing sensitivity to claims that the family is a system in which children influence their parents (Bell, 1968; Danziger, 1971; Lewis & Rosenblum, 1974) as much as parents "socialize" children, and that each part of the system must be understood with reference to the other parts. This has become a dominant theme in contemporary research (McHale, 2007).

Secondly, it has long been recognized that parenting and child development do not take place in a social vacuum. Parents and children interact within a complex system of influences that extend far beyond the household. For example, many infants in industrialized countries spend time in day care from a much earlier age than they did 20 years ago (Lamb & Ahnert, 2006). A few bold researchers, following Bronfenbrenner's (1979) exhortations, have even attempted to view the family in the context of a network of social relationships extending from the child's immediate relationships (such as those with care providers) into communities and the culture at large (e.g., Lamb, 1999b; Pence, 1988).

Thirdly, researchers have made extensive efforts recently to identify the role of **behavior genetics** in understanding parent–child relationships and their effects. Although it emerged in the 1930s, the behavioral genetics approach has become increasingly visible over the past quarter century (Plomin, DeFries, McClearn, & McGuffin, 2000). Researchers in this tradition use comparisons between monozygotic and dizygotic twins or between adopted and non-adopted children to distinguish genetic influences from the effects of both shared and non-shared environmental factors. In childhood, attention has been focused on behavior problems (Moffitt, 2005), especially aggression, and personality development, with researchers such as Deater-Deckard (2000) suggesting that parental responsiveness and affective engagement between parents and children have a genetic component. Such findings and arguments make a compelling case for taking account of the complexities of formative interactions between genes and environmental factors. In a longitudinal study, for example, O'Connor, Neiderhiser, Reiss, Hetherington, and Plomin (1998) compared adoptees at genetic risk for antisocial behavior because their biological mothers had such histories with those not obviously at risk. The researchers found that children at risk for antisocial behavior were treated more negatively by their adoptive parents and that the levels of parental negativity were correlated with the children's levels of behavior problems, even when the children's genetic predispositions were taken into account.

Such provocative findings ensure that the behavior genetics approach to the study of individual differences will remain prominent among researchers, especially because recent analyses assume no incompatibility with the traditional psychological perspectives that still predominate (see Collins, Maccoby, Steinberg, Hetherington, & Bornstein, 2000, for a discussion). At the same time, the literature on parenting has always had its dissenters. Over the past decade, for example, Judith Harris' (1995, 1998) "group socialization" theory has forced us to reconsider the influence of parents on their children's development, by arguing that the peer group has a dominant role. Current analyses continue to reflect on whether and how child care experiences influence children's psychosocial development (Belsky et al., 2007) and are more receptive to the idea that there is great plasticity in the genetic factors that channel development (Belsky, 1997; Belsky & Pluess, 2009).

Partly as a result of the these conceptual developments, the past 20 years has witnessed an explosion of research on the effects of parenting, taking account of some of the complexities of development. No contemporary account of parenting can easily isolate substantial formative associations between individual "determinants" and outcomes:

> In current socialization studies, simple first-order correlations between parenting characteristics and child outcomes are seldom relied on. Indeed, sometimes they are not even reported. Instead, multivariate analyses are used to investigate such questions as whether a given aspect of parenting has different effects on different kinds of children or in families living in different circumstances; or whether different aspects of parenting have independent, additive effects, whether they are interchangeable, or whether they interact so that the effects of one depend on the level of another. (Maccoby, 2000, pp. 6–7)

The analyses hinted at use of mediational analyses within longitudinal research so that the effects of different potential factors can be seen to influence jointly the developmental process (see, e.g., Criss, Shaw, Moilanen, Hitchings, & Ingoldsby, 2009). These new statistical approaches that have been made accessible to psychologists include multilevel (O'Connor, Dunn, Jenkins & Rashbash, 2006), structural equation (e.g., Schudlich & Cummings, 2007), and hierarchical modeling (e.g., Elgar, Mills, McGrath, Waschbusch, & Brownridge, 2007) techniques. These procedures, in turn, allow ever more complex models to be formulated, often (quite wrongly) led by the data rather than by good psychological theory.

Because so many diverse factors shape contemporary research on parenting, it is difficult to summarize what we know about parents' influences on their children's development. It is often noted that there is no "unifying theory" of parenting (e.g., O'Connor, 2002), as if such a theory were possible! Indeed, the diversity of extant perspectives either reflects the complex nature of parenting and its influences on child development or indicates that the field is still in its infancy and has yet to develop a fully fledged and comprehensive theory, as O'Connor suggests. Our task in this chapter is to summarize the major themes that animate and motivate current and future work, recognizing at the outset that psychoanalytic theorizing has clearly influenced current research, theory, and clinical practice, and has helped promote and preserve the multidisciplinary scholarship and research that has been so influential. We begin by examining current portrayals of parent–infant relationships, using attachment theory as a secure base from which to incorporate complementary perspectives. Thereafter, we turn to relationships between preschool-age, elementary school-age, and adolescent children and their parents, discussing the mechanisms by which these relationships are gradually transformed in the course of development. One major message here is that parenting is a dynamic construct—parents relate to babies in fundamentally different ways than parents relate to adolescents—and that such changes in parenting must be mapped. Systemic factors are emphasized throughout by comparing the parenting styles and influences of mothers and fathers. This allows us only to hint at the complexity of the family system—a fuller account would consider, in addition, the influences of siblings, grandparents, and care providers, but this is beyond the scope of our chapter.

A final section of the chapter examines the broader societal factors that affect the adequacy or quality of the relationships between parents and their children, and their impact on child development. In this context, we discuss the possible impact of parent and child gender, sociocultural and socioeconomic variations, divorce and single parenthood, and family violence.

ATTACHMENT THEORY: A FRAMEWORK FOR UNDERSTANDING PARENT–INFANT RELATIONSHIPS

All major theories of emotional development have discussed the development of attachments, but the most influential explanation was provided by John Bowlby (1969), a psychoanalyst who was impressed by ethological theories regarding the early emotional communication between infants and their parents. Bowlby's attachment theory emphasized the way that the infant's innate capacity to emit signals to which adults are biologically predisposed to respond fostered the development of attachments.

Bowlby's theory built on the assumption that the behavioral propensities of infants and parents must be considered in the context of the environment in which our species evolved. In that "environment of evolutionary adaptedness," the survival of infants depended on their ability to maintain proximity to protective adults. Unlike many other species, however, young humans are unable to move closer to or follow adults for several months; they are even incapable of clinging to adults to maintain contact. Human infants must instead rely on signals to entice adults to approach them. For these signals to be effective, adults must be predisposed to respond. The best example of such a *prepotent* signal is the infant cry, which is very effective in attracting adults to approach, pick up, and soothe the crying infant.

Bowlby (1969) described four phases in the development of parent–infant attachments:

1. the newborn phase of indiscriminate social responsiveness (the first one or two months)
2. the phase of discriminating sociability (the second to the seventh months)
3. "maintenance of proximity to a discriminated figure by means of locomotion as well as signals" (from the seventh month through the second year)
4. the phase of goal-corrected partnership (the third year on).

Phase 1: Indiscriminate Social Responsiveness of Newborns (Birth through One or Two Months)

This phase is marked by the development of a repertoire of signals by the infant. Infant cries have a markedly arousing effect on those who hear them: Typically, adults are motivated to relieve the cause of the baby's distress via physiological mechanisms that have long been recognized (e.g., Frodi et al., 1978; Murray, 1979). The most common response to crying is to pick up the infant (Bell & Ainsworth, 1972), and the most effective way of quieting a distressed infant is to hold him or her (Korner & Thoman, 1970, 1972). This illustrates Bowlby's assumption that both infants and adults have biologically determined behavioral predispositions that serve to maximize the infant's chances of survival. Crying is the first example of a class of behaviors labeled *attachment behaviors* by Bowlby. The defining or common characteristic of these behaviors is that they all serve to bring the baby close to protective and caring adults. In the early months, this goal is achieved by getting adults to approach the infant, but responsibility later shifts.

A second potent attachment behavior enters the baby's repertoire in the second month of life—smiling. Like crying, smiling is a signal that affects adults' behavior. However, smiles are effective because they encourage adults to *stay near* and continue interacting with the baby— both find the interaction *pleasant*—whereas cries encourage adults to *approach* the baby in order to terminate a signal that they find *aversive* (Ambrose, 1961; Frodi, Lamb, Leavitt, & Donovan, 1978a).

From birth, therefore, the baby is capable of affecting his or her environment and the people in it, although babies use proximity-promoting signals indiscriminately in this phase. They are satisfied with anyone who responds to their smiles, cries, and other signals, and they do not yet show any preferences for particular people. This is not surprising, because babies do not yet have the capacity to discriminate among or recognize individuals. Toward the end of this phase, the relevant perceptual and cognitive capacities develop, and babies start to recognize people in varied contexts, preferring those with whom they have most consistent interaction. This defines the transition to the second phase of attachment development.

Phase 2: Discriminating Sociability (One or Two Months through Six or Seven Months)

Although Bowlby (1969) suggested that the second phase began in the second or third month of life, infants are able to discriminate visually among people much earlier than this using auditory, visual, olfactory, and kinesthetic cues (Lamb, Bornstein, & Teti, 2002). Very young infants recognize their mothers' faces and also identify them by voice or smell but, of course, this does not imply that they realize that these are different characteristics of the same person (Bushnell, Sai & Mullin, 1989; Field, Cohen, Garcia, & Greenberg, 1984). We do not know when infants develop multimodal concepts of people and thus realize that when they hear their mothers' voices, for example, they will see their mothers' faces if they open their eyes.

Once babies can recognize familiar people, they can start to exhibit preferences among them. Presumably because infants associate particular people with pleasurable experiences (e.g., feeding, cuddling, rocking, play) and the relief of distress from early on, or because familiarity (other things being equal) tends to produce positive feelings, babies soon prefer to interact with familiar people.

During this phase of development, babies are far more coordinated behaviorally than they were earlier. Their arousal level is much less variable, and they spend more time in alert states (Emde & Robinson, 1979). Parent–infant play becomes more frequent, and in many Western cultures face-to-face games become sources of delight for both adults and infants. In early interactions of this sort, the adult assumes major responsibility for keeping the interaction going; the baby coos, smiles, or sticks out his or her tongue and the adult responds with a similar action (Kaye & Marcus, 1981). From repeated experiences of this type, however, the baby seems to learn three things: the rule of *reciprocity* (namely, that in social interaction, partners take turns acting and reacting to the other's behavior); *effectance* (his or her behavior can affect the behavior of others in a consistent and predictable fashion) and *trust* (the caretaker can be counted on to respond when signaled). These concepts are learned not only in the course of face-to-face interactions but also in the interactions centered on infant distress and adults' attempts to soothe them (Lamb, 1981a, 1981b), and their acquisition is a major step in the process of becoming social. Once infants realize that their cries (and later their smiles and coos) elicit predictable responses from others, they begin to develop a coherent view of the social world and perceive themselves as individuals who can significantly affect others. The degree to which babies feel confident of their predictions regarding the behavior of others—that is, their degree of trust or faith in the reliability of specific people—determines the security of their attachment relationships. Obviously, individual differences in the level of trust or perceived effectance each infant develops depend in part on individual differences in the responsiveness of the adults with whom the baby interacts (see below).

Phase 3: Attachments—Specific, Enduring, Affective Bonds (Seven to Twenty-Four Months)

By seven months of age, infants clearly understand and respect the rule of reciprocity in their interactions. Intentional social behavior is also possible. The beginning of Phase 3 is marked by two major behavioral changes. First, the baby now starts to protest (by crying) when left by one of the people to whom he or she is attached—*separation protest*—which signifies the baby's concern about the departure and present whereabouts of an attachment figure. Second, the baby is now able to move from place to place without assistance and this opens up a wealth of opportunities for exploration and allows the infant to assume an increasingly active role in achieving and maintaining proximity to attachment figures. Ainsworth, Blehar, Waters, and Wall (1978) label this as *the* attachment phase, because the proximity of the parent becomes a key concern and the quality of the infant's interactions plays a crucial role in the construction of self (Bowlby, 1969)—a topic discussed below, as well as by Thompson and Goodvin in Chapter 9 of this volume.

Phase 4: Goal-Correlated Partnerships (Twenty-Four to Thirty Months Onward)

For Bowlby (1969), the next major transition occurs at the beginning of the third year of life, although infants become increasingly sophisticated in their abilities to behave intentionally, communicate linguistically, and respond appropriately in a variety of different contexts in the intervening months. As they grow older, children initiate more of their interactions and are therefore respondents in proportionately fewer of them. They can tolerate increasing distance from attachment figures, and become increasingly adept at interacting with peers and unfamiliar adults. For Bowlby, the major qualitative transformation involves the capacity for elementary role taking and the ability to take the parents' needs into account when interacting with them.

Measuring Attachment Relationships

As explained earlier, infants come to trust or count on the adults who respond consistently to their signals; in Bowlby's terminology, differences in the adults' responsiveness shape the child's *internal working models* of them. Not all adults are equivalently responsive or sensitive, however, and so infants should differ with respect to the amount of trust they feel, and thus the way they behave. To explore this question, Ainsworth developed a procedure—the Strange Situation—for assessing the *security of infant–adult attachment* (Ainsworth et al., 1978). The procedure has seven episodes, designed to expose infants to increasing levels of stress in order to observe how they organize their attachment behaviors around their parents when distressed by being in an unfamiliar environment, the entrance of an unfamiliar adult, and brief separations from the parent (Table 10.1).

According to attachment theory, infants should be able to use attachment figures as secure bases from which to explore the novel environment. The stranger's entrance should lead infants to inhibit exploration and draw a little closer to their parents, at least temporarily. In response to their parents' departure, infants should attempt to bring them back by crying or searching, and by limiting exploration and affiliation. Following their parents' return, infants should seek to reengage in interaction and, if distressed, perhaps ask to be cuddled and comforted. The same responses should occur, with somewhat greater intensity, following the second separation and reunion. In fact, this is precisely how about 65% of the infants studied in the United States behave in the Strange Situation (Teti & Teti, 1996; Thompson, 1998). Following the practices of Ainsworth and her colleagues, these infants are regarded as securely attached (they are also called Type B) because their behavior conforms to theoretical predictions about how babies should behave in relation to attachment figures.

By contrast, some infants seem unable to use their parents as secure bases from which to explore, and they are called insecure. Some are distressed by their parents' absence, and behave ambivalently on reunion, both seeking contact and interaction and angrily rejecting it when it is offered. These infants are conventionally labeled insecure–resistant or ambivalent (Type C). They typically account for about 15% of the infants in American research samples (Teti & Teti, 1996; Thompson, 1998). A third group of infants seem little concerned by their parents' absence. Instead of greeting their parents on reunion, they actively avoid interaction and ignore their parents' bids. These infants are said to exhibit insecure–avoidant attachments (Type A), and they typically constitute about 20% of the infants in American samples (Teti &

TABLE 10.1
The Strange Situation Procedure

Episode	Persons Present	Entrances and Exits
1	Parent and child	
2	Parent, stranger, and child	Stranger enters
3	Stranger and child	Parent departs
4	Parent and child	Stranger departs
5	Child	Parent departs
6	Stranger and child	Stranger enters
7	Parent and child	Parent enters; stranger departs

Teti, 1996; Thompson, 1998). Main and her colleagues have also described a fourth group of infants whose behavior is "disoriented" and/or "disorganized" (Type D; Main & Solomon, 1990). These infants simultaneously display contradictory behavior patterns, manifest incomplete or undirected movements, and appear confused or apprehensive about approaching their parents. These infants may be similar in some respects to infants in all three of the other groups, although they tend to be overrepresented in the insecure sub-groups.

Attachment theorists have emphasized the role played by prior infant–mother interactions in shaping these patterns of behavior, which are believed to reflect internal working models shaped by those earlier interactions. There is general support for the notion that sensitive or responsive parenting—that is, nurturant, attentive, nonrestrictive parental care—and synchronous infant–mother interactions are associated with secure infant behavior in the Strange Situation, and this appears to be true of US-based samples as well as samples from cultures outside the United States (De Wolff & van IJzendoorn, 1997; Posada et al., 1999; Thompson, 1998). The mothers of infants who behave in either insecure–avoidant or insecure–resistant fashions manifest less socially desirable patterns of behavior: They may overstimulate or understimulate, fail to make their behaviors contingent on infant behavior, appear cold or rejecting, and sometimes act ineptly. Similar proportions of infants fall into the major categories when assessed interacting with their fathers (Lamb & Lewis, 2010).

Because there is much variability in these results, it is difficult to identify precisely what aspects of parental behavior are important. Some studies identify warmth but not sensitivity, some patterning of stimulation but not warmth or amount of stimulation, and so forth. There is a general belief, however, that insecure–avoidant attachments are associated with intrusive, overstimulating, rejecting parenting, whereas insecure–resistant attachments are linked to inconsistent, unresponsive parenting (Belsky, 1999; De Wolff & van IJzendoorn, 1997). Certainly, programs that make parents more sensitive to their infants do increase the likelihood that those infants will be securely attached (Bakermans-Kranenburg, van IJzendoorn & Juffer, 2003). Although the antecedents of disorganized attachments are less well established, disorganized attachments are more common among abused and maltreated infants and among infants exposed to other pathological caretaking environments (Lyons-Ruth & Jacobvitz, 1999; Teti, Gelfand, Messinger, & Isabella, 1995; for a meta-analysis, see Baer & Martinez, 2006) and may be consequences of parental behaviors that infants find frightening or disturbing (Main & Hesse, 1990; Schuengel, Bakermans-Kranenburg, van IJzendoorn, & Blom, 1999).

To Whom Do Attachments Form?

According to Bowlby, the consistency of an adult's presence and availability during a sensitive period—the first six postnatal months—determines whom the baby will become attached to. If there were no consistent caretaker over this period (as might occur in institutions such as hospitals, for example), the baby would not form an attachment. Ainsworth and Bowlby proposed that most babies have a hierarchy of attachment figures and that their primary caretakers—usually their mothers—become primary attachment figures before any other relationships are formed (Bretherton & Munholland, 1999). Once infants have this foundation, Ainsworth and Bowlby argued, the infants may (and often do) form relationships with others—for example, fathers and older siblings. Obviously, these individuals must regularly spend some minimum amount of time with infants if attachments are to form, but unfortunately we do not know what this minimum level is.

Adult–infant interaction is also important in determining whether infant–adult attachments will form, because infants become attached to those persons whom they associate, over time, with consistent, predictable, and appropriate responses to their signals and needs. The importance of quality of interaction rather than quantity is underscored by the evidence that babies become attached to both of their parents even though most continue to spend much less time with their fathers than with their mothers (Lamb, 2002a; Lamb & Lewis, 2010). In stress-free situations such as the home, babies show no consistent preference for one parent. When stress occurs—whether occasioned by fatigue, the threat or reality of separation, or the entry of a stranger—proximity-seeking attachment behaviors increase and are directed toward whichever parent is with the baby. Research in the 1970s suggested that even with little contact between fathers and their babies, infants become attached to their fathers, although when both parents were present, babies between the ages of 10 and 18 months typically turned to their mothers preferentially when distressed (Lamb, 1976a, 1976c). Such findings confirm that mothers tend to be the primary attachment figures of young infants, and that infants nevertheless become attached to their fathers and mothers at about the same time, contrary to Bowlby's prediction.

Research suggests that even with little contact between fathers and their babies, infants become attached to their fathers.

In many cultures, including the USA and the UK, mothers and fathers interact with babies in distinctly different ways. A detailed analysis of videotaped records of face-to-face play between parents and very young infants (two- to six-month-olds) showed that fathers provided more unpredictable, less rhythmic, and less containing stimulation (both physical and vocal) than mothers did (Yogman, 1981). Naturalistic home observations of older infants and their parents yielded similar findings (Lamb, 1976b). For example, triadic interactions between parents and their 11–15-month-olds showed that mothers seemed set on maintaining the interaction, while fathers show more positive affect (Lindsey & Caldera, 2006). Similarly, Borke, Lamm, Eickhorst and Keller (2007) found that German fathers tended to engage in a more "distal" style of interaction whereas mothers were more proximal (i.e., they used bodily contact).

Fathers are also more likely to engage in physically stimulating or unpredictable types of play than are mothers (Lamb, 1976b, 1977a), while mothers are more likely to initiate games like pat-a-cake and peek-a-boo, or to engage in bouts of play mediated by toys. Importantly, these differences in the types of play are not evident in all social and cultural contexts (Lamb, 1977b, 2002a), suggesting that they reflect social aspects of the parents' roles, rather than intrinsic or biological factors.

Level of Contact, Sensitivity and Attachments

The evidence suggests that, across a variety of cultural settings, about two-thirds of the attachments to either parent are rated secure (e.g., Ahnert, Pinquart & Lamb, 2006; Diener, Mangelsdorf, McHale, & Frosch, 2002; Lamb, Hwang, Frodi, & Frodi, 1982). Most studies, such as that of Monteiro et al. (in press) using an attachment Q-sorting technique, show few differences in the average levels of infant–mother and infant–father security. Yet even today mothers and fathers often spend very different amounts of time with their infants (Korman & Lewis, 2001; Lewis, 1986). This raises an interesting question: How much contact is required to establish a secure attachment and what it is about that contact that is important, particularly given the recent shift towards greater paternal involvement (O'Brien, 2005; Pleck & Masciadrelli, 2004)?

How infants form secure, insecure, and disorganized relationships with their attachment figures has been central to discussion of attachments since the development of the theory. Much emphasis has been placed on the role of **parental sensitivity** (see, e.g., Ainsworth et al., 1978), although others have used terms such as "affect attunement" (Jonsson & Clinton, 2006; Stern, Hofer, Haft, & Dore, 1985), "affect mirroring" (Fonagy, Gergely, Jurist, & Target, 2002), responsiveness (Bornstein, Tamis-LeMonda, Hahn, & Haynes, 2008), and "mutual responsivity" (Kochanska, Aksan, Prisco, & Adams, 2008). In a recent study, Barry, Kochanska, and Philibert (2008) reported that children with a genetic risk for maladaptive development (a short allele in the 5-HTTLPR polymorphism linked to serotonin uptake) had insecure attachments at 15 months if their mothers had been less sensitive, but secure attachments if mothers had earlier been more sensitive. Such results complement other findings showing that the responsivity of parents to their infants' distress at six months predicts both social competence and behavior problems two and a half years later (Leerkes, Blankson, & O'Brien, 2009). We must avoid assuming that the direction of influence simply runs from parent to child (Papousek, 2007), however; each participant affects the other. For example, Pauli-Pott and Mertesacker (2009) found that highly positive maternal affect accompanied by positive affect in the infant at 4 months of age predicted secure relationships in the Strange Situation at 18 months, but when accompanied by negative or neutral infant affect, positive maternal affect predicted later insecure attachment.

As far as fathers are concerned, it seems reasonable to assume that individual differences in paternal sensitivity influence the security of infant–father attachment just as individual differences in maternal sensitivity influence the security of infant–mother attachment (see above). Notaro and Volling (1999), however, found no significant associations between assessments of American mother– and father–infant attachment in the Strange Situation, and near contemporaneous measures of parental responsiveness in a brief (3-minute) session. These findings were consistent with an earlier report that measures of father–infant interaction at home when infants were 6 and 9 months of age were unrelated to the security of infant–father attachment in the Strange Situation at 12 months (Volling & Belsky, 1992) and with Rosen and Rothbaum's (1993) observation that measures of both maternal and paternal behavior were weakly associated with later assessments of attachment security in the Strange Situation. By contrast, Brown, Mangelsdorf, Wong, Shigeto, & Neff, (2009) also reported stability between 1 and 3 years in the security of infant–father attachment, while Goossens and Van IJzendoorn (1990) reported that the sensitivity of fathers in a free-play session was correlated with near-contemporaneous assessments of infant–father attachment in a sample of Dutch fathers, and a meta-analysis of eight studies concerned with the association between paternal sensitivity and the quality of infant–father attachment in the Strange Situation revealed a small but statistically significant association (Van IJzendoorn & DeWolff, 1997) that was significantly weaker than the association between maternal sensitivity and the security of infant–mother attachment (Van IJzendoorn & DeWolff, 1997). Differential patterns of influence for mothers and fathers are evident in mediational analyses (Kochanska et al., 2008) and up to the age of three (Lindsey, Cremeens, Colwell, & Caldera, 2009).

The reasons for such differences between parents are not clear. Cox, Owen, Henderson, and Margand (1992) found that American fathers who were more affectionate, spent more time with their 3-month-olds, and had more positive attitudes were more likely to have infants who were securely attached to them 9 months later. Caldera, Huston, and O'Brien (1995) likewise reported that American infants were more likely to appear insecure in the Strange Situation at 18 months when their fathers appeared more detached in a semi-structured laboratory setting 12 months earlier. Further, Van IJzendoorn (1995) reported an association between the security of infant–father attachment and the Dutch fathers' representation of their own childhood attachments. It could be that the relative amounts of time spent by fathers are important as well, making today's more involved fathers more influential than their predecessors. Such associations raise intriguing questions about whether and how attachment styles in infancy prepare the child for later social-cognitive skills.

Predictive Validity of Attachment Styles in Infancy

The association between Strange Situation behavior and styles of interaction with others has been well documented (Berlin & Cassidy, 1999; Kerns, 1996; Sroufe, 1996; Teti, 2005). Babies with secure attachments to their mothers are later more cooperatively playful than insecure infants when interacting with friendly strangers or peers. Other researchers have examined the relation between Strange Situation classifications and aspects of later achievement motivation in children, reporting that secure infant–mother attachments at 12 or 18 months are associated with superior problem-solving abilities in a variety of stressful and challenging contexts in the preschool years. In particular, children who were securely attached to their mothers as infants persisted longer and more enthusiastically in cognitively challenging situations than did children who had insecure attachments (Frankel & Bates, 1990; Grossmann, Grossmann, & Zimmerman, 1999; Sroufe, 1983). Secure infants also seem to be more resilient and robust when stressed or challenged and appear more socially competent and independent when they later enter preschool (Teti & Teti, 1996). Insecure attachment in infancy, particularly of the disorganized/disoriented type (D), is associated with elevated rates of antisocial and externalized behavior problems in later childhood (Lyons-Ruth, Easterbrooks, & Davidson, 1997; Shaw, Owens, Vondra, & Keenan, 1996).

The effects of infant–father attachment on subsequent behavior have also been studied. Sagi, Lamb, and Gardner (1986) reported that the security of both mother– and father–infant attachment on Israeli kibbutzim was associated with indices of the infants' sociability with strangers: Securely attached infants were more sociable than insecure–resistant infants. Earlier, Lamb et al. (1982) reported that Swedish infants who were securely attached to their fathers were more sociable with strangers, and Main and Weston (1981) found that the security of both mother–infant and father–infant attachments affected American infants' responses to an unfamiliar person (dressed as a clown). Belsky, Garduque, and Hrncir (1984) reported that the security of both attachment relationships, but especially the infant–mother attachment, affected executive capacity, an index of cognitive performance, in a sample of American toddlers.

The results of other studies suggest that infant–mother attachments may have greater and more consistent predictive power than infant–father attachments. Main, Kaplan, and Cassidy (1985) reported that earlier and concurrent assessments of mother–child attachment had greater impact on children's attachment-related responses than earlier and concurrent assessments of child–father attachment. Similar results were reported by Suess, Grossmann, and Sroufe (1992), who studied associations between parent–infant attachment security and the quality of German children's later interactions with peers. Interestingly, although the parents' sensitivity toward their 12-month-olds did not predict later behavior problems in one study (Benzies, Harrison, & Magill-Evans, 1998), Verschueren and Marcoen (1999) reported that the security of child–mother attachments had a greater effect on the positive self-perceptions of 5- and 6-year-olds than did child–father attachments, whereas the security of child–father attachments best predicted whether or not the children would have behavior problems. In both studies, the beneficial effects of secure attachments to one parent partially but not completely offset the adverse effects of insecure attachment to the other, and we might expect the same to be true in infancy. By contrast, Steele, Steele, Croft, and Fonagy (1999) found that the ability of British 6-year-olds to read affective expressions in cartoons was predicted by the security of infant–mother attachments 5 years earlier, but not by infant–father attachments at 18 months or by the parents' feelings of attachment during pregnancy. Later in this chapter, we discuss in greater depth the longer term formative implications of infant–parent attachments.

Attachment within the Family System: Infants, Mothers and Fathers

At the start of the chapter, we emphasized the increasingly popular claim that a full understanding of parenting must take into consideration the system of family relationships and not only individual relationships, and we need to include the role of physiological processes within this system. New fathers interact with their newborns in the same ways as mothers do (Rödholm & Larsson, 1982). Indeed their attentiveness is matched by similar changes in hormonal levels (decreased levels of testosterone and estradiol, coupled with increasing levels of cortisol and prolactin) around the time of their infants' births (Storey, Walsh, Quinton, & Wynne-Edwards, 2000). The female hormone estrogen seems to make younger women more sensitive to "cuteness" in infants than either men or menopausal women (Sprengelmeyer et al., 2009). Fathers also experience postnatal mood swings that may well have biological foundations (Ramchandani, Stein, Evans, O'Connor, & the ALSPAC Study Team, 2005). Such findings might provide a biological explanation for the association between the way expectant parents interact with dolls during pregnancy and their later interactions with infants and toddlers (Favez et al., 2006).

However, it is important to note that "biological parenthood" does not necessarily yield stronger attachments. Indeed, IVF and biological fathers in Sweden showed similar patterns of "prenatal attachment", and the stronger these feelings the easier it was for these men to adjust to early parenthood (Hjelmstedt & Collins, 2008). In stably cohabiting families, fathers' reports of attachment to their infants are also consistent over time (Condon, Corkindale, & Boyce, 2008).

Another influence on the family system is the gender of the participants. Fagot and Kavanagh (1993) reported that both parents found interaction with insecurely attached infants less pleasant, and both tended to become less involved in interactions with insecurely attached boys, a factor that may explain the greater likelihood of behavior problems among boys. Interestingly, fathers had unusually high levels of interaction with insecure–avoidant girls, who received the fewest directive instructions from their mothers. Schoppe-Sullivan, Diener, Mangelsdorf, Brown, McHale, and Frosch (2006) provided further evidence of the complementarity of parental roles. They found that, although fathers and mothers were similarly sensitive to their one-year-old sons, mothers appeared more sensitive to daughters than fathers were and less sensitive to sons than to daughters. At the same time, the fathers were more sensitive to sons when their partners were less sensitive. The complexity of the underlying associations was underscored by Gable, Crnic, and Belsky (1994), who reported robust correlations among marital quality, the quality of parent–child relationships, and child outcomes in a study of 2-year-olds. Infants characterized by negative emotionality early in the first year tended to become more positive when they had active, sensitive, and happily married mothers, whereas some infants became more negative when their fathers were dissatisfied with their marriages, insensitive, and uninvolved in their children's lives (Belsky, Fish, & Isabella, 1991). Davis, Schoppe-Sullivan, Mangelsdorf, and Brown (2009) also found that the infant's temperament influenced the quality of parenting, particularly those aspects shared between the two parents.

Clearly, attachments cannot be treated in isolation from other factors, particularly the relationship between the parents. In a study of 20-month-olds, for example, Easterbrooks and Goldberg (1984) found that the children's adaptation was promoted by both the amount of paternal involvement and, more importantly, the quality or sensitivity of their fathers' behavior. By contrast, the security of neither infant–mother nor infant–father attachment predicted the adjustment at age five of infants reared on traditional kibbutzim (those with central dormitories for children) in Israel, although, in keeping with the ecological model described earlier, the security of the infant–caretaker relationship did predict later behavior (Oppenheim, Sagi, & Lamb, 1988).

Lamb and his colleagues (Lamb, Thompson, Gardner, & Charnov, 1985; Thompson, 1998) have emphasized that the degree of **predictive validity** from measures of attachment security is far from perfect, regardless of whether the child–mother or child–father attachment is studied. Rather, the predictive relationship between Strange Situation behavior in infancy and subsequent child behavior is found only when there is stability in caretaking arrangements and family circumstances that seem to maintain stability in patterns of parent–child inter-action subsequently reflected in similar patterns of Strange Situation behavior. This raises the interesting question: Is the prediction of adjustment over time attributable to individual differences in the quality of early infant–parent attachments, or is it attributable to the con-tinuing quality of child–parent interactions over time? The latter would imply that the quality of early relationships was predictively valuable not because it caused later differences directly, but because it presaged later differences in the quality of relationships that in turn support continuing differences in the child's behavior. In other words, early interactions may shape the initial internal working models that are believed to guide behavior but these internal working models are continually updated and revised in light of later interactions. Such a pattern of findings would place the locus of stability in continuing parent–child interactions rather than in some characteristic of the child fixed by formative interactions with parents early in life. We return to these issues later in the chapter when discussing the long-term implications of individual differences in the quality of early child–parent relationships.

A GRADUAL ENTRANCE INTO THE SOCIAL WORLD: THE PRESCHOOL AND SCHOOL YEARS

The years between infancy and the child's entry into formal educational settings are marked by dramatic developmental changes. Seven areas of change—physical and locomotor growth, language, impulse control, social-cognitive understanding, conceptions of the self, cognitive executive processes, and the desire for autonomy—characterize the years between infancy and school and have significant effects on the nature and quality of parent–child relationships (Maccoby, 1984). Importantly, the transition from infancy to early childhood brings a dra-matic change in the roles of parents because physical, mental, and language development makes new behavioral capacities possible and facilitates the comprehension of more complex parental communication. From the end of infancy, the amount of child care performed by parents also declines progressively (DeLuccie, 1996; Galinsky, 1999). Toward the end of the second year of life, therefore, parents increasingly attempt to shape their children's social lives by directly encouraging children to behave in appropriate ways and discouraging them from inappropriate and socially proscribed behavior. The ability to conceptualize symbolically facilitates another important process—**observational learning**. Initial discussions of the process emphasized the need for observers to store a model's behavior in memory and then recall it for subsequent performance in order for this form of learning to be effective (Bandura, 1969, 1977). More recent theory encompasses not only observational learning but also the system of interactions and relationships, drawing on cognitive models of development and social factors such as attachments (Bandura, 1986, 1997).

The Preschool Child's Understanding of Social Relationships

Research until the 1980s emphasized the preschool child's continuing egocentrism. Over the past 20 years, however, many researchers have studied the understanding of social relationships in terms of the ability to predict others' actions or thoughts using the false belief paradigm in which the child has to make a judgment about another person's beliefs when that person's behavior suggests that he or she has a different conception of reality. In such situations, preschoolers recognize the other's perspective—albeit in a relatively immature manner—by the age of four (Wellman, Cross, & Watson, 2001). Although there is heated controversy about the origins of these skills (see Lewis & Carpendale, 2010, for an introduction), it is likely that the ability to "read minds" emerges gradually in the course of everyday social interaction, particularly with parents and other family members. Thus, 3- to 4-year-olds typically perform better in false belief tests (Figure 10.1) when they have more siblings (Jenkins & Astington, 1996; Lewis et al., 1996; Perner et al., 1994), particularly older siblings (Ruffman et al., 1998). This "sibling effect" suggests that family factors affect the emergence of these perspective-taking skills. The more contact that preschoolers have with extended family members, particularly more socially proficient relatives such as older cousins, uncles, and aunts, the earlier they acquire such skills (Lewis et al., 1996). Presumably, the quality of

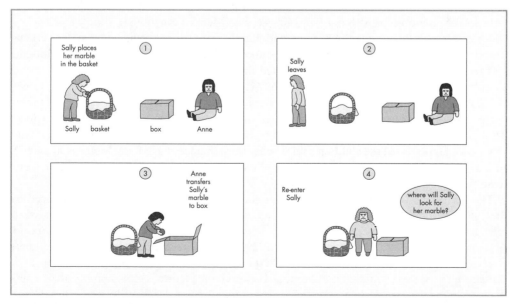

FIGURE 10.1 False-belief test.

interaction between parents and children also predicts the speed at which children come to understand such important aspects of their social world.

Three types of evidence support this hypothesis. In infancy, first of all, children learn how to understand social interactions in the course of everyday experiences, particularly those that involve teasing and shared attention (Reddy, 2003; Tomasello, 1999). Second, variations in parenting style are correlated with differences in the development of **social cognition** (Astington, 1996; Ruffman, Perner, & Parkin, 1999; Sabbagh & Seamans, 2008; Vinden, 2001), indicating that parents stage-manage the toddler's and preschooler's gradual entry into both social interactions and social understanding. For example, Ruffman et al. (1999) found that children scored higher on tests of false belief when their parents dealt with disciplinary events by asking their children to reflect on the victims' feelings. Similarly, maternal talk about the mind and cooperative sibling interaction in the third year predict the age of acquisition of mental state reasoning (Dunn, Brown, & Beardsall, 1991; Dunn, Brown, Slomkowski, Tesla, & Youngblade, 1991). Third, factors within the attachment relationship itself predict concurrent and later psychosocial functioning, as assessed in the child's developing ability to understand mental states (Fonagy & Target, 1997; Hobson, 2002; Meins, 1999). Early evidence of an association between attachment and social understanding in infancy was reported by Bretherton, Bates, Benigni, Camaioni, and Volterra (1979), who found that securely attached 12-month-olds had been more likely to point at objects and look to see whether the parent was looking (known as "proto-declarative" pointing) a month earlier. Securely attached children also did better on diverse "**theory of mind**" tasks (Fonagy, Redfern & Charman, 1997; Symons & Clark, 2000), whereas children who were securely attached at one year of age were more likely to pass a false belief task at 4 years (Meins, 1997) and more complex mind reading tests at 5 years (Meins, Fernyhough, Russell, & Clarke-Carter, 1998).

What accounts for the correlation between secure attachment and more skilled social understanding? Following Bretherton et al. (1979), Fonagy and Target (1997) suggested that there is a close association between the ability to understand that people have mental states and the earlier self-representational skills presumed by the internal working model construct. Fonagy and Target suggested that conceptually related "reflective" functions serve as a basis of later social understanding, emerging as a natural consequence of generalizations from the attachment relationships with parents. Meins (1999; Meins, Fernyhough, Fradley, & Tuckey, 2001; see also Ereky-Stevens, 2008) suggested that the parent's communication style is crucial to this transmission. Describing parents who treat their children as "persons" with thoughts and feelings as "mindminded," Meins argued that such parents tend to "treat their infants as individuals with minds, rather than merely entities with needs that must be met" (1999, p. 332), exposing infants and toddlers to more talk about psychological constructs. From this perspective, exposure to mental state language and secure attachment are highly intertwined. Thus, mothers' language about 5-month-olds' minds (but not mindminded language about other people) predicted the children's false belief performance at age four (Meins et al., 2002). In this way, social understanding is acquired while children learn about and within social relationships (Carpendale & Lewis, 2010).

These links between attachment and later social understanding are surely influenced by the interactional processes that we discussed earlier. For example, "mind-mindedness" is mediated by the processes identified earlier: sensitivity of parents to their infants (Laranjo, Bernier, & Meins, 2008; Ontai & Thompson, 2008), "joint engagement" with their toddlers (Nelson, Adamson & Bakeman, 2008) or responsiveness (Ensor & Hughes, 2008) to their preschoolers' behaviors and later utterances. However, the picture is more complicated. There is cross-cultural evidence that some of the patterns addressed above do not generalize to other settings. For example, Lewis, Huang, and Rooksby (2006) did not find associations between parental styles, family size (interactions with cousins because few families had more than one child) and false belief in mainland China.

Do Mothers and Fathers Differentially Socialize Boys and Girls?

Other than parental attachments and/or the use of forms of language that allow the children to enter into more complex social relationships, are there other identifiable influences on the development of social understanding? Gender has a pervasive influence on socialization in general, and parent–child interaction in particular (Fagot, 1995; Ruble & Martin, 1998), although researchers have documented surprisingly few differences in the ways in which boys and girls are treated by their parents during the first years of life (Lytton & Romney, 1991; Russell & Saebel, 1997; Siegel, 1987). For example, Lytton and Romney's meta-analysis of 172 studies involving over 27,000 children revealed only one consistent difference between mothers and fathers—a significant, but small, tendency for fathers to encourage the use of sex-typed toys more than mothers did. Otherwise, there were insufficient data to support the claim that mothers and fathers differentially affect their children's sex-role development. Lytton and Romney further reported that, beyond the preschool years, the similarities between the behavior of mothers and fathers increased. Later research has confirmed this pattern. For example, French fathers tended to be more directive in play with toddlers than were mothers (Labrell, 1994), but by 42 months, fathers no longer challenged their children more than mothers did (Labrell, Deleau, & Juhel, 2000). Similarly, early differences in parent–child language (Gleason, 1975; Rowe, Coker, & Pan, 2004) are not clearly echoed in patterns of parent–child communication in the preschool period (Pellegrini, Brody & Stoneman, 1987; Welkowitz, Bond, Feldman & Tota, 1990), although preschool teachers seem to convey powerful but subtle sex-differentiating signals to young children (Leaper, 2002; Maccoby, 1998).

Researchers typically observe mothers and fathers in the same context, which may not be equivalently representative of the settings in which they typically interact with their children. Different settings impose different constraints on parents (Lewis & Gregory, 1987; Ross & Taylor, 1989), and most researchers do not sample contexts in a way that would allow them to determine whether some contexts magnify or minimize parental styles or have different effects depending on the parents' styles. This tendency on the part of researchers is likely to obscure discernible differences between the behavior of mothers and fathers, although the results of a few studies suggest that such differences exist in the preschool period. In one recent study, for example, Lindsey and Mize (2001) examined parent–child and child–peer dyads in "pretend" and "physical play" sessions. Not only did mothers engage in more pretend play with their daughters while father–son dyads specialized in physical play, but patterns of parent–child pretend and physical play also predicted the amounts of the same type of play with peers. Similarly, Hagan and Kuebli (2007) explored the way parents assisted their preschoolers on a balance beam. They found that mothers were equally attentive to children of either sex, but fathers were particularly protective of their daughters in this context. Future research needs to examine such subtle differences between parents.

Even in the preschool period, children in a variety of cultures clearly differentiate between the roles of mothers and fathers. For example, Raag and Rackliff (1998) introduced pre-schoolers to a laboratory play room in which a range of sex-neutral and sex-stereotyped toys were laid out, and then asked the children which toys they and their parents thought it was appropriate to play with. Many boys, particularly those who had chosen sex-stereotypical toys, stated that their fathers would consider cross-sex toy play to be "bad." Thus fathers were believed by sons, but not daughters, to have more restrictive rules of conduct than mothers did. By their entry into school, furthermore, children appear to have highly stereotyped views of parental roles. Domestic work is widely described as the mother's prerogative whereas bread winning is seen as the province of fathers throughout the school years (Hartley, 1960; Langford, Lewis, Solomon, & Warin, 2001; Williams, Bennett, & Best, 1975). Interviews with over 800 5- to 15-year-olds in four societies revealed that these beliefs persisted into middle childhood and adolescence (Goldman & Goldman, 1983). Such differences suggest that maternal and paternal styles, while hard to discern in observational studies, may have strong effects on preschoolers, perhaps because they perceive subtle nuances in parental behavior or social stereotypes which underpin sex role differences.

Future research is needed to explore how mothers and fathers influence their preschoolers' development. We need more longitudinal research that straddles the boundaries of social interactions between parents and children and the latter's "cognitive" development. In an exemplary study of this sort, LaBounty, Wellman, Olson, Lagattuta, & Liu (2008) reported that mothers' emotional expressiveness with 3½-year-olds was related to the children's later (5 years) grasp of emotions, whereas fathers' use of "causal explanatory" language in conversation predicted their children's concurrent and later "theory of mind" understanding.

The School-Age Child

Few researchers have focused on parent–child relationships involving children between six and twelve years of age. The school years have been a focus of active research in the past two decades, but researchers have typically emphasized either the roles played by mothers and fathers or the parents' overall parenting styles. In this section, we briefly compare mothers and fathers before describing some fundamental dimensions of parenting.

As their children grow older, mothers continue to spend more time with their children than fathers do (Collins & Russell, 1991; Pleck & Masciadrelli, 2004). When observed together, however, mothers and fathers initiate activities with equal frequency (Noller, 1980), and there are broad similarities in their reactions to their children's play and cognitive styles (Bronstein, 1984). Individual patterns of paternal closeness are relatively stable over time during middle childhood, and there are discernible parental styles in this period (Herman & McHale, 1993). Most research on socialization during this phase has been concerned with the influences of peers, teachers, and educational institutions on children's adjustment (see Eccles and Roeser, Chapter 12, and Rubin and his colleagues, Chapter 11, this volume). Those researchers who have examined parent–child relationships during the elementary school years have focused on achievement and achievement motivation or on the competition between parental and peer influences, rather than on the association between the quality of parent–child relationships and aspects of children's socioemotional development. Parents remain influential and affectively salient throughout this period and into adolescence, however. Interactions with parents allow children to practice, rehearse, and refine skills that later facilitate interactions with peers (MacDonald & Parke, 1984; Parke et al., 2002, 2004). Furthermore, as peers become more important at the end of middle childhood, parents continue to remain central; their role is transformed rather than usurped (Buhrmeister & Furman, 1990; Collins, Harris, & Susman, 1995; Lamborn & Steinberg, 1993; Oosterwegel & Oppenheimer, 1993).

Styles of Parenting in Middle Childhood

Due in part to advances in children's cognitive skills and abilities, school-aged children need less intensive and more subtle monitoring and exert more self-control than younger children. Most parents and professionals, however, believe that parents must continue to assume directive roles, allowing children to express emotions fully, making important norms salient, and setting appropriate limits when necessary (Greenberg & Speltz, 1988). Parental monitoring is still valuable; Crouter, MacDermid, McHale, and Perry-Jenkins (1990) found that less well-monitored boys received lower grades at school than children whose parents monitored them more closely. Successful parents are therefore sensitive to the changing needs of growing children, gradually increasing the children's involvement in such family decisions as the allocation of responsibilities and household chores (Goodnow, 1996). Parent–child relationships continue to be recalibrated and redefined as parents become increasingly involved in anticipatory guidance and emotional support. Parents continue to promote emotional stability by serving as "secure bases," despite the fact that their children begin to shield their emotional and social lives from their parents' view. Conflicts over behavioral control are replaced by a concern with achievement and industriousness, with an explicit focus on helping children make the transition to adult roles. Both parents and children play important roles in the redefinition of their relationships.

As Maccoby (1984, 1992) has argued, "coordination" and "co-regulation" rather than bidirectional patterns of influence increasingly characterize parent–child relationships in middle childhood. Based on new methods of monitoring, guiding, and supporting their children, parents reinforce children's understanding of moral standards, although there is more concern with equity and fairness in the parent–child relationship during middle childhood than there was earlier. Consequently, effective socialization increasingly involves monitoring children rather than directing them (Baumrind, 1991; Hetherington & Clingempeel, 1992).

Parents adjust their demands during middle childhood in accordance with the expectation that, by the time children reach adolescence, they should approach adult standards of behavior. Compared with parents of younger children, for example, parents of school-aged children are less inclined to use physical coercion with their children and are more apt to appeal to their self-esteem or to their sense of humor, and seek to arouse their guilt (Maccoby, 1984, 1992). Verbal mediation of control replaces physical control and this transition affects children's behavior: When mothers rely on reasoning and suggestions, children tend to negotiate, whereas when mothers use direct maternal strategies, children tend to be defiant (Kuczynski, Kochanska, Radke-Yarrow, & Girnius-Brown, 1987). Advances in cognitive development enable children to understand the legitimacy of parental authority (Damon, 1983). Recent theoretical analyses have stressed the need to consider the bidirectional influences of parent–child relationships and the wider contexts in which they take place (Kuczynzki, 2003).

During this phase, the manner in which children interact with their parents also changes. School-aged children do not express anger toward their parents as openly and as often as they did when they were younger, and they are less likely to whine, yell, and hit. In part, this is because parents of school-aged children are less concerned with promoting autonomy and establishing daily routines and more concerned with children's industriousness and achievement. Recent sociological analyses of family communication styles point to a shift towards family "democracy" over successive generations (e.g., Beck & Beck-Gernsheim, 1995; Giddens, 1998). Whereas education was considered to be the responsibility of the schools a generation ago, contemporary parents worry about the extent to which they should become involved in their children's school work (Solomon, Warin & Lewis, 2002), whether they should require children to do chores, what standards of performance they should demand, and the extent to which they should monitor their children's social life (Maccoby, 1984). Anticipatory guidance of the child, monitoring of the child's activities, expressions of affection, and parental teaching during this phase all serve to prevent behavior problems (Holden, 1995; Holden & Miller, 1999). It is not just that children with disengaged parents are more socially incompetent, irresponsible, immature, and alienated from their families; they also have poorer relationships with peers and perform more poorly at school (Baumrind 1991; Patterson, Reid, & Dishion, 1992; Rubin et al., Chapter 11, this volume). Clearly, parental involvement plays an important role in the development of both social and cognitive competence in children, whereas a lack of parental monitoring is strongly associated with the risk of delinquent behavior (Andrews & Dishion, 1994).

According to Freud, the superego begins to become dominant in middle childhood, and, as a result, children become preoccupied with mastering adult standards of behavior. Children want to meet their parents' expectations and feel distressed when they fail, although they may blame the distress on their parents or themselves. This ambiguity may mark the beginning of the intrapersonal and interpersonal conflict that becomes prominent during adolescence (Freud, 1958). As discussed below, however, most research casts doubt on the psychoanalytic depiction of adolescence as a period of significant intrapersonal and interpersonal conflict.

Baumrind's Model of Parental Styles

Some of the most influential research on the ways in which specific childrearing patterns were associated with particular child outcomes was initiated by Baumrind in the 1960s (Baumrind, 1967, 1971, 1973, 1975, 1991; Baumrind & Black, 1967). Baumrind distinguished four patterns of **parenting**, which she labeled **authoritarian, authoritative**, permissive, and nonconformist. According to Baumrind, authoritarian parents value obedience and recommend forceful imposition of the parents' will, permissive parents believe that parents should be nonintrusive but available as resources, whereas nonconformist parents, although opposed to authority, are "less passive and exert more control than permissive parents" (Baumrind, 1975, p. 14). Between the extremes represented by authoritarian and permissive parents fall authoritative parents, who encourage independence and attempt to shape their preschoolers' behavior using rational explanation.

According to Baumrind, authoritative parents are sensitive to and facilitate their children's changing sense of self. Furthermore, by allowing themselves to learn from their children, authoritative parents maximize their positive impact, teaching their children, as authoritarian and permissive parents do not, that social competence emerges within a context of interpersonal give-and-take. Although authoritative parents strive to foster independence, they also inculcate a value system characterized by conformity to cultural and societal norms by balancing the use of both reasoning and punishment.

Authoritative parents, by contrast, value self-assertion, wilfulness, and independence, and foster these goals by assuming active and rational parental roles. Baumrind (1967, 1972) explained that the children of authoritative parents are socially responsible because their parents clearly communicate realistic demands that are intellectually stimulating while generating moderate amounts of tension.

Mothers, Fathers, and Cultural Influences on Parenting Styles

Attempts to compare mothers' and fathers' approaches to parenting have yielded inconclusive findings. Baumrind's analysis underscores the need to study parents' philosophies of childrearing, but Baumrind focused on parents rather than mothers and/or fathers, and she has not explored why parents adopt the strategies they do. Studying the parents of 305 Australian preschoolers, Russell and his colleagues (1998) found that mothers were more likely to identify with the authoritative style of parenting, whereas fathers were more likely to describe themselves as either authoritarian or permissive. Parents were also more often identified with the authoritarian perspective when the child under discussion was a son. These patterns of evidence suggest that we need to consider both the children's impact on the parents' childrearing beliefs and the reasons why mothers and fathers may have differing philosophies, because these may well be colored by the divergent roles they assume in the

Authoritative parents inculcate a value system characterized by conformity to cultural and societal norms by balancing the use of reasoning and punishment.

family. Of course, this assertion needs to be explored empirically in a wide variety of cultural and subcultural settings.

Although authoritative parents foster a sense of independence in their children, they also inculcate a value system characterized by conformity to cultural and societal norms by balancing the use of reasoning and punishment. Many researchers have confirmed Baumrind's original conclusion that firm and responsive parenting seems to promote greater cooperation, less delinquency, and higher social and cognitive competence in children. However, further research into comparisons of different cultural contexts has complicated the picture. In African American families, authoritarian parenting, particularly if associated with physical punishment, may not increase the level of behavior problems, suggesting that the pattern of findings reported by Baumrind is culture-specific (Baumrind, 1972). In addition, Baumrind has yet to document the developmental processes by which authoritative parents facilitate their children's socialization (Darling & Steinberg, 1993).

In the past two decades, however, other researchers have greatly enriched our understanding of socialization processes (Bugental & Goodnow, 1998), with family systems analysts such as Patterson (1976, 1982) documenting the processes by which parents and children shape one another's behavior. For example, some parents unwittingly train their children to use negative gestures manipulatively while others both fail to extinguish their children's undesirable behaviors and may even foster conduct problems (Andrews & Dishion, 1994). **Conduct disordered** teenagers also elicit coercive behavior from adults (Patterson et al., 1992). These insights have been useful in the development of intervention programs designed to help parents exercise more effective control over their children's and adolescents' behavior (Andrews & Dishion, 1994).

MacKinnon(-Lewis) and her colleagues (MacKinnon, Lamb, Belsky, & Baum, 1990; MacKinnon-Lewis, Lamb, Arbuckle, Baradaran, & Volling, 1992; MacKinnon-Lewis et al., 1994; MacKinnon-Lewis, Volling, Lamb, Hattie, & Baradaran, 2001) have also built on Patterson's work, demonstrating that the behavior of both parents and children is affected by their expectations or attributions about one another, and that both attributions and behavioral tendencies are influenced by the dyad's history of interactions. Studies such as these illustrate the role of cognitions in family socialization; values and beliefs are increasingly viewed as both motivators and interpretive lenses through which parents and children of all ages view one another, and analysis of the cognitive facets of parent–child socialization is increasingly prominent (Bugental & Goodnow, 1998).

Parental behaviors and children's cognitive constructions of the world are filtered through the same attachment lens that influences earlier development, with some studies suggesting gender differences in the patterns of attachment. For example, Diener, Isabella, Behunin, and Wong (2008) found that 6- to 10-year-old American boys reported more secure attachments to fathers than to mothers, whereas the reverse was true of girls. Other researchers reported more secure child–mother than child–father attachments (Booth-LaForce et al., 2006). Such patterns have their social and cognitive correlates and sequelae. In keeping with the findings on preschoolers, maternal and paternal closeness are independently related to peer-rated adjustment and perceived self-competence in American 10-year-olds (Rubin et al., 2004). Such findings complement earlier ones in which attachment security with both parents is associated with various indices of positive friendship qualities among preadolescents (Lieberman, Doyle, & Markiewicz, 1999).

Both parents also influence their children's early educational aspirations. Booth-LaForce et al. (2006) found that secure attachments related to superior self-perceived academic competence especially when children had secure attachments to both parents. Martin, Ryan and Brooks-Gunn (2007) likewise found that mothers' and fathers' support for their two-year-olds independently predicted their children's language and arithmetic scores just before school entry at the age of five. Further, fathers who are supportive in their preschoolers' interactions have offspring who do better on cognitive and language assessments (Cabrera, Shannon & Tamis-LeMonda, 2007). The same holds true in the school years. Most research on educational attainment suggests that the levels of parental conversation and parental limit setting affect achievement, with no clear differences between mothers and fathers (e.g., Scott, 2004).

In two large studies, however, Flouri and Buchanan (2004) found that British children with more involved fathers had higher IQs at 7 years of age. Belsky et al. (2008) found that parents' support for their children's independent thinking was related to reading and arithmetic at 6 to 8 years, particularly in boys. In addition, however, fathers' support for independent thinking best predicted changes over this age range. This is consistent with evidence that fathers exert demands on their children, particularly their sons, in the subjects they especially value, such as physics or mathematics (Crowley, Callanan, Tenenbaum, & Allen, 2001; Tenenbaum & Leaper, 2003). When fathers become involved in school activities, this contributes unique variance to their children's educational perfomance (McBride, Schoppe-Sullivan, & Ho, 2005).

Of course, this does not mean that fathers make unique contributions to development in middle childhood. In interpreting longitudinal evidence, Lewis, Newson and Newson (1982) argued that such correlations are more likely to reflect a range of factors, particularly about the relationship between the parents. Recent evidence supports this view. For example, the link between paternal involvement and child outcomes is linked with the quality of the father–mother relationship (Goldman, 2005) as well as to factors outside the family such as the parents' employment patterns (Gottfried, Gottfried, & Bathurst, 2002). We return to these issues later in the chapter.

The Individual's Construction of Relationships: Internal Working Models

Although most of the research on parent–child attachments has concentrated on the interactions between parents and their infants within the reunion episode of the Strange Situation, many theorists have examined the changing nature and function of parent–child attachment relationships, reasoning that these continue to develop and change in ways that require continued coordination and integration as maturing individuals adapt to their changing social contexts (see Greenberg, Cicchetti, & Cummings, 1990; Sroufe, 1988, 1996). As mentioned earlier, ideas within cognitive science concerning the importance of self-representations (e.g., Mandler, 1985), led attachment theorists to propose that infants and young children construct "internal working models" in the course of early interactions that reflect their experience of the self in these relationships and guide their behavior in later relationships (Bowlby, 1969, 1973, 1988; Bretherton, 1990, 1991, 1993). Although internal working models continue to be formed during and after early childhood, maintaining continuity in individual developmental pathways, there exists wide variation across individuals in the degree to which working models reflect the individual's own experiences, as well as his or her cognitive, linguistic, and behavioral skills (Bowlby, 1973).

Internal working models represent children's conceptions of attachment figures as reflected in their interactions and in the feedback they receive from their parents. Working models influence overt demonstrations of attachment behavior as children grow older, but attachment behavior becomes more subtle with age because older children are more capable of evaluating the intentions, motives, and behaviors of attachment figures. Crittenden (1990, 1992, 1994) has further proposed that individuals acquire multiple working models associated with different memory systems. In what she terms the dynamic maturation model of attachment, she argues that we need to consider simultaneously both attachments and the way family processes affect the impact of parental styles on children's internal working models (Crittenden, 2006; Crittenden & Dallos, 2009). These are particularly sensitive to conflict and parental neglect.

The internal working model construct has become central to explanations of the role played by attachment relationships in children's social relationships and individual psychosocial functioning over time. Main, Kaplan, and Cassidy (1985) suggested that emotional openness in discussing imagined parent–child separations and conversations with parents reflected aspects of children's mental representations of relationships with their parents. Specifically, those children who were securely attached at 12 months provided accounts that appeared more coherent, elaborate, and emotionally open at 6 years of age, whereas those children who were insecurely attached at 12 months were more likely to offer sad, irrational, or bizarre responses later, or else were completely silent. Slough (1988) reported similar results. Using a story completion task, furthermore, Cassidy (1988) found that children who behaved securely on reunion with their mothers represented themselves positively in interviews and were better able to acknowledge less than perfect aspects of the self than children who behaved insecurely.

ADOLESCENCE

One prediction of attachment theory is that there will be transgenerational continuities in attachment styles. Main and her colleagues (George, Kaplan, & Main, 1985; Main & Goldwyn, 1994) developed the adult attachment interview (AAI) to assess adults' ability to integrate early memories of their relationships with parents into overarching working models of relationships. According to Main, these working models fall into one of three categories, with adults classified as *autonomous* (free to evaluate their early attachment relationships), *dismissive* of their attachment relationships, or *preoccupied* with their attachment relationships. According to Kobak and Sceery (1988), adolescents in the secure or autonomous group were rated by their peers as more ego resilient, less anxious, and less hostile. These adolescents reported little distress and high levels of social support, whereas those in the dismissive group were rated low on ego resilience and high on hostility by their peers, with whom they had distant relationships. Adolescents in the preoccupied group were viewed as less ego resilient and more anxious by their peers, and they reported higher levels of personal distress and family support than those in the dismissive group. Steinberg (1990) has hypothesized that securely attached adolescents may be more likely than dismissive or preoccupied adolescents to renegotiate healthy relationships with their parents successfully. Autonomous adults appeared more sensitively responsive to their infants than adults in the dismissive and preoccupied groups, and their children were more likely to be securely attached (see van IJzendoorn, 1995, for a review). As mentioned earlier, for example, British mothers' and fathers' perceptions during pregnancy of their attachments to their own parents predicted the security of their infants' later attachments to them (Fonagy, Steele & Steele, 1991; Steele, Steele, & Fonagy, 1996).

These studies on the associations between individual internal working models and parent–child relationships suggest that secure children, adolescents, and adults who see attachment figures as well as themselves as primarily good, though not perfect, are able to communicate with ease, tend to have flexible interpersonal styles, express empathy for others, and discuss attachment relationships coherently without idealizing them.

Many psychologists have made note of qualitative and functional transformations in parent–child relationships in adolescence (Collins, 1990; Hauser et al., 1987; Hill, 1988; Parke & Buriel, 1998; Shulman & Seiffge-Krenke, 1997), with children shifting their dependence first to same-sex and then to opposite-sex peers, while continuing the processes of self-differentiation and individuation which become the major themes of development in adolescence (Collins, 1990; Grotevant, 1998; Hill & Holmbeck, 1987; Steinberg, 1988, 1990). As with previous phases of development, research comparing mothers and fathers reveals few differences between mothers' and fathers' interactional styles (Russell & Saebel, 1997; Silverberg, Tennenbaum, & Jacob, 1992), although parent–adolescent relationships are increasingly marked by self-assertion, distance, and conflict. Steinberg (1987) found that early maturing sons and daughters reported more conflict with their mothers than later maturing children, although these processes may take a different form and have different meaning in mother–child and father–child relationships. The effects of puberty are frequently confounded with the effects of other age-related changes such as the transition from elementary to middle or from middle to high school (Collins & Russell, 1991; Simmons & Blyth, 1987), but whatever their relative importance, the biological, social, and cognitive changes associated with puberty all make early adolescence a critical transitional period during which youngsters are expected to consolidate their knowledge of the norms and roles of adult society and, at least in Western industrialized societies, begin to become emotionally and economically independent of their parents (Grotevant, 1998).

Baumrind (1991) noted that parents of adolescents tend to use increasingly complex variations of the basic patterns described above when faced with the unique challenges and changes characteristic of the adolescent period. She concluded that:

> Adolescents' developmental progress is held back by directive, officious, or unengaged practices and facilitated by reciprocal, balanced interactions characteristic of . . . authoritative . . . parents. Directive parents who are authoritarian generate internalizing problem behaviors and are less successful at curtailing drug use. Directive parents who are not authoritarian effectively promote positive competence. (p. 753)

Similarly, Dornbusch, Ritter, Leiderman, Roberts, and Fraleigh (1987) found that adolescents with authoritative parents had higher grades in school than adolescents whose parents were

Parent–adolescent relationships are increasingly marked by self-assertion, distance, and conflict.

rated authoritarian or permissive. The relationship between parental styles and school performance, however, may be mediated by adolescent psychosocial maturity, work orientation, and socioemotional adjustment (Steinberg, Elmen, & Mounts, 1989). Studies of the links between attachments and peer relationships also show clear links in adolescence. For example, Dykas, Ziv and Cassidy (2008) found that 17-year-olds rated as securely attached on the AAI were seen by their contemporaries as more prosocial and less aggressive.

Mothers, Fathers, and Adolescents

Researchers have also described some interesting differences between the ways in which mothers and fathers relate to male and female adolescents (Collins & Russell, 1991; Steinberg, 1987, 1990). Collins and Russell focused on three dimensions of parent–child relationships in middle-class families: interactions (measured by frequency, extent and structure), affect (indexed by the degree of positive affect, closeness, and cohesion), and cognition (indexed by discrepancies between parents' and children's perceptions of their relationships). They concluded that, as in infancy, mothers engage in more frequent interaction with children in middle childhood and adolescence (especially interactions involving caretaking and routine family tasks) than fathers do, and that most father–child interactions involve play, recreation, and goal-oriented actions and tasks (see also Lamb, 1997; Montemayor & Brownlee, 1987; Russell & Russell, 1987). When dyadic and systemic aspects of parent–adolescent relationships are examined (Larson & Richards, 1994; Steinberg, 1990), mothers appear to engage in more shared activities with daughters than with sons, although both relationships are marked by relatively high levels of both closeness and discord. Fathers, by contrast, tend to be more engaged with their sons, have little contact with daughters, and generally have more distant relationships with their children than mothers do (Hosley & Montemayor, 1997; Montemayor & Brownlee, 1987; Youniss & Ketterlinus, 1987). Mothers and fathers become equivalently involved in activities related to their children's scholastic and extracurricular performance and achievement (Youniss & Smollar, 1985), however, and both parents continue to engage in frequent nurturant caretaking (Russell & Russell, 1987). In most interactional domains, in fact, the differences between mothers and fathers are neither as large nor as consistent as many theorists have hypothesized (Lamb, 1997) although adolescents in North America (Hosley & Montemayor, 1997) and Britain (Langford et al., 2001) consistently report being closer to their mothers than to their fathers. Adolescents believe that their mothers know them better than their fathers do, and, although they care about both mothers and fathers, daughters are more likely than sons to differ with parents regarding the degree of closeness

(Langford et al., 2001, Hosley & Montemayor, 1997; Youniss & Ketterlinus, 1987). Korean daughters see their fathers as distant and controlling (Rohner & Pettengill, 1985).

Because fathers spend less time with, have fewer conversations with, and are less affectively salient to their adolescent children, one might expect them to be less influential. Consistent with this, daughters report being relatively uninfluenced by their fathers (Larson & Richards, 1994) and even sons feel that mothers provide more support than fathers do (Youniss & Smollar, 1985). On the other hand, there is clear evidence that some fathers have positive influences on their children's academic performance (Chen, Liu, & Li, 2000) and achievement, particularly in sports (Jodl, Michael, Malanchuk, Eccles, & Sameroff, 2001). One recent analysis of almost 1300 Taiwanese eighth graders found that their attachments to their mothers and fathers independently predicted differences in their psychosocial adjustment (Liu, 2008). In addition, Phares (1996, 1997) concluded a review of the literature on child psychopathology by noting that fathers have powerful direct and indirect effects on their children's adjustment. For example, Brennan, Hammen, Katz, and Le Brocque (2002) reported that maternal and paternal depression had additive adverse effects on adolescents' adjustment, and maternal depression had a more reliable effect on adolescents when the fathers were substance abusers.

As in earlier years, of course, some patterns of influence in adolescence are quite complex and indirect. In an observational study, for example, Gjerde (1986) found that mother–son interactions were less stormy when fathers were present than when mothers and sons were observed alone, whereas father–son interactions were of poorer quality in triadic than in dyadic settings. Parents and adolescents may view their interaction quite differently as well. Noller and Callan (1988) videotaped 41 mother–father–adolescent triads discussing the adolescents' behavior and then had trained observers, the interactants, and members of other mother–father–child triads rate the degree of anxiety, dominance, involvement, and friendliness shown by each of the interactants. The ratings made by the experts were very similar to those made by members of other families. Interactants rated other members of their families more negatively than they rated themselves, although the ratings by participating and non-participating parents were more divergent than ratings by adolescents who were and were not involved.

Both Gjerde's and Noller and Callan's studies illustrate innovative techniques for studying parent–adolescent relationships, and underscore the importance of obtaining data from multiple informants. Further amplifying this point, Sternberg and her colleagues (Sternberg et al., 1993; Sternberg, Lamb, & Dawud-Noursi, 1998; Sternberg, Lamb, Guterman, & Abbott 2006b) showed that mothers' and adolescents' views of children's behavior problems varied depending on the informants' experiences and perspectives.

Tensions in the Parent–Adolescent Relationship

Tension is inevitable as parents try to maintain attachments and dependency while teenagers strive for independence. Until the mid-1970s, in fact, adolescence was viewed as a period during which parental influence was gradually usurped by the influence of the peer group as a result of intergenerational conflict over values, norms, and behavior (Coleman, 1961). Research on parent–adolescent relationships was largely influenced by psychoanalysts such as Anna Freud (1958) who believed that the biological changes associated with puberty cause emotional distress which in turn leads to rebelliousness and family conflict in the context of a second Oedipal constellation (see also Blos, 1979; Josselson, 1980; Sebald, 1977). These normative processes allegedly drove an emotional wedge between adolescents and their parents and this in turn was believed to facilitate the successful transition from childhood to adulthood. In fact, Anna Freud thought that adolescents who had close respectful relationships with their parents were probably at greatest risk for later psychopathology, a hypothesis that has not been supported empirically (Steinberg, 1990). Indeed, the notion that adolescence is typically characterized by conflict and turmoil rather than by closeness and harmony has been replaced by the realization that most children make the transition to adulthood without significant ego instability. Large-scale surveys show that the vast majority of adolescents continue to rely on their parents for advice, support, and emotional intimacy (Maccoby & Martin, 1983; McGrellis, Henderson, Holland, Sharpe, & Thomson, 2000; Noller & Callan, 1986; Offer, Ostrov, & Howard, 1981), suggesting that parent–adolescent relationships are marked by increasing interdependence and mutuality rather than by detachment and conflict. In contrast to the traditional "storm and stress" model, Coleman and Hendry (1990) theorized that adolescence is a phase of development in which, as with every other stage, individuals come to terms with successive shifts—in parental, peer, and heterosexual relationships.

Solomon, Warin, Lewis, and Langford (2002) explored the ways in which family members describe the patterns of closeness and responsibility between adolescents and their parents, noting that, in a gesture of intergenerational solidarity, many parents (especially mothers) and teenagers describe each other as friends or "mates." Such patterns echo McGrellis et al.'s (2000) large survey of British teenagers in which parents, particularly mothers, were listed high on the adolescents' list of "heroes"—consistently above sports, TV, and pop idols. However, the detailed interviews and qualitative analyses performed by Solomon and his colleagues indicated that these reports obscured underlying paradoxes and contradictions in parent–adolescent relationships as the partners strived for mutuality. As an extreme example, some parents, particularly mothers, reported that they would let their young teenagers go into town on the bus to meet friends, but might follow in their car to ensure their safety. Or, they might allow their children to spend many hours with their boyfriends/girlfriends, but check their teenager's diaries to ensure that they were not sexually active.

Although parent–adolescent relationships are not typically characterized by conflict and turmoil, there is a significant amount of minor but persistent conflict between parents and adolescents (Collins, 1991, 1997; Holmbeck & O'Donnell, 1991; Smetana, 1995), which reaches a peak in mid-adolescence and then declines (Offer et al., 1981; Steinberg, 1981). It has been estimated that families with adolescent children on average argue approximately twice a week (Montemayor, 1983), but this bickering or quarrelling over everyday issues (school work, chores, quarrels with siblings, personal hygiene and grooming, activities, friends, and mundane disobedience) is rarely severe enough to interfere with the development of healthy parent–adolescent relationships and seldom escalates into conflict (Acock & Bengtson, 1978; Youniss & Smollar, 1985). Steinberg (1990) estimated that conflict severe enough to yield a drastic deterioration in the quality of family relationships occurs in only about 5% to 10% of families. The types of issues that are the focus of family arguments change little from preadolescence through late adolescence (Hosley & Montemayor, 1997; Smetana, 1989), although disputes over household responsibilities become more frequent in late adolescence whereas disputes about academic performance peak in early adolescence with the transition to junior high school (Hamburg, 1985).

Preadolescents and adolescents seldom dispute parents' authority to make rules although they argue that parents should not impose such rules unilaterally, and should not have such low expectations of their abilities to comply (Damon, 1977; Hunter, 1984). Perhaps, therefore, family conflicts facilitate communication and adolescent autonomy by promoting open discussions of the parents' reasons and adolescents' protests over their parents' unilateral authority and demands (Youniss, 1989; Youniss & Smollar, 1985). The fact that children contest the basis of their parents' authority also underscores the fact that parent–adolescent conflict may be interpreted differently by parents and children (Larson & Richards, 1994). Parents are more likely to offer conventional interpretations of conflict whereas adolescents are more likely to interpret conflict in terms of personal jurisdiction (Smetana, 1988, 1989, 1995).

Summary

The preadolescent and adolescent periods mark the beginning of the biological changes associated with puberty which parallel transformations in the quality and meaning of parent–child relationships. Self-differentiation and individuation are linked to children's growing sexuality, and they may bring distance and conflict to parent–child relationships. Unfortunately, researchers studying the transformations of relationships during this period have not yet successfully disentangled the effects of puberty from the effects of contemporaneous role transitions.

During adolescence, children are expected to consolidate and apply their knowledge about the roles and rules of adult society, begin to achieve emotional and economic independence from parents, and complete the biological and physical changes that began in the pre-adolescent period. Psychoanalysts such as Anna Freud believe that intrapsychic forces associated with a "second Oedipal" event, interacting with the biological changes associated with pubertal development, disrupt emotional functioning, thereby producing adolescent rebelliousness and intrafamilial strife. This view has been challenged by the results of large-scale surveys showing no widespread psychopathology among adolescents, with only about 5% to 10% of families experiencing a dramatic decline in the quality of parent–child relationships during adolescence. Contrary to the psychoanalytic view, furthermore, adolescents do not become disengaged from their parents; instead parent–child relationships are qualitatively and functionally transformed. Some scholars have hypothesized that adolescents increasingly distance themselves from their parents, with the result that parent–offspring relationships are increasingly marked by self-assertion and conflict over family decisions. Other social scientists have suggested that parent–child relationships characterized by unilateral authority become parent–adolescent relationships marked by cooperative negotiations (mutuality), emotional closeness, and continuing parental support and influence.

THE LONGER VIEW: PARENTS' INFLUENCES ON TEENAGERS AND YOUNG ADULTS

It is relatively difficult to conduct longitudinal research following individuals into adulthood because families may move, or may not be eager for repeated contact with researchers, but the few existing studies have yielded interesting patterns. For a start, the "children" in these families appear to learn from particular experiences in the teenage years. For example, adults' feelings about their relationships and peer interactions are positively correlated with their experiences of parental care in the adolescent years (Burns & Dunlop, 1998), a finding that is consistent with findings showing continuities between adults' attachment feelings in pregnancy and their children's behavior in the Strange Situation (see above). Early paternal involvement also predicts adult children's feelings of satisfaction in spousal relationships and self-reported parenting skills (Franz, McClelland, & Weinberger, 1991). Likewise, fathers' expressions of hostility towards their 16-year-olds and the extent to which they undermined their teenagers' autonomy predicted the degree of hostility and low ego-resiliency reported in the "child" by close friends at age 25 (Allen, Hauser, O'Connor, & Bell, 2002). Measures of teenager–mother hostility also predicted adjustment at age 25.

Other researchers have examined paternal involvement in children's lives in relation to both concurrent parent–child measures and the children's later psychosocial functioning. For example, Lewis, Newson, and Newson (1982) found that the reported involvement of British fathers in two-parent households at ages 7 and 11 predicted the children's performance in national examinations at age 16 as well as whether or not they had a criminal record by age 21. Likewise, in their analyses of data from the UK National Child Development Study, Flouri and Buchanan (2002a, 2002b) have reported a variety of positive predictive associations between patterns of paternal involvement and later indices (when the "children" were 33 years of age) of psychosocial adjustment even when a range of possible mediating factors (e.g., gender, parental socioeconomic status (SES), family structure, parental mental health, maternal involvement) were controlled. Maternally reported father-involvement at age 7 predicted the child's self-reported closeness to father at 16 and lower levels of police contact as reported by the child's mother and teacher (Flouri & Buchanan, 2002a). This in turn predicted marital satisfaction and diminished psychological distress at age 33 (Flouri & Buchanan, 2002b). At the same time, self-reported closeness to mother at age 16 predicted only marital satisfaction 17 years later. Furthermore, Koestner, Franz, and Weinberger (1990) reported significant associations between paternal involvement at age five and the children's feelings when they were in their early thirties—more than 25 years later. Similarly, Franz, McClelland, Weinberger, and Peterson (1994) re-contacted children initially studied by Sears, Maccoby and Levin (1957) and reported that "Over a period of 36 years, the children of warm, affectionate fathers, and boys with warm mothers and less stressful childhood years were more likely to be well adjusted adults who, at age 41, were mentally healthy, coping adequately, and psychosocially mature" (p. 141). Results such as these suggest that, in the long term, patterns of father–child closeness might be crucial predictors of later psychosocial adjustment although the patterns of maternal and paternal influence remain to be explored in depth.

These longitudinal studies relied predominantly on maternal reports of early paternal involvement and warmth, however, and we must be cautious in inferring paternal influences from these data, particularly as marital closeness is a strong predictor of children's psychological well-being as well (Cummings, Goeke-Morey, & Raymond, 2004; Davies & Cummings, 1994; Grych & Fincham, 1990). It could be that maternal reports of high paternal involvement reflect something else, such as family harmony or the mother's own psychological well-being, and this would explain why levels of paternal involvement are often unrelated to contemporaneous indices of adjustment. For example, Israeli teenagers' academic performance was related to their descriptions of maternal, but not paternal, involvement (Feldman, Guttfreund, & Yerushalmi, 1998).

Further work needs to be conducted to tease apart the reasons for these links between paternal relationships with children and later psychological functioning. At present, the evidence seems to suggest that some features of father–child relationships might be more influential than expected given the amounts of time men in two-parent households typically spend with their children. It could be that paternal influences are epiphenomenal—involved men might for example have better adjusted adult children because 50% of their genetic make-up is shared. The theoretical debates summarized at the start of the chapter underscore the need to avoid simplistic interpretations of associations that are likely to be complex as well as simplistic comparisons between father-present and father-absent families.

On the other hand, although it is clear that some fathers (like mothers) can have adverse effects on their children's adjustment, on balance the literature shows positive effects of paternal involvement with children. For example, Sarkadi, Kristiansson, Oberklaid, and Bremberg (2008) conducted a systematic review of 24 longitudinal studies involving 22,300 children; 22 reported significant paternal influences on child development. Of these, 21 recorded "positive" influences and only one negative. Although in some studies the paternal effect was no longer significant when SES was controlled, and factors such as cohabitation were most important, the authors concluded that paternal involvement appears to affect the frequency both of behavior problems in boys and of psychological problems in girls. Paternal involvement was related to decreased delinquency and economic disadvantage in low SES families and showed a general association with enhanced cognitive development.

How do these effects of fathering work? Clearly, we need sophisticated models that take account of the complexities of factors in the family and social systems, including each parent's psychosocial adjustment, their relationship, wider social processes and the child's own developmental status. In an exemplary study, Boyce and his colleagues (2006) found that the effects of paternal involvement in infancy on behavior problems at the age of nine were moderated by measures of the children's psycho-physiological sensitivity at the age of seven. Children with high autonomic reactivity who had experienced both low father involvement in infancy and maternal depression later had the most pronounced problems.

DIVERSITY IN FAMILY PATTERNS AND RELATIONSHIPS

In this final section, we aim to illustrate the need for researchers to address the issue of diversity more completely by briefly describing research on cultural variation, the effects of divorce and single parenting, and the effects of family violence on children and adolescents. The research on single parent and divorcing families underlines not only the importance of parenting relationships in children's development, but also the factors that influence these so poignantly—the relationship between parents, economic and social factors that influence the family system and, importantly, the ways in which these factors change continuously through time. Family violence is discussed because the research has identified some important themes that are relevant to our broader understanding of family influences on child and adolescent development.

Cultural and Subcultural Variation

Despite the multicultural nature of contemporary societies, most information on the socioemotional development of children has been derived from studies of white, middle-class North Americans. Ethnocentricity in developmental science has limited the generalizability and universality of developmental principles and norms, while restricting our understanding of the variations in human behavior and experiences across cultures and subcultures (Bornstein, 2009). It is all too easy to make assumptions about the similarities and differences between family types and members of different ethnic groups. Social scientists frequently assume, for example, that most households include two adult parents living with their children, although it has long been clear that such households are in the minority (Lamb, 1999b; Rapoport, Rapoport, & Strellitz, 1975).

Researchers are also somewhat blind to ethnic differences, particularly given the dramatic international migration that took place in the second half of the twentieth century. For example, more than 30% of all young Americans today come from minority backgrounds and ethnic minority families constitute the fastest growing segment of the US population (Cabrera & Garcia Coll, 2004; Parke & Buriel, 1998; Roopnarine, 2004). African Americans make up an increasing proportion of the total population of young people in the USA, while the numbers of Hispanic youths and of children born to immigrants are growing rapidly. In addition, children in the United States are increasingly likely to grow up in poverty, which has harmful effects on the nature and quality of parent–child relationships (Brooks-Gunn, Britto, & Brady, 1999; Duncan & Brooks-Gunn, 1997). Conditions of family hardship, for example, are associated with less responsive, patient, and nurturant parental behavior toward children and adolescents (Brooks-Gunn & Chase-Lansdale, 1995; Lempers, Clark-Lempers & Simons,

1989; Osofsky, Hann, & Peebles, 1993; Tamis-Lemonda & McFadden, 2010). Because socio-economic and sociocultural factors appear to have such a powerful effect on the processes and outcomes of socialization (Parke & Buriel, 1998), there have been increasing demands by social scientists to include culture and cultural experiences as critical variables in research on human development. Recent years have witnessed increased attention to African American (McHale et al., 2006) and Latin American (Cabrera, Shannon, West, & Brooks-Gunn, 2006) parenting on the part of researchers. This research has elucidated differences between African American, European American, and Latino American families (Foster & Kalil, 2007; Roopnarine, Fouts, Lamb, & Lewis-Elligan, 2005; Fouts, Roopnarine, & Lamb, 2007; Fouts et al., in press; Vogel, Bradley, Raikes, Boller, & Shears,, 2006), but most researchers have focused on problems in development (Coley & Medeiros, 2007) and there is sill insufficient analysis of normative family patterns, let alone the cultural diversity around the world (Bornstein, 2009), particularly because the effects of culture and ethnicity are often confounded with the effects of SES and poverty (Tamis LeMonda & McFadden, 2010).

Even though their practices deviate massively from those that characterize industrialized countries, studies of child care among hunter-gatherers, such as the !Kung, Bofi, or Aka, have also contributed significantly to our understanding of the causes of variation in child rearing practices. In these countries, for example, the amount of child care performed by fathers varies depending on the availability of other care providers (Konner, 2005; Hewlett, 1987, 2005; Hewlett & MacFarlan, 2010). More generally, Hrdy's (2005; see also Lamb & Ahnert, 2006) examination of "allo-mothering" underscores not only the extent to which allo-mothering is nearly universal but also how the identity of "allo-mothers" varies as individuals opportunistically exploit the human resources available to them.

Forest dwelling hunter-gatherers such as the Aka and the Bofi are characterized by extremely egalitarian norms and minimal gender differentiation, whereas hunter-gatherers such as the Hadza of East Africa are more gender stratified and, not coincidentally, not characterized by equivalently high levels of paternal participation in child care (Marlowe, 2005). Paternal participation in infant care is also lower among agricultural groups in Africa than among the forest hunter-gatherers such as the Aka and Bofi, although fathers in these cultures begin providing care, guidance, and tutelage to their offspring much earlier in development than Western fathers became involved in childcare in the middle part of the twentieth century.

The physical and social ecologies occupied by these African groups and by parents in industrialized societies are dramatically different, yet the relevant research shows that variability, change, adaptability, and opportunism are key features when we examine parenting (perhaps especially fathering) and child care in cross-cultural and/or historical perspective (Hewlett & Macfarlan, 2010).

The significance of sociocultural factors is also evident in research on parental disciplinary styles. Steinberg and Darling (1994; Steinberg, Darling & Fletcher, 1995), for example, found that although authoritative rearing was always beneficial or at least not harmful and that disengaged parenting was always harmful or at least not beneficial, the impact of parenting style varied across sociocultural groups. Authoritative parenting was beneficial and neglectful parenting was disadvantageous for European American and Latin youth, but authoritarian parenting was more advantageous for Asian American adolescents and more disadvantageous for European American adolescents than for adolescents in the other groups.

Few researchers have compared parent–adolescent relationships in different countries. Kroger (1985) found that American, New Zealand, and British adolescents from Grades 6, 8, 10, and 12 all had similar attitudes towards parental authority. Although American girls of all ages felt more favorably about their parents, girls in New Zealand, who had positive attitudes toward their parents in the early grades, became less positive as they grew older. Feldman and her colleagues (Feldman & Rosenthal, 1991; Feldman, Rosenthal, Mont-Reynaud, Leung, & Lau, 1991) found that although Hong Kong Chinese adolescents reported more misbehavior and expected to achieve behavioral autonomy later that did Australian and American youth, levels of misconduct and expectations of behavioral autonomy were related in similar ways to family environments and adolescent values in Chinese and Western cultures. More studies of this sort may be especially informative as we seek to distinguish the effects of broad cultural factors from the effects of parental socialization strategies. Recent studies of parenting and child development among immigrants promise to be especially informative in this regard (see Lamb & Bougher, 2009, for a brief review of some recent research on this topic).

Divorce and Single Parenthood

Although the rates of divorce have leveled recently, about half of the children in the United States and northern Europe are still likely to experience the separation of their parents before they reach adulthood (Amato, in press). Interestingly, geographical and/or cultural factors influence the contact between parents and their children after their parents' divorce. In North America, many children lose meaningful contact with their fathers, whereas in the geographically more compact UK, in which the term "custody" was abolished over a decade ago, children usually reengage with their fathers to some (often limited) degree after an initially difficult period (Maclean & Eekelaar, 1997). Nevertheless, common sense and scientific research tell us that the experience of divorce and continuing parental separation are experiences likely to have psychological costs, demonstrably with respect to psychosocial adjustment, behavior and achievement at school, educational attainment, employment trajectories, income generation, involvement in antisocial and even criminal behavior, and the ability to establish and maintain intimate relationships. Controversy and ideology bedeviled acknowledgment and analysis of these costs in the 1970s and 1980s, but there is substantial consensus today that children are better off psychologically and developmentally in two- rather than single-parent families (Amato, in press; see also Malloy, Lamb, and Katz, Chapter 13, this volume) and that the effects of father loss due to the parents' separation/divorce are greater and more reliable than the effects of father absence due to paternal death (Amato & Keith, 1991; Maier & Lachman, 2000).

The first challenge, of course, was to determine why these differences emerge. Whereas social scientists and commentators such as Biller (1981, 1993) and Blankenhorn (1995) proposed that child adjustment was adversely affected when children lacked father figures in their lives, most social scientists questioned this interpretation both because it failed to acknowledge the many other salient and potentially harmful conditions or events experienced by children whose parents do not live together and because it cannot account for the diversity of responses to separation and divorce (Lamb, 1999b, 2002b; Lamb & Kelly, 2009). Notwithstanding group differences between children in single- and two-parent families, only a minority of children in single-parent families are maladjusted; the majority evince no psychopathology or behavioral symptoms, whether or not they experience psychic pain (Emery, 1999; Hetherington & Kelly, 2002).

A variety of factors account for individual differences in children's adjustment following the divorce/separation of their parents (Lamb, 2002a; Lamb & Kelly, 2009), as Malloy and her colleagues explain in Chapter 13. Typically, first of all, single parenthood is associated with a variety of social and financial stresses with which custodial parents must cope, largely on their own. Second, because single mothers need to work more extensively outside the home than married mothers do, parents spend less time with children in single-parent families and the levels of supervision and guidance are lower and less reliable than in two-parent families (Hetherington & Kelly, 2002; McLanahan, 1999). Thirdly, divorce commonly disrupts one of the child's most important and enduring relationships, that with his or her father (Lamb & Kelly, 2009). Children's well-being is significantly enhanced when their relationships with nonresidential fathers are positive and when nonresident fathers are actively engaged in their lives (Fabricius, Braver, Diaz, & Velez, 2010). (Positive relationships with custodial mothers were also beneficial, of course.) Finally, conflict between parents commonly precedes, emerges during, or increases during the separation and divorce processes, and often continues beyond them (Cummings, Merrilees, & Ward George, 2010; Kelly, 2000).

The level of involvement and quality of relationships between both parents and their children, the level of conflict between the two parents, and the socioeconomic circumstances in which children reside all affect adjustment to divorce/single parenthood and in the absence of intensive and reliable longitudinal data, it is often difficult either to discern causal relationships unambiguously or to establish the relative importance of different factors. For example, child adjustment, paternal involvement in decision-making, the level of high-quality contact children have with non-custodial parents and the amount of child support received are all correlated (Amato & Gilbreth, 1999; Braver & O'Connell, 1998; Braver et al., 1993; Furstenberg & Cherlin, 1991; McLanahan & Sandefur, 1994; Seltzer, 1991, 1994, 1998; Zill & Nord, 1996), making it difficult to determine which factor is most important.

Family Violence

Surprising as it may seem, most incidents of serious and less physical violence in the United States and other industrial nations occur among family members in the home (Straus & Gelles, 1986, 1990; Straus, Gelles, & Steinmetz, 1980). Because no standardized data collection techniques or consensual definitions exist, however, estimates of the prevalence of child maltreatment in the US vary between 200,000 and 4 million cases per year, with as many as 1 million cases of "serious abuse" and 2,000 to 5,000 fatalities per year (Finkelhor & Dziuba-Leatherman, 1994; Sedlak & Broadhurst, 1996; Straus & Gelles, 1990). In addition, the parents of 10% to 30% of the children in the US treat one another violently (Geffner & Pagelow, 1990; Hughes & Luke, 1998; Straus & Gelles, 1986, 1990), often in the presence of their children (Hughes, Parkinson & Vargo, 1989; O'Brien, John, Margolin, & Erel, 1994). Various factors (such as the child's age, gender, and sociodemographic status) are related to the reported incidence of domestic violence, as is the source of information about the reported abuse (Sternberg & Lamb, 1999).

The consequences of domestic violence are pervasive, although no single behavioral or emotional characteristics are common to abused children, and other aspects of the child's environment may be highly influential (Emery, 1989). In addition, many of the earlier studies had particularly severe methodological problems (such as the failure to include appropriate comparison groups, or to obtain objective measures of the violence, or children's adjustment) and researchers still commonly fail to document all possible types of family violence in the studies they conduct (National Research Council, 1993). In comparison with non-abused children, abused children of all ages manifest many psychological deviations, but there is no one-to-one relation between incidents and symptoms (Ammerman, Cassisi, Herson, & Van Hasselt, 1986; Cicchetti, in press; Emery & Billings, 1998). In addition to possible neurodevelopmental and psychological impairment (Lynch & Roberts, 1982; Oates, Peacock, & Forrest, 1984), socioemotional and psychological damage is also common. Social learning theorists contend that physical abuse leads to later aggression because aggressive responses are frequently modeled and often have desirable consequences (Dodge, Bates, & Pettit, 1990; Emery, 1989). Not surprisingly, maltreated children have poor relations with peers (Dodge et al., 1990; Dodge, Pettit, & Bates, 1994; George & Main, 1979; Salzinger, Feldman, Hammer, & Rosario, 1993; Wolfe & Mosk, 1983) with whom they behave aggressively (Bousha &

Twentyman, 1984; Dodge et al., 1990; Egeland & Sroufe, 1981; George & Main, 1979; Kaufman & Cicchetti, 1989; Price & Van Slyke, 1991), suffer from deficits in social cognition (Barahal, Waterman, & Martin, 1981), lack empathy (Main & George, 1985), appear depressed (Kazdin, Moser, Colbus, & Bell, 1985; Sternberg et al., 1993), and perform poorly on cognitive tasks and in school (Eckenrode, Laird, & Doris, 1993; Hoffman-Plotkin & Twentyman, 1984; Kendall-Tackett & Eckenrode, 1996). Abused children are also more likely to manifest aggressive, non-compliant acting-out (Pianta, Egeland, & Erickson, 1989; Sternberg et al., 1993). Abused children may become overly attentive to hostile cues, mis-interpreting the behavior of others and responding with aggression (Dodge et al., 1990; Price & Van Slyke, 1991) and to develop insecure attachments (Carlson, Cicchetti, Barnett, & Braumwald, 1989; Crittenden, 1988; Crittenden & Ainsworth, 1989; Lamb, Gaensbauer, Malkin, & Shultz, 1985) because they have come to see the world as a threatening place, although most abused children remain attached to abusive parents and see positive aspects to their relationships (Sternberg et al., 1994, 2005). Abused and neglected children are also more likely than are matched controls to be arrested for delinquency, to become adult criminals, and to exhibit violent criminal behavior (Widom, 1989, 1994). Not all abused or neglected children suffer these negative consequences, however, although researchers have yet to discern why some adolescents are more resilient than others. Factors such as age of onset and seriousness of abuse and neglect probably play a role in determining long-term outcomes (Sternberg, Baradaran, Abbott, Lamb, & Guterman, 2006a). On the other hand, there is increasing evidence that children can be affected adversely by family violence even when they "merely" witness violence and are not themselves directly assaulted or neglected (Holden, Geffner, & Jouriles, 1998).

CONCLUSIONS

Thanks in large part to Freud's insightful focus on the formative significance of parent–child relationships, students of social and personality development have studied these relationships throughout much of the past century. Over time, they have come to place less emphasis on the "critical" importance of early experiences and relationships, choosing instead to view relationships at various stages of the lifespan as significant, albeit changing, aspects of the formative social environment. As we have noted in this chapter, the focal contents of parent–child relationships change as children grow older and, presumably, as their parents mature as well. Initially, parents provide a context in which children learn that their behaviors have consequences, developing conceptions of their own effectance and trust in others' reliable responsiveness. Thereafter, parents instill standards of behavior and self-control, before becoming foils for their children's pursuit of independence and autonomy as adolescence unfolds. Needless to say, parents differ in their ability to respond sensitively to their children's individual needs and characteristics, and in the way in which they strive to discipline and socialize their children. These differences affect the quality of parent–child relationships and may in turn have long-term influences on children's behavior and adjustment, although their relative importance, in the context of the many other influential events children experience, remain to be determined. Certainly, researchers today see parent–child relationships as dynamic systems that vary in quality depending on individual, familial, societal, and cultural circumstances.

Although some research topics (especially parent–infant and, to a lesser extent, parent–adolescent relationships) have been very well studied, others (e.g., "parenting" young adults or children in middle childhood) have been relatively neglected. The need to address these topics remains. Much current scholarship is focused on connections among previously unrelated areas. For example, Parke and his colleagues (2002, 2004) have made extensive efforts to unravel the patterns of influence between the family and peer systems, having shown that they are highly interrelated. At the same time, researchers in the behavioral genetics and social learning traditions have combined forces to examine the complexity of interactions between genetic and social factors (Hetherington, Bridges, & Insabella, 1998). Only by combining approaches in this manner will we obtain a broader understanding of the ways in which parents shape their children's development.

Although we have made considerable progress in our attempts to understand the complexities of parenting, three key issues will need especially close attention in the immediate future. First, there are many gaps in our understanding of research methods. As O'Connor (2002) suggests, reliance on diverse methods is virtuous, but brings with it particular problems, especially when different methods produce incompatible results! Second, we persist in treating "parenting" as "mothering," because mothers continue to take the major role in child care and socialization and are more available to study, whereas research continues to suggest that we should distinguish father–child and mother–child relationships and their influences. Finally, as Hay and Nash (2002) and Lamb (1999b) pointed out, we continue to assume that the "traditional" nuclear family is the blueprint against which all other types of family should be compared—usually unfavorably. The challenge for future research is to acknowledge that psychologists tend to focus rather narrowly on households typical of their white, predominantly Anglo-Saxon backgrounds, even though such families are in the minority, and that their studies poorly reflect and represent the diversity and complexity of contemporary family life.

REFERENCES AND SUGGESTED READINGS (📖)

Acock, A. C., & Bengtson, V. L. (1978). On the relative influence of mothers and fathers: A covariance analysis of political and religious socialization. *Journal of Marriage and the Family*, *40*, 519–530.

Ahnert, L., Pinquart, M., & Lamb, M. E. (2006). Security of children's relationships with nonparental care providers: A meta-analysis. *Child Development*, *74*, 664–679.

Ainsworth, M. D. S., Blehar, M. C., Waters, E., & Wall, S. (1978). *Patterns of attachment: A psychological study of the strange situation*. Hillsdale, NJ: Lawrence Erlbaum Associates.

Allen, S. M., Hauser, S. T., O'Connor, T. G., & Bell, K. L. (2002). Prediction of peer-rated adult hostility from autonomy struggles in adolescent–family interactions. *Development and Psychopathology*, *14*, 123–137.

Amato, P. R. (1993). Children's adjustment to divorce: Theories, hypotheses, and empirical support. *Journal of Marriage and the Family*, *55*, 23–38.

Amato, P. R. (2000). Diversity within single-parent families. In D. H. Demo, K. R. Allen, & M. A. Fine (Eds.), *Handbook of family diversity* (pp. 149–172). Oxford, UK: Oxford University Press.

Amato, P. R., & Gilbreth, J. G. (1999). Nonresident fathers and children's well-being: A meta-analysis. *Journal of Marriage & the Family*, *61*, 557–573.

Amato, P. R., & Keith, B. (1991). Parental divorce and the well-being of children: A meta-analysis. *Psychological Bulletin*, *110*, 26–46.

Amato, P. R., & Rezac, S. J. (1994). Contact with nonresidential parents, interparental conflict, and children's behavior. *Journal of Family Issues*, *15*, 191–207.

Amato, P. R., & Sobelewski, J. M. (2004). The effects of divorce on fathers and children: Nonresidential father and stepfathers. In M. E. Lamb (Ed.), *The role of the father in child development* (4th ed., pp. 341–367). New York: Wiley.

Ambrose, J. A. (1961). The development of the smiling response in early infancy. In B. M. Foss (Ed.), *Determinants of infant behavior* (pp. 179–196). London: Methuen.

Ammerman, R. T., Cassisi, J. E., Herson, M., & Van Hasselt, V. B. (1986). Consequences of physical abuse and neglect in children. *Clinical Psychology Review*, *6*, 291–310.

Andrews, D. W., & Dishion, T. J. (1994). The microsocial structure underpinnings of adolescent problem behavior. In R. D. Ketterlinus & M. E. Lamb (Eds.), *Adolescent problem behaviors: Issues and research* (pp. 187–207). Hillsdale, NJ: Lawrence Erlbaum Associates.

Astington, J. W. (1996). What is theoretical about the child's understanding of mind? A Vygotskian view of its development. In P. Carruthers & P. K. Smith (Eds.), *Theories of theories of mind* (pp. 184–199). Cambridge, UK: Cambridge University Press.

Baer, J., & Martinez, C. D. (2006). Child maltreatment and insecure attachment: A meta-analysis. *Journal of Reproductive & Infant Psychology, 24,* 187–197.

Bakermans-Kranenburg, M. J., van IJzendoorn, M. H., & Juffer, F. (2003). Less is more: Meta-analyses of sensitivity and attachment interventions in early childhood. *Psychological Bulletin, 129,* 195–216.

Bandura, A. (1969). *Principles of behavior modification.* New York: Holt, Rinehart, & Winston.

Bandura, A. (1977). Self-efficacy: Toward a unifying theory of behavioral change. *Psychological Review, 84,* 191–215.

Bandura, A. (1986). *Social foundations of thought and action: A social cognitive theory.* Englewood Cliffs, NJ: Prentice Hall.

Bandura, A. (1997). *Self-efficacy: The exercise of control.* New York: Freeman.

Barahal, R. M., Waterman, J., & Martin, H. P. (1981). The social cognitive development of abused children. *Journal of Consulting and Clinical Psychology, 49,* 508–516.

Barry, R. A., Kochanska, G., & Philibert, R. A. (2008). G–E interaction in the organization of attachment: mothers' responsiveness as a moderator of children's genotypes. *Journal of Child Psychology and Psychiatry, 49,* 1313–1320.

Baumrind, D. (1967). Child care practices anteceding three patterns of preschool behavior. *Genetic Psychology Monographs, 75,* 43–88.

Baumrind, D. (1971). Current patterns of parental authority. *Developmental Psychology Monographs, 4,* 1–103.

Baumrind, D. (1972). An exploratory study of socialization effects on black children: Some black–white comparisons. *Child Development, 43,* 261–267.

Baumrind, D. (1973). The development of instrumental competence through socialization. In A. Pick (Ed.), *Minnesota symposia on child psychology* (Vol. 7, pp. 3–46). Minneapolis, MN: University of Minnesota.

Baumrind, D. (1975). *Early socialization and the discipline controversy.* Morristown, NJ: General Learning.

Baumrind, D. (1991). Parenting styles and adolescent development. In R. M. Lerner, A. C. Petersen, & J. Brooks-Gunn (Eds.), *Encyclopedia of adolescence* (Vol. 2, pp.746–758). New York: Garland Publishing.

Baumrind, D., & Black, A. E. (1967). Socialization practices associated with dimensions of competence in preschool boys and girls. *Child Development, 38,* 291–327.

Beck, U., & Beck-Gernsheim, E. (1995). *The normal chaos of love.* Cambridge, UK: Polity.

Bell, R. Q. (1968). A reinterpretation of the direction of effects in studies of socialization. *Psychological Review, 75,* 81–95.

Bell, S. M., & Ainsworth, M. D. (1972). Infant crying and maternal responsiveness. *Child Development, 43,* 1171–1190.

Belsky, J. (1997). Variation in susceptibility to rearing influence: An evolutionary argument. *Psychological Inquiry, 8,* 182–186.

Belsky, J. (1999). Interactional and contextual determinants of attachment security. In J. Cassidy & P. R. Shaver (Eds.), *Handbook of attachment: Theory, research, and clinical applications* (pp. 249–264). New York: Guilford Press.

Belsky, J., Booth-LaForce, C., Bradley, R., Brownell, C. A., Burchinal, M., Campbell, S. B., et al. (2008). Mothers' and fathers' support for child autonomy and early school achievement. *Developmental Psychology, 44,* 895–907.

Belsky, J., Fish, M., & Isabella, R. A. (1991). Continuity and discontinuity in infant negative and positive emotionality: Family antecedents and attachment consequences. *Developmental Psychology, 27,* 421–431.

Belsky, J., Garduque, L., & Hrncir, E. (1984). Assessing performance, competence, and executive capacity in infant play: Relations to home environment and security of attachment. *Developmental Psychology, 20,* 406–417.

Belsky, J., & Pluess, M. (2009). The nature (and nurture?) of plasticity in early human development. *Perspectives on Psychological Science, 4,* 345–351.

Belsky. J., Vandell, D. L., Burchinal, M., Clarke-Stewart, K., McCartney, K., & Owen, M. T. (2007). Are there long-term effects of early child care? *Child Development, 78,* 681–701.

Benzies, K. M., Harrison, M. J., & Magill-Evans, J. (1998). Impact of marital quality and parent–infant interaction on preschool behavior problems. *Public Health Nursing, 15,* 35–43.

Berlin, L. J., & Cassidy, J. (1999). Relations among relationships: Contributions from attachment theory and research. In J. Cassidy & P. R. Shaver (Eds.), *Handbook of attachment: Theory, research, and clinical applications* (pp. 688–712). New York: Guilford Press.

Biller, H. B. (1981). Father absence, divorce, and personality development. In M. E. Lamb (Ed.), *The role of the father in child development* (2nd ed., pp. 489–552). New York: Wiley.

Biller, H. B. (1993). *Fathers and families: Paternal factors in child development.* Westport, CT: Auburn House.

Blankenhorn, D. (1995). *Fatherless America.* New York: Basic Books.

Blos, P. (1979). *The adolescent passage.* New York: International Universities Press.

Booth-LaForce, C., Oh, W., Kim, A., Rubin, K. H., Rose-Krasnor, L., & Burgess, K. (2006). Attachment, self-worth, and peer-group functioning in middle childhood. *Attachment and Human Development, 8,* 309–325.

Borke, J., Lamm, B., Eickhorst, A., & Keller, H. (2007). Father–infant interaction, paternal ideas about early child care, and their consequences for the development of children's self-recognition. *Journal of Genetic Psychology, 168,* 365–379.

Bornstein, M. H. (Ed.) (2009). *Handbook of cultural developmental science.* New York: Psychology Press.

Bornstein M. H., Tamis-LeMonda C. S., Hahn C. S., & Haynes, O. M. (2008). Maternal responsiveness to young children at three ages: Longitudinal analysis of a multidimensional, modular, and specific parenting construct. *Developmental Psychology*, *44*, 867–874.

Bousha, D. M., & Twentyman, C. T. (1984). Mother–child interactional style in abuse, neglect, and control groups: Naturalistic observations in the home. *Journal of Abnormal Psychology*, *93*, 106–144.

Bowlby, J. (1969). *Attachment and loss: Vol. 1. Attachment*. New York: Basic Books.

Bowlby, J. (1973). *Attachment and loss: Vol. 2. Separation: Anxiety and anger*. New York: Basic Books.

Bowlby, J. (1988). *A secure base: Parent–child attachment and healthy human development*. New York: Basic Books.

Boyce, W. T., Essex, M. J., Alkon, A., Goldsmith, H. H., Kraemer, H. C., & Kupfer, D. J. (2006). Early father involvement moderates biobehavioral susceptibility to mental health problems in middle childhood. *Journal of the American Academy of Child and Adolescent Psychiatry*, *45*, 1510–1520.

Braver, S. H., Wolchik, S. A., Sandler, I. N., Fogas, B. S., & Zvetina, D. (1991). Frequency of visitation by divorced fathers: Differences in reports by fathers and mothers. *American Journal of Orthopsychiatry*, *61*, 448–454.

Braver, S. L., & O'Connell, E. (1998). *Divorced dads: Shattering the myths*. New York: Thatcher Putnam.

Braver, S. L., Wolchik, S. A., Sandler, I. N., Sheets, V. L., Fogas, B., & Bay, R.C. (1993). A longitudinal study of noncustodial parents: Parents without children. *Journal of Family Psychology*, *7*, 9–23.

Brennan, P. A., Hammen, C., Katz, A. R., & Le Brocque, R. M. (2002). Maternal depression, paternal psychopathology, and adolescent diagnostic outcomes. *Journal of Consulting & Clinical Psychology*, *70*, 1075–1085.

Bretherton, I. (1990). Open communication and internal working models: Their role in the development of attachment relationships. In R. A. Thompson (Ed.), *Socioemotional development* (pp. 57–114). Lincoln, NE: University of Nebraska.

Bretherton, I. (1991). Pouring new wine into old bottles: The social self as internal working model. In M. R. Gunnar & L. A. Sroufe (Eds.), *Self process and development: Minnesota symposia on child psychology* (Vol. 23, pp. 1–41). Hillsdale, NJ: Lawrence Erlbaum Associates.

Bretherton, I. (1993). From dialogue to internal working models: The co-construction of self relationships. In C. A. Nelson (Ed.), *Memory and affect in development* (pp. 237–263). Hillsdale, NJ: Lawrence Erlbaum Associates.

Bretherton, I., Bates, E., Benigni, L., Camaioni, L., & Volterra, V. (1979). Relations between cognition, communication, and quality of attachment. In E. Bates (Ed.), *The emergence of symbols: Cognition and communication in infancy* (pp. 223–269). New York: Academic Press.

Bretherton, I., & Munholland, K. A. (1999). Internal working models in attachment relationships: A construct revisited. In J. Cassidy & P. R. Shaver (Eds.), *Handbook of attachment: Theory, research, and clinical applications* (pp. 89–111). New York: Guilford Press.

Bronfenbrenner, U. (1979). Contexts of child rearing: Problems and prospects. *American Psychologist*, *34*, 844–850.

Bronstein, P. (1984). Differences in mothers' and fathers' behaviors toward children: A cross-cultural comparison. *Developmental Psychology*, *20*, 995–1003.

Brooks-Gunn, J., Britto, P. R., & Brady, C. (1999). Struggling to make ends meet: Poverty and child development. In M. E. Lamb (Ed.), *Parenting and child development in "nontraditional" families* (pp. 279–304). Mahwah, NJ: Lawrence Erlbaum Associates.

Brooks-Gunn, J., & Chase-Lansdale, P. L. (1995). Adolescent parenthood. In M. H. Bornstein (Ed.), *Handbook of parenting* (pp. 113–150). Hillsdale, NJ: Lawrence Erlbaum Associates.

Brown, G. L., Mangelsdorf, S. C., Wong, M. S., Shigeto, A. & Neff, C. (2009, April). *Fathering and father–child attachment across the first three years: Stability and longitudinal links*. Poster presented at the Society for Research in Child Development, Denver, CO.

Bugental, D. B., & Goodnow, J. S. (1998). Socialization processes. In W. Damon & N. Eisenberg (Eds.), *Handbook of child psychology: Vol. 3. Social, emotional and personality development* (5th ed., pp. 289–463). New York: Wiley.

Buhrmeister, D. P., & Furman, W. C. (1990). Perceptions of sibling relationships during middle childhood and adolescence. *Child Development*, *61*, 1387–1398.

Burns, A., & Dunlop, R. (1998). Parental divorce, parent–child relations, and early adult relationships: A longitudinal Australian study. *Personal Relationships*, *5*, 393–407.

Bushnell, I. W. R., Sai, F., & Mullin, J. T. (1989). Neonatal recognition of the mother's face. *British Journal of Developmental Psychology*, *7*, 3–15.

Cabrera, N., & Garcia Coll, C. (2004). Latino fathers: Uncharted territory in need of much exploration. In M. E. Lamb (Ed.), *The role of the father in child development* (4th ed., pp. 98–120). Hoboken, NJ: Wiley.

Cabrera, N. J., Shannon, J. D., & Tamis-LeMonda, C. S. (2007). Fathers' influence on their children's cognitive and emotional development: From toddlers to pre-K. *Journal of Applied Developmental Science*, *11*, 208–213.

Cabrera, N. J., Shannon, J. D., West, J., & Brooks-Gunn, J. (2006). Parental interactions with Latino infants: Variation by country of origin and English proficiency. *Child Development*, *77*, 1190–1207.

Caldera, Y. M., Huston, A. C., & O'Brien, M. (1995). *Antecedents of father–infant attachment: A longitudinal study*. Paper presented at the Society for Research in Child Development, Indianapolis, IN.

Carlson, V., Cicchetti, D., Barnett, D., & Braunwald, K. G. (1989). Finding order in disorganization: Lessons from research on maltreated infants' attachment to their caregivers. In D. Cicchetti & V. Carlson (Eds.), *Child *maltreatment: Theory and research on the causes and consequences of child abuse and neglect* (pp. 494–528). New York: Cambridge University Press.

Carpendale, J. I. M., & Lewis, C. (2006). *How children develop social understanding*. Oxford, UK: Blackwell.

Carpendale, J. I. M., & Lewis, C. (2010). The development of social understanding: A relational perspective. In W. Overton & R. M. Lerner (Eds.), *The handbook of lifespan developmental psychology* (Vol. 1). Chichester, UK: Wiley.

Cassidy, J. (1988). Child–mother attachment and the self in six-year-olds. *Child Development, 59*, 121–134.

Chen, X., Liu, M., & Li, D. (2000). Parental warmth, control and indulgence and their relations to adjustment in Chinese children. *Journal of Family Psychology, 14*, 401–409.

Clarke-Stewart, K. A., & Hayward, C. (1996). Advantages of father custody and contact for the psychological well-being of school-age children. *Journal of Applied Developmental Psychology, 17*, 239–270.

Coleman, J. C., & Hendry, L. (1990). *The nature of adolescence* (2nd ed.). London: Routledge.

Coleman, J. S. (1961). *The adolescent society: The social life of the teenager and its impact on education*. New York: Basic Books.

Coley, R. L., & Medeiros, B. L. (2007). Reciprocal longitudinal relations between nonresident father involvement and adolescent delinquency, *Child Development, 78*, 132–147.

Collins, W. A. (1990). Parent–child relationships in the transition to adolescence: Continuity and change in interaction, affect, and cognition. In R. Montemayor, G. R. Adams, & T. Gullotta (Eds.), *From childhood to adolescence: A transitional period? Advances in adolescent development*. (Vol. 2, pp. 85–106). Beverly Hills, CA: Sage.

Collins, W. A. (1991). Shared views and parent–adolescent relationships. In R. L. Paikoff (Ed.), *Shared views in the family during adolescence: New directions for child development* (Vol. 51, pp. 103–110). San Francisco: Jossey-Bass.

Collins, W. A. (1997). Relationships and development during adolescence: Interpersonal adaptation to individual change. *Personal Relationships, 4*, 1–14.

Collins, W. A., Harris, M. L., & Susman, A. (1995). Parenting during middle childhood. In M. H. Bornstein (Ed.), *Handbook of parenting* (Vol. 1, pp. 65–89). Mahwah, NJ: Lawrence Erlbaum Associates.

Collins, W. A., Maccoby, E. E., Steinberg, L., Hetherington, E. M., & Bornstein, M. H. (2000). Contemporary research on parenting: The case for nature and nurture. *American Psychologist, 55*, 218–232.

Collins, W. A., & Russell, G. (1991). Mother–child and father–child relationships in middle childhood and adolescence: A developmental analysis. *Developmental Review, 11*, 99–136.

Condon, J. T., Corkindale, C. K., & Boyce, P. (2008). Assessment of postnatal paternal–infant attachment: Development of a questionnaire instrument. *Journal of Reproductive and Infant Psychology, 26*, 195–210.

Cooksey, E. C. (1997). Consequences of young mothers' marital histories for children's cognitive development. *Journal of Marriage and the Family, 59*, 245–261.

Cooksey, E. C., & Fondell, M. M. (1996). Spending time with his kids: Effects of family structure on fathers' and children's lives. *Journal of Marriage and the Family, 58*, 693–707.

Cox, M. J., Owen, M. T., Henderson, V. K., & Margand, N. A. (1992). Prediction of infant–father and infant–mother attachment. *Developmental Psychology, 28*, 474–483.

Criss, M., Shaw, D. S., Moilanen, K. L., Hitchings, J. E., & Ingoldsby, E. M. (2009). Family, neighborhood, and peer characteristics as predictors of child adjustment: A longitudinal analysis of additive and mediation models. *Social Development, 18*, 511–535.

Crittenden, P. M. (1988). Relationship at risk. In J. Belsky & T. J. Nezworski (Eds.), *Clinical implications of attachment* (pp. 136–176). Hillsdale, NJ: Lawrence Erlbaum Associates.

Crittenden, P. M. (1990). Internal representational models of attachment relationships. *Infant Mental Health Journal, 11*, 259–277.

Crittenden, P. M. (1992). Treatment of anxious attachment in infancy and early childhood. *Development and Psychopathology, 4*, 575–602.

Crittenden, P. M. (1994). Peering into the black box: An exploratory treatise on the development of self in young children. In D. Cicchetti & S. L. Toth (Eds.), *Disorders and dysfunctions of the self* (pp. 79–148). Rochester, NY: University of Rochester.

Crittenden, P. M. (2006). A dynamic-maturational model of attachment. *Australian and New Zealand Journal of Family Therapy, 27*, 105–115.

Crittenden, P. M., & Ainsworth, M. D. S. (1989). Child maltreatment and attachment theory. In D. Cicchetti & V. Carlson (Eds.), *Child maltreatment: Theory and research on the causes and consequences of child abuse and neglect* (pp. 432–463). New York: Cambridge University Press.

Crittenden, P. M., & Dallos, R. (2009). All in the family: Integrating attachment and family systems theories. *Clinical Child Psychology & Psychiatry, 14*, 389–409.

Crouter, A. C., MacDermid, S. M., McHale, S. M., & Perry-Jenkins, M. (1990). Parental monitoring and perceptions of children's school performance and conduct in dual- and single-earner families. *Developmental Psychology, 26*, 649–657.

Crowley, K., Callanan, M. A., Tenenbaum, H. R., & Allen, E. (2001). Parents explain more often to boys than to girls during shared scientific thinking. *Psychological Science, 12*, 258–261.

Cummings, E. M., & Davies, P. T. (1994). *Children and marital conflict: The impact of family dispute and resolution*. New York and London: Guilford.

Cummings, E. M., Goeke-Morey, M. C., & Raymond, J. (2004). Fathers in family context: Effects of marital quality and marital conflict. In M. E. Lamb (Ed.), *The role of the father in child development* (4th ed., pp. 196–221). Hoboken, NJ: Wiley.

Cummings, E. M., Merrilees, C. E., & Ward George, M. (2010). Fathers, marriages and families: Revisiting and updating the framework for fathering in family context. In M. E. Lamb (Ed.), *The role of the father in child development* (5th ed., pp. 154–176). Hoboken, NJ: Wiley.

Cummings, E. M., & O'Reilly, A. W. (1997). Fathers in family context: Effects of marital quality on child adjustment. In M. E. Lamb (Ed.), *The role of the father in child development* (3rd ed., pp. 49–65). New York: Wiley.

Damon, W. (1977). Measurement and social development. *Counseling Psychologist, 6*, 13–15.

Damon, W. (1983). *Social and personality development*. New York: Norton.

Danziger, K. (1971). *Socialization*. Hamondsworth, UK: Penguin.

Darling, N., & Steinberg, L. (1993). Parenting style context: An integrative model. *Psychological Bulletin, 113*, 487–496.

Davies, P. T., & Cummings, E. M. (1994). Marital conflict and child adjustment: An emotional security hypothesis. *Psychological Bulletin, 116*, 387–411.

Davis, E., Schoppe-Sullivan, S. J., Mangelsdorf, S. C., & Brown, G. L. (2009). The role of infant temperament in stability and change in coparenting behavior across the first year of life. *Parenting: Science and Practice, 9*, 143–159.

Deater-Deckard, K. (2000). Parenting and child behavioral adjustment in early childhood: A quantitative genetic approach to studying family processes. *Child Development, 71*, 468–484.

DeLuccie, M. (1996). Predictors of paternal involvement and satisfaction. *Psychological Reports, 79*, 1351–1359.

De Wolff, M. S., & van IJzendoorn, M. H. (1997). Sensitivity and attachment: A meta-analysis on parental antecedents of infant attachment. *Child Development, 68*, 571–591.

Diener, M. L., Isabella, R. A., Behunin, M. G., & Wong, M. S. (2008). Attachment to mothers and fathers during middle childhood: Associations with child gender, grade, and competence. *Social Development, 17*, 84–101.

Diener, M., Mangelsdorf, C., McHale, J., & Frosch, C. (2002). Infants' behavioral strategies for emotion regulation with fathers and mothers: Associations with emotional expressions and attachment quality. *Infancy, 5*, 151–172.

Dodge, K. A., Bates, J. E., & Pettit, G. S. (1990). Mechanisms in the cycle of violence. *Science, 250*, 1678–1683.

Dodge, K. A., Pettit, G. S., & Bates, J. E. (1994). Effects of physical maltreatment on the development of peer relations. *Development and Psychopathology, 6*, 43–55.

Dornbusch, S. M., Ritter, R. L., Liederman, H., Roberts, D., & Fraleigh, M. (1987). The relation of parenting style to adolescent school performance. *Child Development, 58*, 1244–1257.

Downey, D. B. (1994). The school performance of children from single-mother and single-father families: Economic or interpersonal deprivation? *Journal of Family Issues, 15*, 129–147.

Duncan, G., & Brooks-Gunn, J. (Eds.). (1997). *Consequences of growing up poor*. New York: Russell Sage Foundation.

Dunn, J., Brown, J., & Beardsall, L. (1991). Family talk about feeling states and children's later understanding of others' emotions. *Developmental Psychology, 27*, 448–455.

Dunn, J., Brown, J., Slomkowki, C., Tesla, C., & Youngblade, L. (1991). Young children's understanding of other people's feelings and beliefs: Individual differences and their antecedents. *Child Development, 62*, 1352–1366.

Dykas, M. J., Ziv, Y., & Cassidy, J. (2008). Attachment and peer relations in adolescence. *Attachment & Human Development, 10*, 123–141.

Easterbrooks, M. A., & Goldberg, W. A. (1984). Toddler development in the family: Impact of father involvement and parenting characteristics. *Child Development, 55*, 740–752.

Eckenrode, J., Laird, M., & Doris, J. (1993). School performance and disciplinary problems among abused and neglected children. *Developmental Psychology, 29*, 53–62.

Egeland, B., & Sroufe, L. A. (1981). Attachment and early maltreatment. *Child Development, 52*, 44–52.

Elgar, F. J., Mills, R. S. L., McGrath, P. J., Waschbusch, D. A., & Brownridge, D. A. (2007). Maternal and paternal depressive symptoms and child maladjustment: The mediating role of parental behavior. *Journal of Abnormal Child Psychology, 35*, 943–955.

Emde, R. N., & Robinson, J. (1979). The first two months: Recent research in developmental psychology and the changing view of the newborn. In J. Noshpitz & J. Call (Eds.), *Basic handbook of child psychiatry*. New York: Basic Books.

Emery, R. E. (1989). Family violence. *American Psychologist, 44*, 312–329.

Emery, R. E. (1994). *Renegotiating family relationships: Divorce, child custody, and mediation*. New York: Guilford.

Emery, R. E. (1999). *Marriage, divorce, and children's adjustment* (2nd ed.). Thousand Oaks, CA: Sage Publications.

Emery, R. E., & Billings, L. L. (1998). An overview of the nature, causes, and consequences of abusive family relationships. *American Psychologist, 53*, 121–135.

Ensor, R., & Hughes, C. (2008). Content or connectedness? Mother–child talk and early social understanding. *Child Development, 79,* 201–216.

Ereky-Stevens, K. (2008). Associations between mothers' sensitivity to their infants' internal states and children's later understanding of mind and emotion. *Infant and Child Development, 17,* 527–543.

Fabricius, W. V., Braver, S. L., Diaz, P., & Velez, C. F. (2010). Custody and parenting time: Links to family relationships and well-being after divorce. In M. E. Lamb (Ed.), *The role of the father in child development* (5th ed., pp. 201–240). Hoboken, NJ: Wiley.

Fagot, B. I. (1995). Parenting boys and girls. In M. H. Bornstein (Ed.), *Handbook of parenting* (Vol. 1, pp. 163–183). Mahwah, NJ: Lawrence Erlbaum Associates.

Fagot, B. I., & Kavanagh, K. (1993). Parenting during the second year: Effects of children's age, sex and attachment classification. *Child Development, 64,* 258–271.

Favez, N., Frascarolo, F., Carneiro, C., Montfort, V., Corboz-Warnery, A. & Fivaz-Depeursinge, E. (2006). The development of the family alliance from pregnancy to toddlerhood and children outcomes at 18 months. *Infant and Child Development, 15,* 59–73.

Feldman, R., Guttfreund, D., & Yerushalmi, H. (1998). Parental care and intrusiveness as predictors of the abilities– achievement gap in adolescence. *Journal of Child Psychology & Psychiatry & Allied Disciplines, 39,* 721–730.

Feldman, S. S., & Rosenthal, D. A. (1991). Age expectations of behavioral autonomy in Hong Kong, Australian, and American youth: The influence of family variables and adolescents' values. *International Journal of Psychology, 26,* 1–23.

Feldman, S. S., Rosenthal, D. A., Mont-Reynaud, R., Leung, K., & Lau, S. (1991). Ain't misbehavin': Adolescent values and family environments as correlates of misconduct in Australia, Hong Kong, and the United States. *Journal of Research on Adolescence, 1,* 109–134.

Field, T. M., Cohen, D., Garcia, R., & Greenberg, R. (1984). Mother–stranger face discrimination by the newborn. *Infant Behavior and Development, 7,* 19–25.

Finkelhor, D., & Dziuba-Leatherman, J. (1994). Children as victims of violence: A national survey. *Pediatrics, 91,* 413–420.

Flouri, E., & Buchanan, A. (2002a). Father involvement in childhood and trouble with the police in adolescence: Findings from the 1958 British cohort. *Journal of Interpersonal Violence, 17,* 689–701.

Flouri, E., & Buchanan, A. (2002b). What predicts good relationships with parents in adolescence and partners in adult life: Findings from the 1958 British birth cohort. *Journal of Family Psychology, 16,* 186–198.

Flouri, E., & Buchanan, A. (2004). Early fathers' and mothers' involvement and child's later educational outcomes. *British Journal of Educational Psychology, 74,* 141–153.

Fonagy, P., Gergely, G., Jurist, E., & Target, M. (2002). *Affect regulation, mentalization, and the development of the self.* New York: Other Press.

Fonagy, P., Redfern, S., & Charman, T. (1997). The relationship between belief–desire reasoning and a projective measure of attachment security (SAT). *British Journal of Developmental Psychology, 15,* 51–61.

Fonagy, P., Steele, H., & Steele, M. (1991). Maternal representations of attachment during pregnancy predict the organization of infant–mother attachment at one year of age. *Child Development, 62,* 891–905.

Fonagy, P., & Target, M. (1997). Attachment and reflective function: Their role in self-organization. *Development and Psychopathology, 9,* 679–700.

Foster, E. M., & Kalil, A. (2007). Living arrangements and children's development in low-income white, black, and Latino families. *Child Development, 78,* 1657–1674.

Fouts, H., Roopnarine, J. L., & Lamb, M. E. (2007). Social experiences and daily routines of African-American infants in different socioeconomic contexts. *Journal of Family Psychology, 21,* 655–664.

Frankel, K. A., & Bates, J. E. (1990). Mother–toddler problem solving: Antecedents in attachment, home behavior, and temperament. *Child Development, 61,* 810–819.

Franz, C. E., McClelland, D. C., & Weinberger, J. (1991). Childhood antecedents of conventional social accomplishment in midlife adults: A 36-year prospective study. *Journal of Personality & Social Psychology, 60,* 586–595.

Franz, C. E., McClelland, D. C., Weinberger, J., & Peterson, C. (1994). Parenting antecedents of adult adjustment: A longitudinal study. In C. Perris, W. A. Arrindell, & M. Eisemann (Eds.), *Parenting and psychopathology* (pp. 127–144). New York: Wiley.

Freud, A. (1958). Adolescence. *Psychoanalytic Study of the Child, 13,* 255–278.

Freud, S. (1940). *An outline of psychoanalysis.* New York: Norton.

Frodi, A. M., Lamb, M. E., Leavitt, L. A., & Donovan, W. L. (1978a). Fathers' and mothers' responses to infant smiles and cries. *Infant Behavior and Development, 1,* 187–198.

Frodi, A. M., Lamb, M. E., Leavitt, L. A., Donovan, W. L., Neff, C., & Sherry, D. (1978b). Fathers' and mothers' responses to the faces and cries of normal and premature infants. *Developmental Psychology, 14,* 490–498.

Furstenberg, F. F., Jr., & Cherlin, A. J. (1991). *Divided families: What happens to children when parents part.* Cambridge, MA: Harvard University Press.

Gable, S., Crnic, K., & Belsky, J. (1994). Coparenting within the family system: Influences on children's development. *Family Relations: Journal of Applied Family & Child Studies, 43*, 380–386.

Gadsden, V. L. (1999). Black families in intergenerational and cultural perspective. In M. E. Lamb (Ed.), *Parenting and child development in "nontraditional" families* (pp. 221–246). Mahwah, NJ: Lawrence Erlbaum Associates.

Galinsky, E. (1999). *Ask the children: What America's children really think about paternal employment.* New York: Morrow.

Geffner, R., & Pagelow, M. D. (1990). Victims of spouse abuse. In R. T. Ammerman & M. Hersch (Eds.), *Treatment of family violence* (pp. 113–135). New York: Wiley.

George, C., Kaplan, N., & Main, M. (1985). *Adult attachment interview.* Unpublished manuscript, University of California, Berkeley.

George, C., & Main, M. (1979). Social interactions of young abused children: Approach, avoidance, and aggression. *Child Development, 50*, 306–318.

Giddens, A. (1998). *The third way.* Cambridge, UK: Polity.

Gjerde, P. F. (1986). The interpersonal structure of family interaction settings: Parent–adolescent relations in dyads and triads. *Developmental Psychology, 22*, 297–304.

Gleason, J. B. (1975). Fathers and other strangers: Men's speech to young children. In D. P. Dato (Ed.), *Language and linguistics* (pp. 289–297). Washington, DC: Georgetown University Press.

Goldman, J. D. C., & Goldman, R. J. (1983). Children's perceptions of parents and their roles: A cross-national study in Australia, England, North America and Sweden. *Sex Roles, 9*, 791–812.

Goldman, R. (2005). *Fathers' involvement in their children's education.* London: National Family and Parenting Institute.

Goodman, G. S., Emery, R. E., & Haugaard, J. J. (1998). Developmental psychology and law: Divorce, child maltreatment, foster care, and adoption. In W. Damon, I. Siegel, & A. Renninger (Eds.), *Handbook of child psychology: Vol. 4. Child psychology in practice* (5th ed., pp. 775–875). New York: Wiley.

Goodnow, J. J. (1996). From household practices to parents' ideas about work and interpersonal relationships. In S. Harkness & C. Super (Eds.), *Parents' cultural belief systems* (pp. 313–344). New York: Guilford.

Goossens, F. A., & van IJzendoorn, M. H. (1990). Quality of infants' attachments to professional caregivers: Relation to infant–parent attachment and day-care characteristics. *Child Development, 61*, 832–837.

Gottfried, A. E., Gottfried, A. W., & Bathurst, K. (2002). Maternal and dual earner employment status and parenting. In M. H. Bornstein (Ed.), *Handbook of parenting* (Vol. 2, pp. 207–230). Mahwah, NJ: Lawrence Erlbaum Associates.

Greenberg, M. T., Cicchetti, D., & Cummings, E. M. (Eds.). (1990). *Attachment in the preschool years: Theory, research, and intervention.* Chicago: University of Chicago Press.

Greenberg, M. T., & Speltz, M. (1988). Attachment and the ontogeny of conduct problems. In J. Belsky & T. J. Nezworski (Eds.), *Clinical implications of attachment* (pp. 177–218). Hillsdale, NJ: Lawrence Erlbaum Associates.

Grossmann, K. E., Grossmann, K., & Zimmermann, P. (1999). A wider view of attachment and exploration: Stability and change during the years of immaturity. In J. Cassidy & P. R. Shaver (Eds.), *Handbook of attachment: Theory, research, and clinical applications* (pp. 760–786). New York: Guilford.

Grotevant, H. D. (1998). Adolescent development in family contexts. In W. Damon & N. Eisenberg (Eds.), *Handbook of child psychology: Vol. 3. Social, personality, and emotional development* (5th ed., pp. 1097–1149). New York: Wiley.

Grych, J. H., & Fincham, F. D. (1990). Marital conflict and children's adjustment: A cognitive–contextual framework. *Psychological Bulletin, 108*, 267–290.

Hagan, L. K., & Kuebli, J. (2007). Mothers' and fathers' socialization of preschoolers' physical risk taking. *Journal of Applied Developmental Psychology, 28*, 2–14.

Hamburg, B. A. (1985). Early adolescence: A time of transition and stress. *Journal of Early Adolescence, 78*, 158–167.

Hanson, T. L., McLanahan, S. S., & Thomson, E. (1996). Double jeopardy: Parental conflict and stepfamily outcomes for children. *Journal of Marriage & the Family, 58*, 141–154.

Harris, J. R. (1995). Where is the child's environment? A group socialization theory of development. *Psychological Review, 102*, 458–489.

Harris, J. R. (1998). The *nurture assumption: Why children turn out the way they do.* Glencoe, IL: Free Press.

Hartley, R. (1960). Children's concepts of male and female roles. *Merrill-Palmer Quarterly, 6*, 83–91.

Hauser, S., Book, B., Houlihan, J., Powers, S., Weiss-Perry, B., Follansbee, D., et al. (1987). Sex differences within the family: Studies of adolescent and parent family interactions. *Journal of Youth and Adolescence, 16*, 199–220.

Hay, D., & Nash, A. (2002). Social development in different family arrangements. In P. K. Smith & C. Hart (Eds.), *Blackwell handbook of childhood social development* (pp. 238–261). Oxford, UK: Blackwell.

Herman, M. A., & McHale, S. M. (1993). Coping with parental negativity: Links with parental warmth and marital adjustment. *Journal of Applied Developmental Psychology, 14*, 121–130.

Herzog, E., & Sudia, C. E. (1973). Children in fatherless families. In B. M. Caldwell & H. N. Ricciuti (Eds.), *Review of child development research* (Vol. 3, pp. 141–232). Chicago: University of Chicago Press.

Hetherington, E. M., Bridges, M., & Insabella, G. M. (1998). What matters? What does not? Five perspectives on the association between marital transitions and children's adjustment. *American Psychologist, 53,* 167–184.

Hetherington, E. M., & Clingempeel, G. (1992). Coping with marital transitions. *Monographs of the Society for Research in Child Development, 57* (Serial No. 227).

Hetherington, E. M., & Henderson, S. H. (1997). Fathers in stepfamilies. In M. E. Lamb (Ed.), *The role of the father in child development* (3rd ed., pp. 212–226). New York: Wiley.

Hetherington, E. M., & Kelly, J. (2002). *For better or for worse: Divorce reconsidered.* New York: Norton.

Hetherington, E. M., & Stanley-Hagan, M. M. (1999). Stepfamilies. In M. E. Lamb (Ed.), *Parenting and child development in "nontraditional" families.* (pp. 137–159). Mahwah, NJ: Lawrence Erlbaum Associates.

Hewlett, B. S. (1987). Intimate fathers: Patterns of paternal holding among Aka pygmies. In M. E. Lamb (Ed.), *The father's role: Cross-cultural perspectives* (pp. 295–330). Hillsdale, NJ: Lawrence Erlbaum Associates.

Hewlett, B. S. (2005). Who cares for hunter-gatherer children? In B. S. Hewlett & M. E. Lamb (Eds.), *Hunter-gatherer childhoods* (pp. 175–176). New Brunswick, NJ: Aldine/Transaction.

Hewlett, B. S., & MacFarlan, S. J. (2010). Fathers' roles in hunter-gatherer and other small-scale cultures. In M. E. Lamb (Ed.), *The role of the father in child development* (5th ed., pp. 413–434). Hoboken, NJ: Wiley.

Hill, J. (1988). Adapting to menarche: Familial control and conflict. In M. Gunnar (Ed.), *Minnesota symposium on child psychology* (Vol. 21, pp. 43–77). Hillsdale, NJ: Lawrence Erlbaum Associates.

Hill, J., & Holmbeck, G. N. (1987). Familial adaptation to biological change during adolescence. In R. M. Lerner & T. Foch (Eds.), *Biological–psychological interactions in early adolescence: A life-span perspective* (pp. 207–223). Hillsdale, NJ: Lawrence Erlbaum Associates.

Hjetmstedt, A., & Collins, A. (2008). Psychological functioning and predictions of relationships in IVF fathers and controls. *Scandinavian Journal of Caring Science, 22,* 72–78.

Hobson, P. (2002). *The cradle of thought: Explorations of the origins of thinking.* London: Macmillan.

Hoffman-Plotkin, D., & Twentyman, C. T. (1984). A multimodal assessment of behavioral and cognitive deficits in abused and neglected preschoolers. *Child Development, 55,* 794–802.

Holden, G. W. (1995). Parental attitudes towards childrearing. In M. H. Bornstein (Ed.), *Handbook of parenting* (Vol. 3, pp. 359–392). Mahwah, NJ: Lawrence Erlbaum Associates.

Holden, G. W., Geffner, R., & Jouriles, E. W. (Eds.). (1998). *Children exposed to marital violence: Theory, research, and applied issues.* Washington, DC: American Psychological Association.

Holden, G. W., & Miller, P. C. (1999). Enduring and different: A meta-analysis of the similarity in parents' child rearing. *Psychological Bulletin, 125,* 223–254.

Holmbeck, G. N., & O'Donnell, K. (1991). Discrepancies between perceptions of decision making behavioral autonomy. In R. Paikoff (Ed.), *Shared views in the family during adolescence: New directions for child development* (pp. 51–69). San Francisco: Jossey-Bass.

Hosley, C. A., & Montemayor, R. (1997). Fathers and adolescents. In M. E. Lamb (Ed.), *The role of the father in child development* (3rd ed., pp. 162–178). New York: Wiley.

Hrdy, S. B. (2005). Comes the child before man: How cooperative breeding and prolonged post weaning dependence shaped human potential. In B. S. Hewlett & M. E. Lamb (Eds.), *Hunter-gatherer childhoods* (pp. 65–91). New Brunswick, NJ: Transaction/Aldine.

Hrdy, S. B. (2009). *Mothers and others.* Cambridge, MA: Harvard University Press.

Hughes, H. M., & Luke, D. A. (1998). Heterogeneity of adjustment among children of battered women. In G. W. Holden, R. Geffner, & E. W. Jouriles (Eds.), *Children exposed to marital violence: Theory, research, and applied issues* (pp. 185–221). Washington, DC: American Psychological Association.

Hughes, H. M., Parkinson, D. L., & Vargo, M. C. (1989). Witnessing spouse abuse and experiencing physical abuse: A "double whammy"? *Journal of Family Violence, 4,* 197–209.

Hunter, F. T. (1984). Socializing procedures in parent–child and friendship relations during adolescence. *Developmental Psychology, 20,* 1092–1099.

Isaacs, M. B., & Leon, G. H. (1988). Remarriage and its alternatives following divorce: Mother and child adjustment. *Journal of Marital & Family Therapy, 14,* 163–173.

Jarvis, P. A., & Creasey, G. L. (1991). Parental stress, coping, and attachment in families with an 18-month-old infant. *Infant Behavior & Development, 14,* 383–395.

Jenkins, J. M. (2000). Marital conflict and children's emotions: The development of an anger organization. *Journal of Marriage and the Family, 62,* 723–736.

Jenkins, J. M., & Astington, J. W. (1996). Cognitive factors and family structure associated with theory of mind development in young children. *Developmental Psychology, 32,* 70–78.

Jodl, K. M., Michael, A., Malanchuk, O., Eccles, J. S., & Sameroff, A. (2001). Parents' roles in shaping early adolescents' occupational aspirations. *Child Development, 72,* 1247–1265.

Johnson, J. R. (1994). High conflict divorce. *Future of Children, 4,* 165–182.

Johnston, J. R., Kline, M., & Tschann, J. M. (1989). Ongoing postdivorce conflict: Effects on children of joint custody and frequent access. *American Journal of Orthopsychiatry, 59,* 576–592.

Jonsson, C.-O., & Clinton, D. (2006). What do mothers attune to during interactions with their infants? *Infant and Child Development*, *15*, 387–402.

Josselson, R. (1980). Ego development in adolescence. In J. Adelson (Ed.), *Handbook of adolescent psychology* (pp. 188–210). New York: Wiley.

Jouriles, E. N., Norwood, W. D., McDonald, R., Vincent, J. P., & Mahoney, A. (1996). Physical violence and other forms of marital aggression: Links with children's behavior problems. *Journal of Family Psychology*, *10*, 223–234.

Katz, L. F., & Gottman, J. M. (1993). Patterns of marital conflict predict children's internalizing and externalizing behaviors. *Developmental Psychology*, *29*, 940–950.

Kaufman, J., & Cicchetti, D. (1989). Effects of maltreatment of school-age children's socioemotional development: Assessments in a day-camp setting. *Developmental Psychology*, *4*, 516–524.

Kaye, K., & Marcus, J. (1981). Infant imitation: The sensory-motor agenda. *Developmental Psychology*, *17*, 258–265.

Kazdin, A. E., Moser, J., Colbus, D., & Bell, R. (1985). Depressive symptoms among psychically abused and psychiatrically disturbed children. *Journal of Abnormal Psychology*, *94*, 298–307.

Kelly, J. B. (2000). Children's adjustments in conflicted marriage and divorce: A decade review of research. *Journal of the American Academy of Child and Adolescent Psychiatry*, *39*, 963–973.

Kendall-Tackett, K. A., & Eckenrode, J. (1996). The effects of neglect on academic achievement and disciplinary problems: A developmental perspective. *Child Abuse & Neglect*, *20*, 161–169.

Kerns, K. A. (1996). Individual differences in friendship quality: Links to child–mother attachment. In W. M. Bukowski, W. W. Hartup, & A. F. Newcomb (Eds.), *The company they keep: Friendship in childhood and adolescence* (pp. 137–157). New York: Cambridge University Press.

Kiernan, K. E. (2006). Non-residential fatherhood and child involvement: Evidence from the Millennium Cohort Study. *Journal of Social Policy*, *35*, 651–669.

Kobak, R., & Sceery, A. (1988). Attachment in late adolescence: Working models, affect regulation, and representation of self and others. *Child Development*, *59*, 135–146.

Kochanska, K., Aksan, N., Prisco, T. R., & Adams E. E. (2008). Mother–child and father–child mutually responsive orientation in the first 2 years and children's outcomes at preschool age: Mechanisms of influence. *Child Development*, *79*, 30–44.

Koestner, R., Franz, C., & Weinberger, J. (1990). The family origins of empathic concern: A 26-year longitudinal study. *Journal of Personality & Social Psychology*, *58*, 709–717.

Konner, M. (2005). Hunter-gatherer infancy and childhood: The !Kung and others. In B. S. Hewlett & S. E. Lamb (Eds.), *Hunter-gatherer childhoods: Evolutionary, developmental and cultural perspectives*. New Brunswick, NJ: Aldine/Transaction.

Korman, M., & Lewis, C. (2001). Mothers' and fathers' speech to infants: Explorations of the complexity of context. In M. Almgren et al. (Eds.), *Research on child language* (pp. 431–453). Somerville, MA: Cascadilla Press.

Korner, A. F., & Thoman, E. G. (1970). Visual alertness in neonates as evoked by maternal care. *Journal of Experimental Child Psychology*, *10*, 67–78.

Korner, A. F., & Thoman, E. G. (1972). The relative efficacy of contact and vestibular–proprioceptive stimulation in soothing neonates. *Child Development*, *43*, 443–453.

Kroger, J. (1985). Relationships during adolescence: A cross-national study of New Zealand and United States teenagers. *Journal of Adolescence*, *8*, 47–56.

Kuczynski, L. (2003). Beyond directionality: Bilateral conceptual frameworks for studying dynamics in parent–child relations. In L. Kuczynski (Ed.), *Handbook of dynamics in parent–child relations* (pp. 3–24). Thousand Oaks, CA: Sage.

Kuczynski, L., Kochanska, G., Radke-Yarrow, M., & Girnius-Brown, O. (1987). A developmental interpretation of young children's noncompliance. *Developmental Psychology*, *23*, 799–806.

LaBounty, J., Wellman, H. M., Olson, S., Lagattuta, K., & Liu, D. (2008). Mothers' and fathers' use of internal state talk with their young children. *Social Development*, *17*, 757–775.

Labrell, F. (1994). A typical interaction behavior between fathers and toddlers: Teasing. *Early Development and Parenting*, *3*, 125–130.

Labrell, F., Deleau, M., & Juhel, J. (2000). Father's and mother's distancing strategies towards toddlers. *International Journal of Behavioral Development*, *24*, 356–361.

Lamb, M. E. (1976a). Effects of stress and cohort on mother– and father–infant interaction. *Developmental Psychology*, *12*, 435–443

Lamb, M. E. (1976b). Interactions between eight-month-old children and their fathers and mothers. In M. E. Lamb (Ed.), *The role of the father in child development* (1st ed., pp. 307–328). New York: Wiley.

Lamb, M. E. (1976c). Twelve-month-olds and their parents: Interaction in a laboratory playroom. *Developmental Psychology*, *12*, 237–244.

Lamb, M. E. (1977a). The development of mother–infant and father–infant attachments in the second year of life. *Developmental Psychology*, *13*, 637–648.

Lamb, M. E. (1977b). Father–infant and mother–infant interaction in the first year of life. *Child Development, 48,* 167–181.

Lamb, M. E. (1981a). Developing trust and perceived effectance in infancy. In L. P. Lipsitt (Ed.), *Advances in infancy research* (Vol. 1, pp. 101–130). Norwood, NJ: Ablex.

Lamb, M. E. (1981b). The development of social expectation in the first year of life. In M. E. Lamb & L. R. Sherrod (Eds.), *Infant social cognition* (pp. 155–175). Hillsdale, NJ: Lawrence Erlbaum Associates.

Lamb, M. E. (1997). The development of father infant relationships. In M. E. Lamb (Ed.), *The role of the father in child development* (3rd ed., pp. 104–120, 332–342). New York: Wiley.

Lamb, M. E. (1999a). Noncustodial fathers and their impact on the children of divorce. In R. A. Thompson & P. R. Amato (Eds.), *The post-divorce family: Research and policy issues* (pp. 105–125). Thousand Oaks, CA: Sage.

Lamb, M. E. (Ed.) (1999b). *Parenting and child development in "nontraditional" families.* Mahwah, NJ: Lawrence Erlbaum Associates.

Lamb, M. E. (2002a). Infant–father attachments and their impact on child development. In C. S. Tamis-LeMonda & N. Cabrera (Eds.), *Handbook of father involvement* (pp. 93–118). Mahwah, NJ: Lawrence Erlbaum Associates.

Lamb, M. E. (2002b). Nonresidential fathers and their children. In C. S. Tamis-LeMonda & N. Cabrera (Eds.), *Handbook of father involvement* (pp. 169–184). Mahwah, NJ: Lawrence Erlbaum Associates.

Lamb, M. E., & Ahnert, L. (2006). Nonparental child care: Context, concepts, correlates, and consequences. In W. Damon et al. (Eds.), *Handbook of child psychology* (Vol. 4, 6th ed., pp. 950–1016). Hoboken, NJ: Wiley.

Lamb, M. E., Bornstein, M. H., & Teti, D. M. (2002). *Development in infancy* (4th ed.). Mahwah, NJ: Lawrence Erlbaum Associates.

Lamb, M. E., & Bougher, L. D. (2009). How does migration affect mothers' and fathers' roles within their families? Reflections on some recent research. *Sex Roles, 60,* 611–614.

Lamb, M. E., Gaensbauer, T. J., Malkin, C. M., & Shultz, L. (1985). The effects of abuse and neglect on security of infant–adult attachment. *Infant Behavior and Development, 8,* 35–45.

Lamb, M. E., Hwang, C. P., Frodi, A. M., & Frodi, M. (1982). Security of mother and father–infant attachment and its relation to sociability with strangers in traditional and nontraditional Swedish families. *Infant Behavior & Development, 5,* 355–367.

📖 Lamb, M. E., & Kelly, J. B. (2009). Improving the quality of parent–child contact in separating families with infants and young children: Empirical research foundations. In R. M. Galatzer-Levy, L. Kraus, & J. Galatzer-Levy (Eds.), *The scientific basis of child custody decisions* (2nd ed., pp. 187–214). Hoboken, NJ: Wiley.

📖 Lamb, M. E., & Lewis, C. (2010). The development and significance of father–child relationships in two-parent families. In M. E. Lamb (Ed.), *The role of the father in child development* (5th ed.). Chichester, UK: Wiley.

Lamb, M. E., Thompson, R. W., Gardner, E. L., & Charnov, E. L. (1985). *Infant–mother attachment: The origins and development significance of individual differences in Strange Situation behavior.* Hillsdale, NJ: Lawrence Erlbaum Associates.

Lamborn, S. D., & Steinberg, L. (1993). Emotional autonomy redux: Revisiting Ryan and Lynch. *Child Development, 64,* 483–499.

Langford, W., Lewis, C., Solomon, Y. & Warin, J. (2001). *Family understandings: Closeness, authority and independence in families with teenagers.* London: Family Policy Study Centre & Joseph Rowntree Foundation.

Laranjo, J., Bernier, A., & Meins, E. (2008). Associations between maternal mind-mindedness and infant attachment security: Investigating the mediating role of maternal sensitivity, *Infant Behavior and Development, 31,* 688–695.

Larson, R., & Richards, M. H. (1994). *Divergent realities: The emotional lives of mothers, fathers, and adolescents.* New York: Basic Books.

Leaper, C. (2002). Parenting girls and boys. In M. Bornstein (Ed.), *Handbook of parenting: Children and parenting* (2nd ed., Vol. 1, pp. 189–225). Mahwah, NJ: Lawrence Erlbaum Associates.

Leerkes, E. M., Blankson, A. N. & O'Brien, M. (2009). Differential effects of maternal sensitivity to infant distress and nondistress on social–emotional functioning. *Child Development, 80,* 762–775.

Lempers, J. D., Clark-Lempers, D., & Simons, R. L. (1989). Economic hardship, parenting, and distress in adolescence. *Child Development, 60,* 25–39.

Lewis, C. (1986). *Becoming a father.* Milton Keynes, UK: Open University Press.

Lewis, C., & Carpendale, J. I. M. (2010). Social cognition. In P. K. Smith & C. Hart (Eds.), *The handbook of social development* (2nd ed.). Oxford, UK: Blackwell.

Lewis, C., Freeman, N. H., Kyriakidou, C., Maridaki-Kassotaki, K., & Berridge, D. (1996). Social influences on false belief access: Specific sibling influences or general apprenticeship? *Child Development, 67,* 2930–2947.

Lewis, C., & Gregory, S. (1987). Parents' talk to their infants: The importance of context. *First Language, 7,* 201–216.

Lewis, C., Huang, Z. & Rooksby, M. (2006). Chinese preschoolers' false belief understanding: Is social knowledge underpinned by parental styles, social interactions or executive functions? *Psychologia, 49,* 252–266.

Lewis, C., Newson, J., & Newson, E. (1982). Father participation throughout childhood. In N. Beail & J. McGuire (Eds.), *Fathers: Psychological perspectives* (pp. 174–793). London: Junction.

Lewis, M. & Rosenblum, L. (Eds.) (1974). *The effect of the infant on its caregiver.* New York: Wiley.

Leyendecker, B., & Lamb, M. E. (1999). Latino families. In M. E. Lamb (Ed.), *Parenting and child development in "nontraditional" families* (pp. 247–262). Mahwah, NJ: Lawrence Erlbaum Associates.

Lieberman, M., Doyle, A. B., & Markiewicz, D. (1999). Developmental patterns in security of attachment to mother and father in late childhood and early adolescence: Associations with peer relations. *Child Development, 70,* 202–213.

Lindsey, E. W., & Caldera, Y. M. (2006). Mother–father–child triadic interaction and mother–child dyadic interaction: Gender differences within and between contexts. *Sex Roles, 55,* 511–521.

Lindsey, E. W., Campbell, J., MacKinnon-Lewis, C., Frabutt, J. M., & Lamb, M. E. (2002). Marital conflict and boys' peer relationships: The mediating role of mother–son emotional reciprocity. *Journal of Family Psychology, 16,* 466–477.

Lindsey, E. W., Colwell, M. J., Frabutt, J. M., Chambers, J. C., & MacKinnon-Lewis, C. (2008). Mother–child dyadic synchrony in European American and African American families during early adolescence. *Merrill-Palmer Quarterly, 54,* 289–315.

Lindsey, E. W., Cremeens, P. R., Colwell, M. J., & Caldera, Y. M. (2009). The structure of parent–child dyadic synchrony in toddlerhood and children's communication competence and self-control. *Social Development, 18,* 375–396.

Lindsey, E. W., & Mize, J. (2001). Contextual differences in parent–child play: Implications for children's gender role development. *Sex Roles, 44,* 155–176.

Liu, Y.-L. (2008). An examination of three models of the relationships between parental attachments and adolescents' social functioning and depressive symptoms. *Journal of Youth & Adolescence, 37,* 941–952.

Lynch, M., & Roberts, J. (1982). *Consequences of child abuse.* London: Academic Press.

Lyons-Ruth, K., Easterbrooks, M. A., & Davidson, C. C. (1997). Infant attachment strategies, infant mental lag, and maternal depressive symptoms: Predictors of internalizing and externalizing problems at age 7. *Developmental Psychology, 33,* 681–692.

Lyons-Ruth, K., & Jacobvitz, D. (1999). Attachment disorganization: Unresolved loss, relational violence, and lapses in behavioral and attentional strategies. In J. Cassidy & P. R. Shaver (Eds.), *Handbook of attachment: Theory, research, and clinical applications* (pp. 520–554). New York: Guilford.

Lytton, H., & Romney, D. M. (1991). Parents' differential socialisation of boys and girls: A meta-analysis. *Psychological Bulletin, 109,* 267–296.

Maccoby, E. (1984). Middle childhood in the context of the family. In W. A. Collins (Ed.), *Development during middle childhood: The years from six to twelve* (pp. 184–239). Washington, DC: National Academy of Sciences.

Maccoby, E. E. (1992). The role of parents in the socialization of children: A historical overview. *Developmental Psychology, 28,* 1006–1017.

Maccoby, E. E. (1998). *The two sexes: Growing up apart, coming together.* Cambridge, MA: Harvard University Press.

Maccoby, E. E. (2000). Parenting and its effects on children: On reading and misreading behavior genetics. *Annual Review of Psychology, 51,* 1–27.

Maccoby, E. E., & Martin, J. (1983). Socialization in the context of the family: Parent–child interaction. In P. H. Mussen & E. M. Hetherington (Eds.), *Handbook of child psychology: Vol. 4. Socialization, personality, and social development* (4th ed., pp. 1–101). New York: Wiley.

MacDonald, R. H., & Parke, R. D. (1984). Bridging the gap. Parent–child play interaction and peer competence. *Child Development, 55,* 1265–1277.

MacKinnon, C., Lamb, M. E., Belsky, J., & Baum, C. (1990). An affective–cognitive model of mother–child aggression. *Development and Psychopathology, 2,* 1–14.

MacKinnon-Lewis, C., Lamb, M. E., Arbuckle, B., Baradaran, L. P., & Volling, B. (1992). The relationship between biased maternal and filial attributions and the aggressiveness of their interactions. *Development and Psychopathology, 2,* 1–14.

MacKinnon-Lewis, C., Volling, B. L., Lamb, M. E., Dechman, K., Rabiner, D., & Curtner, M. E. (1994). A cross-contextual analysis of children's social competence: From family to school. *Developmental Psychology, 30,* 325–333.

MacKinnon-Lewis, C., Volling, B. L., Lamb, M. E., Hattie, J., & Baradaran, I. (2001). A longitudinal examination of the associations between mothers' and children's attributions and their aggression. *Development and Psychopathology, 13,* 69–81.

Maclean, M., & Eekelaar, J. (1997). *The parental obligation: A study of parenthood across households.* Oxford, UK: Hart.

Maier, E. H., & Lachman, M. E. (2000). Consequences of early parental loss and separation for health and well-being in midlife. *International Journal of Behavioral Development, 24,* 183–189.

Main, M., & George, C. (1985). Response of abused and disadvantaged toddlers to distress in age mates: A study in the day care setting. *Developmental Psychology, 21,* 407–412.

Main, M., & Goldwyn, R. (1994). *Adult attachment classification system.* Unpublished manuscript, University of California, Berkeley.

Main, M., & Hesse, E. (1990). Parents' unresolved traumatic experiences are related to infant disorganized attachment status: Is frightened and/or frightening parental behavior the linking mechanism? In M. T. Greenberg, D. Cicchetti, & E. M. Cummings (Eds.), *Attachment in the preschool years: Theory, research, and intervention* (pp. 161–182). Chicago: University of Chicago Press.

Main, M., Kaplan, N., & Cassidy, J. (1985). Security in infancy, childhood, and adulthood: A move to the level of representation. In I. Bretherton & E. Waters (Eds.), Growing points of attachment theory and research. *Monographs of the Society for Research in Child Development, 50* (1/2, Serial No. 209), 66–104.

Main, M., & Solomon, J. (1990). Procedures for identifying infants as disorganized/disoriented during the Ainsworth Strange Situation. In M. T. Greenberg, D. Cicchetti, & E. M. Cummings (Eds.), *Attachment in the preschool years: Theory, research, and intervention* (pp. 121–160). Chicago: University of Chicago Press.

Main, M., & Weston, D. R. (1981). Security of attachment to mother and father: Related to conflict behavior and the readiness to establish new relationships. *Child Development, 52,* 932–940.

Mandler, G. (1985). *Cognitive psychology: An essay in cognitive science.* Hillsdale, NJ: Lawrence Erlbaum Associates.

Marlowe, F. W. (2005). Who tends Hadza children? In B. S. Hewlett & M. E. Lamb (Eds.), *Hunter-gatherer childhoods* (pp. 177–190). New Brunswick, NJ: Aldine/Transaction.

Martin, A., Ryan, R. M., & Brooks-Gunn, J. (2007). The joint influence of mother and father parenting on child cognitive outcomes at age 5. *Early Childhood Research Quarterly, 22,* 423–439.

McAdoo, H. P. (1993). Ethnic families: Strengths that are found in diversity. In H. P. McAdoo (Ed.), *Ethnic families: Strength in diversity* (pp. 3–14). Newbury Park, CA: Sage.

McBride, B. A., Schoppe-Sullivan, S. J., & Ho, M. H. (2005). The mediating role of fathers' school involvement on student achievement. *Journal of Applied Developmental Psychology, 26,* 201–216.

McGrellis, S., Henderson, S., Holland, J., Sharpe, S., & Thomson, R. (2000). *Beyond the moral maze: A quantitative study of young people's values.* London: Tuffnell.

McHale, J. P. (2007) When infants grow up in multiperson relationship systems. *Infant Mental Health Journal, 28,* 370–392.

McHale, S. M., Crouter, A. C., Kim, J. Y., Burton, L. M., Davis, K. D., Dotterer, A. M., et al. (2006). Mothers' and fathers' racial socialization in African American families: Implications for youth. *Child Development, 77,* 1387–1402.

McLanahan, S. S. (1999). Father absence and the welfare of children. In E. M. Hetherington (Ed.), *Coping with divorce, single parenting, and remarriage: A risk and resiliency perspective* (pp. 117–145). Mahwah, NJ: Lawrence Erlbaum Associates.

McLanahan, S. S., & Sandefur, G. (1994). *Growing up with a single parent: What hurts, what helps?* Cambridge, MA: Harvard University Press.

McLanahan, S., & Teitler, J. (1999). The consequences of father absence. In M. E. Lamb (Ed.), *Parenting and child development in "nontraditional" families* (pp. 83–102). Mahwah, NJ: Lawrence Erlbaum Associates.

McNeal, C., & Amato, P. R. (1998). Parents' marital violence: Long-term consequences for children. *Journal of Family Issues, 19,* 123–139.

Meins, E. (1997). Security of attachment and maternal tutoring strategies: Interaction within the zone of proximal development. *British Journal of Developmental Psychology, 15,* 129–144.

Meins, E. (1999). Sensitivity, security and internal working models: Bridging the transmission gap. *Attachment & Human Development, 1,* 325–342.

Meins, E., Fernyhough, C., Fradley, E., & Tuckey, M. (2001). Rethinking maternal sensitivity: Mothers' comments on infants' mental processes predict security of attachment at 12 months. *Journal of Child Psychology and Psychiatry, 42,* 637–648.

Meins, E., Fernyhough, C., Russell, J., & Clark-Carter, D. (1998). Security of attachment as a predictor of symbolic and mentalising abilities: A longitudinal study. *Social Development, 7,* 1–24.

Meins, E., Fernyhough, C., Wainwright, R., Das Gupta, M., Fradley, E., & Tuckey, M. (2002). Maternal mind-mindedness and attachment security as predictors of theory of mind understanding. *Child Development, 73,* 1715–1726.

Moffitt, T. E. (2005). The new look of behavioral genetics in developmental psychopathology: Gene–environment interplay in antisocial behaviors. *Psychological Bulletin, 131,* 533–554.

Monteiro, L., Verissimo, M., Vaughn, B. E., Santos, A. J., Torres, N., & Fernandes, M. (in press). The organization of children's secure base behaviour in two parent Portuguese families and father's participation in child related activities. *European Journal of Developmental Psychology.*

Montemayor, R. (1983). Parents and adolescents in conflict: All families some of the time and some families most of the time. *Journal of Early Adolescence, 3,* 83–103.

Montemayor, R., & Brownlee, J. (1987). Fathers, mothers, and adolescents: Gender based differences in parental roles during adolescence. *Journal of Youth and Adolescence, 16,* 281–291.

Murray, A. D. (1979). Infant crying as an elicitor of parental behavior: An examination of two models. *Psychological Bulletin, 86,* 191–215.

National Research Council. (1993). *Understanding child abuse and neglect.* Washington, DC: National Academy.

Nelson, P. B., Adamson, L. B., & Bakeman, R. (2008). Toddlers' joint engagement experience facilitates pre-schoolers' acquisition of theory of mind. *Developmental Science, 11*, 840–845.

Noller, P. (1980). Cross-gender effect in two-child families. *Developmental Psychology, 16*, 159–160.

Noller, P., & Callan, V. J. (1986). Adolescent and parent perceptions of family cohesion and adaptability. *Journal of Adolescence, 9*, 97–106.

Noller, P., & Callan, V. J. (1988). Understanding parent–adolescent interactions: Perceptions of family members and outsiders. *Developmental Psychology, 24*, 707–714.

Notaro, P. C., & Volling, B. L. (1999). Parental responsiveness and infant–parent attachment: A replication study with fathers and mothers. *Infant Behavior & Development, 22*, 345–352.

Oates, K., Peacock, A., & Forrest, D. (1984). The development of abused children. *Developmental Medicine and Child Neurology, 26*, 649–659.

O'Brien, M. (2005). *Shared caring: Bringing fathers into the frame*. Manchester, UK: Equal Opportunities Commission.

O'Brien, M., John, R. S., Margolin, G., & Erel, O. (1994). Reliability and diagnostic efficacy of parents' reports regarding children's exposure to marital aggression. *Violence and Victims, 9*, 45–62.

O'Connor, T. G. (2002). The effects of parenting reconsidered: Findings, challenges and applications. *Journal of Child Psychology and Psychiatry, 43*, 555–572.

O'Connor, T. G., Dunn, J., Jenkins, J. M., & Rasbash, J. (2006). Predictors of between-family and within-family variation in parent–child relationships. *Journal of Child Psychology and Psychiatry, 47*, 498–510.

O'Connor, T. G., Neiderhiser, J. M., Reiss, D., Hetherington, E. M., & Plomin, R. (1998). Genetic contributions to continuity, change, and co-occurrence of antisocial and depressive symptoms in adolescence. *Journal of Child Psychology & Psychiatry & Allied Disciplines, 39*, 323–336.

Offer, D., Ostrov, E., & Howard, K. (1981). *The adolescent: A psychological self-portrait*. New York: Basic Books.

Ontai, L. L., & Thompson, R. A. (2008). Attachment, parent–child discourse and theory-of-mind development. *Social Development, 17*, 47–60.

Oosterwegel, A., & Oppenheimer, L. (1993). *The self-system: Developmental changes between and within self-concepts*. Hillsdale, NJ: Lawrence Erlbaum Associates.

Oppenheim, D., Sagi, A., & Lamb, M. E. (1988). Infant–adult attachments on the kibbutz and their relation to socioemotional development 4 years later. *Developmental Psychology, 24*, 427–433.

Osofsky, J. D., Hann, D. M., & Peebles, C. (1993). Adolescent parenthood: Risks and opportunities for parent and infants. In C. Zeanah (Ed.), *Handbook of infant mental health* (pp. 106–119). New York: Guilford.

Overton, W. F. (2006). Developmental psychology: Philosophy, concepts, methodology. In W. Damon & R. M. Lerner (Series Eds.) and R. M. Lerner (Volume Ed.), *Handbook of child psychology. Vol. 1. Theoretical models of human development* (6th ed., pp. 18–88). Hoboken, NJ: Wiley.

Papousek, M. (2007). Communication in early infancy: An arena of intersubjective learning. *Infant Behavior and Development, 30*, 258–266.

Parke, R. D., & Buriel, R. (1998). Socialization in the family: Ethnic and ecological perspectives. In W. Damon & N. Eisenberg (Eds.), *Handbook of child psychology: Vol. 3. Social, emotional, and personality development* (5th ed., pp. 463–552). New York: Wiley.

Parke, R. D., Dennis, J., Flyr, M., Morris, K. L., Killian, C., McDowell, D. J., et al. (2004). Fathering and children's peer relationships. In M. E. Lamb (Ed.), *The role of the father in child development* (4th ed., pp. 32–57). New York: Wiley.

Parke, R. D., Simpkins, S. D., McDowell, D. J., Kim, M., Killian, C., Dennis, J., et al. (2002). Relative contributions of families and peers to children's social development. In P. K. Smith & C. Hart (Eds.), *Blackwell handbook of childhood social development* (pp. 156–177). Oxford, UK: Blackwell.

Patterson, G. R. (1976). The aggressive child: Victim and architect of a coercive system. In L. A. Hamelynch, L. C. Handy, & E. J. March (Eds.), *Behavior modification and families* (pp. 267–316). New York: Brunner/Mazel.

Patterson, G. R. (1982). *Coercive family processes*. Eugene, OR: Castalia.

Patterson, G. R., Reid, J. B., & Dishion, T. J. (1992). *A social learning approach IV: Antisocial boys*. Eugene, OR: Castalia.

Pauli-Pott, U., & Mertesacker, B. (2009). Affect expression in mother–infant interaction and subsequent attachment development. *Infant Behavior & Development, 32*, 208–215.

Pellegrini, A. D., Brody, G. H., & Stoneman, Z. (1987). Children's conversational competence with their parents. *Discourse Processes, 10*, 93–106.

Pence, A. R. (Ed.) (1988). *Ecological research with children and families: From concepts to methodology*. New York: Teachers College Press.

Perner, J., Ruffman, T., & Leekam, S. R. (1994). Theory of mind is contagious: You catch it from your sibs. *Child Development, 65*, 1228–1238.

Phares, V. (1996). *Fathers and developmental psychopathology*. New York: Wiley.

Phares, V. (1997). Psychological adjustment, maladjustment, and father–child relationships. In M. E. Lamb (Ed.), *The role of the father in child development* (3rd ed., pp. 261–283). New York: Wiley.

Pianta, R., Egeland, B., & Erickson, M. F. (1989). The antecedents of maltreatment: Results of the Mother–Child Interaction Research Project. In D. Cicchetti & V. Carlson (Eds.), *Child maltreatment: Theory and research on the causes and consequences of child abuse and neglect* (pp. 203–253). New York: Cambridge University Press.

Pleck, E. (2004). The dimensions of fatherhood: A history of the good dad–bad dad complex. In M. E. Lamb (Ed.), *The role of the father in child development* (4th ed., pp. 32–57). New York: Wiley.

Pleck, J. H., & Masciadrelli, B. P. (2004). Paternal involvement by U.S. residential fathers: Levels, sources and consequences. In M. E. Lamb (Ed.), *The role of the father in child development* (4th ed., pp. 222–270). New York: Wiley.

Plomin, R., DeFries, J. C., McClearn, G. E., & McGuffin, P. (2000). *Behavioral genetics* (4th ed.). New York: Worth.

Posada, G., Jacobs, A., Carbonell, O. A., Alzate, G., Bustamante, M. R., & Arenas, A. (1999). Maternal care and attachment security in ordinary and emergency contexts. *Developmental Psychology, 35*, 1379–1388.

Price, J. M., & Van Slyke, D. (1991, April). *Social information processing patterns and social adjustment of maltreated children.* Paper presented to the Society for Research in Child Development, Seattle, WA.

Raag, T., & Rackliff, C. L. (1998). Preschoolers' awareness of social expectations of gender: Relationships to toy choices. *Sex Roles, 38*, 685–700.

Ramchandani, P., Stein, A., Evans, J., O'Connor, T. G., & the ALSPAC Study Team (2005). Paternal depression in the postnatal period and child development: A prospective population study. *The Lancet, 365*, 3201–3205.

Rapoport, R., Rapoport, R., & Strellitz, Z. (1975). *Fathers, mothers and others.* London: Routledge.

Reddy, V. (2003). On being the object of attention: Implications for self–other consciousness. *Trends in Cognitive Sciences, 7*, 397–402.

Rödholm, M., & Larsson, K. (1982). The behavior of human male adults at their first contact with a newborn. *Infant Behavior and Development, 5*, 121–130.

Rohner, R. P., & Pettengill, S. M. (1985). Perceived parental acceptance–rejection and parental control among Korean adolescents. *Child Development, 56*, 524–528.

Roopnarine, J. L. (2004). African American and African Caribbean fathers: Level, quality and meaning of involvement. In M. E. Lamb (Ed.), *The role of the father in child development* (4th ed., pp. 58–97). Hoboken, NJ: Wiley.

Roopnarine, J. L., Fouts, H. N., Lamb, M. E., & Lewis-Elligan T. Y. (2005). Mothers' and fathers' behaviors toward their 3–4 month-old infants in low-, middle-, and upper-socioeconomic African American families. *Developmental Psychology, 41*, 723–731.

Rosen, K. S., & Rothbaum, F. (1993). Quality of parental caregiving and security of attachment. *Developmental Psychology, 29*, 358–367.

Ross, H., & Taylor, H. (1989). Do boys prefer daddy or his physical style of play? *Sex Roles, 20*, 23–33.

Rowe, M. L., Coker, D., & Pan, B. A. (2004). A comparison of fathers' and mothers' talk to toddlers in low-income families. *Social Development, 13*, 278–291.

Rubin, K. H., Coplan, R. J., Chen, X., Buskirk, A. A., & Wojslawowicz, J. C. (2004). Peer relationships in childhood. In M. H. Bornstein & M. E. Lamb (Eds.), *Developmental science: An advanced textbook* (5th ed., pp. 469–512). Mahwah, NJ: Lawrence Erlbaum Associates.

Ruble, D. N., & Martin, C. L. (1998). Gender development. In W. Damon and N. Eisenberg (Eds.), *Handbook of child psychology: Vol. 3. Social, emotional, and personality development* (5th ed., pp. 933–1016). New York: Wiley.

Ruffman, T., Perner, J., Naito, M., Parkin, L., & Clements, W. A. (1998). Older (but not younger) siblings facilitate false belief understanding. *Developmental Psychology, 34*, 161–174.

Ruffman, T., Perner, J., & Parkin, L. (1999). How parenting style affects false belief understanding. *Social Development, 8*, 395–411.

Russell, A., Aloa, V., Feder, Y., Glover, A., Miller, H., & Palmer, G. (1998). Sex-based differences in parenting styles in a sample with preschool children. *Australian Journal of Psychology, 50*, 89–99.

Russell, G., & Russell, A. (1987). Mother–child and father–child relationships in middle childhood. *Child Development, 58*, 1573–1585.

Russell, A., & Saebel, J. (1997). Mother–son, mother–daughter, father–son, and father–daughter: Are they distinct relationships? *Developmental Review, 17*, 111–147.

Sabbagh, M. A., & Seamans, E. L. (2008). Intergenerational transmission of theory-of-mind. *Developmental Science, 11*, 354–360.

Sagi, A., Lamb, M. E., & Gardner, W. (1986). Relations between Strange Situation behavior and stranger sociability among infants on Israel kibbutzim. *Infant Behavior & Development, 9*, 271–282.

Salzinger, S., Feldman, R., Hammer, M., & Rosario, M. (1993). The effects of physical abuse on children's social relationships. *Child Development, 64*, 169–187.

Sarkadi, A., Kristiansson, R., Oberklaid, F., & Bremberg, S. (2008). Fathers' involvement and children's developmental outcomes: A systematic review of longitudinal studies. *Acta Paediatrica, 97*(2), 153–158.

Schoppe-Sullivan, S. J., Diener, M. L., Mangelsdorf, S. C., Brown, G. L., McHale, J. L., & Frosch, C. A. (2006). Attachment and sensitivity in family context: The roles of parent and infant gender. *Infant & Child Development, 15*, 367–385.

Schudlich, T. D. D. R., & Cummings, E. M. (2007). Parental dysphoria and children's adjustment: Marital conflict styles, children's emotional security, and parenting as mediators of risk. *Journal of Abnormal Child Psychology*, *35*, 627–639.

Schuengel, C., Bakermans-Kranenburg, M., van IJzendoorn, M. H., & Blom, M. (1999). Unresolved loss and infant disorganization: Links to frightening maternal behavior. In J. Solomon & C. George (Eds.), *Attachment disorganization* (pp. 71–94). New York: Guilford.

Scott, J. (2004). Family, gender and educational attainment in Britain: A longitudinal study. *Journal of Comparative Family Studies*, *35*, 565–589.

Sears, R. R., Maccoby, E. E., & Levin, H. (1957). *Patterns of child rearing*. Palo Alto, CA: Stanford University.

Sebald, H. (1977). *Adolescence: A social psychological analysis* (2nd ed.). Englewood Cliffs, NJ: Prentice Hall.

Sedlak, A. J., & Broadhurst, D. D. (1996). *Third national incidence study of child abuse and neglect: Final report*. Washington, DC: US Department of Health and Human Services.

Seltzer, J. A. (1991). Relationships between fathers and children who live apart: The father's role after separation. *Journal of Marriage & the Family*, *53*, 79–101.

Seltzer, J. A. (1994). Consequences of marital dissolution for children. *Annual Review of Sociology*, *20*, 235–266.

Seltzer, J. A. (1998). Men's contributions to children and social policy. In A. Booth & A. C. Crouter (Eds.), *Men in families: When do they get involved? What difference does it make?* (pp. 303–314). Hillsdale, NJ: Lawrence Erlbaum Associates.

Shaw, D. S., Owens, E. B., Vondra, J. I., & Keenan, K. (1996). Early risk factors and pathways in the development of early disruptive behavior problems. *Development & Psychopathology*, *8*, 679–699.

Shulman, S., & Seiffge-Krenke, I. (1997). *Fathers and adolescents: Developmental and clinical perspectives*. London: Routledge.

Siegel, A. U. (1987). Are sons and daughters more differently treated by fathers than by mothers? *Developmental Review*, *7*, 183–209.

Silverberg, S. B., Tennenbaum, D. L., & Jacob, T. (1992). Adolescence and family interaction. In V. B. Van Hasselt & M. Hersen (Eds.), *Handbook of social development: A lifespan perspective* (pp. 347–370). New York: Plenum.

Simmons, R. G., & Blyth, D. A. (1987). *Moving into adolescence: The impact of pubertal change and school context*. New York: Aldine DeGruyter.

Simons, R. L. & Associates (1996). *Understanding differences between divorced and intact families: Stress, interaction, and child outcome*. Thousand Oaks, CA: Sage.

Slough, N. (1988). *Assessment of attachment in five-year-olds: Relationship among separation, the internal representation, and mother–child functioning*. Unpublished doctoral dissertation, University of Washington, Seattle.

Smetana, J. G. (1988). Adolescents' and parents' conceptions of parental authority. *Child Development*, *59*, 321–335.

Smetana, J. G. (1989). Adolescents' and parents' reasoning about actual family conflicts. *Child Development*, *60*, 1052–1067.

Smetana, J. G. (1995). Context, conflict, and constraint in adolescent–parent authority relationships. In M. Killen & D. Hart (Eds.), *Morality in everyday life: Developmental perspectives* (pp. 225–255). Cambridge, UK: Cambridge University Press.

Solomon, Y., Warin, J. & Lewis, C. (2002). Helping with homework? Homework as a site of tension for parents and teenagers. *British Educational Research Journal*, *28*, 603–622.

Solomon, Y., Warin, J., Lewis, C. & Langford, W. (2002). Intimate talk between parents and their teenage children: Democratic openness of covert control. *Sociology*, *36*, 965–983.

Sprenglemeyer, R., Perrett, D. I., Fagan, E. C., Coinwell, R. E., Lobmaier, J. S., Sprengelmeyor, A., et al. (2009). The cutest little baby face: A hormonal link to sensitivity to cuteness in infant faces. *Psychological Science*, *20*, 149–154.

Sroufe, L. A. (1983). Individual patterns of adaptation from infancy to preschool. In M. Perlmutter (Ed.), *Development and policy concerning children with special needs* (pp. 41–83). Hillsdale, NJ: Lawrence Erlbaum Associates.

Sroufe, L. A. (1988). The role of infant–caregiver attachment in development. In J. Belsky & T. J. Nezworski (Eds.), *Clinical implications of attachment* (pp. 18–40). Hillsdale, NJ: Lawrence Erlbaum Associates.

Sroufe, L. A. (1996). *Emotional development*. Cambridge, UK: Cambridge University Press.

Steele, H., Steele, M., Croft, C., & Fonagy, P. (1999). Infant–mother attachment at one year predicts children's understanding of mixed emotions at six years. *Social Development*, *8*, 161–178.

Steele, H., Steele, M., & Fonagy, P. (1996). Associations among attachment classifications of mothers, fathers, and their infants. *Child Development*, *67*, 541–555.

Steinberg, L. (1981). Transformation in family relationships at puberty. *Developmental Psychology*, *17*, 833–840.

Steinberg, L. (1987). Impact of puberty on family relations: Effects of pubertal status and pubertal timing. *Developmental Psychology*, *23*, 451–460.

Steinberg, L. (1988). Reciprocal relations between parent–child distance and pubertal maturation. *Developmental Psychology*, *24*, 122–128.

Steinberg, L. (1990). Interdependence in the family: Autonomy, conflict, and harmony in the parent–adolescent relationships. In S. S. Feldman & G. Elliott (Eds.), *At the threshold: The developing adolescent* (pp. 255–276). Cambridge, MA: Harvard University Press.

Steinberg, L. D., & Darling, N. E. (1994). The broader context of social influence in adolescence. In R. K. Silbereisen & E. Todt (Eds.), *Adolescence in context* (pp. 25–45). New York: Springer-Verlag.

Steinberg, L. D., Darling, N. E., & Fletcher, A. C. (1995). Authoritative parenting and adolescent development: An ecological journey. In P. Moen, G. H. Elder, & K. Luscher (Eds.), *Examining lives in context* (pp. 423–466). Washington, DC: American Psychological Association.

Steinberg, L., Elmen, J. D., & Mounts, N. S. (1989). Authoritative parenting, psychosocial maturity, and academic success among adolescents. *Child Development, 60,* 1424–1436.

Stern, D. N., Hofer, L., Haft, W., & Dore, J. (1985). Affect attunement: The sharing of feeling states between mother and infant by means of inter-modal fluency. In T. Field, & N. Fox (Eds.), *Social perception in infants* (pp. 249–268). Norwood, NJ: Ablex.

Sternberg, K. J., Baradaran, L., Abbott, C. B., Lamb, M. E., & Guterman, E. (2006a). Type of violence, age, and gender differences in the effects of family violence on children's behavior problems: A mega analysis. *Developmental Review, 26,* 89–112.

Sternberg, K. J., & Lamb, M. E. (1999). Violent families. In M. E. Lamb (Ed.), *Parenting and child development in "nontraditional" families* (pp. 305–325). Mahwah, NJ: Lawrence Erlbaum Associates.

Sternberg, K. J., Lamb, M. E., & Dawud-Noursi, S. (1998). Understanding domestic violence and its effects: Making sense of divergent reports and perspectives. In G. W. Holden, R. Geffner, & E. W. Jouriles (Eds.), *Children exposed to family violence* (pp. 121–156). Washington, DC: American Psychological Association.

Sternberg, K. J., Lamb, M. E., Greenbaum, C., Cicchetti, D., Dawud, D., Cortes, R. M., et al. (1993). Effects of domestic violence on children's behavior problems and depression. *Developmental Psychology, 29,* 44–52.

Sternberg, K. J., Lamb, M. E., Greenbaum, C., Dawud, S., Cortes, R. M., & Lorey, F. (1994). The effects of domestic violence on children's perceptions of their perpetrating and nonperpetrating parents. *International Journal of Behavioral Development, 17,* 779–795.

Sternberg, K. J., Lamb, M. E., Guterman, E., & Abbott, C. B. (2006). Effects of early and later family violence on children's behavior problems and depression: A longitudinal, multi-informant perspective. *Child Abuse and Neglect, 30,* 283–306.

Sternberg, K. J., Lamb, M. E., Guterman, E., Abbott, C. B., & Dawud-Noursi, S. (2005). Adolescents' perceptions of attachments to their mothers and fathers in families with histories of domestic violence: A longitudinal perspective. *Child Abuse and Neglect, 29,* 853–869.

Storey, A. E., Walsh, C. J., Quinton, R. L., & Wynne-Edwards, R. E. (2000). Hormonal correlates of paternal responsiveness in new and expectant fathers. *Evolution and Human Behavior, 21,* 79–95.

Straus, M. A., & Gelles, R. J. (1986). Change in family violence from 1975–1985. *Journal of Marriage and the Family, 48,* 465–479.

Straus, M. A., & Gelles, R. J. (1990). How violent are American families? Estimates from the national family violence resurvey and other studies. In M. A. Straus & R. J. Gelles (Eds.), *Physical violence in American families* (pp. 95–108). New Brunswick, NJ: Transaction Books.

Straus, M. A., Gelles, R. J., & Steinmetz, S. (1980). *Behind closed doors: Violence in the American family*. New York: Doubleday/Anchor.

Suess, G. J., Grossmann, K. E., & Sroufe, L. A. (1992). Effects of infant attachment to mother and father on quality of adaptation in preschool: From dyadic to individual organisation of self. *International Journal of Behavioral Development, 15,* 43–65.

Symons, D. K., & Clark, S. E. (2000). A longitudinal study of mother–child relationships and theory of mind in the preschool period. *Social Development, 9,* 3–23.

Tamis-LeMonda, C. S., & McFadden, K. E. (2010). Fathers from low-income backgrounds: Myths and evidence. In M. E. Lamb (Ed.), *The role of the father in child development* (5th ed., pp. 296–318). Hoboken, NJ: Wiley.

Tenenbaum, H. R., & Leaper, C. (2003). Parent–child conversations about science: The socialization of gender inequities? *Developmental Psychology, 39,* 34–47.

Teti, D. M. (Ed.) (2005). *Handbook of research methods in developmental psychology*. Oxford, UK: Blackwell.

Teti, D. M., Gelfand, D. M, Messinger, D. S., & Isabella, R. (1995). Maternal depression and the quality of early attachment: An examination of infants, preschoolers, and their mothers. *Developmental Psychology, 31,* 364–376.

Teti, D. M., & Teti, L. O. (1996). Infant–parent relationships. In N. Vanzetti & S. Duck (Eds.), *A lifetime of relationships* (pp. 77–104). Belmont, CA: Brooks/Cole.

Thompson, R. A. (1998). Early sociopersonality development. In W. Damon & N. Eisenberg (Eds.), *Handbook of child psychology: Vol. 3. Social, emotional, and personality development* (5th ed., pp. 25–104). New York: Wiley.

Tomasello, M. (1999). *The cultural origins of human cognition*. Cambridge, MA: Harvard University Press.

van IJzendoorn, M. H. (1995). The association between adult attachment representations and infant attachment, parental responsiveness, and clinical status: A meta-analysis on the predictive validity of the Adult Attachment Interview. *Psychological Bulletin, 113,* 404–410.

van IJzendoorn, M. H., & Juffer, F. (2006). Meta-analytic evidence for massive catch-up and plasticity in physical, socio-emotional, and cognitive development. *Journal of Child Psychology & Psychiatry*, *47*, 1228–1245.

van IJzendoorn, M. H., & De Wolff, M. S. (1997). In search of the absent father–meta-analysis of infant–father attachment: A rejoinder to our discussants. *Child Development*, *68*, 604–609.

Verschueren, K., & Marcoen, A. (1999). Representation of self and socioemotional competence in kindergartners: Differential and combined effects of attachment to mother and father. *Child Development*, *70*, 183–201.

Vinden, P. G. (2001). Parenting attitudes and children's understanding of mind. A comparison of Korean American and Anglo-American families. *Cognitive Development*, *16*, 793–809.

Vogel, C. A., Bradley, R. H., Raikes, H. H., Boller, K., & Shears, J. K. (2006). Relation between father connectedness and child outcomes. *Parenting: Science and Practice*, *6*, 189–209.

Volling, B. L., & Belsky, J. (1992). Infant, father, and marital antecedents of infant–father attachment security in dual-earner and single-earner families. *Journal of Behavioral Development*, *15*, 83–100.

Welkowitz, J., Bond, R. N., Feldman, L., & Tota, M. E. (1990). Conversational time patterns and mutual influence in parent–child interactions: A time series approach. *Journal of Psycholinguistic Research*, *19*, 221–243.

Wellman, H. M., Cross, D., & Watson, J. (2001). Meta-analysis of theory of mind development: The truth about false belief. *Child Development*, *72*, 655–684.

Widom, C. S. (1989). The cycle of violence. *Science*, *244*, 160–166.

Widom, C. S. (1994). Childhood victimization and risk for adolescent problem behaviors. In M. E. Lamb & R. D. Ketterlinus (Eds.), *Adolescent problem behaviors* (pp. 127–164). Hillsdale, NJ: Lawrence Erlbaum Associates.

Williams, J., Bennett, S., & Best, D. (1975). Awareness and expression of sex stereotypes in young children. *Developmental Psychology*, *11*, 635–642.

Wolfe, D. A., & Mosk, M. D. (1983). Behavioral comparisons of children from abusive and distressed families. *Journal of Consulting and Clinical Psychology*, *51*, 702–708.

Yogman, M. (1981). Games fathers and mothers play with their infants. *Infant Mental Health Journal*, *2*, 241–248.

Youniss, J. (1989). Parent–adolescent relationships. In W. Damon (Ed.), *Child development today and tomorrow* (pp. 379–392). Hoboken, NJ: Jossey-Bass.

Youniss, J., & Ketterlinus, R. D. (1987). Communication and connectedness in mother and father–adolescent relationships. *Journal of Youth and Adolescence*, *16*, 265–280.

Youniss, J., & Smollar, J. (1985). *Adolescent relations with mothers, fathers, and friends*. Chicago: University of Chicago Press.

Zill, N., & Nord, C. W. (1996). *Causes and consequences of involvement by non-custodial parents in their children's lives: Evidence from a national longitudinal study*. Paper presented to the National Center on Fathers and Families Roundtable, New York.

❖ 11 ❖

PEER RELATIONSHIPS IN CHILDHOOD

Kenneth H. Rubin
University of Maryland
Robert Coplan
Carleton University
Xinyin Chen
University of Western Ontario
Julie Bowker
University at Buffalo, the State University of New York
Kristina L. McDonald
University of Maryland

INTRODUCTION

An early view of the development of adaptive and maladaptive behaviors during childhood and adolescence suggested that such outcomes stemmed largely from the quality of the child's relationship with his or her parents and from the types of socialization practices that the parents engaged in. This primary focus on the developmental significance of the parent–child relationship and of parenting practices was proposed early by Freud (1933) in his theory of psychosexual development, by Sears, Maccoby, and Levin (1957) in their seminal research on the significance of discipline variability and social learning, and by Bowlby (1958) in his influential writings on the long-term developmental importance of the mother–infant attachment relationship. Without denying the veracity of these claims, it is nevertheless the case that adjustment and maladjustment in childhood stem from a wide variety of sources including genetic and biological underpinnings and social influences other than parents. For example, children and adolescents spend enormous amounts of time, both in and out of home, relating to and interacting with many other people of potential influence. These significant others include their siblings, teachers or out-of-home caregivers, and peers. Children's **peers** are the focus of the present chapter.

To examine the significance of peers in children's lives, this chapter is organized as follows. We begin with a discussion of the theory that has brought the study of peers to its present status. Next, we describe normative patterns of peer interaction from infancy through late childhood and early adolescence. In the following section, we review the literature on children's **friendships**; we examine what it is that draws children together as friends and the qualitative dimensions of children's behavior displayed during interaction with friends. Next, we describe the functions of the peer group, the processes involved in peer group formation, and peer group norms and organization. This section leads to a discussion of the correlates, proximal determinants, and consequences of being accepted or rejected by the peer group. The distal processes (e.g., family factors, cultural factors) by which children become accepted or rejected by their peers are described in another section. Our chapter concludes with a discussion of some of the directions that future research might productively follow.

The purpose of this chapter is to describe the nature and significance of children's peer relationships. It is our intention to argue that such relationships represent contexts within which a significant degree of adaptive development occurs, and that without the experience of normal peer relationships, maladaptive development is likely to follow.

THEORETICAL PERSPECTIVES ON PEER RELATIONSHIPS RESEARCH

The theoretical groundwork for modern research on children's peer relationships can be traced back over 75 years. Piaget (1932) suggested that children's relationships with peers could be clearly distinguished from their relationships with adults. Adult–child relationships could be construed as being asymmetrical and falling along a vertical plane of dominance and power assertion. Children normally accept adults' rules, not necessarily because they understand them, but rather because obedience is required. By contrast, children's relationships with peers were portrayed as being balanced, egalitarian, and as falling along a more or less horizontal plane of power assertion and dominance. It was within the context of peer interaction that Piaget believed children could experience opportunities to examine conflicting ideas and explanations, to negotiate and discuss multiple perspectives, and to decide to compromise with or to reject notions held by peers. Piaget influenced a good deal of contemporary research concerning children's peer relationships, particularly regarding relations among how children think about their social worlds (social-cognition), their social behaviors, and the quality of their peer relationships (e.g., Rose-Krasnor & Denham, 2009).

Another early theoretical perspective on peer relationships stems from the writings of Sullivan (1953). Like Piaget, Sullivan believed that the concepts of mutual respect, equality, and reciprocity developed from peer relationships. Sullivan, however, emphasized the significance of "special" relationships—chumships and friendships—for the emergence of these concepts. In the early school years, whether friends or not, Sullivan thought children were basically insensitive to their peers. During the juvenile years (late elementary school), however, children were thought to be able to recognize and value each other's personal qualities; as a consequence, peers gained power as personality shaping agents. Sullivan's theory has proved influential in terms of the contemporary study of children's friendships (e.g., Vitaro, Boivin, & Bukowski, 2009) as well as in understanding loneliness as a significant motivational force in development and adjustment (e.g., Asher & Paquette, 2003).

Building on the turn-of-the-century notions of Cooley (1902), George Herbert Mead (1934) developed a third influential theory in which he suggested that the ability to reflect on the *self* developed gradually over the early years of life, primarily as a function of peer play and peer interaction. This theoretical position has been highly influential in contemporary research concerning relations between the quality of children's peer relationships and the organization of the self-system (e.g., Boivin & Hymel, 1997).

Learning and social learning theory is yet another approach that has guided current research on children's peer relationships. The basic tenet of the social learning approach to development is that children learn about their social worlds, and how to behave within these contexts, through direct peer tutelage and observation of peers "in action" (Bandura & Walters, 1963). From this perspective, peers are viewed as behavior control and behavior change agents for each other. In this regard, children punish or ignore non-normative social behavior and reward or reinforce positively those behaviors viewed as culturally appropriate and competent.

Ethological theory has also provided a novel and substantial influence on the study of children's peer relationships. From an ethological perspective, it is argued that there is a relation between biology and the ability to initiate, maintain, or disassemble particular relationships. It is a central tenet of ethological theory that social behavior and organizational structure are limited by biological constraints, and that they serve an adaptive evolutionary function (Hinde & Stevenson-Hinde, 1976). A basic focus of contemporary human ethological research has been the provision of detailed descriptions of the organization and structure of social behaviors and groups (Vaughn & Santos, 2009). Moreover, with the assumption that behavior is best understood when observed in natural settings, ethological theory has had a major impact on how children's peer interactions and relationships are studied.

Finally, there is the *group socialization theory* of Harris (1995, 1999, 2009). In a series of literature reviews, Harris challenged the view that primarily their parents mold children's personalities; rather, in her view, the peer group plays a more significant role in personality and social development. Briefly, she proposed that, once children find themselves outside the home, they take on the norms prevalent in the groups within which they spend their time . . . and, for the most part, those groups comprise other children! Drawing from social psychological perspectives on the significance of group norms (a motivation to "fit in"), in-group biases and out-group hostilities, and social cognitive views of group processes, she argued that children's identities develop primarily from their experiences within peer groups. Although Harris' view that parents and such dyadic relationships as friendship are relatively unimportant for individual development has drawn many criticisms (e.g., Collins, Maccoby, Steinberg, Hetherington, & Bornstein, 2000), publication of her work could have met with unanimous applause on the parts of those researchers who have attempted to demonstrate the significance of peer interactions, relationships, and groups for normal and abnormal development. For decades, theorists, researchers, and policy makers who have cited the primacy of parenting and the parent–child relationship have challenged those who have attempted to establish the significance of children's peer experiences. With Harris' counterchallenge, a gauntlet was thrown down—researchers must now begin to address some central questions about the causal roles that genes, biology, family, and peers play in child and adolescent adjustment and maladjustment.

THE DEVELOPMENTAL COURSE OF PEER INTERACTION

Infancy and the Toddler Period

Not surprisingly, children become increasingly interactive and competent at initiating and maintaining social exchanges as they grow older. What might be surprising is how very young children are when they can be first observed to engage in socially directed behaviors toward peers.

Given obvious motoric, cognitive, and verbal limitations, one might not expect much peer interaction when observing young infants. Indeed, Buhler (1935), in one of the first studies of peer interaction in infancy, suggested that prior to 6 months, babies were fairly oblivious to each other's presence. However, there is now reason to believe that the social awareness of very young infants has been grossly underestimated. For example, Eckerman (1979) reported that infants as young as 2 months of age are aroused by the presence of peers and engage in mutual gaze. Other signs of socially oriented interest during the first half-year of life include smiling, vocalizing, and reaching toward peers (Fogel, 1979). By 6 to 9 months, infants direct looks, vocalizations, and smiles at one another—and often return such gestures in kind (Hay, Pederson, & Nash, 1982).

Babies show signs of socially oriented interest such as smiling and reaching towards peers from the age of 2 months.

These socially oriented behaviors increase steadily with age over the first year of life. Moreover, the tendency to *respond* to social overtures increases dramatically during the last quarter of the first year (Jacobson, 1981). Responses are often in the form of imitative acts, focused on objects. Mueller and Silverman (1989) argued that these imitations represent the first evidence of shared meanings between peers, an important precursor for cooperative peer activities. Despite the apparent sociability of the infant, it seems fairly clear that social interaction with peers occurs relatively rarely and that when interactive bouts do occur, they are not for lengthy periods of time.

During the second year, toddlers take giant steps in advancing their social repertoires (Brownell & Kopp, 2007). With the emergence of locomotion and the ability to speak (Adolph & Berger, Chapter 5, and MacWhinney, Chapter 8, this textbook), social interchanges become increasingly complex. From the somewhat unpredictable social response sequences observed between infants, interactive exchanges and sequences in the toddler period can be characterized as more predictable, complex, coordinated, and lengthy (Ross & Conant, 1992; Verba, 1994). These interactions typically take the form of simple "games," which are marked by reciprocal imitative acts and the emergence of turn-taking (Howes, 1988; Ross, Lollis, & Elliot, 1982; Warneken, Chen, & Tomasello, 2006). Hay and Cook (2007) argued that these prototypical social games are characterized by a "playful, nonliteral quality" (p. 103) that distinguishes them from more "literal" interaction (e.g., interpersonal conflict). Importantly, by the toddler period, children are more likely to socially imitate peers than to imitate adults (Ryalls, Gull, & Ryalls, 2000).

The Preschool Years

The major social interactive advance in the third year of life is the ability for children to share symbolic meanings through social pretense (Howes & Matheson, 1992). Children begin to spontaneously take on complementary roles, none of which "matches" their real-world situations, and to agree on the adoption of these imaginary roles within a rule-governed context. These remarkable accomplishments can be seen in the peer play of many 24- to 48-month-olds. The ability to share meaning during pretense has been referred to as *intersubjectivity* (Trevarthen, 1979). Goncu (1993) reported a systematic change in the inter-subjective quality of the social interchanges of 3- versus 4½-year-olds. For example, the social interactions of older preschoolers involve longer sequences and turns and incorporate a more coordinated agreement among partners in terms of the roles, rules, and themes of pretend play.

In summary, despite the advances noted above, it is clearly the case that when infants and toddlers are brought together in social groups, they spend most of their time alone, or near or watching others, and *not* in coordinated, complex social exchanges.

Social participation. In 1932, Parten described six sequential **social participation** categories: unoccupied behavior, solitary play, onlooker behavior (the child observes others but does not participate in the activity), parallel play (plays beside but not with other children), associative play (plays and shares with others), and cooperative play (social play in which there is a defined division of labor). Parten concluded that children between the ages of 2 and 5 engage in increasing frequencies of associative and cooperative play and in decreasing frequencies of idle, solitary, and onlooker behavior. Parten's social participation scale and her findings dominated the literature concerning children's play and sociability for almost 50 years. Yet her database derived from a sample of only 40 children attending a single university laboratory preschool. Furthermore, conclusions based on her data were simplistic. For example, the 3-year-old preschooler was characterized as a solitary or parallel player and the 5-year-old was described as spending the most time in associative or cooperative play.

A more critical reading of Parten's study suggests a more complex set of conclusions. To begin with, children at all ages engage in unoccupied, onlooking, solitary, parallel, and group play activities (Howes & Matheson, 1992). Even at 5 years, children spend less of their free play time in classroom settings interacting with others than being alone or near others. Moreover, the major developmental changes in the play of preschoolers concern the cognitive maturity of their solitary, parallel, and group interactive activities (Rubin, Watson, & Jambor, 1978). Solitary-sensorimotor behaviors become increasingly rare over the preschool years, and the relative frequency of solitary-construction or exploration remains the same. Furthermore, the only types of social interactive activity to increase with age are sociodramatic play and games-with-rules. Taken together, the extant data reveal *age differences* only for particular forms of solitary and group behaviors.

Other early developmental differences. There are developmental differences not only on the prevalence or level of social participation, but also on the nature (e.g., prosocial versus aggressive) of social interaction. On the prosocial side, helping and sharing behaviors with peers are observed to increase from the early toddler to the early preschool years (Benenson, Markovits, Roy, & Denko, 2003; Eisenberg, Fabes, & Spinrad, 2006). This is likely a result of increasing social-cognitive and affective perspective-taking abilities. A more sophisticated understanding of how others think and feel promotes the development of empathy, which may in turn lead to more prosocial behaviors (Vaish, Carpenter, & Tomasello, 2009). This also facilitates more "mature" peer interactions. For example, Brownell, Ramani, and Zerwas (2006) reported age-related changes in children's social understanding and cooperation over the first three years of life. Whereas coordinated activities between younger toddlers were sporadic and more likely to be coincidental in nature, during the second year children were considerably more skilled at cooperating towards a common goal.

Finally, throughout the preschool years, children also demonstrate age-related increases in social-communicative competence (Goldstein, Kaczmarek, & English, 2002). For example, from toddlerhood to preschool-age, children develop the ability to use gestures to represent absent objects and to explicitly coordinate roles in pretend play (Sawyer, 1997). Moreover, older preschool age children direct more speech to their peers than do their younger counterparts and their communication with peers is more likely to include indirect (i.e., declaratives, interrogatives, inferred requests) than direct (imperatives) requests (Garvey, 1984). Genyue

Sharing behavior increases from the early toddler to the early preschool years.

and Lee (2007) described the emergence of *flattery* behavior between the ages of 3 and 6 years, with older preschoolers appropriately moderating their display of such behavior in keeping with the familiarity and presence/absence of the intended target. However, regardless of age, two-thirds of preschoolers' socially directed speech is comprehensible and has a successful outcome (Levin & Rubin, 1983). These data raise questions concerning Piaget's assumption that the speech of preschoolers is characterized primarily by egocentric utterances.

Notwithstanding these increases in prosocial and sociable behaviors, preschoolers' interactions with peers also evolve in terms of more negative social interchanges. For example, although aggression tends to decline overall from toddlerhood to the preschool years (particularly instrumental aggression such as fights over toys and possessions; NICHD Early Child Care Research Network, 2001), an increasing proportion of aggression becomes *hostile* in intent. This may be due to preschoolers' increased understanding of social motives and peer intentions (e.g., Lee & Cameron, 2000), which may also contribute toward an accompanying increase in social-cognitively "advanced" forms of *social* and *relational* aggression (Crick, Casas, & Mosher, 1997).

Development beyond the Preschool Period

In middle childhood, children's interactions with peers become increasingly complex and multifaceted. In many respects, these developments can be attributed to continued advances in the abilities to understand and appreciate others' thoughts, intentions, and emotions (Izard, 2009; Selman & Schultz, 1990). Thus, social communicative competence continues to improve with age, and children become more adept at establishing shared meanings with their peers (Goldstein et al., 2002). Continued improvement in **social skills** allows for children to more competently achieve their social goals and resolve interpersonal dilemmas (Rubin & Rose-Krasnor, 1992). Furthermore, with age children become better able to engage in rule-governed competitive games (Hartup, Brady, & Newcomb, 1983). Finally, there continue to be age-related increases in altruistic behavior from early to middle and late childhood (Eisenberg et al., 2006).

In summary, we have described the developmental progression of children's interactive skills with peers. These skills aid children to initiate and maintain dyadic relationships with non-familial others. These special dyadic relationships have been posited to serve many adaptive functions throughout the childhood and adolescent years; indeed, throughout life! We turn now to a discussion of children's friendships.

CHILDREN AND THEIR FRIENDS

The establishment and maintenance of close friendships with peers represent challenging yet rewarding endeavors throughout childhood. In childhood, however, the constituent factors associated with friendship formation and maintenance vary with age; indeed, the very meaning of friendship undergoes developmental change. In the following sections we discuss the functions of friendship, children's changing understandings of friendship, prevalence and stability of friendship during childhood and adolescence, issues of friendship measurement, the friendship formation processes, similarities between friends, children's interactive behaviors with friends and non-friends, gender-related issues in children's friendships, children without friends, and friendship and adjustment. An overriding theme is the significance of friendship in children's psychosocial development.

Functions of Friendship

A friendship is a close, mutual, and voluntary dyadic relationship. This definition distinguishes friendship from such peer-group level constructs as popularity, which refers to the experience of being liked or accepted by or well-known among one's peers. Defining features of friendship include reciprocity and a feeling of perceived equality between individuals. In its simplest definition, *reciprocity* refers to the return of like behavior and affection between partners and is an essential component of any definition of friendship.

Friendships in childhood serve to (1) provide support, self-esteem enhancement, and positive self-evaluation; (2) provide emotional security; (3) provide affection and opportunities for intimate disclosure; (4) provide intimacy and affection; (5) offer consensual validation of interests, hopes, and fears; (6) provide instrumental and informational assistance; (7) promote the growth of interpersonal sensitivity; and (8) offer prototypes for later romantic, marital, and parental relationships (Newcomb & Bagwell, 1995; Sullivan, 1953). Perhaps the most important function of friendship is to offer children an extra-familial base of security from which they may explore the effects of their behaviors on themselves, their peers, and their environments.

From a developmental perspective, Parker and Gottman (1989) argued that friendship serves different functions for children at different points in their development. For the *young child*, friendship serves to maximize excitement and amusement levels in play, and helps to organize behavior in the face of arousal. In *middle childhood*, friendships aid in acquiring knowledge about behavioral norms and help children learn the skills necessary for successful self-presentation and impression management. These skills become crucial in middle childhood when anxiety about peer relationships develops. Finally, in *adolescence*, friendships serve to assist individuals in their quest for self-exploration and identity formation and to help them integrate logic and emotions.

Children's Conceptions of Friendship

One of the most productive areas of developmental inquiry has been the study of how children think about and define friendship. In general, friendship conceptions have been assessed by asking children such questions as "What is a best friend?" or "What do you expect from a best friend?" In response to these questions and others, children of all ages describe best-friendships as relationships that are characterized by reciprocity or mutual "give and take" (Hartup & Stevens, 1999). Beyond this general agreement about the importance of reciprocity, however, developmental differences exist in children's conceptions of friendship. For instance, during early and middle childhood (7 to 8 years), children describe friends as companions who live nearby, have nice toys, and share the child's expectations about play activities (Bigelow & LaGaipa, 1980). During late childhood (10 to 11 years) shared values and rules become more important, and friends are expected to stick up for, and be loyal to, each other. Finally, by early adolescence (11 to 13 years), friends are seen as sharing similar interests, making active attempts to understand each other, and willing to engage in intimate self-disclosure (Schneider & Tessier, 2007). Taken together, it appears that children's understanding of friendship become increasingly sophisticated and their expectations become increasingly linked to intimacy with age.

Why do such developmental changes occur? Selman and Schultz (1990) argued that the key to developmental change in children's friendship conceptions is *perspective taking* ability. Young children do not yet realize that other people feel or think about things differently from themselves. As children grow older, they gradually take on the viewpoints of others, moving from egocentrism to a mutual perspective. As a final step, children/adolescents are able to mentally stand outside of the social system comprising their social interactions and relationships and to view themselves and their relationships with others from the perspective of someone who is not involved in the relationship, that is from a "third person perspective". This shift in how children "see" themselves and others is thought to be manifested in their understanding of friendships.

Other researchers have argued that children's friendship expectations develop in conjunction with the child's understanding of reciprocity (e.g., Youniss, 1980). Young children who believe that their own contribution toward a friendship is the most important are more likely to understand friendship in terms of momentary interactions and how they themselves are affected. By adolescence, friendship is perceived as an ongoing relationship, and friends are people on whom children can count for continuing understanding and intimate social support. In contrast, Berndt (1981) argued that friendship conceptions represent the cumulative assimilation of basically unrelated themes or dimensions, such as commonalities in play interests and self-disclosure. According to Berndt, children do not abandon initial notions about play and mutual association when they eventually recognize the importance of intimacy and loyalty.

Although the jury is still out in terms of what may be the underlying mechanisms by which the understanding of friendships develops, speculation is plausible. Essentially, children's conceptions about friendship reflect their own transitions from the world of the concrete to the world of the abstract. What children may require and desire in a friendship develops as a function of their growing understanding of the world and in conjunction with their own expanding social needs. Beginning in early childhood, the social world is increasingly cognitively differentiated. Eventually, children begin to realize that a friendship can serve potentially as both a resource and a context that differ from the conditions that exist with non-friends.

The Prevalence and Stability of Friendship

Perspectives on the development of children's friendship conceptions generate several predictions about the nature of such friendships at various ages, along with how children will behave in the company of their friends. For example, it would be consistent with these perspectives if children's friendships were seen to demonstrate more stability, prosocial responding, psychological similarity, and intimate personal knowledge over time and age. As it happens, most children and adolescents have at least one mutual friend (Hartup & Stevens, 1999). Beginning in the elementary school years, children's friendships are identified by way of friendship nominations. For example, children may be asked to nominate their "best" three same-gender friends in their class, grade, and school. The *mutuality* of nominations is then evaluated; thus, a child who receives a reciprocal best friendship nomination is considered to have a mutual best friend. According to Parker and Asher (1993), approximately 75% to 80% of children have at least one mutual *best* friendship, although prevalence varies across studies due to variability in the measurement of "best" friendship (e.g., when the number of best friendship nominations permitted differs; Berndt & McCandless, 2009).

Identifying a child's friends is not as easy a task as one may surmise. Simply asking a child to name her or his best friend(s) may lead to the production of a socially desirable response or the unilateral choice of a partner who does not reciprocate the friendship nomination. Furthermore, the child may misinterpret the "meaning" of a friend, and may provide an overinclusive set of responses (e.g., by naming "chums" or "acquaintances" rather than a "best friend"). Historically, most peer relationships researchers have limited friendship nominations to same-gender friends "in your class" or "in your grade" primarily because the majority of children only nominate same-gender, same-grade, and same-school peers as their best friends (Hartup & Stevens, 1999). But growing evidence that a sizable number of children and adolescents have friends from outside-school contexts (neighborhood, different school, sports team, out of town, online, and so forth; e.g., Mesch & Talmud, 2007) and who are of the other gender, and that these friendships can strongly influence adjustment (e.g., Chan & Poulin, 2007; Kiesner, Poulin, & Nicotra, 2003; Poulin & Pedersen, 2007), has led to a recent shift toward relaxing these friendship nomination restrictions in studies of child and adolescent friendships.

Once mutual friendships are formed, friendships at all ages show remarkable stability. During the preschool years, two-thirds of children who identify one another as friends do so again 4 to 6 months later (Gershman & Hayes, 1983). Berndt and Hoyle (1985) found an increase in the stability of mutual friendships from age 5 years (50%) to age 10 years (75%), but not from age 10 years to age 14 years. In fact, it has been consistently found that only half of all young adolescent friendships are stable across one academic school year (Bowker, 2004; Wojslawowicz Bowker, Rubin, Burgess, Booth-LaForce, & Rose-Krasnor, 2006). This lack of increased stability during early adolescence can be accounted for by two factors. To begin with, friendships tend to become more exclusive with age—as such, children may allow some friendships to dissolve. As well, as children approach puberty, rapid changes in interests, and varying rates of development may result in a period of change in friendships choices (Berndt, 1985; Bowker, 2004). However, the trend toward increased stability in friendships continues into older age (Cairns, Leung, Buchanan, & Cairns, 1995). There is also evidence suggesting that boys are more likely than girls to have stable same-gender (Benenson & Christakos, 2003; Hardy, Bukowski, & Sippola, 2002) and other-gender friendships (Chan & Poulin, 2007). Multi-context friendships (friendships that comprise individuals who interact both inside and outside of school) also appear to be more stable than single-context friendships (Chan & Poulin, 2007).

Similarities between Friends

What are some of the factors that influence the formation of children's friendships? A facile first response is that age and gender are important magnets that pull children together. In addition, friends tend to be of the same ethnic background (Aboud & Mendelson, 1996). Thus, from an early age, children are attracted to and choose friends who are like themselves in *observable* characteristics. For example, it has been reported that children are attracted to peers whose behavioral tendencies are similar to their own (Rubin, Lynch, Coplan, Rose-Krasnor, & Booth, 1994). Greater behavioral similarities exist between friends than non-friends, and children share friendships with other children who resemble themselves in terms of prosocial and delinquent/antisocial behaviors (Haselager, Hartup, van Lieshout, & Riksen Walraven, 1998; Popp, Laursen, Kerr, Burk, & Stattin, 2008), shyness and internalized distress (e.g., Hogue & Steinberg, 1995; Rubin, Wojslawowicz, Rose-Krasnor, Booth-LaForce, & Burgess, 2006b), popularity and acceptance (Kupersmidt, DeRosier, & Patterson, 1995), peer group difficulties (e.g., victimization; Bowker et al., 2009), academic achievement and motivation (Altermatt & Pomerantz, 2003), and hobbies or interests (e.g., Selfhout, Branje, ter Bogt, & Meeus, 2009). In addition to similarity in behavior and peer group functioning, friends are more similar in their targets for aggression than nonfriends (Card & Hodges, 2006).

Similarity has been associated not only with friendship formation (Kupersmidt et al., 1995), but also with friendship maintenance. For instance, by adolescence, stable friendship pairs, in comparison to those members of friendships that dissolve, are more likely to be similar to each other in their *attitudes* about school and academic aspirations; the use of drugs and alcohol; and that which is considered to be normal teen behavior (e.g., Urberg, Degirmencioglu, & Piligrim, 1997; Vitaro, Tremblay, Kerr, Pagani, & Bukowski, 1997).

Behaviors between Friends

Friends interact with each other differently than do non-friends. In general, children of all ages engage in more talk, task orientation, cooperation, positive affect, and effective conflict management during social interactions with friends than with non-friends (Hartup, 1996; Simpkins & Parke, 2002). In this regard, friendship is not only a social and positive relational context, but it also provides for the expression and regulation of affect (Parker & Gottman, 1989).

From a developmental perspective, children as young as 3½ years direct more social overtures, engage in more social interaction, and play in more complex ways with friends than with non-friends (Doyle, 1982). Preschool-aged friends tend to be more cooperative with each other during play (Charlesworth & LaFreniere, 1983), and 4th and 5th grade friends demonstrate greater play sophistication (e.g., positive fantasy play, negotiation) when interacting with their friends than with non-friends (Simpkins & Parke, 2002). By adolescence, friend/non-friend behavioral differences are even stronger than in middle childhood or the early preschool years. Altruistic acts, particularly generosity, cooperation, and helpfulness between friends, increase with age and continue well into adolescence (Berndt, 1985; Windle, 1994).

Research involving **conflict** between friends and non-friends is somewhat contradictory. Friends differ from non-friends not only by engaging in more friendly interactions, but also by demonstrating more quarreling, active hostility (assaults and threats) and reactive hostility (refusals and resistance) between pairs. For example, Hartup and his colleagues (Hartup & Laursen, 1995; Hartup, Laursen, Stewart, & Eastenson, 1998) observed that nursery school children engaged in more conflicts overall with their friends than with neutral associates. Simpkins and Parke (2002) also reported greater levels of negative affect and guilty coercion within dyads of friends than non-friends. Most likely, these findings can be attributed to the fact that friends spend more time actually interacting with each other than do non-friends.

There are important differences, however, in the ways in which friends and non-friends *resolve* conflicts that arise, and in what the outcomes of those conflicts are likely to be. For example, friends, as compared with non-friends, make more use of negotiation and disengagement, relative to standing firm, in their resolution of conflicts. In terms of conflict outcomes, friends are more likely to reach equitable resolutions (Newcomb & Bagwell, 1995) and agreements (Tomada, Schneider, & Fonzi, 2002). Thus, although the amount of conflict is greater between friends than non-friends, friends resolve conflicts in ways that help ensure that their relationships persist beyond the conflict and continue into the future (Laursen, Hartup, & Keplas, 1996).

In summary, children appear to behave differently in the company of friends than non-friends. When interacting with friends, children engage in more prosocial behaviors as well as more conflicts than when with non-friends. These conflicts are more likely to be resolved through negotiation, and the outcomes are usually equitable and involve mutual agreement. The differences described suggest that children view friendship as a unique context, separate and qualitatively different from their experiences with non-friends.

Gender-Related Issues

There appear to be some similarities in the ways that boys and girls think about friendship; for example, both boys and girls emphasize that they depend on friends for company, approval, and support (Craft, 1994). However, gender differences emerge when boys and girls are asked the question "What do you expect from a good friend?" Girls tend to respond by referring to that which they may *receive* from a good friend; boys emphasize *reciprocity*, or provisions that they expect to receive from, as well as give to, a friend (Craft, 1994). Differences also are revealed when children are asked to describe their same-gender peers. Girls often describe them as being nice. In contrast, boys are more likely to describe their male classmates in terms of their interests; fighting, artistic, and athletic abilities; goofiness; and academic performance (Benenson, 1990). These findings provide some support for the proposition that boys are more concerned with status within the peer group, whereas girls are more concerned with friendship and affiliations.

Studies of children's friendships also reveal gender differences in the *quality* of boys' and girls' friendships. Girls report more intimate exchange, conflict resolution, validation and caring, and help and guidance within their friendships than do boys (Parker & Asher, 1993; Rubin et al., 2004). These findings might be explained by girls' greater orientation toward dyadic relationships. Girls may be more emotionally invested in their friendships, which in turn, may help to foster intimacy and feelings of closeness. Gender differences are not typically found, however, in levels of relationship satisfaction (Parker & Asher, 1993; Rose & Rudolph, 2006), suggesting that the abovementioned positive features of friendship may carry different "meaning" for boys and girls (Rose, Swenson, & Robert, 2009). And there is growing evidence that girls' friendships can be psychologically stressful relationship experiences. For instance, girls report greater distress when imagining the termination of their friendships than do boys (Benenson & Christakos, 2003). Also, girls report more **co-rumination**, or intimate self-disclosure done in a "ruminative" fashion (e.g., negative dwelling on emotionally charged and intimate everyday occurrences and feelings), within their friendships than do boys (Rose, 2002), which in turn, is concurrently and predictively associated with **internalizing problems** (Rose, 2002; Rose, Carlson, & Waller, 2007).

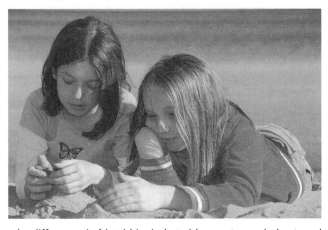

One of the main gender differences in friendships is that girls report more intimate exchange than boys.

Children without Friends

Some children may be unsuccessful in their attempts to make friends. Indeed, researchers have found that approximately 15% to 20% of children and young adolescents are *friendless*, or without any mutual friends (Parker & Asher, 1993; Parker & Seal, 1996). Importantly, a similar percentage of youth have been found to be consistently or *chronically* friendless (Wojslawowicz Bowker et al., 2006). Friendless children may lack social skills or may demonstrate behaviors that their peers judge to be unattractive (Parker & Seal, 1996). Regardless of the reason for friendlessness, however, children without mutual friends report more loneliness than do children with mutual friendships (e.g., Parker & Seal, 1996; Parker & Asher, 1993), and chronic friendlessness has been associated with increasing internalizing difficulties and peer victimization (Ladd & Troop-Gordon, 2003; Wojslawowicz Bowker et al., 2006) Moreover, Bagwell, Newcomb, and Bukowski (1998) found that being without a mutual friend during the 5th grade was a negative predictor of feelings of general self-worth during adulthood.

It should be noted that children who are *rejected* by their peers are not necessarily friendless (Cairns, Cairns, Neckerman, Gest, & Gariepy, 1988). Relatedly, not all highly and average accepted children have mutual friendships (Parker & Asher, 1993). This leads to a number of interesting questions regarding the possible effects of having a close friendship. Laursen, Bukowski, Aunola, and Nurmi (2007) found, for example, that initial social isolation predicted increases in internalizing and **externalizing problems** and initial internalizing and externalizing problems predicted increases in isolation, *but only for those children who did not have a mutual friendship*. Thus, a single close friend may serve to alleviate the negative "costs" of being disliked and isolated by the majority of one's peers.

Friendship and Adjustment

Considerable evidence has accumulated that having a friend can promote or support positive adjustment, particularly during potentially stressful times of transition and peer difficulty (e.g., Berndt & Keefe, 1995). For example, as children make the transition into elementary school, those who enter school with a mutual friend report higher levels of school satisfaction and academic interest than those children who begin the school years without a friend. Hodges and colleagues found that simply having a mutual best friend protected youth from the internalizing and externalizing "costs" of peer victimization (Hodges, Boivin, Vitaro, & Bukowski, 1999).

The associations between friendship and adjustment, however, are more complex when the stability and quality of the friendship is considered, along with the characteristics of the best friend. In one study, Berndt, Hawkins, and Jiao (1999) found that ratings of sociability and leadership increased across the transition from elementary to middle school, but only for those children who had high-quality, stable friendships. Behavior problems were found to increase from sixth to seventh grade only for those children who had stable friendships with children who had behavior problems themselves. Furthermore, having a high-quality, positive friendship has been linked to positive psychological well-being (Berndt & Keefe, 1995). But results from a few studies suggest that there may also be a "dark" side to some high-quality friendships (Bowker & Rubin, 2009; Rose, 2002; Rose et al., 2007). For instance, Rose and colleagues found that co-rumination is associated with both positive friendship quality and such emotional difficulties as anxiety and depression. Taking such findings together, it appears critical to consider more than one friendship "factor" in studies of friendship and adjustment.

Friendship and shy/withdrawn children.   Children who are shy, socially wary, and anx-ious might be expected to have difficulties forming and maintaining friendships. After all, social timidity may preclude opportunities to establish friendships to begin with, and social skills deficits associated with social wariness may prove to inhibit the formation and mainten-ance of friendship over time. However, no differences have been reported in the proportions of friendship prevalence and friendship stability for shy/withdrawn children relative to non-shy/non-withdrawn children. For example, the prevalence of best friendships among *young* socially withdrawn children is not significantly different from that among non-withdrawn children (Ladd & Burgess, 1999), and approximately 60% of withdrawn 8-, 9-, and 10-year-olds have reciprocated friendships, a percentage that is nearly identical to that of non-withdrawn age-mates (Schneider, 1999; Rubin et al., 2006b). Rubin and colleagues also found that withdrawn children were as likely as non-withdrawn children to have a stable best friend-ship during late childhood and early adolescence (Rubin et al., 2006b). It appears that social withdrawal and shyness are individual characteristics that do not influence the formation, prevalence, and maintenance of friendship in childhood.

Beyond prevalence and stability, however, there is some evidence that the friendship experi-ences of many shy/withdrawn children may be less than positive relationship experiences. For example, there is some evidence that withdrawn children tend to form friendships with simi-larly withdrawn and victimized peers, and that their friendships are relatively poor in relation-ship quality (Rubin et al., 2006b; Schneider, 1999). These findings suggest a "misery loves company" scenario for withdrawn children and their best friends. One may conjure up images of victimized friends coping poorly in the world of peers . . . images reflected in recent newspaper and television accounts of peer victimization and its untimely consequences. In support of this notion, having a withdrawn friend has been associated with increased social withdrawal across the middle school transition (Oh et al., 2008). Yet *any* mutual best friend-ship, even if it is a "miserable" one, but especially if it is stable (Oh et al., 2008), may help withdrawn children navigate difficult times of transition and school change (Rubin et al., 2004).

Friendship and externalizing children.   Similar to shy/withdrawn children, those who act "against" their social worlds through **aggression**, opposition, and impulsivity also do *not* have difficulty *forming* friendships. Although they tend to be more disliked than other chil-dren (Newcomb, Bukowski, & Pattee, 1993), the majority of aggressive children have a mutual best friendship and are as likely as well-adjusted children to have mutual friends (e.g.,Vitaro, Brendgen, & Tremblay, 2000).

Aggression, however, seems to be negatively related to friendship stability (e.g., Hektner, August, & Realmuto, 2000), a finding that is not too surprising considering the adverse nature of aggression. Moreover, aggressive children have friends who are more aggressive or their relationships are more confrontational and antisocial in quality (Dishion, Andrews, & Crosby, 1995; Dishion, Eddy, Haas, Li, & Spracklen, 1997). High levels of relational aggres-sion (e.g., threatening friendship withdrawal) *within* the friendship, and high levels of exclusiv-ity, jealousy, and intimacy characterize the friendships of relationally aggressive children. In contrast, overtly aggressive children direct their overt aggression *outside* their friendship dyads, and report low levels of intimacy (Grotpeter & Crick, 1996).

Perhaps alarmingly, it has been reported that aggressive behaviors become more acceptable to peers and attractive with age (e.g., Bukowski, Sippola, & Newcomb, 2000), and more strongly associated with perceived popularity (Cillessen & Mayeux, 2004). Moreover, it is well known that a child's association with deviant friends and peers often leads to subsequent behavioral and social difficulties (Berndt & Keefe, 1995; Dishion, McCord, & Poulin, 1999). As such, researchers would do well to examine the processes by which aggressive behavior becomes increasingly acceptable and whether friendship serves to exacerbate difficulties rather than ameliorate them during the late childhood and early adolescent years.

Summary

Most children have at least one friend. Children become friends with other children who are like themselves in terms of "surface" characteristics and behavioral characteristics, and, during the adolescent years, with others who share similar attitudes, opinions, and values. Children's *conceptions* of friendship progress from the concrete to the abstract with age, and this change is reflected in their behavior with their friends. With age, children's friendships demonstrate more stability, more reciprocal altruism, and more intimate personal knowledge. Friends engage in qualitatively different types of interactions than non-friends at all ages, and the characteristics of these interactions can be used to describe and predict the friendship formation process. Children who are in the process of becoming friends are more likely to communicate clearly, self-disclose more often, and resolve conflicts more effectively than children who do not become friends. Although conflict often occurs within friendships, friends resolve conflicts in ways that *enhance* the likelihood that the relationship will persist or continue. There are also notable gender differences in the qualities of boys' and girls' friendships, and research on children who are without mutual best friends supports the hypothesis that friendship plays a significant role in social development by providing children with settings and contexts within which to learn about themselves, their peers, and the world around them.

CHILDREN'S GROUPS

Thus far, we have emphasized developmental trends in social interaction and the significance of dyadic peer relationships. However, children also spend a large proportion of their time in formal and informal group settings where membership is not defined solely by friendship. In the following sections we explore the structural and functional characteristics of the peer group, the processes that are involved in group formation, and group norms and organization.

The Peer Group as a Social Context

It is not uncommon to see groups of preschool children playing together in the classroom, the schoolyard, or the neighborhood. When children of this young age are observed together, for the most part, their behaviors are independently oriented, and their concerns are with their own immediate ends (Isaacs, 1933). Somewhere in middle childhood, however, a change occurs. This change can be characterized as a transformation from a *group of peers* to a *peer group*.

Peer groups usually range in size from three to over 10 children, with an average of five or six members, and mostly comprise same-gender peers (Chen, Chang, & He, 2003a; Kindermann, McCollom, & Gibson, 1995). In childhood, relatively small and intimate cliques predominate. However, children's involvements in cliques tend to decline in adolescence, whereas affiliation with larger crowds becomes a salient feature of adolescent social life (e.g., Brown, Eicher & Petrie, 1986). These developmental shifts may result from broader changes in social-cognitive abilities and social-ecological conditions. Whereas young children may seek support from intimate groups as a source of psychological dependence in an effort to establish personal autonomy from parents, adolescents may strive to acquire a sense of identity in a peer context with different lifestyles and value systems (Brown, 1990). Moreover, with increasing age, more sophisticated social skills allow adolescents to maintain extensive and different types of peer relationships.

There are mixed findings in the literature concerning gender differences in group characteristics. Although some researchers have reported that boys are more likely than girls to engage in group activities and that boys' groups are larger than girls' groups (Benenson, Apostoleris & Parnass, 1997; Maccoby, 1995; Ruble & Martin, 1998; Thorne & Luria, 2001), others have failed to find significant gender differences in the extensivity of peer networks (e.g., Cairns et al., 1995; Tarrant, 2002).

Insofar as the *nature* of the peer group is concerned, some researchers (e.g., Strayer & Strayer, 1976) have argued that the characteristics of a group can be represented by the additive effects of a specific behavior (e.g., dominance) from each member on each other member. It has also been argued that the group may develop on the basis of dyadic social relationships and thus may be best conceived of as an aggregation of relationships (e.g., Hinde, 1987). Nevertheless, many researchers have agreed that the characteristics of a group are emergent, that is, not reducible to the characteristics of the individuals who compose the group (Cairns & Cairns, 1994; Chen, Chen, & Kaspar, 2001). Unlike such dyadic social relationships as friendship, the peer group represents a social context that is developed through the collective functioning of members based on group norms and values (Brown, 1990; Cairns & Cairns, 1994). Children in the group are "tied together" and, at the same time, constrained by common interests and group norms. As a result, the "character" of the group may serve to guide how children react to various tasks and thus function as a context for social interactions and individual behaviors (Brown, 1990).

Peer Group Functions

In peer group interactions, children learn a variety of specific skills that are required for group functioning. Fine (1987) argued that peer groups teach children (1) how to engage in cooperative activity aimed at collective rather than individual goals; (2) about social structures; (3) the skills associated with leading and following others; (4) the control of hostile impulses towards fellow members; and (5) to mobilize aggression in the service of group loyalty by directing it towards "outsiders". In addition, social networks and emotional connections that children establish and maintain with other members may constitute a major source of social support for children to cope with stress and adjustment difficulties (Hartup, 1992). In short, frequent contact, common activities and interpersonal affective connectedness among group members may make children's groups a strong socialization influence (Kindermann, 1993).

It has been argued that whereas experiences with friends may be specific to dyadic social situations, peer groups may have pervasive impact on individual social, emotional, and behavioral functioning and adjustment in larger social settings. Findings from empirical research are consistent with these arguments (e.g., Cairns & Cairns, 1994; Chen, Chang, Liu, & He, 2008; Kindermann, McCollom, & Gibson, 1995). For example, whereas natural peer groups might be formed based on children's motivational factors, the profile of peer networks significantly predicts subsequent changes in individual motivation in school (Kindermann, 1993). Similar findings have been reported concerning the contributions of peer groups to such matters as school drop-out, teenage pregnancy, and delinquency (e.g., Cairns & Cairns, 1994; Chen et al., 2001; Dekovic, Engels, Shirai, De Kort, & Anker, 2002; Kiesner, Poulin, & Nicotra, 2003; Xie, Cairns & Cairns, 2001).

Cliques and Crowds

According to Brown (1990), there are two main types of peer groups: *cliques* and *crowds*. Whereas cliques are relatively smaller friendship-based groups, crowds are reputation-based collectives of similarly stereotyped individuals who are defined by the primary attitudes or activities their members share. Clique activities are often represented by relatively intensive interactions and emotional involvement of group members. Crowds are more loosely organized and less intimate than cliques; members of a crowd may not even interact with one another. However, crowds often grant adolescents an identity embedded within a larger social structure. In high school, identifiable crowds include "normals," "jocks," "brains," "populars," "greasers," "partyers," "loners," and "druggies" (Brown, Mounts, Lamborn, & Steinberg, 1993). For example, "jocks" are very involved in athletics and tend to be popular; "brains" worry about their grades and have marginal standing with peers; and "druggies" do poorly in school, are hostile towards authority figures, and engage in risky health behaviors such as unsafe sex and binge drinking (Eccles & Roeser, Chapter 12, this volume; La Greca, Prinstein, & Fetter, 2001).

Crowd membership is an important contributor to an adolescent's social functioning because of its influence on social contacts and relationships with peers. For example, the stigma that is placed on members of a particular crowd channels adolescents into relationships and dating patterns with those sharing a similar crowd label. These negative reputations may prevent adolescents from exploring new identities and discourages a shift to other crowd memberships. There is evidence that the stigma associated with some large peer groups or crowds influences the judgments that adolescents form about their peers (Horn, 2003). Consistent with the findings from research focused on individuals' aggressive reputations and social cognitions (e.g., Dodge, 1980), Horn (2003) found that adolescents are biased in their use of reputational or stereotypical information about particular groups, especially when presented with ambiguous situations. It is likely that these crowd-specific evaluations help to perpetuate group stereotypes and the structure of peer groups within a school.

Methodological Issues in the Study of Peer Groups

Until recently, the measurement or quantification of peer groups was difficult, if not ineffective. Traditionally, researchers relied on self-report data by asking children or young adolescents to create a list of their closest friends or group members. This single-informant approach raised psychometric concerns with regard to the reliability and validity of the data.

Assessing peer groups. Two techniques, social network analysis (SNA, Richards, 1995) and the social cognitive map (SCM, Cairns, Gariepy, & Kindermann, 1989) were introduced to assess peer groups. SNA is based on friendship nominations. Children are typically asked to list up to 10 friends with whom they hang out most often in the school. Through the analysis of a computer program, NEGOPY (Richards, 1995), clusters of students who report having relatively high contact with one another are identified. NEGOPY can detect group members, liaisons, dyads, and isolates based on patterns of friendship links and the strengths of the links; participants are assigned membership in one of the social network positions. *Group members* are those individuals who belong to a rather exclusive social group that comprises at least three individuals who have most (>50%) of their links with other members in the same group and who are all connected by some paths entirely within the group. *Liaisons* are individuals who have friendships with group members, but are not group members themselves. *Dyads* are individuals who have one reciprocated friendship link, either to each other or to another individual. These individuals do not belong to a group *per se*, but have mutual friendships. Finally, *isolates* are those children who have no reciprocated friendships. It should be noted that because SNA is based on friendship (either reciprocal or non-reciprocal) links, groups identified through the program represent *friendship networks*.

Compared with SNA, the "composite social cognitive map" (SCM) technique, developed by Cairns et al. (1989), assesses peer groups more directly. Children are first asked "Are there people in school who hang around together a lot? Who are they?" To ensure that the respondents include themselves, a follow-up question is asked: "What about you? Do you hang around together a lot with a group? Who are these people you hang around with?" Children are expected to report on groups about which they are most knowledgeable. Based on the reports of all participants, a matrix is constructed from the number of occasions that any two persons co-occurred in the same group. Specifically, each participant's group-membership profile is first generated based on the frequencies of nominations of group membership with every other child in the class. Then a profile similarity index is derived by correlating pairs of individual group-membership profiles. Children with similar group-membership profiles are clustered into the same group (Cairns & Cairns, 1994).

This latter methodology offers several advantages. To begin with, not all children are required as respondents in order to obtain an accurate representation of naturally occurring peer groups. Obtaining nominations from half of the children in a particular setting seems to be sufficient. As well, the examination of individual connectedness provides information beyond public consensus about rejected or popular children. Popular children are not necessarily popular in all social groups, and "social maps" provide a vehicle to determine this aspect of peer groups.

Examining the contextual effect of the peer group.   Researchers have used multilevel modeling to examine the significance of the peer group for individual social behaviors and school performance in several studies (Espelage, Holt, & Henkel, 2003; Ryan, 2001). Chen et al. (Chen, Chang, & He, 2003; Chen et al., 2008), for example, investigated group effects on social functioning and academic achievement in Chinese children. Individual-level relations between academic achievement and social functioning might be *mediated* and facilitated by the group context. By providing a social context for the selection and socialization processes (e.g., establishing the group profile and reputation, mutual regulation based on group norms), the peer group served to promote the formation of relations between academic achievement and social functioning. Moreover, depending on specific group norms, peer group functioning might *moderate* the relations between individual academic achievement and social adjustment. Compared with their counterparts in other groups, for example, children who had academic difficulties and were affiliated with low-achieving groups were more likely to display social problems. The low-achieving groups exacerbated social and behavioral problems of academically poor children and placed them at heightened risk for maladaptive social development. High-achieving groups, however, served a buffering function that protected academically poor children from developing social problems. As a result, academically weak children in high-achieving groups developed fewer social problems than their counterparts in low-achieving groups.

Summary

Peer groups offer children a unique context for learning about themselves and others (see Vaughn & Santos, 2009 for a review). Children's initial dyadic experiences with friends assist them in acquiring the appropriate social skills necessary for peer acceptance. Once children are accepted by their peers, a variety of different cliques is formed, and members are afforded the opportunity to explore the group setting. Sometimes adolescents assume membership in "crowds." Through membership in cliques and crowds adolescents learn about common goals, cooperation, the complex interrelationships that make up a group's structure, and importantly, social skills and qualities that are required for effective functioning in a collective context. Cliques and crowds offer distinct social opportunities to adolescents. The former provides a context for adolescents to test and develop values and roles in the absence of adult monitoring; the latter offers extra-familial support in the development of a sense of self.

PEER ACCEPTANCE, REJECTION, AND PERCEIVED POPULARITY

The experience of being liked and accepted by the peer group-at-large is known as **peer acceptance** and the experience of being disliked by peers has been termed **peer rejection**. The construct of **perceived popularity**, or who it is that children think are "popular," cool, central, or highly visible, has gained research attention with the acknowledgment that children who are perceived by the larger peer group to be popular may not always be well-liked by the larger peer group (e.g., Merten, 1997; Parkhurst & Hopmeyer, 1998). In the following sections, we examine the methods used by researchers to assess acceptance, rejection, and perceived popularity within the peer group. We also describe findings concerning the possible determinants of peer acceptance, rejection, and perceived popularity and the outcomes that persistent difficulties with peers may entail.

Assessing the Quality of Children's Peer Relationships

There are myriad procedures designed to assess the quality of children's peer relationships (see Asher & McDonald, 2009 and Cillessen, 2009 for more descriptions). Basically, these procedures can be subdivided into categories corresponding to two questions: "Is the child liked?" and "What is the child like?" (Parker & Asher, 1987). To answer these questions, researchers have relied on several sources of information concerning the valence and nature of children's peer interactions, including parents, clinicians, and archival data. However, the most common sources employed have involved children, teachers, and direct behavioral observations. Children are excellent informants about who it is in their peer group that has qualitatively good or poor relationships. As "insiders," peers recognize and identify characteristics of children and their relationships that are ultimately relevant in the determination of the child's social status and integration within the peer group. Moreover, the judgments of peers are based on many extended and varied experiences with those being evaluated. For example, as "insiders" peers are privy to low frequency, but psychologically significant events (e.g., a punch in the nose or taking someone's valued possession), which lead to the establishment and maintenance of particular social reputations. Finally, peer assessments of children's behaviors and relationships represent the perspectives of many observers with whom the target child has had a variety of relationships (Rubin, Bukowski, & Parker, 2006a). Taken together, it is not surprising that most contemporary research concerning the quality, the correlates, and the determinants of children's peer relationships is dominated by peer assessment methodology.

Like peers, teachers may provide useful and rich data concerning low frequency social exchanges that contribute to the quality of a child's peer relationships. One advantage that teacher assessments have over peer assessments is that the data collection process is much more efficient and less time consuming. Classroom time is not necessary to gather the assessment data. A second advantage is that teachers may prove to be more objective than peers in their assessments of social behavior. Teachers are not part and parcel of the group structure or behavioral schemes being evaluated; thus, they may be valuable, objective sources of information. However, teachers may bring with them an "adultomorphic" perspective that carries with it value judgments about social behaviors that might differ from those of children. As well, their judgments may be biased by their relations with children and children's gender (e.g., Ladd & Profilet, 1996).

Assessments of Peer Acceptance

Sociometric nominations trace their origins through Moreno (1934), who originally used it to examine attraction and repulsion within the peer group. Coie, Dodge, and Coppotelli (1983) furthered Moreno's work, creating a method of assessment still widely used today. This method of assessing **sociometric popularity** and rejection is to have children nominate three to five peers whom they "like" and "dislike." From these nominations children are categorized into status groups based on the number of positive and negative nominations they received from peers. To control for class size, nominations are standardized within each classroom (or grade). Usually, only same-gender nominations are used to control for the opposite gender negative biases that occur in childhood.

Based on these nominations, children are classified into five sociometric categories. Children who receive many "like" and few "dislike" nominations are labeled (sociometrically) *popular*, those who receive many "like" and many "dislike" nominations are *controversial*. The other categories are *rejected* (liked by few and disliked by many), *neglected* (liked by few and disliked by few), and *average* (near the midrange of liked and disliked nominations). Over the years, researchers have found that the more extreme sociometric classifications are moderately stable over time; popular children tend to remain popular, and rejected children tend to remain rejected, although this stability declines over longer intervals (e.g., Cillessen, Bukowski, & Haselager, 2000). However, when one examines the relation between peer rejection and associated negative outcomes, a significant amount of variance remains unexplained. Recent work has explored the construct of "classification strength" to increase the sensitivity of sociometric measurement (DeRosier & Thomas, 2003). Classification strength refers to the degree to which a child falls within a prescribed status group. For example, classification strength would distinguish between children in the same status group by differentiating between borderline-rejected and extremely rejected children. DeRosier and Thomas's (2003) work indicates that using classification strength results in greater concurrent validity with sociobehavioral adjustment.

A second method to capture peer acceptance is a rating-scale measure. Rating-scale methods involve children rating each of their classmates (or a randomly selected group of grade-mates) on a scale (e.g., 1 = *not at all* to 5 *very much*) of how much they like to play or work with that person. This method can be used to yield a continuous indicator of peer acceptance or to classify children into groups based on low, average, or high acceptance. An advantage of rating-scale measures is that each child in a class or grade receives an equal number of ratings rather than information just being gathered on the prominent or salient children, as may be the case when nominations are used.

Similar to the measurement of peer acceptance and rejection, perceived popularity is often measured with peer nominations. Researchers have asked children to nominate peers they believe to be most popular and peers they believe to be least popular (e.g., Cillessen & Mayeux, 2004; Rose, Swenson, & Waller, 2004). As with the sociometric nominations technique, nominations of peer-perceived popularity are standardized and children are assigned to one of three possible groups: popular, unpopular, or average (all others). Other researchers have measured a similar construct to perceived popularity by asking teachers to nominate students who they believe are "popular" and have many friends (Rodkin, Farmer, Pearl, &

Van Acker, 2000, 2006). Those who have simultaneously examined sociometric popularity and peer-perceived popularity have found that these two types of measurement may identify distinct groups of children and that correlations between acceptance and perceived popularity are moderate to strong (Cillessen & Mayeux, 2004; Hawley, 2003; LaFontana & Cillessen, 2002; Parkhurst & Hopmeyer, 1998; Vaillancourt & Hymel, 2006). When examining the sociometrically assessed *controversial* group in terms of perceived popularity, results differ by study. Parkhurst and Hopmeyer (1998) found that children identified as controversial were the most likely group to be labeled as popular by a peer-perception measure. However, LaFontana and Cillessen (1999) found that controversial children were more likely to be perceived as "average." All in all, it seems that traditional assessments of likeability may portray different pictures than do peer group perceptions of popularity.

Despite its "popularity" as a measurement tool, the use of sociometric techniques carries with it some potential disadvantages. For example, some researchers have suggested that the use of sociometric nominations and ratings may be ethically problematic. The use of negative nomination measures may implicitly sanction negative judgments about peers and lead children to view disliked peers even more negatively (Bell-Dolan, Foster, & Sikora, 1989). To address this issue, Iverson, Barton, and Iverson (1997) conducted interviews with 10- and 11-year-olds regarding their reactions to completing group-administered sociometric nominations. Some children reported that a few of the low-status peers were talked about "behind their backs" but that these negative comments were never revealed to the low-status children. However, no child reported having hurt feelings or having knowledge of anyone else having hurt feelings. Iverson and colleagues maintain that sociometric assessments do not breach the ethical condition of minimal risk of harm—harm not greater than children might encounter in daily life.

Sociometric techniques have other limitations, such as practicality. Sociometric assessments are most often made in schools, because this is where children spend a majority of their time in the company of peers (Eccles & Roeser, Chapter 12, this volume). However, obtaining consent from everyone involved (i.e., school administrators, parents, teachers, children) is often difficult. If children nominate a classmate who has not agreed to participate, researchers are ethically bound not to use the data. Thus, for a researcher to obtain an accurate picture of a school's social structure there is strong need to obtain consent from a large majority of the school-attending children.

Nevertheless, a great deal can be learned about normative child development through the use of sociometric techniques and the simultaneous assessment of social behavior. The methods designed to identify the behavioral characteristics of children are examined below.

Assessment of Child Behaviors

Peer assessments of social behavior. In general, peer assessment procedures involve asking children to nominate peers on the basis of a variety of behavioral roles or character descriptions provided (e.g., "Who in your class is a good leader?", "Who gets into fights?", or "Who likes to play alone?"). Nominations received from peers are summed in various ways to provide indices of a child's typical social behavior or reputation within the peer group (Asher & McDonald, 2009). A commonly used peer assessment technique is the *Revised Class Play* (Masten, Morison, & Pellegrini, 1985) and its subsequent adaptations (e.g., Rubin et al., 2006b). Factor analysis of children's nominations using these measures has yielded dimensions of aggression, shyness/withdrawal, exclusion/victimization, sociability-leadership, and prosocial behaviors.

As mentioned above, the use of peers as informants carries with it many advantages, the most important of which may be that peers can identify children who engage in behaviors that are salient to other children but too infrequent or too subtle for researchers to observe with any reliability (Rubin et al., 2006a). However, a disadvantage of peer assessments involves potential reputational biases (Hymel, Wagner, & Butler, 1990b). In this regard, even though a child's behaviors may change over time, her "reputation" may persist with peers. In particular, reputations are likely to be influenced by infrequent but salient events (e.g., aggressive outbursts, social gaffes). In addition, peer ratings are affected by the characteristics of the "rater," including behavioral reputation, peer status, age, and liking of the target (Younger & Boyko, 1987).

Finally, the *type* of behavior being described appears to impact on peer nominations and ratings. For example, peer assessments of sociability and aggression are more stable than those of social withdrawal (e.g., Moskowitz, Schwartzman, & Ledingham, 1985). From very early in childhood, aggression is viewed as deviant and unacceptable. Social withdrawal, however, is not viewed negatively by peers until the later years of childhood (e.g., Younger, Gentile, & Burgess, 1993). Consequently, the instability of peer assessments of social withdrawal may be attributed to the inability of young children to conceptualize these behaviors accurately.

Teacher assessments of social behavior. It is not uncommon for researchers to request teachers to assess the social and emotional characteristics of their students. Many standardized measures exist at present. Generally, these measures can be broken down into several socioemotional clusters or factors that fall along dimensions of positive child behaviors, aggression, hyperactivity, and anxiety (Coplan & Rubin, 1998; Ladd & Profilet, 1996).

Relations between teacher and peer assessments of children's social behavior are quite strong, especially concerning aggression and sociability (Ledingham, Younger, Schwartzman, & Bergeron, 1982). The relations between teacher and peer assessments of behavior increase from early to late childhood, but more so for externalizing behaviors than for internalizing behaviors (Hymel, Rubin, Rowden, & LeMare, 1990a). The increased correspondence between peer- and teacher-derived ratings of social withdrawal with age also mirrors the age-related increase in the association between peer rejection and social withdrawal (Rubin & Mills, 1988; Younger et al., 1993).

Behavioral observations of social behavior. Behavioral observations represent the standard against which all other forms of social behavioral assessment must be measured. In this regard, a "true" face-valid picture of aggression, withdrawal, or socially competent behavior is probably best captured from observations of children in naturalistic settings. Laboratory or analog methods are also useful for carefully observing socially important behaviors that may be hard to capture or may occur less frequently in natural settings (e.g., Hubbard, 2001; McDonald, Putallaz, Grimes, Kupersmidt, & Coie, 2006; Putallaz & Wasserman, 1990). From these observations, age and gender "norms" can be established for the production of particular forms of social behavior. From these "norms," procedures may be developed to identify children who deviate from their age-mates or from children of the same gender.

Several observational taxonomies have been developed to assess the frequency of occurrence of various behavior styles, relationship roles, and levels of social competence. For example, Rubin (2001) developed the *Play Observation Scale* (POS), a norm-based time-sampling procedure to assess free play behaviors in early and middle childhood. During free play (either in a class or in a laboratory play room), behaviors with and without peers are coded on a checklist that includes the cognitive play categories of functional-sensorimotor, exploratory, constructive, dramatic, and games-with-rules behaviors nested within the abovementioned social participation categories of solitary, parallel, and group activities

(Figure 11.1). In addition, overt and relational aggression, rough-and-tumble play, unoccupied and onlooker behaviors, and conversations with peers are recorded. Observational procedures such as the *Play Observation Scale* are useful in targeting children whose behaviors (e.g., aggression, social withdrawal) deviate from age-group norms. Additionally such procedures can be used to validate peer and teacher assessments of children's social behavior.

Play Observation Scale Coding Sheet (2001)

Name of Child:_____   ID_____   Cohort____   Age____

Free Play Session _____

Time Sample

	:10	:20	:30	:40	:50	:60
uncodable						
out of room						
transitional						
unoccupied						
onlooker						

Solitary Behaviors:

	:10	:20	:30	:40	:50	:60
Occupied						
Constructive						
Exploratory						
Functional						
Dramatic						
Games						

Parallel Behaviors:

	:10	:20	:30	:40	:50	:60
Occupied						
Constructive						
Exploratory						
Functional						
Dramatic						
Games						

Group Behaviors:

	:10	:20	:30	:40	:50	:60
Occupied						
Constructive						
Exploratory						
Functional						
Dramatic						
Games						

Peer Conversation_____

Double Coded Behaviors:

	:10	:20	:30	:40	:50	:60
Anxious Behaviors						
Hovering						
Aggression						
Rough-and-Tumble						

Conversation/Interacting With: 1_____ 2_____ 3_____ 4_____ 5_____ 6_____

FIGURE 11.1   The play observation scale coding sheet used by Rubin (2001).

Unfortunately, several factors conspire against the use of observational methodology. To begin with, observations are time-, energy-, and money-consuming. Whereas peer and teacher assessments can be conducted in minutes or hours, observations can require weeks or months of data collection. Second, as children get older, it becomes increasingly difficult to observe them during "free play"—although technological advances in remote audiovisual recording have allowed researchers to observe children's interactions and conversations from afar (e.g., Asher, Rose, & Gabriel, 2001; Pepler & Craig, 1995). Finally, observations may be reactive; for example, children who are aware that they are being observed may behave in atypical manners, perhaps suppressing negative behaviors or increasing the production of prosocial behaviors.

To summarize, many different methods have been used to assess children's functioning in their peer group. Sociometric techniques are useful indications of how children feel about a specific child, that is, "Is the child liked?" This does not, however, inform us about the behaviors associated with, or contributing to, these assessments. Conversely, assessments and behavioral observations of children's social behaviors describe "what the child is like" but fail to inform us about their standing in the peer group. In the following section, we examine relations between peer acceptance and children's social behaviors.

CORRELATES AND DETERMINANTS OF PEER ACCEPTANCE

Which children are liked or disliked by peers? What are these children like? These two questions have been subjected to countless studies for more than half a century (e.g., Bonney, 1942; Northway, 1944). From the start, we must issue two cautions. Because many of the data on these questions stem from correlational studies, one must not assume that the behaviors associated with peer acceptance or rejection necessarily *cause* children's social status. Second, not all correlates and potential causes of peer acceptance and rejection are behavioral in nature. For example, sociometric popularity is positively associated with academic competence, physical attractiveness, and having a good sense of humor (e.g., Daniels & Leaper, 2006); it is negatively associated with having an uncommon name (see Hartup, 1983, for a relevant review). Importantly, however, physical appearance and uncommon names are not particularly strong correlates of peer acceptance. The variables most highly associated with status in the peer group include children's social behaviors and their ways of thinking about social phenomena.

Behavioral Correlates of Peer Acceptance

If one is to accept the classification scheme currently in vogue *vis-à-vis* the study of children's peer relationships, one might expect to find different and distinct behaviors associated with popular, rejected, neglected, and average peer status. However, the reality is that membership in each of the sociometrically classified groups may be acquired in a multitude of ways.

Sociometrically popular children are generally prosocial, skilled at initiating and maintaining qualitatively positive relationships, and are assertive and named as leaders by peers (e.g., Asher & McDonald, 2009; Chen & Tse, 2008; Gazelle, 2008; Pakaslahti, Karjalainen, & Keltikangas-Jarvinen, 2002; Tomada & Schneider, 1997). When entering new peer situations, popular children are more likely than members of other sociometric status groups to consider the frame of reference common to the ongoing playgroup and to establish themselves as sharing in this frame of reference (Putallaz & Wasserman, 1990). It is as if they ask themselves "What's going on?" and "How can I fit in?" Sociometrically popular children are also less likely to draw unwarranted attention to themselves when entering ongoing playgroups.

That is, they do not talk exclusively or arrogantly about themselves and their own social goals or desires, and they do not disrupt ongoing group activities (Dodge, Schlundt, Schocken, & Delugach, 1983). When entering playgroups, and during other social activities, sociometrically popular children speak clearly and respond contingently to the social overtures of others (Black & Logan, 1995). In short, sociometrically popular children appear to be socially competent.

Children *perceived* as popular are characteristically dominant but otherwise are not as easily "summed up." Indeed, perceived popularity has been linked to a varied list of characteristics. For example, perceived popularity has been associated with both physical and relational aggression, the latter of which is intended to harm relationships and friendships, especially for older children (Cillessen & Mayeux, 2004; Rose et al., 2004), as well as prosocial behavior (Cillessen & Mayeux, 2004; LaFontana & Cillessen, 2002). Perceived popularity has also been associated with having a good sense of humor, academic competence, athletic ability, being attractive, and being stylish and wealthy (Vaillancourt & Hymel, 2006). *Controversial* children display a combination of positive and negative social behaviors, perhaps because they may be the same children perceived as popular (see above).

To understand the discrepant characteristics that are related to being perceived as popular, researchers have investigated whether there may be separate and distinct groups of perceived popular children. Researchers have found two such groups: "model" and "tough" children (Rodkin et al., 2000, 2006). "Model" children are perceived as being "cool" and at the same time are academically competent, physically skilled, sociable, and not rated as aggressive by teachers. "Tough" children are also perceived as "cool" but are highly aggressive and physically competent. Rubin (2002) also distinguished between these groups of children by applying the labels of "popular-as-decent" and "popular-as-dominant."

Relations between forms of aggression and perceived popularity have been investigated, as the causal nature between status and aggression are questioned. Examinations of these associations reveal that relational aggression may be more central than physical or overt aggression to the establishment and maintenance of perceived popularity. In a longitudinal investigation of acceptance, perceived popularity, and aggression, Cillessen and Mayeux (2004) found evidence to suggest that children who are perceived as popular subsequently increase their use of relational aggression. They hypothesize that relational aggression may serve as a means to maintain social prominence during adolescence, especially for girls (Cillessen & Mayeux, 2004; Rose et al., 2004). Furthermore, Rose et al. (2004) found that the association between overt aggression and perceived popularity was fully explained through the association of both constructs with relational aggression.

Neglected children have been shown to interact with their peers less frequently than average children, and to be less sociable and less aggressive, disruptive, and negative than other children, including those in the average group (Coie & Dodge, 1988). Neglected children have often been characterized as shy and withdrawn (e.g., Coie & Kupersmidt, 1983; Dodge, Murphy, & Buchsbaum, 1984), yet this is still up for debate (Rubin, LeMare, & Lollis, 1990). Although, as indicated, neglected children appear to interact with peers less frequently than do other children, no consistent evidence has emerged to suggest that neglected children display the psychological and emotional characteristics of social anxiety and extreme social wariness that are concomitants of social withdrawal. Furthermore, many researchers have failed to find sociometrically neglected children to be more withdrawn than average children (e.g., Rubin, Chen, & Hymel, 1993).

In summary, few behaviors have been found to be distinctive of sociometrically neglected children. Indeed, neglected children appear to be low on nearly every dimension of behavior (see Newcomb et al., 1993). Significantly, this sociometric classification is also relatively unstable, even over short periods (e.g., Newcomb & Bukowski, 1984). Furthermore, the defining characteristic of this group—a lack of "noticeability"—makes it very difficult to obtain good peer assessments of their behaviors. With this in mind, the fact that there appear to be few strong associations between neglected status and specific behaviors is unsurprising.

Rejected children are also quite heterogeneous in their behavioral characteristics. The most commonly cited correlate of peer *rejection* is aggression. Three forms of aggression appear to be associated clearly and strongly with sociometric rejection—instrumental aggression, bullying, and relational aggression. Instrumental aggression is directed at others for the purpose of obtaining desired objects, territories, or privilege. Bullying is directed toward the harming (or the threatening thereof), either physically or verbally, of particular intimidated victims (Olweus, 1993). As noted above, the goal of relational aggression is to manipulate or disrupt relationships and friendships, and its form can be overt or covert, but is usually covert (Archer & Coyne, 2005; Crick et al., 1997). Social aggression has also been linked with peer rejection; social aggression has been defined as aggression meant to manipulate group acceptance and damage others' social standing (Galen & Underwood, 1997). Regardless of type of aggression and regardless of type of measurement (peer ratings, observations, teacher ratings) aggression is highly correlated with peer dislike (Crick et al., 1997; Haselager, Cillessen, Van Lieshout, Riksen-Walraven, & Hartup, 2002; McNeilley-Choque, Hart, Robinson, Nelson, and Olsen, 1996).

Most of the data we have described above are correlational. In two studies, however, Dodge (1983) and Coie and Kupersmidt (1983) observed the interactions of *unfamiliar* peers with one another. These interactions took place over several days. Gradually some of the children became popular while others were rejected. The behaviors that most clearly predicted peer rejection were instrumental and reactive aggression. Crick (1996) has obtained similar results over the course of a school year.

Not all aggressive children are rejected. Aggressive children make up only 40% to 50% of the rejected group. Newcomb and colleagues (1993) proposed that aggression may not necessarily lead to peer rejection if it is balanced by a set of positive qualities that facilitate interactions and positive relations with other children. When aggressive behavior co-occurs with disruptive, hyperactive, or inattentive and immature behavior it is more likely to be associated with rejection than when it does not (e.g., Miller-Johnson, Coie, Maumary-Gremaud, Bierman, & The Conduct Problems Prevention Research Group, 2002). Furthermore, with increasing age, it appears as if aggression becomes decreasingly associated with rejection, especially among boys (e.g., Sandstrom & Coie, 1999). The negative association between physical aggression and peer acceptance decreases in strength as children progress through junior high school (Cillessen & Mayeux, 2004), perhaps as children form groups with similar peers (Cairns et al., 1988) or as they develop more differentiated views of their social world (Rubin et al., 2006a).

Socially anxious, timid, and withdrawn children have likewise been reported as rejected. Withdrawn children make up 10% to 20% of the rejected group (e.g., Parkhurst & Asher, 1992; Volling, MacKinnon-Lewis, Rabiner, & Baradaran, 1993), but peer rejection, in this case, may depend on the form of withdrawal displayed and, as mentioned previously, the age of the child. Solitary-passive behavior comprises solitary exploratory and/or constructive activity in the company of others; this activity appears relatively benign in early childhood, but becomes increasingly associated with peer rejection with increasing age (Rubin & Mills, 1988). Solitary-active behavior comprises solitary sensorimotor activity and/or dramatic play in the company of others (Coplan, Rubin, Fox, Calkins, & Stewart, 1994) and is associated with rejection throughout childhood (Rubin & Mills, 1988). Lastly, social reticence comprises behaviors such as watching others from afar and avoiding activity altogether (Coplan et al., 1994) and may reflect internalized feelings of social anxiety (Rubin, Coplan, & Bowker, 2009).

Reticence appears to elicit peer rejection and exclusion, *in vivo*, from very early through late childhood (Gazelle & Ladd, 2003; Hart et al., 2000; Stewart & Rubin, 1995).

There are also gender differences in how social withdrawal is related to peer rejection. Socially withdrawn boys are more likely to be rejected than similarly behaved girls (Coplan, Gavinsky-Molina, Lagace-Seguin, & Wichmann, 2001; Gazelle, 2008; Gazelle & Ladd, 2003), perhaps because withdrawn behaviors violate male gender norms (Caspi, Elder, & Bem, 1988). However, Gazelle (2008) found that this gender difference did not hold if children were attention-seeking or aggressive in addition to being anxious and solitary. Agreeable anxious-solitary and normative anxious-solitary girls were less rejected than their male counterparts; however, if children were disruptive or aggressive in addition to being anxious and solitary, they were equally likely to be rejected by peers, regardless of gender. It would appear that any form of social behavior considered deviant from normalcy is likely to be associated with peer rejection. The extant studies have been carried out mostly in Western cultures. Given that "normalcy" may have different definitions in non-Western cultures, it may be that the behaviors associated with peer rejection in the West are not those typically associated with rejection in other cultures. We discuss this possibility, especially as it relates to social withdrawal, in a later section.

Social Cognitive Correlates of Peer Acceptance

Researchers have hypothesized that the ways in which children interpret and process information about their social worlds play a causal role in determining their social behaviors (Crick & Dodge, 1994; Lemerise & Arsenio, 2000), and in turn, peer acceptance and/or rejection. An example of how social cognition may be implicated in establishing particular types of peer relationships is taken from a **social information-processing** model described by Rubin and Rose-Krasnor (1992). These authors speculated that when children face an interpersonal dilemma (e.g., making new friends or acquiring an object from someone else), their thinking follows a particular sequence. First, children may select a *social goal*. This entails establishing a representation of the desired *end state* of the problem solving process. Second, they *examine the task environment*; this involves reading and interpreting all the relevant social cues. For example, boys and girls are likely to produce different solutions when faced with a social dilemma involving same-gender as opposed to opposite-gender peers (Rubin & Krasnor, 1986). As well, the social status, familiarity, and age of the participants in the task environment are likely to influence the child's goal and strategy selection (Krasnor & Rubin, 1983). Third, they *access and select strategies*; this process involves generating possible plans of action for achieving the perceived social goal and choosing the most appropriate one for the specific situation. Fourth, they *implement the chosen strategy*. Finally, it is proposed that children *evaluate the outcome of the strategy*; this step involves assessing the situation to determine the relative success of the chosen course of action in achieving the social goal. If the initial strategy is unsuccessful, the child may repeat it, or select and enact a new strategy, or abandon the situation entirely. Crick and Dodge (1994) proposed a similar social-cognitive model designed to account for *aggression* in children. This model consists of six stages, namely, (1) encoding of social cues; (2) interpreting of encoded cues; (3) clarifying goals; (4) accessing and generating potential responses; (5) evaluating and selecting responses; and (6) enacting chosen responses. The social competence model is outlined in Figure 11.2.

Lemerise and Arsenio (2000) integrated *emotional* experiences into the Crick and Dodge (1994) social information-processing model. For example, aggressive children's emotional reactions to problematic social situations might include frustration or anger; anxious/withdrawn children may react with fear. These emotions, in turn, may influence the information that is attended to and the information that is recalled. This mood-congruent information

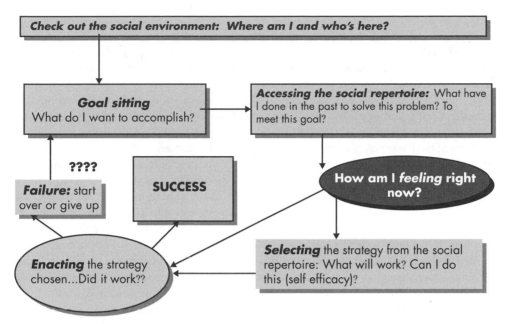

FIGURE 11.2   An information processing model of social competence and social problem solving.

processing might reinforce aggressive children's social schemas or "working models" that the social world is hostile or withdrawn children's notions that the social world is fear inducing. These emotional responses may explain, in part, why aggressive and withdrawn children respond in predictable ways to negative events befalling them.

Aggressive-rejected children demonstrate characteristic deficits or qualitative differences in performance at various stages of these models. They are more likely than their non-aggressive and more popular counterparts to assume malevolent intent when they are faced with negative circumstances, even when the social cues are ambiguous (e.g., Dodge et al., 2003; Orobio de Castro, Veerman, Koops, Bosch, & Monshouwer, 2002). When selecting social goals, rejected children tend to have motives that undermine, rather than establish or enhance, their social relationships. For example, their goals might comprise "getting even" with or "defeating" their peers (e.g., Rabiner & Gordon, 1992; Rose & Asher, 1999). In contrast, sociometrically popular children believe that negotiation and compromise will help them reach their social goals while simultaneously maintaining positive relationships with peers (Hart, DeWolf, Wozniak, & Burts, 1992; Hart, Ladd, & Burleson, 1990; Rose & Asher, 1999; Troop-Gordon & Asher, 2005).

As noted above, children must have access to a broad repertoire of strategies to meet their social goals. Researchers have found that aggressive and rejected children have smaller strategic repertoires, generate more hostile or dominant strategies, and generally assess these strategies differently from their non-aggressive or nonrejected peers (e.g., Chung & Asher, 1996; Dodge & Price, 1994). For example, they are more inclined to select solutions as agonistic or bribe strategies, and they are less likely than their non-aggressive or more popular counterparts to suggest prosocial strategies in response to social problems concerning object acquisition or friendship initiation (e.g., Crick, Grotpeter, & Bigbee, 2002; Orobio de Castro et al., 2002). Furthermore, aggressive children are more likely to view aggression as a viable or appropriate response (e.g., Erdley & Asher, 1998) and anticipate greater rewards for aggressive behavior (Boldizar, Perry, & Perry, 1989; Perry, Perry, & Rasmussen, 1986).

During interviews, young *withdrawn* children suggest during interviews that they would use more adult-dependent and non-assertive social strategies to solve their interpersonal dilemmas (Rubin, 1982). Examining their attributions, withdrawn children are also more likely than aggressive or comparison children to feel as if they will fail in social situations and to attribute their social failures to dispositional characteristics rather than to external circumstances (Wichmann, Coplan, & Daniels, 2004).

Also of relevance to understanding how social cognitions are related to peer acceptance is the construct of **rejection sensitivity**, the tendency to defensively expect, readily perceive, and overreact to rejection (Downey, Lebolt, Rincon, & Freitas, 1998). Rejection sensitivity has been defined as the tendency to defensively expect, readily perceive, and overreact to rejection (Downey et al., 1998). It is typically assessed by presenting children with hypothetical scenarios and asking them how nervous or angry they would feel and how much they expect to be rejected in each situation. Downey and colleagues have hypothesized that expectations of rejection that are accompanied by anger may lead to aggressive behavior with peers and that (nervous or) anxious expectations of rejection may lead to internalizing or anxious behaviors with peers. In support of this hypothesis, Downey et al. (1998) found that angry expectations of rejection were positively associated with teacher-rated aggression and negatively linked with social competence. Furthermore, child and adolescent anxious expectations have been linked with social anxiety and social withdrawal (London, Downey, Bonica, & Paltin, 2007). Longitudinal evidence also suggests that peer rejection predicts increases in rejection sensitivity over time (Sandstrom, Cillessen, & Eisenhower, 2003); however, research on the processes by which peer rejection and rejection sensitivity are linked across time is currently in its infancy.

Thus, the social-cognitive profiles of rejected withdrawn and aggressive children are quite distinct. The latter group is likely to interpret ambiguous social stimuli as hostile and threatening, misattribute blame to others, and respond with inappropriate anger-aggravated hostility. There can be no doubt why such cognition-behavior sequences are associated with peer rejection. Withdrawn children are more likely to generate adult-dependent strategies and unassertive strategies, as well as blame themselves for their social failures. Social dilemmas may evoke emotionally anxious-fearful reactions in withdrawn children; their inability to regulate and overcome their wariness is thought to result in an unassertive, submissive social problem solving style.

Cognitions and Feelings about the Self and Peer Acceptance

Do children feel and think better about themselves when they experience positive peer relationships? Is there a relation between negative self-perceptions and peer rejection? These important questions have attracted much research attention.

Perceived social competence was first defined and assessed by Harter (1998) as an index of children's awareness of their own peer acceptance or social skillfulness. In general, children with higher perceived social competence tend to be more popular with peers, and there is also a trend for the magnitude of this relation to increase with age (Ladd & Price, 1986).

Rejected children think more poorly of their own social competencies than do their more popular age-mates. Longitudinal evidence shows that being rejected in school predicts later negative social self-concept (Hymel et al., 1990a; Ladd & Troop-Gordon, 2003). It may also be that negative self-perceptions predict increases in peer rejection (Salmivalli & Isaacs, 2005), although it is likely that peer rejection and negative self-perceptions mutually reinforce one another. However, this general association may be true only for that group of rejected children described as anxious-withdrawn, submissive, sensitive, and/or wary (e.g., Boivin & Hymel, 1997). As indicated above, withdrawn children display a pattern of self-defeating attributions for social situations (i.e., they attribute their social failures to stable and internal causes and their social successes to unstable and external causes; Rubin & Krasnor, 1986; Wichmann et al., 2004). In contrast, rejected-aggressive children do not report thinking poorly about their social relationships with peers; indeed, rejected-aggressive children appear to overestimate their social competence and peer acceptance (Boivin, Poulin, & Vitaro, 1994; Zakriski & Coie, 1996). These findings are in keeping with the results of studies concerning extremely withdrawn and extremely aggressive children; it is only the former group that reports having difficulty with their social skills and peer relationships (Rubin et al., 1993).

Self-efficacy is the degree to which children believe they can successfully perform behaviors that are necessary for achieving desired outcomes (Bandura, 1977). In general, positive correlations have been found between children's social self-efficacy perceptions and positive sociometric nomination scores (Wheeler & Ladd, 1982). Aggressive and socially withdrawn children differ with regard to their perceived social self-efficacy. First, aggressive and non-aggressive children do not differ from each other concerning their self-efficacy perceptions of prosocial behaviors; aggressive children, however, report higher efficacy for enacting verbally and physically aggressive acts than do their peers (Erdley & Asher, 1996). In contrast, withdrawn children report lower efficacy for enacting verbally and physically aggressive behaviors relative to peers (Quiggle, Garber, Panak, & Dodge, 1992).

It should not be surprising to learn that children who feel socially incompetent, and who believe that others dislike them, come to develop feelings of isolation and loneliness. Indeed, researchers have consistently reported that it is only the sociometrically rejected group that discloses strong feelings of loneliness relative to average and popular children; neglected children are no more lonely or dissatisfied with their social circumstances than sociometrically average children (Asher & Wheeler, 1985). Chronic peer rejection may also lead to increases in loneliness over time (Burks, Dodge, & Price, 1995). Importantly, only rejected-submissive/timid/withdrawn children report being lonelier than their more accepted peers; rejected-aggressive children do not express negative feelings in this regard. These relations have been found throughout childhood (Boivin & Hymel, 1997; Cassidy & Asher, 1992; Crick & Ladd, 1993) and early adolescence (Parkhurst & Asher, 1992).

The data described above lead to two clear conclusions. First, rejected children internalize their social difficulties with peers; they report that they are less competent, less efficacious, and less satisfied *vis-à-vis* their social skills and peer relationships. Second, this conclusion is more likely for that subset of rejected children who can be described as withdrawn, timid, or submissive.

Finally, it may be that having a good friend can go a long way in preventing the development of negative feelings about one's social life. For example, friendship *quality* is associated with indices of psychosocial adjustment and functioning, such as self-esteem (Berndt, 1996; Rubin et al., 2009). These data help to explain the finding that rejected-aggressive children do not report difficulties with the self-system. Although classmates generally dislike this group, aggressive children tend to affiliate with others like them (Cairns & Cairns, 1991). The social support available to them, albeit from a deviant subgroup, may buffer aggressive children from developing negative self-perceptions and loneliness.

In summary we have described the characteristics of sociometrically popular, rejected, neglected, controversial, and perceived popular children. Of these groups, only rejected, controversial, and perceived popular children appear to have substantive behavioral problems. Furthermore, the difficulties associated with peer rejection appear to differ markedly from those who are characteristically aggressive and those who are submissive, wary, and withdrawn. Rejected-*aggressive* children can best be characterized as behaviorally hostile and as having a limited social-cognitive repertoire insofar as resolving their interpersonal problems is concerned. Indeed, they believe that they can "get things done" (meet their social goals) by behaving in an aggressive manner. Furthermore, they do not seem to understand that their behaviors lead others to dislike them; they do not report feeling poorly about their social skills or relationships. Rejected-*withdrawn* children, by contrast, can best be characterized as behaviorally submissive and as thinking and feeling poorly about themselves and their social relationships; they also suffer feelings of isolation and loneliness. Given these characterizations, it behooves us to ask whether peer rejection can be used as a "red flag" to identify children who may be at risk for developing negative psychological "outcomes" as adolescents or adults. We address this question in the following section.

OUTCOMES OF PEER RELATIONSHIPS DIFFICULTIES

There is some debate among researchers as to the "causal" nature implied by the relations typically reported between peer rejection and psychological maladjustment. For example, it is possible that underlying behavioral tendencies that may account for children being rejected by peers (i.e., aggression) also contribute toward later negative outcomes (i.e., juvenile delinquency). In this regard, the experience of peer rejection itself does not actually lead to adjustment difficulties. However, results from a series of recent longitudinal studies have provided compelling support for the notion that peer rejection itself provides a unique contribution toward later maladjustment.

Peer Rejection and Externalizing Problems

Results of longitudinal studies have indicated that peer rejection in childhood is associated with a wide range of **externalizing problems** in adolescence, including delinquency, conduct disorder, attentional difficulties, and substance abuse (Kupersmidt & Coie, 1990). These findings are not particularly surprising given the well-established link between aggression and peer rejection, and especially given that aggressive-rejected children are more likely to remain rejected over time.

However, other studies have indicated that *early* peer rejection provides a unique increment in the prediction of later antisocial outcomes, even when controlling for previous levels of aggression and externalizing problems (e.g., Ladd & Burgess, 2001; Miller-Johnson et al., 2002; Miller-Johnson, Coie, Maumary-Gremaud, Lochman, & Terry, 1999; Wentzel, 2003). For example, Laird, Jordan, Dodge, Pettit, and Bates (2001) followed 400 children from early childhood through to adolescence. They reported that peer-rated sociometric rejection at ages 6 to 9 years predicted externalizing problems in adolescence, even when controlling for the stability of externalizing problems over this age period.

The development of new statistical and methodological techniques has also allowed researchers to deconstruct the relation between peer rejection and subsequent maladjustment. For example, Dodge and colleagues (2003) reported that peer rejection predicted longitudinal "growth" in aggression over time (controlling for original levels of aggression) from early to middle childhood, and from middle childhood to adolescence. These researchers also found a developmental pathway in which peer rejection led to more negative information processing patterns (i.e., hostile cue interpretation), which in turn led to increased aggression. Additionally, Prinstein and La Greca (2004) found that girls' childhood aggression predicted later substance use and sexual risk behavior, but only for those girls who were disliked or rejected in junior high school. Given that changes in peer acceptance tend to precede changes in aggression over time, but not vice versa (Haselager et al., 2002), one can begin to understand the truly *transactional* nature of the relation between peer rejection and the development of externalizing problems over time.

Peer Rejection and Internalizing Problems

Results from a growing number of studies have indicated that anxious withdrawal is contemporaneously and predictively associated with **internalizing problems** across the lifespan, including low self-esteem, anxiety problems, loneliness, and depressive symptoms (e.g., Coplan, Prakash, O'Neil, & Armer, 2004; Coplan, Arbeau, & Armer, 2008; Crozier, 1995; Gest, 1997; Prior, Smart, Sanson, & Oberklaid, 2000). Rubin and colleagues followed a group of children from kindergarten (age 5 years) to the ninth grade (age 15 years). They reported that withdrawal in kindergarten and Grade 2 predicted self-reported feelings of depression, loneliness, and negative self-worth, and teacher ratings of anxiety in the fifth grade (age 11 years; Hymel et al., 1990a; Rubin & Mills, 1988). In turn, social withdrawal in the fifth grade predicted self-reports of loneliness, depression, negative self-evaluations of social competence, feelings of not belonging to a peer group that could be counted on for social support, and parental assessments of internalizing problems in the ninth grade (Rubin, Chen, McDougall, Bowker, & McKinnon, 1995a).

Researchers have also begun to explore the *unique* role of peer rejection in the prediction of internalizing problems. For example, in a longitudinal study following 405 children from kindergarten to Grade 7, Kraatz-Keily, Bates, Dodge, and Pettit (2000) reported that peer rejection predicted increases in both internalizing and externalizing problems over time. Relatedly, Gazelle and Ladd (2003) found that shy-anxious kindergarteners who were also excluded by peers displayed a greater stability in anxious solitude through the fourth grade. Anxious-solitary children who were not excluded by peers displayed decreased anxious solitude over time. In this regard, there appears to be a dialectic or transactional relation between anxious-solitude and rejection (Rubin et al., 2009).

In understanding the link between peer rejection and psychosocial adjustment, it may also be important to consider the role of children's *perceptions* of their *own* peer rejection. Children's perceived rejection has been associated with increases in depression over time (e.g., Kistner, Balthazor, Risi, & Burton, 1999). Moreover, Sandstrom, Cillessen, and Eisenhower (2003) found that children's self-appraisal of peer rejection was associated with increased internalizing and externalizing problems even after controlling for actual peer rejection. Thus, children's *beliefs* that they are rejected may play an influential role in the development of psychosocial maladjustment.

Summary

In this section, we presented evidence that supported the premise that peer rejection can directly cause such negative outcomes as internalizing and externalizing problems. Furthermore, believing that one is rejected by the peer group can also affect negative outcomes. As we have already noted, two major causes of peer rejection are the demonstration of aggressive and withdrawn behavior. The display of socially competent behavior protects children from peer rejection. Thus, it would appear important to understand the underlying causes of both competent and incompetent social behavior and, based on this information, develop prevention and intervention programs that may protect children from peer rejection and its negative consequences. We consider the developmental origins of children's peer relationships and social skills in the following section.

ORIGINS OF CHILDREN'S PEER RELATIONSHIPS AND SOCIAL SKILLS

By now, it should be obvious that children's peer relationships and social skills are of central importance to their experience of everyday life. Popular and socially competent children feel and think well of themselves, and they fare better in school than their less popular and skilled age-mates. Rejected children tend to lead less successful lives, both academically and personally.

It seems reasonable to ask questions about the origins of children's peer relationships and social skills. There is growing evidence that biological or dispositional factors (e.g., child temperament) directly and indirectly impact on the quality of children's peer relationships. The social well-being of children also appears to be influenced by parent–child relationships and parents' socialization beliefs and behaviors. Here we review dispositional, parenting, and ecological factors that have been associated with children's peer relationships.

Temperament and Peer Relationships

Temperament can be broadly defined as the biological basis for the affective arousal, expression, and regulatory components of personality (Goldsmith et al., 1987). Variability in these components contributes to differences in individual personality characteristics, and is associated with a wide range of developmental outcomes (see Wachs & Kohstamm, 2001). There is compelling evidence to suggest that child temperament plays a particularly powerful role in children's social interactions with peers. For example, in a longitudinal study from early childhood to adolescence, Prior and colleagues (2000) reported that almost half the variation in children's social skills could be explained by temperamental traits.

Researchers have focused on three broad groups of temperamental traits that appear to be differentially associated with children's social functioning in the peer group. The first of these is related to *resistance to control* (sometimes labeled *manageability*). These characteristics encompass lack of attention, low agreeableness, and strong attention to rewarding stimuli. These "difficult to manage" children tend to be boisterous and socially immature, and unresponsive to parents' and teachers' attempts to modulate their activities (Bates, 2001). In the peer group, such children tend to have poorer social skills, and are more likely to "act out" and display other externalizing problems (Coplan, Bowker, & Cooper, 2003; Fabes et al., 1999; Patterson & Sanson, 1999).

The second broadly defined group of temperamental traits that has been related to children's peer relationships concerns *negative affect* (sometimes labeled *reactivity*) and includes negative emotional reactivity and difficulty-to-regulate or difficulty-to-control affect. Children who are highly reactive and poorly regulated are easily angered, frustrated, and provoked by peers, and do not adequately control the expression of these negative emotions. These children tend to have poorer social skills, and display both internalizing and externalizing problems (Eisenberg et al., 2001; Guerin, Gottfried, & Thomas, 1997; Rubin, Burgess, Dwyer, & Hastings, 2003). Clearly, these constellations of dispositionally based behaviors mark children for peer rejection.

There is also some indication that emotion regulation may be a risk/protective factor in the relation between children's sociability and social adjustment. Rubin, Coplan, Fox, and Calkins (1995b) reported that temperamentally *sociable* children who lacked emotion regulatory control were disruptive and aggressive among peers, yet their sociable counterparts who could regulate their emotions were socially competent. Dispositionally unsociable children, who were good emotion regulators, appeared to suffer no ill effects of their lack of social behavior. These children were productive engagers of constructive and exploratory play when in the peer group. Unsociable children who were poor emotion regulators, however, demonstrated anxious and wary behaviors and were more behaviorally reticent in a peer play setting. Furthermore, these unsociable, poor emotion-regulating children were viewed by parents as having more internalizing problems than their age-mates. Thus, preschoolers who are emotionally dysregulated appear to behave in ways that will result in peer rejection, regardless of sociability. Moreover, difficulties in **emotion regulation** can contribute toward the development of both internalizing and externalizing problems.

Finally, the third group of temperamental traits constitutes shyness/inhibition and involves wary responses to social situations and novelty. Temperamentally shy children may want to play with other children, but tend to refrain from talking and interacting with peers because of social fear and anxiety (Coplan et al., 2004; Henderson, Marshall, Fox, & Rubin, 2004; Rubin, Burgess, & Hastings, 2002). With peers, shy children display less socially competent and prosocial behaviors, employ less positive coping strategies, and are more likely to develop anxiety problems (see Rubin, Bowker, & Kennedy, 2009 for a review). Moreover, as noted above, shy and socially withdrawn children become increasingly rejected and victimized by peers over time (Gazelle & Rudolph, 2004).

Parenting and Peer Relationships

Children usually grow up living with their parents and one or more siblings. Moreover, their families bring with them societal and cultural expectations and values, and stressors and supports that must assuredly influence children's social repertoires. Parents serve at least three roles or functions in the child's development of social competence and qualitatively positive peer relationships. First, parent–child interaction represents a context within which many competencies necessary for social interaction with others develop. Second, the parent–child relationship provides a safety net permitting the child the freedom to examine the features of the social universe, thereby enhancing the development of social skills. Third, it is within the parent–child relationships that the child begins to develop expectations and assumptions about interactions and relationships with other people (Booth-LaForce & Kerns, 2009).

Parent–child attachment relationships precede peer relationships, and because this is normally the case, formative experiences in the family may play an important role in influencing the development of peer relationships (e.g., Booth-LaForce & Kerns, 2009). *Attachment theory* has provided a framework and a methodology for making predictions from parent–child relationships to peer relationships. According to attachment theorists, parents who are able and willing to recognize their infants' or toddlers' emotional signals, to consider their children's perspectives, and to respond promptly and appropriately according to their children's needs help their children develop a belief system that incorporates the parent as one who can be relied on for protection, nurturance, comfort, and security (Belsky & Cassidy, 1995). A sense of trust in relationships results from the secure infant/toddler–parent bond. Furthermore, the child forms a belief that the self is competent and worthy of positive response from others.

The securely attached young child feels secure, confident, and self-assured when introduced to novel settings; this sense of felt security fosters the child's exploration of the social environment. Exploration of the social milieu leads to peer interaction and play, which, in turn, leads to the development of skills essential for the establishment and maintenance of positive peer relationships. Alternatively, the insecurely attached child believes that interpersonal relationships are rejecting or neglectful. Such conceptions of relationships are thought to result in the child's attempting to strike out aggressively at peers or avoid peer interaction; both of these behavioral styles preclude the child from the benefits of peer interaction.

There are, in fact, considerable data documenting the relations between the quality of infant–parent attachment relationships and the quality of children's social interactions with peers throughout the first 5 years of life (see Booth-LaForce & Kerns, 2009 for a review). For example, insecure-avoidant (A) babies later exhibit more hostility, anger, and distancing and aggressive behavior in preschool settings than their secure (B) counterparts (e.g., Egeland, Pianta, & O'Brien, 1993). Insecure-ambivalent (C) infants are more whiney, easily frustrated, and socially inhibited at 2 years than their secure age-mates (e.g., Fox & Calkins, 1993; Spangler & Schieche, 1998). Insecure-disorganized-disoriented (D) attachment status in infancy predicts the subsequent display of aggression among preschool and elementary school peers (e.g., Lyons-Ruth, Easterbrooks, & Cibelli, 1997). Finally, research also indicates that infants with secure attachment histories are later more popular and socially competent in the peer group in elementary school than their insecurely attached peers (see Booth-LaForce & Kerns, 2009 and Sroufe, Egeland, Carlson, & Collins, 2005 for reviews).

Studies of the contemporaneous relations between attachment and children's social behaviors and relationships support the longitudinal data just described. For example, in early and middle childhood as well in early adolescence, youngsters who experience a secure relationship with their mothers have been found to be more popular, sociable, and competent with peers than their insecure counterparts, whereas those who are insecure exhibit more aggressive and/or withdrawn behaviors (Booth-LaForce et al., 2006; Granot & Mayseless, 2001; Rose-Krasnor, Rubin, Booth, & Coplan, 1996).

In support of the notion that the child's *internal working model* provides substance for his or her social cognitions and behaviors, Cassidy, Scolton, Kirsh, and Parke (1996) found that children assessed as securely attached at 3½ years of age provided more prosocial responses to negative events and had more positive representations than insecure children about peer intentions during ambiguous negative acts when they were 10 years old. In concert with attachment theory, the authors speculated that securely attached children develop representations of their mothers as sensitive and responsive, and thus are unlikely to do something that would intentionally harm them. These internal representations guide children to develop similar conceptions of their peers.

Finally, given that the parent–child attachment relationship is a *dyadic* one, it would suggest that the dyadic friendship relationships of securely attached children should differ from those of insecurely attached children. Support for this notion stems from studies in which children with secure attachment relationships, in contrast to those with insecure attachments, are found (1) to report having one or more good friends; (2) to indicate fewer problems with peers such as being ridiculed or excluded from group activities; (3) to have fewer negative and asynchronous friendships; and (4) to be capable of establishing and maintaining close and intimate friendships with peers (Kerns, Klepac, & Cole, 1996; McElwain & Volling, 2004; Lieberman, Doyle, & Markiewicz, 1999; Rubin et al., 2004).

Parenting Behaviors and Peer Relationships

Parents may influence the development of social behaviors, and ultimately, the quality of their children's peer relationships by (1) providing opportunities for their children to have contact with peers; (2) monitoring their children's peer encounters when necessary; (3) coaching their children to deal competently with interpersonal peer-related tasks; and (4) disciplining unacceptable, maladaptive peer-directed behaviors (Parke, Burks, Carson, Neville, & Boyum, 1994; Parke & O'Neill, 1999; Pettit & Mize, 1993). For example, Ladd and Golter (1988) reported that mothers who arranged child–peer engagements had preschoolers who (1) had a larger number of playmates; (2) had more consistent play companions in their informal non-school networks; and (3) were better liked by peers. Mothers who initiated peer activities were likely to have children who spent more time playing in peers' homes; this variable was associated with peer acceptance (Ladd, Hart, Wadsworth, & Golter, 1988). Furthermore, parents who initiated peer opportunities for their children were more likely to have children

Parenting behavior affects a child's peer relationships; parents who provide opportunities for peer contact help their children to initiate and manage their own peer relationships.

who were socially competent (Kerns, Cole, & Andrews, 1998; Ladd & Hart, 1992). From these findings, it would appear that parents' provision of opportunities for peer interaction help empower their children with the abilities to initiate and manage their own peer relationships.

Parents also regularly monitor, supervise, and coach their children during peer activities. Lack of parental monitoring has generally been linked to children's externalizing behavior difficulties and adolescent delinquency (Barber, 2002). Furthermore, children whose parents rely on indirect rather than direct monitoring of their peer contacts are less hostile towards others (Ladd & Golter, 1988). Moreover, children whose mothers and fathers offer advice on how to manage their social dilemmas are viewed by parents and teachers as socially competent (McDowell, Parke, & Wang, 2003). And mothers' over- as well as under-involvement in orchestrating and monitoring peer contacts is detrimental to children's social success, at least among boys (Ladd & Hart, 1992).

Mothers of more popular children are more active and effective in supervising their children's peer-related behaviors during free play than mothers of less well accepted children. Furthermore, mothers of less popular children suggest that they would coach their children to be more avoidant in response to hypothetical problems involving peers, whereas mothers of more popular children encourage their children to employ positive and assertive strategies for handling interpersonal problems involving peers (Finnie & Russell, 1988).

In summary, when parents provide their children with opportunities to play with peers, coach their children through difficulties with peers, and facilitate their children's peer interactions, their children are more popular among their age-mates.

With respect to parental behaviors much of the research on parenting and peer relationships has focused on the importance of two dimensions of parenting: warmth and control. Warmth typically denotes parental behaviors such as praise, encouragement, physical affection, physical and psychological availability, and approval. Control has been defined as consistent enforcement of rules accompanied by an ability to make age-appropriate demands on the child. Parents of unpopular and/or peer-rejected children have been reported to use inept, harsh, and authoritarian disciplinary and socialization practices more frequently than those of their more popular counterparts (e.g., Bierman & Smoot, 1991). These findings seem to hold for preschoolers and elementary schoolers. Alternatively, parents of popular and socially competent children use more feelings-oriented reasoning and induction, warm control, and more positivity during communication (Mize & Pettit, 1997).

As noted above, children's behaviors influence the extent to which they may be accepted or rejected by peers. In this regard, studies that simply correlate parenting behaviors and cognitions with peer acceptance appear to miss a "step" in the link between these two phenomena. However, researchers who study links between parenting and children's social behaviors provide the information necessary to understand the links between parenting and peer acceptance. For example, with regard to the socialization of socially incompetent behaviors, parents who may be characterized as physically punitive, cold, rejecting, overly critical, and inconsistent in their discipline practices have children who behave aggressively during peer interaction (e.g., Dishion, 1990; Dishion & Patterson, 2006). In this regard, parents who are cold, rejecting, and punitive provide substantive models of hostility to their children (Patterson, 1983). Researchers have also consistently shown that parents of aggressive children inadvertently reinforce aggressive and impulsive behaviors (Dishion & Patterson, 2006). Importantly, it is not only cold, hostile, authoritarian parenting that promotes childhood aggression. Parents of aggressive children have also been found to be emotionally neglectful and lacking in responsiveness (Greenberg, Speltz, & Deklyen, 1993). Thus, parental permissiveness, indulgence, and lack of supervision appear connected to children's demonstrating aggressive behavior in the peer group (see Rubin & Burgess, 2002, for a review). Taken together, punitive, rejecting, cold, and overly permissive parenting behaviors are associated with, and predictive of, childhood aggression, which in turn is associated with, and predictive of, peer rejection.

Research concerning parenting behaviors and styles associated with social withdrawal (the other major behavioral correlate of peer rejection) focus on overcontrol and overprotection (see Hastings, Nuselovici, Rubin, & Cheah, 2010 for a review). Parents who use high power assertive strategies and who place many constraints on their children's independence and exploration appear to hinder the development of social competence and interaction with peers (Degnan, Henderson, Fox, & Rubin, 2008). Furthermore, children who are socially withdrawn are on the receiving end of parental overcontrol and overprotection (Hane, Cheah, Rubin, & Fox, 2008). There is also some evidence to suggest that parents may inadvertently exacerbate childhood shyness and social anxiety by modeling or reinforcing children's socially anxious behaviors (e.g., Barrett, Dadds, & Rapee, 1996).

CULTURE AND PEER RELATIONSHIPS

What we know about the development and correlates, causes, and outcomes of children's social behaviors and relationships is constrained by the cultures in which we study these phenomena (Cole & Packer, Chapter 2, this volume). The vast majority of the published data on children's peer experiences are derived from studies conducted in North America and Western Europe. Simply put, we know very little about the development and significance of peer acceptance, rejection, and friendship in non-Western cultures. Among the many aspects of socioemotional and cognitive functioning in human development, children's experiences in the peer group are perhaps most sensitive to **cultural influences** (Hinde, 1987). Children's behaviors in the peer context, peer evaluations and responses in interactions, the formation and function of peer relationships, and the organization of peer groups are likely to be culture-bound because they are often directed by cultural conventions, norms, and values (Chen & French, 2008).

Cultural influence may be reflected in children's peer interaction styles, peer acceptance and rejection, friendships and social networks. At the *behavioral* level, socialization pressures resulting from cultural endorsement and constraint may be directly associated with the prevalence and development of specific behaviors such as cooperation (Domino, 1992), compliance

(Chen et al., 2003), and emotional expressivity (e.g., Schneider, 1998). At the *overall peer acceptance* level, cultural value systems determine, to a great extent, standards for peer acceptance and rejection of children who are prototypically assertive (Chen, Li, Li, Li, & Liu, 2000) and aggressive (Casiglia, Lo Coco & Zappulla, 1998) among their peers. Finally, the functional roles that children's *friendships* and *peer groups* fulfill may vary across culture (e.g., French, Jansen, Rianasari, & Setiono, 2003; French, Setiono, & Eddy, 1999). For example, whereas the enhancement of self-esteem is regarded as particularly significant among friends in Western cultures, it is not highly appreciated among children in other cultures (e.g., China; Chen, Kaspar, Zhang, Wang, & Zheng, 2004). Similarly, whereas group affiliation is viewed in Western cultures as fulfilling individual psychological needs, such as the development of self-identity and enhancement of feelings about self-worth (Sullivan, 1953), Chinese culture places great emphasis on the role of the peer group to socialize members in appropriate *collective* behavior. In this regard, Eastern cultures may pay more attention to the *nature* of peer group networks ("good" or "bad" in terms of the consistency between group goals and activities and collectivistic orientations) than to individual functioning (Chen et al., 2008).

A central issue concerning cultural influence on peer interactions and relationships is the role of cultural norms and values in defining the "meanings" of social behaviors. Culture may not only affect the development and prevalence of particular social behaviors, but may also provide guidance for social judgment and evaluation of those behaviors that serve as a basis of social acceptance and rejection (Chen & French, 2008). Specifically, cultural patterns, especially those concerning socialization goals and expectations, are likely to affect group and individual beliefs, attitudes, and value systems. For example, one important socialization goal in Western cultures is the development of individual autonomy, assertiveness, and independence. These characteristics are highly emphasized during social interaction (Triandis, 1990). In contrast, social connectedness, interdependence, and conformity are valued social characteristics in most Asian and Latino collectivistic cultures (Greenfield, 1994). These different cultural beliefs and norms provide a frame of reference for the social evaluation of adaptive and maladaptive behaviors (Bornstein, 1995). Social evaluations may, in turn, affect how children interpret and react to each other's behaviors, and eventually determine whether a child is accepted by peers or the types of relationships the child develops with others.

The argument that different cultures draw different meanings from given social behaviors and interaction patterns in different ways has received empirical support in a series of cross-cultural studies by Chen and colleagues (Chen et al., 1998; Chen, Chen, Li, & Wang, 2009). Consistent with the findings of Western researchers, the frequent display of prosocial and cooperative behaviors was positively associated with peer acceptance and teacher-rated competence; the frequent display of aggressive or disruptive behavior was related to peer rejection in Chinese children (Chen, Rubin, & Li, 1995). In China, however, aggressive children experience feelings of loneliness and depression; this is not typically the case among aggressive children in North America (Chen et al., 1995). This finding may emanate from the strict prohibition of disruptive and aggressive behavior among Chinese children; students who display such deviant behaviors are often publicly criticized and even humiliated by teachers and peers in Chinese schools.

The role of culture as a context is also evident in the social interpretations of shy-inhibited behavior. In the Western literature, the display of shy, socially inhibited behavior is thought to derive from an approach–avoidance conflict in social situations; thus, socially withdrawn, restrained behaviors are taken to reflect internal fearfulness and a lack of social confidence (see Rubin et al., 2003). Children who display shy-inhibited behavior are believed to be socially incompetent, immature, and maladaptive in cultural contexts within which individual characteristics of assertiveness, expressiveness, and competitiveness are valued and encouraged (Triandis, 1990). However, shy-inhibited behavior is considered an indication of accomplishment and maturity in traditional Chinese culture; shy, wary, and inhibited children are perceived as well-behaved and understanding (e.g., Chen, in press; Luo, 1996). The social and cultural endorsement of their behavior is likely to help shy-sensitive children obtain social support and develop self-confidence in social situations. Accordingly, it has been found that whereas shy-inhibited children in Canada and the United States experience social and psychological difficulties, shy children in China are accepted by peers, well adjusted to the school environment, and less likely than others to report loneliness and depression (e.g., Chen, Rubin, Li, & Li, 1999). In an observational study, for example, when shy-inhibited children made initiations to their peers, they were likely to receive positive, supportive responses such as approval, cooperation, and compliance in China, but negative responses such as rejection and neglect in Canada (Chen, DeSouza, Chen, & Wang, 2006). Moreover, peers were more likely to voluntarily initiate positive interactions such as sharing and helping behaviors with shy children in China than in Canada. These findings indicate the significance of cultural norms for the development of social behaviors and peer relationships.

In summary, cross-cultural studies, especially those conducted in China and other Asian countries, have indicated that some behaviors viewed as maladaptive and abnormal in Western cultures are viewed as adaptive and acceptable therein. Peer acceptance is associated with behaviors that are viewed as acceptable within a culture, and behaviors regarded as culturally maladaptive are associated with peer rejection. Unfortunately, there has been little work, longitudinal or otherwise, in which researchers have examined the distal predictors (e.g., temperament, family factors) that may help explain cultural differences in the prediction and long-term outcome of peer acceptance and rejection. Such studies would enrich our knowledge of the cultural "meanings" of children's social behaviors and relationships.

CONCLUSIONS

In this chapter, we have reviewed literature concerning children's peer relationships. It should be clear that experiences garnered by children in the peer group and with their friends represent significant development phenomena. Thus, children who are accepted by peers and who have qualitatively rich friendships appear to fare better, throughout childhood, than children who are rejected and excluded by the peer group or who are lacking in friendship.

In this chapter, we have attempted to document those factors responsible, in part, for children's peer and friendship status. Influences include such intraindividual factors as temperament, emotion regulation, and social cognitive prowess as well as such interindividual factors as family relationships (e.g., attachment), quality of parenting style experienced, and cultural norms and values.

Although we have learned a great deal about the significance of children's peer interactions, relationships, and groups, there remain some rather interesting and important questions to address. For example, little research has focused on individual differences in the extent to which very young children (toddlers) demonstrate socially competent and incompetent behavior. Indeed, what does competent social behavior look like at age one or two? We indicated that by the end of the second year of life toddlers are able to engage in complementary and reciprocal interactive behaviors with peers. But do individual differences in such behaviors predict social competence, peer acceptance, and the ability to make and keep friends in later years? If dispositional and socialization factors vary in infancy, it seems likely that individual differences in social skills may be present in the second and third years of life—differences that may predict and/or lead to adaptation to the developmental milestone of preschool or kindergarten entry.

In this chapter we also presented a brief overview of the significance of children's friendships. We indicated that children's friendships serve a variety of functions including the provision of emotional and social support. We noted that children's ideas about friendship become increasingly abstract with age. Furthermore, children's friendships are posited to play an increasingly important role with age. Yet little is known about when it is in childhood that friendship can first serve as a promoter or inhibitor of adaptation or as a buffer against the ill-effects of parental or peer neglect or rejection. This issue of the functional significance of friendship may prove very helpful in planning intervention programs for children who demonstrate poorly developed social skills and peer relationships as early as the preschool years.

We indicated that from as early as 3 years of age, children's groups can be characterized by stable and rigid dominance hierarchies. The main function of these hierarchies appears to be to reduce conflict and aggression among peer group members. In the early years of childhood, the most dominant members of the peer group are the most popular and most highly imitated in their peer group. Yet dominance status in these earliest years of childhood is gained through consistent victory in interpersonal conflict. The route to dominance status in the middle and later years of childhood is, as yet, uncharted. It remains to be seen whether the relations between dominance status and peer acceptance remain consistent throughout childhood. Indeed, is it the case that dominance status, as assessed in early childhood, predicts perceived power and popularity when children move into middle school? This is a time when many of those perceived as popular are also viewed by peers as somewhat aggressive, assertive, and as boastful "show-offs." The early origins of young adolescent perceived popularity, dominance, and leadership represent areas that require the attention of researchers.

The topic of children's peer relationships has caught the attention of the lay public. Not a day goes by without a major newspaper, magazine article, or even films appearing on such matters as popularity, rejection, friendship, bullying, conflict, meanness, and peer pressure. With the eyes of the public attending to such matters, it remains up to the researcher to provide the consumer with a research-based picture of the roles played by the peer group in childhood and adolescence. It would be timely, indeed, to offer policy makers and educators the suggestion that "no child left behind" movements in public schools should incorporate children's social skills and relationships into the academic curriculum. After all, if children are rejected or victimized by peers in their schools, they may find it rather difficult to concentrate on learning to read, write, or solve mathematical problems (Wentzel & Asher, 1995; Wentzel, McNamara-Barry, & Caldwell, 2004). If children are lacking friends in school, or if they are lacking in social skills, what is the likelihood that they would feel comfortable working on group projects? Children's peer interactions, relationships, and groups are not only relevant insofar as psychological and emotional adjustment is concerned; they are clearly important entities as children attempt to make their ways through their everyday lives.

ACKNOWLEDGMENTS

This chapter was supported by National Institute of Mental Health grant 1R01MH58116 to Kenneth H. Rubin.

REFERENCES AND SUGGESTED READINGS (📖)

Aboud, F., & Mendelson, M. (1996). Determinants of friendship selection and quality: Developmental perspectives. In W. Bukowski & A. Newcomb (Eds.), *The company they keep: Friendship in childhood and adolescence* (pp. 87–112). Cambridge, UK: Cambridge University Press.

Adler, P. A., Kless, S. J., & Adler, P. (1992). Socialization to gender roles: Popularity among elementary school boys and girls. *Sociology of Education, 65*, 169–187.

Altermatt, E., & Pomerantz, E. (2003). The development of competence-related and motivational beliefs: An investigation of similarity and influence among friends. *Journal of Educational Psychology, 95*(1), 111–123.

Archer, J., & Coyne, S. M. (2005). An integrated review of indirect, relational, and social aggression. *Personality and Social Psychology Review, 9*, 212–230.

Asher, S. R., & McDonald, K. L. (2009). The behavioral basis of acceptance, rejection, and perceived popularity. In K. H. Rubin, W. M. Bukowski, & B. Laursen (Eds.), *Handbook of peer interactions, relationships, and groups* (pp. 232–248). New York: Guilford Press.

Asher. S. R., & Paquette, J. (2003). Loneliness and peer relations in childhood. *Current Directions in Psychological Science, 12*, 75–78.

Asher, S. R., Rose, A. J., & Gabriel, S. W. (2001). Peer rejection in everyday life. In M. R. Leary (Ed.), *Interpersonal rejection* (pp. 105–142). New York: Oxford University Press.

Asher, S. R., & Wheeler, V. A. (1985). Children's loneliness: A comparison of rejected and neglected peer status. *Journal of Consulting and Clinical Psychology, 53*, 500–505.

Bagwell, C. L., Newcomb, A. F., & Bukowski, W. M. (1998). Preadolescent friendship and peer rejection as predictors of adult adjustment. *Child Development, 69*, 140–153.

Bandura, A. (1977). *Social learning theory*. Englewood Cliffs, NJ: Prentice Hall.

Bandura, A., & Walters, R. H. (1963). *Social learning and personality development*. New York: Holt, Rinehart, & Winston.

Barber, B. K. (2002). *Intrusive parenting: How psychological control affects children and adolescents*. Washington, DC: American Psychological Association.

Barrett, P. M., Dadds, M. R., & Rapee, R. M. (1996). Family treatment of childhood anxiety disorders: A controlled trial. *Journal of Consulting and Clinical Psychology, 64*, 333–342.

Bates, J. E. (2001). Adjustment style in childhood as a product of parenting and temperament. In T. D. Wachs & G. A. Kohstamm (Eds.), *Temperament in context* (pp. 173–200). Mahwah, NJ: Lawrence Erlbaum Associates.

Bell-Dolan, D., Foster, S., & Sikora, D. (1989). Effects of sociometric testing on children's behavior and loneliness in school. *Developmental Psychology, 25*, 306–311.

Belsky, J., & Cassidy, J. (1995). Attachment: Theory and evidence. In M. L. Rutter, D. F. Hay, & S. Baron-Cohen (Eds.), *Developmental principles and clinical issues in psychology and psychiatry* (pp. 373–402). Oxford, UK: Blackwell.

Benenson, J. F. (1990). Gender differences in social networks. *Journal of Early Adolescence, 10*, 472–495.

Benenson, J. F., Apostoleris, N. H., & Parnass, J. (1997). Age and sex differences in dyadic and group interaction. *Developmental Psychology, 33*, 538–543.

Benenson, J. F., & Christakos, A. (2003). The greater fragility of females' versus males' closest same-sex friendships. *Child Development, 74*, 1123–1129.

Benenson, J. F., Markovits, H., Roy, R., & Denko, P. (2003). Behavioural rules underlying learning to share: Effects of development and context. *International Journal of Behavioural Development, 27*, 116–121.

Berndt, T. J. (1981). Relations between social cognition, nonsocial cognition, and social behavior: The case of friendship. In J. H. Flavell & L. Ross (Eds.), *Social cognitive development* (pp. 176–199). Cambridge, UK: Cambridge University Press.

Berndt, T. J. (1985). Prosocial behavior between friends in middle childhood and early adolescence. *Journal of Adolescence, 5*, 307–313.

Berndt, T. J. (1996). Friendship quality affects adolescents' self esteem and social behavior. In W. M. Bukowski, A. F. Newcomb, & W. W. Hartup (Eds.), *The company they keep: Friendship during childhood and adolescence*. New York: Cambridge University Press.

Berndt, T. J., Hawkins, J. A., & Jiao, Z. (1999). Influences of friends and friendships on adjustment to junior high school. *Merrill-Palmer Quarterly, 45*, 13–41.

Berndt, T. J., & Hoyle, S. G. (1985). Stability and change in childhood and adolescent friendships. *Developmental Psychology, 21*, 1007–1015.

Berndt, T. J., & Keefe, K. (1995). Friends' influence on adolescents' adjustment to school. *Child Development, 66*, 1313–1329.

Berndt, T. J., & McCandless, M. A. (2009). Methods of investigating children's relationships with friends. In K. H. Rubin, W. M. Bukowski, & B. Laursen (Eds.), *Handbook of peer interactions, relationships, and groups* (pp. 63–81). New York: Guilford Press.

Bierman, K. L., & Smoot, D. L. (1991). Linking family characteristics with poor peer relations: The mediating role of conduct problems. *Journal of Abnormal Child Psychology, 19*, 341–356.

Bigelow, B. J., & LaGaipa, J. J. (1980). The development of friendship values and choice. In H. Foot & A. Chapman (Eds.), *Friendship and social relations in children* (pp. 15–44). New Brunswick, NJ: Transaction.

Black, B., & Logan, A. (1995). Links between communication patterns in mother–child, father child, and child–peer interactions and children's social status. *Child Development, 66*, 255–271.

Boivin, M., & Hymel, S. (1997). Peer experiences and social self-perceptions: A sequential model. *Developmental Psychology, 33*, 135–145.

Boivin, M., Poulin, F., & Vitaro, F. (1994). Depressed mood and peer rejection in childhood. *Development and Psychopathology, 6*, 483–498.

Boldizar, J. P., Perry, D. G., & Perry, L. C. (1989). Outcome values and aggression. *Child Development, 60*, 571–579.

Bonney, M. E. (1942). A study of social status on the second grade level. *Journal of Genetic Psychology, 60*, 271–305.

Booth-LaForce, C., & Kerns, K. A. (2009). Family influences on children's peer relationships. In K. H. Rubin, W. Bukowski, & B. Laursen (Eds.), *Peer interactions, relationships, and groups* (pp. 508–530). New York: Guilford Press.

Booth-LaForce, C., Oh, W., Kim, A. H., Rubin, K. H., Rose-Krasnor, L., & Burgess, K. (2006). Attachment, self-worth, and peer-group functioning in middle childhood. *Attachment & Human Development, 8*, 309–325.

Bornstein, M. H. (1995). Form and function: Implications for studies of culture and human development. *Culture and Psychology, 1*(1), 123–138.

Bowker, A. (2004). Predicting friendship stability during early adolescence. *Journal of Early Adolescence, 24*, 85–112.

Bowker, J., Fredstrom, B., Rubin, K., Rose-Krasnor, L., Booth-LaForce, C., & Laursen, B. (2009). *Distinguishing those children who form new best friends from those who do not.* Unpublished manuscript.

Bowker, J. C., & Rubin, K. H. (2009). Self-consciousness, friendship quality, and internalizing problems during early adolescence. *British Journal of Developmental Psychology, 19*, 249–268.

Bowlby, J. (1958). The nature of the child's tie to his mother. *International Journal of Psychoanalysis, 39*, 350–373.

Brendgen, M., Little, T. D., & Krappmann, L. (2000). Rejected children and their friends: A shared evaluation of friendship quality? *Merrill-Palmer Quarterly, 46* (1), 45–70.

Brown, B. B. (1990). Peer groups and peer cultures. In S. S. Feldman & G. R. Elliott (Eds.), *At the threshold* (pp. 171–196). Cambridge, MA: Harvard University Press.

Brown, B. B., Eicher, S. A., & Petrie, S. (1986). The importance of peer group ("crowd") affiliation in adolescence. *Journal of Adolescence, 9*, 73–96.

Brown, S. B., Mounts, N., Lamborn, S. D., & Steinberg, L. (1993). Parenting practices and peer group affiliation in adolescence. *Child Development, 64*, 467–482.

Brownell, C. A. & Kopp, C. B. (2007). *Socioemotional development in the toddler years: Transitions and transformations.* New York: Guilford Press.

Brownell, C. A., Ramani, G. B., & Zerwas, S. (2006). Becoming a social partner with peers: Cooperation and social understanding in one- and two-year-olds. *Child Development, 77*, 803–821.

Buhler, C. (1935). *From birth to maturity: An outline of the psychological development of the child.* London: Routledge & Kegan Paul.

Bukowski, W. M., Sippola, L. K., & Newcomb, A. F. (2000). Variations in patterns of attraction to same- and other-sex peers during early adolescence. *Developmental Psychology, 36*(2), 147–154.

Burks, V. S., Dodge, K. A., & Price, J. M. (1995). Models of internalizing outcomes of early rejection. *Development & Psychopathology, 7*, 683–695.

Cairns, R. B., & Cairns, B. D. (1991). Social cognition and social networks: A developmental perspective. In D. J. Pepler & K. H. Rubin (Eds.), *The development and treatment of childhood aggression* (pp. 249–278). Hillsdale, NJ: Lawrence Erlbaum Associates.

Cairns, R. B., & Cairns, B. D. (1994). *Lifelines and risks: Pathways of youth in our time.* Cambridge, UK: University Press.

Cairns, R. B., Cairns, B. D., Neckerman, H. J., Gest, S., & Gariepy, J. L. (1988). Peer networks and aggressive behavior: Peer support or peer rejection? *Developmental Psychology, 24*, 815–823.

Cairns, R. B., Gariepy, J. L., & Kindermann, T. (1989). *Identifying social clusters in natural settings.* Unpublished manuscript, University of North Carolina at Chapel Hill.

Cairns, R. B., Leung, M. C., Buchanan, L. & Cairns, B. (1995). Friendships and social networks in childhood and adolescence: Fluidity, reliability, and interrelations. *Child Development, 66*, 1330–1345.

Card, N., & Hodges, E. (2006). Shared targets for aggression by early adolescent friends. *Developmental Psychology, 42*, 1327–1338.

Casiglia, A. C., Lo Coco, A., & Zappulla, C. (1998). Aspects of social reputation and peer relationships in Italian children: A cross-cultural perspective. *Developmental Psychology, 34*, 723–730.

Caspi, A., Elder, G. H., Jr., & Bem, D. J. (1988). Moving away from the world: Life-course patterns of shy children. *Developmental Psychology, 24*, 824–831.

Cassidy, J., & Asher, S. R. (1992). Loneliness and peer relations in young children. *Child Development, 63*, 350–365.

Cassidy, J., Scolton, K. L., Kirsh, S. J., & Parke, R. D. (1996). Attachment and representations of peer relationships. *Developmental Psychology, 32*, 892–904.

Chan, A. & Poulin, F. (2007). Monthly changes in the composition of friendship networks in early adolescence. *Merrill-Palmer Quarterly*, *53*(4), 578–602.

Charlesworth, W. R., & LaFreniere, P. (1983). Dominance, friendship, and resource utilization in preschool children's groups. *Ethology and Sociobiology*, *4*, 175–186.

Chen, X. (in press). Shyness-inhibition in childhood and adolescence: A cross-cultural perspective. In K. H. Rubin & R. Coplan (Eds.), *The development of shyness and social withdrawal*. New York: Guilford Press.

Chen, X., Chang, L., & He, Y. (2003a). The peer group as a context: Mediating and moderating effects on the relations between academic achievement and social functioning in Chinese children. *Child Development*, *74*, 710–727.

📖 Chen, X., Chang, L., Liu, H., & He, Y. (2008). Effects of the peer group on the development of social functioning and academic achievement: A longitudinal study in Chinese children. *Child Development*, *79*, 235–251.

Chen, X., Chen, H., & Kaspar, V. (2001). Group social functioning and individual socio-emotional and school adjustment in Chinese children. *Merrill-Palmer Quarterly*, *47*, 264–299.

Chen, X., Chen, H., Li, D., & Wang, L. (2009). Early childhood behavioral inhibition and social and school adjustment in Chinese children: A 5-year longitudinal study. *Child Development*, *80*, 1692–1704.

Chen, X., DeSouza, A., Chen, H., & Wang, L. (2006). Reticent behavior and experiences in peer interactions in Canadian and Chinese children. *Developmental Psychology*, *42*, 656–665.

Chen, X. & French, D. (2008). Children's social competence in cultural context. *Annual Review of Psychology*, *59*, 591–616.

Chen, X., Hastings, P., Rubin, K. H., Chen, H., Cen, G., & Stewart, S. L. (1998). Childrearing attitudes and behavioral inhibition in Chinese and Canadian toddlers: A cross-cultural study. *Developmental Psychology*, *34*, 677–686.

Chen, X., Kaspar, V., Zhang, Y., Wang, L., & Zheng, S. (2004). Peer relationships among Chinese and North American boys: A cross-cultural perspective. In N. Way & J. Chu (Eds.), *Adolescent boys in context* (pp. 197–218). New York: New York University Press.

Chen, X., Li, D., Li, Z., Li, B., & Liu, M. (2000). Sociable and prosocial dimensions of social competence in Chinese children: Common and unique contributions to social, academic and psychological adjustment. *Developmental Psychology*, *36*, 302–314.

Chen, X., Rubin, K. H., & Li, B. (1995) Social and school adjustment of shy and aggressive children in China. *Development and Psychopathology*, *7*, 337–349.

Chen, X., Rubin, K. H., Li, B., & Li, Z. (1999). Adolescent outcomes of social functioning in Chinese children. *International Journal of Behavioural Development*, *23*, 199–223.

Chen, X., Rubin, K. H., Liu, M., Chen, H., Wang, L., Li, D., et al. (2003b). Compliance in Chinese and Canadian toddlers. *International Journal of Behavioral Development*, *27*, 428–436.

Chen, X. & Tse, H. C. (2008). Social functioning and adjustment in Canadian-born children with Chinese and European backgrounds. *Developmental Psychology*, *44*, 1184–1189.

Chung, T., & Asher, S. R. (1996). Children's goals and strategies in peer conflict situations. *Merrill-Palmer Quarterly*, *42*, 125–147.

Cillessen, A. H. N. (2009). Sociometric methods. In K. Rubin, W. Bukowski, & B. Laursen (Eds.), *Handbook of peer interactions, relationships, and groups* (pp. 82–99). New York: Guilford Press.

Cillessen, A., Bukowski, W., & Haselager, G. (2000). Stability of sociometric categories. *New Directions for Child and Adolescent Development*, *88*, 75–93.

📖 Cillessen, A. H. N., & Mayeux, L. (2004). From censure to reinforcement: Developmental changes in the association between aggression and social status. *Child Development*, *75*, 147–163.

Coie, J. D. & Dodge, K. A. (1988). Multiple sources of data on social behavior and social status. *Child Development*, *59*, 815–829.

Coie, J. D. & Dodge, K. A. (1998). Aggression and anti-social behavior. In N. Eisenberg (Ed.), *Handbook of child psychology: Social, emotional, and personality development* (5th ed., pp. 779–862). New York: Wiley.

Coie, J. D., Dodge, K. A., & Coppotelli, H. (1983). Continuities and changes in children's social status: A five-year longitudinal study. *Merrill-Palmer Quarterly*, *29*, 261–282.

Coie, J. D., & Krehbiehl, G. (1984). Effects of academic tutoring on the social status of low-achieving, socially rejected children. *Child Development*, *55*, 1465–1478.

📖 Coie, J. D., & Kupersmidt, J. (1983). A behavioral analysis of emerging social status in boys' groups. *Child Development*, *54*, 1400–1416.

Collins, W., Maccoby, E. E, Steinberg, L., Hetherington, E. M., & Bornstein, M. H. (2000). Contemporary research on parenting: The case for nature and nurture. *American Psychologist*, *55*, 218–232.

Cooley, C. H. (1902). *Human nature and the social order*. New York: Scribner.

Coplan, R. J., Arbeau, K. A., & Armer, M. (2008). Don't fret, be supportive! Maternal characteristics linking child shyness to psychosocial and school adjustment in kindergarten. *Journal of Abnormal Child Psychology*, *36*, 359–371.

Coplan, R. J., Bowker, A., & Cooper, S. (2003). Parenting stress, child temperament, and social adjustment in preschool. *Early Childhood Research Quarterly*, *18*, 376–395.

Coplan, R. J., Gavinsky-Molina, M. H., Lagace-Seguin, D., & Wichmann, C. (2001). When girls versus boys play alone: Gender differences in the associates of nonsocial play in kindergarten. *Developmental Psychology*, *37*, 464–474.

Coplan, R. J., Prakash, K., O'Neil, K., & Armer, M. (2004). Do you "want" to play? Distinguishing between conflicted-shyness and social disinterest in early childhood. *Developmental Psychology, 40*, 244–258.

Coplan, R. J., & Rubin, K. H. (1998). Exploring and assessing non-social play in the preschool: The development and validation of the Preschool Play Behavior Scale. *Social Development, 7*, 72–91.

Coplan, R. J., Rubin, K. H., Fox, N. A., Calkins, S. D., & Stewart, S. L. (1994). Being alone, playing alone, and acting alone: Distinguishing among reticence and passive and active solitude in young children. *Child Development, 65*, 129–137.

Craft, A. (1994). Five and six year-olds' views of friendship. *Educational Studies, 20*(2), 181–194.

Crick, N. R. (1996). The role of overt aggression, relational aggression, and prosocial behavior in the prediction of children's future social adjustment. *Child Development, 67*, 2317–2327.

Crick, N. R., Casas, J. F., & Mosher, M. (1997). Relational and overt aggression in preschool. *Developmental Psychology, 33*, 579–588.

Crick, N. R., & Dodge, K. A. (1994). A review and reformulation of social information-processing mechanisms in children's social adjustment. *Psychological Bulletin, 115*, 74–101.

Crick, N. R., Grotpeter, J. K., & Bigbee, M. A. (2002). Relationally and physically aggressive children's intent attributions and feelings of distress for relational and instrumental peer provocations. *Child Development, 73*(4), 1134–1142.

Crick, N. R., & Ladd, G. W. (1993). Children's perceptions of their peer experiences: Attributions, loneliness, social anxiety, and social avoidance. *Developmental Psychology, 29*(2), 244–254.

Crozier, W. R. (1995). Shyness and self-esteem in middle childhood. *British Journal of Educational Psychology, 65*, 85–95.

Daniels, E. & Leaper, C. (2006). A longitudinal investigation of sport participation, peer acceptance, and self-esteem among adolescent girls and boys. *Sex Roles, 55*, 878–880.

Degnan, K. A., Henderson, H. A., Fox, N. A., & Rubin, K. H. (2008). Predicting social wariness in middle childhood: The moderating roles of childcare history, maternal personality and maternal behavior. *Social Development, 17*, 471–487.

Dekovic, M., Engels, R. C. M. E., Shirai, T., De Kort, G., & Anker, A. L. (2002). The role of peer relations in adolescent development in two cultures: The Netherlands and Japan. *Journal of Cross-Cultural Psychology, 33*, 577–595.

DeRosier, M. E., & Thomas, J. M. (2003). Strengthening sociometric prediction: Scientific advances in the assessment of children's peer relations. *Child Development, 74*, 1379–1392.

DeSouza, A., & Chen, X. (2002, July). *Social initiative and responses of shy and non-shy children in China and Canada*. Presented at the Biennial Conference of the International Society for the Study of Behavioral Development (ISSBD), Ottawa, Canada.

Dishion, T. J. (1990). The family ecology of boys' peer relations in middle childhood. *Child Development, 61*, 874–892.

Dishion, T. J., Andrews, D. W., & Crosby, L. (1995). Antisocial boys and their friends in early adolescence: Relationship characteristics, quality, and interactional process. *Child Development, 66*, 139–151.

Dishion, T. J., Eddy, M., Haas, E., Li, F., & Spracklen, K. (1997). Friendships and violent behavior during adolescence. *Social Development, 6*(2), 207–223.

Dishion, T. J., McCord, J., & Poulin, F. (1999). When interventions harm: Peer groups and problem behavior. *American Psychologist, 54*(9), 755–764.

Dishion, T. J., & Patterson, G. R. (2006). The development and ecology of antisocial behavior. In D. Cicchetti & D. J. Cohen (Eds.), *Developmental psychopathology, Vol. 3: Risk, disorder, and adaptation* (pp. 503–541). New York: Wiley.

Dodge, K. A. (1980). Social cognition and children's aggressive behavior. *Child Development, 51*, 162–170.

Dodge, K. A. (1983). Behavioral antecedents of peer social status. *Child Development, 54*, 1386–1399.

Dodge, K. A., Lansford, J., Burks, V., Bates, J. E., Pettit, G., Fontaine, R., et al. (2003). Peer rejection and social information-processing factors in the development of aggressive behavior problems in children. *Child Development, 74*, 374–393.

Dodge, K. A., Murphy, R. R., & Buchsbaum, K. (1984). The assessment of intention-cue detection skills in children: Implications for developmental psychopathology. *Child Development, 55*, 163–173.

Dodge, K. A., & Price, J. M. (1994). On the relation between social information processing and socially competence behavior in early school-aged children. *Child Development, 65*, 1385–1397.

Dodge, K. A., Schlundt, D. G., Schocken, I., & Delugach, J. D. (1983). Social competence and children's social status: The role of peer group entry strategies. *Merrill-Palmer Quarterly, 29*, 309–336.

Domino, G. (1992). Cooperation and competition in Chinese and American children. *Journal of Cross-Cultural Psychology, 23*, 456–467.

Downey, G., Lebolt, A., Rincon, C., & Freitas, A. L. (1998). Rejection sensitivity and children's interpersonal difficulties. *Child Development, 69*, 1074–1091.

Doyle, A. (1982). Friends, acquaintances, and strangers: The influence of familiarity and ethnolinguistic background on social interaction. In K. H. Rubin & H. S. Ross (Eds.), *Peer relations and social skills in childhood.* New York: Springer-Verlag.

Eckerman, C. O. (1979). The human infant in social interaction. In R. Cairns (Ed.), *The analysis of social interactions: Methods, issues, and illustrations* (pp. 163–178). Hillsdale, NJ: Lawrence Erlbaum Associates.

Egeland, B., Pianta, R., & O'Brien, M. A. (1993). Maternal intrusiveness in infancy and child maladaptation in early school years. *Development & Psychopathology, 5*(3), 359–370.

Eisenberg, N., Cumberland, A., Spinrad, T. L., Fabes, R. A., Shepard, S. A., Reiser, M., et al. (2001). The relations of regulation and emotionality to children's externalizing and internalizing problem behavior. *Child Development, 72*, 1112–1134.

Eisenberg, N., Fabes, R. A., & Spinrad, T. L (2006). Prosocial development. In W. Damon & R. M. Lerner (Series Ed.) & N. Eisenberg (Vol. Ed.), *Handbook of child psychology: Vol. 3. Social, emotional, and personality development* (6th ed., pp. 646–718). New York: Wiley.

Erdley, C. A., & Asher, S. R. (1996). Children's social goals and self-efficacy perceptions as influences on their responses to ambiguous provocation. *Child Development, 67*, 1329–1344.

Espelage, D. L., Holt, M. K., & Henkel, R. R. (2003). Examination of peer-group contextual effects on aggression during early adolescence. *Child Development, 74*, 205–220.

Fabes, R.A., Eisenberg, N., Jones, S., Smith, M., Guthrie, I., Poulin, R., et al. (1999). Regulation, emotionality, and preschoolers' socially competent peer interactions. *Child Development, 70*, 432–442.

Fine, G. A. (1987). *With the boys: Little league baseball and preadolescent culture.* Chicago: University of Chicago Press.

Finnie, V., & Russell, A. (1988). Preschool children's social status and their mothers' behavior and knowledge in the supervisory role. *Developmental Psychology, 24*, 789–801.

Fogel, A. (1979). Peer- vs. mother-directed behavior in 1- to 3-month old infants. *Infant Behavior and Development, 2*, 215–226.

Fox, N. A. & Calkins, S. (1993). Relations between temperament, attachment, and behavioral inhibition: Two possible pathways to extroversion and social withdrawal. In K. H. Rubin & J. Asendorpf (Eds.), *Social withdrawal, inhibition, and shyness in childhood* (pp. 81–100). Chicago: University of Chicago Press.

Franzoi, S. L., Davis, M. H., & Vasquez-Suson, K.A. (1994). Two social worlds: Social correlates and stability of adolescent status groups. *Journal of Personality and Social Psychology, 67*, 462–473.

French, D. C., Jansen, E. A., Rianasari, M., & Setiono, K. (2003). Friendships of Indonesian children: Adjustment of children who differ in friendship presence and similarity between mutual friends. *Social Development, 12*, 605–621.

French, D. C., Setiono, K., & Eddy, J. M. (1999). Bootstrapping through the cultural comparison minefield: Childhood social status and friendship in the United States and Indonesia. In W. A. Collins & B. Laursen (Eds.). *Relationships as developmental contexts: Minnesota symposium on child psychology* (Vol. 30, pp. 109–131). Hillsdale, NJ: Lawrence Erlbaum Associates.

Freud, S. (1933). *New introductory lectures on psychoanalysis.* New York: Norton.

Furman, W., Simon, V., Shaffer, L., & Bouchey, H. A. (2002). Adolescents' working models and styles for relationships with parents, friends, and romantic partners. *Child Development, 73*, 241–255.

Galen, B. R. & Underwood, M. K. (1997). A developmental investigation of social aggression among children. *Developmental Psychology, 33*, 589–600.

Garvey, C. (1984). Children's talk. Cambridge, MA: Harvard University Press.

Gazelle, H. (2008). Behavioral profiles of anxious solitary children and heterogeneity in peer relations. *Developmental Psychology, 44*, 1604–1624.

Gazelle, H., & Ladd, G. W. (2003). Anxious solitude and peer exclusion: A diathesis-stress model of internalizing trajectories in childhood. *Child Development, 74*, 257–278.

Gazelle, H., & Rudolph, K. D. (2004). Moving toward and away from the world: Social approach and avoidance trajectories in anxious solitary youth. *Child Development, 75*, 1–21.

Genyue, F., & Lee, K. (2007). Social grooming in the kindergarten: The emergence of flattery behavior. *Developmental Science, 10*, 255–265.

Gershman, E. S., & Hayes, D. S. (1983). Differential stability of reciprocal friendships and unilateral relationships among preschool children. *Merrill-Palmer Quarterly, 29*, 169–177.

Gest, S. D. (1997). Behavioral inhibition: Stability and association with adaptation from childhood to early adulthood. *Journal of Personality and Social Psychology, 72*, 467–475.

Goldsmith, H. H., Buss, A., Plomin, R., Rothbart, M. K., Thomas, A., Chess, S., et al. (1987). What is temperament? Four approaches. *Child Development, 58*, 505–529.

Goldstein, H., Kaczmarek, L. A., & English, K. M. (2002). *Promoting social communication: Children with developmental disabilities from birth to adolescence*. Baltimore: Brookes.

Goncu, A. (1993). Development of intersubjectivity in the dyadic play of preschoolers. *Early Childhood Research Quarterly, 8*, 99–116.

Granot, D., & Mayseless, O. (2001). Attachment security and adjustment to school in middle childhood. *International Journal of Behavioral Development, 25*(6), 530–541.

Greenberg, M. T., Speltz, M. L., and Deklyen, M. (1993). The role of attachment in the early development of disruptive behavior problems. *Development and Psychopathology, 5*, 191–213.

Greenfield, P. M. (1994). Independence and interdependence as developmental scripts: Implications for theory, research, and practice. In P. M. Greenfield & R. R. Cocking (Eds.), *Cross-cultural roots of minority child development* (pp. 1–40). Hillsdale, NJ: Lawrence Erlbaum Associates.

Grotpeter, J. K., & Crick, N. R. (1996). Relational aggression, overt aggression, and friendship. *Child Development, 67*, 2328–2338.

Guerin, D. W., Gottfried, A. W., & Thomas, C. W. (1997). Difficult temperament and behavior problems: A longitudinal study from 1.5 to 12 years. *International Journal of Behavioural Development, 21*, 71–90.

Hane, A. A., Cheah, C. S. L., Rubin, K. H., & Fox, N. A. (2008). The role of maternal behavior in the relation between shyness and social withdrawal in early childhood and social withdrawal in middle childhood. *Social Development, 17*, 795–811.

Hardy, C. L., Bukowski, W. M., & Sippola, L. K. (2002). Stability and change in peer relationships during the transition to middle-level school. *Journal of Early Adolescence, 22*(2), 117–142.

Harris, J. R. (1995). Where is the child's environment? A group socialization theory of development. *Psychological Review, 102*(3), 458–489.

Harris, J. R. (1999). How to succeed in childhood. In S.J. Ceci & W. Williams (Eds.), The nature–nurture debate: The essential readings (pp. 84–95). Malden, MA: Blackwell.

Harris, J. R. (2009). *The nurture assumption: Why children turn out the way they do*. New York: Free Press.

Hart, C. H., DeWolf, M. D., Wozniak, P., & Burts, D. C. (1992). Maternal and paternal disciplinary styles: Relations with preschoolers' playground behavioral orientations and peer status. *Child Development, 63*, 879–892.

Hart, C. H., Ladd, G. W., & Burleson, B. R. (1990). Children's expectations of the outcomes of social strategies: Relations with sociometric status and maternal disciplinary styles. *Child Development, 61*, 127–137.

Hart, C. H., Yang, C., Nelson, L. J., Robinson, C. C., Olsen, J. A., Nelson, D. A., et al. (2000). Peer acceptance in early childhood and subtypes of socially withdrawn behaviour in China, Russia and the United States. *International Journal of Behavioral Development, 24*, 73–81.

Harter, S. (1998). The development of self-representations. In N. Eisenberg (Ed), *Handbook of child psychology: Social, emotional, and personality development* (5th ed., pp. 553–618). New York: Wiley.

Hartup, W. W. (1983). Peer relations. In E. M. Hetherington (Ed.), *Handbook of child psychology: Vol. 4. Socialization, personality and social development* (4th ed., pp. 103–196). New York: Wiley.

Hartup, W. W. (1992). Social relationships and their developmental significance. *American Psychologist, 44*, 120–126.

Hartup, W. W. (1996). The company they keep: Friendships and their developmental significance. *Child Development, 67*, 1–13.

Hartup, W. W., Brady, J. E., & Newcomb, A. F. (1983). Social cognition and social interaction in childhood. In E. T. Higgins, D. N. Ruble, & W. W. Hartup (Eds.), *Social cognition and social development*. New York: Cambridge University Press.

Hartup, W. W., & Laursen, B. (1995). Conflict and context in peer relations. In C. H. Hart (Ed.), *Children on playgrounds*. Ithaca, NY: State University of New York Press.

Hartup, W. W., Laursen, B., Stewart, M. A., & Eastenson, A. (1998). Conflicts and the friendship relations of young children. *Child Development, 69*, 1590–1600.

Hartup, W. H., & Stevens, N. (1999). Friendships and adaptation across the life span. *Current Directions in Psychological Science, 8*, 76–79.

Haselager, G. J. T., Cillissen, H. N., Van Lieshout, C. F. M., Riksen-Walraven, J. M. A., & Hartup, W. W. (2002). Heterogeneity among peer-rejected boys across middle childhood: Developmental pathways of social behavior. *Child Development, 73*, 446–456.

Haselager, G. J. T., Hartup, W. M., van Lieshout, C. F. M., & Riksen-Walraven, J. M. (1998). Similarities between friends and nonfriends in middle childhood. *Child Development, 69*(4), 1198–1208.

Hastings, P. D., Nuselovici, J. N., Rubin, K. H., & Cheah, C. S. L. (2010). Shyness, parenting, and parent–child relationships. In K. H. Rubin & R. J. Coplan (Eds), *The development of shyness and social withdrawal in childhood and adolescence* (pp. 107–130). New York: Guilford.

Hawley, P. H. (2003). Prosocial and coercive configurations of resource control in early adolescence: A case for the well-adapted Machiavellian. *Merrill-Palmer Quarterly, 49*, 279–309.

Hay, D. F. & Cook, K. V. (2007). The transformation of prosocial behavior from infancy to childhood. In

C. A. Brownell & C. B. Kopp (Eds.), *Socioemotional development in the toddler years: Transitions and transformations* (100–131). New York: Guilford Press.

Hay, D. F., Pederson, J., & Nash, A. (1982). Dyadic interaction in the first year of life. In K. H. Rubin & H. S. Ross (Eds.), *Peer relationships and social skills in childhood*. New York: Springer-Verlag.

Hektner, J. M., August, G. J., & Realmuto, G. M. (2000). Patterns and temporal changes in peer affiliation among aggressive and nonaggressive children participating in a summer school program. *Journal of Clinical Child Psychology*, *29*(4), 603–614.

Henderson, H. A., Marshall, P. J., Fox, N. A., & Rubin, K. H. (2004). Psychophysiological and behavioral evidence for varying forms and functions of nonsocial behavior in preschoolers. *Child Development*, *75*, 251–263.

Hinde, R. A. (1987). *Individuals, relationships and culture*. Cambridge, UK: Cambridge University Press.

Hinde, R. R. & Stevenson-Hinde, J. (1976). Toward understanding relationships: Dynamic stability. In P. Bateson & R. Hinde (Eds.), *Growing points in ethology* (pp. 451–479). Cambridge, UK: Cambridge University Press.

Hodges, E. V. E., Boivin, M., Vitaro, F., & Bukowksi, W. M. (1999). The power of friendship protection against an escalating cycle of peer victimization. *Developmental Psychology*, *35*(1), 94–101.

Hogue, A., & Steinberg, L. (1995). Homophily of internalized distress in adolescent peer groups. *Developmental Psychology*, *31*(6), 897–906.

Horn, S. (2003). Adolescents' reasoning about exclusion from social groups. *Developmental Psychology*, *39*(1), 71–84.

Howes, C. (1988). Peer interaction of young children. *Monographs of the Society for Research in Child Development*, *53* (No. 217).

Howes, C., & Matheson, C. C. (1992). Sequences in the development of competent play with peers: Social and social-pretend play. *Developmental Psychology*, *28*, 961–974.

Hubbard, J. A. (2001). Emotion expression processes in children's peer interaction: The role of peer rejection, aggression, and gender. *Child Development*, *72*, 1426–1438.

Hubbard, J. A., Dodge, K. A., Cillessen, A. H. N., Coie, J. D., & Schwartz, D. (2001). The dyadic nature of social information processing in boys' reactive and proactive aggression. *Journal of Personality and Social Psychology*, *80*, 268–280.

Hymel, S., Rubin, K. H., Rowden, L., & LeMare, L. (1990a). Children's peer relationships: Longitudinal predictions of internalizing and externalizing problems from middle to late childhood. *Child Development*, *61*, 2004–2021.

Hymel, S., Wagner, E., & Butler, L. (1990b). Reputational bias: View from the peer group. In S. R. Asher & J. Coie (Eds.), *Peer rejection in childhood* (pp. 156–186). Cambridge, UK: Cambridge University Press.

Isaacs, S. (1933). *Social development in young children: A study of beginnings*. London: Routledge.

Iverson, A. M., Barton, E. A., & Iverson, G. L (1997). Analysis of risk to children participating in a sociometric task. *Developmental Psychology*, *33*, 104–112.

Izard, C. E. (2009). Emotion theory and research: Highlights, unanswered questions, and emerging issues. *Annual Review of Psychology*, *60*, 1–25.

Jacobson, J. L. (1981). The role of inanimate objects in early peer interaction. *Child Development*, *52*, 618–626.

Kerns, K. A., Cole, A. K., & Andrews, P. B. (1998). Attachment security, parent peer management practices, and peer relationships in preschoolers. *Merrill-Palmer Quarterly*, *44*, 504–522.

Kerns, K. A., Klepac, L., & Cole, A. (1996). Peer relationships and preadolescents' perceptions of security in the child–mother relationship. *Developmental Psychology*, *33*, 703–710.

Kiesner, J., Poulin, F., & Nicotra, E. (2003). Peer relations across contexts: Individual–network homophily and network inclusion in and after school. *Child Development*, *74*(5), 1328–1343.

Kindermann, T. A. (1993). Natural peer groups as contexts for individual development: The case of children's motivation in school. *Developmental Psychology*, *29*, 970–977.

Kindermann, T. A., McCollom, T. L., & Gibson, E., Jr. (1995). Peer networks and students' classroom engagement during childhood and adolescence. In K. Wentzel & J. Juvonen (Eds.), *Social motivation: Understanding children's school adjustment*. New York: Cambridge University Press.

Kistner, J., Balthazor, M., Risi, S., & Burton, C. (1999). Predicting dysphoria from actual and perceived acceptance in childhood. *Journal of Clinical Child Psychology*, *28*, 94–104.

Kraatz-Keily, M., Bates, J. E., Dodge, K. A., & Pettit, G. S. (2000). A cross-domain analysis: Externalizing and internalizing behaviors during 8 years of childhood. *Journal of Abnormal Child Psychology*, *28*, 161–179.

Krasnor, L., & Rubin, K. H. (1983). Preschool social problem solving: Attempts and outcomes in naturalistic interaction. *Child Development*, *54*, 1545–1558.

Kupersmidt, J. B., & Coie, J. D. (1990). Preadolescent peer status, aggression, and school adjustment as predictors of externalizing problems in adolescence. *Child Development*, *61*, 1350–1362.

Kupersmidt, J., DeRosier, M., & Patterson, C. (1995). Similarity as the basis for children's friendships: The roles of sociometric status, aggressive and withdrawn behavior, academic achievement and demographic characteristics. *Journal of Social and Personal Relationships*, *12*, 439–452.

Ladd, G. W., & Burgess, K. B. (1999). Charting the relationship trajectories of aggressive, withdrawn, and aggressive/withdrawn children during early grade school. *Child Development*, *70*(4), 910–929.

Ladd, G. W., & Burgess, K. B. (2001). Do relational risks and protective factors moderate the linkages between childhood aggression and early psychological and school adjustment? *Child Development, 72*, 1579–1601.

Ladd, G. W., & Golter, B. (1988). Parents' initiation and monitoring of children's peer contacts: Predictive of children's peer relations in nonschool and school settings? *Developmental Psychology, 24*, 109–117.

Ladd, G. W., & Hart, C. H. (1992). Creating informal play opportunities: Are parents' and preschoolers' initations related to children's competence with peers? *Developmental Psychology, 28*, 1179–1187.

Ladd, G. W., Hart, C. H., Wadsworth, E. M., & Golter, B. S. (1988) Preschoolers' peer networks in nonschool settings: Relationship to family characteristics and school adjustment. In S. Salzinger, J. Antrobus, & M. Hammer (Eds.), *Social networks of children, adolescents, and college students.* Hillsdale, NJ: Lawrence Erlbaum Associates.

Ladd, G. W., & Price, J. M. (1986). Promoting children's cognitive and social competence: The relation between parents' perceptions of task difficulty and children's perceived and actual competence. *Child Development, 57*, 446–460.

Ladd, G. W., & Profilet, S. M. (1996). The child behavior scale: A teacher report measure of young children's aggressive, withdrawn, and prosocial behaviors. *Developmental Psychology, 32*, 1008–1024.

Ladd, G. W., & Troop-Gordon, W. (2003). The role of chronic peer difficulties in the development of children's psychological adjustment problems. *Child Development, 74*, 1344–1367.

Laird, R. D., Jordan, K. Y., Dodge, K. A., Pettit, G. S., & Bates, J. E. (2001). Peer rejection in childhood, involvement with antisocial peers in early adolescence, and the development of externalizing behavior problems. *Development and Psychopathology, 13*, 337–354.

LaFontana, K. M., & Cillessen, A. H. N. (1998). The nature of children's stereotypes of popularity. *Social Development, 7*, 301–320.

LaFontana, K. M., & Cillessen, A. H. N. (1999). Children's interpersonal perceptions as a function of sociometric and peer-perceived popularity. *Journal of Genetic Psychology, 160*, 225–242.

LaFontana, K. M., & Cillessen, A. H. N. (2002). Children's perceptions of popular and unpopular peers: A multimethod assessment. *Developmental Psychology, 38*, 635–647.

La Greca, A., Prinstein, M., & Fetter, M. (2001). Adolescent peer crowd affiliation: Linkages with health-risk behaviors and close friendships. *Journal of Pediatric Psychology, 26*(3), 131–143.

Langlois, J. H., & Stephan, C. W. (1981). Beauty and the beast: The role of physical attraction in peer relationships and social behavior. In S. S. Brehm, S. M. Kassin, & S. X. Gibbans (Eds.), *Developmental social psychology: Theory and research* (pp. 152–168). New York: Oxford University Press.

Laursen, B., Bukowski, W., Aunola, K., & Nurmi, J. (2007). Friendship moderates prospective associations between social isolation and adjustment problems in young children. *Child Development, 78*, 1395–1404.

Laursen, B., Hartup, W. W., & Keplas, A. L. (1996). Towards understanding peer conflict. *Merrill-Palmer Quarterly, 42*, 76–102.

Ledingham, J., Younger, A., Schwartzman, A., & Bergeron, G. (1982). Agreement among teacher, peer and self-ratings of children's aggression, withdrawal and likeability. *Journal of Abnormal Child Psychology, 10*, 363–372.

Lee, K., & Cameron, A. (2000). Extracting truthful information from lies: Emergence of the expression–representation distinction. *Merrill-Palmer Quarterly, 46*, 1–20.

Lemerise, E. A., & Arsenio, W. F. (2000). An integrated model of emotion processes and cognition in social information processing. *Child Development, 71*, 107–108.

Levin, E., & Rubin, K. H. (1983). Getting others to do what you wanted them to do: The development of children's requestive strategies. In K. Nelson (Ed.), *Child language* (Vol. 4). Hillsdale, NJ: Lawrence Erlbaum Associates.

Lieberman, M., Doyle, A., & Markiewicz, D. (1999). Developmental patterns in security of attachment to mother and father in late childhood and early adolescence: Associations with peer relations. *Child Development, 70*(1), 202–213.

London, B., Downey, G., Bonica, C., & Paltin, I. (2007). Social causes and consequences of rejection sensitivity. *Journal of Research on Adolescence, 17*, 481–506.

Luo, G. (1996). *Chinese traditional social and moral ideas and rules.* Beijing, China: The University of Chinese People Press.

Lyons-Ruth, K., Easterbrooks, M. A., & Cibelli, C. D. (1997). Infant attachment strategies, infant mental lag, and maternal depressive symptoms: Predictors of internalizing and externalizing problems at age 7. *Developmental Psychology, 33*(4), 681–692.

Maccoby, E. E. (1995). The two sexes and their social systems. In P. Moen, G. H. Elder, Jr., & K. Luescher (Eds.), *Examining lives in context: Perspectives on the ecology of human development* (pp. 347–364). Washington, DC: American Psychological Association.

Masten, A. S., Morison, P., & Pellegrini, D. S. (1985). A Revised Class Play method of peer assessment. *Developmental Psychology, 3*, 523–533.

McDonald, K. L., Putallaz, M., Grimes, C. L., Kupersmidt, J. B., & Coie, J. D. (2006). Girl talk: Gossip, friendship, and sociometric status. *Merrill-Palmer Quarterly, 53*, 381–411.

McDowell, D. J., Parke, R. D., & Wang, S. (2003). Differences between mothers' and fathers' advice-giving style and content: Relations with social competence and psychological functioning in middle childhood. *Merrill-Palmer Quarterly*, *49*, 55–76.

McElwain, N. L., & Volling, B. L. (2004). Attachment security and parental sensitivity during infancy: Associations with friendship quality and false belief understanding at age four. *Journal of Social and Personal Relationships*, *21*, 639–667.

McNeilley-Choque, M. K., Hart, C. H., Robinson, C. C., Nelson, L. J., & Olsen, S. F. (1996). Overt and relational aggression on the playground: Correspondence among different informants. *Journal of Research in Childhood Education*, *11*, 47–67.

Mead, G. H. (1934). *Mind, self, and society*. Chicago: University of Chicago Press.

Merten, D. E. (1997). The meaning of meanness: popularity, competition, and conflict among junior high school girls. *Sociology of Education*, *70*, 175–191.

Mesch, G., & Talmud, I. (2007). Similarity and the quality of online and offline social relationships among adolescents in Israel. *Journal of Research on Adolescence*, *17*, 455–466.

Miller-Johnson, S., Coie, J. D., Maumary-Gremaud, A., Bierman, K. & The Conduct Problems Prevention Research Group (2002). Peer rejection and aggression and early starter models of conduct disorder. *Journal of Abnormal Child Psychology*, *30*, 217–230.

Miller-Johnson, S., Coie, J., Maumary-Gremaud, A., Lochman, J., & Terry, R. (1999). Relationship between childhood peer rejection and aggression and adolescent delinquency severity and type among African-American youth. *Journal of Emotional and Behavioral Disorders*, *7*, 137–146.

Mize, J., & Pettit, G. S. (1997). Mother's social coaching, mother–child relationship style, and children's peer competence: Is the medium the message? *Child Development*, *68*(2), 312–332.

Moreno, J. L. (1934). *Who shall survive? A new approach to the problem of human inter-relations*. Washington, DC: Nervous and Mental Disease Publishing Co.

Moskowitz, D. S., Schwartzman, A. E., & Ledingham, J. E. (1985). Stability and change in aggression and withdrawal in middle childhood and early adolescence. *Journal of Abnormal Psychology*, *94*, 30–41.

Mueller, E., & Silverman, N. (1989). Peer relations in maltreated children. In D. Cicchetti & V. Carlson (Eds.), *Child mistreatment: Theory and research on the causes and consequences of child abuse and neglect* (pp. 529–578). New York: Cambridge University Press.

Newcomb, A. F. & Bagwell, C. (1995). Children's friendship relations: A meta-analytic review. *Psychological Bulletin*, *117*, 306–347.

Newcomb, A. F. & Bukowski, W. M. (1984). A longitudinal study of the utility of social preference and social impact sociometric classification schemes. *Child Development*, *55*, 1434–1447.

Newcomb, A. F., & Bukowski, W. M., & Pattee, L. (1993). Children's peer relations: A meta-analyic review of popular, rejected, neglected, controversial, and average sociometric status. *Psychological Bulletin*, *113*, 99–128.

NICHD Early Child Care Research Network (2001). Child care and children's peer interaction at 24 and 36 months: The NICHD study of early child care. *Child Development*, *72*, 1478–1500.

Northway, M. L. (1944). Outsiders: A study of the personality patterns of children least acceptable to their age mates. *Sociometry*, *7*, 10–25.

Oh, W., Rubin, K. H., Bowker, J. C., Booth-LaForce, C., Rose-Krasnor, L., & Laursen, B. (2008). Trajectories of social withdrawal from middle childhood to early adolescence. *Journal of Abnormal Child Psychology*, *36*(4), 553–566.

Olweus, D. (1993) Victimization by peers: Antecedents and long-term outcomes. In K. H. Rubin & J. B. Asendorf (Eds.), *Social withdrawal, inhibition, and shyness in childhood*. Hillsdale, NJ: Lawrence Erlbaum Associates.

Orobio de Castro, B., Veerman, J. W., Koops, W., Bosch, J. D., & Monshouwer, H. J. (2002). Hostile attribution of intent and aggressive behavior: A meta-analysis. *Child Development*, *73*(3), 916–934.

Pakaslahti, L., Karjalainen, A., & Keltikangas-Jarvinen, L. (2002). Relationships between adolescent prosocial problem-solving strategies, prosocial behaviour, and social acceptance. *International Journal of Behavioral Development*, *26*, 137–144.

Parke, R. D., Burks, V. M., Carson, J. L., Neville, B., & Boyum, L.A. (1994). Family–peer relationships: A tripartite model. In R. D. Parke & S. G. Kellam (Eds.), *Exploring family relationships with other social contexts*. Hillsdale, NJ: Lawrence Erlbaum Associates.

Parke, R. D., & O'Neil, R. (1999). Social relationships across contexts: Family–peer linkages. In W. A. Collins & B. Laursen (Eds.), *Minnesota symposium on child psychology* (Vol. 30, pp. 211–239). Hillsdale, NJ: Lawrence Erlbaum Associates.

Parker, J. G., & Asher, S. R. (1987). Peer relations and later personal adjustment: Are low-accepted children at risk? *Psychological Bulletin*, *102*, 357–389.

Parker, J. G., & Asher, S. R. (1993). Friendship and friendship quality in middle childhood: Links with peer group acceptance and feelings of loneliness and social dissatisfaction. *Developmental Psychology*, *29*, 611–621.

Parker, J. G., & Gottman, J. M. (1989). Social and emotional development in a relational context: Friendship interaction from early childhood to adolescence. In T. J. Berndt & G. W. Ladd (Eds.), *Peer relations in child development* (pp. 15–45). New York: Wiley-Interscience.

Parker, J. G. & Seal, J. (1996). Forming, losing, renewing, and replacing friendships: Applying temporal parameters to the assessment of children's friendship experiences. *Child Development, 67*, 2248–2268.

Parkhurst, J. T., & Asher, S. R. (1992). Peer rejection in middle school: Subgroup differences in behavior, loneliness, and interpersonal concerns. *Developmental Psychology, 28*, 231–241.

Parkhurst, J. T., & Hopmeyer, A. (1998). Sociometric popularity and peer-perceived popularity: Two distinct dimensions of peer status. *Journal of Early Adolescence, 18*, 125–144.

Parten, M. B. (1932). Social participation among preschool children. *Journal of Abnormal and Social Psychology, 27*, 243–269.

Patterson, G. R. (1983). Stress: A change agent for family process. In N. Garmezy & M. Rutter (Eds.) *Stress, coping, and development in children* (pp. 235–264). Baltimore: Johns Hopkins University Press.

Patterson, G., & Sanson, A. (1999). The association of behavioral adjustment to temperament, parenting and family characteristics among 5-year-old children. *Social Development, 8*, 293–309.

Pepler, D. J., & Craig, W. (1995). A peek behind the fence: Naturalistic observations of aggressive behavior with remote audiovisual recording. *Developmental Psychology, 31*, 548–553.

Perry, D. G., Perry, L. C., & Rasmussen, P. (1986). Cognitive social learning mediators of aggression. *Child Development, 57*, 700–711.

Pettit, G. S., and Mize, J. (1993). Substance and style: Understanding the ways in which parents teach children about social relationships. In S. Duck (Ed.), *Learning about relationships* (pp. 118–151). Newbury Park, CA: Sage.

Piaget, J. (1932). *The moral judgment of the child.* Glencoe, IL: Free Press.

Popp, D., Laursen, B., Kerr, M., Burk, W., & Stattin, H. (2008). Modeling homophily over time with an actor–partner interdependence model. *Developmental Psychology, 44*, 1028–1039.

Poulin, F., & Pedersen, S. (2007). Developmental changes in gender composition of friendship networks in adolescent girls and boys. *Developmental Psychology, 43*(6), 1484–1496.

Prinstein, M. J., & La Greca, A. M. (2004). Childhood rejection, aggression, and depression as predictors of adolescent girls' externalizing and health risk behaviors: A six-year longitudinal study. *Journal of Consulting and Clinical Psychology, 72*, 103–112.

Prior, M., Smart, D., Sanson, A., & Oberklaid, F. (2000). Does shy-inhibited temperament in childhood lead to anxiety problems in adolescence? *Journal of the American Academy of Child and Adolescent Psychiatry, 39*, 461–468.

Putallaz, M., & Wasserman, A. (1990). Children's entry behaviors. In S. R. Asher & J. D. Coie (Eds.), *Peer rejection in childhood.* New York: Cambridge University Press.

Quiggle, N., Garber, J., Panak, W., & Dodge, K. A. (1992). Social-information processing in aggressive and depressed children. *Child Development, 63*, 1305–1320.

Rabiner, D., & Gordon, L. (1992). The coordination of conflicting social goals: Differences between rejected and nonrejected boys. *Child Development, 63*, 1344–1350.

Raudenbush, S. W., & Bryk, A. S. (2002). *Hierarchical linear models: Applications and data analysis methods.* Thousand Oaks, CA: Sage.

Richards, W. D. (1995). *NEGOPY 4.30 manual and user's guide.* Burnaby, Canada: Simon Fraser University.

Rodkin, P. C., Farmer, T. W., Pearl, R., & Van Acker, R. (2000). Heterogeneity of popular boys: Antisocial and prosocial configurations. *Developmental Psychology, 36*, 14–24.

Rodkin, P. C., Farmer, T. W., Pearl, R., & Van Acker, R. (2006). They're cool: Social status and peer group supports for aggressive boys and girls. *Social Development, 15*, 175–204.

Rose, A. J. (2002). Co-rumination in the friendships of girls and boys. *Child Development, 73*, 1830–1843.

Rose, A. J., & Asher, S. R. (1999). Children's goals and strategies in response to conflicts within a friendship. *Developmental Psychology, 35*, 69–79.

Rose, A. J., Carlson, W., & Waller, E. M. (2007). Prospective associations of co-rumination with friendship and emotional adjustment: Considering the socioemotional trade-offs of co-rumination. *Developmental Psychology, 43*(4), 1019–1031.

Rose, A. J., & Rudolph, K. D. (2006). A review of sex differences in peer relationship processes: Potential trade-offs for the emotional and behavioral development of girls and boys. *Psychological Bulletin, 132*, 98–131.

Rose, A., Swenson, L., & Robert, C. (2009). Boys' and girls' motivations for refraining from prompting friends to talk about problems. *International Journal of Behavioral Development, 33*, 178–184.

Rose, A., Swenson, L., & Waller, E. (2004). Overt and relational aggression and perceived popularity: Developmental differences in concurrent and prospective relations. *Developmental Psychology, 40*, 378–387.

Rose-Krasnor, L., & Denham, S. (2009). Social and emotional competence in early childhood. In K. H. Rubin, W. Bukowski, & B. Laursen (Eds.), *Peer interactions, relationships, and groups* (pp. 162–179). New York: Guilford Press.

Rose-Krasnor, L., Rubin, K. H., Booth, C. L., and Coplan, R. (1996). Maternal directiveness and child attachment security as predictors of social competence in preschoolers. *International Journal of Behavioral Development*, *19*, 309–325.

Ross, H. S., & Conant, C. L. (1992). The social structure of early conflict: Interactions, relationships, and alliances. In C. U. Shantz & W. W. Hartup (Eds.), *Conflict in child and adolescent development*. Cambridge, UK: Cambridge University Press.

Ross, H. S., Lollis, S. P., & Elliot, C. (1982). Toddler–peer communication. In K. H. Rubin & H. S. Ross (Eds.), *Peer relationships and social skills in childhood*. New York: Springer-Verlag.

Rubin, K. H. (1982). Social and social-cognitive developmental characteristics of young isolate, normal and sociable children. In K. H. Rubin & H. S. Ross (Eds.), *Peer relationships and social skills in childhood* (pp. 353–374). New York: Springer-Verlag.

Rubin, K. H. (2001). *The Play Observation Scale (POS)*. University of Maryland, College Park. Available from author.

Rubin, K. H. (2002). *The friendship factor: Helping our children navigate their social world—and why it matters for their success and happiness*. New York: Viking Penguin.

Rubin, K. H., Bowker, J., & Kennedy, A. (2009). Avoiding and withdrawing from the peer group in middle childhood and early adolescence. In K. H. Rubin, W. Bukowski, & B. Laursen (Eds.), *Handbook of peer interactions, relationships, and groups* (pp. 303–321). New York: Guilford Press.

Rubin, K., Bukowski, W., & Parker, J. (2006a). Peer interactions, relationships, and groups. In W. Damon, R. Lerner, & N. Eisenberg (Eds.,) *Handbook of child psychology: Vol. 3. Social, emotional, and personality development* (6th ed., pp. 571–645). New York: Wiley.

Rubin, K. H. & Burgess, K. (2002). Parents of aggressive and withdrawn children. In M. Bornstein (Ed.), *Handbook of parenting* (2nd ed., Vol. 1, pp. 383–418). Hillsdale, NJ: Lawrence Erlbaum Associates.

Rubin, K. H., Burgess, K. B., Dwyer, K. D., & Hastings, P. (2003). Predicting preschoolers' externalizing behaviors from toddler temperament, conflict, and maternal negativity. *Developmental Psychology*, *39*, 164–176.

Rubin, K. H., Burgess, K. B., & Hastings, P. D. (2002). Stability and social–behavioral consequences of toddlers' inhibited temperament and parenting behaviors. *Child Development*, *73*, 483–495.

Rubin, K. H., Cheah, C. S. L., & Fox, N. (2001). Emotion regulation, parenting and display of social reticence in preschoolers. *Early Education & Development*, *12*, 97–115.

Rubin, K. H., Chen, X., & Hymel, S. (1993). Socioemotional characteristics of withdrawn and aggressive children. *Merrill-Palmer Quarterly*, *39*, 518–534.

Rubin, K. H., Chen, X., McDougall, P., Bowker, A., & McKinnon, J. (1995a). The Waterloo Longitudinal Project: Predicting internalizing and externalizing problems in adolescence. *Development and Psychopathology*, *7*, 751–764.

Rubin, K. H., Coplan, R. J., & Bowker, J. C. (2009). Social withdrawal in childhood. *Annual Review of Psychology*, *60*, 141–171.

Rubin, K. H., Coplan, R. J., Fox, N. A., & Calkins, S. (1995b). Emotionality, emotion regulation, and preschoolers' social adaptation. *Development and Psychopathology*, *7*, 49–62.

Rubin, K. H., Dwyer, K. M., Booth, C. L., Kim, A. H., Burgess, K. B., & Rose-Krasnor, L. (2004) Attachment, friendship, and psychosocial functioning in early adolescence. *Journal of Early Adolescence*, *24*, 326–356.

Rubin, K. H., & Krasnor, L. R. (1986). Social-cognitive and social behavioral perspectives on problem solving. In M. Perlmutter (Ed.), *Cognitive perspectives on children's social and behavioral development. The Minnesota symposia on child psychology* (Vol. 18, pp. 1–68). Hillsdale, NJ: Lawrence Erlbaum Associates.

Rubin, K. H., LeMare, L. & Lollis, S. (1990). Social withdrawal in childhood: Developmental pathways to peer rejection. In S. Asher & J. Coie (Eds.), *Peer rejection in childhood*. New York: Cambridge University Press (pp. 217–249).

Rubin, K. H., Lynch, D., Coplan, R., Rose-Krasnor, L., & Booth, C. L. (1994). "Birds of a feather . . .": Behavioral concordances and preferential personal attraction in children. *Child Development*, *65*, 1778–1785.

Rubin, K. H., & Mills, R. S. L. (1988). The many faces of social isolation in childhood. *Journal of Consulting and Clinical Psychology*, *6*, 916–924.

Rubin, K. H. & Rose-Krasnor, L. (1992). Interpersonal problem solving. In V. B. Van Hassat & M. Hersen (Eds.), *Handbook of social development* (pp. 283–323). New York: Plenum.

Rubin, K. H., Watson, K., & Jambor, T. (1978). Free play behaviors in preschool and kindergarten children. *Child Development*, *49*, 534–536.

Rubin, K. H., Wojslawowicz, J. C., Rose-Krasnor, L., Booth-LaForce, C., & Burgess, K. B. (2006b). The best friendships of shy/withdrawn children: Prevalence, stability, and relationship quality. *Journal of Abnormal Child Psychology*, *34*, 139–153.

Ruble, D. N., & Martin, C. L. (1998). Gender development. In N. Eisenberg (Ed.), *Handbook of child psychology: Vol 3. Social, emotional, and personality development* (pp. 933–1016). New York: Wiley.

Ryalls, B. O., Gull, R. E., & Ryalls, K. R. (2000). Infant imitation of peer and adult models: Evidence for a peer model advantage. *Merrill-Palmer-Quarterly*, *46*, 188–202.

Ryan, A. M. (2001). The peer group as a context for the development of young adolescent motivation and achievement. *Child Development*, *72*, 1135–1150.

Salmivalli, C. & Isaacs, J. (2005). Prospective relations among victimization, rejection, friendlessness, and children's self- and peer-perceptions. *Child Development*, *76*(6), 1161–1171.

Sandstrom, M. J., Cillessen, A. H. N., & Eisenhower, A. (2003). Children's appraisal of peer rejection experiences: Impact on social and emotional adjustment. *Social Development*, *12*, 530–550.

Sandstrom, M. J., & Coie, J. D. (1999). A developmental perspective on peer rejection: Mechanisms of stability and change. *Child Development*, *70*, 955–966.

Sawyer, R. K. (1997). *Pretend play as improvisation: Conversation in the preschool classroom*. Mahwah, NJ: Lawrence Erlbaum Associates.

Schneider, B. H. (1998). Cross-cultural comparison as doorkeeper in research on the social and emotional adjustment of children and adolescents. *Developmental Psychology*, *34*, 793–797.

Schneider, B. (1999). A multimethod exploration of the friendships of children considered socially withdrawn by their school peers. *Journal of Abnormal Child Psychology*, *27*, 115–123.

Schneider, B., & Tessier, N. (2007). Close friendship as understood by socially withdrawn, anxious early adolescents. *Child Psychiatry & Human Development*, *38*(4), 339–351.

Sears, R. R., Maccoby, E., & Levin, H. (1957). *Patterns of child rearing*. White Plains, NY: Peterson.

Selfhout, M., Branje, S., ter Bogt, T., & Meeus, W. H. J. (2009). The role of music preferences in early adolescents' friendship formation and stability. *Journal of Adolescence*, *32*, 95–107.

Selman, R.L. (1980). *The growth of interpersonal understanding*. New York: Cambridge University Press.

Selman, R. & Schultz, L. (1990). *Making a friend in youth: Developmental theory and pair therapy*. Chicago: University of Chicago Press.

Simpkins, S., & Parke, R. (2002). Do friends and nonfriends behave differently? A social relations analysis of children's behavior. *Merrill-Palmer Quarterly*, *48*, 263–283.

Spangler, G., & Schieche, M. (1998). Emotional and adrenocortical responses of infants to the strange situation: The differential function of emotional expression. *International Journal of Behavioral Development*, *22*, 681–706.

Sroufe, L. A., Egeland, B., Carlson, E. A., & Collins, W. A. (2005). Placing early attachment experiences in developmental context. In K. E. Grossmann, K. Grossmann, & E. Waters (Eds.), *Attachment from infancy to adulthood* (pp. 48–70). New York: Guilford Press.

Stewart, S. L. & Rubin, K. H. (1995). The social problem solving skills of anxious-withdrawn children. *Development and Psychopathology*, *7*, 323–336.

Strayer, F. F. & Santos, A. J. (1996). Affiliative structures in preschool peer groups. *Social Development*, *5*, 117–130.

Strayer, F. F., & Strayer, J. (1976). An ethological analysis of social agonism and dominance relations among preschool children. *Child Development*, *47*, 980–989.

Sullivan, H. S. (1953). *The interpersonal theory of psychiatry*. New York: Norton.

Tarrant, M. (2002). Adolescent peer groups and social identity. *Social Development*, *11*, 110–123.

Thorne, B., & Luria, Z. (2001). Sexuality and gender in children's daily worlds. In J. M. Henslin (Ed.), *Down to earth sociology: Introductory readings* (11th ed., pp. 156–167). New York: The Free Press.

Tomada, G., & Schneider, B. H. (1997). Relational aggression, gender, and peer acceptance: Invariance across culture, stability over time, and concordance among informants. *Developmental Psychology*, *33*, 601–609.

Tomada, G., Schneider, B., & Fonzi, A. (2002). Verbal and nonverbal interactions of four- and five-year-old friends in potential conflict situations. *Journal of Genetic Psychology*, *163*, 327–339.

Trevarthen, C. (1979). Communication and cooperation in early infancy: A description of primary intersubjectivity. In M. Bullowa (Ed.), *Before speech* (pp. 321–347). Cambridge, UK: Cambridge University Press.

Triandis, H. C. (1990). Cross-cultural studies of individualism and collectivism. *Nebraska Symposium on Motivation* (Vol. 37, pp. 41–133). Lincoln, NE: University of Nebraska Press.

Troop-Gordon, W. P., & Asher, S. R. (2005). Modifications in children's goals when encountering obstacles to conflict resolution. *Child Development*, *76*, 568–582.

Urberg, K. A., Degirmencioglu, S. M., & Pilgrim, C. (1997). Close friend and group influence on adolescent cigarette smoking and alcohol use. *Developmental Psychology*, *33*, 834–844.

Vaillancourt, T., & Hymel, S. (2006). Aggression and social status: The moderating roles of sex and peer-valued characteristics. *Aggressive Behavior*, *32*, 396–408.

Vaish, A., Carpenter, M., & Tomasello, M. (2009). Sympathy through affective perspective taking and its relation to prosocial behavior in toddlers. *Developmental Psychology*, *45*(2), 534–543.

Vaughn, B. E., & Santos, A. J. (2009). Structural descriptions of social transactions among young children: Affiliation and dominance in preschool groups. In K. H. Rubin, W. Bukowski, & B. Laursen (Eds.), *Handbook of peer interactions, relationships, and groups* (pp. 195–214). New York: Guilford Press.

Verba, M. (1994). The beginnings of collaboration in peer interaction. *Human Development*, *37*, 125–139.

Vitaro, F., Boivin, M., & Bukowski, W. M. (2009). The role of friendship in child and adolescent psychosocial development. In K. H. Rubin, W. Bukowski, & B. Laursen (Eds.), *Peer interactions, relationships, and groups* (pp. 568–588). New York: Guilford Press.

Vitaro, F., Brendgen, M., & Tremblay, R. (2000). Influence of deviant friends on delinquency: Searching for moderator variables. *Journal of Abnormal Child Psychology, 28*, 313–325.

Vitaro, F., Tremblay, R. E., Kerr, M., Pagani, L., & Bukowski, W. M. (1997). Disruptiveness, friends' characteristics, and delinquency in early adolescence: A test of two competing models of development. *Child Development, 68*, 676–689.

Volling, B. L., MacKinnon-Lewis, C., Rabiner, D., & Baradaran, L. P. (1993). Children's social competence and sociometric status: Further exploration of aggression, social withdrawal, and peer rejection. *Development and Psychopathology, 5*, 459–483.

Wachs, T. D., & Kohstamm, G. A. (2001). *Temperament in context*. Mahwah, NJ: Lawrence Erlbaum Associates.

Warneken, F., Chen, F., & Tomasello, M. (2006). Cooperative activities in young children and chimpanzees. *Child Development, 77*, 640–663.

Wentzel, K. R. (2003). Sociometric status and adjustment in middle school: A longitudinal study. *Journal of Early Adolescence, 23*, 5–28.

Wentzel, K. R., & Asher, S. R. (1995). The academic lives of neglected, rejected, popular, and controversial children *Child Development, 66*, 754–763.

Wentzel, K. R., McNamara-Barry, C., & Caldwell, K. A. (2004). Friendships in middle school: Influences on motivation and school adjustment. *Journal of Educational Psychology, 96*(2), 195–203.

Wheeler, V. A., & Ladd, G. W. (1982). Assessment of children's self-efficacy for social interactions with peers. *Developmental Psychology, 18*, 795–805.

Wichmann, C., Coplan, R. J., & Daniels, T. (2004). The social cognitions of socially withdrawn children. *Social Development, 13*, 377–392.

Windle, M. A. (1994). A study of friendship characteristics and problem behaviors among middle adolescents. *Child Development, 65*, 1764–1777.

Wojslawowicz Bowker, J. C., Rubin, K. H., Burgess, K. B., Booth-LaForce, C., & Rose-Krasnor, L. (2006). Behavioral characteristics associated with stable and fluid best friendship patterns in middle childhood. *Merrill-Palmer Quarterly, 52*(4), 671–693.

Xie, H., Cairns, B. D., & Cairns, R. B. (2001). Predicting teen motherhood and teen fatherhood: Individual characteristics and peer affiliations. *Social Development, 10*, 488–511.

Younger, A. J., & Boyko, K. A. (1987). Aggression and withdrawal as social schemas underlying chidlren's peer perceptions. *Child Development, 58*, 1094–1100.

Younger, A., Gentile, C., & Burgess, K. (1993). Children's perceptions of social withdrawal: Changes accross age. In K. H. Rubin & J. Asendorpf (Eds.), *Social withdrawal, inhibition, and shyness in childhood*. Hillsdale, NJ: Lawrence Erlbaum Associates.

Youniss, J. (1980). *Parents and peers in social development: A Piaget–Sullivan perspective*. Chicago: University of Chicago Press.

Zakriski, A. L., & Coie, J. D. (1996). A comparison of aggressive-rejected and nonaggressive-rejected children's interpretations of self-directed and other-directed rejection. *Child Development, 67*, 1048–1070.

❖ 12 ❖

SCHOOL AND COMMUNITY INFLUENCES ON HUMAN DEVELOPMENT

Jacquelynne S. Eccles
University of Michigan
Robert W. Roeser
Portland State University

INTRODUCTION

In 1979, Bronfenbrenner published the first of a series of works charging developmental psychology with the need to study human development from more naturalistic and contextual points of view. He stressed that humans develop within a set of embedded physical and sociocultural contexts of influence beginning with their own biological make-up and ending with the political/historical contexts into which they are born and raised. Bronfenbrenner emphasized that we cannot understand human development without understanding the multidimensional forces that operate across time both within and across these levels of influence—biological, psychological, social, cultural, economic, and political. Although it is true that children are most directly influenced by their immediate relationships and face-to-face interactions with other human beings, particularly their parents, siblings, extended family members, friends, peers and teachers, these proximal human relationships are nonetheless shaped by more distal social, cultural, economic, and political forces in the contemporary societal context. For example, workplace experiences affect parents' mental health and economic resources, which in turn affect parenting behaviors and child outcomes (e.g., Whitbeck et al., 1997). Similarly, neighborhoods structure the types of opportunities and risks children are exposed to whenever they leave their home, and thereby, to the extent their parents adapt their parenting behaviors to the neighborhood environment outside of the home, also affect parent–child interactions in the home (e.g., Furstenberg, Cook, Eccles, Elder, & Sameroff, 1999). Finally, schools are elaborate multilevel institutions that influence children's academic, social–emotional and behavioral development in a wide variety of ways—ranging from teacher influences on student **achievement** associated with the quality of instruction, to physical influences on student mood and motivation associated with the school building itself in terms of noise, light, cleanliness, and overcrowding, to peer influences on students' behavioral conduct based on the social composition of a school's student body (e.g., Rutter & Maughan, 2002).

Since 1979, there has been growing interest in the influences of these extra-familial contexts of human development. Researchers have begun looking at of the contributions of neighborhoods, communities, religious institutions and schools, as well as larger, political, societal, cultural, and historical forces, on young people's academic, social–emotional and behavioral development. In this chapter, we focus on two of these contexts: schools and community-based settings (such as churches, synagogues or mosques; playgrounds; afterschool clubs; and neighborhood streets). Young people spend many of their waking hours in such settings, and this is increasingly true as they move into adolescence. Although these extra-familial settings afford opportunities and present various risks for healthy development, they have been researched less than the family by developmental scientists until relatively recently. As a result, much of the current work on how school and community settings influence child and adolescent development has been done by scholars from a broad range of disciplines outside of developmental psychology, including educational psychology, sociology, anthropology, applied linguistics, history, and so on. We draw on a variety of these disciplinary resources in this chapter. This kind of interdisciplinary perspective on the role of schools and community settings in child and adolescent development is a necessary dimension of the kind of ecologically oriented and culturally and historically informed developmental science that Bronfenbrenner outlined.

We focus first on schools, because they occupy a central place in the developmental agenda set forth for children in almost every nation of the world. Thus, in the majority of nations, from the time children first enter school in early or middle childhood until they complete their formal education sometime in adolescence, children and youth spend more time in schools than in any other context outside their homes. By virtue of their central role in lives of children and families, schools are increasingly playing a role in the education of children and youth not only in terms of the traditional "three Rs" of reading, writing and arithmetic, but also in terms of moral and character development, the cultivation of motivation to learn and a desire for lifelong learning, the promotion of social–emotional skills and well-being, and the prevention and remediation of emotional–behavioral problems (Greenberg et al., 2003; Roeser & Eccles, 2000).

Exploring all the possible ways in which educational institutions influence the various domains of child and adolescent development is beyond the scope of a single chapter. Instead, we present a developmental systems framework for conceptualizing the context of schooling, and provide a set of examples of pathways of influence by which the multilevel and multidimensional nature of the context of school can influence child and adolescent development. Specifically, we focus on three normative developmental moments when the influences of various dimensions of the context of school on students' motivation, achievement, and well-being are most evident: the transitions into elementary (ages 5–10), middle (ages 10–14), and high school (ages 14–18). We begin this section by describing schools as multilevel social organizations that can influence children's cognitive, socio-emotional, and behavioral development through organizational, social, and instructional processes that operate at several different levels of the overall *school system*. These levels range from the immediate, very proximal relationships between students, tasks, and teachers in the classroom; to quasi-proximal influences in terms of principals and school boards in setting school-level policies; to distal national level policies mandating particular kinds of assessments and funding structures for schools. After providing a descriptive account of these various levels of the school system, we present three examples of how chains of causal processes can operate across multiple levels of the school system to influence students' daily experiences of teaching and learning in school and, thereby, their longer-term educational lifepaths as they enter and pass through elementary and secondary school and beyond (Roeser & Peck, 2003). The first example focuses on the transition into elementary school, the second on the transition from elementary school into either junior high school or middle school, and the third on the transition into high school. In these examples, we try to highlight the important reciprocal relations that exist between students and the people and conditions of their school environments (e.g., Skinner & Belmont, 1993). We also discuss how different students, characterized by different profiles of personal and socioeconomic risks and assets, fare differentially across these **school transitions**. We focus on schools in the first section of this chapter.

In addition to schools, we also focus on community and neighborhoods as central contexts of human development. Developmental science's interest in community and neighborhood influences has evolved more recently than its interest in schools. Prior to about two decades ago, it was rare to find an article on neighborhood influences in any of the major developmental psychology journals. Since that time, there has been a dramatic rise in their prevalence. Much of this increase reflected initial concerns with children growing up in poverty. In 1987, a sociologist, William Julius Wilson, published an influential book, *The Truly Disadvantaged*, which spotlighted the potential role of neighborhood effects on human development. Since then, various interdisciplinary teams of researchers have initiated large-scale projects to study the impact of neighborhood and community forces on human development. We summarize the results of this work in the second part of this chapter.

We end the chapter with a discussion of how both school and community contexts can affect child and adolescent development through their structuring of peer groups and social networks more generally, and through affordances for participation in organized activities that impart skills, meaning, and satisfying relationships. Schools and communities have a large influence on the nature of the peers with whom individuals spend the most time. Schools also structure the nature of these interactions through grouping and instructional practices. We elaborate on these influences. We also summarize the indirect influence of schools and communities on children's and adolescents' involvement in community-based and after-school extracurricular activities. Children and adolescents also spend a great deal of time out of school. As they get older, much of this time is spent outside the home. Does it matter what they do during this time? Does participating in organized activities such as team sports, volunteer service, or faith-based organizations influence development? How? We summarize emerging theory and research evidence regarding these questions towards the end of the chapter.

SCHOOLS AS CENTRAL CONTEXTS OF DEVELOPMENT

What constitutes the developmental context of schooling? Drawing on developmental contextual perspectives (e.g., Bronfenbrenner, 1979; Ford & Lerner, 1992; Sameroff, 1983), we conceptualize the context of schooling as one that bridges between the macro-levels of society and culture that shape the practice of education from afar, and the middle levels and micro-levels of the school as an organization, its *classrooms* and the people that inhabit these settings whose daily acts of leadership, teaching, and social interaction affect children's learning and development in immediate ways (Cole, 1996). Figure 12.1 depicts the school environment as encompassing such a span of interdependent contexts spanning from the very macro (e.g., national educational policies) to the very micro (design of particular academic tasks) in relation to a given child within the school system. This descriptive model of the context of schooling is guided by seven basic assumptions derived from developmental systems thinking, as follows.

1. The context of schooling involves a complex nested social system, characterized by multiple levels of structure and organization and associated with particular kinds of processes aimed at shaping acts of leadership, teaching and learning.
2. It is the complex configurations of factors across levels, operating through both indirect and direct chains of effects involving people, resources, and educational practices, that exert important influences on children's academic, socioemotional, and behavioral development.

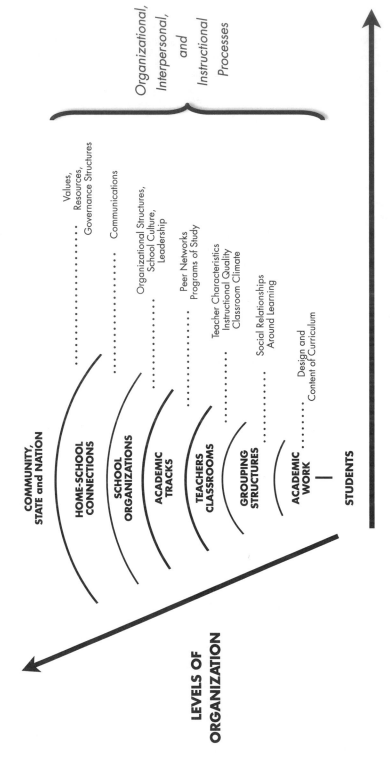

FIGURE 12.1 Model of the context of schooling.

3. The kinds of structures and processes associated with the school system "develop" from both the first-person perspective of, and a third-person perspective on, the growing child as he or she moves through the various institutions that compose the system (elementary, middle, and high schools).

4. The study of human development in contexts such as schools today requires a focus on cultural diversity and the fact that young people from different racial, ethnic, linguistic, and socioeconomic backgrounds face different kinds of barriers and opportunities with respect to education.

5. As whole persons encompassing social, emotional, moral, behavioral and cognitive–intellectual dimensions of being, humans both learn and are affected by acts of teaching and learning across multiple dimensions—not just the cognitive/intellectual one.

6. School socialization effects are mediated to some significant degree by young people's subjective perceptions of their developmental contexts as well as by their own **agentic** behavior that co-constitutes these contexts in ways that feed back to shape their own development.

7. Education in free and democratic societies is not only about enculturation and a trajectory of increasing participation of cultural ways of knowing, feeling and doing; it is also ideally about the development of qualities of mindful awareness and concern for others that allow for freedom of thought, creativity, harmonious relations among diverse peoples, and myriad forms of social and personal renewal (Roeser & Peck, 2009). In the next section, we elaborate on these assumptions.

Assumption 1: The Context of Schooling Involves Multiple Nested Levels of Organization Generically Called a "School System"

From the location of the school within macro-level government systems characterized by laws and the educational policies of the nation, state, and local school district, "down" to the micro-level of the classroom and the social dynamics between teachers and students from different ethnic and racial backgrounds, the context of schooling in human development can be conceptualized as a multilevel system characterized by an array of political, cultural, economic, organizational, interpersonal, and instructional processes that both directly and indirectly shape the development of educators and students alike (Sarason, 1990; Zalantino & Sleeman, 1975). The different levels of context of schooling can be conceptualized as moving out from the child in a series of temporally and spatially "larger" contexts with their associated processes and webs of influence (see Figure 12.1). Examples of such nested contexts and their related causal processes include the nature of academic work (Level 1); the structure of classroom activities and groups (Level 2); the quality of teachers' professional preparation, their classroom pedagogy and the **classroom climate** (Level 3); the existence of academic tracks composed of particular types of students and teachers (Level 4); the nature of school organizational structure and culture (Level 5); the presence or absence of linkages between schools and other institutions in the local community (home, community-based organizations; Level 6), and location of the school within district, state, and national governance systems (Level 7). Thus, understanding the context of schooling requires considerable interdisciplinary expertise in order to address the complexity of these seven interdependent levels of school systems and to assess the influences of such complexity on child and youth outcomes. It also requires the measurement of both "etic" and "emic" features of the context of schooling to capture both the tacit and tangible dimensions of these nested levels (Roeser, Urdan, & Stephens, 2009).

Assumption 2: Causal Chains of Influence Operate Within and Across Levels of the Context of Schooling to Affect Child and Adolescent Development

From a developmental science perspective, complex causal chains of effect across multiple levels and involving various organizational, interpersonal and instructional resources and practices are usually necessary to understand a "school effect" on student outcomes (Rutter & Maughan, 2002). For example, imagine a situation in which, due to concerns about equity in achievement among students from different socioeconomic backgrounds, a superintendent mandates that all schools in the district implement a new, equity-producing pedagogical practice called cooperative learning (district level). Principals in this district would presumably then organize their teachers to learn the new pedagogical technique (school level) and to apply it in their classrooms (classroom level). If it were implemented well, all children within classrooms in this school would be seen working in groups (group level) on fairly complex, conceptual problems for which cooperative techniques were designed (academic work level; e.g., Cohen & Lotan, 1997). Research suggests this would lead to increases in self-esteem, inter-ethnic relationships, and achievement among the children, especially for those of low ability or status (student level; Stevens & Slavin, 1995). In contrast, if the policy were implemented in a way that did not prepare the teachers adequately to implement cooperative learning techniques properly in the classroom, it could harm teachers and students by creating groups that actually reinforce preexisting status differences among students as well as peer segregation of students along socioeconomic lines. Such an outcome might affect not only students, but also teachers. It could, hypothetically, undermine their sense of **efficacy** with regard to effectively teaching students with varying abilities and statuses (Cohen & Lotan, 1997) and thereby lead to diminishing efforts to do so over time (e.g., Tschannen-Moran, Woolfolk Hoy, & Hoy, 1998).

As a second example, consider the influences on both teachers and students that the No Child Left Behind policy, originally designed to increase teacher accountability for student learning and enhance student performance in the core subjects, has actually had (e.g., No Child Left Behind (NCLB) legislation; Nichols & Berliner, 2007). Frustrated with the relatively poor performance of many of America's children compared to children in other modern societies, NCLB was put into place with the goal of holding schools, teachers, and students responsible for greater gains in learning as assessed by standardized tests. It was hoped that by enacting an accountability regime involving frequent and ongoing testing, by providing testing results to parents, and by tying the test results to a series of incentives and punishments for schools, the policy would motivate principals, teachers, parents, and students to work together towards academic improvement. Testing has now been in place since 2003, and there is little evidence of any marked improvements in the performance of America's students on standardized achievement tests in math, reading, and science (Nichols & Berliner, 2007, 2008). Why? How can a developmental science perspective help to analyze this situation? What are the complex webs and chains of causal influences that may lie behind the results of NCLB as an educational policy?

A developmental perspective on this policy focuses attention on issues of context and how well policy-mandated changes might affect the context of schooling, as well as how well those contexts meet or fail to meet the needs and goals of those involved—in this case, teachers and students (e.g., Boyce et al., 1998). For instance, there is growing evidence that mandated testing has a number of unintended negative effects on teachers and students. At the most basic level, high-stakes testing puts extraordinary pressure on teachers to teach to the test and sometimes even engage in less than ethical practices to insure student success on such tests (Berliner, 2003). That is, some teachers, under pressure, act in ways that are actually contrary to their professional ideals. The power of situations in this regard, as social psychology has repeatedly demonstrated, is considerable (Ross & Nisbett, 1981). Furthermore, mandated testing often leads to the use of particular classroom instructional methods such as drill and practice on test-like items; and that such practices, necessary to address national mandates as assessed by standardized multiple choice tests, are often at odds with teachers' own preferred instructional strategies and assessment practices (Ball, 2002; Nichols & Berliner, 2007). This discrepancy between the kinds of teaching that are mandated through the testing system and related incentives and punishments of NCLB, and the intrinsic desires of teachers themselves with regard to teaching and assessment practices, may lead to diminished motivation for teachers to do this work in the short term and the long term (Deci & Ryan, 2002). Such a dampening of teacher enthusiasm could, in turn, adversely affect students' own motivation, effort, and achievement in the classroom (Brophy, 1988). In this example, one can see how a motivational and developmental science lens on schooling can begin to disclose insights into how a well-intended mandate from the nation, state, or district can have both intended and unintended consequences for teacher and student behavior.

Assumption 3: The Structures, Processes, and Webs of Influence Associated With the Context of Schooling Change Across Development

From both a first-person and a third-person perspective, we can say that the structures and processes of the school system develop as children move into and progress through elementary school, middle school, high school, and on to post-secondary educational settings. That is, not only are children developing, but so too is the whole nature of the context of schooling that they experience over time. The inclusion of a time dimension along the bottom of Figure 12.1 emphasizes this point. For example, Eccles and her colleagues (1993) documented a cluster of grade-related changes in various organizational, social, and instructional processes in schools as students transition from elementary to middle school. They found, for instance, that school size increases, the closeness of relationships between teachers and students declines, and social comparison and competition become more prevalent motivational strategies in classrooms. These changes have been linked to declines in young people's motivation to learn and well-being as they move into and through secondary-school environments in a variety of developmental studies now (see Roeser et al., 2009). Understanding the interaction of different school features on children at different ages of development is a critical component of a developmental science approach to understanding the role of schooling in human development (Eccles & Roeser, 2009; Finn, 2006; Perry & Weinstein, 1998).

Assumption 4: The Study of Development in School Contexts is also the Study of Cultural Diversity and Issues of Equity in Education

Currently, the school-aged population in the US (ages 5 to 18 years) is growing and includes approximately 49 million individuals (Sable & Garofano, 2007). Since 1965, the number of Asian- and Latin-American immigrants to the United States has steadily increased (National Research Council, 1997). These ongoing trends, in conjunction with variations in birth rates among different ethnic populations, have had the effect of increasing the racial, ethnic, and linguistic diversity of the school-aged population in the US (National Center for Education Statistics (NCES), 2005). Racially and ethnically, the school-aged population today is approximately 57% European-American; 20% Latin-American; 17% African-American; 5% Asian-American/Pacific-Islander; and 1% Native American (Sable & Garofano, 2007). The percentage of Latin-American students increased rapidly since the early 1990s and is expected to continue to rise over the next decade. Culturally and linguistically, approximately one in five in the school-aged population is either an immigrant or the child of recent immigrants

(Garcia, Jensen, & Cuellar, 2006; Suarez-Orozco & Saurez-Orozco, 2001); and one in five speak a language other than English (mostly Spanish) in their homes (NCES, 2006). These "new Americans" are primarily from Latin America, Asia and the Caribbean—particularly Mexico, followed by the Philippines, Vietnam, the Dominican Republic, and China (Camarota & McArdle, 2003).

Racial, ethnic, and linguistic background, as well as immigrant generational status, intersects with poverty in the lives of school-aged children and adolescents. Data show that European-American and Asian-American children and adolescents are the least likely to grow up in poverty, regardless of their (immigrant) generational status. In contrast, between a quarter and a third of all African-Americans and Native Americans, and over a third of Latin Americans (especially Mexican immigrants and children of immigrants) between the ages of 5 and 18 years old grow up in poverty in the US today (NCES, 2005).

Due to factors such as poverty and its correlates, data also show ongoing achievement gaps between young people from different racial, ethnic, linguistic and socioeconomic backgrounds. Despite impressive gains over the past 30 years, for example, African-American children continue to score less well on achievement tests than their European-American counterparts (Wigfield et al., 2006). Latin-American and Native-American students have shown less educational progress over the decades compared to European-Americans and still achieve at lower levels, whereas Asian-Americans perform at levels comparable to or exceeding those of Whites (NCES, 2007). For instance, Asian-Americans are much more likely to complete advanced placement courses in math and science before high-school graduation that European-Americans, who in turn were more likely to do so than their African-, Latin-, and Native-American peers (NCES, 2007).

Of particular concern today is the educational progress of native and foreign-born children and youth of Mexican descent. Latinos, especially those with familial roots in Mexico, are the largest and most rapidly growing ethnic "minority" group in the United States. Because of their rapid growth, the aggregate level of education of Latin Americans will strongly affect the quality of the future labor force, as well as future demand for public services (Vernez, Abrahamse & Quigley, 1996). Unfortunately, immigrants from Mexico and the next generation experience downward assimilation in the United States due to factors such as low human capital, negative cultural contexts of reception, and curtailed educational attainments (Portes & Rumbaut, 2001). Mexican immigrants are the least likely of all immigrants to attend high school or college, and the same is true for the native-born same-ethnic peers (Slavin & Calderon, 2001). Furthermore, among those who do enroll in post-secondary education, Mexican-descent youth are overrepresented in those who attend 2-year community colleges (Kao & Thompson, 2003).

Differences in school resources: The issue of educational equity is an important part of the study of schooling and development.

In summary, statistics on the demographic composition of the school-aged population, as well as those on differences in educational outcomes among different sub-groups, highlight that an inquiry into the role of schools as early and long-term contexts of child and adolescent development is also an inquiry into cultural diversity in human development. Such an inquiry is also necessarily about significant and longstanding issues of inequality in educational opportunities and outcomes for young people from different racial, ethnic, and socioeconomic backgrounds. Attention to issues of cultural diversity, and issues of educational equity, are an important, if oftentimes implicit, part of the study of schooling and development (Entwisle, Alexander, & Olson, 1997).

Assumption 5: Acts of Teaching and Learning Involve and Affect "Whole Persons"

Acts of teaching and learning are inherently social, emotional, moral, behavioral, and cognitive affairs, simultaneously (Noddings, 2005a; Shulman, 2005). In short, teacher and learning involve whole persons (Roeser & Galloway, 2002). Additionally, good teaching has a lot in common with good parenting and the kind of security for exploration and learning that effective parents afford their young. In both cases, more capable adults need to provide the younger learner with both a safe social–emotional base from which they can start out and return to in times of uncertainty, and scaffolded opportunities for exploration and autonomous skill development that, when feeling safe, the young can take advantage of in the service of learning (Wentzel, 2002). This breadth of the goals in education is illustrated in Table 12.1, where we list various aims of educational training and the kinds of developmental outcomes one would expect to see in the students if these skills are taught effectively. This assumption implies that the social, emotional, and moral dimensions of the teaching and the overall context of schooling need to be made explicit and measured as key components of school and classroom environments (e.g., Jennings & Greenberg, 2009; Pianta & Hamre, 2009; Roeser, Urdan, & Stephens, 2009). In addition, the social, emotional, and moral outcomes of schooling, in addition to cognitive intellectual ones, need to be made explicit and studied in future research studies as well (e.g., Mind and Life Educational Research Network (submitted);

TABLE 12.1

Non-subject matter aims and outcomes of education involving "whole children" and "whole adolescents"

Domains and Skills	Motive Dispositions	Action Tendencies
Self-regulation		
Emotion regulation	Self-control and resilience	Behavioral inhibition and recovery
Attention regulation	Will power and stick-to-itiveness	Behavioral focus and persistence
	Self-confidence and efficacy	Behavioral initiative and persistence
Prosociality		
Social skills	Cooperation and conscientiousness	Helping and rule-abiding behavior
Conflict resolution skills	Agreeableness	Civil behavior
Mindful awareness		
Self-awareness	Personal responsibility and curiosity	Moral living and lifelong learning
Social awareness	Social responsibility and empathy	Contributions to community
Cultural awareness	Mutual respect and openmindedness	Non-discrimination/celebration of diversity
Global awareness	Universal responsibility and compassion	Contributions to peaceful world change

Noddings, 2005b; Roeser et al., 2009). In summary, the holistic conceptualization of both educational contexts and outcomes in terms of multiple domains of development (e.g., the intellectual, the social, the moral, and the emotional) is an important valued-added perspective that developmental science can add to the study of schooling and its influences on human development.

Assumption 6: Children Co-construct Their Educational Lifepaths Through School by Making Meaning of Schools in Subjective Ways and Through Their Own Agency and Characteristics

Another assumption of a developmental science approach to schooling is that the socialization effects of schooling are mediated to some degree by young people themselves through their subjective perceptions, agentic actions, and evocative characteristics. First, young people shape their own school experiences based on their subjective perceptions of the socialization context and socializing agents in schools. The assumption is that children and adolescents appraise and make meaning of their developmental contexts in terms of how well they "fit" or are "mismatched" with fundamental biological, psychological, and social needs (Boyce et al., 1998; Eccles & Midgley, 1989; Roeser, Eccles, & Strobel, 1998b). Depending on how well the instructional and interpersonal features of school contexts "fit with" or are "mismatched" with the needs of students at various ages, and to the extent that students perceive such fits or mismatches, the theory predicts either positive or negative changes in motivation, well-being and behavior, respectively (Eccles & Roeser, 2009). Of course, students' perceptions are biased or shaped by their previous domain-relevant experiences, so this form of memory-appraisal of present-action sequence forms one way in which students "create" their own developmental life-space.

Another mechanism by which students contribute to their own development in school is through their intrinsic curiosity, competence motivation, exploratory behaviors, and **agency** in general (Deci & Ryan, 2002). Organisms are active in their own development from the very beginnings of life, and to talk about school effects without an understanding of the transactional nature of such effects is to explore only half of the picture. The notion of person–environment transactions in the determination of achievement and educational lifepaths more generally remains a challenging but important theoretical approach to the study of schooling (e.g., Roeser et al., 2002b).

A third way in which students contribute to their own development in schools is through their evocative characteristics, including both physical (e.g., attractiveness) and personality-based (e.g., extraversion) characteristics, which, by either intentionally or unintentionally eliciting certain kinds of reactions from others, can contribute to the nature of the socializing context and its reciprocal effects on the person (e.g., Caspi & Roberts, 2001).

Although there is a rather large research literature examining the unidirectional effects of "contexts on kids," relatively few studies attend to understanding the conjoint role that students, their perceptions, their own agentic acts, and their evocative characteristics, in conjunction with the nature of their physical and social environments in school, play in their own learning and development there (e.g., Skinner & Belmont, 1993). Understanding such person–environment contributions to educational lifepaths is a clear goal of a developmental science perspective on schooling (Eccles & Midgley, 1989, Roeser & Peck, 2003; Rutter & Maughan, 2002). As Boyce and colleagues (1998) put it with regard to the study of development and psychopathology—and the same applies to the study of development and education—the next phase of research needs to attend to both "the actual *transactions* between children and contexts and the *transduction* of contextual influences into pathways of biological mediation" (p. 143; emphasis in original).

Education in free and democratic societies is not only about enculturation and a trajectory of increasing participation of cultural ways of knowing, feeling and doing; it is also ideally about the development of qualities of mindful awareness and concern for others.

Assumption 7: Education is About Cultural Ways of Knowing *and* Qualities of Awareness

In addition to socializing young people in culturally sanctioned ways of thinking and feeling (i.e., *civic education*) and scaffolding their development of knowledge and disciplined ways of knowing (i.e., *subject-matter education*), we propose that public education in free and democratic societies necessarily ought to be in places that educate for mindful awareness and related volitional modes of attending, thinking, feeling, perceiving, acting, and interacting. The means by which the public education system can do this we term *contemplative education* (Roeser & Peck, 2009). Whereas the cultivation of civic-mindedness and the acquisition of subject-matter knowledge are essential outcomes of education related to sociocultural participation, the cultivation of awareness and willful self-regulation are preconditions for deep learning, freedom of thought, creativity, harmonious social relationships, and myriad forms of personal and social renewal.

In the next section, we describe the various levels and associated processes that comprise the context of schooling (see Figure 12.1) and provide some examples of research linking these various levels and processes to aspects of children's academic, social–emotional, and behavioral development. After this, we summarize what we know about developmental changes in these various aspects of schooling as children progress through different school types (elementary, middle, and high school), as well as how such changes influence aspects of children's and adolescents' development.

LEVELS OF THE CONTEXT OF SCHOOLING

Level 1: Academic Work

The nature of the academic work students are asked to do is at the heart of their school experience. At a fundamental level, the nature of school work affects not only what children may come to know about themselves and the world, but also their capacities to pay attention (e.g., listening to stories), their interests and passions, and their morals and ethics (Dewey, 1902; Doyle, 1983). Two key aspects of academic work that can influence students' emotional, cognitive, and moral development are (a) the content of the curriculum in terms of its intellectual substance and its consideration of global social–historical realities (e.g., Noddings, 2005a, 2005b; Partnership for 21st Century Skills, 2008; Zins, Weissberg, Wang, & Walberg, 2004); and (b) the design of instruction in terms of scaffolding knowledge development, and also in terms of its capacity to cultivate interest, meaningfulness, challenge, and deep cognitive, emotional, and behavioral engagement with the material (Blumenfeld, 1992; Blumenfeld, Mergendoller, & Swartout, 1987).

Both the content and the design of academic tasks can be conceptualized in terms of their relative attunement or mismatch with the developmental needs and capacities of students of a particular age and social background, and the needs of society at a particular time in history. Some evidence supports the notion that academic work that is meaningful to the developmental and historical reality of children's experience promotes motivation to learn and helps to "bond" young people with the institution of school (e.g., Burchinal, Roberts, Zeisel, & Rowley, 2008; Roeser, Eccles & Sameroff, 2000). Curricula that represent the "voices," images, role models, and historical experiences of traditionally underrepresented groups may be particularly important for helping students from such groups to identify with school and success in school, and for students from the majority cultural group to develop a broader understanding of the diversity, as well as the experiences and contributions, of minority groups in history (Ball, 2002; Fine, 1991; Graham & Taylor, 2002; Romo & Falbo, 1996; Valencia, 1991). The challenge of providing curricula that address developmentally and historically meaningful topics to a diverse and large school population is a central and ongoing challenge in education in the United States and many developed nations today (Meier, 2008). For instance, studies show that boredom in school, low interest, and perceived irrelevance of the curriculum are associated with diminished engagement and learning and, for some, can be part of the reason for withdrawing from school (Assor, Kaplan, & Roth, 2002; Eccles, 1983; Finn, 2006; Jackson & Davis, 2000; Larson & Richards, 1989; National Research Council and Institute of Medicine (NRC/IOM), 2004; Newmann, Wehlage, & Lamborn, 1992).

Although there exist many innovative curriculum movements today that are reinvigorating the teaching of subject matter (e.g., the Facing History and Ourselves Project: Sleeper & Strom, 2006), we want to draw attention to one emerging movement that aims to provide a new kind of curriculum into public school education: the **social–emotional learning** movement (SEL; Elias et al, 1997). SEL programs focus on teaching content and skills related to learning in five core "non-subject matter" domains: self-awareness, social awareness, responsible decision-making, self-management, and relationship management (Collaborative for Academic, Social, and Emotional Learning, 2003). Reviews and meta-analyses of social and emotional learning programs delivered in classrooms provide evidence that SEL programs can prevent substance abuse (Gottfredson & Wilson, 2003), antisocial behavior (Wilson, Gottfredson, & Najaka, 2001) and mental health problems (Durlak & Wells, 1997). Furthermore, a recent meta-analysis (Durlak, Weissberg, Taylor & Dymnicki, in press) examined the outcomes of over 250 experimental studies of social and emotional learning programs for all students. Of the 27 programs that examined indicators of academic achievement at the post-intervention period, students receiving SEL programs showed significant and meaningful improvements on achievement test performance; the effect was equivalent to approximately a 10 percentage point gain on achievement testing. Further, program students were significantly more likely to attend school, less likely to be disciplined for misbehavior, and received better grades. Thus, evidence is accruing to suggest that by broadening the academic curriculum to include social–emotional learning, dividends for behavioral, social–emotional, and intellectual development can be achieved.

In addition to the "what is taught" in schools, the "how things are taught," including the design of academic tasks, also can influence children's motivation, engagement, and learning (Ball, 2002; Blumenfeld, 1992; Deci & Ryan, 2002; Fredricks, Blumenfeld, & Paris, 2004). Choosing materials that provide an appropriate level of challenge for a given class, designing learning activities that require diverse cognitive operations (e.g., opinion, following routines, memory, comprehension), structuring lessons so they build on each other in a systematic fashion, using multiple representations of a given problem, and explicitly teaching children strategies that assist in learning (e.g., asking oneself if one has understood what was just read) are but a few of the design features that can "scaffold" learning and promote interest, engagement and learning. Work on the role of interest in learning, engagement, and intrinsic motivation highlights the important role of the design of academic tasks in this regard (Renninger, 2000). Increased interest is associated with greater engagement in the task and higher levels of mastery of the material (Fredricks et al., 2004; Renninger, 2000; Wigfield, Eccles, Schiefele, Roeser, & Davis-Kean, 2006). Even more importantly, interesting tasks increase intrinsic motivation to do well (Deci & Ryan, 2002) and increase the likelihood that students develop a strong personal identity as a committed school student (Eccles, 2009). Thus, at this level of analysis, one can see that the nature of academic work plays a central role in a chain of related educational outcomes, including task interest to task engagement, to mastery and learning, to intrinsic motivation to learn, to identification of oneself as a learner who is bonded to school.

From a developmental perspective, there is evidence that the content and design of academic work may not change over time in ways that reflect the increasing cognitive sophistication, diverse life experiences, and identity-linked motivational needs of children and adolescents as they move from the elementary into the secondary-school years (Eccles, 2009; Wigfield et al., 2006). As one indication, middle-school children report the highest rates of boredom when doing schoolwork, especially passive work (e.g., listening to lectures) and in particular classes such as social studies, mathematics, and science (Larson, 2000; Larson & Richards, 1989). Academic work becomes less, rather than more, complex in terms of the cognitive demands as children move from elementary to junior high school (Juvonen, 2007; Juvonen, Le, Kaganoff, Augustine, & Constant, 2004). It may be that declines in children's motivation during the transition to secondary school in part reflect academic work that lacks challenge and meaning commensurate with children's cognitive and emotional needs (Eccles & Midgley, 1989). For instance, Roeser, Eccles, and Sameroff (1998) found that curricular meaningfulness, as perceived by middle-school students, was a positive predictor of longitudinal changes in their valuing of and commitment to school from the beginning to the end of middle school. The findings showed that the more meaningful students found their work in English, science, and social studies, the more they valued their education and learning over time. Efforts at middle-school reform also support this hypothesis: Adolescents' motivation to learn is maintained and does not decline when secondary schools introduce more challenging and developmentally and historically meaningful academic work (Eccles, Wigfield, & Schiefele, 1998; Jackson & Davis, 2000; Lee & Smith, 2001).

In sum, although research in this area is still relatively sparse, some evidence shows that as children develop cognitively and emotionally, and as they begin to take a greater interest in understanding the world and their identity within that world, schools often provide repetitive, low-level tasks that are unimaginative in content and design. This seems particularly true in an age in which learning is increasingly seen as synonymous with performance on multiple choice standardized tests. The nature of these changes in academic work is likely to undermine motivation in most children, as well as to exacerbate motivational and behavioral difficulties in those children who had trouble with academic work earlier in their development during elementary school (see Roeser, Eccles, & Freedman-Doan, 1999). In addition, although more evidence is needed here as well, there is some indication that teaching children about social and emotional issues may be an important new addition to classroom curriculum in the twenty-first century.

LEVEL 2: GROUPS AND ACTIVITY STRUCTURES

The next level of the context of schooling that can influence child and adolescent development concerns the social structure of learning activities in the classroom. Classroom instruction is delivered through different grouping and activity structures, including whole-group instruction, individualized instruction, and small-group instruction. Groups are often formed on the basis of children's ability level; alternatively, groups can be formed from students representing a diverse array of abilities brought together in a cooperative work arrangement (Oakes, 2005; Stevens & Slavin, 1995). Thus, some classroom grouping strategies are associated with individualistic activity structures, in which individuals work alone and their behavior is independent of others; other foster social comparison in which there is competition; and still others foster collaboration and cooperation. In these ways, different classroom social structures communicate quite different implicit messages about relationships with others, the goals of learning, and children's abilities—messages that, in turn, influence children's perceptions of students' own academic competence and social acceptability, as well as their perceptions of the characteristics of their classmates (Roseth, Johnson, & Johnson, 2008).

Different group structures also elicit different patterns of teacher behaviors and peer group associations. For instance, research has shown that the use of either whole-class instruction or within-class ability groups can highlight ability differences among students, can lead to increased social comparison by students and teachers, and can make salient differential teacher treatment of high and low achievers in the classroom (Oakes, 2005; Wigfield et al., 2006). When this happens, activity structures in the classroom are serving to reinforce rather than disrupt achievement status hierarchies, differentiated competence beliefs between low and high achievers, and friendship selection patterns based primarily on similarities in academic abilities. Given the equation of achievement with intelligence and worth in American society (Covington, 2000), low-ability children often show diminished self-perceptions of competence and feelings of self-worth in classrooms where status differences are made salient by the kinds of activity structures and teaching strategies described above (Oakes, 2005; Rosenholtz & Simpson, 1984). Research also indicates that children positioned as "low ability" in the classroom are more likely perceived by their classmates as less desirable friends than their high-achieving peers (Karweit & Hansell, 1983). In this case, activity structures are exerting influences on the formation of social networks or patterns of social isolation among students. We say more about these processes later when we discuss ability **tracking**.

The use of collaborative or cooperative groups is a popular alternative to either whole-group, ability-grouped, or individualized instruction at the elementary-school level. Stevens and Slavin (1995) concluded that cooperative learning techniques in which students work in small groups and receive rewards or recognition based on group performance lead to increases in student achievement, self-esteem, and social acceptance among students of different social statuses and ethnic backgrounds. With proper instruction in the social skills necessary for group work, cooperative groups can provide numerous "niches" for students with different strengths to participate in the learning process, can increase the amount of social support and reinforcement available in the classroom for learning complex material, can increase contact among students of different abilities and, thus, can foster a broader network of friendship patterns in the classroom and fewer instances of social isolation (Roseth et al., 2008).

From a developmental perspective, the use of whole-group and within-class ability-grouped instruction increases in frequency as children progress from elementary to middle and high school. Within-class ability grouping in reading is widespread even in the early grades; the use of between-class ability grouping in mathematics, English, and science classes increases considerably as children move into and through secondary school (Feldlaufer, Midgley, & Eccles, 1988; Eccles, et al., 1993, 1998; NRC/IOM, 2004). At the same time, the use of both individualized instruction and cooperative grouping declines. This is a good example of a change in educational environment that is mismatched with the needs of youth. A recent meta-analysis of over eight decades of research on approximately 17,000 early adolescents from 11 different countries showed that higher achievement and more positive peer relationships were associated with cooperative rather than competitive or individualistic activity structures in the middle-school classroom (Roseth et al., 2008). We discuss the implications of these grade-related changes in activity structures further below when we address the transition into secondary school.

LEVEL 3: TEACHERS, INSTRUCTION, AND CLASSROOM CLIMATE

The next level of the context of school that is important to consider in developmental research is that of teachers and their beliefs and pedagogical practices, as well as the social and instructional atmosphere of the classroom they create through their presence and practice. With regard to the kinds of teacher beliefs that are consequential for their pedagogical decisions, practices, and interpersonal behavior in the classroom, teachers' professional identity beliefs about themselves as a teacher, as well as their pedagogical beliefs about the kinds of teaching practices that work best in motivating and supporting learning, are important (Roeser, Marachi, & Gehlbach, 2002a). Due in part to these beliefs and the actions they motivate and regulate, the hypothesis is that teachers create particular kinds of classroom learning environments for and with students. Dimensions of learning environments have historically been conceptualized in terms of the order and management of the classroom, the nature of social relationships among peers and between teachers and students, and the instructional climate in terms of ways of motivating learning, providing instruction and support for student learning, and giving feedback to students (Moos, 1979). In the next section, we provide examples of research on key processes operating at the level of teacher identity and pedagogical beliefs, instructional practices, and the classroom climate as a whole that have, independently and interdependently, been shown to affect children's and adolescents' development in school.

Teacher Professional Identity and Pedagogical Beliefs

Social cognitive and sociocultural approaches to the study of teaching and learning have demonstrated the important role that teachers' beliefs play in shaping their pedagogical decisions and strategies in the classroom (Calderhead, 1996; Shulman, 2005). The kinds of beliefs that have been found to motivate teachers' instructional decisions and interpersonal behavior in the classroom include their efficacy beliefs regarding their teaching and interpersonal capabilities, their instructional goals and styles of managing classrooms and motivating students, and the kinds of expectations and beliefs that teachers may have about individual—or even groups of—students they teach, and their views about what it means and takes to "learn" something. More recently, scholars have begun to examine how teachers' social–emotional competencies are also key determinants of their behavior in the classroom (Jennings & Greenberg, 2009).

Efficacy for teaching beliefs.   Teachers' efficacy beliefs regarding their ability to perform the core tasks of teaching—managing a classroom, teaching for understanding and assisting students who need additional support, and maintaining emotional balance while doing these—are key processes affecting not only teaching-related behaviors in the classroom, but also the regulation of emotion and well-being. Tschannen-Moran, Woolfolk Hoy, and Hoy (1998), for instance, found that teachers' efficacy beliefs were positively related to their investment of effort in teaching, their persistence in working with students with academic difficulties, and their willingness to experiment with new teaching strategies. Other studies have shown that when teachers hold high generalized expectations for student learning and students perceive these expectations, students achieve more and experience a greater sense of competence as learners (Ashton, 1985; Brophy, 2004; Eccles et al., 1998; Lee & Smith, 2001; Midgley, Feldlaufer, & Eccles, 1989; NRC/IOM, 2004, Weinstein, 1989). Unfortunately, as we discuss later, the proportion of teachers with a high sense of teacher efficacy decreases as children move from elementary into secondary school. In addition, the proportion of teachers with a strong sense of teaching efficacy is lower in schools that educate a predominance of poor and minority children (Darling-Hammond, 1997; Eccles et al., 1993; Juvonen, 2007; Juvonen et al., 2004; NRC/IOM, 2004; Roeser & Midgley, 1997).

With respect to emotional well-being and regulation, Roeser and Midgley (1997) found that elementary-school teachers who felt more efficacious with regard to their ability to successfully teach all of their students also reported less stress in dealing with the emotional–behavioral problems that some of their students displayed in their classrooms. This makes sense because efficacy indexes confidence to be successful at a task given current resources and supports (Bandura, 1994), whereas stress results when environmental challenges overcome individuals' ability to cope given current resources and supports (Folkman & Lazarus, 1984). Self-efficacy beliefs and subjective stress go hand-in-glove.

Role beliefs.   Teachers' beliefs about what their professional role entails are another important component of their professional identities. Two common role definitions that teachers identify with are that of the "academic instructor" (oriented toward teaching academic content) and that of the "socializer" (oriented toward addressing children's social–emotional and behavioral needs; fosterer of the "good citizen"). In a study of 98 elementary-school teachers, Brophy (1988, 2004) found that an endorsement of the "instructor" role was critical for teachers' ability to ensure student achievement, but that some of the most effective teachers were those who blended an academic with a socializing focus. In addition, he found that teachers who saw themselves primarily as "instructors" responded much more negatively to those students who were under-achievers, academically unmotivated, or disruptive during learning activities than to the other students in the class; in contrast, "socializers" responded most negatively to either the hostile aggressive and defiant students or the children who thwarted the teachers' efforts to form close personal relationships. In this study, one can see how different role beliefs are associated with both instructional outcomes and interpersonal processes in the classroom, insofar as role beliefs seem to index the kinds of sensitivities teachers have to being "triggered" emotionally in the classroom.

Differential expectations for student success.   Another set of teacher beliefs that have been studied in relation to student outcomes is the differential expectations that teachers have regarding the likelihood of success of different students within the same classroom. Most of the studies linking differential teacher expectations to either their own behaviors or to their students' achievement and motivation have been done under the rubric of teacher expectancy effects. The issue is whether teacher expectancies about different students' prospects for success, and the related differential patterns of student interaction that can flow from these expectancies, translate into levels of student achievement that "live up" or "live down" to the teachers' initial expectancies (Rosenthal, 1974). In developmental science, this kind of "self-fulfilling prophecy" is an example of how hypothesized "interactional continuity," operating here through differential teacher expectancies and related behavior that reinforces students' present ability level, can influence students' achievement trajectories in school over time (Caspi & Roberts, 2001).

The history of research in this area has been controversial and contested, but it appears that teacher-expectancy effects depend on whether teachers structure activities differently for, and interact differently with, high- and low-expectancy students, as well as on whether the students perceive these differences (Jussim, Eccles, & Madon, 1996; Weinstein, 1989). A great deal of the work on teacher-expectancy effects has focused on differential treatment related to gender, ethnic group, and/or social class. Most of this work has investigated the potential undermining effects of low teacher expectations on girls (for mathematics and science), on minority children (for all subject areas), and on children from lower social class family backgrounds (again for all subject areas) (Eccles & Wigfield, 1985; Jussim et al., 1996; Parsons, Kaczala, & Meece, 1982; Rists, 1970).

Weinstein (1989) and her colleagues, for instance, found that both high- and low-achieving students report perceiving differential teacher treatment of students on the basis of ability in most elementary-school classrooms. High achievers are seen by students of all ability levels as receiving higher expectations, more opportunities to participate in class, and more choice about work, whereas low achievers are seen as receiving more negative feedback, more control, and more feedback concerning work completion and following rules. The greater the perceived differential treatment in a classroom, the greater is the impact that teachers' expectations will have on achievement and children's self-perceptions of competence (Weinstein, 1989). Observational studies of teacher behavior validate these perceptions: Teachers often do treat high and low achievers differently in these ways (Brophy, 1988; NRC/IOM, 2004).

Other work, however, suggests that teacher expectancy effects may not be as negative as once believed. For the effect to be of great concern, one needs to demonstrate that it has a negative biasing effect (i.e., that teachers' expectations lead to changes in motivation and performance over time beyond what would be expected given knowledge of the characteristics of the specific students; Jussim et al., 1996; Jussim, Palumbo, Chatman, Madon, & Smith, 2000; Madon et al., 2001). Evidence for such negative biasing effects is minimal in the short run. Much of the association between teacher expectations for individual students and subsequent student motivation and performance reflects the "accurate" association between teacher expectations and student characteristics, such as prior achievement levels and behavioral patterns (Jussim et al., 1996; Madon et al., 2001). In addition, not all teachers respond to their expectations with behaviors that undermine the motivation and performance of the low-expectancy students. Some teachers respond to low expectations with increased instructional and motivational efforts for particular students and succeed in increasing both student motivation and learning (Goldenberg, 1992). Nonetheless, small but consistent teacher expectancy effects over time can have a large cumulative effect on students' motivation and achievement (Jussim et al., 1996; Smith, Jussim, & Eccles, 1999), particularly if these effects begin in kindergarten and the first grade (Entwisle & Alexander, 1993). Finally, Jussim et al. (1996) found that girls, low-socioeconomic status students, and minority students are more susceptible to these effects than European American, middle-class boys.

Weiner (1991) and Graham (1991) studied a slightly different aspect of within-classroom variations in the teacher–student interaction linked to teacher expectancy effects. Weiner (1991) hypothesized that teachers' emotional reactions may convey their expectations to students. Specifically, it was hypothesized that teachers may display pity in providing negative feedback to those students for whom they have low expectations. In contrast, it was hypothesized that teachers would display anger in providing negative feedback to those students for whom they have high expectations. Such a difference in effect could underlie teacher expectancy effects. Graham (1991) investigated this hypothesis by manipulating bogus instructors' emotional reactions to experimental participants' (learners') performance on a laboratory task: "Instructors" who showed pity and offered excessive help, for example, produced "learners" who either attributed their "failures" to lack of ability and lowered their expectations for success (Graham & Barker, 1990) or engaged in a variety of behaviors (e.g., making excuses for their poor performance) designed to maintain the learners' sense of self-worth (Covington, 1992). Similarly, Parsons, Kaczala, and Meece (1982) demonstrated that, when praise is used in a way that conveys low teacher expectations (i.e., patronizing praise for low-level successes), it undermines junior high-school students' confidence in their abilities as well as their expectations for success. In contrast, when overt criticism conveys high teacher expectations (i.e., when the teacher uses public criticism only with high-performing students to protect the low-performing students' egos), high rates of criticism are associated with higher than predicted confidence in one's ability.

Researchers such as Steele and Aronson (Aronson & Steele, 2005; see Nisbett, 2008, for a review) have linked perceptions of differential expectations, particularly for African-American students, to school disengagement and disidentification (the separation of one's self-esteem from all forms of school-related feedback). Steele and Aronson argue that when African-American students believe that teachers and other adults have negative **stereotypes** of African-American children's academic abilities and this belief is made salient, the African-American students' performance anxieties increase and their academic confidence decreases, which, in turn, lead them to disidentify with the school context to protect their self-esteem. It is interesting that other studies using the same theoretical notions and experimental techniques have shown that Asian-American students believe that teachers and adults expect them to perform very well and that belief leads Asian students to perform better on tests when their ethnicity is made salient (Shih, Pittinsky, & Ambady, 1999). Furthermore in very similar studies, Shih and her colleagues have found that Asian-American females perform better on tests of math ability when their Asian identity is made salient and worse on the same tests when their female identity is made salient (Ambady, Shih, Kim & Pittinsky, 2001; Shih et al., 1999).

Researchers interested in the relatively poor academic performance of adolescents from some ethnic groups have suggested another classroom-based experience linked to teachers' expectations, beliefs, and prejudices: **discrimination**, specifically, the impugning of one's intellectual ability based on ethnicity, race, or gender (Brody et al., 2006; Chavous, Rivas-Drake, Smalls, Griffin, & Cogburn, 2008; Fordham & Ogbu, 1986; Garcia Coll et al., 1996; Graham & Taylor, 2002; Ruggiero & Taylor, 1995; Roeser et al., 1998a; Wong, Eccles, & Sameroff, 2003). Two types of discrimination have been discussed: (1) anticipation of future discrimination in the labor market, which might be seen as undermining the long-term benefits of education (Fordham & Ogbu, 1986), and (2) the impact of daily experiences of discrimination in school and other settings that can affect mental health and academic motivation (Chavous et al., 2008; Sellers, Caldwell, Schmeelk-Cine & Zimmerman, 2003; Roeser et al., 1998a; Wong et al., 2003). Both types have been shown to adversely affect the development of ethnic-minority adolescents.

For instance, in a 2-year longitudinal analysis of African-American early adolescents across seventh to ninth grade of junior high, Wong et al. (2003) found that adolescents who perceived more incidents of racial discrimination with teachers, school staff, and classmates in Grade 8 also showed declines in their academic self-concept and teacher-reported grades and increases in their self-reported psychological distress for Grade 7 to Grade 9. Furthermore, they found that African-American youth who had a positive connection to their ethnic group showed less of a decline in school motivation, achievement, and well-being over time in relation to level of perceived discrimination. In this sample, anticipated future discrimination appeared to motivate the youth to do their very best so that they would be maximally equipped to deal with future discrimination. Similarly, in a study of Puerto Rican 13- to 14-year-old early adolescents, Szalacha et al. (2003) found that adolescents who perceived more incidents of racial discrimination with classmates, store clerks, teachers, and neighbors also reported lower global self-worth. Several researchers have pointed out that the impact of experiences of racism may be particularly salient during middle childhood and early adolescence as children begin to solidify their ethnic identities and are often exposed to more heterogeneous student populations in terms of ethnic, religion, and other social categories (Rowley, Burchinal, Roberts, & Zeisel, 2008; Wong et al., 2003).

In a large study of Asian, Mexican, and Central and South American immigrant high-school students growing up in major metropolitan areas of the United States, Portes and Rumbaut (2001) found that a majority of youth in their sample reported feeling discriminated against at school and in other settings. The major sources of this perceived discrimination were European-American classmates, teachers, and neighbors. Such experiences were associated with greater feelings of depression among the youth in the study.

Rosenbloom and Way (2004) also studied the dynamics of discrimination in multiracial urban high schools. Asian-American students reported harassment by peers, whereas African-American and Latin-American students were more likely to report discrimination by adults such as teachers. The authors linked the experiences of discrimination among different groups: when teachers preferred Asian-American students and saw "model minority," the African-American and Latino adolescents resented this differential teacher treatment and thus harassed the Asian-American students.

One interesting finding is beginning to emerge for this work on discrimination: it appears that when youth have a strong positive ethnic identity, it has protective effects against the potential aversive effects of daily experiences of ethnic discrimination. Several researchers have found that those African-American youth who have strong and positive ethnic identities are much less negatively affected by experiences of racial discrimination than their less strongly identified peers (Burchinal et al., 2008; Chavous et al., 2003; Harris-Britt, Valrie, Kurtz-Costes, & Rowley, 2007; Wong et al., 2003). Thus, educating for diversity and redressing discrimination are two goals that educators might pursue in their efforts to reduce the persistent ethnic group differences in school achievement.

Pedagogical Goals

Another key set of cognitions that are associated with teachers' classroom behavior concerns their beliefs about the purposes or goals of instruction and learning in school (e.g., Covington, 2000). **Achievement goal theory** is a social–cognitive approach to the study of motivated behavior in achievement settings that posits that cognitive *purposes* or goals organize the quality of individual's attention, emotion, cognition, and consequently, behavior during teaching or learning (Ames, 1992; Maehr & Midgley, 1996). Ames (1992) has used goal theory to describe how mastery- or performance-oriented classrooms can emerge from the goals that teachers hold implicitly about the purposes of learning and related ways of teaching and motivating learning. Specifically, Ames linked teachers' pedagogical goals to the ways that teachers use time in their classrooms; distribute authority; recognize, group and evaluate students; and design classroom tasks. She focused on two particular achievement goals that teachers can espouse that then shape their pedagogical practice—a relative ability or a mastery goal orientation (Roeser, Midgley, & Urdan, 1996). These two goal orientations are hypothesized to lead to two different patterns of instruction.

The first pattern, called a "relative ability-goal orientation," is one in which teachers believe that the goal of learning is demonstrating one's abilities, especially relative to others. Grouping by ability, differential rewards for high achievers, public evaluative feedback, academic competitions, and other practices promoting the notion that academic success means out-performing others and proving one's superior ability are practices employed by such teachers that are consistent with this goal orientation (Ames, 1992; Midgley, 2002). Unfortunately, most youth, by definition, are not "the best" and thus may not receive rewards and recognition in classrooms that emphasize relative ability. We know that in ability-oriented classrooms, children are more likely to use low-level strategies to learn, experience more anxiety and negative affect, and devote attentional resources to making themselves look smarter or avoiding looking dumber than other students rather than learning the material (Ames, 1992; Midgley, 2002). Urdan, Midgley, and Anderman (1998) found that fifth grade teachers' reports of their performance-oriented approaches to instruction (e.g., helping students see how their performance compares to others, pointing out students who do well academically as models for other students) were positively associated with students' reported use of self-handicapping in the classroom (purposefully withdrawing effort in order to protect self-worth). This study and others suggest that children who lack confidence in their academic competence are particularly vulnerable in such environments (Covington, 2000). Although few studies have looked at this, it seems plausible that learned helpless responses to academic failure, the avoidance of engaging in work, negative emotional experiences, and stereotype threat effects are more likely to beset low-ability students in ability-focused environments (Dweck, 2002; Roeser, 2004).

On the other hand, some teachers hold the view that mastery, self-improvement, and progressive skill development are the valued ends of learning in the classroom. These beliefs "show through" in terms of greater efforts to acknowledge individual effort and improvement regardless of a child's current ability level, provisions of choice and collaborative work in which social comparison and status differences are de-emphasized, and more teacher talk to students about the idea that mastering new content, learning from mistakes, and continuing to try despite setbacks are more highly valued hallmarks of learning and being successful (e.g., Turner et al., 2002). For example, using observational data, Meece (1991) found that upper elementary teachers in classrooms rated by students as more mastery-oriented than other classrooms were more likely to promote meaningful learning, adapt instruction to the developmental levels and interests of students, support student autonomy and peer collaboration, and emphasize the intrinsic value of learning. Other studies have shown that ninth grade teachers' self-reported mastery-oriented approaches to instruction (e.g., stressing to students the importance of understanding work and not just memorizing it, making an effort to provide students with work that has meaning in their everyday lives) were positively associated with students' aggregate perceptions of their classrooms as mastery-oriented. These aggregate perceptions were related, in turn, to lower incidences of student-reported disruptive behavior in the classroom. Mastery-oriented pedagogical practices have also been linked to reductions in students' concerns about their ability relative to peers and the feelings of self-consciousness, anxiety, or disenfranchisement that can accompany such concerns (Assor, Vansteenkiste, & Kaplan, 2009; Maehr & Midgley, 1996; Midgley, 2002; Murayama & Elliot, 2009; NRC/IOM, 2004; Roeser et al., 1996). In addition, mastery-focused classrooms can foster children's use of deeper processing strategies to learn, positive affective around learning, and more of an intrinsic, task-mastery-oriented motivation approach to learning in the students (Covington, 2000).

For developmental changes in teachers' professional identity, beliefs, and goals, grade-level changes have been documented for all of these types of teacher beliefs. For example, grade-level differences in teachers' efficacy beliefs regarding their ability to teach and influence all of the students in their classes have been found. Midgley, Feldlaufer, and Eccles (1989a) showed that teachers in junior high-school environments feel less efficacious than their colleagues who teach in elementary-school settings. These results are not surprising due to the larger number of students, the lack of extended contact with students during the day, and the content-focused educational training that secondary teachers experience in comparison to their elementary-school colleagues. Nonetheless, this decline in teacher efficacy can have a major impact on child development, particularly for the low-performing children. As discussed more fully later in this chapter, students' experiencing a decline in their teachers' sense of efficacy as they transition into secondary school is associated with declines in aspects of motivation and school engagement. Early adolescents need role models who provide supportive feedback about their ability to be successful academically. If teachers do not feel particularly efficacious in relation to their teaching, their students are likely to lose confidence in their ability to learn.

There are also grade-related differences in teachers' role beliefs. Compared to teachers in elementary-school settings, teachers in secondary-school settings see their role more in relation to content instruction than to socialization (McPartland, 1990). This difference likely reflects two factors: First, secondary teachers' education is more focused on particular content areas than on child development. Second, aspects of teachers' work in secondary schools such as departmentalization by academic discipline and large student loads also promote a focus on academic content issues rather than individual mental health concerns. Similarly, Roeser et al. (2002a) found that secondary-school teachers are less likely to endorse the notion that students' mental health concerns are part of the teacher role than elementary-school teachers. An important implication of such findings is that, at a time when adolescents need academic and socioemotional guidance and support from both parents and non-parental adults (i.e., during early adolescence), teachers may be less likely to provide such support given the number of students they teach, their educational training, and the size of secondary schools (Eccles et al., 1993). Although elementary teachers seem sensitive to both internalized and externalized distress in children (Roeser & Midgley, 1997), secondary-school teachers may fail to notice children who are experiencing internalized distress and having difficulty adjusting to the transition to middle or high school. This seems especially true of children who struggle emotionally but continue to perform at an acceptable academic level (Juvonen et al., 2004; Lord, Eccles, & McCarthy, 1994). Consequently, because secondary teachers have so many students, they may not be able to be sensitive to mental health issues until these problems severely undermine academic performance or disrupt classroom activities. This creates a hole in the "safety net" available to children at a time when they are in particularly acute need of adult support and guidance (Simmons & Blyth, 1987).

Grade-level differences have also been identified for teachers' endorsement of mastery versus ability goals and related pedagogical practices. For example, Midgley and her colleagues (Midgley, 2002; Midgley, Anderman, & Hicks, 1995; Roeser et al., 1998a; Roeser, Midgley, & Maehr, 1994) found that, as children progress from elementary to middle school, both teachers (in reflecting on their own work environments and the learning environments for students in the school) and students (in reflecting on their school environments) report that their school environment is more focused on competition, relative ability, and social comparison than on learning, task mastery, and individual improvement. These changes occur during a time when adolescents are particularly vulnerable to social comparisons with peers. They are beginning to differentiate ability from effort and also are starting to view ability more as a "fixed capacity" than an incremental skill. Not measuring up to one's peers in terms of academic ability in school settings that increasingly emphasize ability differences is very likely to undermine academic motivation and well-being among students generally and vulnerable students in particular (Roeser & Eccles, 2000; Roeser et al., 1998b).

Finally, from the students' perspective, experiences of ethnic discrimination increase with grade level as well. Greene, Way, and Pahl (2006) found that African-American and Asian-American adolescents report increasing levels of discrimination from adults as they move through high school. African-American students also report an increasing amount of discrimination from peers during this same time period, suggesting that for African-American students, experiences of discrimination in general increase as they progress through high school. Interestingly, the Latino and Puerto Rican students in the same study did not show these same patterns; if anything these groups reported less ethnic discrimination as they moved through high school (Burchinal et al., 2008).

In summary, teachers' beliefs about themselves as a teacher and about the teaching role, about the students they teach, and about the goals and purposes of learning are all important factors that constitute a "psychological environment" that accompanies the pedagogical practices and forms of interaction related to these teacher beliefs. As such, these beliefs represent one important factor that can shape student outcomes in school indirectly through effects on teacher behavior as students move through the school system. In addition, many teacher beliefs "change" from the perspective of the developing child in ways that may be contraindicated with respect to the kinds of supports and learning environments young people need during adolescence. Next, we turn to the qualifications and quality of instruction that teachers deliver as a related set of factors that are consequential for child development at the teacher/classroom level of analysis.

Teacher Qualifications and Quality of Instruction

Teacher qualifications, in terms of their educational preparation and training, as well as teachers' ability to deliver high-quality classroom instruction, are the next school context factors we discuss that are important for child and adolescent development in schools.

Teacher qualifications. Research on teacher qualifications and student achievement outcomes has revealed that the qualifications of the teachers that children encounter, especially in the early years of school when foundational literacy and numeracy skills are the focus of the curriculum, have substantial effects on students' academic growth and subsequent educational trajectories through high school (Hill, Rowan, & Ball, 2005; Rowan, Correnti & Miller, 2002). In a review of evidence from three different national data sources, Darling-Hammond (1999) concluded that teacher preparation and certification are by far the strongest correlates of student achievement in reading and mathematics, even after taking account of students' socioeconomic and sociolinguistic background. The importance of teacher qualifications for student achievement has now been demonstrated in 46 countries that participated in the Trends in International Mathematics and Science Study (TIMMS) in 2003: Greater teacher qualifications were associated with increased mathematical achievement across nations (Akiba, LeTendre, & Scribner, 2007). In addition, evidence shows that teachers with greater qualifications also are more likely to use reform-oriented teaching practices in middle-school math classrooms (Smith, Desimone, & Ueno, 2005). Thus, it appears that teacher preparation and qualifications can improve instructional quality, which in turn can affect student achievement.

Darling-Hammond (1999) reviewed evidence showing that knowledge of the subject matter to be taught is essential to good teaching, but also that the returns of subject matter expertise in terms of improvements in student learning diminish as that expertise grows well beyond the curriculum to be taught. That is, beyond some basic mastery of the curricular content to be taught, other teacher qualifications such as the complexity of a teachers' pedagogical content knowledge (e.g., knowing how to teach a particular subject), developmental knowledge (e.g., knowing how to teach a particular subject to students of a particular age), and skill in bringing these to bear collectively on instruction matter more for student outcomes. For instance, research on effective teaching has shown that the most effective teachers are those who are flexible and able to adapt their teaching approaches to fit the needs of different students and the demands of different instructional goals or content (Doyle, 1985).

In addition, Darling-Hammond (1999) noted the troubling tendency of poor and ethnic-minority children to be over-exposed to "out-of-field" teachers teaching their subject matter classes. For instance, in Grades 5 through 8, it is estimated that 70% of poor and ethnic-minority adolescents have "math" teachers who do not possess even a college minor in math or a math-related field; the percentage is 50% during the high-school years (Peske & Haycock, 2006). Research among high-school students has demonstrated the negative achievement-related impact of having an out-of-field teacher on mathematics in particular (Goldhaber & Brewer, 2000). Research shows that not only are large proportions of the teaching staff in poor schools made up of non-credentialed or unqualified teachers, but substitutes also regularly fill the places of full-time teachers in these schools, there is little support for English-language learners (ELLs), and staff turnover is high (Darling-Hammond, 1997, 2000).

ELLs for whom English is a second language (ESL students) are also disproportionately exposed to unqualified teachers in US schools. Approximately 75% of ELLs in US schools speak Spanish (Fashola, Slavin, Calderon & Duran, 2001). Integrated language and subject matter courses that emphasize both receptive skills in listening and reading and production skills in speaking and writing are needed to assist ESL students in mastering both English and the subject matter (August & Hakuta, 1998; Valdes, 2001). Resistance to native language programs nationally and a shortage of teachers who are proficient in English and Spanish and who know how to prepare content instruction for ELL students hamper these efforts nationwide (Fashola et al., 2001).

In summary, teacher qualifications are an important source of educational inequality in US schools generally and the educational lifepaths and so-called "achievement gaps" involving poor and ethnic-minority children from particular racial/ethnic groups (African-, Latin-, and Native-American youth in particular). Although the NCLB Act of 2002 included a provision to redress inequality in teacher qualifications in high-concentration poor and ethnic-minority schools, such provisions did little to remedy the inequities. The lack of effect NCLB had on redressing real inequalities in teacher qualifications has been attributed in part to the relatively low standards for what constituted a highly qualified teacher in NCLB, and in part to the relatively low resources that were dedicated to teacher training by the law (Darling-Hammond, 2007; Peske & Haycock, 2006).

Instructional quality. As noted above, closely related to teacher qualifications is the quality of instruction that teachers deliver in the classroom. Research on instructional quality in both developed and developing nations has shown that it matters for students' learning and achievement (Heyneman & Loxly, 1983; Pianta & Hamre, 2009). Given the research reviewed above linking teacher qualifications and student outcomes, this research also suggests that instructional quality and teaching practices are important mediators between teacher qualifications and student achievement (e.g., Smith et al., 2005).

Although valid assessments of instructional quality remain a complex challenge in this area of research, recent research has shown that instructional quality is often mediocre in US public schools, especially if the students are poor (Pianta, Belsky, Houts & Morrison, 2007; Quint, 2006). Mashburn et al. (2008), for instance, in a study of over 2000 children enrolled in public pre-school programs, found that the quality of teachers' instruction predicted gains in academic and language skills. These authors also found that teacher quality was lower in classrooms with more than 60% low-income children, when teachers lacked a degree in early childhood education, and when they held less child-centered and more adult control-oriented beliefs concerning child development (Pianta et al., 2005).

Similarly, a study of elementary schools showed that teachers in high-poverty and high-minority schools are more likely to use certain kinds of pedagogical practices more than others, including the exercise of strong control over students and the limiting of their use of constructivist teaching practices, because, in part, they believe that poor children lack the inner control necessary to play a responsible role in their own learning (Solomon, Battistich, & Hom, 1996). Furthermore, because a substantial minority of low-income students are perceived as arriving to school with social–emotional and behavioral problems that compromise their readiness to learn (Adelman & Taylor, 1998), their teachers are more likely to experience feelings of burden in relation to their level of emotional needs (Roeser & Midgley, 1997); feel a need to distance themselves from their students emotionally (Solomon et al., 1996); and feel less efficacious as a teacher (Bandura, 2006). The use of heavy extrinsic inducements and controlling, teacher-centered forms of instruction in these environments may be a function of teachers' feeling overwhelmed and inefficacious in such settings and also the relative inexperience and high turnover of teachers in high-poverty, high-minority schools (Darling-Hammond, 1997, 2007). As these selected research studies indicate, at both elementary- and secondary-school levels, improvements in instructional quality remain a critical challenge for reform efforts (e.g., Pianta & Hamre, 2009; Quint, 2006). However, improvements in instructional quality often require other kinds of contingent reforms to be maximally effective (see Quint, 2006). For instance, Greenwald, Hedges, and Laine (1996) found that teachers' education, ability, and experience, in conjunction with being in small schools and lower teacher–student ratios, were the constellation of factors that mattered most for aggregate achievement at the school and district levels.

Changes in teacher qualifications and instructional quality.   Very little research has looked at how the nature of teacher qualifications or instructional quality changes over time from the perspectives of students as they progress through the school system. This represents one fruitful area for future research on human development in the contexts of schools.

Teacher–Student Relationships, Climate and Management

The nature of the classroom climate, referring to the general social-relational atmosphere of the classroom and its basis in teacher–student relationships, as well as how the classroom is organized and managed, is an important context feature at this level of analysis that can affect child and adolescent development.

Classroom climate and teacher–student relationships.   Research suggests that the quality of teacher–student relationships in terms of instrumental and social support, trust, and caring, and the fostering of a sense that all students are valued members of a learning community who belong in the classroom, is essential for the development of students' academic motivation, engagement, learning, and social–emotional well-being in school (Burchinal et al., 2008; Deci & Ryan, 2002; Eccles et al., 1998; Goodenow, 1993; NRC/IOM, 2004; Pianta, 1999; Roeser et al., 1996; Wentzel, 2002). Perceptions of teacher social support and sense of belonging and membership in a learning community are especially important precursors to individuals' motivation to learn (Osterman, 2000). Sense of belonging is perhaps especially critical for young people who must traverse significant ethnic and racial, socio-economic, and sociolinguistic borders to feel fully part of a school in which middle-class, majority cultural norms often predominate (Davidson & Phelan, 1999; Garcia-Reid, Reid, & Peterson, 2005; Lucas, Henze, & Donato, 1990). Correlational studies with adolescents show that students' perceptions of caring teachers enhance their feelings of self-esteem, school belonging, and positive affect in school (NRC/IOM, 2004; Roeser & Eccles, 1998; Roeser et al., 1996). In a naturalistic longitudinal study, Pianta et al. (2008) found that emotional supportive interactions in pre-school predicted trajectories of reading and math development across elementary school, though the associations were small. In sum, emotionally supportive teachers are a critical foundation for motivation to learn. The importance of relationships for reinvigorating education and reengaging disenfranchised students is at the heart of many of the most innovative approaches to school reform over the past couple of decades (Brown, 1997; Connell, 2003; Quint, 2006; Schaps, 2003).

Several researchers are studying how classroom climate is related to students' emotions in the classroom, and in turn their motivation and learning (Frenzel, Goetz, Ludtke, Pekrun, & Sutton, 2009; Frenzel, Pekrun, & Goetz, 2007; Goetz, Frenzel, Hall, & Pekrun, 2007; Goetz, Frenzel, Pekrun, Hall, & Ludtke, 2007; Goetz, Pekrun, Hall, & Haag, 2006; Pekrun, Goetz, Titz, & Perry, 2002). These researchers argue that emotional reactions to experiences in the classroom have a large impact on student engagement and learning; and have separated individual emotional reactions to classroom experiences from shared emotional reactions. Findings have revealed that shared emotional reactions across students within the same classroom are influenced by shared perceptions of teachers' enthusiasm and enjoyment (Frenzel et al., 2007). Furthermore, these shared positive and negative emotions were linked to the general level of achievement in the classroom: As a group, students in high-achieving classrooms reported more positive emotions (pride and enjoyment) and less extreme negative emotions (anxiety, shame, and hopelessness). Interestingly, at the individual level, there was a negative association between the average achievement level of the class and the individual student's positive emotional reactions during the class: Individual students reported more positive emotions if they were in a lower-achieving than a higher-achieving classroom, in part because they felt less pressure and a greater sense of control over their own achievements in the lower-achieving classroom (Pekrun, Goetz, & Frenzel, 2007).

Developmental changes in classroom climate and teacher–student relationships. Declines in perception of emotional support from their teachers and in a sense of belonging in the classrooms are quite common as students move from elementary into secondary schools (Burchinal et al., 2008; NRC/IOM, 2004; Roeser et al., 1994; Wigfield, Byrnes, & Eccles, 2006). This shift is particularly troublesome in our highly mobile society in which teachers represent one of the last stable sources of non-parental role models for adolescents. In addition to teaching, teachers in mobile societies such as the United States can provide guidance and assistance when socioemotional or academic problems arise. This role is especially important for promoting developmental competence when conditions in the family and neighborhood cannot or do not provide such supports (Eccles, Lord, & Roeser, 1996; NRC/IOM, 2004; Simmons & Blyth, 1987). Research on the importance of adult mentors in adolescents' lives, particularly in high-risk and very mobile communities, supports this point of view (DuBois, Holloway, Valentine, & Cooper, 2002). Although the positive effects are quite weak, adult mentors do provide stability for their mentees, and their mentees fare better in terms of school achievement, staying out of trouble, and maintaining positive mental health.

Classroom management. Work related to classroom management has focused on two general issues: orderliness/predictability and control/autonomy. With regard to orderliness and predictability, the evidence is quite clear: Student achievement and conduct are enhanced when teachers establish smoothly running and efficient procedures for monitoring student progress, providing feedback, enforcing accountability for work completion, and organizing group activities (e.g., Darling-Hammond & Bransford, 2005; Lee, 2000; Pintrich & Schunk, 2003). Unfortunately, such conditions are often absent, particularly in highly stressed and underfunded schools with inexperienced teachers (Darling-Hammond, 1997; Darling-Hammond & Bransford, 2005; NRC/IOM, 2004).

Research on autonomy versus control is equally compelling. Many researchers believe that classroom practices that support student autonomy are critical for fostering intrinsic motivation to learn and for supporting socioemotional development during childhood and adolescence (Deci & Ryan, 2002; Grolnick, Gurland, Jacob, & Decourcey, 2002; Ruthig et al., 2008). Support for this hypothesis has been found in both laboratory and field-based studies (Deci & Ryan, 2002; Grolnick & Ryan, 1987; NRC/IOM, 2004; Patall, Cooper, & Robinson, 2008; Roeser et al., 1998a). Pekrun and his colleagues have argued that students' perceptions of being in control of their academic outcomes lead to positive emotions, which, in turn, lead to increased engagement (e.g., Pekrun, 2006).

Other researchers have shown how student autonomy support needs to co-occur with other classroom management and instructional features such as adequate structure, orderliness, and relevant curriculum for its benefits on student motivation, engagement, and learning to be fruitful (Assor et al., 2002; Skinner & Belmont, 1993). The issue appears to be one of finding a proper balance between autonomy and structure (Deci & Ryan, 2002). This need for teachers to balance autonomy support and scaffolding and structure during learning activities is further complicated by the fact that the right balance between adult-guided structure and opportunities for student autonomy changes as the students mature: Older students desire more opportunities for autonomy and less adult-controlled structure, but teachers often are less trustful of older students and therefore look to control them more (Eccles et al., 1993). To the extent that students do not experience developmentally appropriate changes in the balance between structure and opportunities for autonomy as they pass through the K-12 school years, their school motivation should decline as they get older (Eccles et al., 1993).

Developmental changes in classroom management. Contrary to what one might expect to happen given the increasing developmental maturity of the children, secondary-school teachers, compared to elementary-school teachers, use more control-oriented strategies, enforce stricter discipline, and provide fewer opportunities for student autonomy and decision-making in the classroom (Midgley, 2002; Midgley & Feldlaufer, 1987; Midgley, Feldlaufer, & Eccles, 1988). Apparently, as children move from elementary to junior high-school environments, their teachers believe that they are less trustworthy and need to be controlled more. To explain this pattern, Willower and Lawrence (1979) suggested that, as children grow older, bigger, and more mature, and as peer subcultures become stronger during adolescence, teachers are increasingly likely to see students as a threat to their authority and thus respond with more control and discipline. Stereotypes about adolescents as unruly and out of control are likely to reinforce such beliefs and strategies. High-profile school violence cases likely increase teachers' concerns about their own safety as well as the safety of other school personnel and students, leading to even tighter controls over high-school students' behaviors (Elliott, Hamburg, & Williams, 1998; Lee & Smith, 2001). Finally, the demands of secondary-school environments, in which teachers have to deal with many students, may predispose them to use more controlling strategies as a way of coping with so many students.

Practices that provide less support for autonomy are likely to be especially problematic at early adolescence when children express an increased desire for opportunities to make choices and have their voices expressed in the classroom (Assor et al., 2009; Eccles et al., 1993). This may be particularly true for students who, because they are poor or have a history of academic or behavioral problems, are placed in low-ability tracks and classrooms where controlling strategies are particularly prevalent (Oakes, 2005). We discuss this further later. In summary, the set of research studies presented provides an example, collectively, of how complex causal chains across different levels of the school system, in this case involving organizational factors (large student loads), teacher beliefs (e.g., adolescents need to be controlled), and related teacher practices (less student autonomy in the classroom), can impact students' motivation, learning and achievement.

Motivational person–environment fit. The work on understanding group differences in achievement and achievement choices as a function of person (students)–environment (school context) configurations is another example of an attempt to identify a broad set of classroom characteristics that can affect child and adolescent motivation and development over time. Many investigators have suggested that students are maximally motivated to learn in situations that fit well with their interests, current skill levels, and psychological needs (e.g., Csikszentmihalyi, Rathunde, & Whalen, 1993; Eccles et al., 1993; Krapp, Hidi, & Renninger, 1992; NRC/IOM, 2004). Research on female participation and achievement in mathematics in the classroom is one example of this approach. There are sex differences in adolescents' preference for different types of learning contexts that likely interact with subject area to produce sex differences in interest in different subject areas (Eccles, 1994, 2009; Hoffmann, 2002; Wigfield et al., 2006). Females appear to respond more positively to math and science instruction if taught in a cooperative or individualized manner rather than a competitive manner, if taught from an applied or person-centered perspective rather than a theoretical or abstract perspective, if taught using a hands-on approach rather than a book-learning approach, and if the teacher avoids sexism in its many subtle forms. The reason given for these effects is the student–classroom fit between the teaching style, the instructional focus, and females' own values, goals, motivational orientations, and learning styles. The few relevant studies support this hypothesis (Eccles & Harold, 1993; Hoffmann, 2002). If such classroom practices are more prevalent in one subject area (e.g., physical science or math) than another (e.g., biological or social science), one would expect sex differences in motivation to learn and subsequent pursuit of courses in these subject areas. The good news is that math and physical science do not have to be taught in these ways; more girl-friendly instructional approaches can be used. When they are, girls, as well as boys, are more likely to continue taking courses in these fields and to consider working in these fields when they become adults (Eccles, 1994, 2009).

Variations on this theme of **person–environment fit** being important in understanding classroom effects on students include research studies on aptitude by treatment interactions in the determination of student achievement (e.g., Roeser et al., 2002b) and theories stressing cultural match or mismatch as one explanation for group differences in school achievement and activity choices (e.g., Fordham & Ogbu, 1986; Suarez-Orozco & Suarez-Orozco, 2001). For example, Valencia (1991) concluded that a mismatch of the values of the school and the materials being taught contributed to the poor performance and high dropout rates among the Latino youth in the high school he and his colleagues studied. Dehyle and LeCompte (1999) made a similar argument in their discussion of the poor performance of Native-American youth in traditional middle-school contexts (see also Burchinal et al., 2008). The misfit between the needs of young adolescents and the nature of junior high-school environments is another example of these person–environment fit dynamics (Eccles et al., 1993; Konings, Brand-Gruwel, van Merrienboer, & Broers, 2008).

Summary of Teacher and Classroom Level of Analysis

In this section, we summarized studies of classroom- and teacher-related factors that suggest that development is optimized when students are provided with challenging tasks in a mastery-oriented environment that provides good emotional and cognitive support, meaningful material to learn and master, and sufficient support for their own autonomy and initiative. Furthermore, there is some evidence that quality instruction is related to teacher preparation and qualifications. Connell and Wellborn (1991) and Deci and Ryan (2002), in their **Self-Determination Theory**, suggested that humans have three basic needs: to feel competent, to feel socially attached, and to have autonomous control in one's life. Further, both sets of authors hypothesized that individuals develop best in contexts that provide opportunities for each of these needs to be met under the guidance of more-expert, qualified, and caring individuals. The types of classroom characteristics that emerge as important for both socioemotional and intellectual development characteristically seem to provide opportunities for students to meet these three basic needs and thereby to flourish more in their development. In addition, in their **Expectancy Value Theory** of achievement choices, Eccles and her colleagues argue that teacher and classroom characteristics like those discussed in this section influence the students' motivation to engage in learning through their impact on the students' expectations for success and the subjective value they attach to engaging in the learning activities provided by the teacher. We will see examples of such influences throughout this chapter.

LEVEL 4: ACADEMIC TRACKS AND CURRICULAR DIFFERENTIATION

The next level of influences is that of academic tracks or "curriculum differentiation policies." These terms refer to the regularities in the ways in which schools structure sets of learning experiences for different types of student (Oakes, 2005). The process of providing different educational experiences for students of different ability levels is a widespread yet very controversial practice in American schools.

Tracking takes different forms at different grade levels. It includes within-class ability grouping for different subject matters or between-class ability grouping in which different types of children are assigned to different teachers. Within-classroom ability grouping for reading and mathematics is quite common in elementary school. In the middle- and high-school years, between-class tracking becomes both more widespread and more broadly linked to the sequencing of specific courses for students bound for different post-secondary-school trajectories (college prep, general, vocational). Differentiated curricular experiences for students of different ability levels structure experience and behavior in three major ways: First, tracking determines the quality and kinds of opportunities to learn the child receives (Oakes, 2005); second, it determines exposure to different peers and thus, to a certain degree, the nature of social relationships that youths form in school (Fuligni, Eccles, & Barber, 1995); and, finally, it determines the social comparison group students use in assessing their own abilities and developing their academic identities (Marsh, Trautwein, Ludtke, Baumert, & Koller, 2007; Marsh, Trautwein, Ludtke, & Brettschneider, 2008).

Despite years of research on the impact of tracking practices, few strong and definitive answers have emerged (Fuligni et al., 1995). The results of these studies vary depending on the outcome assessed, the group studied, the length of the study, the control groups used for comparison, and the specific nature of the context in which these practices are manifest. The research situation is complicated by the fact that conflicting hypotheses about the likely direction and the magnitude of the effects of tracking emerge depending on the theoretical lens one uses to evaluate the practice. The strongest justification for tracking practices derives from a person–environment fit perspective. Children will be more motivated to learn if their educational materials and experiences can be adapted to their current competence level. There is some evidence consistent with this perspective for children placed in high-ability classrooms, high within-class ability groups, and college tracks (Fuligni et al., 1995; Gamoran & Mare, 1989; Kulik & Kulik, 1987; Pallas, Entwisle, Alexander, & Stluka, 1994).

The results for children placed in low-ability and non-college tracks do not confirm this hypothesis. By and large, when long-term effects are found for this group of children, they are usually negative primarily because these children are typically provided with inferior educational experience and support (e.g., Jackson & Davis, 2000; Lee & Smith, 2001; Pallas et al., 1994; Vanfossen, Jones, & Spade, 1987). Low track placements have been related to poor attitudes towards school, feelings of incompetence, and problem behaviors both within school (non-attendance, crime, misconduct) and in the broader community (drug use, arrests) as well as to educational attainments (Oakes, 2005). But whether academic tracks promote such outcomes or reflect preexisting differences remains a matter of considerable debate. It is also important to note that these negative effects result from the stereotypically biased implementation of ability-grouping programs. A different result might emerge for the low-competence students if the teachers implemented the ability tracking program more in keeping with the goals inherent in the person–environment fit perspective—that is, by providing *high*-quality instruction and motivational practices tailored to the current competence level of the students.

Social comparison theory leads to a different prediction regarding the effect of ability grouping and tracking on one aspect of development: ability self-concepts. People often compare their own performance with the performances of others to determine how well they are doing (Marsh, Chessor, Craven, & Roche, 1995; Marsh et al., 2007; Reuman, 1989). They typically conclude they are doing well, and that they have high ability, if they are doing better those around them. In turn, this conclusion should bolster their confidence in their ability to master the material being taught.

Ability grouping should narrow the range of possible social comparisons in such a way as to lead to declines in the ability self-perceptions of higher-ability individuals and to increases in the ability self-perceptions of lower-ability individuals. Marsh and his colleagues refer to this effect as the big fish in a small pond effect (BFSPE). Evidence supports this prediction. For example, Reuman (1989) found that being placed in a low-ability mathematics class in the seventh grade led to an increase in self-concept of mathematics ability and a decrease in test anxiety; and conversely, being placed in a high-ability mathematics class led to a decrease in self-concept of mathematics ability. Similarly, Marsh et al. (1995) found that being placed in a gifted and talented program led to a decline over time in the students' academic self-concepts. Additionally, Marsh and his colleagues have shown consistent evidence that attending a more academically elite high school leads to reductions in students' academic ability self-concepts that persist over time (Marsh et al., 2007). These results have led Marsh and his colleagues to conclude that academic tracking comes at a cost to confidence in one's academic abilities for academically able students. Similarly, Frenzel, Pekrun, and their colleagues have found that individual students experience slightly more negative emotions (anxiety, hopelessness, and shame) and slightly fewer positive emotions (enjoyment and pride) when they are in higher achieving classrooms (Pekrun et al., 2007).

Whether such reductions in students' academic self-confidence and increases in negative emotions actually undermine these students' academic achievement remains to be tested. The main educational argument for having such elite tracks and schools is that such educational environments provide more challenging and engaging educational experiences for academically able and gifted students—experiences that should lead to increased learning, performance, and motivational engagement. Consistent with this perspective, classic achievement motivation theorists predict, and have found supporting evidence, that individuals with a high need for achievement are most motivated to do their best work when the odds of success are at about .5 (Atkinson, 1957). If this is true then lowering the academic self-concepts of high-achieving students should actually increase their motivation to do their very best. The impact of these changes on other aspects of development likely depends on a variety of individual and contextual factors. If the net result of the BFSPE is to bring both low and high performers closer to the .5 probability level, then ability grouping should have a positive impact on all of the students in both ability groups who are highly motivated and a negative impact on all of the individuals in both ability groups who have low motivation to succeed. Theories focused on the importance of challenging material in a supportive environment suggest an increase in motivation for everyone provided that the quality of instruction leads to equally challenging material for all ability levels. Conversely, if the social comparison context also increases the salience of an entity view rather than an incremental view of ability (earlier discussion of teacher's views about intellectual ability; Dweck, 2002), then the decline in ability self-concepts of the high-ability individuals might lead them to engage in more failure-avoidant and ego-protective strategies.

Yet another way to think about the impact of ability grouping on development is in terms of its impact on peer groups: Between-classroom ability grouping and curricular differentiation promotes continuity of contact among children and adolescents with similar levels of achievement and engagement with school. For those doing poorly in school, such practices can structure and promote friendships among students who are similarly alienated from school and are more likely to engage in risky or delinquent behaviors (Dryfoos, 1990). The "collecting" of children with poor achievement or adjustment histories also places additional burdens on teachers who teach these classes (Oakes, 2005).

Tracking and ability grouping can also lead to the concentration of children with similar behavioral vulnerabilities. For instance, Kellam, Rebok, Wilson, and Mayer (1994) found that proportions of moderately to severely aggressive children ranged from 7–8% to 63% among two first-grade classrooms in the same elementary school. They found that these differing rates were a direct result of between-class ability grouping policy. As a result of this policy, children in these two classrooms were exposed to very different environments: one in which aggression was deviant (only 7–8% of students were aggressive) and one in which it was pretty much the norm (63% aggressive students). It seems likely that aggressive behavior would not necessarily lead to peer rejection in the classroom with high rates of aggression. On the contrary, in such an environment, aggression might confer status and social rewards among peers and thus be reinforced. By placing children with similar vulnerabilities in the same environment, both the reinforcement of negative behavior and promotion of friendships among similarly troubled children are more likely. This phenomenon has been well documented by Dishon and colleagues (Dishon, Poulin, & Burraston, 2001) in their intervention work with aggressive children and adolescents. They have found that aggressive and delinquent behavior often increases rather than decreases when aggressive youth are put together in an intervention group designed to decrease problem behavior.

In summary, between-class ability grouping and curriculum differentiation provide examples of how school policy, teacher beliefs and instruction, and student characteristics can all conspire to create maladaptive transactions that perpetuate poor achievement and behavior among low-ability children. Such a hypothetical sequence is depicted in Figure 12.2. The placement of many low-ability children in lower academic track classrooms may cause some teachers to feel overwhelmed and inefficacious. This might translate into poor instructional quality, a lowering of expectations for student success, and use of controlling strategies on the part of such teachers. These factors, in turn, could promote student disengagement (e.g., Kagan, 1990), which then feeds back into the teachers' beliefs and practices. Eventually, academic failure of certain low-ability children can result from these reciprocal processes. The BFSPE studied by Marsh and his colleagues demonstrates that there can also be disadvantages of tracking for high-ability students.

Another important and controversial aspect of curriculum differentiation involves how

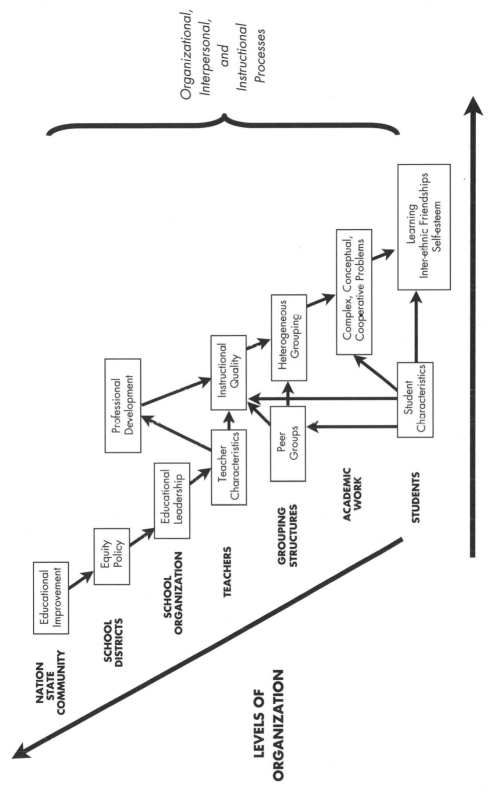

FIGURE 12.2 Causal chains of influence on child/adolescent development within a school system: The hypothesized case of using heterogeneous grouping and complex instruction as a means of increasing educational equity.

students get placed in different classes and how difficult it is for students to move between class levels as their academic needs and competencies change once initial placements have been made. These issues are important both early in a child's school career (e.g., Entwisle & Alexander, 1993) and later in adolescence when course placement is linked directly to the kinds of educational options that are available to the student after high school. Dornbusch (1994) described the impact of tracking on a large, ethnically diverse sample of high-school students in northern California. Analyzing the data course by course, Dornbusch found that 85% of his sample stayed in the same track during high school—there was little mobility. Furthermore, Dornbusch found that many average students were incorrectly assigned to lower track courses. This mistake had long-term consequences for these students, in effect putting them on the wrong path toward meeting the requirements for getting into California's higher educational system. Of particular concern was the fact that these youth and their parents, who were more likely to be of lower socioeconomic background and African- or Latin-American, were not informed of the potential consequences of course decisions made by school personnel during the child's early high-school career. In this case curricular differentiation practices and the absence of school–home communication exerted a profound influence on the lifepaths of these average students who, though able, were placed in lower-ability classrooms in high school.

Similar concerns have been raised about the marginalization and segregation of ESL students on middle- and high-school campuses (Valdes, 2001). There is also some evidence that students with limited English proficiency who are otherwise capable are placed in lower track classes (see Kao & Thompson, 2003). ESL programs are often housed on the periphery of regular school campuses and often fail to provide real opportunities for interaction with native English speakers. Furthermore, similar to the misassignment of African-American and Latino students to, and lack of mobility out of, low academic tracks (e.g., Dornbusch, 1994), there is some evidence that ESL students often get reassigned (downwardly) to ESL programs following school transition events even though they may have graduated from such programs into mainstream classes in their previous schools (Valdes, 2001).

A different perspective on tracking and educational equity comes from national studies using multilevel modeling analyses to examine how between-school differences in the extent of tracking and other reforms relate to student motivation and achievement. For instance, in a study of middle schools, Lee and Smith (1993) found that the extent to which middle schools had engaged in restructuring practices (less departmentalization, more team teaching, more heterogeneous grouping, etc.), students were more engaged in learning and learned more, and there was a more equitable social distribution of these outcomes. Studies of religious schools and high schools have shown similar results—the more that all students in a school are expected to learn a core curriculum, the less inequality there is in student achievement by social background factors (Bryk, Lee, & Holland, 1993; Lee & Bryk, 1989; Lee, Croninger, & Smith, 1997a; Lee & Smith, 1993, 1995; Lee, Smith, & Croninger, 1997b).

LEVEL 5: SCHOOLS AS ORGANIZATIONS WITH CULTURES

Schools also function as formal organizations that are characterized by various "cultures"—including a management/work culture for teachers and a learning culture for students. The effective schools research unequivocally established that features of the internal life of the school culture matter for student outcomes above and beyond students' initial social background characteristics (Good & Weinstein, 1986; Rutter & Maughan, 2002). As Lee (2000) summarized it: "Effective schools have strong leadership focused on academic outcomes. They closely monitor student work. In such schools, teachers hold high expectations for all students. Their social environments are purposeful. Their climates are orderly" (p. 126). These aspects of the school culture impact children's intellectual, socioemotional, and behavioral development. Below we review works on school organizational factors including fiscal resources and student characteristics (Lee, Bryk, & Smith, 1993; Lee & Smith, 2001); school size (Wyse, Keesler, & Schneider, 2008); the social, moral, and academic culture of the school as a whole (e.g, Roeser et al., 2009); unsupervised spaces in a school (Astor, Benbenishty, Zeira, and Vinokur, 2002; Bryk et al., 1993; Goodenow, 1993; Lee & Smith, 2001; Roeser et al., 2009); and school-wide practices such as school start and end times (Carskadon, 1990, 1997) and the yearly school calendar (Alexander, Entwisle, & Olson, 2007).

School Resources

School resources have been studied in various ways with respect to school, including in terms of per-pupil expenditures, the qualifications of the workforce (reviewed above), and the characteristics of the student body itself in terms of social capital. All of these forms of resources can affect developmental outcomes in schools (Greenwald et al., 1996). For instance, the schools attended by African- and Latin-American students generally, as well those attended by rural students in at least a dozen states, are schools with particularly high concentrations of impoverished students (Adelman & Taylor, 1998; Johnson & Strange, 2005). In terms of financial resources, these schools receive fewer state and local resources in terms of per-pupil expenditures than schools in more wealthy communities (Darling-Hammond, 2000; Johnson & Strange, 2005). This is due to the fact that K-12 education is largely funded at the state and local levels. Thus, the resources of a school or district are inextricably linked to where people live and the property wealth of their neighbors. Those in poor communities tend to go to schools with fewer resources, and those in affluent communities tend to go to well-resourced schools (Sawhill, 2006). Although the direct effect of per-pupil expenditures on achievement remains unclear, what is becoming clearer is how the lack of resources for hiring and retaining qualified teachers is a major way that under-resourced schools affect child and adolescent development through the qualifications of the teachers they hire (e.g., Loeb, Darling-Hammond, & Luczak, 2005).

In addition to the resource–teacher qualifications link, other studies have examined how the "mix" of socially disadvantaged students or those with significant emotional–behavioral difficulties has been associated with the educational outcomes of all students in a given school (Rutter & Maughan, 2002). In general, as the ratio of students who are socially disadvantaged goes up in a school, its aggregate achievement goes down. The aggregate behavioral histories of a school's student body also matter. LeBlanc, Swisher, Vitaro, and Tremblay (2007) found that between-school variation in the proportion of students with histories of disruptive problems predicted subsequent rates of classroom behavior problems among high-school students. A variety of mechanisms, including those of peer influences on motivation understood in the context of tracking, and social environments in which maladaptive norms develop, have been proposed to account for these influences (e.g., Rutter & Maughan, 2002).

School resources in terms of adequate materials, a safe environment, and qualifications of the teaching staff are important for students' learning and well being. School district level variations in such school resources are a major contributor to the continuing inequity in educational outcomes for several minority groups in the United States. Thirty-seven percent of African-American youth and 32% of Latin-American youth, compared to 5% of European-American and 22% of Asian-American youth, are enrolled in the 47 largest city school districts in this country; in addition, African-American and Hispanic youth attend some of the poorest school districts in the United States. Twenty-eight percent of the youth enrolled in city schools live in poverty, and 55% are eligible for free or reduced cost lunch, suggesting that class may be as important as (or more important than) ethnicity in the differences in achievement that emerge. Teachers in these schools report feeling less safe than teachers in other school districts, dropout rates are highest, and achievement levels at all grades are the lowest (Council of the Great City Schools, 1992; Lee & Smith, 2001). Finally, schools that serve these populations are less likely than schools serving more advantaged populations to offer either high-quality remedial services or advanced courses and courses that facilitate the acquisition of higher-order thinking skills and active learning strategies. Even adolescents who are extremely motivated may find it difficult to perform well under these educational circumstances.

School Size

Early studies of schools focused primarily on objective characteristics of schools such as school size, teacher–student ratios, number of books in the library, and per-pupil expenditures (Barker & Gump, 1964). School size emerges as one of the most important of these structural characteristics. Barker and Gump (1964) proposed that smaller secondary schools afford young people various opportunities not available in larger schools, opportunities that foster engagement and achievement. Such opportunities included (a) closer relationships between teachers and students, (b) greater adult monitoring of and responsibility for student progress; and (c) a particularly favorable roles-to-people ratio with respect to school extracurricular activities and the need for many students in the school to participate to fulfill those roles. By affecting these mediating processes, school size was hypothesized to affect student outcomes. Subsequent research has consistently verified these hypotheses.

For instance, in a national probability study of high-school students, Crosnoe, Johnson, and Elder (2004) found that students' attachment to school in general and to their teachers in particular was significantly negatively correlated with school size. Lee and Loeb (2000), in an urban Chicago sample of 264 (K-8) schools, found that in smaller schools (<400 students), teachers took greater responsibility for fostering students' learning and students showed greater 1-year gains in mathematics achievement.

Positive relationships, opportunities to participate in the life of the school, and closer monitoring by teachers are key mechanisms in translating school size into greater student bonding with school, motivation to learn and engagement (e.g., Hawkins, 1997; Hawkins, Kosterman, Catalano, Hill & Abbott, 2008). In a national study of high schools, Lee and Smith (1995) found that the greater the school size, the less positive were students' attitudes towards classes, investment of effort in school, and feelings of challenge. In summarizing the work on school size, Lee and Smith (1997) proposed that the most effective K-8 elementary schools with respect to student achievement gains are those that enroll 400 students or less, whereas the ideal 9–12 secondary school in this regard enrolls between 600 and 900 students. Students in elementary/middle schools that are larger than 400, and those in high schools smaller than 600 or larger than 1200, learn less in reading and mathematics. Findings regarding optimal size were consistent regardless of the social class and racial composition of the school. This work and studies by others suggest that the impact of school size on achievement depends on quality of instruction provided. If the schools focus primarily on social climate and devote limited focus to academic press, the students feel quite good about attending the school but their academic achievement is no higher than that of students attending much larger schools (Wyse et al., 2008). Again, this work provides a nice illustration of how complex configurations of factors in school systems, not single factors in isolation, account for "school effects" *per se* on students.

Others have studied issues of school size in the context of the schools-within-schools or small learning community approaches (Maroulis & Gomez, 2008; Ready & Lee, 2008). The schools-within-schools approach grew out of two concerns: reducing the size of each student's learning community without having to build new schools, and providing students with greater choice over their high-school curriculum. Educators decided that they could create several smaller learning communities within the existing large high-school buildings. Furthermore, they decided that they could increase student choice and sense of autonomy by focusing these smaller learning communities on specific subject matter or career topics such as math/science, the arts, health, and vocational education. Unfortunately, unless school administrators are very careful, these smaller learning communities often end up creating the same problems that we discussed under academic tracking; namely, tracking highly linked to the students' social class, which can then exacerbate problems of inequity in educational experiences (Ready & Lee, 2008). The students like these smaller learning communities and report feeling that their educational options fit better with their own career and educational goals, even though they acknowledge the status hierarchies associated with the different communities that can be created along social class lines in certain schools-within-schools programs.

Connell (2003; Connell & Klem, 2000) has created a major school reform model, *First Things First*, which uses small learning communities as a key component. He also requires that the schools create these communities in ways that do not segregate students based on current ability levels and social class. Finally, he provides the schools with major academic learning supports to keep the focus on learning rather than social climate. The results of his reform efforts in risk schools are quite promising. Not only has the reform succeeded in raising the academic performance of the schools, it has also reduced the differentials in performance across social class groups and increased both attendance and high-school graduation rates.

School Culture

The concept of the culture of the school as a whole, and the fact that different schools, like different communities, vary in their interpersonal, moral and academic cultures, expectations and goals for students, has made an important contribution to our understanding of school effects (e.g., Bandura, 2006; Bryk et al., 1993; Comer, 1980; Lee & Smith, 2001; NRC/IOM, 2004; Rutter, Maughan, Mortimore, & Ouston, 1979; Sarason, 1990). For example, in their analysis of why students achieve more in Catholic public schools, Bryk et al. (1993) discuss how both the academic and social cultures of Catholic schools fundamentally differ from those within most public schools in ways that positively affect the motivation of students, parents, and teachers. These cultures or general school climate are characterized by high value placed on learning, high expectations that all children can learn and master a core curriculum, and affirm the belief that though the business of school is learning, each person has inherent value and dignity and each person is a valued member of a social community (see also Lee & Smith, 2001). As a second example of general school culture factors that are consequential for student achievement, Bandura and his colleagues documented between-school differences in the aggregate level of teachers' efficacy beliefs (Bandura, 1994), a concept called collective efficacy. School-level differences in the collective efficacy of elementary-school teachers have been related to differences in students' aggregate reading and mathematics achievement (e.g., Goddard, Hoy, & Woolfolk Hoy, 2000).

Research and intervention work has also been done on how to create positive moral cultures in schools. This work, done by the Child Development Project (CDP) in Oakland, California, takes a school-level approach to fostering students' social and ethical development as well as their cognitive and academic development. Critically important to this approach are practices that directly engage students in cooperative and community-building activities at school. These include the use of cooperative learning techniques in classrooms, classroom management strategies that rely on student participation in norm setting and decision-making, teaching of conflict resolution skills, and curricula that focus students on themes of care. Research and intervention studies have shown that such practices foster a "community of care" that positively influences students' self-understanding, motivational beliefs and feelings of belonging, and in-school behavior (Battistich et al., 1999; Schaps, 2003).

Work in the area of school violence has also focused on the social and moral cultures of the school as a whole. Astor and his colleagues (Astor Meyer, & Behre, 1999; Astor et al., 2002; Benbenishty & Astor, 2007; Benbenishty, Astor, Zeira, & Vinokus, 2002) have shown that both the levels of school violence and students' concerns about their safety at school decrease as the social climate in the schools increases. It is likely that these two aspects of schools are reciprocally related: as climate decreases, violence increases, and as violence and bullying increase, the general social climate in the school further deteriorates.

In addition to the social and moral dimensions of the school culture, Maehr and Midgley (1996) argued that schools can be characterized by *academic* cultures as well. Just as teachers' instructional strategies are associated with and give rise to certain achievement goals in students, so too, these authors argue, do schools as a whole through their particular policies and practices (see also Midgely, 2002). The argument is that schools, through practices such as how they recognize students, create school-level emphasis on different achievement goals that then affect students' own goals and beliefs in their engagement and behavior (Midgley, 2002; Roeser et al., 1996; Urdan & Roeser, 1993). For example, schools' use of public honor rolls and assemblies for the highest achieving students, class rankings on report cards, differential curricular offerings for students of various ability levels, and so on are all practices that emphasize relative ability, competition, and social comparison in the school ("school ability orientation"). In contrast, through the recognition of academic effort and improvement, rewards for different competencies that extend to all students, and through practices that emphasize learning and task mastery (block scheduling, interdisciplinary curricular teams, cooperative learning), schools can promote a focus on discovery, effort and improvement, and academic mastery ("school task orientation"). Maehr and Midgley (1996) spent 3 years working with one middle school to test these ideas. Although it was quite difficult to actually change the school's practices, student motivation did increase as the school became more task-focused and less ability-focused (see also NRC/IOM, 2004).

Anderman, Maehr, and Midgley (1999) presented evidence that Maehr and Midgley's attempts to alter the school-level goal structure in their school improvement work influenced the goal structures students perceived in their classrooms. Anderman and his colleagues (1999) found that when students moved from elementary schools into the treatment middle school (where efforts were underway to create a mastery goal structure), they reported a slight decrease in personal performance goals whereas students entering the control middle school reported an increase in performance goals. In addition, students moving to the treatment school reported no change in their perceptions of a performance goal structure in their classrooms whereas those moving into the comparison middle school reported increased emphasis on performance goals.

The academic goal focus of a school has important implications for students' mental health as well. In a series of studies, Roeser and Eccles found that middle-school adolescents' belief that their school was ability-focused was associated with declines in their educational values, achievement, and self-esteem, and increases in their anger, depressive symptoms, and school truancy from seventh to eighth grade. These effects were found after controlling for prior levels of each adjustment outcome, adolescents' prior academic ability, and their demographic background (ethnicity, gender, family income; Roeser & Eccles, 1998; Roeser, Eccles, & Sameroff, 1998a). These results support the idea that schools that emphasize ability are likely to alienate a significant number of students who cannot perform at the highest levels, leading to anxiety, anger, disenchantment, and self-selection out of the school environment (Eccles & Midgley, 1989; Finn, 1989; Maehr & Midgley, 1996; Midgley, 2002). In contrast, schools that emphasize effort, improvement, task mastery, and the expectation that all students can learn appear to enfranchise more children in the learning process, promote adaptive attributions (e.g., achievement is based on effort and is therefore malleable), reduce depression, and decrease the frustration and anxiety that can be generated in achievement settings.

An extension of this work on academic climates with high-school students comes from a study by Fiqueira-McDonough (1986). She studied two high schools that were similar in intake characteristics and achievement outcomes, but differed in their academic orientation and rates of delinquent behavior. The high school characterized by a greater emphasis on competition and high grades (ability orientation) had higher delinquency rates, particularly among low-achieving students, than the school that was "more diverse in its goals and [took] a greater interest in students' non-academic needs," where school attachment (valuing of school, liking teachers) was greater on average. Furthermore, individual differences in school attachment were a primary predictor of delinquent activity: Students with lower school attachment were more involved in delinquency than students with higher school attachment. Fiqueira-McDonough (1986) concluded that the broader concern of this school with motivation and diverse needs of students enhanced adolescents' attachment to school, which, in turn, discouraged involvement in delinquency.

Research using students' perceptions of the school culture has documented that perception of the school academic culture is correlated with perception of the teacher–student relationships. For instance, adolescents who perceive a task orientation in their school also report that their teachers are friendly, caring, and respectful. These factors, in turn, predict an increased sense of belonging in school among adolescents (Roeser et al., 1996). In contrast, perceptions of a school ability orientation are negatively correlated with adolescents' perceptions of caring teachers (Roeser et al., 1996). From the adolescents' perspective, a de-emphasis on comparison and competition and an emphasis on effort and improvement are intertwined with their view of caring teachers. Other research has documented that adolescents' perceptions of a school performance goal structure are positively correlated with perceptions of racial discrimination in school among African- and Latin-American youth (Roeser & Peck, 2003; Roeser, 2004). It may be that by adolescence, certain ethnic-minority students become more aware of the differential reward structures and opportunities in the school, who the primary benefactors of these structures and opportunities are, and how such disparities in opportunities and outcomes mirror what youth see between racial/ethnic groups in the wider society. Focusing on task-oriented motivational strategies in schools may thereby reduce the salience and potentially debilitating effects of racial/ethnic stereotypes and relative ability-oriented rewards structures on the achievement of particular groups of students.

Research on school cultures has revealed that school-wide policies and practices can influence not only students' motivation and achievement, but also teachers' professional identities, work motivation, and pedagogy. As studies of "effective schools" have shown, competent leadership and a sense of mutual support among school staff are two important ingredients in effective schools (Good & Weinstein, 1986). However, not all schools have work environments in which there is equitable treatment of teachers, democratic decision-making processes, a spirit of innovation, and opportunities for the professional development of all teachers. From a goal theory perspective, it is hypothetically possible to describe the work environment of a school as emphasizing competition, social comparison, and differential treatment of teachers (e.g., a performance goal structure); cooperation, equity, and a spirit of innovation (e.g., a mastery goal structure); or to some degree, both. Roeser, Marachi, and Gehlbach (2000) found that when teachers perceived differential treatment of teachers by their administrators, and a sense of competitiveness among the teaching staff in the school, they were more likely to endorse classroom practices that highlighted ability differences and competition between students. On the other hand, when teachers in elementary and middle schools perceived support for innovation, experimentation, and even acceptance of "failure" when innovating from school leaders and their colleagues, they were more likely to emphasize these values and goals through their own classroom pedagogy. Together, these findings underscore the possibility that real change in students' motivation and learning through reform efforts may turn on whether or not a supportive work culture for teachers in which cooperation, innovation, and experimentation are valued exists in a school (Good & Weinstein, 1986; Maehr, 1991; Maehr & Midgley, 1996; Sarason, 1990). Again, this set of findings underscores interdependencies across levels of the school system when one is trying to understand the influence of schooling on child and adolescent development. As Sarason (1990, pp. xiii–xiv) put it:

> Schools have been intractable to change and the attainment of goals by reformers ... the unreflective acceptance of the belief that schools exist only or primarily for children is one of the root causes of this intractability. Schools should exist equally for the development of both faculty and students ... teachers cannot create and sustain the conditions for the productive development of children if those conditions do not exist for the teachers.

Unsupervised School Spaces

Another important physical dimension of school buildings is the non-instructional spaces that adolescents move in and through before school, after school, and between classes. These spaces include the parking lots and the school grounds, the hallways and the bathrooms, the sports fields (if any), and the cafeteria(s). One example of the importance of such spaces in the study of schooling and development comes from the work of Astor and his colleagues (1999) on school violence. These authors have found that even though students may respond affirmatively to a series of questions about how safe they feel in school in general, they still can show strong fears in particular areas of the school or school grounds at particular times of the day where violence is most likely to occur. For example, in a study of students in five high-school settings in southeastern Michigan, Astor and his colleagues (1999) found that most violent events reported by students occurred in what the authors called the "undefined public spaces" of the school—parking lots, bathrooms, particular hallways, and so on where no adults assumed supervisory jurisdiction. These spaces were undefined in terms of adult monitoring of behavior in them, and thus were the frequent sites for fights, unwanted sexual attention, and other negative behaviors.

School violence and bullying can have a negative impact on the target victims' and observing students' motivation and well-being (Nishina & Juvonen, 2005). In terms of the perpetrators, Fagan and Wilkinson (1998) reviewed theory and evidence that suggest several different functional goals that violence can serve for youth. These included the securing of high status among peers, acquisition of material goods, dominance of others and retribution for insults to the self, defiance of authority, and a form of "rough justice" in situations in which there is little legitimate adult authority. Thus, understanding the origins of school violence requires that we look at how school organizational factors and the psychological processes of the perpetrators co-contribute to school violence and its impacts on victims. In addition, understanding how undefined school spaces may offer disenfranchised students a venue to express themselves in antisocial ways at school may lead to new insights into how to reduce antisocial behavior by providing additional monitoring in unsupervised areas, as well as providing young people with more constructive opportunities for autonomy, belonging, status, competence, and well-being in the context of school and the way classrooms and the school as a whole are run.

School Hours and Schedules

Scholars have looked at two aspects of school schedules in terms of their impact on human development: school start and ending times, and the nature of the annual school calendar.

School start and end times. School start time is yet another example of how regulatory processes associated with schools can interact with individual regulatory processes, here biological ones, to influence development. Research conducted by Carskadon (1990, 1997) has shown that as children progress through puberty they actually need more, not less, sleep. During this same period, as children move through elementary to middle and high school, schools typically begin earlier and earlier in the morning, necessitating earlier rise times for adolescents (Carskadon, 1997). In concert with other changes, such as the later hours at which adolescents go to bed, the earlier school start times of the middle and high school create a "developmental mismatch" that can both promote daytime sleepiness and undermine adolescents' ability to make it to school on time, alert, and ready to learn.

The "developmental mismatch" of increased need for sleep and earlier school start time can promote daytime sleepiness in adolescents.

The time at which school ends also has implications for child and adolescent adjustment. In communities where few structured opportunities for after-school activities exist, especially impoverished communities, children are more likely to be involved in high-risk behaviors such as substance use, crime, violence, and sexual activity during the period between 2 and 8 p.m. Providing structured activities either at school or within community organizations after school, when many children have no adults at home to supervise them, is an important consideration in preventing children and adolescents from engaging in high-risk behaviors (Carnegie Council on Adolescent Development, 1989; Eccles & Templeton, 2002) and for keeping educationally vulnerable students on track academically (Mahoney, Lord, & Carryl, 2005b; Peck, Roeser, Zarrett, & Eccles, 2008).

School calendar. American schools typically are in session from September into June. This calendar reflects the historical need for students to be available to work on family farms during the summer. Such need is no longer typical for the vast majority of America's students. What is the consequence of this calendar for learning? This question has become highly salient in educational policy discussions due to increasing evidence that social class differences in school achievement result in large part because of social class differences in the "summer learning gap." Most recently, work by Alexander, Entwisle, and their colleagues showed that much of the social class differential in school achievement reflects differences that already exist when the students enter kindergarten and differences that accumulate over the elementary-school years in learning over the summer vacations. On average, children living in poor families learn less and forget more over the summer vacation than children living in middle-class and upper-class families, in part because these families are able to provide their children with a variety of structured learning experiences over the summer (Alexander et al., 2007). When they compared the actual rate of learning over the course of the school year across social class lines in the Baltimore school district, Alexander and his colleagues found little if any social class difference; in contrast, they found a substantial difference over the summer time. Work on summer schools has shown that well-designed summer school programs can help ameliorate this social-class differential (Alexander et al., 2007).

LEVEL 6: SCHOOL–HOME–COMMUNITY CONNECTIONS

Home–School Connections

Parent involvement in their child's schooling has consistently emerged as an important factor in promoting both academic achievement and socioemotional well-being (Comer, 1980; Eccles & Harold, 1993). Parent involvement in the form of monitoring academic activities and homework, providing assistance with homework, engaging children in educational enrichment activities outside of school, and active participation in classroom activities and in school organizations (e.g., governance, parent–teacher associations) (Epstein, 1992) communicates positive educational expectations, interest, and support to the child. Parent involvement also helps to establish a "safety net" of concerned adults (parents and teachers) that can support children's academic and socioemotional development and assist children if adjustment problems should arise (Jackson & Davis 2000; NRC/IOM, 2004).

Evidence also suggests that home–school connections are relatively infrequent during the elementary years and become almost non-existent during the middle- and high-school years (e.g., Carnegie Council on Adolescent Development, 1989; Eccles & Harold, 1993; Epstein, 1992; Stevenson & Stigler, 1992). This lack of involvement has been attributed to few efforts on the part of schools to involve parents, especially as children transition out of neighborhood-based elementary schools into the larger, more impersonal middle- and high-school environments (Eccles & Harold, 1993). The cultural belief that teachers are in charge of children's learning also contributes to the low levels of parent involvement in schools in the United States (Stevenson & Stigler, 1992). Other characteristics and experiences of parents that reduce involvement include a lack of time, energy, and/or economic resources, lack of knowledge, feelings of incompetence, failure to understand the role parents can play in education, or a long history of negative interactions of parents with the schools (Eccles & Harold, 1993; NRC/IOM, 2004).

School–Community Connections

Comer (1980) stressed the importance of school–community connections and partnerships. He argued that schools are a part of the larger community and that they will be successful only to the extent that they are well integrated into that community at all levels. For example, schools need to be well connected to the communities' social services so that schools can play a cooperative role in furthering children's and their families' well-being. Conversely, communities need to be invested in their schools in ways that stimulate active engagement across these two societal units. For example, when the business community is well connected to the school, there are likely to be increased opportunities for students to develop both the skills and knowledge necessary to make a smooth transition from school into the world of work. Such opportunities can range from frequent field trips to various employment settings to apprenticeships to direct involvement of employees in the instructional program of the school.

Concern about a stronger link between communities and schools has led to a recent increase in opportunities for students to be involved in community service-learning opportunities. In 1989, the Turning Points report (Carnegie Council on Adolescent Development, 1989) recommended that every middle school include supervised youth service in the community or school as part of the core academic curriculum. Today 25% of elementary schools, 38% of middle schools, and 46% of all high schools have students participating in either mandatory or voluntary service-learning activities (NCES, 2004).

Evidence for a positive impact of service-learning on various indicators of child and adolescent development is accumulating (NRC/IOM, 2004). For example, participants in well-designed service-learning programs do better than comparison groups on measures of problem-solving ability, reading and mathematics achievement, and course failure (Eyler, Root, & Giles, 1998; Fisher, 2001; Melchior & Bailis, 2002; Moore & Allen, 1996). Participation in service-learning programs is also linked to positive social assets, civic engagement, community involvement, and increased social and personal responsibility (e.g., Kahne, Chi, & Middaugh, 2002; Scales, Blyth, Berkas, & Kielsmeier, 2000), empathetic understanding (Scales et al., 2000), improved attitudes toward diverse groups in society (Yates & Youniss, 1996), altruistic motivation (Scales et al., 2000), closer communication with one's parents (Scales et al., 2000), more positive or mastery-oriented motivation for school work (Scales et al., 2000), greater commitment to academic learning (Scales et al., 2000), increased feelings of personal efficacy and self-esteem (Kahne et al., 2002; Yates & Youniss, 1996), and a better sense of oneself (Hamilton & Fenzel, 1988; Hart, Yates, Fegley, & Wilson, 1995). Finally, service-learning has also been related to reductions in problem behaviors. In a review of programs aimed at reducing adolescent pregnancy and unprotected sex, Kirby (2002) concluded that service-learning is an effective approach. Service-learning has also been linked to decreases in problem behavior in terms of lower course failure, school suspension, and school dropout (Allen, Philliber, Herrling & Kuperminc, 1997), fewer discipline problems (Calabrese & Schumer, 1986), and reduced absenteeism (Melchior & Bailis, 2002).

Part-time employment is another example of school–community linkage that relates to the quality of adolescents' adjustment. Although part-time work outside of school hours can promote developmental competence by providing structured, safe opportunities in which adolescents can acquire skills, learn to follow structured routines, work cooperatively with others, and serve others (Mortimer, Shanahan, & Ryu, 1994), some have suggested that too much employment can undermine school success and promote engagement in problem behaviors. For instance, Steinberg, Fegley, and Dornbusch (1993) found that adolescents who work 20 hours or more per week show poor grades, lower school commitment, and less engagement in class activities than their non-working peers. One possible reason for these relations is that adolescents who work long hours are getting insufficient sleep. Steinberg et al. (1993) found that about one-third of the adolescents in their study who worked 20 hours a week or more also reported they were frequently too tired to do their homework and often chose easier classes to accommodate their heavy employment schedules. Although it is true that academically disengaged adolescents are more likely to seek out other settings such as part-time work to get their needs met, it is also true that increased work hours predict academic disengagement (Steinberg et al., 1993).

Mortimer and her colleagues found a much more positive association between working during the high-school years and successful adolescent development. In their multiyear longitudinal study of 1000 adolescents, they found that working an average of 20 hours a week or less bolsters self-confidence, time management skills, career exploration, and responsibility. It also was associated with increased likelihood of attending and completing college (Mortimer et al., 1994; Staff, Mortimer, & Uggen, 2004). Two issues are critical in explaining the differences in these two major studies: amount of time worked and prior academic and psychological functioning. Adolescents who take near full-time jobs while they are in high school, in part because they are already alienated from school, are likely to become further disengaged from schooling as they find a more rewarding niche at work. In contrast, working 10–20 hours per week is a positive growth experience for those adolescents who are doing adequately in other aspects of their development (Zimmer-Gembeck & Mortimer, 2006).

Closer ties between schools and communities may be especially important in high-risk neighborhoods. Both researchers and policy makers have become concerned with the lack of structured opportunities for youth after school (e.g., Carnegie Corporation of New York, 1992; Eccles & Gootman, 2002; Eccles & Templeton, 2002). In most communities, adolescents finish their school day by 2 or 3 in the afternoon. Also in most communities there are few structured activities available for these youths other than work. And typically, their parents are working until early evening—leaving the adolescents largely unsupervised. Such a situation is worrisome for two reasons: First, communities are missing an opportunity to foster positive development through meaningful activities and, second, adolescents are most likely to engage in problem behaviors during this unsupervised period. A closer collaboration between communities and schools could help solve this dilemma. At the most basic level, school buildings could be used as activity centers. At a more cooperative level, school and community personnel could work together to design a variety of programs to meet the multiple needs of their youth. We discuss this issue more extensively later in the chapter.

In this section, we summarized the multiple ways through which schools as complex organizations can influence child development. We stressed the fact that the various levels of organization interact in ways that shape the day-to-day experiences of children, adolescents, and teachers. We also stressed that there are systematic differences in these organizational features and that these differences help to explain differences in both teachers' behaviors and children's development within the school context. In the next sections, we provide three more specific examples of how these processes interact with each other and with the developmental level of the child to influence human development. The first focuses on transition into elementary school; the second and third focus on the transition from elementary school to either middle or junior high school and then on to high school. Both of these examples illustrate how children are exposed to systematic age-related changes in their out-of-family contexts of development and how these changes can impact their development.

SCHOOL TRANSITIONS AS WINDOWS ON THE INFLUENCE OF SCHOOL CONTEXT EFFECTS

Because they involve simultaneous changes in the school context and child developmental outcomes, school transitions provide a unique opportunity to assess school context effects on human development. All school districts must decide both when they allow children to begin school and how they will group the grade levels within the various school buildings. One common arrangement is to group children in kindergarten through sixth grade in elementary schools, children in Grades 7 through 9 in junior high schools, and children in Grades 10 through 12 in senior high schools. The other most common arrangement places the transitions after Grades 5 and 8—creating elementary schools, middle schools, and senior high schools. In both of these arrangements, children typically begin public schooling at age 5 with the entry into kindergarten. In addition, children typically move to a new and often larger building at each of the major school transition points (e.g., the move to middle or junior high school). These school transitions typically also involve increased bussing and exposure to a much more diverse student body. Despite sound theoretical reasons to expect that such transitions should influence children's development (Eccles, Midgley, & Adler, 1984), until recently there has been little empirical work on school transition effects. Because most of the empirical work has focused on the junior high-/middle-school transition, we emphasize this transition after briefly reviewing the work on the entry to elementary school.

Transition into Elementary School

Entrance into elementary school and then the transition from kindergarten to first grade introduces several systematic changes in children's social worlds (Perry & Weinstein, 1998). First, classes are age stratified, making age-independent ability social comparison much easier. Second, formal evaluations of competence by "experts" begin. Third, formal ability grouping begins usually with reading group assignment. Fourth, peers have the opportunity to play a much more constant and salient role in children's lives. Each of these changes should affect children's development. We know that first grade children modify both their expectations and their behavior more to failure feedback than children in preschool and kindergarten (Parsons & Ruble, 1977; Stipek & Hoffman, 1980). Changes such as those described above could certainly contribute to these changes in children's response to failure. We also know that parents' expectations for, and perceptions of, their children's academic competence are influenced by report card marks and standardized test scores given out during the early elementary-school years, particularly for mathematics (Alexander & Entwisle, 1988; Arbreton & Eccles, 1994).

Morrison and his colleagues have exploited the fact that schools have cut-off ages for eligibility to start school to examine the effects of age versus schooling on student development. As a result of these cut-offs, there is a group of children whose ages fall very near to the cut-off point (e.g., needing to be 5 years of age by September 1 of the school year). Those who make this cut-off get to start school; those who don't have to wait another year to begin formal schooling. By comparing the performance of these children on a variety of indicators, Morrison and his colleagues are able to estimate the effects of schooling versus maturing on various aspects of cognitive development (e.g., Christian, Morrison, Frazier, & Massetti, 2000). In general, they have found that the impacts of schooling are quite specific: Those children who attended kindergarten and first grade did better than children near in age who did not start school on tests of reading and letter recognition, mathematical skills, general information, and phonemic segmentation. In contrast, they did not do better on tests of receptive vocabulary and subsyllabic segmentation.

Evidence is emerging of significant long-term consequences of children's experiences in the first grade (Schulting, Malone, & Dodge, 2005). This is particularly true for experiences associated with ability grouping and within-class differential teacher treatment. Studies have shown that teachers use a variety of information in assigning first-grade students to reading groups, including temperamental characteristics (such as interest and persistence), ethnicity, gender, and social class (e.g., Alexander, Entwisle, & Dauber, 1994; Rist, 1970). Alexander et al. (1994) demonstrated that differences in first-grade reading group placement and teacher–student interactions have a significant and substantial effect (even after controlling for beginning differences in competence) on motivation, achievement, and behavior many years later. Furthermore, Pallas et al. (1994) demonstrated that these effects are mediated in part by differential instruction and in part by the exaggerating impact of ability group placement on parents' and teachers' views of the children's abilities, talents, and motivation.

The Middle Grades School Transition

There is substantial evidence of declines in academic motivation, interest in school, and achievement across the early adolescence years; particularly as these adolescents make the transition to middle or junior high school (approximately ages 11–14; see Anderman & Maehr, 1994; Anderman et al., 1999; Eccles et al., 1993; Juvonen et al., 2004; Rumberger, 1995; Wigfield, Eccles, & Pintrich, 1996). There are also increases in test anxiety (Wigfield & Eccles, 1989), focus on self-evaluation rather than task mastery (Nicholls, 1990), and both truancy and school dropout (NRC/IOM, 2004; Rosenbaum, 1976, 1991). Although these changes are not extreme for most adolescents, there is sufficient evidence of declines in various indicators of academic motivation, behavior, and self-perceptions and values over the early adolescent years to make one wonder what is happening. And although few studies have gathered information on ethnic or social class differences in these declines, academic failure and dropout are especially problematic among some ethnic groups and among youth from low-SES communities and families. It is probable then that these groups are particularly likely to show these declines in academic motivation and self-perceptions as they move into and through the secondary-school years (e.g., Roeser & Eccles, 1998; Roeser et al., 1999; Roeser & Peck, 2003).

Several explanations have been offered for these "negative" changes in academic motivation: Some point to the intraspsychic upheaval associated with early adolescent development (Blos, 1965). Others point to the simultaneous occurrence of several life changes. For example, Simmons and Blyth (1987) attributed these declines, particularly among females, to the coincidence of the junior high-school transition with pubertal development. Still others point to the nature of the junior high-school environment itself rather than the transition *per se*. Extending person–environment fit theory (Hunt, 1975) into a developmental perspective (stage–environment fit theory), Eccles and Midgley (1989) proposed that these negative developmental changes result from the fact that traditional junior high schools do not provide developmentally appropriate educational environments for early adolescents. They suggested that different types of educational environment are needed for different age groups to meet individual developmental needs and foster continued developmental growth. Exposure to the developmentally appropriate environment would facilitate both motivation and continued growth; in contrast, exposure to developmentally inappropriate environments, especially developmentally regressive environments, should create a particularly poor person–environment fit, which should lead to declines in motivation as well as detachment from the goals of the institution.

This analysis suggests several important developmental questions. First, what are the developmental needs of the early adolescent? Second, what kinds of educational environments are developmentally appropriate for meeting these needs and stimulating further development? Third, what are the most common school environmental changes before and after the transition to middle or junior high school? Fourth, and most importantly, are these changes compatible with the physiological, cognitive, and psychological changes early adolescents are experiencing? Or is there a developmental mismatch between maturing early adolescents and the classroom environments they experience before and after the transition to middle or junior high school that leads to a deterioration in academic and socioemotional development and performance for some children?

Stage–environment fit and the transition to junior high or middle school. Until quite recently, few empirical studies focused on differences in the classroom or school environment across grades or school levels (Juvonen et al., 2004). Most descriptions focused on school-level characteristics such as school size, degree of departmentalization, and extent of bureaucratization. For example, Simmons and Blyth (1987) pointed out that most junior high schools are substantially larger than elementary schools and instruction is more likely to be organized departmentally. As a result, junior high-school teachers typically teach several different groups of students, making it very difficult for students to form a close relationship with any school-affiliated adult precisely at the point in development when there is a great need for guidance and support from non-familial adults. Such changes in student–teacher relationships are also likely to undermine the sense of community and trust between students and teachers, leading to a lowered sense of efficacy among the teachers, an increased reliance on authoritarian control practices by the teachers, and an increased sense of alienation among the students. Finally, such changes are likely to decrease the probability that any particular student's difficulties will be noticed early enough to get the student necessary help, thus increasing the likelihood that students on the edge will be allowed to slip onto negative motivational and performance trajectories leading to increased school failure and dropout. In the next sections, we discuss these issues in more detail.

Teacher control.   First, despite the increasing maturity of students, junior high-school classrooms, compared to elementary-school classrooms, are characterized by a greater emphasis on teacher control and discipline, and fewer opportunities for student decision-making, choice, and self-management (e.g., Jackson & Davis, 2000; Juvonen et al., 2004; Midgley, 2002; Midgley & Feldlaufer, 1987). As outlined earlier, stage–environment fit theory suggests that the mismatch between young adolescents' desires for autonomy and control and their perceptions of the opportunities in their learning environments should result in a decline in the adolescents' intrinsic motivation and interest in school. Mac Iver and Reuman (1988) provided some support for this prediction: They compared the changes in intrinsic interest in mathematics for adolescents reporting different patterns of change in their opportunities for participation in classroom decision-making questions across the junior high-school transition. Those adolescents who perceived their seventh-grade mathematics classrooms as providing fewer opportunities for decision-making than had been available in their sixth-grade mathematics classrooms reported the largest declines in their intrinsic interest in mathematics as they moved from the sixth grade into the seventh grade.

Teacher–student relationships.   As noted earlier, junior high-school classrooms are characterized by a less personal and positive teacher–student relationship than elementary-school classrooms. Given the association of classroom climate and student motivation reviewed earlier, it should not surprising that moving into a less supportive classroom leads to a decline in these early adolescents' interest in the subject matter being taught in that classroom, particularly among the low-achieving students (Dotterer, McHale, & Crouter, 2009; Juvonen et al., 2004; Midgley et al., 1988).

Teacher efficacy.   Junior high-school teachers also feel less effective as teachers than elementary-school teachers, especially for low-ability students (Juvonen et al., 2004; Midgley et al., 1988). Given the association of teacher efficacy and students' beliefs, attitudes, motivation, and achievement (Ashton, 1985; NRC/IOM, 2004), it is again not surprising that these differences in teachers' sense of efficacy before and after the transition to junior high school contributed to the decline in early adolescents', particularly low-achieving adolescents', confidence in their academic abilities and potential (Midgley, Feldlaufer, & Eccles, 1989).

Groups and activity structures.   The shift to junior high school is also associated with an increase in practices such as whole-class task organization and between-classroom ability grouping (Jackson & Davis, 2000; Juvonen et al., 2004; Oakes, Gamoran, & Page, 1992). As noted earlier, such changes should increase social comparison, concerns about evaluation, and competitiveness (Eccles et al., 1984; Rosenholtz & Simpson, 1984). They are also likely to increase teachers' use of normative grading criteria and more public forms of evaluation, both of which have been shown to have a negative effect on early adolescents' self-perceptions and motivation.

Grading practices.   There is no stronger predictor of students' self-confidence and efficacy than the grades they receive. If academic marks decline with the junior high-school transition, then adolescents' self-perceptions and academic motivation should also decline. In fact, junior high-school teachers use stricter and more social comparison-based standards than elementary-school teachers to assess student competency and to evaluate student performance, leading to a drop in grades for many early adolescents as they make the junior high-school transition (Eccles & Midgley, 1989; Roderick, 1993; Simmons & Blyth, 1987). This decline in grades is not matched by a decline in the adolescents' scores on standardized achievement tests, suggesting that the decline reflects a change in grading practices rather than a change in the rate of the students' learning (Kavrell & Petersen, 1984). Imagine what such decline in grades might do to early adolescents' self-confidence and motivation. Although Simmons and Blyth (1987) did not look at this specific question, they did document the impact of this grade drop on subsequent school performance and dropout. Even controlling for a youth's performance prior to the school transition, the magnitude of the grade drop following the transition into either junior high school or middle school was a major predictor of early school leaving (see also Roderick, 1993).

Pedagogical goals.   Several of the changes noted above are linked together in goal theory. Classroom practices related to grading practices, support for autonomy, and instructional organization affect the relative salience of mastery versus performance goals that students adopt as they engage in learning tasks at school. The types of change associated with the middle grades school transition should precipitate greater focus on performance goals. As noted earlier, Midgley and her colleagues found support for this prediction (Midgley, 2002; Midgley et al., 1995). In this study, both teachers and students indicated that performance-focused goals were more prevalent and task-focused goals were less prevalent in the middle-school classrooms than in the elementary-school classrooms. In addition, the elementary-school teachers reported using task-focused instructional strategies more frequently than did the middle-school teachers. Finally, at both grade levels the extent to which teachers were task-focused predicted the students' and the teachers' sense of personal efficacy. Not surprisingly, personal efficacy was lower among the middle-school participants than among the elementary-school participants.

Anderman et al. (1999) extended this work by comparing two groups of young adolescents: a group who moved into a middle school that emphasized task-focused instructional practices and a group who moved into a middle school that emphasized more traditional performance/ability focused instructional practices. Although these two groups of students did not differ in their motivational goals prior to the school transition, they did after the transition. As predicted, the adolescents who moved into the first type of middle school were less likely to show an increase in their extrinsic motivational and performance-oriented motivational goals.

School reform efforts.   Jackson and Davis (2000) summarized many middle-school reform efforts. They concluded that the following middle-school characteristics support both learning and positive youth development:

1. a curriculum grounded in rigorous academic standards and current knowledge about how students learn best, which is relevant to the concerns of adolescents
2. instructional methods designed to prepare all students to achieve at the highest standards
3. organizational structures that support a climate of intellectual development and a caring community with shared educational goals
4. staff who are trained experts at teaching young adolescents
5. ongoing professional development opportunities for the staff
6. democratic governance that involves both the adults and the adolescents
7. extensive involvement of parents and the community
8. high levels of safety and practices that support good health.

Similar conclusions were reached by Juvonen and her colleagues (2004).

Summary.   Changes such as those just reviewed are likely to have a negative effect on many children's motivational orientation toward school at any grade level. But Eccles and Midgley (1989) have argued that these types of school environmental changes are particularly harmful at early adolescence given what is known about psychological development during this stage of life. Evidence from a variety of sources suggests that early adolescent development is characterized by increases in desire for autonomy, peer orientation, self-focus and self-consciousness, salience of identity issues, concern over heterosexual relationships, and capacity for abstract cognitive activity (Brown, 2004; Eccles & Midgley, 1989; Keating, 1990; Simmons & Blyth, 1987; Wigfield et al., 1996). Simmons and Blyth (1987) argued that adolescents need safe, intellectually challenging environments to adapt to these shifts. In light of these needs, the environmental changes often associated with transition to junior high school seem especially harmful in that they emphasize competition, social comparison, and ability self-assessment at a time of heightened self-focus; they decrease decision-making and choice at a time when the desire for control is growing; they emphasize lower-level cognitive strategies at a time when the ability to use higher level strategies is increasing; and they disrupt social networks at a time when adolescents are especially concerned with peer relationships and may be in special need of close adult relationships outside of the home. The nature of these environmental changes, coupled with the normal course of individual development, is likely to result in a developmental mismatch so that the "fit" between the early adolescent and the classroom environment is particularly poor, increasing the risk of negative motivational outcomes, especially for adolescents who are having difficulty succeeding in school academically.

The High-School Transition

Although there is less work on the transition to high school, the existing work suggests quite similar problems (Coleman & Hoffer, 1987; Jackson & Davis, 2000; Lee & Smith, 2001; NRC/IOM, 2004; Wehlage, Rutter, Smith, Lesko, & Fernandez, 1989). For example, high schools are typically even larger and more bureaucratic than junior high schools and middle schools. Lee and Smith (2001) provide numerous examples of how the sense of community among teachers and students is undermined by the size and bureaucratic structure of most high schools. There is little opportunity for students and teachers to get to know each other and, likely as a consequence, there is distrust between them and little attachment to a common set of goals and values. There is also little opportunity for the students to form mentor-like relationships with a non-familial adult and little effort is made to make instruction relevant to the students. Such environments are likely to further undermine the motivation and involvement of many students, especially those not doing particularly well academically, those not enrolled in the favored classes, and those who are alienated from the values of the adults in the high school. These hypotheses need to be tested.

Most large public high schools also organize instruction around curricular tracks that sort students into different groups. As a result, there is even greater diversity in the educational experiences of high-school students than in those of middle grades students; unfortunately, this diversity is often associated more with the students' social class and ethnic group than with differences in their talents and interests (Bryk et al., 1993; Lee et al., 1993; Lee & Smith, 2001). As a result, curricular tracking has served to reinforce social stratification rather than foster optimal education for all students, particularly in large schools (Dornbusch, 1994; Bryk et al., 1993; Lee et al., 1993; Lee & Smith, 2001). Bryk et al. (1993) documented that average school achievement levels do not benefit from this curricular tracking. Quite the contrary—evidence comparing Catholic high schools with public high schools suggests that average school achievement levels are increased when all students are required to take the same challenging curriculum. This conclusion is true even after one has controlled for student selectivity factors. A more thorough examination of how the organization and structure of our high schools influences cognitive, motivational, and achievement outcomes is needed.

Summary of School Transitions Research

In this section, we summarized the evidence related to the impact of school transitions on development. As one would expect, given what we now know about the ecological nature of the junior high-school transition, many early adolescents, particularly the low achievers and the highly anxious, experience great difficulty with this transition. In many ways, this transition can be characterized as a developmentally regressive shift in one's school context. Consistent with our stage–environment fit perspective, such a shift has negative consequences for many youths' school engagement and performance. Also consistent with our stage–environment fit perspective, there is an increasing number of intervention studies showing that the junior high-school transition does not have to yield negative consequences for vulnerable youth. Middle grades educational institutions can be designed in a developmentally progressive manner, and when they are, the majority of early adolescents gain from this school transition.

We have now completed our discussion of school influences on development. In this section, we outlined the many ways in which schools affect the socioemotional development and achievement of children and adolescents. We stressed the need to take both a systems level and a developmental perspective on the school. We now turn to a similar discussion of neighborhood influences. Like schools, neighborhoods are complex places in which children and adolescents spend a great deal of time. Unlike schools, much of this time is unstructured and unorganized. In addition, neighborhoods are far less well integrated contexts than schools. They include a wide array of people, contexts, and both opportunities and risks. Consequently, both the theoretical and the empirical research on neighborhood effects is much more diverse and scattered. It is also more recent, and therefore less voluminous. The major themes in this work are summarized in the next section.

NEIGHBORHOOD AND COMMUNITY INFLUENCES

Recent interest in the potential impact of neighborhoods and communities on human development has grown out of two major lines of work: Bronfenbrenner's articulation of an ecological view of development and renewed concerns with the impact of poverty on children and adolescents.

The publication of Wilson's book *The Truly Disadvantaged* in 1987 was probably the biggest single impetus to the study of poverty in the past 50 years. He outlined the problems of inner-city neighborhoods with unusually high concentrations of poverty, arguing that such neighborhoods pose major threats for socializing the next generation. According to Wilson, inner-city poverty of the 1980s and 1990s is quite different from inner-city poverty in previous generations because employment opportunities have moved out of these neighborhoods, leaving behind a situation in which the adults cannot find employment within their neighborhoods and communities. This in turn leads to high rates of unemployment, demoralization, and drug use, along with the deterioration of both the two-parent family and community well-being. Together these characteristics create a situation in which children have few successful role models and little obvious incentive to do well in school. Instead, they have many models of hopelessness and illegal behaviors. They also live in run-down housing with abundant health risks. Parents who do not have the economic means to leave these neighborhoods must cope with these conditions as they try to rear their children to become hopeful, healthy, and fully functioning members of the larger society. Wilson stressed just how difficult this task is if one lives in these truly disadvantaged neighborhoods.

Research related to Wilson's hypotheses, as well as to work by Bronfenbrenner and his colleagues (Bronfenbrenner & Morris, 1998) and the growing interest in the effects of poverty on human development (e.g., McLoyd, 1990; Sharkey, 2009), is accumulating. First and foremost, all researchers acknowledge the importance of studying both direct and indirect effects of neighborhood characteristics (Brooks-Gunn, Duncan, & Aber, 1997a, 1997b; Elder & Conger, 2000; Furstenberg et al., 1999; Runyan et al., 2009; Sampson, Raudenbush, & Earls, 1997). Most attention has been focused on the indirect effects of neighborhood characteristics mediated through the family, school, and peer networks. For example, the stresses on parents of living in poor, under-resourced neighborhoods are assumed to undermine effective parenting, especially for vulnerable parents (e.g., those who are unemployed or who have other major problems). In addition, the realities of the neighborhood are assumed to influence parents' goals and interactions with neighborhood institutions and residents (e.g., parents are likely to keep their children in the house or apartment as much as possible if the streets and parks in their community are dangerous). Similarly, because schools are funded to a great extent from neighborhood resources, the quality of the schools children attend is directly related to the incomes of the families living in their neighborhood. Finally, the kinds of peers children are likely to associate with are directly influenced by the types of children and families who live in their neighborhood. As noted below, work assessing these types of indirect influence is just beginning. Thus far, results support their importance (Brooks-Gunn et al., 1997a, 1997b).

Second, the nature and range of neighborhood influences on development differ by age. Infants and preschoolers are affected most by the indirect effects of neighborhood characteristics on their parents' behaviors and by the direct effects of varying health hazards associated with living in different types of communities. As children get older, they are affected more directly by the other institutions in the neighborhood, such as the schools and community recreational facilitates, and by the peers and adults who reside in their neighborhood. These out-of-home neighborhood influences are especially influential during adolescence and young adulthood (Brooks-Gunn et al., 1997a, 1997b).

Third, we are just beginning to study the influences of neighborhood culture on development. Most work has focused on the establishing that there are neighborhood effects; that is, that children's development is affected by the characteristics of the neighborhoods in which they grow up independent of the characteristics of their families. This is not an easy thing to demonstrate because families living in different neighborhoods are also quite different from each other (Firkowska et al., 1978). The best example of this problem is family income. Poor families live in poor neighborhoods; rich families live in rich neighborhoods. How, then, does a researcher know if the relation of neighborhood poverty to children's school grades is due to "neighborhood effects" or to their parents' income? Researchers are still working out exactly how to answer this question.

An attempt to separate out these influences is the work by Rosenbaum and his associates (e.g., Rosenbaum, 1980, 1991; Rosenbaum, Kulieke, & Rubinowitz, 1988). In 1976, the courts in Chicago ordered the Chicago Housing Authority to redress ethnic discrimination in housing placement by offering poor families the opportunity to move to better housing. Families who accepted this offer were randomly assigned to housing either in a better inner-city neighborhood or in a middle-class suburban community outside of Chicago. Rosenbaum and his colleagues studied the long-term differences in developmental outcomes for the children in these two types of families. Youths reared in the suburbs were much more likely to graduate from high school, to complete a college track high-school academic program, and to attend college than youths reared in the alternative inner-city neighborhood. Given the experimental design of this study, it provides the strongest empirical support available that the neighborhood in which a child grows up has an impact on that child's developmental outcomes. The source of this effect, however, was not identifiable in this study. Researchers are now shifting their focus to understanding the processes that might account for such a neighborhood effect.

The US government enacted a major social policy experiment by providing a randomly selected group of very poor families in several large cities with the opportunity to move to middle-class neighborhoods in nearby suburbs (The Move to Opportunity Program—MTO). Researchers from several different disciplines are studying the consequences of this experiment for children's development. So far the evidence looks quite good for elementary-school-aged children and for mothers: The children are doing better in school and in general social functioning that the control group children, and the mothers are doing better on both schooling and employment outcomes than the control group mothers (Leventhal & Brooks-Gunn, 2004). The MTO adolescents are also less involved in criminal behavior than the control group adolescents.

These studies support the hypothesis that neighborhood characteristics should influence the course of human development for residents. But how do neighborhood characteristics influence development? Jencks and Mayer (1990) suggested three likely sources of influence that are of particular importance to this chapter: contagion, collective socialization, and resource exposure. By *contagion*, Jencks and Mayer (1990) were referring to the impact primarily of peer groups and young adults on children's behaviors, goals, and values. They argued that both good and bad behaviors are easily modeled and picked up by younger children as they watch the older children, adolescents, and young adults in their neighborhood. If most of the adolescents in a neighborhood drop out of school and use drugs and alcohol, then younger children are likely to adopt similar behavior patterns and values as they grow up. In addition, the older individuals in the neighborhood often actively recruit younger children and adolescents into the most typical activity settings (e.g., either gangs or more positive settings linked to faith-based or prosocial activity-based organizations such as Girl Scouts), further increasing the likelihood of children adopting the behavior patterns and values of the older residents in their communities. By and large, evidence supports this hypothesis (Brooks-Gunn et al., 1997a, 1997b; Furstenberg et al., 1999).

By *collective socialization*, Jencks and Mayer (1990) meant the collaborative efforts in the community to socialize the next generation. Somewhat like the recruitment component of the contagion effect discussed above, adults in a community sometimes have common goals for their children. If they are able to implement these goals with common strategies and socialization practices, they should be able to increase the likelihood of the children becoming the types of individuals they want them to become. Having abundant and consistent role models of the desired kinds of adult outcomes in the neighborhood should also increase this likelihood. Although work assessing this hypothesis is just beginning, initial findings provide promising support (Brooks-Gunn et al., 1997a, 1997b).

Closely related to this perspective is the work by Sampson et al. (1997) on collective efficacy. These researchers defined *collective efficacy* in terms of two components: social cohesion (shared values and goals) and confidence in shared social control mechanisms. After controlling for family-level characteristics such as income, education, and employment, and neighborhood-demographic characteristics such as the percentage of families living below the poverty line, the percentage of immigrant and African-American families, and the instability of the resident structure, Sampson et al. found that neighborhoods with a high sense of collective efficacy among the residents had lower rates of crime and delinquency. These investigators are also gathering extensive developmental data on the children in these neighborhoods. In the future, we will learn whether living in a neighborhood with a high sense of collective efficacy also serves as a protective factor in children's development.

By *resource exposure*, Jencks and Mayer (1990) meant the availability of opportunities versus dangers and risks. Communities vary in the presence and quality of such good things as schools, faith-based institutions, and other types of activity-base organization, recreational facilities, health facilities, access to affordable stores and markets, and police monitoring, as well as such risky things as the presence of liquor stores and drug outlets, the proportion of run-down versus quality housing, and both gang and police harassment. Jencks and Mayer argued that exposure to these types of risks and opportunities should influence the behaviors of all members of the community. The little available evidence is supportive of these predictions, but the effects of these general neighborhood characteristics are quite weak and, by and large, appear to be mediated through their impact of families and peer groups (Brooks-Gunn et al., 1997a, 1997b). In the next section we discuss the evidence for more positive effects of participating in organized activities, which are, typically, differentially available across various types of neighborhoods.

Furstenberg and his colleagues (1999) have suggested another mechanism of influence: *family management*. They suggested that the impact of neighborhoods on development would be moderated by the quality of parenting to which the children were exposed. Effective parents should adjust both their childrearing practices and the nature of their children's exposure to opportunities and risks outside the home depending on the type of community in which they live. In turn, these practices should either buffer the children from exposure to potential risks or facilitate their growth through exposure to positive opportunities. They referred to this set of practices as family management. The little available evidence suggests that many well-functioning parents do vary their practices depending on their community and that successfully implementing locally effective strategies does buffer against the negative impact of neighborhood risks on development, particularly in early and middle childhood periods (Brooks-Gunn et al., 1997a, 1997b; Duncan & Brooks-Gunn, 1997; Furstenberg, et al, 1999).

Summary of Neighborhood and Community Influences

There has been an increase in the amount and quality of work being done on neighborhood and community effects on human development. Although still in its infancy, this work has documented the influence of community characteristics on community members. As Bronfenbrenner (1979) predicted, communities influence the development of children primarily through their influence on the microsystem (i.e., through their influence on parenting practices, teacher behavior, school resources, and peer group behaviors). Because of the importance of the microsystem, the magnitude of neighborhood effects is quite small. Effective parents are able to buffer their children's development from the risks and dangers in many neighborhoods. Nonetheless, the impact of the neighborhood on development increases as children get older (Elliott et al., in preparation), partly because parental control and influences decrease as children move into adolescence and young adulthood. During these periods of life, individuals have much more control over their own behaviors and, consequently, their interactions with larger social units outside the home. This increasing independence can put them at greater risk to out-of-family influences on their development.

COMMUNITY- AND SCHOOL-BASED FREE-TIME ACTIVITIES

Communities and schools may also affect human development through their influence on the availability of structured leisure time activities. The release of *A Matter of Time* by the Carnegie Corporation of New York (1992) put the spotlight on the role of productive use of time in successful development. It illustrated how much discretionary time children and adolescents have and how much of this time is spent on unstructured activities such as "hanging out" with one's friends, watching television, and listening to music. The report stressed that constructive, organized activities are a good use of children's and adolescents' time because (1) doing good things with one's time takes time away from opportunities to get involved in risky activities; (2) one can learn good things (such as specific competencies, prosocial values and attitudes) while engaged in constructive activities; and (3) involvement in organized activity settings increases the possibility of establishing positive social supports and networks. To date, there has been relatively little longitudinal, developmentally oriented research focused on either the benefits or the costs of how children and adolescents spend their discretionary time. Most of the relevant research has been done in sociology and leisure studies, and most of the work has focused on adolescents.

Most of the sociological and psychological research on activity involvement has focused on extracurricular school activities. This research has documented a link between adolescents' extracurricular activities and adult educational attainment, occupation, and income, after controlling for social class and ability (Eccles & Templeton, 2002). This work also documented the protective value of extracurricular activity participation in reducing involvement in delinquent and other risky behaviors (e.g., Eccles, Barber, Stone, & Hunt, 2003; Mahoney, Larson, & Eccles, 2005a).

Research within leisure studies has taken a slightly different path, focusing on the differences between relaxed leisure and constructive, organized activities: Relaxed leisure is characterized as enjoyable, but not demanding (watching TV). In contrast, constructive, organized leisure activities (such as team sports, performing arts, and organized volunteer activities) require effort and commitment and provide a forum in which to express one's identity or passion (e.g., Larson, Hansen, & Moneta, 2006; Larson & Kleiber, 1993). These activities are assumed to have more developmentally beneficial outcomes than relaxed, unstructured leisure because they provide the opportunity (1) to acquire and practice specific social, physical, and intellectual skills that may be useful in a wide variety of settings; (2) to contribute to the well-being of one's community and develop a sense of agency as a member of one's community; (3) to belong to a socially recognized and valued group; (4) to establish supportive social networks of both peers and adults that can help one in both the present and the future; and (5) to experience and deal with challenges.

Recent research supports these assumptions about the positive effects of participation in organized activities (Larson & Hansen, 2005; Mahoney et al., 2005a, 2005b). For example,

Mahoney and Cairns (1997) and McNeal (1995) found that participation in extracurricular activities is related to lower rates of school dropout, particularly for high-risk youth. Mahoney (1997) also showed a connection to reduced rates of criminal offending. In addition, adolescents involved in a broad range of adult-endorsed activities report lower rates of substance use than their non-involved peers (Youniss, Yates, & Su, 1997b). Sport, in particular, has been linked to lower likelihood of school dropout and higher rates of college attendance (Eccles et al., 2003; McNeal, 1995), especially among low-achieving and blue-collar male athletes (Holland & Andre, 1987).

Participation in school-based extracurricular activities has also been linked to increases on such positive developmental outcomes as high-school grade point average, strong school engagement, and high educational aspirations (Barber, Eccles & Stone, 2001; Eccles & Barber, 1999; Lamborn, Brown, Mounts, & Steinberg 1992). Similarly, participation in high-school extracurricular activities and out-of-school volunteer activities predicts high levels of adult participation in the political process and other types of volunteer activities, continued sport engagement, and better physical and mental health (Barber et al., 2001; Glancy, Willits, & Farrell, 1986; Youniss, McLellan, & Yates, 1997a; Youniss et al., 1997b).

In contrast to these positive associations, sport has also been linked to increased rates of school deviance and drug and alcohol use (e.g., Eccles & Barber, 1999; Lamborn et al., 1992). These results suggest that participation in organized activities can have both positive and negative effects. Why? Several explanations for the positive results associated with participation have been offered: Rehberg (1969) suggested the importance of association with academically oriented peers, exposure to academic values, enhanced self-esteem, generalization of a high sense of personal efficacy, and superior career guidance and encouragement. Coleman (1961) stressed the values and norms associated with the different peer clusters engaged in various types of extracurricular activities. Otto and Alwin (1977) added skill and attitude acquisition (both interpersonal and personal) and increased membership in important social networks. Other investigators have focused on links among peer group formation, identity formation, and activity involvement (Eccles & Barber, 1999; Eccles & Templeton, 2002; Eckert, 1989; Mahoney et al., 2005a). For example, Fine (1992) stressed how participation in something like Little League shapes both the child's definition of himself as a "jock" and the child's most salient peer group. In turn, these characteristics (one's identity and one's peer group) influence subsequent activity choices, creating a synergistic system that marks out a clear pathway into a particular kind of adolescence.

Involvement in sports links an adolescent to a set of similar peers, provides shared experiences and goals, and can reinforce friendships.

This strong link between activity participation and peer group membership also provides an explanation for the negative influences of sports participation on drug and alcohol use. Knowing what an adolescent is doing often tells us a lot about whom the adolescent is with: It is very likely that participation in organized activity settings directly affects adolescents' peer group precisely because such participation structures a substantial amount of peer group interaction. One's co-participants become one's peer crowd. And such peer crowds often develop an activity-based "culture," providing adolescents with the opportunity to identify with a group having a shared sense of "style." Involvement in a school organization or sport links an adolescent to a set of similar peers, provides shared experiences and goals, and can reinforce friendships between peers (Larson, 1994; Mahoney et al., 2005a).

Participation in religious institutions, often called "congregations," and their affiliated youth groups is another important context of development that has been under-researched in the developmental sciences (King & Roeser, 2009; Roehlkepartain & Patel, 2006). A national study on religion showed that approximately half of all American adolescents attend religious services at a congregation weekly, with another quarter of youth attending services less than weekly but more frequently than just on the major religious holidays of their tradition (Smith & Denton, 2005). Furthermore, about half of all US adolescents (ages 13–17 years) indicate a strong, positive orientation to matters of religion, faith, and religious experience in their lives (Smith & Denton, 2005). With regard to this half of the youth population, a growing body of evidence shows links between religious participation/development and better health and well-being, as well as between religious participation and reduced rates of emotional distress and antisocial behavior (see King & Roeser, 2009; Oser, Scarlett, & Bucher, 2006).

Smith (2003) theorizes that religious institutions exert constructive influences on youth development, for instance by providing youth with three types of capital, including: (1) *spiritual capital* in the form of religious mentors and role models, moral and religious worldviews, and contexts for reflection and spiritual contemplation; (2) *cultural capital* in the form of opportunities for skill development (i.e., leadership skills) and for learning core cultural knowledge (e.g., Biblical events); and (3) *social capital* in the form of social ties across differently aged peers, non-parental adults, and members of wider communities and society. Such forms of capital, in turn, inform identity, activity choices, and the nature of one's social networks in positive and prosocial ways (King & Roeser, 2009). For instance, participation in religious congregational contexts has been linked to faith development (Roehlkepartain & Patel, 2006), defined as the degree to which a young person comes to internalize the priorities, commitments, and perspectives of their religious tradition (Benson, Donahue, & Erickson, 1989), and less contact with deviant peers and more contact with parents, non-parental adults, and non-deviant peers (King & Furrow, 2004; Larson et al., 2006; Martin, White, & Perlman, 2001).

PEER CULTURE AS A PRIMARY MEDIATOR OF SCHOOL, COMMUNITY, AND FREE-TIME ACTIVITY EFFECTS

Throughout our discussion of school, community, and organized activity effects on development, we have suggested ways in which particular characteristics might influence peer interactions. In this section, we discuss these connections in more detail. As discussed earlier, schools, activity settings, and communities provide the places in which a great deal of peer interaction takes place. Peer groups are often formed from among the residents in communities and the participants in organized activities. This geographical clustering of peer networks can have either positive or negative effects on development, depending on the nature of the individuals involved and the shared values and norms of the groups that emerge.

Researchers are just beginning to explore the full range of such influences. In this section, we explore this issue. We focus on those aspects of peer relations closely linked with the school, activity setting, and community contexts. Specifically, we focus on peers as co-learners, on the reinforcing and socializing mechanism within peer groups, and on the individual children's attempts to coordinate multiple goals.

Peers as Co-Learners

The extensive work on the advantages of cooperative learning provides one lens on the link between peers and schooling. This work has stressed several roles of peers as co-learners. Most directly, doing learning activities in a social context is usually more fun and, thus, intrinsically interesting (Slavin, 1990). Peers can also help each other understand and learn the material through group discussion, sharing of resources, modeling academic skills, and interpreting and clarifying the tasks for each other (NRC/IOM, 2004; Schunk, 1987). Each of these characteristics should influence achievement through its impact of the children's expectations for success, their valuing of the activity, and their focus on learning rather than performance goals. One way in which positive social interactions have been facilitated in classrooms is through cooperative learning (Slavin, 1990). Finally, cooperative learning is also linked to the mechanism discussed earlier: When cooperative learning is used in classrooms, children are more accepting of one another, and fewer children are socially isolated. Thus, greater use of such techniques can mitigate the effects of peer rejection and lack of belonging on students' academic motivation.

Closely related to the work on cooperative learning is the work on peer tutoring. Children learn a great deal from teaching other children (Eccles & Templeton, 2002; Jackson & Davis, 2000; McLaughlin, 2000; Sieber, 1979). Such an arrangement benefits both the tutor and the tutee. An interesting variant on peer tutoring is described in *Turning Points* (Carnegie Council on Adolescent Development, 1989): cross-age tutoring. A special group of eighth graders was trained and then allowed to tutor first graders in reading. What made the eighth graders special was the fact that all of them were doing quite poorly in school and were reading substantially below grade level. Nonetheless, they did read better than the first graders. It was hoped that the intervention would help both the eighth and first graders; and it did! Both the school engagement and performance of the group of eighth graders increased dramatically—so much so that they stayed in school and were reading at grade level when they graduated from high school. In addition, their tutees continued to read at grade level as long as they interacted with their older student tutor. This intervention demonstrates the power of cross-age tutoring as a way to provide older students with a meaningful and fulfilling task as well as younger children with the extra help they need to avoid falling behind.

Similar cross-age dynamics operate in communities. As noted earlier, older children and adolescents sometimes recruit younger children in the dominant peer group activity settings in particular neighborhoods; these can be either positive settings such as faith-based institutions or recreational centers or more negative settings such as gangs. Some of the most successful youth development programs discussed in *A Matter of Time* (Carnegie Corporation, 1992) involve cross-age mentoring programs like the one described earlier (see also McLaughlin, 2000).

Peer Group Influences

Much of the classic work on peer influences on development focused on the negative effects of peer groups on adolescents' commitment to doing well in school. Investigators have now turned their attention to understanding the specific mechanisms by which peer groups can either support or undermine positive development through their impact on both school engagement and involvement in other positive activities. This research has documented that children tend to cluster together in peer groups that share the same motivational orientations and activity preferences and that such clustering serves to reinforce their existing motivational orientation and activity preferences, leading to a strengthening of these individual differences over time (e.g., Berndt & Keefe, 1995; Berndt, Laychak, & Park, 1990; Epstein, 1983; Kindermann, McCollam, & Gibson, 1996; Youniss, 1980). But whether such effects are positive or negative depends on the nature of the peer groups' motivational values and behavioral orientations (Eccles et al., 2003). For example, high-achieving children who seek out other high achievers as friends should end up with more positive academic motivation as a result of their interactions with like motivated children. In contrast, low achievers who become involved with a group of friends who are also low achievers should become even less motivated to do school work and more interested in other activity settings (Fuligni et al., 1995; Kindermann, 1993; Kindermann et al., 1996).

The role of peer group influences is likely to vary across different ages. For example, peers may play an especially important role during adolescence. There are two major differences between children and adolescents in peer-group processes. Adolescents are more aware of, and concerned about, peer-group acceptance, and adolescents spend much more unsupervised time with peer groups in social, sports, and other extracurricular activities (Eccles & Templeton, 2002). For example, early adolescents rate social activities as very important to them, and like them better than most of the other activities they do, particularly academic activities (Brown, 2004; Wigfield, Eccles, Mac Iver, Reuman, & Midgley, 1991). Furthermore, Harter (1990) found that early adolescents' physical appearance and social acceptance are the most important predictors of their general self-esteem, much more important than their perceptions of their own cognitive competence. These results suggest that the potential role of peer groups should be greater during adolescence and that the nature of the effect should depend on the values of the peer group and the specific domains being considered. Hanging out with a group of friends highly motivated for school achievement should facilitate academic motivation and achievement, perhaps to the detriment of motivational commitment in other domains. Similarly, although hanging out with a low academic motivation group should undermine academic motivation, it may facilitate motivation and involvement in some other arena depending on the values of the peer group.

The work by Stattin and Magnusson (1990) provides an example of this process. They reported that some young women (early maturers) are particularly likely to be channeled into early heterosocial peer groups and activities. Because these females look sexually mature, they are more likely to become involved with older peers, particularly with older male peers who interact with them in a gender-role stereotypic manner. As these young women get caught up in this peer social system, they shift their attention away from academic activities and into heterosocial activities and roles. As a result, they lower their educational aspirations, shift the value they attach to academic pursuits and, in fact, end up obtaining less education than one would have predicted based on their prepubertal academic performance and motivation. Instead, they often marry and become parents earlier than their female classmates.

Work by Stattin, Kerr, Mahoney, Persson, and Magnusson (2005) elaborates on these early findings. They follow a sample of adolescents as they move through adolescence and into adulthood. Just like the girls in the Stattin and Magnusson study, these early maturing girls were likely to drop out of school earlier and then to both marry and have children earlier than their later maturing peers. But this was true for only a subset of the early maturing girls: those who attended community recreation centers, where they met and then began dating older males. Thus, Stattin et al. (2005) were able to document the pathway by which these early maturing girls moved into a risky older peer group. The recreation centers in their communities provided the setting in which these peer influences were able to be manifest.

Peers' Role in the Coordination of Multiple Goals

The work by Stattin et al. is also illustrative of the importance of coordinating multiple goals. Just as schools and communities are complex organizations with multiple purposes and goals, so individuals have multiple goals. Learning to coordinate and manage one's goals is a key developmental task. Peers can play a central role in this process by making various goals and activities more or less salient and more or less desirable. Adolescence is an ideal time in which to observe the dynamics of this process. Similar processes have been suggested for various ethnic groups. Several investigators have suggested that some groups are likely to receive less peer support for academic achievement than affluent European-American youth (e.g., Fordham & Ogbu, 1986; Willis, 1977). Steinberg, Dornbusch, and Brown (1992) concluded that both the lower performance of African-Americans and Latin-Americans and the higher performance of European-Americans and Asian-Americans are due more to ethnic differences in peer support for academic achievement than ethnic differences in either the value parents attach to education or the youths' beliefs regarding the likely occupational payoff for academic success. Even though the adolescents in each of these groups reported strong support for school achievement from their parents, the Latin-American and African-American students reported less support for school achievement among their peers than either the European-American or Asian-American students. Consequently there was less congruence between parents and peers in the valuing of school achievement. Some of the African-Americans indicated that they had great difficulty finding a peer group that would encourage them to comply with their parents' valuing of educational success. As a result, they reported that they had to be very careful in selecting which of their African-American peers to have as close friends. European-American and Asian-American students are much less likely to report this kind of peer dilemma.

Summary of Peer Effects

Peer influences are an integral part of both school and neighborhood effects. Spending time with one's peers is a major activity in both of these extra-familial contexts: In fact, the opportunity to spend so much time with one's peers is one of their major distinguishing characteristics. In this section, we have stressed that the impact of peers in these settings depends on the nature of the individuals and the inherent activities. Characteristics of both schools and neighborhoods influence the types of peers to whom, and the types of peer-group activities to which, children and adolescents will be exposed. If these peers have positive, prosocial values and behaviors, these associations are likely to facilitate positive developmental outcomes; if these peers have more problematic values and behaviors, these associations are likely to put the children's development at risk. Schools and neighborhoods also structure the kinds of activities individuals have the opportunity to engage in during their free time.

CONCLUSIONS

In this chapter, we have summarized the many ways in which schools, activity settings, and communities can influence child and adolescent development. We began by pointing out how the multiple levels of school organization interact to shape the day-to-day experiences of children and teachers. We stressed how one must think of schools as complex organizations to understand how decisions and regulatory processes at each level impact on schools as a context for development. We also stressed the interface of schools, as complex changing institutions, with the developmental trajectories of individuals. To understand how schools influence development, one needs to understand change at both the individual and the institutional level. The stage–environment fit theory provides an excellent example of the linking of these two developmental trajectories. Imagine two trajectories: one at the school level and one at the individual level. Schools change in many ways over the grade levels. The nature of these changes can be developmentally appropriate or inappropriate in terms of the extent to which they foster continued development toward the transition into adulthood and maturity. (The changes can also be developmentally irrelevant, but we did not discuss these types of changes.) Children move through this changing context as they move from grade to grade and from school to school. Similarly, children develop and change as they get older. They also have assumptions about their increasing maturity and the privileges it ought to afford them. We believe optimal development occurs when these two trajectories of change are in synchrony with each other; that is, when the changes in the context mesh well with, and perhaps even slightly precede, the patterns of change occurring at the individual level. Furthermore, we summarized evidence that the risk of negative developmental outcomes is increased when these two trajectories are out of synchrony—particularly when the context changes in a developmental regressive pattern.

We also discussed the relation of school characteristics to other contexts of development, particularly the community and the peer group. We then discussed how neighborhood characteristics can influence development independent of its association with schools. We summarized how both school and neighborhood influences are mediated by their impact on peer interactions and activity involvement. Throughout we stressed the need to look at interactions among these various contextual influences. Researchers seldom consider interactions across contexts of development. Instead, they tend to specialize in one context—for example, the family or the peer group. But people live in multiple contexts. Making sense of, and coordinating the demands of, these multiple contexts are among the more challenging developmental tasks. We know very little about how individuals manage these tasks and about how the ability to manage these tasks develops over time. We know relatively little about how characteristics of one context influence the characteristics of other contexts. We summarized some of the ways in which school, peer, leisure activity setting, and neighborhood characteristics influence the nature of children's peer groups and peer interactions. Much more such work and theorizing are needed.

Another way to think about multiple contexts is in terms of their relative ability to meet human needs. As we noted earlier, Connell and Wellborn (1991) suggested that individuals develop best in contexts that provide opportunities to feel competent, to feel socially connected and valued, and to exercise control over their own destiny. If this is true, then individuals ought to be drawn toward those contexts that provide these opportunities in developmentally appropriate doses. Variations across contexts on these characteristics could explain why individuals come to prefer one context over another—for example, adolescents who are not doing well in school or who are having difficulty getting along with their parents might turn to their peer group to find a sense of competence and positive self-esteem. Essentially, we are arguing that when individuals have some choice over where to spend their time, they will choose to spend the most time in those social contexts that best fulfill their needs for a sense of competence, for high-quality social relationship, for respect from others for their autonomy and individuality, and for a sense of being valued by one's social partners. If they can fulfill these needs within social contexts that reinforce normative behavior, they are likely to do well in school and other culturally valued institutions. If they cannot fulfill their needs in these types of social contexts, they are likely to seek out other social contexts, which, in turn, may reinforce more norm-breaking and problematic behaviors. Thus, if we want to support positive, normative developmental pathways for our children and adolescents, it is critical that we provide them with ample opportunities to fulfill their basic human needs in social contexts that reinforce positive normative developmental pathways.

ACKNOWLEDGMENTS

We would like to thank our colleagues and students for helping us think through the issues raised in this chapter and for helping us in preparing the manuscript. We would also like to thank the editors of this book for their comments and editorial suggestions.

REFERENCES AND SUGGESTED READINGS (📖)

Adelman, H. S., & Taylor, L. (1998). Reframing mental health in schools and expanding school reform. *Educational Psychologist, 33*, 135–152.

Akiba, M., LeTendre, G. K., & Scribner, J. P. (2007). Teacher quality, opportunity gap, and national achievement in 46 countries. *Educational Researcher, 36*, 369–387.

Alexander, K. L., & Entwisle, D. (1988). Achievement in the first two years of school: Patterns and processes. *Monographs of the Society for Research in Child Development, 53* (2, Serial No. 218).

Alexander, K. L., Entwisle, D. R., & Dauber, S. L. (1994). *On the success of failure: A reassessment of the effects of retention in primary grades.* Cambridge, UK: Cambridge University Press.

Alexander, K. L., Entwisle, D. R., & Olson, L. S. (2007). Lasting consequences of the summer learning gap. *Sociology of Education, 72*, 167–180.

Allen, J. P., Philliber, S., Herrling, S., & Kuperminc, G. P. (1997). Preventing teen pregnancy and academic failure: Experimental evaluation of a developmentally-based approach. *Child Development, 64*, 729–742.

Ambady, N., Shih, M., Kim, A., & Pittinsky, T. L. (2001). Stereotype susceptibility in children: Effects of identity activation on quantitative performance. *Psychological Science, 12*(5), 385–390.

Ames, C. (1992). Classrooms: Goals, structures, and student motivation. *Journal of Educational Psychology, 84*, 261–271.

Anderman, E. M., & Maehr, M. L. (1994). Motivation and schooling in the middle grades. *Review of Educational Research, 64*, 287–309.

Anderman, E. M., Maehr, M. L., & Midgley, C. (1999). Declining motivation after the transition to middle school: Schools can make a difference. *Journal of Research and Development in Education, 32*, 131–147.

Arbreton, A. J. A., & Eccles, J. S. (1994, April). *Mothers' perceptions of their children during the transition from kindergarten to formal schooling: The effect of teacher evaluations on parents' expectations for their early elementary school children.* Paper presented at the American Educational Research Association Conference, New Orleans, LA.

📖 Aronson, J., & Steele, C. M. (2005). Stereotypes and the fragility of academic competence, motivation, and self-concept. In A. J. Elliot & C. S. Dweck (Eds.), *Handbook of competence and motivation.* New York: Guilford.

Ashton, P. (1985). Motivation and the teacher's sense of efficacy. In C. Ames & R. Ames (Eds.), *Research on motivation in education, Vol. 2: The classroom milieu* (pp. 141–171). Orlando, FL: Academic Press.

Assor, A., Kaplan, H., & Roth, G. (2002). Choice is good but relevance is excellent: Autonomy-enhancing and suppressing teacher behaviors predicting students' engagement in schoolwork. *British Journal of Educational Psychology, 72*, 261–278.

Assor, A., Vansteenkiste, M., & Kaplan, A. (2009). Identified versus introjected approach and introjected avoidance motivation in school and in sports: The limited benefits of self-worth striving. *Journal of Educational Psychology, 101*(2), 482–487.

Astor, R. A., Meyer, H. A., Behre, W. J. (1999). Unowned places and times: Maps and interviews about violence in high schools. *American Educational Research Journal, 36*, 3–42.

Astor, R. A., Benbenishty, R., Zeira, A., & Vinokur, A. (2002). School climate, observed risky behaviors, and victimization as predictors of high school students' fear and judgments of school violence as a problem. *Health Education & Behavior, 29*, 716–730.

Atkinson, J. W. (1957). Motivational determinants of risk taking behavior. *Psychological Review*, *64*, 359–372.

August, D., & Hakuta, K. (Eds.). (1998). *Educating language minority children*. Washington, DC: National Academy Press.

Ball, A. F. (2002). Three decades of research on classroom life: Illuminating the classroom communicative lives of America's at-risk students. In W. G. Secada (Ed.), *Review of research in education* (Vol. 26, pp. 71–112). Washington, DC: American Educational Research Association Press.

Bandura, A. (1994). *Self-efficacy: The exercise of control*. New York: W. H. Freeman.

Bandura, A. (2006). Toward a psychology of human agency. *Psychological Science*, *1*, 164–180.

Barber, B. L., Eccles, J. S., & Stone, M. R. (2001). Whatever happened to the Jock, the Brain, and the Princess?: Young adult pathways linked to adolescent activity involvement and social identity. *Journal of Adolescent Research*, *16*, 429–455.

Barker, R., & Gump, P. (1964). *Big school, small school: High school size and student behavior*. Stanford, CA: Stanford University Press.

Baumrind, D. (1971). Current patterns of parental authority. *Developmental Psychology Monograph*, *4*(1).

Battistich, V., Watson, M., Solomon, D., Lewis, C., & Schaps, E. (1999). Beyond the three R's: A broader agenda for school reform. *Elementary School Journal*, *99*, 415–432.

Benbenishty, R., & Astor, R. A. (2007). Monitoring indicators of children's victimization in school: Linking national-, regional-, and site-level indicators. *Social Indicators Research*, *84*, 333–348.

Benbenishty, R., Astor, R. A., Zeira, A., & Vinokus, A. D. (2002). Perceptions of violence and fear of school attendance among junior high school students in Israel. *Social Work Research*, *2*, 71–87.

Benson, P. L., Donahue, M. J., & Erickson, J. A. (1989). Adolescence and religion: A review of the literature from 1970 to 1986. *Research in the Social Scientific Study of Religion*, *1*, 153–181.

Berliner, D. (2003, May). *Heisenberg, high-stakes testing, and the honor of teachers*. Lecture at Stanford University School of Education, Stanford, CA.

Berndt, T. J., & Keefe, K. (1995). Friends' influence on adolescents' adjustment to school. *Child Development*, *66*, 1312–1329.

Berndt, T. J., Laychak, A. E., & Park, K. (1990). Friends' influence on adolescents' academic achievement motivation: An experimental study. *Journal of Educational Psychology*, *82*(4), 664–670.

Blos, P. (1965). The initial stage of male adolescence. *Psychoanalytic Study of the Child*, *20*, 145–164.

Blumenfeld, P. C. (1992). Classroom learning and motivation: Clarifying and expanding goal theory. *Journal of Educational Psychology*, *84*, 272–281.

Blumenfeld, P. C., Mergendoller, J., & Swartout, D. (1987). Task as a heuristic for understanding student learning and motivation. *Journal of Curriculum Studies*, *19*, 135–148.

Boyce, W. T., Frank, E., Jensen, P. S., Kessler, R. C., Nelson, C. A., Steinberg, L., et al. (1998). Social context in developmental psychopathology: Recommendations for future research from the MacArthur Network on Psychopathology and Development. *Development and Psychopathology*, *10*, 143–164.

Brody, G. H., Chen, Y.-F., Murry, V. M., Simons, R. L., Ge, X., Gibbons, F. X., et al. (2006). Perceived discrimination and the adjustment of African American youths: A five-year longitudinal analysis with contextual moderation effects. *Child Development*, *77*(5), 1170–1189.

Bronfenbrenner, U. (1979). *The ecology of human development: Experiments by nature and design*. Cambridge, MA: Harvard University Press.

Bronfenbrenner, U., & Morris, P. A. (1998). The ecology of environmental processes. In W. Damon (Series Ed.) & R. M. Lerner (Vol. Ed.), *Handbook of child psychology* (5th ed., Vol. 1, pp. 993–1028). New York: Wiley.

Brooks-Gunn, J., Duncan, G. J., & Aber, J. L. (Eds.) (1997a). *Neighborhood poverty* (Vol. 1). New York: Russell Sage Foundation.

Brooks-Gunn, J., Duncan, G. J., & Aber, J. L. (Eds.) (1997b). *Neighborhood Poverty* (Vol. 2). New York: Russell Sage Foundation.

Brophy, J. (1988). Research linking teacher behavior to student achievement: Potential implications for instruction of Chapter 1 students. *Educational Psychologist*, *23*, 235–286.

Brophy, J. E. (2004). *Motivating students to learn* (2nd ed.). Mahwah, NJ: Lawrence Erlbaum Associates.

Brown, A. L. (1997). Transforming schools into communities of thinking and learning about serious matters. *American Psychologist*, *52*, 399–413.

Brown, B. B. (2004). Adolescents' relationships. New York: Holt, Rinehart & Winston.

Bryk, A. S., Lee, V. E., & Holland, P. B. (1993). *Catholic schools and the common good*. Cambridge, MA: Harvard University Press.

Burchinal, M. R., Roberts, J. E., Zeisel, S. A., & Rowley, S. J. (2008). Social risk and protective factors for African American children academic achievement and adjustment during the transition to middle school. *Developmental Psychology*, *44*(1), 286–292.

Calabrese, R., & Schumer, H. (1986). The effects of service activities on adolescent alienation. *Adolescence*, *21*(83), 675–687.

Calderhead, J. (1996). Teachers, beliefs, and knowledge. In D. C. Berliner & R. C. Calfee (Eds.), *Handbook of educational psychology* (pp. 709–725). New York: Simon & Schuster Macmillan.

Camarota, S. A., & McArdle, N. (2003). *Where immigrants live: An examination of state residency of the foreign born by country of origin in 1990 and 2000*. Washington, DC: Center for Immigration Studies.

Carnegie Corporation of New York (1992). *A matter of time: Risk and opportunity in the non school hours*. New York: Carnegie Corporation.

Carnegie Council on Adolescent Development (1989). *Turning points: Preparing American youth for the 21st century*. New York: Carnegie Corporation.

Carskadon, M. A. (1990). Patterns of sleep and sleepiness in adolescents. *Pediatrician, 17*, 5–12.

Carskadon, M. A. (1997, April). *Adolescent sleep: Can we reconcile biological needs with societal demands?* Lecture given at Stanford University, Stanford, CA.

Caspi, A., & Roberts, B. W. (2001). Personality development across the life course: The argument for continuity and change. *Psychological Inquiry, 12*, 49–66.

Cauce, A. M., Comer, J. P., & Schwartz, D. (1987). Long term effects of a systems oriented school prevention program. *American Journal of Orthopsychiatric Association, 57*, 127–131.

Chavous, T. M., Bernat, D. H., Schmeelk-Cone, K., Caldwell, C. H. Kohn-Wood, L., & Zimmerman, M. A. (2003). Racial identity and academic attainment among African American adolescents. *Child Development, 74*(4), 1076–1090.

Chavous, T. M., Rivas-Drake, D., Smalls, C., Griffin, T., & Cogburn, C. (2008). Gender matters, too: The influences of school racial discrimination and racial identity on academic engagement outcomes among African American adolescents. *Developmental Psychology, 44*, 637–654.

Christian, M. K., Morrison, F. J., Frazier, J. A., & Massetti, F. (2000). Specificity in the nature and timing of cognitive change. *Journal of Cognition and Development, 1*(4), 429–448.

Cohen, E. G., & Lotan, R. A. (Eds.). (1997). *Working for equity in heterogeneous classrooms: Sociological theory in practice*. New York: Teachers College Press.

Cole, M. (1996). *Cultural psychology: A once and future discipline*. Cambridge, MA: Harvard University Press.

Coleman, J. S. (1961). *The adolescent society*. New York: Free Press.

Coleman, J. S., & Hoffer, T. (1987). *Public and private high schools: The impact of communities*. New York: Basic Books.

Collaborative for Academic, Social, and Emotional Learning (CASEL). (2003). *Safe and sound: An educational leader's guide to evidence-based social and emotional learning programs*. Chicago: CASEL. Retrieved October 1, 2003, from www.casel.org

Comer, J. (1980). *School power*. New York: Free Press.

Connell, J. P. (2003). *Getting off the dime: First steps toward implementing First Things First*. Report prepared for the US Department of Education. Philadelphia: Institute for Research and Reform in Education.

Connell, J. P., & Klem, A. M. (2000), You can get there from here: Using a theory of change approach to plan urban education reform. *Journal of Educational and Psychological Consultation, 11*, 93 120.

Connell, J. P., & Wellborn, J. G. (1991). Competence, autonomy, and relatedness: A motivational analysis of self-system processes. In R. Gunnar & L. A. Sroufe (Eds.), *Minnesota symposia on child psychology* (Vol. 23, pp. 43–77). Hillsdale, NJ: Lawrence Erlbaum Associates.

Council of the Great City Schools (1992). *National urban education goals: Baseline indicators, 1990–91*. Washington, DC: Council of the Great City Schools.

Covington, M. V. (1992). *Making the grade: A self-worth perspective on motivation and school reform*. New York: Cambridge University Press.

Covington, M. V. (2000). Goal theory, motivation, and school achievement: An integrative review. *Annual Review of Psychology, 51*, 171–200.

Crosnoe, R., Johnson, M. K., & Elder, G. H. (2004). School size and the interpersonal side of education: An examination of race/ethnicity and organizational context. *Social Science Quarterly, 85*(5), 1259–1274.

Csikszentmihalyi, M., Rathunde, K., & Whalen, S. (1993). *Talented teenagers: The roots of success and failure*. New York: Cambridge University Press.

Daniels, L. M., Haynes, T. L., Stupnisky, R. H., Perry, R. P., Newall, N. E., & Pekrun, R. (2007). *Contemporary Educational Psychology, 33*, 584–608.

Darling-Hammond, L. (1997). *The right to learn: A blueprint for creating schools that work*. San Francisco: Jossey-Bass.

Darling-Hammond, L. (1999). *Teacher quality and student achievement: A review of state policy evidence* (Document R-99-1). University of Washington: Center for the Study of Teaching and Policy.

Darling-Hammond, L. (2000). New standards and old inequalities: School reform and the education of African American students. *Journal of Negro Education, 69*, 263–287.

Darling-Hammond, L. (2007). Evaluating "No Child Left Behind". *The Nation*, May 21.

Darling-Hammond, L., & Bransford, J. (Eds.). (2005). *Preparing teachers for a changing world: What teachers should learn and be able to do*. San Francisco: Jossey-Bass.

Davidson, A. L., & Phelan, P. (1999). Students' multiple worlds: An anthropological approach to understanding students' engagement with school. In Urdan, T. C. (Ed.), *Advances in motivation: The role of context, Volume 11* (pp. 233–273). Stamford, CT: JAI Press.

Deci, E. L., & Ryan, R. M. (2002). Self-determination research: Reflections and future directions. In E. L. Deci & R. M. Ryan (Eds.), *Handbook of self-determination theory research* (pp. 431–441). Rochester, NY: University of Rochester Press.

Dehyle, D., & LeCompte, M. (1999). Cultural differences in child development: Navaho adolescents in middle schools. In R. H. Sheets & E. R. Hollins (Eds.), *Racial and ethnic identity in school practices: Aspects of human development* (pp. 123–140). Mahwah, NJ: Lawrence Erlbaum Associates.

Dewey, J. (1902/1990). *The child and the curriculum.* Chicago: University of Chicago Press.

Dishon, T. J, Poulin, F., & Burraston, B. (2001). Peer group dynamics associated with iatrogenic effect in group interventions with high-risk young adolescents. *New Directions for Child and Adolescent Development, 91,* 79–82.

Dornbusch, S. M. (1994). *Off the track.* Presidential address at the biennial meeting of the Society for Research on Adolescence, San Diego, CA.

Dotterer, A. M., McHale, S. M., & Crouter, A. C. (2009). The development and correlates of academic interests from childhood through adolescence. *Journal of Educational Psychology, 101*(2), 509–519.

Doyle, W. (1983). Academic work. *Review of Educational Research, 53,* 159–200.

Doyle, W. (1985). Recent research on classroom management: Implications for teacher preparation. *Journal of Teacher Education, 36,* 31–35.

Dryfoos, J. G. (1990). *Adolescents at risk: Prevalence and prevention.* Oxford, UK: Oxford University Press.

DuBois, D. L., Holloway, B. E., Valentine, J. C., & Cooper, H. (2002). Effectiveness of mentoring programs for youth: A meta-analytic review. *American Journal of Community Psychology, 30*(2), 157–198.

Duncan, G. J., & Brooks-Gunn, J. (Eds.). (1997). *Consequences of growing up poor.* New York: Russell Sage Foundation.

Durlak, J. A., & Wells, A. M. (1997). Primary prevention mental health programs for children and adolescents: A meta-analytic review. *American Journal of Community Psychology, 25,* 115–152.

Durlak, J. A., Weissberg, R. P., Taylor, R. D., & Dymnicki, A. B. (in press). The effects of school-based social and emotional learning: A meta-analytic review. *Child Development.*

Dweck, C. S. (2002). The development of ability conceptions. In A. Wigfield & J. S. Eccles (Eds.), *Development of achievement motivation* (pp. 57–88). San Diego, CA: Academic Press.

Dweck, C. S. (1992). The study of goals in psychology. *Psychological Science, 3,* 165–166.

Eccles, J.S. (1983). Expectancies, values, and academic behavior. In J. Spence (Ed.), *Achievement and achievement motivation.* San Francisco: W.H. Freeman.

Eccles, J. S. (1984). Sex differences in achievement patterns. In T. Sonderegger (Ed.), *Nebraska symposium on motivation* (Vol. 32, pp. 97–132). Lincoln, NE: University of Nebraska Press.

Eccles, J. S. (1994). Understanding women's educational and occupational choices: Applying the Eccles et al. model of achievement-related choices. *Psychology of Women Quarterly, 18,* 585–609.

Eccles, J. S. (2009). Who am I and what am I going to do with my life? Personal and collective identities as motivators of action. *Educational Psychologist, 44*(2), 78–89.

Eccles, J. S., & Barber, B. L. (1999). Student council, volunteering, basketball, or marching band: What kind of extracurricular involvement matters? *Journal of Adolescent Research, 14,* 10–43.

Eccles, J. S., Barber, B. L., Stone, M., & Hunt, J. (2003). Extracurricular activities and adolescent development. *Journal of Social Issues, 59,* 865–889.

Eccles, J. S., & Gootman, J. A. (Eds.). (2002). *Community programs to promote youth development.* Washington, DC: National Academy Press.

Eccles, J. S., & Harold, R. D. (1993). Parent–school involvement during the early adolescent years. *Teachers' College Record, 94,* 568–587.

Eccles, J., Lord, S., & Roeser, R. (1996). Round holes, square pegs, rocky roads, and sore feet: The impact of stage/environment fit on young adolescents' experiences in schools and families. In D. Cicchetti & S. L. Toth (Eds.), *Rochester symposium on developmental psychopathology, Volume VIII: Adolescence: opportunities and challenges* (pp. 47–93). Rochester, NY: University of Rochester Press.

Eccles, J. S., & Midgley, C. (1989). Stage/environment fit: Developmentally appropriate classrooms for early adolescents. In R. Ames & C. Ames (Eds.), *Research on motivation in education* (Vol. 3, pp. 139–181). New York: Academic Press.

Eccles, J., Midgley, C., & Adler, T. (1984). Grade-related changes in the school environment: Effects on achievement motivation. In J. G. Nicholls (Ed.), *The development of achievement motivation* (pp. 283–331). Greenwich, CT: JAI Press.

Eccles, J. S., Midgley, C., Wigfield, A., Buchanan, C. M., Reuman, D., Flanagan, C., & MacIver, D. (1993). Development during adolescence: The impact of stage–environment fit on adolescents' experiences in schools and families. *American Psychologist, 48,* 90–101.

Eccles, J. S., & Roeser, R. (2009). Schools, academic motivation and stage–environment fit. In R. M. Lerner & L. Steinberg (Eds.), *Handbook of adolescent psychology* (3rd ed., pp. 404–434). Hoboken, NJ: Wiley.

Eccles, J. S., & Templeton, J. (2002). Extracurricular and other after-school activities for youth. In W. S. Secada (Ed.), *Review of Educational Research* (Vol. 26, pp. 113–180). Washington DC: American Educational Research Association Press.

Eccles, J., & Wigfield, A. (1985). Teacher expectations and student motivation. In J. B. Dusek (Ed.), *Teacher expectations* (pp. 185–217). Hillsdale, NJ: Lawrence Erlbaum Associates.

Eccles, J. S., Wigfield, A., & Schiefele, U. (1998). Motivation. In N. Eisenberg (Ed.), *Handbook of child psychology* (5th ed., Vol. 3, pp. 1017–1095). New York: Wiley.

Eckert, P. (1989). *Jocks and burnouts: Social categories and identity in the high school.* New York: Teacher College Press.

Elder, G. H., & Conger, R. D. (2000). *Children of the land.* Chicago: University of Chicago Press.

Elias, M. J., Zins, J. E., Weissberg, R. P., Frey, K. S., Greenberg, M. T., Haynes, N. M., et al. (1997). *Promoting social and emotional learning: Guidelines for educators.* Alexandria, VA: Association for Supervision and Curriculum Development.

Elliott, D. S., Hamburg, B. A., & Williams, K. R. (1998). *Violence in American schools.* Cambridge, UK: Cambridge University Press.

Elliott, D. S., Menard, S., Rankin, B., Elliott, A., Wilson, W. J., & Huizinga, D. (in preparation). *Overcoming disadvantage: Successful youth development in high risk neighborhoods.*

Entwisle, D. R., & Alexander, K. L. (1993). Entry into school: The beginning school transition and educational stratification in the United States. *Annual Review of Sociology, 19,* 401–423.

Entwisle, D. R., Alexander, K. L. & Olson, L. S. (1997). *Children, schools and inequality.* Boulder, CO: Westview.

Epstein, J. L. (1983). The influence of friends on achievement and affective outcomes. In J. L. Epstein & N.L. Karweit (Eds.), *Friends in school* (pp. 177–200). New York: McGraw-Hill.

Epstein, J. L. (1992). School and family partnerships. In M. Alkin (Ed.), *Encyclopedia of educational research* (pp. 1139–1151). New York: Macmillan.

Eyler, J., Root, S., and Giles, D. E., Jr. (1998). Service-learning and the development of expert citizens: Service-learning and cognitive science. In R. Bingle and D. Duffey (Eds.), *With service in mind.* Washington, DC: American Association of Higher Education.

Fagan, J., & Wilkinson, D. L. (1998). Guns, youth violence and social identity. In M. Tonry & M. H. Moore (Eds.), *Youth violence* (pp. 373–456). Chicago: University of Chicago Press.

Fashola, O. S., Slavin, R. E., Calderon, M., & Duran, R. (2001). Effective programs for Latino students in elementary and middle schools. In R. E. Slavin & M. Calderon (Eds.), *Effective programs for Latino students* (pp. 1–66). Mahwah, NJ: Lawrence Erlbaum Associates.

Feldlaufer, H., Midgley, C., & Eccles, J. S. (1988). Student, teacher, and observer perceptions of the classroom environment before and after the transition to junior high school. *Journal of Early Adolescence, 8,* 133–156.

Fine, G. A. (1992). *With the boys: Little League baseball and preadolescent culture.* Chicago: University of Chicago Press.

Fine, M. (1991). *Framing dropouts: Notes on the politics of an urban public high school.* Albany, NY: State University of New York Press.

Finn, J. D. (1989). Withdrawing from school. *Review of Educational Research, 59,* 117–142.

Finn, J. D., (2006). *The adult lives of at-risk students: The roles of attainment and engagement in high school.* Report NCES 2006–328 to National Center of Educational Statistics. Washington, DC: US Department of Education.

Fiqueira-McDonough, J. (1986). School context, gender, and delinquency. *Journal of Youth and Adolescence, 15,* 79–98.

Firkowska, A., Ostrowska, A., Sokolowksa, M., Stein, Z., Susser, M., & Wald, I. (1978). Cognitive development and social policy. *Science, 200*(23), 1357–1362.

Fisher, D. (2001). "We're moving on up": Creating a schoolwide literacy effort in an urban high school. *Journal of Adolescent & Adult Literacy, 45*(2), 92–101.

Folkman, S., & Lazarus, R. S. (1984). If it changes it must be a process: A study of emotion and coping during three stages of a college examination. *Journal of Personality and Social Psychology, 48,* 150–170.

Ford, D. H., & Lerner, R. M. (1992). *Developmental systems theory: An integrative approach.* Newbury Park, CA: Sage.

Fordham, S., & Ogbu, J. U. (1986). Black students' school success: Coping with "the burden of 'acting white' ". *Urban Review, 18,* 176–206.

Fredricks, J. A., Blumenfeld, P. C., & Paris, A. H. (2004). School engagement: Potential of the concept, state of the evidence. *Review of Educational Research, 74,* 59–109.

Frenzel, A. C., Goetz, T., Ludtke, O., Pekrun, R., & Sutton, R. E. (2009). Emotional transmission in the classroom: Exploring the relationship between teacher and student enjoyment. *Journal of Educational Psychology, 101,* 705–716.

Frenzel, A. C., Pekrun, R., & Goetz, T. (2007). Perceived learning environments and students' emotional experiences: A multilevel analysis of mathematics classrooms. *Learning and Instruction*, *17*(5), 478–493.

Fuligni, A. J., Eccles, J. S., & Barber, B. L. (1995). The long-term effects of seventh-grade ability grouping in
mathematics. *Journal of Early Adolescence*, *15*(1), 58–89.

Furstenberg, F. F., Cook, T., Eccles, J. S., Elder, G., & Sameroff, A. (1999). *Managing to succeed*. Chicago:
University of Chicago Press.

Gamoran, A., & Mare, R. D. (1989). Secondary school tracking and educational inequality: Compensation,
reinforcement, or neutrality? *American Journal of Sociology*, *94*, 1146–1183.

Garcia, E. E., Jensen, B., & Cuellar, D. (2006). Early academic achievement of Hispanics in the United States:
Implications for teacher preparation. *New Educator*, *2*, 123–147.

Garcia Coll, C. T., Crnic, K., Hamerty, G., Wasik, B. H., Jenkins, R., Vazquez Garcia, H., & McAdoo, H. P. (1996).
An integrative model for the study of developmental competencies in minority children. *Child Development*, *20*,
1891–1914.

Garcia-Reid, P., Reid, R. J., & Peterson, N. A. (2005). School engagement among Latino youth in an urban middle
school context: Valuing the role of social support. *Education and Urban Society*, *37*(3), 257–275.

Glancy, M., Willits, F. K., & Farrell, P. (1986). Adolescent activities and adult success and happiness: Twenty-four
years later. *Sociology and Social Research*, *70*, 242–250.

Goddard, R. D., Hoy, W. K., & Woolfolk Hoy, A. (2000). Collective teacher efficacy: Its meaning, measure and
impact on student achievement. *American Educational Research Journal*, *37*, 479–507.

Goetz, T., Frenzel, A. C., Hall, N. C., & Pekrun, R. (2007). Antecedents of academic emotions: Testing the
internal/external frame of reference model for academic enjoyment. *Contemporary Educational Psychology*,
33, 9–33.

Goetz, T., Frenzel, A. C., Pekrun, R., Hall, N. C., & Ludtke, O. (2007). Between- and within-domain relations of
students' academic emotions. *Journal of Educational Psychology*, *99*, 715–733.

Goetz, T., Pekrun, R., Hall, N., & Haag, L. (2006). Academic emotions from a social-cognitive perspective:
Antecedents and domain specificity of students' affect in the context of Latin instruction. *British Journal of
Educational Psychology*, *76*, 289–308.

Goldenberg, C. (1992). The limits of expectations: A case for case knowledge about teacher expectancy effects.
American Educational Research Journal, *29*, 517–544.

Goldhaber, D. D. & Brewer, D. J. (2000). Does teacher certification matter? High school teacher certification status
and student achievement. *Educational Evaluation and Policy Analysis*, *22*, 129–145.

Good, T., & Weinstein, R. (1986). Teacher expectations: A framework for exploring classrooms. In K. Zumwalt
(Ed.), *Improving teaching* (pp. 63–85). Alexandria, VA: Association for Supervision and Curriculum Development.

Goodenow, C. (1993). Classroom belonging among early adolescent students: Relationships to motivation and
achievement. *Journal of Early Adolescence*, *13*(1), 21–43.

Gottfredson, D. C., & Wilson, D. B. (2003). Characteristics of effective school-based substance abuse prevention.
Prevention Science, *4*, 27–38.

Graham, S. (1991). A review of attribution theory in achievement contexts. *Educational Psychology Review*, *3*, 5–39.

Graham, S., & Barker, G. (1990). The downside of help: An attributional–developmental analysis of helping
behavior as a low ability cue. *Journal of Educational Psychology*, *82*, 7–14.

Graham, S., & Taylor, A. Z. (2002). Ethnicity, gender, and the development of achievement values. In A. Wigfield &
J. S. Eccles (Eds.), *Development of achievement motivation* (pp. 123–146). San Diego: Academic Press.

Greenberg, M. T., Weissberg, R. P., Utne O'Brien, M., Zins, J. E., Fredericks, L., Resnik, H., et al. (2003).
Enhancing school-based prevention and youth development through coordinated social, emotional, and academic
learning. *American Psychologist*, *58*, 466–474.

Greene, M. L., Way, N., & Pahl, K. (2006). Trajectories of perceived adult and peer discrimination among Black,
Latino, and Asian American adolescents: Patterns and psychological correlates. *Developmental Psychology*, *42*,
218–238.

Greenwald, R., Hedges, L. V., & Laine, R. D. (1996). The effect of school resources on student achievement. *Review
of Educational Research*, *66*, 361–396.

Grolnick, W. S., & Ryan, R. M. (1987). Autonomy in children's learning: An experimental and individual difference
investigation. *Journal of Personality & Social Psychology*, *52*, 890–898.

Grolnick, W. S., Gurland, S. T., Jacob, K. F., & Decourcey, W. (2002). The development of self-determination in
middle childhood and adolescence. In A. Wigfield & J. S. Eccles (Eds.), *Development of achievement motivation*
(pp. 147–171). San Diego, CA: Academic Press.

Hamilton S. F., & Fenzel, L M. (1988). The impact of volunteer experience on adolescent social development:
Evidence of program effects. *Journal of Adolescent Research*, *3*(1), 65–80.

Harris-Britt, A., Valrie, C.R., Kurtz-Costes, B., & Rowley, S. J. (2007). Perceived racial discrimination and self-
esteem in African American youth: Racial socialization as a protective factor. *Journal of Research on Adolescence*,
17(4), 669–682.

Hart, D., Yates, M., Fegley, S., & Wilson, G. (1995). Moral commitment in inner-city adolescents. In M. Killen & D. Hart (Eds.), *Morality in everyday life: Developmental perspectives*. New York: Cambridge University Press.

Harter, S. (1990). Causes, correlates and the functional role of global self-worth: A life-span perspective. In J. Kolligian & R. Sternberg (Eds.), *Perceptions of competence and incompetence across the life-span* (pp. 67–98). New Haven, CT: Yale University Press.

Hawkins, J. D. (1997). Academic performance and school success: Sources and consequences. In R. P. Weissberg et al. (Eds.), *Enhancing children's wellness, Volume 8: Issues in children's and family's lives* (pp. 278–305). Thousand Oaks, CA: Sage.

Hawkins, J. D., Kosterman, R., Catalano, R. F., Hill, K. G., & Abbott, R. D. (2008). Effects of social development intervention in childhood 15 years later. *Archives of Pediatrics and Adolescent Medicine, 162*, 1133–1141.

Heyneman, S. P., & Loxley, W. A. (1983). The effect of primary-school quality on academic achievement across twenty-nine high- and low-income countries. *American Journal of Sociology, 88*, 1162–1194.

Hill, H. C., Rowan, B., & Ball, D. L. (2005). Effects of teachers' mathematical knowledge for teaching on student achievement. *American Educational Research Journal, 42*, 371–406.

Hoffmann, L. (2002). Promoting girls' interest and achievement in physics classes for beginners. *Learning and Instruction, 12*, 447–465.

Holland, A., & Andre, T. (1987). Participation in extracurricular activities in secondary school: What is known, what needs to be known? *Review of Educational Research, 57*, 437–466.

Hunt, D. E. (1975). Person–environment interaction: A challenge found wanting before it was tried. *Review of Educational Research, 57*, 437–466.

Jackson, A. W., & Davis, G. A. (2000). *Turning points 2000: Educating adolescents in the 21st century*. New York: Teachers College Press.

Jencks, C., & Mayer, S. E. (1990). The social consequences of growing up in a poor neighborhood. In L. E. Lynn, Jr. and M. G. H. McGeary (Eds.), *Inner-city poverty in the United States*. Washington, DC: National Academy Press.

Jennings, P. A., & Greenberg, M. (2009). The prosocial classroom: Teacher social and emotional competence in relation to child and classroom outcomes. *Review of Educational Research, 79*, 491–525.

Johnson, J., & Strange, M. (2005). *Why rural matters 2005: The facts about rural education in the 50 states*. Randolph, VT: The Rural School and Community Trust.

Jussim, L., Eccles, J. S., & Madon, S. (1996). Social perception, social stereotypes, and teacher expectations: Accuracy and the quest for the powerful self-fulfilling prophecy. In L. Berkowitz (Ed.), *Advances in experimental social psychology* (pp. 281–388). New York: Academic Press.

Jussim, L., Palumbo, P., Chatman, C., Madon, S., & Smith, A. (2000). Stigma and self-fulfilling prophecies. In T. F. Heatherton et al. (Eds.), *The social psychology of stigma* (pp. 374–418). New York: Guilford Press.

Juvonen, J. (2007). Reforming middle schools: Focus on continuity, social connectedness, and engagement. *Educational Psychologist, 42*(4), 197–208.

Juvonen, J., Le, V. N., Kaganoff, T., Augustine, C., & Constant, L. (2004). *Focus on the wonder years: Challenges facing the American middle school*. Santa Monica, CA: Rand.

Juvonen, J., Nishina, A., & Graham, S. (2006). Ethnic diversity and perceptions of safety in urban middle schools. *Psychological Science, 17*(5), 393–400.

Kagan, D. M. (1990). How schools alienate students at risk: A model for examining proximal classroom variables. *Educational Psychologist, 25*, 105–125.

Kahne, J., Chi, B., and Middaugh, E. (2002), *Cityworks evaluation summary, Surdna Foundation and Mills College*. Oakland, CA: CERG.

Kao, G., & Thompson, J. S. (2003). Racial and ethnic stratification in educational achievement and attainment. *Annual Review of Sociology, 29*, 417–442.

Karweit, N., & Hansell, S. (1983). School organization and friendship selection. In J. L. Epstein & N. Karweit (Eds.), *Friends in school: Patterns of selection and influence in secondary schools* (pp. 29–38). New York: Academic Press.

Kavrell, S. M., & Petersen, A. C. (1984). Patterns of achievement in early adolescence. In M. L. Maehr (Ed.), *Advances in motivation and achievement* (pp. 1–35). Greenwich, CT: JAI Press.

Keating, D. P. (1990). Adolescent thinking. In S. S. Feldman & G. R. Elliott (Eds.), *At the threshold: The developing adolescent* (pp. 54–89). Cambridge, MA: Harvard University Press.

Kellam, S. G., Rebok, G. W., Wilson, R., & Mayer, L. S. (1994). The social field of the classroom: Context for the developmental epidemiological study of aggressive behavior. In R. K. Silbereisen & E. Todt (Eds.), *Adolescence in context: The interplay of family, school, peers, and work in adjustment* (pp. 390–408). New York: Springer-Verlag.

Kindermann, T. A. (1993). Natural peer groups as contexts for individual development: The case of children's motivation in school. *Developmental Psychology, 29*(6), 970–977.

Kindermann, T. A., McCollam, T. L., & Gibson, E., Jr. (1996). Peer networks and students' classroom engagement during childhood and adolescence. In K. Wentzel & J. Juvonen (Eds.), *Social motivation: Understanding children's school adjustment*. (pp. 279–312). Boston: Cambridge University Press.

King, P. D., & Roeser, R. W. (2009). Religion and spirituality in adolescent development. In R. M. Lerner & L. Steinberg (Eds.), *Handbook of adolescent psychology* (3rd ed.). Hoboken, NJ: Wiley.

King, P. E., & Furrow, J. L. (2004). Religion as a resource for positive youth development: Religion, social capital, and moral outcomes. *Developmental Psychology*, *40*(5), 703–713.

Kirby, D. B. (2002). Effective approaches to reducing adolescent unprotected sex, pregnancy, and childbearing. *Journal of Sex Research*, *39*, 51–57.

Konings, K. D., Brand-Gruwel, S., van Merrienboer, J. J. G., & Broers, N. J. (2008). Does a new learning environment come up to students' expectations? A longitudinal study. *Journal of Educational Psychology*, *100*(3), 535–548.

Krapp, A., Hidi, S. & Renninger, K. A. (1992). Interest, learning and development. In K. A. Renninger, S. Hidi, & A. Krapp (Eds.), *The role of interest in learning and development* (pp. 3–25). Hillsdale, NJ: Lawrence Erlbaum Associates.

Kulik, J. A., & Kulik, C. L. (1987). Effects of ability grouping on student achievement. *Equity & Excellence*, *23*, 22–30.

Lamborn, S. D., Brown, B. B., Mounts, N. S., & Steinberg, L. (1992). Putting school in perspective: The influence of family, peers, extracurricular participation, and part-time work on academic engagement (pp. 153–181). In F. M. Newmann (Ed.), *Student engagement and achievement in American secondary schools*. New York: Teachers College Press.

Larson, R. (1994). Youth organizations, hobbies, and sports as developmental contexts. In R. K. Silberiesen & E. Todt (Eds.), *Adolescence in context*. New York: Springer-Verlag.

Larson, R. W. (2000). Toward a psychology of positive youth development. *American Psychologist*, *55*, 170–183.

Larson, R., & Hansen, D. (2005). The development of strategic thinking: Learning to impact human systems in a youth activism program. *Human Development*, *48*, 237–349.

Larson, R., Hansen, D., & Moneta, G. (2006). Differing profiles of developmental experiences across types of organized youth activities. *Developmental Psychology*, *42*, 849–863.

Larson, R., & Kleiber, D. (1993). Free time activities as factors in adolescent adjustment. In P. Tolan & B. Cohler (Eds.), *Handbook of clinical research and practice with adolescents* (pp. 125–145). New York: Wiley.

Larson, R., & Richards, M. (Eds.). (1989). Introduction: The changing life space of early adolescence. *Journal of Youth and Adolescence*, *18*, 501–509.

Lazarus, R. S. & Folkman, S. (1984). *Stress, appraisal and coping*. New York: Springer.

LeBlanc, L., Swisher, R., Vitaro, F., & Tremblay, R. E. (2007). School social climate and teachers' perceptions of classroom behavior problems: A ten-year longitudinal and multilevel study. *Social Psychology in Education*, *10*, 429–442.

Lee, V. E. (2000). Using hierarchical linear modeling to study social contexts: The case of school effects. *Educational Psychologist*, *35*, 125–142.

Lee, V. E. & Bryk, A. S. (1989). A multilevel model of the social distribution of high school achievement. *Sociology of Education*, *62*, 172–192.

Lee, V. E., Bryk, A. S., & Smith, J. B. (1993). The organization of effective secondary schools. In L. Darling-Hammond (Ed.), *Review of research in education* (Vol. 19, pp. 171–267). Washington, DC: American Educational Research Association.

Lee, V. E., Croninger, R. G., & Smith, J. B. (1997a). Course taking, equity, and mathematics learning: Testing the constrained curriculum hypothesis in U.S. secondary schools. *Educational Evaluation and Policy Analysis*, *19*, 99–121.

Lee, V. E., & Loeb, S. (2000). School size in Chicago Elementary Schools: Effects on teacher attitudes and student achievement. *American Educational Research Journal*, *37*, 3–31.

Lee, V. E., & Smith, J. B. (1993). Effects of restructuring on the achievement and engagement of midde-grade students. *Sociology of Education*, *66*, 164–187.

Lee, V. E., & Smith, J. B. (1995). Effects of high school restructuring and size on early gains in achievement and engagement. *Sociology of Education*, *68*, 241–270.

Lee, V. E., & Smith, J. B. (1997). High school size: Which works best for whom? *Educational Evaluation and Policy Analysis*, *19*, 205–227.

Lee, V. E., & Smith, J. (2001). *Restructuring high schools for equity and excellence: What works*. New York: Teachers College Press.

Lee, V. E., Smith, J. B., & Croninger, R. G. (1997b). How high school organization influences the equitable distribution of learning in mathematics and science. *Sociology of Education*, *70*, 128–150.

Leventhal, T., & Brooks-Gunn, J. (2004). Diversity in developmental trajectories across adolescence: Neighborhood influences. In R. L. Lerner & L Steinberg, *Handbook of adolescent psychology* (2nd ed., pp. 451–486). Hoboken, NJ: Wiley.

Loeb, S., Darling-Hammond, L., & Luczak, J. (2005). How teaching conditions predict teacher turnover in California schools. *Peabody Journal of Education*, *80*, 44–70.

Lord, S., Eccles, J. S., & McCarthy, K. (1994). Risk and protective factors in the transition to junior high school. *Journal of Early Adolescence*, *14*, 162–199.

Lucas, T., Henze, R., & Donato, R. (1990). Promoting the success of Latino language-minority students: An exploratory study of six high schools. *Harvard Educational Review*, *60*, 315–340.

Mac Iver, D. J., Reuman, D. A., & Main, S. R. (1995). Social structuring of school: Studying what is, illuminating what could be. In M. R. Rosenzweig & L. W. Porter (Eds.), *Annual review of psychology* (Vol. 46). Palo Alto, CA: Annual Reviews.

Mac Iver, D., & Reuman, D. A. (1988, April). *Decision-making in the classroom and early adolescents' valuing of mathematics*. Paper presented at the annual meeting of the American Educational Research Association, New Orleans, LA.

Madon, S., Smith, A., Jussim, L., Russell, D. W., Eccles, J. Palumbo, P., et al. (2001). Am I as you see me or do you see me as I am? Self-fulfilling prophecies and self-verification. *Personality and Social Psychological Bulletin*, *27*, 1214–1224.

Maehr, M. L. (1991). The "psychological environment" of the school: A focus for school leadership. In P. Thurstone & P. Zodhiates (Eds.), *Advances in educational administration* (Vol. 2, pp. 51–81). Greenwich, CT: JAI Press.

Maehr, M. L., & Midgley, C. (1996). *Transforming school cultures to enhance student motivation and learning*. Boulder, CO: Westview Press.

Mahoney, J. L. (1997, April). *From companions to convictions: Peer groups, school engagement, and the development of criminality*. Paper presented at the Biennial Meeting of the Society for Research on Child Development, Washington, DC.

Mahoney, J. L., & Cairns, R. B. (1997). Do extracurricular activities protect against early school dropout? *Developmental Psychology*, *33*, 241–253.

Mahoney, J. L., Larson, R., & Eccles, J. (Eds.). (2005a). *Organized activities as contexts of development: Extracurricular activities, after-school and community programs*. Hillsdale, NJ: Lawrence Erlbaum Associates.

Mahoney, J. L., Lord, H., & Carryl, E. (2005b). An ecological analysis of after-school program participation and the development of academic performance and motivational attributes for disadvantaged children. *Child Development*, *76*, 811–825.

Maroulis, S., & Gomez, L. M. (2008). Does "connectedness" matter? Evidence from a social network analysis within a small-school reform. *Teachers College Record*, *110*, 1901–1929.

Marsh, H. W., Chessor, D., Craven, R., & Roche, L. (1995). The effects of gifts and talented programs on academic self-concept: The big fish strikes again. *American Educational Research Journal*, *32*, 285–319.

Marsh, H. W., Trautwein, U., Ludtke, O., Baumert, J., & Koller, O. (2007). The big-fish–little-pond effect: Persistent negative effects of selective high schools on self-concept after graduation. *American Educational Research Journal*, *44*, 631–669.

Marsh, H. W., Trautwein, U., Ludtke, O., & Brettschneider, W. (2008). Social comparison and big-fish–little-pond effects on self-concept and other self-belief constructs: Role of generalized and specific others. *Journal of Educational Psychology*, *100*, 510–524.

Martin, T. F., White, J. M., & Perlman, D. (2001). Religious socialization: A test of the channeling hypothesis of parental influence on adolescent faith maturity. *Journal of Adolescent Research*, *18*(2), 169–187.

Mashburn, A. J., Pianta, R. C., Hamre, B. K., Downer, J. T., Barbarin, O. A., Bryant, D., et al. (2008). Measures of classroom quality in prekindergarten and children's development of academic, language, and social skills. *Child Development*, *79*(3), 732–749.

McLaughlin, M. W. (2000). *Community counts: How youth organizations matter for youth development*. Washington, DC: Public Education Network.

McLoyd, V. C. (1990). The impact of economic hardship on Black families and development. *Child Development*, *61*, 311–346.

McNeal, R. B. (1995). Extracurricular activities and high school dropouts. *Sociology of Education*, *68*, 62–81.

McPartland, J. M. (1990). Staffing decisions in the middle grades. *Phi Delta Kappan*, *71*(6), 465–469.

Meece, J. (1991). The classroom context and students' motivational goals. In M. Maehr & P. Pintrich (Eds.), *Advances in motivation and achievement* (Vol. 7, pp. 261–286). Greenwich, CT: JAI.

Meece, J. L., Glienke, B. B., & Burg, S. (2006). Gender and motivation. *Journal of Social Psychology*, *44*, 351–373.

Meier, J. (2008). Introduction to the special section on European perspectives on the role of education in increasingly diverse European societies. *Child Development Perspectives*, *2*, 92.

Melchior, A. & Bailis, L. N. (2002). Impact of service-learning on civic attitudes and behaviors of middle and high school youth: Findings from three national evaluations. In A. Furco & S. H. Billig (Eds.), *Service-learning: The essence of the pedagogy* (pp. 201–222). Greenwich, CT: Information Age.

Midgley, C. (2002). *Goals, goal structures, and patterns of adaptive learning*. Mahwah, NJ: Lawrence Erlbaum Associates.

Midgley, C., Anderman, E., & Hicks, L. (1995). Differences between elementary and middle school teachers and students: A goal theory approach. *Journal of Early Adolescence*, *15*, 90–113.

Midgley, C., & Feldlaufer, H. (1987). Students' and teachers' decision-making fit before and after the transition to junior high school. *Journal of Early Adolescence*, *7*, 225–241.

Midgley, C., Feldlaufer, H., &, Eccles, J. S. (1988). The transition to junior high school: Beliefs of pre- and post-transition teachers. *Journal of Youth and Adolescence, 17*, 543–562.

Midgley, C. M., Feldlaufer, H., & Eccles, J. S. (1989a). Changes in teacher efficacy and student self- and task-related beliefs during the transition to junior high school. *Journal of Educational Psychology, 81*, 247–258.

Midgley, C., Feldlaufer, H., & Eccles, J. S. (1989b). Student/teacher relations and attitudes toward mathematics before and after the transition to junior high school. *Child Development, 60*, 981–992.

Mind and Life Educational Research Network (submitted for publication). *Contemplative practices and mental training: Prospects for American education.*

Moore, C., & Allen, J. P. (1996). The effects of volunteering on the young volunteer. *Journal of Primary Prevention, 17*, 231–258.

Moos, R. H. (1979). *Evaluating educational environments.* San Francisco: Jossey-Bass.

Mortimer, J. T., Shanahan, M., & Ryu, S. (1994). The effects of adolescent employment on school-related orientation and behavior. In R. K. Silbereisen & E. Todt (Eds.), *Adolescence in context: The interplay of family, school, peers, and work in adjustment* (pp. 304–326). New York: Springer-Verlag.

Murayama, K., & Elliot, A. J. (2009). The joint influence of personal achievement goals and classroom goal structures on achievement-relevant outcomes. *Journal of Educational Psychology, 101*, 432–447.

National Center for Education Statistics (2004). *Service-learning and community service in K-12 public schools.* Washington, DC: US Department of Education.

National Center for Education Statistics (2005). *The condition of education 2005* (NCES 2005–094). Washington, DC: US Department of Education.

National Center for Education Statistics (2006). *The condition of education 2006* (NCES 2006–071). Washington, DC: US Department of Education.

National Center for Education Statistics (2007). *Status and trends in the education of racial and ethnic minorities* (NCES 2007–039). Washington, DC: US Department of Education.

National Research Council (1997). *The new Americans: Economic, demographic, and fiscal effects of immigrations.* Washington, DC: National Academy Press.

National Research Council and Institute of Medicine (2004). *Engaging schools.* Washington, DC: National Academies Press.

Newmann, F. M., Wehlage, G. G., & Lamborn, S. D. (1992). The significance and sources of student engagement. In F. M. Newmann (Ed.), *Student engagement and achievement* in *American secondary schools* (pp. 11–39). New York: Teachers College Press.

Nicholls, J. G. (1990). What is ability and why are we mindful of it? A developmental perspective. In R. J. Sternberg & J. Kolligian (Eds.), *Competence considered.* New Haven, CT: Yale University Press.

Nichols, S. L., & Berliner, D. C. (2007). *Collateral damage: How high stakes testing corrupts America's school.* Boston: Harvard Education Press.

Nichols, S. L., & Berliner, D. C. (2008). Testing the joy out of learning. *Educational Leadership, 65*, 14–18.

Nisbett, R. E. (2008). *Intelligence and how to get it.* New York: W. W. Norton.

Nishina, A., & Juvonen, J. (2005). Daily reports of witnessing and experiencing peer harassment in middle school. *Child Development, 76*(2), 435–450.

Noddings, N. (2005a). *The challenge to care in schools: An alternative approach to education.* New York: Teachers College Press.

Noddings, N. (Ed.) (2005b). *Educating citizens for global awareness.* New York: Teachers College Press.

Oakes, J. (2005). *Keeping track: How schools structure inequality* (2nd ed.). New Haven: CT: Yale University Press.

Oakes, J., Gamoran, A., & Page, R. N. (1992). Curriculum differentiation: Opportunities, outcomes, and meanings. In P. Jackson (Ed.), *Handbook of research on curriculum* (pp. 570–608). New York: Macmillan.

Orfield, G. (1999). *Resegregation in American schools.* Cambridge, MA: Harvard University Press.

Oser, F. K., Scarlett, W. G., & Bucher, A. (2006). Religious and spiritual development throughout the lifespan. In W. Damon & R. M. Lerner (Series Eds.) & R. M. Lerner (Volume Ed.), *Handbook of child psychology, Vol. 1: Theoretical models of human development* (6th ed., pp. 942–998). New York: Wiley.

Osterman, K. F. (2000). Students' need for belonging in the school community. *Review of Educational Research, 70*(3), 323–367.

Otto, L. B., & Alwin, D. (1977). Athletics, aspirations and attainments. *Sociology of Education, 50*, 102–113.

Pallas, A. M., Entwisle, D. R., Alexander, K. L., & Stluka, M. F. (1994). Ability-group effects: Instructional, social, or institutional? *Sociology of Education, 67*, 27–46.

Parsons, J. E., & Ruble, D. N. (1977). The development of achievement–related expectancies. *Child Development, 48*, 1075–1079.

Parsons, J. S., Kaczala, C. M., & Meece, J. L. (1982). Socialization of achievement attitudes and beliefs: Classroom influences. *Child Development, 53*, 322–339.

Partnership for 21st Century Skills (2008). See www.21stcenturyskills.org

Patall, E. A., Cooper, H., & Robinson, J. C. (2008). The effects of choice on intrinsic motivation and related outcomes: A meta–analysis of research findings. *Psychological Bulletin, 134*, 270–300.

Pearce, N. J., & Larson, R. W. (2006). How teens become engaged in youth development programs: The process of motivational change in a civic activism organization. *Applied Developmental Science, 10*, 121–131.

Peck, S., Roeser, R. W., Zarrett, N. R. & Eccles, J. S. (2008). Exploring the role of extracurricular activity involvement in the educational resilience of vulnerable adolescents: Pattern- and variable-centered approaches. *Journal of Social Issues, 64*, 135–156.

Pekrun, R. (2006). The control-value theory of achievement emotions: Assumptions, corollaries, and implications for educational research and practice. *Educational Psychology Review, 18*, 315–341.

Pekrun, R., Goetz, T., & Frenzel, A.C. (2007, April). *Achievement and individual emotion: A multi-level analyses.* Symposium paper presented at American Educational Research Association, San Diego, CA.

Pekrun, R., Goetz, T., Titz, W., & Perry, R. P. (2002). Academic emotions in students' self-regulated learning and achievement: A program of qualitative and quantitative research. *Educational Psychologist, 37*, 91–105.

Perry, K. E., & Weinstein, R. S. (1998). The social context of early schooling and children's school adjustment. *Educational Psychologist, 33*, 177–194.

Peske, H. G., & Haycock, K. (2006). *Teaching inequality: How poor and minority students are shortchanged on teacher quality.* Washington, DC: Education Trust.

Pianta, R. C. (1999). *Enhancing relationships between children and teachers.* Washington, DC: American Psychological Association.

Pianta, R. C., Belsky, J., Houts, R., & Morrison, F. (2007). Opportunities to learn in America's elementary classrooms. *Science, 5820*, 1795–1796.

Pianta, R., Belsky, J., Vandergrift, N., Houts, R., & Morrison, F. J. (2008). Classroom effects on children's achievement trajectories in elementary school. *American Educational Research Journal, 45*, 365–398.

Pianta, R. C., & Hamre, B. K. (2009). Conceptualization, measurement and improvement of classroom processes: Standardized observation can leverage capacity. *Educational Researcher, 38*, 109–119.

Pianta, R., Howes, C., Burchinal, M., Bryant, D., Clifford, R., Early, D., et al. (2005). Features of pre-kindergarten programs, classrooms, and teachers: Do they predict observed classroom quality and child–teacher interactions? *Journal of Applied Developmental Science, 3*, 144–159.

Pianta, R. C. & Shuhlman, M. W. (2004). Teacher–child relationships and children's success in the first years of school. *School Psychology Review, 33*, 444–458.

Pintrich, P. R., & Schunk, D. H. (2003). *Motivation in education: Theory, research, and application* (2nd ed.). Englewood Cliffs, NJ: Merrill-Prentice Hall.

Portes, A., & Rumbaut, R. G. (2001). *Legacies: The story of the immigrant second generation.* Berkeley, CA: University of California Press.

Quint, J. (2006). *Meeting five critical challenges of high school reform: Lessons from research on three reform models.* New York: Manpower Demonstration Research Corporation. Retrieved November 11, 2009, from www.mdrc.org/publications/428/execsum.pdf

Ready, D. D., & Lee, V. E. (2008). Choice, equity, and schools-within-schools reform. *Teachers College Record, 110*(9), 1930–1958.

Rehberg, R. A. (1969). Behavioral and attitudinal consequences of high school interscholastic sports: A speculative consideration. *Adolescence, 4*, 69–88.

Renninger, K. A. (2000). Individual interest and its implications for understanding intrinsic motivation. In C. Sansone & J. M. Harackiewicz (Eds.), *Intrinsic and extrinsic motivation* (pp. 373–404). San Diego, CA: Academic Press.

Reuman, D. A. (1989). How social comparison mediates the relation between ability-grouping practices and students' achievement expectancies in mathematics. *Journal of Educational Psychology, 81*, 178–189.

Rist, R. C. (1970). Student social class and teacher expectations: The self-fulfilling prophecy in ghetto education. *Harvard Educational Review, 40*, 411–451.

Roderick, M. (1993). *The path to dropping out.* Westport, CT: Auburn House.

Roehlkepartain, E. C., & Patel, E. (2006). Congregations: Unexamined crucibles for spiritual development. In E. C. Roehlkepartain et al. (Eds.), *The handbook of spiritual development in childhood and adolescence* (pp. 324–336). Thousand Oaks, CA: Sage.

Roeser, R. W. (2004). Competing schools of thought in achievement goal theory? In M. L. Maehr & P. R. Pintrich (Eds.), *Advances in motivation and achievement, Volume 13: Motivating students, improving schools* (pp. 265–299). New York: Elsevier.

Roeser, R. W., & Eccles, J. S. (1998). Adolescents' perceptions of middle school: Relation to longitudinal changes in academic and psychological adjustment. *Journal of Research on Adolescence, 88*, 123–158.

Roeser, R. W., & Eccles, J. S. (2000). Schooling and mental health. In A. J. Sameroff, M. Lewis, & S. M. Miller (Eds.), *Handbook of developmental psychopathology* (2nd ed., pp. 135–156). New York: Plenum.

Roeser, R. W., Eccles, J. S., & Freedman-Doan, C. (1999). Academic and emotional functioning in middle adolescence: Patterns, progressions, and routes from childhood. *Journal of Adolescent Research, 14*, 135–174.

Roeser, R. W., Eccles, J. S., & Sameroff, J. (1998a). Academic and emotional functioning in early adolescence. Longitudinal relations, patterns, and prediction by experience in middle school. *Development and Psychopathology, 10*, 321–352.

Roeser, R. W., Eccles, J. S., & Strobel, K. (1998b). Linking the study of schooling and mental health: Selected issues and empirical illustrations at the level of the individual. *Educational Psychologist, 33*, 153–176.

Roeser, R. W., & Galloway, M. G. (2002). Studying motivation to learn in early adolescence: A holistic perspective. In T. Urdan & F. Pajares (Eds.), *Academic motivation of adolescents: Adolescence and education* (Vol. 2, pp. 331–372). Greenwich, CT: Information Age Publishing.

Roeser, R. W., Marachi, R., & Gehlbach, H. (2002a). A goal theory perspective on teachers' professional identities and the contexts of teaching. In C. Midgley (Ed.), *Goals, goal structure, and patterns of adaptive learning* (pp. 204–239). Mahwah, NJ: Lawrence Erlbaum Associates.

Roeser, R. W., & Midgley, C. M. (1997). Teachers' views of aspects of student mental health. *Elementary School Journal, 98*(2), 115–133.

Roeser, R. W., Midgley, C. M., & Maehr, M. L. (1994, February). *Unfolding and enfolding youth: A development study of school culture and student well-being.* Paper presented at the Society for Research on Adolescence, San Diego, CA.

Roeser, R. W., Midgley, C., & Urdan, T. C. (1996). Perceptions of the school psychological environment and early adolescents' psychological and behavioral functioning in school: The mediating role of goals and belonging. *Journal of Educational Psychology, 88*, 408–422.

Roeser, R. W., & Peck, S. C. (2003). Patterns and pathways of educational achievement across adolescence: A holistic–developmental perspective. *New Directions for Child and Adolescent Development, 101*, 39–62.

📖 Roeser, R. W., & Peck, S. C. (2009). An education in awareness: Self, motivation, and self-regulated learning in contemplative perspective. *Educational Psychologist, 44*, 119–136.

Roeser, R. W., Shavelson, R. J., Kupermintz, H., Lau, S., Ayala, C., Haydel, A., et al. (2002b). The concept of aptitude and multidimensional validity revisited. *Educational Assessment, 8*, 191–205.

Roeser, R. W., Stephens, J. C., & Urdan, T. (2009). School as a context of motivation and development. In K. Wentzel & A. Wigfield (Eds.), *Handbook of motivation.* Mahwah, NJ: Lawrence Erlbaum Associates.

Roeser, R. W., Strobel, K. R., & Quihuis, G. (2002c). Studying early academic motivation, social–emotional functioning, and engagement in learning: Variable- and person-centered approaches. *Anxiety, Stress, and Coping, 15*(4), 345–368.

Roeser, R. W., Urdan, T. C., & Stephens, J. M. (2009). School as a context of motivation and development. In K. R. Wentzel & A. Wigfield (Eds.), *Handbook of motivation at school* (pp. 381–410). New York: Routledge.

Romo, H. D., & Falbo, T. (1996). *Latino high school graduation.* Austin, TX: University of Texas Press.

Rosenbaum, J. E. (1976). *Making inequality: The hidden curriculum of high school tracking.* New York: Wiley.

Rosenbaum, J. E. (1980). Social implications of educational grouping. *Review of Research in Education, 7*, 361–401.

Rosenbaum, J. E. (1991). Black pioneers: Do their moves to the suburbs increase economic opportunity for mothers and children? *Housing Policy Debate, 2*(4), 1179–1213.

Rosenbaum, J. E., Kulieke, M. J., & Rubinowitz, L. S. (1988). White suburban schools' responses to low-income Black children: Sources of successes and problems. *Urban Review, 20*, 28–41.

Rosenbloom, S. R., & Way, N. (2004) Experiences of discrimination among African American, Asian American, and Latino adolescents in an urban high school. *Youth and Society, 35*, 420–451.

Rosenholtz, S. J., & Simpson, C. (1984). The formation of ability conceptions: Developmental trend or social construction? *Review of Educational Research, 54*, 301–325.

Rosenthal, R. (1969). Interpersonal expectations effects of the experimenter's hypothesis. In R. Rosenthal & R. L. Rosnow (Eds.), *Artifacts in behavioral research* (pp. 182–279). New York: Academic Press.

Rosenthal, R. (1974). *On the social psychology of the self-fulfilling prophecy: Further evidence for Pygmalion effects and their mediating mechanisms.* New York: MSS Modular Publications.

Roseth, C. J., Johnson, D. W., & Johnson, R. T. (2008). Promoting early adolescents' achievement and peer relationships: The effects of cooperative, competitive and individualistic goal structures. *Psychological Bulletin, 134*, 223–246.

Ross, L., & Nisbett, R. E. (1991). *The person and the situation: Perspectives of social psychology.* New York: McGraw-Hill.

Rowan, B., Correnti, R., & Miller, R. J. (2002). What large-scale, survey research tells us about teacher effects on student achievement: Insights from the Prospects Study of Elementary Schools. *Teachers College Record, 104*, 1525–1567.

📖 Rowley, S. J., Burchinal, M. R., Roberts, J. E., & Zeisel, S. A., (2008). Racial identity, social context, and race-related social cognition in African Americans during middle childhood. *Developmental Psychology, 44*, 1537–1546.

Ruggiero, K. M., & Taylor, D. M. (1995). Coping with discrimination: How disadvantaged group members perceive the discrimination that confronts them. *Journal of Personality and Social Psychology, 68*, 826–838.

Rumberger, R. W. (1995). Dropping out of middle school: A multilevel analysis of students and schools. *American Educational Research Journal, 32*, 583–625.

Runyan, D. K., Hunter, W. M., Socolar, R. R. S., Amaya-Jackson, L., English, D., Landswerk, J., et al. (2009). Children who prosper in unfavorable environments: The relationship to social capital. *Pediatrics, 101*(1), 12–18.

Ruthig, J. C., Perry, R. P., Hladkyj, S., Hall, N. C., Pekrun, R., & Chipperfield, J. G. (2008). Perceived control and emotions: Interactive effects on performance in achievement settings. *Social Psychology Education, 11*, 161–180.

Rutter, M. (1983). School effects on pupil progress: Research findings and policy implications. *Child Development, 54*, 1–29.

Rutter, M., & Maughan, B. (2002). School effectiveness findings 1979–2002. *Journal of School Psychology, 40*, 451–475.

Rutter, M., Maughan, B., Mortimore, P., & Ouston, J. (1979). *Fifteen thousand hours: Secondary schools and their effects on children.* Cambridge, MA: Harvard University Press.

Sable, J., and Garofano, A. (2007). *Public elementary and secondary school student enrollment, high school completions, and staff from the common core of data: School year 2005–06* (NCES 2007–352). Washington, DC: National Center for Education Statistics. Retrieved June 18, 2007, from http://nces.ed.gov/pubsearch/pubsinfo.asp?pubid=2007352

Sameroff, A. (1983). Developmental systems: Contexts and evolution. In W. Kessen (Ed.) and P. H. Mussen (Series Ed.), *Handbook of child psychology: Volume 1. History, theory, and methods* (pp. 237–294). New York: Wiley.

Sampson, R. J., Raudenbush, S. W., & Earls, F. (1997). Neighborhoods and violent crime: A multilevel study of collective efficacy. *Science, 277*, 918–924.

Sarason, S. B. (1990). *The predictable failure of school reform.* San Francisco: Jossey-Bass.

Sawhill, I. V. (2006). Opportunity in America: The role of education. *Future of Children Policy Brief*, Fall, 1–7.

Scales, P. C., Blyth, D. A., Berkas, T. H., & Kielsmeier, J. C. (2000). The effects of service-learning on middle school students' social responsibility and academic success. *Journal of Early Adolescence, 20*(3), 332–358.

Schaps, E. (2003). The heart of a caring school. *Educational Leadership, 60*, 31–33.

Schulting, A. B., Malone, P. S., & Dodge, K. A. (2005). The effect of school-based kindergarten transition policies and practices on child academic outcomes. *Developmental Psychology, 41*(6), 860–871.

Schunk, D. H. (1987). Peer models and children's behavioral change. *Review of Educational Research, 57*, 149–174.

Sellers, R. M., Caldwell, C. H., Schmeelk-Cone, K. H., & Zimmerman, M. A. (2003). Racial identity, racial discrimination, perceived stress, and psychological distress among African American young adults. *Journal of Health and Social Behavior, 44*(3), 302–317.

Sharkey, P. (2009). *Neighborhoods and the Black–White mobility gap.* Report to Economic Mobility Project of the Pew Charitable Trusts, Washington, DC. See www.economicmobility.org

Shih, M., Pittinsky, T. L., & Ambady, N. (1999). Stereotype susceptibility: Identity salience and shifts in quantitative performance. *Psychological Science, 10*(1), 80–83.

Shulman, L. S. (2005). Signature pedagogies in the professions. *Daedalus, 134*, 52–59.

Sieber, R. T. (1979). Classmates as workmates: In formal peer activity in the elementary school. *Anthropology and Education Quarterly, 10*, 207–235.

Simmons, R. G., & Blyth, D. A. (1987). *Moving into adolescence: The impact of pubertal change and school context.* Hawthorn, NY: Aldine de Gruyter.

Skinner, E. A., & Belmont, M. J. (1993). Motivation in the classroom: Reciprocal effects of teacher behavior and student engagement across the school year. *Journal of Educational Psychology, 85*, 571–581.

Slavin, R. E. (1990). Achievement effects of ability grouping in secondary schools: A best-evidence synthesis. *Review of Educational Research, 60*, 471–499.

Slavin, R. E. & Calderon, M. (2001). *Effective programs for Latino students.* Mahwah, NJ: Lawrence Erlbaum Associates.

Sleeper, M. E. & Strom, M. S. (2006). Facing history and ourselves. In M. J. Elias & H. Arnold (Eds.), *The educators' guide to emotional intelligence and academic achievement: Social–emotional learning in the classroom* (pp. 240–246). Thousand Oaks, CA: Corwin Press.

Smith, A. E., Jussim, L., & Eccles, J. S. (1999). Do self-fulfilling prophecies accumulate, dissipate, or remain stable over time? *Journal of Personality and Social Psychology, 77*, 548–565.

Smith, C. (2003). Theorizing religious effects among American adolescents. *Journal for the Scientific Study of Religion, 42*, 17–30.

Smith, C., & Denton, M. L. (2005). *Soul searching: The religious and spiritual lives of American teenagers.* Oxford, UK: Oxford University Press.

Smith, T. M., Desimone, L. M. & Ueno, K. (2005). "Highly qualified" to do what? The relationship of NCLB teacher quality mandates and the use of reform-oriented instruction in middle school mathematics. *Educational Evaluation and Policy Analysis, 27*, 75–109.

Solomon, D., Battistich, V., & Hom, A. (1996). Teacher beliefs and practices in schools serving communities that differ in socioeconomic level. *Journal of Experimental Education, 64*, 327–347.

Staff, J., Mortimer, J. T., & Uggen, C. (2004). Work and leisure in adolescence. In R. L. Lerner & L. Steinberg (2004). *Handbook of adolescent psychology* (2nd ed., pp. 429–450). Hoboken, NJ: Wiley.

Stattin, H., Kerr, M., Mahoney, J., Persson, A., & Magnusson, D. (2005). Explaining why a leisure context is bad for some girls and not for others. In J. L Mahoney, R. W. Larson, & J. S. Eccles. (Eds.). *Organized activities as contexts of development: Extracurricular activities, after-school and community programs* (pp. 211–234). Hillsdale, NJ: Lawrence Erlbaum Associates.

Stattin, H., & Magnusson, D. (1990). *Pubertal maturation in female development*. Hillsdale, NJ: Lawrence Erlbaum Associates.

Steinberg, L., Dornbusch, S., & Brown, B. (1992). Ethnic differences in adolescents' achievements: An ecological perspective. *American Psychologist, 47*, 723–729.

Steinberg, L., Fegley, S., & Dornbusch, S. M. (1993). Negative impact of part-time work on adolescent adjustment: Evidence from a longitudinal study. *Developmental Psychology, 29*, 171–180.

Stevens, R. J., & Slavin, R. E. (1995). The cooperative elementary school: Effects on students' achievement, attitudes, and social relations. *American Educational Research Journal, 32*, 321–351.

Stevenson, H. W., & Stigler, J. W. (1992). *The learning gap: Why our schools are failing and what we can learn from Japanese and Chinese education*. New York: Summit Books.

Stipek, D. J., & Hoffman, J. M. (1980). Children's achievement-related expectancies as a function of academic performance histories and sex. *Journal of Educational Psychology, 72*, 861–865.

Strobel, K., & Roeser, R. W. (1998, April). *Patterns of motivation and mental health in middle school: Relation to academic and emotional regulation strategies*. Paper presented at the Annual Meeting of the American Educational Research Association, San Diego.

Suarez-Orozco, C., & Suarez-Orozco, M. (2001). *Children of immigration*. Cambridge, MA: Harvard University Press.

Szalacha, L. A., Erkut, S., Garcia Coll, C., Alarcon, O., Fields, J. P., & Ceder, I. (2003). Discrimination and Puerto Rican children's and adolescents' mental health. *Cultural Diversity and Ethnic Minority Psychology, 9*, 141–155.

Tschannen-Moran, M., Woolfolk Hoy, A., & Hoy, W. K. (1998). Teacher efficacy: Its meaning and measure. *Review of Educational Research, 68*, 202–248.

Turner, J. C., Midgley, C., Meyer, D. K., Ghenn, M., Anderman, E. M., Kang, Y., et al. (2002). The classroom environment and students' reports of avoidance strategies in mathematics: A multimethod study. *Journal of Educational Psychology, 94*, 88–106.

Urdan, T., Midgley, C., & Anderman, E. (1998). The role of classroom goal structure in students' use of self-handicapping strategies. *American Educational Research Journal, 35*, 101–122.

Urdan, T. C., & Roeser, R. W. (1993, April). *The relations among adolescents' social cognitions, affect, and academic self-schemas*. Paper presented at the annual meeting of the American Educational Research Association, Atlanta, GA.

Valdes, G. (2001). *Learning and not learning English: Latino students in American schools*. New York: Teachers College Press.

Valencia, R. R. (Ed.) (1991). *Chicano school failure and success: Research and policy agendas for the 1990s*. London: Falmer Press.

Vanfossen, B. E., Jones, J. D., & Spade, J. Z. (1987). Curriculum tracking and status maintenance. *Sociology of Education, 60*, 104–122.

Vernez, G., Abrahamse, A., & Quigley, D. D. (1996). *How immigrants fare in U.S. education*. Santa Monica, CA: Rand Corporation.

Wehlage, G., Rutter, R., Smith, G., Lesko, N., & Fernandez, R. (1989). *Reducing the risk: Schools as communities of support*. Philadelphia: Falmer Press.

Weiner, B. (1991). On perceiving the other as responsible. In R. A. Dienstbier (Ed.), *Perspectives on motivation: Nebraska symposium on motivation, 1990* (pp. 165–236). Lincoln, NE: University of Nebraska Press.

Weinstein, R. (1989). Perceptions of classroom processes and student motivation: Children's views of self-fulfilling prophecies. In C. Ames & R. Ames (Eds.), *Research on motivation in education: Vol. 3: Goals and cognitions* (pp. 13–44). New York: Academic Press.

Wentzel, K. (2002). Are effective teachers like good parents? Teaching styles and student adjustment in early adolescence. *Child Development, 73*, 287–301.

Whitbeck, L. B., Simons, R. L., Conger, R. D., Wickrama, K. A. S., Ackley, K. A. & Elder, G. H. (1997). The effects of parents' working conditions and family economic hardship on parenting behaviors and children's self-efficacy. *Social Psychology Quarterly, 60*, 291–303.

Wigfield, A., Byrnes, J. B., & Eccles, J. S. (2006). Adolescent development. In P. A. Alexander & P. Winne (Eds.), *Handbook of educational psychology* (2nd ed.). Mahwah, NJ: Lawrence Erlbaum Associates.

Wigfield, A., & Eccles, J. S. (1989). Test anxiety in elementary and secondary school students. *Educational Psychologist, 24*, 159–183.

Wigfield, A., Eccles, J. S., & Pintrich, P. R. (1996). Development between the ages of eleven and twenty-five. In D. C. Berliner and R. C. Calfee (Eds.), *The handbook of educational psychology* (pp. 148–185). New York: Macmillan.

Wigfield, A., Eccles, J. S., Schiefele, U., Roeser, R., Davis-Kean, P. (2006). Motivation. In N. Eisenberg (Ed.), *Handbook of child psychology* (6th ed., Vol. 3, pp. 933–1002). New York: Wiley.

Wigfield, A., Eccles, J., Mac Iver, D., Reuman, D., & Midgley, C. (1991). Transitions at early adolescence: Changes in children's domain-specific self-perceptions and general self-esteem across the transition to junior high school. *Developmental Psychology*, *27*, 552–565.

Willis, P. L. (1977). *Learning to labor: How working class kids get working class jobs*. Driffield, UK: Nafferton.

Willower, D. J., & Lawrence, J. D. (1979). Teachers' perceptions of student threat to teacher status and teacher pupil control ideology. *Psychology in the Schools*, *16*, 586–590.

Wilson, D. B., Gottfredson, D. C., & Najaka, S. S. (2001). School-based prevention of problem behaviors: A meta-analysis. *Journal of Quantitative Criminology*, *17*, 247–272.

Wilson, W. J. (1987). *The truly disadvantaged: The inner city, the underclass and public policy*. Chicago: University of Chicago Press.

Wong, C. A., Eccles, J. S., & Sameroff, A. J. (2003). The influence of ethnic discrimination and ethnic identification on African-Americans adolescents' school and socioemotional adjustment. *Journal of Personality*, *71*, 1197–1232.

Wyse, A. E., Keesler, V., & Schneider, B. (2008). Assessing the effects of small school size on mathematics achievement: A propensity score-matching approach. *Teachers College Record*, *110*(9), 1879–1900.

Yates, M., & Youniss, M. (1996). A developmental perspective on community service in adolescence. *Social Development*, *5*(1), 85–111.

Youniss, J. (1980). *Parents and peers in social development*. Chicago: University of Chicago.

Youniss, J., McLellan, J. A., & Yates, M., (1997a). What we know about engendering civic identity. *American Behavioral Scientist*, *40*, 619–630.

Youniss, J., Yates, M., & Su, Y. (1997b). Social integration: Community service and marijuana use in high school seniors. *Journal of Adolescent Research*, *12*, 245–262.

Zalantino, S. D., & Sleeman, P. J. (1975). *A systems approach to learning environments*. Pleasantville, NY: Redgrave.

Zimmer-Gembeck, M. J., & Mortimer, J. T. (2006). Adolescent work, vocational development, and education. *Review of Educational Research*, *76*, 537–566.

Zins, J. E., Weissberg, R. P., Wang, M. C., & Walberg, H. J. (2004). *Building academic success on social and emotional learning*. New York: Teachers College Press.

CHILDREN AND THE LAW: EXAMPLES OF APPLIED DEVELOPMENTAL PSYCHOLOGY IN ACTION

Lindsay C. Malloy, Michael E. Lamb, and Carmit Katz
University of Cambridge

INTRODUCTION

Each year, increasing numbers of children come into contact with the legal, social service, and child welfare systems around the world, often as a result of child maltreatment, parental separation/divorce, and delinquent behavior. As a result, children represent "a large and growing legal constituency, one that possesses a special set of constraints involving basic developmental competencies, including cognitive, social, and emotional, that may constrain their effective participation" (Bruck, Ceci, & Principe, 2006, p. 777). In response to these trends, the amount of research concerning children and the law has grown rapidly and continues to grow, making it one of the fastest-growing areas in all of developmental psychology (Bruck et al., 2006). Lawyers, judges, social workers, jurors, parents, and others must make important (often life-transforming) decisions about children's lives in different contexts every day. Psychological research can and should guide these crucial decisions. But does it?

Although legal and social service intervention is often justified by reference to children's best interests, the interventions themselves are seldom informed by reference to developmental theory or the results of scientific research. Instead, political, ideological, and cultural values may guide the development of policies such as those that allow the prosecution of juvenile offenders in adult courts or emphasize family preservation rather than the termination of parental rights when children have been severely and persistently abused by their parents. It is unfortunate that policy makers sometimes fail to take advantage of a burgeoning and increasingly sophisticated understanding of child development in this way because superior public policy and law would surely emerge if policies and practices were better informed.

Psychological research can be and has been used to guide the treatment of children in legal contexts, however, and we use these instances to demonstrate in this chapter how applied and basic psychological research can complement one another, with researchers helping guide practitioners and the latter in turn offering insights and asking questions that foster a more complete understanding of developmental processes. Our discussion focuses on the role and relevance of psychological research in relation to child maltreatment, divorce, and juvenile justice.

When developmental psychology emerged as a distinct discipline about a century ago, it focused very heavily on applied issues, with psychologists regularly providing advice to parents, teachers, and paediatricians (Clarke-Stewart, 1998; Sears, 1975). By the middle of the twentieth century, however, psychologists shifted their focus to basic research questions, apparently fearing that a concern with applied issues made developmental psychology less credible as a science. Today, we see a new appreciation for applied research simultaneously enhancing children's welfare while yielding insights into normative developmental processes that could not be obtained by basic research alone.

As far back as 1843, British psychologists used the "insanity defence" in a case involving a man who attempted to assassinate the Prime Minister of the United Kingdom (Brigham, 1999). Psychology and the legal system thus share a long (and often tumultuous) history. The first legal brief to cite social science evidence was filed in 1908 (*Muller v. Oregon*) and perhaps the best known legal brief informed by psychologists was submitted to the US Supreme Court in 1954 to demonstrate the effects of racial segregation on children's education (*Brown v. Board of Education*, 1954).

More than a century ago, Munsterberg (1908) argued that "The time for such applied psychology is surely near . . . all are ready to see that certain chapters of Applied Psychology are sources of help and strength for them. The lawyer alone is obdurate [pp. 9–10]. . . . It is surprising and seems unjustifiable that lawyers and laymen alike should not have given any attention, so far, to the . . . many . . . methods of the psychological laboratory—methods in the study of memory and attention, feeling and will, perception and judgment, suggestion and emotion. In every one of these fields, the psychological experiment could be made helpful to the purposes of court and law" (p. 76). Munsterberg's claims were met with skepticism and hostility from some legal professionals (e.g., Wigmore, 1909), and even some social scientists (e.g., Cairns, 1935), who reflected opinions and sentiments that prevail to this day, despite considerable evidence that applied psychologists have made substantial contributions with respect to policy concerning children's eyewitness testimony, divorce, and juvenile justice, as shown in the next section.

We begin by defining applied and basic psychology, and then discuss the ways in which both types of research have informed policy and practice regarding these three topics, while also highlighting challenges that were overcome, lessons learned along the way, and issues of continued concern.

APPLIED VERSUS BASIC RESEARCH

What better place to start than with the common misconceptions about applied and basic research? Applied psychological research is often (mis)characterized as atheoretical and methodologically inferior to basic research, while basic research is often (mis)characterized as "that which sits on shelves for other academics to read." Although this may be true in some cases, neither of these characterizations is fair. Furthermore, although applied and basic research may be differently motivated, the distinction need not be framed in an "either/or" format (e.g., Should my research attempt to understand natural phenomena, *or* solve a social problem? Should I make a contribution to theory *or* improve lives?). Both types of research can and often do improve the quality of individuals' lives significantly but, according to Groark and McCall (2005, p. 558), the issue is "how soon, how directly, and what other information is needed before such knowledge guides practice and action."

Applied research has been defined as "research conducted to solve a problem or in order to provide information that can be put to some specific use," whereas basic research is defined as "research motivated by the desire to expand knowledge" (Zigler & Finn-Stevenson, 1999, p. 555). Often basic research is thought of as "knowledge for the sake of knowledge" with unknown but potentially broader implications than applied research aimed at solving a particular problem, usually in a specific setting or context (Campbell, 1978; Cialdini, 1980; Lewin, 1946). Because applied psychology's goal is to provide knowledge relevant to particular circumstances in real-world contexts, it is often conceptualized as "action scholarship" (Groark & McCall, 2005). As such, applied psychology defines and addresses, and aims to solve real-world problems as well as related research questions.

Differences between applied and basic research are also evident in the associated research and dissemination processes including such features as timing, speed, criterion, control, and methodology (Groark & McCall, 2005). For example, applied research faces more stringent deadlines: It must be completed fast enough that the information gleaned is still relevant to the real-world problem at hand. Applied psychologists may take advantage of methods that appear applicable rather than those that might be considered "scientifically ideal" under other circumstances (McCall & Green, 2004). Psychologists conducting applied research also look beyond traditional avenues, such as academic journals, for dissemination, engaging in dialogues with practitioners, policy makers, and other end-users. Because they must simultaneously ensure that they are conducting rigorous empirical research while being aware of concerns and practices in the field, psychologists conducting applied research may find themselves making difficult decisions and choosing among contradictory options more often than psychologists conducting basic research.

As mentioned earlier, applied research and basic psychological research are not mutually exclusive. Not only is there considerable overlap, but they need and complement one another in unique and important ways. For instance, applied psychology typically involves assessing the generalizability of basic theories or findings (Groark & McCall, 2005). In addition, field findings can be understood by putting them in the context of basic research. For example, we show later how applied research has promoted children's welfare, but also how the close study of children's experiences and performance in real-world settings has enhanced our understanding of developmental processes. This point deserves emphasis because psychologists often view applied research as intellectually and methodologically inferior, unlikely to enhance our broader understanding.

While basic research has the "presumed advantage of being guided by and contributing to theory" (Groark & McCall, 2005, p. 558), research concerning children and the law is solidly grounded in developmental theory while still addressing applied issues. There is much to gain, methodologically and substantively, from studying children in both experimental analog and real-world contexts. Grappling with real-world problems and contexts, applied psychology has also "produced innovative developmental paradigms, theories, and frameworks" that augment and enhance the tools available for future research (Bruck et al., 2006, p. 776). Through various outlets, the answers to these questions are then conveyed to the field and public at large. In the following pages, we illustrate these processes in relation to three topics: children's eyewitness testimony, parental separation and divorce, and juvenile justice issues. For each topic, we review (a) the impetus for this line of work, (b) successful applications of applied and basic research, including problems encountered and solutions devised along the way, and (c) areas that reflect further challenges.

CHILD MALTREATMENT AND CHILDREN'S EYEWITNESS TESTIMONY

Although we try, as a society, to protect children, the prevalence of child maltreatment (physical, sexual, and psychological abuse, as well as neglect) makes clear that too many children do not live in safe and secure circumstances. For example, in the United States, about 3.5 million investigations or assessments are carried out annually following reports of suspected child maltreatment. Following these investigations, nearly 800,000 children were classified as victims of maltreatment in 2007 (US Department of Health and Human Services, Administration on Children, Youth, and Families, 2009). The situation is alarming elsewhere as well. In 2003, approximately 235,000 child maltreatment investigations were conducted in Canada, and almost half of these cases were substantiated by child protection workers (Trocmé et al., 2001). Between 2001–02 and 2005–06, the number of child protection notifications in Australia almost doubled from 138,000 to 267,000, with increases in the number of substantiated cases as well (Australian Institute of Health and Welfare, 2007). In England, 570,000 cases were referred in 2002–2003, and over 30,000 of these cases were registered or substantiated (Creighton, 2004).

Although many factors affect children's adjustment, maltreatment can profoundly affect children's cognitive, socioemotional, and even physical development (Celano, Hazzard, Campbell, & Lang, 2002; Cicchetti, in press; Dodge, Pettit, Bates, & Valente, 1995; Egeland, Yates, Appleyard, & van Dulmen, 2002; Feiring, Taska, & Lewis, 1998; Lyon & Saywitz, 1999; National Research Council, 1993; Shonk & Cicchetti, 2001; Sternberg, Baradaran, Abbott, Lamb, & Guterman, 2006a; Valle & Silovsky, 2002). Importantly, these effects can be long-lasting: Child maltreatment is a major risk factor for short- and long-term adjustment problems, including adult psychopathology (see reviews by Alexander, 1992; Beitchman, Zucker, Hood, DaCosta, Akman, & Cassavia, 1992; Briere & Runtz, 1993; Cicchetti, in press; Finkelhor, 1990; Finkelhor & Browne, 1988; Green, 1993; Sternberg, Lamb, Guterman, & Abbott, 2006b). Early identification of maltreatment is critical for ending victimization, protecting children, and providing children, families, and potentially perpetrators with appropriate services and treatment.

Early identification is easier said than done, however, because child maltreatment is a crime that is extremely difficult to investigate. For one thing, the crimes often occur behind closed doors and are shrouded in secrecy. Especially in the case of sexual abuse, furthermore, corroborative evidence rarely exists either because the nature of the abuse does not lend itself to physical evidence (e.g., fondling), or physical evidence has disappeared due to delayed reporting, which is quite common (Goodman-Brown, Edelstein, Goodman, Jones, & Gordon, 2003; London, Bruck, Ceci, & Shuman, 2005; Pipe, Lamb, Orbach, & Cederborg, 2007). Even in the rare cases where physical evidence exists, it may not identify the perpetrator. As a result, children's eyewitness testimony is often critical. Without it, justice will not be served, children will not be protected, and victims will not be treated. Thus, it is imperative that children's reports are clear, consistent, detailed, and accurate. When children's accounts are vague, inconsistent, and/or incomplete, their reports tend to be met with skepticism (e.g., Leippe, Manion, & Romanczyk, 1992; see Myers, 1992), whereas "aside from a smoking pistol, nothing carries as much weight with a jury as the testimony of an actual witness" (Loftus & Ketcham, 1991, p. 16).

Children most often testify about maltreatment, but they can also be called upon to provide statements as victims or witnesses to other crimes (domestic violence, murder, etc.) or in civil proceedings (e.g., custodial disputes, removals of children or adults from their homes) (Bruck et al., 2006; Lamb, 2003; Lamb, Hershkowitz, Orbach, & Esplin, 2008). As a result, research on children's eyewitness testimony has mushroomed.

Impetus for This Line of Research

Coinciding with and in response to the growing awareness of child maltreatment and a desire to see it dealt with aggressively (Bruck et al., 2006; Lamb, 2003), several barriers to children's participation in the legal system were removed in the 1980s. For example, in the United States, Canada, and the UK, most jurisdictions ceased requiring corroborative evidence when children alleged that they had been sexually abused. These changes made it possible for children to participate in the legal system, which they had rarely done before (Ceci & Bruck, 1995), in part because they were thought to be incompetent witnesses. Unfortunately, several well-publicized but controversial child sexual abuse cases have certainly contributed to the persistence of this reputation (e.g., *California v. Raymond Buckey et al., Commonwealth of Massachusetts v. Cheryl Amirault LeFave; New Jersey v. Michaels, Lillie and Reed v. Newcastle City Council & Ors, North Carolina v. Robert Fulton Kelly Jr., State v. Fijnje*).

In the McMartin Preschool Abuse case in California, for example, dozens of children alleged that Raymond Buckey and colleagues working in the preschool subjected children to months of ritual sexual abuse (*California v. Raymond Buckey et al.*). Alleged victims claimed bizarre experiences (e.g., they were taken into tunnels underneath the school; they saw witches fly; they went on hot air balloon rides; and they witnessed human and animal sacrifice) but no physical evidence confirming the allegations ever emerged. The charges were eventually dropped after years of investigation and criminal trials. Defendants in other cases were not so lucky, often serving time in jail before their convictions were overturned (Ceci & Bruck, 1995; Nathan & Snedeker, 1995).

In these cases, which rested almost entirely on children's allegations, it was the jury's task to determine whether the children could be believed. Juries had to make such decisions in the face of contradictory claims by prosecutors that children never lie about sexual abuse, and by defence attorneys that children were easily led to provide false reports following repeated suggestive interviews by zealous therapists. At the time, there was virtually no relevant scientific evidence (Bruck et al., 2006) so research on children's eyewitness testimony was nudged into existence. It has continued to flourish in response to a continuing stream of high-profile cases. Of note, some of these cases (as described above) highlight children's vulnerabilities and susceptibility to suggestion (i.e., **suggestibility**) while others demonstrate the ability of even young children to provide accurate and detailed testimony. In one widely publicized case, for example, 5-year-old Sarah Ahn described both the driver who had abducted her friend, Samantha Runnion, while they were playing at their apartment complex, and his vehicle. The girl's description was critical in the arrest of the perpetrator and subsequent trial, which ended in the perpetrator being sentenced to death for the abduction, sexual assault, and murder of Samantha Runnion (Lewin, 2002; Luna, 2005).

How Did Psychologists Respond to the Need for Research on Children's Eyewitness Testimony?

Certainly, research relevant to some of the issues raised by these cases already existed, but there was uncertainty about the extent to which psychologists could use the basic developmental literature to understand children's eyewitness testimony, how the results could be translated into practical guidelines and conclusions, and how unanswered questions might best be framed and addressed.

Basic research on some topics, the development of memory and language in particular, clearly informed our understanding of children's eyewitness testimony. For example, psychologists had long been aware of age-related improvements in children's memory capacity and ability to structure narrative accounts of remembered events (Bauer, 2006; Fivush & Haden, 2003; Nelson & Fivush, 2004; Schneider & Bjorklund, 1998), but researchers now faced real-world problems that could not be addressed using the results of studies largely focused on children's memories for number lists and other non-stressful events. Researchers thus began the arduous task of developing innovative methods and paradigms balancing the need for **ecological validity** with ethical concerns.

To increase ecological validity (i.e., relevance to memories of abuse), researchers began studying children's ability to remember stressful medical procedures, inoculations, and medical examinations (e.g., Baker-Ward, Gordon, Ornstein, Larus, & Clubb, 1993; Goodman, Hirschman, Hepps, & Rudy, 1991b; Goodman, Quas, Batterman-Faunce, Riddlesberger, & Kuhn, 1997; Howe, Courage, & Peterson, 1996; Ornstein, Baker-Ward, Gordon, & Merritt, 1997; Pipe et al., 1997; Quas et al., 1999; Saywitz, Goodman, Nicholas, & Moan, 1991). Such events included some abuse-relevant elements (e.g., stress, bodily touch, salience) and thus increased ecological validity without exposing children to unnecessary distressing events. Furthermore, unlike most instances of abuse, the events in these studies were objectively verifiable, allowing researchers to investigate children's accuracy in response to different types of question.

In a further effort to increase ecological validity, some researchers began testing some of the relevant issues specifically among maltreated children (e.g., Eisen, Qin, Goodman, & Davis, 2002; Howe, Cicchetti, Toth, & Cerrito, 2004; Lyon, Malloy, Quas, & Ahern, in press; Lyon, Malloy, Quas, & Talwar, 2008; Lyon & Saywitz, 1999) whereas most research on child witnesses has involved children who have not been maltreated (e.g., Bruck et al., 2006; see Lyon, 2007). By creatively making research more applicable and ecologically valid, psychologists have obtained an increasingly clear picture of children's capacities and limitations.

Even if some elements are similar, however, medical examinations and procedures are not the same as maltreatment, so some researchers began to conduct field studies to determine systematically (a) how children were actually interviewed in investigative settings, and (b) how children responded to different types of questions when asked by investigators about possible experiences of abuse. This research represented a shift from simply labeling children as competent or incompetent as well as recognition of the importance of field research for true progress in this area. Instead, researchers sought to identify the most effective ways of interviewing children in order to capitalize on their capabilities and competencies while also recognizing their limitations. In other words, given what had been learned about children's abilities, capacities, limitations and the factors that influence them, how might they be interviewed to best effect? This research on investigative interviewing illustrates the contributions of both applied and basic psychologists to the development of knowledge and its dissemination, resulting in improved investigative techniques around the world.

The Investigative Interview

For the reasons described above (e.g., lack of corroborative evidence), suspected victims (and other witnesses) of maltreatment are typically interviewed about their experiences, and these **investigative interviews** typically set into motion criminal proceedings and a variety of interventions for children and families, making the encounters between children and investigative interviewers critically important.

Despite variations in legal traditions and social welfare policies, there is substantial international consensus about the types of forensic interviews that elicit the most accurate and complete information, a consensus fuelled by mounting evidence regarding children's linguistic, communicative, social, and memorial capacities (e.g., American Professional Society on the Abuse of Children, 1990, 1997; Home Office, 1992, 2007; Lamb et al., 2008; Poole & Lamb, 1998). First, there is an agreement among researchers that interviewers should first establish a supportive relationship ("rapport") with children, and encourage them to correct the interviewers and/or seek clarification when necessary before questioning them about the alleged criminal incidents. Second, many experts recommend that interviewers should allow children to practice providing narrative descriptions of events and should introduce them to the interviewing style before starting to explore possible abuse. Most professionals also agree that investigative interviews should be conducted using **open-ended questions** (e.g., "Tell me about everything that happened to you") with focused but not suggestive (e.g., "When did it happen?") questions used as seldom and as late in the interview as possible. Such recommendations are supported by experimental evidence suggesting that open-ended questions are preferable because they access free recall memory which is more likely to be accurate, whereas focused questions tend to engage both memory processes that are more prone to error *and* narrow information retrieval.

Reaching the End-Users of Results

This research has been used to craft best-practice guidelines (e.g., Achieving Best Evidence, Home Office, 2007; Memorandum of Good Practice, 1992; NICHD Investigative Interview Protocol, 2000—see below) in the hope that these guidelines would reform interview practice, although consensus about the manner in which interviews should be conducted does not mean that interviews are typically conducted in accordance with these recommendations. As is common in other fields (see Grol & Grimshaw, 2003 for a review of implementing best-practice guidelines in the medical field), practitioners often fail to abide by best-practice guidelines and recommendations (Aldridge & Cameron, 1999; Memon, Wark, Holley, Bull, & Köhnken, 1996; Warren, Woodall, Hunt, & Perry, 1996).

For example, Sternberg, Lamb, Davies, & Westcott (2001a) evaluated the effect of the Memorandum of Good Practice on the investigative interview conducted by police officers in the UK interviewing children about alleged abuse. Despite the Memorandum's call for open questions, forensic interviewers relied heavily on **closed questions** (47%) (e.g., "Where did he touch you?"), option-posing utterances (29%) (e.g., "Did he touch you over or under your clothes?"), and suggestive prompts (5%) (e.g., "He hurt you, right?"). Open-ended questions (e.g., "Tell me what happened when you were with X") were infrequently (6%) employed to elicit information from children. As a result, the information obtained was of uncertain quality: 40% of the information that children provided was obtained using option-posing and suggestive questions, which yield less reliable information than open-ended questions do (Dent, 1982, 1986; Goodman, Bottoms, Schwartz-Kenney, & Rudy, 1991a; Hutcheson, Baxter, Telfer, & Warden, 1995; Lamb et al., 1996).

Studies conducted in Israel, the US, and Sweden similarly revealed that many interviewers did not adhere to best-practice guidelines. The widespread similarities in interview practices across countries and cultures was noteworthy and alarming primarily because the extant practices were at considerable odds with practices recommended by researchers and professional advisory groups around the world (e.g., American Professional Society on the Abuse of Children, 1990; Home Office, 1992, 2007). In other words, despite consistent research documenting the superiority of certain ways of obtaining information, interviewers around the world continued to employ inferior and potentially dangerous practices when they interviewed alleged victims. Such findings raised questions about the effectiveness of guidelines that are not rigorously evaluated in the field and underscored the need for greater investment in ongoing training and supervision to bring about major changes in the quality of investigative interviewing (Lamb, Orbach, Hershkowitz, Esplin, & Horowitz, 2007). This was a difficult but useful lesson to learn, one that has been painstakingly learned by psychologists and professionals in other fields as well (e.g., Grol & Grimshaw, 2003; Hohmann & Shear, 2002).

Why don't forensic interviewers adhere to recommended interview practices? There are many potential reasons. A good investigative interview demands a great deal of interviewers. Among other things, it requires accommodating children's limited language abilities and vocabulary, asking appropriate questions, obtaining detailed evidence about sensitive topics, and maintaining children's often limited attention. Furthermore, the daily routines of investigative interviewers typically leave no time to access the latest findings. In addition, some interviewers sincerely believe that they are following best-practice guidelines (e.g., Aldridge & Cameron, 1999; Powell & Wright, 2008; Warren et al., 1999) despite evidence to the contrary.

In response to interviewer needs, researchers developed detailed guidelines to make it easier for interviewers to achieve best practice (e.g., Cognitive Interview, Fisher, Brennan, & McCauley, 2002; Finding Words technique or the RATAC (Rapport, Anatomy Identification, Touch Inquiry, Abuse, and Closure) protocol, Walters, Holmes, Bauer, & Vieth, 2003; NICHD Investigative Interview Protocol, Lamb et al., 2008). Only the NICHD Protocol has been extensively and internationally validated in the field, however, so we discuss it in detail, describing how it was developed, implemented, evaluated, revised, and maintained.

NICHD Investigative Interview Protocol

The NICHD Protocol was designed to translate professional recommendations into operational guidelines (Lamb et al., 2008; Orbach, Hershkowitz, Lamb, Esplin, & Horowitz, 2000) and guide interviewers to use prompts and techniques that maximize the amount of information elicited from free-recall memory. It covers all phases of the investigative interview.

Pre-substantive phase. In the *introductory phase*, the interviewer introduces himself/herself, clarifies the child's task (the need to describe events in detail and to tell the truth), and explains the ground rules and expectations (i.e., that the child can and should say "I don't remember," "I don't know," "I don't understand," or correct the interviewer when appropriate). This phase was developed with sensitivity to the fact that children are usually unused to being the sole source of information and often fail to ask for clarification when they do not understand (e.g., Lamb, Sternberg, Orbach, Hershkowitz, & Esplin, 1999; Saywitz, Snyder, & Nathanson, 1999; Sternberg et al., 1997; Waterman, Blades, & Spencer, 2000, 2004). This phase also reflects the legal system's demands that interviewers include questions designed to establish that children understand the difference between true and false statements. In the NICHD Protocol, this is done in a developmentally appropriate manner that takes account of young children's difficulty defining abstract concepts (e.g., truth, lies) (Lyon, 2000; Lyon et al., 2008; Lyon & Saywitz, 1999).

The *rapport-building phase* was designed to create a relaxed, supportive environment for children and to establish rapport between children and interviewers in light of evidence that children are more likely to be cooperative when interviewers are friendly (e.g., Bottoms, Quas, & Davis, 2007; Quas, Wallin, Papini, Lench, & Scullin, 2005; Roberts, Lamb, & Sternberg, 2004). Also, children are prompted to describe a recently experienced neutral event in detail. This "training" is designed to familiarize children with the open-ended investigative strategies and techniques used in the substantive phase while demonstrating the specific level of detail expected of them.

In a *transitional part* between the pre-substantive and the substantive phases of the interview, a series of prompts are used to identify the target event/s under investigation non-suggestively and with prompts that are as open as possible. The interviewer only moves on to some carefully worded and increasingly focused prompts (in sequence) if the child fails to identify the target event/s.

Substantive phase. If the child makes an allegation, the *free-recall phase* begins with an invitation ("Tell me everything . . ."), followed by other free-recall prompts or invitations (see Table 13.1). As soon as the first narrative is completed, the interviewer asks whether the incident occurred "one time or more than one time" and then proceeds to secure incident-specific information using follow-up ("Then what happened?") and cued (e.g., "Earlier you mentioned a [person/object/action]. Tell me everything about that") invitations, making reference to details mentioned by the child to elicit uncontaminated free-recall accounts of the alleged incident/s.

Only after exhaustive free-recall prompting do interviewers proceed to directive questions (focused recall questions that address details previously mentioned by the child and request information within specific categories [e.g., time, appearance] such as "When did it happen?" or "What color was that [mentioned] car?" If crucial details are still missing, interviewers then ask limited option-posing questions (mostly yes/no or forced-choice questions referencing new issues that the child failed to address previously). Suggestive utterances, which communicate to the child what response is expected, are strongly discouraged.

Implementation. Although the Protocol took advantage of mounting psychological evidence about children's abilities, researchers next had to determine whether it would "work" in the field. Israel was the first country to ask this question (Orbach et al., 2000), and the implementation was difficult. As is common in other fields, practitioners in the field were reluctant to admit that their methods were not useful and found it difficult to make changes to rely on the new guidelines. Through intensive efforts to create and maintain a constructive relationship based on mutual respect and good faith, however, the Protocol was evaluated. In

TABLE 13.1
Interviewer Prompt Types and Examples

Prompt Type	Examples
Invitation	Tell me everything that happened as well as you can remember.
	Then what happened?
	Tell me more about that.
Cued invitation	Think back to that [day/night] and tell me everything that happened from [some action mentioned by the child] until [a later action described by the child].
	Tell me more about [person/object/activity mentioned by the child].
	You mentioned [person/object/activity mentioned by the child]; tell me everything about that.
Direct/Focused	You mentioned [person/object/activity], When/what/where [completion of the direct question]?
	You mentioned you were at the shops. Where exactly were you? [pause for response] Tell me about that shop.
	Earlier you mentioned that your mother "hit you with this long thing." What is that thing? [pause for response] Tell me about that thing.
Questions to AVOID	Yes/No questions (e.g., Did he touch you?)
	Option posing questions (e.g., Was that over or under your clothes?)
	Questions that encourage children to imagine events (e.g., Tell me what might have happened.)
	Suggestive questions (e.g., He hurt you, didn't he?)

These and other examples can be found in Lamb et al. (2008).

light of the successes outlined below, the Israeli Department of Youth Investigation made the Protocol mandatory. Since 1998, every investigative interview of young alleged victims, witnesses, or suspects has been conducted using the Protocol.

Evaluation.   Findings obtained in independent field studies in four countries (Cyr & Lamb, 2009; Lamb et al., 2008; Orbach et al., 2000; Sternberg, Lamb, Orbach, Esplin, & Mitchell, 2001b) showed dramatic improvements in the quality of their interviews once they began using the Protocol. Simply publishing best-practice guidelines may not work, but interviewers can be trained to conduct better interviews, regardless of their jurisdiction or profession (e.g., social workers, police officers; Sternberg et al., 1997; Sternberg, Lamb, Esplin, & Baradaran, 1999).

When using the Protocol, interviewers use at least three times more open-ended and approximately half as many option-posing and suggestive prompts as they do when exploring comparable incidents, involving children of the same age, without the Protocol. Interviewers using the Protocol also introduce option-posing and suggestive questions later in the interview process than do peers not using the Protocol. Because option-posing and suggestive questions by definition involve the introduction of information by investigators, they may contaminate later phases of the children's reports, especially when younger children are involved (Bjorklund, Bjorklund, Brown, & Cassel, 1998; Ceci & Bruck, 1995; Memon et al., 1996), and thus their delayed utilization is forensically important. When priority was given to open-ended strategies and techniques in Protocol interviews, there were also significant increases in the number of facilitators and other supportive comments addressed to child witnesses (Hershkowitz, Orbach, Lamb, Sternberg, & Horowitz, 2006); this further enhanced the recall and reporting of information by encouraging children to be more cooperative.

When forensic investigators follow the structured NICHD Protocol, they thus obtain better information from alleged victims. In each study, about half of the informative and forensically relevant details and more than 80% of the initial disclosures of sexual abuse were provided in response to free-recall prompts. This is important because, as noted earlier, details elicited using free recall or open-ended prompts are more likely to be accurate than details elicited using more focused prompts in both field and laboratory analog contexts (Dale, Loftus, & Rathbun, 1978; Dent, 1986; Dent & Stephenson, 1979; Goodman et al., 1991a; Hutcheson et al., 1995; Lamb & Fauchier, 2001; Lamb et al., 2007; Orbach & Lamb, 2001).

Interestingly, all of the above findings were replicated in the US, the UK, Israel, and Canada, without differences in the proportions of prompts that were open-ended, differences in the proportions of details elicited using open-ended prompts, age differences, or differences in the proportion of the interviews completed before the first use of option-posing questions. The lack of age differences raised doubts about the interpretation and generalization of the results obtained in experimental laboratory analog settings, illustrating how applied research can lead basic researchers to re-evaluate their findings and interpretations.

Of course, it is important to consider multiple perspectives and goals when conducting applied research, and researchers must decide carefully how to determine whether an intervention was successful (Westmaas, Gil-Rivas, & Silver, 2007). As described above, the Protocol was evaluated in terms of how it changed interviewer practice and questioning and also how it improved children's reports. Subsequent research asked whether introduction of the Protocol made a difference to the ways in which cases were evaluated and adjudicated. As predicted by the developers of the Protocol, Pipe, Orbach, & Lamb (2008) found that, following introduction of the Protocol, proportionally more cases were referred for prosecution and more were resolved by conviction.

The Importance of Long-Term Evaluation and Training

As mentioned above, professional consensus alone did not yield changes in interviewers' behavior even when they knew what they should do and believed that they were following those recommendations (Aldridge & Cameron, 1999; Warren et al., 1999). Studies on the effective interviewing of children have also demonstrated how difficult it is to alter the ways in which interviewers typically perform. Practitioner training and even education of the public often yields improvement in trainees' knowledge but no meaningful changes in the ways in which they actually behave (see Grol & Grimshaw, 2003; Westmaas et al., 2007 for public health examples).

Recognizing this, training in use of the Protocol has always been accompanied by efforts to provide continued support, guidance, and feedback after interviewers start using the Protocol; these strategies are supported by the results of experimental research in other contexts (Adams, Field, & Verhave, 1999; Clark, 1971; Frayer & Klausmeier, 1971; Gully, 1998; Sweet, 1966). In the case of the NICHD Protocol, improvements occurred only after interviewers started reviewing and receiving critical feedback from expert consultants and fellow interviewers (Lamb et al., 2002c). Unfortunately, improvements derived from this close monitoring and feedback rapidly diminished when the interviewers stopped attending regular feedback sessions. Within 6 months after the training/supervision ended, police officers in the US were conducting interviews that resembled their original interviews more than when they were getting the expert feedback (i.e., fewer open-ended prompts, earlier introduction of more focused prompts) (Lamb et al., 2002b).

The adverse effects of termination of supervision and feedback have important, although somewhat sobering, implications for those attempting to apply information gleaned from research in the real world. Clearly, it is possible to employ professionals' accumulated knowledge of memory and communicative development to improve the quality of information elicited from alleged victims of child abuse, but these benefits are obtained only when extensive efforts are made not only to train interviewers to adopt recommended practices, but to ensure the maintenance of these practices as well. Regardless of their skillfulness, interviewers continue to maintain or improve their skills only when they regularly review their own and others' interviews closely, discussing their strategies, successes, and mistakes with other interviewers. In Israel, for example, all interviewers are required to continue attending regular peer-review sessions of this sort and this seems to have ensured that the investigative interviews conducted there are of high quality (87% of all substantive questions were open according to a recent study by Katz & Hershkowitz, in press), suggesting that good interviewers can continue to get better in the right circumstances.

In all, the NICHD Protocol and its training model illustrate an effective collaboration between academia and the field, with researchers and practitioners working together to generate solutions to real-world problems (Lamb et al., 2008). This model, which has been applied with success in Israel, Canada, the US, and parts of the UK, has led to improvements in the quality of interviews with children who are alleged victims of sexual or physical abuse. It is an influential example of collaboration between researchers and practitioners. Continued evaluation of the Protocol, its components, and its implementations highlight the importance of a continuous feedback loop between applied researchers, basic researchers, and the field.

How Does the Protocol Continue to Influence Research and Practice?

The continued collaboration between practitioners and academia not only has allowed for the evaluation and validation of the Protocol but also has cast light on further research questions and problems for research psychologists to address. For example, a more recent version of the

Protocol can be used when interviewing witnesses who are not victims (Lamb, Sternberg, Orbach, Hershkowitz, & Horowitz, 2003b), and another version has been developed and used to interview youthful suspects (Hershkowitz, Horowitz, Lamb, Orbach, & Sternberg, 2004); this is discussed further below. Currently, Lamb and his colleagues are field-testing a revision designed to provide additional reassurance for children who are unusually reluctant to talk about their experiences (Hershkowitz, Horowitz, & Lamb, 2005; Hershkowitz et al., 2006; Hershkowitz, Lamb, & Horowitz, 2007; Pipe et al., 2007), and are trying to determine whether the Protocol can be used effectively to interview children with learning or mental difficulties— an important question because such individuals are disproportionally likely to be abused (Crosse, Kaye, & Ratnofsky, 1993; Hershkowitz et al., 2007; Sullivan & Knutson, 2000).

Furthermore, those who study linguistic, communicative, and memory development among young children have long believed that preschoolers were incapable of providing narrative responses to invitations (Bourg et al., 1999; Hewitt, 1999; Kuehnle, 1996). However, applied research demonstrated that, when invitations were carefully formulated and children appropriately prepared for their roles as informants, even children as young as four years of age were capable of providing detailed responses (Lamb et al., 2003a). The fact that the Protocol is effective with preschoolers is not of interest only to interviewers who often have difficulty interviewing very young children but also to those who conduct basic developmental research. Of course, such findings also prompt questions about the most effective techniques to use with even younger children.

Through a combination of applied and basic research, it has been possible to enhance our understanding of normative developmental processes *and* improve the quality of investigative interviewing of children. This careful research has made it possible to enhance the value of children's testimony in ways that should enable law enforcement, child protection, and judicial agencies to protect children better from maltreatment.

Summary

In the past few decades, literally hundreds of studies conducted by an internationally and disciplinarily diverse group of researchers have shed light on children's abilities, capacities, and limitations while elucidating the factors that influence children's eyewitness testimony. By identifying children's strengths, weaknesses, and characteristics, researchers have fostered improvements in the quality of forensic interviewing and the evaluation of the information elicited from children. Clearly, it is possible to obtain valuable information from children, but doing so requires careful investigative procedures, a realistic awareness of children's capacities and limitations, and an appreciation of the restrictions imposed on interviews by real-world characteristics. Ongoing feedback and training is critical to ensure that interviewers continue to adhere to the Protocol and do not drift back.

THE EFFECTS OF PARENTAL SEPARATION AND DIVORCE

Forensic interviewing is not the only real-world problem to have been illuminated by applied developmental science, of course. Many social scientists have documented the extent to which children's development can be affected by their parents' separation, and applied developmental psychologists have, in turn, shown how psychological research not only helps explain these effects, but also informs the development of social policies and practices that can help ameliorate the more negative effects.

Divorce and parental separation clearly affect more children than child maltreatment; about half the children in the US spend at least part of their childhood living with a single parent, and similar experiences affect considerable (though slightly smaller) numbers of children in most other industrialized countries. Researchers have clearly demonstrated that, on average, children benefit from being raised in two-[biological or adoptive]parent families rather than separated, divorced, or never-married single-parent households (Amato, 2000; Aquilino, 1996; Carlson, 2006; Clarke-Stewart & Brentano, 2006; Clarke-Stewart, Vandell, McCartney, Owen, & Booth, 2000; Hetherington, 1999; Hetherington & Kelly, 2002; McLanahan, 1999; McLanahan & Teitler, 1999; Simons, Lin, Gordon, Conger, & Lorenz, 1999), although there is considerable variability within groups, and the differences between groups are relatively small. Indeed, although children growing up in fatherless families are, on average, disadvantaged relative to peers growing up in two-parent families with respect to psychosocial adjustment, behavior and achievement at school, educational attainment, employment trajectories, income generation, involvement in antisocial and even criminal behavior, and the ability to establish and maintain intimate relationships, the majority of children with divorced parents enjoy average or better-than-average social and emotional adjustment as young adults (Booth & Amato, 2001; Clarke-Stewart & Brentano, 2006; Hetherington & Kelly, 2002; Kelly & Emery, 2003). Approximately 25% of children in post-separation and divorced families give evidence of adjustment problems, compared to 12–15% in married families. Thus, the majority of children from separated families evince no psychopathology or behavioral symptoms, although they are likely to experience psychic pain for at least some period of time (Emery, 1998; Hetherington & Kelly, 2002; Laumann-Billings & Emery, 2000; Schwartz & Finley, in press).

Such individual differences in outcomes force us to identify more precisely both the ways in which divorce/single parenthood may affect children's lives and the factors that might account for individual differences in children's adjustment following their parents' separation. Several interrelated factors appear to be especially significant.

Economic Stresses

Typically, single parenthood is associated with a variety of social and financial stresses with which custodial parents must cope, largely on their own. Single-parent families are more economically stressed than two-parent families, and economic stresses or poverty appear to account (statistically speaking) for many effects of single parenthood (Hetherington & Kelly, 2002; McLanahan, 1999).

Reductions in the Quality of Relationships with Children

Because single mothers need to work more extensively outside the home than married or partnered mothers do, parents spend less time with children in single-parent families and the levels of supervision and guidance are lower and less reliable than in two-parent families (Hetherington & Kelly, 2002; McLanahan, 1999). Reductions in the level and quality of parental stimulation and attention may affect achievement, compliance, and social skills while diminished supervision makes antisocial behavior and misbehavior more likely (Hetherington & Kelly, 2002).

Conflict between Parents

Conflict between the parents commonly precedes, emerges during, or increases during the separation and divorce processes, and often continues for some time beyond them. Inter-parental conflict is an important correlate of children's psychosocial adjustment just as marital harmony, its conceptual inverse, appears to be a reliable correlate of positive adjustment

(Cummings Goeke-Morey, M. C., & Raymond, 2004; Cummings, Merrilees, & George 2010; Johnston, 1994; Kelly, 2000). The negative impacts of high levels of marital conflict on the quality of parenting of both mothers and fathers have been well documented. In general, parental conflict is associated with more rejecting, less warm and nurturing parenting by mothers, and with fathers' withdrawal from parenting and engagement in more intrusive interactions with their children (Cummings & Davies, 1994; Grych, 2005). Anger-based marital conflict is associated with filial aggression and externalizing behavior problems, perhaps because such parents and children have similar difficulty regulating negative affect (Katz & Gottman, 1993). These and other data support the observation that some of the "effects of divorce" are better viewed as the effects of marital or parental conflict and violence (Kelly, 2000).

The adversarial legal system tends to promote conflict between already vulnerable parents because of its win–lose orientation and the way it fosters hostile behaviors and demands. Although the adversarial process purports to focus on children's "best interests," parents' psychologically driven legal strategies more often represent their own needs and perceived entitlements, and the effect is to diminish the possibility of future civility, productive communication, and cooperation (Kelly, 2003).

Quality and Type of Parenting

The quality and type of parenting have emerged as important influences on the post-separation/divorce adjustment of school-aged children and adolescents. Deterioration in the quality of parenting after separation has long been recognized (Belsky, Youngblade, Rovine, & Volling, 1991; Clarke-Stewart & Brentano, 2006; Hetherington, 1999; Sturge-Apple, Davies, & Commings, 2006; Wallerstein & Kelly, 1980). Many parents are preoccupied, stressed, emotionally labile, angry, and depressed following separation, and their "diminished parenting" includes less positive involvement and affection expressed with their children, and more coercive and harsh forms of discipline. External factors such as absorption in dating, new partners, cohabitation, remarriage, and poverty and financial instability are also associated with reductions in the quality of parenting (Amato, 2000; Hetherington, 1999; Kelly, 2000; Pruett, Williams, Insabella, & Little, 2003; Simons et al., 1999; Wallerstein & Kelly, 1980).

By the same token, specific aspects of parenting can moderate the impact of separation and divorce on children's social, emotional, and academic adjustment, and potentially protect children against the harmful impacts of high conflict. Such effective parenting is characterized by warmth and engagement, authoritative discipline (setting limits, non-coercive discipline and control, enforcement of rules, appropriate expectations), academic skill encouragement, and monitoring of the children's activities (Amato & Fowler, 2002; Amato & Gilbreth, 1999; Finley & Schwartz, 2007; Hetherington, 1999; Martinez & Forgatch, 2002; Simons et al., 1999).

Disruptions in Relationships with Fathers

Divorce commonly disrupts one of the child's most important and enduring relationships, that with his or her father. As Amato (1993; Amato & Gilbreth, 1999) has shown with particular clarity, however, the bivariate associations between father absence and children's adjustment are much weaker than one might expect. Indeed, Amato and Gilbreth's (1999) meta-analysis revealed no significant association between the frequency of father–child contact and child outcomes, largely because of the great diversity in the types of "father-present" relationships. We might predict that contacts with abusive, incompetent, or disinterested fathers are likely to have much different effects than relationships with devoted, committed, and sensitive fathers. As expected, Amato and Gilbreth (1999) found that children's well-being was significantly enhanced when their relationships with nonresident fathers were positive, when the nonresident fathers engaged in active parenting, and when contact was frequent. Clarke-Stewart and Hayward (1996), Dunn, Cheng, O'Connor, and Bridges (2004), Finley and Schwartz (2007), Hetherington, Bridges, and Insabella (1998), and Simons and Associates (1996) likewise reported that children benefited when their nonresident fathers were actively involved in routine everyday activities, and the conclusion was clearly supported in recent analyses by Carlson (2006) of data from the National Longitudinal Study of Youth. Carlson showed that father involvement was associated with better adolescent adjustment and that paternal involvement partially mediated the effects of family structure (notably divorce or single parenthood) on adolescents' behavioral outcomes. Similarly, higher levels of paternal involvement in their children's schools were associated with better grades, better adjustment, fewer suspensions, and lower dropout rates than were lower levels of involvement (Nord, Brimhall, & West, 1997). Active engagement in a variety of specific activities and ongoing school-related discussions between fathers and their adolescents significantly lowered the probability of school failure when compared to adolescents with less actively engaged fathers.

Another meta-analysis indicated that, on multiple measures of emotional and behavioral adjustment and academic achievement by mothers, fathers, teachers, and clinicians, children in joint physical **custody** were better adjusted than children in sole custody arrangements. In fact, children in shared custody were as well adjusted as children whose parents remained married (Bauserman, 2002). Although joint physical custody parents reported less past and current conflict than did sole physical custody parents, conflict did not explain the superiority of the children in joint custody arrangements. Again, the clear implication is that active paternal involvement, not simply the number or length of meetings between fathers and children, predicts child adjustment. This suggests that post-divorce arrangements should specifically seek to maximize positive and meaningful paternal involvement rather than simply allow minimal levels of visitation. As in non-divorced families, in other words, the quality of continued relationships with the parents—both parents—is crucial (Kelly & Lamb, 2000; Lamb & Kelly, 2009). Stated differently and succinctly, the better (richer, deeper, and more secure) the parent–child relationships, the better the children's adjustment, whether or not the parents live together (Lamb, 2002a, 2002b; Lamb & Kelly, 2009).

Unfortunately, those conducting custody and visitation awards do not always appear to understand what sort of interaction is needed to consolidate and maintain parent–child relationships. As a result, their decisions seldom ensure either sufficient amounts of time or adequate distributions of that time for children and parents. Decision makers have typically failed to recognize and take advantage of the knowledge of children's psychological needs and the developmental trajectories that have been compiled over the past few decades of intensive research. This research is invaluable both because an understanding of normative developmental phases helps us understand how parental separation and divorce may affect children's development and adjustment, and because it can be useful when designing post-divorce living arrangements most likely to benefit children (Kelly & Lamb, 2000; Lamb & Kelly, 2009). Basic research on early social development and descriptive research on the multifaceted correlates of divorce combine to yield a clearer understanding of the ways in which divorce affects children and of how the welfare of many children could be enhanced by changes in common practices. Furthermore, research on the impacts of divorce enhances our understanding of developmental processes by providing a new context in which to examine children's social development.

In the next paragraphs, we briefly review attachment research. Then we demonstrate how it has been applied successfully by the legal and child welfare systems before identifying areas of continued concern and challenge.

Attachment

Attachment is one of the most frequently researched aspects of child development, and researchers have documented long-lasting effects of attachment styles (Cassidy & Shaver, 2008; Thompson, 1999, 2006). According to attachment theorists, infants form attachments to those who have been available regularly and have responded to the infants' signals and needs (Lamb, Thompson, Gardner, & Charnov, 1985; Thompson, 2006; see also Lamb & Lewis, Chapter 10, this volume). As described by Bowlby (1969), and largely confirmed by subsequent research (for detailed review, see Thompson, 2006), infant–parent attachments pass through four broad developmental phases, during the first three of which infants learn to discriminate among adult carers and gradually develop emotional attachments to them.

Responses to separation become increasingly intense as attachments to parents and other important carers strengthen between 6 and 24 months of age (Yarrow; 1963; Yarrow & Goodwin, 1973). Most infants initially prefer the parent who provides most of their care and are more likely to seek out their preferred parents for comfort when distressed (Lamb, 2002a). Non-preferred parents remain emotionally important, however, and are sought out for other social and emotional needs, and, when primary carers are not available, for comfort. Although infants and toddlers may resist transitions between parents in the second year, just as they sometimes protest (even more strongly) daily transitions to out-of-home care providers, they generally comfort quite quickly once the transition is accomplished. This is particularly likely when both parents have the opportunity to engage in normal parenting activities (feeding, playing, soothing, putting to bed, etc.) while attachments are being established and consolidated.

Infants and toddlers need regular interaction with their "attachment figures" in order to foster, maintain, and strengthen their relationships (Lamb, Bornstein, & Teti, 2002a; Thompson, 2006). This means that young children need to interact with both parents in a variety of contexts (feeding, playing, diapering, soothing, reading, putting to bed, etc.) to ensure that the relationships are consolidated and strengthened. In the absence of such opportunities for regular interaction across a broad range of contexts, infant–parent relationships may weaken rather than grow stronger. Relationships with parents continue to play a crucial role in shaping children's social, emotional, personal, and cognitive development into middle childhood and adolescence (Lamb & Lewis, Chapter 10, this volume).

Attachment and Implications for Parental Separation and Divorce

When parents divorce, do judges and legal practitioners incorporate and apply this information about attachment and early relationships when making decisions? The answer is complex and perhaps best given as "sometimes" or "increasingly."

Attachment research tells us that the ideal post-divorce situation is one in which children with separated parents have opportunities to interact with both parents frequently in a variety of functional contexts (feeding, play, discipline, basic care, limit-setting, putting to bed, etc.) (Kelly & Lamb, 2000; Lamb, 2002b; Lamb & Kelly, 2001, 2009). However, even though children's best interests are usually served by keeping both parents actively involved in their children's lives, many custody and access arrangements do not foster the maintenance of relationships between children and their nonresident parents. Unfortunately, policy makers, judges, and lawyers in many jurisdictions have not been very attentive to the importance of promoting children's relationships with both of their parents. Arbitrary and one-size-fits-all restrictions on the amounts of time children spend with their fathers have been the norm regardless of the quality of the father–child relationships. Traditional "visiting guidelines" in many jurisdictions assign every other weekend to the nonresident parent (with perhaps a brief midweek visit), and mental health professionals often rely on unsubstantiated beliefs that every other weekend is best for children because it ensures that children continue to have only one "real home."

These plans have left much to be desired for many families, and have caused great dissatisfaction and sense of loss to the majority of children in post-divorce arrangements (Fabricius, Braver, Diaz, & Schenck, 2010). Research on children's and young adults' retrospective views of their post-divorce living arrangements indicates that the majority express strong wishes and longing for more time with their fathers, a desire for more closeness, and favorable views of shared physical custody arrangements (Fabricius et al., 2010; Fabricius & Hall, 2000; Laumann-Billings & Emery, 2000; Smith & Gallop, 2001).

What Recommendations Follow from the Attachment Research?

In order to ensure that both parents become or remain attached to their children, post-divorce **parenting plans** need to encourage participation by both parents in as broad as possible an array of social contexts on a regular basis. That is, brief dinners and occasional weekend visits do not provide a broad enough or extensive enough basis for such relationships to be fostered, whereas weekday and weekend daytime and nighttime activities are important for children of all ages. Even young children should spend overnight periods with both parents when both have been involved in their care prior to separation, even though neo-analysts have long counseled against this (Kelly & Lamb, 2000; Lamb & Kelly, 2009). When both parents have established significant attachments and both have been actively involved in the child's care, overnight "visits" will consolidate attachments and child adjustment, not work against them. Consistent with this reasoning, the results of research by Pruett, Insabella, and Gustafson (2005) show that regular overnight visits were associated with better adjustment on the part of toddlers and young children. Parents who have been actively involved before divorce but are then denied overnight access to their children are thereby excluded from an important array of activities, and the strength or depth of their relationships suffers as a result. In the absence of sufficiently broad and extensive interactions, many fathers drift out of their children's lives, and children see their fathers as increasingly peripheral, placing these children at risk psychologically and materially (Fabricius et al., 2010).

Furthermore, to minimize the deleterious impact of extended separations from either parent when children are young, and still consolidating their attachments, attachment theory tells us that there should be more frequent transitions than would perhaps be desirable with older children (Lamb & Kelly, 2009). To be responsive to young children's psychological needs, in other words, the parenting schedules adopted for children under age two or three should actually involve more transitions, rather than fewer, to ensure the continuity of both relationships and to promote the children's security and comfort. Although no empirical research exists testing specific parenting plans following separation, it is likely, for example, that infants and toddlers who are attached to committed and competent fathers would remain most comfortable and secure with a schedule that allowed them to see their fathers at least three times a week, including at least one extended overnight stay, so that there is no separation of greater than 2–3 days. From the third year of life, the ability to tolerate longer separations begins to increase, so that most toddlers can manage two consecutive overnights with each parent without stress.

Best Practices in the Case of Parental Separation and Divorce

There are a number of empirically based practices that mental health professionals can provide to help separating parents reduce the risks that children face. Firstly, they can prepare parents to talk to their children about those aspects of the separation and divorce that directly affect them. Remarkably, most children are not informed about the details and meaning of the parental separation for them, are not invited to ask questions nor allowed an opportunity to give suggestions regarding their new living arrangements, and are not consulted regarding schedule changes (Dunn, Davies, O'Connor, & Sturgess, 2001; Smart, 2002; Smart & Neale, 2000), which leaves children to cope with these major changes in their lives without either emotional support or cognitive clarity.

Many jurisdictions have introduced education programs that explain to separating parents the effects of divorce on children, the impact of parent conflict, the particular risk when parents use their children to express their anger and disagreement, the need to separate children's needs from adult needs, and parenting skills, and often provide skill-based training to minimize conflict and promote more effective communication. At least in the short term, these courses appear to be effective (e.g., Arbuthnot & Gordon, 1996; Bacon & McKenzie, 2004; Ellis & Anderson, 2003; Pedro-Carroll, Nakhnikian, & Montes, 2001), particularly when the content is empirically based and includes skill-based training and role-play exercises. More extensive research-based parent education programs appear to bring about meaningful behavioral changes in both mothers and fathers (for reviews, see Braver, Griffin, Cookston, Sandler, & Williams, 2005; Haine, Sandler, Wolchik, Tein, & Dawson-McClure, 2003).

Secondly, because transitions between households provide opportunities for discussion and argument, it is important to ensure that these exchanges take place in neutral settings and at times that limit contact between the parents when there is a history of conflict. For example, one parent might drop the children off at school or day care, with the other parent picking them up at the end of the day. Parenting coordinators report that many children benefit from the elimination of face-to-face parent confrontations at the family residence or other meeting places, and conflict becomes a much less frequent experience. Similarly, visitation exchange centers allow children to be brought by one parent without making it necessary for the parents to encounter one another directly. Such arrangements may be especially helpful when either the parents or children are fearful, and have been shown to increase the frequency of contact between nonresident parents and their children while reducing levels of conflict between the parents (Flory, Dunn, Berg-Weger, & Milstead, 2001).

Other practices have also been developed to address conflict between separating parents. Of these, custody and divorce mediation has been best evaluated and validated (Emery, 1994; Emery, Laumann-Billings, Waldron, Sbarra, & Dillon, 2001; Kelly, 2002, 2004). The potential benefits are substantial in both the short term (e.g., earlier settlement of parenting disputes, reduced parental conflict, improved parental support) and the longer term (e.g., more sustained contact between nonresident fathers and children 12 years later), relative to parents using the traditional adversarial system (Emery et al., 2001; Kelly, 2004).

Parenting coordinators are also increasingly used in the United States, representing an effort to address the needs of children where there is very high conflict between the parents. Parenting coordination is a child-focused dispute resolution process designed to help parents settle disputes regarding their children in a timely manner, while facilitating compliance with parenting plans and related court orders. A non-adversarial intervention, the parenting coordination role combines case and conflict management, relevant parent education, mediation, and sometimes arbitration of certain child-related disputes that the parents cannot settle on their own. Parenting coordination is generally viewed as a post-decree process for parents who have demonstrated a continuing inability to settle child-specific disputes through other means, including private negotiations, mediation, specialized parent education groups, settlement conferences, or following trial. Most parenting coordinators serve by stipulation of the parents and court order, or by private consent agreements. In general, the judiciary has been supportive and enthusiastic; other professionals involved with these families have also indicated in surveys that parent coordinators can be very effective, especially in reducing the frequency and intensity of disputes (Coates, Deutsch, Starnes, Sullivan, & Sydlik, 2004). The Guidelines for Parenting Coordination (2006) were developed by an AFCC task force, and their value, as well as the need for extensive training, has been discussed at length by Kelly (in press). Although there has been no systematic research on long-term effectiveness, dramatic decreases in the rates of litigation (court appearances) in the first year after parenting coordinators were appointed were reported in one unpublished dissertation (Johnston, 1994). Several articles on the most problematic post-divorce families make clear that parenting coordinators are among the most important interventions available to smooth the post-separation and divorce transitions (Coates et al., 2004; *Family Courts Review*, 2001).

Thirdly, professionals can become familiar with and promote awareness of various models for parenting plans that have been informed by applied research. Instead of one standard visiting pattern, a menu of different time-sharing options for children of different ages would encourage parents, professionals, and courts to consider children's ages and developmental needs and achievements; the quality of parent–child relationships; parents' interest and capacity to be involved in their children's lives; and children's voices and input when appropriate. Model parenting plans typically include multiple options for various living arrangements that range from traditional visiting, expanded access involving more midweek and weekend time, and various shared physical custody arrangements. Many model plans available include highly detailed templates to guide parental choices with respect to legal decision-making and parental responsibilities. It is important that agreements and court orders are sufficiently detailed so that both parents know when, where, and how their children will make the transitions between households, eliminating the ambiguity that angry parents exploit and which often cause one or both parents to argue in front of their children. Orders that make vague references to "liberal visitation" invite sustained argument, and, when mothers remain angry, do not sufficiently protect children's relationships with their fathers. Even in legal cultures that emphasize "private ordering," lawyers, therapists, and custody evaluators should help parents develop specific schedules for children's time with each parent, and courts should routinely expect such language and detail.

Fourth, custody evaluators should become familiar and stay current with the empirical literature regarding attachment, child development, parent–child relationships, parental separation, and children's adjustment. If they are to make recommendations to the court—a subject currently generating some controversy (Tippins & Wittmann, 2005)—these recommendations should be grounded in and supported by the current research literature, rather than theory or subjective bias (Kelly & Johnston, 2005; Lamb & Kelly, 2009; Warshak, 2000).

Overall, decisions following divorce/separation, especially those involving custody and parenting plans, should be attentive to individual circumstances and sensitive to the parents' and children's strengths, schedules, and needs (Kelly, 2005, 2007; Smyth & Chisholm, 2006). And, of course, practitioners should make use of the wealth of psychological research relevant to attachment and parental separation/divorce.

Why Aren't These Best Practices Followed More Often?

As in the case of investigative interviewing, practitioners making decisions about children's lives in the context of parental separation may sincerely believe that they are doing the "right" thing. However, many of their beliefs are unfounded, and unsupported by empirical research.

For example, the prohibition of overnight "visitation" has been justified by prejudices and beliefs rather than by any empirical evidence (Warshak, 2000), which has demonstrated benefits of overnight visitation for many children. Such beliefs are often rooted in stereotypes about the traditional role of fathers in children's lives. For example, the lingering resistance to overnights among professionals working with divorcing families appears to reflect the view that fathers are not important attachment figures. Thus, even psychologists who have long recognized the need to minimize the length of separations from attachment figures when devising parenting plans have typically focused only on separations from mothers, thereby revealing the presumption that young children are not meaningfully attached to their fathers.

The adversarial legal system in the United States may also be partly responsible for the plans devised and decisions made following parental separation, encouraging rather than reducing conflict in the process. Although the adversarial process purports to focus on children's "best interests," parents' psychologically driven legal strategies more often represent their own needs and perceived entitlements, and the effect is to diminish the possibility of future civility, productive communication, and cooperation (Kelly, 2003). Our focus should remain on the children's best interests, not "fairness" to the parents.

Summary

Both applied research on divorce and basic research on attachment point to the central importance of maintaining meaningful relationships with both parents. Many innovative practices and programs have been developed over the past few decades as increasing numbers of professionals have come to recognize the importance of promoting continued relationships between children and both of their separating parents. There is a still long way to go, however. Unfortunately, reasoned discussion about the potential benefits of greater involvement by nonresident parents has often been drowned out by poisonous rhetoric from groups and individuals mired in gendered concerns about fairness for parents rather than children's best interests. Also, long-held beliefs and stereotypes about parents, particularly fathers, have influenced the uptake of psychological research in this arena.

Interestingly, although decisions about the disposition and living arrangements of children in the case of divorce appear to downplay the importance of the parents' involvement, family preservation programs in the case of child maltreatment tend to overstate the importance of family involvement. In fact, the legal system tends to privilege family relationships in some situations where it is deleterious (Gelles, 1996) while failing to strengthen and promote parent–child relationships when parents separate in divorce, despite being committed and competent parents. Because so many children are affected by their parents' separation or by social service interventions, it is critical to determine which decisions are in the best interests of children and how best to apply what we know about the importance of children's relationships.

JUVENILE JUSTICE

Psychological research has also made significant contributions to juvenile justice, particularly with respect to **culpability** and **competence to stand trial**. In this section, we discuss the seminal role that developmental research played in the US Supreme Court decision to abolish the death penalty for adolescents (*Roper v. Simmons*, 2005), and then turn to an issue that has not yet been much affected by psychological research—interrogating juvenile suspects. As discussed above, basic and applied psychological research played a significant role in informing and changing the ways that young victims and witnesses are interviewed, but despite similarities in the developmental principles, research on capacities and limitations has not been taken into account where young suspects are concerned.

A Brief History

When the juvenile justice system in the United States was designed, there was clear recognition of developmental differences between adults and juveniles. With these differences (e.g., maturity of judgment, malleability) in mind, the system emphasized **rehabilitation** rather than punishment. Following a dramatic shift in policy and public concern about juvenile crime in the 1980s, however, a very different system is evident today (see Fagan, 2008; Scott & Steinberg, 2008; Steinberg, 2009; Steinberg & Scott, 2003 for reviews). Adolescents are increasingly adjudicated in adult court where they face more severe punishments including, up to a few years ago, the death penalty. Harsher and more punitive sanctions are being levied on adolescents who are found guilty of committing crimes, leading some to refer to the "criminalization" of the juvenile justice system (Feld, 1993). Indeed, Fagan writes (2008, p. 82), "As adolescents came increasingly to be feared as perpetrators of the most serious and violent crimes, the principles of rehabilitation that were essential to the juvenile court were largely abandoned."

Role of Developmental Research in the Juvenile Justice System

The juvenile justice system is characterized by difficult and distinct decisions and judgments (e.g., status or age-defined offenses; judgments concerning adolescents' competency to stand trial, risk for future harm, and potential response to treatment) made by individuals who would surely benefit from an understanding of child and adolescent development. For example, judges might thus weigh information about immaturity of judgment and behavior regulation when sentencing; defence attorneys could learn how better to communicate with and represent clients who are faced with important decisions (e.g., whether to accept a plea bargain); and prosecutors could consider developmental issues when deciding whether to charge young suspects as juveniles or adults (Steinberg, 2009). Although, as Steinberg notes, the consideration of developmental psychology in decisions concerning juvenile justice is not a "panacea," decision-making can and should be informed by the lessons learned by developmental psychologists. The US Supreme Court's decision to abolish the death penalty for adolescents is illustrative.

Abolition of the Death Penalty for Adolescents

In *Roper v. Simmons* (2005), the United States Supreme Court ruled that the execution of offenders for crimes committed at the age of 16 or 17 constituted cruel and unusual punishment in violation of the Eighth Amendment to the Constitution. In prior decisions, the death penalty had already been deemed unsuitable for those under 15 in *Thompson v. Oklahoma* (1988), but left standing for 16- and 17-year-olds in *Stanford v. Kentucky* (1989). The court's decision in *Roper v. Simmons* was based on evidence mitigating adolescents' culpability as a result of their developmental status summarized in an amicus curiae brief (American Medical Association et al., 2004) submitted by a coalition of academic professional bodies (i.e., the American Medical Association, the American Psychiatric Association, the American Society for Adolescent Psychiatry, the American Academy of Child & Adolescent Psychiatry, the American Academy of Psychiatry and the Law, the National Association of Social Workers, the Missouri Chapter of the National Association of Social Workers, and the National Mental Health Association). The brief outlined decades of research on adolescent development and adolescent offending conducted by those who study cognitive, social, and moral development; criminology; and even neuroscience. Much of the research was basic in nature, while some was conducted specifically to test certain aspects of adolescent offending, as is typically done when applied psychologists address a specific problem. The overarching claim was that "Older adolescents behave differently than adults because their minds operate differently, their emotions are more volatile, and their brains are anatomically immature" (p. 4), as explained in the following paragraphs.

Basic Research Relevant to Juvenile Justice

In terms of cognitive and psychosocial development, laboratory research using several paradigms (e.g., gambling tasks, computerized driving games; Cauffman et al., in press; Steinberg et al., 2008) finds that adolescents are more impulsive and less future-oriented than adults, even young adults (e.g., Steinberg et al., 2009). Adolescents live for the moment. If they consider the future consequences of their actions at all, they tend to focus on potential short- rather than long-term consequences, perhaps because their greater sensitivity to rewards than to risks makes their judgements immature (Cauffman & Steinberg, 2000; Steinberg & Cauffman, 1996; Steinberg et al., 2008, 2009). In the amicus brief, researchers claimed that "Adolescents are inherently more prone to risk-taking behavior and less capable of resisting impulses because of cognitive and other deficiencies" (p. 5). One of these "other" deficiencies is related to their **emotional regulation**. Adolescents often let their emotions "get the better of them" and tend to be more emotionally volatile even in comparison to young adults who are just a few years older. For example, Steinberg notes (2009, pp. 480–481), "Although basic cognitive competence matures by the time individuals reach age 16, many of the social and emotional capacities that influence adolescents' judgment and decision making, especially outside the psychologist's laboratory, continue to mature into late adolescence and beyond."

Socially, adolescents are more affected by peer pressure or peer influence—especially when they are in groups. For example, adolescents take more chances and make more risky decisions when in groups (e.g., Gardner & Steinberg, 2005). When their choices involve clothing or music, the increased susceptibility to peer influence may have limited long-term consequences for themselves or others, but when choices involve whether to commit an illegal act or engage in other risky behavior, the susceptibility to peer influence becomes more problematic.

In recent years, impressive technological advances have allowed researchers to explore the biological basis of these changes (see Johnson, Chapter 4, this volume). Anatomical differences between the brains of adolescents and adults demonstrate that adolescents are not fully mature until after the age of 18 (see Scott & Steinberg, 2008; Steinberg, 2007, 2008, for reviews). Important differences are evident in the frontal lobes, for example—areas of the brain known to play critical roles in executive function, planning, and decision making. The frontal lobes are underdeveloped in terms of myelination and pruning, both of which affect how the brain functions. As noted in the amicus brief (p. 12), "Research shows that adolescent brains are more active in regions related to aggression, anger, and fear, and less active in regions related to impulse control, risk assessment, and moral reasoning than adult brains." This basic neuroscience research thus confirms what research psychologists have learned about adolescent behavior.

Applied Research Concerning Juvenile Justice

Applied research also helped the authors of the amicus brief to reach an important conclusion, "Executing adolescents does not serve the recognized purposes of the death penalty"

(p. 21). One such purpose is to deter future crime. However, research on the increasingly punitive orientation of the juvenile justice system shows that these policies (e.g., transfer to adult criminal court) fail to deter future crime and may actually increase recidivism (Bishop & Frazier, 2000; Singer & McDowall, 1988; see Fagan, 2008 for review). Reporting on the consistent failure of harsher sanctions to deter juvenile offending, Fagan (2008, pp. 100–101) writes, "Rarely do social scientists or policy analysts report such consistency and agreement under such widely varying sampling, measurement, and analytic conditions . . . Few modern criminologists or correctional administrators maintain the illusion that incarceration has either broad therapeutic benefits or a strong deterrent effect." Not only does more severe treatment fail to achieve its intended purpose (e.g., increasing public safety), but it is also extensively costly to taxpayers (Greenwood, 2006), and it jeopardizes the safety, mental health, and future prospects of many juveniles (e.g., Bishop & Frazier, 2000; Cesaroni & Peterson-Badali, 2005; Forst, Fagan, & Vivona, 1989; see Fagan, 2008). This is critical because mental illness and mental health symptoms are very common among juvenile offenders, especially female offenders, upon entering the juvenile justice system (e.g., Cauffman, 2004; Cauffman, Lexcen, Goldweber, Shulman, & Grisso, 2007; Teplin, Abram, McClelland, Dulcan, & Mericle, 2002; Wasserman, McReynolds, Lucas, Fisher, & Santos, 2002).

Applied research in this field has also helped to document the **age–crime curve** and has led to the delineation of two primary groups of offenders—adolescent limited and life-course persistent (Moffitt, 1993). Decades of research conducted around the world demonstrates that most juvenile offenders cease offending after adolescence, whether or not they come into contact with the legal system; a very small proportion of adolescent offenders continue committing crimes later in life (e.g., Moffitt & Caspi, 2001; Moffitt, Caspi, Harrington, & Milne, 2002; Odgers et al., 2008). Complementing the basic research on adolescence discussed above, this real-world research has (or should have) critical implications for the treatment and punishment of juvenile offenders.

The Death Penalty Decision

In 2002 (*Atkins v. Virginia*), the US Supreme Court abolished the death penalty for individuals with intellectual disabilities, in part because of their "disabilities in areas of reasoning, judgment, and control of their impulses." Of course, adolescents share these characteristics, and this influenced the Supreme Court's later decision to abolish the death penalty for adolescents as well.

Writing for the majority, Justice Kennedy referred to important characteristics of adolescence that had been described in the amicus brief, including adolescents' diminished decision-making capacity and their related tendency to engage in risky and irresponsible behaviour; their increased susceptibility to external pressure, especially from peers; and the changing nature of their identity. In reference to the developing adolescent character, Justice Kennedy wrote that it was "less supportable to conclude that even a heinous crime committed by a juvenile is evidence of irretrievably depraved character." In fact, because of considerable and rapid changes in adolescent character, researchers have referred to adolescents as "moving targets" (Grisso, 1998). When trying to conduct psychological assessments and predictions about future behavior, it is quite difficult to "hit" such moving targets, but, the court opined, adolescents would most likely "outgrow" their criminal behavior as they matured.

What Else Have We Learned from Research Concerning Juvenile Justice?

Certainly, basic and applied developmental researchers have made significant contributions in the field of juvenile justice: The abolition of the death penalty for juvenile offenders is literally a matter of life and death for some young people. Importantly, research pertaining to adolescent development and juvenile justice has done more than merely inform legal practices; it has informed our understanding of normative developmental processes as well, again demonstrating the reciprocal relationship between basic and applied research.

Developmental psychologists clearly recognize adolescence as a formative period during which rapid change is apparent while adolescents "make substantial progress in acquiring and coordinating skills that are essential to filling the conventional roles of adulthood" (Steinberg, 2009, p. 480). Certain developmental "tasks" (e.g., education, vocational training, dating and intimate relationships, goal setting, cooperation in groups) help adolescents to both develop psychologically and transition successfully into young adulthood and the new roles that may await them (e.g., parent, member of the work force). Steinberg (2009, p. 480) notes that:

> This process of development toward psychosocial maturity is one of reciprocal interaction between the individual and her social context. Several environmental conditions are particularly important, such as the presence of an authoritative parent or guardian, association with prosocial peers, and participation in educational, extracurricular, or employment activities that facilitate the development of autonomous decision making and critical thinking.

It is clear that juveniles in the justice system, particularly those who are incarcerated, are accomplishing (or not accomplishing) these developmental tasks in a very different environment than other youths. Their environment primarily includes peers, with less opportunity for education and vocational training than would be available "on the outside." They also lack the influence of caring adult role models, including parents/guardians and older siblings. Such differences likely influence their developmental trajectories at least in comparison with those spending their formative years in more normative contexts such as schools, neighbourhoods, and families.

Researchers have studied these youth to learn about basic psychological processes in different developmental contexts. For example, this research has allowed us to understand better peer influence and the potential iatrogenic effects of incarceration and other interventions for problematic behavior. Several studies have found that surrounding delinquent teenagers with other delinquent teenagers actually escalates their bad behavior, especially among those considered "high risk" or most in need of intervention (e.g., Dishion, Spracklen, Andrews, & Patterson, 1996; Patterson, Dishion, & Yoerger, 2000; Poulin, Dishion, & Burraston, 2001; see Cécile & Born, 2009; Dishion, McCord, & Poulin, 1999, for reviews). In intervention settings, incarceration in particular, adolescents may literally learn how to be better offenders—a phenomenon that Dishion et al. (1999, p. 756) term "deviancy training." This work has implications not only for the legal system but also for mental health professionals who may conduct or recommend group therapy.

Interrogation of Juvenile Suspects

In the section on investigative interviewing, we discussed decades of research on children's eyewitness testimony and the many steps that have been taken to help ensure that they provide accurate testimony. There is much at stake when juvenile suspects are questioned as well. Oddly, while the legal and child protection systems have responded to developmental research with policies and protocols for interviewing young people who are victims or witnesses to crime, research has not similarly affected practice where juveniles are suspected of committing crimes. Noting the neglect of relevant research in this area, Owen-Kostelnik, Reppucci, and Meyer (2006, p. 286) wrote: "Our assumption is that 'kids are kids' no matter the context in which they find themselves; being suspected of committing a crime does not make a child an adult."

False Confessions

In what is commonly known as "the Central Park jogger case," five teenage boys confessed to the brutal assault and rape of a woman in New York City (Kassin, 2002). Twelve years into their prison sentence, DNA and confession evidence confirmed the identity of the actual rapist—Matias Reyes (*People of the State of New York v. Kharey Wise et al.*, 2002). The boys, who were now young men, were exonerated and released from prison. Although this case is extremely well known, it is unfortunately not an isolated incident. False confessions are more common than people realize.

Left: Kharey Wise as he looked in court when he was arraigned in the Central Park jogger rape case. (Photo by John Pedin/NY Daily News Archive via Getty Images). Right: Kharey Wise testifies against the death penalty at a hearing before the New York State Assembly at Pace University. Wise, who was wrongfully convicted of beating and raping a woman jogger in Central Park in 1989, spent 15 years in prison. He was released when the real assailant confessed to the crime. (Photo by Debbie Egan-Chin/NY Daily News Archive via Getty Images.)

Over the past 20 years, advances in DNA testing have exonerated over 200 individuals in the United States, some of whom were on death row at the time. Although it is difficult to determine precisely, a surprising 15% to 25% of all DNA exonerations included a false confession or admission which contributed, at least in part, to the wrongful conviction (Garrett, 2008; Scheck, Neufeld, & Dwyer, 2000; Innocence Project, www.innocenceproject.org, last accessed September 1, 2009). Unfortunately, false confessions do not result from a particular legal system or set of procedures—proven false confessions have been documented in England, Australia, New Zealand, China, Japan, Norway, Finland, Germany, Iceland, the Netherlands, and Canada (Kassin et al., 2010). Researchers have identified dispositional and situational factors associated with the risk that individuals will make a false confession (see Kassin & Gudjonsson, 2004; Kassin et al., 2010 for reviews). Although false confessions, whether in the real world or in the laboratory, occur at all ages, young people appear disproportionately likely to confess falsely.

Youth as a Dispositional Risk Factor for False Confession

Field research.   In the Central Park Jogger case, each of the five boys recanted his confession immediately, claiming that he had confessed in order to be allowed home. This exemplifies some of the principles of adolescent development discussed above, including immaturity of judgment, focus on short-term consequences, and impulsivity.

In a study of individuals whose innocence had been verified using DNA evidence, Gross, Jacoby, Matheson, Montgomery, and Patel (2005) found that whereas only 13% of the adults had confessed falsely, 42% of the juveniles had done so, with the youngest exonerees (12 to 15 years old) confessing to murder or rape at an alarming rate (69%). In a study of "proven false confession cases," mostly involving serious crimes, Drizin and Leo (2004) found that 33% involved false confessions from juveniles, and 55% of these were from juveniles who were 15 and under—even though juveniles typically represent only 8% and 16% of all arrests for murder and rape, respectively (Snyder, 2006).

Self-report data also speak to the frequency with which juveniles confess falsely (of those interrogated, 6% in Viljoen, Klaver, & Roesch, 2005; 7.3% in Gudjonsson, Sigurdsson, Asgeirsdottir, & Sigfusdottir, 2006; 8.8% in Gudjonsson, Sigurdsson, Sigfusdottir, & Asgeirsdottir, 2008). Furthermore, more frequent interrogation is associated with greater risk (Gudjonsson et al., 2006). In a large international study, youth from various parts of Europe (i.e., Iceland, Norway, Finland, Latvia, Lithuania, Russia, and Bulgaria) were asked about their experience of interrogation and false confession. Of the 11.5% (2,726) interrogated by the police, 14% claimed to have falsely confessed (Gudjonsson, Sigurdsson, Asgeirsdottir, & Sigfusdottir, in press).

Responses to hypothetical vignettes have also been studied. For example, when presented with hypothetical interrogation situations, 25% of male juvenile offenders indicated that they would choose to confess falsely in at least one of the scenarios (Goldstein, Condie, Kalbeitzer, Osman, & Geier, 2003). Grisso et al. (2003) presented community and justice-system-involved juveniles and young adults with vignettes describing police interrogation situations and asked participants to indicate the "best choice" for the suspect—confess, remain silent, or deny the offense. Younger individuals were more likely to choose the "confess" option: over half of 11- to 13-year-olds and approximately one-fifth of adults did so. Although the vignettes did not indicate that suspects were innocent and that confessions were necessarily false, this research is consistent with youths' propensity to confess. For instance, Viljoen et al. (2005) found that 55% of juvenile defendants confessed when questioned as suspects by the police, with confessors significantly younger than those who remained silent.

In addition to false confessions, field research indicates that juveniles also make other decisions in the interrogation room that put them at risk. For example, younger suspects are more likely to misunderstand or to waive their Miranda rights and/or right to counsel and rarely ask for attorneys to be present (Grisso, 1980; Viljoen et al., 2005; see Grisso, 1981, 1997 for reviews).

Laboratory research.   As in the case of children's eyewitness testimony, researchers have struggled to develop ecologically valid *and* ethical research paradigms to mimic interrogation situations. For example, Kassin and Kiechel (1996) introduced a creative solution—the "Alt key" methodology. In this paradigm, participants complete a reaction time task after being warned that data will be lost and the computer will crash if they press the "Alt" key. Inevitably, the computer crashes and participants are accused of pressing the forbidden key. They are asked to sign a statement indicating that their actions caused the computer to crash.

To increase the ecological validity of this paradigm, Redlich and Goodman (2003) added heftier consequences to the equation—participants would have to complete 10 hours of data entry after the experiment finished if they admitted pressing the forbidden key, and the study revealed clear linear developmental differences in the risk of making false confessions. Young adults were the least likely to take responsibility for crashing the computer (59%). Twelve and 13-year-olds were the most likely (78%) to sign the statement; 15- and 16-year-olds did so 72%

of the time. Similar developmental differences were found in the participants' willingness to question authority—the majority (65%) of 12- and 13-year-olds were willing to sign the statement taking responsibility for crashing the computer without asking a single question, but this tendency decreased with age (46% of the 15- and 16-year-olds and 33% of the young adults).

Hypothetical vignette studies have also been conducted with normative populations. These studies show similar improvements in legal decision making and legal reasoning with age (e.g., Grisso et al., 2003; Peterson-Badali & Abramovitch, 1993; Redlich, Silverman, & Steiner, 2003). This research confirms the importance of developmental status in legal decision making, regardless of whether youth are involved in the justice system.

Developmental Influences in the Interrogation Room

Several of the basic psychological principles that influence young people's ability to provide eyewitness testimony (discussed in the "Child Maltreatment and Children's Eyewitness Testimony" section above) and make them ineligible for the death penalty also increase their vulnerability in the interrogation room. Several of these characteristics also pertain to individuals with intellectual disabilities (Gudjonsson, 2003; Gudjonsson & MacKeith, 1994). Specifically, adolescents are characterized by immature decision making, and impulsivity; they also are less future-oriented, are more suggestible, are more compliant with authority, tend to emphasize short- over long-term consequences, and are more susceptible to pressure from peers and other external influences (e.g., lawyers, parents) (e.g., Cauffman & Steinberg, 2000; Gardner & Steinberg, 2005; Gudjonsson & Singh, 1984; Richardson, Gudjonsson, & Kelly, 1995; Richardson & Kelly, 2004; Singh & Gudjonsson, 1992; Steinberg et al., 2008, 2009). Perhaps not surprisingly, then, exactly half (19) of the proven multiple false confession cases examined by Drizin and Leo (2004) involved false confessions from multiple juvenile suspects to the same crime. As discussed above, youth involved in the justice system are disproportionately affected by mental impairments, including mental health issues and impairments in intellectual ability (e.g., Cauffman, 2004; Closson & Rogers, 2007; Quinn, Rutherford, Leone, Osher, & Poirier, 2005). Given that individuals with mental impairments are also at increased risk for false confession (e.g., Gudjonsson, 1990; Redlich, Summers, & Hoover, 2010), juveniles may be in "double jeopardy" (Redlich, 2007, p. 610) when questioned as suspects. Redlich adds (p. 610), "The fact that all juveniles have one false confession risk factor (young age) and that most have two risk factors (young age and mental impairment) underscores the need for immediate reforms in the interrogation of minors." Youths' developmental capacities and limitations are of importance in the interrogation room, although they have been largely ignored and even exploited to date.

In the Interrogation Room

The "Reid Technique" (Inbau, Reid, Buckley, & Jayne, 2001), now in its fourth edition, is taught and used by interrogators around the world. The website claims to have trained over 500,000 investigators in the United States, Canada, Europe, Asia, and the Middle East (Reid & Associates, 2009). Also, self-report studies of investigators in the US and Canada indicate the high prevalence of Reid-like techniques (e.g., Kassin et al., 2007; Leo, 1996; Meyer & Reppucci, 2007). This technique involves creating a confrontational environment in which the ultimate goal is to obtain a confession because detectives have already concluded that the suspect is guilty; the "interview" has thus become an "interrogation." The technique includes such tactics as lying to suspects, presenting false evidence, minimizing and justifying the crime and its consequences, interrupting and disallowing denials, asking suspects to report hypothetical details of the crime, and other tactics known to increase false reports among children and adults in other contexts (e.g., Garven, Wood, Malpass, & Shaw, 1998; Libby, 2003; Wade, Garry, Read, & Lindsay, 2002; see Loftus, 1997, 2003 for reviews).

Despite the developmental differences discussed earlier in this chapter, proponents of Reid-like techniques (the most prevalent method in the United States; Kassin et al., 2010) pay little or no attention to the age of the suspect being interviewed. In fact, when interrogating adolescents, the Reid training manual recommends, "the same general rules prevail as for adults" (Inbau et al., 2001, p. 99). This is evident in the use of Reid-like techniques with juveniles in self-report and observational studies (Feld, 2006; Meyer & Reppucci, 2007), even at the same rates that they claim to use the techniques with adult suspects (Meyer & Reppucci, 2007).

Regarding young suspects, the Reid technique actually recommends outright exploitation of their developmental characteristics. For example, Inbau et al. (2001) recommended exploiting juveniles' "restless energy, boredom, low resistance to temptation, and lack of supervision" (Kassin et al., 2010, p. 20). They also suggest that police "play one [suspect] against the other." Given what we know about adolescents and peer pressure, they are right in concluding that this tactic may work especially well with young, first-time offenders (Inbau et al., 2001, pp. 292–293).

Recognizing that juveniles (and others with intellectual vulnerabilities) are at increased risk for false confession, recent versions of the training manual (Inbau et al., 2001) do recommend taking some precautions concerning juvenile suspects, however. In discussing the presentation of fictitious evidence, for example, they note, "This technique should be avoided when interrogating a youthful suspect with low social maturity" (p. 429) and with those with diminished mental capacity (e.g., mental retardation), but it is not clear that police interrogators are capable of making judgments about adolescents' social maturity.

Of course, even if they are not recommended, these methods remain perfectly legal, regardless of the suspect's age! And, in several high-profile cases, these tactics have been extremely effective in obtaining confessions from juvenile suspects (see Drizin & Colgan, 2004; Firstman & Salpeter, 2008; Kassin et al., 2010; and Lambert, 2008 for more details of these cases). Michael Crowe, a 14-year-old boy who confessed falsely to murdering his sister, was told several lies by police before confessing, including that his hair was found in her hands, his blood found in her room, and that he had failed a lie detector test. Marty Tankleff, a 17-year-old boy who discovered his stabbed parents, confessed after several hours of denial. He was presented with false evidence against him; most persuasive of all was when the police told him that his father had awoken from his coma and accused his son of the crime. It took almost two decades before Marty was released from prison.

Where to Go From Here?

Kassin et al. (2010, p. 30) state, "There is a strong consensus among psychologists, legal scholars, and practitioners that juveniles and individuals with cognitive impairments or psychological disorders are particularly susceptible to false confession under pressure. Yet little action has been taken to modulate the methods by which these vulnerable groups are questioned when placed into custody as crime suspects." The authors thus recommend that, for one thing, individuals who conduct interviews and interrogations with juveniles should receive special training, concerning the risks associated with youthful age (as well as the risks associated with other vulnerabilities such as mental retardation and mental illness). Ideally, this training would cover relevant principles of developmental psychology and interview strategies and structure.

Recent attempts at revising the NICHD Investigative Interview Protocol for use with suspects are promising in this regard. Hershkowitz et al. (2004) used a modified version of the protocol to interview alleged perpetrators of sexual abuse between the ages of 9 and 14. Surprisingly, suspects who fully or partially admitted their involvement were very responsive to open-ended prompts. In fact, the total number of details provided by the suspects did not vary depending on whether they fully or partially admitted the allegations. Kassin et al.'s (2010) call for more systematic research on such alternatives to typical interrogations should be heeded.

Summary

Although suspects are considered "innocent until proven guilty," juveniles cannot be considered "vulnerable until suspected of a crime." If children and adolescents need certain protections or techniques when interviewed as victims or witnesses, they should not be treated like adults when suspected of criminal behavior. The legal system cannot have it both ways.

As we have seen, adolescents have several characteristics that reduce their culpability but increase their risk when they come into contact with the law. These "moving targets" are difficult to study, yet basic and applied psychological researchers have produced mounting evidence of key differences between adolescents and adults that should affect how they are treated in the legal system. When writing about these "fundamental differences," Steinberg (2009, p. 481) concludes, "Taken together, the lessons of developmental science offer strong support for the maintenance of a separate juvenile justice system in which adolescents are judged, tried, and sanctioned in developmentally appropriate ways."

Crucial reforms, most notably the US Supreme Court abolition of the death penalty for adolescents, have used developmental knowledge successfully. Other areas, however, are still in need of reform. The interrogation of juveniles is one arena in which we could make better use of current knowledge and also heed calls for more research on alternative interviewing strategies. As Kassin et al. (2010, p. 30) point out, in light of existing research, "It is uniformly clear to all parties that vulnerable suspect populations—namely, juveniles and people who are cognitively impaired or psychologically disordered—need to be protected in the interrogation room."

CONCLUSIONS

By using examples regarding children and the law, this chapter illustrates the richness and multifaceted value of applied developmental science. In the areas of children's eyewitness testimony, parental separation/divorce, and juvenile offending, basic and applied psychological research have combined to offer creative and empirically based solutions to real-world problems. Furthermore, applied research has not only promoted children's welfare in these various contexts, but also advanced our understanding of developmental processes and theories more generally, helped test the validity and generalizability of findings obtained previously through experimental research, and led to the creation of new and creative research methodologies.

The road has not been easily travelled, and much work remains to be done. Due to the "large and growing legal constituency" of youth (Bruck et al., 2006, p. 777), we chose to focus on examples from children and the law to illustrate both successes and challenges. Unfortunately, many decision-makers in the legal community fail to take advantage of a burgeoning and increasingly sophisticated understanding of child development when making crucial decisions about children's lives. However, as we have shown in this chapter, psychological research has been used to guide the treatment of children in some legal contexts. We have used these examples to demonstrate how applied and basic psychological research can inform and complement one another, with researchers helping guide practitioners and the latter in turn offering insights and asking questions that foster a more complete understanding of developmental processes.

In the field of children's eyewitness testimony, basic research on children's cognitive and social development has allowed researchers to devise and implement forensic interview practices that have enhanced the quality of forensic interviewing around the world. Through a combination of applied and basic research, it has been possible to improve the value of children's testimony in ways that should allow society to protect children better from maltreatment *and* further our understanding of normative developmental processes. Also, this research has illustrated an important lesson: Simply publishing best-practice guidelines may not be enough to change practice in the field, at least in the long term, highlighting the importance of ongoing training and continued evaluation. The NICHD Protocol and its training model illustrate an effective and influential example of collaboration between academia and the field to generate and disseminate solutions to real-world problems.

In the field of divorce, basic research on attachment and applied research on the impact of parental divorce/separation on children have informed the development of social policies and practices that can help ameliorate the more negative effects of divorce while providing a new context in which to examine children's social development. Unfortunately, decisions about custody and visitation (e.g., amount and distributions of parent–child time) often reflect a lack of knowledge or long-held biases about parent–child relationships, especially concerning father–child relationships. Although several innovative practices have been developed over the past few decades, there is still a long way to go in devising ways to promote children's best interests and their continued relationships with both of their separating parents.

In the field of juvenile justice, basic and applied psychological researchers have clarified how adolescents should be evaluated and treated in the legal system. This research not only has influenced the US Supreme Court's decision to abolish the death penalty for adolescents, but has informed our understanding of normative developmental processes as well (e.g., peer influence), again demonstrating the reciprocal relationship between basic and applied research. Although the death penalty is now off the table for juveniles, they are increasingly being transferred to adult criminal court where they face a more punitive environment. Discussing this trend, Fagan (2008, p. 93) writes, "While the law has moved toward waiving increasingly younger teens to adult criminal court, social and biological evidence suggests moving in the other direction. Perhaps it's time for the law to change course and follow the science."

The interrogation of juveniles is another area in which we could make better use of current knowledge. Several of the basic psychological principles that influence youths' ability to provide eyewitness testimony and make them ineligible for the death penalty also increase their vulnerability in the interrogation room. However, these vulnerabilities are largely ignored or even exploited when juveniles are interrogated about suspected crimes. Additional research and reforms are needed.

The Importance of Influencing Legal Practice with Science (and Vice Versa)

Why should we, as social scientists, care whether our work has implications for the legal system? Ogloff provides an answer (2000, p. 459): "The law is among the most pervasive forces in society. For psychology to have an impact on society, it is crucial for psychology to have an impact on the law."

This is easier said than done, of course. Psychology and the legal system share a long (and often tumultuous) history. Conflict between two disciplines is quite common (e.g., behavioral science and public health; Muehrer et al., 2002), and professionals in academia and the field alike must make efforts toward mutual respect and collaboration. We must strive to inform practice with science (and vice versa) so that the best information can be obtained and disseminated. This may mean greater awareness of and sensitivity to differences in training, motivations, goals, and professional "cultures." Scholars have observed that those in the psychology and legal professions come from two different "cultures" (Brigham, 1999), which may be, in part, responsible for the doubt and even suspicion on both sides. Certainly, the chance of successful collaboration is enhanced by overcoming barriers, including differences in training and communication.

This should be "a two-way street." Psychologists must work to understand the law and the legal system if they wish to make an impact—they cannot expect the field to operate exactly as it does in the laboratory. Those who fail to consider the applied context in which they are working risk making inappropriate conclusions or recommendations. Because legal professionals must operate within the context and confines of *their* own field, guidelines that ignore real-world conditions and are impractical will be disregarded and may also discourage future relationships and research uptake. In response to Munsterberg's (1908) claims that psychologists could help address difficult legal questions, Wigmore (1940, p. 367) responded, "Whenever the Psychologist is ready for the Courts, the Courts are ready for him."

Importantly, psychologists cannot expect to be the "ones with all the answers," dispensing information and advice to those in the legal community. They must be prepared for the feedback loop and the reciprocal relationships which can enhance their research, right down to the identification of new and timely research questions (Ogloff, 2000).

Dissemination

For applied psychological research to have an impact, the findings need to reach the field. Most academics conduct research in the laboratory, present it to other academics at conferences, and publish it in academic journals, which are inaccessible literally or figuratively to most non-psychologists. Most psychological studies will *remain* inaccessible unless psychologists attempt to reach other audiences. Even some of the books that have addressed issues discussed in this chapter accessibly (e.g., Ceci & Bruck, 1995; Scheck et al., 2000; Warshak, 2001) have had limited success bringing those in academia and the field together to debate relevant issues. Conferences aimed at practitioners and academics have perhaps had more success in facilitating the exchange of ideas and knowledge and encouraging debate (e.g., American Psychology Law Society, International Investigative Interviewing Research Group).

Applied psychologists must engage in dialogues with practitioners, policy makers, and other end-users. To this end, Sommer (2006) calls for "dual dissemination," which involves psychologists writing their own articles for publication to more general audiences in parallel to their publications for more specialized academic audiences. In so doing, psychologists must retrain themselves to write for or speak to other audiences. When writing for judges and other legal practitioners, for example, it is important to keep publications focused and practical. Jargon should be eliminated completely, and simple rather than technical language should be used whenever possible. When research findings are disseminated to new and different audiences, they may reach individuals who can apply and test the findings in new contexts, potentially leading to novel research questions.

The amount of research concerning children and the law has grown rapidly and continues to grow. While promoting children's welfare and legal reform, this research has contributed to developmental knowledge, theory, and methodology more generally. Applied developmental psychology has a long and rich history and continues to influence the legal system and other realms. This is critical because "How are we as psychologists to regard a discipline that succeeds primarily in speaking to itself?" (Gergen, 1995).

REFERENCES AND SUGGESTED READINGS (☐)

Adams, B. J., Field, L., & Verhave, T. (1999). Effects of unreinforced conditional selection training, multiple negative comparison training, and feedback on equivalence class formation. *Psychological Record, 49,* 685–702.

Aldridge, J., & Cameron, S. (1999). Interviewing child witnesses: Questioning techniques and the role of training. *Applied Developmental Science, 3,* 136–147.

Alexander, P. C. (1992). Application of attachment theory to the study of sexual abuse. *Journal of Consulting and Clinical Psychology, 60,* 185–195.

Amato, P. R. (1993). Children's adjustment to divorce: Theories, hypotheses, and empirical support. *Journal of Marriage and the Family, 55,* 23–38.

Amato, P. R. (2000). The consequences of divorce for adults and children. *Journal of Marriage and the Family, 62,* 1269–1287.

Amato, P. R., & Dorius, C. (2010). Fathers, children, and divorce. In M. E. Lamb (Ed.), *The role of the father in child development* (5th ed.). Hoboken, NJ: Wiley.

Amato, P. R., & Fowler, F. (2002). Parenting practices, child adjustment, and family diversity. *Journal of Marriage and Family, 64,* 703–716.

Amato, P. R., & Gilbreth, J. G. (1999). Non-resident fathers and children's well-being: A meta-analysis. *Journal of Marriage and the Family, 61,* 557–573.

American Medical Association, American Psychiatric Association, American Society for Adolescent Psychiatry, American Academy of Child & Adolescent Psychiatry, American Academy of Psychiatry and the Law, National Association of Social Workers, Missouri Chapter of the National Association of Social Workers, & National Mental Health Association. (2004, July). *Amici curiae brief submitted to Roper v. Simmons, 543 U.S. 551 (2005).*

American Professional Society on the Abuse of Children (1990). *Guidelines for psychosocial evaluation of suspected sexual abuse in young children.* Chicago, IL: APSAC.

American Professional Society on the Abuse of Children (1997). *Guidelines for psychosocial evaluation of suspected sexual abuse in young children* (revised). Chicago, IL: APSAC.

Aquilino, W. S. (1996). The life course of children born to unmarried mothers: Childhood living arrangements and young adult outcomes. *Journal of Marriage and the Family, 58,* 293–310.

Arbuthnot, J., & Gordon, D. A. (1996). Does mandatory divorce education for parents work? A six-month outcome evaluation. *Family & Conciliation Courts Review, 34,* 60–81.

Atkins v. Virginia, 536, U.S. 304. (2002).

Australian Institute of Health and Welfare (2007). *Child protection Australia 2005–06.* Child welfare series no. 40, Cat. no. CWS 28. Canberra, Australia: AIHW.

Bacon, B. L., & McKenzie, B. (2004). Parent education after separation/divorce: Impact of the level of parental conflict on outcomes. *Family Court Review, 42,* 85–98.

Baker-Ward, L., Gordon, B. N., Ornstein, P. A., Larus, D. M., & Clubb, P. A. (1993). Young children's long-term retention of a pediatric examination. *Child Development, 64,* 1519–1533.

Bauer, P. J. (2006). Event memory. In D. Kuhn & R. Siegler (Volume Eds.), W. Damon & R. M. Lerner (Eds. in Chief), *Handbook of child psychology, Volume 2: Cognition, perception, and language* (6th ed., pp. 373–425). Hoboken, NJ: Wiley.

Bauserman, R. (2002). Child adjustment in joint-custody versus sole-custody arrangements: A meta-analytic review. *Journal of Family Psychology, 16,* 91–102.

Beitchman, J. H., Zucker, K. J., Hood, J. E., DaCosta, G. A., Akman, D., & Cassavia, E. (1992). A review of the long term effects of child sexual abuse. *Child Abuse & Neglect, 16,* 101–118.

Belsky, J., Youngblade, L., Rovine, M., & Volling, B. (1991). Patterns of marital change and parent–child interaction. *Journal of Marriage and the Family, 53,* 487–498.

Bishop, D., & Frazier, C. (2000). Consequences of transfer. In J. Fagan & F. Zimring (Eds.), *The changing borders of juvenile justice* (pp. 227–277). Chicago: University of Chicago Press.

Bjorklund, D., Bjorklund, B., Brown, R., & Cassel, W. (1998). Children's susceptibility to repeated questions: How misinformation changes children's answers and their minds. *Applied Developmental Science, 2,* 99–111.

Booth, A., & Amato, P. R. (2001). Parental predivorce relations and offspring postdivorce well-being. *Journal of Marriage and the Family*, *63*, 197–212.

Bottoms, B. L., Quas, J. A., & Davis, S. L. (2007). The influence of the interviewer-provided social support on children's memory, suggestibility, and disclosures. In M. E. Pipe et al. (Eds.), *Child sexual abuse: Disclosure, delay, and denial* (pp. 135–157). Mahwah, NJ: Lawrence Erlbaum Associates.

Bourg, W., Broderick, R., Flagor, R., Kelly, D. M., Ervin, D. L., & Butler, J. (1999). *A child interviewer's guidebook*. Thousand Oaks, CA: Sage.

Bowlby, J. (1969). *Attachment and loss: Vol. 1. Attachment*. New York: Basic Books.

Braver, S. L., Griffin, W. A., Cookston, J. T., Sandler, I. N., & Williams, J. (2005). Promoting better fathering among divorced nonresident fathers. In W. M. Pinsof & J. Lebow (Eds.), *Family psychology: The art of the science* (pp. 295–325). New York: Oxford University Press.

Briere, J., & Runtz, M. (1993). Childhood sexual abuse: Long-term sequelae and implications for psychological assessment. *Journal of Interpersonal Violence*, *8*, 312–330.

Brigham, J. (1999). What is forensic psychology anyway? *Law and Human Behavior*, *23*, 273–298.

Brown v. Board of Education, 375 U.S. 483. (1954).

Bruck, M., Ceci, S. J., & Principe, G. F. (2006). The child and the law. In K. A. Renninger, I. E. Sigel, W. Damon, & R. M. Lerner (Eds.), *Handbook of child psychology* (6th ed., Vol. 4, pp. 776–816). Hoboken, NJ: Wiley.

Cairns, H. (1935). *Law and the social sciences*. London: Kegan Paul, Trench Trubner and Co.

California v. Raymond Buckey et al., Los Angeles County Sup. Ct. #A750900.

Campbell, D. T. (1978). Qualitative knowing in action research. In M. Brenner, P. March, & M. Brenner (Eds.), *The social contexts of method* (pp. 184–209). London: Croom Helm.

Carlson, M. J. (2006). Family structure, father involvement, and adolescent behavioural outcomes. *Journal of Marriage and the Family*, *68*, 137–154.

Cassidy, J., & Shaver, P. R. (Eds.) (2008). *Handbook of attachment: Theory, research, and clinical applications* (2nd ed.). New York: Guilford Press.

Cauffman, E. (2004). A statewide screening of mental health symptoms among juvenile offenders in detention. *Journal of the American Academy of Child and Adolescent Psychiatry*, *43*, 430–439.

Cauffman, E., Lexcen, F. J., Goldweber, A., Shulman, E. P., & Grisso, T. (2007). Gender differences in mental health symptoms among delinquent and community youth. *Youth Violence and Juvenile Justice*, *5*, 288–307.

Cauffman, E., Shulman, E. P., Steinberg, L., Claus, E., Banich, M., Graham, S., et al. (in press). Age differences in affective decision making as indexed by performance on the Iowa Gambling Task. *Developmental Psychology*.

Cauffman, E., & Steinberg, L. (2000). (Im)maturity of judgment in adolescence: Why adolescents may be less culpable than adults. *Behavioral Sciences and the Law*, *18*, 741–760.

Ceci, S. J., & Bruck, M. (1995). *Jeopardy in the courtroom: A scientific analysis of children's testimony*. Washington, DC: APA Books.

Cécile, M., & Born, M. (2009). Intervention in juvenile delinquency: Danger of iatrogenic effects? *Children and Youth Services Review*, *31*, 1217–1221.

Celano, M., Hazzard, A., Campbell, S. K., & Lang, C. B. (2002). Attribution retraining with sexually abused children: Review of techniques. *Child Maltreatment*, *7*, 65–76.

Cesaroni, C., & Peterson-Badali, M. (2005). Young offenders in custody: Risk and assessment. *Criminal Justice and Behavior*, *32*, 251–277.

Cialdini, R. B. (1980). Full cycle social psychology. In L. Bickman (Ed.), *Applied social psychology annual*. Newbury Park, CA: Sage.

Cicchetti, D. (in press) Developmental psychopathology. In R. M. Lerner (Gen. Ed.), M. E. Lamb & A. Freund (Vol. Eds.), *Handbook of lifespan development, Volume 2: Social and personality development*. Hoboken, NJ: Wiley.

Clark, D. C. (1971). Teaching concepts in the classroom: A set of prescriptions derived from experimental research. *Journal of Educational Psychology Monograph*, *62*, 253–278.

Clarke-Stewart, K. A. (1998). Historical shifts and underlying themes in ideas about rearing young children in the United States: Where have we been? Where are we going? *Early Development & Parenting*, *7*, 101–117.

Clarke-Stewart, A. & Brentano, C. (2006). *Divorce: Causes and consequences*. New Haven, CT: Yale University Press.

Clarke-Stewart, K. A., & Hayward, C. (1996). Advantages of father custody and contact for the psychological well-being of school-age children. *Journal of Applied Developmental Psychology*, *17*, 239–270.

Clarke-Stewart, K. A., Vandell, D. L., McCartney, K., Owen, M. T., & Booth, C. (2000). Effects of parental separation and divorce on very young children. *Journal of Family Psychology*, *13*, 304–326.

Closson, M., & Rogers, K. M. (2007). Educational needs of youth in the juvenile justice system. In C. L. Kessler & L. J. Kraus (Eds.), *The mental health needs of young offenders: Forging paths toward reintegration and rehabilitation* (pp. 229–240). New York: Cambridge University Press.

Coates, C. A., Deutsch, R., Starnes, H., Sullivan, M. J., & Sydlik, B. (2004). Parenting coordination for high-conflict families. *Family Court Review*, *42*, 246–262.

Commonwealth of Massachusetts v. Cheryl Amirault LeFave, 1999.

Creighton, S. J. (2004). Prevalence and incidence of child abuse: International comparisons. *National Society for the Prevention of Cruelty to Children*. Retrieved September 5, 2009, from www.nspcc.org.uk/Inform/research/Briefings/prevalenceandincidenceofchildabuse_wda48217.html

Crosse, S. B., Kaye, E., & Ratnofsky, A. C. (1993). *A report on the maltreatment of children with disabilities*. Washington, DC: National Center of Child Abuse and Neglect.

Cummings, E. M., & Davies, P. T. (1994). Maternal depression and child development. *Journal of Child Psychology and Psychiatry and Allied Disciplines, 35*, 73–112.

Cummings, E. M., Goeke-Morey, M. C., & Raymond, J. (2004). Fathers in family context: Effects of marital quality and marital conflict. In M. E. Lamb (Ed.), *The role of the father in child development* (4th ed., pp. 196–221). Hoboken, NJ: Wiley.

Cummings, E. M., Merrilees, C. E., & George, M. R. W. (2010). Fathers, marriages, and families: Revisiting and updating the framework for fathering in the family context. In M. E. Lamb (Ed.), *The role of the father in child development* (5th ed.). Hoboken, NJ: Wiley.

Cyr, M., & Lamb, M. E. (2009). Assessing the effectiveness of the NICHD investigative interview protocol when interviewing French-speaking alleged victims of child sexual abuse in Quebec. *Child Abuse & Neglect, 33*, 257–268.

Dale, P. S., Loftus, E. F., & Rathbun, L. (1978). The influence of the form of the question on the eyewitness testimony of preschool children. *Journal of Psycholinguistic Research, 74*, 269–277.

Dent, H. R. (1982). The effects of interviewing strategies on the results of interviews with child witnesses. In A. Trankell (Ed.), *Reconstructing the past: The role of psychologists in criminal trials* (pp. 279–297). Stockholm: Norstedt.

Dent, H. R. (1986). Experimental study of the effectiveness of different techniques of questioning child witnesses. *British Journal of Social and Clinical Psychology, 18*, 41–51.

Dent, H. R., & Stephenson, G. M. (1979). An experimental study of the effectiveness of different techniques of questioning child witnesses. *British Journal of Social and Clinical Psychology, 18*, 41–51.

Dishion, T. J., McCord, J., & Poulin, F. (1999). When interventions harm: Peer groups and problem behavior. *American Psychologist, 54*, 755–764.

Dishion, T. J., Spracklen, K. M., Andrews, D. W., & Patterson, G. R. (1996). Deviancy training in male adolescent friendships. *Behavior Therapy, 27*, 373–390.

Dodge, K. A., Pettit, G. S., Bates, J. E., & Valente, E. (1995). Social information-processing patterns partially mediate the effect of early physical abuse on later conduct problems. *Journal of Abnormal Psychology, 104*, 632–643.

Drizin, S. A., & Colgan, B. (2004). Tales from the juvenile confession front: A guide to how standard police interrogation tactics can produce coerced and false confessions from juvenile suspects. In G. D. Lassiter (Ed.), *Interrogations, confessions, and entrapment* (pp. 127–162). New York: Kluwer Academic/Plenum.

Drizin, S. A., & Leo, R. A. (2004). The problem of false confessions in the post-DNA world. *North Carolina Law Review, 82*, 891–1007.

Dunn, J., Cheng, H., O'Connor, T. G. & Bridges, L. (2004). Children's perspectives on their relationships with their nonresident fathers: Influences, outcomes and implications. *Journal of Child Psychology and Psychiatry, 45*, 553–566.

Dunn, J., Davies, L., O'Connor, T., & Sturgess, W. (2001). Family lives and friendships: The perspectives of children in step-, single-parent, and two-parent families. *Journal of Family Psychology, 15*, 272–287.

Egeland, B., Yates, T., Appleyard, K., & van Dulmen, M. (2002). The long-term consequences of maltreatment in the early years: A developmental pathway model to antisocial behavior. *Children's Services: Social Policy, Research, & Practice, 5*, 249–260.

Eisen, M. L., Goodman, G. S., Qin, J., Davis, S., & Crayton, J. (2007). Maltreated children's memory: Accuracy, suggestibility, and psychopathology. *Developmental Psychology, 43*, 1275–1294.

Eisen, M. L., Qin, J., Goodman, G. S., & Davis, S. L. (2002). Memory and suggestibility in maltreated children: Age, stress arousal, dissociation, and psychopathology. *Journal of Experimental Child Psychology, 83*, 167–212.

Ellis, D., & Anderson, D. Y. (2003). The impact of participation in a parent education program for divorcing parents on the use of court resources: An evaluation study. *Conflict Resolution Quarterly*, 169–187.

Emery, R. E. (1994). *Renegotiating family relationships: Divorce, child custody, and mediation*. New York: Guilford Press.

Emery, R. E. (1998). *Marriage, divorce, and children's adjustment* (2nd ed.). Thousand Oaks, CA: Sage.

Emery, R. E., Laumann-Billings, L., Waldron, M. C., Sbarra, D. A., Dillon, P. (2001). Child custody mediation and litigation: Custody, contact, and coparenting 12 years after initial dispute resolution. *Journal of Consulting and Clinical Psychology, 69*, 323–332.

Fabricius, W. V., Braver, S. L., Diaz, P., & Schenck, C. (2010). Custody and parenting time: Links to family relationships and well-being after divorce. In M. E. Lamb (Ed.), *The role of the father in child development* (5th ed.). Hoboken, NJ: Wiley.

Fabricius, W. V., & Hall, J. (2000). Young adults' perspectives on divorce: Living arrangements. *Family & Conciliation Courts Review, 38*, 446–461.

Fagan, J. (2008). Juvenile crime and criminal justice: Resolving border disputes. *Future of Children, 18*, 81–118.

Family Courts Review (2001). Special issue, *39*(3).

Feiring, C., Taska, L., & Lewis, M. (1998). The role of shame and attributional style in children's and adolescents' adaptation to sexual abuse. *Child Maltreatment, 3*, 129–142.

Feld, B. C. (1993). Criminalizing the American juvenile court. *Crime & Justice, 17*, 197–280.

Feld, B. (2006). Police interrogations of juveniles: An empirical study of policy and practice. *Journal of Criminal Law and Criminology, 97*, 219–316.

Finkelhor, D. (1990). Early and long-term effects of child sexual abuse: An update. *Professional Psychology: Research and Practice, 21*, 325–330.

Finkelhor, D., & Browne, A. (1988). Assessing the long-term impact of child sexual abuse: A review and conceptualization. In G. T. Hotaling et al. (Eds.), *Family abuse and its consequences: New directions in research* (pp. 270–284). Thousand Oaks, CA: Sage.

Finley, G. E., & Schwartz, S. J. (2007). Father involvement and young adult outcomes: The differential contributions of divorce and gender. *Family Court Review, 45*, 573–587.

Firstman, R., & Salpeter, J. (2008). *A criminal injustice: A true crime, a false confession, and the fight to free Marty Tankleff*. New York: Ballantine Books.

Fisher, R. P., Brennan, K. H., & McCauley, M. R. (2002). The cognitive interview method to enhance eyewitness recall. In M. Eisen, G. Goodman, & J. Quas (Eds.), *Memory and suggestibility in the forensic interview* (pp. 265–286). Mahwah, NJ: Lawrence Erlbaum Associates.

Fivush, R., & Haden, C. A. (Eds.). (2003). *Autobiographical memory and the construction of a narrative self: Developmental and cultural perspectives*. Mahwah, NJ: Lawrence Erlbaum Associates.

Flory, B. E., Dunn, J., Berg-Weger, M., & Milstead, M. (2001). An exploratory study of supervised access and custody exchange services. *Family Court Review, 39*, 469–482.

Forst, M. A., Fagan, J., & Vivona, T. S. (1989). Some paradoxical effects of the treatment—custody dichotomy for adolescents in adult prisons. *Juvenile and Family Court Journal, 40*, 1–15.

Frayer, D. A., & Klausmeier, H. J. (1971). *Variables on concept learning: Task variables*. Theoretical paper No. 28. Madison, WI: Wisconsin Research and Development Center for Cognitive Learning.

Gardner, M., & Steinberg, L. (2005). Peer influence on risk-taking, risk preference, and risky decision-making in adolescence and adulthood: An experimental study. *Developmental Psychology, 41*, 625–635.

Garrett, B. (2008). Judging innocence. *Columbia Law Review, 108*, 55–142.

Garven, S., Wood, J. M., Malpass, R. S., & Shaw, J. S., III. (1998). More than suggestion: The effect of interviewing techniques from the McMartin Preschool case. *Journal of Applied Psychology, 83*, 347–359.

Gelles, R. J. (1996). *The book of David: How preserving families can cost children's lives*. New York: Basic Books.

Gergen, K. J. (1995). Postmodern psychology: Resonance and reflection. *American Psychologist, 50*, 394.

Goldstein, N., Condie, L., Kalbeitzer, R., Osman, D., & Geier, J. (2003). Juvenile offenders' Miranda rights comprehension and self-reported likelihood of false confessions. *Assessment, 10*, 359–369.

Goodman, G. S., Bottoms, B. L., Schwartz-Kenney, B. M., & Rudy, L. (1991a). Children's testimony about a stressful event: Improving children's reports. *Journal of Narrative and Life History, 1*, 69–99.

Goodman, G. S., Hirschman, J. E., Hepps, D., & Rudy, L. (1991b). Children's memory for stressful events. *Merrill-Palmer Quarterly, 37*, 109–157.

Goodman, G. S., Quas, J. A., Batterman-Faunce, J. M., Riddlesberger, M. M., & Kuhn, J. (1997). Children's reactions to and memory for a stressful event: Influences of age, anatomical dolls, knowledge, and parental attachment. *Applied Developmental Science, 1*, 54–75.

Goodman-Brown, T. B., Edelstein, R. S., Goodman, G. S., Jones, D. P. H., & Gordon, D. S. (2003). Why children tell: A model of children's disclosure of sexual abuse. *Child Abuse & Neglect, 27*, 525–540.

Green, A. H. (1993). Child sexual abuse: Immediate and long-term effects and intervention. *Journal of the American Academy of Child & Adolescent Psychiatry, 32*, 890–902.

Greenwood, P. (2006). *Changing lives: Delinquency prevention as crime control policy*. Chicago: University of Chicago Press.

Grisso, T. (1980). Juveniles' capacities to waive Miranda rights: An empirical analysis. *California Law Review, 68*, 1134–1166.

Grisso, T. (1981). *Juveniles' waiver of rights: Legal and psychological competence*. New York: Plenum.

Grisso, T. (1997). The competence of adolescents as trial defendants. *Psychology, Public Policy, and Law, 3*, 3–32.

Grisso, T. (1998). *Forensic evaluation of juveniles*. Sarasota, FL: Professional Resource Press.

Grisso, T., Steinberg, L., Woolard, J., Cauffman, E., Scott, E., Graham, S., et al. (2003). Juveniles' competence to stand trial: A comparison of adolescents' and adults' capacities as trial defendants. *Law and Human Behavior, 27*, 333–363.

Groark, C. J., & McCall, R. B. (2005). Integrating developmental scholarship into practice and policy. In

M. H. Bornstein & M. E. Lamb (Eds.), *Developmental science: An advanced textbook* (5th ed., pp. 557–601). Mahwah, NJ: Lawrence Erlbaum Associates.

Grol, R., & Grimshaw, J. (2003). From best evidence to best practice: Effective implementation of change in patients' care. *Lancet, 362*, 1225–1230.

Gross, S. R., Jacoby, K., Matheson, D. J., Montgomery, N., & Patel, S. (2005). Exonerations in the United States, 1989 through 2003. *Journal of Criminal Law & Criminology, 95*, 523–553.

Grych, J. H. (2005). Interparental conflict as a risk factor for child maladjustment: Implications for the development of prevention programs. *Family Court Review, 43*, 97–108.

Gudjonsson, G. H. (1990). One hundred alleged false confession cases: Some normative data. *British Journal of Clinical Psychology, 29*, 249–250.

Gudjonsson, G. H. (2003). *The psychology of interrogations and confessions: A handbook*. Chichester, UK: Wiley.

Gudjonsson, G. H., & MacKeith, J. A. C. (1994). Learning disability and the Police and Criminal Evidence Act of 1984. Protection during investigative interviewing: A video-recorded false confession to double murder. *Journal of Forensic Psychiatry, 5*, 35–49.

Gudjonsson, G. H., Sigurdsson, J. F., Asgeirsdottir, B. B., & Sigfusdottir, I. D. (2006). Custodial interrogation, false confession, and individual differences: A national study among Icelandic youth. *Personality and Individual Differences, 41*, 49–59.

Gudjonsson, G. H., Sigurdsson, J. F., Sigfusdottir, I. D., & Asgeirsdottir, B. B. (2008). False confessions and individual differences: The importance of victimization among youth. *Personality and Individual Differences, 45*, 801–805.

Gudjonsson, G. H., Sigurdsson, J. F., Asgeirsdottir, B. B., & Sigfusdottir, I. D. (in press). Interrogation and false confession among adolescents in seven European countries: What background and psychological variables best discriminate between false confessors and non-false confessors? *Psychology, Crime, and Law*.

Gudjonsson, G. H., & Singh, K. K. (1984). Interrogative suggestibility and delinquent boys: An empirical validation study. *Personality & Individual Differences, 5*, 425–430.

Guidelines for Parenting Coordination (2006). AFCC Task Force on Parenting Coordination. *Family Court Review, 44*, 164–181.

Gully, S. M. (1998). The influences of self-regulation processes on learning and performance in a team training context. *Dissertation Abstracts International: Section B: the Sciences & Engineering, 58* (9-B), 5175.

Haine, R. A., Sandler, I. N., Wolchik, S. A., Tein, J.-U., & Dawson-McClure, S. R. (2003). Changing the legacy of divorce: Evidence from prevention programs and future directions. *Family Relations, 52*, 397–405.

Hershkowitz, I., Horowitz, D., & Lamb, M. E. (2005). Trends in children's disclosure of abuse in Israel: A national study. *Child Abuse and Neglect, 29*, 1203–1214.

Hershkowitz, I., Horowitz, D., Lamb, M. E., Orbach, Y., & Sternberg, K. J. (2004). Interviewing youthful suspects in alleged sex crimes: A descriptive analysis. *Child Abuse and Neglect, 28*, 423–438.

Hershkowitz, I., Lamb, M. E., & Horowitz, D. (2007). Victimization of children with disabilities. *American Journal of Orthopsychiatry, 77*, 629–635.

Hershkowitz, I., Orbach, Y., Lamb, M. E., Sternberg, K. J., & Horowitz, D. (2006). Dynamics of forensic interviews with suspected abuse victims who do not disclose abuse. *Child Abuse and Neglect, 30*, 753–769.

Hetherington, E. M. (Ed.). (1999). Should we stay together for the sake of the children? In E. M. Hetherington (Ed.), *Coping with divorce, single parenting, and remarriage* (pp. 93–116). Mahwah, NJ: Lawrence Erlbaum Associates.

Hetherington, E. M., Bridges, M., & Insabella, G. M. (1998). What matters? What does not? Five perspectives on the association between marital transitions and children's adjustment. *American Psychologist, 53*, 167–184.

Hetherington, E. M., & Kelly, J. (2002). *For better or for worse: Divorce reconsidered*. New York: Norton.

Hewitt, S. D. (1999). *Assessing allegations of sexual abuse in preschool children*. Thousand Oaks, CA: Sage.

Hohmann, A. A., & Shear, M. K. (2002). Community-based intervention research: Coping with the "noise" of real life in study design. *American Journal of Psychiatry, 159*, 201–207.

Home Office. (1992). *Memorandum of good practice on video recorded interviews with child witnesses for criminal proceedings*. London: Home Office with Department of Health.

Home Office. (2007). *Achieving best evidence in criminal proceedings: Guidance on interviewing victims and witnesses, and using special measures*. London: Home Office.

Howe, M. L., Cicchetti, D., Toth, S. L., & Cerrito, B. M. (2004). True and false memories in maltreated children. *Child Development, 75*, 1402–1417.

Howe, M. L., Courage, M. L., & Peterson, C. (1996). "How can I remember when I wasn't there?": Long term retention of traumatic experiences and emergence of the cognitive self. In K. Pezdek & W. P. Banks (Eds.), *The recovered memory/false memory debate* (pp. 121–149). San Diego, CA: Academic Press.

Hutcheson, G. D., Baxter, J. S., Telfer, K., & Warden, D. (1995). Child witness statement quality: Question type and errors of omission. *Law and Human Behavior, 19*, 631–648.

Inbau, F. E., Reid, J. E., Buckley, J. P., & Jayne, B. C. (2001). *Criminal interrogation and confessions* (4th ed.). Gaithersberg, MD: Aspen.

Innocence Project. (2009). Understand the causes: False confessions. Retrieved September 4, 2009, from www.innocenceproject.org/understand/False-Confessions.php

Johnston, T. (1994). *Analysis of Santa Clara County, CA case files*. Unpublished dissertation.

Kassin, S. M. (2002, November 1). False confessions and the jogger case. *New York Times*, p. A31.

Kassin, S. M., Drizin, S. A., Grisso, T., Gudjonsson, G. H., Leo, R. A., & Redlich, A. D. (2010). Police-induced confessions: Risk factors and recommendations. *Law and Human Behavior*, *34*, 3–38.

Kassin, S. M., & Gudjonsson, G. H. (2004). The psychology of confessions: A review of the literature and issues. *Psychological Science in the Public Interest*, *5*, 35–69.

Kassin, S. M., & Kiechel, K. L. (1996). The social psychology of false confessions: Compliance, internalization, and confabulation. *Psychological Science*, *7*, 125–128.

Kassin, S. M., Leo, R. A., Meissner, C. A., Richman, K. D., Colwell, L. H., Leach, A.-M., et al. (2007). Police interviewing and interrogation: A self-report survey of police practices and beliefs. *Law and Human Behavior*, *31*, 381–400.

Katz, L. F., & Gottman, J. M. (1993). Patterns of marital conflict predict children's internalizing and externalizing behaviors. *Developmental Psychology*, *29*, 940–950.

Katz, C., & Hershkowitz, I. (in press). The effect of drawing on the richness of accounts provided by alleged victims of child sexual abuse. *Child Maltreatment*.

Kelly, J. B. (2000). Children's adjustment in conflicted marriage and divorce: A decade review of research. *Journal of the American Academy of Child Psychiatry*, *39*, 963–973.

Kelly, J. (2002). Psychological and legal interventions for parents and children in custody and access disputes: Current research and practice. *Virginia Journal of Social Policy and Law*, *10*, 129–163.

Kelly, J. (2003). Parents with enduring child disputes: Multiple pathways to enduring disputes. *Journal of Family Studies*, *9*, 37–50.

Kelly, J. B. (2004). Family mediation research: Is there support for the field? *Conflict Resolution Quarterly*, *22*, 3–35.

Kelly, J. B. (2005). Developing beneficial parenting plan models for children following separation and divorce. *Journal of American Academy of Matrimonial Lawyers*, *19*, 237–254.

Kelly, J. B. (2007). Children's living arrangements following separation and divorce: Insights from empirical and clinical research. *Family Process*, *46*, 35–52.

Kelly, J. B. (in press). Training for the parenting coordinator role. *Journal of Child Custody*.

Kelly, J. B., & Emery, R. E. (2003). Children's adjustment following divorce: Risk and resilience perspectives. *Family Relations*, *52*, 352–362.

Kelly, J. B. & Johnston, J. R. (2005). Commentary on Tippins and Whitmann's "Empirical and ethical problems with custody recommendations: A call for clinical humility and judicial vigilance". *Family Court Review*, *4*, 233–241.

Kelly, J. B., & Lamb, M. E. (2000). Using child development research to make appropriate custody and access decisions for young children. *Family and Conciliation Courts Review*, *38*, 297–311.

Kelly, J. B., & Lamb, M. E. (2003). Developmental issues in relocation cases involving young children: When, whether, and how? *Journal of Family Psychology*, *17*, 193–205.

Kuehnle, K. (1996). *Assessing allegations of child sexual abuse*. Sarasota, FL: Professional Resource Press/Professional Resource Exchange.

Lamb, M. E. (2002a). Infant–father attachments and their impact on child development. In C. S. Tamis-LeMonda & N. Cabrera (Eds.), *Handbook of father involvement: Multidisciplinary perspectives* (pp. 93–117). Mahwah, NJ: Lawrence Erlbaum Associates.

Lamb, M. E. (2002b). Placing children's interests first: Developmentally appropriate parenting plans. *Virginia Journal of Social Policy and the Law*, *10*, 98–119.

Lamb, M. E. (2003). Child development and the law. In R. M. Lerner, M. A. Easterbrooks, & J. Mistry (Eds.), *Handbook of psychology, Volume 6: Developmental psychology* (pp. 559–577). Hoboken, NJ: Wiley.

Lamb, M. E., Bornstein, M. H., & Teti, D. M. (2002a). *Development in infancy* (4th ed.). Mahwah, NJ: Lawrence Erlbaum Associates.

Lamb, M. E., & Fauchier, A. (2001). The effects of question type on self-contradictions by children in the course of forensic interviews. *Applied Cognitive Psychology*, *15*, 483–491.

Lamb, M. E., Hershkowitz, I., Orbach, Y., & Esplin, P. W. (2008). *Tell me what happened: Structured investigative interviews of child victims and witnesses*. Hoboken, NJ: Wiley.

Lamb, M. E., Hershkowitz, I., Sternberg, K. J., Esplin, P. W., Hovav, M., Manor, T., et al. (1996). Effects of investigative utterance types on Israeli children's responses. *International Journal of Behavioural Development*, *19*, 627–637.

Lamb, M. E., & Kelly, J. B. (2001). Using the empirical literature to guide the development of parenting plans for young children: A rejoinder to Solomon and Biringen. *Family Court Review*, *39*, 365–371.

Lamb, M. E., & Kelly, J. B. (2009). Improving the quality of parent–child contact in separating families with infants and young children: Empirical research foundations. In R. M. Gatalzer Levy, L. Kraus, & J. Galatzer-Levy (Eds.), *The scientific basis of child custody decisions* (2nd ed., pp. 187–214). Hoboken, NJ: Wiley.

Lamb, M. E., & Lewis, C. (2010). The development and significance of father–child relationships in two parent families. In M. E. Lamb (Ed.), *The role of the father in child development* (5th ed.). Hoboken, NJ: Wiley.

Lamb, M. E., Orbach, Y., Hershkowitz, I., Esplin, P. W., & Horowitz, D. (2007). A structured forensic interview protocol improves the quality and informativeness of investigative interviews with children: A review of the research using the NICHD Investigative Interview Protocol. *Child Abuse & Neglect, 31*, 1201–1231.

Lamb, M. E., Sternberg, K. J., & Esplin, P. W. (1998). Conducting investigative interviews of alleged sexual abuse victims. *Child Abuse and Neglect, 22*, 813–823.

Lamb, M. E., Sternberg, K. J., Orbach, Y., Esplin, P. W., & Mitchell, S. (2002b). Is ongoing feedback necessary to maintain the quality of investigative interviews with allegedly abused children? *Applied Developmental Science, 6*, 35–41.

Lamb, M. E., Sternberg, K. J., Orbach, Y., Esplin, P. W., Stewart, H., & Mitchell, S. (2003a). Age differences in young children's responses to open-ended invitations in the course of forensic interviews. *Journal of Consulting and Clinical Psychology, 71*, 926–934.

Lamb, M. E., Sternberg, K. J., Orbach, Y., Hershkowitz, I., & Esplin, P. W. (1999). Forensic interviews of children. In R. Bull & A. Memon (Eds.), *The psychology of interviewing: A handbook* (pp. 253–278). New York: Wiley.

Lamb, M. E., Sternberg, K. J., Orbach, Y., Hershkowitz, I., & Horowitz, D. (2003b). Differences between accounts provided by witnesses and alleged victims of child sexual abuse. *Child Abuse and Neglect, 27*, 1019–1031.

Lamb, M. E., Sternberg, K. J., Orbach, Y., Hershkowitz, I., Horowitz, D., & Esplin, P. W. (2002c). The effects of intensive training and ongoing supervision on the quality of investigative with alleged sex abuse victims. *Applied Developmental Science, 6*, 114–125.

Lamb, M. E., Thompson, R. A., Gardner, W. P., & Charnov, E. L. (1985). *Infant–mother attachment*. Hillsdale, NJ: Lawrence Erlbaum Associates.

Lambert, B. (2008, July 1). Freed after 17 years in prison, L.I. man will not face new trial. *New York Times*, p. A1.

Laumann-Billings, L., & Emery, R. E. (2000). Distress among young adults in divorced families. *Journal of Family Psychology, 14*, 671–687.

Leippe, M. R., Manion, A. P., & Romanczyk, A. (1992). Eyewitness persuasion: How and how well do fact finders judge the accuracy of adults' and children's memory reports? *Journal of Personality and Social Psychology, 63*, 181–197.

Leo, R. A. (1996). Inside the interrogation room. *Journal of Criminal Law and Criminology, 86*, 266–303.

Lewin, K. (1946). Action research and minority problems. *Journal of Social Issues, 2*, 34–35.

Lewin, T. (2002, July 22). Ideas & trends; above expectation: A child as witness. *New York Times*, section 4, p. 3.

Libby, L. K. (2003). Imagery perspective and source monitoring in imagination inflation. *Memory and Cognition, 7*, 1072–1081.

Lillie and Reed v. Newcastle City Council & Ors [2002] EWHC 1600 (QB).

Loftus, E. F. (1997). Creating false memories. *Scientific American, 277*, 70–75.

Loftus, E. F. (2003). Make-believe memories. *American Psychologist, 58*, 864–873.

Loftus, E. F., & Ketcham, K. (1991). *Witness for the defense: The accused, the eyewitness, and the expert who puts memory on trial*. New York: St Martin's Press.

London, K. L., Bruck, M., Ceci, S. J., & Shuman, D. W. (2005). Disclosure of child sexual abuse: What does the research tell us about the ways that children tell? *Psychology, Public Policy, and Law, 11*, 194–226.

Luna, C. (2005, July 23). Girl's killer gets death. *Los Angeles Times*, p. B1.

Lyon, T. D. (2000). Child witnesses and the oath: Empirical evidence. *Southern California Law Review, 73*, 1017–1074.

Lyon, T. D. (2007). False denials: Overcoming methodological biases in abuse disclosure research. In M. E. Pipe et al. (Eds.), *Disclosing abuse: Delays, denials, retractions and incomplete accounts*. Mahwah, NJ: Lawrence Erlbaum Associates.

Lyon, T. D., Malloy, L. C., Quas, J. A., & Ahern, E.C. (in press). Children's reasoning about adult transgression secrecy: Effects of adult identity, child age, and maltreatment. *Child Development*.

Lyon, T. D., Malloy, L. C., Quas, J. A., & Talwar, V. (2008). Coaching, truth induction, and young maltreated children's false allegations and false denials. *Child Development, 79*, 914–929.

Lyon, T. D., & Saywitz, K. J. (1999). Young maltreated children's competence to take the oath. *Applied Developmental Science, 3*, 16–27.

Martinez, C. R., & Forgatch, M. S. (2002). Adjusting to change: Linking family structure transitions with parenting and boys' adjustment. *Journal of Family Psychology, 16*, 107–117.

McCall, R. B. & Green, B. L. (2004). Beyond the methodological gold standards of behavioral research: Considerations for practice and policy. *Society for Research in Child Development Social Policy Reports, 18*, 1–19.

McCall, R. B., Green, B. L., Strauss, M. S., & Groark, C. J. (1997). Issues in community-based research and program evaluation. In I. E. Sigel & K. A. Renninger (Eds.), *Handbook of child psychology* (Vol. 4, 5th ed., pp. 955–997). New York: Wiley.

McLanahan, S. S. (1999). Father absence and the welfare of children. In E. M. Hetherington (Ed.), *Coping with divorce, single parenting, and remarriage* (pp. 117–146). Mahwah, NJ: Lawrence Erlbaum Associates.

McLanahan, S. S., & Sandefur, G. (1994). *Growing up with a single parent: What hurts, what helps.* Cambridge, MA: Harvard University Press.

McLanahan, S. S., & Teitler, J. (1999). The consequences of father absence. In M. E. Lamb (Ed.), *Parenting and child development in "nontraditional" families* (pp. 83–102). Mahwah, NJ: Lawrence Erlbaum Associates.

Memon, A., Wark, L., Holley, A., Bull, R., & Köhnken, G. (1996). Reducing suggestibility in child witness interviews. *Applied Cognitive Psychology, 10*, 503–518.

Memorandum of Good Practice (1992). London: Her Majesty's Stationery Office.

Meyer, J. R., & Reppucci, N. D. (2007). Police practices and perceptions regarding juvenile interrogations and interrogative suggestibility. *Behavioral Sciences and the Law, 25*, 757–780.

Moffitt, T. (1993). Adolescence-limited and life-course persistent antisocial behavior: A developmental taxonomy. *Psychological Review, 100*, 674–701.

Moffitt, T. E., & Caspi, A. (2001). Childhood predictors differentiate life-course persistent and adolescence-limited antisocial pathways among males and females. *Development & Psychopathology, 13*, 355–375.

Moffitt, T. E., Caspi, A., Harrington, H., & Milne, B. J. (2002). Males on the life-course-persistent and adolescence-limited antisocial pathways: Follow-up at age 26 years. *Development & Psychopathology, 14*, 179–207.

Muehrer, P. R., Salovey, P., Abdelmonem, A. A., Coyne, J. C., Kring, A. M., Merson, M. H., et al. (2002). Overcoming barriers to collaboration between basic behavioral scientists and public health scientists in research on mental disorders. *Journal of Clinical Psychology in Medical Settings, 9*, 253–265.

Muller v. Oregon, 208 U.S. 412 (1908).

Munsterberg, H. (1908). *On the witness stand.* Garden City, NY: Doubleday.

Myers, J. E. B. (1992). *Legal issues in child abuse and neglect.* Newbury Park, CA: Sage.

Nathan, D., & Snedeker, M. (1995). *Satan's silence: Ritual abuse and the making of a modern American witch hunt.* New York: Basic Books.

National Research Council (1993). *Understanding child abuse and neglect.* Washington, DC: National Academy Press.

Nelson, K., & Fivush, R. (2004). The emergence of autobiographical memory: A social cultural developmental theory. *Psychological Review, 111*, 486–511.

Nord, C., Brimhall, D., & West, J. (1997). *Fathers' involvement in their children's schools.* Washington, DC: National Center for Education Statistics.

New Jersey v. Michaels, 625 A.2d 579 aff'd 642 A.2d 1372 (1994).

North Carolina v. Robert Fulton Kelly Jr., 456 S.E.2d 861 (1995).

Odgers, C. L., Moffitt, T. E., Broadbent, J. M., Dickson, N., Hancox, R. J., Harrington, H., et al. (2008). Female and male antisocial trajectories: From childhood origins to adult outcomes. *Development and Psychopathology, 20*, 673–716.

Ogloff, J. R. P. (2000). Two steps forward and one step backward: The law and psychology movement(s) in the 20th century. *Law and Human Behavior, 24*, 457–483.

Orbach, Y., Hershkowitz, I., Lamb, M. E., Esplin, P. W., & Horowitz, D. (2000). Assessing the value of structured protocols for forensic interviews of alleged child abuse victims. *Child Abuse and Neglect, 24*, 733–752.

Orbach, Y., & Lamb, M. E. (2001). The relationship between within-interview contradictions and eliciting interviewer utterances. *Child Abuse and Neglect, 25*, 323–333.

Ornstein, P. A., Baker-Ward, L., Gordon, B. N., & Merritt, K. A. (1997). Children's memory for medical experiences: Implications for testimony. *Applied Cognitive Psychology, 11*, S87–S104.

Ornstein, P. A., Gordon, B. N., & Larus, D. M. (1992). Children's memory for a personally experienced event: Implications for testimony. *Applied Cognitive Psychology, 6*, 49–60.

Owen-Kostelnik, J., Reppucci, N. D., & Meyer, J. D. (2006). Testimony and interrogation of minors: Assumptions about maturity and morality. *American Psychologist, 61*, 286–304.

Patterson, G. R., Dishion, T. J., & Yoerger, K. (2000). Adolescent growth in new forms of problem behavior: Macro- and micro-peer dynamics. *Prevention Science, 1*, 3–13.

Pedro-Carroll, J., Nakhnikian, E., & Montes, G. (2001). Assisting children through transition: Helping parents protect their children from the toxic effects of ongoing conflict in the aftermath of divorce. *Family Court Review, 39*, 377–392.

People of the State of New York v. Kharey Wise, Kevin Richardson, Antron McCray, Yusef Salaam, & Raymond Santana: Affirmation in Response to Motion to Vacate Judgment of Conviction (2002). Indictment No. 4762/89, December 5, 2002.

Peterson-Badali, M., & Abramovitch, R. (1993). Grade related changes in young people's reasoning about plea decisions. *Law & Human Behavior, 17*, 537–552.

Pipe, M. E., Goodman, G. S., Quas, J., Bidrose, S., Ablin, D., & Craw, S. (1997). Remembering early experiences during childhood: Are traumatic events special? In J. D. Read & D. S. Lindsay (Eds.), *Recollections of trauma: Scientific evidence and clinical practice* (pp. 417–423). New York: Plenum Press.

Pipe, M. E., Lamb, M. E., Orbach, Y., & Cederborg, A.-C. (2007). *Child sexual abuse: Disclosure, delay and denial.* Mahwah, NJ: Lawrence Erlbaum Associates.

Pipe, M. E., Orbach, Y., & Lamb, M. E. (2008, March). The effect of the NICHD Interview Protocol on the outcomes of child sexual abuse investigations. In M. E. Lamb, *How does the quality of interviews with alleged victims of child abuse affect investigation and intervention?* Symposium presented at the annual meeting of the American Psychology Law Society, Jacksonville, FL.

Poole, D. A., & Lamb, M. E. (1998). *Investigative interviews of children: A guide for helping professionals.* Washington, DC: American Psychological Association.

Poulin, F., Dishion, T. J., & Burraston, B. (2001). 3-Year iatrogenic effects associated with aggregating high-risk adolescents in cognitive–behavioral preventive interventions. *Applied Developmental Science, 5,* 214–224.

Powell, M. B., & Wright, R. (2008). Investigative interviewers' perceptions of the value of different training tasks on their adherence to open-ended questions with children. *Psychiatry, Psychology and Law, 15,* 272–283.

Prohaska, T. R., & Rozensky, R. H. (2002). Overcoming barriers to collaboration between basic behavioral scientists and public health scientists in research on mental disorders. *Journal of Clinical Psychology in Medical Settings, 9,* 253–265.

Pruett, M. K., Insabella, G. M., & Gustafson, K. (2005). The Collaborative Divorce Project: A court-based intervention for separating parents with young children. *Family Courts Review, 43,* 38–51.

Pruett, M. K., Williams, T. Y., Insabella, G., & Little, T. D. (2003). Family and legal indicators of child adjustment to divorce among families with young children. *Journal of Family Psychology, 17,* 169–180.

Quas, J. A., Goodman, G. S., Bidrose, S., Pipe, M. E., Craw, S. & Ablin, D. S. (1999). Emotion and memory: Children's long-term remembering, forgetting, and suggestibility. *Journal of Experimental Child Psychology, 72,* 235–270.

Quas, J. A., Wallin, A. R., Papini, S., Lench, H., & Scullin, M. H. (2005). Suggestibility, social support, and memory for a novel experience in young children. *Journal of Experimental Child Psychology, 91,* 315–341.

Quinn, M. M., Rutherford, R. B., Leone, P. E., Osher, D. M., & Poirier, J. M. (2005). Youth with disabilities in juvenile corrections: A national survey. *Exceptional Children, 71,* 339–345.

Redlich, A. D. (2007). Double jeopardy in the interrogation room: Young age and mental illness. *American Psychologist, 62,* 609–611.

Redlich, A. D., & Goodman, G. S. (2003). Taking responsibility for an act not committed: Influence of age and suggestibility. *Law and Human Behavior, 27,* 141–156.

Redlich, A. D., Silverman, M., & Steiner, H. (2003). Pre-adjudicative and adjudicative competence in juveniles and young adults. *Behavioral Sciences and the Law, 21,* 393–410.

Redlich, A. D., Summers, A., & Hoover, S. (2010). Self-reported false confessions and false guilty pleas among offenders with mental illness. *Law & Human Behavior, 34,* 79–90.

Reid & Associates (2009). Interviewing and interrogation. Retrieved September 1, 2009, from www.reid.com/training_programs/interview_overview.html

Richardson, G., Gudjonsson, G. H., & Kelly, T. P. (1995). Interrogative suggestibility in an adolescent forensic population. *Journal of Adolescence, 18,* 211–216.

Richardson, G., & Kelly, T. P. (2004). A study in the relationship between interrogative suggestibility, compliance and social desirability in institutionalised adolescents. *Personality and Individual differences, 36,* 485–494.

Roberts, K. P., Lamb, M. E., & Sternberg, K. J. (2004). The effects of rapport building style on children's reports of a staged event. *Applied Cognitive Psychology, 18,* 189–202.

Roper v. Simmons, 543 U.S. 551 (2005).

Saywitz, K. J., Goodman, G. S., Nicholas, E., & Moan, S. F. (1991). Children's memories of a physical examination involving genital touch: Implications for reports of child sexual abuse. *Journal of Consulting and Clinical Psychology, 59,* 682–691.

Saywitz, K. J., Snyder, L., & Nathanson, R. (1999). Faciliating the communicative competence of the child witness. *Applied Developmental Science, 3,* 58–68.

Scheck, B., Neufeld, P., & Dwyer, J. (2000). *Actual innocence.* Garden City, NY: Doubleday.

Schneider, W., & Bjorklund, D. F. (1998). Memory. In W. Damon (Series Ed.) and D. Kuhn & R. S. Siegler (Vol. Eds.), *Handbook of child psychology: Volume 2. Cognition, perception, and language* (pp. 467–521). New York: Wiley.

Schwartz, S. J., & Finley, G. E. (in press). Mothering, fathering, and divorce: The influence of divorce on reports of and desires for maternal and paternal involvement. *Family Court Review.*

Scott, E., & Steinberg, L. (2008). *Rethinking juvenile justice.* Cambridge, MA: Harvard University Press.

Sears, R. R. (1975). Your ancients revisited: A history of child development. In E. M. Hetherington (Ed.), *Review of child development research.* Oxford, UK: University of Chicago Press.

Shonk, S. M., & Cicchetti, D. (2001). Maltreatment, competency deficits, and risk for academic and behavioral maladjustment. *Developmental Psychology, 37,* 3–17.

Sigurdsson, J. F., & Gudjonsson, G. H. (2004). Forensic psychology in Iceland: A survey of members of the Icelandic Psychological Society. *Scandinavian Journal of Psychology*, *45*, 325–329.

Simons, R. L. and Associates (Eds.). (1996). *Understanding differences between divorced and intact families.* Thousand Oaks, CA: Sage Publications.

Simons, R. L., Lin, K. H., Gordon, L. C., Conger, R. D., & Lorenz, F. O. (1999). Explaining the higher incidence of adjustment problems among children of divorce compared with those in two parent families. *Journal of Marriage and the Family*, *61*, 1020–1033.

Singer, S. I., & McDowall, D. (1988). Criminalizing delinquency: The deterrent effects of the New York Juvenile Offender Law. *Law and Society Review*, *22*, 521–536.

Singh, K., & Gudjonsson, G. H. (1992). Interrogative suggestibility among adolescent boys and its relationship to intelligence, memory, and cognitive set. *Journal of Adolescence*, *15*, 155–161.

Smart, C. (2002). From children's shoes to children's voices. *Family Court Review*, *40*, 307–319.

Smart, C. & Neale, B. (2000). "It's my life too"—Children's perspectives on post-divorce parenting. *Family Law*, March, 163–169.

Smith, A. B., & Gallop, M. M. (2001). What children think separating parents should know. *New Zealand Journal of Psychology*, *30*, 23–31.

Smyth, B. M., & Chisholm, R. (2006). Exploring options for parental care of children following separation: A primer for family law specialists. *Australian Journal of Family Law*, *20*, 193–218.

Snyder, H. (2006). *Juvenile arrests 2004.* Washington, DC: Office of Juvenile Justice and Delinquency Prevention, Office of Justice Programs.

Sommer, R. (2006). Dual dissemination: Writing for colleagues and the public. *American Psychologist*, *61*, 955–958.

Sroufe, L. A. (1979). The coherence of individual development: Early care, attachment, and subsequent developmental issues. *American Psychologist*, *34*, 834–841.

Stanford v. Kentucky, 492 U.S. 361 (1989).

State v. Fijnje, 11th Judicial Circuit Court, Dade Country, Florida, #84–19728 (1995).

State of New Jersey v. Michaels, 136 N.J. 299, 642 A.2d 1372 (1994).

State of Washington v. Manuel Hidalgo Rodriguez, Washington Court of Appeals No. 17600–2-III (Sept. 22, 1999).

State of Washington v. Carol M.D. and Mark A.D., 983 P.2d 1165 (Wash. Ct. App. 1999).

Steinberg, L. (2007). Risk-taking in adolescence: New perspectives from brain and behavioral science. *Current Directions in Psychological Science*, *16*, 55–59.

Steinberg, L. (2008). A social neuroscience perspective on adolescent risk-taking. *Developmental Review*, *28*, 78–106.

Steinberg, L. (2009). Adolescent development and juvenile justice. *Annual Review of Clinical Psychology*, *5*, 459–485.

Steinberg, L., Albert, D., Cauffman, E., Banich, M., Graham, S., & Woolard, J. (2008). Age differences in sensation seeking and impulsivity as indexed by behavior and self-report: Evidence for a dual systems model. *Developmental Psychology*, *44*, 1764–1778.

Steinberg, L., & Cauffman, E. (1996). Maturity of judgment in adolescence: Psychosocial factors in adolescent decision making. *Law and Human Behavior*, *20*, 249–272.

Steinberg, L., Graham, S., O'Brien, L., Woolard, J., Cauffman, E., & Banich, M. (2009). Age differences in future orientation and delay discounting. *Child Development*, *80*, 28–44.

Steinberg, L., & Scott, E. (2003). Less guilty by reason of adolescence: Developmental immaturity, diminished responsibility, and the juvenile death penalty. *American Psychologist*, *58*, 1009–1018.

Sternberg, K. J., Baradaran, L. P., Abbott, C. B., Lamb, M. E., & Guterman, E. (2006a). Type of violence, age, and gender differences in the effects of family violence on children's behavior problems: A mega-analysis. *Developmental Review*, *26*, 89–112.

Sternberg, K. J., Lamb, M. E., Davies, G. M., & Westcott, H. L. (2001a). The Memorandum of Good Practice: Theory versus application. *Child Abuse & Neglect*, *25*, 669–681.

Sternberg, K. J., Lamb, M. E., Esplin, P. W., & Baradaran, L. P. (1999). Using a scripted protocol in investigative interviews: A pilot study. *Applied Developmental Science*, *3*, 70–76.

Sternberg, K. J., Lamb, M. E., Guterman, E., & Abbott, C. B. (2006b). Effects of early and later family violence on children's behavior problems and depression: A longitudinal, multi-informant perspective. *Child Abuse & Neglect*, *30*, 283–306.

Sternberg, K. J., Lamb, M. E., Hershkowitz, I., Yudilevitch, L., Orbach, Y., Esplin, P. W., et al. (1997). Effects of introductory style on children's abilities to describe experience of sexual abuse. *Child Abuse and Neglect*, *21*, 1133–1146.

Sternberg, K. J., Lamb, M. E., Orbach, Y., Esplin, P. W., & Mitchell, S. (2001b). Use of a structured investigative protocol enhances young children's responses to free-recall prompts in the course of forensic interviews. *Journal of Applied Psychology*, *86*, 997–1005.

Sturge-Apple, M. L., Davies, P. T., & Cummings, E. M. (2006). Hostility and withdrawal in marital conflict: Effects on parental emotional unavailability and inconsistent discipline. *Journal of Family Psychology*, *20*, 227–238.

Sullivan, P. M., & Knutson, J. F. (2000). Maltreatment and disabilities: A population-based epidemiological study. *Child Abuse and Neglect*, *24*, 1257–1273.

Sweet, R. C. (1966). *Educational attainment and attitude toward school as a function of feedback in the form of teachers' written comments*. Technical Report No. 15. Madison, WI: Wisconsin Research and Development Center for Cognitive Learning.

Teplin, L., Abram, K., McClelland, G., Dulcan, M., & Mericle, A. (2002). Psychiatric disorders in youth in juvenile detention. *Archives of General Psychiatry*, *59*, 1133–1143.

Thompson v. Oklahoma, 487 U.S. 815 (1988).

Thompson, R. A. (1999). Early attachment and later development. In J. Cassidy & P. R. Shaver, *Handbook of attachment: Theory, research, and clinical applications* (pp. 265–286). New York: Guilford Press.

Thompson, R. A. (2006). Early sociopersonality development. In W. Damon, R. A. Lerner, & N. Eisenberg (Eds.), *Handbook of child development, Volume 3: Social, emotional, and personality development* (6th ed.). Hoboken, NJ: Wiley.

Tippins, T. M. & Wittmann, J. P. (2005). Empirical and ethical problems with custody recommendations: A call for clinical humility and judicial vigilance. *Family Court Review*, *43*, 193–222.

Trinder, L. & Lamb, M. E. (2005). Measuring up? The relationship between correlates of children's adjustment and both family law and policy in England. *Louisiana Law Review*, *65*, 1509–1537.

Trocmé, N., MacLaurin, B., Fallon, B., Daciuk, J., Billingsley, D., Tourigny, M., et al. (2001). *Canadian Incidence Study of Reported Child Abuse and Neglect: Final Report*. Ottawa, Canada: Minister of Public Works and Government Services.

US Department of Health and Human Services, Administration on Children, Youth, and Families (2009). *Child maltreatment 2007*. Washington, DC: US Government Printing Office.

Valle, L. A., & Silovsky, J. F. (2002). Attributions and adjustment following child sexual and physical abuse. *Child Maltreatment*, *7*, 9–25.

Viljoen, J., Klaver, J., & Roesch, R. (2005). Legal decisions of preadolescent and adolescent defendants: Predictors of confessions, pleas, communication with attorneys, and appeals. *Law and Human Behavior*, *29*, 253–278.

Wade, K. A., Garry, M., Read, J. D., & Lindsay, D. S. (2002). A picture is worth a thousand lies: Using false photographs. *Psychonomic Bulletin and Review*, *9*, 597–603.

Wallerstein, J. & Kelly, J. (1980). *Surviving the breakup: How children and parents cope with divorce*. New York: Basic Books.

Walters, S., Holmes, L., Bauer, G., & Vieth, V. (2003). *Finding words: Half a nation by 2010: Interviewing children and preparing for court*. Alexandria, VA: National Center for Prosecution of Child Abuse.

Warren, A. R., Woodall, C. E., Hunt, J. S., & Perry, N. W. (1996). "It sounds good in theory, but . . .": Do investigative interviewers follow guidelines based on memory research? *Child Maltreatment*, *1*, 231–245.

Warren, A. R., Woodall, C. E., Thomas, M., Nunno, M., Keeney, J. M., Larson, S. M., et al. (1999). Assessing the effectiveness of a training program for interviewing child witnesses. *Applied Developmental Science*, *3*, 128–135.

Warshak, R. A. (2000). Blanket restrictions: Overnight contact between parents and young children. *Family and Conciliation Courts Review*, *38*, 422–445.

Warshak, R. A. (2001). *Divorce poison*. New York: Regan Books.

Wasserman, G. A., McReynolds, L., Lucas, C., Fisher, P. W., & Santos, L. (2002). The Voice DISC–IV with incarcerated male youth: Prevalence of disorder. *Journal of the American Academy of Child and Adolescent Psychiatry*, *41*, 314–321.

Waterman, A. H., Blades, M., & Spencer, C. P. (2000). Do children try to answer nonsensical questions? *British Journal of Developmental Psychology*, *18*, 211–226.

Waterman, A. H., Blades, M., & Spencer, C. P. (2004). Indicating when you do not know the answer: The effect of question format and interviewer knowledge on children's "don't know" responses. *British Journal of Developmental Psychology*, *22*, 335–348.

Westmaas, J. L., Gil-Rivas, V., & Silver, R. C. (2007). Designing and implementing interventions to promote health and prevent illness. In H. S. Friedman & R. C. Silver (Eds.), *Foundations of health psychology* (pp. 52–70). New York: Oxford University Press.

Wigmore, J. H. (1909). Professor Munsterberg and the psychology of testimony. *Illinois Law Review*, *3*, 399–434.

Wigmore, J. H. (1940). *Evidence in trials at common law* (3rd ed.). Boston: Little, Brown.

Yarrow, L. J. (1963). Research in dimensions of early maternal care. *Merrill-Palmer Quarterly*, *9*, 101–114.

Yarrow, L. J., & Goodwin, M. (1973). The immediate impact of separation: Reactions of infants to a change in mother figures. In L. J. Stone, H. T. Smith, & L. B. Murphy (Eds.), *The competent infant* (pp. 1032–1040). New York: Basic Books.

Zigler, E. F., & Finn-Stevenson, M. (1999). Applied developmental psychology. In M. H. Bornstein & M. E. Lamb (Eds.), *Developmental science: An advanced textbook* (4th ed.) (pp. 555–598). Mahwah, NJ: Lawrence Erlbaum Associates.

GLOSSARY

Absolute threshold: Psychophysical term denoting the level at which a stimulus is detected by an observer.

Achievement: The attainment of specific academic and educational goals.

Achievement goal theory: A social–cognitive understanding of motivated behavior in achievement settings that posits that students' responses to success and failure depend on the achievement goals they have. Students who have performance goals are most concerned with how well they do compared to others and are likely to select tasks on which they are certain they can succeed. In contrast, students with mastery goals are most concerned about learning and so are likely to select tasks from which they can learn the most even if they have difficulty succeeding.

Action theory: A conceptualization of human development as an intentional, dynamic, and reciprocal process of "action-feedback-self-organization-further action" in which individuals create behavioral regulators that moderate exchanges occurring between them and the context.

Adaptation: According to Piaget, a basic inherited tendency that governs interactions of the individual with the environment in which existing cognitive structures are assimilated or accommodated in response to experience.

Affordance: Possibility for action, based on the fit between an organism and the environment.

Age–crime curve: The robust empirical finding that the onset of criminal offending is between ages 8–14, peaks in prevalence between ages 15–19, and declines towards adult levels between ages 20–29.

Agency: Individuals' intrinsic curiosity, competence, motivation, and exploratory behaviors that promote their capacity to act in the world and contribute to their own development in school.

Agentic: A characteristic of a person who feels that they can influence their world and the behaviors of those around them and then acts accordingly.

Aggression: High levels of relational aggression (e.g., threatening friendship withdrawal) *within* the friendship, and high levels of exclusivity, jealously, and intimacy, characterize the friendships of relationally aggressive children. In contrast, overtly aggressive children direct their overt aggression *outside* their friendship dyads, and report low levels of intimacy (Grotpeter & Crick, 1996).

Analogy: The process that allows children to produce new grammatical forms by generalizing the structure of forms they already know.

Analysis of variance (ANOVA): Statistical technique based on the general linear model used to assess differences among group means that can accommodate a wide variety of experimental designs, including between-subject effects, within-subject effects, or within-and between-subject (or mixed) effects.

Artifact: Species-specific features of shared and inherited material culture that mediate and coordinate human beings with the physical world and with each other.

Attachment: Biologically and culturally influenced system of interrelated social behaviors between caregiver and child that provide emotional security and encourage environmental exploration.

Attachment theory: Conceptual framework for describing and explaining normative and individual differences in caregiver–child interactions first developed by Bowlby, stressing the foundational influence of the social and emotional qualities of this dyadic relationship (typically mother–infant) in the healthy development of later interpersonal relationships.

Authoritarian parenting: Parenting style, described by Baumrind, characterized by valuing obedience and the forceful imposition of the parents' will; this parenting style has been found more commonly among fathers than mothers, when the child under discussion was a son, and within some cultural contexts to be associated with increased levels of behavior problems.

Authoritative parenting: Parenting style, described by Baumrind, characterized by the encouragement of independence and the influencing of children's behavior using rational explanation that is sensitive to, and facilitates, children's changing sense of self; this parenting style is associated with social competence and conformity to cultural and societal norms.

Autobiographical memory: Emerging after the third birthday, personal memories of past events of one's life that rely upon a sense of self that is central to the narrative account, organizing and giving meaning to the events that are remembered.

Autonomic nervous system: The part of the peripheral nervous system, functioning largely below the level of consciousness, that controls visceral functions like heart rate, digestion, respiration rate, salivation, and sexual arousal.

Babbling: The increased production of structured syllable-like vocalizations in the shape of the consonant–vowel syllables like /ta/ or /pe/ that appears around 6 months.

Behavior genetics: The quantitative study of the degree to which genotypic variability is associated with phenotypic variability in a population; historically behavior genetic studies have focused on estimating the heritability of an observed behavioral trait (e.g., intelligence, personality, psychopathology) by comparing samples of monozygotic (identical) and dizygotic (fraternal) twins.

Behavioral inhibition: A moderately stable self-regulatory response that causes some children to withdraw from unfamiliar people and situations.

Bimanual coordination: Intentional use of differential and complementary manual actions involving both hands to explore objects or assist with motor activity.

Bioecological theory: Bronfenbrenner's conceptualization of human development within the context of four interrelated and nested ecological levels (i.e., *microsystem, mesosystem, exosystem*, and *macrosystem*) which influence individual developmental outcomes in relation to the chronosystem.

Bio-social-behavioral shifts: Qualitative rearrangements in the emergence and organization of behavior resulting from the synthesis of biological and social factors interacting over time within cultural contexts.

Bio-social-cultural change: A generalized cultural (or cultural-mediational) alternative to classical theories in which human development is seen as an emergent process of biological and social changes that interact within and are mediated by culture, the accumulated knowledge, experience, and learning of prior generations.

Categorical data analysis: Class of statistical procedures used to determine whether observed proportions or frequencies differ significantly or are correlated with one another. Examples include chi-square analysis, logistic regression, and log-linear analysis.

Categorization: Grouping of objects that are discriminable based on a shared set of features or properties.

Central nervous system: The part of the nervous system that consists of the brain and the spinal cord and has a fundamental role in the control of behavior.

Classroom climate: The general social-relational atmosphere of the classroom resulting from the organization and management of the learning environment as well as the character of teacher–student relationships.

Closed questions: Queries for information posed to interviewees that specify a response or set of particular responses (e.g., "Did he touch you over or under your clothes?", "Who did you tell?"). These types of questions are typically regarded as less preferable to open-ended questions in investigative interviews in part because they restrict the memory search to certain aspects of the event.

Competence to stand trial: The judgment that a person has the capacity to assist counsel in preparing his or her legal defense and to understand the nature of the proceeding sufficiently to participate in and make decisions about rights afforded to defendants; one of the areas of juvenile justice developmental science has contributed significantly to informing legal statutes and practice.

Computational models: The formalization of cognitive theories using advanced mathematics and statistics that attempt to model the effect of task characteristics on reasoning and problem solving while taking into consideration plausible psychological limitations, such as working memory capacity or available knowledge.

Conceptual splits: Instances in which questions about the nature of human development are framed in terms of opposing explanations such as nature versus nurture, continuity versus discontinuity, and stability versus instability.

Conduct disorder: Repetitive and persistent pattern of behaviors in which social norms or the basic rights of others are violated. These can include aggressive conduct towards other people or animals, behavior that causes property loss or damage, deceitfulness, theft, and serious violations of rules.

Confidence interval: Estimated range of values that surround the point-estimate of a population parameter and indicates the precision, or likely accuracy, of the point estimate.

Conflict: Interpersonal interactions characterized by quarreling, active hostility (assaults and threats) and reactive hostility (refusals and resistance) among individuals.

Conscience: Relationally influenced cognitive and affective processes which govern how young children construct and act consistently with generalizable, internal standards of conduct.

Constraints: Limitations placed upon the possible meanings of words.

Construct validity: Degree to which a variable, as operationally defined, represents an intended theoretical construct; threats to construct validity occur when variables either underrepresent the intended construct or include extraneous factors.

Continuity: Consistency in group-based, normative perceptual abilities between time points.

Continuity–discontinuity issue: A conceptual split that stresses qualitative or quantitative similarity (continuity) or dissimilarity (discontinuity) of the description or explanation of behaviors at different points in the life span.

Co-regulation: "A form of coordinated action between participants that involves a continuous mutual adjustment of actions and intentions" (Fogel & Garvey, 2007) in which participants (e.g., child and adult) are best described as a single system rather than as two separate individuals.

Co-rumination: Intimate self-disclosure characterized by dwelling on emotionally charged and intimate everyday occurrences and feelings in negative ways.

Crawling: A quadrupedal form of locomotion typically accomplished on hands and knees, but also characterized by a variety of idiosyncratic forms of mobility.

Cross-cultural psychology: Research that explores the causes and consequences of cultural differences in which culture is treated as an antecedent or independent variable that acts on psychological processes.

Cruising: A type of upright mobility in which infants move sideways using stationary objects (furniture, hand rails, window ledges, etc.) for support.

Culpability: The judgment that a person is sufficiently responsible for a criminal act or negligence to be at fault and liable for the conduct; one of the areas of juvenile justice developmental science has contributed significantly to informing legal statutes and practice.

Cultural evolution: Nineteenth-century anthropologists' belief that cultures could be classified according to their level of development—characterized by the sophistication of their technology and the complexity of their social organization—which represented progressively advanced stages of the development of humankind.

Cultural influence: The impact of cultural norms and values in defining the "meanings" of social behaviors that affect group and individual beliefs, attitudes, and value systems.

Cultural practice: Recurrent ways of accomplishing valued social activities in concert with some group of one's proximally circumscribed social unit.

Cultural psychology: An approach in which culture is treated as the species-specific medium of human life within which people acquire and share symbolic meanings and practices that contribute to the development of psychological processes within a given cultural group.

Culture: The residue in the present of past human activity in which human beings have variously transformed nature to suit their own ends and passed the cumulated artifacts down to succeeding generations in the form of tools, rituals, beliefs, and ways of conceiving of the world. Psychological and material aspects of culture are inextricably interconnected in a medium of conceptual systems, social institutions.

Custody (child): A legal finding in which the care, control, and maintenance of a child is awarded to one or both parents following a divorce or separation proceeding.

Declarative information: New information in the form of facts that are used in early stages of skill acquisition that can be used with general problem-solving procedures (e.g., means–ends analyses) in an interpretative fashion to facilitate successful problem solving without the need to access (or possess) context-specific strategies.

Design: The structure or plan of investigations that defines the extent and means by which investigators exercise control over their independent, and all other variables, that may be operating in an investigative context. Design variations guard against different threats to the validity of the investigation and determine the conclusions that can be appropriately drawn from the research.

Developmental contextualism: Lerner's conceptualization of human development that emphasizes bidirectional, changing relations among multiple levels of organization involved in human life (e.g., biology, psychology, social groups, culture, history).

Developmental niche: An individual's "life world" in which the complex set of socio-cultural-ecological relations form the proximal environment of development. Developmental niches consist of (1) the physical and social settings in which a child lives, (2) the culturally regulated childrearing and socialization practices of a child's society, and (3) the psychological characteristics of a child's parents, including parental theories about the process of child development and their affective orientation to the tasks of childrearing.

Developmental regulation: The processes of dynamic person-context relations that are a shared feature of systems theories of human development.

Developmental systems theories: a family of related theories of human development that share four components: (1) change and relative plasticity; (2) relationism and the integration of levels of organization; (3) historical embeddedness and temporality; and (4) an emphasis on the limits of generalizability, diversity, and individual differences.

Difference threshold: Psychophysical term denoting the level at which an observer detects a difference between perceptible stimuli.

Differential susceptibility hypothesis: The view that some temperamental or genetic characteristics render children more susceptible to positive as well as negative environmental influences.

Discrimination: The impugning of an individual's intellectual ability based on ethnicity, race, or gender that may undermine the benefits of education by increasing mental health concerns and decreasing academic motivation and by anticipation of future discrimination in the labor market.

Display rules: Social rules governing the appropriate expression of emotion in social situations.

Dual-task deficit: A type of behavioral interference in which cognitive tasks are assumed to require a common system of resources such that freeing up resources in one task should result in better performance in the other.

Dynamic systems theory: A conceptualization of human development combining biological and psychological systems approaches with those of complex and nonlinear systems in physics and mathematics in which systematic changes over time can be explained across different species, age levels, or domains of development.

Ecological validity: The degree to which empirical findings obtained under experimentally controlled conditions are generalizable to real-world situations and settings.

Effect size: An estimate of the magnitude of a population difference or association often obtained by a standardized mean difference statistic or correlation coefficient and used to convey the importance or strength of a statistical result.

Efficacy: Generally, individual beliefs regarding the personal capability to causally effect a desired outcome. Teachers' efficacy beliefs regarding their ability to perform the core tasks of teaching have been shown to be associated with their teaching behaviors in the classroom, professional achievement, and psychological well-being. Students' confidence in their ability to succeed at a task predicts their engagement in that task.

Effortful control: A temperamental quality that concerns the ability to focus and/or shift attention, thinking, or behavior to accomplish one's goals.

Embodied action: The functional outcome of motor actions is constrained by the physical and biomechanical limits and capabilities of the body.

Emotion(al) regulation: The management of emotions to accomplish one's goals.

Empiricist: Philosophical assertion that all perceptual knowledge derives from the senses and grows by way of experience.

Episodic growth: Brief periods of rapid body growth interspersed with longer periods of stasis during which no growth occurs, typically observable only in individual growth data.

Equilibration: According to Piaget, the back-and-forth movement from cognitive equilibrium (characterized by the use of assimilation over accommodation) to cognitive disequilibrium (characterized by the use of accommodation over assimilation) that produces efficient schemes.

Ethics: Principles of right and wrong behavior that govern the conduct of research. Ethical standards are established to maximize benefits and minimize harms; and to ensure the rights, protection, and fair treatment of all who conduct, participate in, and use the results of, research.

Event-related potentials (ERPs): Method of studying neural activity in the brain in which the electrical activation is induced by the presentation of a stimulus and recorded by electrodes that rest on the scalp surface.

Excitatory: Response to a synaptic input which increases the probability that a cell will fire an action potential.

Expectancy Value Theory: A theory of human motivation in which individuals' choice, persistence, and performance are explained by their expectations for success, and the extent to which they value the activity.

Exploratory data analysis: Informal data analysis techniques for understanding the characteristics and meaning of data. Examples include constructing graphs, charts, and plots, and calculating simple descriptive statistics.

External validity: The extent to which the study results are applicable (or generalizable) to individuals, settings, treatments, and times different from those characterizing the original study.

Externalizing problems: Behavioral difficulties in adolescence such as delinquency, conduct disorder, attentional difficulties, and substance abuse associated with peer rejection in childhood.

First words: Emerging typically at 12 months, the production of vocalizations resulting from the infant's growing ability to record the sounds of words, the control vocal productions, and represent the meanings of words.

Fisherian analysis: Class of statistical procedures addressing research questions involving longitudinal changes or cross-sectional differences in average performance. Examples include *t*-tests and various types of analysis of variance (ANOVA).

Friendships: Close, mutual, and voluntary dyadic relationships characterized by reciprocity and a feeling of perceived equality between individuals that provide children with support, security, intimacy, affection, and both instrumental and informational assistance. Outcomes of friendships include consensual validation of interests, hopes, and fears, the creation of prototypes for later romantic, marital, and parental relationships, and growth in interpersonal sensitivity.

Functional Magnetic Resonance Imaging (fMRI): Method of studying the relationship of brain activity and behavior or mental processes by the non-invasive measurement of cerebral blood oxygen using high spatial resolution, and temporal resolution on the order of seconds.

Functionalist approach: Explains emotion in terms of goal attainment in everyday experience: "(e)motion is thus the person's attempt or readiness to establish, maintain, or change the relation between the person and his or her changing circumstances, on matters of significance to that person" (Saarni, et al., 2006, p. 227).

Garden metaphor of culture: A variant of the culture-as-medium view in which the heuristic value of conceiving of culture as the holistic and internally organized artificial environment-for-growing-living things based on that incorporates knowledge, beliefs, and material tools.

Generalized linear model: Broad class of analytic techniques that apply to both quantitative and categorical data and extend the basic concepts of regression and ANOVA to settings where the response variables are discrete and are not assumed to have a normal distribution.

Grammatical development: The progressive transition in the child from the first words to full-blown sentences. During this process children's sentences will differ from the adult standard in various ways that indicate the shape of the patterns they are using.

Growth curve: Age and gender-referenced normative percentiles for height, weight, and other body measures, typically representing mathematically smoothed group data.

Holistic person–context interaction theory: Magnusson's conceptualization of human development emphasizing the individual as an active, intentional part of a complex and continuous dynamic person–environment system of interdependent mental, behavioral, and biological components of the individual (person) and of social, cultural, and physical components of the environment (context).

Inference: The degree to which an observer's psychological experience of a sensory event is interpreted from direct behavioral and physiological measurements.

Inhibitory: Response to a synaptic input which decreases the probability that a cell will fire an action potential.

Innate: Historically, the description of preexisting as opposed to "experiential" contributions to behavior; more recent conceptualizations of innateness hold only to the notion that some brain and cognitive systems are more impervious to experience during development than others.

Internal validity: Correct inferences about the causal connectedness between independent variable and dependent variable in a particular investigation; factors that threaten internal validity are commonly referred to as *confounds*.

Internal working models: Mental representations of the self, other people, and relationships that young children construct from their interactions with attachment figures.

Internalizing problems: Behavioral and emotional problems across the lifespan such as low self-esteem, anxiety problems, loneliness, and depressive symptoms that are associated with peer rejection in childhood.

Investigative interviews: Interviews conducted with witnesses or suspected victims of maltreatment concerning their experiences, the outcomes of which typically set into motion criminal proceedings and a variety of interventions for children and families. Empirical research on the impact of various features of investigative interviews has been used to craft best-practice guidelines for professionals overseeing and conducting investigative interviews.

Item-based patterns: Patterns that determine how particular lexical items or words may combine with other words to produce meaningful syntactic combinations.

Joint attention: A child's shared attention with another via eye contact, often established through referential pointing and shared emotional expression.

Language development: The successful acquisition of language involving six features of communication: auditory development (receptive language), articulatory development (speech production), lexical development (word learning), grammatical development (learning systematic rules of sentences), pragmatic development (learning social-communicative competence), and the development of literacy. The study of each feature requires a unique set of methods, produces standard age-linked milestones in acquisition for normal development, and identifies related mental and physical processes that support its acquisition.

Life-course theory: A conceptualization of human development emphasizing the integrated and dynamic view of the entire course of human life that encompasses growth and decline and integrates individual ontogenies with their changing historical and social contexts.

Life-span developmental theory: Baltes' conceptualization of human development emphasizing life-long adaptive processes from conception through old age.

Longitudinal design: Developmental design in which individuals are studied over time in order to study normative changes and individual differences in development.

Measurement: The research operations that are used to obtain relevant and high quality—standardized, reliable, and valid—scores for analysis. Measurement is sometimes called *scaling*.

Measurement validity: The degree to which an observed variable accurately measures a theorized construct, examples of measurement validity include face, content, factorial, predictive, concurrent, and construct.

Metacognition: Being aware of one's own thought processes, including identifying problems, formulating solutions to solve problems, and allocating resources to the solution of these problems, and so forth.

Molecular genetics: The study of the structure and function of specific gene polymorphisms and their behavioral correlates.

Multivariate analysis: Type of statistical procedure used to analyze multiple scores obtained from the same individual (or other unit of sampling).

Myelinization: Process of brain development involving the lipid coating of neural fibers, and resulting in changes in the speed and fidelity of neural conduction.

Nativist: Philosophical assertion that some kinds of knowledge do not rely on experience and thus that human beings enter the world with a sensory apparatus equipped (at the very least) to order and organize their percepts.

Nature–nurture: A conceptual split in which development is explained by predetermined, inherent factors (e.g., heredity, maturation, or genes as "nature") or by external influences (e.g., environment, experience, or learning as "nurture").

Neurotransmitters: Biochemical substance which is released by the presynaptic neuron at synapses that transmits information to another neuron.

Newborn reflexes: Behaviors appearing at birth and soon after that were traditionally considered to be non-voluntary, hard-wired responses to particular eliciting stimuli.

Nonexperimental designs: Research designs that employ neither randomization nor adequate control conditions and produce results from which causal inferences cannot be made.

Null hypothesis testing: Multistep procedure for judging the statistical significance of data relative to a research question.

Object manipulation: Hand-guided motor actions such as coordinated looking, rotating, transferring, and fingering that facilitate infants' understanding of objects and about events involving objects.

Observational learning: Socialization processes that do not involve the intentional and direct action of parents but occur through children's observations of the parents' social behaviors.

Ontogenesis: The developmental history of an individual, typically the object of psychological theory and research.

Ontological attributes: Features of structures of knowledge that have an entire hierarchy of categories (ontological trees) that are fundamentally different from each other.

Open-ended questions: Queries for information posed to interviewees that do not specify a response or set of particular responses (e.g., "Tell me what happened"). These types of questions are typically regarded as preferable to closed questions in investigative interviews in part because they allow for an extensive memory search.

Optic flow: Visual information from the structure of light reflecting off surfaces in the environment that specifies the direction and velocity of locomotion as an organism moves through the environment.

Overgeneralization: The extension of word meanings beyond their conventional boundaries. These errors often arise because children have not yet learned the name for something and therefore use some near match.

Parental sensitivity: Individual differences in mothers' or fathers' perception of, and responsiveness to, the affective needs of children that can influence attachment security.

Parenting: The dynamic construct of how parents relate to their children across the lifespan that includes similarities and differences in parenting styles of both mothers and fathers within the context of larger family, social, and cultural contexts.

Parenting plans: Legal provision in the case of parental separation or divorce created to ensure that both parents become or remain attached to their children by encouraging parental participation by both parents in as broad as possible an array of social contexts on a regular basis.

Pearsonian analysis: Class of correlation-based statistical procedures addressing research questions involving the correlates of individual differences or the consistency of individual differences across time, settings, or behaviors. Examples include correlation, regression, factor analysis, and structural equation modeling.

Peer acceptance: The experience of being liked and accepted by peers.

Peer rejection: The experience of being disliked and not accepted by peers.

Peers: Similar-age individuals with whom children socialize.

Perceived popularity: The degree to which children are regarded as are "popular," cool, central, or highly visible by their peers.

Perceived social competence: An awareness of one's own peer acceptance or social skillfulness; children with higher perceived social competence tend to be more popular with peers.

Perception: The interpretation and organization of sensory information representing and reflecting characteristics of a physical event or stimulus.

Person–environment fit: A theory of human motivation that suggests students are maximally motivated to learn in situations that fit well with their own interests, current skill levels, and psychological needs.

Phylogenesis: The developmental history of life on earth or, more specifically, a species that constitutes the biological history of the newborn individual.

Plasticity: The potential for relative systematic change in human development across the life span and the multiple levels of organization comprising the ecology of human development (see Ch. 1). In the context of neurological development, the state of not yet having achieved specialization at some level that is an inherent property of brain growth and development, rather than simply the recovery of function after early brain damage (see Ch. 4).

Posture: The position and carriage of the limbs or the body as a whole.

Power: The probability of correctly rejecting a false null hypothesis that depends on various factors including the size of the effect, Type I error rate, and sample size.

Predictive validity: The degree to which experiences in early childhood are associated with aspects of social and emotional development later in the lifespan.

Preference: Behavior directed at one stimulus over another in a choice situation, irrespective of the spatial location of the two stimuli.

Privileged domain: A core area of development believed to be largely innate that provide the basis for domain-specific knowledge and behavior.

Procedural knowledge: Learning governed by condition–action units (production rules) that specify cognitive actions in response to certain problem-solving conditions and are represented by a large number of rule-like units.

Proprioception: Perception of the position and movements of the body.

Prospective control: Using perceptual information from the environment and feedback from prior actions to prepare and guide future actions in an anticipatory and adaptive manner.

Prototype: A generalized conceptualization of an entity that consists of the typical attributes associated with the most commonly found instances of the entity.

Qualitative research methods: Approaches aimed at capturing, describing, and interpreting developmental phenomena through language or other non-quantifiable modalities rather than through statistical analyses. Qualitative approaches are grounded in epistemologies other than positivism.

Quantitative data analysis: Class of statistical procedures used to analyze continuous, multipoint, and ordered data that include ratio, interval, and near-interval scores. Examples include correlation, regression, and various ANOVA techniques.

Quasi-experiments: Research designs in which control procedures are applied but assignment to conditions is not random, limiting the degree to which causal inferences can be made of results.

Reciprocity: Behaviors in which partners take turns acting and reacting to another's behavior.

Regression analysis: General approach, based on the general linear model, to analyzing quantitative data that can be used to answer research questions regarding group trends and those involving individual differences.

Rehabilitation: A central feature of juvenile justice that focuses on preparing youthful offenders for a productive life upon release from detention that is based upon both historical assumptions about adolescents (e.g., maturity of judgment, malleability) as well as more recent empirical research on risk-taking, impulse control, and emotional regulation.

Rejection sensitivity: The tendency to defensively expect, readily perceive, and overreact to peer rejection.

Relational complexity: The complexity of the relationship between pieces of information that must be maintained and manipulated in working memory for a given reasoning process. The peak complexity of relationships one can process is thought to be subject to capacity limitations.

Reliability: The dependability, consistency, or generalizability of a measured variable or score based upon its stability over time, across situations, among observers, or across items comprising a scale.

Repeated measures analysis: Type of statistical procedure used to analyze a score repeatedly assessed over time or setting.

Saccades: Measureable eye movements related to planning and attention (anticipatory saccades), or elicited by visual targets (reactive saccades).

School transitions: Changes in one's school building that typically occur at elementary (ages 5–10), middle (ages 10–14), and high school (ages 14–18) that may result in either progressive or regressive developmental shifts.

Schooling: Based on a nineteenth-century European model of education, a widely practiced and organized form of socialization typified by teaching-learning activities that are removed from contexts of practical activity, involve a distinct social structure, value system, and mediational means (writing).

Schooling effects: Research findings in which children who schooling experience exhibit behavior and levels of performance different than that children without schooling experience.

Security of attachment: According to attachment theory, the degree to which infants use attachment figures as secure bases from which to explore the novel environment.

Self-Determination Theory: A theory of human motivation and personality emphasizing individuals' inherent growth tendencies and their innate psychological needs as well as the motivation behind their choices apart from external influences.

Skeletal principle: Biological constraints that serve to bias developing children's attention to relevant features of a behavioral domain yet also require infusion of cultural input to develop past a rudimentary starting point.

Social cognition: Reasoning about the mental states and processes of others—including goals, intentions, and beliefs—based on their verbal and non-verbal behaviors.

Social information-processing: Rubin and Rose-Krasnor's model of interpersonal problem-solving in which children sequentially select a social goal, examine the task environment, access and implement a chosen strategy, and then evaluate the outcome relative to the initial social goal.

Social participation: Parten's description of six developmentally sequential categories of social interactions, including unoccupied behavior, solitary play, onlooker behavior, parallel play, associative play, and cooperative play.

Social skills: Behaviors and abilities that promote successful initiation and maintenance of social interactions.

Socialization: The developmental process of acquiring interpersonal skills, abilities, and understanding that influence social behavior and interactions across the lifespan.

Social-emotional learning: Inter- and intrapersonal "non-content" domains—including self-awareness, social awareness, responsible decision making, self-management, and relationship management—that relate to content learning. Research findings suggest that social and emotional learning programs delivered in classrooms are positively associated with a wide range of educational and developmental outcomes.

Sociometric popularity: Method of categorizing children into status groups based on the number of positive ("like") and negative ("dislike") nominations received from peers.

Stability: Consistency in individual-order perceptual abilities between time points.

Stability–instability issue: A conceptual split that distinguishes similarities and differences that arise between people within groups as a consequence of within-person change: a person's position relative to his or her reference group may remain the same (stability) or change (instability) with development.

Standardization: Measurement procedures intended to ensure that the assessed scores for all participants are procedurally comparable.

Statistical conclusion validity: The validity of the outcome of a statistical test resulting in a correct or incorrect decision; the latter result can be represented as a threat to validity when a researcher mistakenly rejects a true null hypothesis or fails to reject a false null hypothesis (Type II error).

Stereotype: Commonly held beliefs about groups of people that may or may not be accurate, e.g., the belief that males are better at sports than females.

Stereotypies: Movements performed for their own sake that appear repetitive and uniform, but are actually shown to be variable and unique when measured with high-speed motion tracking devices.

Subcortical: Brain regions such as the basal nuclei, cerebellum, hippocampus, and thalamus, that lay under the cerebral cortex.

Successful intelligence: Sternberg's formalization of the ability to achieve success in life in terms of one's personal standards and sociocultural context, through a balance of analytical, creative, and practical skills. Success depends on the ability to recognize and capitalize on one's strengths and to compensate for one's weaknesses.

Suggestibility: The degree to which a person is susceptible or vulnerable to suggestive influences based upon individual traits or situational demands.

Temperament: The biological basis of the affective arousal, expression, and regulatory components of personality that contribute to a wide range of developmental outcomes, including individual personality characteristics.

Theory of mind: A type of social cognition in which individuals construe others in terms of their mental states and traits, often investigated through the use of "false-belief" tasks.

Tool use: Behaviors in which infants perceive a gap between their own motor abilities and a desired goal, find an alternative means to bridge that gap, and implement a tool or object successfully to achieve the desired goal.

Tracking: The educational practice of grouping students by ability level within or between classroom settings which determines their educational opportunities, social relationships with peers, and self-evaluation of academic abilities.

True experiments: Research designs that include manipulation of the independent variable by the investigator and control of extraneous variables by random assignment of participants to conditions.

Undergeneralization: The failure to use a new word in a fully general fashion. These errors arise because children first acquire words in limited concrete contexts and do not yet know how widely they can be extended.

Univariate analysis: Type of statistical procedure used to analyze a single score from each sampling unit (e.g., individual).

Visual cliff: Glass-topped experimental apparatus giving the impression of a slight drop-off (0.6 cm) on one side and a deep drop-off (102 cm) on the other side, resulting in conflicting visual and haptic information.

AUTHOR INDEX

SUBJECT INDEX

ABOUT THE AUTHORS

Craig B. Abbott is a Senior Research Assistant and Statistician in the Comparative Behavioral Genetics Section at the Eunice Kennedy Shriver National Institute of Child Health and Human Development. He received his B.S. from Brigham Young University and his M.S. and Ph.D. from the University of Utah. His research interests are in the effects of family violence on the social and emotional development of children and adolescents; the development and assessment of techniques for interviewing child witnesses and victims of alleged sexual abuse; and parent–adolescent relationships.

Karen E. Adolph is Professor in the Department of Psychology and the Center for Neuroscience at New York University. She received her B.A. from Sarah Lawrence College and her M.A. and Ph.D. from Emory University, and completed a postdoctoral fellowship at the Albert Einstein College of Medicine. Adolph was previously on the faculty at Carnegie Mellon University. She received a James McKeen Cattell Sabbatical Award, the Robert L. Fantz Memorial Award from the American Psychological Foundation, the Boyd McCandless Award from the American Psychological Association, the Young Investigator Award from the International Society for Infant Studies, and FIRST and MERIT awards from the National Institutes of Health. Her research examines learning and development in the context of infant motor skill acquisition. Adolph is author of SRCD monograph *Learning in the Development of Infant Locomotion*. She chairs the NIH study section on Motor Function and Speech Rehabilitation, is on the Advisory Board of the James S. McDonnell Foundation, and is on the editorial boards of *Developmental Psychobiology, Ecological Psychology*, and *Infancy*.

Martha E. Arterberry is Professor of Psychology at Colby College. She received her B.A. from Pomona College and her Ph.D. from the University of Minnesota. Arterberry currently serves as a consulting editor for *Developmental Psychology*, and she is a coauthor of *The Cradle of Knowledge: Development of Perception in Infancy*. Her research interests in perceptual and cognitive development include the study of depth perception, three-dimensional object perception, categorization, and memory.

Sarah E. Berger is Associate Professor in the Department of Psychology at the College of Staten Island and the Graduate Center, City University of New York. She received her B.A. from the University of Texas at Austin and her M.A. and Ph.D. from New York University. She was awarded the U.S. Fulbright Scholarship Grant to Israel for the 2010–2011 scholastic year and is a recipient of the Martin D. Braine Memorial Award. She is a member of the Association for Psychological Science, the American Psychological Association, the International Society for Infant Studies, the Society for Research in Child Development, and the Cognitive Development Society. Her research interests include the development of problem-solving skills in the context of locomotion and the impact of social and contextual factors on infants' locomotor development.

Damian P. Birney is a Senior Lecturer in the Australian School of Business and Associate Director of the Accelerated Learning Laboratory at the University of New South Wales, Australia. He was awarded his Ph.D. from the University of Queensland, Australia. Birney was an Associate Research Scientist in the Center for the Psychology of Abilities, Competencies, and Expertise at Yale University and holds an Honorary Senior Lecturer position at the University of Sydney. He is a Chief Investigator on the Australian Research Council Linkage Project: Flexible Expertise in Senior Executives. His research interests include the study of cognitive complexity, working memory and intelligence, and related measurement issues.

Marc H. Bornstein is Senior Investigator and Head of Child and Family Research in the Program in Developmental Neuroscience at the Eunice Kennedy Shriver National Institute of Child Health and Human Development. He holds a B.A. from Columbia College, M.S. and Ph.D. degrees from Yale University, and an honorary doctorate from the University of Padua. Bornstein was a Guggenheim Foundation Fellow and has received awards from the Human Relations Area Files, National Institutes of Health, American Psychological Association, the Theodor Hellbrügge Foundation, the American Mensa Education and Research Foundation, the Japan Society for Promotion of Science, and the Society for Research in Child Development. Bornstein has held faculty positions at Princeton University and New York University as well as visiting academic appointments in Bamenda, London, Munich, New York, Paris, Santiago, Seoul, Tokyo, and Trento. He sits on the Governing Council of the SRCD and the Executive Committee of ISIS. Bornstein is coauthor of *Development in Infancy* (5 editions), *Development: Infancy through Adolescence*, and *Lifespan Development* and general editor of the *Crosscurrents in Contemporary Psychology Series* (10 volumes) and the *Monographs in Parenting* (8 volumes). He has also edited the *Handbook of Parenting* (Vols. I–V, 2 editions) and the *Handbook of Cultural Developmental Science*, and he coedited *Developmental Psychology: An Advanced Textbook* (6 editions) as well as numerous other volumes. He is author of several children's books, videos, and puzzles in *The Child's World* and *Baby Explorer* series. Bornstein is Editor Emeritus of *Child Development* and Founding Editor of *Parenting: Science and Practice*. He has contributed scientific papers in the areas of human experimental, methodological, comparative, developmental, crosscultural, neuroscientific, pediatric, and aesthetic psychology.

Julie Bowker is an Assistant Professor of Psychology in the Department of Human Development at the University at Buffalo, the State University of New York. She received her B.S. in Human Development and Family Studies at Cornell University and her Ph.D. in Human Development from the University of Maryland, College Park. Her research program focuses on the roles that peer relationships, particularly friendships, play in social and emotional development during late childhood and early adolescence.

Xinyin Chen is Professor of Psychology at the University of Western Ontario. Chen received his B.A. at East China Normal University and M.A. and Ph.D. at the University of Waterloo. He was a William T. Grant Scholar. Chen's research interests include children's and adolescents' socioemotional functioning (e.g., shyness-inhibition, aggression, and social competence), peer relationships including groups and networks, and family influences, with a focus on crosscultural issues.

Michael Cole is Professor of Communication and Psychology at the University of California —San Diego, where he is director of the Laboratory of Comparative Human Cognition. He received his B.A. at UCLA and his Ph.D. at Indiana University. After spending a postdoctoral year in Moscow where he worked with Alexander Luria and Eugene Sokolov, he became involved in crosscultural research focused on cognitive development and the consequences of engaging in cultural practices associated with literacy and schooling. This work is published in *The Cultural Context of Learning and Thinking* and *The Psychology of Literacy*. He is a Fellow of the American Academy of Arts and Sciences, the Society of Experimental Psychologists, and the Academies of Education of the United States and Russia. He has engaged in research creating model cultural systems and studying the consequences of participation for children of varying ages and backgrounds. His books include *Cultural Psychology: A Once and Future Discipline* and *The Development of Children*.

Robert Coplan is a Professor of Psychology at Carleton University (Ottawa, Canada) and Editor of the journal *Social Development*. He received his B.Sc. at McGill University and his M.A. and Ph.D. at the University of Waterloo. Coplan conducts research and publishes in the area of children's peer relationships and social development, with a specific focus on the development of anxiety and internalizing problems in childhood. He is coauthor of *The Development of Shyness and Social Withdrawal* and *Social Development in Childhood and Adolescence: A Contemporary Reader* and author of *What Teachers Needs to Know about Shy Children at School*.

Jacquelynne S. Eccles is McKeachie/Pintrich Distinguished University Professor of Psychology and Education at the University of Michigan. Eccles received her Ph.D. from UCLA and has served on the faculty at Smith College, the University of Colorado, and the University of Michigan. At the University of Michigan, she served as Chair of the Combined Program in Education and Psychology as well as acting chair of the Psychology Department. She is also a Research Scientist at the Institute for Social Research at the University of Michigan and a visiting World Scholar at the Institute of Education, University of London, UK. She chaired the MacArthur Foundation Network on Successful Pathways through Middle Childhood and was a member of the MacArthur Research Network on Successful Pathways through Adolescence. She is past-president of the Society for Research on Adolescence and Division 35 of APA. Her awards include a Spencer Foundation Fellowship, the Sarah Goddard Power Award, the APS Cattell Fellows Award, SPSSI's Kurt Lewin Award, Distinguished Life Time Career awards from APA Division 15 and from the Society for the Study of Human Development, and the University of Michigan Faculty Recognition Award for Outstanding Scholarship. She is a Fellow in the American Psychological Association, American Psychological Society, American Educational Research Association, and Society for the Psychological Study of Social Issues. She has conducted research on gender-role socialization, identity formation and action, classroom influences on motivation, social development in the family, school, peer, and wider cultural contexts. Her recent work focuses on the ways in which ethnicity and gender become part of the self and influence experiences with others and the relation of self-beliefs and identity to the transition from mid to late adolescence and then into adulthood. She is coeditor of books focused mostly on topics linked to motivation and to gender, and is Editor of the *Journal of Research on Adolescence* and incoming Editor of *Developmental Psychology*.

Rebecca Goodvin is an Assistant Professor of Psychology at Western Washington University. She received her B.A. from Gonzaga University and her M.A. and Ph.D. from the University of Nebraska—Lincoln. Her research focuses on children's emotional and social-cognitive development in the context of parent–child relationships, and in particular on the development of self-concept in early childhood. She has focused on attachment theory and parent–child communication as frameworks for understanding this development, and seeks to integrate the concept of internal working models in attachment theory with a growing understanding of young children's social cognition. In addition, she has a strong interest in the social and institutional contexts surrounding and supporting child development, and worked for the University of Nebraska's Center on Children, Youth, Families, and Schools, and for the University of Nebraska's Center on Children, Families, and the Law on projects including an Early Head Start evaluation, the Midwest Child Care Consortium, and an NIH funded study addressing the context of child neglect in Nebraska.

Donald P. Hartmann is Emeritus Professor of Psychology in the Department of Psychology at the University of Utah. He received his Ph.D. from Stanford University. He is a fellow of three APA divisions: Developmental, Clinical, and Applied Behavior Analysis. He previously served as Editor or Associate Editor of *Behavioral Assessment, Behavior Therapy*, and *Journal of Applied Behavior Analysis*. His writings include *Child Behavior Analysis and Therapy* and *Using Observers to Study Behavior*. His research interests have been in children's friendship loss and MAD (measurement, analysis, and design).

Mark H. Johnson is Professor of Psychology and Director of the Centre for Brain & Cognitive Development at Birkbeck College, University of London, and a Medical Research Council Scientific Team Leader. He received his B.Sc. at the University of Edinburgh, UK and his Ph.D. from the University of Cambridge. He was appointed Research Scientist (1985–89) and then Senior Research Scientist (1994–98) at the Medical Research Council's Cognitive Development Unit, London. From 1990 to 1995 he was Visiting Assistant Professor at the University of Oregon, Eugene, and Associate Professor of Psychology at Carnegie Mellon University. Johnson has published over 200 scholarly articles and books on brain and cognitive development in human infants and other species, and is Co-Editor in Chief of *Developmental Science*. His laboratory currently focuses on typical and atypical functional brain development in human infants and toddlers using several imaging, behavioral, and modeling techniques. Along with his collaborators, he was awarded the Queen's Anniversary Prize for Higher Education in 2006. He received the British Psychological Society President's Award in 2008, and the Experimental Psychology Society Mid-Career Award in 2009.

Carmit Katz is a Research Associate within the Department of Social and Developmental Psychology at Cambridge University, UK. She received her Ph.D. from the School of Social Work at Haifa University in Israel. Katz has conducted several studies with the Unit of Investigative Interviewers in Israel; she has also conducted individual and group training sessions with investigative interviewers. Katz's main professional interest is in promoting the well-being of children who are involved in the legal system. In the course of conducting field studies, Katz is intensively involved in writing and disseminating practical guidelines for investigative interviewers (e.g., the integration of drawings into interviews, interviewing reluctant children about alleged abuse). Katz is coeditor of *Children's Testimony: A Handbook of Psychological Research and Forensic Practice*.

Michael E. Lamb is Professor and Head of the Department of Social and Developmental Psychology at the University of Cambridge, UK. He received his Ph.D. from Yale University, honorary doctorates from the University of Goteborg, Sweden, and the University of East Anglia, UK, and the Association for Psychological Science's James McKeen Cattell Award for Lifetime Contributions to Applied Psychological Research. Lamb is coauthor of *Development in Infancy, Socialization and Personality Development, Infant–Mother Attachment, Child Psychology Today, Investigative Interviews of Children*, and *Tell Me What Happened: Structured Investigative Interviews of Child Victims and Witnesses*. He has edited books on fathers and father–child relationships, including *The Role of the Father in Child Development*, founded and coedited *Advances in Developmental Psychology*, as well as *Developmental Science: An Advanced Textbook*, and has edited other books on child abuse, children's testimony, day care, infant social cognition, social and personality development, sibling relationships, social policy, and parent–child relationships in diverse social and cultural circumstances.

Richard M. Lerner is the Bergstrom Chair in Applied Developmental Science and the Director of the Institute for Applied Research in Youth Development at Tufts University. He went from kindergarten through Ph.D. within the New York City public schools, completing his doctorate at the City University of New York. Lerner was the founding editor of *Journal of Research on Adolescence* and of *Applied Developmental Science*, which he continues to edit. He was a fellow at the Center for Advanced Study in the Behavioral Sciences and is a fellow of the American Association for the Advancement of Science, the American Psychological Association, and the Association for Psychological Science. Prior to joining Tufts University, he was on the faculty and held administrative posts at The Pennsylvania State University, Michigan State University, and Boston College, where he was the Anita L. Brennan Professor of Education and the Director of the Center for Child, Family, and Community Partnerships. Lerner serves on the Advisory Board of the John Templeton Foundation, and held the Tyner Eminent Scholar Chair in the Human Sciences at Florida State University. He is known for his theory of relations between lifespan human development and social change and for his research about relations between adolescents and their peers, families, schools, and communities. As illustrated by his *Liberty: Thriving and Civic Engagement among America's Youth* and *The Good Teen: Rescuing Adolescence from the Myth of the Storm and Stress Years*, his work integrates the study of public policies and community-based programs with the promotion of positive youth development and youth contributions to civil society.

Selva Lewin-Bizan is a Post-Doctoral Fellow at the Institute for Applied Research in Youth Development at Tufts University, working in the 4-H Study. She received a B.A. from Tel-Aviv University, an M.A. from University of Chicago, and a Ph.D. from Boston College. Lewin-Bizan has clinical experience with children, adolescents, and parents in the United States and abroad, in both civilian and military settings. Her research explores how family dynamics and monetary resources affect the lives of children and parents, with special emphasis on fatherhood. This research has a threefold purpose: first, to understand how fathers parent and why; second, to understand how fathering affects fathers themselves; and third, to understand the role of fathers in children's and adolescents' development. Lewin-Bizan's research focuses on policy implications, particularly for economically disadvantaged families.

Charlie Lewis is Professor of Family and Developmental Psychology at Lancaster University. He trained as a clinical psychologist and gained a Ph.D. from Nottingham University. He is the author or coauthor of *Becoming a Father, Fathers, Work and Family Life, Family Understandings*, and *How Children Develop Social Understanding*. He has edited *Reassessing Fatherhood, Children's Early Understanding of Mind*, and a six-volume series on *Developmental Psychology*. His research is focused on children's social-cognitive development, particularly in constructing accounts of social understanding in infants and preschoolers that contrast with the "theory of mind" hypothesis; fathering; the influences of advertising and product placement on children; children's testimony, particularly in those in special education; social and language development of children with autism; and theory in cognitive developmental psychology.

Brian MacWhinney is a Professor of Psychology at Carnegie Mellon University. He received a Ph.D. from the University of California at Berkeley. He has spent sabbatical years as a

Visiting Distinguished Professor at Hong Kong University, Southern Denmark University, and the Hong Kong Institute of Education. MacWhinney's work with Elizabeth Bates on crosslinguistic studies of language processing led to the formulation of the Competition Model. More recently, MacWhinney has incorporated the core assumptions of the Competition Model into a Unified Competition Model that links various forms of language learning and processing to emergentist theories, including the theory of embodied cognition. To facilitate the empirical study of language learning and loss, MacWhinney has constructed a system of computer programs and database called the CHILDES (Child Language Data Exchange System) Project that is used by over 3000 child language researchers in 46 countries. MacWhinney's books include *The CHILDES Project: Tools for Analyzing Talk, The Emergence of Language*, and *The Crosslinguistic Study of Sentence Processing*.

Lindsay C. Malloy is a Postdoctoral Research Associate in the Department of Social and Developmental Psychology at the University of Cambridge, UK. She received her Ph.D. from the University of California, Irvine. Malloy has published in *Developmental Psychology, Child Development*, and *Journal of the American Academy of Child and Adolescent Psychiatry*. She received a dissertation award from the American Psychology Law Society and a Regional Research Award from Psi Chi. She is coeditor of *Children's Testimony: A Handbook of Psychological Research and Forensic Practice*. Her research is concerned with developmental and sociocontextual factors on children's memory and suggestibility, including the effects of cognitive, social, and emotional factors on their reports, and children's and adolescents' disclosure of traumatic or negative experiences.

Clay Mash is a Research Psychologist at the Eunice Kennedy Shriver National Institute of Child Health and Human Development. His B.A. is from Oklahoma State University, and his graduate training was conducted at Indiana University and the University of Pittsburgh. Prior to the NICHD, he completed a postdoctoral fellowship at the University of Massachusetts. At the NICHD, he serves as Principal Investigator of the Early Learning and Development Project and as Co-Investigator of several other research protocols within the Section on Child and Family Research. He has published research on the early development of perception, action, and cognition in infants and young children, is a member of the International Society on Infant Studies and the Society for Research in Child Development, and has served on the editorial board of *Child Development*.

Kristina L. McDonald is a Postdoctoral Research Associate in the Department of Human Development, University of Maryland, College Park. She received her B.A. from Illinois Wesleyan University and her M.S. and Ph.D. from Duke University. Her research interests include the social relationships of children, adolescents, and emerging adults, with a particular focus on how individuals handle conflict with relationship partners, cultural and contextual influences on social interaction, and the socioemotional experiences (e.g., loneliness) associated with characteristics of social relationships.

Martin Packer is Associate Professor of Psychology at Duquesne University and at the University of the Andes, in Bogotá, Colombia. He received his B.A. at Cambridge University, UK and his Ph.D. at the University of California, Berkeley. His research has explored interactions between neonates and their mothers, early childhood peer relationships, conflict among adolescents, and the way schools change the kind of person a child becomes. He has taught at the University of California, Berkeley and the University of Michigan. He is coeditor of *Entering the Circle: Hermeneutic Investigation in Psychology* and *Cultural and Critical Perspectives on Human Development* and is author of *The Structure of Moral Action, Changing*

Classes: School Reform and the New Economy, and *The Science of Qualitative Research: Towards a Historical Ontology*. He is one of the founding coeditors of the journal *Qualitative Research in Psychology*.

Kelly E. Pelzel is a licensed psychologist at the University of Iowa Hospitals and Clinics Center for Disabilities and Development, which is affiliated with the University of Iowa Children's Hospital. She received her B.A. from the University of Northern Iowa and her Ph.D. from the University of Utah. She is a member of the Society for Research in Child Development and the World Association for Infant Mental Health. Her professional interests include social perspective-taking, early childhood mental health, and autism spectrum disorders.

Robert W. Roeser is an Associate Professor in the Department of Psychology and Senior Program Coordinator for the Mind and Life Institute at Portland State University. He received his B.A. from Cornell University, an M.A. from Holy Names College, and M.A. and Ph.D. from the University of Michigan. Roeser has been a William T. Grant Faculty Scholar and a William J. Fulbright Scholar in India. His research focuses on school as a central cultural context of human development, with a special emphasis on how educational program and environments shape outcomes such as motivation to learn, well-being, identity, and self-regulatory capacity.

Kenneth H. Rubin is Director and Professor, Center for Children, Relationships, and Culture in the Department of Human Development, University of Maryland. He received his B.A. from McGill University and his M.S. and Ph.D. from the Pennsylvania State University. Rubin is a fellow of the Canadian and American Psychological Associations and the Association of Psychological Science; he has been a recipient of the International Society for the Study of Behavioral Development Award for Distinguished Contributions to the International Advancement of Research and Theory in Behavioral Development and the American Psychological Association Mentor Award in Developmental Psychology. He twice served as an Associate Editor of *Child Development* and is past-president of the International Society for the Study of Behavioral Development. Rubin's research interests include the study of children's peer and family relationships and their social and emotional development. He is the senior author of three chapters that have appeared in *The Handbook of Child Psychology—Play* and *Peer Interactions, Relationships, and Groups*.

Robert J. Sternberg is Dean of the School of Arts and Sciences and Professor of Psychology and Education at Tufts University, as well as Honorary Professor of Psychology at the University of Heidelberg, Germany. Prior to going to Tufts, he was IBM Professor of Psychology and Education at Yale. Sternberg's Ph.D. is from Stanford and he holds 11 honorary doctorates. Sternberg is President-Elect of the Federation of Associations of Behavioral and Brain Sciences and President of the International Association for Cognitive Education and Psychology. He is past-president of the American Psychological Association and the Eastern Psychological Association. Sternberg is the author of numerous books and articles and has received many professional awards.

Ross A. Thompson is Professor of Psychology at the University of California, Davis. He received his A.B. from Occidental College and his A.M. and Ph.D. from the University of Michigan. Thompson was previously the Carl Happold Distinguished Professor of Psychology at the University of Nebraska. He has been a Visiting Scientist at the Max Planck Institute for Human Development and Education in Berlin, Germany, a Senior NIMH

Fellow in Law and Psychology at Stanford University, and a Harris Visiting Professor at the University of Chicago. He received the Ann L. Brown Award for Excellence in Developmental Research, the Outstanding Research and Creative Activity Award from the University of Nebraska system, and the Boyd McCandless Young Scientist Award for Early Distinguished Achievement from the American Psychological Association, as well as many teaching awards. Thompson is a founding member of the National Scientific Council on the Developing Child, and was a member of the Committee on Integrating the Science of Early Childhood Development of the National Academy of Sciences that wrote *From Neurons to Neighborhoods: The Science of Early Childhood Development*. He has twice been Associate Editor of *Child Development*. His books include *Preventing Child Maltreatment through Social Support: A Critical Analysis, The Postdivorce Family: Children, Families, and Society*, and *Toward a Child-Centered, Neighborhood-Based Child Protection System*. He also edited *Socioemotional Development* and is coauthor of *Infant–Mother Attachment*. His research interests are in early parent–child relationships, the development of emotional understanding and emotion regulation, conscience development, and the growth of self-understanding as well as the applications of developmental research to public policy concerns, including school readiness and its development, early childhood investments, and early mental health.

Amy Eva Alberts Warren is a Post-Doctoral Fellow at the Institute for Applied Research in Youth Development and Project Director of the John Templeton Foundation funded study, The Role of Spiritual Development in Growth of Purpose, Generosity, and Psychological Health in Adolescence. She received a B.A. Clark University and M.A. and Ph.D. from Tufts University. Warren is interested in how people come to be compassionate, socially just, and peaceful. She is particularly interested in the role that parents and educators play in nurturing such development and in how social policies and popular beliefs shape these roles.

Abby C. Winer is a doctoral student at the University of California, Davis and a research assistant at the Social and Emotional Development Lab. She received her A.B. from Georgetown University. While at Georgetown, she assisted with the Early Care and Education Lab assessing the quality of early child care environments and experiences as part of a longitudinal investigation of child care and children's temperaments over time. She was also involved with the Parent–Child Health Project at the George Washington University, examining familial influences on early infant and toddler mental health and temperament. Her current work examines relational influences of attachment, parent–child conversations, and social representations on preschoolers' prosocial and conscience development. Her research interests include the study of the relational contexts and ecologies of children's social and emotional development, both constructive and deconstructive behaviors, as well as the implications and applications of this research to public policy and intervention programs.